PETERSON'S®

ACT® PREP GUIDE:
THE ULTIMATE GUIDE TO MASTERING THE ACT®
2019

PETERSON'S

PETERSON'S

About Peterson's®

Peterson's has been your trusted educational publisher for over 50 years. It's a milestone we're quite proud of, as we continue to offer the most accurate, dependable, high-quality educational content in the field, providing you with everything you need to succeed. No matter where you are on your academic or professional path, you can rely on Peterson's for its books, online information, expert test-prep tools, the most up-to-date education exploration data, and the highest quality career success resources—everything you need to achieve your education goals. For our complete line of products, visit **www.petersons.com**.

Since 2005, Peterson's has been the leading publisher of prep guides for the ACT®. During that time, more than one million students across 60 countries have prepared for the ACT® with Peterson's titles.

For more information, contact Peterson's, 8740 Lucent Blvd., Suite 400, Highlands Ranch, CO 80129; or find us online at **www.petersons.com**.

Peterson's ACT® Prep Guide 2019
ISBN 978-0-7689-4337-5

Printed in the United States of America

10 9 8 7 6 5 4 3 2 1 21 20 19

Fourth Edition

Peterson's Updates

Check out our website at **www.petersonspublishing.com/publishingupdates** to see if there is any new information regarding the test and any revisions or corrections to the content of this book. We've made sure the information in this book is accurate and up-to-date; however, the test format or content may have changed since the time of publication.

TABLE OF CONTENTS

INTRODUCTION TO *PETERSON'S® ACT® PREP GUIDE*

Are you ready for ACT exam success? We hope so, and if you are, then you've come to the right place. You are holding in your hands the perfect ACT study guide to help you reach your target scores on exam day. Why? Because wherever your test skills are at today, and however ambitious your goals are for the official exam, this book is designed to help you reach your goals. With *Peterson's ACT® Prep Guide*, you get the following:

- **Top-to-bottom exam information:** We cover everything you need to know about the exam, including key details like how to register, how the test is scored, what the test costs, what to bring (and not to bring) on test day—all the things you need to know to feel confident that you're ready and have left nothing to chance.

- **Complete exam coverage:** We'll get you up to speed with an overview of the entire structure and format of the ACT exam and each subject test—with this book, there'll be no unwelcome surprises on test day.

- **Step-by step review:** We'll guide you carefully through every section of the test—including the Mathematics, English, Reading, Science, and optional Writing tests—and provide you with proven tips, strategies, and advice from ACT exam experts to help you do your absolute best on the actual exam.

- **Lots of helpful practice:** When it comes to the ACT exam, nothing beats practice with questions that are modeled on the ones you'll encounter on test day. This book has plenty of practice for every question type, along with thorough answer explanations, so you can build your skills and get into peak test-taking shape.

- **Practice designed for *you*:** There's no "one-size-fits-all" approach to preparing for the ACT—you're a unique individual with unique strengths and weaknesses and a unique schedule. No one knows better than you what approach to getting ready for test day will work best. We get it and we want to help you reach your specific test goals, which is why we developed ACT preparation with *you* in mind—we'll take you step-by-step through the prep material at a pace and schedule that works for you Whether you prefer to grab the book whenever you have some time to devote to test preparation and turn to where you last left off or jump to a section or subject you want to focus on, you can go as slow or as fast as you like, review the material as many times as it takes to master a concept or subject, and be confident that each time you prepare, you're moving closer and closer to test-day success.

The bottom line is that the road to achieving your ACT exam goals might not be an easy one—it may require lots of hard work, practice, and dedication. But rest assured, using this book to guide you along your journey to test success means you're off to a great start.

How This Book Is Organized

Peterson's ACT® Prep Guide is organized to give you a clear and thorough understanding of the ACT exam and the skills tested on each of the ACT's five tests.

- **Chapters 1 and 2** tell you everything you need to know about the ACT exam and how to prepare for it: what it includes, how to register for the test, how to decide where and when to take it, how it is scored, and how those scores are reported to the colleges of your choice. Chapter 2 includes study tips that will come in handy as you prepare for the ACT exam.

- **Chapter 3** introduces you to your first full-length ACT practice exam—**the diagnostic test**. This section shows you how to approach this important test, which will help you identify your strengths and weaknesses in all the subjects covered on the ACT exam. You will then take the diagnostic test and complete a self-assessment to help you plan your study path.

- **Chapters 4–14** comprise the review chapters—the meat of the book. These chapters explain every skill you'll need to sharpen to master the ACT's English, Mathematics, Reading, Science, and Writing tests. In addition to the review sections and practice exercises, select chapters feature College Readiness Benchmark Learning Path Practice, which helps you focus on troublesome question types.

- **Chapter 15** gives you more opportunities to prepare with **four full-length practice tests**. Each test features detailed explanations for each question, designed to help you understand *why* an answer choice is correct or incorrect.

- **Chapter 16** shows you how to score your tests. Here you will find answer keys to each test broken down into subject areas and subscores. Included also are conversion charts to help you approximate what your scale scores would be, based on the number of questions you answer correctly on the test. This information is vital to helping you work toward reaching your goal score.

Special Study Features

You will find four kinds of special study features scattered throughout the book. In addition to providing insight into how to best use this guide for test-prep success, each study feature highlights specific types of information:

College Readiness Benchmark Learning Path Exercises provide extra practice to sharpen your skills in subjects considered vital to first-year college course success (as determined by ACT, Inc.)

TIP

Tips point out valuable information you need to know when taking the ACT exam. Tips provide quick and simple hints for selecting the correct answers for the most common ACT question types.

Alerts identify potential pitfalls in the testing format or question types that can cause common mistakes in selecting answers.

NOTE:

Notes address information about the test structure itself.

CAUTION

Cautions provide warnings about possible errors in computation or formulas that can result in choosing incorrect answers on the math test.

How to Use This Book

It's understandable that all of the information you'll be reading about the ACT might seem a little overwhelming. But even if you are feeling confused by everything the ACT requires, take some comfort in the knowledge that you are holding the best resource guide to help you do well on the test. This book's job is not to make you a genius; its job is to make sure you are prepared to take the ACT. If you become a genius in the process, consider that a bonus.

Following the four steps listed below will help you get the most out of using this guide.

Step 1: First Things First—Get to Know the Exam

You will get the most out of *Peterson's ACT® Prep Guide* by using this book as it is organized. You may feel compelled to skip Chapter 1 because you're anxious to get right to the lessons, since that's where the real preparation begins. However, Chapter 1 is very useful for giving you a picture of the exam's content as a whole. There is also important information in it about what you need to do to qualify to take the exam.

ALERT: If you skip Chapter 1, you may not realize that you neglected some important steps in registration or forgot to pay a particular testing fee. Chapter 1 will not prepare you to answer science or math questions, but it is as important as any other chapter in this book.

Step 2: The Diagnostic Test Is Your Friend—Don't Skip It!

Once you've learned all the essential information about the ACT in general, you will need to take the first step toward getting your scores where you want them to be by taking the diagnostic test. The diagnostic test is a full-length practice test that you should take before you start studying or reviewing any subject material.

Understandably, taking a long diagnostic test may not be your ideal way of getting started on your test preparation path. However, the point of a diagnostic test is to give you an idea of what your strengths and weaknesses are before you dive in to your ACT preparation. By taking the diagnostic test and analyzing your answers, you may discover that you retained more information from your English classes than you realized. You might also learn that you aren't quite the science expert you thought you were. Or maybe you'll find that most of your math skills are really strong, but you need some help when it comes to quadratic equations. Getting a clear idea of your strengths and weaknesses will help you to know which chapters of this book really demand your focus. The diagnostic test will help you get that clear idea.

Step 3: Build Your Skills—Practice, Practice, Practice!

After evaluating your diagnostic test results, you should know the skills on which you need to focus. By diligently studying the information presented, you will become familiar with not only the question types that will appear on the ACT, but also the language of the exam to help you be prepared for how the test will be worded.

TIP: Familiarizing yourself with the way particular questions are worded on the ACT exam may help you figure out the kind of question you are answering, which may help you select the best answer.

Practice With the Most Test-Like Questions Available

Sprinkled throughout each review chapter are practice questions related to the ACT-specific skill they assess—these questions will familiarize you with the language and presentation of the ACT exam.

Chapters 4–13 each end with a 20-question, multiple-choice quiz that tests your understanding of each skill assessed on the English, Mathematics, Science, and Reading portions of the ACT exam. Thorough explanations of why the given answer choices are correct and incorrect follow. **Don't skip over these explanations; understanding why an answer is right or wrong can stop you from repeating the same mistakes.** These explanations also function as mini-refresher courses, as they often repeat information you learned in the lessons that precede the practice tests.

Chapter 14, "Mastering the ACT® Writing Test," concludes with a set of practice essay prompts, each one followed by examples of both a poor and an excellent essay response.

Be sure to answer the questions scattered throughout the book as they appear. These questions test your understanding of the skills you just learned, and answering those questions reinforces concepts while the skills are still fresh in your mind. Similarly, taking the short quizzes at the end of each chapter will make the most of all the knowledge you gained while reading those chapters.

Step 4: See What You Have Learned—Test Yourself Again

At the end of the book, you will have the opportunity to take four complete ACT practice tests. With each practice test, you should see an improvement in your score since taking the diagnostic test. After all, you've now read all of the lessons and answered all the questions scattered throughout the book. However, you may still feel you can make improvements. So before taking the final full-length test, you might want to dive back into the book to review and study the skills you need to improve.

You should take these tests under the same circumstances you will encounter on test day. That means completing the English test in 45 minutes, the Math in 60 minutes, and so on. Official test times will be listed on the first page of every practice test. It also means using a calculator on the Math test if you so choose, but not using it on the Science test, which does not allow calculators. We'll talk more about test day rules in Chapter 1.

TIP: If you begin using this book to prepare for the ACT well in advance of test day, you might want to hold off on taking the final practice test until a few days before taking the actual ACT to refamiliarize yourself with its format and contents.

THE PETERSON'S SUITE OF ACT® PRODUCTS

Peterson's has an array of cutting-edge ACT preparation resources designed to give you the best test preparation possible. The following can be used alone or combined with other Peterson's ACT-focused products to help you succeed and achieve the scores you want. Take a few minutes to discover what's available in Peterson's suite of ACT products or visit our website at **www.petersons.com/testprep/act**.

Peterson's ACT® Prep Guide

Peterson's ACT® Prep Guide features content and strategies that will help you master the ACT. It contains a full-length diagnostic test and access to six full-length practice tests (four within the book and two accessible online). *Peterson's ACT® Prep Guide's* skill-specific drills and practice quizzes help familiarize you with the ACT's unique content, structure, and format. Test-taking tips and advice guide you smoothly from registration to test day.

Peterson's ACT® Prep Guide Online Companion

Peterson's ACT® Prep Guide Online Companion gives you access to more test-prep power! In addition to the two online tests included with your book purchase, the choice of how to take the diagnostic and practice tests in *Peterson's ACT Prep Guide* is yours. Take them on paper to simulate the actual ACT test-taking experience, or online for an interactive experience with automated timing and instant feedback and scoring results. Take all the tests on paper, all online, or in a combination of the two. You also will be able to improve your English Language Arts skills with full-length English and Reading College Readiness Benchmark Learning Path practice tests.

To access all your free online tests, go to **www.petersons.com/testprep/act** and select *Peterson's ACT Prep Guide Online Companion*. Enter the coupon code **ACT2019** at check out.

Peterson's ACT® Online Practice Tests

If you find you enjoy the online test-taking experience, you can extend your preparation sessions with *Peterson's ACT® Online Practice Tests for the ACT®*. This set of three full-length practice tests allows you to first diagnose your readiness for the exam and focus your studies on areas in which you need to improve your score. After studying, you can take the second practice test to measure how much you have improved. If further study is needed, a third practice test is provided to gauge your final readiness prior to taking the actual ACT test.

Peterson's ACT® Online Course

Peterson's Online Course for the ACT® is a comprehensive test-prep course that is customized for you. In addition to practice tests, the online course allows access to supplemental content, including additional subject-specific strategies and lessons, tips and college search options tailored to your projected test scores and interests.

Here's how the course works:

1) An initial diagnostic pretest determines your strengths and weaknesses.

2) Based on your diagnostic test results, interactive lessons teach you the subject areas you need to learn.

3) Quizzes after each lesson gauge how well you have learned the materials just taught.

4) Full-length practice tests allow you to apply all the skills you've learned and monitor your progress.

Peterson's Online Course for the ACT® provides short, medium, and full-length options to enable you to get the most out of the course—no matter how close it is to test day!

Give Us Your Feedback

Peterson's publishes a full line of books—test prep, career preparation, education exploration, and financial aid. Peterson's publications can be found at high school guidance offices, college libraries and career centers, and your local bookstore and library. Peterson's books are also available online at **www.petersons.com**.

We welcome any comments or suggestions you may have about this publication. Your feedback will help us make educational dreams possible for you—and others like you.

GOOD LUCK!

Now that you know why *Peterson's ACT® Prep Guide* is an essential resource to prepare you to take a very important test, it's time to make the most of this powerful preparation tool. Turn the page and find out everything you need to know about the ACT!

PART I: BASIC FACTS ABOUT THE ACT® EXAM

CHAPTER 1:
LEARN ABOUT THE ACT® EXAM

OVERVIEW

- An Overview of the ACT® Exam
- Scoring
- When to Take the ACT® Exam
- Registering for the ACT® Exam
- Getting Ready for Test Day
- Next Steps
- Summing It Up

AN OVERVIEW OF THE ACT® EXAM

Before you jump straight into the review sections and test practice in the chapters that follow, it's worth your time and attention to get to know some of the ACT fundamentals first. The truth is, the more you know about the exam and its different components, the more prepared you'll be on the big day, and the greater your advantage will be over the test takers who are less prepared and knowledgeable than you are.

First things first—why should you take the ACT exam so seriously? Along with your academic record, which includes your GPA, your record of extracurricular activities, and any awards, distinctions, and letters of recommendation written on your behalf, your scores on the ACT exam will be an important variable that college admissions staff will use to help determine whether or not you're a good fit for their school and are ready to handle college-level subject material.

So if college is in your long-range plans and the schools you're planning on applying to require the ACT, then it's certainly in your best interest to take the exam seriously.

Should you take the ACT exam?
Each college and university has a unique set of requirements to be considered for admission—know the rules of the schools to which you plan to apply so you can determine if you need to take the ACT exam.

Don't forget—overlooking a key part of your college admissions application like the ACT exam will not help you when decisions regarding acceptance are being made.

The ACT exam is designed to test your knowledge and abilities in the following core subjects, which you've studied throughout your academic career: **English**, **Mathematics**, **Reading**, **Science**, and **Writing**. Here's the official exam breakdown:

ACT® Exam Breakdown		
Test Section	**Number of Questions**	**Time to Complete**
English	75 multiple-choice questions	45 minutes
Mathematics	60 multiple-choice questions	60 minutes
Reading	40 multiple-choice questions	35 minutes
Science	40 multiple-choice questions	35 minutes
Writing*	1 essay	40 minutes

*This test section is optional; to help you decide if you should take this test, check the admissions requirements of the colleges to which you are planning to apply.

You'll see that nearly all the questions on the ACT exam are multiple-choice (except for the optional Writing exam essay). These are the kinds of questions where you'll be tasked with selecting the best available option from a set of possible choices.

The ACT exam (no writing) takes 3 hours and 30 minutes. The ACT with writing takes an additional 40 minutes. There is a break scheduled between the first two tests; if you choose to take the Writing test, you will have another break before this subject test begins.

In the sections and chapters that follow, we'll take a deeper dive into each subject test with helpful practice and review, along with effective test-taking strategies, all designed to help you earn your best possible score. The resources in this book are built around the specifications of the official test, to help you get comfortable with the structure, format, and timing of the exam.

NOTE: For additional information on the ACT exam, visit the official test website: **www.act.org**.

THE ENGLISH TEST

The ACT English Test consists of a set of five essays accompanied by 75 multiple-choice questions. The essays you'll encounter on the exam will span a variety of genres and rhetorical situations, each designed to test your language and writing skills. Each essay will contain underlined portions that are numbered and match up to a numbered set of questions that offer alternatives to how it is currently written. It is your job to determine if each underlined portion is correct as written or requires a revision to accomplish one of the following goals:

- Improve clarity or cohesion
- Promote consistency in author style or tone
- Correct an error in standard English grammar, usage, or mechanics

For each question, if there is an error or multiple errors, you'll select the best correction offered from among the available answer choices. If there are no errors, you'll select the choice that reads NO CHANGE.

You'll also encounter questions that target the following:

- Specific sections of the essay
- Ideas covered or based on the essay
- The structure and organization of the essay

These questions will typically ask you about the best way to think about, organize, or style a specific portion of each essay, or perhaps an entire essay. The relevant portion in each passage will be numbered and those numbers will refer to the corresponding questions that relate to those portions. The focus of these questions is to test your ability to analyze and comprehend a piece of writing, determine if the author was effective in achieving their goals, recognize the key effects of making text revisions, and to make determinations regarding potential improvements.

Your scores on the English test will include a total test score, which is based on how well you answer the entire set of 75 questions, as well as scores for three individual reporting categories, described below.

Conventions of Standard English (51–56% of English exam questions): These questions will test your ability to demonstrate your understanding and mastery of standard English grammar conventions, usage, and mechanics. You'll make determinations regarding revising, editing, and improving the essays presented in the following key areas:

- Punctuation
- Usage
- Sentence structure and formation

Production of Writing (29–32% of English exam questions): These questions will test your understanding and mastery regarding the focus and purpose of a given piece of writing, in the following key areas:

- **Organization, cohesion, and unity:** Does the text utilize a coherent and consistent structure and flow? Is there a logical organization, both among the various elements of the piece and as a whole (including an appropriate introduction, body, and conclusion)?
- **Topic development:** Are the rhetorical elements of the text sound? You'll be tasked with recognizing if the author has achieved their intended goal for the piece, analyzing the author's purpose for various parts of the text, and evaluating the relevance of the material presented within the larger text's focus.

Knowledge of Language (13–19% of English exam questions): These questions will test your understanding and mastery of appropriate language use, effective concision and precision regarding an author's word choice, and how well an author maintains a consistent tone and style within a given piece of writing.

The Mathematics Test

The Mathematics test on the ACT exam is a 60-minute test that consists of 60 multiple-choice questions that span the following five key math subcategories, which you'll have encountered during high school and are typically covered in entry-level college mathematics courses. Your scores on the Mathematics test will include a total test score, which is based on how well you answer the entire set of 60 questions, as well as scores for eight individual reporting categories:

Preparing for Higher Mathematics (57–60% of Math exam questions): These questions will include the following math subcategories:

- **Algebra (12–15% of Math exam questions):** Questions in this subcategory will ask you to use and interpret equations including polynomial, linear, radical, and exponential relationships; graph, model, and solve various types of expressions; solve systems of equations; and apply various results to real-world contexts.
- **Number and quantity (7–10% of Math exam questions):** Questions in this subcategory will test your understanding and knowledge of numerical quantities including expressions with integer and rational exponents; real and complex number systems; and vectors and matrices.
- **Geometry (12–15% of Math exam questions):** Questions in this subcategory will test your understanding of various solids and shapes; your ability to apply such concepts as surface area, congruence, similarity relationships, and volume measurement; your knowledge of composite objects; solving for missing values in circles, triangles, and other figures; trigonometric ratios; and equations of conic sections.
- **Functions (12–15% of Math exam questions):** Questions in this subcategory extend to the application, notation, definition, manipulation, translation, and representation of functions including linear, radical, polynomial, logarithmic, and piecewise functions. Your ability to interpret and utilize key features of graphs will also be tested.

- **Statistics and probability (8–12% of Math exam questions):** Questions in this subcategory will test your understanding of various data collection methods and center and spread of distributions; as well as your ability to model bivariate data relationships and to calculate probabilities that require you to recognize related sample spaces.

Integrating Essential Skills (40–43% of Math exam questions): Your ability to apply and synthesize your aggregate mathematical knowledge and skills to solve more complex problems will be tested here; you'll be tasked with addressing such concepts as:

- Proportional relationships
- Area, volume, and surface area
- Percentages and rates
- Average and median
- Expressing numbers
- Solving multi-step, nonroutine problems that require combining skills
- Applying skills in varied contexts
- Demonstrating fluency
- Understanding important mathematical connections

Modeling: Questions in this category span the other test sections and are designed to measure your ability to work with models and apply concepts of modeling across the math topics presented on the ACT exam. You will be asked to do the following:

- Evaluate models
- Understand models
- Produce models
- Interpret models
- Improve models

While you will have to know basic formulas and computations for the Math section, you will *not* be expected to remember more complex ones—they'll be provided for you along with the questions.

Although most of the questions on the ACT Math test will be self-contained, there will be some that may be part of a set of questions. Be sure to read each question and its associated instructions carefully to earn your best possible score.

TIP: Most of the questions on the ACT Mathematics test will be self-contained, but some may be part of a set of questions—so be sure to read each question and its associated instructions carefully to earn your best possible score.

Using a Calculator on the ACT® Math Test

You'll be permitted to use certain calculators on the Math test, though a calculator is not required and may not always be the best approach to solving a problem. Use your best judgment and the skills you've developed when tackling a math question in order to determine the best route to the correct answer. Review the ACT Calculator Policy at **www.act.org/content/dam/act/unsecured/documents/ACT-calculator-policy.pdf**.

The Reading Test

The Reading test of the ACT exam is a 35-minute test consisting of 40 multiple-choice questions that test your ability to read critically, integrate information from multiple text sources, and apply logical reasoning skills regarding the texts using evidence.

The texts you will encounter on exam day represent those typically encountered in a student's first-year college coursework and will span a variety of subject areas; of the four sections on the ACT Reading test, one will contain two short prose passages and three will include one longer prose passages each. For each passage, you'll be provided with key supporting information, including the type of passage it is, the author and source, and any other relevant supporting information required to help you answer the associated questions correctly.

Your scores on the Reading test will include a total test score, which is based on how well you answer the entire set of 40 questions, an Understanding Complex Texts indicator, and scores for three individual reporting categories:

1) **Key Ideas and Details (55–60% of exam questions):** Questions in this category are designed to measure your ability to do the following:

- Accurately summarize key information and ideas
- Draw logical inferences and conclusions
- Understand relationships (including sequential, comparative, and cause-effect relationships)
- Read texts critically
- Determine central themes and ideas

2) **Craft and Structure (25–30% of exam questions):** Questions in this category will assess your ability to do the following:

- Determine the meanings of words and phrases
- Analyze text structure
- Analyze an author's decisions regarding word choice
- Understand an author's perspective and purpose
- Analyze various points of view and perspectives
- Determine the effectiveness of an author's rhetorical decisions
- Differentiate and analyze sources of information

3) **Integration of Knowledge and Ideas (25–30% of exam questions):** Questions in this category will assess your ability to do the following:

- Differentiate between opinion and fact
- Make key connections between different yet related facts using evidence
- Understand author claims
- Analyze how authors construct their arguments
- Evaluate reasoning and evidence from a variety of sources

Make sure you *carefully* read each passage, its supporting documentation, and all instructions, as the questions on the ACT Reading test questions require you to think critically about the texts, determine meanings that are stated both explicitly and implicitly, recognize main ideas, and identify the meanings of words as they are used in context. You'll also have to locate and interpret significant details, understand the correct sequence of events, comprehend cause-effect relationships, analyze tone and mood, and draw generalizations.

The Science Test

The ACT Science test is a 35-minute test consisting of 40 multiple-choice questions. The test includes various authentic scientific scenarios and is designed to measure your ability to reason, evaluate, analyze, problem solve, and interpret key college-level scientific information. The science skills tested cover the following core topic areas: biology, chemistry, physics, and Earth/space science (meteorology, astronomy, geology, etc.).

The scientific information you'll encounter on test day will appear in three distinct formats:

1) **Data representation (30–40%):** These questions require you to read and interpret information on graphs, scatterplots, and tables.

2) **Research summary (45–55%):** These questions require you to read about experiments and draw conclusions about their designs and results.

3) **Conflicting viewpoints (15–20%):** These questions feature pairs of contrasting hypotheses about data or premises and require you to understand, analyze, compare, and contrast those viewpoints.

Your scores on the Science test will include a total test score, which is based on how well you answer the entire set of 40 questions, as well as scores for three individual reporting categories:

1) **Interpretation of Data (45–55%):** Questions in this category will assess your ability to do the following:
   - Recognize key trends when analyzing scientific data
   - Manipulate scientific data in diagram, graphical, and tabular forms
   - Apply reasoning skills to understanding scientific data and drawing conclusions

2) **Evaluation of Models, Inferences, and Experimental Results (25–35%):** Questions in this category will assess your ability to do the following:
   - Judge the validity of scientific information
   - Draw conclusions and make predictions based on scientific information
   - Determine the validity of explanations for scientific phenomena based on information provided

3) **Scientific Investigation (20–30%):** Questions in this category will assess your ability to do the following:
   - Analyze and understand experimental design, procedures, and tools
   - Identify variables and controls within a scientific experiment
   - Modify, compare, and extend experiments as needed, including predicting the results of additional experimental trials

ALERT: Calculators are not allowed on the Science test, and you will not be required to make any calculations on this test.

The Optional Writing Test

The optional Writing section of the ACT exam is a 40-minute test consisting of a single essay writing task. The test is designed to assess your current writing skills and abilities that are typically taught at the high school and college entry levels. The writing test is administered after the four mandatory multiple-choice sections

NOTE: Your score on the optional Writing test will not affect your composite score or your scores on the individual multiple-choice tests.

You'll receive an essay prompt that covers a specific complex issue, alongside three different perspectives on that particular issue. After reading the prompt and each perspective carefully, you'll compose an essay that evaluates the issue in the prompt and supports your distinct perspective on the issue, while also considering the other perspectives. Your perspective can build off one of the perspectives presented, or it can be a wholly unique perspective on the issue at hand.

Your scores on the Writing test will include four domain scores that are based on an analytic scoring rubric, and a subject-level writing score, ranging from 2–12, which is the rounded average of your four domain scores. The four domains on the ACT Writing test are as follows:

NOTE: Your opinions will *not* affect your score—only the quality of your ideas and writing will.

1) **Language Use and Conventions:** Your ability to communicate a clear and effective written argument will be tested here. This includes your ability to use the standard English-language conventions of word usage, grammar, syntax, and mechanics. Your ability to develop and deploy an appropriate, consistent, and compelling style and tone will also be assessed.
2) **Development and Support:** Your ability to develop cogent ideas, support your point of view, and offer clear reasoning will be measured here. This includes offering evidence, demonstrating clear and sound logic and reasoning, exploring ideas, illustrating through examples, and discussing potential impacts and implications, all designed to help the audience think fully about the issue provided.
3) **Organization:** Your ability to galvanize and deploy your thoughts and ideas in a cohesive, consistent, and effective manner will be assessed here. This includes your adherence to sound essay format and structure, as well as your ability to logically develop and present your thoughts on the issue provided in a clear and logical fashion, to maximum effect.
4) **Ideas and Analysis**: Your ability to effectively generate ideas on the topic provided and to engage critically and thoughtfully with multiple perspectives will be measured here. This includes your ability to understand the topic and its relevance and purpose, as well as the audience, and to generate and develop ideas accordingly.

Again, this is an optional exam section and not every college requires that you take it. You can find the Writing section requirements for your target college(s) on the official ACT website: **www.act.org**.

Your Target ACT Score and Test Goals

Don't forget that you're a unique individual with unique goals for the ACT exam. Do not feel pressured to compete with other students—determine what your goals are for the ACT and then work towards achieving them.

The best path to hitting your target score on the ACT exam is to fully understand and get comfortable with the structure, timing, and format of the test, and to make sure your skills on each test are razor sharp.

The most effective approach for ACT exam success is thorough practice and review with your individual strengths and weaknesses in mind. Make the most of the material presented in this book between now and test day to make your test goals a reality!

SCORING

Let's take a closer look at how the ACT exam is scored, and what it all means for you.

For each of the four multiple-choice tests—English, Mathematics, Reading, and Science—the number of questions you answered correctly are tabulated, which will be your **raw scores** for each test. Your raw scores are then converted into **scale scores**, to give you a test score for each subject test that ranges from 1 (low) to 36 (high). Your total score, also known as your **composite score**, is the average score of these four tests.

You'll also receive a score in each reporting category (covered previously), which will include the total number of questions in the category and the number of questions you answered correctly, as well as the percentage of questions in that category that you answered correctly.

ALERT: The ACT is a multiple-choice test (the optional Writing test is an essay writing task), which does *not* penalize you for selecting a wrong answer. However, a blank answer will be marked as incorrect. Therefore, it is important to answer *every* question on the test, even if you only guess. *Never* leave a question blank!

The optional Writing section is scored a bit differently. Two official essay readers will score your essay independently on a scale from 1 to 6 in each of the following four writing domains:

- Development and Support
- Ideas and Analysis
- Language Use and Conventions
- Organization

If you choose to take the ACT Writing test, you will receive a total of five scores—four domain scores, which will range from 2–12, and a subject-level writing score, which will also range from 2–12 and will be the rounded average of your four domain scores.

Viewing Your Scores

The official ACT test administrators prepare three types of score reports for students:

1) The **student report**, which includes your ACT scores and college and career planning information, is delivered to your online web account. Scores for the multiple-choice tests are generally available for online viewing approximately two weeks after your test date but can take up to eight weeks. If you've decided to take the optional Writing test, your scores (with writing score) will typically be released approximately two weeks after your multiple-choice scores.
2) The **high school report**, which is delivered to your high school, includes your ACT scores and college and career planning information. Scores for the multiple-choice tests are generally available for online viewing approximately two weeks after your test date but can take up to eight weeks. If you've decided to take the optional Writing test, your scores (with writing score) will typically be released approximately two weeks after your multiple-choice scores.
3) The **college report**, which is delivered to the colleges you selected prior to taking the ACT exam, includes your ACT scores and college and career planning information, as well as your reported high school course grades. Delivery varies based on the colleges you selected.

Please note: You may need to be patient when waiting for your scores. Just keep checking back once a week, since scores are posted on a weekly basis.

For a complete breakdown of scoring on the ACT exam and what it all means, visit **www.act.org/content/act/en/products-and-services/the-act/scores.html**.

NOTE: If you think you may have earned low scores on your exam, you can choose to cancel them. However, you will have to make the decision to cancel your scores by 12 p.m. (CT) the Thursday immediately after your Saturday test date without knowing your actual scores.

WHEN TO TAKE THE ACT® EXAM

In the Unites States, the ACT is given several times a year—in September, October, December, February, April, June, and July. Select the test date that works best for you and your specific goals.

NOTE: Starting in 2019, the ACT has added a February ACT test date for students in the state of New York. State students now have six opportunities to take the ACT exam.

No test centers are scheduled in New York or California for the July 2019 test date, so plan accordingly.

If you are preparing to take the ACT for the first time, try setting a goal for yourself after reading through this book and making your way through the practice quizzes, practice tests, and benchmark questions, which should give you an idea of how well you will do on the actual test. If you reach that goal the first time you take the ACT, you may not want to take it again, but it's good to have the option of a do over if you need it.

For a complete list of key dates, registration requirements and deadlines, options regarding special circumstances, and to sign up for test update alerts, go to **www.act.org/content/act/en/products-and-services/the-act/registration.html**.

REGISTERING FOR THE ACT® EXAM

Now that you have a better understanding of the structure, format, timing, and scoring of the ACT exam—and have determined that taking the ACT is right for you—the next important step is signing up for the exam.

Registering online for the ACT exam is the quickest method—go to **www.act.org/content/act/en/products-and-services/the-act/registration.html**, and follow the instructions to create an online account to get started and register. Once you have your ACT web account, you can make any necessary test changes and updates.

Registration will take approximately 40 minutes to complete, and here's what you'll need to have handy to finish the process:

- A valid credit card or other form of payment
- A computer with internet accessibility
- School codes (high school and colleges for sending your score reports to; a code lookup is available on the ACT website)
- A headshot photo, for test security purposes (see the official ACT website for photo file requirements and upload deadlines); please note that you'll also need to bring a valid photo ID with you on test day, along with your printed test ticket, which will contain your uploaded photo
- Information regarding any special accommodations, including English Learner (EL) supports
- Your decision regarding whether or not you're taking the optional Writing test
- Your parent's email address (an optional but helpful tool for communicating information regarding the ACT exam)

If you are under age 13 or cannot pay with a credit card, don't worry—you can request a Register-By-Mail packet by filling out a form online at **https://forms.act.org/student/stud_req.html?_ga=2.136527152.1295897193.1543097273-287684495.1541621411**.

You can also use the official ACT website to locate a convenient test center near you to take the exam, or to find out more information about arranged testing (if you're located at a significant distance from an ACT test center) and standby testing.

Registration Fees

The fee for taking the ACT exam without the optional Writing test is $50.50, which includes having your score report sent to you, your high school, and as many as four colleges of your choice. If you're taking the optional Writing test, the total fee is $67 (the extra $16.50 fee is refundable in the event you either cannot make it to test day or you decide to take the ACT without the Writing test before the test begins).

If you decide to have your score report sent to a fifth and sixth college, there is a $13 fee for each additional school (this must be requested online before your test date).

Other options and fees include:

- Standby testing: $53
- Late registration (available only in the United States and Canada): $30
- Changing the date of your test: $30
- Changing the location of your test: $30
- Requesting a copy of your test and answers (Test Information Release): $20
- Telephone registration fee: $15

You may be eligible for a **fee waiver** or a **state voucher** to help cover the cost of the exam. To find out if you're eligible, and for additional fee information, check out the official ACT website: **www.act.org/content/act/en/products-and-services/the-act/registration/fees.html**.

GETTING READY FOR TEST DAY

In addition to thoroughly preparing for each of the subject tests on the ACT exam, knowing the test day fundamentals and preparing for the big day—including selecting a test day and location, what to expect when you arrive at your test center, what to bring, and what to leave home—will help you avoid surprises, reduce anxiety, and stay ahead of the competition.

Getting ready for the ACT exam is essential, but getting ready for what you'll encounter on exam day is just as important to achieve success.

What to Expect, What to Bring, and What to Leave Home

Test time *always* begins at 8:00 a.m., and by this time you should be present and in your seat. Plan to arrive a little early, giving you time to relax, get comfortable, and get settled into test-taking mode; you *definitely* don't want to have to deal with the stress of racing the clock to avoid missing the start of the test, and you will *not* be admitted to take the test if you arrive late. Consider making a practice run to the test center in advance of test day, so you'll know just how long you'll need on the big morning.

When you arrive at your test center, the staff will check your photo ID and ticket, admit you into the room, bring you to your seat, and provide you with the required test materials.

ALERT: All students need to be present at their test centers no later than 8:00 a.m. Individuals taking the ACT exam without the Writing test are generally dismissed at 12:35 p.m. Those taking the optional Writing test are generally dismissed at 1:35 p.m.

Your Test Day Checklist

Make absolutely certain that you bring the following items with you on test day:

- A printed copy of your test admission ticket
- Acceptable photo ID (visit the official ACT website for what constitutes acceptable ID)
- Sharpened No. 2 pencils with erasers

Consider bringing the following optional items to help maximize your test-taking experience:

- A permissible calculator for the Mathematics test (review the official ACT Calculator Policy at **www.act.org/content/dam/act/unsecured/documents/ACT-calculator-policy.pdf**)
- A watch (without an alarm) to help you pace yourself through each test section
- Comfortable clothing that will allow you to adapt to the test center temperature—whatever it may be
- Snacks, which can be consumed only outside of the test room during the break

Do not bring the following items with you to the test room, or keep them completely silent and out of sight while taking the exam—you will absolutely not be able to use them:

- The following electronic devices: smartphone, cell phone, mobile digital device (e.g., iPad® or tablet), camera, headphones, smart watches, and fitness bands
- Reading material, textbooks, reference materials (including dictionaries and other study aids), scratch paper, and any other outside notes
- Highlighters, colored pens and pencils, or correction tape/fluid
- Tobacco
- Outside reading material

An Additional ACT® Test?
The makers of the ACT like to test out their questions when developing future versions of the test. You should expect to be tasked with taking an additional shorter, multiple-choice test following your standard scored test in one of the four subject areas, to help shape future tests. This additional test will not count towards your score.

NEXT STEPS

Okay—so now you have a better understanding of the ACT fundamentals, including the structure, format, and timing of the exam, how it's all scored, what you need to do to register, and what you should expect on the day of the exam—this is powerful information that will help set you up for test-day success!

Now it's time to move on to building your ACT study plan and making the most of the time you have between now and test day to study, practice, and review each test section as you work towards achieving you best possible scores. And remember—we'll be with you every step of the way. Let's keep going!

SUMMING IT UP

- **The ACT consists of four multiple-choice tests on English, Mathematics, Reading, and Science with a total of 215 questions.** You will have 3 hours and 30 minutes to complete the tests. There is also an optional Writing test that takes an additional 40 minutes to complete. Some colleges do not require the Writing test.
- **The English test** consists of a set of 5 essays accompanied by 75 multiple-choice questions that test your skills in conventions of standard English, production of writing, and knowledge of language. Questions focus on testing your ability to do the following:
  - Analyze and comprehend a piece of writing
  - Determine if the author was effective in achieving their goals
  - Recognize the key effects of making text revisions
  - Make determinations regarding potential improvements
- **The Mathematics test** consists of 60 multiple-choice questions that test your knowledge of higher mathematics (algebra, number and quantity, geometry, functions, and statistics and probability), integrating essential skills (solving complex problems with mathematical knowledge), and modeling.
- **The Reading test** consists of 40 multiple-choice questions that test your ability to read critically, integrate information from multiple text sources, and apply logical reasoning skills regarding the texts using evidence.
- **The Science test** consists of 40 questions assessing your reasoning and problem-solving skills and your ability to interpret, analyze, and evaluate data representation, research summaries, and conflicting viewpoints. These questions are derived from information taught in the natural sciences: biology, chemistry, physics, and Earth/space science (meteorology, astronomy, geology, etc.)
- **The optional Writing test** consists of an essay that requires you to evaluate three perspectives on an issue, create your own perspective on that issue, and explain how your perspective relates to the ones provided. There are no multiple-choice questions. Scoring is based on the following:
  - Language use and conventions
  - Development and support
  - Organization
  - Ideas and analysis
- **When to take the ACT exam:** The ACT is given several times a year—in September, October, December, February, April, June, and July. Select the test date that works best for you.
- **Register for the test online at www.act.org/content/act/en/products-and-services/the-act/registration.html.** During registration, you will choose where and when you will take the test. You will also receive a registration ticket that you MUST bring with you on test day. Registration fees apply.

- **Scoring:** Your scores on the ACT exam will be an important variable that college admissions staff will use to help determine whether or not you're a good fit for their school and are ready to handle college-level subject material.
    - For each of the four multiple-choice tests—English, Mathematics, Reading, and Science—the number of questions you answered correctly are tabulated, which will be your **raw scores** for each test.
    - Your raw scores are then converted into **scale scores**, to give you a test score for each subject test that ranges from 1 (low) to 36 (high).
    - Your total score, also known as your **composite score**, is the average score of these four tests. **The maximum score you can get on the ACT is 36.**
    - **The maximum score you can get on the Writing test is 12**, and that score is determined from the average of the four domain scores awarded by two essay readers.
- **Scores are posted online for you to view within two to eight weeks after the test date.** Reports for the multiple-choice scores are released and mailed within three to eight weeks after the test dates. If you take the Writing test, your score reports will be released approximately two weeks after the multiple-choice scores.

CHAPTER 2: TEST-TAKING STRATEGIES FOR THE ACT® EXAM

OVERVIEW

- Core Study Strategies
- Building Your ACT® Exam Study Plan
- Test-taking Strategies
- Summing It Up

We know why you're reading this book—you're committed to getting your best possible score on the ACT exam and are looking for some effective strategies to build a practical and realistic study plan and prepare for test day. After all, you know how important this exam is, and you're determined to take it seriously.

Smart move!

We also take preparing for the ACT exam very seriously—and our team of test experts has designed this chapter to highlight some proven approaches to preparing for test-day success. As you go through this chapter, keep your unique learning style, schedule, and goals in mind as you develop your personal ACT test-prep strategy—and don't forget that we'll be with you every step of the way!

It's also important to remember that your ACT prep plan should be *flexible*, which means the following:

1) As you prepare for the test, you'll discover that some strategies or techniques work better for you than others; your study plan should remain flexible enough to allow you to adjust to changes that will better help you prepare. Here's an example:

   You organized your weekly study schedule to include a dedicated hour of test prep every weekday morning, but as time progresses you discover that you're actually more focused and productive at night. Make sure you adjust your schedule accordingly rather than sticking blindly to the less effective original plan.

2) As you study and practice for the ACT exam, your strengths and weaknesses will change over time, and your study plan should evolve. Here's another example:

   When you first started preparing, you were really strong in math but were struggling with science. After some extra intensive science practice and review, your science skills got stronger, but you noticed some weaknesses in your English abilities. If this happens, reconsider how much time you're devoting to preparing for the English and science subtests so that you're always giving sufficient attention to your weak areas.

The bottom line is that you need to be smart, dedicated, and flexible as you develop and implement your ACT study plan, in order to maximize the time you have between now and test day. If you're starting to feel anxious or overwhelmed, you *shouldn't*—the great news is that you're already making smart decisions by choosing to use this book to help you prepare. This chapter, and the practice and review chapters throughout this book, are your tools for achieving test-day success. Use them wisely as you develop and implement your ACT study plan and work towards achieving your test goals!

CORE STUDY STRATEGIES

The ACT may not be like any other test you've encountered before—it's a long, high-stakes exam made up of different subject areas, some of which you're likely stronger in than others, so your best bet for preparing for test day is to devise a study plan that incorporates the following:

- Your subject-specific strengths and weaknesses
- The study skills that have proven to work for you thus far in your academic career
- The strategies and tools in this book that are specifically tailored for this unique test
- Your ACT goals, backed by the confidence from knowing that we'll be guiding you through every step of your test prep journey!

First things first—if you're going to prepare effectively for the ACT exam, you have to have a study environment conducive for doing so.

CREATING THE PERFECT STUDY ENVIRONMENT

How and *where* you prep for the ACT matters. Your first step in building a study plan is to set the perfect study conditions that will help keep you focused and motivated. This is largely dictated by what has worked for you in the past, but your current life and schedule will also factor into the equation: busy students who are always on the go may have fewer options for when and where they can study, and students who have plenty of time between now and test day and can set aside several hours a day to prep may have more leeway.

That said, when you're designing your perfect study environment, keep the following suggestions in mind.

Keep distractions to a minimum

Your study space should be free of anything that will distract you from the task at hand—preparing for the ACT. This means that cell phones, tablets, TVs, and other brain drains or items that make it difficult to focus should be kept elsewhere.

Get comfortable—but not too comfortable

Your study space should be comfortable, so you can relax and focus on practice and review without fidgeting, but it shouldn't be so comfortable that you find yourself napping whenever you sit down to study. A good chair and uncluttered desk is often a better choice than lying down in bed.

Find a location that works for you

Do you prepare better alone in your bedroom or in a bustling coffee shop or library? This choice is totally up to you and should be based on what has worked for you in the past.

Adjust your background noise and lighting

Do you tend to work better in total quiet, or do you find it helpful to have some relaxing music playing in the background? Make sure your study space has the perfect level of sound that will help you stay focused and alert.

Then, make sure your study environment contains the right level of light to keep you engaged. Many people find natural light is ideal; if you agree, then try to set up a study space near a window or select an outdoor environment if feasible. If a desk lamp or overhead lighting works best for you, then make sure your study space is suitably equipped. If dimmer lighting works best, then great—just be sure not to study in a dark place that will only serve to put you to sleep!

Decide if you'd rather prep alone or in a group

There are potential benefits and drawbacks to both studying alone and in a group.

- Studying alone may help you stay focused, but if you're struggling in a certain area, then working with others whose strengths and weaknesses complement each other may be a great way to help you improve.
- Studying in a group may be distracting for you, but it can also help keep you more motivated and engaged than studying alone.

Again, use what works for you; trial and error might be a useful approach here.

Find your ideal time of day

The time of day during which you study best is an important part of your study environment. Do you work best first thing in the morning, or are you a nighttime study owl? If possible, schedule your study sessions at the time of day that matches what naturally works best for you.

Fuel up

Are you at optimum levels of study power when you have some coffee and a full stomach? Or does food only make you sleepy? Make sure to approach each study session well-rested, energized, and with the appropriate levels of fuel. Keep in mind that nutritious foods tend to keep your energy levels higher for longer, but things like sugary snacks, sodas, and caffeine tend to create spikes in energy levels that will eventually send you crashing back down.

Gather your tools

Just as important as the things you don't keep around while you study and prepare are the tools you do keep around—like this book! Make sure you have all of your most effective study tools at hand in your work space, including paper and pens/pencils, a calculator, a highlighter, and a watch or clock if you're taking a timed practice test. The last thing you want to do every time you sit down to study is waste time searching for your study tools. Also, keeping organized will help you stay focused, serious, and motivated.

Pay attention to your mental environment

Just as important as having the perfect physical environment to study in is having the right mindset during each study session. Try to leave external worries, stress, or anxieties, which will only drain your energy and focus, outside of your ACT prep. A great way to do this is to take a few minutes before each study session to relax, breathe, and clear your mind and thoughts. Yoga and meditation are great tools for this and are highly recommended. Sometimes just a minute or two is enough and can make a big difference. When your mind is clear and free from distractions, you'll be much more likely to devote yourself to effective ACT test preparation.

BUILDING YOUR ACT® EXAM STUDY PLAN

Now that you have the perfect mental and physical study environments to prepare for the ACT exam, the next step is to build an effective study plan to make the most of your time between now and test day. As you develop your initial study plan, there are two primary factors to consider.

Your Strengths and Weaknesses

Before you develop your study plan, you should have a good idea of your strengths and weaknesses in each subject tested on the ACT exam. This information can come from the following areas:

1) **Your academic history**—Have you always done well in math and science but struggled in English and reading? Perhaps the opposite is true. Your track record in school will help you determine the subjects that you'll need to devote more study time to.
2) **Your results on the diagnostic test**—This book comes equipped with a handy diagnostic test, which will help you figure out which areas you're strong in and which need work. Make sure you take the test under timed, test-like conditions and use your results to help structure your test preparation.

College Readiness Benchmark Exercises

The official makers of the ACT exam recognize the importance of getting ready for success in college—and have created a serles of ACT assessment score benchmarks that demonstrate a high school student's likely readiness for success in credit-bearing two-year and four-year college coursework.

The college-level courses identified by the makers of the ACT that have been designated as key indicators of probable success in college are English composition, college algebra, biology, and social science.

Why have they targeted these course subjects? They're among the most commonly taken credit-bearing courses by first-year college students, and available data indicates that they're highly correlated with academic success.

The following table indicates the ACT exam benchmark scores in each of the designated course areas:

ACT Subject Test	College Course Subject	ACT College Readiness Benchmark Score
Mathematics	College Algebra	22
Science	Biology	23
English	English Composition	18
Reading	Social Sciences	22

What do these scores indicate? ACT, Inc. has analyzed available benchmark and testing data, along with patterns and data regarding student academic coursework performance and has determined that if a student meets an indicated benchmark score, she or he has approximately a 50 percent chance of earning a grade of B or better in the college course it corresponds to and around a 75 percent chance of earning a grade of C or better.

ACT makes its testing and benchmark data available to academic institutions, who can utilize the information in a variety of ways—including admissions and course placement decision making, as well as for evaluating student progress and making determinations regarding appropriate intervention.

Sharpen Your Skills with Our College Readiness Benchmark Learning Path

We've recognized a critical need to prepare students for success in both the ACT Math and Science tests, and to help set them up for success in their coursework upon entering college. These subjects are critical for both academic and professional goal achievement—which is why you'll notice that this book includes helpful science and math College Readiness Benchmark Learning Path exercises at the end of each math and science review chapter. We're also now offering College Readiness Benchmark practice via full-length online Reading and English tests. You can opt to take the College Readiness Benchmark Learning Path for any subject in this book where you need targeted review and practice.

These exercises are designed to provide extra test practice and to help you assess your strengths and weaknesses along the way, which will help keep your ACT study plan on target between now and the big day. Every question will include a thorough, step-by-step breakdown and answer explanation to guide you through the logic and reasoning required to reach the correct solution. Make sure you take full advantage of these benchmark exercises and include them in your study plan schedule to set yourself up for test-day success. In the pages that follow, we'll give you advice on the best way to incorporate the College Readiness Benchmark Learning Path into the time leading up to your ACT exam.

Your Time and Life

As you structure your ACT study plan and think about all the things going on in your life between now and test day, it might be helpful to place things in two categories: essential and nonessential.

- **Essential** things are those you cannot put off until after the ACT exam.
- **Nonessential** things are those that can feasibly be put on hold until after test day.

If you can delay worrying about nonessential things until after you take the ACT, you can potentially help open up some valuable study time in your schedule!

Notice that we referred earlier to your initial study plan—don't forget that your study plan should be flexible and evolve over time, as your skills develop and available time changes (because life happens!).

The following sample study plans can help you construct an effective plan of attack for the ACT.

TIP: Although preparing for the ACT is important, staying on top of your schoolwork is just as high a priority. A responsible ACT study plan makes time for schoolwork and all the other important things you have going on in your life.

The Balanced Study Plan

Are your skills on each subject covered on the ACT—math, English, reading, science, and writing—pretty well balanced? Or maybe you just want to divide the time you've committed to test prep equally among subjects, to ensure that you're covered across the board for test day. The balanced study plan approach is designed to split the time you have between now and test day evenly across all the test sections, so you'll get equal prep and review time for the entire ACT exam.

Follow these steps to develop your own personal balanced study plan:

Step 1: Break down each calendar week you have between now and test day in a chart—here's an example:

Week 1						
Monday	**Tuesday**	**Wednesday**	**Thursday**	**Friday**	**Saturday**	**Sunday**

Step 2: Consider devoting one day each week to practicing and reviewing a specific test subject, and fill in your weekly calendar as follows:

Week 1						
Monday	**Tuesday**	**Wednesday**	**Thursday**	**Friday**	**Saturday**	**Sunday**
Math	General test info	English		English	Writing	Science

You'll notice a couple of things about the calendar above.

First off, there's an empty day (Thursday). Depending on your study needs and goals, and how much time you have between now and test day, you may want to give yourself one day to rest—but that's totally up to you. If you want, you can make this a "test drill" day and give yourself the chance to practice taking the ACT under timed and test-like conditions.

The sample assumes that you're taking the optional writing test; If you're not planning on taking it, you can revise your schedule to four days of prep per week, or use the additional day for test drills.

You'll notice a day for "general test info"—for the first week, devote time to reading Chapter 1 *thoroughly*, to learn what you need to know about the ACT, including registration, scoring, what to expect on test day, and getting comfortable with the general format of each test section. Once you have this down cold, you can remove it from your weekly schedule and use that extra day for Benchmark Practice if you find you need it (see later in the chapter for information on this) or for another day off.

Step 3: Consider refining your calendar even further—breaking down your schedule into subject review and question practice. Here's an example for the first two weeks:

Week 1						
Monday	**Tuesday**	**Wednesday**	**Thursday**	**Friday**	**Saturday**	**Sunday**
Math (subject review)	General test info	English (subject review)		Reading (subject review)	Writing (subject review)	Science (subject review)

Week 2						
Monday	**Tuesday**	**Wednesday**	**Thursday**	**Friday**	**Saturday**	**Sunday**
Math (question practice)		English (question practice)	Test Drill	Reading (question practice)	Writing (question practice)	Science (question practice)

Here's another option: You can break down your schedule even further, dividing the time you have each day to a mix of subject review and question. Let's take a look at another sample:

Week 1						
Monday	**Tuesday**	**Wednesday**	**Thursday**	**Friday**	**Saturday**	**Sunday**
Math (2 hours)	General test info (1 hour)	English (1.5 hours)		Reading (2 hours)	Writing (1 hour)	Science (1.5 hours)
Subject review: 1 hour **Question practice (or Benchmark exercises):** 1 hour		**Subject review:** 30 minutes **Question practice:** 1 hour		**Subject review:** 1 hour **Question practice:** 1 hour	**Essay writing practice:** 1 hour	**Subject review:** 1 hour **Question practice (or Benchmark exercises):** 30 minutes

The bottom line when using this study plan approach—or any study plan you decide to use—is to tailor it and make it work for you and your specific needs. Creating a study plan that isn't helpful or realistic is just a waste of your time. You have options—so make the most of them!

The College Readiness Benchmark Learning Path

Are you looking to devote your study time between now and test day to building your skills in the areas where you most need to? If so, then consider adopting a study plan that takes your specific strengths and weaknesses into consideration when allocating your prep time.

You can take our College Readiness Benchmark Learning Path for all exam topics, or just for the ones where you need that extra boost of review and practice in order to really understand the topic and how it's presented on the ACT exam.

Here is a great approach to determine if you should take this path.

Start by ranking your perceived abilities in the subjects tested on the ACT exam. You can use your academic performance in school to help guide your ranking, or you can take the diagnostic test in this book to help diagnose your strengths and weaknesses—or feel free to use both. Rank the following from 1 (your strongest subject) to 5 (your weakest subject):

Mathematics: ______

Reading: ______

English: ______

Science: ______

***Writing (Optional):** ______

**If you're not taking the optional Writing test, you can devote the extra 10% of your time to your weakest test area.*

Let's assume, for this example, that your rankings are as follows:

Mathematics: 5

Reading: 2

English: 3

Science: 4

***Writing (Optional):** 1

Next, determine the number of hours you have each week to devote for test prep. For example, let's assume you have 15 hours available for test prep this week. Use the following scale to break down the number of hours you should devote to each section:

30% of your time for the section you ranked 5 (Math): 30% of 15 hours is 4.5 hours

25% of your time for the section you ranked 4 (Science): 25% of 15 hours is 3.75 hours

20% of your time for the section you ranked 3 (English): 20% of 15 hours is 3 hours

15% of your time for the section you ranked 2 (Reading): 15% of 15 hours is 2.25 hours

10% of your time for the section you ranked 1 (Writing): 10% of 15 hours is 1.5 hours

Okay, so now you know just how many hours you have this week to devote to each subject. For the topics where you have more time to devote to study, you will add in College Readiness Benchmark Learning Path review as part of your plan.

Let's look at how to fill up your weekly calendar. Decide how you want to divide your time for each section between chapter review, College Readiness Benchmark Learning Path review, and end-of-chapter question practice. Is your math knowledge strong but your test-taking skills shaky and you need more question practice? Is the reverse true? Use this information to structure your study time.

You can spread your time across your schedule in any way that works for you.

Here's a sample of Week 1 of a College Readiness Benchmark Learning Path plan if you need some extra help with your math skills.

Week 1						
Monday	**Tuesday**	**Wednesday**	**Thursday**	**Friday**	**Saturday**	**Sunday**
Math (2 hours)	General test info (1 hour)	English (1.5 hours)		Reading and Math (3 hours)	Writing (1.5 hours)	Science (2 hours)
Subject review: Chapter 6 (1 hour to review 3 topics) **Benchmark exercises**: Chapter 6 (1 hour to review 3 topics)		**Subject review**: 1 hour **Question practice**: 30 minutes		**Reading subject review**: 30 minutes **Reading question practice**: 30 minutes **Math subject review**: Chapter 6 (1 hour to review 3 topics) **Benchmark exercises**: Chapter 6 (1 hour to review 3 topics)	**Essay writing practice:** 1.5 hours	**Subject review**: 1 hour **Question practice**: 1 hour

Then, here's how Week 2 of a Benchmark Learning Path plan might look if you need some extra help with your math skills.

Week 2						
Monday	**Tuesday**	**Wednesday**	**Thursday**	**Friday**	**Saturday**	**Sunday**
Math (2 hours)	Math (2 hours)	English (1.5 hours)		Reading and Math (3 hours)	Math (2 hours)	Science (2 hours)
Subject review: Chapter 6 (1 hour to review 3 topics) **Benchmark exercises**: Chapter 6 (1 hour to review 3 topics)	**Subject review**: Chapter 6 (1 hour to review 3 topics) **Benchmark exercises**: Chapter 6 (1 hour to review 3 topics)	**Subject review**: 1 hour **Question practice**: 30 minutes		**Reading subject review**: 30 minutes **Reading question practice**: 30 minutes **Math subject review**: Chapter 6 (1 hour to review 3 topics) **Benchmark exercises**: Chapter 6 (1 hour to review 3 topics)	**Subject review**: Chapter 6 (1 hour to review 3 topics) **Benchmark exercises**: Chapter 6 (1 hour to review 3 topics)	**Subject review**: 1 hour **Question practice**: 1 hour

If it's science giving you the most trouble, you can dedicate the majority of your time to science Benchmark exercises instead of math—the same with reading or English.

You might need to take the Benchmark Path for all topics. If that's the case, here's what a weekly study plan might look like.

Week 1						
Monday	**Tuesday**	**Wednesday**	**Thursday**	**Friday**	**Saturday**	**Sunday**
Math (2 hours)	General test info (1 hour)	English (2.5 hours)		Reading and Math (2.5 hours)	Writing (1.5 hours)	Science (2 hours)
Subject review: Chapter 6 (1 hour to review 3 topics) **Benchmark exercises:** Chapter 6 (1 hour for 3 topics)		**Subject review:** 1 hour **Benchmark online exercises:** 1.5 hours		**Subject review:** 1 hour **Benchmark online exercises:** 1.5 hours	**Essay writing practice:** 1.5 hours	**Subject review:** 1 hour **Benchmark exercises:** 1 hour for one passage + question set

In the weeks that follow, you would replace the general test info review on Tuesday with the subject of your choice: chapter review + Benchmark exercises.

You might not even know yet where you're struggling, and that's okay! As you make your way through the review chapters of the book, you will see where you need more prep. Throughout, we'll remind you of how to take this College Readiness Benchmark Learning Path and direct you to the appropriate place, whether it be at the end of the chapter for math and science or online for English and reading.

Be sure to revisit your strengths and weaknesses on a weekly basis, and adjust your rankings as needed. Your skill levels will likely shift as you study and practice, and your weekly study plan should follow suit so that you're always spending enough time working on building your weakest areas.

Time-Based Study Plans: For General Prep and a Benchmark Learning Path

Does your brain work best by having a time-based study plan that includes an overview of what you need to accomplish each week? If that sounds like you, then consider using a time-based study plan, which allocates the review chapters in this book and the practice questions for each subject area across your weekly schedule between now and test day.

To build a time-based study plan, first determine how long you have until the big day arrives, and keep your schedule updated with all of the essential and nonessential things you have going on in your life between now and then. As time goes on, feel free to add and/or subtract things to or from your schedule as needed, or reshuffle your daily plans—just remember to always make time to achieve your test-prep goals for the week!

Keep in mind that the breakdown of material in this book that we suggest each week is just that—suggestions. Build your schedule in a way that works best for you and takes your unique needs and goals into account. We created the following plans with the student who needs to tackle all the test sections in mind, but if you find you have already mastered the math covered on the ACT, for example, feel free to review just the math practice questions instead of making your way through the entire chapters. Instead, spend your time on English, reading, science, and writing. Also remember to keep things flexible and continue to update and modify your schedule based on your needs and life!

Four-Month Plan

The following four-month study plan structures each week with ACT preparation and also includes sample essential and nonessential responsibilities to reflect the sort of obligations that might arise in an average test taker's life. One approach to consider is to de-prioritize or postpone some of the nonessential things you have going on to make time for ACT prep and other essential life responsibilities.

Feel free to structure your study plan with the amount of detail that works best for you—some people appreciate seeing every detail of their lives laid out on a very structured daily calendar, while others get overwhelmed by this approach and don't write everything down. Also, note that this study plan focuses on the essential tests on the ACT—if you've decided to take the optional ACT Writing test, then feel free to incorporate review and practice into your study plan as you see fit.

Once again, your primary guiding principle should be to do what works best for you.

Month 1	
Week 1	**ACT Prep**: • Review Chapter 1 "Learn About the ACT Exam" to get familiar with the test. • Take the Diagnostic Test" (Chapter 3) to diagnose your strengths and weaknesses. • Assess whether you want to take the College Readiness Benchmark Learning Path for any test topic at this point. **Essentials**: • Swim team practice • Walk dog • Take out garbage **Nonessentials**: • Guitar lessons • Dinner with friends
Week 2	**ACT Prep**: • Review Part IV: Mathematics Strategies (Chapters 6, 7, and 8). • Note where you're having trouble. Do you need any Benchmark practice before you move on to the end-of-chapter practice questions? **Essentials**: • Debate team • Walk dog • Clean room **Nonessentials**: • Work on bicycle repair project
Week 3	**ACT Prep**: • Complete the ACT Math practice questions in the review chapters. • Note your math strengths and weaknesses in key topic areas. **Essentials**: • Swim team practice • Walk dog • Take out garbage **Nonessentials**: • Jog with mom

Week 3 ***College Readiness Benchmark Learning Path***	**ACT Prep**: • Benchmark Learning Path: Focus on the Mathematics Benchmark exercises at the end of each chapter before moving on to end-of-chapter questions. • Reread chapter reviews in areas where you need more study. **Essentials**: • Swim team practice • Walk dog • Take out garbage **Nonessentials**: • Jog with mom
Week 4	**ACT Prep**: • Review weak math areas in review chapters. • If you have time and need more practice, review the Benchmark Exercises at the end of every chapter. **Essentials**: • Chess club • Walk dog • Clean room **Nonessentials**: • Help dad wash car
Week 4 ***College Readiness Benchmark Learning Path***	**ACT Prep**: • Complete Math practice questions in review chapters. • Note your math strengths and weaknesses in key topic areas. • Review weak math areas in review chapters. **Essentials**: • Chess club • Walk dog • Clean room **Nonessentials**: • Help dad wash car
Month 2	
Week 5	**ACT Prep**: • Review Part V: Reading Strategies (Chapters 9 and 10). • Note where you're having trouble. Do you need any Benchmark practice before you move on to the end-of-chapter practice questions? **Essentials**: • Swim team practice • Walk dog • Take out garbage **Nonessentials**: • Dinner with friends

Week 6	**ACT Prep**: • Complete Reading practice questions in review chapters. • Note your reading strengths and weaknesses in key topic areas. • Review weak reading areas in review chapters. **Essentials**: • Swim team practice • Walk dog • Take out garbage **Nonessentials**: • Help James fix his computer
Week 6 College Readiness Benchmark Learning Path	**ACT Prep**: • Take the online Reading Benchmark practice exam. • Review weak reading areas in review chapters. • Complete Reading practice questions in review chapters. **Essentials**: • Swim team practice • Walk dog • Take out garbage **Nonessentials**: • Help James fix his computer
Week 7	**ACT Prep**: • Review Part III: English Strategies (Chapters 4 and 5). • Note where you're having trouble. Do you need any Benchmark practice before you move on to the end-of-chapter practice questions? **Essentials**: • Debate team • Walk dog • Clean room **Nonessentials**: • Concert downtown
Week 8	**ACT Prep**: • Complete English practice questions in review chapters. • Note your English strengths and weaknesses in key topic areas. • Review weak English areas in review chapters. **Essentials**: • Swim team practice • Walk dog • Take out garbage **Nonessentials**: • Plan graduation trip with friends

<table>
<tr><td>Week 8
College Readiness
Benchmark
Learning Path</td><td>ACT Prep:
• Take the online English Benchmark practice exam.
• Review weak English areas in review chapters.
• Complete English practice questions in review chapters.

Essentials:
• Swim team practice
• Walk dog
• Take out garbage

Nonessentials:
• Plan graduation trip with friends</td></tr>
<tr><td colspan="2" align="center">Month 3</td></tr>
<tr><td>Week 9</td><td>ACT Prep:
• Review Part VI: Science Strategies (Chapters 11, 12, and 13).
• Note where you're having trouble. Do you need any Benchmark practice before you move on to the end-of-chapter practice questions?

Essentials:
• Chess club
• Walk dog
• Wash dishes and clean basement

Nonessentials:
• Dinner with friends</td></tr>
<tr><td>Week 10</td><td>ACT Prep:
• Complete Science practice questions in review chapters.
• Note your science strengths and weaknesses in key topic areas.

Essentials:
• Debate team
• Walk dog
• Clean room

Nonessentials:
• Jog with mom</td></tr>
<tr><td>Week 10
College Readiness
Benchmark
Learning Path</td><td>ACT Prep:
• Benchmark Learning Path: Focus on Science Benchmark exercises at the end of each chapter before you move on to end-of-chapter questions.
• Reread chapter reviews in areas where you need more study.

Essentials:
• Debate team
• Walk dog
• Clean room

Nonessentials:
• Jog with mom</td></tr>
</table>

Week 11	**ACT Prep**: • Review weak science areas in review chapters. • If you have time and need more practice, you can review the Benchmark Exercises at the end of every chapter. **Essentials:** • Swim team practice • Walk dog • Take out garbage **Nonessentials:** • Buy new sneakers
Week 11 College Readiness Benchmark Learning Path	**ACT Prep**: • Complete Science practice questions in review chapters. • Note your math strengths and weaknesses in key topic areas. • Review weak math areas in review chapters. **Essentials:** • Swim team practice • Walk dog • Take out garbage **Nonessentials:** • Buy new sneakers
Week 12	**ACT Prep**: • Complete Practice Test 1 (Chapter 15). • Score your test and note your strong and weak areas (Chapter 16). • Spend time focusing on reviewing weak test areas in review chapters. **Essentials:** • Chess club • Walk dog • Wash dishes and clean basement **Nonessentials:** • Help Sharon with book report
Month 4	
Week 13	**ACT Prep**: • Complete Practice Test 2 (Chapter 15). • Score your test and note your strong and weak areas (Chapter 16). • Spend time focusing on reviewing weak test areas in review chapters. **Essentials:** • Debate team • Walk dog • Clean room **Nonessentials:** • Gym with Derek

Week 14	**ACT Prep**: • Complete Practice Test 3 (Chapter 15). • Score your test and note your strong and weak areas (Chapter 16). • Spend time focusing on reviewing weak test areas in review chapters. **Essentials**: • Swim team practice • Walk dog • Take out garbage **Nonessentials**: • Visit Uncle Jerome
Week 15	**ACT Prep**: • Complete Practice Test 4 (Chapter 15). • Score your test and note your strong and weak areas (Chapter 16). • Spend time focusing on reviewing weak test areas in review chapters. **Essentials**: • Chess club • Walk dog • Wash dishes and clean basement **Nonessentials**: • Movies with Robin
Week 16	**ACT Prep**: • Final week before the exam! Focus on reviewing your remaining weak areas and getting comfortable with the format and timing of the test. Make sure to get plenty of rest the night before the big day! **Essentials**: • Debate team • Walk dog • Clean room **Nonessentials**: • Organize and clean closet

TWO-MONTH PLAN

Perhaps you have two months between now and test day. The following two-month plan spreads the subject review and question practice in this book across the weeks you have available between now and test day.

Month 1	
Week 1 College Readiness Benchmark Learning Path	**ACT Prep**: • Review Chapter 1 "Learn About the ACT Exam" to get familiar with the test. • Review Part IV: Mathematics Strategies (Chapters 6, 7, and 8). • For topics giving you trouble, before you go to the end-of-chapter practice questions, review the College Readiness Benchmark Learning Path practice at the end of each chapter. • If you have time, complete the math practice questions in each review chapter—if not, you can revisit later in the plan. • Note your strengths and weaknesses in key topic areas. • Review weak areas in review chapters. **Essentials**: • Swim team practice • Walk dog • Take out garbage **Nonessentials**: • Guitar lessons • Dinner with friends
Week 2	**ACT Prep**: • Review Part V: Reading Strategies (Chapters 9 and 10). • Complete the reading practice questions in the review chapters. • Note your strengths and weaknesses in key topic areas. • Review weak areas in review chapters. **Essentials**: • Debate team • Walk dog • Clean room **Nonessentials**: • Organize and clean closet
Week 2 College Readiness Benchmark Learning Path	**ACT Prep**: • Review Part V: Reading Strategies (Chapters 9 and 10). • Before you go to the end-of-chapter practice questions, take the online Reading College Readiness Benchmark Learning Path Practice Test. • If you have time, complete the reading practice questions in each review chapter—if not, you can revisit later in the plan. • Note your strengths and weaknesses in key topic areas. • Review weak areas in review chapters. **Essentials**: • Debate team • Walk dog • Clean room **Nonessentials**: • Organize and clean closet

Week 3	**ACT Prep**: • Review Part III: English Strategies (Chapters 4 and 5). • Complete the English practice questions in the review chapters. • Note your strengths and weaknesses in key topic areas. • Review weak areas in review chapters. **Essentials**: • Chess club • Walk dog • Wash dishes and clean basement **Nonessentials**: • Movies with Robin
Week 3 College Readiness Benchmark Learning Path	**ACT Prep**: • Review Part III: English Strategies (Chapters 4 and 5). • Before you go to the end-of-chapter practice questions, take the online English College Readiness Benchmark Learning Path Practice Test. Note your strengths and weaknesses in key topic areas. • If you have time, complete the reading practice questions in each review chapter—if not, you can revisit later in the plan. • Note your strengths and weaknesses in key topic areas. • Review your weak areas in review chapters. **Essentials**: • Chess club • Walk dog • Wash dishes and clean basement **Nonessentials**: • Movies with Robin
Week 4	**ACT Prep**: • Review Part VI: Science Strategies (Chapters 11, 12, and 13). • Complete the science practice questions in the review chapters. • Note your strengths and weaknesses in key topic areas. • Review your weak areas in review chapters. **Essentials**: • Swim team practice • Walk dog • Take out garbage **Nonessentials**: • Buy new sneakers

Week 4 College Readiness Benchmark Learning Path	**ACT Prep**: • Review Part VI: Science Strategies (Chapters 11, 12, and 13). • For topics giving you trouble, before you go to the end-of-chapter practice questions, review the College Readiness Benchmark Learning Path Practice at the end of each chapter. • If you have time, complete the science practice questions in each review chapter—if not, you can revisit later in the plan. • Note your strengths and weaknesses in key topic areas. • Review your weak areas in review chapters. **Essentials**: • Swim team practice • Walk dog • Take out garbage **Nonessentials**: • Buy new sneakers
Month 2	
Week 5 College Readiness Benchmark Learning Path	**ACT Prep**: • Complete Practice Test 1 (Chapter 15). • Score your test and note your strong and weak areas (Chapter 16). • Review the end-of-chapter practice questions for one math chapter, one reading chapter, one English chapter, and one science chapter if you haven't yet. • Spend time focusing on reviewing weak test areas in review chapters. **Essentials**: • Debate team • Walk dog • Clean room **Nonessentials**: • Gym with Derek
Week 6 College Readiness Benchmark Learning Path	**ACT Prep**: • Complete Practice Test 2 (Chapter 15). • Score your test and note your strong and weak areas (Chapter 16). • Review the end-of-chapter practice questions for one math chapter, one reading chapter, one English chapter, and one science chapter if you haven't yet. • Spend time focusing on reviewing weak test areas in review chapters. **Essentials**: • Chess club • Walk dog • Wash dishes and clean basement **Nonessentials**: • Help Sharon with book report

Week 7	**ACT Prep**: • Complete Practice Test 3 (Chapter 15). • Score your test and note your strong and weak areas (Chapter 16). • Spend time focusing on reviewing weak test areas in review chapters. **Essentials**: • Swim team practice • Walk dog • Take out garbage **Nonessentials**: • Visit Uncle Jerome
Week 7 College Readiness Benchmark Learning Path	**ACT Prep**: • Complete Practice Test 3 (Chapter 15). • Score your test and note your strong and weak areas (Chapter 16). • Finish any remaining end-of-chapter review questions you have not yet studied. • Spend time focusing on reviewing weak test areas in review chapters. **Essentials**: • Swim team practice • Walk dog • Take out garbage **Nonessentials**: • Visit Uncle Jerome
Week 8	**ACT Prep**: • Complete Practice Test 3 (Chapter 15). • Score your test and note your strong and weak areas (Chapter 16). • Spend time focusing on reviewing weak test areas in review chapters. • Final week before the exam! Focus on reviewing your remaining weak areas and getting comfortable with the format and timing of the test. Make sure to get plenty of rest the night before the big day! **Essentials**: • Debate team • Walk dog • Clean room **Nonessentials**: • Jog with mom

Two-Week Plan

If you're down to just a few weeks between now and the day of your test, don't despair! There's still time for you to incorporate test preparation into your schedule. Make the most of each day you have between now and test day to prep for success.

Week 1	**ACT Prep—Topic review week:** • **Monday**: Review Part IV: Mathematics Strategies (Chapters 6, 7, and 8) • **Tuesday**: Review Part III: English Strategies (Chapters 4 and 5) • **Wednesday**: Review Part V: Reading Strategies (Chapters 9 and 10) • **Thursday**: Review Part VI: Science Strategies (Chapters 11, 12, and 13) • **Friday**: Take the Diagnostic Test (Chapter 3) to diagnose your strengths and weaknesses • **Saturday**: Review topic chapters, focusing on your weak areas • **Sunday**: Day off—remember to give yourself a break to avoid burnout! **Essentials**: • Debate team • Walk dog • Clean room **Nonessentials**: • Dinner with friends
Week 1 College Readiness Benchmark Learning Path	**ACT Prep—Topic review week:** • **Monday**: Review Part IV: Mathematics Strategies (Chapters 6, 7, and 8). Do you need extra help? Skip ahead to the College Readiness Benchmark Learning Path Review for the topics giving you the most trouble before you take the end-of-chapter questions. • **Tuesday**: Review Part III: English Strategies (Chapters 4 and 5). Need extra help? Go straight to the College Readiness Benchmark Learning Path online test before you take the end-of-chapter questions. • **Wednesday**: Review Part V: Reading Strategies (Chapters 9 and 10). Need extra help? Go straight to the College Readiness Benchmark Learning Path online test before you take the end-of-chapter questions. • **Thursday**: Review Part VI: Science Strategies (Chapters 11, 12, and 13). Need extra help? Skip ahead to the College Readiness Benchmark Learning Path Review for the topics giving you the most trouble before you take the end-of-chapter questions. • **Friday**: Take the Diagnostic Test (Chapter 3) to diagnose your strengths and weaknesses. • **Saturday**: Review topic chapters, focusing on your weak areas. • **Sunday**: Day off—remember to give yourself a break to avoid burnout! **Essentials**: • Debate team • Walk dog • Clean room **Nonessentials**: • Dinner with friends

Week 2	**ACT Prep—Test practice week**: • **Monday**: Complete and score Practice Test 1 (Chapters 15 and 16).) • **Tuesday**: Complete and score Practice Test 2 (Chapters 15 and 16). • **Wednesday**: Complete and score Practice Test 3 (Chapters 15 and 16). • **Thursday**: Complete and score Practice Test 4 (Chapters 15 and 16). • **Friday**: Complete any remaining chapter quizzes in math and science. • **Saturday**: Complete any remaining chapter quizzes in English and reading. • **Sunday**: Night before exam—be sure to relax and get plenty of sleep! **Essentials**: • Swim team practice • Walk dog • Take out garbage **Nonessentials**: • Visit Uncle Jerome
Week 2 College Readiness Benchmark Learning Path	**ACT Prep—Question practice week**: • **Monday**: Complete Practice Test 1 (Chapters 15 and 16); also review the end-of-chapter practice questions for one math chapter, one reading chapter, one English chapter, and one science chapter if you haven't yet. • **Tuesday**: Complete Practice Test 2 (Chapters 15 and 16); also review the end-of-chapter practice questions for one math chapter, one reading chapter, one English chapter, and one science chapter if you haven't yet. • **Wednesday**: Complete Practice Test 3 (Chapters 15 and 16); review any remaining end-of-chapter questions. • **Thursday**: Complete Practice Test 4 (Chapters 15 and 16). • **Friday**: Reread any review chapters and review any Benchmark questions in any topics still giving you trouble. • **Saturday**: Reread any review chapters and review any College Readiness Benchmark Learning Path questions in any topics still giving you trouble. • **Sunday**: Night before exam—be sure to relax and get plenty of sleep! **Essentials**: • Swim team practice • Walk dog • Take out garbage **Nonessentials**: • Visit Uncle Jerome

The Night Before

There are some simple things you can do to ensure test day goes as smoothly as possible. It's probably not very helpful to say "Relax! Don't let the test stress you out!" Look, taking tests is stressful, and it's natural to feel anxious about test day. However, there are things you can do to make things a little less nerve-wracking.

Our first helpful hint about how to handle the night before test day may actually be the exact thing you want to hear: don't study. Well, at least don't study too much. If you try to cram all night before the test, you're only going to be exhausted during the test, and trust us—a night of studying is not worth taking the test half awake. So give yourself the night before test day off. Do something fun and relaxing. Spend time with a friend. Watch a movie. Read a book. Just don't stay up too late; make sure you get plenty of sleep the night before the ACT. However, if you must do some last-minute study and review, just don't overdo it.

Instead of cramming, a better use of your time the night before test day would be to organize your supplies. You'll need at least two sharpened No. 2 pencils with fresh erasers (pens and mechanical pencils are not allowed). Pack your calculator, and triple check to make sure it meets the ACT requirements. Review your route to the testing site one last time to make sure you know how to get there and are familiar enough with the area to adjust your route if there are unexpected detours or an accident. Make sure you have your admission ticket and photo ID. If you think you'll need a snack during your test break, pack it now. If you think you might need a light jacket or sweatshirt in case the testing site is cool, set it aside so you're not scrambling in the morning.

Once again, the most important thing you can do the night before test day is to get a good night's sleep. Minimize distractions if you can, turn out the lights early, and set an alarm (or two, if you need them). Finally, rest assured—if you followed the advice, strategies, review, and practice outlined in this book, then you're well prepared, have everything you need to take with you, and are well rested. You are now primed for success on the ACT!

TEST-TAKING STRATEGIES

It wouldn't be surprising if thinking about the ACT causes you some level of worry or anxiety—after all, it's a high-stakes exam that covers a lot of material. Try your best to relax—if you use this book responsibly, you'll have a real edge over the test-taking competition. Each test-specific chapter in this book covers strategies for tackling the Math, Science, Reading, English, and Writing tests on the ACT exam.

The following are some proven ACT test-taking strategies that you can use to your advantage.

Learn from your mistakes: Unless you're perfect (and if you are, congratulations!), chances are you'll make some mistakes during your prep for the ACT. First, don't let these moments discourage you. Instead, look at them as temporary obstacles that you can overcome with a little effort. Second, make sure you approach these as learning opportunities. If you answer a practice question incorrectly, don't run away from it! Instead, face it bravely and work your way through the answer explanation, and figure out where you went wrong. Use this newfound knowledge to make sure you don't make the same mistake twice!

Use the test-prep dynamic duo—topic review and question practice: Many test takers find that an effective way to approach ACT prep is to focus on subject review for a particular topic alongside targeted question practice based on that particular topic. For example, they'll spend a Tuesday working on reviewing fractions and answering questions based only on fractions. If this type of targeted test prep works for you, then be sure to take full advantage of it. Also, be sure to take full advantage of the benchmark exercises for the math and science sections of the exam that you'll find in this book—this additional, thorough test prep will help you build your skills in these key subjects and set you up for test-day success.

Remember the ACT is *not* a cram exam: Preparing for a high score on the ACT is not a race to memorize as many facts, figures, and formulas as possible between now and test day. The ACT exam is designed to test your ability to process, analyze, and apply real-world information in various practical applications, on top of the knowledge you've acquired throughout your academic career—simply put, it's testing to see that you possess the everyday tools you'll need to succeed in college! Not only will cramming likely *not* work, it may work *against* you, leaving you frustrated and exhausted for the real exam.

Build an effective test-taking pace: The ACT contains multiple timed test sections—if you're going to get through the exam before the clock runs out for each test section, you'll need to establish a good test-taking pace before the big day. Make sure you're comfortable with the format and timing of the ACT exam and each test section before test day, and practice working in simulated timed conditions in order to develop an effective test-taking pace.

Make educated guesses: Since the majority of questions on the ACT are multiple-choice questions, educated guessing is a powerful tool you can use to your advantage. When you are faced with a tough question and are unsure of the answer, try your best to eliminate answer choices that you know are incorrect and take an educated guess based on your knowledge of the topic area.

Don't leave any question blank: *There are no penalties for wrong answers.* This means that you should make every effort to leave no question unanswered. When you aren't sure of an answer, educated guesses are best, but even a completely wild guess is better than an unanswered question.

Practice under test-like conditions: The most effective ACT practice you can have is practice that simulates actual test conditions. Take your practice tests seriously and take them in a distraction-free environment. Use a timer or alarm clock to simulate the actual time allowed for each test section. This way, you'll know exactly what to expect on test day!

Avoid tricky traps: When you're tackling test questions, be on the lookout for tricky answer-choice distractors—these are choices that look and/or sound similar to the correct answers, and they're designed to confuse and challenge you! If you're careful and vigilant, you'll see these distractors coming from a mile away, and they won't slow you down!

Don't get hung up: When you confront a difficult question on the exam, don't let it slow you down or derail you from maintaining your test-taking pace. Instead, either take an educated guess and move on or make a note to revisit it after completing the rest of the questions in the test section. Remember, easy and hard questions are worth the same amount on the ACT, and you don't want to lose guaranteed points on an easy question you never get to because you spent too much time on a hard question.

Conquer anxiety during the test: While you're in the middle of a test, it's not uncommon to experience unexpected bursts of anxiety, and trying to pretend it's not there might just make it worse. Instead, take a moment—just a few seconds—to stop, take a deep breath, and remind yourself that you're prepared and ready to do your best on this exam. Trust us, it's time well spent!

Be accountable: Hold yourself accountable to sticking to your ACT prep study plan. A system of penalties and rewards works well for many test takers: reward yourself for achieving certain test-prep milestones you've set for yourself, and penalize yourself for failing to stick to your plan. It can be an effective way to stay on track!

Use the power of positivity: A positive mindset can go a long way toward keeping you motivated and energized as you work through your study plan between now and test day. It won't always be easy, but if you do your best and stay positive, you'll be in your best mental position to achieve real success.

Don't forget the basics: Sure, we know that you're focused on practice and review for the ACT exam, but that doesn't mean you should neglect the fundamentals. A healthy diet, regular exercise, and plenty of sleep will go a long way toward fueling your mind and body and helping you stay on task. Trust us on this one!

Don't procrastinate: If you're asking yourself when you should begin preparing for the ACT, the easy answer is *right now*! The more time you have to prepare, the better off you're likely to be on test day. Procrastination is the enemy of progress, both in life and on test day.

Imagine success: Successful people in all walks of life treat success as an inevitability, the unavoidable result of a journey of hard work and dedication toward a clearly defined goal. From this point forward, imagine that success on the ACT is just waiting for you at the end of your test-prep journey, and if you stick to your plan and work hard, you'll earn it!

Use what works: This is the "golden rule" of test preparation—there are a million tricks and tools for test-day success, but the truth is that everyone is different and what works for some test takers may not work as well for others. The running theme for you and your ACT study plan is that you should adopt the strategies that are proven to work for you, avoid what doesn't, and be flexible during your journey.

Listen to yourself: No, we're not telling you to give in to that destructive little voice telling you to watch TV or go see your friends instead of study. However, we are telling you to listen to your mind and body as you prepare—they will tell you when you should take a break to avoid burnout and when you're feeling energized and ready to take on some unscheduled extra study time.

Mix things up: A great way to keep things fresh and interesting while you prep for the ACT exam is to mix things up. Try new study venues and prep tools (e.g., flashcards and mobile apps, etc.) to keep you engaged.

Take notes: You need a system to keep track of what's working, what isn't, what topics you want to revisit or investigate further, and new ideas to incorporate into your study plan. Keep notes along the way (a pencil and paper or a note-taking program on your smartphone work well) so you don't forget anything.

Mark up this book as needed (if it's yours): Use whatever tools you're used to using to study effectively. Highlighters, pens, underlining, notes in the margins, and page flags are all fair game if they help you stay organized and study effectively. Remember, this book is designed to be used!

Master the test format and instructions: A great little time-saver on exam day is to get comfortable with the format and instructions you'll encounter on the ACT before test day. Being prepared for what you'll encounter will also give you an added boost of confidence!

Diagnose your strengths and weaknesses: We've said this before, but it bears repeating. You should be aware of your ACT strengths and weaknesses throughout your test prep, and you and your study schedule should remain flexible and evolve to adjust to this changing information.

Always have prep resources on hand: You never know when you'll have some unexpected downtime that you can use to study (in a car, on a train, in between classes or activities, etc.). Always having some mobile ACT prep on hand can help you make the most of your downtime.

Know what kind of learner you are: Successful test takers understand what type of learners they are and craft their test prep accordingly. Visual learners learn best by seeing and utilize visual tools and techniques to study. Auditory learners tend to absorb new concepts and ideas by hearing them and create audio techniques to study. Kinesthetic learners learn best by doing. Whatever type of learner you are, try crafting tools that best match how you and your brain work.

Ask for help when needed: There's no shame in asking for help from others as you prepare for the ACT exam. If you get stuck on a challenging topic or question, reach out to someone you trust for help—a friend, a family member, or teacher can prove helpful. You should also see if there are test-prep resources available to you through your school or community. Remember, you're not alone during your journey to ACT success!

SUMMING IT UP

- Create the perfect study environment to help prepare effectively for the ACT, keeping the following in mind:
  - Keep distractions to a minimum.
  - Get comfortable—but not too comfortable.
  - Choose the location—at home or away—where you work best.
  - Control background noise in your study area.
  - Decide if you study best alone or in a group.
  - Have adequate lighting in your study area.
  - Select a time of day that matches your peak studying ability.
  - Have some nutritious study fuel on hand.
  - Have the tools you need to study effectively at the ready.
  - Create a positive and productive mental environment.
- Build an effective ACT study plan to make the most of your time between now and test day. Skills-based or time-based study plans can be effective; be sure to have your study plan written down and always on hand, and make sure you stick with it.
- Your ACT study plan should be flexible enough to incorporate everything else you have going on in your life.

- Use proven test-taking strategies to help you achieve your ACT score goals:
  - Learn from your mistakes.
  - Topic review and question practice are a powerful combination.
  - Remember the ACT exam is not a cram exam.
  - Build an effective test-taking pace.
  - Utilize educated guessing.
  - Don't leave any question blank.
  - Practice under test-like conditions.
  - Avoid tricky-question traps.
  - Don't get hung-up on difficult questions.
  - Face anxiety head on if it arises during the exam.
  - Hold yourself accountable for sticking to your study plan.
  - Stay positive throughout your ACT preparation.
  - Don't forget the basics, including a healthy diet, regular exercise, and plenty of sleep.
  - Don't procrastinate—start your ACT preparation as soon as possible!
  - Envision ACT success as the inevitable end of your test-prep journey.
  - Adopt the strategies that are proven to work for you, avoid what doesn't, and be flexible during your journey.
  - Listen to your mind and body as you prepare.
  - Mix things up to keep your test prep fresh and interesting.
  - Take notes and mark up this book as needed (if it's yours).
  - Master the ACT format and instructions before test day.
  - Diagnose your strengths and weaknesses and use them to maintain your study plan.
  - Always have prep resources on hand.
  - Know what kind of learner you are.
  - Ask for help when needed.

PART II:
The Diagnostic Test

Chapter 3: The Diagnostic Test

DIAGNOSTIC TEST INTRODUCTION

Now that you are familiar with the format of the ACT exam and how to approach your study plan, it's time to assess your skills in all test areas using the diagnostic test. This test mirrors the ACT exam you will see on test day—it has the exact number of questions as the ACT, and the questions presented reflect the subject matter you will see on the actual ACT. Use your diagnostic test results to determine the subject areas giving you the most trouble—then focus your most intensive studying there first.

We suggest that you take this exam under conditions that mimic the test as closely as possible. Find a quiet spot where you will have limited or, ideally, no interruptions. As hard as it may be, silence your phone and put it in another room so you're not tempted to look at it. It should go without saying, but turn off the television and don't listen to any music. Treat this like you would an actual exam.

Each subject test will note a time limit at its start. Set a timer and try to answer all of the section's questions in the allotted time. If you find you can't, make a note—time management is an issue you will have to practice before test day. See? That's what this diagnostic test is for—to see where your strengths and weaknesses lie so you can work on them.

Here are a few more suggestions before you start.

- **Get your answer sheets ready.** The answer grid sheets and the pages on which you can plan and write your essay are provided on the next several pages. Cut them out (or if you prefer, photocopy them) and get them organized before you begin your test session.
- **Include breaks in your test session.** Be sure to include a 30-minute break after you take the math test. If you plan on taking the writing test, take a 10-minute break after completing the science test before you begin. That way, you will give yourself the same mental breaks you will get on test day.
- **Use the calculator you will take with you to the ACT.** Be sure that the calculator you intend to use on test day is allowed (see the list of prohibited calculators in Chapter 1).
- **Don't look for answer choice patterns.** There is no correct answer letter quota on the ACT exam. Do not feel you have to select a particular answer choice letter (A, B, C, D, etc.) just because you have not selected it in a while.

After the diagnostic test you will find full answers and explanations for each test question, sample essays at different levels, and a chart that explains where you can find preparation to help you learn the info in every single test question.

GOOD LUCK!

CONTINUE

Chapter 3: The Diagnostic Test

OVERVIEW

- Answer Sheets
- English Test
- Mathematics Test
- Reading Test
- Science Test
- Writing Test
- Answer Keys and Explanations
- Diagnostic Test Assessment Grid
- Diagnostic Test Conclusion

English Test

1. Ⓐ Ⓑ Ⓒ Ⓓ	16. Ⓕ Ⓖ Ⓗ Ⓙ	31. Ⓐ Ⓑ Ⓒ Ⓓ	46. Ⓕ Ⓖ Ⓗ Ⓙ	61. Ⓐ Ⓑ Ⓒ Ⓓ
2. Ⓕ Ⓖ Ⓗ Ⓙ	17. Ⓐ Ⓑ Ⓒ Ⓓ	32. Ⓕ Ⓖ Ⓗ Ⓙ	47. Ⓐ Ⓑ Ⓒ Ⓓ	62. Ⓕ Ⓖ Ⓗ Ⓙ
3. Ⓐ Ⓑ Ⓒ Ⓓ	18. Ⓕ Ⓖ Ⓗ Ⓙ	33. Ⓐ Ⓑ Ⓒ Ⓓ	48. Ⓕ Ⓖ Ⓗ Ⓙ	63. Ⓐ Ⓑ Ⓒ Ⓓ
4. Ⓕ Ⓖ Ⓗ Ⓙ	19. Ⓐ Ⓑ Ⓒ Ⓓ	34. Ⓕ Ⓖ Ⓗ Ⓙ	49. Ⓐ Ⓑ Ⓒ Ⓓ	64. Ⓕ Ⓖ Ⓗ Ⓙ
5. Ⓐ Ⓑ Ⓒ Ⓓ	20. Ⓕ Ⓖ Ⓗ Ⓙ	35. Ⓐ Ⓑ Ⓒ Ⓓ	50. Ⓕ Ⓖ Ⓗ Ⓙ	65. Ⓐ Ⓑ Ⓒ Ⓓ
6. Ⓕ Ⓖ Ⓗ Ⓙ	21. Ⓐ Ⓑ Ⓒ Ⓓ	36. Ⓕ Ⓖ Ⓗ Ⓙ	51. Ⓐ Ⓑ Ⓒ Ⓓ	66. Ⓕ Ⓖ Ⓗ Ⓙ
7. Ⓐ Ⓑ Ⓒ Ⓓ	22. Ⓕ Ⓖ Ⓗ Ⓙ	37. Ⓐ Ⓑ Ⓒ Ⓓ	52. Ⓕ Ⓖ Ⓗ Ⓙ	67. Ⓐ Ⓑ Ⓒ Ⓓ
8. Ⓕ Ⓖ Ⓗ Ⓙ	23. Ⓐ Ⓑ Ⓒ Ⓓ	38. Ⓕ Ⓖ Ⓗ Ⓙ	53. Ⓐ Ⓑ Ⓒ Ⓓ	68. Ⓕ Ⓖ Ⓗ Ⓙ
9. Ⓐ Ⓑ Ⓒ Ⓓ	24. Ⓕ Ⓖ Ⓗ Ⓙ	39. Ⓐ Ⓑ Ⓒ Ⓓ	54. Ⓕ Ⓖ Ⓗ Ⓙ	69. Ⓐ Ⓑ Ⓒ Ⓓ
10. Ⓕ Ⓖ Ⓗ Ⓙ	25. Ⓐ Ⓑ Ⓒ Ⓓ	40. Ⓕ Ⓖ Ⓗ Ⓙ	55. Ⓐ Ⓑ Ⓒ Ⓓ	70. Ⓕ Ⓖ Ⓗ Ⓙ
11. Ⓐ Ⓑ Ⓒ Ⓓ	26. Ⓕ Ⓖ Ⓗ Ⓙ	41. Ⓐ Ⓑ Ⓒ Ⓓ	56. Ⓕ Ⓖ Ⓗ Ⓙ	71. Ⓐ Ⓑ Ⓒ Ⓓ
12. Ⓕ Ⓖ Ⓗ Ⓙ	27. Ⓐ Ⓑ Ⓒ Ⓓ	42. Ⓕ Ⓖ Ⓗ Ⓙ	57. Ⓐ Ⓑ Ⓒ Ⓓ	72. Ⓕ Ⓖ Ⓗ Ⓙ
13. Ⓐ Ⓑ Ⓒ Ⓓ	28. Ⓕ Ⓖ Ⓗ Ⓙ	43. Ⓐ Ⓑ Ⓒ Ⓓ	58. Ⓕ Ⓖ Ⓗ Ⓙ	73. Ⓐ Ⓑ Ⓒ Ⓓ
14. Ⓕ Ⓖ Ⓗ Ⓙ	29. Ⓐ Ⓑ Ⓒ Ⓓ	44. Ⓕ Ⓖ Ⓗ Ⓙ	59. Ⓐ Ⓑ Ⓒ Ⓓ	74. Ⓕ Ⓖ Ⓗ Ⓙ
15. Ⓐ Ⓑ Ⓒ Ⓓ	30. Ⓕ Ⓖ Ⓗ Ⓙ	45. Ⓐ Ⓑ Ⓒ Ⓓ	60. Ⓕ Ⓖ Ⓗ Ⓙ	75. Ⓐ Ⓑ Ⓒ Ⓓ

Mathematics Test

1. Ⓐ Ⓑ Ⓒ Ⓓ Ⓔ	16. Ⓕ Ⓖ Ⓗ Ⓙ Ⓚ	31. Ⓐ Ⓑ Ⓒ Ⓓ Ⓔ	46. Ⓕ Ⓖ Ⓗ Ⓙ Ⓚ
2. Ⓕ Ⓖ Ⓗ Ⓙ Ⓚ	17. Ⓐ Ⓑ Ⓒ Ⓓ Ⓔ	32. Ⓕ Ⓖ Ⓗ Ⓙ Ⓚ	47. Ⓐ Ⓑ Ⓒ Ⓓ Ⓔ
3. Ⓐ Ⓑ Ⓒ Ⓓ Ⓔ	18. Ⓕ Ⓖ Ⓗ Ⓙ Ⓚ	33. Ⓐ Ⓑ Ⓒ Ⓓ Ⓔ	48. Ⓕ Ⓖ Ⓗ Ⓙ Ⓚ
4. Ⓕ Ⓖ Ⓗ Ⓙ Ⓚ	19. Ⓐ Ⓑ Ⓒ Ⓓ Ⓔ	34. Ⓕ Ⓖ Ⓗ Ⓙ Ⓚ	49. Ⓐ Ⓑ Ⓒ Ⓓ Ⓔ
5. Ⓐ Ⓑ Ⓒ Ⓓ Ⓔ	20. Ⓕ Ⓖ Ⓗ Ⓙ Ⓚ	35. Ⓐ Ⓑ Ⓒ Ⓓ Ⓔ	50. Ⓕ Ⓖ Ⓗ Ⓙ Ⓚ
6. Ⓕ Ⓖ Ⓗ Ⓙ Ⓚ	21. Ⓐ Ⓑ Ⓒ Ⓓ Ⓔ	36. Ⓕ Ⓖ Ⓗ Ⓙ Ⓚ	51. Ⓐ Ⓑ Ⓒ Ⓓ Ⓔ
7. Ⓐ Ⓑ Ⓒ Ⓓ Ⓔ	22. Ⓕ Ⓖ Ⓗ Ⓙ Ⓚ	37. Ⓐ Ⓑ Ⓒ Ⓓ Ⓔ	52. Ⓕ Ⓖ Ⓗ Ⓙ Ⓚ
8. Ⓕ Ⓖ Ⓗ Ⓙ Ⓚ	23. Ⓐ Ⓑ Ⓒ Ⓓ Ⓔ	38. Ⓕ Ⓖ Ⓗ Ⓙ Ⓚ	53. Ⓐ Ⓑ Ⓒ Ⓓ Ⓔ
9. Ⓐ Ⓑ Ⓒ Ⓓ Ⓔ	24. Ⓕ Ⓖ Ⓗ Ⓙ Ⓚ	39. Ⓐ Ⓑ Ⓒ Ⓓ Ⓔ	54. Ⓕ Ⓖ Ⓗ Ⓙ Ⓚ
10. Ⓕ Ⓖ Ⓗ Ⓙ Ⓚ	25. Ⓐ Ⓑ Ⓒ Ⓓ Ⓔ	40. Ⓕ Ⓖ Ⓗ Ⓙ Ⓚ	55. Ⓐ Ⓑ Ⓒ Ⓓ Ⓔ
11. Ⓐ Ⓑ Ⓒ Ⓓ Ⓔ	26. Ⓕ Ⓖ Ⓗ Ⓙ Ⓚ	41. Ⓐ Ⓑ Ⓒ Ⓓ Ⓔ	56. Ⓕ Ⓖ Ⓗ Ⓙ Ⓚ
12. Ⓕ Ⓖ Ⓗ Ⓙ Ⓚ	27. Ⓐ Ⓑ Ⓒ Ⓓ Ⓔ	42. Ⓕ Ⓖ Ⓗ Ⓙ Ⓚ	57. Ⓐ Ⓑ Ⓒ Ⓓ Ⓔ
13. Ⓐ Ⓑ Ⓒ Ⓓ Ⓔ	28. Ⓕ Ⓖ Ⓗ Ⓙ Ⓚ	43. Ⓐ Ⓑ Ⓒ Ⓓ Ⓔ	58. Ⓕ Ⓖ Ⓗ Ⓙ Ⓚ
14. Ⓕ Ⓖ Ⓗ Ⓙ Ⓚ	29. Ⓐ Ⓑ Ⓒ Ⓓ Ⓔ	44. Ⓕ Ⓖ Ⓗ Ⓙ Ⓚ	59. Ⓐ Ⓑ Ⓒ Ⓓ Ⓔ
15. Ⓐ Ⓑ Ⓒ Ⓓ Ⓔ	30. Ⓕ Ⓖ Ⓗ Ⓙ Ⓚ	45. Ⓐ Ⓑ Ⓒ Ⓓ Ⓔ	60. Ⓕ Ⓖ Ⓗ Ⓙ Ⓚ

CONTINUE

Reading Test

1. Ⓐ Ⓑ Ⓒ Ⓓ	11. Ⓐ Ⓑ Ⓒ Ⓓ	21. Ⓐ Ⓑ Ⓒ Ⓓ	31. Ⓐ Ⓑ Ⓒ Ⓓ
2. Ⓕ Ⓖ Ⓗ Ⓙ	12. Ⓕ Ⓖ Ⓗ Ⓙ	22. Ⓕ Ⓖ Ⓗ Ⓙ	32. Ⓕ Ⓖ Ⓗ Ⓙ
3. Ⓐ Ⓑ Ⓒ Ⓓ	13. Ⓐ Ⓑ Ⓒ Ⓓ	23. Ⓐ Ⓑ Ⓒ Ⓓ	33. Ⓐ Ⓑ Ⓒ Ⓓ
4. Ⓕ Ⓖ Ⓗ Ⓙ	14. Ⓕ Ⓖ Ⓗ Ⓙ	24. Ⓕ Ⓖ Ⓗ Ⓙ	34. Ⓕ Ⓖ Ⓗ Ⓙ
5. Ⓐ Ⓑ Ⓒ Ⓓ	15. Ⓐ Ⓑ Ⓒ Ⓓ	25. Ⓐ Ⓑ Ⓒ Ⓓ	35. Ⓐ Ⓑ Ⓒ Ⓓ
6. Ⓕ Ⓖ Ⓗ Ⓙ	16. Ⓕ Ⓖ Ⓗ Ⓙ	26. Ⓕ Ⓖ Ⓗ Ⓙ	36. Ⓕ Ⓖ Ⓗ Ⓙ
7. Ⓐ Ⓑ Ⓒ Ⓓ	17. Ⓐ Ⓑ Ⓒ Ⓓ	27. Ⓐ Ⓑ Ⓒ Ⓓ	37. Ⓐ Ⓑ Ⓒ Ⓓ
8. Ⓕ Ⓖ Ⓗ Ⓙ	18. Ⓕ Ⓖ Ⓗ Ⓙ	28. Ⓕ Ⓖ Ⓗ Ⓙ	38. Ⓕ Ⓖ Ⓗ Ⓙ
9. Ⓐ Ⓑ Ⓒ Ⓓ	19. Ⓐ Ⓑ Ⓒ Ⓓ	29. Ⓐ Ⓑ Ⓒ Ⓓ	39. Ⓐ Ⓑ Ⓒ Ⓓ
10. Ⓕ Ⓖ Ⓗ Ⓙ	20. Ⓕ Ⓖ Ⓗ Ⓙ	30. Ⓕ Ⓖ Ⓗ Ⓙ	40. Ⓕ Ⓖ Ⓗ Ⓙ

Science Test

1. Ⓐ Ⓑ Ⓒ Ⓓ	11. Ⓐ Ⓑ Ⓒ Ⓓ	21. Ⓐ Ⓑ Ⓒ Ⓓ	31. Ⓐ Ⓑ Ⓒ Ⓓ
2. Ⓕ Ⓖ Ⓗ Ⓙ	12. Ⓕ Ⓖ Ⓗ Ⓙ	22. Ⓕ Ⓖ Ⓗ Ⓙ	32. Ⓕ Ⓖ Ⓗ Ⓙ
3. Ⓐ Ⓑ Ⓒ Ⓓ	13. Ⓐ Ⓑ Ⓒ Ⓓ	23. Ⓐ Ⓑ Ⓒ Ⓓ	33. Ⓐ Ⓑ Ⓒ Ⓓ
4. Ⓕ Ⓖ Ⓗ Ⓙ	14. Ⓕ Ⓖ Ⓗ Ⓙ	24. Ⓕ Ⓖ Ⓗ Ⓙ	34. Ⓕ Ⓖ Ⓗ Ⓙ
5. Ⓐ Ⓑ Ⓒ Ⓓ	15. Ⓐ Ⓑ Ⓒ Ⓓ	25. Ⓐ Ⓑ Ⓒ Ⓓ	35. Ⓐ Ⓑ Ⓒ Ⓓ
6. Ⓕ Ⓖ Ⓗ Ⓙ	16. Ⓕ Ⓖ Ⓗ Ⓙ	26. Ⓕ Ⓖ Ⓗ Ⓙ	36. Ⓕ Ⓖ Ⓗ Ⓙ
7. Ⓐ Ⓑ Ⓒ Ⓓ	17. Ⓐ Ⓑ Ⓒ Ⓓ	27. Ⓐ Ⓑ Ⓒ Ⓓ	37. Ⓐ Ⓑ Ⓒ Ⓓ
8. Ⓕ Ⓖ Ⓗ Ⓙ	18. Ⓕ Ⓖ Ⓗ Ⓙ	28. Ⓕ Ⓖ Ⓗ Ⓙ	38. Ⓕ Ⓖ Ⓗ Ⓙ
9. Ⓐ Ⓑ Ⓒ Ⓓ	19. Ⓐ Ⓑ Ⓒ Ⓓ	29. Ⓐ Ⓑ Ⓒ Ⓓ	39. Ⓐ Ⓑ Ⓒ Ⓓ
10. Ⓕ Ⓖ Ⓗ Ⓙ	20. Ⓕ Ⓖ Ⓗ Ⓙ	30. Ⓕ Ⓖ Ⓗ Ⓙ	40. Ⓕ Ⓖ Ⓗ Ⓙ

WRITING TEST

Plan Your Essay

Write Your Essay

ENGLISH TEST

45 Minutes—75 Questions

DIRECTIONS: In this section, you will see passages with words and phrases that are underlined and numbered. In the right-hand column you will see a question corresponding to each number that provides alternatives to the underlined part. In most of the items, you are to choose the best alternative. If no change is needed, choose NO CHANGE.

In other items, there will be either a question about an underlined portion of the passage, or a question about a section of the passage, or about the passage as a whole. This question type will correspond to a number or numbers in a box.

For each question, choose the best alternative or answer and fill in the corresponding circle on the answer sheet.

PASSAGE I

Code Talking

[1]

In September of 1992, a group of <u>American hero</u> (1) who had gone unrecognized for many years was honored by the United States Pentagon.

[2]

During World War II, the United States Marines needed to develop a <u>code, for communicating</u> (2) top-secret information. <u>It being the case that they would then have access to information about United States Marines tactics and troop movements, it was crucial that enemy forces not be able to decipher the code.</u> (3)

1. A. NO CHANGE
   B. hero
   C. hero's
   D. heroes

2. F. NO CHANGE
   G. code for communicating
   H. code, for communicating,
   J. code for communicating,

3. A. NO CHANGE
   B. It was crucial to the United States, that enemy forces not be able to decipher the code, having access to information about Marines tactics and troop movements.
   C. It was crucial that enemy forces not be able to decipher the code, because if they did they would have access to information about the Marines' tactics and troop movements.
   D. Crucially, the enemy forces were not able to decipher the code, which would have access to the Marines' tactics and troop movements.

CONTINUE

[3]

The military recruited a small group of Navajos to create a code based on their language. Unfortunately, the Navajo language made an excellent code for several essential reasons. First, it was extremely difficult to learn and virtually unknown outside the Navajo community in the American Southwest. Second, the Navajo language does not have a written form; it uses no alphabet. Its complexity and obscurity made it the perfect basis for a code.

4. F. NO CHANGE
   G. As a result,
   H. However,
   J. OMIT the underlined portion.

[4]

The first group of Navajo recruits attended boot camp in 1942. Afterward, they set to work developing a vast dictionary of code words for military terms, based on the Navajo language. Each code talker had to memorize the dictionary before being sent to a Marine unit. Using telephones and radios to transmit encoded orders and information, once the code talkers were stationed with a unit.

5. A. NO CHANGE
   B. As a result
   C. However
   D. OMIT the underlined portion.

6. F. NO CHANGE
   G. Once, the code talkers used telephones and radios to transmit encoded orders and information, when they were stationed with a unit.
   H. Once stationed with a unit, using telephones and radios to transmit encoded orders and information.
   J. Once they were stationed with a unit, the code talkers used telephones and radios to transmit encoded orders and information.

[5]

While the Navajo language was complicated The code was even more complex. A code talker receiving a message heard a stream of Navajo words. The receiver had to translate the words into English, and then use the first letter of each English equivalent to spell out a word. Adding to the difficulty, of breaking the

7. A. NO CHANGE
   B. complicated the.
   C. Complicated the
   D. complicated, the

8. F. NO CHANGE
   G. (Begin new paragraph) Adding to the difficulty
   H. (Do NOT begin new paragraph) More difficulty,
   J. (Do NOT begin new paragraph) Adding to the difficulty

code was the fact that most letters could be indicated by the code talkers with more than one Navajo word. Also, there were certain military terms that were not spelled out letter by letter, so although the military terms did not translate to words, the creators of the code matched Navajo words to them. [9]

9. At this point, the writer would like to help readers understand how the code worked. Which of the following sentences, if added here, would most effectively accomplish this?

A. The code was not like Morse code, which used a system of dots and dashes to signify letters of the alphabet.

B. For example, *besh-lo*, Navajo for "iron fish," was the code word for submarine.

C. Prior to this, other Native American languages had been used in military codes.

D. The code, which was so difficult, should have been acknowledged earlier by the Pentagon.

[6]

Though able to crack the codes of other military branches, enemy forces never managed to decipher what the Marines' Navajo code talkers said. The code talkers were renowned for the <u>speed, and accuracy,</u> (10) with which they worked,

10. **F.** NO CHANGE
G. speed, and accuracy
H. speed and accuracy
J. speed and accuracy,

<u>and also they were credited by officers</u> (11) for the U.S. Marines' success in World War II.

11. **A.** NO CHANGE
B. and officers credited them
C. they were credited by officers
D. OMIT the underlined portion.

[7]

The code talkers were not acknowledged until quite recently because the Navajo language remained part of a security classified code. At last, though, half a century later, thirty-five former code talkers and their families attended the dedication of the Navajo code talker exhibit at the United States Pentagon, officially taking <u>its places</u> (12) in military history. [13]

12. **F.** NO CHANGE
G. their place
H. our places
J. his placement

CONTINUE

13. Assuming that each of the following statements is true, which would make the most effective concluding sentence to this essay?

A. Code breaking has been an integral part of wartime intelligence gathering for centuries.

B. Today, a statue commemorating the brave contributions of the Navajo code talkers exists in Arizona.

C. Over 400,000 American soldiers lost their lives fighting in World War II.

D. Today, there are approximately 182,000 active members in the United States Marines.

Questions 14 and 15 ask about the essay as a whole.

14. The writer is planning to add the following sentence to the essay:

So complicated was the code that even a Navajo soldier who had been taken prisoner by the enemy was unable to understand it.

This sentence would best be placed after the last sentence in Paragraph:

F. 4.

G. 5.

H. 6.

J. 7.

15. Suppose the writer had been assigned to write an essay describing the contributions of minority soldiers in World War II. Would this essay successfully fulfill the assignment?

A. Yes, because it describes the contributions of Navajo soldiers.

B. Yes, because it describes a military maneuver that was crucial to the success of the war.

C. No, because it discusses the contributions of only one minority group of soldiers.

D. No, because the essay does not focus on the positive effects of the Navajo soldiers' work.

PASSAGE II

The Real World

[1]

Our college employment counseling center recommended that students have mock interviews before setting out into the world for the real thing. For some reason, I believed that this applied to other people but not to me. Midway through my senior year of college, she sent (16) out resumes to several law firms in the area. Nobody was consulted (17) about how to begin seeking a job. My plan was to work at a law firm for a couple of years before attending law school. I received a couple of responses and was thrilled to set up my first interview at a prestigious law firm that had offices all over the world. It was (18) exactly the type of environment in which I envisioned myself.

[2]

The position for which I was interviewing; was (19) a clerical job that, the interviewer made clear from the outset, would require long hours, late nights, and a great deal of filing and photocopying. I confidently announced to the interviewer that I didn't mind long hours and thankless assignments. After all, I happily informed him my aim (20) was to work my way up and

16.
- **F.** NO CHANGE
- **G.** I sent
- **H.** we send
- **J.** I'm sending

17.
- **A.** NO CHANGE
- **B.** With nobody I consulted
- **C.** Nobody consulted me
- **D.** I didn't consult with anybody

18.
- **F.** NO CHANGE
- **G.** There was
- **H.** Here is
- **J.** And so it was

19.
- **A.** NO CHANGE
- **B.** interviewing, was
- **C.** interviewing—was
- **D.** interviewing was

20.
- **F.** NO CHANGE
- **G.** informed him, my aim
- **H.** informed, him my aim
- **J.** informed him my aim,

CONTINUE

someday be his boss. I figured the surprised look on his face was because he wasn't used to seeing young men as ambitious and articulate as I was. 21

21. The writer considered deleting the previous sentence and instead writing, "I can't believe I made such a foolish mistake." If the writer had done this, it would have diminished the reader's understanding of:

I. the narrator's point of view at the time of the interview.
II. what type of job the narrator wished to obtain.
III. the interviewer's opinion of the narrator.

A. I only
B. II only
C. I and III only
D. I, II, and III

I would of (22) kept going, had he not suggested moving on to another topic.

22. **F.** NO CHANGE
G. could of
H. would have
J. would to have

[3]

In the next phase of the interview, I was asked to list my strengths and weaknesses. I'm sorry to say that here I left nothing to the imagination. I believed (23) that my interviewer would value my stark honesty when I told him that my greatest weaknesses included not getting along with other people very well and a tendency to make more enemies than friends. The interviewer raises (24) his eyebrows but said nothing, and I was certain that he

23. **A.** NO CHANGE
B. We believed
C. They believed
D. Our belief

24. **F.** NO CHANGE
G. was raising
H. had raised
J. raised

knew he'd found his candidate. After all, I figured, (25) I wouldn't need to get along with people to photocopy and file, so I'd hit upon the perfect answer to a tricky question.

25. **A.** NO CHANGE
B. all I figured,
C. all I, figured
D. all I figured

[4]

[1] I did not get offered that job, nor the next several firms at which I interviewed for one. 26

27 [2] Eventually I paid a long-overdue trip to the college job counseling office and got a few pointers on my technique.

[3] I am happy to say that while I never did end up going to law school, I have become a high school guidance counselor who specializes in helping students find internships in community businesses. 28

26. **F.** NO CHANGE
G. ones for interviewing from the next several firms
H. the next several for which I interviewed at other firms
J. any interviews from the next several jobs at firms

27. Which of the following sentences, if added here, would most effectively signal the shift in focus that occurs at this point in the essay?

A. I felt very angry at the firms that rejected me as a job candidate.
B. Time and time again, I tried and failed to get a job.
C. Every interview I gave ended much like the first one had: with no promise of a job.
D. After a few months, I finally had to admit that the problem might be with my approach.

28. The writer wants to add a sentence here that would give the essay a sense of completion by tying the ending back to the beginning. Which choice would best accomplish this?

F. Not all of my students are interested in an internship, but I encourage them to give it a try.
G. I conduct practice interviews with every student because, as I tell them, it's a lot harder to give a good interview than one might think!
H. I can't believe that so many of my students have never interviewed for a job before!
J. I can only hope that one of my students will accomplish my early dreams of becoming a lawyer.

29. The writer is considering adding a concluding sentence to Paragraph 4. Which of the following would be the most effective addition?

A. I quickly realized that college just wasn't a good fit for me.
B. I knew I had the interview game all figured out from the beginning.
C. I learned a valuable lesson from my interviewing experience.
D. I should have insisted that the law firm give me an internship on the spot.

CONTINUE

PASSAGE III

All About Aardvarks

[1]

What do you know about the aardvark—a curious animal with an even more curious name. (30) If you're like the average person, the answer is likely "not much," which stands to reason—unless you're in a zoo or happen to be wandering in sub-Saharan Africa, you're not likely to run across an aardvark any time soon. [31]

[2]

The name *aardvark* itself is attributed to the Afrikaans language, a South African language that evolved from the dutch, (32) and the closest English translation is "earth pig," which seems like an apt description of this snout-faced creature.

[3]

Aardvarks are furry, nocturnal-feeding mammals that are native to southern portions of Africa, which provides a suitable climate and habitat of grassland, bushland, and savanna (33) for aardvarks to thrive. The aardvark is certainly no newcomer—fossils have been found across the African and; (34) European continents that date back nearly 5 million years.

[4]

If you ever did come face to face with an aardvark, you probably wouldn't forget it they (35) have an instantly recognizable appearance,

30.
- **F.** NO CHANGE
- **G.** name?
- **H.** name!
- **J.** name;

31. Which of the following sentences would make an effective transition between paragraphs 1 and 2?
- **A.** The aardvark typically flips onto its back when attacked.
- **B.** That sums up what is currently known about the noble aardvark.
- **C.** Let's take a closer look at the history and habits of this interesting mammal.
- **D.** There are a few types of ants and termites that aardvarks will shy away from eating, including poisonous varieties.

32.
- **F.** NO CHANGE
- **G.** Dutch,
- **H.** dutch;
- **J.** Dutch.

33.
- **A.** NO CHANGE
- **B.** grassland bushland and savanna
- **C.** grassland bushland, and savanna
- **D.** grassland; bushland and; savanna

34.
- **F.** NO CHANGE
- **G.** and.
- **H.** and,
- **J.** and

35.
- **A.** NO CHANGE
- **B.** forget, it they
- **C.** forget it—they
- **D.** forget it they;

with a stout body covered in coarse gray hair, an arched back, prominent ears that are keenly sensitive and used to aid hunting, and a long snout <u>thats</u> 36 used to forage and track food. Aardvarks typically grow to around 3–4 feet in length, not including their tails, with an average weight of around 150 pounds.

36. **F.** NO CHANGE
G. that
H. that's
J. that was

[5]

Aardvarks are solitary creatures by nature. During the day, they typically can be found lounging in a cool, damp, dark, and dank underground burrow (<u>they are expert and really good diggers</u>) 37 created in an effort to escape the blistering sunlight.

37. **A.** NO CHANGE
B. they are both good and expert diggers
C. they are expert diggers
D. they are really expert and really good diggers

[6]

After the sun sets, they emerge from their burrows and <u>have begun</u> 38 hunting for food, relying on their sensitive snouts to sniff out their meals. If you see an aardvark with its snout pressed firmly against the ground, grunting softly as it lurches forward, you'll know it's searching for food. Those prominent and sensitive aardvark ears mentioned earlier also help the aardvark track food, with hearing and smelling being the two primary senses it relies on to find sufficient food for survival. The average aardvark diet consists almost exclusively of termites and ants, and its <u>weak</u> 39 snout skin helps protect it from the bites and stings of its insect prey.

38. **F.** NO CHANGE
G. had began
H. will be beginning
J. begin

39. **A.** whispery
B. tough
C. smooth
D. thin

[7]

The aardvark possesses a variety of tools designed to protect itself from enemies out in the wild. In addition to their keen senses of hearing and smell, which helps them to become aware of approaching predators quickly, they are surprisingly speedy creatures when they need to be, and have been known to run in unpredictable zig-zag patterns to <u>encounter</u> 40 its enemies. They

40. **F.** entice
G. envelope
H. embrace
J. escape

CONTINUE

are also excellent swimmers, helping them flee from other creatures when danger is sensed. <u>Her</u> [41] digging skills are also a huge asset when trying to avoid other animals, and they have been known to burrow their way to a quick escape when threatened. Aardvarks also possess a thick, tough skin beneath their fur and have claws that are capable of causing considerable damage.

[8]

Although the average aardvark lives <u>20 or 25 years</u> [42], you can conclude that its ingenious survival tactics and specialized tools have contributed to its longevity as a species. Perhaps one day your path will cross with an aardvark, although it's likely that will happen only at a zoo or wildlife exhibit. [43]

41. **A.** NO CHANGE
B. Our
C. His
D. Their

42. **F.** NO CHANGE
G. 20 years or 25 years
H. 25–20 years
J. 20–25 years

43. Which of the following would make an effective concluding statement to this essay?

A. If you do encounter one, be sure to pay this creature the respect it deserves!
B. There are zoos all around the country that you can visit.
C. If you ever travel to Africa from the United States, make sure you bring your passport!
D. Try digging a burrow in the dirt when you have some extra time to spare!

Questions 44 and 45 ask about the essay as a whole.

44. Imagine that you were given an assignment by your school newspaper to write an informative article about animals indigenous to the African continent. Does this essay successfully fulfill the assignment?

F. Yes, because aardvarks are indigenous to the African continent.
G. Yes, because you mentioned Africa in the article.
H. No, because the aardvark has also been found to dwell in other continents.
J. No, because your focus on the aardvark is too narrow for the scope of the assignment.

45. The writer is considering adding the following sentence to the essay:

The rhinoceros is a creature native to Africa, and it feeds off the indigenous plant life it encounters, including trees, bushes, and grasses.

Given that this statement is true, should it be added to the essay, and, if so, where?

A. Yes, at the end of paragraph 6, because both animals have skin that serves to protect them.
B. Yes, at the beginning of the second paragraph, because both animals are indigenous to Africa.
C. No, because the passage is not about any animals other than the aardvark.
D. No, because aardvarks are carnivores, and the rhinoceros is an herbivore.

PASSAGE IV

Defied Expectations

[1]

On January 23, 1849, in the town of Geneva, New York, Elizabeth Blackwell stepped onto the altar, of the Presbyterian church. And [46] received her Doctor of Medicine degree from the president of Geneva Medical College. The effect was, [47] she took her place in history. Blackwell had defied the expectations of most of her teachers and classmates to become the countries first female [48] doctor.

[2]

As a young woman, Blackwell had worked as a teacher, but she found herself unsatisfied. Once she realized that her dream was to be a doctor, she faced tremendous obstacles. There had never before been a female physician in America; girls [49] often didn't even receive the same basic education that boys did. Blackwell's education did not prepare her for the challenges of

46. **F.** NO CHANGE
G. altar of the Presbyterian church and
H. altar of the Presbyterian church; and
J. altar of the Presbyterian church, and

47. **A.** NO CHANGE
B. Therefore
C. In doing so
D. Even so

48. **F.** NO CHANGE
G. countries' first female
H. first female country's
J. country's first female

49. **A.** NO CHANGE
B. America; as a result, girls
C. America and therefore girls
D. America, but girls

CONTINUE

medical school, and <u>to catch up she had to do much</u>[50]. To make up for the gaps in her education, she arranged to live in the household of a physician, where <u>having access</u>[51] to educational resources and received some medical training.

50. **F.** NO CHANGE
G. to catch up she would have
H. there was for her to do much catching up
J. she had to catch up

51. **A.** NO CHANGE
B. she had access
C. she has access
D. she did have access

[3]

As she prepared to apply to medical school, Blackwell sought advice from physicians in New York and Philadelphia. She found that they <u>doubted</u>[52] she would be admitted to medical school; at least one advisor went so far as to suggest that she might disguise herself as a man in order to gain admittance. Her advisors were not far from wrong in their prediction. Blackwell <u>applies</u>[53] to well over a dozen medical <u>colleges; and received admission to only one. Geneva Medical College.</u>[54]

52. **F.** NO CHANGE
G. debated
H. insisted
J. supposed

53. **A.** NO CHANGE
B. applied
C. has applied
D. applying

54. **F.** NO CHANGE
G. colleges, and received admission to only one, Geneva Medical College.
H. colleges but received admission to only one: Geneva Medical College.
J. colleges. But received admission to only one: Geneva Medical College.

[4]

Gaining admission to the college <u>became</u>[55] the first in a long line of obstacles. Blackwell discovered that her fellow <u>students who were all men and had</u>[56] elected as a joke to admit her and were <u>astonishing</u>[57] and bewildered when she actually showed up. The students were embarrassed by her presence in lectures on topics—such as human anatomy—that they considered unsuitable for mixed company.

55. **A.** NO CHANGE
B. was not
C. becomes
D. were

56. **F.** NO CHANGE
G. students were all men and they
H. men students had
J. students, all of whom were men, had

57. **A.** NO CHANGE
B. astonished
C. astonishment
D. having astonishment

[5]

Steadily, and with perseverance, Blackwell gained acceptance among the students and faculty. After, (58) she completed her degree, she continued to face prejudice and outright barriers to her career. (59) She was unable to establish the private practice she had hoped for, but she had the chance to do other things instead. (60)

58. F. NO CHANGE
G. Afterward,
H. After
J. After to

59. A. NO CHANGE
B. face outright barriers to her career, that was prejudice
C. face outright prejudice that was a barrier to her career
D. face barriers that were outright prejudice to her career

60. Which of these choices, assuming they are all accurate, should the writer use here to show that Elizabeth Blackwell found success as a doctor?
F. NO CHANGE
G. and she is remembered for having been the first woman in America to receive a medical degree
H. but she had a distinguished career as a promoter of preventative medicine and as a champion of medical opportunities for women
J. and when she went to study at a hospital in Paris, she was assigned the same duties as young girls with no education at all

PASSAGE V

Form and Function in the Roman Aqueducts

[1]

The use of a system of pipes to carry water from its source to the place where it is needed is an imperious (61) idea, one that can be traced back to several ancient civilizations including, Persia, India, and Egypt (62). The Roman Empire is generally considered to

61. A. NO CHANGE
B. unsettling
C. inimitable
D. ingenious

62. F. NO CHANGE
G. civilizations, including Persia, India, and Egypt
H. civilizations including Persia, India and Egypt
J. civilizations, including: Persia and India and Egypt

CONTINUE

have created the most advancing system of water transport in the ancient world, roughly two thousand years ago.
63

63. A. NO CHANGE
B. created the most advanced system
C. created in advance of the system
D. created a system of the most superlative advancement

[2]

The Roman Empire's water transport—or aqueduct—system was a feat of engineering it combined form and function. The
64

64. F. NO CHANGE
G. which had been combining
H. that made a combination of
J. that combined

aqueducts were built in Italy, Greece, Spain, France, and other regions that were within the vast reach of the Roman Empire. The original Roman aqueducts were quite truly tunnels that ran down hillsides to transport water used to irrigate the plains. Later, the
65

65. A. NO CHANGE
B. simply
C. actually
D. quickly

structures became more elaborate, they were able to conduct
66

66. F. NO CHANGE
G. elaborate but they
H. elaborate; they
J. elaborate! So they

water over distances in excess of fifty miles. 67

67. Which of the following sentences, if inserted here, would best support the writer's point that the aqueducts were an impressive accomplishment?

A. Today's water transport systems, of course, are far more effective.
B. The Roman Empire's accomplishments also included finely engineered roads, bridges, and buildings.
C. Several modern European countries still contain evidence of the aqueducts.
D. Amazingly, some of these aqueducts are still in use.

[3]

The most famous Roman aqueducts are those that consisted of tiers of granite arches reaching across valleys. The Romans used a trial-and-error system; some of their aqueducts
68

68. F. NO CHANGE
G. system, some
H. system: some
J. system! Some

failed, for those that succeeded were used as models for subsequent ones. The principles of engineering that held up the
69

69. A. NO CHANGE
B. failed, but
C. failed, so
D. fail, but

successful arches are the same ones that <u>will be applied</u> [70] in modern <u>architecture (for example on many impressive American landmarks)</u> [71].

[4]

The stone <u>arches':</u> [72] while well-known, actually were a relatively small portion of the aqueduct system. <u>The rest of the aqueducts were different</u> [73]. The system took advantage of the force of gravity, which caused the water to flow from the source to the city, passing through a series of distribution tanks along the way, providing water to the people of the cities and to the famous majestic fountains of the Roman Empire.

[5]

Water conduit systems have, of course, undergone hundreds of decades' worth of modernization. While modern-day aqueduct systems <u>would</u> [74] transport far more water over far greater distances, they lack the grandeur of the arched Roman aqueducts. [75]

70. **F.** NO CHANGE
G. are applied
H. had been applied
J. were applying

71. **A.** NO CHANGE
B. architecture, for example, on many impressive American landmarks
C. architecture
D. architecture—for example—on many, impressive American landmarks

72. **F.** NO CHANGE
G. arches
H. arches;
J. arches,

73. Which choice best supports the paragraph by giving the most specific details?

A. NO CHANGE
B. The rest of the aqueduct consisted of a series of underground pipes that were made mostly of stone and terra cotta.
C. The graceful curves of the stone arches are, of course, much more interesting than the rest of the aqueducts.
D. The rest of the system was different, made of several kinds of materials.

74. **F.** NO CHANGE
G. should
H. will
J. OMIT the underlined portion.

75. The writer wants the final sentence of the last paragraph to reflect the main idea of the whole essay. Which of the following sentences would best accomplish this?

A. NO CHANGE
B. It's too bad that modern technology is not as aesthetically pleasing as it was during the days of the Roman Empire.
C. The Roman Empire will long be remembered for its aqueducts, as well as for its advanced system of political governance.
D. As far as modern technology advances, it will always be indebted to the aesthetic and mechanical achievements of the Roman Empire.

STOP

MATHEMATICS TEST

60 Minutes—60 Questions

DIRECTIONS: For each of the following items, solve each problem, choose the correct answer, and then fill in the corresponding circle on the answer sheet.

If you encounter problems that take too much time to solve, move on. Solve as many problems as you can; then return to the others in the time remaining for the test.

You may use a calculator on this test for any problems you choose, but some of the problems may best be solved without the use of a calculator.

SHOW YOUR WORK HERE

Note: Unless otherwise stated, assume the following:

1. Illustrative figures are NOT necessarily drawn to scale.
2. Geometric figures lie in a plane.
3. The word *line* indicates a straight line.
4. The word *average* indicates arithmetic mean.

1. If $-3(2 - x) = 4 - (3x + 1)$, what is x?

A. $\frac{3}{2}$

B. $\frac{2}{3}$

C. 3

D. $\frac{11}{2}$

E. $-\frac{1}{3}$

2. If 3 out of a package of 25 batteries were defective, what percentage of the batteries in the package worked?

F. $\frac{3}{25}\times 100$

G. $\frac{22}{25\times 100}$

H. $\frac{3}{25\times 100}$

J. $\frac{22}{100}\times 25$

K. $\frac{22}{25}\times 100$

CONTINUE

3. At a yoga studio, first-time customers are permitted to borrow equipment for use in the class. There are 6 yoga mats, 4 bolsters, and 3 sets of blocks available for use. If one of each type of equipment is needed in the class, from how many different combinations does a customer have to choose?

A. 12
B. 18
C. 24
D. 72
E. 144

SHOW YOUR WORK HERE

4. In the following diagram, *l* and *m* are lines. Which choice gives the correct measures of $\angle a$ and $\angle b$?

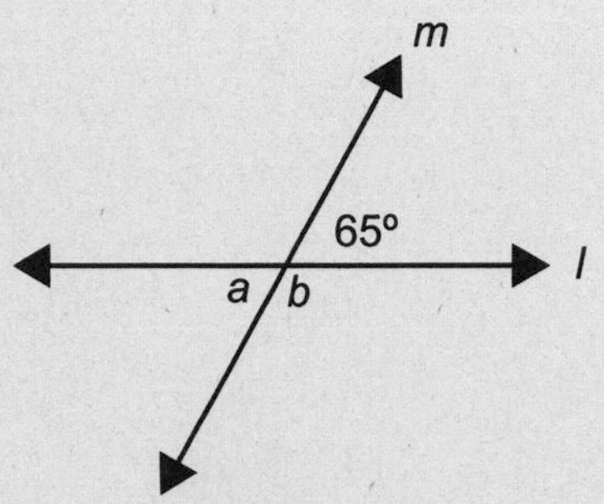

F. m $\angle a$ = 295° and m $\angle b$ = 125°

G. m $\angle a$ = 65° and m $\angle b$ = 65°

H. m $\angle a$ = 25° and m $\angle b$ = 115°

J. m $\angle a$ = 65° and m $\angle b$ = 115°

K. m $\angle a$ = 65° and m $\angle b$ = 50°

5. If 0.65 < x < 85%, which of the following could be x?

A. $\frac{2}{5}$

B. $\frac{5}{12}$

C. $\frac{5}{8}$

D. $\frac{2}{3}$

E. $\frac{7}{8}$

6. The average of set S is 14. If set $S = \{10, 12, 19, x\}$, what is the value of x?

F. 14
G. 15
H. 16
J. 20
K. Cannot be determined

7. A merchant at a farmer's market sells jars of homemade marmalade for $4.50 each. To encourage patrons to purchase in bulk, he offers a 10% discount on packages of 5 jars and a 15% discount on packages of 10 jars. If a customer buys 15 jars, what is her total cost?

A. $20.25
B. $38.25
C. $50.63
D. $58.50
E. $67.50

8. Which of these expressions is equivalent to $\frac{2x+6}{(x+3)(3x-9)}$?

F. $\frac{4}{3x-9}$

G. $\frac{2(x+6)}{3(x+3)(x-9)}$

H. $\frac{2(x+1)}{3x(x-3)}$

J. $\frac{2}{3(x-3)}$

K. $\frac{2}{3(x-9)}$

9. Zarley spends 22 minutes of a 50-minute workout on strength training. What percentage of the workout does he devote to other exercises?

A. 14%
B. 22%
C. 28%
D. 44%
E. 56%

SHOW YOUR WORK HERE

CONTINUE

SHOW YOUR WORK HERE

10. The perimeter of an encampment in an African village is equipped with an alarm designed to sound when predatory animals come within 2 feet of it. Using a web camera, it was determined that 6 of 25 times the alarm sounded were false alarms. What percentage was due to actual animals encountering the alarm?

F. $\dfrac{19}{25\times100}$

G. $\dfrac{19}{100}\times25$

H. $\dfrac{6}{25}\times100$

J. $\dfrac{19}{25}\times100$

K. $\dfrac{6}{25\times100}$

11. If $z=-3$, then what is the value of $\dfrac{6}{-z}+z(1-2z)$?

A. −22
B. −19
C. −7
D. 17
E. 23

12. When 64 is divided by *x*, the quotient is a negative integer. Which of the following could be *x*?

F. 16
G. 6
H. 1
J. −8
K. −12

13. If $\dfrac{5-x}{5}=20$, then $x=$ __________.

A. −105
B. −95
C. −20
D. 30
E. 95

14. A group of students fills an entire row in the school auditorium. Counting from the left, Matt is seated in the fourth chair in the row; counting from the right, he is seated in the fifteenth chair in the row. What is the total number of chairs in this row?

F. 11
G. 12
H. 18
J. 19
K. 20

SHOW YOUR WORK HERE

15. Let $h(x) = 1 - |2 - 3x|$. Evaluate $h(-2)$.

A. −7
B. −3
C. −1
D. 5
E. 9

16. The clock below shows a time of 3:05. What time will the clock show when the minute hand has moved 60° clockwise?

F. 3:00
G. 3:15
H. 3:45
J. 4:05
K. 5:05

17. To which expression is $(3x - 2)(2x + 3)$ equal?

A. $6x^2 - 6$
B. $5x + 1$
C. $6x^2 + 1$
D. $6x^2 + 5x - 6$
E. $6x^2 - 5x + 6$

CONTINUE

SHOW YOUR WORK HERE

18. If, in the figure below, point *A* is the vertex of a square with area 9, which of the following could be another vertex of this square?

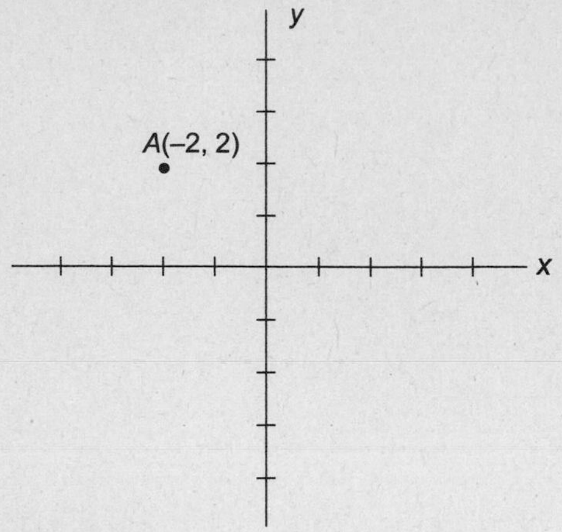

F. (–9, 2)
G. (–5, 5)
H. (–2,–7)
J. (3, 2)
K. (7, 2)

19. The width of the base, length of the base, and height of a rectangular box are in the ratio 1:2:4. If the volume of the box is 4,096 cubic centimeters, what is the length of the base?

A. 8 cm
B. 10 cm
C. 16 cm
D. 32 cm
E. 128 cm

20. How many sections on the spinner below should be colored red in order to make the probability of the arrow NOT landing on red 0.375 in a single spin?

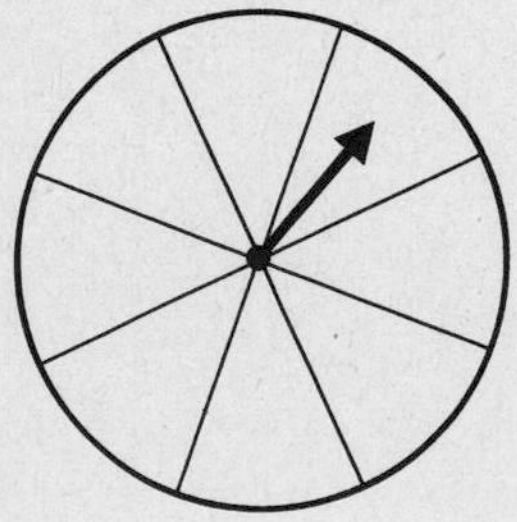

F. 1
G. 3
H. 5
J. 7
K. 8

21. Of the triangles with the side lengths given below, which is a right triangle?

A. 6, 13, 14
B. 8, 10, 12
C. 12, 16, 18
D. 15, 22, 23
E. 20, 21, 29

SHOW YOUR WORK HERE

22. A corner market sells individual cans of soda for $1.25 each. A superstore sells cases of 24 cans of this soda for $19.20. How much more would it cost to buy 24 individual cans at the market instead of a case from the superstore?

F. $0.45
G. $4.80
H. $4.20
J. $10.80
K. $30

23. Which of the following represents the translation of $j(x)=\sqrt{x}$ five units to the right and up two units?

A. $k(x)=\sqrt{x-2}+5$

B. $k(x)=\sqrt{x+5}-2$

C. $k(x)=\sqrt{x-5}-2$

D. $k(x)=\sqrt{x+5}+2$

E. $k(x)=\sqrt{x-5}+2$

24. To which of the following expressions is $\dfrac{z^4}{\left(z^{-2}\right)^5}$ equal?

F. $\dfrac{1}{z^{-6}}$
G. z^7
H. z^{-40}
J. z
K. z^{14}

25. The scale on a city map indicates that $\frac{5}{8}$ inch equals $3\frac{1}{2}$ city blocks. To how many blocks does 4 inches correspond?

A. $7\frac{13}{16}$

B. $8\frac{3}{4}$

C. $9\frac{3}{5}$

D. $22\frac{2}{5}$

E. 20

CONTINUE

26. What are the solutions of $x(3x - 4) = 4$?

SHOW YOUR WORK HERE

F. $x = 4, x = -\frac{1}{3}$

G. $x = 4, x = \frac{8}{3}$

H. $x = \frac{2}{3}, x = -2$

J. $x = 0, x = 4$

K. $x = -\frac{2}{3}, x = 2$

27. Joanie scored 80 on 3 tests, 92 on 2 tests, and 100 on 1 test. What is her average for all the tests, to the nearest tenth of a point?

A. 80.0
B. 86.0
C. 87.3
D. 90.7
E. 92.0

28. What is the domain of the function $h(x) = |x - 4| - 1$?

F. $(-1, \infty]$

G. $(-\infty, -1]$

H. $(-\infty, \infty)$

J. $(-\infty, 4]$

K. $[4, \infty)$

29. What is the complete set of solutions of the equation $\sin 2x = -\frac{1}{2}$ for $0 \le x \le 2\pi$?

A. $\frac{7\pi}{6}, \frac{11\pi}{6}$

B. $\frac{\pi}{12}, \frac{5\pi}{12}, \frac{13\pi}{12}, \frac{17\pi}{12}$

C. $\frac{\pi}{6}, \frac{\pi}{3}, \frac{7\pi}{6}, \frac{4\pi}{3}$

D. $\frac{7\pi}{12}, \frac{11\pi}{12}, \frac{19\pi}{12}, \frac{23\pi}{12}$

E. $\frac{2\pi}{3}, \frac{5\pi}{6}, \frac{8\pi}{3}, \frac{17\pi}{6}$

30. A truck driver earns 35 cents for every mile she drives. How much will she earn if she drives for $9\frac{1}{2}$ hours at an average speed of 55 miles per hour?

F. \$60.45
G. \$149.29
H. \$165.41
J. \$182.88
K. \$202.63

31. Which of the following represents the solution set to the compound inequality $x \leq -2$ or $x > 4$?

A. 

B. 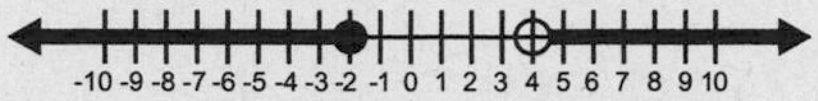

C. 

D. 

E. 

32. A fish tank has a length of 24 inches, a width of 8 inches, and a height of 10 inches. If the tank contains 1,728 cubic inches of water, what is the depth, in inches, of water in the tank?

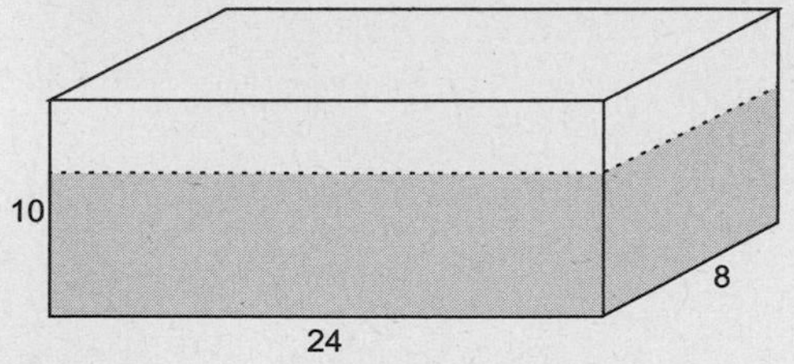

F. 6
G. 7
H. 8
J. 9
K. 10

33. A car rental company charges $20 per day for a rental car, plus $0.50 for each mile driven. If Kecia kept a car for 3 days and was charged $156, how many miles did she drive?

A. 432
B. 312
C. 192
D. 156
E. 96

34. A leg and hypotenuse of a right triangle have lengths 4 meters and 9 meters, respectively. What is the length of the other leg of the triangle?

F. $\sqrt{9^2+4^2}$ meters
G. 9^2+4^2 meters
H. $\sqrt{9^2-4^2}$ meters
J. 9^2-4^2 meters
K. $9-4$ meters

SHOW YOUR WORK HERE

CONTINUE

35. The formula for the surface area of a rectangular box is $S = 2(lw + lh + wh)$. To which expression is w equal?

SHOW YOUR WORK HERE

A. $\frac{S-2lh}{4lh}$

B. $\frac{S-2lh}{2l+2h}$

C. $\frac{S}{2lh}-2l-2h$

D. $\frac{S}{2(l+lh+h)}$

E. $\frac{S-lh}{l+h}$

36. Consider the function $f(x)$ graphed below:

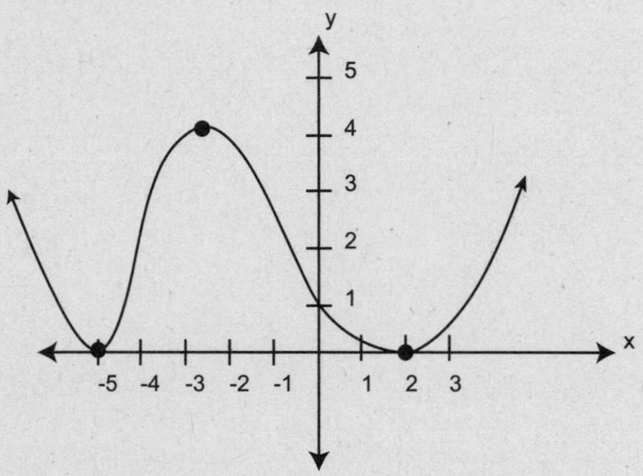

The following statements are true EXCEPT:

F. The solution set of the inequality $f(x) < 0$ is the empty set.

G. The range of $f(x)$ is $[0,\infty)$.

H. The maximum of $f(x)$ is 4.

J. The domain of $f(x)$ is the set of all real numbers.

K. There are two x-intercepts.

37. $\frac{w^2-9}{w} \div \frac{w^2-3w}{3} =$ ________

A. $w(w-3)^2$

B. $\frac{12}{w}$

C. $\frac{3w+3}{w^2}$

D. $\frac{3w+9}{w^2}$

E. $\frac{(w-3)^2(w+3)}{3}$

38. In right triangle *ABC* below, $\cos A = \frac{1}{2}$. What is the value of $\cos B$?

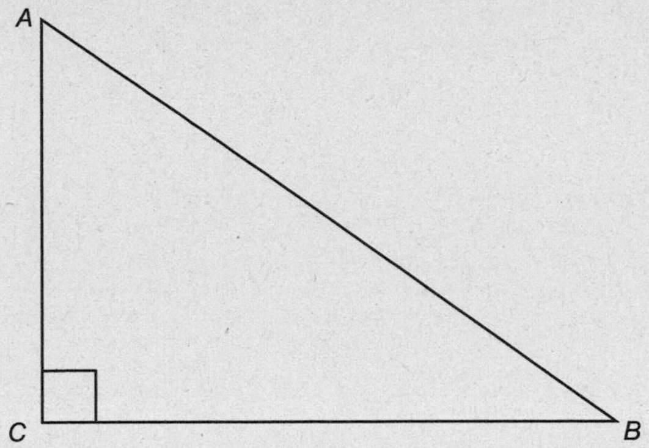

F. 2

G. $\sqrt{3}$

H. $\frac{\sqrt{3}}{2}$

J. $\frac{\sqrt{3}}{3}$

K. $\frac{1}{2}$

39. If $f(x) = \frac{1}{x+2}$ and $g(x) = \frac{3}{x+1}$, what is $(g \circ f)(x)$?

A. $\frac{3x+6}{x+3}$

B. $3(x+2)+1$

C. $\frac{x+2}{x}$

D. $\frac{x+1}{3} + \frac{1}{2}$

E. $\frac{x+1}{2x+5}$

SHOW YOUR WORK HERE

CONTINUE

40. A packing company is looking to reduce costs by changing the size of its boxes. It wants to create a new box that has the same volume as its current box, but a smaller surface area. The current box is shown below. What are the dimensions, in feet, of the box with the same volume and the smallest surface area?

SHOW YOUR WORK HERE

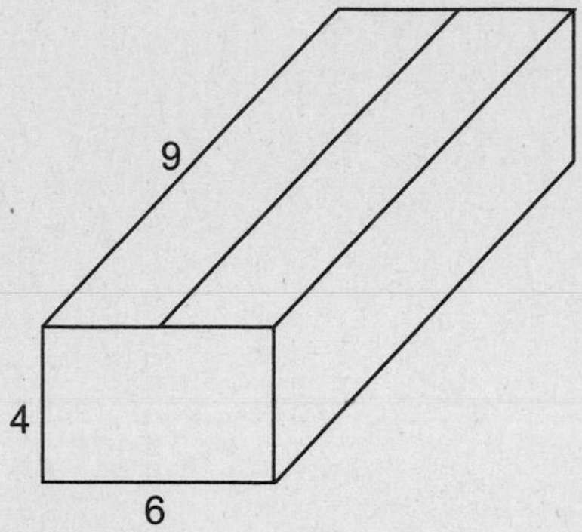

F. $2 \times 3 \times 36$

G. $2 \times 4 \times 27$

H. $3 \times 6 \times 12$

J. $3 \times 8 \times 9$

K. $6 \times 6 \times 6$

41. Which of these lines is parallel to a line with the equation $x = \frac{1}{3}y + 2$?

A. $y = 2$

B. $y = \frac{1}{3}x - 5$

C. $y + 3x = 1$

D. $x = 2$

E. $6y - 18x = 0$

42. A pump can remove water from a swimming pool at a rate of 3.5 gallons per minute. At this rate, how many gallons will be removed after *h* hours?

F. $3.5h$

G. $\frac{h}{3.5}$

H. $210h$

J. $\frac{h}{210}$

K. $h + 3.5$

43. The table shows how the variable y depends on various values of x. Which equation best represents this relationship?

x	–2	0	2	4
y	–3	–2	–1	0

A. $y = x - 1$
B. $y = 2x + 1$
C. $y = -2x - 2$
D. $y = \frac{1}{2}x - 2$
E. $y = -\frac{1}{2}x - 2$

44. If $x > y$ and $z > y$, which of the following MUST be true?

F. $x > z$
G. $z > x$
H. $x^2 > y^2$
J. $z^2 > y^2$
K. $x + z > 2y$

45. If $3x - 2y = 0$ and $2x + 3y = 13$, what is the value of $\frac{y}{x}$?

A. $\frac{2}{3}$
B. $\frac{3}{2}$
C. 5
D. 3
E. 2

46. In the figure below, a circle is inscribed within a square. If the perimeter of the square is 36 feet, what is the area of the shaded region, in square feet?

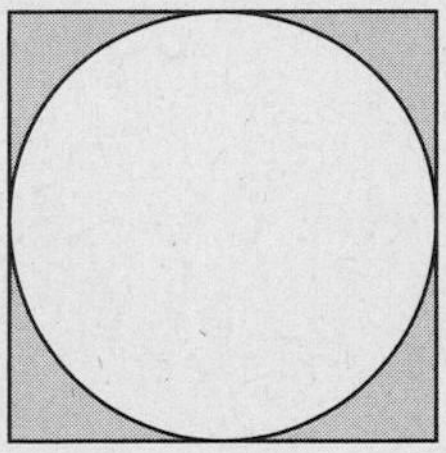

F. $9 - 4.5\pi$
G. $36 - 9\pi$
H. $36 + 9\pi$
J. $81 - 20.25\pi$
K. $81 - 36\pi$

SHOW YOUR WORK HERE

CONTINUE

47. A carnival game involves a spinner with congruent sections numbered 1 through 50. On a given spin, the spinner has an equal chance of landing on any number. If Greg bets on numbers 32 through 46, what is the probability that the spinner will land on one of Greg's numbers?

SHOW YOUR WORK HERE

A. $\frac{1}{50}$

B. $\frac{7}{25}$

C. $\frac{3}{10}$

D. $\frac{7}{10}$

E. $\frac{23}{25}$

48. In the rectangular prism shown below, what is the length of diagonal $\overline{QS}$?

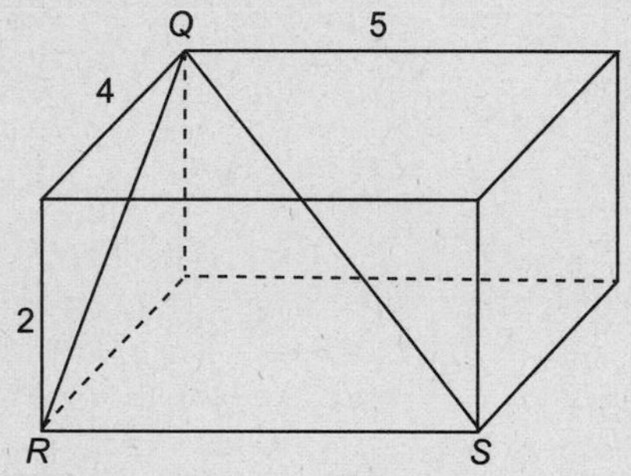

F. $2\sqrt{5}$

G. 5.5

H. $3\sqrt{5}$

J. 11

K. 20

49. What is the maximum value of the function $f(x) = -3x^2 + 18x - 1$?

A. –28

B. –10

C. –1

D. 3

E. 26

50. The length of the radius of circle *A* is 3 times as long as the radius of circle *B*. If the area of circle *A* is *x*, what is the area of circle *B*?

F. $\frac{x}{9}$

G. $\frac{x}{6}$

H. $\frac{x}{3}$

J. $3x$

K. $9x$

51. Which of the following lines is parallel to the line graphed below?

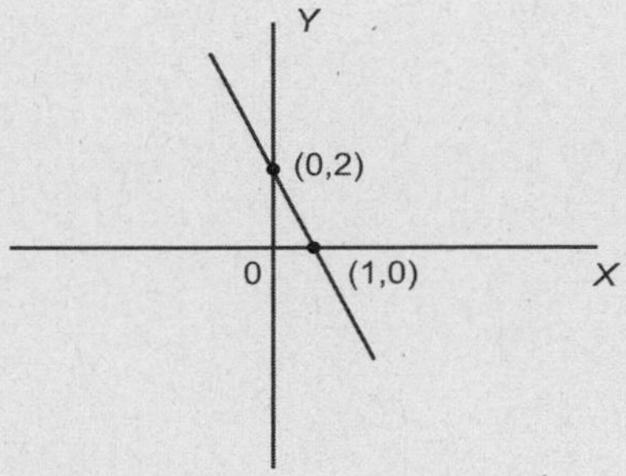

A. $y=x+2$

B. $y=2x-3$

C. $y=-2x+2$

D. $y=\frac{1}{2}x-5$

E. $y=-\frac{1}{2}x+2$

52. If the area of ΔABC is 24 square feet, what is the perimeter of parallelogram *BCED*, in feet?

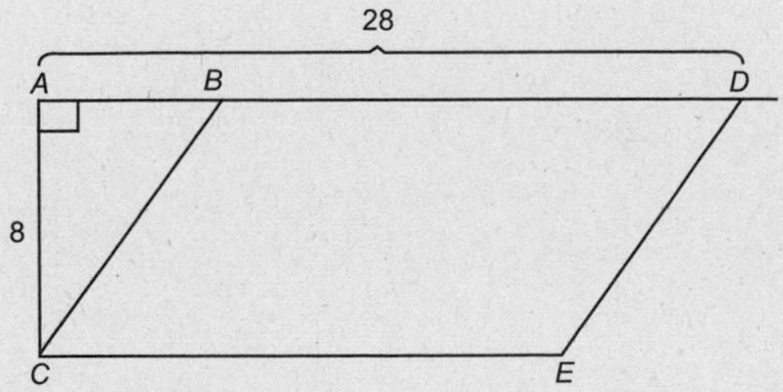

F. 76 feet

G. 72 feet

H. 68 feet

J. 64 feet

K. $44+2\sqrt{73}$ feet

SHOW YOUR WORK HERE

CONTINUE

53. A company is producing outdoor projector systems for use in holiday decorations. The profit function is $p(x) = 2x^2 - 3x - 14$, where x is in hundreds of projectors and $p(x)$ is in thousands of dollars. How many projectors must the company sell to break even?

A. 35
B. 200
C. 350
D. 1,400
E. 3,500

54. Working together, a standard printer and a high-speed printer can complete a certain print job in $3\frac{1}{3}$ hours. If it takes the high-speed printer 5 hours to do the job alone, how many hours would it take the standard printer to do the job alone?

F. $1\frac{2}{3}$
G. $4\frac{1}{6}$
H. $6\frac{2}{3}$
J. $8\frac{1}{3}$
K. 10

55. Increasing a number by 30% and then decreasing the result by 50% is the same as decreasing the number by:

A. 10%
B. 15%
C. 20%
D. 35%
E. 65%

SHOW YOUR WORK HERE

56. In the figure below, if Line 1 is parallel to Line 2, all of the following are true EXCEPT:

SHOW YOUR WORK HERE

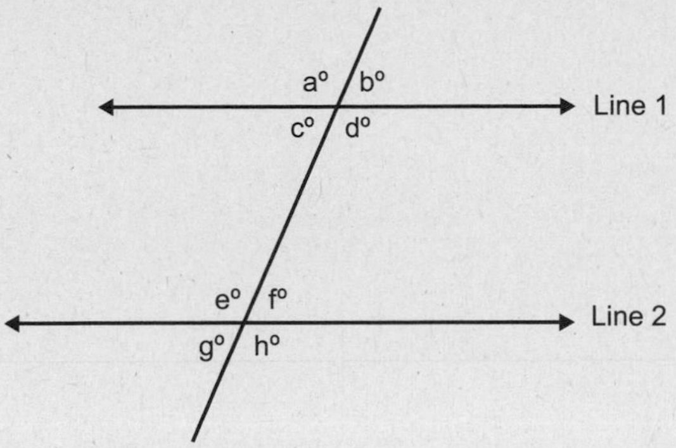

F. $a + b = g + h$
G. $f - h = c - d$
H. $a + h = g + c$
J. $d + b - f = e + c - g$
K. $h - c = d - f$

57. In the figure below, what is the value of *n*?

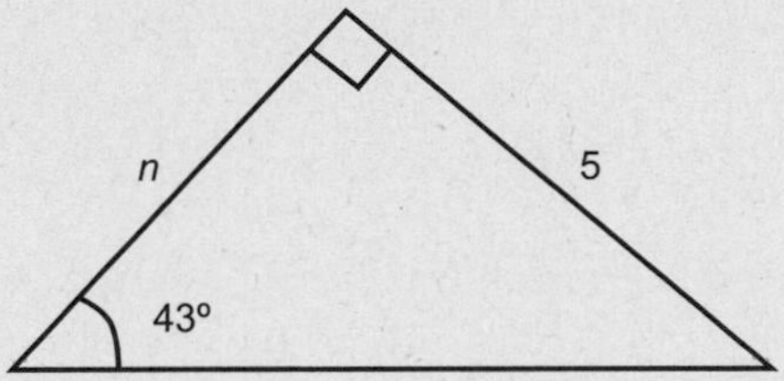

A. $\frac{5}{\sin 43°}$

B. $\frac{5}{\cos 47°}$

C. $\frac{5}{\tan 43°}$

D. 5 sin 47°

E. 5 tan 43°

58. The sum of three consecutive odd integers is 129. What is the average of the two smallest of these integers?

F. 41
G. 42
H. 43
J. 44
K. 45

CONTINUE

59. What is the equation of the parabola graphed below?

SHOW YOUR WORK HERE

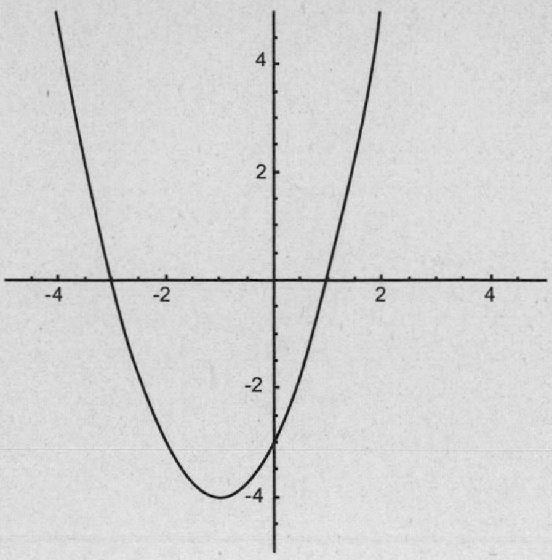

A. $y = x^2 - 2x - 3$
B. $y = x^2 - 2x + 3$
C. $y = x^2 + 2x - 3$
D. $y = x^2 + 2x + 3$
E. $y = -x^2 - 2x - 3$

60. Two fair six-sided dice are rolled. What is the probability that the sum of the two faces on which the dice come to rest is less than 4?

F. $\frac{1}{36}$

G. $\frac{1}{18}$

H. $\frac{1}{12}$

J. $\frac{5}{36}$

K. $\frac{1}{6}$

STOP

READING TEST

35 Minutes—40 Questions

DIRECTIONS: There are four passages in this test. Each passage is followed by several questions. Read each passage, select the best answer to each related question, and fill in the corresponding circle on the answer sheet. You may look back at the passages as often as you need.

PASSAGE I

PROSE FICTION: Passage A is an excerpt from *The Strange Case of Dr. Jekyll and Mr. Hyde*, by Robert Louis Stevenson. Passage B is an excerpt from *The Invisible Man*, by H.G. Wells.

Passage A

by Robert Louis Stevenson

Six o'clock struck on the bells of the church that was so conveniently near to Mr. Utterson's dwelling, and still he was digging at the problem. Hitherto it had touched him on the intellectual side alone; but now his imagination also was engaged, or rather enslaved; and as he lay and tossed in the gross darkness of the night and the curtained room, Mr. Enfield's tale went by before his mind in a scroll of lighted pictures. He would be aware of the great field of lamps of a nocturnal city; then of the figure of a man walking swiftly; then of a child running from the doctor's; and then these met, and that human Juggernaut trod the child down and passed on regardless of her screams. Or else he would see a room in a rich house, where his friend lay asleep, dreaming and smiling at his dreams; and then the door of that room would be opened, the curtains of the bed plucked apart, the sleeper recalled, and lo! there would stand by his side a figure to whom power was given, and even at that dead hour, he must rise and do its bidding. The figure in these two phases haunted the lawyer all night; and if at any time he dozed over, it was but to see it glide more stealthily through sleeping houses, or move the more swiftly and still the more swiftly, even to dizziness, through wider labyrinths of lamplighted city, and at every street corner crush a child and leave her screaming. And still the figure had no face by which he might know it; even in his dreams, it had no face, or one that baffled him and melted before his eyes; and thus it was that there sprang up and grew apace in the lawyer's mind a singularly strong, almost an inordinate, curiosity to behold the features of the real Mr. Hyde. If he could but once set eyes on him, he thought the mystery would lighten and perhaps roll altogether away, as was the habit of mysterious things when well examined. He might see a reason for his friend's strange preference or bondage (call it which you please) and even for the startling clause of the will. At least it would be a face worth seeing: the face of a man who was without bowels of mercy: a face which had but to show itself to raise up, in the mind of the unimpressionable Enfield, a spirit of enduring hatred.

From that time forward, Mr. Utterson began to haunt the door in the by-street of shops. In the morning before office hours, at noon when business was plenty, and time scarce, at night under the face of the fogged city moon, by all lights and at all hours of solitude or concourse, the lawyer was to be found on his chosen post.

"If he be Mr. Hyde," he had thought, "I shall be Mr. Seek."

Passage B

by H.G. Wells

The stranger came early in February one wintry day, through a biting wind and a driving snow, the last snowfall of the year, over the down, walking as it seemed from Bramblehurst railway station and carrying a little black portmanteau in his thickly gloved hand. He was wrapped up from head to foot, and the brim of his soft felt hat hid every inch of his face but the shiny tip of his nose; the snow had piled itself against his shoulders and chest, and added a white crest to the burden he carried. He staggered into the Coach and Horses, more dead than alive as it seemed, and flung his portmanteau down. "A fire," he cried, "in the name of human charity! A room and a fire!" He stamped and shook the snow from off himself in the bar, and followed Mrs. Hall into her guest parlour to strike his bargain. And with that much introduction, that and a ready acquiescence to terms and a couple of sovereigns flung upon the table, he took up his quarters in the inn.

Mrs. Hall lit the fire and left him there while she went to prepare him a meal with her own hands. A guest to stop at Iping in the winter-time was an unheard-of piece of luck, let alone a guest who was no "haggler," and she was resolved to show herself worthy of her good fortune. As soon as the bacon was well under way, and Millie, her lymphatic aid, had been brisked up a bit by a few deftly chosen expressions of contempt, she carried the cloth, plates, and glasses into the parlour and began to lay them with the utmost clat. Although the fire was burning up briskly, she was surprised to see that her visitor still wore his hat and coat, standing with his back to her and staring out of the window at the falling snow in the yard. His gloved

CONTINUE

hands were clasped behind him, and he seemed to be lost in thought. She noticed that the melted snow that still sprinkled his shoulders dripped upon her carpet. "Can I take your hat and coat, sir," she said, "and give them a good dry in the kitchen?"

"No," he said without turning.

She was not sure she had heard him, and was about to repeat her question.

He turned his head and looked at her over his shoulder. "I prefer to keep them on," he said with emphasis, and she noticed that he wore big blue spectacles with side-lights and had a bushy side-whisker over his coat-collar that completely hid his face.

"Very well, sir," she said. "As you like. In a bit the room will be warmer."

He made no answer and had turned his face away from her again; and Mrs. Hall, feeling that her conversational advances were ill-timed, laid the rest of the table things in a quick staccato and whisked out of the room.

Questions 1–3 ask about Passage A.

1. As it is used in line 12, the word *rich* most nearly means:

A. wealthy.
B. affluent.
C. abundant.
D. plush.

2. Mr. Utterson starts spending time by the door in the by-street of shops:

F. while having a nightmare about Mr. Enfield.
G. after deciding he needs to see Mr. Hyde.
H. before talking to his friend about Mr. Hyde.
J. on his way to his place of work.

3. It can be inferred from the passage that the relationship between Mr. Utterson and Mr. Hyde is most similar to that between:

A. two brothers.
B. a police officer and a criminal.
C. an employee and a boss.
D. former co-workers.

Questions 4–7 ask about Passage B.

4. What does the first paragraph (lines 1–16) suggest about the stranger?

F. He has something to hide.
G. He is a wanted criminal.
H. He is the strangest man Mrs. Hall has ever met.
J. He is about to die.

5. As it is used in line 2, the word *biting* most likely means:

A. snapping.
B. freezing.
C. abrasive.
D. hateful.

6. Which of the following statements does NOT describe Mrs. Hall's attitude toward the stranger?

F. She cares about his well-being.
G. She is uneasy in his presence.
H. She is amused by his odd behavior.
J. She feels she is professionally obligated to him.

7. The main purpose of the information in Passage B is to:

A. provide information about the inn management business.
B. characterize Mrs. Hall as a caring and kind person.
C. explain why Mrs. Hall is so attentive to the stranger.
D. list the reasons why Mrs. Hall puts up with the stranger's cruel behavior.

Questions 8–10 ask about both passages.

8. It can be reasonably inferred that one way Mr. Utterson in Passage A is DIFFERENT from Mrs. Hall in Passage B is:

F. he is intrigued by a mysterious person.
G. he finds someone's behavior baffling.
H. he feels concern for other people.
J. he likes to solve mysteries.

9. It can be reasonably inferred that these two passages:

A. occur on the final pages of the novels from which they were excerpted.
B. are the most important incidents in the novels from which they were excerpted.
C. were intended to be humorous tangents in the novels from which they were excerpted.
D. occur early in the novels from which they were excerpted.

10. Paragraph 1 of Passage A and Paragraph 2 of Passage B are both mainly about:

F. the arrivals of mysterious people.
G. the effects mysterious people have on others.
H. the evil deeds mysterious people do.
J. the demanding nature of mysterious people.

PASSAGE II

SOCIAL SCIENCE: This passage is excerpted from a handbook by education pioneer Maria Montessori, who developed a special method for teaching children.

The "Children's House" is the *environment* which is offered to the child that he may be given the opportunity of developing his activities. This kind of school is not of a fixed type, but may vary according to the financial resources at disposal and to the opportunities afforded by the environment. It ought to be a real house; that is to say, a set of rooms with a garden of which the children are the masters. A garden which contains shelters is ideal, because the children can play or sleep under them, and can also bring their tables out to work or dine. In this way they may live almost entirely in the open air, and are protected at the same time from rain and sun.

The central and principal room of the building, often also the only room at the disposal of the children, is the room for "intellectual work." To this central room can be added other smaller rooms according to the means and opportunities of the place: for example, a bathroom, a dining-room, a little parlor or common-room, a room for manual work, a gymnasium and rest-room.

The special characteristic of the equipment of these houses is that it is adapted for children and not adults. They contain not only didactic material specially fitted for the intellectual development of the child, but also a complete equipment for the management of the miniature family. The furniture is light so that the children can move it about, and it is painted in some light color so that the children can wash it with soap and water. There are low tables of various sizes and shapes—square, rectangular and round, large and small. The rectangular shape is the most common as two or more children can work at it together. The seats are small wooden chairs, but there are also small wicker armchairs and sofas.

In the working-room there are two indispensable pieces of furniture. One of these is a very long cupboard with large doors. It is very low so that a small child can set on the top of it small objects such as mats, flowers, etc. Inside this cupboard is kept the didactic material which is the common property of all the children.

The other is a chest of drawers containing two or three columns of little drawers, each of which has a bright handle (or a handle of some color to contrast with the background), and a small card with a name upon it. Every child has his own drawer, in which to put things belonging to him.

Round the walls of the room are fixed blackboards at a low level, so that the children can write or draw on them, and pleasing, artistic pictures, which are changed from time to time as circumstances direct. The pictures represent children, families, landscapes, flowers and fruit, and more often Biblical and historical incidents. Ornamental plants and flowering plants ought always to be placed in the room where the children are at work.

Another part of the working-room's equipment is seen in the pieces of carpet of various colors—red, blue, pink, green and brown. The children spread these rugs upon the floor, sit upon them and work there with the didactic material. A room of this kind is larger than the customary class-rooms, not only because the little tables and separate chairs take up more space, but also because a large part of the floor must be free for the children to spread their rugs and work upon them.

In the sitting-room, or "club-room," a kind of parlor in which the children amuse themselves by conversation, games, or music, etc., the furnishings should be especially tasteful. Little tables of different sizes, little armchairs and sofas should be placed here and there. Many brackets of all kinds and sizes, upon which may be put statuettes, artistic vases or framed photographs, should adorn the walls; and, above all, each child should have a little flower-pot, in which he may sow the seed of some indoor plant, to tend and cultivate it as it grows. On the tables of this sitting-room should be placed large albums of colored pictures, and also games of patience, or various geometric solids, with which the children can play at pleasure, constructing figures, etc. A piano, or, better, other musical instruments, possibly harps of small dimensions, made especially for children, completes the equipment. In this "club-room" the teacher may sometimes entertain the children with stories, which will attract a circle of interested listeners.

The furniture of the dining-room consists, in addition to the tables, of low cupboards accessible to all the children, who can themselves put in their place and take away the crockery, spoons, knives and forks, table-cloth and napkins. The plates are always of china, and the tumblers and water-bottles of glass. Knives are always included in the table equipment.

11. According to the passage, the Children's House is a(n):

- **A.** playground for children.
- **B.** type of school.
- **C.** indoor environment.
- **D.** house to live in.

CONTINUE

12. The author suggests that the equipment in a Children's House should be "adapted for children and not adults" (line 19) because:

F. adults are not allowed in a Children's House.
G. children cannot learn by using adult-sized equipment.
H. it encourages sharing among children.
J. it will help children to be self-sufficient.

13. In the sixth paragraph (lines 41–47), the main point is that the decorations in a Children's House

A. should be varied.
B. must be very religious.
C. teach children about history.
D. force children to be artistic.

14. The passage states that a working room must contain pieces of multicolored carpet because:

F. colorful objects stimulate creativity.
G. this is the area on which the children work.
H. the tables and chairs take up too much space.
J. children must learn how to spread out carpets.

15. As it is used in line 20, the word *didactic* most likely means:

A. educational.
B. enjoyable.
C. teach.
D. small.

16. Which of these statements is supported by the second paragraph (lines 12–17)?

F. Exercise is an element of the educational method the author describes.
G. Children will develop good table manners if they eat in a dining room.
H. Children spend only half of their school day in the central room.
J. Manual work is the most important activity that takes place in the central room.

17. The drawers, in contrast to the cupboard, are described as:

A. a common area.
B. a piece of storage equipment.
C. an element in the working room.
D. a place for personal possessions.

18. The author's attitude toward children is one of:

F. curiosity.
G. trust.
H. admiration.
J. wrath.

19. The passage indicates that the author believes that:

A. adults should not be involved in the education of children.
B. multiple stimuli and freedom are integral to a good education.
C. children need to live apart from adults when learning.
D. unsupervised children tend to get into a lot of trouble.

20. Based on the eighth paragraph (lines 56–72), the author believes that:

F. a child's education is incomplete if the child cannot play a musical instrument.
G. children should not have to participate in activities that do not interest them.
H. it's important for a child to be given a plant to nurture and cultivate.
J. a child will never learn patience without access to a club room.

PASSAGE III

HUMANITIES: This passage is adapted from the introduction to a book in which author Edgar Allan Poe discusses his approach to composing literature.

Charles Dickens, in a note now lying before me, alluding to an examination I once made of the mechanism of "Barnaby Rudge," says—"By the way, are you aware that Godwin wrote his 'Caleb Williams' backwards? He first involved his hero in a web of difficulties, forming the second volume, and then, for the first, cast about him for some mode of accounting for what had been done."

I cannot think this the precise mode of procedure on the part of Godwin—and indeed what he himself acknowledges, is not altogether in accordance with Mr. Dickens' idea—but the author of "Caleb Williams" was too good an artist not to perceive the advantage derivable from at least a somewhat similar process. Nothing is more clear than that every plot, worth the name, must be elaborated to its dénouement before anything be attempted with the pen. It is only with the dénouement constantly in view that we can give a plot its indispensable air of consequence, or causation, by making the incidents, and especially the tone at all points, tend to the development of the intention.

There is a radical error, I think, in the usual mode of constructing a story. Either history affords a thesis—or one is suggested by an incident of the day—or, at best, the author sets himself to work in the combination of striking events to form merely the basis of his narrative—designing, generally, to fill in with description, dialogue, or authorial comment, whatever crevices of fact, or action, may, from page to page, render themselves apparent.

I prefer commencing with the consideration of an effect. Keeping originality always in view—for he is false to himself who ventures to dispense with so obvious and so easily attainable a source of interest—I say to myself, in the first place, "Of the innumerable effects, or impressions, of which the heart, the intellect, or (more generally) the soul is susceptible, what one shall I, on the present occasion, select?" Having chosen a novel, first, and secondly a vivid effect, I consider whether it can be best wrought by incident or tone—whether by ordinary incidents and peculiar tone, or the converse, or by peculiarity both of incident and tone—afterward looking about me (or rather within) for such combinations of event, or tone, as shall best aid me in the construction of the effect.

I have often thought how interesting a magazine paper might be written by any author who would—that is to say who could—detail, step by step, the processes by which any one of his compositions attained its ultimate point of completion. Why such a paper has never been given to the world, I am much at a loss to say—but, perhaps, the authorial vanity has had more to do with the omission than any one other cause. Most writers—poets in especial—prefer having it understood that they compose by a species of fine frenzy—an ecstatic intuition—and would positively shudder at letting the public take a peep behind the scenes, at the elaborate and vacillating crudities of thought—at the true purposes seized only at the last moment—at the innumerable glimpses of idea that arrived not at the maturity of full view—at the fully matured fancies discarded in despair as unmanageable—at the cautious selections and rejections—at the painful erasures and interpolations—in a word, at the wheels and pinions—the tackle for scene-shifting—the stepladders and demon-traps—the cock's feathers, the red paint and the black patches, which, in ninety-nine cases out of the hundred, constitute the properties of the literary histrio.

I am aware, on the other hand, that the case is by no means common, in which an author is at all in condition to retrace the steps by which his conclusions have been attained. In general, suggestions, having arisen pell-mell, are pursued and forgotten in a similar manner.

For my own part, I have neither sympathy with the repugnance alluded to, nor at any time the least difficulty in recalling to mind the progressive steps of any of my compositions; and, since the interest of an analysis, or reconstruction, such as I have considered a desideratum, is quite independent of any real or fancied interest in the thing analyzed, it will not be regarded as a breach of decorum on my part to show the modus operandi by which some one of my own works was put together. I select "The Raven," as most generally known. It is my design to render it manifest that no one point in its composition is referable either to accident or intuition—that the work proceeded, step by step, to its completion with the precision and rigid consequence of a mathematical problem.

Let us dismiss, as irrelevant to the poem, per se, the circumstance—or say the necessity—which, in the first place, gave rise to the intention of composing a poem that should suit at once the popular and the critical taste.

21. Which of the following is NOT characteristic of the way Dickens thought Godwin wrote "Caleb Williams"?

A. Godwin wrote the ending first.
B. Godwin imagined difficulties for his character.
C. Godwin wrote the first part of the story last.
D. Godwin made sure the tone fit the incidents in his story.

22. One can reasonably infer that when the author writes literature, he:

F. always starts with the beginning of his story before working forward.
G. does not pay attention to the process by which he writes.
H. is only concerned with tone and has no interest in plot.
J. is primarily concerned with manipulating the reader.

23. The creation of "The Raven" involved:

I. a precise method.
II. accident.
III. intuition.

A. I only
B. I and III only
C. II and III only
D. I, II, and III

CONTINUE

24. Poe's claim that "There is a radical error, I think, in the usual mode of constructing a story. Either history affords a thesis—or one is suggested by an incident of the day" (lines 18–20) most strongly suggests that during writing sessions, Poe would:

F. use historical events as the basis of a plot he is outlining.
G. completely alter historical events to suit the plot he is devising.
H. set his story in the future so he does not have to rely on history at all.
J. not faithfully base a plot in one of his stories on history.

25. The main point of the fifth paragraph (lines 39–58) is that Poe:

A. intends to write a detailed article about the literary process.
B. thinks there are several reasons why no one has written a valuable article about the literary process.
C. does most of his writing in a frenzied state of ecstatic intuition.
D. has no idea why no one has written an article about the literary process.

26. Poe explains that when writing, he:

F. works in a state of creative frenzy.
G. keeps notes on his writing process.
H. is more concerned with tone than plot.
J. remains very conscious of his writing process.

27. According to the first paragraph (lines 1–6), Dickens expressed his theories about Godwin:

A. in an article entitled "Barnaby Rudge."
B. in a response to Poe's examination of "Barnaby Rudge."
C. after reading Godwin's story "Barnaby Rudge."
D. after Poe criticized Godwin's "Caleb Williams."

28. The author offers all of the following as reasons why no one has written a detailed article about the literary process EXCEPT:

F. Crudity
G. Vanity
H. Forgetfulness
J. Deceptiveness

29. Based on the passage, the author intends to change the way:

A. writers create literature.
B. readers analyze literature.
C. readers perceive the literary process.
D. writers discuss the literary process.

30. The sentence, "Let us dismiss, as irrelevant to the poem, per se, the circumstance—or say the necessity—which, in the first place, gave rise to the intention of composing a poem that should suit at once the popular and the critical taste." (lines 77–80) suggests that the author:

F. admits that his work is fairly irrelevant.
G. is very proud of the popularity of his poem "The Raven."
H. intended "The Raven" to have widespread appeal.
J. does not respect critics even though they praised his poem "The Raven."

PASSAGE IV

NATURAL SCIENCE: The following passage is excerpted from a book about popular science written by scientist Aaron Bernstein in 1869.

One would be well justified in calling the blood "man's body in a liquid state." For the blood is destined to become the living solid body of man.

People were astonished, when Liebig, the great naturalist, called blood the "liquid flesh;" we are correct even in going further and calling the blood "man's body in a liquid state." From blood are prepared not only muscles and flesh, but also bones, brain, fat, teeth, eyes, veins, cartilages, nerves, tendons, and even hair.

It is utterly wrong for anybody to suppose, that the constituents of all these parts are dissolved in the blood, say as sugar is dissolved in water. By no means. Water is something quite different from the sugar dissolved in it; while the blood is itself the material from which all the solid parts of the body are formed.

The blood is received into the heart, and the heart, like a pump, forces it into the lungs. There it absorbs in a remarkable manner the oxygen of the air which comes into the lungs by breathing. This blood, saturated now with oxygen, is then recalled to another part of the heart by an expansive movement of that organ.

This part of the heart contracts again and impels the oxygenated blood into the whole body by means of arteries, which branch out more and more, and become smaller and smaller, until at last they are no longer visible to the naked eye. In this manner the blood penetrates all part of the body, and returns to the heart by means of similar thread-like veins, which gradually join and form larger veins. Having reached the heart, it is again forced into the lungs, and absorbs there more oxygen, returns to the heart, and is again circulated through the whole system.

During this double circulation of the blood from the heart to the lungs and back, and then from the heart to all parts of the body and back again—during all this, the change of particles, so remarkable in itself, is constantly going on: the exchange by which the useless and wasted matter are secreted and new substances distributed. This fact is wonderful, and its cause not yet fully explained by science; but so much is certain, that the blood when being conveyed to all parts of the human body, deposits whatever at the time may be needed there for the renewal of that part.

Thus the blood that has been formed in the child from the mother's milk, contains phosphorus, oxygen, and calcium. These substances, during the circulation of the blood, are deposited in the bones, and form "phosphate of lime," the principal element in the bone. In the same manner fluor and calcium are given to the teeth. The muscles, or flesh, also receive their ingredients from the blood; so do the nerves, veins, membranes, brain, and nails; also the inner organs, such as the heart, lungs, liver, kidneys, intestines, and stomach.

They all, however, in return give to the blood their waste particles, which it carries to that part of the human body where they may be secreted.

If any member of the body is so bound, that the blood cannot circulate, it must decay; for the life of the body consists in its constant change and transformation, in the continual exchange of fresh substances for waste ones. But this vital exchange is only kept up by the constant circulation of the blood, which, while it decreases by being transformed into vital parts of the body, is always formed anew by our daily food.

Food is therefore very justly called "Means of Existence," and the blood may rightly be called the "Juice of Life."

31. What is the main idea of the fourth paragraph (lines 14–18)?

A. Blood journeys from the heart to the lungs.
B. The heart works as a pump.
C. Blood moves from the heart through arteries.
D. Blood is saturated with oxygen in the lungs.

32. The author compares blood with water to prove that:

F. one contains sugars and the other does not.
G. they have different relationships with particular solids.
H. blood dissolves solid materials and water does not.
J. they are both organic liquids.

33. The passage mentions that Liebig is a(n):

A. biologist.
B. naturalist.
C. zoologist.
D. instructor.

34. It can be inferred from the second paragraph (lines 4–8) that:

F. all elements of the human body are blood-based.
G. blood is the only liquid in the human body.
H. a human cannot lose blood and survive.
J. there is more blood in the flesh than there is in the organs.

35. According to the author, during circulation, oxygen:

I. extracts calcium from teeth.
II. is deposited in bones.
III. forms phosphate of lime.

A. I only
B. I and II only
C. II and III only
D. I, II, and III

36. The author claims that blood is the "Juice of Life" (line 58) because:

F. blood is extracted from solid food.
G. it is a clearer term than "Means of Existence."
H. blood contains as many nutrients as a serving of fresh juice.
J. blood cannot circulate if any part of the body is bound.

37. The passage states that waste particles in blood:

A. are deposited in the organs.
B. are secreted from body parts.
C. prevent blood from circulating.
D. decay inside the body.

38. According to the author, the human body:

I. must be in a constant state of change.
II. must constantly break down and repair itself.
III. constantly needs fresh substances.

F. I only
G. II only
H. II and III only
J. I and III only

39. As it is used in line 9, the word *constituents* most nearly means:

A. components.
B. constants.
C. bases.
D. continents.

CONTINUE

40. The author concludes that blood is:

F. a remarkable and mysterious substance.

G. the only substance upon which human life depends.

H. more important than food to the human body.

J. the essential ingredient of human life.

STOP

SCIENCE TEST

35 Minutes—40 Questions

DIRECTIONS: There are seven passages in this test. Each passage is followed by several questions. Read each passage, select the best answer to each related question, and fill in the corresponding circle on the answer sheet. You may look back at the passages as often as you need.

You are NOT allowed to use a calculator on this test.

PASSAGE I

Ecologists studying crabs were examining interactions between three different species of crabs: Crab 1, Crab 2, and Crab 3. They compared the behavior of each crab against both of the other types of crabs, one species at a time, in a series of experiments. Crabs were also compared with a similar-sized competitor from their own species.

Experiment 1

In Experiment 1, two crabs, one from two different species, were put into a tank together with a food item that all three species were known to eat. Each species was compared separately against each other species, so Crab 1 was compared to Crab 2, Crab 1 with Crab 3, and Crab 2 with Crab 3. The experiment examined how often each species of crab ate any food at all, how often each species found the food first, and how often each species of crab found the food after its competitor but still managed to eat something.

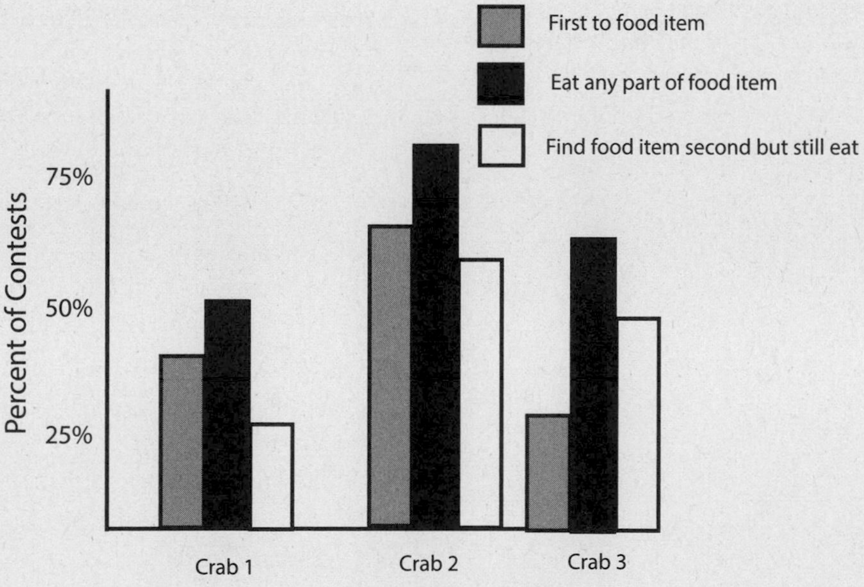

CONTINUE

Experiment 2

Experiment 2 used the same setup and compared each species of crab with each other, as described in Experiment 1. This time, researchers recorded how often each species initiated a conflict with another species and how often each species was the victor in these conflicts.

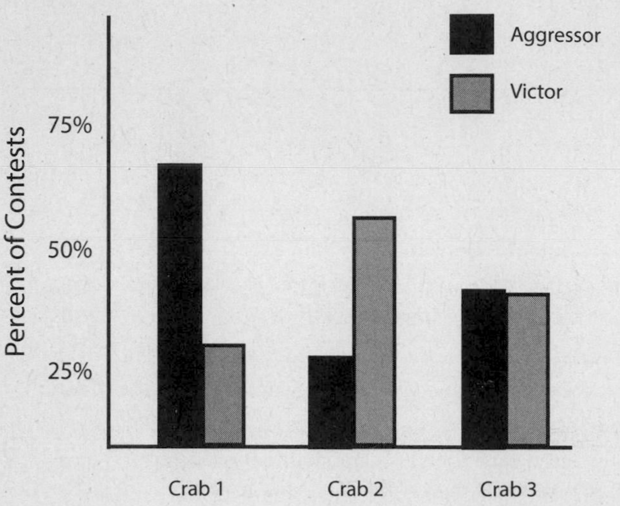

Experiment 3

Experiment 3 used engineering equipment to test how strong each crab's shell was. Shells from crabs of different sizes were placed under stress until they broke.

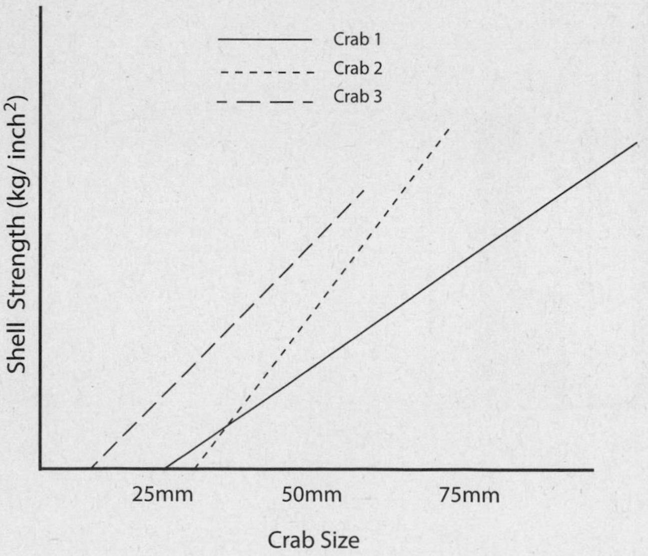

1. Based on the experiments in this study, which crab species is most likely to live a solitary life?

A. Crab 1
B. Crab 2
C. Crab 3
D. No way to tell from the information given

2. What is a possible overall hypothesis for these experiments?

F. Crab 2 is the most skillful fighter of the three species.
G. Crab 3 is the strongest of the three species.
H. One crab is at a disadvantage in contests with other species.
J. Crabs avoid competition with each other.

3. Which statement about Experiment 3 is not accurate?

A. Crab 1 was the largest crab tested.
B. Crab 2's shell increases in strength the most as the crab grows.
C. Crab 3 has the strongest shell.
D. The largest Crab 2 tested was 75mm.

4. What piece of additional information would best help to explain the overall behavior of Crab 1?

F. All three crabs share the same habitat.
G. Crab 1 has a superior sensory system compared to the other two crabs.
H. Crabs 2 and 3 are predators of Crab 1.
J. Crab 1 has more dangerous weapons (claws) than the other two crabs.

5. Which crab has the weakest shell?

A. A 10 mm Crab 3
B. A 20 mm Crab 3
C. A 25 mm Crab 1
D. A 25 mm Crab 2

6. What is one additional experiment the researchers could perform that would help determine the influence of other crabs on each crab's ability to eat?

F. Offer each crab different food items and see which one they prefer.
G. Perform experiments 1 and 2 between 2 crabs of the same species.
H. Test each crab's ability to find a food item separately from one another.
J. Repeat experiments 1 and 2 using larger crabs.

PASSAGE II

Waves are believed to be caused by the transference of energy from wind to a body of water as the wind pushes the water ahead of it. Based on this theory, wave height should be proportional to the speed of the wind that generates the wave. Scientists exploring this hypothesis performed the following experiments.

Experiment 1

A recording station was constructed to measure wind speeds and wave heights at an ocean location. For each wave detected, the height of the wave as it passed the station was recorded, as was the wind speed at the station at the precise moment of crossing. The information recorded by the station's sensors is presented in Figure 1.

FIGURE 1

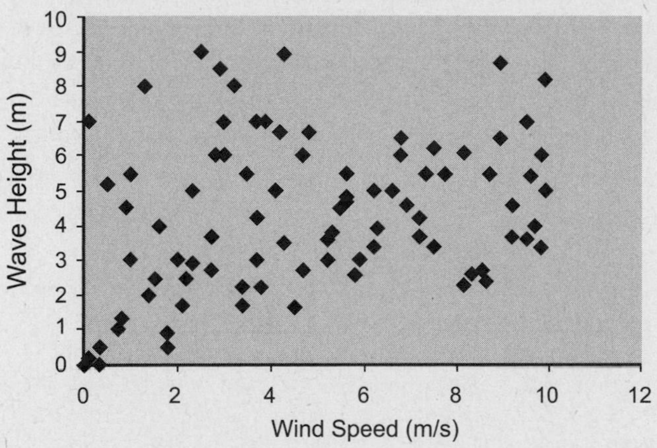

Experiment 2

Swell waves are waves that originate in storm centers. When a swell wave moves faster than the storm that produced it, it often maintains its height and spreads to further regions beyond the storm. Over the course of a week, scientists observed the percentage of waves crossing the recording station used in Experiment 1 that did not originate in the station's vicinity. The results are depicted in Table 1.

Table 1

Day	Percentage of Swell Waves
Monday	13
Tuesday	37
Wednesday	7
Thursday	21
Friday	6
Saturday	3
Sunday	28

Experiment 3

A recording station was constructed to measure the wind speeds and wave heights in a small lake with minimal access to larger water bodies. Wind speed and wave height measurements, collected in the same manner as described in Experiment 1, are represented in Figure 2.

FIGURE 2

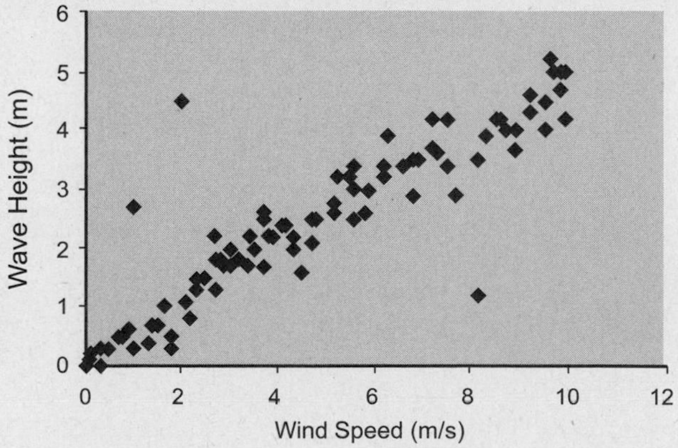

CONTINUE

7. The highest wave height was observed at a wind speed of approximately

   A. 0.0 m/s.
   B. 2.4 m/s.
   C. 8.8 m/s.
   D. 10.0 m/s.

8. How many significant outlier wave heights were observed among the data in Figure 2?

   F. 0
   G. 1
   H. 2
   J. 3

9. What would be a possible alternative explanation, besides the stated hypothesis, for the data shown in the three experiments?

   A. The hypothesis stated in the introduction can be rejected in all cases.
   B. Wind speed correlates with wave height in the ocean but not in small lakes.
   C. Wind speed correlates with wave height in small lakes but not in the ocean.
   D. Swell waves have completely unpredictable wave heights.

10. In science, a null hypothesis is a statement that there is no relationship between variables; if the hypothesis is accepted then the null hypothesis is rejected and vice versa. What is the null hypothesis for this study?

   F. Wind speed directly influences wave height.
   G. Wind speed has no influence on wave height.
   H. Swell waves are more common than wind-driven waves.
   J. Swell waves are rarer than wind-driven waves.

11. Figure 2 suggests that swell waves of which of the following heights crossed the recording station used in Experiment 3?

   A. 1.2 m and 2.7 m
   B. 0.5 m and 2.0 m
   C. 2.7 m and 5.0 m
   D. 1.2 m and 6.0 m

12. In order to lend further support to the hypothesis stated in the passage's introduction, scientists could:

   F. repeat the lake experiment on a day with severe thunderstorms.
   G. repeat the ocean experiment on a perfectly wind-free day.
   H. collect data on wave height and wind speed from an indoor pool exposed to a powerful electronic blower.
   J. collect data on wave height and wind speed from a body of water not as open as an ocean but not as enclosed as a lake.

PASSAGE III

A *projectile* is defined as an object upon which the only force is gravity. In order to observe the parameters of a projectile, a student hit a tennis ball with a racket and filmed the ball's trajectory. She then viewed the film and used equations to simulate the ball's trajectory in terms of its horizontal distance from the point of impact and its corresponding vertical height above the ground. Various readings, presented in chronological order from the beginning of the ball's movement until the end, are recorded in Table 1.

Table 1

Horizontal Distance (m)	Vertical Height (m)	Horizontal Distance (m)	Vertical Height (m)
0	1	15	0.9
1.5	2.3	16.5	1.2
3.0	3.3	18	0
4.5	4.0	19.5	0.5
6.0	4.5	21	0
7.5	4.7	22.5	0
9.0	4.1	24.0	0
10.5	3.2	22.0	0
12.0	2.1	20.0	0
13.5	0	18.0	0

Figure 1 indicates the ball's horizontal distance from the point of impact as plotted against time.

FIGURE 1

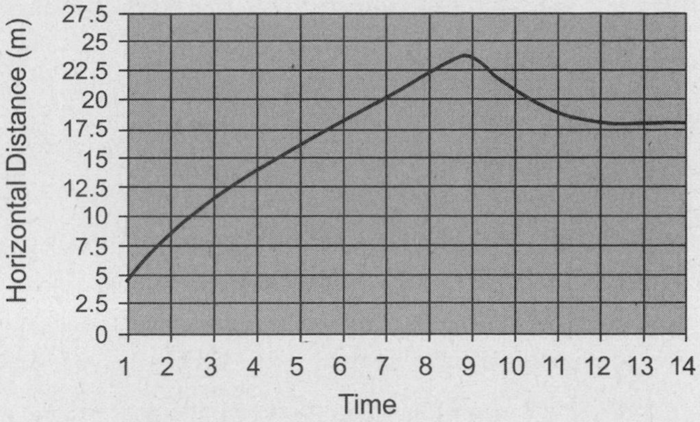

13. What was the ball doing approximately 12.5 seconds after it left the racket?

A. Traveling forward in the air
B. Rolling forward
C. Rolling backward
D. Stopped

14. Approximately how much time passes between the time the ball first lands and when it bounces for the last time?

F. 1.5 seconds
G. 2.5 seconds
H. 6 seconds
J. 8.5 seconds

15. The ball reached its maximal vertical height at which horizontal distance?

A. 7.5 m
B. 16.5 m
C. 19.5 m
D. 24.0 m

16. If the horizontal distance traveled by the ball is plotted against the height of the ball relative to the ground, which graph would most accurately represent the data?

F.

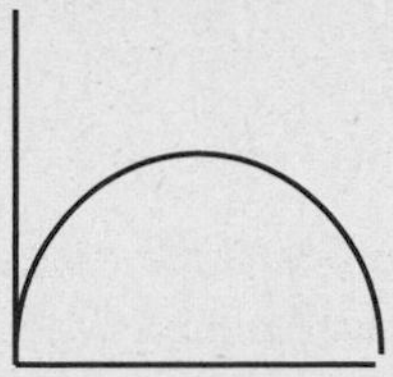

G.

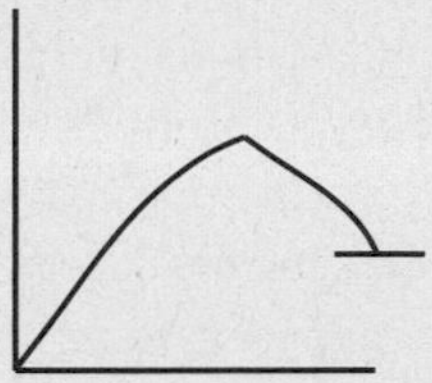

H.

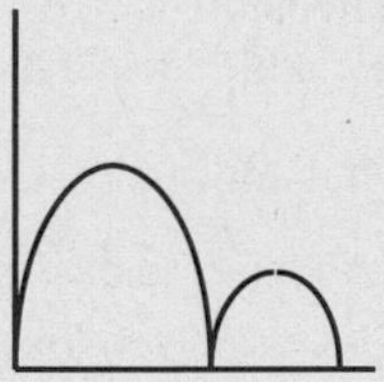

J.

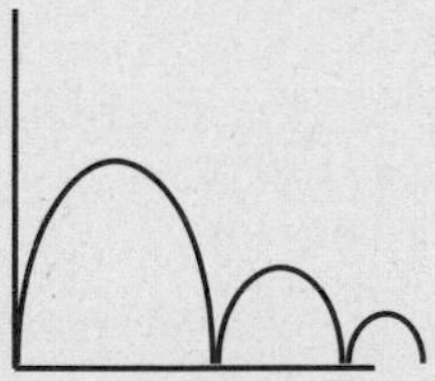

17. Which of the following can be inferred from the data in the passage?

A. The ball rolled on the ground from 8 seconds after the student hit it to 12 seconds after the student hit it.
B. The ball traveled away from the point of impact from 7 seconds after the student hit it to 12 seconds after the student hit it.
C. The ball rolled on the ground from 12 seconds after the student hit it to 14 seconds after the student hit it.
D. The ball flew in the air from 7 seconds after the student hit it to 10 seconds after the student hit it.

CONTINUE

PASSAGE IV

The number of cases of childhood asthma has risen dramatically in the past few decades. The following hypotheses attempt to account for the increasing incidence of this disease among children.

Contaminants Hypothesis

The dramatic increase in childhood asthma in recent decades can be explained by the fact that children today are more exposed to environmental contaminants, including dust, pollen, molds, pesticides, air pollution, second-hand cigarette smoke, and food additives. Taken together, these chemicals form a "toxic soup" that envelops children, either attacking their lungs directly, triggering the wheezing and shortness of breath characteristic of asthma, or compromising their immune systems, making them more susceptible to a wide range of diseases. Moreover, because they spend a greater amount of time indoors watching television, playing video games, or using computers, children today have greater exposure to indoor allergens than in the past.

Hygienic Hypothesis

The dramatic increase in childhood asthma in recent decades can be attributed to the over-obsession with health and cleanliness that has pervaded our culture. We increasingly sanitize our homes with disinfectants, immunize our children to ward off even minor, non-life-threatening diseases, and shield children from "unclean" animals and other children with the slightest sign of a cold. However, the human body evolved over millions of years in close proximity to its natural surroundings, including dirt, germs, and all kinds of noxious elements; the human immune system evolved specifically to recognize and fight such elements. If children have not been sufficiently exposed to germs and impurities at an early age, their underused immune systems become hypersensitized when they do eventually encounter these elements. Such immune system deficiencies predispose children to asthma and other similar diseases.

18. Which of the following are proponents of the two hypotheses likely to agree on, but for different reasons?

F. Asthma is the most common childhood disease in developed countries.
G. Spending too much time indoors is a health risk.
H. Vaccinations are overused.
J. Too many chemicals are added to food these days.

19. If a child who moves from a rural countryside to a congested metropolitan area develops asthma for the first time, this could support:

A. the Contaminants Hypothesis but not the Hygienic Hypothesis.
B. the Hygienic Hypothesis but not the Contaminants Hypothesis.
C. both the Contaminants Hypothesis and the Hygienic Hypothesis.
D. neither the Contaminants Hypothesis nor the Hygienic Hypothesis.

20. Proponents of the Contaminants Hypothesis could use which piece of evidence from the Hygienic Hypothesis to support their own theory?

F. The increase in childhood immunizations, if it could be shown that sometimes these immunizations cause severe side effects
G. The decrease in children's exposure to animals, if it could be shown that this negatively affects the development of such children's immune systems
H. The increased use of household sanitizers, if it could be shown that such products contain chemicals that can trigger asthma attacks
J. The increase in childhood immunizations, if it could be shown that such immunizations are extremely successful in warding off major human diseases, such as polio

21. Which of the following products, if overused, might be condemned by either the Contaminants Hypothesis or the Hygienic Hypothesis?

A. Food additives
B. Unpasteurized cheese
C. Bleach
D. Slightly moldy bread

22. Believers in the Hygienic Hypothesis would be likely to characterize the effect of what they describe as our society's preoccupation with health as:

F. detrimental because it causes us to disregard the effects of the noxious elements of our environment.
G. beneficial because it leads people to immunize their children against a multitude of diseases.
H. unquantifiable because the effects of our society's obsession with health and cleanliness cannot be precisely determined.
J. ironic because current actions intended to promote health actually diminish it.

23. A parent is considering applying a synthetic mosquito repellent to his six-month-old child. Which of the following reactions would be most expected based on the information in the passage?

A. Supporters of the Hygienic Hypothesis would encourage the use of the repellent.

B. Supporters of the Hygienic Hypothesis would discourage the use of the repellent.

C. Supporters of the Hygienic Hypothesis would not have an opinion on the use of the repellent.

D. Supporters of the Contaminants Hypothesis would encourage the use of the repellent.

24. Some scientists believe that an increase in the survival rate of low-birth-weight babies has greatly increased the number of children susceptible to asthma. How does this theory relate to the two theories presented in the passage?

F. It supports the Contaminants Hypothesis but not the Hygienic Hypothesis.

G. It supports the Hygienic Hypothesis but not the Contaminants Hypothesis.

H. It supports both the Contaminants Hypothesis and the Hygienic Hypothesis.

J. It supports neither the Contaminants Hypothesis nor the Hygienic Hypothesis.

PASSAGE V

It has long been hypothesized that the average adult needs 7 to 8 hours of sleep daily to ensure optimal functioning of mind and body, and that sleep deprivation causes not only physical impairments but mental abnormalities as well. Researchers conducted studies to explore the ways in which sleep deprivation affects the performance of mental tasks and the physiological activities of the brain.

Study 1

Ten healthy adults volunteered to remain awake for an entire night and participate in cognitive tests over the course of a 30-hour sleepless period. Each subject was awakened at 7:00 a.m. on Day 1 of the study for the first set of tests and, subsequently, was tested every 3 hours until 1:00 p.m. on Day 2. Each testing trial consisted of verbal, math, and short-term memory tasks, rated at the same difficulty level from trial to trial. The researchers measured both the speed and the accuracy of responses to test items, combining these scores into a mean Proficiency Quotient on a scale from 1 to 10. Results are depicted in Figure 1.

FIGURE 1

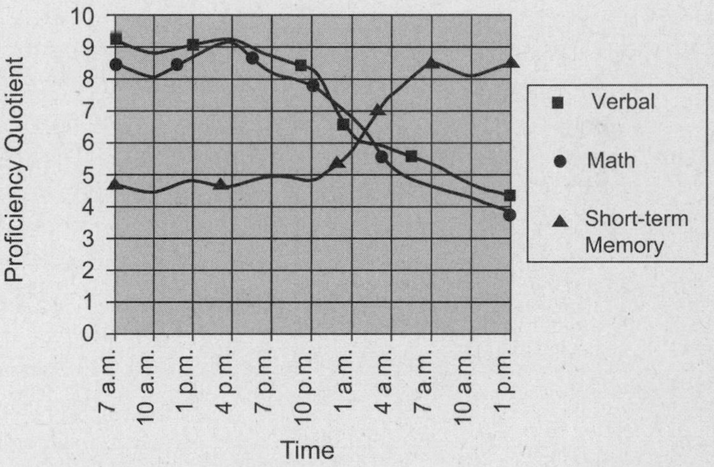

CONTINUE

Study 2

A sleep-deprived volunteer, awake for 25 straight hours, and a fully rested volunteer, observed 1 hour after waking from a restful 8-hour sleep, were monitored while responding to the questions and tasks listed in Table 1. Functional magnetic resonance imaging (MRI) scans were used to indicate brain activity while the subjects responded. The *temporal lobe* and the *parietal lobe* are two regions of the cerebral cortex. The activity status of these regions during the responses to the specific questions and tasks are indicated in Table 1, with a checkmark signifying activity in that lobe and an "X" signifying lack of activity.

Table 1

Question / Task	Sleep-Deprived Subject		Rested Subject	
	Temporal Lobe	Parietal Lobe	Temporal Lobe	Parietal Lobe
What is 642 divided by 27?	X	X	X	✓
Read the following text from Lincoln's Gettysburg Address [text provided].	X	✓	✓	X
Define "loyalty."	X	✓	✓	X
Fill in the blank in the following sequence: 3, 7, 15, 31, __, 127	X	X	X	✓
Describe a memorable dream you had during childhood.	X	✓	✓	X
Calculate: (232 + 464 − 117) × 6	X	X	X	✓

25. Based on the results in Figure 1, the maximal proficiency in math was observed around what time?

A. 7 a.m. on Day 1
B. 10 a.m. on Day 1
C. 4 p.m. on Day 1
D. 7 a.m. on Day 2

26. The tested skill in Figure 1 that showed the greatest range of proficiencies over the provided time course was

F. verbal.
G. math.
H. short-term memory.
J. All three were equal in range.

27. Overall, for both the sleep-deprived and rested subjects, which lobe exhibited more activity in the questions and tasks described in Table 1?

A. The parietal lobe, activated five times for every three times the temporal lobe was activated
B. The parietal lobe, activated two times for every one time the temporal lobe was activated
C. The temporal lobe, activated two times for every one time the parietal lobe was activated
D. The temporal lobe, activated five times for every three times the parietal lobe was activated

28. Which results from Study 2 help explain the short-term memory results in Study 1?

F. The parietal lobe takes over for the temporal lobe when sleep-deprived.
G. Verbal skills improve when sleep-deprived..
H. Sleep-deprived people are unable to perform complex math skills.
J. Study 2 does not explain the short-term memory results.

29. Insomnia is an inability to sleep. The methodology of Study 1 would be most flawed if it were found that:

A. all 10 participants reported experiencing episodes of insomnia at some points in their lives.
B. 5 of the participants reported changes in their sleep patterns during the week following the study.
C. 4 of the 10 participants suffered from severe insomnia during the middle of the night prior to Day 1 of the study.
D. all 10 participants experienced insomnia during the entire 30-hour study.

30. Which of the following is a reasonable generalization that can be made from Study 1?

F. Math and verbal ability are independent from short-term memory.
G. Math and verbal ability are dependent on short-term memory.
H. Short-term memory improves shortly after waking and steadily improves after that.
J. Math and verbal skills are at their worst after being awake for about 24 hours.

PASSAGE VI

Coagulation of the blood—commonly called *clotting*—is the process by which blood solidifies to stop the flow of bleeding. Clotting requires numerous proteins called *clotting factors*, which generally circulate in the bloodstream in an inactive state. These factors are activated in a series of steps when clotting is required.

The clotting process begins with the appearance of Tissue Factor emitted by damaged cells. Tissue Factor binds to activated Factor 7 and forms an enzyme called TF-7, which activates Factor 10; Factor 10, in turn, binds to and activates Factor 5. This creates an enzyme called *prothrombinase*, which converts *prothrombin* to *thrombin*. Thrombin helps to form soluble molecules of fibrin and also activates Factor 13, which converts the soluble fibrin molecules into an insoluble meshwork forming the clot. This process is summarized in Figure 1.

FIGURE 1

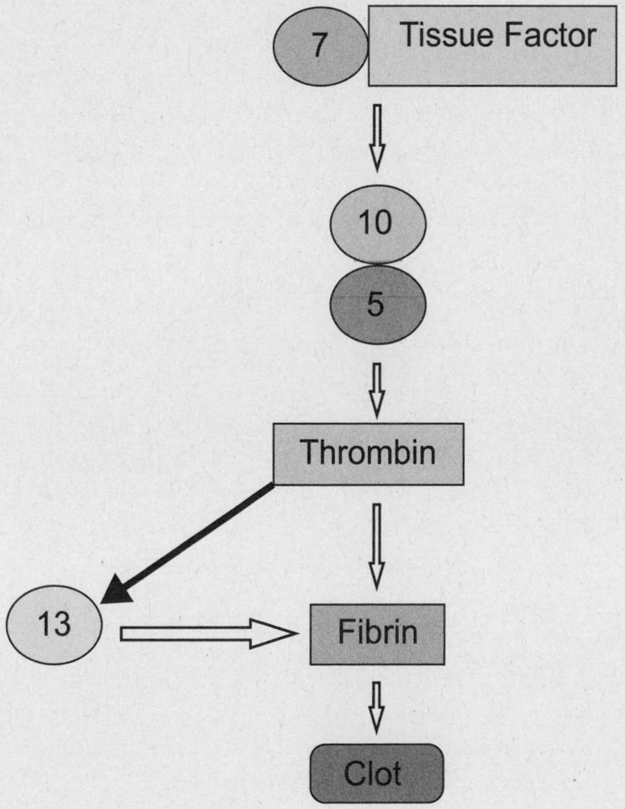

This initial clotting process is *amplified* by the further activation of these and other factors which are inserted back into the clotting process to enhance its effect. Table 1 lists four proteins that play a role in this amplification process.

Table 1

Protein	Activates Factor:
TF-7	9
Thrombin	5, 8, 11
Complex Formed from Factors 8 and 9	10
Factor 11	9

Calcium ions are also required for clotting to take place.

31. A patient has a mutation that affects the origin of otherwise healthy tissue factors. What would be the most likely impact of such a mutation?

A. The patient will be unable to form clots.
B. The patient will form clots in healthy tissue.
C. The patient's tissue factors will be unable to bind with activated 7.
D. Clotting factors in the bloodstream will be permanently activated.

32. What sort of clotting would occur in a situation where a patient produced too much prothrombinase?

F. No clotting would occur.
G. Partial clotting would occur.
H. Normal clotting would occur.
J. Excess clotting would occur.

33. A chelating agent is used to bind calcium ions, rendering them ineffective. Which of the following people would be most likely to benefit from this agent?

A. A doctor treating a bleeding accident victim
B. A technician in a blood donation facility
C. A geneticist researching the molecular makeup of blood
D. A hemophiliac suffering from an inability to form blood clots

CONTINUE

34. A scientist wants to take a closer look at the functioning of Factor 10 in the amplification process. What is an experiment she could perform that would accomplish this goal?

F. Disable the binding ability of Factor 8 in a test mouse.
G. Disable thrombin production in a test mouse.
H. Disable TF-7 in a test mouse.
J. Introduce extra Factor 10 into a test mouse.

PASSAGE VII

Carbon dioxide (CO_2), one of the components of photosynthesis, is essential to the survival and growth of a plant. But what happens if the CO_2 concentration changes from the current level and rises or falls? A series of tests were conducted exposing woody plants to steadily increasing CO_2 concentrations. The impact on nutrients (using nitrogen as an example), growth, and breakdown (decomposition) of dead plant material were all measured under increased CO_2 concentration. The results are shown in Table 1.

Table 1

CO_2 Concentration (mol_{CO_2}/mol_{air})	Nitrogen Content of Wood (% Change)	Growth Rate (mm/week)	Decomposition Rate (% mass/week)
350	–1	0.4	5
370	–2	0.8	4
390	–2.5	1	5
410	–3.5	1.3	6
420	–4.6	1.6	7
440	–5.7	1.9	6
460	–6.8	2.2	2
480	–9	2.6	9
500	–11	2.4	4
520	–25	2.8	9
540	–15	3	8
560	–18	3.1	4
580	–21	3.3	6
600	–24	3.2	4.5
620	–27	3.4	4.5
640	–30	1	5
660	–34	0.7	4
680	–36	0.4	3
700	–38	0.2	5.5

35. Looking at Table 1, what is the relationship between CO_2 and decomposition?

A. As CO_2 concentration increases, decomposition rate decreases.
B. As CO_2 concentration increases, decomposition rate increases.
C. As CO_2 concentration increases, decomposition rate initially increases and then decreases.
D. As CO_2 concentration increases, there is little defined effect on decomposition rate.

36. According to the data in the table, CO_2 concentration and growth rate are, until 620 mol_{CO_2}/mol_{air}:

F. directly proportional.
G. inversely proportional.
H. negatively correlated, in general, but not proportional.
J. positively correlated, in general, but not proportional.

37. What is a plausible explanation for the changes in growth rate that begin at 640 mol_{CO_2}/mol_{air}?

A. It is the threshold above which more CO_2 kills the plant.

B. The plant becomes stressed and vulnerable to insect damage.

C. The plant has insufficient fertilizer beginning at 640 mol_{CO_2}/mol_{air}.

D. The plant has reached its maximum height.

38. What is the most likely explanation for the sudden change in nitrogen content at 520 mol_{CO_2}/mol_{air}?

F. 520 is a threshold concentration where nitrogen begins to drop rapidly.

G. Experiment error occurred.

H. High decomposition rates affect the nitrogen level.

J. Another nutrient must have dropped in concentration as well.

39. When growth rate peaks, the decomposition rate is:

A. at its lowest.

B. lower than average but not at its lowest.

C. higher than average but not at its highest.

D. at its highest.

40. In a hypothetical version of this experiment, decomposition rate steadily decreases as CO_2 concentration increases. What might explain such a finding?

F. CO_2 is removing the oxygen bacteria need to function.

G. Insufficient nutrients inhibit bacteria growth.

H. Wood increases in quality as CO_2 concentration increases.

J. Slower plant growth provides less area for decomposers.

STOP

WRITING TEST

40 Minutes

DIRECTIONS: This is a test of your writing skills. You have forty (40) minutes to write an essay in English. Be sure to carefully read the issue and three perspectives presented before planning and writing your essay so you understand clearly the task you are being asked to do. Your essay will be graded on the evidence it provides of your ability to analyze the issue; evaluate and analyze the perspectives; state and develop a personal perspective; and describe the relationship between the given perspectives and your own, while effectively using organization, logic, and language according to the conventions of standard written English.

The Classroom of the Future

Most of us are accustomed to learning in traditional classrooms—with walls, windows, teachers, and fellow classmates all together in rooms, in pursuit of common educational goals. But advances in technology and online learning may change the shape of the future classroom. We conduct a wide array of important daily tasks online: paying bills, making purchases, maintaining relationships with friends and family, and conducting important research. Online learning opportunities are available for students from the primary through postgraduate level, and they continue to expand. Weighing the potential advantages and disadvantages of a learning environment that makes complete use of modern technology and the internet's capabilities, we must look at the possibility of the physical classroom of the past being replaced by the virtual classroom of the future.

Read and carefully consider these perspectives. Each suggests a particular way of thinking about how the classroom of the future should work.

Perspective One

Physical classrooms will and should always exist. The internet and modern technology clearly provide life-changing and time-saving benefits, but also include too many distractions. Effective, focused learning can only occur in a traditional classroom alongside other students, under the direct guidance of a teacher keeping everyone on task.

Perspective Two

Physical classrooms will and should eventually be replaced by online classrooms. Technological advances have made traditional classrooms unnecessary and have revealed their limitations. In the future, the modern, virtual classroom will be free of the constraints and limitations that inhibit learning and impede the achievement of each student's educational goals.

Perspective Three

The classroom of the future will continue to integrate the best of both worlds—the traditional and the virtual—for a blended, effective learning experience. Students will benefit from guided classroom learning that also takes advantage of technology for additional opportunities to achieve educational goals.

Essay Task

Write a cohesive, logical essay in which you consider multiple perspectives on the classroom of the future. In your essay, be sure to:

- examine and assess the perspectives given
- declare and explain your own perspective on the issue
- discuss the relationship between your perspective and those given

Your perspective may be in full or partial agreement, or in total disagreement, with any of the others. Whatever the case, support your ideas with logical reasoning and detailed, persuasive examples.

Plan and Write Your Essay

Use the first two pages of the Writing test answer sheet (found at the beginning of the test) to generate ideas and plan your essay. Then use the following four pages to write your essay. Consider the following as you compose your essay:

What are the strengths and weaknesses of the three perspectives provided?

- Identify the insights they present and what they fail to consider.
- Ascertain why a given perspective might persuade or fail to persuade.

How can you apply your own experience, knowledge, and values?

- Express your perspective on the issue, identifying the perspective's strengths and weaknesses.
- Formulate a plan to support your perspective in your essay.

STOP

1.	D	**20.**	G	**39.**	B	**58.**	H
2.	G	**21.**	C	**40.**	J	**59.**	A
3.	C	**22.**	H	**41.**	D	**60.**	H
4.	J	**23.**	A	**42.**	J	**61.**	D
5.	A	**24.**	J	**43.**	A	**62.**	G
6.	J	**25.**	A	**44.**	J	**63.**	B
7.	D	**26.**	H	**45.**	C	**64.**	J
8.	J	**27.**	D	**46.**	G	**65.**	B
9.	B	**28.**	G	**47.**	C	**66.**	H
10.	H	**29.**	C	**48.**	J	**67.**	D
11.	B	**30.**	G	**49.**	A	**68.**	F
12.	G	**31.**	C	**50.**	J	**69.**	B
13.	B	**32.**	G	**51.**	B	**70.**	G
14.	G	**33.**	A	**52.**	F	**71.**	C
15.	C	**34.**	J	**53.**	B	**72.**	J
16.	G	**35.**	C	**54.**	H	**73.**	B
17.	D	**36.**	H	**55.**	A	**74.**	J
18.	F	**37.**	C	**56.**	J	**75.**	D
19.	D	**38.**	J	**57.**	B		

1. **The correct answer is D.** In this sentence, the singular *hero* should be plural since it is referring to a group of them, so *heroes* (choice D) is the correct answer. Choice B is an incorrectly spelled plural form of *hero*. Choice C is the possessive form of *hero*, which does not fit in this sentence as written.

2. **The correct answer is G.** The phrase "for communicating" is set off by a comma in the passage, but because the description "for communicating" modifies *code* (defining the purpose of that code), "for communicating" is what is called a restrictive phrase. It should not be separated from the word or phrase it modifies. The same is true for "top secret," which eliminates choices H and J.

3. **The correct answer is C.** Avoid such wordy constructions as "it being the case that they would," especially when good alternatives are available. "It was crucial that enemy forces not be able to decipher the code" puts "enemy forces" (the subject) at the front of the sentence. Choice D also places "enemy forces" near the beginning of the sentence, but the second clause is constructed in such a way as to imply that the *code*, not the enemy forces, would have access to the tactics and troop movements. Choice B's "having access" is ambiguous about who would have that access. Only choice C makes clear who has the access.

4. **The correct answer is J.** As written, the sentence incorrectly uses the transition word *unfortunately*, but there is nothing unfortunate about discovering that the Navajo language made an excellent code. Choices G and H also use transition words that don't fit within the context of this sentence. The only choice that makes sense for this sentence is choice J, which removes the unnecessary transition word.

5. **The correct answer is A.** This sentence shows a simple progression from one event to the next, so *afterward* (choice A) is the best choice. Choice B is a transitional phrase that indicates the completion of a cause and effect relationship, and there is no such relationship in this sentence. *However* (choice C) indicates a contradiction. Omitting *afterward* (choice D) would not alter the sentence's meaning dramatically; however, it would not improve the sentence either.

6. **The correct answer is J.** Choices F and H can be eliminated because neither sentence has a subject ("the code talkers"). In choice G, the comma after *Once* indicates that the action happened only one

time; the sentence implies that the actions of the code talkers were ongoing, so *once* does not make sense in the context. Only choice J is a complete sentence that does not alter the original sentence's meaning incorrectly.

7. **The correct answer is D.** As written, we have a sentence fragment. Connecting the dependent clause "While the Navajo language was complicated" and the independent clause "the code was even more complex" with a comma creates a complete and grammatically correct sentence, so choice D is correct. The other answer choices fail to fix the sentence fragment.

8. **The correct answer is J.** This phrase should not begin a new paragraph, because it does not introduce a new idea, so choice G is incorrect. It lists another supporting detail to the main idea of the paragraph (which is that the code was complicated). No comma is needed because the underlined words do not serve as an introductory phrase. They are part of the larger phrase, "adding to the difficulty of breaking the code," which is the actual full introductory phrase. Choice H is incorrect because "More difficulty" is not a complete transitional phrase and is a grammatically incorrect way to begin a sentence.

9. **The correct answer is B.** The best way to help the reader understand how the code worked would be with a specific example of the code, rather than with general facts about other languages, codes, etc. Only choice B addresses details about the code. Choice A goes off on an unnecessary tangent about Morse code. Choice C confuses the flow by backtracking to discuss military codes used in the past. Choice D contributes to the author's larger argument, but the difficulty of the code is not a detail that will help a reader better understand the specifics of the code itself.

10. **The correct answer is H.** The commas in the original sentence are not needed to separate "speed and accuracy" from the rest of the sentence, as the adverbial phrase does not need to be set off from the verb (the work of the code talkers). Choices G and J fail to delete all of the unnecessary commas.

11. **The correct answer is B.** The current sentence uses both the passive voice and an awkward construction. Choice B corrects the error with a clear, active phrase. Choice C loses the conjunction *and* to create a comma splice, and choice D, omitting the underlined portion entirely, makes no sense.

12. **The correct answer is G.** In this question you're being asked to determine the appropriate pronoun and noun, given the context of the sentence. The antecedent that the pronoun is replacing here is the plural "Navajo code talkers"; therefore, a plural pronoun is required, so it is incorrect as written. In this instance, *their* is the correct pronoun and *place* is the correct noun for this sentence. *Our* is an incorrect pronoun here, since it is safe to assume that neither the author nor the reader is a Navajo code talker. Choice J uses a singular pronoun, which is incorrect.

13. **The correct answer is B.** An effective concluding sentence to an essay effectively ties up the overall message or sentiment of the piece. Choices A, C, and D focus on minor details in the piece, and, thus, are incorrect. Choice B captures the sentiment of the piece, that the Navajo code talkers should be commemorated and memorialized.

14. **The correct answer is G.** The sentence belongs in the paragraph that is about the complexity of the Navajo code, Paragraph 5, in which the author states, "While the Navajo language was complicated, the code was even more complex." Paragraph 4 is about the development and memorization of the code, so choice F is incorrect. Paragraph 6 is about the effectiveness of the code, so choice H is incorrect. Choice J is incorrect because Paragraph 7 is about the code talkers' legacy.

15. **The correct answer is C.** This essay is focused on the specific contributions of one minority group: the Navajos. An essay describing the contributions of minority soldiers would have to be more inclusive by talking about the involvement of various minority groups in the war effort, so choices A and B are incorrect. Choice D is incorrect because the essay does focus on the positive effects of the Navajo soldiers' work. Only choice C explains why this essay does not describe the contributions of various groups of minority soldiers in World War II.

16. **The correct answer is G.** Here, you're being asked to determine the correct pronoun to replace the author, who is both the subject and antecedent of this sentence. As this essay is written from the first person perspective, the pronoun *I* is the correct choice here, and the correct verb form is *sent*. Choices H and J both use incorrect pronouns and verb forms.

17. **The correct answer is D.** "Nobody was consulted" (choice A) is an example of passive voice—giving the action to the object of the sentence, not the author—and it makes the existing sentence very unclear. Only "I

didn't consult with anybody" (choice D) corrects the problem. The reversal of word order in choice B, "With nobody I consulted," makes the sentence awkward. "Nobody consulted me" (choice C) changes the meaning of the sentence, implying that the author should have been consulted about interviewing.

18. **The correct answer is F.** The current sentence correctly uses the pronoun *it* to refer to the environment of the law firm and remains in the past tense like the rest of the paragraph. "There was" (choice G) replaces the pronoun with a vague descriptive that doesn't make sense in context. "Here is" (choice H) incorrectly uses the present tense. "And so it was" (choice J) begins the sentence with an inappropriate transition.

19. **The correct answer is D.** As written, the sentence contains unnecessary punctuation, as semicolons are only used to separate two independent clauses. No punctuation is needed here, so choice D is correct. Choices B and C also include incorrect and unnecessary punctuation.

20. **The correct answer is G.** The narrative phrase, "I happily informed him" should be set off by commas, because it describes the manner in which the speaker announced his aim to the interviewer. Only choice G accomplishes this. Choice F is incorrect because the original sentence lacks the necessary comma after *him*. Choices H and J misplace the comma.

21. **The correct answer is C.** Deleting the previous sentence would eliminate the writer's description of what he believed at the time of the interview (statement I)—that his interviewer was impressed with how ambitious and articulate he was. It would also take away the reference to "the surprised look" on the interviewer's face, which tells the reader something about the interviewer's opinion of the narrator (statement III). The idea that the author is trying to communicate here is the distance between his feelings about himself and the interviewer's feelings about him; statements I and III describe exactly that. Choice A does not encompass everything the reader would not know if the writer had replaced the sentence. Statement II is not relevant to the sentence, so choices B and D can be eliminated.

22. **The correct answer is H.** The correct phrase is "would have." "would of" (choice F) and "could of" (choice G) are never correct, although they are common mistakes due to pronunciation. Choice J is grammatically incorrect in any context.

23. **The correct answer is A.** The sentence uses the correct pronoun and verb forms and is correct as written. The other choices would all introduce pronoun and verb form errors.

24. **The correct answer is J.** The underlined verb should be in the simple past tense, in keeping with the rest of the sentence. Choice F should be used in the present tense. Choice G should only be used if the sentence is in the past continuous tense. Choice H is incorrect since the sentence does not require the simple past perfect tense.

25. **The correct answer is A.** Try reading the sentence without "I figured"; it makes sense, which means "I figured" is an extra informational phrase that needs to be set off by commas. The phrase is correct as written. Choices B and C each eliminate a necessary comma. Choice D eliminates both necessary commas.

26. **The correct answer is H.** This question requires you to figure out the clearest wording to explain that the writer did not get the next several jobs for which he interviewed. The first part of the sentence talks about not being offered "that job," so the *nor* implies that *several* should refer to jobs, not firms, which is the mistake the original sentence makes. Choice H makes this distinction clear. Choice G retains the error, and choice J changes the meaning by suggesting that the author was offered no more interviews.

27. **The correct answer is D.** The shift in focus that the question mentions is the narrator's understanding that his failure to get a job might be his own fault. The best clue to this is the next sentence, in which the author calls his visit to the job counseling office "long overdue." Only choice D shows the narrator realizing that his approach might be to blame. Choices A, B, and C merely recycle information that the author has presented in the first part of the paragraph: that he has failed to get any of the jobs for which he applied.

28. **The correct answer is G.** The essay begins with the narrator saying that his college employment office recommended mock interviews for students about to begin a job search. Choice G ties the ending to the beginning by mentioning the practice interview and implying that the writer is helping his students to learn from his mistakes. Choice J is off topic. Choice F is not necessarily off topic, but it does not tie the end of the essay back to its beginning. Choice H does not tie back to the beginning, and it makes a jarring shift to a less formal tone than the rest of the passage.

29. **The correct answer is C.** An effective concluding sentence should tie up the major themes and purpose of the essay. Here, choice C is the best addition. The sentiment in choice A is not supported by the information provided in the essay. Choices B and D are the opposite of the learning experience the author likely received.

30. **The correct answer is G.** The question word *what* at the beginning of the sentence provides a clue that we are dealing with a question, so a question mark should end the sentence. The sentence as written and choices H and J all utilize incorrect punctuation to end a question.

31. **The correct answer is C.** The first paragraph of this sentence introduces us to the essay topic (aardvarks), and Paragraph 2 delves into factual information regarding the animal. Choice C is the best option to serve as a transition bridge between the two paragraphs. Choice A would fit better in Paragraph 7, which discusses the aardvark's defensive weapons and strategies. Choice B would best serve as a concluding sentence for the entire essay. Choice D would best fit in paragraph 6, which discusses the aardvark's primary food sources.

32. **The correct answer is G.** The word *Dutch* is a proper noun and should therefore be capitalized. Although it is also capitalized in choice J, the addition of the period would create a sentence fragment, so choice J is incorrect.

33. **The correct answer is A.** Items in a list should always be separated by commas, as they are in the underlined portion, or by semicolons in more complex lists. Removing the commas, as in choice B, creates confusion. Choice C incorrectly omits the comma after *grassland*. Choice D uses semicolons, which are not needed here, and incorrectly places one after *and*.

34. **The correct answer is J.** As written, the sentence contains superfluous punctuation after the word *and*. No punctuation is needed, so choice J is correct. Choices G and H contain unnecessary punctuation.

35. **The correct answer is C.** As written, the sentence is a run-on. Em-dashes are used to create necessary long pauses in a sentence, and an em-dash is used effectively in choice C. Choice B inserts a comma incorrectly into the sentence. Choice D incorrectly inserts a semicolon into the sentence.

36. **The correct answer is H.** The sentence as written contains an incorrectly written contraction (*thats*); *that's*, a contraction for *that is*, requires an apostrophe. Choices G and J are incorrect given the context of the sentence.

37. **The correct answer is C.** The sentence as written contains superfluous words; saying that aardvarks are expert diggers implies that they are really good at digging, so it doesn't need to be reiterated. Choice C corrects this error. Choices B and D fail to correct the problem of excessive wordiness.

38. **The correct answer is J.** The sentence as written uses the incorrect verb form of *to begin*. Choice J correctly uses the present tense. Choice G is written in the past tense, which is incorrect here. Choice H is written in the future tense, which is incorrect here.

39. **The correct answer is B.** Context is key when determining the appropriate word choice in a sentence. The adjective used to describe the aardvark's snout skin should reinforce the fact it "helps protect it from the bites and stings of its insect prey." As written, the adjective *weak* would not fit. The word that best supports the sentence is *tough* (choice B). Choices C and D also don't support the notion that the skin serves as a protective barrier, shielding the aardvark from bites and stings.

40. **The correct answer is J.** This sentence discusses the tools that the aardvark possesses to protect it from enemies, including the ability to run in zig-zag patterns. The only choice that appropriately describes how its unpredictable running protects it from enemies is *escape* (choice J).

41. **The correct answer is D.** In order to determine the appropriate pronoun choice, we need to examine the antecedent it is replacing. Here, it is replacing *aardvarks*, a plural noun; thus, the plural pronoun *their* (choice D) is the appropriate choice.

42. **The correct answer is J.** When referring to a specific numerical range, the use of an en-dash is appropriate, with the lower value end of the range on the left and the higher value end of the range on the right; therefore, choice J is correct. The other choices don't appropriately display the numerical range as intended.

43. **The correct answer is A.** Choice A best fits the essay and concluding paragraph, reminding readers that after everything that we've just learned about aardvarks, we should respect them if we encounter one. Choices B and C are out of context, as zoos and Africa are just minor supporting details in the essay. Choice D would be a comical conclusion, and does not fit the tone of the passage.

44. The correct answer is J. The purpose of this question is to determine if the text, as written, has met a specified goal—in this instance, an informative article about animals indigenous to the African continent for your school newspaper. As this essay focuses solely on the aardvark, and no other animals indigenous to Africa, it would be too narrow to fulfill the scope of the assignment, so choice J is correct.

45. The correct answer is C. The sentence in question refers to the eating habits of the rhinoceros; although it is also a native African creature, it is simply not information that fits within an essay that focuses solely on aardvarks, so choice C is correct.

46. The correct answer is G. The words "altar of the Presbyterian church" form one descriptive phrase, so no commas are needed in it—choice F can be eliminated. No comma (choice J) or semicolon (choice H) is needed before the conjunction *and* in this sentence, because receiving her degree is the second of two actions carried out by the same subject (Elizabeth Blackwell).

47. The correct answer is C. You can tell by context that the underlined phrase should mean something like "By receiving her degree," but the original sentence is awkward and contains an unnecessary comma. Choice C best accomplishes this. While the word *therefore* (choice B) implies a cause and effect, the phrase "in doing so" (choice C) communicates that her action had significance. *Even so* (choice D) means "in spite of," which does not make sense in this context.

48. The correct answer is J. The right choice must use the singular possessive form of *country*. Choice F is neither singular nor possessive, choice G is possessive but plural, and choice H scrambles the word order and distorts the meaning. Only choice J does the job.

49. The correct answer is A. Each of the two halves of the sentence can stand on its own, so the semicolon is correct. The other choices provide the wrong links between the two ideas, falsely indicating cause and effect (as in choices B and C) or contrast (as in choice D).

50. The correct answer is J. As it is written, the phrase is confusing, placing the verb awkwardly before the subject. Choices G and H are even more confusingly phrased. The simplest and clearest wording is choice J.

51. The correct answer is B. The sentence only makes sense if the underlined section contains a subject and a verb. "Having access" (choice A) lacks a subject. Choice B includes the subject and employs the correct tense. Choice C has a subject but is the present tense, and choice D is awkward and redundant.

52. The correct answer is F. You can tell from context that the underlined word should be something that means "didn't believe," so *doubted* (choice F) is the best choice. The doctors Blackwell consulted didn't think she would be admitted to medical school because no women had ever been admitted to medical school. Choices G, H, and J do not make any sense in this context.

53. The correct answer is B. This passage is written in the past tense, so *applied* (choice B) is the correct tense. "Has applied" would imply that her applications were pending, but all of the events of this passage are described in the past tense because Elizabeth Blackwell lived in the nineteenth century. Choices A and D would only be used if the passage were written in the present tense. Choice C uses the simple past perfect tense incorrectly.

54. The correct answer is H. Both the semicolon and the period in the underlined portion create new stand-alone sentences, but neither punctuation mark is followed by something that can stand on its own, so choice F is incorrect. While choice G comes close to fixing the problem, the comma after *colleges* is misplaced, and the comma before *Geneva* is not as strong as a colon would be. Choice H works best—the first punctuation mark is gone, *and* is replaced by the more effective *but*, and the colon appropriately denotes the final clarifying example. Choice J creates a fragment.

55. The correct answer is A. The phrase is correctly written in the past tense: *became* implies that her admission to medical school was at the head of a long line of obstacles. Choices C and D are grammatically incorrect, while choice B changes the sentence's meaning.

56. The correct answer is J. The current sentence lacks an action verb; choice J corrects this problem and appropriately sets off the modifying phrase with commas. Choice G changes both the meaning and the tense. Choice H is awkward because the phrase "men students" does not make sense.

57. The correct answer is B. The underlined word must be a past-tense verb. *Astonishing* (choice A) is an adjective, *astonishment* (choice C) is a noun, and "having astonishment" (choice D) is a descriptive phrase. *Astonished* (choice B) is the correct past-tense verb.

58. The correct answer is H. "After she completed her degree" is the correct introductory phrase, because it establishes the time sequence involved (Blackwell faced prejudice after she completed her degree). There is no need to separate the word *after* from the rest of the phrase, so the comma is inappropriate (choice F).

Choice G is not the correct introductory word and reintroduces the unnecessary comma. "After to" is not a proper introductory phrase, so choice J is incorrect.

59. **The correct answer is A.** In this sentence, *prejudice* and "outright barriers to her career" are two distinct items: *prejudice* describes feelings directed against her, and *outright barriers* are actions possibly taken by those who felt that prejudice. Therefore, the sentence should include both items separately to preserve the author's meaning. Choice C makes the mistake of combining these items. Choices B and D do not make grammatical sense.

60. **The correct answer is H.** As it is written, the sentence does not explain what "other things" Blackwell did and does not tell the reader whether or not she had any success as a doctor, both of which would successfully complete the passage. Choice G also does not describe anything that Blackwell went on to do after she got her degree, and choice J describes an occurrence that could not be construed as success. Only choice H describes the successes that Blackwell had after becoming a doctor, despite the obstacles she faced.

61. **The correct answer is D.** *Ingenious* means "clever and inventive," making it the best choice to describe a *brilliant* idea. *Imperious* (choice A) means "arrogant," *unsettling* (choice B) means "disturbing," and *inimitable* (choice C) means "unable to be imitated."

62. **The correct answer is G.** The comma in this sentence belongs in the place where it will distinguish the start of the list from the rest of the sentence. Putting the comma after "ancient civilizations" and before *including* indicates that Persia, India, and Egypt are items included on the list of ancient civilizations. The original sentence (choice F) and choice H are missing the comma after *civilizations*. Choice J uses a colon, which is not needed before a list when *including* is used. It also should link the first two items in the list with a comma and not the conjunction *and*.

63. **The correct answer is B.** The sentence as written contains the incorrect form of the adverb *advance*. To describe something technologically complex, you would say that it is *advanced*, not *advancing*. Choice C implies that something was created in advance of, or before, the system, but this choice doesn't make sense in the context. "Superlative advancement" is, in fact, superlative: it doesn't provide additional understanding of the high level of technology used by the Romans to create the aqueducts, so choice D is incorrect. On the ACT exam, always err on the side of the least complex construction with the fewest words.

64. **The correct answer is J.** As it is written, this is a run-on sentence. Using *that* instead of *it* (choice F) makes it clear that you are describing what the aqueduct system combined (form and function) and not adding a separate thought that describes the aqueduct system in this manner. Choices G and H are awkward and wordy.

65. **The correct answer is B.** *Simply* is the idiom that works with *quite*. It also manages to convey the author's meaning: that the first aqueducts were not complicated. Choices A and C are awkward in this context, and choice D does not make sense.

66. **The correct answer is H.** A semicolon, not a comma, should separate two stand-alone phrases. The fact that the structures were elaborate is related to the fact that they could conduct water over large distances, but each thought can stand alone. The conjunctions *but* and *so* in choices G and J are inappropriate, because the relationship between the two parts of the sentence is not one of contrast or of cause and effect.

67. **The correct answer is D.** Choice A makes the aqueducts seem less impressive by highlighting the superiority of today's systems. Choice B might indicate that the Roman Empire was impressive, but it doesn't say anything about aqueducts. Choice C indicates that the aqueducts might still stand, which is impressive enough, but choice D adds the fact that the aqueducts are still in use, which is even more impressive.

68. **The correct answer is F.** The existing sentence correctly uses a semicolon to separate two phrases that each form a complete sentence. A comma (choice G) or colon (choice H) does not perform this function. The first phrase is not an exclamation, so choice J does not make sense.

69. **The correct answer is B.** *Failed* is the correct verb form (it corresponds with the use of the past tense in the rest of the passage), which allows you to eliminate choice D. Choices A and C imply cause and effect, which isn't the most suitable relationship. The better choice offers a contrast: some aqueducts failed, but those that didn't were used as models. This implies a difference between the failing models and the successful models, and the Romans' different response to each situation.

70. **The correct answer is G.** This sentence compares the past to the present. The application of principles in modern architecture takes place in the present, so it should be written as *are applied* (choice G). The original phrase indicates an action that will happen in the future. Choices H and J indicate actions that happened in the past.

71. **The correct answer is C.** In the original sentence, the information in the parentheses does not add to our understanding of the Roman aqueducts, so it should be eliminated entirely (choice C). Choices B and D fail to eliminate that information.

72. **The correct answer is J.** *Arches* is plural. Because it is not a possessive, it does not need an apostrophe (choice F). It should be followed by a comma to set off the informational phrase ("while well-known"), and not a semicolon (choice H), which separates two complete clauses. Choice G fails use any punctuation at all.

73. **The correct answer is B.** Choice B provides specific information about the aqueducts that didn't fall into the category of the famous stone-arch aqueducts. Choice C discusses one feature of the stone arches but adds nothing about their role in the greater system. Choice D explains that the other aqueducts were made of different materials but doesn't specify what these materials were, making it a less desirable possibility than choice B.

74. **The correct answer is J.** The best way to maintain the proper tense and appropriately contrast the technologies of past and present is to omit the underlined word altogether, as choice J suggests. Leaving it as is (choice F) or changing it to another word (choices G and H) does not correct the error.

75. **The correct answer is D.** A main theme of the essay is the legacy of ancient Roman aqueducts in modern architecture. Choice C is close, but it mentions the Romans' advanced system of government, which is an idea not mentioned in the essay. Choices A and B do not reflect the main idea.

Mathematics

1.	A	**16.**	G	**31.**	B	**46.**	J
2.	K	**17.**	D	**32.**	J	**47.**	C
3.	D	**18.**	G	**33.**	C	**48.**	H
4.	J	**19.**	C	**34.**	H	**49.**	E
5.	D	**20.**	H	**35.**	B	**50.**	F
6.	G	**21.**	E	**36.**	H	**51.**	C
7.	D	**22.**	J	**37.**	D	**52.**	J
8.	J	**23.**	E	**38.**	H	**53.**	C
9.	E	**24.**	K	**39.**	A	**54.**	K
10.	J	**25.**	D	**40.**	K	**55.**	D
11.	B	**26.**	K	**41.**	E	**56.**	H
12.	J	**27.**	C	**42.**	H	**57.**	C
13.	B	**28.**	H	**43.**	D	**58.**	G
14.	H	**29.**	D	**44.**	K	**59.**	C
15.	A	**30.**	J	**45.**	B	**60.**	H

1. **The correct answer is A.** Solve the equation, as follows:

$$\begin{aligned}-3(2-x)&=4-(3x+1)\\ -6+3x&=4-3x-1\\ -6+3x&=3-3x\\ 6x&=9\\ x&=\frac{9}{6}=\frac{3}{2}\end{aligned}$$

Choices B and C are results of solving an equation of the form $ax = b$ incorrectly; you must divide both sides by a. Choice D is wrong because the distributive property was not applied correctly. Choice E arises from solving an equation of the form $ax + b = c$ incorrectly; you must subtract b from both sides, not add it.

2. **The correct answer is K.** Since 3 of 25 batteries were defective, it follows that 22 of 25 batteries worked. So the percentage that worked is $\frac{22}{25}\times 100$. Choice F is the percentage that is defective. Choices G and J have terms misplaced in the formula. Choice H is an attempt at computing the percentage of defective batteries, but has the 100 in the wrong place in the formula.

3. **The correct answer is D.** To get the number of combinations, simply multiply the numbers of each type of item: $3 \bullet 4 \bullet 6 = 72$ different combinations. Choice A does not account for the different number of mats available. Choice B does not account for the different number of bolsters available. Choice C does not account for the different number of blocks available. Choice E counted each combination twice.

4. **The correct answer is J.** $\angle a$ is vertical to the given 65° angle, and vertical angles always have the same measure. $\angle b$ is supplementary to 65° and to $\angle a$, and supplementary angles have measures that add up to 180°. Subtract 65° from 180° to find $m\angle b$: $180° - 65° = 115°$.

Choice F has an incorrect measure of $\angle a$, which likely results from assuming that vertical angles must have measures that add up to 360°, and an incorrect measure of $\angle b$, which likely results from an arithmetic error. Choice G assumes that all four angles must have the same measure; this would only be true if they were all right angles. Choice H has the correct measure of $\angle b$ but an incorrect measure of $\angle a$, which likely results from incorrectly assuming that vertical angles have measures that add up to 90°. Choice K has a correct measure of $\angle a$, but an incorrect measure for $\angle b$, which likely results from assuming that the measures of the three angles must add up to 180°.

5. **The correct answer is D.** To compare fractions, decimals, and percentages, convert them all to the same form. Since $85\% = 0.85$, $0.65 < x < 0.85$. Choices A and B are both less than $\frac{1}{2}$, or 0.5, so they can be eliminated. As a decimal, $\frac{5}{8} = 0.625$, so choice C can also be eliminated as too small. As a decimal, $\frac{2}{3}=0.\overline{66}$. This does fall between 0.65 and 0.85, so choice D is correct. For the record, $\frac{7}{8}=0.875$, so it is too big.

6. **The correct answer is G.** If the mean, or average, of a set of numbers is known, the sum of the numbers can be found by multiplying the mean by the number of values. With four numbers in the set, the sum of the numbers must be 4 × 14 = 56. Subtract the sum of the known numbers from this sum to find the unknown value: 56 – (10 + 12 + 19) = 15. Choice F is the average of the set, but it is not the value of the unknown number. Choice H would make the median of the set 14, not the mean. Choice J is too high, resulting in a mean that is higher than 14; numbers in a set do not necessarily need to be listed in order.

7. **The correct answer is D.** The price for 5 jars is $4.50(5) = $22.50. The 10% discount on this amount is 0.10($22.50) = $2.25, so the price for a 5-jar package is $22.50 – $2.25 = $20.25. The price for 10 jars is $4.50(10) = $45.00. The 15% discount on this amount is 0.15($45.00) = $6.75, so the price of a 10-jar package is $45.00 - $6.75 = $38.25. The total cost for 15 jars is $20.25 + $38.25 = $58.50. Choice A is the charge for 5 jars with the discount. Choice C is the result of applying a 25% discount to 15 jars; this is not the correct way to deal with percent discounts. Choice B is the charge for 10 jars with the discount. Choice E is the total cost without the discount applied.

8. **The correct answer is J.** Factor the numerator and denominator, and then cancel factors common to both:

$$\frac{2x+6}{(x+3)(3x-9)}=\frac{2\cancel{(x+3)}}{3\cancel{(x+3)}(x-3)}=\frac{2}{3(x-3)}$$

Choices F and H are the results of incorrectly canceling common terms, not factors, in the numerator and denominator. Choices G and K are the results of incorrectly factoring out a common factor from a binomial; make certain to factor it out of *both* terms.

9. **The correct answer is E.** The number of minutes spent on other exercises is 50 – 22 = 28. To get the percentage of the entire workout for which this accounts, compute $\frac{28}{50}\times 100 = 56\%$. Choice A is incorrect because you need to multiply 28 by 2, not divide by 2, when computing the percentage. Choice B is incorrect because $\frac{22}{50}\neq 22\%$, and this would be the percentage of the workout dedicated to strength training, not other exercises. Choice C is incorrect because $\frac{28}{50}\neq 28\%$. Choice D is the percentage of the workout dedicated to strength training.

10. **The correct answer is J.** Since 6 of 25 times were false alarms, the difference, 19, must be the number of times the alarm sounded correctly. The percentage of the time that the alarm sounded correctly is $\frac{19}{25}\times 100$. Choice F is incorrect because you should multiply by 100 instead of dividing by 100. Choice G is incorrect because you need to interchange 100 and 25. Choice H is incorrect because it is the percentage of the time that the alarm sounded incorrectly. Choice K is an incorrect attempt at computing the percentage of the time that the alarm sounded incorrectly; you should multiply by 100, not divide by it.

11. **The correct answer is B.** Substitute in $z = -3$ and simplify:

$$\begin{aligned}&\frac{6}{-(-3)}+(-3)(1-2(-3))\\&=\frac{6}{3}-3(1+6)\\&=2-3(7)\\&=2-21=-19\end{aligned}$$

Choice A is incorrect because $\frac{6}{-(-3)}=2$, not –2. Choice C is incorrect because the order of operations was not followed: 2 – 3(7) does not equal (2 – 3)(7). Choice D is incorrect because 1 –2(–3) = 1 + 6 = 7, not –5. Choice E is incorrect because 2 – 3(7) = 2 – 21, not 2 + 21.

12. **The correct answer is J.** A negative times a negative is positive, so a positive divided by a negative is negative. Therefore, *x* must be negative, and you can eliminate choices F, G, and H. In order for the quotient to be an integer, 64 must be divisible by *x*; only –8 divides evenly into 64, so choice J is correct. Choice K is not possible because 64 is not divisible by –12.

13. **The correct answer is B.** Solve for *x*, as follows:

$$\begin{aligned}\frac{5-x}{5}&=20\\5-x&=100\\5-100&=x\\-95&=x\end{aligned}$$

Choice A is the result of an error involving negative signs. Choices C and D are incorrect because you should multiply both sides of the equation by 5 to clear the fractions, not add 5 to both sides. Choices D and E involve errors when solving equations of the form $a + x = b$.

14. **The correct answer is H.** Counting from the right side, Matt is in the fifteenth chair, so you know that there are at least 15 seats; eliminate choices F and G. Counting from the left side, he's in the fourth chair, so there must be three seats to the left of him. That means that there are a total of 15 + 3 = 18 seats.

15. **The correct answer is A.** $h(-2) = 1 - |2 - 3(-2)| = 1 - |2 + 6| = 1 - 8 = -7$. Choice B is incorrect because (–3)(–2) = 6, not –6. Choice C is the result of not applying the order of operations correctly. Choice D is incorrect because (–3)(–2) = 6, not –6, and you ignored the absolute value bars. Choice E is incorrect because the absolute value does not apply to the negative outside the bars.

16. **The correct answer is G.** There are 12 numbers on the clock. A circle contains 360°, so the distance between each pair of consecutive numbers is 360° ÷ 12 = 30°. If the minute hand moves 60°, it will move from 1 to 2 to 3. That means that both the hour hand and minute hand will be on 3, which represents a time of 3:15 (choice G). Choice F represents a move 30° counter-clockwise, and choice H is 240° clockwise. Choice J is 360° clockwise, and choice K is 720° clockwise.

17. **The correct answer is D.** Apply the FOIL method to multiply these binomials:

$$(3x - 2)(2x + 3) = (3x)(2x) + (3x)(3) - 2(2x) - 2(3)$$

$$= 6x^2 + 9x - 4x - 6$$

$$= 6x^2 + 5x - 6$$

Choice A does not include the middle terms of the product. Choice B is the result of adding the binomials instead of multiplying them. Choice C has the wrong constant term and no middle term of the product. Choice E is incorrect because the signs of the last two terms are wrong.

18. **The correct answer is G.** The area of a square is equal to s^2, where s is a side of the square. Since the area of this square is 9, s must be 3. Point A has coordinates (–2, 2), so any other vertex of the same square must have an x-coordinate that is either equal to or 3 units away from –2.

This means that the x-coordinate can be –5, – 2, or 1; eliminate choices F, J, and K. The vertex must also have a y-coordinate that is either equal to or 3 units away from 2. This means that the y-coordinate can be –1, 2, or 5; eliminate choice H. Only choice G, (–5, 5), meets both conditions.

19. **The correct answer is C.** Let x represent the width. Then, the length is $2x$ and the height is $4x$. So the volume formula yields the equation $x(2x)(4x) = 4{,}096$. This simplifies to $8x^3 = 4{,}096$. Dividing both sides by 8 yields $x^3 = 512$. So $x = 8$ cm. Thus, the length is 2(8 cm) = 16 cm. Choice A is the width. Choice B is the result of adding 2 cm to the width instead of doubling the width. Choice D is the height. Choice E is the area of the base.

20. **The correct answer is H.** The spinner is divided into 8 equal sections. As a fraction, $0.375 = \frac{3}{8}$. For the probability of NOT landing on red on a single spin to be $\frac{3}{8}$, then 3 of the sections must NOT be red. That means that the remaining 8 – 3 = 5 sections must be red. Choice F is incorrect because there are 8 congruent wedges, so this would imply that the probability of not landing on red is 0.875. Choice J would make the probability of not landing on red 0.125. Choice K would make the probability of not landing on red 0.

21. **The correct answer is E.** The sides of any right triangle are related by the Pythagorean theorem, which states that the sum of the squares of the legs is equal to the square of the hypotenuse. This is often written as $a^2 + b^2 = c^2$, where a and b are the legs, and c is the hypotenuse. Test each set of sides to see which satisfies the Pythagorean theorem and is therefore a right triangle:

Choice A: (6, 13, 14)

$$6^2 + 13^2 = 14^2$$
$$36 + 169 = 196$$
$$205 \neq 196\text{; eliminate}$$

Choice B: (8, 10, 12)

$$8^2 + 10^2 = 12^2$$
$$64 + 100 = 144$$
$$164 \neq 144\text{; eliminate}$$

Choice C: (12, 16, 18)

$$12^2 + 16^2 = 18^2$$
$$144 + 256 = 324$$
$$400 \neq 324\text{; eliminate}$$

Choice D: (15, 22, 23)

$15^2 + 22^2 = 23^2$

$225 + 484 = 529$

$709 \neq 529$; eliminate

Choice E: (20, 21, 29)

$20^2 + 21^2 = 29^2$

$400 + 441 = 841$

$841 = 841 \therefore$ right triangle

22. **The correct answer is J.** 24 cans at $1.25 each would cost a total of $30. The superstore sells a case of 24 cans for $19.20, which is a savings of $30 – $19.20 = $10.80. Choice F is the savings per can, not per case. For choice G, you have incorrectly multiplied 12 times $1.25 to get the cost of a case from the corner store. For choice H, you used $1 per can instead of $1.25 per can at the corner store. Choice K is the cost of 24 cans.

23. **The correct answer is E.** To move a function to the right 5 units, you subtract 5 from the input, meaning you replace *x* by *x* – 5. Then, to move the function up 2 units, you add 2 to the output. Doing so yields the function in choice E. Choice A is incorrect because the 2 and 5 are interchanged. Choice B is incorrect because it is down 2 units and left 5 units. Choice C is down 2 units, and choice D is left 5 units.

24. **The correct answer is K.** Use the exponent rules to simplify the expression:

$$\frac{z^4}{\left(z^{-2}\right)^5} = \frac{z^4}{z^{-10}} = z^4 \bullet z^{10} = z^{4+10} = z^{14}$$

Choices F, G, and H are the result of using the wrong rule for simplifying the quotient of powers of the same base. Choice J is the result of using the wrong rule for simplifying the power of a power.

25. **The correct answer is D.** Let *x* be the number of city blocks corresponding to 4 inches. Set up and solve the following proportion:

$$\frac{\frac{5}{8}\text{ inch}}{3\frac{1}{2}\text{ city blocks}} = \frac{4\text{ inches}}{x\text{ city blocks}}$$

$$\frac{5}{8}x = 4\left(3\frac{1}{2}\right)$$

$$\frac{5}{8}x = 4\left(\frac{7}{2}\right)$$

$$\frac{5}{8}x = 14$$

$$x = 14 \bullet \frac{8}{5}$$

$$x = \frac{112}{5} = 22\frac{2}{5}$$

26. **The correct answer is K.** Multiply the terms on the left side, bring all terms to the left, factor, and solve for *x*:

$$x(3x-4) = 4$$

$$3x^2 - 4x = 4$$

$$3x^2 - 4x - 4 = 0$$

$$(3x+2)(x-2) = 0$$

$$x = -\frac{2}{3}, x = 2$$

Choices F and H represent errors in factoring. Choice G is the result of setting each factor in the original equation equal to 4, but you can only do this when one side is 0. Choice J represents the same error made in Choice G, with an additional error of solving the resulting linear equations incorrectly.

27. **The correct answer is C.** To find the average, add up all the test scores, and divide by the number of tests. Some of the scores repeated more than once, so this must be taken into account. There were 6 tests, so the average is:

$$\frac{80+80+80+92+92+100}{6} = \frac{524}{6} = 87.3$$

Choice A is the mode, the most common score. Choice B is the median of the six test scores, which is the average of the middle two values (80 and 92). Choice D is the average of the three different scores, which does not account for some scores occurring more times than others. Choice E is the median of the three scores, which is neither the median nor the mean of the set of all six scores.

28. **The correct answer is H.** The graph of $h(x)$ is obtained by translating the graph of $y = |x|$ to the right 4 units and down 1 unit. Since the domain of $y = |x|$ is $(-\infty, \infty)$, such a translation does not affect the domain. So the domain of $h(x)$ is also $(-\infty, \infty)$. Choice F is incorrect because it is the range of $h(x)$. Choice G is incorrect because this would be the range of $y = -1 - |x - 4|$. Choice J is incorrect because this is just the set of inputs that generates the left part of the graph of $h(x)$. Choice K is incorrect because this is just the set of inputs that generates the right part of the graph of $h(x)$.

29. **The correct answer is D.** Using the unit circle, it follows that $2x = \frac{7\pi}{6}, \frac{11\pi}{6}, \frac{19\pi}{6}, \frac{23\pi}{6}$. Dividing by 2 yields the solutions $x = \frac{7\pi}{12}, \frac{11\pi}{12}, \frac{19\pi}{12}, \frac{23\pi}{12}$. Choice A is incorrect because the values must be divided by 2. Choice B shows the values where $\sin(2x) = \frac{1}{2}$, not $-\frac{1}{2}$. Choice C shows the values where $\sin(2x) = \frac{\sqrt{3}}{2}$. Choice E shows the values where $\sin(2x) = -\frac{\sqrt{3}}{2}$.

30. **The correct answer is J.** To find the total earnings, multiply the 35 cents earned per mile by the total number of miles. To find the total number of miles, multiply the speed by the amount of time:

Distance = 55 miles per hour × 9.5 hours = 522.5 miles

Total earnings = 522.5 miles × 35 cents per mile = \$182.88. Choice F is the result of multiplying 9.5 by 35, then dividing by 55, with a place value error. Choice G is the result of multiplying 9.5 by 55, then dividing by 35, with a place value error. Choice H is the result of dividing 55 by both 9.5 and 35, with a place value error. Choice K is the result of multiplying 55 by 35, then dividing by 9.5, with a place value error.

31. **The correct answer is B.** The inequality states that x is *less than or equal to* –2 or *greater than* 4. Therefore, the endpoints should be -2 and 4, and the shading should be outside the region between those values. Since –2 is included in the solution set, it should be marked with a closed circle, and since 4 is not included in the solution set, it should be marked with an open circle.

Choice A has the correct endpoints, but the wrong region is shaded. Choice C has the endpoints in the correct locations, but filled in incorrectly, and the wrong region is shaded. Choice D has the correct regions shaded, but the filling in of the endpoints is incorrect. Choice E mixes up the signs of the endpoints, as well as their filling in, and the region that is shaded.

32. **The correct answer is J.** The length and width of the water are the same as those of the tank. Therefore, the water's volume is equal to the area of the tank's base (length × width) times the water's depth. Since you are given the water's volume and the length and width of the tank's base, you can solve for the water depth d:

$$1{,}728 = (24)(8)(d)$$
$$1{,}728 = 192d$$
$$\frac{1{,}728}{192} = d$$
$$d = 9$$

The dimensions for depth in choices F, G, and H result in a volume less than 1,728 cubic inches, since the 8 and 24 are fixed. For choice K, this would mean the tank was full, which would result in a volume of 1,920 cubic inches.

33. **The correct answer is C.** Kecia had the car for 3 days, so 3(\$20) = \$60 of the charges were due to the daily fee. That means that the remaining \$156 – \$60 = \$96 were mileage charges. Each mile is charged at \$0.50, so Kecia must have driven \$96 ÷ \$0.50 = 192 miles. For choice A, you have incorrectly added \$156 and \$60 (charge for a 3-day rental) instead of subtracting \$60 from \$156. For choice B, you did not subtract \$60 from \$156. Choice D, 156, is a dollar amount and not the mileage driven. For choice E, you forgot to divide by \$0.50.

34. **The correct answer is H.** Let x be the missing side. Use the Pythagorean theorem:

$$9^2 = 4^2 + x^2$$
$$x^2 = 9^2 - 4^2$$
$$x = \sqrt{9^2 - 4^2}$$

Choice F is incorrect because the terms inside the radical should be subtracted. Choice G is incorrect because the terms should be subtracted and the radical sign is missing. Choice J is missing the radical sign. Choice K is the result of incorrectly distributing the radical sign through a difference—specifically, $\sqrt{a-b} \neq \sqrt{a} - \sqrt{b}$.

35. **The correct answer is B.** Isolate w on the right side, as follows:

$$S = 2(lw + lh + wh)$$
$$S = 2lw + 2lh + 2wh$$
$$S = w(2l + 2h) + 2lh$$
$$S - 2lh = w(2l + 2h)$$
$$w = \frac{S - 2lh}{2l + 2h}$$

Choice A is incorrect because $2lw + 2wh$ does not equal $(4lh)w$. Choices C and D are the result of making errors when solving a linear equation of the form $ax + b = c$; you subtract b from both sides and divide by a. Choice E is incorrect because you canceled terms, not factors, common to the numerator and denominator.

36. **The correct answer is H.** The arrowheads affixed to the ends of the graph, pointing upward, suggest that the range extends to plus infinity. So the local maximum value of 4 occurring at $x = -3$ is not the maximum of the function. Choice F is incorrect because this is true since the graph of $f(x)$ never dips below the x-axis. Choice G is incorrect because this is true since the smallest y-value on the graph is 0, and the arrowheads affixed to the ends of the graph, pointing upward, suggest that the range extends to plus infinity. Choice J is incorrect because this is true since every real number x is a viable input for this function, as seen by the fact that there is a point on the graph corresponding to each real number x. Choice K is incorrect because this is true since both –5 and 2 are x-intercepts of the graph.

37. **The correct answer is D.** Factor, convert the quotient to a product, and simplify, as follows:

$$\frac{w^2 - 9}{w} \div \frac{w^2 - 3w}{3} = \frac{(w-3)(w+3)}{w} \div \frac{w(w-3)}{3}$$
$$= \frac{\cancel{(w-3)}(w+3)}{w} \bullet \frac{3}{w\cancel{(w-3)}}$$
$$= \frac{3w + 9}{w^2}$$

Choices A and E did not convert the quotient to a product, and terms, not factors, were incorrectly canceled in choice A. Choice B is the result of canceling terms, not factors, common to the numerator and denominator. Choice C does not have the distributive property applied correctly.

38. **The correct answer is H.** Cosine is equal to $\frac{\text{adjacent side}}{\text{hypotenuse}}$, so $\frac{AC}{AB} = \frac{1}{2}$ as shown in the figure below.

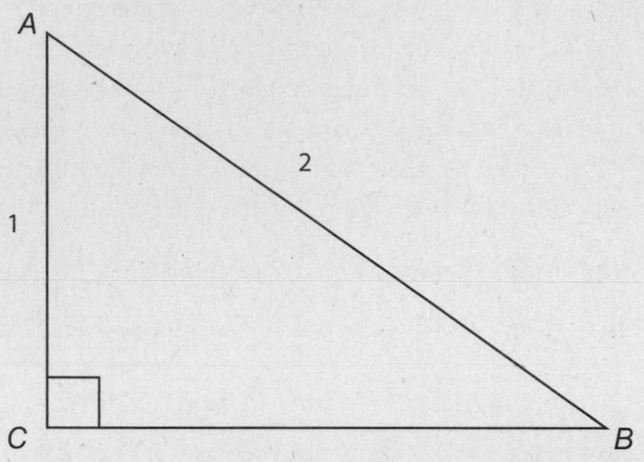

To find the cosine of angle B, you need to know the length of the side adjacent to it, segment BC. Since the length of a leg of this triangle is related to the length of its hypotenuse in the ratio of 1:2, this is a 30-60-90 right triangle, whose three sides are related in the ratio of $1:\sqrt{3}:2$. This means that $BC = \sqrt{3}$ and $\cos B = \frac{\sqrt{3}}{2}$, choice H. Choice F is csc$B$. Choice G is cot$B$. Choice J is tan$B$. Choice K is sin$B$.

39. **The correct answer is A.** Calculate as follows:

$$(g \circ f)(x) = g(f(x)) = \frac{3}{\frac{1}{x+2} + 1}$$
$$= \frac{3}{\frac{1 + x + 2}{x+2}} = \frac{3}{\frac{x+3}{x+2}} = \frac{3(x+2)}{x+3} = \frac{3x+6}{x+3}$$

Choice B is incorrect because $\frac{1}{a+b} \neq \frac{1}{a} + \frac{1}{b}$. Choice C is incorrect because you cannot cancel terms common to the numerator and denominator of a fraction like this; you can only cancel like *factors*. Choice D is incorrect because you initially computed $(f \circ g)(x)$, and when simplifying, note that $\frac{1}{a+b} \neq \frac{1}{a} + \frac{1}{b}$. Choice E is incorrect because you initially computed $(f \circ g)(x)$.

40. **The correct answer is K.** Start by finding the volume and surface area of the current box:

$$V = lwh$$
$$= 6 \times 9 \times 4$$
$$= 216$$

$$SA = 2lw + 2lh$$
$$= 2(6)(9) + 2(8)(4) + 2(6)(4)$$
$$= 108 + 72 + 48$$
$$= 228$$

Now find the answer choice with a volume of 216 and a surface area less than 228.

Choice F:

$V = 2 \times 3 \times 36 = 216$

$SA = 2(6) + 2(108) + 2(72) = 372$; eliminate

Choice G:

$V = 2 \times 4 \times 27 = 216$

$SA = 2(8) + 2(108) + 2(54) = 340$; eliminate

Choice H:

$V = 3 \times 6 \times 12 = 216$

$SA = 2(18) + 2(72) + 2(36) = 252$; eliminate

Choice J:

$V = 3 \times 8 \times 9 = 216$

$SA = 2(24) + 2(72) + 2(27) = 246$; eliminate

Choice K:

$V = 6 \times 6 \times 6 = 216$

$SA = 2(36) + 2(36) + 2(36) = 216$

This is the only surface area smaller than 228, so it is correct.

41. The correct answer is E. Write the given equation in slope-intercept form: $y = 3x - 6$. The slope is 3. So any line with a slope 3 is parallel to this line. Since $6y - 18x = 0$ as $y = 3x$, it is parallel to the given line. Choice A has slope 0, not 3. Choice B has slope $\frac{1}{3}$, not 3. Choice C has slope –3, not 3. Choice D is vertical and therefore not parallel to a diagonal line with slope 3.

42. The correct answer is H. Since 1 hour equals 60 minutes, it follows that *h* hours equals 60*h* minutes. Now, multiply *rate* times *time* get the number of gallons removed:

$$\frac{3.5 \text{ gallons}}{1 \text{ minute}} \times 60h \text{ minutes} = 210h \text{ gallons}$$

Choices F, G, and K are the result of not converting hours to minutes when computing the number of gallons. The answers in choices G and J divided rate by time instead of multiplying the quantities.

43. The correct answer is D. The table lists coordinates of points on the line. All of the answer choices are in slope-intercept form, $y = mx + b$, where m is the slope and b is the y-intercept. The second pair of coordinates listed in the table is (0, –2), giving the y-intercept of the line as –2. Choices A and B can be eliminated, since neither equation has a y-intercept of –2. The slope of a line is equal to the change in its y-coordinates divided by the change in its x-coordinates. Looking at the row of x-coordinates, you can see that they change in increments of 2; the y-coordinates change in increments of 1. This means that the slope of the line is $\frac{1}{2}$, so choice D, $y = \frac{1}{2}x - 2$, correctly represents the relationship in the table. In choice A, the point (–2, –3) does not satisfy this equation. In choice B, (0, –2) does not satisfy this equation. In choice C, (–2, –3) does not satisfy this equation. In choice E, (2, –1) does not satisfy this equation.

44. The correct answer is K. You know that both x and z are greater than y, but you aren't given any information about how they relate to one another. This means that you cannot tell which, if either of them, is greater than the other, so choices F and G can be eliminated. You might assume that since $x > y$, $x^2 > y^2$, but this is not necessarily true. If $x = 2$ and $y = -3$, for example, then $2^2 < (-3)^2$, making $x^2 < y^2$. This allows you to eliminate choices H and J, leaving choice K as correct. It must be true that $x + z > 2y$; since both x and z are greater than y, their sum must be greater than $2y$.

45. The correct answer is B. To solve this system of equations simultaneously, use the elimination method:

$$\begin{aligned} 2(3x - 2y) &= 2(0) \\ -3(2x + 3y) &= -3(13) \end{aligned} \quad \text{is equivalent to} \quad \begin{aligned} 6x - 4y &= 0 \\ -6x - 9y &= -39 \end{aligned}$$

Add the equations to get $-13y = -39$. Dividing both sides by –13 yields $y = 3$. Substituting this value back into the first original equation, gives $3x - 2(3) = 0$, so that $3x = 6$ and $x = 2$. Thus, the value of $\frac{y}{x}$ is $\frac{3}{2}$. Choice A is the value of $\frac{x}{y}$. Choice C is the value of $x + y$. Choice D is y. Choice E is x.

46. The correct answer is J. The area of the shaded region is the difference between the area of the square and the area of the circle. The perimeter of the square is 36 feet, so each of its sides is $36 \div 4 = 9$ feet. If you draw a diameter through the center of the circle, you will see that it is equal to a side of the square, so the diameter of the circle is also 9 feet, as shown in the figure.

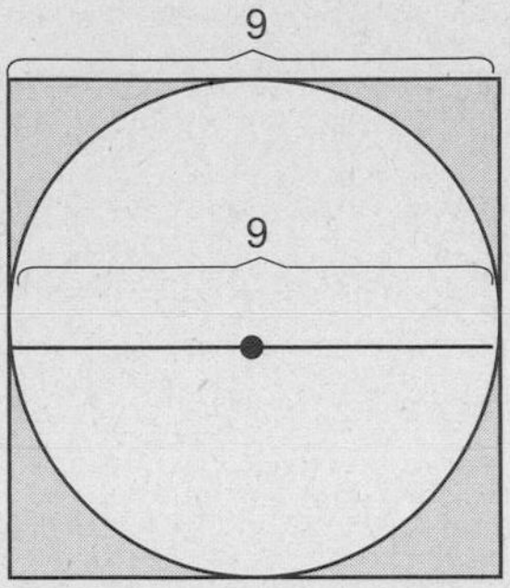

Now find the areas of both known regions. Area of a square is equal to s^2, so the area of this square is $9^2 =$ 81 square feet. Area of a circle is equal to πr^2. Since the diameter of the circle is 9, its radius is 4.5, making its area $\pi(4.5)^2 = 20.25\pi$ square feet. Therefore, the area of the shaded region is $81 - 20.25\pi$ square feet. For choice F, you have forgotten to square the side and the radius when finding the area of the square and circle, respectively. Choice G is incorrect because the area of the square is 81 square feet, not 36 square feet, and the radius of the circle is 4.5 feet, not 3 feet. Choice H is the perimeter of the shaded region, not its area. Choice K is incorrect because the radius of the circle is 4.5 feet, not 6 feet.

47. The correct answer is C. There are a total of 50 numbers on the wheel, so figure out how many of these 50 will make Greg win. Greg bets on numbers 32 through 46. Be careful not to settle for 46 – 32, because this difference does not include both 32 and 46 as possibilities. To include both endpoints, add one to the difference between them; that means there are $46 - 32 + 1 = 15$ winning numbers. Therefore, the probability that the spinner will land on one of Greg's numbers is $\frac{15}{50} = \frac{3}{10}$. Choice A is the probability of landing on any given number, but Greg placed his bet on 15 of the 50 numbers. Choice B is incorrect because there are 15 numbers on which Greg placed his bet, not 14. Choice D is the probability that the spinner does not land on one of Greg's numbers. Choice E is incorrect because Greg did not bet on 46 numbers; he only bet on 15 of them.

48. The correct answer is H. $\overline{QS}$ is the hypotenuse of right triangle *QRS*, so use the Pythagorean theorem, starting with the lengths of legs $\overline{QR}$ and $\overline{RS}$. $RS = 5$, and $\overline{QR}$ is the hypotenuse of a right triangle with legs lengths 2 and 4, so:

$$QR^2 = 2^2 + 4^2$$
$$QR^2 = 4 + 16$$
$$QR = \sqrt{20} = 2\sqrt{5}$$

Now find the length of $\overline{QS}$:

$$QS^2 = 5^2 + (2\sqrt{5})^2$$
$$QS^2 = 25 + 20$$
$$QS = \sqrt{45} = 3\sqrt{5}$$

Choice F is the length of *QR*. Choice G is half the sum of the three given dimensions. Choice J is the sum of the three given dimensions. Choice K is half the volume of the box.

49. The correct answer is E. The maximum of a quadratic function that opens downward is the *y*-coordinate of the vertex. Complete the square to identify the vertex:

$$\begin{aligned} f(x) &= -3x^2 + 18x - 1 \\ &= -3(x^2 - 6x) - 1 \\ &= -3(x^2 - 6x + 9) - 1 + 27 \\ &= -3(x - 3)^2 + 26 \end{aligned}$$

The maximum is 26. Choices A and B are the result of not balancing the expression correctly when completing the square. Choice C did not complete the square; –1 is not the *y*-coordinate of the vertex. Choice D is the *x*-coordinate, not the *y*-coordinate, of the vertex.

50. The correct answer is F. The ratio of the areas of two figures is equal to the *square* of the ratios of their corresponding linear measurements. Since the ratio of the radius of circle *A* to the radius of circle *B* is 3:1, the ratio of their areas must be $3^2{:}1^2 = 9{:}1$. That means that the area of circle *B* is $\frac{1}{9}$ the area of circle *A*, or $\frac{x}{9}$.

Choice G is incorrect because $3^2 = 9$, not 6. Choice H is incorrect because you must square the 3 for the denominator. Choices J and K are incorrect because circle *A* is larger than circle *B*, so its area must be larger.

51. The correct answer is C. Parallel lines have equal slopes. Plugging into the slope formula, you'll find that the slope of the line shown is $\frac{2-0}{0-1} = \frac{2}{-1} = -2$. Since all of the answer choices are already in slope-intercept form $y = mx + b$, where *m* is the slope, a quick scan reveals that the only line with a slope of –2 is $y = -2x + 2$, choice C. Choices A, B, and D are incorrect because the graphed line falls from left to right, so it must have a negative slope—each of these lines has a positive slope. In choice E, the slope is wrong; remember that the slope of a line is the change in *y* divided by the change in *x*.

52. **The correct answer is J.** The area of a triangle is equal to $\frac{1}{2}bh$. The area of ΔABC is 24 and its height, segment *AC*, has a length of 8, so its base, segment *AB*, must have a length of 6. Given that $AD = 28$, it follows that $BD = 28 - 6 = 22$. Now that you have the length of a pair of sides of the parallelogram, you just need the length of the other pair of sides to solve. Since segment *BC* happens to be the hypotenuse of a right triangle with legs of 6 and 8, its length must be 10. That makes the perimeter of parallelogram *BCED* equal to $2(22 + 10) = 2(32) = 64$ feet. For choice F, you likely used *AD* in place of *BD* when computing the perimeter. For choice G, you likely used the length of *AC* instead of the length of *BC*, and *AD* instead of *BD*, when computing the perimeter. For choice H, you likely used *AD* in place of *BD* and *AB* instead of *BC* when computing the perimeter. For choice K, you miscomputed the length of *BC*.

53. **The correct answer is C.** Solve the equation $p(x) = 0$:

$$2x^2 - 3x - 14 = 0$$
$$(x + 2)(2x - 7) = 0$$
$$x = -2, \frac{7}{2}$$

Since *x* represents a number of projectors, –2 can be discarded. Using $x = \frac{7}{2}$, the number of projectors that must be sold is $\frac{7}{2} \times 100 = 350$. Choices A and E used the wrong conversion; *x* is measured in hundreds of projectors. Choice B factored the expression incorrectly. Choice D used the constant term of $p(x)$ only; you must factor and use the roots.

54. **The correct answer is K.** Let *x* equal the number of hours it takes the standard printer to do the job alone. That means that every hour it does $\frac{1}{x}$ of the job. The high-speed printer can complete the job alone in 5 hours, so every hour it does $\frac{1}{5}$ of the job. Working together, the two printers complete the job in $3\frac{1}{3} = \frac{10}{3}$ hours, so each hour they do $\frac{1}{\left(\frac{10}{3}\right)} = \frac{3}{10}$ of the job. The sum of the individual rates is equal to the rate working together, so you can write the following equation and solve for *x*:

$$\frac{1}{x} + \frac{1}{5} = \frac{3}{10}$$
$$\frac{1}{x} = \frac{3}{10} - \frac{1}{5}$$
$$\frac{1}{x} = \frac{1}{10}$$
$$x = 10$$

Choices F and G cannot be correct because the standard printer would take longer than the high-speed printer to do the job alone. If you selected choice H, you likely made an arithmetic error. Choice J is the result of adding the rates, which is incorrect—these two printers are going to work *together*, which does not accurately portray the comparison of job completion rates of the two printers.

55. **The correct answer is D.** Pick a number, then apply the percent changes to it and see what happens. Use 100, since it's the easiest number for which to find percentages. 30% of 100 is 30, so increasing 100 by 30% results in $100 + 30 = 130$. 50% of 130 is 65, so decreasing 130 by 50% results in $130 - 65 = 65$. Since you started with 100, this is a net decrease of $100 - 65 = 35$. As a percent of 100, 35 represents 35%, so choice D is correct. Choice A is too low and likely the result of an arithmetic error. Choice B is the result of multiplying 0.30 times 0.50, but this implies that the percentages both serve to increase a quantity or decrease a quantity to which they are being applied; here, one percentage is an increase and the other is a decrease. Choice C is incorrect because you cannot simply add or subtract percentages unless they are being applied to the same amount; in this case, the percentages are being applied in succession and hence, to different amounts. You must subtract choice E from 100% to get the correct percentage.

56. **The correct answer is H.** When parallel lines are crossed by a transversal, 8 angles are formed. Unless the transversal is perpendicular to the pair of parallel lines (and it isn't in this case), 4 of the angles are acute and 4 of the angles are obtuse. All of the acute angles are equal to each other, all of the obtuse angles are equal to each other, and each acute angle is supplementary to each obtuse angle. Evaluate the expression in each choice to see which is NOT true:

Choice F: ($a + b = g + h$):

obtuse + acute = acute + obtuse

True; eliminate

Choice G: ($f - h = c - d$):

acute – obtuse = acute – obtuse

True; eliminate

Choice H: ($a + h = g + c$):

obtuse + obtuse = acute + acute

NOT true; CORRECT

Choice J: ($d + b - f = e + c - g$):

obtuse + acute – acute = obtuse + acute – acute

True; eliminate

Choice K: ($h - c = d - f$):

obtuse – acute = obtuse – acute

True; eliminate

57. **The correct answer is C.** You're given the side opposite the 43° angle, as well as the side adjacent to it. Choose the trig function that uses both the opposite and adjacent sides to an angle in a right triangle. Since $\text{tangent} = \dfrac{\text{opposite side}}{\text{adjacent side}}$, $\tan 43° = \dfrac{5}{n}$. To solve for n, isolate it on one side of the equation:

$$\tan 43° = \frac{5}{n}$$
$$n(\tan 43°) = 5$$
$$n = \frac{5}{\tan 43°}$$

Choices A and B are the hypotenuse, not n. In choice D, you are not using the correct definition of sine of an angle. For choice E, you should divide by tan 43°, not multiply by it.

58. **The correct answer is G.** Let x be the smallest of the three integers. Then, the other two are $x + 2$ and $x + 4$. The fact that their sum must be 129 yields the equation $x + (x + 2) + (x + 4) = 129$. This is equivalent to $3x + 6 = 129$, so that $3x = 123$. Thus, $x = 41$. So the three integers are 41, 43, and 45. The average of the two smallest of these integers is $\dfrac{41+43}{2} = 42$. Choice F is the smallest of the three integers. Choice H is the average of all three integers. Choice J is the average of the largest two of the integers. Choice K is the largest of the three integers.

59. **The correct answer is C.** The graph opens upward, which means that the coefficient of x^2 must be positive, so you can eliminate choice E immediately. The graph also indicates a y-intercept of –3, which means that $y = -3$ when $x = 0$, so you can eliminate choices B and D as well. Now pick a specific point from the graph and plug its coordinates into the remaining answer choices. Since the x-intercept (1, 0) is easily identifiable and makes the arithmetic simplest, let $x = 1$ and $y = 0$ to see which equation works:

Choice A: $y = x^2 - 2x - 3$ for (0):

$$0 = 1^2 - 2(1) - 3$$
$$0 = 1 - 2 - 3$$
$$0 \neq -4$$

Eliminate choice A.

Choice C: $y = x^2 + 2x - 3$ for (0):

$$0 = 1^2 + 2(1) - 3$$
$$0 = 1 + 2 - 3$$
$$0 = 0$$

This is the correct answer.

60. **The correct answer is H.** There are 36 possible outcomes. The only ones that satisfy the condition are (1,1), (1, 2), and (2, 1), where the first number represents the face of Die 1 and the second number represents the face of Die 2. So the probability of this event is $\dfrac{3}{36} = \dfrac{1}{12}$. Choice F is the probability that the sum of the two dice is 2, but you should also include the outcomes for which the sum is 3. The answer in choice G excludes one of the possible outcomes from consideration; there are *two* ways to get a sum of 3. Choice J is the probability that the sum is 3 or 4. Choice K includes the outcomes that result in a sum of 4.

Reading

1.	D	**11.**	B	**21.**	D	**31.**	A
2.	G	**12.**	J	**22.**	J	**32.**	G
3.	B	**13.**	A	**23.**	A	**33.**	B
4.	F	**14.**	G	**24.**	J	**34.**	F
5.	B	**15.**	A	**25.**	B	**35.**	C
6.	H	**16.**	F	**26.**	J	**36.**	F
7.	C	**17.**	D	**27.**	B	**37.**	B
8.	J	**18.**	G	**28.**	F	**38.**	J
9.	D	**19.**	B	**29.**	C	**39.**	A
10.	G	**20.**	H	**30.**	H	**40.**	J

1. **The correct answer is D.** This is a vocabulary-in-context question about the word *rich*, which appears in the fourth sentence of the first paragraph. While choices A, B, and C are all definitions of the word, only choice D makes sense in this context. The synonyms *wealthy* (choice A) and *affluent* (choice B) can only describe people, not houses. *Abundant* (choice C) cannot describe a house on its own; what is the house abundant in? *Plush* (choice D), however, can describe a house, so it best captures the meaning of *rich* as it is used in the context of Paragraph 1.

2. **The correct answer is G.** This is a detail question that requires a close reading of the first paragraph in which Mr. Utterson decides that the only way to understand why his friend feels compelled to do the bidding of Mr. Hyde is to see Mr. Hyde for himself. The first sentence of the second paragraph says, "From that time forward, Mr. Utterson began to haunt the door in the by-street of shops." Although Mr. Utterson has a dream about Mr. Hyde in the story, he does not have a nightmare about Mr. Enfield, so choice F is not correct. You can eliminate choice H since there is no mention of who, exactly, is Mr. Utterson's friend who feels compelled to do the bidding of Mr. Hyde, and there is no mention of whether or not Mr. Utterson ever discussed Mr. Hyde with that friend. The reader only knows that he discussed Mr. Hyde with someone named Mr. Enfield. There is also no indication that the door in the by-street of shops is on the way to Mr. Utterson's place of work, so choice J is incorrect.

3. **The correct answer is B.** This is an inference question about Mr. Utterson and Mr. Hyde. Based on information in this passage, the reader can conclude that Mr. Hyde is evil and, at the end of the passage, Mr. Utterson decides to pursue him. Choice B is correct because this relationship is most similar to that of a police officer pursuing a criminal. Some brothers and former co-workers do not get along, but that is not enough to conclude that choice A or choice D is correct. Although there is a sense that Mr. Hyde has a certain amount of power over Mr. Utterson's thoughts, the relationship is not like that of an employee and a boss, so choice C does not make sense.

4. **The correct answer is F.** This is an inference question. The stranger who comes to the Coach and Horses seems to want to keep his face and body hidden in his outerwear and is making a conscious effort to conceal his identity from Mrs. Hall. Clearly, he has something to hide, so choice F is the best answer. However, there is not enough information in this passage to conclude that he is a criminal (choice G), and there is not enough information about Mrs. Hall to conclude that the stranger is the strangest man she has ever met (choice H). Although the stranger seemed "more dead than alive," this is merely a colorful description of him and not a concrete indication that he was actually about to die, so choice J is not the best answer.

5. **The correct answer is B.** This is a vocabulary-in-context question for the word *biting*, which appears in the first sentence of the passage. In this sentence, *biting* describes the wind on a wintry day, so *freezing* is the best definition of the word in this particular context. Although the other answer choices are synonyms for *biting*, none of them describes how the word is used in this context. Wind cannot really be *snapping* (choice A) or *abrasive* (choice C). Wind cannot express emotions, so *hateful* (choice D) does not make sense in this context.

6. **The correct answer is H.** This is an EXCEPT question, so eliminate choices that *are* supported by the passage. Mrs. Hall does her best to make the stranger comfortable, so she does seem to care about his well-being, which eliminates choice F.

However, she also works at the Coach and Horses, so it is probably her job to care about his well-being. Therefore, you can conclude that she feels professionally obligated to see to his comfort (choice J). Based on the way she sets his table quickly before rushing out of the room, you can conclude that she feels uneasy in his presence, which eliminates choice G. However, as odd as the stranger is, his behavior never seems to amuse Mrs. Hall, so choice H is the best answer.

7. **The correct answer is C.** The sentence in lines 18-21 explains that Mrs. Hall intends to be particularly attentive to the stranger because he does not haggle over the price of the room and he arrives at a time of year when her inn does not do much business. Therefore, choice C is the best answer. Choice A implies that the author is concerned with giving general information about the inn business, when the main purpose of the passage is to tell the personal story of its characters. The lines imply that Mrs. Hall plans to be attentive to the stranger because it will help her business, not because she is necessarily a kind person who cares about the well-being of others, so choice B is not the best answer. The stranger's behavior may be odd, but this passage does not suggest that he is particularly cruel, so choice D is not the best answer.

8. **The correct answer is J.** This question is asking you to make an inference by contrasting two characters in similar situations. Since it is asking you to find a difference between those two people, you should try to eliminate all the answer choices that suggest ways they are similar. Mr. Utterson is intrigued by the mysterious Mr. Hyde and Mrs. Hall is intrigued by the mysterious stranger who comes to the Coach and Horses, so this is one way they are similar. Therefore, you can eliminate choice F. Both Mr. Utterson and Mrs. Hall find the behavior of those two mysterious people baffling, so choice G is wrong. Mr. Utterson seems to care about his friend who is obsessed with Mr. Hyde and Mrs. Hall cares about the troubled stranger who comes to the Coach and Horses, so choice H does not describe a way they are different. However, only Mr.Utterson wants to seek out a mysterious person to learn more about him, and Mr. Utterson's enthusiasm about it makes it seem as though he likes to solve mysteries. Even though the stranger who comes to the Coach and Horses intrigues Mrs. Hall, she wants to flee from him, not solve the mystery that apparently surrounds him. So choice J describes a difference between Mr. Utterson and Mrs. Hall.

9. **The correct answer is D.** This is an inference question about how these passages function in the novels from which they were excerpted. Since each passage seems to set up something—Passage A sets up Mr. Utterson's pursuit of Mr. Hyde, and Passage B sets up the arrival of a mysterious stranger at the Coach and Horses—it is unlikely they occur on the final pages of the novels from which they were excerpted (choice A). A passage that merely sets up a plot thread probably won't be the most important incident in a novel, no matter how important the plot thread that follows will be, so you can eliminate choice B. However, since both passages set up plot threads that will likely be important, it is more likely that they occur early in the novels from which they were excerpted, so choice D is the best answer. Neither passage is particularly humorous, so choice C does not make sense.

10. **The correct answer is G.** This is a main idea question about Paragraph 1 of Passage A and Paragraph 2 of Passage B. Choice F is incorrect because Mr. Hyde does not actually arrive anywhere in Passage 1. However, only he seems particularly evil, so choice H cannot apply to Passage 2. Mr. Hyde may demand things of Mr. Utterson's friend, and the stranger who comes to the Coach and Horses demands that Mrs. Hall light a fire and get him a room at the inn, but neither captures the main idea of the paragraphs in question. Therefore, choice J is not the best answer. The only choice that really captures the main ideas of the paragraphs is choice G, since Paragraph 1 of Passage A describes how Mr. Hyde is affecting Mr. Utterson's thoughts and dreams, and Paragraph 2 of Passage B describes how the stranger affects Mrs. Hall's behavior, since she is working to attend to the stranger's needs.

11. **The correct answer is B.** In the second sentence of the passage, the author identifies the Children's House as a "kind of school." While play may be performed in a Children's House as part of the educational process, it is more of a place of learning than a place of play, so choice A is not the best answer. While the author does identify a Children's House as an environment, she indicates that it is important for it to include an outdoor space, so choice C is incorrect. The author also identifies the Children's House as "a real house," but it is not one to live in (choice D) but rather a house to learn in during school hours.

12. **The correct answer is J.** The author refers to how equipment adapted for children will allow them to do

such things as move furniture around by themselves, which implies that it fosters self-sufficiency rather than reliance on adult assistance, so choice J is the best answer. While a Children's House is specially adapted for children, the author never suggests that adults are not allowed in a Children's House (choice F) and does mention the presence of a teacher in the house. Choice G is too extreme: while the child-sized equipment in a Children's House may make it easier for children to learn, there is no suggestion that they cannot learn at all when using adult-sized equipment. Although the author does reference how the educational equipment is the common property of all the children, she never implies that the fact that it is adapted specifically for children encourages sharing (choice H).

13. **The correct answer is A.** The sixth paragraph describes a variety of decorations in a Children's House, including a blackboard for drawing, pictures, and plants, so choice A is the best answer. Choice B is both too extreme and too focused on the indication that some of the pictures in the room can be biblical. Choice C makes the same mistake, but focuses on the pictures of historical incidents instead of biblical stories. Choice D focuses on the line about blackboards rather than on the main idea of the paragraph as a whole.

14. **The correct answer is G.** In the seventh paragraph, the author states, "The children spread these rugs upon the floor, sit upon them and work there," so choice G is the correct answer. The author never explains why the pieces of carpet should be multicolored, so choice F is not the best answer. While the author does mention that the table and chairs take up space in the working room (choice H), this does not have anything to do with why pieces of carpet are necessary in a working room. The author also states that the children are responsible for spreading out the pieces of carpet, but she does not imply that this is a necessary skill to learn, so choice J is not the best answer either.

15. **The correct answer is A.** The author uses the word *didactic* to describe materials intended to assist "the intellectual development of the child," so choice A, *educational*, is the best answer. While children might enjoy the materials with which they work, the author is more concerned with children's intellectual development than their enjoyment here, so choice B can be eliminated. Choice C can be eliminated, since the author uses *didactic* as an adjective to describe material in the passage and *teach* is a verb. While the materials with which children work are often small to suit their small size, the author's concern with intellectual development in line 20 makes choice A a better answer than choice D.

16. **The correct answer is F.** The author indicates that there should be a gymnasium in the central room described in the second paragraph, and since gymnasiums are places for exercise, choice F is a reasonable conclusion. The paragraph also mentions the need for a dining room in the central room, but choice G reaches a conclusion that the paragraph does not really support. The paragraph mentions that the central room is often also the only room at the disposal of the children, which contradicts the conclusion in choice H. While the author mentions a number of activities that can be performed in the central room, she does not apply any kind of hierarchy to these activities, so there is no support for the conclusion in choice J.

17. **The correct answer is D.** In the fifth paragraph, the author explains that the drawers are where a student puts "things belonging to him," so choice D is the best answer. Choice A mixes up the roles of the drawers and the cupboard. Both are pieces of storage equipment, so choice B is incorrect. Both are also elements of the working room, so choice C is also incorrect.

18. **The correct answer is G.** The author's educational method seems to be built on trust, as the house she describes is designed to trust children to take measures to educate themselves. While such a place may depend on the curiosity of the children, the author does not seem particularly curious about children in this passage, so choice F is not the best answer. While the ability to trust someone may imply admiration for that person, the author is not emotional enough to support the conclusion in choice H. Choice J, *wrath*, means "extreme anger," and the author certainly never expresses anger toward children.

19. **The correct answer is B.** Throughout the passage, the author advocates a learning environment with multiple stimuli that allows children the freedom to learn in their own ways, so choice B is the best answer. Choice A, however, is an extreme conclusion and one that ignores mention of a teacher in the passage. Choice C is incorrect for the same reason. Choice D reaches a conclusion contradicted by all of the details in this passage.

20. **The correct answer is H.** In the eighth paragraph, the author indicates that "above all," a child should have a flower pot in which to to sow and cultivate a plant, which supports the conclusion in choice H. The other answer choices all lack enough specific support for their

extreme conclusions. While the author indicates that a club room should contain musical instruments, she never implies that a child's education is incomplete if the child cannot play an instrument (choice F). She also mentions that only those children who are interested would gather to listen to a teacher read stories but does not imply that those who aren't interested should never participate in a specific activity (choice G). The author states that a club room should contain "games of patience," but she never implies that a child will never learn patience without access to a club room (choice J).

21. **The correct answer is D.** Choice D is the only answer choice that does not describe one of Dickens's theories about how Godwin wrote "Caleb Williams"; it describes one of Poe's theories ("It is only with the dénouement constantly in view that we can give a plot its indispensable air of consequence, or causation, by making the incidents, and especially the tone at all points, tend to the development of the intention."). In the first paragraph, the author explains that Dickens believed that Godwin "...wrote his 'Caleb Williams' backwards. ..." (choice A). The passage notes, "He first involved his hero in a web of difficulties (choice B) and then, for the first, cast about him for some mode of accounting for what had been done" (choice C).

22. **The correct answer is J.** In the fourth paragraph, the author describes how he is first concerned with creating an effect to manipulate the heart, intellect, or soul when writing, so choice J is the best answer. In the second paragraph, the author admits that he agrees with Williams that a story should be written backward, which contradicts choice F. Since the author is introducing an explanation of the process by which he wrote "The Raven," choice G cannot be correct. While the author seems very concerned with tone when writing, choice H reaches an extreme conclusion that the passage contradicts.

23. **The correct answer is A.** In the seventh paragraph, the author explains that "...that no one point in its composition is referable either to accident or intuition—that the work proceeded, step by step, to its completion with the precision and rigid consequence of a mathematical problem." This reveals that the creation of "The Raven" only involved a precise method and never involved accident or intuition.

24. **The correct answer is J.** By following the opinion, "There is a radical error, I think, in the usual mode of constructing a story" with "Either history affords a thesis," Poe implies that he believes that faithfully basing a story's thesis on historical events is an error. This supports the conclusion in choice J and contradicts the one in choice F. Choice G is too extreme: Poe only implies that basing a plot on history is an error, not that a writer should completely disregard historical events. Choice H is too specific and reaching this conclusion would require more evidence than this passage provides.

25. **The correct answer is B.** As a whole, the fifth paragraph relates the author's theories about why no one has written an article about the literary process, even though such an article would be valuable. The author does not make his own intention to write such an article known until the seventh paragraph, so choice A is incorrect. Choice C describes a misconception about the literary process and not the author's own process. Although the author states, "Why such a paper has never been given to the world, I am much at a loss to say," he then goes on to present multiple theories about why no one has written such an article, so choice D is incorrect.

26. **The correct answer is J.** Poe's statement that "For my own part, I have neither sympathy with the repugnance alluded to, nor at any time the least difficulty in recalling to mind the progressive steps of any of my compositions" supports the conclusion in choice J and contradicts the one in choice F. While Poe does claim to always remember his creative process, he does not suggest that he needs to take notes to remember it, so choice G is not the likeliest answer. Earlier in the passage, Poe states that he is more concerned with plot than tone, which contradicts choice H.

27. **The correct answer is B.** In the first line of the passage, Poe states that Dickens expressed his theories about Godwin "... in a note now lying before me, alluding to an examination I once made of the mechanism of 'Barnaby Rudge.'" That line contradicts choice A. Poe never indicates who wrote "Barnaby Rudge," so choice C is not correct. There is no indication that Poe criticized "Caleb Williams" either, so choice D is incorrect as well.

28. **The correct answer is F.** The author refers to the crudities of thought, but does not imply that crudity is at all responsible for the lack of an article on the literary process. However, he does blame vanity (choice G) in the fifth paragraph and forgetfulness (choice H) in the sixth paragraph. Since the author describes the desire to deceive readers into believing literature is composed "in a frenzy" in the fifth paragraph, choice J is incorrect as well.

29. **The correct answer is C.** The author's main goal seems to be to clarify the ways writers create their work, so choice C is the best answer. The author never implies that he expects his study will change the way writers create literature, so choice A is not the best answer. Clarifying the literary process, not clarifying the meaning of literature itself, is the author's goal, so choice B is not correct. The author does not indicate that his clarification will necessarily change what writers say about their own processes, so the conclusion in choice D does not have as much support as does the one in choice C.

30. **The correct answer is H.** Since the author is about to discuss his poem "The Raven," and he refers to how he will not discuss his intention to make it "a poem that should suit at once the popular and the critical taste," he implies that he did intend for it to have widespread appeal for both readers and critics. So choice H is the best answer. The author only indicates the irrelevance of a particular question, not his own work, so choice F is incorrect. The author may indicate that he intended "The Raven" to have popular appeal, but he does not refer to or imply the success of that intention, so choice G is not the best answer. The author never comments on his feelings toward critics; he only implies that he wanted "The Raven" to appeal to them, so choice J is incorrect.

31. **The correct answer is A.** The main idea captures the most important overall idea of a paragraph, and only choice A accomplishes this. Choices B and D focus on individual details that support that main idea, but they fail to capture the most important idea of the fourth paragraph as a whole. Choice C contains an idea from the fifth paragraph, not the fourth one.

32. **The correct answer is G.** In the third paragraph, the author compares blood with water to illustrate how certain solid materials dissolve in water, while blood is the very material that *forms* other solids. Choice F is incorrect because the author never indicates that blood does not contain sugar, which it does. Choice H mixes up the functions of water and blood in the comparison. While it is true that water and blood are both organic liquids, this fact has nothing to do with the information in the third paragraph.

33. **The correct answer is B.** In the first line of the second paragraph, the author explicitly identifies Liebig as a naturalist. While that general term could mean that he is either a biologist (choice A), a zoologist (choice C), or even an instructor (choice D), the explicitness or specificity of the statement means that choice B remains the best answer.

34. **The correct answer is F.** Based on the second paragraph's list of body parts that are formed from blood, choice F is a very reasonable conclusion to draw from the paragraph. While the paragraph focuses on the liquid blood, it does not support the erroneous inference in choice G. Choice H is too extreme; while one could reasonably infer that a human could not survive after losing a great deal of blood, this answer choice implies that even the slightest loss of blood would cause death. Choice J reaches a conclusion that is simply not supported by evidence in the second paragraph.

35. **The correct answer is C.** According to the seventh paragraph, during circulation, oxygen in blood is deposited in bones (statement II) and helps forms phosphate of lime (statement III). However, calcium is given to teeth during circulation, which is the opposite of calcium being *extracted* from teeth during circulation (statement I). Therefore, the correct answer must account for only statements II and III and eliminate statement I. Only choice C accomplishes this. Choices A, B, and D all include the false statement I.

36. **The correct answer is F.** In the ninth paragraph, the author explains how the body extracts new blood from food, and juice is extracted from solid foods such as fruits and vegetables, so choice F is the most logical answer. The terms "Means of Existence" and "Juice of Life" describe two different things, so one is not used to clarify the other, which means choice G is not the best answer. While juice and blood contain nutrients, choice H reaches a very specific conclusion that is not supported by details in the passage. Choice J is a true statement from the ninth paragraph, but it has nothing to do with why the author describes blood as "Juice of Life."

37. **The correct answer is B.** The answer to this question is revealed in the eighth paragraph, which states that waste particles are carried "…to that part of the human body where they may be secreted." This statement proves that choice B is the correct answer. Since depositing is the opposite of secreting, choice A can be eliminated. Choice C is an effect of the binding of body parts, not an effect of waste particles in the blood. The fact that waste particles are secreted means they cannot remain in the body to decay (choice D).

38. **The correct answer is J.** The answer to this question can be found in the ninth paragraph which states that "… the life of the body consists in its constant change (statement I) and transformation, in the continual exchange of fresh substances for waste ones (statement III)." However, it never suggests that the human body must constantly break down (statement II), which implies an unhealthy body. So the correct answer choice must include statements I and III and eliminate statement II, which is what choice J does. Choice F is incorrect because it fails to include statement III. Choice G is incorrect because it includes only the false statement. Choice H is incorrect because it includes the false statement and only one of the two true statements.

39. **The correct answer is A.** When replacing the word *constituents* in line 9 with each of the answer choices, only *components* (choice A) makes sense in the sentence's context. *Constants* (choice B) and *continents* (choice D) may look similar to *constituents*, but neither word makes sense in the context of line 9. *Bases* (choice C) might refer to the most important components of the body parts, but not all of the components, so choice C is not the best answer.

40. **The correct answer is J.** After explaining how integral blood is to the formation and functioning of every part of the human body, the author concludes that it is the "Juice of Life," all of which supports the conclusion in choice J. In the sixth paragraph, the author does imply that blood can be both remarkable and mysterious, but its mystery certainly is not important enough to this passage to be an essential ingredient of the author's overall conclusion, so choice F is not the best answer. The author certainly understands the importance of blood, but choice G reaches an extreme conclusion that the passage does not really support. Choice H makes a comparison and judgment that the passage's details do not support, either.

Science

1.	A	**11.**	A	**21.**	A	**31.**	B
2.	H	**12.**	H	**22.**	J	**32.**	H
3.	C	**13.**	D	**23.**	B	**33.**	B
4.	J	**14.**	G	**24.**	J	**34.**	F
5.	D	**15.**	A	**25.**	C	**35.**	D
6.	H	**16.**	J	**26.**	G	**36.**	J
7.	B	**17.**	A	**27.**	B	**37.**	B
8.	J	**18.**	G	**28.**	J	**38.**	G
9.	C	**19.**	C	**29.**	C	**39.**	B
10.	G	**20.**	H	**30.**	F	**40.**	G

1. **The correct answer is A.** To answer this question, focus on Experiments 1 and 2. Looking at Experiment 2, when Crab 1 is faced with a competitor of any species, it is almost twice as likely to eat if it finds the food first. This species rarely gets anything at all if it is second to find the food item, and this is true even when competing against members of the same species. Those results imply that this species is less likely to eat if it is in a group, encouraging solitude. Second, this species is the most aggressive of the three species. Such tendencies would be a disadvantage if constantly surrounded by other crabs. Constant aggression would pose risks, endangering the crab and distracting from survival behaviors such as eating. Taken together, Crab 1 is the most likely of the three to live alone instead of in a group. Crabs 2 and 3 (choices B and C) both have lower aggression and are more likely to eat even if they find the food second, suggesting that these species are well adapted to group living. Choice D is incorrect, for while it is not possible to be absolutely certain about how these crabs live from this data alone, there is enough information to make an educated guess.

2. **The correct answer is H.** The three experiments are all focused on how crabs compare to one another. The first two experiments compare how crabs compete in two important areas: successful acquisition of food and the ability to win contests. The third experiment compares shell strength, and a stronger shell is a possible advantage when it comes to fights over food or other resources. Taken together, the experiments seem to be examining the relative competitive standing of each species of crab. Choices F and G are possible hypotheses for individual experiments, 2 and 3 respectively, but neither choice encompasses the entire breadth of experiments being performed. Choice J might possibly be a hypothesis for the first two experiments combined but does not explain why Experiment 3 is included.

3. **The correct answer is C.** Looking at the graph, Crab 3's line is above the other two, indicating that it has the strongest shell based on the size of the crab. However, Crab 2, followed closely by Crab 1, has the highest breaking strength overall, since its line reaches the highest. This can be explained if Crabs 1 and 2 grow larger than Crab 3 or at least some larger individuals were tested. Choice A is incorrect since the Crab 1 line goes much farther along the x-axis, which represents size, than either Crabs 2 or 3. Crab 2's strength-to-size line has the steepest slope, indicating that its shell grows stronger more quickly as the crab's size increases. The line for Crab 2 stops around 75 mm (choice D) suggesting that either Crab 2 doesn't get any larger or that was the largest size examined in the study.

4. **The correct answer is J.** The most notable difference in behavior among the three crabs is that Crab 1 is much more aggressive and likely to instigate a conflict than the other two crabs. Why this is so isn't explained, but the crab must have some reason to expect that it will benefit from the contest. To benefit from the contest it must expect to win the contest, which suggests that this crab has evolved ways to win such contests. The fact that it does not win implies that it is following its instinct into an unknown situation that is not working the way the crab expects. One possible explanation for this is that Crab 1 has never seen either of these crabs before and acts as it normally would but meets an unexpected response. If they shared a habitat (choice F), Crab 1 would have known under which circumstances fighting was likely to pay off and avoid losing battles. Fighting costs energy that the crab could use for other purposes and which the crab will seek to conserve. Choice G is not supported by the results of Experiment 1, where Crab 1 finds food first more often than Crab 3. Choice H likewise makes little sense, as animals do not attack their own predators unprovoked, nor is there any evidence presented that losing crabs are killed or eaten.

5. **The correct answer is D.** The strength versus size line crosses the *x*-axis at about 25mm in size. Crab 3 intersects the *x*-axis at around 10 mm, and Crab 2 around 30 mm. The *y*-axis (Breaking Strength) has no scale, so there is no indication that the bottom of the *y*-axis is zero. To determine which crab is lowest on the vertical axis, estimate what the line for each crab would look like if extended downward past the *x*-axis. If the line for Crab 2 is extended to 25 mm, it will be below the *x*-axis, while Crab 1 is right on it (choice C). At 20 mm (choice B), Crab 2 is below the *x*-axis, while Crab 3 is above it, and at 10 mm breaking strength, Crab 2 is even farther below the *x*-axis, while Crab 3's breaking strength is right on it (choice A). That leaves only choice D.

6. **The correct answer is H.** In order to determine how each crab influences the others, that influence must be removed. Testing each species of crab separately, for example recording how often a hungry crab of each type finds food on its own or how quickly it finds it, would be one way to see if it behaves differently when it is alone. Testing their preference for different foods (choice F) would provide insight into the behavior of each crab but would not explain how each species is influenced by the others. According to the passage, the experiments in choice G were already performed, so it is part of the information provided. Choice J would expand the understanding of how these crabs interact but would do nothing to examine how they behave in isolation.

7. **The correct answer is B.** The highest *y* value (wave height) was observed at an *x* value (wind speed) of about 2.4 m/s. Choice A is incorrect because one of the lowest wave heights was observed at 0.0 m/s. Choice C is incorrect because a high wave height was observed around 8.8 m/s, but it wasn't the highest. Choice D is incorrect because this was the highest tested wind speed.

8. **The correct answer is J.** There are three points that significantly deviate from the general positively sloped line that develops from the relationship between wave height and wind speed. These are outliers.

9. **The correct answer is C.** Figure 2 shows a very clear correlation between wind speed and wave height in small lakes; as wind speed increases, wave height increases in a very linear pattern. This in and of itself does not prove the hypothesis that wind speed drives wave height, but it is strongly suggestive that it is true in small lakes. The data in the ocean is much more highly variable, with no clear pattern in the relationship between wind speed and wave height; the scatterplot points are almost random. Experiment 2 tries to explain this pattern by showing that swell waves are common, and swell waves are determined by the distant storm instead of local wind. However, there were days that had few swell waves, and there is no indication which data points represent a swell wave. From Figure 1 alone, the swell waves might well have a clear relationship with wind speed, while the other waves do not; there is no way to tell. Therefore, the data can also be reasonably interpreted to mean that the hypothesis might simply not be true in the ocean. Choice A is incorrect since the lake data is quite convincing. Choice B can be rejected on the basis of Figure 1 alone. The characteristics of swell waves are not tested in any of the experiments, so choice D can be rejected.

10. **The correct answer is G.** The entire experiment is set up to test the relationship between wind speed and wave height. The stated hypothesis is given in choice F, that wind speed directly influences wave height. A null hypothesis for this experiment, then, is that wave height and wind speed are not related; the experiment is disproving that idea. While experiment 2 is measuring the frequency of swell waves, it makes no hypothesis about their relative frequency and so has no null hypothesis. Therefore both H and J are incorrect.

11. **The correct answer is A.** Any of the waves indicated in the graph could, in theory, be a swell wave, but there's no way to tell which points on the general upward curve represent waves that originated elsewhere. However, the three very noticeable outlying points on the graph are most likely swell waves, since there's no other way to explain why their heights would be so different from the mass of other waves recorded at those same wind speeds. The first outlying point corresponds to a wave with a height of a little under 3 meters, while the third outlying point, on the right side of the graph corresponding to a wind speed of a little over 8 m/s, comes in at just over 1 meter. The waves that are 1.2 and 2.7 meters high are good approximations for

these outlying points that are likely to represent swell waves. Choices B, C, and D do not represent outlying points.

12. **The correct answer is H.** Experiment 3 added validity to the original hypothesis by using a lake setting, which significantly reduced the number of swell waves that might obscure the relationship between wave height and wind speed. Still, in addition to outlying values, there was some variation even among the points composing the solidly upward trend. Observing the effect of a wind blower on an indoor pool would eliminate possible outside interference even more, thus providing an excellent opportunity to further support the original hypothesis. In the absence of any mitigating factors, one could determine whether the resulting graph is precisely linear as the theory would suggest. Choice F is incorrect, as thunderstorms would likely only complicate the data by introducing additional variables into the experiment. Choice G is incorrect, as the point of the experiments is to observe the effect of wind on wave height. Not much would be gained, therefore, by conducting trials during a wind-free period. Choice J leans in the opposite direction of correct choice H. Rather than reduce the chance of swell waves even further in order to observe the pure effect of wind on wave height, choice J proposes to observe a body of water likely to have even more swell waves than the lake. One would expect the results to be somewhat in between those recorded in the ocean and those recorded at the lake, which is not likely to lend additional support to the hypothesis.

13. **The correct answer is D.** According to Figure 1, the horizontal distance between the ball and the racket stops changing (i.e., it is neither increasing nor decreasing), around 12.5 seconds after it leaves the racket. From the table, the ball has a consistent vertical height of zero, meaning it has hit the ground and staying there, before it has returned to 18 m, as shown in the graph. Therefore, the ball must be standing still and any answer choice that indicates the ball is still moving is incorrect.

14. **The correct answer is G.** The ball first hits the ground (vertical height is zero in the table) and bounces when it has traveled 13.5 meters; this corresponds to a time of approximately 3.5 seconds on the graph. It hits the ground again for a second bounce when it has traveled 18 meters in total; this is the second time in the table that the height is zero. This corresponds to approximately 6 seconds on the graph, so 2.5 seconds elapse between the time the ball bounces once and when it bounces again. Choice F is the total time elapsed between the ball's second bounce and when it bounces for good. Choice H is the total time elapsed before the ball bounces twice, not the time between bounces. Choice J, 8.5 seconds, does represent the time between the ball first reaching 13.5 meters and bouncing and then traveling 18 meters, or the distance of the second bounce. But look carefully at the graph: 8.5 seconds is the difference between 11 seconds and 2.5 seconds. At 11 seconds the ball is indeed 18 meters from its starting point but, at that point, it has started traveling backward. The ball has stopped bouncing and is rolling.

15. **The correct answer is A.** This is the horizontal distance at which the largest vertical height was observed. Choice B is incorrect because this was the horizontal distance for the maximal height during the first bounce, but not overall. Choice C is incorrect because this was the horizontal distance for the maximal height during the second bounce, but not overall. Choice D is incorrect because this was the largest observed horizontal distance.

16. **The correct answer is J.** From the information in the table, the ball travels forward while rising higher before the ball's height starts to decrease. The ball hits zero and rises then falls twice before finally settling on the ground. Each time the height reaches zero and then increases indicates a bounce, each one of lesser height than the one before. The data will resemble a row of humps, each one smaller than the one before, until height stays at zero. Choice F represents a ball that does not bounce. Choice G looks a lot like Figure 1, which is horizontal distance plotted by time, not vertical distance. Choice H is close, but it depicts a ball that only bounces once instead of twice.

17. **The correct answer is A.** Figure 1 shows that at the 8-second mark, the ball was roughly 22.5 meters from the point of impact. Table 1 shows that at this horizontal distance, the vertical height of the ball was 0 and had been for a few meters. The height of the ball continues to be 0 for the rest of the way, meaning that it was on the ground at this point. The horizontal distance continues to increase to a maximum of 24 meters from the student, whereupon it decreases back to 18 meters away, which corresponds to the point at which the distance curve flattens out on Figure 1 at the 12-second mark. So between 8 and 12 seconds, the ball was moving with a height of 0, meaning it was rolling on the ground. Choice B is incorrect, because Figure 1 indicates that from 9 to 12 seconds after impact, the ball's distance from the student decreased, meaning that it

traveled back toward the point of impact for part of the time period mentioned in this choice. Choice C is incorrect, because Figure 1 indicates that after 12 seconds, the ball's horizontal distance remained unchanged, which means the ball stopped moving between 12 and 14 seconds after the point of impact. Choice D is incorrect, because at the 7-second mark, the ball was roughly 20 meters from the start point, and from there traversed the distances (listed at the end of Table 1) that correspond to vertical heights of 0. Figure 1 shows the ball moving back toward the point of impact at the 10-second mark. So between 7 and 10 seconds, the ball must have been rolling on the ground, not flying through the air.

18. **The correct answer is G.** Both hypotheses find risks in spending too much time indoors. For proponents of the Contaminants Hypothesis, too much time indoors exposes children to potentially dangerous indoor contaminants. For proponents of the Hygienic Hypothesis, too much time indoors deprives children of exposure to minor threats that will help them build a healthy immune system. Both hypotheses agree it's a problem but not on the reason. Choice F is incorrect, since neither hypothesis discusses how common asthma is relative to other illnesses. Choices H and J only apply to the Hygienic and Contaminants hypotheses, respectively, so form no point of agreement.

19. **The correct answer is C.** Since environmental contaminants are more likely to be present in larger quantities in a congested metropolitan area than a rural countryside, it's possible that the child in question, upon moving, would be significantly exposed to them for the first time. The Contaminants Hypothesis is based on the assertion that environmental impurities (such as smoke and pollution) may be a contributing factor in the development of asthma, so the evidence presented in this case could support this theory. This means you can eliminate choice D. Yet it could also support the Hygienic Hypothesis, since it's possible that the child's immune system has been compromised by a lack of exposure to environmental contaminants, and the move to the congested city atmosphere has overwhelmed his underdeveloped immune system, making him susceptible to the disease. Choice C is correct because both hypotheses could be supported, making choices A and B incorrect.

20. **The correct answer is H.** Supporters of the Hygienic Hypothesis argue that household sanitizers are bad because they eliminate the type of contaminants with which children's immune systems need to come in contact in order to develop. However, if these sanitizers themselves contain the kind of chemicals included in the "toxic soup" that supporters of the Contaminants Hypothesis cite, these supporters could claim that sanitizers contribute to asthma for the reason *they* state, not the reason put forth by supporters of the Hygienic Hypothesis. Choice F is incorrect, because potential side effects of immunizations are beyond the scope of both hypotheses. Nothing about side effects speaks to the main issue of rising asthma rates. Choice G is incorrect, because the result it states—the negative effect on the development of children's immune systems—is exactly what proponents of the Hygienic Hypothesis predict will happen when children are less exposed to animals and other natural environmental elements. Choice J is incorrect, as the Hygienic Hypothesis does not maintain that immunizations are entirely unnecessary or state that warding off major diseases is not beneficial to children. Proponents of the hypothesis take issue with the overuse of immunizations to ward off minor, non-fatal diseases. It is this overuse of immunizations that Hygienic theorists believe may prevent the kind of contact with germs necessary for the proper development of the immune system.

21. **The correct answer is A.** Food additives are specifically mentioned in the passage as a problem for people who favor the Contaminants Hypothesis. Most food additives are preservatives, and proponents of the Hygienic Hypothesis might object to over-preservation of food, which does not let developing immune systems encounter mold or other germs in old food. Non-preservative food additives are not specifically connected to the Hygienic Hypothesis but would certainly be objectionable to proponents of the Contaminants Hypothesis. Unpasteurized cheese (choice B) might raise objections from those who favor the Hygienic Hypothesis, since pasteurization kills all the natural bacteria in dairy products. Bleach (choice C) would most likely appeal to those who favor the Contaminants Hypothesis, since it can clean away dust and mold and other environmental risks. Proponents of the Hygienic Hypothesis object to excessive cleaning. Slightly moldy bread (choice D) would likely not bother proponents of the Hygienic Hypothesis, who would argue that a little mold might not be bad.

22. **The correct answer is J.** Our obsession with health and cleanliness is clearly intended to make us healthier, but supporters of the Hygienic Hypothesis believe it can also have the opposite effect on children by stunting the development of their immune systems. It's reasonable to say that this qualifies as ironic (that is, peculiar or paradoxical). Choice F is incorrect, considering that our obsession with health and cleanliness has an effect contrary to the one stated in this choice. We don't disregard the noxious elements of our environment; we attempt to stamp them out, much to the consternation of the Hygienic Hypothesis supporters. Choice G is incorrect, because proponents of the Hygienic Hypothesis believe that excessive reliance on immunizations is detrimental, not beneficial. Choice H is incorrect, as the Hygienic Hypothesis does cite a specific effect of our obsession with health and cleanliness: it negatively impacts our immune systems by underexposing us to natural elements.

23. **The correct answer is B.** Supporters of the Hygienic Hypothesis believe that some steps we're taking to sanitize our lives are weakening children's immune systems. They feel that the overuse of immunizations and excessive sanitizing of our living spaces have a negative effect on health. They also consider natural elements of our environment, presumably even noxious ones like mosquitoes, to play a part in the proper development of our immune systems. Therefore, it is reasonable to infer that they would not be in favor of protecting a child from mosquitoes with a man-made repellent; this is, most likely, an example of the kind of thing they would believe to have negative consequences in the long run. This eliminates choices A and C in favor of choice B. Choice D is incorrect, because it would be reasonable to infer that bug spray is similar to pesticides and other chemicals contributing to the "toxic soup" the supporters of the Contaminants Hypothesis loathe; therefore, they would be more likely to oppose its use than to encourage it.

24. **The correct answer is J.** At the heart of both theories lies the idea that environmental factors are responsible for the dramatic increase in childhood asthma. The first theory states that the environment has become too dirty; the second argues that the environment has become too clean. Both, however, relate the rise in asthma directly to environmental changes. The theory presented in this question ignores environmental factors altogether, while citing a biological factor that may account for the increased susceptibility to asthma. It thus supports neither theory presented in the passage, making choices F, G, and H incorrect.

25. **The correct answer is C.** 4 p.m. on Day 1 is the time at which the graph for math proficiency, represented by the line with circles, reaches its highest point. Choice A is incorrect because this was one of the times at which maximal verbal proficiency was observed. Choice B is incorrect because this is the time at which minimal short-term memory proficiency was observed. Choice D is incorrect because this is the time at which minimal verbal and math proficiencies were observed.

26. **The correct answer is G.** The maximum math skill proficiency matched that of verbal skill proficiency, but its minimum was significantly lower. Choice F is incorrect because verbal and math skills were nearly identical in maxima, but the minimum for math was lower than that for verbal. Choice H is incorrect because the minimum for short-term memory was higher than the minima for the other two skills, and the maximum was lower than the maxima for the other two skills. Choice J is incorrect because according to the data, the three skills did not exhibit the same ranges of proficiency.

27. **The correct answer is B.** According to Table 1, the parietal lobe was activated 6 times, while the temporal lobe was activated 3 times. That means that the parietal lobe was activated more, by a 2:1 ratio (the reduced version of the 6:3 ratio). Choice C is incorrect because it misidentifies the ratio, while Choices A and D are incorrect because they describe (correctly and incorrectly) the ratio between the lobes' inactivity status.

28. **The correct answer is J.** A major flaw of Study 2, at least as it connects to Study 1, is that it does not test short-term memory. All of the questions are either acquired skills (math, reading) or long-term memory recall (recalling a dream, defining loyalty). As a result, Study 2 does not provide significant insight as to why short-term memory improved during sleep deprivation in Study 1. Choice F might be true in some cases but does not address the question of short-term memory. Choice G is clearly not true, and in the case of H, math ability declines but does not seem to end, nor would such a result explain short-term memory performance.

29. **The correct answer is C.** Note that Study 2 explicitly indicates that the rested volunteer received 8 hours of quality sleep, something never indicated in regard to Study 1's subjects, who were awakened for tests at 7 a.m. If nearly half of them slept terribly just prior to the study, then the study, which supposedly differentiates between performances while rested and performances while sleep-deprived, would already be questionable. If the designers of a sleep-deprivation study wish to compare rested subjects with sleep-deprived ones, they must be sure that the rested subjects are truly rested. Choice A is incorrect. The study is designed to show how performance after rest might differ from performance while sleep-deprived. As long as the subjects tested didn't suffer major bouts of insomnia immediately preceding the study, it would make little difference whether they had experienced insomnia sometime in the past. Choice B is incorrect because results following the study are irrelevant to the methodology of the study itself. It would not be unusual for some subjects to experience changes in sleep patterns after participating in such a study, but that has no bearing on what the study set out to show and whether it was designed properly to show it. Choice D in no way invalidates the study's methodology, since the point all along was to keep participants awake for 30 straight hours.

30. **The correct answer is F.** Math and verbal skills decline after about 14 hours; at the same time, short-term memory skills seem to improve. If short-term memory were essential for math and verbal tasks, the three measures should follow a similar pattern. All three should decrease or increase (choice G). Choice H is not true since short-term memory remains more or less the same for hours before it starts to improve. Choice J is also not correct since, while math and verbal skills have declined considerably after 24 hours, the graph of these skills is not quite at its lowest point until 30 hours have passed. Math and verbal skills can still decrease after 24 hours.

31. **The correct answer is B.** Tissue factors are produced by damaged cells. These then bind with TF-7 to start the chain of events that results in clotting. If the origin of the tissue factors is affected by the mutation, then these tissue factors are being produced in the wrong place. The clotting sequence can still take place, but not only in damaged areas. Choices A and C can be ruled out, since the mutation does not disable the tissue factors themselves. Choice D can be eliminated, since circulating inactive clotting factors are different from the tissue factors that are produced in the event of injury.

32. **The correct answer is H.** The role of prothrombinase is to convert prothrombin into thrombin. Thrombin forms fibrin, the first part of the clot, and activates Factor 13. Too much prothrombinase will convert all of the prothrombin available, but without extra prothrombin there is nothing for the excess prothrombinase to act on. Same for the extra activated Factor 13: unless there is excess fibrin to be converted into the impermeable matrix, the excess Factor 13 will have no effect. Normal clotting will result. No clotting (choice F) would occur if there were no prothrombinase at all. Choice G is impossible, since an excess still means there is enough prothrombinase and factor 13 to complete the clotting process; the excess has no way to create excess clots (choice J).

33. **The correct answer is B.** This is inferable if we closely follow the chain of cause and effect. The chelating agent interferes with the effectiveness of calcium ions. Since calcium ions are required for clotting, we can deduce that the chelating agent would prevent clotting. Of the people in the choices, only the technician in choice B would benefit from *preventing* clotting, since he or she would not want donated blood stored for later use to clot in the storage bags. In contrast, the doctor and the hemophiliac in choices A and D would presumably want to aid, not inhibit, clotting. It's also difficult to see any reason for the researcher in choice C to be interested in clotting in anything other than a theoretical sense, so without further information, we cannot presume that this person would have a use for the chelating agent.

34. **The correct answer is F.** The best way to specifically examine the role of any one factor is to isolate the activity of that particular factor. The best way to isolate its function is to remove Factor 10 in a test organism. As the information in the passage demonstrates, isolating Factor 10 is a little bit tricky because it is formed from a complex composed of two different factors, 8 and 9, each of which may have their own independent role to play in amplification of the clotting process. Preventing that complex from forming by disabling the ability of 8 and 9 to bind together is the only way to remove 10 and only 10. Removing thrombin (choice G) would prevent formation of 10 by eliminating Factor 8, but it would also remove Factors 5 and 11, making it impossible to isolate the effects of Factor 10. Disabling TF-7 (choice H) would also eliminate factor 10 by removing some production of Factor 9. However, it is not clear if Factor 9 plays a role in amplification beyond helping make Factor 10, so again, Factor 10 may not be isolated. Introducing extra Factor 10 (choice J) might not be successful because an amplification factor needs clots to amplify. Extra Factor 10 may simply go unused, so the specific role of Factor 10 would still be uncertain.

35. **The correct answer is D.** There are clearly some changes in the rate of decomposition as the CO_2 concentration increases, but it is difficult to see a definite pattern in the changes. If you visualize the decomposition data presented as a graph instead of a table, the plot would resemble a mountain range, with different peaks and valleys, some higher than the starting value, some below the starting value, but ending up pretty close to the starting value. You can conclude from such a pattern that the effect on decomposition rate from CO_2 concentration is not dramatic, since there are no huge departures from the starting value, and that the decomposition rate changes almost at random as the CO_2 concentration increases. The relationship between them, if any, is extremely weak. No definite pattern such as described in choices A, B, or C can be seen.

36. The correct answer is J. CO_2 concentration and growth rate are generally correlated in a positive manner, but they are not proportional values. Choice F is incorrect because as CO_2 concentration increases, growth rate also increases, but the two values are not proportional. Choice G is incorrect because as CO_2 concentration increases, the growth rate also increases, so they cannot be inversely proportional. Choice H is incorrect because there is a clear positive correlation between the two variables, according to the table.

37. The correct answer is B. At this point the plant continues to grow, but more slowly. That suggests conditions that damage but do not kill the plant, such as insect damage. If the plant were dead, or had reached its maximum height (choices A or D), it could not continue to grow, even at a slower rate. Choice C is at first glance plausible but at 660 mol_{CO_2}/mol_{air} the growth rate is still about what it is at around 360 mol_{CO_2}/mol_{air}, before there was any loss of nitrogen at all. That suggests that whatever is causing the reduced growth is connected directly to CO_2 concentration and not to the nitrogen.

38. The correct answer is G. The key is that only the nitrogen reading is odd. Plant growth is normal according the trend established so far, and so is decomposition. That suggests that whatever the problem is only affects nitrogen and nothing else. Then notice that a pretty steady decline occurred with each increase in concentration before 520 mol_{CO_2}/mol_{air}, then the anomalous reading, then at 530 mol_{CO_2}/mol_{air}, the previous pattern immediately reestablishes itself as if the anomalous result never happened (eliminating choice F). All of these clues suggest a problem that only applies to that one data point. The most likely answer is an error of some kind (choice G). Choice H is not supported by evidence, since similar decomposition rates in other parts of the data set do not have that effect. There is no evidence for choice J nor an explanation as to why it might be true.

39. The correct answer is B. When growth rate peaks, at 620 mol_{CO_2}/mol_{air}, the decomposition rate is 4.5% mass/week. Given the range of decomposition rates provided in the table, this is lower than average, but it is not at its minimum.

40. The correct answer is G. Bacteria are the primary agents of decomposition. If the rate is slowing, then something must be interfering with bacteria. Nitrogen, which according to the passage represents several nutrients, is steadily dropping. Decomposers derive their nutrition from the material they decompose. If that material supplies insufficient nutrition, it can feed fewer bacteria. As the nutrient levels drop with increasing CO_2 concentration, the rate of decomposition would drop as fewer and fewer bacteria are supported. Choice F is unlikely for two reasons. One is that if the bacteria needed oxygen, and if at some point there wasn't enough, then rather than a gradual decline at some point the decomposition rate should plummet to zero. The other reason is that many bacteria can function without oxygen. Choice H might account for the findings as better wood might be more resistant to decomposition. However, as the wood is continuing to lose vital nutrients, the quality is clearly decreasing, not increasing. Choice J does not work, since the plant continues to grow rather than shrink, even if the rate slows eventually.

Sample Essay: Score 1

Ideas and Analysis:	Score = 1
Development and Support:	Score = 1
Organization:	Score = 1
Language Use and Conventions:	Score = 1

I already learn what I need to know online from the websites I go to, Facebook and Twitter and more they have everything that's going on. I can get everything from a book or teacher that I can get from them on my laptop or phone, so why bother going into school and wasting my time? I can even play games and listen to my music and show off all my photos to my friends and whoever so why cant I skip school and do what I need to do on my own schedule and finally live like adults? I get really bored in school anyway and so do my friends and we'd all be much rather spending our time doing almost anything else. My school's a waste of money too so they can stop paying the teachers and everyone there and maybe they can start paying the students for a change?

Scoring Explanation

Ideas and Analysis: Score = 1

This essay fails to establish a unifying thesis that addresses the given prompt. The writer provides some ideas regarding the value of traditional classrooms (a waste of time and money) but fails to utilize them in a cohesive or effective manner. There is little or no effort to create a piece of writing that responds to the specific essay task.

Development and Support: Score = 1

The writer of this piece does little to develop the few ideas provided into an effective argument that addresses the essay task. As a result, we do not get the writer's perspective on the future of the classroom or the impact technology will have on it. Furthermore, the writer doesn't provide any additional external support for his or her ideas, and the resulting essay lacks depth, authority, or credence.

Organization: Score = 1

This essay response lacks a coherent, effective flow of ideas connected to an overarching theme. Instead, we are given a disjointed set of thoughts that are at best tangentially related to the writing task. The response indicates that the author believes traditional school is a waste of money and time, time that is better spent on a computer or phone, but it lacks an effective overall structure and doesn't progress toward a central idea regarding the future of the classroom.

Language Use and Conventions: Score = 1

The response demonstrates a significant skill deficit in the effective use of language mechanics and conventions. The essay contains several errors in grammar and usage and uses a limited word-choice range, which adversely impact a reader's ability to comprehend the author's intent.

Sample Essay: Score 6

Ideas and Analysis:	Score = 6
Development and Support:	Score = 6
Organization:	Score = 6
Language Use and Conventions:	Score = 6

It can be argued that technological advances in recent decades have helped us learn as much about the classroom as we learn inside the classroom. Although it's certainly clear that the traditional classroom has equipped generations of students with the knowledge and skills required to lead America and other countries around the world into the modern technological era, with great change comes the responsibility to pause and reflect. What should happen now? We need to take a hard and thoughtful look at the current design of the average classroom, at both its strengths and its limitations, and design a new and unabashedly modern learning environment—one that takes full advantage of modern technological innovations while retaining the healthy structural roots that have allowed us to flourish thus far.

The traditional classroom does provide educational nourishment for fertile minds that are eager to learn. A skilled and motivated teacher, equipped with an effective lesson plan and learning goals, can make a real and measurable difference in the minds of students inside of these rooms. But the technological advances that have flooded into our everyday lives have changed the way we live, and in turn are changing how we think and learn. These are just a few examples: More of us now get our news from our phones instead of newspapers. Most of us stay in touch with the people in our lives through social media websites as much or more than in person. If we need to handle our daily responsibilities we go over to our computers as often as we roll up our sleeves and head out the front door. With so much of our lives unfolding online, why shouldn't the modern classroom follow suit?

As previously mentioned, the way we learn has already changed. We read on tablets and phones, consume information through websites, communicate online as much as in person—an effective learning environment (the word *classroom* even feels outdated) takes this into consideration and mirrors the society and culture in which it exists.

What should the classroom of the future look like? An effective modern classroom will integrate the best of both worlds. It will acknowledge that real learning objectives can be met when students gather together in rooms under the direct guidance of qualified, capable teachers. It will also acknowledge that technology has advanced to the level where each student can use modern tools to address his or her individual educational goals in a virtual learning environment, wherever they are. Envision less time spent in an actual classroom but just as much time spent learning, only in a more effective fashion that takes into consideration each student's individual skill set and goals. Modified classroom learning can be supplemented with time spent on a tablet, phone, or laptop, at home or anywhere else, in pursuit of customized academic objectives. Students can use emails, texts, chats, tweets, or Skype to contact trained educators for guidance and feedback. Students can collaborate using these tools as well. Assignments, research, and projects can use modern computer applications—the same tools used in a wide range of professions—further preparing students for life beyond the classroom. In schools across the country and around the world this has already happened, though in limited ways. We're squarely in the middle of an "educational evolution," and if logic and forward-thinking were allowed to lead the way, this evolution will continue to follow this path. It has or is occurring in nearly every facet of society, from medicine and banking, to shopping and entertainment—and far beyond—don't our classrooms deserve the same respect, resources, and consideration?

Scoring Explanation

Ideas and Analysis: Score = 6

The writer provides a nuanced, thoughtful argument regarding the future of the classroom. From its insightful and engaging opening to its provocative closing question, the essay presents a wealth of ideas on why the traditional classroom needs to "evolve," as well as ideas for how this can occur. It's clear that the writer of this piece has thoughtfully analyzed the issue and framed it within a larger societal context (learning environments should mirror societal modes of consuming information), lending credence to the balanced, carefully considered perspective provided.

Development and Support: Score = 6

The writer begins the argument with an insightful perspective on the value of technology in learning about effective classroom operation and progresses with a well-reasoned development of ideas that support a clear perspective on the issue. The argument includes a historical perspective that supports the notion that traditional classrooms once had a clear purpose and provides compelling details on how an evolving society needs an evolving learning environment for its fertile and hungry minds. An intriguing set of ideas on how this evolution might occur is provided as the argument moves forward, culminating in an inspirational call to action.

Organization: Score = 6

The writer demonstrates a command of effective essay structure, organization, and flow. A clear perspective on what the classroom of the future should be like is provided, and an array of persuasive material is galvanized and carefully presented in support of this viewpoint. It progresses from a thought-provoking introduction to a well-reasoned argument in support of a blended (traditional and virtual) learning environment and ends with an urgent—and moving—call for change.

Language Use and Conventions: Score = 6

The writer employs an impressive use of language and nuance in the development of a compelling essay. Strong and varied word choices and effective transitions are used throughout, alongside a wealth of emotion, to convince the reader that this perspective on the complex issue of the future of learning is a worthy one. The writer also displays an impressive command of grammar and syntax, lending authority to this argument.

DIAGNOSTIC TEST ASSESSMENT GRID

Now that you've completed the diagnostic test and read through the answer explanations, you can use your results to target your studying. The following tables show you exactly where you can find thorough coverage for every single subject area on the multiple-choice portion of the test. Find the question numbers from the diagnostic test that gave you trouble and highlight or circle them below. The chapters with the most markings are your ideal starting points on your preparation journey.

English Test

ACT® Reporting Category	Question Number	Chapter Reference
Conventions of Standard English	1, 2, 7, 10, 11, 16–20, 22, 24–26, 31–33, 35–37, 39, 41, 46, 48, 50, 51, 53–55, 57, 58, 62–64, 66, 68–70, 72, 74	**Chapter 4**
Production of Writing	4, 5, 8, 9, 13–15, 21, 27–30, 40, 42–45, 60, 67, 73, 75	**Chapter 5**
Knowledge of Language	3, 6, 12, 23, 34, 38, 47, 49, 52, 56, 59, 61, 65, 71	**Chapter 5**

What English test question types gave you the most trouble?

Conventions of Standard English ☐

Production of Writing ☐

Knowledge of Language ☐

Chapters to focus on first: ________________

Math Test

ACT® Reporting Category	Question Number	Chapter Reference
Preparing for Higher Math	1, 2, 7, 10, 11, 16–20, 22, 24–26, 31–33, 35–37, 39, 41, 46, 48, 50, 51, 53–55, 57, 58, 62–64, 66, 68–70, 72, 74	**Pre-Algebra and Elementary Algebra (Chapter 6)**
	11, 13, 15, 17, 23, 24, 26, 28, 36, 37, 39, 41, 44, 45, 49, 56, 59	**Intermediate Algebra and Coordinate Geometry (Chapter 7)**
	16, 29, 32, 38, 40, 46, 48, 50, 52, 57	**Plane Geometry and Trigonometry (Chapter 8)**
Integrating Essential Skills	2, 5, 6–10, 14, 22, 25, 27, 30, 33, 42, 51, 55 5	**Pre-Algebra and Elementary Algebra (Chapter 6)**
	18, 35, 51, 53, 54	**Intermediate Algebra and Coordinate Geometry (Chapter 7)**
	4, 19, 21, 34	**Plane Geometry and Trigonometry (Chapter 8)**
Modeling	2, 3, 9, 25, 32, 33, 50, 52, 53, 56, 59, 30	**Intermediate Algebra and Coordinate Geometry (Chapter 7)**

Which Mathematics test question types gave you the most trouble?

Preparing for Higher Math

- ☐ Pre-Algebra/Elementary Algebra
- ☐ Intermediate Algebra/Coordinate Geometry
- ☐ Plane Geometry/Trigonometry

Integrating Essential Skills

- ☐ Pre-Algebra/Elementary Algebra
- ☐ Intermediate Algebra/Coordinate Geometry
- ☐ Plane Geometry/Trigonometry

Modeling

- ☐ Intermediate Algebra/Coordinate Geometry

Chapters to focus on first: ______________

Reading Test

ACT® Reporting Category	Question Number	Chapter Reference
Key Ideas and Details *(for Social Studies and Science questions)*	11, 13, 14, 16, 17, 31, 35, 37, 38, 40	**Social Studies/Natural Sciences Passages (Chapter 9)**
Key Ideas and Details *(for Literary Narrative/Prose Fiction and Humanities questions)*	2, 4, 6, 7, 19, 21, 24–29	**Literary Narrative/Prose Fiction and Humanities Passages (Chapter 10)**
Craft and Structure *(for Social Studies and Science questions)*	12, 15, 20, 32, 33, 36, 39	**Social Studies/Natural Sciences Passages (Chapter 9)**
Craft and Structure *(for Literary Narrative/Prose Fiction and Humanities questions)*	1, 5, 23, 30	**Literary Narrative/Prose Fiction and Humanities Passages (Chapter 10)**
Integration of Knowledge and Ideas *(for Social Studies and Science questions)*	18, 34	**Social Studies/Natural Sciences Passages (Chapter 9)**
Integration of Knowledge and Ideas *(for Literary Narrative/Prose Fiction and Humanities questions)*	3, 8–10, 22	**Literary Narrative/Prose Fiction and Humanities Passages (Chapter 10)**

Which Reading test question types gave you the most trouble?

Key Ideas and Details
- ☐ Social Studies/Natural Science Passages
- ☐ Literary Narrative/Prose Fiction and Humanities Passages

Craft and Structure
- ☐ Social Studies/Natural Sciences Passages
- ☐ Literary Narrative/Prose Fiction and Humanities Passages

Integration of Knowledge and Ideas
- ☐ Social Studies/Natural Sciences Passages
- ☐ Literary Narrative/Prose Fiction and Humanities Passages

Chapters to focus on first: ______________

Science Test

ACT® Reporting Category	Question Number	Chapter Reference
Interpretation of Data	1, 5, 25–27, 36, 39	**Data Representation (Chapter 11)**
	13–16, 19, 20, 23, 35	**Research Summaries (Chapter 12)**
	7, 8, 11	**Conflicting Viewpoints (Chapter 13)**
Evaluation of Experiments	3, 28, 37, 38, 40	**Data Representation (Chapter 11)**
	17, 18, 22, 24, 30, 31	**Research Summaries (Chapter 12)**
	9, 10	**Conflicting Viewpoints (Chapter 13)**
Scientific Investigation	2, 4, 29	**Data Representation (Chapter 11)**
	21, 32–34	**Research Summaries (Chapter 12)**
	6, 12	**Conflicting Viewpoints (Chapter 13)**

What Science test question types gave you the most trouble?

Interpretation of Data
- ☐ Data Representation
- ☐ Research Summaries
- ☐ Conflicting Viewpoints

Evaluation of Experiments
- ☐ Data Representation
- ☐ Research Summaries
- ☐ Conflicting Viewpoints

Scientific Investigation
- ☐ Data Representation
- ☐ Research Summaries
- ☐ Conflicting Viewpoints

Chapters to focus on first: _______________

A Word About the Writing Test

If you took the Writing test and found that your essay did not compare well to the level 6 essay sample, don't worry. We're here to help you with that too. Chapter 14, "Mastering the ACT® Writing Test," has the information you need to strengthen your writing skills. It also includes a full essay grading rubric, which tells you what the graders are looking for in a high-quality essay. Use the rubric as you would use the grids to help you focus on the areas you need to work on.

DIAGNOSTIC TEST CONCLUSION

Taking the diagnostic test should have given you more insight into the ACT exam: what it feels like to take such a long test, how you perform on a timed exam, and where you now need to focus your energy in the days, weeks, and months leading up to your test day.

Here are some questions to keep in mind as you move on to the preparation part of your ACT study plan:

How did I do under timed conditions?

Did you find yourself rushing to answer the final questions in every test section? Did one particular section give you more problems than others? Take note of how timing affected you in this test, and see if you can make small changes to your test-taking approach. For example, maybe you spent too much time reading the passages in the Reading test and then didn't actually have time to answer all the questions. The good news? Every section in this book offers tips on how to efficiently and quickly answer ACT questions. Study up and, when you take Practice Test 1, you can see if your method improves.

Did I make careless mistakes or second-guess myself?

Well, first of all, you're not alone. Testing is *hard*—you're under timed conditions and you want to do very well. The best part about taking on a plan of study with this book is that when you are done, you will be *prepared*. First, you will know the test inside and out. This is a very important bit of knowledge, as you won't even have to stop to read directions or familiarize yourself with the test come exam day—you will be ready to go! Second, you will have a deeper understanding not only of all the different topics tested on the ACT, but also how the exam presents them (the language it uses and how it asks questions). The key to excelling on the ACT exam is to speak the language of the test maker, and that's what we're here to help you do.

Did I just not know how to answer questions in a particular section?

Maybe you sailed through the Math test but could barely get through a Science test passage. Or maybe the Reading test was a breeze, but you couldn't for the life of you remember anything about trigonometry. Whatever your situation, this book has extensive preparation for it. Now that you have a better understanding of your strengths and weaknesses as they relate to the ACT, you can customize your study plan. To that end, we've added a feature to help. To that end, we've added a feature to help.

COLLEGE READINESS BENCHMARK LEARNING PATH PRACTICE

After taking this Diagnostic Test and reviewing the results, you might find you need an extra boost of preparation and study to get your math, science, reading, or English skills where they need to be to do well on the ACT. First, visit the chapters listed in the assessment grids to review the material for each test topic. Then, consider taking the College Readiness Benchmark Learning Path, which you will find mentioned throughout the chapters.

The College Readiness Benchmark Learning Path gives you the test-like ACT practice in the sections you need to get up to speed on all you should know before test day. For each chapter, we've created sets of passages (where applicable) and questions that look just like those you will see on the ACT exam. By taking this path, you will get intensive practice on all the math, science, reading, or English passage and question types, accompanied by detailed answer explanations that tell you why each choice is correct or incorrect.

Take the College Readiness Benchmark Learning Path to focus your study and become confident in your test-taking skills!

No matter what challenges you faced on the diagnostic test, there's a section in this book to help you overcome them. Stay focused, commit the time, and take your practice tests—if you do that, you give yourself the best chance to excel to the best of your abilities and obtain your target score on the ACT exam.

PART III: ENGLISH STRATEGIES FOR THE ACT® EXAM

Chapter 4: Conventions of Standard English

Chapter 5: Production of Writing and Knowledge of Language

ENGLISH STRATEGIES FOR THE ACT® EXAM

Do you know what an editor does? After a writer finishes a book or article, that piece of writing goes to the editor, who checks it over for errors in usage and mechanics, as well as rhetoric. That's basically what you're going to do on the ACT English test. You'll play the role of editor by reading and editing brief passages that can be made better by correcting errors or deleting, adding, or moving details. Don't worry, though. Your job will be easier than the job of a professional editor since you'll have four possible corrections to choose from. The next two chapters will help you to select the best answer choices.

First of all, you need to become familiar with the style of the passages and questions on the ACT English test, since you may not have taken a test quite like this one before. Each passage is fairly short, about 350 to 450 words. Each paragraph in that passage is numbered, and each paragraph contains underlined phrases followed by numbers. Those numbers refer to a corresponding question.

Sometimes, several complete sentences in a paragraph will begin with a number in brackets. These numbers are used for identification when you have to decide the best way to reorganize sentences or choose which sentence needs to be deleted. The question that asks you to do this task will correspond to a number in a box. This number soup may sound a little confusing, but it will be less confusing when you see what an English passage on the ACT exam looks like. So let's look at one:

PASSAGE 1

Sample ACT English Passage

[1]

This is a sample of a passage in the English section of the ACT test. Isn't it fabulous? Watch out, though, because this passage contains some errors. Remember, <u>it's your job to find them errors</u> (10) and figure out the best way to correct them.

[2]

[1] This is the second paragraph of the sample passage. [2] You may notice that it's a bit different from the first paragraph. [3] However, <u>your job is still the same; you still have to</u> (11) find the errors and choose the answers that best correct them. [4] I like pancakes. [5] This is the final sentence in this sample passage—aren't you sorry it's finished? [12]

10. **A.** NO CHANGE
B. it's your job to find those errors
C. it's your job to find this errors
D. it's your job to find that errors

11. **F.** NO CHANGE
G. your job is still the same you still have to
H. your job is still the same, you still have to
J. your job is still the same) you still have to

12. For the sake of the unity and coherence of this paragraph, which sentence should be omitted?
A. Sentence 1
B. Sentence 2
C. Sentence 3
D. Sentence 4

As you probably noticed, this extra-short sample passage contains two underlined portions with a number beneath each of them. That means two multiple-choice questions will ask about it. However, unlike most multiple-choice questions you've probably answered throughout your school career, in Usage/Mechanics questions, the first answer choice is always the same: NO CHANGE. You see, the underlined words in an ACT English passage will not always contain errors, and if they don't, you should select NO CHANGE. Pretty tricky!

Still confused about what all the numbers mean? Let's take a closer look.

Boldfaced numbers in brackets identify the paragraph order.

[2]

[1] This is the second paragraph of the sample passage. [2] You may notice that it's a bit different from the first paragraph. [3] However, <u>your job is still the same; you still have to</u> find the
11
errors and choose the answers that best correct them. [4] I like pancakes. [5] This is the final sentence in this sample passage—aren't you sorry it's finished? [12]

Numbers that appear below the <u>underlined</u> portion of the passage correspond to specific usage questions.

Numbers in brackets before each sentence within a paragraph identify sentence order.

Numbers that appear in a box correspond to questions that relate to a paragraph's strategy, organization, or style.

Now that you have the key to ACT English by the numbers, we can focus on the answers and explanations that go with the sample passage. Something to keep in mind—when you are answering questions on the ACT English test, be sure to read the entire sentences as they appear in the passage and not just the short portions in the answer choices. Seeing how the words in the answer choices work in the greater context of the passage may help you to answer the questions. Now—on to the explanations!

Did you see the error in question 10? There is a lack of agreement between the pronoun *them* and the noun *errors*. Try saying the sentence out loud. Doesn't it sound wrong to say "them errors"? It does, because it is grammatically incorrect. The sentence should read "it's your job to find *those* errors." Therefore, you can conclude that **choice B is the best answer** to question 10. Just remember that when you actually take the ACT exam, you should only think of how the sentence sounds and not actually say it out loud. A room full of babbling test takers can be a little distracting.

> **NOTE:** Most rhetorical skills questions will probably be a bit more familiar since they tend to contain an actual question and the first answer choice will not always be NO CHANGE.

Question 11 is a different story. This is one of those tricky questions about underlined words that don't actually contain any errors. Choices G, H, and J actually introduce new punctuation errors to a sentence that is already written correctly. Therefore, **the best answer choice is F:** NO CHANGE.

Question 12 is yet another story because, as you can see, it begins with a direct question and the first answer choice is not NO CHANGE. Those clues should help you conclude that question 12 is a rhetorical skills question. This particular question tests your ability to find the sentence that does not belong in the paragraph. This particular paragraph is about how ACT English passages look. It isn't about food. So what is a sentence about the author's preference for pancakes doing in it? The clever editor will select **answer choice D** to omit this irrelevant sentence about pancakes—even though pancakes are really tasty.

The next two chapters will get deeper into the two main categories of errors you will find on the ACT English test. You will look for mistakes in punctuation, grammar, sentence structure, strategy, organization, and style. Each of these errors falls into one of two categories: Conventions of Standard English and Production of Writing/Knowledge of Language. First up—Conventions of Standard English!

COLLEGE READINESS BENCHMARK LEARNING PATH PRACTICE

As you make your way through Part III and review all the English conventions, writing, and language strategies you'll need to excel on the ACT, you might find you need some more in-depth practice to feel comfortable with the topic. If you feel you fall into this category, follow our College Readiness Benchmark Learning Path for a whole test's worth of ACT English practice. To access this full-length English practice test, go to **www.petersons.com/testprep/act** and enter the code **ACT2019** where directed.

The practice tests are designed to give you the targeted ACT review you need for the topics where you need to focus. Each question is accompanied by an in-depth answer explanation that addresses every answer option, so you can see why it is correct or incorrect.

Follow the College Readiness Benchmark Learning Path to get up to speed on your English skills!

CHAPTER 4: CONVENTIONS OF STANDARD ENGLISH

OVERVIEW

- Punctuation
- Usage
- Sentence Structure and Formation
- Summing It Up
- Practice

On the ACT exam, errors on questions that test your knowledge of the category called Conventions of Standard English may really jump out at you. For example, a sentence that asks a question but ends in an exclamation point *(Is that your sock!)* just looks wrong. Of course, you'll need to know a little more than "find the sentences that look wrong" to correctly answer these questions, which comprise from 51–56% of all the questions you'll see on your exam. The good news is that you've probably learned most of the rules discussed in this chapter already.

The official subcategories covered in this section are Sentence Structure and Formation, Punctuation, and Usage. First of all, we should probably define the terms *usage* and *mechanics*. **Usage** refers to the way words are used in a sentence. Obviously, you'll want to make sure they're used correctly to select the best answers on the ACT exam. But first, let's start with the more technical components of sentences, such as punctuation, which will be the first topic in this chapter.

PUNCTUATION

Periods. Commas. Semicolons. Apostrophes. There are quite a few different kinds of punctuation, and each punctuation mark has its own purpose. Punctuation questions will test your ability to recognize the correct way to use these little symbols.

End-of-Sentence Punctuation

Every sentence must come to an end. That means the one form of punctuation you will see in every complete sentence is end-of-sentence punctuation. These were probably the very first punctuation marks you learned about.

- **The period (.):** good for ending most sentences.
- **The exclamation point (!):** handy for ending exclamations, which indicate extreme excitement.
- **The question mark (?):** absolutely necessary for ending questions.

> **TIP** A question can be asked excitedly, but it still needs to end with a question mark, not an exclamation point.

End-of-sentence marks are relatively clear-cut. You probably already know that you shouldn't end a question with a period or an exclamation with a question mark. These marks become slightly tricky only when quotation marks are added to the punctuation mix.

For the most part, end-of-sentence punctuation belongs *within* the quotation marks. Like this:

Tessa asked, "Have you seen my superhero costume?"

The only exception occurs when the quotation marks indicate a title and placing end-of-sentence punctuation within the marks might give the false impression that the mark is part of the title:

Have you read Tessa's article, "I Am a Superhero"?

Commas

Let's continue with one of the most common forms of punctuation and one of the most misused: the **comma**. Some writers use commas like salt—they sprinkle them all over their sentences. And just as sprinkling around too much salt will make your food taste pretty bad, sprinkling around too many commas without rhyme or reason will make sentences pretty bad too. Here's an example of a sentence with way too many commas:

If there is one thing I love, it's fresh bread, straight from the oven, of Gomer's Bakery.

While there is the odd situation in which the use of a comma is up to the writer, there are almost always very definite rules for comma use.

Introductory or Transitional Words and Phrases

Commas should be used to offset introductory words or phrases from the words that follow. Here are some examples:

Suddenly, I realized I was locked out of the house.

At that moment, the entire room began to shake.

My alarm never went off. Therefore, I missed my job interview.

Compound Sentences

Compound sentences consist of two independent clauses, which means both parts of the sentence would be complete sentences on their own. When independent clauses are joined by a conjunction to form a compound sentence, a comma is used before the conjunction to separate the clauses. For example:

> *Chandra is going to see that new movie at the theater, but Mason is going to watch it on demand.*

Chandra is going to see that new movie at the theater is the first independent clause. *Mason is going to watch it on demand* is the second. The conjunction is *but,* and a comma is used to separate those clauses correctly.

> **TIP** Commas are not used to separate compound predicates, which explain more than one thing about the subject.
>
> For example: *Adriana rides the bus, and reads a book.* (Incorrect!)
> *Adriana rides the bus and reads a book.* (Correct!)

Nonrestrictive Words, Phrases, and Clauses

A **nonrestrictive** word, phrase, or clause is not essential to the meaning of the sentence and should be separated with one comma if it comes at the beginning or end of the sentence and two commas if it is placed in the middle.

> **Nonrestrictive phrase at the beginning of the sentence:** *The most delicious of all fruits, apples grow in orchards.*

> **Nonrestrictive phrase in the middle of the sentence:** *Apples, the most delicious of all fruits, grow in orchards.*

> **Nonrestrictive phrase at the end of the sentence:** *In the orchard I grew apples, the most delicious of all fruits.*

Read this sentence:

> *My pants, which I bought at the mall, are too tight.*

This sentence would still make sense without the clause *which I bought at the mall.* It would read *My pants are too tight*, which is a perfectly fine sentence. That means the clause is nonrestrictive and should be enclosed in commas like it is in the sentence above. However, if that clause were **restrictive**—essential to the meaning of the sentence—no commas would be needed (Example: *The pants I bought at the mall are too tight.*).

Series

Each item in a series of three or more in a list should be separated with a comma. For example:

> *I keep my cell phone, e-reader, pens, and wallet in my desk drawer.*

In this sentence a comma also precedes the conjunction *and*, although this is not a hard-and-fast rule. Some writers prefer not to use that extra comma. So the following sentence is also technically correct:

> *I keep my cell phone, e-reader, pens and wallet in my desk drawer.*

> **TIP** The decision to place a comma before the conjunction in a series of items is up to the writer. Passages on the ACT exam use the comma before the conjunction, but you will not be expected to answer questions about such situations without concrete rules.

Appositives

An **appositive** is a noun, noun phrase, or noun clause that describes or renames a noun. An appositive contains a noun or pronoun and often one or more modifiers, and it appears directly before or after the noun it describes. Appositives need to be set off with commas.

For example:

My car, a real piece of garbage, keeps breaking down on the highway.

In this sentence, the appositive is *a real piece of garbage*, and commas are used to set it off correctly.

Quotations

When quoting a complete phrase someone said, one or more commas are needed to separate it from the rest of the sentence. See how the commas are used in these examples:

Buddy said, "That sandwich made me feel sick."

"That sandwich made me feel sick," Buddy said.

"That sandwich," Buddy began, "made me feel sick."

However, if that quotation includes end-of-sentence punctuation, a comma is not needed.

For example:

"That sandwich made me feel sick!," Buddy said. **(Incorrect)**

"That sandwich made me feel sick!" Buddy said. **(Correct)**

Now answer this quick exercise question. Keep in mind that all questions on the ACT exam will relate to a larger passage and not a stand-alone statement like this one. You will get the chance to answer questions that relate to passages at the end of each English chapter and in the practice tests.

This story a medieval thriller written by Shirley Jackson, is really scary.
(1)

1. **A.** NO CHANGE
   B. This story, a medieval thriller written by Shirley Jackson,
   C. This story a medieval thriller written by Shirley Jackson
   D. This story, a medieval thriller written by Shirley Jackson

The correct answer is B. The appositive phrase *a medieval thriller written by Shirley Jackson* must be set off from the rest of the sentence with commas.

Apostrophes

Apostrophes look like commas that have floated up to the top of words, but they serve very different functions from commas. Apostrophes are most often used to indicate that a word is a contraction or to show possession.

Correct use of apostrophes in **contractions** mostly depends on placing the apostrophe in the right place (*Do'nt*—**incorrect!** *Don't*—**correct!**) and recognizing when a word that looks like a contraction is not a contraction (for example, *it's* is a contraction of *it is*; *its* is the possessive form of *it*).

Using apostrophes in possessive words is a little trickier. For the most part, the apostrophe will be placed before the letter *s*.

Madison's keys

the dog's bone

the car's headlights

the sun's beams

However, if the possessive word ends with an *s*, the apostrophe belongs after the *s*.

the glasses' lenses

the two kittens' guardian

the brass' gleam

the lens' reflection

This rule is different when a specifically named person is doing the possessing. For people whose names end in *s*, an apostrophe and an extra *s* is required.

Mavis's hair

Augustus's shoes

Venus's lunch

Charles's smile

When more than one noun is doing the possessing, only the last noun in the pair or list needs an apostrophe.

my father and mother's favorite restaurant

the bedspread and the curtains' pattern

Cherie and Gladys's address

the bass and drums' sounds

Colons

Colons look like a stack of two periods, though they are always used within a sentence. Colons are usually used to introduce a list or series of examples:

My pack contains everything I need for school: books, pens, a calculator, and a lunch bag.

Colons are also used to offset and emphasize an example:

That book taught me the most important lesson of all: true friendship never dies.

Colons can also be placed after a salutation in a letter (*To whom it may concern:*) or used to separate a title from a subtitle (*Green Peas: The Movie*). However, colons should not be used to separate objects and verbs (**Incorrect:** *My opinion is: irrelevant*) or prepositions and objects (**Incorrect:** *Gluten is found in: bread, pasta, and many other basic foods.*).

Semicolons

A **semicolon** looks like a period floating over a comma, and it should not be confused with a colon. Semicolons can be used in place of conjunctions in compound sentences, joining the independent clauses just as *and*, *or*, *but*, or *because* would:

I spent the day reorganizing my bedroom; it was a complete mess.

Semicolons are also necessary in lists that contain items with commas. To keep all those commas from becoming confusing, semicolons separate each individual item.

This meal contains only the freshest ingredients: tomatoes and onions, which I bought at the farmer's market; basil, which I grew in a pot in the kitchen; and peppers, which I grew in the backyard garden.

ALERT: Colons and semicolons are not interchangeable. Each punctuation mark has its own function.

Now answer this quick exercise question.

There are a variety of creatures other than fish in this book about sea animals: dolphins and whales, which are mammals; crabs and lobsters, which are crustaceans; and octopi and squid, which are mollusks. (2)

2. **F.** NO CHANGE
   G. sea animals; dolphins and whales, which are mammals; crabs and lobsters, which are crustaceans; and octopi and squid, which are mollusks.
   H. sea animals: dolphins and whales, which are mammals, crabs and lobsters, which are crustaceans, and octopi and squid, which are mollusks.
   J. sea animals: dolphins and whales; which are mammals; crabs and lobsters; which are crustaceans; and octopi and squid; which are mollusks.

The correct answer is F. The sentence is correct as is. The colon is used properly to signal a list of upcoming examples. Since the items listed contain commas, it is best to separate them using semicolons.

Dashes

Much like the comma, the dash tends to get overused and misused. A big problem with dashes is that they're almost never needed according to the rules of mechanics, so a lot of writers just aren't sure what to do with them. You're about to become one of the lucky few who do know when to use the pesky dash.

Like the colon, a **dash** can be used to offset and emphasize a single example:

In trying times, I knew I could always turn to the one individual who understood me—my dog, Blinky.

A dash can also be used to separate an example or examples in the middle of a sentence:

Everything—boxes, hats, and games—came tumbling from the top shelf during the earthquake.

Dashes are also useful for indicating a pause or interruption in dialogue:

Marcus asked, "Can I borrow your—"

"Sure! Whatever! Take what you want!" Paulette enthused before Marcus could complete his question.

Parentheses

Sometimes, a few extra details are needed to make a sentence as informative as it can be, but those details aren't always easy to cram into the natural flow of the sentence. In such cases, parentheses are in order. Like dashes, **parentheses** are used to enclose bonus examples, but the examples in parentheses tend to be a little less relevant to the sentence than the ones you'd place between dashes.

> **TIP** Watch out for sentences that overuse parentheses. They clutter sentences with too much nonessential information. You may be expected to delete unnecessary parenthetical information on the ACT exam.

Mrs. Gale (my brother's high school Earth Science teacher) is going to be teaching biology next quarter.

Now you will put everything you have learned about punctuation to the test by reading this sample passage and answering the questions that follow.

An avalanche occurs when a mass of <u>snow, rock, soil, or ice, breaks</u> [3] away from a mountainside and slides down the slope. Factors such as seasonal thawing, wind, and vibrations can cause avalanches. <u>Consequently, avalanches can make numerous</u> [4] recreations very <u>dangerous; skiing, mountain climbing, and hiking.</u> [5] However, there are methods for preventing major avalanches before they happen. One such approach is accomplished

3. **A.** NO CHANGE
   B. snow rock, soil, or ice, breaks
   C. snow, rock, soil or ice, breaks
   D. snow, rock, soil, or ice breaks

The correct answer is D. There is no comma needed between *ice* and *breaks*.

4. **F.** NO CHANGE
   G. Consequently avalanches can make numerous
   H. Consequently— avalanches can make numerous
   J. Consequently; avalanches can make numerous

The correct answer is F. The sentence is correct as is. A comma is the correct punctuation here.

5. **A.** NO CHANGE
   B. dangerous skiing, mountain climbing, and hiking.
   C. dangerous: skiing, mountain climbing, and hiking.
   D. dangerous, skiing, mountain climbing, and hiking.

The correct answer is C. A colon is needed after *dangerous* because it introduces a list of examples.

with <u>explosives (deployed from helicopters or shot from small howitzers) that trigger</u> (6) minor avalanches before major ones can occur.

6. F. NO CHANGE
G. explosives, deployed from helicopters or shot from small howitzers, that trigger
H. explosives deployed from helicopters or shot from small howitzers that trigger
J. explosives' deployed from helicopters or shot from small howitzers that trigger

The correct answer is H. The fragment *deployed from helicopters or shot from small howitzers* is important to the sentence, so it should not be set off by parentheses or commas.

ALERT: You should not skip portions of English passages just because they are not numbered. Sentences that do not correspond to questions directly may still help you to select correct answers.

USAGE

Do subjects and verbs agree? Answering usage questions can be a bit more complicated than answering punctuation questions, but knowing the rules is still key. And while incorrect punctuation won't necessarily make a sentence sound wrong, poor usage will. So thinking about how these sentences sound can help you select the best answers to usage questions. How about pronouns and their antecedents or modifiers and the words they modify? Does the writer use idioms correctly?

Nouns

If a sentence is like a galaxy, then the subject of that sentence is the sun around which all the other words revolve. The subject is always a **noun**: the person, place, or thing doing the action the sentence describes. A number of grammar and usage questions on the ACT exam will involve a sentence's subject, often in terms of how it agrees with verbs or pronouns. However, before we discuss how nouns interact with other words, let's look at some special forms of nouns.

Plural Nouns

The nice thing about nouns is that they really have only two essential forms: the singular and the plural. The **singular noun** form requires nothing fancy at all. *Cat, dog, otter, lampshade, avocado, eyebrow*—these are all nouns in their most basic singular form. Making nouns plural is often as simple as adding the letter *s* to the end. Stick an *s* to the end of *cat*; now you have many *cats*. Done.

Plural nouns get tricky only when they are irregular—hard-and-fast rules are often tough to apply to a language as complicated as English. Ideally, we could say that you're always safe adding *-es* to the end of all nouns that end in *o* to make them plural. Unfortunately, this is not always the case. For example, the plural of *avocado* is *avocados*.

While you cannot be expected to memorize every single irregular plural noun for the ACT exam, you can familiarize yourself with some of the most common. Take a look at this table:

Noun ends with-	Creating the plural form	Examples	
-f	change *f* to *v* and add *-es*	**singular:** calf	**plural:** calves
		singular: elf	**plural:** elves
		singular: half	**plural:** halves
		singular: leaf	**plural:** leaves
		singular: shelf	**plural:** shelves
		singular: thief	**plural:** thieves
		singular: wolf	**plural:** wolves
-fe	change *f* to *v* and add *-s*	**singular:** knife	**plural:** knives
		singular: wife	**plural:** wives
		singular: life	**plural:** lives
-is	change to *-es*	**singular:** axis	**plural:** axes
		singular: analysis	**plural:** analyses
		singular: parenthesis	**plural:** parentheses
-o	add *-es*	**singular:** echo	**plural:** echoes
		singular: hero	**plural:** heroes
		singular: potato	**plural:** potatoes
		singular: tomato	**plural:** tomatoes
-ouse	change to *-ice*	**singular:** louse	**plural:** lice
		singular: mouse	**plural:** mice
-s	add *-es*	**singular:** class	**plural:** classes
		singular: boss	**plural:** bosses
-us	*change to -i*	**singular:** alumnus	**plural:** alumni
		singular: fungus	**plural:** fungi

There are a few other variations of irregular plural nouns that do not involve changing the last letter or two of the singular form. Fortunately, most of these should be very familiar to you.

Nouns that require *-oo-* to be changed to *-ee-* for their plural form:

singular: foot	**plural:** feet
singular: goose	**plural:** geese
singular: tooth	**plural:** teeth

Nouns that require the addition or substitution of *-en* for their plural form:

singular: man	**plural:** men
singular: ox	**plural:** oxen
singular: woman	**plural:** women
singular: child	**plural:** children

Finally, there are the nouns that require no change whatsoever to become plural:

singular: deer	**plural:** deer
singular: fish	**plural:** fish
singular: offspring	**plural:** offspring
singular: series	**plural:** series
singular: sheep	**plural:** sheep
singular: species	**plural:** species

Now answer this quick exercise question.

There are <u>mouses</u> living under the foliage.
7

7. **A.** NO CHANGE
B. mouse's
C. mice
D. mices

The correct answer is C. The plural of *mouse* is *mice*.

Collective Nouns

Collective nouns are interesting because they have some of the flavor of plural nouns since they seem to describe more than one thing: a bunch of students in a *class*, a group of sailors in a *navy*, several fish in a *school*, etc. However, while the individuals (*students*, *sailors*, *fish*) in these collections are plural, the collections themselves (*class*, *navy*, *school*) are singular. Recognizing when a collective noun is used as a singular or plural subject will be particularly important when we deal with subject-verb agreement and noun-pronoun agreement in the next section of this book.

First, you should familiarize yourself with some common collective nouns.

army	audience	band	board	class
committee	company	corporation	council	department
faculty	family	firm	flock	group
herd	jury	majority	navy	public
school	senate	society	team	unit

Agreement

Words in a sentence are a little like people. When they agree, things go smoothly. When they don't, there might be trouble. You can ensure that the elements in sentences don't clash by recognizing when they aren't in agreement. Subjects and verbs need to be on the same page in terms of number. The same is true of pronouns and antecedents, which also need to agree in terms of gender.

Subject/Verb Agreement

Every complete sentence has a **subject** and a **verb.** The subject is the noun doing the action. The verb is the action the subject is doing. Simple, right? Actually, it is fairly simple, and a sentence with just a subject and a verb can be really simple.

The dog growls.

That sentence only has three words, but it's still a complete sentence because it has a subject and a verb. Just as important, the subject and verb agree: the singular subject *dog* agrees with the singular verb *growls*. That's right: the verb is singular even though it ends with the letter *s*. Okay, maybe it's slightly complicated. Nevertheless, if you can remember that rule, you're on your way to identifying when subjects and verbs are in agreement. Furthermore, you can say the sentence out loud. Does *The dog growl* sound right to you?

Determining whether or not subjects and verbs are in agreement can get a little more complicated in sentences with compound subjects.

The dog and the bear growl.

Neither *dog* nor *bear* ends with an *s*, so they may not look plural, but they work together as a compound subject when joined with a conjunction such as *and*. That means they require a plural verb, and as you may have guessed, a plural verb does not end in an extra *s*. The compound subject and verb are in agreement in the sentence above. However, if the conjunction were *or* or *nor*, a singular verb would be required.

Neither the dog nor the bear growls.

Once again, the compound subject and verb are in agreement.

When dealing with collective nouns, the agreement rule depends on what the collective noun is doing. If every member of the collective noun is doing the exact same thing, it is operating as a single unit and the verb should be singular:

TIP: Subject-verb agreement can get confusing when there is a word or phrase between the subject and verb. Make sure you have identified the entire subject and verb correctly before figuring out whether or not they agree.

*The city council **agrees** that Wednesday is the best day to meet.*

However, if all the members of that collective noun are doing their own things, those members should be specified and a plural verb is required.

The city council **disagree** *on the best day to meet; they may never hold another meeting.*

Although the sentence above is grammatically correct, many writers will avoid the awkward construction of using a collective noun with a plural verb by adding the word *members* to the sentence:

The city council members **disagree** *on the best day to meet; they may never hold another meeting.*

Pronoun/Antecedent Agreement

Pronouns and **antecedents** also need to agree. A pronoun replaces a specific noun. Its antecedent is the noun the pronoun replaces. To illustrate, look at a simple example with the following sentences.

Luisa lives in the red house. She has lived there for nearly 20 years.

The subject of both sentences is *Luisa*. But rather than repeat Luisa's name, which might sound awkward, we can use a subject pronoun for the second reference. In the example, the antecedent to the pronoun *she* is *Luisa*. The noun and pronoun agree, both in number (*Luisa* is a singular subject; *she* is a singular pronoun) and gender (*Luisa* is a female; *she* is a female pronoun). Perfect!

Let's look at another example, but this time, we'll use a possessive pronoun instead of a personal pronoun. Since it would be redundant to say *Luisa drives Luisa's car*, most writers would replace the second *Luisa* with a possessive pronoun.

Luisa drives her car.

Much better, right? In this sentence, *Luisa* is the antecedent and the pronoun is *her*. Both are in agreement in this sentence if we understand that Luisa is female. *Her* is a female possessive pronoun. It is also singular, which is appropriate since Luisa is only one woman. Now, if the sentence read *Luisa drives his car*, it would lack pronoun-antecedent agreement in terms of gender (unless, of course, if Luisa was borrowing some guy's car). If it read *Luisa drives their car*, it would sound as if Luisa were driving a car owned by two or more people other than herself.

However, *their* would be necessary in a sentence with a **compound antecedent**. For example, maybe Luisa co-owns her car with a friend named Ginnie. Then the sentence should read, *Luisa and Ginnie drive their car on alternating days.* Compound antecedents are a bit more complicated when the conjunction is *or* or *nor* instead of *and*. In such cases, you will select your pronoun based on the antecedent to which it is nearest.

1) *Neither my wife nor my daughters brought* **their** *luggage out to the car.*

2) *Neither my daughters nor my wife brought* **her** *luggage out to the car.*

Both of these sentences are written correctly. Since the plural antecedent *daughters* is closer to the pronoun in sentence 1, the plural pronoun *their* is required. Since the singular antecedent *wife* is closer to the pronoun in sentence 2, the singular pronoun *her* is required.

Now, if your antecedent is a collective noun, selecting the right pronoun depends on what the collective noun is doing and how it is doing it. If every member of the collective noun is doing the exact same thing as a single unit, the singular pronoun is needed.

The soccer team played **its** *game magnificently.*

In this example, everyone on the team is playing the same game, and the singular pronoun *its* is used correctly. However, if all of the members of that collective noun are doing their own thing, a singular pronoun is in order.

The soccer team played **their** *individual positions magnificently.*

This example describes how the members of the team handled their individual positions (goalkeeper, defenders, midfielders, forwards), and it uses the plural pronoun *their* correctly.

Now answer this quick exercise question.

Neither Henrietta nor Alexandra has <u>their</u> ticket to the show.
8

8. **F.** NO CHANGE
G. its
H. she
J. her

The correct answer is J. This is a compound antecedent using the word *nor*. The verb must agree with the subject closest to it.

Selecting Pronouns

Person will be another factor when figuring out the best way to use pronouns on the ACT exam. A first-person pronoun (*I*, *me*, *we*, *us*) is necessary when a writer is referring to herself.

A second-person pronoun (*you*) is needed when the writer is addressing the reader. When the pronoun refers to a third person who is neither writing nor reading the passage, a third-person pronoun (*she*, *he*, *her*, *him*, *they*, *them*) is needed.

Choosing the right pronoun can be tricky in sentences that pair them with nouns. Is *Ricky and I went to the game* or *Ricky and me went to the game* correct?

In such cases, try removing the noun and saying the sentence with just the pronoun (*I went to the game*; *me went to the game*). Chances are the wrong pronoun will now sound wrong.

Relative Pronouns

Relative clauses are like adjectives: they exist to describe. You can recognize a relative clause from the presence of a **relative pronoun**. The relative pronouns *who*, *whom*, *whose*, and *that* refer to people; the relative pronouns *that* and *which* refer to things.

The relative clauses in the following sentences are underlined:

Mr. Marshall, <u>who used to live next door to me</u>, is the head manager at my new job.

The person <u>whom you are seeking</u> is not at home.

Florida, <u>which is where I went on vacation last year</u>, is located in the southern region of the United States.

The truck <u>that is parked across the street</u> belongs to Francois.

Reflexive Pronouns

When a subject needs a pronoun to refer to itself, a **reflexive pronoun** fits the bill. In fact, *itself* is a reflexive pronoun, as is any pronoun that ends with *-self* or *-selves*. There are five singular reflexive pronouns (*myself, yourself, himself, herself, itself)* and three plural reflexive pronouns (*ourselves, yourselves, themselves*).

Reflexive pronouns are often misused when included as part of a list of subjects. For example:

Feel free to contact Bob, Jerry, and ***myself****.*

Don't do it! The best way to tell if a reflexive pronoun is needed is to write or say the sentence as if you were the only subject:

Feel free to contact ***me****.*

A good rule of thumb is to use the reflexive pronoun when the subject and the object of the sentence are the same (***I*** heard ***myself***.), and the regular object pronoun when they are different **(*****You*** heard ***me***.).

Interrogative Pronouns

To interrogate is to question, and **interrogative pronouns** are used to ask questions. There are five main interrogative pronouns: *whose, who,* and *whom* refer to people exclusively; *what* refers to things exclusively; and *which* can refer to people or things.

The addition of the suffix *-ever* also creates five less common interrogative pronouns. These are *whatever, whichever, whoever, whomever,* and *whosoever.*

TIP

Perhaps the most common confusion regarding interrogative pronouns is when to use *who* and when to use *whom.*

- *Who* is used as the subject of a question. (Example: *Who called at 3 a.m. this morning?*)
- *Whom* is used as the object of a question. (Example: *To whom am I speaking?*)

Possessive Pronouns

In an earlier section of this book, you learned a thing or two about apostrophes. As you may recall, they are important elements when indicating that a noun possesses something. More often than not, you can just pop an apostrophe and an *s* onto the end of a word to make it possessive.

That guitar is Jimi's.

There is a goldfish in Jess's bathtub.

You also learned that the extra *s* is not necessary with a possessive noun that already ends in *s* but is not someone's name.

The lions' cubs played in the grass.

Those books' covers are falling apart.

Pronouns, however, usually have their very own forms to show possession. Since pronouns such as *his, her, its, their, my, mine, yours, their,* and *theirs* already show possession, they don't need an apostrophe or an extra *s*.

*The game is **mine.***

***Their** friend is coming to the beach with us.*

***Her** father is coaching the team.*

*The cat licked **its** paws.*

The only pronouns that do need that apostrophe and extra *s* are the indefinite pronouns an*ybody, anyone, everybody, everyone, no one*, and *nobody*.

***Anybody's** guess is as good as mine.*

***Everybody's** weekend will be spent studying.*

ALERT: Remember that *it's* is not the possessive form of *it*; it is a contraction of *it is*.

Verb Tense

Verbs are words that refer to actions, and their tense indicates when that action happened. Is the action happening now? The verb is in the present tense. Did the action already happen? Well, then the verb is in the past tense. Are you still waiting for it to happen? Then the verb is in the future tense.

Past, present, and future are the most basic points in time. However, there are quite a few more than three verb tenses.

- **Simple present tense** indicates an action happening now: *I am here.*
- **Present progressive tense** indicates an action happening now that will continue into the future: *I am walking.*
- **Present perfect progressive tense** indicates an unfinished action: *I have been studying all day.*
- **Present perfect simple tense** indicates an action that occurred in the past but continues to be relevant: *I have eaten artichokes.*
- **Past perfect simple tense** indicates an action that occurred in the past but is now complete: *When I woke up this morning, I realized that it had rained last night.*
- **Past simple tense** indicates an action that happened already: *I was asleep.*
- **Past progressive tense** pairs a past tense verb with a continuous verb ending in *-ing*: *I was dreaming.*
- **Past perfect progressive tense** reflects on an ongoing action from the past: *By the 1990s, hip-hop had been a popular form of music for several years.*
- **Future simple tense** indicates an action that will happen later: *I will be home by 5:00.*
- **Future progressive tense** indicates an action that will happen later and continue: *I will be working all day tomorrow.*
- **Future perfect simple tense** indicates the completion of an action that will happen later: *I will have finished cleaning the house by noon today.*
- **Future perfect progressive tense** indicates an incomplete action that will happen later: *I will have been cooking for three hours by the time my guests arrive.*

NOTE: You will not be expected to identify the various verb tenses on the ACT exam, but familiarizing yourself with them will help you to spot errors and select the best answer choices.

Adjectives and Adverbs

As we've already established, the only completely essential elements of a sentence are its subject and verb.

The dog barks.

Once again, that is a complete sentence. But is it a particularly interesting sentence? Writing a sentence with nothing but a subject and a verb is like making soup with nothing but water and tomatoes. Where are the other flavors? In a sentence, **adjectives** (words that describe nouns) and **adverbs** (words that describe verbs) add some extra flavor. Think of them as the spices of a sentence.

The furious dog barks uncontrollably.

Now there's a sentence that paints a picture! The adjective *furious* shows the dog is not barking playfully. The adverb *uncontrollably* shows that the dog is really worked up and probably won't calm down anytime soon. In this section, we will take a look at the different forms of adjectives and adverbs you have to know before taking the ACT exam.

Comparative and Superlative

Big! Bigger! Biggest! Adjectives and adverbs change form when they are used to make a comparison.

The **comparative** form is used when comparing two things.

Comparative adjectives:

This street is wider than the last one.

I feel more limber than I did before I stretched.

Comparative adverbs:

This week seemed to go by more quickly than last week did.

I am taking my studies more seriously than I ever have before.

The **superlative** form is used when comparing three or more things.

Superlative adjectives:

This is the longest book I own.

Alshad is the politest boy in my class.

Craig is the most ambitious candidate.

Superlative adverbs:

Out of everyone in the office, Peri works the hardest.

This is the quickest I have ever run.

As you may have noticed, simply adding *-er* to the end of comparative and *-est* to the end of superlative adjectives is not always enough. Once again, there are a number of exceptions you need to understand to use comparative and superlative adjectives correctly.

Case	Adjective	Comparative	Superlative
One- and two-syllable adjectives ending in *-e* do not need an extra *-e*.	*close* *large* *simple*	*closer* *larger* *simpler*	*closest* *largest* *simplest*
One-syllable adjectives ending in a consonant need to have that consonant doubled.	*big* *sad* *thin*	*bigger* *sadder* *thinner*	*biggest* *saddest* *thinnest*
One- and two-syllable adjectives ending in *-y* change the *-y* to an *-i*.	*dry* *heavy* *tiny*	*drier* *heavier* *tinier*	*driest* *heaviest* *tiniest*
Certain adjectives with two or more syllables remain the same but need the addition of *more* for comparatives and *most* for superlatives.	*beautiful* *complete* *important*	*more beautiful* *more complete* *more important*	*most beautiful* *most complete* *most important*
Irregular adjectives require their own special alterations in the comparative and superlative forms.	*bad* *far* *good* *many*	*worse* *farther* *better* *more*	*worst* *farthest* *best* *most*

For comparative adverbs, adding *more* is usually enough, and superlative adverbs usually only need *most*.

I sang <u>more quietly</u> than Enid did.

The car runs <u>most smoothly</u> on paved roads.

As you may have guessed, there are exceptions to this rule, but don't worry because there aren't as many exceptions for adverbs as there are for adjectives. Basically, any adverb that does not end in *-ly* should be treated the same way you would treat it if it were being used to modify a noun instead of a verb.

Adverb	Comparative	Superlative
bad	worse	worst
far	farther	farthest
fast	faster	fastest
good	better	best
hard	harder	hardest
little	less	least
long	longer	longest
loud	louder	loudest
many	more	most
quick	quicker	quickest

Another thing you need to make sure of on the ACT exam is that comparatives and superlatives are actually being used to make a comparison. You may have seen an advertisement that boasts, "Our product is better!" You might ask, "Better than *what*?" Obviously, the implication is that the product is better than other similar products, but the comparison is not correct and complete if that information is not stated directly.

Our product is better than other similar products!

Maybe that isn't the catchiest slogan in the world, but it is a complete comparison. Remember that incomplete comparisons are incorrect when you're reading English passages on the ACT exam.

TIP: Incomplete comparisons involving superlatives may not sound as awkward as incomplete comparisons involving comparatives, but they are still grammatically incorrect. For example, it is grammatically incorrect to say *"You're the best."*

Idioms

A recurring theme in this book so far has been "the English language can be tricky." For nonnative English speakers, there are few things trickier than idioms. Idioms are so confusing because they use words to mean something other than their literal meanings. If you were to "pull the wool over someone's eyes," you probably would not literally grab a wool scarf and pull it over that person's eyes. However, you may deceive them, which is the idiomatic meaning of "pull the wool over someone's eyes." See what we mean? Idioms are tricky.

English is a rich language, and it is very, very rich with idioms. There is no way to address all of them in this book. Be prepared for the possibility that you may encounter completely unfamiliar idioms on the ACT exam. Even if you are not 100 percent familiar with the meaning of a particular idiom, you may still recognize it as an idiom if it sounds a bit familiar and does not make literal sense in the context of the passage. Idiom questions on the ACT exam often require you to identify mistakes in their wording. So even if you don't know what the idiom "bite off more than you can chew" means, you may still have heard it. Therefore, you should be able to recognize that "bite off more than you can see" is not a correctly composed idiom. You may also deduce that biting with your eyes, which you use for seeing, is both difficult and uncomfortable.

NOTE: A good way to become familiar with a wide variety of idioms is to read a lot. Writers love to use idioms!

Here are some other common idioms:

Idiom	Meaning
Actions speak louder than words.	What one does is more important than what one says.
Add insult to injury	To make an already bad situation worse
A perfect storm	The absolute worst situation possible
Bite the bullet	Get something done because there's no getting out of it
Break the ice	Help people feel more at ease in social situations
Comparing apples and oranges	To compare two things that can't be compared
Feel under the weather	Feel ill
Give the cold shoulder	Intentionally ignore or treat with indifference
Is on the ball	Is very competent
Hit the sack	Go to bed
Kill two birds with one stone	Accomplish two tasks with a single action
Let sleeping dogs lie	Do not provoke a potentially unpleasant situation

Idiom	Meaning
Let the cat out of the bag	Reveal a secret
Once in a blue moon	Rarely
Take with a grain of salt	Not to take something too seriously
The elephant in the room	The big issue or problem that nobody wants to address

Prepositional Phrases

As the old lesson goes, a preposition is anywhere a mouse can go: *over, under, sideways, down, in, out, at, from, above, to, inside, outside, before, after, forward, toward,* etc. **Prepositions** indicate time and direction, and—pun intended—are pretty straightforward. Prepositional phrases, however, are less straightforward. In fact, they're very similar to idioms in that they cannot be explained with simple rules. You just have to get familiar with them and decide what sounds the best.

A **prepositional phrase** combines a preposition with one or more words. For example, *at home* is a common prepositional phrase. You will need to be aware of the most commonly used prepositional phrases on the ACT exam. Here are a few common prepositions you should remember:

among friends	at school	in the family	in the yard
at home	at work	in the grass	in your mind
at the office	at the beach	in the room	on the lawn
at play	in my heart	in the tree	on the road
	in the doorway	in the window	on the roof

NOTE: Sometimes, you may have to read a sentence more than once to figure out whether or not it contains an error.

Now you will put everything you have learned about grammar and usage to the test by reading this sample passage and answering the questions that follow.

By the time you attend college, you probably have a very clear idea of what your interests, strengths, and weakness are, which [9] means you probably also have an idea of what your ideal major is. However, you may discover that idea can evolve once you actually start taking classes.

9. **A.** NO CHANGE
B. interests, strengths, and weaknesss are
C. interests, strengths, and weakness's are
D. interests, strengths, and weaknesses are

The correct answer is D. The plural of *weakness* is *weaknesses.*

When I began our undergraduate studies, [10] I was a journalism major. I loved writing, and journalism seemed like a practical writing career. However, after taking a couple of journalism classes, I realized that I simply did not have much aptitude for interviewing people and "rooting out the story." Since I was already part of the communications department as a journalism major, I decided to stay within that department but attempt my hand at a totally different major. [11]

10. **F.** NO CHANGE
G. When I began my undergraduate studies
H. When we began our undergraduate studies
J. When you began our undergraduate studies

The correct answer is G. The passage takes on a first-person point of view, so all parts should be singular.

11. **A.** NO CHANGE
B. try my hand at a totally different major
C. try my mind at a totally different major
D. attempt my hand in a totally different major

The correct answer is B. The correct idiom is *try my hand.*

Realizing I had most interest in movies than journalism, [12] I decided to major in film studies. I'm happy to say that it was a perfect fit, and I ended up getting my bachelor's degree in film studies. When I started college, I never imagined I would get a degree in watching and writing about movies!

12. **F.** NO CHANGE
G. the most interest in movies than journalism
H. more interest in movies than journalism
J. many interest in movies than journalism

The correct answer is H. When comparing two items, the correct word to use is *more.*

SENTENCE STRUCTURE AND FORMATION

We started this chapter with a close-up look at tiny punctuation marks. Then our scope widened a bit to examine how words relate to each other by studying grammar and usage. Now we're going to explore entire sentences. Are you ready to take a look at the big picture?

Sentence structure and formation questions will test your ability to understand the relationships between and among clauses, the placement of modifiers, and shifts in construction. You will have to spot little bits of sentences known as *fragments* and sentences that go on and on and on, known as *run-ons*.

Clauses

Just as you can't have a sentence without a subject and verb that express a complete thought, you can't have a sentence without clauses. We'll let you in on a little secret: a phrase that contains a subject and verb is a **clause**. If the clause expresses a complete thought, it's an **independent clause**, because it can stand on its own. A clause that has its own subject and verb but cannot stand on its own is a **dependent (or subordinate) clause**.

> **Independent clause:** *The rooster crows.*
>
> **Dependent clause:** *when the sun rises*

A dependent clause needs to be paired with an independent clause to be part of a complete sentence.

> *When the sun rises, the rooster crows.*

In English writing, there are four different sentence structures. Notice that each one always includes at least one independent clause.

A **simple sentence** has only one independent clause:

> *The dog barks.*

A **compound sentence** has two or more independent clauses joined with a conjunction or semicolon:

> *The dog barks, and the cat meows.*
>
> *The dog barks; the cat meows.*

A **complex sentence** has one independent clause and at least one subordinate clause:

> *When the mail carrier arrives, the dog barks.*

A **compound-complex sentence** has at least two independent clauses and at least one subordinate clause:

> *When the mail carrier arrives, the dog barks; the cat meows.*

ALERT: A semicolon is the most used punctuation mark that can join independent clauses without a conjunction. Using only a comma to join independent clauses without a conjunction creates a **comma splice**, which is considered incorrect punctuation usage.

You may have noticed the important role conjunctions play in these various sentence structures. When a conjunction joins independent clauses of equal importance, it is known as a **coordinating conjunction**.

> *The movie was very good, but the book was terrible.*

In this compound sentence, *but* is the coordinating conjunction. If you divide the sentence before and after the coordinating conjunction, you will still have two independent clauses of equal importance:

The movie was very good.

The book was terrible.

However, if a conjunction joins a subordinate clause to an independent clause, it is known as a **subordinating conjunction**.

The movie that I didn't want to see was actually very good.

In this sentence, the subordinate clause is *that I didn't want to see*, which is not a complete sentence on its own. The subordinating conjunction is *that*. Here are some other coordinating and subordinating conjunctions:

Coordinating Conjunctions
and
but
for
nor
or
so
yet

Subordinating Conjunctions	
after	until
although	when
as	whenever
because	whereas
before	wherever
even though	whether
if	which
since	while
that	who
though	why
unless	

Now answer this quick exercise question.

The jacket, I bought this afternoon, fits me perfectly.
13

13. **A.** NO CHANGE
B. jacket those I bought this afternoon fits
C. jacket I bought this afternoon, fits
D. jacket that I bought this afternoon fits

The correct answer is D. The subordinate clause in this sentence is *that I bought this afternoon*.

Fragments and Run-ons

Two of the most common sentence structure errors are fragments and run-ons. The names of these writing errors say a lot about what they are. A fragment is a piece of a complete object. The same is true in English. A **fragment** is a piece of a sentence, but it is not a complete one.

Bouncing on the waves.

What was bouncing on the waves? This phrase needs a subject. Otherwise, it's nothing more than a fragment.

The little boat is bouncing on the waves.

Ah, that's more like it. The subject-verb pair *The little boat* and *is* rescued this sentence from the fragment heap.

Run-on sentences are the opposite of fragments, but they are just as incorrect. They combine two or more independent clauses without using a coordinating conjunction or proper punctuation. In effect, the sentences "run on" (and into each other) without stopping. Unlike a fragment, in which there is a shortage of words, run-on sentences have too many words improperly joined together.

NOTE: Sometimes, writers use fragments and run-on sentences on purpose to achieve a particular effect. However, as far as the ACT English test is concerned, fragments and run-on sentences are always wrong.

The sea is rough and stormy the little boat is bouncing on the waves.

This run-on sentence needs the correct punctuation, but adding a comma is not quite enough:

The sea is rough and stormy, the little boat is bouncing on the waves.

Now the sentence has graduated from a run-on sentence to a comma splice. It needs one more element to make it grammatically correct. However, that little boat need not fear. This comma splice can be repaired by adding a coordinating conjunction.

The sea is rough and stormy, and the little boat is bouncing on the waves.

Run-on sentences can also be corrected without adding a conjunction by using the correct punctuation, such as a semicolon, a dash, or a period.

TIP: The ACT will never ask you to choose between stylistic differences such as the different ways to correct a run-on sentence. There will be only *one* correct answer.

Semicolon: *The sea is rough and stormy; the little boat is bouncing on the waves.*

Dash: *The sea is rough and stormy—the little boat is bouncing on the waves.*

Period: *The sea is rough and stormy. The little boat is bouncing on the waves.*

You could also make one of the clauses dependent on the other by adding a subordinate conjunction.

Because the sea is rough and stormy, the little boat is bouncing on the waves.

As you can see, there are several ways to express the thought clearly.

Now answer this quick exercise question.

Irina was surfing a jellyfish stung her.
14

14. **F.** NO CHANGE
G. was surfing, a jellyfish
H. surfing when a jellyfish
J. was surfing when a jellyfish

The correct answer is J. The original run-on sentence has been corrected by making the second clause (*a jellyfish stung her*) dependent on the first (*Irina was surfing*).

Modifiers and Their Problems

As we said while discussing adjectives and adverbs, descriptive parts of speech add spice to sentences. However, you cannot just sprinkle these particular spices anywhere. **Modifiers** such as adjectives, adverbs, and descriptive phrases and clauses need to be placed correctly in sentences. Otherwise, you can end up with a very bewildering brew.

The two most common modifier issues are misplaced modifiers and dangling modifiers. A **misplaced modifier** is not placed next to the word it is supposed to modify.

I tiptoed across the floor because I didn't want to wake the people sleeping in the room below mine carefully.

In this sentence, the modifier *carefully* is a long way from home. In fact, its placement makes it seem as though the people were sleeping carefully. How do you sleep carefully? You have to be conscious to be careful. The adverb *carefully* would be put to better use modifying *tiptoed*. The best way is to pluck it from the end of the sentence and drop it immediately after *tiptoed*.

I tiptoed carefully across the floor because I didn't want to wake the people sleeping in the room below mine.

Excellent! In this sentence, the modifier *carefully* is no longer misplaced.

Dangling modifiers are even more confusing than misplaced ones. They don't modify anything at all because there's nothing in the sentence for them to modify. Take a look at this sentence:

Worried about the time, breakfast was left on the table.

The modifier in this sentence is *Worried about the time*. The problem is we don't know exactly who was worried about the time—it certainly can't be breakfast! This sentence leaves the modifier dangling without anything to modify. Someone needs to add a subject to give the modifier something to do. We'll handle this one.

Worried about the time, Greta left her breakfast on the table.

The addition of the subject *Greta* gives the phrase *worried about the time* something to modify.

NOTE: On the ACT exam, make sure you choose the right noun to give the modifier something to modify. You will make the best selection by reading the passage very carefully.

Now answer this quick exercise question.

The man did not show up to work today who runs the store.
15

15. **A.** NO CHANGE
B. did not show up to work who runs the store today.
C. did not show up who runs the store to work today.
D. who runs the store did not show up to work today.

The correct answer is D. The modifier *who runs the store* should directly follow the word it describes: *man*.

Parallel Structure

When two things are parallel, they are moving in the same direction. All parts of a group of words in a sentence need to move in the same direction too. You can't place a word or phrase that's going backward into the past alongside one that's moving into the future. In fact, you cannot combine different tenses into any single group. Parallel structure crumbles when groups of words combine different types of phrases, clauses, and parts of speech.

I start my day by brushing my teeth, eating breakfast, and then head to school.

This sentence describes something that is happening in the present, and the writer uses the present continuous tense to indicate that she is brushing her teeth and eating breakfast. Everything is smooth until that final phrase: *then head to school*. It is written in the simple present tense, which violates the parallel structure of a sentence otherwise written in the present continuous tense.

I start my day by brushing my teeth, eating breakfast, and heading to school.

This sentence corrects the parallel structure by putting that pesky final verb in its present continuous tense. Now all parts of the sentence are moving in the same direction.

TIP: A sentence does not need to be written entirely in the same tense to be correct. It just needs to be structured correctly. The sentence *I ate an apple yesterday, and I am going to eat an orange tonight* does not violate parallel structure.

You need to be aware of parallel structure when using other parts of speech in lists as well. To be grammatically correct, the words have to be the same part of speech and used correctly in the structure of the sentence.

Incorrect: *Sean was brave, courage, and kind.* (*Courage* is a noun; *brave* and *kind* are adjectives.)

Correct: *Sean was brave, courageous, and kind.*

Incorrect: *In the snow I drive carefully, defensively, and slow.* (*Slow* is an adjective; *carefully* and *defensively* are adverbs.)

Correct: *In the snow I drive carefully, defensively, and slowly.*

Correlative Conjunctions

You must also be mindful of parallel structure when dealing with correlative conjunctions. These are conjunctions that work in pairs: *either . . . or*, *neither . . . nor*, and *not only . . . but also*. Mixing your correlative conjunctions is another way to violate parallel structure.

Neither the pants or the shirt suit my taste in clothing.

Oops! *Neither* indicates a negative, and *or* indicates a positive. So what does this sentence mean? Do the pants and shirt suit the writer's very particular tastes, or don't they? We will know only if the parallel structure is repaired.

Neither the pants nor the shirt suit my taste in clothing.

Oh, the writer doesn't like either piece of clothing! Too bad!

ALERT: To say something like *I am not only a son, but a brother* is incorrect because the *not only...but also* conjunction is missing the word *also* in this instance.

Now you will put everything you have learned about grammar and usage to the test by reading this sample passage and answering the questions that follow.

Back in the 1970s, few members of the movie industry believed <u>in a strange, little, movie called *Star Wars*</u> [16]. George Lucas's <u>outer space fantasy. It was full</u> [17] of odd robots and creatures very out of step with the vogue for gritty, realistic, and rather pessimistic movies. However, <u>it has outlasted most of the movies of its day and continuing</u> [18] to delight audiences well into the twenty-first century. In fact, *Star Wars* seems more popular than ever lately, spawning

16.
F. NO CHANGE
G. in a strange little movie called *Star Wars*
H. in a movie strange, little movie called *Star Wars*
J. in a strange called *Star Wars*

The correct answer is G. No commas are needed to set off the adjectives modifying *movie*.

17.
A. NO CHANGE
B. outer space fantasy was full
C. outer space fantasy; it was full
D. outer space fantasy will be fulls

The correct answer is B. *George Lucas's outer space fantasy* is a fragment that cannot be a stand-alone sentence or set off by a semicolon.

18.
F. NO CHANGE
G. it has outlasted most of the movies of its day; and continues
H. it has outlasted most of the movies of its day and continues
J. it has outlasted most of the movies of its day, continues

The correct answer is H. Since *has outlasted* and *continues* are the compound predicate to the subject pronoun *it*, no punctuation is needed before the coordinating conjunction *and.*

a recent stream of feature films and <u>television series, as well as all of the merchandise</u> (19) that has been an important part of this pop-culture juggernaut since its inception some four decades ago.

19. **A.** NO CHANGE
B. television series. As well as all of the merchandise
C. television series, all of the merchandise
D. television series all of the merchandise

The correct answer is A. The section is correct as is.

SUMMING IT UP

- **End-of-sentence punctuation** includes the period, the exclamation point, and the question mark. When a sentence ends with quotation marks used to indicate dialogue, the end-of-sentence punctuation is placed within the quotation marks. If the quotation marks indicate a title and placing end-of-sentence punctuation within the marks might give the false impression that the mark is part of the title, the end-of-sentence punctuation is placed outside of the closing quotation marks.
- **Commas** are used to separate introductory words, phrases, and clauses; clauses in compound sentences, nonrestrictive phrases, items in series, appositives, and quotations.
- **Apostrophes** are used to separate letters in contractions and indicate possession. When indicating possession, an apostrophe is usually followed by the letter *s*. However, no extra *s* is necessary if the possessing word ends in *s* and is not someone's name.
- **Colons** are used to introduce a list of items or offset an example.
- **Dashes** are used to offset examples and indicate a pause or interruption in dialogue.
- **Parentheses** enclose bonus information that cannot be fit into a sentence naturally.
- **Plural nouns** do not always end with *s*; there are several variations among plural nouns depending on the words' letters. **Collective nouns** are singular nouns in most cases; they act as plural nouns only when individual members are not acting in unison.
- **Subjects and verbs** are in agreement when they are in the same form. They both need to be either singular or plural.
- **Pronouns and antecedents** (the words for which the pronouns stand in) need to be in agreement. They need to agree in terms of number, gender, and person.
- **Relative pronouns** signal relative clauses, which are used to describe nouns; **reflexive pronouns** refer back to their subjects; **interrogative pronouns** are used when asking a question; **possessive pronouns** show ownership.
- **Verb tense** indicates when the action the verb describes takes place.
- **Comparative adjectives and adverbs** are used when comparing two things. They usually end in *-er*. **Superlative adjectives and adverbs** are used when comparing three or more things. They usually end in *-est*.
- **Idioms** use words to mean something other than their literal meanings.
- **Prepositional phrases** combine a preposition with other words to indicate direction and time.
- **Independent clauses** contain a subject and a verb and make sense on their own. **Subordinate clauses** contain a subject-verb pair but must be linked to an independent clause to be correct.
- **Fragments** are partial sentences that lack either a subject or a verb. They are grammatically incorrect.
- **Run-on sentences** are complete sentences that are connected without the necessary conjunction or punctuation.
- **Modifiers** are words and phrases that describe something. **Misplaced modifiers** are not placed next to the words they are supposed to modify. They are grammatically incorrect. **Dangling modifiers** fail to modify any word at all.
- **Parallel structure** occurs when all groups of words in a sentence are written in the same tense and form. When such words are not in the same tense or form, the sentence is grammatically incorrect. Failing to pair correlative conjunctions correctly also violates parallel structure.

ONLINE PREP

WANT TO KNOW MORE?

Pump up your test prep power with *Peterson's Online Course for the ACT® Exam.* The course will give you access to customized lessons designed to strengthen your skills in the Grammar and Usage topics covered on the ACT English test:

- Pronouns, Nouns, and Verbs
- Adjectives and Adverbs
- Connection Words
- What Makes a Sentence?
- Using Modifiers
- Common Sentence Mistakes
- Sentence Enders
- Setting off Phrases
- Apostrophes
- Agreement
- Verb Tenses
- Shift in Person

To purchase and access the course, go to **www.petersons.com/testprep/act**.

PRACTICE

Now it's time to take your first English practice quiz. The passages in this quiz are similar in length to those that will appear on the actual ACT exam. Read each one very carefully before answering the questions. When you've finished answering all 20 questions, check the answers and explanations that follow to figure out how well you did and why you may have selected some incorrect answer choices.

PASSAGE I

The Great Chicago Fire

[1]

On October 8, 1871, a fire ignited in Chicago, Illinois, and continued to engulf the city for the next two days. One of the most monumental disasters on U.S. soil, the Great Chicago Fire ultimately killed as <u>many as 300 people left more</u> [1] than 100,000 others without homes, and ravaged 3.3 square miles of land. This is a tragic story, yet not one without hope, <u>as anyone which has visited</u> [2] or lived in the city of Chicago can confirm today.

[2]

The <u>most famous tale of the Great Chicago Fire's cause almost seem</u> [3] like something out of a children's story: a cow owned by Patrick and Catherine O'Leary had kicked over a lantern in their barn. The lantern set <u>fire to the barn, and then the fire swept</u> [4] through the entire city. However, this story has no more validity than the average children's story.

1. A. NO CHANGE
   B. many as 300, people left more
   C. many as 300 people; left more
   D. many as 300 people, left more

2. F. NO CHANGE
   G. as anyone who has visited
   H. as anyone those has visited
   J. as anyone which have visited

3. A. NO CHANGE
   B. most famous tale of the Great Chicago Fire's cause almost seeming
   C. most famous tale of the Great Chicago Fire's cause almost seems
   D. most famous tale of the Great Chicago Fire's cause almost will seem

4. F. NO CHANGE
   G. fire to the barn, though then the fire swept
   H. fire to the barn, after then the fire swept
   J. fire to the barn, until then the fire swept

A dozen years after the fire, Michael Ahern admitted he made up the story, a reporter from the *Chicago Republican,* because he thought people would find it interesting. The truth is that no one knows exactly how the Great Chicago Fire started, though it did indeed begin in the O'Leary's barn.

5.
A. NO CHANGE
B. Michael Ahern, a reporter from the *Chicago Republican*, admitted he made up the story
C. reporter Michael Ahern admitted he from the *Chicago Republican* made up the story
D. Michael Ahern, a reporter from the *Chicago Republican*

[3]

What is known is how rapidly and ruthlessly the fire spun out of control. Since most of the buildings in Chicago were constructed of wood at the time, the fire had a lot of material to consume. Even the sidewalks in Chicago were made of wood. As the wind lifted up burning debris and carried it throughout the city, new conflagrations broke out.

6.
F. NO CHANGE
G. how much rapider and more ruthless the fire
H. how rapider and ruthlesser the fire
J. how rapid and ruthless the fire

7.
A. NO CHANGE
B. lifted up burning debris and carries
C. lifted up burning debris and carrying
D. Lifts up burning debris and carries

[4]

Chicagos' mayor Roswell B. Mason sent out a distress call to get help from neighboring towns while his own fire department continued to fight the flames. However, the end of the Great Chicago Fire was mostly brought about naturally as it died down on its own. The rainfall that began on October 9 helped drown the already dying fire. It was out by the morning of October 10, 1871.

8.
F. NO CHANGE
G. Chicagos mayor Roswell B. Mason
H. Chicago is mayor Roswell B. Mason
J. Chicago's mayor Roswell B. Mason

[5]

The Great Chicago Fire was now over Chicago's troubles had barely begun. With many people dead and homeless, and many buildings destroyed including the courthouse and waterworks a difficult period of repairs lay ahead. Reconstruction began immediately, though another major fire in 1874 was a tremendous setback. However, the use of terra cotta tiles in many newly constructed buildings would make Chicago one of the most

9.
A. NO CHANGE
B. Fire was now over, Chicago's troubles had barely begun
C. Fire was now over, but Chicago's troubles had barely begun
D. Fire was now and Chicago's troubles had barely begun

10.
F. NO CHANGE
G. destroyed; including the courthouse and waterworks; a difficult period
H. destroyed. Including the courthouse and waterworks. A difficult period
J. destroyed—including the courthouse and waterworks—a difficult period

fireproof cities in the United States. By 1893, it was ready to host a major international fair called the World's Columbian Exposition. Today, Chicago is one of the most popular cities in the United States. Its fire department training academy is now located on the site where the O'Leary's barn once stood. It is a reminder of how much Chicago has endured and how much it has overcome.

PASSAGE II

Rock Opera

[1]

Are there two kinds of music more different than opera and rock music. Opera is [11] an artful form of music sung by professionally trained singers that conveys complex stories. Rock music is rough and raw and is played on loud electric guitars by people who often don't even know how to read music. Opera is for serious and cultured. [12] Rock music is for everyone, and the less serious and cultured they are, the better. [13]

11.
- **A.** NO CHANGE
- **B.** opera and rock music: opera is
- **C.** opera and rock music? Opera is
- **D.** opera and rock music, opera is

12.
- **F.** NO CHANGE
- **G.** Opera is for serious and cultured people.
- **H.** Opera is for serious, cultured.
- **J.** Opera is for serious and culture.

13.
- **A.** NO CHANGE
- **B.** cultured they be, the better
- **C.** cultured they was, the better
- **D.** cultured they is, the better

[2]

Of course, these stereotypes were shattered in the 1960s when several rock musicians schemed to unite that most serious of music forms with the wildest pop music around. It all began with a British called The Who [14] and their manager Kit Lambert. Rock bands of the time did not get any wilder than The Who. The band was known to smash his instruments [15] to pieces at the end of concerts so loud they actually broke world records for volume. Lambert was more of a serious music lover, and his father, Constant Lambert, was the musical director of the Royal Ballet at England's Covent Garden.

14.
- **F.** NO CHANGE
- **G.** The Who
- **H.** popular called The Who
- **J.** rock band called The Who

15.
- **A.** NO CHANGE
- **B.** The band was known to smash their instruments
- **C.** The band was known to smash its instruments
- **D.** The band was known to smash our instruments

[3]

Feeling the band he managed needed a good gimmick as if smashing instruments was not a good enough gimmick on its own (16), Lambert encouraged The Who's main songwriter, Pete Townshend, to try putting more complex stories into his songs.

16.
- **F.** NO CHANGE
- **G.** gimmick. As if smashing instruments was not a good enough gimmick on its own.
- **H.** gimmick (as if smashing instruments was not a good enough gimmick on its own)
- **J.** gimmick (as if smashing instruments was not a good enough gimmick on its own

Realizing The Who's second album was neither long enough or progressive enough (17) to compete with what the most interesting

17.
- **A.** NO CHANGE
- **B.** was neither long enough and progressive enough
- **C.** was either long enough or progressive enough
- **D.** was neither long enough nor progressive enough

other bands of the time were doing, Townshend strung together six unfinished songs, gave them a storyline, had his first (18) "mini-opera."

18.
- **F.** NO CHANGE
- **G.** unfinished songs, gave them a storyline, and had his first
- **H.** unfinished songs, had his first
- **J.** unfinished songs, gave them a storyline, as had his first

[4]

However it was The Who's full-length opera (19) that made them

19.
- **A.** NO CHANGE
- **B.** However, it was The Who's full-length opera
- **C.** However: it was The Who's full-length opera
- **D.** It was The Who's full-length opera

international celebrities and made "rock opera" a household word (20). The opera was called *Tommy* and told the story of a boy with multiple disabilities who ends up becoming a pinball champion and reluctant religious leader. As strange as the story was, the public loved it. Artists such as Andrew Lloyd Webber, Pink Floyd, Green Day, and The Decemberists would follow, making their own successful unions of opera and rock and roll.

20.
- **F.** NO CHANGE
- **G.** made "rock opera" a house word
- **H.** made "rock opera" a holding word
- **J.** made "rock opera" a household

Answers and Explanations

Be sure to read each explanation thoroughly to help you understand why the incorrect answer choices are incorrect, why you may have selected them, and how to avoid making the same errors on the actual ACT exam.

1. **The correct answer is D.** Items in a series need to be separated with commas, even if those items consist of phrases. This particular series describes the various disastrous results of the Great Chicago Fire. As the sentence is originally written, the first two items in that list—the number of people who died in the fire, and the number of people who were left homeless—are not separated with any punctuation, so choice A is incorrect. Items in a list should be separated with semicolons only if those items already contain commas. Since this is not the case, choice C is incorrect. Choice B includes a comma, which is the correct punctuation for separating the items in this particular series, but it is misplaced in the middle of the first item, so this choice is incorrect. Only choice D correctly places the comma after the first item (*killed as many as 300 people*).

2. **The correct answer is G.** As it is written, the sentence uses the wrong relative pronoun. The antecedent is the indefinite pronoun *anyone*, which indicates a person, yet the relative pronoun *which* should be used only to replace a thing. So you can eliminate choices F and J. Choice J makes the additional error of matching the plural verb *have* with the singular pronoun *anyone*. Choice H mistakenly uses the plural pronoun *those* to indicate the singular antecedent *anyone*. Only choice G offers the relative pronoun *who* and the correct agreement.

3. **The correct answer is C.** This is a somewhat tricky subject-verb agreement question because of all the words that appear between the subject *tale* and the verb *seem*. However, a careful reading of the sentence reveals that these words are, indeed, its subject and verb. It should also reveal that the singular noun *tale* needs a singular verb, and *seem* is a plural verb. Therefore, you can eliminate choice A. Rewriting the verb in the progressive tense (*seeming*) does not correct the error, so go ahead and eliminate choice B too. The same is true of rewriting it in the future tense (*will seem*), so you can rule out choice D. That leaves choice C, which correctly rewrites the verb in the singular form (*seems*).

4. **The correct answer is F.** This sentence contains two ideas of equal importance: the lantern set fire to the barn, and then the fire swept through the entire city. That means it needs a coordinating conjunction to join those two ideas, and since *and* is a coordinating conjunction, the sentence is correct as it is written. Choices G, H, and J all replace the correct coordinating conjunction with various incorrect subordinating conjunctions.

5. **The correct answer is B.** There is a misplaced modifier in this sentence as it is written. The modifier is *a reporter from the Chicago Republican*, and it needs to modify the subject *Michael Ahern*. However, the way it is placed in the original sentence makes it seem as though the story about the O'Leary's cow was a reporter from the *Chicago Republican*. That means choice A is incorrect. Only choice B moves the modifier so it follows the subject directly. Choice C is worded confusingly, and choice D deletes words, which would turn the sentence into a fragment, so these two answer choices are both incorrect.

6. **The correct answer is F.** In this sentence, the words *rapidly* and *ruthlessly* modify the verb *spun*. Since they are written in the adverb form, and adverbs modify verbs, the sentence is correct as written, and choice F is the best answer. Since nothing is being compared in this sentence, the comparative form is not required, so choice G is incorrect. That answer choice makes the additional error of transforming the adverbs into adjectives. Choice H further misuses the comparative form with the word *ruthlesser*, which is not a real word. Choice J does not attempt to use the comparative form, but it is still wrong since *rapid* and *ruthless* are adjectives, not adverbs.

7. **The correct answer is A.** The underlined portion in this sentence uses parallel structure, and it is balanced since both *lifted* and *carried* are written in the past tense. Since this is correct as written, choice A is the best answer. Choices B and C violate that parallel structure by mixing the past and present tenses (choice B), and the past and progressive tenses (choice C). Choice D is parallel, but it rewrites the two verbs in the present tense, and this is incorrect since the sentence describes something that happened in the past.

8. **The correct answer is J.** This question tests your knowledge of how to use apostrophes to show possession. As the sentence is originally written, the apostrophe is used incorrectly. It makes it seem as though there is more than one Chicago, or that the name of the city ends with the letter *s*. Choice G fails to use the apostrophe, and choice H deletes the apostrophe and the *s*. Both elements are needed when a singular word that does not end with *s* is in its possessive form. Only choice J uses both essential elements in their correct places.

9. **The correct answer is C.** This is a run-on sentence as written. The two clauses in this compound sentence—*The Great Chicago Fire was now over* and *Chicago's troubles had barely begun*—need to be joined with a coordinating conjunction. Choice B uses a comma instead of a conjunction; that is known as a comma splice, and comma splices are always incorrect. Choice D uses a coordinating conjunction, but it is not the right coordinating conjunction. The choice also randomly deletes the adjective *over*, and the comma before the conjunction is missing. Since the second clause is a counterpoint to the first, the coordinating conjunction *but* is in order, making choice C the best answer.

10. **The correct answer is J.** In this sentence, *including the courthouse and waterworks* is an example, and it needs to be offset from the rest of the sentence. The best way to accomplish this is with dashes, so choice J is the best answer. As the sentence is originally written, there is no offsetting punctuation at all, so choice F is incorrect. Choice G mistakenly uses semicolons instead of dashes. Choice H not only uses periods, which is the wrong punctuation to use to offset examples, but also turns the example into a fragment.

11. **The correct answer is C.** The first sentence of the passage asks a question, and, therefore, it should end with a question mark. As originally written, it ends with a period, which belongs at the end of a statement. Choice A is incorrect. Choice B attempts to correct the problem by joining the first two sentences of the passage with a colon, yet the colon would be appropriate only if placed before both parts of the example. Since only the example relating to opera follows the first sentence (the example relating to rock music is in its own sentence that comes next), the colon is not the right punctuation for this particular circumstance, which makes choice B incorrect. Choice D creates a comma splice, which is never a correct solution. Choice C offers the simplest solution to a fairly simple problem by replacing the period with a question mark.

12. **The correct answer is G.** Opera is for serious and cultured *what*? As this sentence is written, we simply do not know because it lacks an object for the preposition *for*. Therefore it is incomplete, and you can eliminate choice F. Choice H fails to correct the problem; it only replaces the coordinating conjunction with a comma. Choice J turns the adjective *cultured* into a noun, leaving the sentence nonsensical. To correct this sentence, you need to make an assumption about what or who is serious and cultured. *People* is a good guess that makes sense within the context of the passage, so choice G is the best answer.

13. **The correct answer is A.** This underlined portion contains a variation of the idiomatic expression *the less . . . the better*. The idiom is used correctly and everything is in agreement, so choice A is the best answer. Choices B, C, and D ruin a perfectly good sentence with various verbs that fail to agree with the subject pronoun *they*.

14. **The correct answer is J.** In this sentence, *called The Who* is a modifier; it explains what something is called. But what is that thing? We do not know because it is a dangling modifier, making choice F incorrect. Introducing a subject for the modifier to modify will correct this sentence. Since this passage makes it clear that The Who is a rock band, introducing that information to the sentence will correct it. Choice J accomplishes this task well. Choice G makes it seem as though there are several *The Whos*, and it just so happens that the British one invented the rock opera. Eliminate choice G. *Popular* is an adjective, not a noun, and though The Who became popular, this adjective does not correct the dangling modifier problem, so choice H is incorrect.

15. **The correct answer is B.** This is a pronoun-antecedent question, and the sentence as written makes it seem as though The Who was one person. It was actually a band of four people, so choice A does not make sense. Since The Who is a band, it is a collective noun, so collective noun rules apply here. Think about what The Who are doing in this sentence: they are smashing their instruments. Chances are every member of the Who does not play the same instrument; otherwise the sentence might read something like *the band was known to smash its guitars*. Since most band members play different instruments, each member of The Who is doing something a little different, even though they

are all smashing something. Therefore, the best way to write this sentence is as it is written in choice B, not choice C. Choice D makes it sound as if you, the reader, and the writer of this passage owned instruments that The Who took away and smashed.

16. **The correct answer is H.** This sentence contains a little bonus information about how The Who already had a gimmick before inventing the rock opera. Bonus information should not be dropped in the middle of a sentence without any punctuation to separate it. This is how it appears in the sentence as originally written, so choice F is incorrect. It belongs within a set of parentheses, as it appears in choice H. Choice J has the right idea but fails to close up the parentheses. Choice G creates a fragment by splitting off the subordinate clause before the bonus information with a period.

17. **The correct answer is D.** As it is written, this sentence mismatches the words in a correlative conjunction. The negative *neither* does not belong with the positive *or*, so choice A is incorrect. Now, your job is to figure out if this sentence requires the *neither . . . nor* correlative conjunction or the *either . . . or* one. Since the sentence indicates that Pete Townshend made an effort to make The Who's second album something that it was not (long enough or progressive enough to compete with what the most interesting other bands of the time were doing), you can conclude that this sentence requires the *neither . . . nor* combination. That means you can eliminate choice C and select choice D as the best answer. There is no *neither . . . and* correlative conjunction, so you should have eliminated choice B.

18. **The correct answer is G.** The sentence as originally written is incorrect because it lacks a conjunction between the two final items in the series of things Pete Townshend did to make his first "mini-opera." Since these items are of equal importance, a coordinating conjunction is needed, and choice G contains the best option. Choice H senselessly eliminates one of the important items in this series. Choice J uses a subordinating conjunction that makes no sense in this context.

19. **The correct answer is B.** *However* is a transitional word, and a transitional word needs to be offset with a comma. Since the sentence as written fails to do this, you can eliminate choice A. Since choice B does do this, you can select it as the best answer. Choice C uses the wrong punctuation. Choice D deletes the transitional word completely. While this is not grammatically incorrect, the transitional word improves the flow of ideas between the final two paragraphs, so choice D is not the very best option.

20. **The correct answer is F.** This question expects you to be familiar with the idiom "household word," which is a word or term so common that people seem to use it in every household. The sentence as originally written uses the idiom correctly, so choice F is correct. Choices G and J delete elements necessary to the idiom's common use. There is no such idiom as "a holding word," so choice H is incorrect.

Chapter 5: Production of Writing and Knowledge of Language

OVERVIEW

- Topic Development
- Organization, Unity, and Cohesion
- Knowledge of Language and Style
- Summing It Up
- Practice

Now that you know everything you need about the questions on the ACT English test that cover conventions of standard English, it's time to get familiar with the test's other question types. Production of Writing questions and Knowledge of Language questions are a bit trickier than straightforward conventions of English questions because the error may not be quite as obvious. Questions in these categories deal with subtler matters of strategy, organization, and style. Specifically, Production of Writing questions (which make up 29–32% of the test) cover the development of a topic, as well as the organization, cohesion, and unity of a piece of writing. Knowledge of Language questions (which make up 13–19% of the test) focus on proper word choice and keeping the tone and style consistent. Together, these question types deal with making sure a piece of writing is as clear and convincing as it can be.

Take a look at this paragraph.

Have you ever heard the song of a prairie warbler? The bird makes a buzzing sound that rises and falls, changing pitch. Male cardinals appear to have red feathers because of the way the light catches them and not because the feathers contain red pigment. The prairie warbler's song is quite enchanting.

NOTE: Production of Writing and Knowledge of Language questions may sometimes seem as though they have more than one correct answer. That will never be the case, so be sure to contrast those answers against each other to select the very best one.

Grammatically speaking, there's nothing wrong with this paragraph. The punctuation is in the right place. The sentences are well constructed. However, there is definitely something wrong with it. What's a sentence about cardinal feathers doing in a paragraph about a prairie warbler's song? Your guess is as good as ours, because the inclusion of that sentence about cardinals and their lovely feathers has nothing to do with the paragraph's topic. In fact, it is downright distracting—it weakens the author's attempt to convince you that the prairie warbler's song is unique and enchanting. This is the kind of subtle error you will have to recognize when answering rhetorical skills questions on the ACT exam.

Obviously, all Production of Writing and Knowledge of Language questions do not deal with off-topic details. They also involve making sure that the tone and mood of a piece of writing are consistent and appropriate, deleting redundant details, making sure the transitions between ideas are strong, avoiding wordiness, and so on. You basically learned how to fix the major errors in a piece of writing in the previous chapter. In this chapter you will learn how to make a piece of writing really worth reading, which is something that all the best editors do.

TOPIC DEVELOPMENT

Just as a well-prepared team studies the competing team's strategies to plot out its moves as effectively as possible, a strong writer plots out her or his ideas to reach an audience as effectively as possible. Writers choose the expressions that will best affect their particular readers. They delete, revise, and delete again the details most likely to fall flat with that audience. They choose only the most relevant and convincing details to support their writing. All of this is part of the writer's topic development.

Supporting Examples and Evidence

A piece of writing has two main elements: 1) a topic; and 2) the examples and evidence that support that topic. You can't have one without the other. Simply stating a topic is neither very informative nor convincing.

> *Hawaii is the best place to take a vacation. That's it! I'm sure you'll start planning your vacation right now!*

We're sure Hawaii is a lovely state and a great place to vacation, but it's going to take a bit more convincing than that.

> *Hawaii is the best place to take a vacation. The weather is warm and sunny. The Pacific Ocean is clear, blue, and perfect for swimming or surfing. The local cuisine and music are unique and fabulous. Once you go to Hawaii, you may never want to go home again!*

We were right! Hawaii *is* a lovely state and a great place to vacation! All it took to convince us were a few relevant pieces of evidence to explain why Hawaii is so nice.

Not everything that is remotely related to a topic is actually relevant. Had the above paragraph boasted about how great the snowy Swiss Alps are for skiers, it would not belong in this paragraph just because it relates to the topic of a great vacation spot. The vacation spot in this paragraph is very specific, and all of the paragraph's details need to be relevant to that spot: Hawaii.

As another way to access your ability to recognize relevant details, supporting examples and evidence questions may ask you to identify what kind of information the passage would lose if a particular example or piece of evidence was deleted.

NOTE: Some questions may ask you to assess the author's use of particular strategies and details. For such questions, you should think about whether those elements improve or harm the passage, and why.

ACT English questions may ask you to select examples and evidence to support a piece of writing that needs to be more convincing. You can get a good idea of how those questions will look by trying the following exercise question. Start by reading the paragraph.

[1] There is an ongoing debate about the use of practical special effects versus computer-generated effects in movies. [2] Practical effects are physical props and models built by expert craftspeople. [3] Computer-generated effects are complex visuals made by digital animators. [4] Supporters of practical effects feel that they bring a sense of realism to a film. [5] Those who prefer computer-generated effects do so because such effects are on the cutting edge of technology, and therefore look more modern and realistic to their eyes. [1]

1. Which of the following sentences, when inserted after Sentence 4, would provide a concrete example of a statement made by the author?
   - **A.** Practical effects might also include masks and costumes that might otherwise be created digitally by a computer effects department.
   - **B.** Practical effects do not require actors and actresses to interact with animated characters and objects that are not really there.
   - **C.** Before computer-generated effects came into use in the 1980s, almost all movie special effects were created by practical means.
   - **D.** Even though most modern audiences seem to prefer computer-generated effects, some filmmakers continue to use practical ones.

The correct answer is B. The new sentence is to be inserted into the paragraph after a sentence about those who support practical special effects. Choice B provides evidence and explanation for this preceding sentence.

Off-Topic and Redundant Details

Building an argument is a bit like making a dish. If you were making a salad, you probably wouldn't toss chocolate chips into it just because chocolate chips are food and you happen to have a bag of them lying around. You would choose only the ingredients that belong in the particular salad you're making: some fresh lettuce, a few ripe tomatoes, maybe a nice sprinkling of dill, etc. You'd probably have a hard time convincing anyone to eat that salad if it were also full of chocolate chips.

Similarly, you would not just toss any old idea into a piece of writing simply because it happened to pop into your head. You would select only the ideas, details, and examples most relevant to your topic.

Remember that paragraph about what a wonderful vacation spot Hawaii is? Do you also remember how a sentence about how wonderful a vacation spot the Swiss Alps are would not belong in that paragraph? That's because details about the Swiss Alps are **off-topic** in a paragraph about Hawaii. If you see such an off-topic detail in a passage on the ACT test, you'll probably be expected to delete it.

> **TIP:** Pay attention to the precise location of details you are going to add to a passage. Just because a detail might be relevant in the passage, it might not be relevant in the particular spot designated in the question.

You'll have to make a similar tough decision if you find **redundant** details. These are details that repeat information already stated in the passage. A writer does not need to keep saying the same thing over and over again. He or she does not need to include the same ideas over and over and...oops. Our apologies. The information in this paragraph is starting to get a bit redundant. Well, think of these redundant details as examples of the kinds you will have to delete on the ACT exam.

Take a look at the following example question to get familiar with ACT questions that require you to delete details.

[1] Thunderstorms, powerful winds, relentless rain, and dangerous ocean waves are all by-products of tropical cyclones. [2] The cyclones themselves are storm systems that rotate with great speed. [3] They spin in circular movements. [4] They usually form over warm bodies of water, and gain their power as surface water evaporates and builds saturated storm clouds. [2]

2. For the sake of unity and coherence, which of the following sentences does NOT belong in the paragraph?

F. Sentence 1
G. Sentence 2
H. Sentence 3
J. Sentence 4

The correct answer is H. Sentence 3 is redundant—the preceding sentence already says that storm systems *rotate with great speed.*

Appropriate Expressions

When a writer is plotting out a piece of writing, he or she has to think about who is going to be reading that piece of writing. If it is going to be an article in a science journal, it probably shouldn't contain expressions like "I was totally *crushing it* in the chemistry lab!" Such journals are aimed at professional people in a particular field who know all the technical jargon and expect the articles they read to be formal and written at an academic level. To those readers, informal language seems unprofessional and indicates that the writer probably isn't taking her or his work very seriously. However, using slang like *crushing it* might be completely appropriate to use in a blog post for a wide audience that doesn't have the patience to decode a lot of technical language.

ALERT: Not every kind of writing demands either formal or informal language. The most important factor is consistency. No matter what kind of writing it is, the entire piece should be written entirely either in formal or informal language and not a haphazard combination of both.

This strategy involves knowing exactly who your audience is and choosing the most appropriate language to reach them. Take a look at the following table to see examples of the kinds of writing in which it's usually appropriate to use informal expressions and the kinds that usually utilize formal expressions.

Formal	Informal
Academic journal	Blog post
Academic paper	Entertainment magazine article
Newspaper article	Fictional story
Scientific studies	Novel
Sociological studies	Personal essay
Textbook	Post on social media site

Passages on the ACT exam won't necessarily announce the kinds of writing they are, but you will be able to tell if they require formal or informal language based on how they are written, the topic being discussed, and the overall tone. Chances are if you're reading a formally written passage that suddenly includes a single slang expression, that slang expression does not belong, and there will be a question requiring you to delete it from the passage … kind of like this example question:

[1] Everybody these days seems obsessed with wasting every waking moment blathering away on social media sites. [2] These are computer-mediated tools for the creation and exchange of information. [3] People seem to think their every thought and item of personal business is so precious that it needs to be announced to the entire world. [4] Personally, I think that people need to consider their own privacy a little more. [3]

3. For the sake of unity and coherence, which of the following sentences does NOT belong in the paragraph?

   A. Sentence 1
   B. Sentence 2
   C. Sentence 3
   D. Sentence 4

The correct answer is B. The tone of Sentence 2 is too formal for the rest of the paragraph, which seems like a personal essay or blog post on social media.

ORGANIZATION, UNITY, AND COHESION

Now that we've discussed the kinds of ideas that belong in a particular piece of writing, we're going to examine the best ways to put those ideas together. Nothing undermines a piece of writing like bad organization—no matter how solid its ideas may be. Imagine building a brick house by sticking those bricks together with chewing gum. Bricks are nice and sturdy, but that chewing gum isn't going to hold them together very well. Good organization is more like using good old cement to adhere those bricks together.

The Production of Language subcategory on the ACT English test evaluates how well you understand the "cement" of a piece of writing. These organizational techniques that cement ideas in a piece of writing include choosing effective opening, transitional, and closing sentences. Just as you would not build a house with the smallest bricks on the bottom, writers also need to make sure their ideas are in the right order, and reorganizing for the sake of clarity and logic is another important organizational skill.

NOTE: Production of Writing questions may ask you the best way to improve paragraphs by moving sentences to the spots where they are most logical.

Strong Opening Sentences

All journeys begin with a single step, and all pieces of writing begin with a single sentence. It's okay to stumble on the first step of that journey, but it is not okay to stumble when composing an opening sentence. The opening sentence sets the tone for all the other sentences that follow. It is also the sentence that most needs to hook the reader's interest. Imagine reading an article with a long, boring, meandering opening sentence. How much will you want to keep reading after that? However, an opening sentence that hooks your interest will make you want to keep reading.

TIP: A strong opening sentence does not just grab the reader's interest. It is also relevant to the topic of the passage as a whole and leads into the second sentence naturally.

Here are a few suggestions for making an opening sentence that really grabs the reader's attention.

- State the topic of the piece briefly and clearly. (Example: *Without question, Shakespeare was the finest playwright who ever lived.*)
- Use exciting words. (Example: *Although William Shakespeare wrote his plays four hundred years ago, they still have the **power** to **thrill** and **dazzle** audiences today.*)
- Ask a question. (Example: *Who is generally considered to be the finest playwright who ever lived?*)
- Use a point-counterpoint structure. (Example: *Most people think William Shakespeare is the finest playwright who ever lived. However…*)

- Use a surprising fact or theory. (Example: *William Shakespeare is generally regarded as the finest playwright who ever lived, but there is a pervasive theory that he didn't actually write some of his most well-known plays.)*
- If appropriate, try using a bit of humor. (Example: *If William Shakespeare is the great playwright everyone seems to think he is, why do I fall asleep every time I have to sit through one of his plays?)*
- Start with a quotation. (Example: *"The remarkable thing about Shakespeare is that he is really very good — in spite of all the people who say he is very good." –poet Robert Graves in "Sayings of the Week,"* The Observer, *1964*).

Now read this paragraph and answer the example question that follows.

The problem began when the state decided to use butterfly ballots. These are paper ballots that require voters to punch out perforated dots known as *chads*. However, a lot of voters had difficulty punching out these chads, leaving the dots hanging out of the ballots. Consequently, the press questioned whether or not Florida had tallied its votes correctly. This was an important issue, since Florida's votes were the deciding factor in who would be the next president of the United States. [4]

4. The writer wishes to open the essay with a sentence that will set its theme and tone. Which of the following would most effectively accomplish this?

A. In 2000, United States voters had to decide who the next president would be, and their choice was either George W. Bush, a Republican, or Al Gore, a Democrat who'd been the Vice President of the United States for the past eight years.

B. Have you ever wondered how different states count the votes of their citizens in a presidential election?

C. The 2000 U.S. presidential election was thrown into turmoil when Florida decided to recount its votes.

D. Supporters of 2000 presidential candidate Al Gore were really hoping a recount in Florida would put him in the White House

The correct answer is C. It is the most ideal introduction and topic sentence for the sentences that follow.

Organizing for Clarity

Now you know what writers need to do to hook their readers, but no piece of writing can rest on its opening sentence alone. Every sentence and paragraph that follows needs to be strong too, and they also need to be well organized. Let's continue our comparison of a piece of writing to a brick house. Imagine you walked into the entry hallway and the first room you entered was…the attic? Doesn't the attic belong at the very *top* of the house? Yes, it does.

Every part of a piece of writing needs to be in a sensible place so that the piece is clear, logical, and completely readable. This is true of both sentences and paragraphs. Basically, the ideas in a piece of writing should not jump out of closets and yell "Surprise!" Writers need to lead up to their ideas with each one linking to the next in a sensible order. Take a look at the following sentences:

1) In the window was the cutest puppy I'd ever seen.

2) I decided she was the right puppy for me, and I've been happy ever since I brought her home.

3) When I woke up this morning, I thought to myself, "I wish I had a dog."

4) So after eating breakfast and getting dressed, I went to the pet shop.

Isn't that an adorable experience? Well, maybe it isn't that adorable in the order it is written. Take a second to see if you can put these sentences in their correct order.

Are you ready for the solution? These sentences belong in the following order: 3, 4, 1, 2. They simply do not make any sense in any other order.

Organization questions on the ACT exam may not be as clear-cut as this rather simplistic example. However, there will always be a *best* way to organize sentences in paragraphs. There will also be a *best* way to organize paragraphs, since some questions may require you to consider the organization of the passage as a whole. Just as the sentences in a paragraph need to be ordered clearly and logically, paragraphs need to follow each other in the same manner.

TIP: Keep an eye out for transitional words when answering organization questions. For example, a word like *however* should signify an idea contrary to the one before, or a word like *also* should signify an idea that builds on the one before it.

The most obvious paragraph organization errors occur when the opening and closing paragraphs are incorrectly placed. The reason this error is obvious is that there are very clear ways to identify these paragraphs: the opening paragraph will include its topic statement, and the closing paragraph will include the concluding statement. If the topic statement or concluding statement suddenly pops up in the middle of a passage and basically yells "Surprise!" you know those paragraphs are not in the correct order. However, when the body paragraphs—the ones in the middle—are out of order, it may be a little tougher to recognize the problem.

The key is to read the paragraphs carefully to make sure that there are no surprise details in them. Each detail needs to be introduced clearly. If the introduction of a detail in one paragraph follows a deeper explanation or description of that detail in a previous paragraph, then those body paragraphs are probably out of order. If you read carefully and yet continue to find a passage confusing, that might also be a clue that the paragraphs are not in the right order. Just as our little example about the adorable puppy had a very definite order, the sentences and paragraphs in a passage will always have a definite order too. They simply won't make sense if they aren't in that order.

See if you can select the best order for the following paragraph by answering this example question.

[1] Anoles all have slender bodies with long, thin tails. [2] There are 165 species of the small lizard known as the anole. [3] However, each species is so similar that scientists often have a tough time distinguishing them. [4] They also all have adhesive pads at the ends of their claws, which help them climb and stick to flat surfaces. [5]

5. Which of the following sentence sequences will make the paragraph most logical?

F. NO CHANGE
G. 3, 4, 2, 1
H. 2, 3, 1, 4
J. 2, 4, 1, 2

The correct answer is H. It is the only order that makes sense. Starting the paragraph introducing the topic, the anole, with information about the number of species, and then following with a sentence with contradictory information, and then adding details about the lizard's appearance with the third and fourth sentences presents the topic in a clear and logical order.

Transitional Words and Phrases

As we've learned, an important factor in strong organization is how ideas connect to each other. Transitional words and phrases are the fasteners that link ideas. Without transitional words and phrases, you could end up with something like this:

> *I met Rahul in front of the movie theater. We were supposed to see* Avengers: Age of Ultron. *We decided to see* Ant-Man *instead. We made the right decision. It was great.*

Who went to see this movie, a robot? There has to be a less choppy way to express these thoughts. Adding a few transitional words and phrases should do the trick.

> *I met Rahul in front of the movie theater* ***since*** *we were supposed to see* Avengers: Age of Ultron. ***However****, we decided to see* Ant-Man *instead.* ***Ultimately****, we made the right decision* ***because*** *it was great.*

Different transitional words and phrases perform different functions. Take a look at the following table:

Function	Transitional Words and Phrases
introduction	to begin, first of all, to start with
an addition	additionally, also, furthermore, in addition, moreover, secondly
clarification	in other words, that is to say, to put it another way
the passage of time	afterwards, later, meanwhile, next, subsequently
examples	for example, for instance, to demonstrate, specifically, to illustrate
cause	because, since
effect	as a result, consequently, therefore
comparison	comparatively, in comparison, in similar fashion, likewise, similarly
contrast	at the same time, however, in contrast, nevertheless, notwithstanding, on the contrary, yet
conclusion	in conclusion, in short, to conclude, to sum up, to summarize, ultimately

Sometimes writers use entire sentences to transition between ideas. The transitional sentence in the following example is underlined.

> *People currently understand that the earth is spherical. <u>However, this was not always the case.</u> The common belief used to be that the world was flat.*

Although this sentence makes complete sense without the transitional sentence, that transitional sentence helps connect the contrasting ideas *(people now know the earth is spherical; people once thought the earth was flat)* in a way that holds the reader's interest.

[1] There is an attitude in our culture that certain art forms qualify as "high art" and others qualify as "low art." [2] European films are often distinguished as "high art" for the most sophisticated and intellectual people, while comic books are "low art" aimed at children and people with average or below-average educations. 6 [3] Many European films are as silly and insubstantial as the worst American movies, while there have been comic books with incredibly rich characterizations and plot developments.

6. Which of the following sentences would provide the most effective transition between the second and third sentences of the paragraph?

   A. Subsequently, there has been a great explosion in the number of comic books on the market.
   B. In contrast, fine literature is considered to be a "high art" and is taught in classes around the world.
   C. For example, people who did not attend a college might be thought of as uneducated.
   D. However, a closer look at this stereotype reveals that it is both patronizing and untrue.

The correct answer is D. It transitions from one point of view (thoughts on how all European films are "high art" and comic books are "low art") to another (thoughts on how many European films are silly and many comic books are complex).

Strong Endings

So we've covered the best ways to get a piece of writing started and moving through its details and ideas. All that's left is to wrap it up. That's where the closing sentence comes in. It's the cap on a piece of writing, and it should leave the reader feeling satisfied.

A closing sentence doesn't have to be too fancy. At this point, the writer has already introduced and discussed all necessary topics and supporting details. There shouldn't be anything new that requires further explanation in the closing sentence. Here are some different qualities of a strong closing sentence:

- It is short and clear.
- It repeats key words or phrases from the first paragraph to provide satisfying continuity.
- It uses compound structure for the sake of clarity and balance after what may have been a complicated collection of details.
- It redefines an important idea or detail in the passage.
- It captures an accepted attitude regarding the topic.

TIP: Beginning a concluding sentence with "In conclusion" is technically appropriate, but it is not a very interesting way to signal the conclusion of a piece of writing.

To close this section on organization questions, try another practice paragraph-question pair.

When construction of the Empire State Building concluded and Governor Al Smith declared it open on May 1, 1931, New York City had become the home to the tallest building in the world. In subsequent years, more than 20 taller buildings would be constructed across the globe, stripping the Empire State Building of its tallest building status. [7]

7. The writer wishes to improve the conclusion of this paragraph. Which of the following would most effectively accomplish this if placed after the final sentence?

   F. One such building is the Burj Khalifa in Dubai, which stands 2,717 feet tall.

   G. The Empire State Building began construction on March 17, 1930, two months after the excavation crew broke the ground of its site.

   H. The Empire State Building has been an iconic location in such films as *King Kong, An Affair to Remember,* and *Sleepless in Seattle*.

   J. However, for the impact the building has made on our culture and its sheer iconic design, it will forever be one of the most recognizable and celebrated skyscrapers in the world.

The correct answer is J. It ties up all the information in the paragraph and leaves a lasting impression.

KNOWLEDGE OF LANGUAGE AND STYLE

Style: everyone wants to have some, and pieces of writing are no different. Style does not necessarily mean making everything tidy and neat or putting everything in its proper place. That is organization. Style means achieving something with a bit of flair; it means eliminating the elements that do not work and taking advantage of the ones that really add some interest...maybe even a little excitement. Style also requires knowing exactly who the audience is and the best way to reach that audience. Style involves tailoring the images, words, tone, and mood of a piece of writing to that audience's particular specifications.

Elements such as ambiguous pronoun references, wordiness, and redundancy are likely to distract any audience and need to be cleaned up or cut out. Knowledge of Language category questions test you on how well you recognize effective language use. How well does the language presented adhere to a cohesive tone and style?

Tone and Mood

When you read a piece of writing, you should be able to tell what the writer feels about the topic. Does she or he seem against it or in favor of it? A good piece of writing should also make you feel something. Does it make you happy or sad, angry or soothed?

A piece of writing with style should be written with feeling *and* stir feelings. If it does, then the writer has mastered the tone and mood of the piece.

- **Tone** is the author's attitude toward the subject she or he is discussing.
- **Mood** is the author's way of making the reader feel certain emotions.

> **TIP:** Contractions can help create an informal tone.

Sometimes it is very easy to recognize the tone of a piece. If a writer declares, "I think soft cheeses are disgusting!" it doesn't take a genius to figure out that he is not a fan of soft cheeses. A lot of writers opt for greater subtlety than this.

For some reason, many people have developed a taste for soft cheese.

This writer does not do anything as blunt as declaring soft cheeses "disgusting," but she still makes her opinion known by using the subtle phrase *For some reason*. This phrase indicates that she does not understand the reason many people have developed a taste for soft cheeses, which indicates that she is not one of those soft-cheese-loving people. With that phrase, she makes the tone of her argument clear.

Despite the writer's intentions, different people may react to a piece of writing differently. One person may find an article to be inspirational, while another might think it is utterly boring. Nevertheless, a writer will still put forth his or her best effort to make you feel a particular emotion by manipulating the mood of a piece. Carefully chosen words help establish a particular atmosphere. Let's think of something as mundane as a dog. What if a writer described that dog like this:

NOTE: Rhetorical skills questions may ask you to identify the audience for a particular piece of writing. To answer such questions, you should think about its tone and mood.

The mutt's mile-long tongue dripped drool puddles the size of the Atlantic Ocean.

Have you stopped rolling all over the floor in a fit of laughter yet? Okay, maybe it wasn't that funny, but you can probably tell that the writer was going for a humorous mood by focusing on a sillier aspect of the dog (its drooling) and using absurdly exaggerated descriptions (the dog's tongue was a mile long; the puddles of drool were the size of the Atlantic Ocean).

Another writer may see the same dog and decide to describe it like this:

The snarling mongrel dripped rank saliva from its powerful, snapping jaws.

Well, there's a dog we hope we never have to meet. Although the dog is basically doing the same thing it was in the previous example (drooling), the writer has completely altered the humorous mood by using unpleasant words like *snarling* and *rank* and focusing on the powerful snapping of the dog's *jaws*. Even the decision to refer to the dog as a *mongrel* instead of the somewhat more comical (and slightly affectionate) *mutt* contributes to the threatening mood of this second example.

Writers often signal the tone or mood of their work by using certain key words. The following table provides a small sampling of words they use to indicate negative and positive tones and moods.

Positive Words	Negative Words
adorable	abhorrent
celebratory	annoying
cheerful	angering
comforting	belligerent
comic	bitter
compassionate	boring
confident	cold
delightful	condescending
ebullient	contemptuous
fascinating	derogatory
friendly	despairing
funny	desperate
hilarious	disrespectful
hopeful	dull
joyful	embarrassing
laudatory	frustrating
lively	harsh
passionate	hopeless
playful	lethargic
respectful	melancholy
reverent	miserable
romantic	pathetic
sympathetic	pretentious
whimsical	solemn
	upsetting

One of your many jobs on the ACT English test is to ensure that the tone or mood of a passage is consistent. If a writer seems like he is in favor of a particular topic, and then suddenly seems to take a negative stance without rhyme or reason, this is an error in style and you have to correct it. If a writer seems to be establishing a jolly mood, then suddenly starts dropping in negative words—possibly because she doesn't really understand what they mean—you're going to have to correct that too. Get started by reading this example passage and deciding what to do with its underlined portion in the question that follows:

NOTE: While many types of rhetorical skills questions refer to entire sentences or paragraphs, some use the same underlined portion format of usage/mechanics questions.

When my mother told me she wanted to move in with my wife and me, I was knocked two ways from Sunday. You see: my wife and I had established a quiet little existence in our small suburban house. We were perfectly happy gardening, reading, and doing other activities that would probably bore most normal people to tears. The idea of my <u>tornado of a mom</u> (8) living with us would basically take that happy existence and stomp all over its head.

8. **A.** NO CHANGE
B. dear mother
C. maternal caregiver
D. most beloved family member

The correct answer is A. The underlined portion is ideal as is. *Tornado of a mom* is an interesting and descriptive phrase that precisely describes the image and feel the author wants to convey.

Precise and Appropriate Images and Words

Gigi asked, "Steve, can you please put my stuff in the thing?"

Huh? What exactly is Gigi asking Steve to do? What stuff? What thing? Gigi needs to choose her words more precisely!

Gigi asked, "Steve, can you please put my luggage in the overhead compartment?"

Oh, they're on an airplane! See how much clearer an image we get when reading precise words?

Precise words and images make writing come alive. They help the reader to know exactly what is being discussed and give the reader a clear picture of how things look, sound, feel, and smell.

The moon came up.

So what? The moon comes up all the time. Why should we care that it came up again?

The full moon arose and emitted a glow that bathed the landscape in a soft, enchanting glow.

Wow! That is an image that would get us up off the sofa and go outside to see it for ourselves. So do you see how precise images can make writing really sparkle?

On the ACT exam, you will examine passages to determine whether more precise words and images will make them clearer and more stylish. If a writer lapses into describing specific items as *stuff* and *things*, it's your job as editor to clarify what that writer is trying to say. You will determine the most appropriate words and images by reading the passage carefully and completely.

TIP: You will also consider tone and mood when answering questions about precise and appropriate words and images, since the most appropriate ones should suit the overall mood and tone of the passage.

Try this next example question:

No other artist did more to propel surrealism into the mainstream than Salvador Dali. Dali's bizarre images of melting clocks crawling with ants and elephants with legs as long and thin as stilts can be seen on wall posters, T-shirts, coffee mugs, and calendars throughout the world. Perhaps this is because people respond to the playfulness of his images or the way they resemble the odd dreams that someone experiences (9) while sleeping.

9. **F.** NO CHANGE
   G. all the strangest people experience
   H. even the most straight-laced person experiences
   J. a few students experience

The correct answer is H. *Someone* is not a precise enough word. You'll want to look for the most specific and appropriate replacement for words that don't convey any information about a person or thing.

Ambiguous Pronoun References

As we've just seen, using imprecise words and images can really confound readers. Another baffling mistake is the ambiguous pronoun reference.

I spent the morning searching for my keys and my wallet, but I found only it.

Once again, we are going to need some clarification. Specifically, what is *it*? There are two possible antecedents in this sentence: *keys* and *wallet*. The pronoun *it* can refer to only one of them. As this sentence is written, the pronoun reference is ambiguous. The best way to clarify this ambiguity is to get rid of the pronoun completely:

I spent the morning searching for my keys, which I found, and my wallet, which I didn't. (**Correct!**)

I spent the morning searching for my keys and my wallet, but I found only my wallet. (**Also correct!**)

Multiple pronouns can make the ambiguous pronoun situation even more confusing:

Solveig and Jelynne were supposed to meet me at 3:00 p.m., but she was stuck in traffic, and she overslept.

Who was stuck in traffic and who overslept? We can't tell from this sentence.

Solveig and Jelynne were supposed to meet me at 3:00 p.m., but Jelynne was stuck in traffic, and Solveig overslept. (**Correct!**)

Now we know who might need a wake-up call next time.

ALERT: Using the passive voice weakens style. Passive voice is when the action is being done by the subject *(The book was read by me.)* instead of having the subject do the action *(I read the book)*.

Ambiguous pronoun references also occur when there is no antecedent at all.

I called her, but she wasn't home.

Called who? There are two pronouns in this sentence and no antecedent. We need a specific idea of who is being called for this sentence to be clear.

I called my sister, but she wasn't home. (**Correct!**)

So once again, precise words save the day. Now it's your chance to put on the superhero cape and tights and save the day by fixing an example that desperately needs your help:

The plot of this novel is riveting, but <u>their</u> (10) prose style was not very involving.

10. **A.** NO CHANGE
B. the pages'
C. the author's
D. the plot's

The correct answer is C. The prose style of a novel belongs to its author.

A Word on Wordiness

This is the final lesson section of this rhetorical skills chapter of this book, which is a kind of publication, and it discusses an error called wordiness.

In case you didn't notice, the above sentence is an example of that error!

Wordiness occurs when writers get a little overenthusiastic about words. They use more words than necessary. Maybe that's a good strategy if you're a professional writer who gets paid by the word, but you probably won't get a lot of jobs if all your work suffers from wordiness. The simplest way is often the best way. So let's see what we can do to simplify that mess of a sentence that began this lesson. Unfortunately, that means we're going to have to read it again. Here it is:

> *This is the final lesson section of this rhetorical skills chapter of this book, which is a kind of publication, and it discusses an error called wordiness.*

Let's examine the various problems with the sentence.

- You could probably already tell that the lessons in this book are divided into sections. Eliminate the word *section*.
- The second instance of the pronoun *this* is unnecessary. It implies that there is more than one rhetorical skills chapter in this book. Don't worry, there is only one rhetorical skills chapter, and it's almost finished. Eliminate *this*.
- We trust that you already know what a book is. There is no reason to define it as *a kind of publication*.
- In fact, you already know the rhetorical skills chapter is in this particular book, so let's eliminate the mention of this *book* altogether. Eliminating that also eliminates the pronoun *it* that refers to the antecedent *book*.
- The words *lesson* and *rhetorical skills* can be consolidated. This is a rhetorical skills lesson, after all. That eliminates the need for *chapter*.

By making those eliminations, you can construct a clearer and more concise sentence like this:

> *This final rhetorical skills lesson discusses an error called wordiness.*

It's time to answer another example question.

There are 120 species of pine trees in the Northern Hemisphere, <u>but only one species, the Sumatran pine, can</u> [11] be found below the equator.

11. F. NO CHANGE
G. but only the Sumatran pine can
H. but only one species, a species called the Sumatran pine, can
J. but only one can

The correct answer is G. Deleting one species, which is not needed, is the most clear and concise way to revise the sentence.

ALERT: Some incorrect answer choices in wordiness questions may delete necessary words as well as unnecessary ones. The correct answers will address the wordiness without depriving the original sentence of its details and meaning.

SUMMING IT UP

- **Supporting examples** and **evidence** support the topic of a passage, but **off-topic** and **redundant details** need to be deleted. Off-topic details are distracting because they introduce ideas that have little or nothing to do with the topic being discussed. Redundant details repeat information needlessly.
- **Appropriate expressions** suit the formal or informal style of a particular piece of writing. Expressions too informal for a formal piece of writing need to be revised. Expressions too formal for an informal piece of writing also need to be revised.
- **Strong opening sentences** hook the reader's interest and set the tone for the rest of the passage.
- **Organizing for clarity** involves placing sentences and paragraphs in the clearest and most logical order. Ideas should flow into each other naturally.
- **Transitional words and phrases** improve the connection of ideas between sentences and paragraphs.
- **Strong closing sentences** bring passages to satisfying conclusions with clarity, impact, and relevance to the overall passage.
- **Tone** is the author's attitude toward the subject she or he is discussing, which is apparent from the words the author chooses. Tone needs to be consistent throughout a piece of writing.
- **Mood** is the author's way of making the reader feel certain emotions, which the author achieves by the use of either positive or negative descriptive words. Mood needs to be consistent throughout a piece of writing.
- **Precise and appropriate images and words** need to be used in place of vague language. Vague language can render ideas and details unclear and uninteresting.
- **Ambiguous pronoun references** occur when a pronoun's antecedent is unclear or missing. A noun needs to be used in place of the ambiguous pronoun.
- **Wordiness** occurs when writers use more words than is necessary, and it renders writing cluttered and unclear. Correcting wordiness involves picking out all of the unnecessary words without deleting any essential details and reconstructing the sentence.

ONLINE PREP

Want to Know More?

Access more practice questions, lessons, helpful hints, and strategies for the following Rhetorical Skills topics in *Peterson's Online Course for the ACT® Exam*:

- Strategy
- Style
- Organization
- Using Modifiers

To purchase and access the course, go to **www.petersons.com/testprep/act**.

COLLEGE READINESS BENCHMARK LEARNING PATH PRACTICE

Need more in-depth practice? Go to **www.petersons.com/testprep/act** to take the College Readiness Benchmark Learning Path full-length English practice test. To access this test, select the *Peterson's ACT® Prep Guide Online Companion* and enter the coupon code **ACT2019** at checkout.

PRACTICE

Now it's time to take your second English practice quiz. Read each passage very carefully before answering each question. When you're finished answering all 20 questions, check the answers and explanations that follow to figure out how well you did and why you may have selected some incorrect answer choices.

Feathered Dinosaurs

[1]

[1] [1] The image of the dinosaur changed in 1995 when a surprising discovery was made in Liaoning, China. [2] Paleontologists found dinosaur fossils with well-preserved feathers. [2] [3] The iconic lizard-like appearance of the dinosaur had morphed into a more bird-like creature. [4] Some of the common birds include sparrows, pigeons, and seagulls. [3]

1. The writer wishes to open Paragraph 1 with a sentence that will set the theme and tone of the passage. Which of the following would most effectively accomplish this?

A. Most people think of dinosaurs as big scary monsters covered in scales a lot like the ones you can see on an alligator in your local zoo!
B. For a century and half, the most common concept of the dinosaur was a giant creature with scales not unlike those of an alligator or iguana.
C. The common image of dinosaurs as large beasts covered in scales was completely changed when scientists realized several dinosaurs actually have feathers.
D. Dinosaurs in movies always seem to be covered in lizard-like scales, but you'll never see another dinosaur like that after the discovery scientists made in 1995.

2. The writer wishes to improve the transition between Sentences 2 and 3 in Paragraph 1. Which of the following would most effectively accomplish this if placed at the beginning of Sentence 3?

F. Consequently,
G. In conclusion,
H. Suddenly,
J. In similar fashion,

3. For the sake of unity and coherence, which of the following sentences does NOT belong in Paragraph 1?

A. Sentence 1
B. Sentence 2
C. Sentence 3
D. Sentence 4

[2]

[1] One dissimilarity Huxley noted was that the *Archaeopteryx* had feathers while the *Compsognathus* did not. [2] However, Huxley may have been wrong on that matter. [3] Actually, scientists had been drawing connections between birds and dinosaurs since the mid-nineteenth century when biologist Thomas Henry Huxley suggested that birds had evolved from dinosaurs. [4] <u>He based his thing</u> (4) on the skeletal similarities between the dinosaur *Campsognathus* and *Archaeopteryx*, the creature generally regarded as the first bird. [5]

4. **F.** NO CHANGE
   G. He based his idea
   H. He based his theory
   J. He made his thing

5. Which of the following sentence sequences will make Paragraph 2 most logical?
   A. NO CHANGE
   B. 3, 4, 1, 2
   C. 2, 1, 4, 3
   D. 1, 2, 4, 3

[3]

The Liaoning discovery of 1995 led to a deeper exploration of the possibility that several dinosaur species had feathers, and *Compsognathus* is believed to be one such dinosaur. Others include the more iconic *Velociraptor* and the mighty *Tyrannosaurus rex*. You heard me right: the *Velociraptor* and the *Tyrannosaurus* had feathers! [6] Considered two of the most threatening dinosaurs, <u>these fearsome beasts took on a somewhat comic appearance when artists began creating conceptual renderings of them with the feathers scientists believe they sported.</u> (7) However, feathered dinosaurs still did not dominate pre-history. In fact, recent studies indicate that the original concept of the creatures was the most common: most dinosaurs were covered in scales, not feathers. The current theory is that feathers evolved throughout dinosaur history, and though there was the odd

6. For the sake of unity and coherence, what should the writer do with the preceding sentence?
   F. move it to the beginning of the paragraph
   G. move it to the end of the paragraph
   H. delete it entirely
   J. divide it into two sentences at the colon

7. **A.** NO CHANGE
   B. these fearsome beasts took on a somewhat comic appearance when artists began creating conceptual renderings of them with all the feathers professional scientists believe they sported all over their bodies.
   C. these fearsome beasts took on a somewhat comic appearance when artists began creating conceptual renderings of them, which are drawings and other kinds of pictures that artists make, with the feathers scientists believe they sported.
   D. these beasts took on a somewhat comic appearance when artists began creating them with feathers.

early dinosaur with feathers, feathers did not become more common until closer to the end of the dinosaur age. [8]

[4]

Still, there is much to learn about which dinosaurs were feathered and when feathers evolved to the point that they were most common. Scientists believe dinosaurs grew feathers because they (9) provided warmth and attracted mates. So feathers may also have much to teach about basic dinosaur biology. Regardless of which dinosaurs had feathers, when those feathers evolved, and the functions those feathers performed, there is no question that feathered velociraptors and tyrannosauruses have transformed our concept of these fascinating, extinct creatures completely.

8. Which of the following parenthetical statements, when inserted in the preceding sentence, would provide a concrete example of a statement made by the author?
   - **F.** (dinosaurs lived between 230 million years ago and 65 million years ago)
   - **G.** (the Cretaceous period was the final one to see the existence of dinosaurs)
   - **H.** (among the last dinosaurs to walk the earth were the iguanodon, the centrosaurus, the triceratops, and the troodon)
   - **J.** (2014 saw the discovery of the feathered *Kulindadromeus*, a 150 million-year-old herbivore)

9.
   - **A.** NO CHANGE
   - **B.** that
   - **C.** dinosaurs
   - **D.** those feathers

Question 10 asks about the passage as a whole.

10. Is the writer's decision not to use contractions appropriate in the passage?
   - **F.** No, because it makes the passage inaccessible to a general audience.
   - **G.** No, because it creates an informal tone that is inappropriate for the subject.
   - **H.** Yes, because it creates a formal tone that is appropriate for the nature of the subject.
   - **J.** Yes, because it helps to focus the essay on the feathered dinosaurs.

Goodbye, Car!

[1]

[1]You do not realize how much of a car-culture exists in the suburbs until you move to an urban environment. [2] I lived in the suburbs of Long Island for most of my life. [3] I was born on this little island by (11) Manhattan, and continued to live there when I got my driver's license as a teenager. [4] Like many a suburban dweller, I was hooked on my car. [5] That changed drastically after I moved to the city. [6] That's when I went from being a suburban dweller to a city boy. [12]

11.
   - **A.** NO CHANGE
   - **B.** a stone's throw from
   - **C.** around
   - **D.** somewhere near

12. For the sake of unity and coherence, which of the following sentences does NOT belong in the paragraph?
   - **F.** Sentence 1
   - **G.** Sentence 4
   - **H.** Sentence 5
   - **J.** Sentence 6

[2]

Long Island was not without public transportation for getting around on [13]. It had buses and the famous Long Island railroad. However, without any subway system; plenty of garages, driveways, free parking lots, and street parking spots; and a gas station on every corner, Long Islanders were much more likely to own and drive their own cars [14] than take advantage of the buses and trains. I was no different, and the way I used my car now makes me cringe. If I had to pop a letter in the mailbox a block away, I'd literally get into my car and drive it. [15] It was as if I didn't have a pair of functioning legs!

[3]

[1] When I moved to New York City's borough of Brooklyn at the age of 25, I arrived in my car. [2] Yet I discovered a very different environment from that of Long Island. [3] Instead of bucolic streets lined with houses, there were bustling blocks of apartment buildings. [16] [4] Parking was hard to come by, and street-sweeping laws meant I had to find a new parking spot almost every day even if I'd found the perfect parking spot and didn't need to use my car again for a while. [5] Those laws meant I could get a parking ticket for leaving my car on the wrong side of the street, and I received my share of tickets during my first year in Brooklyn. [17] [6] Furthermore, the abundance of public transportation meant I usually didn't have to use my car anyway. [7] I took the subway to work in Manhattan, and the cost of subway fare was much less than the price of gas. [8] Plus, the less often I drove my car, the less often I needed to get it repaired at an expensive auto shop.

[4]

[1] Since then I have never considered getting another car. [2] Ultimately, I decided my car was more trouble than it was worth and gave it up completely. [3] Aside from the amount of

13.
- **A.** NO CHANGE
- **B.** without public transportation
- **C.** without public transportation for getting around Long Island
- **D.** without transportation

14.
- **F.** NO CHANGE
- **G.** much more likely to own their own cars
- **H.** much more likely to own cars
- **J.** much more likely to own and drive their cars

15.
- **A.** NO CHANGE
- **B.** that
- **C.** that one block
- **D.** my car

16. For the sake of unity and coherence, Sentence 3 in Paragraph 3 should be:
- **F.** where it is now.
- **G.** placed at the end of Paragraph 3.
- **H.** placed at the beginning of Paragraph 4.
- **J.** deleted altogether.

17. The writer is considering eliminating Sentence 5 in Paragraph 3. If the writer removed this sentence, the essay would primarily lose:
- **A.** an example of how laws are created to hurt people, not help them.
- **B.** the main point of the author's argument against car ownership.
- **C.** evidence to support the idea that street sweeping laws can cause problems for car owners.
- **D.** an explanation of what made him finally decide to give up his car and never get another one.

money I save [let's not forget about the costs of car insurance or annual inspections, either!], there is also the safety and environmental benefits of using public transportation exclusively. [4] One is much less likely to get injured or worse in a bus or subway than a car. [5] Buses that carry many people cause less air pollution than all the private cars needed to transport those individuals would. [18] [19]

18. The writer wishes to improve the organization of Paragraph 4. Which of the following would most improve the paragraph?

- **F.** Moving the second sentence to the end of the paragraph
- **G.** Moving the second sentence in front of the first sentence
- **H.** Introducing a new sentence about how cars are more dangerous than buses
- **J.** Deleting the second sentence altogether

19. The writer wishes to improve the conclusion of this paragraph. Which of the following would most effectively accomplish this if placed after the final sentence?

- **A.** I am not trying to convince anyone else to travel the same route that I did, but I can attest that my life has improved in several ways since I decided to say "goodbye" to my car!
- **B.** As Booth Tarkington wrote in the novel *The Magnificent Ambersons*, "I'm not sure he's wrong about automobiles…With all their speed forward they may be a step backward in civilization – that is, in spiritual civilization."
- **C.** I have also begun taking taxicabs more often, though they can actually be very expensive if I'm going a long distance.
- **D.** But since buses do create some pollution, the very best to get around is to use your feet and walk everywhere.

Question 20 asks about the passage as a whole.

20. Which of the following assignments would this essay most clearly fulfill?

- **F.** Write a persuasive essay for a general audience about the pros and cons of car ownership.
- **G.** Write a persuasive essay for an audience of children about road safety.
- **H.** Write a persuasive essay for an audience of automotive manufacturers about the changing attitudes about car ownership.
- **J.** Write a persuasive essay for a general audience about something you decided to give up.

1. **The correct answer is B.** This question tests your ability to select the very best opening sentence for the passage. Since the mood of the passage is formal, and referring to dinosaurs as *big scary monsters* is pretty informal, choice A is not the best opening sentence and you can eliminate it. Choice C reveals too much since the paragraph builds to the discovery that some dinosaurs had feathers. Choice D is not the most relevant opening sentence since it dwells on the way dinosaurs look in movies, and this is not something the rest of the passage discusses. Only choice B is a completely relevant opening sentence that suits the tone of the rest of the passage.

2. **The correct answer is H.** This question expects you to choose the best transitional phrase or word. For such questions, it is important to think about what each sentence is doing. Sentence 2 describes a discovery. Sentence 3 describes how that discovery changed long-held perceptions. That change was pretty sudden, so *suddenly* is the best transitional word, and choice H is correct. Choice F would be correct only if there were a cause-and-effect relationship between the sentences. Choice G indicates the drawing of a conclusion when the passage has barely begun. Choice J indicates a comparison, and the author does not compare ideas between Sentences 2 and 3 in Paragraph 1.

3. **The correct answer is D.** This question asks you to eliminate an off-topic sentence from Paragraph 1, which is about how paleontologists discovered that some dinosaurs have feathers. Although birds are related to feathered dinosaurs, they are not the main topic of the paragraph, and a list of types of birds does not belong in it. That means choice D is the best answer. The sentences indicated in choices A, B, and C are all relevant to the topic of the discovery of feathered dinosaurs.

4. **The correct answer is H.** As written, the sentence lacks precise wording. The word *thing* is much too vague, which means choices F and J are incorrect. Choice G is more precise, but it is not the best choice since scientists do not devise scientific *ideas*; they devise scientific *theories*. Choice H is the most precise answer.

5. **The correct answer is B.** This question tests your ability to organize sentences in their most logical order. As Paragraph 2 is originally written, Thomas Henry Huxley's conclusions are discussed before he has been introduced. A good signal that the paragraph is disorganized is the fact that Huxley's full name does not appear until the third sentence. You can also conclude that the first two sentences of the paragraph belong after Sentence 4 since those first two sentences discuss the dinosaur *Compsognathus* and the bird *Archaeopteryx*, which are introduced in Sentence 4. Therefore, choice B describes the best sequence of sentences for the paragraph. Choices A, C, and D do not organize the paragraph effectively.

6. **The correct answer is H.** This question expects you to deal with an inappropriate expression. This is a formal scientific passage, and the expression *you heard me right* is very informal. It also shifts the third-person point of view of the overall passage to the second person. Deleting it altogether is the best approach, so choice H is correct. Neither moving the sentence (choices F and G) nor dividing it into two sentences (choice J) makes it any more appropriate.

7. **The correct answer is A.** This sentence is correct as written, so choice A is the best answer. Choices B and C take a perfectly fine sentence and make it wordy. Choice B wastes space by distinguishing that the scientists are *professional* and that the feathers were *all over the bodies of the dinosaurs*. The reader can probably assume that the scientists in question were professional and the feathers were on the dinosaurs' bodies. Choice C wastes space by overexplaining conceptual renderings when the reader can probably figure out what conceptual renderings are from the information in the sentence. Choice D makes the opposite error by deleting necessary details, making it seem as though feathered dinosaurs were fictional monsters created by artists.

8. **The correct answer is J.** The sentence in Paragraph 3 mentions that some early dinosaurs had feathers, and choice J provides an example of one such early, feathered dinosaur. Choice F goes off topic by explaining when dinosaurs lived. Choice G mentions the final dinosaur period, not an early one. Choice H lists an assortment of dinosaurs that lived at the end of the dinosaur era, and we do not even know whether or not they had feathers.

9. **The correct answer is D.** Choice A is incorrect because there is an ambiguous pronoun reference in the sentence as it is originally written. Does *they* refer to

feathers or *dinosaurs*? Since it does not make much sense that dinosaurs provided warmth to dinosaurs (were the dinosaurs snuggling with each other?), you can conclude that the best substitute for *they* is *those feathers* (choice D) and not *dinosaurs* (choice C). Choice B just substitutes one ambiguous pronoun for another, and it also introduces a pronoun-antecedent agreement error since *dinosaurs* and *feathers* are both plural, and *that* is a singular pronoun.

10. **The correct answer is H.** The tone of this passage is fairly formal, and since contractions contribute to an informal tone, choice H is the best answer, and choice G can be eliminated. Formal writing does not have to be inaccessible to a general audience, and a general audience will probably grasp this passage with or without contractions, so choice F is not the best answer. Contractions do not create focus, so choice J does not make sense.

11. **The correct answer is B.** As the sentence is originally written, it lacks precise wording. *By* is too vague a word to clearly indicate the relative positions of Manhattan and Long Island, so choice A is not the best answer. Choices C and D are equally vague and can be eliminated. Choice B uses a descriptive idiom to indicate that Long Island is very close to Manhattan. It is the best answer choice.

12. **The correct answer is J.** In Sentence 4, the author explains that he was once a suburban dweller. In Sentence 5, he explains that he moved to the city. He does not need to immediately repeat that information in Sentence 6. It is redundant, which means choice J is the best answer. Choices F, G, and H would all deprive the paragraph of essential details.

13. **The correct answer is B.** As originally written, the sentence is too wordy. The reader should already know the purpose of public transportation, so the additional phrase for *getting around on* is unnecessary and awkward. Therefore, choice A is incorrect. Choice C introduces redundant information to an already wordy sentence by mentioning Long Island a second time. Choice D removes an important detail. Without the word *public* we do not know if the writer is discussing public transportation like buses and trains, or private transportation like a car. Only choice B corrects the wordiness of the original sentence without deleting important information.

14. **The correct answer is H.** As it is originally written, the sentence contains redundant information, so choice F is not the correct answer. The ownership of cars is mentioned twice (Long Islanders were much more likely to *own* and drive their *own* cars). Also, the reader can assume that these car owners also drive their cars, so that detail can be deleted. Only choice H corrects this redundant and wordy sentence. Choice G fails to correct the redundancy. Choice J fails to correct the wordiness.

15. **The correct answer is C.** Choice A is incorrect because there is an ambiguous pronoun reference in the sentence as it is originally written. Is the writer driving the car or the block? We do not know, because he uses the ambiguous pronoun *it*. Choice B is just another ambiguous pronoun, so you can eliminate it. Replacing *it* with the best concrete noun clears up the ambiguity, so you have to decide if the writer intended the pronoun to refer to the car or the block. Try replacing *it* with choices C and D to get a better idea of the best answer. Choice D makes it unclear where or why the writer was driving his car. Choice C makes it clear that he was driving that one block to mail a letter. Choice C is the best answer choice.

16. **The correct answer is J.** Think about what the sentence contributes to the topic of owning a car in the city. Does it contribute anything by explaining how homes in the city were different from the ones in the suburbs? This passage is not about general differences between suburban and urban life; it is very specifically about owning a car in those environments. The sentence does not belong in this passage, and should be deleted as per the instructions in choice J. Leaving it where it is (choice F) or moving it elsewhere in the passage (choices G and H) does not make the sentence any less off topic.

17. **The correct answer is C.** This sentence describes how street sweeping laws often caused the writer to receive parking tickets. Without Sentence 5, the essay would lose supporting evidence. Therefore, choice C is the best answer. While the writer probably didn't enjoy getting those tickets, choice A is an extreme conclusion to draw. The sentence describes only one of many reasons the writer decided to give up his car; it is not significant enough to conclude that choices B or D are correct.

18. **The correct answer is G.** The second sentence of Paragraph 4 finds the writer deciding to give up his car once and for all. The rest of the paragraph deals with the consequences of that decision. Therefore, it belongs at the beginning of the paragraph (choice G). Moving the sentence even further from the beginning of the paragraph, as choice F suggests, would make the paragraph even less organized. Since the sentence can function as a strong introduction to the paragraph, deleting it (choice J) is not the best approach. Introducing an extra sentence describing information that already appears later in the passage does not make much sense either, so choice H is wrong.

19. **The correct answer is A.** This question asks you to choose the best closing sentence for a passage that lacks one. Choice A sums up the writer's attitude about car ownership while also tying in the title of the passage, so it is a very effective closing sentence. Good closing sentences often contain quotes, but the one in choice B doesn't suit this passage's friendly, informal tone, and its spiritual element has nothing to do with the rest of the passage. Choice C suddenly introduces a new detail about taxicabs, which is something not discussed elsewhere in the passage, so this answer choice fails to wrap up the discussion well. Choice D contradicts the writer's argument in favor of public transportation and would be a very odd way to close the passage.

20. **The correct answer is J.** Think about what the writer is explaining and the words he uses to explain that. Is this passage particularly technical? It isn't, so it is unlikely he wrote it for an audience of automotive manufacturers (choice H). However, the passage is not particularly simplistic. The complex sentence structure and relatively advanced vocabulary the writer uses suggests he did not write his essay for children. Furthermore, road safety is a very minor discussion point in this passage, so choice G is not the best answer. While the writer's approachable language indicates that he wrote his essay for a general adult audience, he does not describe the pros and cons of car ownership; he discusses only the cons. Therefore, choice F cannot be correct. That leaves choice J as the best answer.

PART IV: MATHEMATICS STRATEGIES FOR THE ACT® EXAM

Chapter 6: Pre-Algebra and Elementary Algebra

Chapter 7: Intermediate Algebra and Coordinate Geometry

Chapter 8: Plane Geometry and Trigonometry

MATHEMATICS STRATEGIES FOR THE ACT® EXAM

The ACT Mathematics test covers the main concepts from the high school mathematics curriculum, including pre-algebra, elementary algebra, intermediate algebra, coordinate geometry, basic plane geometry, and elementary trigonometry. On test day, you will have 60 minutes to answer 60 multiple-choice questions.

ACT Math questions fall into two main categories: Integrating Essential Skills and Preparing for Higher Math. Integrating Essential Skills questions make up 40–43 percent of the ACT Math test, and cover the math you learned up through middle school, including percentages, proportions, basic geometry, and averages. These topics are the building blocks of the tougher math you study now. Preparing for Higher Math questions cover algebra and beyond. This category includes the following official subtopics:

- Number & Quantity
- Algebra
- Functions
- Geometry
- Statistics & Probability

Finally, Modeling questions span both of the above categories, and test your understanding of models and how they represent mathematical concepts.

Think of math as a construction project you have to tackle, beam by beam, nail by nail. Your job is to get to the end result—but in order to do so, you need to have the proper tools and to know the most efficient way to use them. This section of *Peterson's ACT® Prep Guide* is your toolkit and your instruction manual. We'll walk you through the nitty-gritty of all the math you will encounter on the exam and show you the best method to find an answer, prove it is right, and move on to the next question.

COLLEGE READINESS BENCHMARK LEARNING PATH PRACTICE

As you make your way through Chapters 6, 7, and 8 and review all the math you should know to do well on your ACT, you may encounter some topics that give you extra trouble. That's where our extra College Readiness Benchmark Practice comes in.

Take the College Readiness Benchmark Learning Path if, after making your way through the review, you need an extra boost before you tackle the more straightforward practice questions at the end of every chapter and the practice tests at the end of the book.

Accompanying each topic, a special icon will guide you along the College Readiness Benchmark Learning Path, leading you to a special section at the end of each math chapter. There, you will find ACT Math practice exercises that look like the questions you will see on test day. Following each question is a very detailed answer explanation that walks you not only through the right answer, but also how to get there and why all of the other choices are incorrect.

These College Readiness Benchmark practice exercises really get into the thought processes you should follow when you take your ACT exam—they'll give you the boost you need to review the solving process before you approach the rest of the review.

CHAPTER 6: PRE-ALGEBRA AND ELEMENTARY ALGEBRA

OVERVIEW

- Basic Arithmetic Operations
- Exponents, Radicals, and Approximation
- Basic Logarithms
- Ratios, Proportions, and Percentages
- Linear Equations in One Variable
- Absolute Value
- Algebraic Expressions
- Introduction to Quadratic Equations
- Counting Techniques
- Simple Probability
- Basic Statistics and Data Collection
- Summing It Up
- College Readiness Benchmark Learning Path Practice
- Practice

The exam is very skills-oriented, so while there are indeed many concepts to review, the exam doesn't include tricky questions involving obscure facts or convoluted reasoning. You'll need to know your rules and how to apply them—and that's where this chapter will come in handy as you prepare for your exam.

The three chapters in this section will review the main concepts, formulas, and techniques you should be comfortable with before you take the ACT exam. In addition to the math review, we'll also give you lots of tips and problem-solving strategies that you can use to efficiently attack problems on this exam, as well as cautionary remarks highlighting potential pitfalls and the most common errors that students make. At the end of each chapter, you will find a 20-question practice exam reviewing the main concepts with test-like questions. Make sure to read through the explanations—each one not only explains why the correct answer is right, but also why you might have arrived at one of the incorrect choices.

COLLEGE READINESS BENCHMARK LEARNING PATH PRACTICE

If you're still having trouble with any topic after you've made your way through the chapter review, take the Benchmark Learning Path—turn to page 252 for our College Readiness Benchmark Learning Path practice, which will walk you step-by-step through three practice questions for every topic in this chapter.

We've created these questions for you after studying years of ACT tests. Each of these Benchmark questions gives you an idea of the most common question types you'll see in each math category on test day. We don't only want you to be familiar with how to solve these questions—we also want you to know what to expect. The more familiar you are with ACT exam language, the less nervous you'll be and the better you'll do when you're taking the real thing.

Upon completing these three chapters, you will be armed with the tools and strategies to be victorious on the ACT Mathematics test! So, without further delay, let's begin.

This chapter focuses on the main elements of pre-algebra and elementary algebra. It may have been a very long time since you actually considered some of these topics, and you are likely on autopilot when working with numbers and expressions. But there are many subtleties that you may have forgotten, and the majority of questions on the ACT Mathematics test will require you to call upon these concepts. So, even if this material *seems* easy and you feel the urge to skip it, we encourage you to reconsider! It will be worth your time to review, even if just one single concept is made clearer as a result.

BASIC ARITHMETIC OPERATIONS

The study of mathematics begins with the set of **whole numbers**, namely 1, 2, 3, 4... The table below provides a quick way to determine if a number can divide evenly into another whole number—that is, no remainder is produced when dividing.

These are the most common divisibility rules:

Whole Number	A whole number *n* is divisible by the number in the left column if...
2	the number *n* ends in 0, 2, 4, 6, or 8.
3	the digit sum of *n* is divisible by 3.
4	the last two numbers of *n*, taken as a number in and of itself, is divisible by 4.
5	the number *n* ends in 0 or 5.
6	the number *n* is divisible by both 2 and 3.
9	the digit sum of *n* is divisible by 9.
10	the number *n* ends in 0.

These rules are useful when determining the factors of a whole number. A whole number *n* whose only factors are the numbers 1 and *n* is called **prime**; if it has other factors, it is called **composite**. Every composite number can be written as a product of prime numbers, which is called its **prime factorization**. For instance, $90 = 2 \times 3 \times 3 \times 5$.

TIP

The **digit sum** is the sum of all digits in the numeral *n*. For example, the digit sum of 234 is $2 + 3 + 4 = 9$, which means it is divisible by both 3 and 9.

Two related concepts are the **greatest common factor (GCF)** and the **least common multiple (LCM)** of two or more whole numbers. The GCF of two whole numbers *n* and *m* is the largest whole number that **divides *into both* n and m evenly**. The LCM of two whole numbers *n* and *m* is the smallest whole number ***into which* both n and m divide**.

For instance, consider the whole numbers 8 and 28. Even though 2 is a common factor of both 8 and 28, it is not the *greatest* common factor. Rather, 4 is the GCF. Also, the smallest whole number into which both 8 and 28 divide is 56—this is their LCM. These definitions also apply to three or more whole numbers. See if you can identify the GCF and LCM in this sample question.

Which of the following sets contains two elements with a greatest common factor of 6 and a least common multiple of 72?

F. {6, 30}
G. {12, 18}
H. {18, 24}
J. {24, 72}
K. {6, 144}

The correct answer is H. You should use the answer choices provided to you and test them all out to find the pair of numbers with a greatest common factor of 6 and a least common multiple of 72. If a choice does not meet one of the two conditions, stop and move on—do not bother testing for the other condition.

Choice F: {6, 30}
GCF = 6; LCM = 30; eliminate
Choice G: {12, 18}
GCF = 6; LCM = 36; eliminate
Choice H: {18, 24}
GCF = 6; LCM = 72; DONE!

The set of **integers** is comprised of the whole numbers, their negatives, and 0. We write this as the set {... –4, –3, –2, –1, 0, 1, 2, 3, 4 ...}. Arithmetic involving integers is similar to the arithmetic involving whole numbers, but with the caveat that you must learn how to take negative signs into consideration.

The following rules and terminology are useful when working with integers:

1. $-(-a) = a$, for any integer a	**5.** Sums of positive integers are positive.
2. $a - (-b) = a + b$, for any integers a, b	**6.** Sums of negative integers are negative.
3. An integer is *even* if it is a multiple of 2.	**7.** A product of two negative integers is positive.
4. An integer is *odd* if it is not a multiple of 2.	**8.** A product of one positive and one negative integer is negative.

Here's a handy rule to keep in mind. If you have a product or quotient of more than two integers, count the number of negative signs to determine the sign of the product or quotient. If there is an even number of negative signs, the product or quotient is positive; if there is an odd number of negative signs, the product or quotient is negative.

Fractions and Decimals

A **fraction** is a quotient of two whole numbers, denoted by $\frac{a}{b}$, where $b \neq 0$. The top number is called the **numerator**, and the bottom number is the **denominator**. A fraction is *simplified* or *in reduced form* if the numerator and denominator do not share any common factors.

An important fact to remember through the ACT Mathematics test, which will likely come up in the form of an incorrect answer choice, is that you can never divide by 0! If an answer choice results in a denominator of 0, you know for sure it cannot be correct.

TIP: When performing arithmetic operations involving fractions, simplifying all fractions *first* will lead to smaller numbers that are easier to work with.

With that in mind, the **reciprocal** of $\frac{a}{b}$ can be computed by flipping the fraction over to get $\frac{b}{a}$, if, and only if, $a \neq 0$!

Here is a quick reference chart that shows how to handle arithmetic operations involving fractions. You can bookmark this page and come back to it if you get caught on a fraction problem and are unsure of the rules and how to apply them.

Arithmetic Operation	Rule (in Symbols)	Interpretation
Adding/Subtracting	$\frac{a}{b} \pm \frac{c}{d} = \frac{ad \pm cb}{bd}$	When fractions have different denominators, first find a common denominator. Apply it to the fractions and then add or subtract the numerators.
Simplifying/Reducing	$\frac{a \bullet c}{b \bullet c} = \frac{a}{b}$	You can cancel like factors in the numerator and denominator of a fraction to reduce it to lowest terms.
Multiplying by –1	$-\frac{a}{b} = \frac{-a}{b} = \frac{a}{-b}$	When multiplying a fraction by –1, you can multiply either the numerator or the denominator by –1, but NOT both.
Multiplying	$\frac{a}{b} \bullet \frac{c}{d} = \frac{ac}{bd}$	When multiplying two fractions, you can simply multiply their numerators and their denominators.
Dividing	$\frac{a}{b} \div \frac{c}{d} = \frac{a}{b} \bullet \frac{d}{c} = \frac{ad}{bc}$ $\frac{\frac{a}{b}}{\frac{c}{d}}$ means $\frac{a}{b} \div \frac{c}{d}$	When dividing two fractions, start by converting the quotient into a multiplication problem.

CAUTION There are several errors test-takers often make when working with fractions. You can prevent yourself from choosing incorrect answers on the ACT exam by avoiding these inequality errors.

Error	Comment
$\frac{a}{b+c} \neq \frac{a}{b} + \frac{a}{c}$	You cannot pull a fraction apart as a sum of two fractions when the sum occurs in the denominator.
$\frac{a}{b} + \frac{c}{d} \neq \frac{a+c}{b+d}$	When adding fractions, do not simply add the numerators and denominators. First, get a common denominator.
$\frac{a}{a+b} \neq \frac{\not{a}}{\not{a}+b}$	You cannot cancel *terms* that are the same in the numerator and denominator. You can only cancel *factors* common to both.

Sometimes, fractions will be written as **mixed numbers**. Often, it is easier to convert such a number to an **improper fraction**, or one whose numerator is larger than the denominator. For instance: $4\frac{2}{5} = \frac{4 \bullet 5 + 2}{5} = \frac{22}{5}$.

Don't lose all sense of your rules of arithmetic when a decimal point is introduced into the mix. Arithmetic involving decimal numbers is just like arithmetic involving integers, with the extra step of correctly positioning the decimal point. The same sign conventions for integers (your rules for positives and negatives from page 226) apply here.

The following are some rules of thumb to apply when working with decimal numbers:

- When *adding or subtracting decimal numbers*, line up the decimal points and add or subtract as you would whole numbers, simply keeping the decimal point in the same position.
- When *multiplying* decimal numbers, remove the decimal points and then multiply the numbers as you would whole numbers. Then, to determine the position of the decimal point, count the number of digits after the decimal point in all original numbers being multiplied. Move that number of steps left from the far right of the product, and place the decimal point there.

Any fraction can be converted into a decimal number by dividing the numerator by the denominator. All such decimal numbers will either terminate or repeat. Any decimal number that neither repeats nor terminates is called **irrational**. A **real number** is any number that is either rational or irrational.

TIP Some common irrational numbers are $\sqrt{2}$, π, and *e*.

When performing arithmetic operations on numbers expressed in different ways (e.g., fractions, mixed numbers, and decimal numbers), convert all numbers to the same format and then proceed as usual.

Let's look at some problems in action.

Examples:

Perform the following computations:

1. $3\frac{5}{8} \div \frac{3}{4} =$ ___________

2. $(0.02)(-1.4)(-0.3) =$ ___________

3. $\frac{3}{5} - 1.2 - 4\frac{1}{2} =$ ___________

Solutions:

1. $3\frac{5}{8} \div \frac{3}{4} = \frac{29}{8} \div \frac{3}{4} = \frac{29}{8} \bullet \frac{4}{3} = \frac{29}{\cancel{4} \bullet 2} \bullet \frac{\cancel{4}}{3} = \frac{29}{6}$

2. $(0.02)(-1.4)(-0.3) = 0.0084$

3. $\frac{3}{5} - 1.2 - 4\frac{1}{2} = 0.6 - 1.2 - 4.5 = -5.1$

Now let's look at a conversion question as it might appear on the ACT exam.

$\frac{0.0378}{0.21}$ is equal to how many thousandths?

A. 0.180

B. 1.8

C. 18

D. 180

E. 7,938

The correct answer is D. Convert the fraction: $\frac{0.0378}{0.21}$, or 180 thousandths. The problem asks how many thousandths, not simply the value of the decimal number to which the quotient is equal. Be careful to read *exactly* what the question is asking for; all of the natural wrong answers will be included among the choices!

Scientific Notation

Decimals with several digits before and/or after the decimal point are often expressed using **scientific notation**, a way of writing a complicated decimal as a product of a simpler decimal and a power of 10. For example:

$2{,}345 = 2.345 \times 10^3$ (digits before the decimal point)

$0.00000342 = 3.42 \times 10^{-6}$ (digits after the decimal point)

The "simpler decimal" has only one place *before* the decimal point. The power of 10 then tells you how many places the decimal point must move in the simpler decimal to get the original one. For instance, in the first example above, we used the power 3 because the decimal point must move 3 places *to the right* to get from 2.345 back to the original number 2,345. Likewise, in the second example, we used the power –6 because the decimal point must move 6 places *to the left* to get from 3.42 back to the original number 0.00000342.

Now, try some on your own.

Examples:

Rewrite the following two numbers using scientific notation:

1. 0.06054 = ________
2. 231.2 = ________

Solutions:

1. 6.054×10^{-2}
2. 2.312×10^{2}

TIP: Some answers (possibly the correct answer!) on the ACT exam might be expressed in scientific notation in place of the decimal you originally calculate.

Real Number Properties

The following properties apply for *all* real numbers *a*, *b*, and *c*:

Property Name	Rule (in symbols)	Interpretation
Commutative	$a+b=b+a$ $a \bullet b=b \bullet a$	You can add or multiply real numbers in any order.
Associative	$(a+b)+c=a+(b+c)$ $(a \bullet b) \bullet c=a \bullet (b \bullet c)$	You can group the terms of a sum or a product of more than two terms in any manner you like.
Distributive	$a \bullet (b \pm c)=a \bullet b \pm a \bullet c$	To multiply a sum or difference by a real number, first multiply each term by the number and then add/subtract the results.
FOIL	$(a+b) \bullet (c+d)=$ $a \bullet c+a \bullet d+b \bullet c+b \bullet d$	The acronym FOIL means "First, Outer, Inner, Last" and represents all combinations of terms to be multiplied. FOILing means using the distributive property twice.
Zero Factor Property	If $a \bullet b=0$, then either $a=0$ or $b=0$, or both.	If a product of real numbers is zero, then at least one of the factors must be zero.

The ACT exam will often ask you to simplify an arithmetic expression involving all types of numbers and operations. In order to do so correctly, you must use the following rules: the **order of operations**.

Step 1: Simplify all expressions contained within parentheses.

Step 2: Simplify all expressions involving exponents.

Step 3: Perform all multiplication and division as it arises from left to right.

Step 4: Perform all addition and subtraction as it arises from left to right.

TIP: To help you remember the correct order of operations, try using the acronym PEMDAS: **P**arentheses, **E**xponents, **M**ultiplication and **D**ivision, **A**ddition, and **S**ubtraction.

If there are multiple groupings, apply the same steps *within* each grouping.

Try your hand with these problems.

Examples:

Simplify the following arithmetic expressions using the order of operations.

1. $-2(3-1)+4\times3-2=$ __________

2. $-3[10-(2+3)\times(1-(-1))]=$ __________

Solutions:

1. $-2(3-1)+4\times3-2=-2(2)+4\times3-2=-4+12-2=8-2=6$

2. $-3[10-(2+3)\times(1-(-1))]=-3(10-5\times2)=-3(0)=0$

Don't rush when faced with what looks like basic arithmetic! Work slowly and methodically, and make sure you stick to the rules. Some of the answer choices provided on the ACT exam are sure to be incorrect solutions that would result if you perform operations in the wrong order.

Read word problems just as you would numerical expressions—carefully, making sure to interpret each sentence so you know what's being asked of you. There will be a question or two on the ACT exam that is a word problem whose solution requires only basic arithmetic. The trick is to carefully extract the given information and answer the question being asked.

See if you can figure out what's being asked in the word problem below.

A car rental company charges \$40 per day for a rental car, plus \$0.25 for each mile driven. If Dan kept a car for 5 days and drove 248 miles, what was the cost of the rental?

A. \$445
B. \$262
C. \$200
D. \$150
E. \$62

The correct answer is B. Dan had the car for 5 days, so 5(\$40) = \$200 for the daily fee. Since he drove 248 miles, the cost of the mileage is 248(\$0.25) = \$62. So the cost of the rental is \$200 + \$62 = \$262.

Turn to page 252 to follow the College Readiness Benchmark Learning Path questions covering Basic Arithmetic Operations.

EXPONENTS, RADICALS, AND APPROXIMATION

On the ACT exam, exponents, radicals, and approximation fall under the category of Preparing for Higher Math. The questions in this section fall under the subcategory Number & Quantity. It is convenient to express a product involving multiple identical terms, such as $2\times3\times3\times3\times5$, in a more compact manner. This is where exponents come into play. If *b* and *n* are natural numbers, then $b^n=\underbrace{b\times\ldots\times b}_{n\text{ times}}$. Here, *b* is called the **base** and *n* is the **exponent**.

The table on the following page outlines the properties of exponents that will be useful to know when solving various algebra problems. Again, this is a good table to bookmark and return to as you work to remember exponent rules.

For the following, assume that the bases *a* and *b* are greater than 1, and that the exponents *n* and *m* are real numbers.

Exponent Rule (in symbols)	Interpretation
$a^0 = 1$	The result of raising any nonzero real number to the zero power is 1.
$a^{-n} = \frac{1}{a^n}, \quad a^n = \frac{1}{a^{-n}}$	A term in the numerator that is raised to a negative exponent is equivalent to a term in the denominator with the same base, but positive exponent, and vice versa.
$a^n \bullet a^m = a^{n+m}$	When multiplying terms with the same base raised to powers, add the powers.
$\frac{a^n}{a^m} = a^{n-m}$	When dividing terms with the same base raised to powers, subtract the powers.
$\left(a^n\right)^m = a^{n \bullet m}$	When raising a term that is already raised to a power to another power, multiply the powers.
$(a \bullet b)^n = a^n \bullet b^n$	When raising a product to a power, apply the power to each term and multiply the results.
$\left(\frac{a}{b}\right)^n = \frac{a^n}{b^n}$	When raising a quotient to a power, apply the power to each term and divide the results.
If $a = b$, then $a^n = b^n$, for any exponent n.	If two real numbers are equal, then their powers are also equal.

CAUTION

When you are rushing, it is very common to apply the exponent rules incorrectly and even to make up rules that do not exist! The following are some common misapplications of rules to avoid when working with exponents.

Error	Interpretation
$-a^2 \neq (-a)^2$	If the negative sign is *outside* the parentheses of a quantity being squared, then the square does not apply to it.
$(a+b)^n \neq a^n + b^n$	The power of a sum is not equal to the sum of the powers.
$\frac{a^n}{b^m} \neq \left(\frac{a}{b}\right)^{n-m}$	You cannot write the quotient of terms with different bases raised to different powers as a single quotient raised to a power.
$a^n \bullet b^m \neq (a \bullet b)^{n+m}$	You cannot write the product of terms with different bases raised to different powers as a single product raised to a power.

Let's do some practice with exponents.

Examples:

Simplify the following expressions using the appropriate exponent rule(s):

1. $(-2)^3 \times 3^{-2} =$ ____________

2. $\left(\frac{2}{3}\right)^{-3} \bullet \left(2^{-1}\right)^{-2} =$ ____________

Solutions:

1. $(-2)^3 \bullet 3^{-2} = \frac{(-1)^3 \bullet 2^3}{3^2} = \frac{-8}{9} = -\frac{8}{9}$

2. $\left(\frac{2}{3}\right)^{-3} \bullet \left(2^{-1}\right)^{-2} = \frac{2^{-3}}{3^{-3}} \bullet 2^{(-1)(-2)} = \frac{3^3}{2^3} \bullet 2^2 = \frac{27}{8} \bullet 4 = \frac{27}{2}$

The **square root** of a nonnegative real number a is another number b whose square is a—that is $b^2 = a$. In such case, we write. For instance, $\sqrt{36} = 6$, and $\sqrt{121} = 11$. Note that $(-6)^2$ also equals 36, and $(-11)^2$ also equals 121; therefore –6 and –11 are also square roots of 36 and 121, respectively.

A **cube root** of a real number a is another number b whose cube is a—that is $b^3 = a$. In such case, we write $\sqrt[3]{a} = b$. For instance, $\sqrt[3]{27} = 3$ and $\sqrt[3]{-64} = -4$.

Square roots and cube roots are called **radicals.** In both cases, the a in $\sqrt{a}$ and in $\sqrt[3]{a}$ is called the **radicand.**

The following are useful properties of radicals to master before you take the ACT.

Radical Rule (in symbols)	Interpretation
$\left(\sqrt{a}\right)^2 = a,\ \left(\sqrt[3]{a}\right)^3 = a$	Raising an *n*th root to the *n*th power gives back the original radicand.
$\sqrt{a \bullet b} = \sqrt{a} \bullet \sqrt{b}$, when $a \geq 0$ and $b \geq 0$.	The square root of a product is the product of the square roots.
$\sqrt{\frac{a}{b}} = \frac{\sqrt{a}}{\sqrt{b}}$, when $a \geq 0$ and $b > 0$.	The square root of a quotient is the quotient of the square roots.
$\frac{1}{\sqrt{a}} = \frac{1}{\sqrt{a}} \bullet \frac{\sqrt{a}}{\sqrt{a}} = \frac{\sqrt{a}}{a}$, when $a > 0$.	You can clear a square root from the denominator of a fraction by multiplying the numerator and denominator of the fraction by the square root. (This is often called "multiplying by the *conjugate*" or "*rationalizing* the denominator.")
If $0 < a < b$, then $\sqrt{a} < \sqrt{b}$.	If a is less than b, then you can take the square root on both sides of the inequality without having to reverse the sign.

These properties can be used to simplify radicals. For instance:

$$\sqrt{72}=\sqrt{2\bullet4\bullet9}=\sqrt{2}\bullet\sqrt{4}\bullet\sqrt{9}=\sqrt{2}\bullet2\bullet3=6\sqrt{2}$$

Adding and Subtracting Radical Expressions

If the terms you want to add have the *same* radical parts, just add or subtract the coefficients:

$$2\sqrt{5}-6\sqrt{5}=$$
$$(2-6)\sqrt{5}=-4\sqrt{5}$$

However, terms that have *different* radical parts cannot be combined:

$$3\sqrt{5}+4\sqrt{7}-9\sqrt{5}=$$
$$(3-9)\sqrt{5}+4\sqrt{7}=-6\sqrt{5}+4\sqrt{7}$$

ALERT: A common error is to apply the radical to each individual term of a sum. Note that the square root of a sum is *not* the sum of the square roots. In this example, note that $-6\sqrt{5}+4\sqrt{7}\neq(-6+4)\sqrt{5+7}$! The same goes for cube roots.

Let's work through a problem together.

Example:

Simplify $\dfrac{56\sqrt{7}}{28\sqrt{42}}$.

Solution:

Let's use the properties of radicals and apply the rules of multiplying fractions to simplify this expression:

$$\frac{56\sqrt{7}}{28\sqrt{42}}=\frac{2\bullet\cancel{28}\sqrt{7}}{\cancel{28}\sqrt{7\bullet6}}=\frac{2\cancel{\sqrt{7}}}{\cancel{\sqrt{7}}\bullet\sqrt{6}}=\frac{2}{\sqrt{6}}$$

Finally, we rationalize the denominator (removing its root symbol) by multiplying the numerator and denominator by $\sqrt{6}$:

$$\underbrace{\frac{56\sqrt{7}}{28\sqrt{42}}=\frac{2}{\sqrt{6}}}_{\text{From above}}=\underbrace{\frac{2}{\sqrt{6}}\bullet\frac{\sqrt{6}}{\sqrt{6}}}_{\text{Rationalizing the denominator}}=\frac{2\sqrt{6}}{6}=\frac{\sqrt{6}}{3}$$

Approximation

Computations often arise in which either numbers are so large that working with them directly is difficult or expressions involve roots or irrational numbers that can make you stop in your tracks and not be able to proceed. In these cases, you should resort to approximation, where you round a number to one that is easier to manipulate. There are a couple of methods that can help you arrive at an answer more quickly when approximating or estimating real numbers.

A common technique is to round large numbers to the nearest thousand, ten thousand, etc. Suppose you want to round a whole number to the nearest thousand. Look at the digit to the immediate right, which in this case is the hundreds place. If that digit is 5 or greater, increase the digit in the thousands place by 1 and replace all digits to its right with zeros; if the digit is 4 or less, keep the thousands place as is and replace all digits to its right with zeros.

For example, 343,783 rounded to the nearest thousand is 344,000, while 214,332,499 rounded to the nearest thousand is 214,332,000. The same technique works when rounding any real number expressed as a decimal number to any place desired.

1,	0	0	0,	0	0	0	.	0	0	0	0
Millions	Hundred thousands	Ten thousands	Thousands	Hundreds	Tens	Ones		Tenths	Hundredths	Thousandths	Ten thousandths

Decimal number place values from millions to ten thousandths.

Estimating roots, such as $\sqrt{47}$ and $\sqrt[3]{11}$, can be tricky. Sometimes, though it's not easy to provide a single estimate, providing a range of values is easier. For instance, it's not easy to compute $\sqrt{47}$. In a case like this, you can determine numbers with more obvious square roots on either side of 47.

> **TIP:** Rounding the numbers involved in a problem can help you to eliminate some choices right off the bat!

You know $6^2 = 36$ and $7^2 = 49$ and that $36 < 47 < 49$. Therefore, you know $\underbrace{\sqrt{36}}_{=6} < \sqrt{47} < \underbrace{\sqrt{49}}_{=7}$, so that $6 < \sqrt{47} < 7$. The answer to $\sqrt{47}$ must lie somewhere between 6 and 7.

The same trick works for estimating cube roots, except in that case you want to find two numbers for which the cube root, not square root, is easily computed.

Other irrational numbers, such as π and e, enter into computations. Common approximations for these are $\pi \approx 3.14$ and $e \approx 2.718$.

Try this question working with irrational numbers.

What is the smallest positive integer value of x for which $x - \sqrt{7} > 7$ is true?

F. 11
G. 10
H. 9
J. 8
K. 7

The correct answer is G. Rewrite the inequality to solve for the range of x:

$$\begin{aligned} x - \sqrt{7} &> 7 \\ x &> 7 + \sqrt{7} \end{aligned}$$

Since $\sqrt{7}$ is between 2 and 3, $7 + \sqrt{7}$ must be between 9 and 10. Therefore, the smallest positive integer value of x is 10.

Ordering Real Numbers by Value

A real number p is *less than* another real number q, written $p < q$, if q lies further to the right along the real number line than p. We also say that q is *greater than* p. The same process can be used to compare whole numbers, decimals, and fractions—you can compare two fractions by first converting them to decimal numbers and using the same process.

For instance, $-2 < -\frac{7}{5}$, $3 \le 4.102$, $\pi \ge 3.14$, and $0 > -0.001$.

The questions related to ordering on the ACT Mathematics test can be a bit tricky, primarily because they are often asked in a more abstract manner. That is, they usually involve variables rather than numbers.

> **TIP:** When dealing with problems involving variables and inequalities, it is always a good idea to plug in actual numbers to eliminate choices. Always try to find a way to make the problem less abstract!

The following important properties will be very helpful to know when handling these types of questions.

Rule	Explanation
If $0 < a < b$, then $a^n < b^n$, for any positive exponent n.	If a is less than b, then you can raise both sides of the inequality to a positive exponent without reversing the inequality sign. (Note: You reverse the inequality sign whenever you multiply or divide both sides by a negative number.)
If $0 < a < b$, then $-b < -a < 0$.	If a and b are both positive, and a is less than b, then the reverse inequality is true for the negatives of a and b.
If $a < b$ and $c < d$, then $a + c < b + d$.	You can add the left sides and right sides of inequalities that have the same signs; the resulting sums satisfy the same inequality.
If $0 < a < 1$, then $a^2 < a$.	Squaring a real number between 0 and 1 produces a smaller real number.
If $a > 1$, then $a^2 > a$.	Squaring a real number greater than 1 produces a larger real number.
If $0 < a < b$, then $\frac{1}{b} < \frac{1}{a}$.	If a and b are both positive, and a is less than b, then the reverse inequality is true for the reciprocals of a and b.

See if you can solve these ACT-style sample questions.

If $x > y$ and $z > y$, which of the following MUST be true?

F. $z^2 > y^2$
G. $x^2 > y^2$
H. $x > z$
J. $x + z > 2y$
K. $z > x$

The correct answer is J. You know that both x and z are greater than y, but you are not given any information about how they relate to one another. This means that you cannot tell which, if either of them, is greater than the other. So you can eliminate choices H and K. You might assume that since $x > y$, $x^2 > y^2$, but this is not necessarily true. If $x = 2$ and $y = -3$, for example, then $2^2 < (-3)^2$, making $x^2 < y^2$. This allows you to eliminate choices F and G, leaving choice J as correct. It must be true that $x + z > 2y$; since both x and z are greater than y, their sum must be greater than $2y$.

If $65\% < x < 0.85$, which of the following could be x?

A. $\frac{5}{12}$
B. $\frac{5}{8}$
C. $\frac{2}{5}$
D. $\frac{2}{3}$
E. $\frac{7}{8}$

The correct answer is D. To compare fractions, decimal numbers, and percentages, convert all the numbers to the same form. Since $65\% = 0.65$, $0.65 < x < 0.85$.

Convert the fractions in the answer choices to decimal form to solve. Choices A and C are both less than 0.5, so they can be eliminated. Choice B can also be eliminated as too small since $\frac{5}{8}$ equals 0.625 in decimal form.

Choice D converts to 0.66 in decimal form. This number falls between 0.65 and 0.85 and is therefore correct.

As a decimal number, choice B can also be eliminated as too small. As a decimal number, $\frac{2}{3} = 0.\overline{66}$. This number does fall between 0.65 and 0.85, so choice D is correct.

Turn to page 254 to follow the College Readiness Benchmark Learning Path questions covering Exponents, Radicals, and Approximation.

BASIC LOGARITHMS

Logarithms are not tested heavily on the ACT Mathematics test, but they do arise occasionally under the category of Preparing for Higher Math (and the subcategory of Functions), so it's best to be prepared. A logarithm is simply an exponent. The key formula to remember is $y = \log_a x$ means the same thing as $x = a^y$. So, for instance, $\log_4 64 = x$ can be written as $4^x = 64$, and the answer is, of course, $x = 3$. So $\log_4 64 = 3$, meaning the quantity $\log_4 64$, is the exponent to which you raise 4 in order to get 64.

Try these logarithm problems on your own.

Examples:

Compute the following logarithms.

1. $\log_2 128 =$ ______
2. $\log_6 1 =$ ______
3. $\log_3 \sqrt{3} =$ ______

Solutions:

1. $\log_2 128 = 7$
2. $\log_6 1 = 0$
3. $\log_3 \sqrt{3} = \frac{1}{2}$

Turn to page 257 to follow the College Readiness Benchmark Learning Path questions covering Basic Logarithms.

RATIOS, PROPORTIONS, AND PERCENTAGES

On the ACT exam, ratios, proportions, and percentages are tested under the category of Integrating Essential Skills. A **ratio** is a comparison of one quantity x to another quantity y, expressed as a fraction $\frac{x}{y}$, or sometimes using the notation $x{:}y$ (read "x to y"). In plain English, this is interpreted as, "For every x of one type, there are y of the second type."

For example, if there are 3 girls to every 1 boy in a class, we say that the ratio of girls to boys is 3:1, or 3 to 1, and write the fraction $\frac{3}{1}$. Similarly, if there are 5 dogs for every 2 cats in an animal shelter, we say that the ratio of dogs to cats is 5:2, or 5 to 2, and write the fraction $\frac{5}{2}$. We could have instead described the ratio as 2 cats for every 5 dogs, and say the ratio of cats to dogs is 2:5 and write the fraction $\frac{2}{5}$. This conveys the same information. However, since $\frac{2}{5} \neq \frac{5}{2}$, the two ratios are not equal. The order in which the quantities appear in a ratio is important because we represent the ratio as a fraction.

A **proportion** is an equation relating two ratios. In symbols, a proportion is expressed by setting two fractions equal to each other, say $\frac{a}{b} = \frac{c}{d}$. Proportions arise when solving many different types of problems—you'll use them in problems that ask you to change units of measure and find side lengths of similar triangles.

Proportions are often formulated when one ratio is known and one of the two quantities in an equivalent ratio is unknown. Here is an example of a simple scenario you might see on the ACT:

There are 3 binders for every 5 boxes of pens in a supply closet. If the last count was 80 boxes of pens, how many binders are in the supply closet?

To solve this problem, let b denote the number of binders in the supply closet. You can set up the proportion $\frac{3}{5}=\frac{b}{80}$.

To solve for b, cross-multiply to get $3(80) = 5b$, or $240 = 5b$. Dividing both sides by 5 then yields $b = 48$. So there are 48 binders in the supply closet.

Now, look at this sample question.

A new unit of measure called the *wobble* is a unit of length equivalent to 8 inches. If the length of a giraffe's neck is 6 feet, what is the length of the giraffe's neck in wobbles?

F. 0.11
G. 7.5
H. 8
J. 9
K. 64

The correct answer is J. First, you know that 1 foot = 12 inches, so 6 feet is equivalent to 6(12) = 72 inches. You are given that 1 wobble = 8 inches, and you want to determine how many wobbles are in 72 inches. Let x be the number of wobbles in 72 inches and set up a proportion:

$$\frac{1}{8}=\frac{x}{72}$$
$$8x=72$$
$$x=\frac{72}{8}$$
$$x=9$$

ALERT: The answer obtained by reversing the ratio is sure to be one of the wrong answer choices for ratio and proportion problems!

The word **percent** means "per hundred." A percentage is used to express the number of *parts* of a *whole*. For instance, 34 percent means "34 parts of 100," which can be expressed as the fraction $\frac{34}{100}$ and as the decimal 0.34. It is also denoted as 34%. These three representations are all equivalent.

TIP: To convert from decimal form to percent form, you simply move the decimal point two units to the right and affix the % sign; to convert in the opposite manner, move the decimal point two units to the left, insert a decimal point, and drop the % sign.

Problems involving percentages on the ACT exam can be whittled down to three basic calculations:

Problem Type	Method Used to Solve the Problem	Example
Compute x% of y.	Convert x% to a decimal and multiply by y.	**Q:** Compute 54% of 8. **A:** $0.54(8) = 4.32$
What percent of x is y?	Divide x by y.	**Q:** What percent of 150 is 45? **A:** $\frac{45}{150} = 0.30 = 30\%$
x is y% of what number z?	Convert y% to a decimal, multiply it by z, and set equal to x. Solve for z.	**Q:** 18 is 40% of what number z? **A:** Solve $0.40z = 18$ for z to get $z = 45$.

Sometimes, questions on the ACT exam will be as straightforward as one of the examples above. But more likely, you will be given a word problem involving percentages, and you will need to identify which of these scenarios applies. For instance, consider the following problem.

Max went out to dinner and paid a total of \$36, which included the amount due plus a \$9 tip. What percentage of the amount due does this tip represent?

A. 9%

B. 20%

C. 25%

D. $33\frac{1}{3}\%$

E. 40%

The correct answer is D. If \$36 included the amount due plus a \$9 tip, the amount due must have been \$36 – \$9 = \$27. As a percentage of the amount due, \$9 represents the following:

$$\frac{\$9}{\$27} \times 100\% = 33\frac{1}{3}\%$$

Make certain to read the problem carefully! You are asked for the percent of the amount *due*, not the amount *paid*.

Turn to page 258 to follow the College Readiness Benchmark Learning Path questions covering Ratios, Proportions, and Percentages.

LINEAR EQUATIONS IN ONE VARIABLE

On the ACT exam, linear equations are tested under the category of Preparing for Higher Math (and the subcategory of Algebra). **Linear equations** are equations in which the variable is raised to the first power, like $5x = 13$ and $4(y-1) = 5$. The process of solving linear equations involves simplifying expressions by clearing fractions and using the order of operations and the distributive property of multiplication to get the variable on one side of the equation.

The basic rule to remember is *balance both sides of the equation*. If you add or subtract a number from one side, you MUST do so to the other; if you divide or multiply one side by a number, you MUST do it to the other.

Let's solve an example problem together.

Example:

If $3(1 - 2x) + 4(2x - 1) = -x$, what is the value of x^2? _________

Solution:

First, you must solve the given equation. The order of operations applies to solving linear equations—after all, the variable x represents a real number. Simplify the left side and then get the x-terms on the left side and constants on the right. Combine like terms, and then divide by the coefficient of x:

$$\begin{aligned} 3(1-2x)+4(2x-1) &= -x \\ 3-6x+8x-4 &= -x \\ 2x-1 &= -x \\ 2x+x &= 1 \\ 3x &= 1 \\ x &= \frac{1}{3} \end{aligned}$$

Remember to read carefully! Note that you were not asked for the solution, but rather an expression involving it.

The final step here is to compute x^2, which is $\left(\frac{1}{3}\right)^2 = \frac{1}{9}$.

TIP If you are asked to solve a linear equation like this, a quick way to get the solution is to substitute the given choices for the variable. Whichever one results in a true statement, like 1 = 1, is the solution.

Sometimes, a linear equation can involve more than one variable, and you can be asked to solve for one of them in terms of the others. The same exact procedure applies! For instance, you can solve the equation $y - y_1 = m(x - x_1)$ for x_1 as follows:

$$\begin{aligned} y-y_1 &= m(x-x_1) \\ y-y_1 &= mx-mx_1 \\ y-y_1-mx &= -mx_1 \\ \frac{y-y_1-mx}{-m} &= x_1 \end{aligned}$$

The fraction on the left side can be expressed in various equivalent ways, and often the correct choice listed will not be the solution you come up with, but rather a variant of your solution. Using the properties of fractions, all of the following are equivalent to this fraction. All of these answers would be correct:

$$\frac{-y+y_1+mx}{m},\ \frac{y_1-y+mx}{m},\ \frac{y_1}{m}-\frac{y}{m}+x$$

TIP If a linear equation involves fractions, first multiply both sides of the equation by the LCD of all fractions occurring in the equation. Then, you can just deal with arithmetic involving integers, which is quicker than working with fractions!

See how this method is put into practice in the following problem.

If $\frac{1}{4}y-\frac{1}{12}=\frac{5}{8}y+\frac{3}{4}$, then what is the value of $\frac{1}{y}$?

- **A.** 20
- **B.** −11
- **C.** 11
- **D.** $-\frac{20}{9}$
- **E.** $-\frac{9}{20}$

The correct answer is E. Multiply both sides of the equation by the LCD, 24, to eliminate the fractions. Then solve the equation for *y*:

$$\frac{1}{4}y-\frac{1}{12}=\frac{5}{8}y+\frac{3}{4}$$
$$24\bullet\left(\frac{1}{4}y-\frac{1}{12}\right)=24\bullet\left(\frac{5}{8}y+\frac{3}{4}\right)$$
$$6y-2=15y+18$$
$$-20=9y$$
$$-\frac{20}{9}=y$$

Therefore, $\frac{1}{y}=-\frac{9}{20}$

Turn to page 260 to follow the College Readiness Benchmark Learning Path questions covering Linear Equations in One Variable.

ABSOLUTE VALUE

Absolute value falls under the category of Integrating Essential Skills. A **number line** is a convenient way of illustrating the position of real numbers with respect to zero. The integers 7 and –7 are both 7 units away from 0, even though they exist on either side of 0. For any real number *a*, we use the **absolute value** of *a*, denoted $|a|$, to measure the distance between *a* and 0. Since distance is a nonnegative quantity, the definition has two parts:

$$|a|=\begin{cases} a, \text{ if } a\geq 0 \\ -a, \text{ if } a<0 \end{cases}$$

For instance, |8| = 8 and |–8| = –(–8) = 8. This definition works for any type of real number: integers, fractions, decimal numbers, or irrational numbers.

The following are some useful properties of absolute value you should master before taking the ACT exam:

Property (in symbols)	Property (in words)
$\lvert a\rvert=b$ whenever $a=b$ or $a=-b$	The real numbers *b* and –*b* are both $\lvert b\rvert$ units from the origin.
$\lvert a\bullet b\rvert=\lvert a\rvert\bullet\lvert b\rvert$	The absolute value of a product is the product of the absolute values.
$\left\lvert\frac{a}{b}\right\rvert=\frac{\lvert a\rvert}{\lvert b\rvert}$, whenever $b\neq 0$	The absolute value of a quotient is the quotient of the absolute values.

CAUTION

Remember, when a and b have opposite signs, $|a+b| \neq |a|+|b|$.

For example, $|-5+4| \neq |-5|+|4|$.

The correct way of simplifying $|-5 + 4|$ is by first simplifying the whole expression inside the absolute value bars (much like parentheses). Then, when there is a single number enclosed by the absolute value bars, compute the absolute value.

So $|-5 + 4| = |-1| = 1$. This is not equivalent to $|-5| + |4|$, which equals 9.

Let's try some practice problems.

Examples:

Simplify these expressions involving absolute value:

1. $-5-|2-6| =$ ________
2. $|-5|^{-1}-|-1|^{3} =$ ________

TIP When applying the order of operations, treat absolute values like parentheses. Remember PEMDAS: what's inside the parentheses (or in this case, absolute value bars) is always simplified first.

Solutions:

1. $-5-|2-6| = -5-|-4| = -5-4 = -9$
2. $|-5|^{-1}-|-1|^{3} = (5)^{-1}-(1)^{3} = \frac{1}{5}-(1)^{3} = \frac{1}{5}-1 = -\frac{4}{5}$

Question 2 may look a bit intimidating, but just remember—compute the absolute values first. Then, apply the order of operations as usual.

Turn to page 262 to follow the College Readiness Benchmark Learning Path questions covering Absolute Value.

ALGEBRAIC EXPRESSIONS

On the ACT exam, algebraic expressions are tested under the category of Preparing for Higher Math. A **variable** is an unknown quantity represented by a letter, like x, y, or z. A **constant** is a real number whose value does not change. A **term** is a variable or constant, or products of powers thereof, and an **algebraic expression** is an arithmetic combination of terms, like $5x - 3yz$ or $2xy^3 - 5xz + 3$.

If two terms have the same variables, they are called **like terms**. For instance, $21a^5$ and $-8a^5$ are like terms because they have the same variable: a^5. Likewise, if two terms have different variables—such as $10zy$ and $10xy$—then they are not like terms. Different powers of the same variable—such as $3m^3$ and $4m^6$—are also not like terms. The powers must also be the same.

When evaluating algebraic expressions for specific values of the variables, simply substitute the values in and simplify the arithmetic expression, as in the problem below.

If $a = 4$, then $3a(a - 1)^2 + a \div 2 = ?$

- **A.** 56
- **B.** 108
- **C.** 110
- **D.** 194
- **E.** 216

The correct answer is C. Plug $a = 4$ into the expression:

$$3a(a - 1)^2 + a \div 2 = 3(4)(4 - 1)^2 + 4 \div 2$$

Note that at this point, it is just an **arithmetic expression**, so you follow those rules (specifically the order of operations) to simplify it:

$$\begin{aligned} 3(4)(4-1)^2 + 4 \div 2 &= 3(4)(3)^2 + 4 \div 2 \\ &= 3(4)(9) + 4 \div 2 \\ &= 108 + 2 \\ &= 110 \end{aligned}$$

Since variables represent real numbers, all of the rules (exponent rules, order of operations, etc.) and properties of arithmetic (commutative property, associative property, etc.) must apply to algebraic expressions.

To add (or subtract) like terms, you add (or subtract) the coefficients of the terms and keep the variable parts the same. For instance: $5x^6 + 8x^6 = 13x^6$.

When multiplying or dividing terms, use the exponent rules just as when simplifying arithmetic expressions. Remember the FOIL method when multiplying two binomials? It is often used when multiplying algebraic expressions. For example:

$$(2x + 3y)(x - 5) = 2x(x) + 2x(-5) + 3y(x) + 3y(-5) = 2x^2 - 10x + 3xy - 15y.$$

This same process works for multiplying trinomials and polynomials with even more terms.

CAUTION

When expanding the square of a binomial, like $(a + b)^2$, remember that this means $(a + b)(a + b)$, and you must apply the FOIL method. A common error is to distribute the exponent to get $a^2 + b^2$. This is incorrect! If you FOIL as in the above example, you get $a^2 + \boxed{2ab} + b^2$!

Observe this polynomial term.

What is the sum of the polynomials $4ab^3 + 3a^2b^3$ and $-a^2b - 2a^2b^3$?

- **F.** $4ab^3 - a^2b + 5a^2b^3$
- **G.** $3ab^3 + a^2b^3$
- **H.** $3ab^3 + 5a^2b^3$
- **J.** $4ab^3 - a^2b + a^2b^3$
- **K.** $4ab^3 + a^3b + 5a^3b^3$

The correct answer is J. Do not be thrown by the variables—simply combine like terms. In the expression $(4ab^3 + 3a^2b^3) + (-a^2b - 2a^2b^3)$, there are two multiples of a^2b^3. Since $3a^2b^3 + (-2a^2b^3) = a^2b3$, the entire expression simplifies to $4ab^3 - a^2b + a^2b^3$.

SIMPLIFYING EXPRESSIONS

The basic rules of factoring are important to review, including factoring out a GCF and factoring differences of squares and basic trinomials. More sophisticated factoring techniques (like factoring differences/sums of cubes, factoring by regrouping, etc.) are not covered on the exam, so you do not need to sweat those! Try the following problems as a quick review of factoring.

Examples:

Factor the following expressions completely:

1. $12x^2y^3 - 4xy^2 + 16x^3y^3 =$ ____________
2. $6x^2 + x - 2 =$ ____________
3. $2x^2 - 8x - 10 =$ ____________
4. $x^2 - 81 =$ ____________

Solutions:

1. $12x^2y^3 - 4xy^2 + 16x^3y^3 = 4xy^2(3xy - 1 + 4x^2y)$
2. $6x^2 + x - 2 = (3x + 2)(2x - 1)$
3. $2x^2 - 8x - 10 = 2(x + 1)(x - 5)$
4. $x^2 - 81 = (x - 9)(x + 9)$

The exponent rules are also applicable when simplifying algebraic expressions. Try the following problems to practice manipulating exponents when working with variables instead of whole numbers.

Examples:

Simplify the following algebraic expressions:

1. $(3a^2b)^2 =$ ____________
2. $\dfrac{v^{-3}\left(wx^2\right)^3}{w^2xv^2} =$ ____________

Solutions:

1. $(3a^2b)^2 = 3^2a^4b^2 = 9a^4b^2$
2. $\dfrac{v^{-3}\left(wx^2\right)^3}{w^2xv^2} = \dfrac{v^{-3}w^3x^6}{w^2xv^2} = \dfrac{w^3x^6}{v^3w^2xv^2} = \dfrac{w^3x^6}{w^2xv^2} = \dfrac{1}{v^{-1}} \bullet \dfrac{w^3x^6}{w^2xv^5} \bullet \dfrac{wx^5}{v^5} = vwx^5$

Expressions in Word Problems

One of the most challenging parts of algebra, and a major part of the ACT Mathematics test, is translating words describing a math scenario into symbols. Several word problems involving arithmetic, linear equations, systems of equations, basic geometry, and elementary triangle trigonometry are typically included on the ACT exam, so it is definitely in your best interest to practice solving them.

When creating an algebraic expression, equation, or inequality that describes a relationship between one or more quantities, you must first identify what the unknowns are and how many of them you have. Use a different letter for each unknown. Then, identify common words and phrases (*is*, *of*, *less than*, *greater than*, etc.) and translate them, piece by piece, into algebraic expressions.

Let's try some practice problems.

Example:

Translate the following statements into algebraic expressions.

1. A number is three less than two times another number. ____________

2. The square of the sum of two numbers is greater than 4. ____________

3. The sum of two numbers is twice the product of two other numbers. ____________

Solutions:

1. $x = 2y - 3$
2. $(x + y)^2 > 4$
3. $x + y = 2wz$

Turn to page 264 to follow the College Readiness Benchmark Learning Path questions covering Algebraic Expressions.

INTRODUCTION TO QUADRATIC EQUATIONS

On the ACT exam, quadratic equations are tested under the category of Preparing for Higher Math. Another common type of equation is a **quadratic equation**, which is an equation in the form $\mathbf{ax^2 + bx + c = 0}$, where a, b, and c are real numbers and $a \neq 0$. There can be 0, 1, or 2 solutions to a quadratic equation. The methods you can use to solve these equations include factoring, the quadratic formula, and completing the square. We will give you an in-depth look at factoring in this section.

To master the process of solving a quadratic equation by factoring, it's important to follow these steps in order every time. First, put the equation into the standard form $ax^2 + bx + c = 0$. Take note! Do NOT factor until you put the equation in this form—zero MUST be on one side of the equation before you proceed.

Next, if possible, factor the quadratic expression into a product of two factors. Once factored, set each factor equal to zero and solve for x.

For example, let's look at $6x^2 + x = 2$.

First, rewrite the equation in the correct form: $6x^2 + x - 2 = 0$.

Next, factor the left side to get an equivalent equation that is the product of two factors: $(3x + 2)(2x - 1) = 0$.

Finally, set each factor equal to zero and solve for x:

$$3x+2=0 \Rightarrow x=-\frac{2}{3}$$

$$2x-1=0 \Rightarrow x=\frac{1}{2}$$

So the solutions of the equation are $-\frac{2}{3}$ and $\frac{1}{2}$.

TIP: When you are able to factor the expression into a product of two factors, it is possible that there is only one factor, but it will be squared.

Examples:

Determine the real solutions of the following quadratic equations.

1. $5x^2 + 35x = 0$ ____________
2. $x^2 + 11x + 10 = 0$ ____________
3. $9x^2 + 6x + 1 = 0$ ____________
4. $x^2 - 144 = 0$ ____________
5. $x^2 + 4 = 0$ ____________

Solutions:

1. $5x^2 + 35x = 5x(x + 7) = 0$, so $x = 0, -7$
2. $x^2 + 11x + 10 = (x + 10)(x + 1) = 0$, so $x = -10, -1$
3. $9x^2 + 6x + 1 = (3x + 1)^2 = 0$, so $x = -\frac{1}{3}$ (NOTE! Only one solution!)
4. $x^2 - 144 = (x - 12)(x + 12) = 0$, so $x = -12, 12$
5. $x^2 + 4 = 0$ does not have real solutions.

ALERT: The expression $a^2 + b^2$ does NOT factor!

Turn to page 266 to follow the College Readiness Benchmark Learning Path questions covering Quadratic Equations.

COUNTING TECHNIQUES

There are two main types of counting problems that commonly occur on the ACT Mathematics test.

One type of problem will ask you to determine the number of combinations that can be formed from a of quantity 1, b of quantity 2, c of quantity 3, etc. Assuming that order is not important and that all of the quantities are different, you simply need to multiply a, b, c, etc. together.

Example:

A deli offers a lunch special composed of a salad, a beverage, and a dessert. The deli serves 7 kinds of salads, 5 kinds of beverages, and 3 kinds of desserts. How many different lunch special combinations are possible?

Solution:

There are 7 kinds of salads, 5 kinds of beverages, and 3 kinds of desserts, so there are a total of $7 \times 5 \times 3 = 105$ possible lunch combinations.

In another type of counting problem, you will be asked to find the number of ordered arrangements of n objects.

Example:

At a track meet, five athletes are running a relay race, and the coach records the order in which they cross the finish line. In how many different orderings can these five athletes cross the finish line, assuming that ties are not allowed?

Solution:

To get started, note there are five possible people that could cross the finish line first. Now that one athlete is out of the running, how about the second place? Well, there are 4 remaining athletes, any of whom can come in second. So, at this point, there are 5×4 ways of getting the first- and second-place winners. We are not yet done! There are 3 remaining athletes, any of whom can come in third place. So there are $5 \times 4 \times 3$ different ways of getting the first-, second-, and third-place winners. Continuing in a similar way, there are $5 \times 4 \times 3 \times 2$ different ways in which the first four athletes can cross the finish line, leaving the fifth athlete as the only one who can come in fifth place. So, all told, there are $5 \times 4 \times 3 \times 2 \times 1$ such orderings. We write this expression more compactly using **factorials**; that is, we write $5! = 5 \times 4 \times 3 \times 2 \times 1$.

Try a practice problem much like one you might see on the exam.

A group of four friends meets four days a week to study. For each meeting, a different friend is responsible for bringing snacks, and nobody is allowed to bring snacks on more than one day. In how many different ways can the friends be matched up with the day on which they are each responsible to bring the snacks?

A. 10
B. 12
C. 24
D. 64
E. 120

The correct answer is C. Let us call the days A, B, C, and D. There are four different ways to assign the friend responsible for bringing snacks on day A. Once that is decided, that friend can no longer bring snacks on the remaining three days, leaving three choices for day B. Similarly, there are then two options for day C, and only one for day D. As such, just as in the example, we multiply $4 \times 3 \times 2 \times 1$ to get the total number of orderings. This product is 24.

Turn to page 268 to follow the College Readiness Benchmark Learning Path questions covering Counting Techniques.

SIMPLE PROBABILITY

All experiments that involve uncertainty or chance (e.g., predicting the stock market or weather, guessing the percentage of votes a candidate will receive, or simply flipping a coin) involve probability. Probability falls under the category of Preparing for Higher Math.

The result of a single trial of a probability experiment is called an **outcome**. The collection of all outcomes is the **sample space**, which is written as a set. For instance, if you roll a typical six-sided die and record the number of the face on which it comes to rest, the outcomes are the labels on the faces: $S = \{1, 2, 3, 4, 5, 6\}$. An **event** is a subset of the sample space and is usually described using one or more conditions. For instance, the event that "the die lands on an odd number" is the subset $E = \{1, 3, 5\}$.

Suppose E and F represent events of some probability experiment. Some common events formed using them are as follows:

Event	Description in Words
E or F	All outcomes in E or in F or in both
E and F	All outcomes in common to E and F
Complement of E	All outcomes NOT in E

You are likely familiar with the notion of chance, such as the percent chance of snow today or the likelihood that a professional baseball player will hit a home run. The **probability** of an event A, denoted by $P(A)$, is a number between 0 and 1, inclusive, that describes the percent chance that event A has of occurring.

How do you determine the probability of an event? The answer can be rather complicated, but for most of the experiments you will encounter, each outcome in the sample space is *equally likely*. So if the sample space contains N outcomes, then the probability of any *one* of them occurring is $\frac{1}{N}$.

This can be extended to events in the sense that if A contains k elements, then $P(A) = \frac{\text{Number of outcomes in } A}{\text{Number of possible outcomes}} = \frac{k}{N}$.

For the above dice experiment, since the event "the die lands on an odd number" is the subset $E = \{1, 3, 5\}$, and all outcomes are equally likely, $P(E) = \frac{3}{6} = \frac{1}{2}$. So there's a 50 percent chance of the die landing on an odd number, which is intuitive!

Take a look at this probability question.

A board game involves a spinner with congruent sections numbered 1 through 25. On a given spin, the spinner has an equal chance of landing on any number. What is the probability that the spinner will land on a number that is divisible by 3?

A. $\frac{17}{25}$

B. $\frac{14}{25}$

C. $\frac{8}{25}$

D. $\frac{7}{25}$

E. $\frac{3}{25}$

The correct answer is C. There are a total of 25 numbers on the wheel, so we must determine how many of these 25 numbers are divisible by 3. Writing them down, we see that 3, 6, 9, 12, 15, 18, 21, and 24 are precisely the numbers from 1 to 25 that are divisible by 3. Since there are 8 of them and 25 numbers in all, the probability that the number on which the spinner lands is divisible by 3 is $\frac{8}{25}$.

Turn to page 269 to follow the College Readiness Benchmark Learning Path questions covering Simple Probability.

BASIC STATISTICS AND DATA COLLECTION

As part of the Preparing for Higher Math category, the ACT covers statistics and data collection. **Statistics** is a collection of procedures and principles used for gathering data and analyzing information that aids in making decisions and inferences when faced with uncertainty. Suppose you have certain data—such as the number of sit-ups you can do in 75 seconds, or the number of people who attend different yoga classes at a local studio. Each measurement in the data set originates from a distinct source called a **unit**. The complete collection of units about which information is sought is called the **population**. A **variable** is a characteristic of the population of units we are interested in, and the observed values of a variable comprise its **data**.

There are two main types of variables: qualitative and quantitative. A **qualitative** variable is one with values that are categories (e.g., gender, hair color, demographic information). There is not a unique numerical ordering of these outputs. A **quantitative** variable is one whose values are numerical quantities (e.g., height, temperature, number of heads obtained in three flips of a coin).

It is rarely possible to collect data for each and every unit in a population because resources are often limited. So a representative subset of the population of units, called a **sample**, is chosen for which you will attempt to gather information for the variable of interest.

An ideal sample should be reasonably large. For instance, if the population of your study were the entire US population, you would not want to choose your sample to consist of merely eight people from Connecticut. The sample should also be devoid of bias. A study is **biased** if it systematically favors certain outcomes. For instance, suppose you were investigating a question in which females would likely respond differently than males, and that your population was equally split between males and females. In such case, a sample consisting of 98 percent males could potentially yield biased results.

COMPUTING MEAN

Questions involving data and statistics on the ACT exam will sometimes require you to compute the average (or **mean**) of a list of numbers in some applied context. To compute the mean of a list of numbers, simply add the numbers and then divide by how many numbers you added:

$$\text{mean} = \frac{\text{sum of values}}{\text{number of values}}$$

> **CAUTION**
>
> You must include any zeros in the total count when computing a mean.
>
> For instance, the mean of the set {0, 2, 5, 6, 7} is $\frac{0+2+5+6+7}{5}=4$, not $\frac{0+2+5+6+7}{4}=5$.

SUMMING IT UP

- The **greatest common factor (GCF)** of two whole numbers *n* and *m* is the largest whole number that divides into both *n* and *m* evenly. The **least common multiple (LCM)** of two whole numbers *n* and *m* is the smallest whole number into which both *n* and *m* divide.
- The **order of operations** when simplifying an expression is first parentheses, then exponents, then multiplication and division from left to right, and finally addition and subtraction from left to right.
- If *b* and *n* are natural numbers, then $b^n = \underbrace{b \times \ldots \times b}_{n \text{ times}}$. Here, *b* is called the **base** and *n* is the **exponent**.
- **Scientific notation** is simply a way of expressing a number as a product of a decimal number between 1 and 10 and an appropriate power of 10.
- The **square root** of a nonnegative real number *a* is another number *b* whose square is *a*, that is $b^2 = a$. In such case, we write $\sqrt{a} = b$. A **cube root** of a real number *a* is another number *b* whose cube is *a*, that is $b^3 = a$. In such case, we write $\sqrt[3]{a} = b$.
- A **logarithm** is simply an exponent. When working with logarithms, remember that $y = \log_a x$ means the same thing as $x = a^y$.
- A **ratio** is a comparison of one quantity *x* to another quantity *y*, expressed as a fraction $\frac{x}{y}$, or sometimes using the notation *x*:*y*. In words, this is interpreted as, "for every *x* of one type, there are *y* of the second type."
- A **proportion** is an equation relating two ratios. In symbols, a proportion is expressed by setting two fractions equal to each other, say $\frac{a}{b}=\frac{c}{d}$.
- The word **percent** means "per hundred." A **percentage** is used to express the number of *parts* of a *whole*.
- **Linear equations** are equations in which the variable is raised to the first power. The process of solving linear equations involves simplifying various expressions by clearing fractions and using the order of operations and the distributive property of multiplication in order to get the variable on one side of the equation.
- The **absolute value** of *a*, denoted $|a|$, measures the distance between *a* and 0.
- A **variable** is an unknown quantity represented by a letter, like *x*, *y*, or *z*; a **constant** is a real number whose value does not change.
- An **algebraic expression** is an arithmetic combination of terms. All of the rules (exponent rules, order of operations, etc.) and properties of arithmetic (commutative property, associative property, etc.) must apply to algebraic expressions.

- **Like terms** are two or more terms that have the same variables.
- A **quadratic equation** is an equation of the form $ax^2 + bx + c = 0$, where a, b, and c are real numbers, and $a \neq 0$.
- There are two main types of counting problems on the ACT exam:

    1) If you want to determine the number of combinations that can be formed from a of quantity 1, b of quantity 2, c of quantity 3, assuming that order is not important and that all of the quantities are different, you simply need to multiply a, b, c, together.

    2) The number of ordered arrangements of n objects is $n!$
- An **outcome** is the result of a single trial of a probability experiment. The collection of all outcomes is the **sample space.** An **event** is a subset of the sample space and is usually described using one or more conditions.
- The **probability** of an event A, denoted by $P(A)$, is a number between 0 and 1, inclusive, that describes the percent chance that event A has of occurring.
    - If each outcome in the sample space is *equally likely* and the sample space contains N outcomes, then the probability of any *one* of them occurring is $\frac{1}{N}$.

      This can be extended to events in the sense that if A contains k elements, then $P(A) = \frac{\text{Number of outcomes in } A}{\text{Number of possible outcomes}} = \frac{k}{N}$.
    - To compute the **mean** of a list of numbers, simply add the numbers and divide by how many numbers are added:

$$\text{mean} = \frac{\text{sum of values}}{\text{number of values}}.$$

ONLINE PREP

Want to Know More?

Access more practice questions, lessons, helpful hints, and strategies for the following pre-algebra and elementary algebra topics in *Peterson's Online Course for the ACT® Exam*:

- Averages
- Converting Fractions
- Factoring
- Fractions and Decimals
- Inequalities
- Number Properties
- Operations with Fractions
- Percents
- Powers and Roots
- Probability
- Quadratics
- Ratios
- Solving Equations
- Word Problems

To purchase and access the course, go to **www.petersons.com/testprep/act**.

COLLEGE READINESS BENCHMARK LEARNING PATH PRACTICE

Directions: The following practice exercises are designed to provide you with more opportunities to familiarize yourself with the content you will encounter on the ACT exam. Read each question carefully and choose the best answer. As you go through the practice set, review each solution and follow the expanded explanations provided to help strengthen your skills in working with Pre-Algebra and Elementary Algebra topics.

Basic Arithmetic Operations

1. Compute: $12 - 9 \div 3 \times 5 + 5$

SHOW YOUR WORK HERE

A. –8

B. 2

C. 0

D. 10

E. 50

The correct answer is B. You must use the **order of operations** when simplifying an arithmetic expression like this. This is especially important when parentheses are not in the expression because it takes the guesswork out of simplifying the expression. To this end, first perform the division and multiplication from left to right as it arises:

$$12 - 9 \div 3 \times 5 + 5 =$$

$$12 - 3 \times 5 + 5 =$$

$$12 - 15 + 5$$

Now perform subtraction and add from left to right as it arises to further simplify:

$$12 - 15 + 5 = -3 + 5 = 2$$

The key is to follow this set of rules explicitly and not to insert parentheses mentally. Doing so results in a miscalculation. The most frequently occurring error is to perform the operations as they arise from left to right, which would give you an answer of 10 (choice D). The other choices arise when inserting parentheses in different places in the expression.

2. Suppose *m* is a negative odd integer and *n* is a negative even integer. Which of the following expressions must be a positive odd integer?

SHOW YOUR WORK HERE

F. $n + m$

G. $m - n$

H. $\frac{m}{n}$

J. $-(m + n)$

K. $m \bullet n$

The correct answer is J. Questions about the *form* of a number can be intimidating. For these types of question, break down the information into what is given and what is being asked. For this problem:

- "*m* is a negative odd integer" means *m* belongs to the list –1, –3, –5, –7, ...
- "*n* is a negative even integer" means *n* belongs to the list –2, –4, –6, –8, ...
- The result must be a positive odd integer, meaning it belongs to the list 1, 3, 5, 7, ...

To begin, if you add two negative numbers, integers or otherwise, the result is negative; therefore you can eliminate choice F. Next, choice H is a likely candidate to eliminate because quotients are often not integers. To convince yourself of this, use some actual values for m and n. If you use m = −3 and n = −2, the result is $\frac{m}{n}=\frac{-3}{-2}=\frac{3}{2}$, which is not an integer. So you can eliminate choice H.

Choice K can also be eliminated. Using $m=-3$ and $n=-2$ (though *any* pairings will work) shows that $m \bullet n=(-3)\bullet(-2)=6$, which is a positive *even* integer. Do not get stuck trying to reason abstractly here; using actual values can cut to the chase much more quickly.

This leaves choices G and J. First, note that the sum of an even integer and an odd integer is always odd. This is a fact that you should commit to memory. Further, since $n + m = m + n$ by the commutative property, and $m + n$ is negative as we saw earlier, it follows that $m + n$ is an odd negative integer. Multiplying it by −1 yields a positive odd integer. Thus, choice J is the correct answer.

If you did not see this, you could go on to eliminate choice G by using $m = -5$ and $n = -2$.
Then, $m - n = -5 - (-2) = -5 + 2 = -3$, which is negative.

SHOW YOUR WORK HERE

3. Compute: $\dfrac{4+\frac{3}{8}}{2+\frac{3}{8}}$

A. $\frac{35}{19}$

B. $\frac{35}{64}$

C. $\frac{7}{5}$

D. $\frac{565}{64}$

E. 2

The correct answer is A. This problem is a combination of order of operations *in disguise* and properties of fractions. The most common error committed when trying to simplify an expression like this is to cancel like *terms* in the numerator and denominator rather than like *factors*. The former are separated by plus and minus signs, whereas the latter are separated by multiplication signs.

For example, the following calculation is incorrect: $\dfrac{4+\frac{3}{8}}{2+\frac{3}{8}} \neq \dfrac{\cancel{4}\,2+\cancel{\frac{3}{8}}}{\cancel{2}+\cancel{\frac{3}{8}}}$.

Instead, the given expression can be written equivalently as $\dfrac{4+\frac{3}{8}}{2+\frac{3}{8}}=\left(4+\frac{3}{8}\right)\div\left(2+\frac{3}{8}\right)$.

Simplifying this expression requires the use of the order of operations: simplify each of the two sums enclosed in parentheses first by getting a common denominator, then divide the resulting fractions.

The correct steps are as follows:

$$\begin{aligned}\left(4+\frac{3}{8}\right)\div\left(2+\frac{3}{8}\right)&=\left(\frac{32}{8}+\frac{3}{8}\right)\div\left(\frac{16}{8}+\frac{3}{8}\right)\\&=\frac{35}{8}\div\frac{19}{8}\\&=\frac{35}{\not{8}}\bullet\frac{\not{8}}{19}\\&=\frac{35}{19}\end{aligned}$$

The incorrect choices reflect the results of several common errors. Choice C is the result of adding the numerators and fractions without first getting a common denominator, while choice B is the result of doing that *and* forgetting to convert the division problem to an equivalent product. Choice D is the result of forgetting to convert the division problem to an equivalent product (obtained by replacing the fraction after the division sign by its reciprocal). Choice E is the result of the initial cancellation that we pointed to as a common mistake. Being comfortable with computing with fractions will ensure that you will not make these errors.

EXPONENTS, RADICALS, AND APPROXIMATION

1. Simplify: $\left(2^{-1}+3^{-1}\right)^{-2}$

SHOW YOUR WORK HERE

A. $\frac{36}{5}$

B. $\frac{36}{25}$

C. $\frac{25}{36}$

D. 13

E. 25

The correct answer is B. Dealing with exponents in the context of order of operations can be tricky. For this problem, the most common error involves incorrectly applying the –2 exponent. A common mistake is to distribute the –2 power to both terms, but $\left(2^{-1}+3^{-1}\right)^{-2}\neq\left(2^{-1}\right)^{-2}+\left(3^{-1}\right)^{-2}$. Making this incorrect assumption leads to choice D.

Following the order of operations requires that you simplify the expression inside the parentheses first. To do this, convert the terms to fractions (since they each involve a negative power) and then combine the fractions by getting a least common denominator:

$$\left(2^{-1}+3^{-1}\right)^{-2}=\left(\frac{1}{2}+\frac{1}{3}\right)^{-2}=\left(\frac{3}{6}+\frac{2}{6}\right)^{-2}=\left(\frac{5}{6}\right)^{-2}$$

So how do you handle the negative power? In the simplified form above, the effect of the negative power is to flip the fraction inside to obtain $\left(\frac{5}{6}\right)^{-2}=\left(\frac{6}{5}\right)^{2}$. A common error is to apply the negative power too early and flip the fractions in the second step above; that is, $\left(\frac{1}{2}+\frac{1}{3}\right)^{-2}\neq(2+3)^2$. Doing this results in choice E. Another common error is to forget to flip the fraction entirely and square it; this results in choice C.

Complete the simplification by squaring **both** the numerator and denominator to get $\left(\frac{6}{5}\right)^{2}=\frac{36}{25}$. If you only square the numerator, you get choice A.

2. Compute: $\sqrt{91} \bullet \left(\frac{\sqrt{13}}{\sqrt{7}} - \frac{\sqrt{7}}{\sqrt{13}}\right)$

SHOW YOUR WORK HERE

F. $-\sqrt{91}$

G. $\frac{6}{91}$

H. 6

J. $\frac{3}{\sqrt{91}}$

K. 20

The correct answer is H. Often, when students see radicals, the tendency is to pull out the calculator and immediately approximate them. But that is not an option here because none of the choices are decimals. Instead, you should familiarize yourself with the basic rules for simplifying radicals and fractions.

Using the order of operations, you need to simplify the expression inside the parentheses first. To do so, you must combine the fractions into a single fraction. And to do this, you need a common denominator. (If you just subtract the numerators and denominators, you will get choice F). The common denominator is the product $\sqrt{7} \bullet \sqrt{13}$, applied as follows:

$$\sqrt{91} \bullet \left(\frac{\sqrt{13}}{\sqrt{7}} - \frac{\sqrt{7}}{\sqrt{13}}\right) = \sqrt{91} \bullet \left(\frac{\sqrt{13} \bullet \sqrt{13}}{\sqrt{7} \bullet \sqrt{13}} - \frac{\sqrt{7} \bullet \sqrt{7}}{\sqrt{13} \bullet \sqrt{7}}\right)$$
$$= \sqrt{91} \bullet \left(\frac{\sqrt{13} \bullet \sqrt{13} - \sqrt{7} \bullet \sqrt{7}}{\sqrt{7} \bullet \sqrt{13}}\right)$$

Now, use the fact that $\sqrt{a} \bullet \sqrt{a} = a$ to simplify the numerator as follows:

$$\sqrt{91} \bullet \left(\frac{\sqrt{13} \bullet \sqrt{13} - \sqrt{7} \bullet \sqrt{7}}{\sqrt{7} \bullet \sqrt{13}}\right) = \sqrt{91} \bullet \left(\frac{13-7}{\sqrt{7} \bullet \sqrt{13}}\right)$$
$$= \sqrt{91} \bullet \left(\frac{6}{\sqrt{7} \bullet \sqrt{13}}\right)$$

Next, simplify the denominator using the property $\sqrt{a} \bullet \sqrt{b} = \sqrt{a \bullet b}$:

$$\sqrt{91} \bullet \left(\frac{6}{\sqrt{7} \bullet \sqrt{13}}\right) = \cancel{\sqrt{91}} \bullet \left(\frac{6}{\cancel{\sqrt{91}}}\right) = 6$$

The incorrect answer choices will often be the results of some arithmetic error. For example, choice J is the result of saying $\sqrt{a} \bullet \sqrt{a} = 2a$, while choice K is the result of adding inside the parentheses instead of subtracting. If you are careful, these types of errors will be easily avoidable.

3. If $\frac{1}{4} < z < \frac{1}{2}$, which of the following must be greater than 1?

SHOW YOUR WORK HERE

A. 2z

B. z^2

C. z – 1

D. $z + \frac{3}{4}$

E. $\sqrt{z}$

255

Chapter 6
Pre-Algebra and Elementary Algebra

The correct answer is D. Questions like this are among the most difficult you will encounter on the ACT exam. But they are not as bad as you think if you focus on breaking them down and applying a sound strategy.

First, the question asks which of the expressions **must** be greater than 1. This means no matter what value of *z* between $\frac{1}{4}$ and $\frac{1}{2}$ is plugged in, the resulting value must be greater than 1.

To begin, eliminate choice C. This involves subtracting 1 from a positive fraction less than 1, which makes it smaller than 1, not greater.

Next, choices B and E can be eliminated using the following rules:

- If $0 < a < b$, then $a^2 < b^2$.
- If $0 < a < b$, then $\sqrt{a} < \sqrt{b}$.

Since $\frac{1}{4} < z < \frac{1}{2}$, squaring all parts yields the following:

$$\left(\frac{1}{4}\right)^2 < z^2 < \left(\frac{1}{2}\right)^2 = \frac{1}{16} < z^2 < \frac{1}{4}$$

So z^2 must be less than 1.

Finding the square roots of all parts yields the following:

$$\sqrt{\frac{1}{4}} < z < \sqrt{\frac{1}{2}} = \frac{1}{2} < \sqrt{z} < \frac{1}{\sqrt{2}}$$

So $\sqrt{z}$ must be less than 1.

This problem comes down to deciding between choices A and D. At this point, it is often helpful to plug in values for *z* to aid in the decision process. But do not do so sporadically. Choosing values of *z* close to the endpoints of its range (that is, close to $\frac{1}{4}$ and $\frac{1}{2}$) is often the way to go.

To make the value as big as possible when multiplying (as in choice A), choose values at the upper end of the range. No matter what value of *z* you choose between $\frac{1}{4}$ and $\frac{1}{2}$, it will always be less than 1; it only *equals* 1 when *z* is chosen to be $\frac{1}{2}$, and that is not in the range. Therefore, the correct answer cannot be choice A; it must be choice D.

Note: While it is recommended to be familiar with many of the facts stated in the explanation, sometimes the "guess and check" method may be a quicker way to solving a problem or this method may be your only alternative if you forget a formula. In this case, the obvious value between $\frac{1}{4}$ and $\frac{1}{2}$ is $\frac{1}{3}$. When "checked" into all the answer options, it only renders a value greater than 1 for choice D.

Another method is to choose to convert the fractions to decimals and follow a logical approach to solving. Whatever method you choose, it is in your best interest to be comfortable with fractions for this test.

BASIC LOGARITHMS

1. Simplify: $\log_5\left(\frac{1}{125}\right)$

SHOW YOUR WORK HERE

A. –3

B. 3

C. $\frac{1}{625}$

D. $\frac{1}{25}$

E. 25

The correct answer is B. The logarithms you will be asked to compute on the ACT will result in integers or fractions. Even so, students are often alarmed by logarithms, but it is mainly due to the intimidating notation. So let's change the way it looks. Call the expression *x*:

$$\log_5\left(\frac{1}{125}\right) = x$$

This can be written as an equivalent exponential equation obtained by raising the base to the right side and setting it equal to the quantity of which you are taking the logarithm. Here, that equation is $5^x = \frac{1}{125}$.

In words, you want to find the value of *x* for which if you raise 5 to it, you get $\frac{1}{125}$. Rewriting the right side as a power of 5 is helpful in this regard. Observe that $\frac{1}{125} = \frac{1}{5^3} = 5^{-3}$. So *x* must be –3.

There are various common errors committed in this type of problem. For one, from the equation $5^x = \frac{1}{5^3}$, students often conclude that $x = 3$. But, the exponential parts must both be in the numerator before you can equate exponents. Another error stems from reformulating the logarithm equation incorrectly. Specifically, choice C is the result of viewing it as the equation $5x = \frac{1}{125}$, while choice D arises from viewing it as the equation $x = 5\left(\frac{1}{125}\right)$.

2. Compute: $\log_2\left(\frac{2^2 \bullet 2^{-3}}{2^3}\right)$

SHOW YOUR WORK HERE

F. –3

G. –4

H. 2

J. 4

K. Undefined

The correct answer is G. The key to this problem lies in using the property $\log_a\left(a^x\right) = x$. Since the base $a = 2$, you need to express the quantity in the parentheses as a power of 2. This requires the use of the exponent rules:

$$\frac{2^2 \bullet 2^{-3}}{2^3} = \frac{2^2}{2^3 \bullet 2^3} = \frac{2^2}{\left(2^3\right)^2} = \frac{2^2}{2^6} = 2^{2-6} = 2^{-4}$$

So $\log_2\left(\frac{2^2 \bullet 2^{-3}}{2^3}\right) = \log_2\left(2^{-4}\right) = -4$.

The errors often made in this type of problem stem from trouble with computing with exponents and using exponent rules. For instance, $\frac{2^{-3}}{2^3} \neq 1$; making this error leads to choice H. Similarly, $2^{-3} \neq -2^3$; this error leads to $\log_2(-4)$, which is undefined (choice K). Making the error $\log_2\left(\frac{1}{2^4}\right) \neq 4$ leads to choosing choice J. In this case, you must bring the 2 to the numerator before applying the property $\log_a\left(a^x\right) = x$. Finally, $2^3 \bullet 2^3 = \left(2^3\right)^2 = 2^6$, not $2^{3+2} = 2^5$; this error leads to incorrectly choosing choice F.

3. Compute: $\log_3\left(\frac{243}{9}\right)$

SHOW YOUR WORK HERE

A. 10

B. $\frac{5}{2}$

C. 3

D. 9

E. 7

The correct answer is C. This is like the previous problems, but the actual base is not used explicitly in the expression inside the parentheses. So you need to know to express the input as a single power of 3, and *then* use correct properties.

Note that $\frac{243}{9} = 27 = 3^3$. Therefore, $\log_3\left(\frac{243}{9}\right) = \log_3\left(3^3\right) = 3$.

A common error here is to apply the logarithm to the numerator and denominator separately; however, $\log_3\left(\frac{243}{9}\right) \neq \frac{\log_3(243)}{\log_3(9)}$. This leads to incorrectly choosing choice B. Choices A and E arise from typical errors with exponent rules: $\frac{a^b}{a^c} \neq a^{b \cdot c}$ and $\frac{a^b}{a^c} \neq a^{b+c}$. Finally, choice D is the result of dividing the input by the base to conclude incorrectly that $\log_3(27) = \frac{27}{3}$.

Ratios, Proportions, and Percentages

1. Three supporting beams (front, back-left, and back-right) of a tripod hold up a virtual reality simulator with a weight distribution in the ratio 4:6:6. If the back-right beam holds up to 300 pounds, how much weight is supported by the front beam?

SHOW YOUR WORK HERE

A. 200 pounds

B. 300 pounds

C. 500 pounds

D. 800 pounds

E. 600 pounds

The correct answer is A. If 4:6:6 is the ratio of front:back left:back right, then it can be concluded that the back legs are equal and the front leg is less than the back legs. So if the back leg holds up to 300 pounds, then the front leg has to hold up *less* than 300 pounds. The only logical answer among the choices is 200 pounds (choice A).

Another strategy is to determine the number of units involved and then the number of pounds corresponding to a single unit. The number of units is the sum of the components of the ratios, namely $4 + 6 + 6 = 16$. The back-right beam holds up 6 units of weight to the tune of 300 pounds; so each unit is equivalent to $\frac{300}{6} = 50$ pounds. Thus, the front beam holds up $4(50) = 200$ pounds.

The distractor choices for this type of problem often are the correct answers to different questions. For instance, 300 pounds (choice B) is the weight supported by the back-left leg, 500 pounds (choice C) is the total weight supported by the front leg and one back leg, 800 pounds (choice D) is the weight of the simulator, and 600 pounds (choice E) is the combined weight that the back legs hold up.

2. An amateur softball player can pitch the ball at 40 miles per hour. Which of these expressions is this rate expressed in feet per second?

SHOW YOUR WORK HERE

F. $40 \times 60 \times 60 \times 5{,}280$ feet per second

G. $\frac{40 \times 60 \times 60}{5{,}280}$ feet per second

H. $\frac{40 \times 5{,}280}{60}$ feet per second

J. $\frac{40 \times 5{,}280}{60 \times 60}$ feet per second

K. $\frac{40}{60 \times 5{,}280}$ feet per second

The correct answer is J. The method underlying converting units is to ensure the units you want to end up with are correctly placed In the product you create. This amounts to using the correct forms of the conversion factors. If you do, the units with which you begin will cancel, and you will end up with the units you desire.

The conversion factors needed are as follows:

- 1 mile = 5,280 feet
- 1 hour = 60 minutes
- 1 minute = 60 seconds

The word *per* means "divide by." So for conversion purposes, it is convenient to think of "40 miles per hour" as $\frac{40 \text{ miles}}{1 \text{ hour}}$. Convert the units as follows:

$$\frac{40 \cancel{\text{miles}}}{1 \cancel{\text{hour}}} \times \frac{1 \cancel{\text{hour}}}{60 \cancel{\text{minutes}}} \times \frac{1 \cancel{\text{minute}}}{60 \boxed{\text{seconds}}} \times \frac{5{,}280 \boxed{\text{feet}}}{1 \cancel{\text{mile}}}$$

Notice the boxed units are the ones we want to keep. All other intermittent units must cancel. Thus, the equivalent expression is given by choice J. All other choices are the results of not using the correct form of the conversion factors and so, not all the units cancel in the right way.

3. What is the result of reducing $3\frac{3}{10}$ by $2\frac{1}{5}\%$ of itself?

SHOW YOUR WORK HERE

A. $3\frac{1,137}{5,000}$

B. $3\frac{1,863}{5,000}$

C. $6\frac{33}{50}$

D. $\frac{363}{5,000}$

E. $\frac{30}{499}$

The correct answer is A. There are three main steps to solving this problem. First, remember that *p*% means $p \bullet \frac{1}{100}$.

Therefore, $2\frac{1}{5}\% = \frac{11}{5}\% = \frac{11}{5} \bullet \frac{1}{100} = \frac{11}{500}$. A common error here is to forget to multiply by $\frac{1}{100}$.

Next, the word *of* means "multiply." So $2\frac{1}{5}\%$ of $3\frac{3}{10}$ is $\left(3\frac{3}{10}\right) \bullet \left(\frac{11}{500}\right) = \frac{33}{10} \bullet \frac{11}{500} = \frac{363}{5,000}$.

Finally, you are asked to reduce $3\frac{3}{10}$ by this amount, which means you must subtract $\frac{363}{5,000}$ from $3\frac{3}{10}$. If you neglect to do this step, you get choice D, and if you add instead of subtract, you will get choice B. When subtracting, make certain to convert both to equivalent fractions with the LCD 5,000; if you subtract in the wrong order $(a - b) \neq (b - a)$ and without LCDs, you will get choice E:

$$\begin{aligned} 3\frac{3}{10} - \frac{363}{5,000} &= \frac{33}{10} - \frac{363}{5,000} \\ &= \frac{33 \bullet 500}{10 \bullet 500} - \frac{363}{5,000} \\ &= \frac{33 \bullet 500 - 363}{5,000} \\ &= \frac{16,137}{5,000} \\ &= 3\frac{1,137}{5,000} \end{aligned}$$

Another way to look at this problem is to recognize that if you reduce a number by a very small percentage, it should be less than what you start with (choice A). Choices B and C are larger than 3.3, and choices D and E are MUCH smaller than 3.3.

Linear Equations in One Variable

1. Solve for *z*: $2 - [3 - 2(1 - 2z)] = -z$

SHOW YOUR WORK HERE

A. $\frac{1}{3}$

B. 1

C. $-\frac{1}{5}$

D. −2

E. 3

The correct answer is A. Simplifying an expression involving multiple grouping symbols may seem intimidating, but if you work your way from the inside out using the order of operations, you will succeed. Proceed as follows to whittle the left side down to a difference of two terms:

$$2-[3-\underbrace{2(1-2z)}_{\text{Start here.}}]=-z$$

$$2-[\underbrace{3-2+4z}_{\text{Simplify this.}}]=-z$$

$$\underbrace{2\ -[1+4z]}_{\text{Distribute }-1.}=-z$$

$$2-1-4z=-z$$

$$1-4z=-z$$

The most common error involves not applying the distributive property correctly. Remember, you need to apply a multiple in front of a grouping symbol to all terms contained within it. Various errors of this type result in choices B and C.

Isolate the z terms on the right side by adding $4z$ to get the equation $1 = 3z$. Make certain you add the *opposite* of the term you want to move to the other side so that it cancels on the side from which you want to move it; otherwise, you incorrectly arrive at choice C.

Divide both sides by the coefficient of z to get $z=\frac{1}{3}$. Common errors committed in this last step are subtracting the coefficient of z from both sides and dividing the coefficient of z by the constant term on the other side of the equation. These errors result in choices D and E, respectively.

2. Solve for d: $nd = A(be - nd)$.

SHOW YOUR WORK HERE

F. $d=\frac{be}{2n}$

G. $d=\frac{Abe}{n+An}$

H. $d=\frac{Abe}{2n}$

J. $d=\frac{(A+1)n}{Abe}$

K. $d=Abe-(n+An)$

The correct answer is G. The strategy is to gather the d terms on one side and all other terms on the other side of the equation. Then, factor out a d and divide both sides by the resulting coefficient of d:

$$nd = A(be-nd)$$

$$nd = Abe - And$$

$$nd + And = Abe$$

$$d(n+An) = Abe$$

$$d=\frac{Abe}{n+An}$$

Typical mistakes here are incorrect cancelation of terms and not applying the distributive property correctly. Choice F is the result of canceling the *A*s below:

$$\frac{Abe}{n+An}\neq\frac{\cancel{A}be}{n+\cancel{A}n}$$

Choice H is the result of incorrectly adding nd to both sides *before* distributing the A. Choices J and K arise from making errors in the last step; specifically, subtracting the coefficient of d from both sides instead of dividing by it and dividing the coefficient of d by the constant term on the other side instead of the other way around, respectively.

3. Solve for x: $-\frac{1}{3}\left(3-\frac{4}{3}x\right)=-3x$

SHOW YOUR WORK HERE

A. $-\frac{9}{23}$

B. $\frac{9}{23}$

C. $\frac{9}{7}$

D. $\frac{9}{31}$

E. $\frac{9}{13}$

The correct answer is D. Generally, getting rid of fractions in an equation as soon as possible is preferable. Here, multiply both sides by –3 to get rid of the leftmost fraction on the left side:

$$(-3)\bullet-\frac{1}{3}\left(3-\frac{4}{3}x\right)=(-3)\bullet(-3x)$$

$$3-\frac{4}{3}x=9x$$

Now, multiply both sides by 3 again to get rid of the remaining fraction:

$$3\bullet\left(3-\frac{4}{3}x\right)=3\bullet(9x)$$

$$9-4x=27x$$

Make sure you multiply *both* sides by the number needed to eliminate the fraction. The tendency is to multiply on only one side; doing so here results in choice E. Also, be careful with the signs; making a sign error on the right side results in choice A.

Now add $4x$ to both sides to gather the x terms on one side of the equation $9 = 31x$; make sure you do not subtract it, or you will get choice B.

Finally, divide both sides by the coefficient of x to get $x=\frac{9}{31}$.

Absolute Value

1. Suppose x is a negative integer. Which of these has the greatest value?

SHOW YOUR WORK HERE

A. $2x$

B. $\frac{1}{2}x$

C. $|x|$

D. $1-x|$

E. $|x^{-1}|$

The correct answer is D. Try to eliminate as many choices as possible right off the bat. Since we know that x is negative, we can eliminate choices A and B because both $2x$ and $\frac{1}{2}x$ are negative.

The remaining three choices (C, D, and E) are all positive. We can eliminate choice E because $\left|x^{-1}\right| = \left|\frac{1}{x}\right|$, and since x is an integer, it follows that this is no greater than 1 no matter what x-value is chosen, while $|x|$ is at least equal to 1.

How do you choose between choices C and D? Plug in some values of x to help guide your thinking:

x	$\lvert x\rvert$	$\lvert 1 - x\rvert$
–2	2	$\lvert 1 - (-2)\rvert = \lvert 3\rvert = 3$
–4	4	$\lvert 1 - (-4)\rvert = \lvert 1 + 4\rvert = 5$
–9	9	$\lvert 1 - (-9)\rvert = \lvert 1 + 9\rvert = 10$

While you might have instinctively thought that $|x|$ (choice C) was larger because you were subtracting inside $|1 - x|$, it turns out that $|1 - x|$ (choice D) gives the largest value.

2. Compute: $\left(1-\left|8-3\left|-4\right|\right|\right)^2$

SHOW YOUR WORK HERE

F. –6

G. –15

H. 361

J. 9

K. 25

The correct answer is J. Before computing anything, realize that the whole quantity is the square of an expression. Therefore, it cannot be negative. You can eliminate choices F and G right away.

You must use the order of operations when simplifying arithmetic expressions, but where does the absolute value fit into the hierarchy? Treat this as you would any other grouping symbol. Start from the innermost grouping symbol and work your way outward:

$$\left(1-\left|8-3\underbrace{\left|-4\right|}_{\text{Compute this first}}\right|\right)^2 = \left(1-\left|\underbrace{8-3\cdot 4}_{\text{Now, compute this following the order of operations}}\right|\right)^2$$

$$=\left(1-\left|8-12\right|\right)^2$$

$$=\left(1-\underbrace{\left|-4\right|}_{\text{Now this}}\right)^2$$

$$=(1-4)^2$$

$$=(-3)^2$$

$$=9$$

If you don't follow the order of operations in the first step and mistakenly compute $8-3 \bullet 4$ from left to right to get $8-3 \bullet 4=5 \bullet 4=20$, the result is choice H. Similarly, if you make the error of computing $-\left|-4\right|=-4$, and not 4, this results in choice K.

3. Which of the following statements is NOT true?

SHOW YOUR WORK HERE

A. $|(-3) \bullet (-2)| = |(-3) \bullet (2)|$

B. $|-(-3)| = 3$

C. $-|2-8| = -(8-2)$

D. $\left|-\frac{2}{3}\right| = \left|\frac{-2}{-3}\right|$

E. $|(-5)-(-6)| = |-5| + |-6|$

The correct answer is E. The most efficient way to check these statements is to compute each one. Choice A computes as $|(-3) \bullet (-2)| = |6|$ and $|(-3) \bullet (2)| = |-6| = 6$ and is therefore true. Choice B computes as $|-(-3)| = |3| = 3$ and is also true. Choice C is true because $-|2-8| = -|-6| = -(6) = -6$ and $-(8-2) = -(6) = -6$. Choice D is true because $\left|-\frac{2}{3}\right| = \frac{2}{3} = \left|\frac{-2}{-3}\right|$. However, choice E computes as $|(-5)-(-6)| = |-5+6| = |1| = 1$, but $|-5| + |-6| = 5+6 = 11$ which is NOT true.

Algebraic Expressions

1. Simplify: $\dfrac{\frac{x}{x-1} - \frac{x}{x+1}}{\frac{x}{x-1} + \frac{x}{x+1}}$

SHOW YOUR WORK HERE

A. 0

B. $\dfrac{4x^3}{(x-1)^2(x+1)^2}$

C. $-\dfrac{1}{x}$

D. x

E. $\dfrac{1}{x}$

The correct answer is E. By far, the most common error made here is canceling common *terms*, not *factors*, in the numerator and denominator. This error would cause you to select zero (choice A). Specifically:

$$\frac{\frac{x}{x-1} - \frac{x}{x+1}}{\frac{x}{x-1} + \frac{x}{x+1}} \neq \frac{\cancel{\frac{x}{x-1}} - \cancel{\frac{x}{x+1}}}{\cancel{\frac{x}{x-1}} + \cancel{\frac{x}{x+1}}} \neq 0$$

Complex fractions can *look* intimidating, but remember they are just notation for division. The given expression can be written equivalently as follows:

$$\frac{\frac{x}{x-1} - \frac{x}{x+1}}{\frac{x}{x-1} + \frac{x}{x+1}} = \left(\frac{x}{x-1} - \frac{x}{x+1}\right) \div \left(\frac{x}{x-1} + \frac{x}{x+1}\right)$$

It is more apparent in this form how the order of operations applies. Simplify the expressions in each set of parentheses first, then divide the results. To simplify these expressions, you must get a common denominator, which is $(x-1)(x+1)$:

$$\frac{x}{x-1}-\frac{x}{x+1}=\frac{x}{x-1}\bullet\frac{x+1}{x+1}-\frac{x}{x+1}\bullet\frac{x-1}{x-1}=\frac{x(x+1)-x(x-1)}{(x+1)(x-1)}=\frac{x^2+x-x^2+x}{(x+1)(x-1)}=\frac{2x}{(x+1)(x-1)}$$

$$\frac{x}{x-1}+\frac{x}{x+1}=\frac{x}{x-1}\bullet\frac{x+1}{x+1}+\frac{x}{x+1}\bullet\frac{x-1}{x-1}=\frac{x(x+1)+x(x-1)}{(x+1)(x-1)}=\frac{x^2+x+x^2-x}{(x+1)(x-1)}=\frac{2x^2}{(x+1)(x-1)}$$

So $\left(\frac{x}{x-1}-\frac{x}{x+1}\right)\div\left(\frac{x}{x-1}+\frac{x}{x+1}\right)=\frac{2x}{(x+1)(x-1)}\div\frac{2x^2}{(x+1)(x-1)}$.

Now you must convert this to an equivalent product by flipping the fraction after the division sign:

$$\frac{2x}{(x+1)(x-1)}\div\frac{2x^2}{(x+1)(x-1)}=\frac{2x}{(x+1)(x-1)}\bullet\frac{(x+1)(x-1)}{2x^2}$$

If you forget to flip the fraction, you get choice B.

Finally, cancel like factors in the numerators and denominators and simplify:

$$\frac{\cancel{2x}}{\cancel{(x+1)(x-1)}}\bullet\frac{\cancel{(x+1)(x-1)}}{\cancel{2x^2}\,x}=\frac{1}{x}$$

Another common error (that results in selecting choice D), is not keeping track of where a term is located that doesn't cancel. Often the x is accidentally placed in the numerator.

2. Compute: $-2(2-x^2)+x^2(x-4)-2x(1-4x)$.

SHOW YOUR WORK HERE

F. x^3-x^2-6x-8

G. x^3+4x^2-2x-4

H. x^3-6x^2+2x+4

J. x^3+6x^2-2x-4

K. x^3+4x^2+2x-4

The correct answer is J. This problem is all about making proper use of the distributive property and keeping track of negative signs. All distractor choices are the results of making an error in one or both. To begin, apply the distributive property on all three products to get the following:

$$-2(2-x^2)+x^2(x-4)-2x(1-4x)=-4+2x^2+x^3-4x^2-2x+8x^2$$

Make certain to multiply each term in the parentheses by the factor outside.

Next, gather like terms (meaning terms with the exact same variable parts) and add their coefficients. It's convenient to underline like terms using the same marking to ensure you do not miss any:

$$-4+\underline{2x^2}+x^3\underline{-4x^2}-2x+\underline{8x^2}=x^3+\underline{6x^2}-2x-4$$

3. Simplify: $-6 \bullet \left(\frac{3}{x} \bullet x^{-1}\right)^{-2}$

SHOW YOUR WORK HERE

A. $-\frac{2x^4}{3}$

B. $-4x^2$

C. $-\frac{54}{x^4}$

D. $4x^4$

E. $-\frac{2}{3}$

The correct answer is A. Following the order of operations is crucial. Here, you must simplify the quantity inside the parentheses first. Then, you apply the exponent. And finally, you multiply the result by –6.

A very common error is not identifying the quantity to which the exponent applies. The exponent only applies to the quantity enclosed in parentheses, and NOT the –6 in front; if you apply it to the –6 as well, you will get choice D.

Simplify the expression inside the parentheses as follows:

$$-6 \bullet \left(\frac{3}{x} \bullet x^{-1}\right)^{-2} = -6 \bullet \left(\frac{3}{x} \bullet \frac{1}{x}\right)^{-2} = -6 \bullet \left(\frac{3}{x^2}\right)^{-2}$$

Note that $\frac{1}{x} \bullet x^{-1} \neq 1$. Making this error results in choice E.

Next, apply the power –2. Do this in two stages. First, apply the negative portion of the power by flipping the fraction. Then, square both the numerator and denominator of the resulting fraction:

$$-6 \bullet \left(\frac{3}{x^2}\right)^{-2} = -6 \bullet \left(\frac{x^2}{3}\right)^{2} = -6 \bullet \frac{\left(x^2\right)^2}{3^2} = -6 \bullet \frac{x^4}{9}$$

Neglecting to flip the fraction results in choice C. And, multiplying the base times the power instead of applying the exponent as above results in choice B.

Finally, simplify the result by canceling like factors in the 6 and 9. Doing so results in $-\frac{2x^4}{3}$.

Introduction to Quadratic Equations

1. Solve for x: $81 - x^2 = 0$

SHOW YOUR WORK HERE

A. –81 and 81

B. 9

C. 81

D. –9 and 9

E. 0 and 9

The correct answer is D. You *could* substitute the values into the equation directly and see which result in true statements, but there is a faster way. Recognize that the left side factors because it is a so-called *difference of squares*. Remember, $a^2 - b^2 = (a - b)(a + b)$ is a form frequently tested on the ACT math exam; it will enable you to avoid cumbersome calculations.

Factoring the left side of $81 - x^2 = 0$ yields $(9 - x)(9 + x) = 0$. Since the only way a product of two expressions can be zero is for one of the expressions itself to be zero, simply set each factor equal to zero and solve for x to see that $x = 9$ or $x = -9$.

2. Solve for x: $x(2x + 7) = 4$

SHOW YOUR WORK HERE

F. -1 and 2

G. $-\frac{1}{2}$ and 4

H. $\frac{1}{2}$ and -4

J. 0 and $-\frac{7}{2}$

K. 4 and $-\frac{3}{2}$

The correct answer is H. First and foremost, do NOT set each factor on the left side equal to 4. This is a very common error, which would result in choice K. The reason why this error is committed is that students are used to having a product equal to *zero*, where you *do* set each factor equal to zero and solve for *x*. But that is the only instance in which that approach works.

You must proceed by multiplying the terms on the left side and bringing all terms to the left side. Then, factor as shown:

$$x(2x+7)=4$$
$$2x^2+7x=4$$
$$2x^2+7x-4=0$$
$$(2x-1)(x+4)=0$$

Now, you can set each factor equal to zero and solve for *x*:

$$2x - 1 = 0, \text{ so that } x = \frac{1}{2}$$

and

$$x + 4 = 0, \text{ so that } x = -4$$

Incorrect factoring is another common error, which is reflected in the other answer choices.

3. Solve for x: $(2x - 3)^2 - (3x - 2)^2 = 0$

SHOW YOUR WORK HERE

A. -1 and 1

B. $\frac{3}{2}$ and $\frac{2}{3}$

C. $-\sqrt{5}$ and $\sqrt{5}$

D. $-\frac{3}{2}$ and $-\frac{2}{3}$

E. No real solutions

The correct answer is A. A common approach is to move the second squared term to the right side and take the square root of both sides. But students often forget to affix $\pm$ to one side, resulting in missing a solution. The safer approach is to expand both squared terms (by FOILing), simplifying the left side by combining like terms, and then refactoring the entire quadratic expression:

$$(2x-3)^2-(3x-2)^2=0$$
$$\left(4x^2-12x+9\right)-\left(9x^2-12x+4\right)=0$$
$$4x^2-12x+9-9x^2+12x-4=0$$
$$-5x^2+5=0$$
$$-5\left(x^2-1\right)=0$$
$$-5(x-1)(x+1)=0$$

Now set each factor on the left-side equal to zero and solve for x to get $x = -1$ and $x = 1$.

When a problem like this involves several different computations and properties, the wrong answer choices are the results of a whole host of errors. Missing a 5 in the fourth step above results in choice C. Setting each factor being squared in the initial equation equal to zero results in choices B and D, the latter if a sign error is made in addition. Choice E is the result of incorrectly equating $x^2 - 1$ to $(x - 1)^2$.

Counting Techniques

1. Nick wants to bind a report at a local printing company. There are 8 choices for the paper color, 3 choices of paper texture, 10 different cover options, and 4 different binding options. How many combinations, total, are there from which to choose for the finished product?

SHOW YOUR WORK HERE

A. $8 \times 3 \times 10 \times 4$

B. $8! \times 3! \times 10! \times 4!$

C. $8! + 3! + 10! + 4!$

D. $8 + 3 + 10 + 4$

E. $(8 + 3 + 10 + 4)!$

The correct answer is A. This is a typical "number of combinations" problem, in which the order in which you account for each option is not relevant. So you simply multiply the number of choices for each option to get the total number of different combinations. Doing so here yields $8 \times 3 \times 10 \times 4$.

Adding instead of multiplying the number of choices for each option results in choice D. Doing so and incorrectly incorporating factorials into the computation results in choices C and E; multiplying and incorrectly incorporating factorials into the computation results in choice B.

2. In how many ways can six different books be arranged on a shelf?

SHOW YOUR WORK HERE

F. $6 + 5 + 4 + 3 + 2 + 1$

G. $(6 + 5 + 4 + 3 + 2 + 1)!$

H. $6! + 5! + 4! + 3! + 2! + 1!$

J. $6! \times 5! \times 4! \times 3! \times 2! \times 1!$

K. $6 \times 5 \times 4 \times 3 \times 2 \times 1$

The correct answer is K. This is a typical "number of different arrangements" problem in which instead of accounting for different choices for several options, we need to count the number of ways to arrange a fixed number of objects in order.

There are six ways to place the first book on the shelf. For each of these six choices, there are five remaining books from which to choose to place the second book next to it. So there are 6×5 ways to arrange the first two books on the shelf. For each of these 6×5 choices, there are four remaining books from which to choose to place the third book next in line. So there are $6 \times 5 \times 4$ ways to arrange the first three books on the shelf. And so on. Continuing until the last book is placed, we see that there are $6 \times 5 \times 4 \times 3 \times 2 \times 1$ ways to arrange six books in order on a shelf.

Common errors include adding instead of multiplying the number of choices for each option and also incorrectly incorporating factorials into the computation results. Adding instead of multiplying the number of choices for each option results in choice F. Doing so and incorrectly incorporating factorials into the computation results in choices G and H. Multiplying and incorrectly incorporating factorials into the computation results in choice J.

3. There are 13 contestants in a baking competition. Four ribbons will be awarded for first, second, third, and fourth place, and no contestant can receive more than one award. In how many ways can the ribbons be awarded?

SHOW YOUR WORK HERE

A. $13 + 12 + 11 + 10$

B. $13 \times 12 \times 11 \times 10$

C. $(13 + 12 + 11 + 10)!$

D. $13! \times 12! \times 11! \times 10!$

E. $13!$

The correct answer is B. This is a variation of the typical "number of different arrangements" problem. Here, the entire group of objects—the 13 contestants—is not used. We approach this problem the same way as the previous problem but stop after the fourth selection is made. So there are $13 \times 12 \times 11 \times 10$ ways to award the four ribbons.

Simple Probability

1. What is the probability that a randomly selected whole number between 3 and 30, inclusive, is either prime or a multiple of 3?

SHOW YOUR WORK HERE

A. $\frac{9}{15}$

B. $\frac{19}{30}$

C. $\frac{1}{30}$

D. $\frac{19}{28}$

E. $\frac{9}{14}$

The correct answer is E. To answer problems like this, you need to know two things: how many total outcomes there are and how many of them satisfy the conditions specified in the problem. Because the choice is made at random, all outcomes are equally likely to be chosen; you simply divide the number of outcomes satisfying the condition by the total number of outcomes possible to get the desired probability.

There are 28 numbers between 3 and 30, inclusive. Therefore, 28 is the number of total possible outcomes of selecting such a number at random. It is common to think there are 30 outcomes if you overlook the fact that the list starts at 3; error results in choice A if the rest of the problem is done correctly.

The outcomes satisfying each of the conditions are listed next:

Prime: **3**, 5, 7, 11, 13, 17, 19, 23, 29

Multiple of 3: **3**, 6, 9, 12, 15, 18, 21, 24, 27, 30

Note there is overlap between the two lists—the number 3. When counting the number of outcomes that are "either prime or a multiple of 3," make sure not to count this twice. If you do, you will get choice D. There are 18 possible outcomes. Thus, the probability that the whole number selected is either prime or a multiple of 3 is $\frac{18}{28} = \frac{9}{14}$.

Pay careful attention to the words *or* and *and*. Choice C is the probability that the whole number chosen is prime and a multiple of 3.

2. In a box of 200 light bulbs, 5% of the bulbs is known to be defective. What is the probability of selecting a non-defective bulb?

F. 95

G. 5

H. 0.05

J. 0.95

K. 0.005

SHOW YOUR WORK HERE

The correct answer is J. This problem asks for the probability of the complement of an event for which you know the probability. The probability of randomly selecting a defective bulb is 5%, which is equal to 0.05. So the probability that a randomly selected bulb is NOT defective is 1 – 0.05 = 0.95.

Choices F and G represent not understanding that a probability cannot be larger than 1; you must convert the percentages that represent likelihood to the equivalent decimal. Choice H is the probability of randomly-selecting a defective bulb. Choice K is the probability of selecting any single bulb from a batch of 200.

3. A four-sided tetrahedral die has faces marked as A, 1, B, and 2. It is rolled twice, and the results are recorded as ordered pairs of the form (1st roll, 2nd roll). What is the probability that an ordered pair contains at least one 2?

A. $\frac{1}{4}$

B. $\frac{1}{16}$

C. $\frac{9}{16}$

D. $\frac{7}{16}$

E. $\frac{3}{8}$

SHOW YOUR WORK HERE

The correct answer is D. The approach here is to write out the elements of the sample space. Then, identify each of the ones that satisfy the condition "contains at least one 2."

(A, A)	(B, A)	(1, A)	**(2, A)**
(A, B)	(B, B)	(1, B)	**(2, B)**
(A, 1)	(B, 1)	(1, 1)	**(2, 1)**
(A, 2)	**(B, 2)**	**(1, 2)**	**(2, 2)**

There are 16 possible outcomes in the sample space. Of these, 7 contain at least one 2. So the probability of the desired event is $\frac{7}{16}$.

A common error is to exclude the ordered pair (2, 2) from the list of those satisfying the condition "at least one 2." Here, "at least one 2" means that either one or both rolls can be a 2. Making this error results in choice E.

Choice C is the probability of the complement of the specified event, namely that neither roll is a 2. Choice B is the probability of getting "exactly two 2s." And, choice A is the probability of getting a 2 on one roll of the die.

PRACTICE

Now it's time to take your first mathematics practice quiz. When you're finished answering all 20 questions, check the answers and explanations that follow to figure out how well you did and why you may have selected an incorrect answer choice.

SHOW YOUR WORK HERE

1. If $\frac{n}{4}$ and $\frac{n}{14}$ are both integers, all of the following could be *n* EXCEPT:

A. 56
B. 70
C. 112
D. 168
E. 224

2. If $\frac{x^3y^2}{z}$ is negative, then which of the following could be true?

I. *x* and *z* are both negative.
II. *x* is negative and *z* is positive.
III. *x* is zero.

F. I only
G. II only
H. I and II
J. II and III
K. I, II, and III

3. In order to set up the internet connection in a computer lab, the following amounts of cable are needed for each computer in the lab:

2 cables, each measuring 3 feet
3 cables, each measuring 9 inches
1 wire, measuring 5 feet

If the room requires 25 computers and cable costs $0.15 per inch, approximately how much will it cost to set up the computers for the lab?

A. $23.85
B. $72
C. $159
D. $596.25
E. $3,975

4. $(0.01)^{-3} =$

F. 10^{-6}
G. 10^{-5}
H. 10^{-3}
J. 10^{3}
K. 10^{6}

5. What is the largest possible value for the product xy if $x + y = 20$ and x and y are both prime numbers?

SHOW YOUR WORK HERE

A. 19
B. 36
C. 51
D. 91
E. 96

6. Which of the following is the prime factorization of 3,780?

F. $2^2 \times 3^3 \times 35$
G. $2 \times 3 \times 5 \times 7$
H. $2^2 \times 3^3 \times 5 \times 7$
J. $2 \times 3^2 \times 5 \times 6 \times 7$
K. $2^2 \times 3^4 \times 5 \times 7$

7. If x is a real number such that $x^3 = 160$, between which two consecutive integers does x lie on the number line?

A. 2 and 3
B. 3 and 4
C. 4 and 5
D. 5 and 6
E. 6 and 7

8. If $\log_6 216 = x$, then $x =$

F. $\frac{\log 216}{6}$
G. $\sqrt[6]{216}$
H. 36
J. 3
K. 6^{216}

9. Phillip answered 4 of the 35 questions on his driving exam incorrectly. What percentage of the questions did Phillip answer correctly?

A. $\frac{4}{35} \times 100\%$
B. $\frac{31}{35} \times 100\%$
C. $\frac{4}{35 \times 100}\%$
D. $\frac{31}{35 \times 100}\%$
E. $\frac{31}{100\%} \times 35$

10. Increasing a positive number by 40% and then decreasing the result by 30% is the same as which of the following?

F. Increasing the original number by 10%
G. Increasing the original number by 12%
H. Decreasing the original number by 12%
J. Increasing the original number by 2%
K. Decreasing the original number by 2%

SHOW YOUR WORK HERE

11. The ratio of butter to chocolate chips in a cookie recipe is 2:3. If $2\frac{1}{4}$ cups of butter are used, how many cups of chocolate chips are used?

A. $\frac{2}{3}$
B. $1\frac{1}{2}$
C. 3
D. $3\frac{3}{8}$
E. 5

12. If $3x + 2 = 9x + 14$, then $4x^3 =$

F. −108
G. −32
H. −24
J. −2
K. 32

13. $-6-|-6|=$

A. −12
B. −6
C. 0
D. 6
E. 36

14. For real numbers *a*, *b*, and *c*, $a < b$ and $c < 0$. Which of the following inequalities MUST be true?

F. $ab > 0$
G. $ac < 0$
H. $a + c < 0$
J. $\frac{a}{c} > \frac{b}{c}$
K. $\frac{a}{c} < \frac{b}{c}$

15. What is the value of $m^2 - 6mn^3 + n$ when $m = -2$ and $n = -1$?

A. −17
B. −13
C. −9
D. 9
E. 17

16. Which of the following is equivalent to $(-4x^3)^2$?

F. $-4x^5$
G. $-3x^6$
H. $-16x^6$
J. $8x^6$
K. $16x^6$

17. Which of the following is the completely factored form of $6d^4e^2 - 18de^3$?

A. $6(d^4e^2 - 18de^3)$
B. $6de^2(d^3 - 3e)$
C. $6(d^4e^2 - 18de^3)$
D. $6d(d^3e^2 - 3e^3)$
E. $-12d^3e^{-1}$

18. There is only one real solution for x for the equation $4x^2 + 12x = k$. Which of the following could be k?

F. 0
G. 4
H. 9
J. −9
K. −18

19. A bag contains only white, yellow, and purple cubes. There are a total of 40 cubes in the bag, and the probability of NOT selecting a yellow cube is $\frac{3}{4}$. How many yellow cubes are in the bag?

A. 4
B. 5
C. 8
D. 10
E. 30

SHOW YOUR WORK HERE

20. A lab technician took a measurement of new rainfall once a day during a five-day work week. The table below indicates how many inches of new rainfall were recorded on each day.

Day	Inches of New Rainfall
Monday	1.0
Tuesday	1.5
Wednesday	0
Thursday	1.0
Friday	0.5

What is the average number of inches per day for this work week?

A. 4
B. 1
C. 0.8
D. 0.4
E. 0

SHOW YOUR WORK HERE

ANSWERS AND EXPLANATIONS

1. **The correct answer is B.** Since $\frac{n}{4}$ and $\frac{n}{14}$ are both integers, then n must be divisible by both 4 and 14. The question asks for the one value that does *not* satisfy this condition, so you are looking for the one choice that is not divisible by both 4 and 14. Since it is difficult to do this by inspection, start with the first answer choice and move through the list until you find the correct number.

   Choice A: 56

   $56 \div 4 = 14$; $56 \div 14 = 4$; eliminate

   Choice B: 70

   $70 \div 4 = 17$ with remainder 2; $70 \div 14 = 5$; correct

   Once you have determined that B is the correct choice, stop here!

   Each of the remaining choices are numbers that are divisible by both 4 and 14.

2. **The correct answer is G.** In order for the expression to be negative, you must have an odd number of negative signs. Since y is squared, the term y^2 cannot be negative. However, both x^3 and z are negative whenever x and z are negative, respectively.

   Statement I is false because if x and z are both negative, then x^3 and z are both negative, making the quotient positive. Statement II is true because if x is negative, then so is x^3. So you have a quotient with one negative term all told; therefore, it must be negative. Statement III is false because if $x = 0$, the entire quotient is zero and thus not negative. Using this information, you can conclude that choice G is the correct answer and that all other choices are incorrect.

3. **The correct answer is D.** First, get the total inches for each type of cable. Two 3-foot cables are $2 \times 3 = 6$ feet, which converts to $6 \times 12 = 72$ inches. Three 9-inch cables are $3 \times 9 = 27$ inches. And the last cable is $5 \times 12 = 60$ inches. Adding together the inches for all cables gives $72 + 27 + 60 = 159$ inches of cable needed to connect *one* computer to the internet. At a cost of \$0.15 per inch, the cost of connecting one computer in the lab to the internet is 159(\$0.15) = \$23.85. Hence, the cost of connecting all 25 computers to the internet is 25(\$23.85) = \$596.25 (choice D).

   Choice A is the cost of connecting one computer to the internet, not 25 of them. Choice B is only the number of inches for two cables measuring 3 feet each. Choice C is incorrect because each computer requires 159 inches of cable for the internet setup, but this is neither the cost of doing so for one computer nor the cost for doing so for all 25 computers in the lab. Choice E is the number of inches of cable needed to connect all 25 computers in the lab to the internet.

4. **The correct answer is K.** The value in parentheses, 0.01, can be rewritten as 10^{-2}. Therefore, $(0.01)^{-3} = (10^{-2})^{-3} = 10^{(-2)(-3)} = 10^6$.

   Choice F is incorrect because 0.01 equals 10^{-2}, not 10^2. In choice G, you added the exponents, but should have multiplied them. Choice H is incorrect because the value in parentheses is 10^{-2}, not 10. Choice J is incorrect because the value in parentheses is 10^{-2}, not 10^{-1}.

5. **The correct answer is D.** Two pairs of prime numbers sum to 20: $3 + 17$ and $7 + 13$. The largest resulting product is $7 \times 13 = 91$, so 91 is the largest possible value of xy if x and y are both prime numbers for which $x + y = 20$.

   Choice A represents a common math mistake—be careful, because the number 1 is not considered to be prime. Choice B is the result of using 2 and 18, but 18 is not prime. Choice C is the smaller of the two such products. Choice E is the result of using 8 and 12, neither of which is prime.

6. **The correct answer is H.** A prime factorization is the product of the powers of the prime factors of a whole number. The prime factorization of 3,780 is $2^2 \times 3^3 \times 5 \times 7$. The best way to get the prime factorization is by using the divisibility rules. In choice G, although 2, 3, 5, and 7 are the prime factors of 3,780, both 2 and 3 occur more than once in the correct factorization. Choices F and J involve non-prime numbers, and so can be eliminated immediately. Choice K contains one too many factors of 3.

   Try to eliminate as many choices as possible first. Here, since choices F and J involve non-prime numbers and you are looking for the prime factorization, they can be eliminated immediately.

7. **The correct answer is D.** The problem is asking you to find two consecutive integers, the first of which has a cube less than 160, and the second of which has a cube greater than 160. Use the answer choices to help you. The cubes of 2, 3, 4, 5, and 6 are, respectively: 8, 27, 64, 125, and 216. Since 160 falls between 125 and 216, you know that x is between 5 and 6, and you do not need to go any further. As such, the other choices are not possible.

8. **The correct answer is J.** The equation $\log_6 216 = x$ is the same as saying $6^x = 216$. Note that $6^3 = 216$, so that the answer is 3 (choice J).

   Choice F is incorrect because the denominator should be $\log_6$, not just 6. Choice G is incorrect because $\log_6 216 = x$ is equivalent to $6^x = 216$, not $216^{\frac{1}{6}} = \sqrt[6]{216} = x$. For choice H, $6^2 = 36$, not 216. Choice K is incorrect because $\log_6 216 = x$ is equivalent to $6^x = 216$, not $6^{216} = x$.

9. **The correct answer is B.** If Phillip answered 4 of the 35 questions incorrectly, then he answered 35 – 4 = 31 correctly. By definition, the percentage is equal to $\frac{\text{part}}{\text{whole}} \times 100\%$. So Phillip answered $\frac{31}{35} \times 100\%$ of the questions correctly.

   Choice A is the percentage of questions he answered *incorrectly*. Choice C is incorrect because the 100 should be in the numerator so that you are taking a proportion of 100%; even then, the result would be the percentage he answered *incorrectly*. Choice D is incorrect because the 100 should be in the numerator so that you are taking a proportion of 100%. For choice E, you need to interchange the 35 and 100 in this expression.

10. **The correct answer is K.** Let x represent some number. Increasing the number by 40% produces the new number $(1 + 0.40)x = 1.40x$. Now, decreasing this result by 30% means to subtract 30% of $1.40x$ from $1.40x$: $(0.30)(1.40x) = 0.42x$, and subtracting this from $1.40x$ yields $0.98x$. So comparing this to the original number x shows that the end result is $0.02x$ less than x. You could have decreased the number by 2% to arrive at the same result.

   TIP: If thinking with variables is problematic for you, you can follow the same process by using a specific number for x, for example, 100.

   Choice F is incorrect because you cannot simply add or subtract percentages unless they are being applied to the same amount. In choices G and H, you multiplied 0.40 times 0.30, but this implies that the percentages both serve to increase a quantity or decrease a quantity to which they are being applied; here, one percentage is an increase and the other is a decrease. For choice J, your calculations are likely correct, but the end result is $0.98x$, which is smaller than x, not larger—the process described leads to a *decrease*, not an increase.

11. **The correct answer is D.** Set up a proportion to determine the number of cups of chocolate chips needed for the recipe, setting this unknown equal to x. Cross-multiply to solve for x:

$$\frac{2}{3} = \frac{2\frac{1}{4}}{x}$$
$$\frac{2}{3} = \frac{\frac{9}{4}}{x}$$
$$2x = 3\left(\frac{9}{4}\right)$$
$$2x = \frac{27}{4}$$
$$x = \frac{27}{8} = 3\frac{3}{8}$$

   Choice A, the ratio itself, is not the number of cups of chocolate chips needed. You must set up a proportion to solve for this unknown. In choice B, you inverted half of the proportion before solving for x. Choice C is incorrect because you can't round down; you should give the exact answer. In choice E, you simply multiplied the two quantities in the ratio; you must set up a proportion to solve for this unknown.

12. **The correct answer is G.** First, solve the given equation for x:

$$3x + 2 = 9x + 14$$
$$2 = 6x + 14$$
$$-12 = 6x$$
$$-2 = x$$

   Now, evaluate $4x^3$ at $x = -2$ to get $4(-2)^3 = 4(-8) = -32$. So choice G is the correct answer.

   Choice F would imply $x = -3$, not -2. For choice H, when computing $(-2)^3$, you multiplied the base times the exponent, but this is not how you compute a power. Choice J is the value of x, not $4x^3$. Choice K is the opposite of the correct answer; it should be negative, not positive.

13. **The correct answer is A.** First, note that $|-6| = 6$. So $-6-|-6|=-6-6$. Now, just add these integers as usual to get –12.

For choice B, you dropped one of the two terms from the expression. For choice C, $-|-6| = -6$, not 6. For choice D, since $-6-|-6|=-6-6$ and you are adding two negative integers, the result cannot be positive. For choice E, you multiplied –6 and $-|-6|$ instead of adding them.

14. **The correct answer is J.** If you divide both sides of the inequality $a < b$ by c, since c is negative, you must reverse the inequality sign when doing so. This yields the inequality $\frac{a}{c} > \frac{b}{c}$. For choice F, if $a = -3$ and $b = 2$, then $a < b$, but $ab < 0$, not > 0. For choice G, take $a = -5$, $b = -3$, and $c = -1$. Note that $ac > 0$. For choice H, take $a = 4$, $b = 5$, and $c = -1$. Note that $a + c = 3 > 0$. For choice K, you need to reverse the inequality sign.

15. **The correct answer is C.** Plug the given values of m and n into the expression and evaluate:

$$\begin{aligned} m^2-6mn^3+n &= (-2)^2-6(-2)(-1)^3+(-1) \\ &= 4-6(-2)(-1)-1 \\ &= 4-12-1 \\ &= -8-1 \\ &= -9 \end{aligned}$$

In choice A, you said $m^2 = -4$ when it is actually 4. In choice B, you dropped m^2 from the expression. Choice D should be –9, not 9. In choice E, you disregarded all negative signs throughout the expression.

16. **The correct answer is K.** For this problem, it is important to remember the rules of exponents. When a product is raised to a power, each of the terms must be raised to that power. So $(-4x^3)^2$ is equal to $(-4)^2 \times (x^3)^2$. When a power is raised to another power, you multiply the exponents. So $(-4)^2 \times (x^3)^2$ is equal to $(-4)^2 \times (x^6)$. Now evaluate: $(-4)^2 \times (x^6) = 16 \times (x^6) = 16x^6$.

In choice F, note that $\left(a^b\right)^c \neq a^{b+c}$; you must apply the exponent to the coefficient, –4, as well. Choice G is incorrect because you must apply the exponent to the coefficient, –4. In choice H, you forgot to square the –1. In choice J, $(-4)^2 = (-4)(-4)$, you do not multiply the base times the exponent.

17. **The correct answer is B.** To factor the expression, look for terms that are common to both quantities. For example, 6 can be divided out of both terms, as can d and e^2. Thus, you can factor out $6de^2$, leaving $(d^3 - 3e)$. So the completely factored form is: $6de^2(d^3 - 3e)$.

In choice A, you forgot to factor the 6 out of the second term, and the GCF actually consists of more than just 6; it also includes powers of d and e. Choice C is incorrect because the GCF actually consists of more than just 6; it also includes powers of d and e. In choice D, the expression is not *completely* factored; you can still factor out e^2. In choice E, you cannot subtract unlike terms by subtracting their coefficients and exponents in this manner.

18. **The correct answer is J.** If a quadratic equation of the form $ax^2 + bx + c = 0$ has only one solution, or root, it means that the expression on the left can be factored as a binomial squared, or $(Mx + N)^2$. First, put the given equation in standard form:

$$4x^2 + 12x - k = 0$$

If you substitute $k = -9$, you get the expression $4x^2 + 12x + 9 = 0$ on the left side, which factors as $(2x + 3)^2$, which implies the equation has only one real solution: $-\frac{3}{2}$.

All other choices of k lead to an expression that cannot be written in the form $(Mx + N)^2$, so the equations corresponding to the other choices of k either have two real solutions or no real solutions.

19. **The correct answer is D.** If the probability of NOT selecting a yellow cube is $\frac{3}{4}$, then the probability of selecting a yellow cube is $1-\frac{3}{4}=\frac{1}{4}$. Let x represent the number of yellow cubes in the bag. Set up the following proportion to solve for x:

$$\begin{aligned} \frac{1}{4} &= \frac{x}{40} \\ 40 &= 4x \\ 10 &= x \end{aligned}$$

Therefore, there are 10 yellow cubes in the bag. Choice A is incorrect because it would mean that the probability of not selecting a yellow cube is $\frac{9}{10}$, not $\frac{3}{4}$. Choice B is incorrect because it would mean that the probability of not selecting a yellow cube is $\frac{7}{8}$, not

$\frac{3}{4}$. Choice C is incorrect because it would mean that the probability of not selecting a yellow cube is $\frac{4}{5}$, not $\frac{3}{4}$. Choice E is the number of cubes in the bag that are NOT yellow.

20. **The correct answer is C.** Remember that $\text{average} = \frac{\text{sum of values}}{\text{number of values}}$. To find the average number of inches of rainfall per day for this data, divide the total number of inches of rainfall for the week by the number of days, 5:

$$\frac{(1.0+1.5+0+1.0+0.5)}{5} = \frac{4.0}{5} = 0.8$$

So the mean daily rainfall is 0.8 inches.

Choice A is the total number of inches of rain recorded for the entire week; you must divide this by 5 (the number of measurements) to get the mean. In choice B, you divided the total number of inches by 4 instead of 5; remember, you must include "0" data values among the number of measurements. In choice D, you divided the total number of inches by 10, not 5. Choice E is incorrect because it would imply that there was absolutely no rain during this week.

CHAPTER 7: INTERMEDIATE ALGEBRA AND COORDINATE GEOMETRY

OVERVIEW

- Lines
- Rational Expressions
- Radical Expressions
- Complex Numbers
- Quadratic Equations and the Quadratic Formula
- Linear Inequalities
- Systems of Linear Equations
- Basic Coordinate Geometry
- Functions
- Modeling
- Sequences
- Matrices
- Summing It Up
- College Readiness Benchmark Learning Path Practice
- Practice

Now that you have brushed up on your pre- and elementary algebra skills in Chapter 6, we'll start building upon those foundations to tackle the next level of ACT Mathematics: intermediate algebra and coordinate geometry. Before you begin this chapter, you should feel confident about the math we presented in the last chapter—go ahead and give it another review if you still feel shaky on the concepts, because most of the information here will combine many of the rules and practices we covered before.

You'll notice that this chapter contains a lot of formulas that give you a direct path to finding correct answers. As we mentioned before, the ACT exam assumes you have knowledge of basic formulas (which include most of the ones we present in this chapter). Many times, there will be a way to figure out an answer without using a formula—but rest assured, if you study and master the tactics in this chapter, you will be armed with the fastest and most efficient way to answer questions on test day.

COLLEGE READINESS BENCHMARK LEARNING PATH PRACTICE

Remember, if you're still having trouble with any Intermediate Algebra or Coordinate Geometry topic after you've made your way through the chapter review, take the College Readiness Benchmark Learning Path. The Benchmark Practice section begins on page 316. We've created 3 practice questions for every topic, based on our expert knowledge of the ACT exam. Each question is an example of a common question type you'll see in each math category on test day. Through this Benchmark practice, you'll become familiar with typical ACT test language and how to translate it when approaching each math question.

LINES

Knowing how to work with lines and linear equations in two variables is an important part of succeeding on the ACT Mathematics test. Let's review the basic features of lines and look at several common ACT exam problem types.

The Equation of a Line

The two most common forms you will see for the equation of a line are **standard form** ($Ax + By = C$), and **slope-intercept form** ($y = mx + b$). In these, A, B, C, m, and b represent real numbers. The more useful of these is the slope-intercept form, since the two numbers m and b actually tell you something about the graph of the line. First, b is the line's ***y*-intercept,** meaning that the graph of the line crosses the y-axis at the point $(0, b)$. Next, m indicates the **slope** of the line, which measures steepness of the line, or the change in y-value per unit change in x-value.

If you have two points on the line, say (x_1, y_1) (x_2, y_2), the slope is the change in y over the change in x, which we calculate as shown here:

$$m = \frac{y_1 - y_2}{x_1 - x_2} = \frac{y_2 - y_1}{x_2 - x_1}$$

- If m is positive, the graph of the line rises from left to right.
- If m is negative, it falls from left to right.
- If $m = 0$, then the equation becomes $y = b$ and the graph is a horizontal line—all points have a y-coordinate of b.

ALERT: Make certain to always subtract the y-coordinates in the same order as the x-coordinates. Otherwise, you will get the negative of the correct slope.

Likewise, the graph of the equation $x = a$ is a vertical line (where $y = 0$). All points in this line have an x-coordinate of a, and such a line is said to have an **undefined slope**.

If you are given a point (x_1, y_1) on a line and you know its slope m, then you can find the **point-slope** form for the equation using the formula $\mathbf{y - y_1 = m(x - x_1)}$.

TIP There is no reason to first determine the y-intercept of the line if you have these two pieces of information. Note that if you solve this equation for y and simplify, you will get the following: $y = mx + \underbrace{(-mx_1 + y_1)}_{\text{This is the } y\text{-intercept } b.}$

Here are some common ACT math problems that ask you to find the equation of a line, along with the best method of attack for each.

Problem Type	Method of Attack
1. Given a point and a slope (either written or by way of a graph), determine the equation of the line.	Use the point-slope formula immediately.
2. Given two points on a line (either written or by way of a graph), determine the slope or the equation of the line.	First, find the slope of the line. (If this is what the question asks for, you are done.) Use the point-slope formula to find its equation.
3. Given a table of points that describe a linear relationship between variables x and y, determine the equation of the line.	Use any two of the points to find the slope. Then, use any of the points from the table with the slope to find the equation of the line.
4. Given a scenario in which two quantities are related linearly, find the equation of the line, or determine the value of one of the variables given the value of the other.	Identify one quantity as the input (x) and the other as the output (y). Typically, the input variable x is the quantity you change; the output variable y is the quantity you observe. Extract information from the description—either two points or a point and slope. Proceed as above.

For all of the problem types listed in the table, depending on the way the choices are listed, you might then need to put the equation into slope-intercept form or standard form.

Consider the following sample question.

Suppose that the points (1, –5) and (2, –1) lie on a line. Which of the following is the equation of this line?

A. $y = x - 8$

B. $y = 4x - 9$

C. $y = 4x + 9$

D. $y = x + 8$

E. $y = \frac{1}{4}x - 9$

The correct answer is B. First, determine the slope:

$$\text{slope} = m = \frac{-5-(-1)}{1-2} = 4$$

Using the point (2, –1) with the point-slope formula, the equation of the line passing through these two points is $y - (-1) = 4(x - 2)$. This is equivalent to $y = 4x - 9$.

ALERT: Be careful with the negative signs when using a point that has a negative coordinate, as in this case. The equation obtained by subtracting incorrectly will likely be among the choices.

Now, let's look at another question.

What is the *y*-intercept of the line represented by the equation $8x + 4y = 20$?

F. $\frac{1}{2}$

G. 2

H. 4

J. 5

K. 8

The correct answer is J. Put the equation into slope-intercept form, $y = mx + b$, where b is the *y*-intercept:

$$8x + 4y = 20$$
$$4y = -8x + 20$$
$$y = -2x + 5$$

This shows that the *y*-intercept of the line is 5.

Your first step should always be to put the equation into slope-intercept form. A common mistake people make is thinking the constant term 20 in the equation $8x + 4y = 20$ is the *y*-intercept, which is incorrect.

Parallel and Perpendicular Lines

Consider two lines whose equations are $y = m_1x + b_1$ and $y = m_2x + b_2$. The lines are **parallel** if the slopes are the same (i.e., $m_1 = m_2$) and **perpendicular** if the product of the slopes is –1 (i.e., $m_1 \times m_2 = -1$).

By definition, lines are parallel if they lie on a plane, always the same distance apart, and never meet.

Perpendicular lines intersect each other on a plane at right (90-degree) angles.

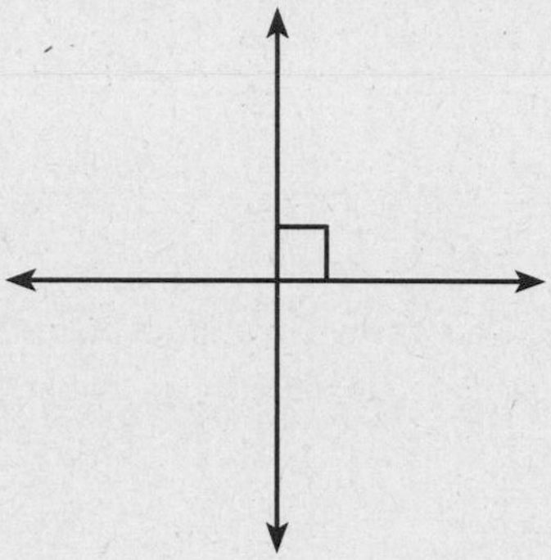

A common type of question on the ACT exam will ask you to compare two lines, or to use information about the relationship between two different lines to determine the equation of one of the lines.

For instance, consider the following problem:

Lines *m* and *n* are perpendicular in the standard (*x*, *y*) coordinate plane below. Which of the following is the equation for line *m*?

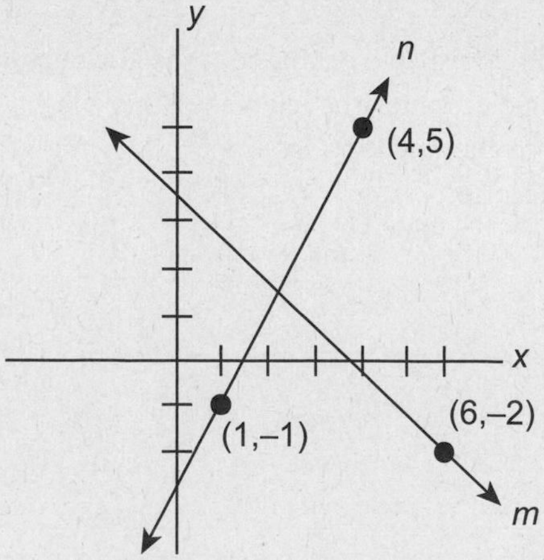

F. $x - 2y = 2$
G. $x + 2y = 1$
H. $x + 2y = 2$
J. $2x + y = -14$
K. $2x - y = 14$

The correct answer is H. First, we need to determine the equation of line *n*. The slope of *n* is $\frac{5-(-1)}{4-1} = 2$. Using the point (4, 5) and this slope with the point-slope formula, we see that the equation of *n* is $y - 5 = 2(x - 4)$, which simplifies to $y = 2x - 3$. Since this line is perpendicular to line *m*, the slope of *m* must be $-\frac{1}{2}$ (since the product of these slopes must be –1).

Using the point (6, –2) on *m* with the point-slope formula yields the equation $y-(-2) = -\frac{1}{2}(x-6)$, which simplifies to $y = -\frac{1}{2}x+1$. Since the choices are given in standard form, we must go one step further to write this as $x + 2y = 2$.

RATIONAL EXPRESSIONS

Do you remember the arithmetic rules for fractions? If you need to brush up on the rules, do a quick review of Chapter 6, because we're going to take the math one step further now—working with fractions that have expressions in the numerator and denominator. Expressions are part of the Preparing for Higher Math category on the ACT exam.

The math here is similar to what you have already seen—you simply add, subtract, multiply, and divide polynomials like you did before and cancel like factors in the top and bottom as you would when simplifying a fraction involving only numbers.

Let's look at a few examples in action and solve the following problems.

Examples:

1. Simplify: $\frac{8x^2+2x-3}{1-2x}$ ________________

2. Add and simplify: $\frac{2x-4}{x^2-1}+\frac{3-x}{x^2-1}$ ________________

3. Subtract and simplify: $\frac{x}{5-2x}-\frac{1}{2+x}$ ________________

4. Multiply and simplify: $\frac{2x^2+2x}{x^2-4}\bullet\frac{x+2}{x^2-1}$ ________________

Solutions:

1. First, factor the numerator and see if anything can be canceled in the top and bottom:

$$\begin{aligned}\frac{8x^2+2x-3}{1-2x} &= \frac{(4x+3)(2x-1)}{-(2x-1)} && \text{Factor!}\\ &= \frac{(4x+3)\cancel{(2x-1)}}{-\cancel{(2x-1)}} && \text{Cancel like factors in top and bottom}\\ &= -(4x+3)\end{aligned}$$

Note that we factored a –1 out of the denominator. Always be on the lookout for negatives when factoring—a common error (and likely one of the incorrect answer choices) is a final expression that drops the –1.

2. In this case, we can simply add the numerators while keeping the denominator the same because the two fractions already have the same denominator. Then, we simplify the result as much as possible:

$$\begin{aligned}\frac{2x-4}{x^2-1}+\frac{3-x}{x^2-1} &= \frac{2x-4+3-x}{x^2-1} && \text{Combine the fractions.}\\ &= \frac{x-1}{x^2-1} && \text{Simplify.}\\ &= \frac{\cancel{x-1}}{\cancel{(x-1)}(x+1)} && \text{Factor and cancel like factors in top and bottom.}\\ &= \frac{1}{x+1}\end{aligned}$$

3. First, find a common denominator—remember, you can't add or subtract without one. You can simply multiply the denominators already present: (5 – 2*x*)(2 + *x*). Express both fractions using this denominator, and then combine and simplify:

$$\frac{x}{5-2x}-\frac{1}{2+x}=\frac{x(2+x)}{(5-2x)(2+x)}-\frac{5-2x}{(5-2x)(2+x)}$$

$$=\frac{x^2+2x}{(5-2x)(2+x)}-\frac{5-2x}{(5-2x)(2+x)}$$

$$=\frac{x^2+2x-5+2x}{(5-2x)(2+x)}$$

$$=\frac{x^2+4x-5}{(5-2x)(2+x)}$$

$$=\frac{(x+5)(x-1)}{(5-2x)(2+x)}$$

Note that the final expression cannot be simplified further since there are no factors common to the top and the bottom.

4. Factor all expressions and then cancel those common to the top and bottom:

$$\frac{2x^2+2x}{x^2-4}\bullet\frac{x+2}{x^2-1}=\frac{2x\cancel{(x+1)}}{(x-2)\cancel{(x+2)}}\bullet\frac{\cancel{x+2}}{\cancel{(x+1)}(x-1)}=\frac{2x}{(x-2)(x-1)}$$

Beware—do not multiply the numerators and the denominators *before* factoring. Doing so will create a huge mess that is nearly impossible to simplify.

TIP If you are asked to *divide* two rational expressions, the process is practically identical to multiplication, with the additional step of first rewriting the division problem as a multiplication problem, just as with division of numerical fractions.

Let's look at three more.

Simplify the following rational expression: $\frac{x^2-y^2}{5x-5y}$.

A. $\frac{x-y}{5}$

B. $\frac{5}{x+y}$

C. $\frac{x+y}{5}$

D. $\frac{1}{5}$

E. $\frac{x^2-5x}{y^2-5y}$

The correct answer is C. First, factor both the numerator and denominator of the fraction, and then cancel any common factors:

$$\frac{x^2-y^2}{5x-5y}=\frac{\cancel{(x-y)}(x+y)}{5\cancel{(x-y)}}=\frac{x+y}{5}$$

If x and y are positive numbers, $\frac{x}{5}-\frac{2}{y}=$

F. $\frac{xy-2}{5y}$

G. $\frac{xy-10}{5+y}$

H. $-\frac{2x}{5y}$

J. $\frac{xy-10}{5y}$

K. $\frac{x-2}{5-y}$

The correct answer is J. To solve, you need a common denominator. The common denominator is $5y$. Write the first fraction, $\frac{x}{5}$, as an equivalent one with a denominator of $5y$: $\frac{y}{y}\bullet\frac{x}{5}=\frac{xy}{5y}$.

Likewise, rewrite the fraction after the minus sign as one with a denominator of $5y$: $\frac{5}{5}\times\frac{2}{y}=\frac{10}{5y}$.

Since the denominators are now the same, you can subtract: $\frac{xy}{5y}-\frac{10}{5y}=\frac{xy-10}{5y}$.

If $a=xy$ and $b=y^2z$, what is $\frac{b}{a}$ in terms of x, y, and z?

A. $\frac{yz}{x}$

B. $\frac{x}{z}$

C. $\frac{x}{yz}$

D. $\frac{xy}{z}$

E. xy^3z

The correct answer is A. You are given the values of a and b in terms of x, y, and z, so substitute these into the expression $\frac{b}{a}$.

Then you have $\frac{b}{a}=\frac{y^2z}{xy}$, which reduces to $\frac{yz}{x}$ using exponent rules.

CAUTION

Make certain you divide in the correct order. A common error is to compute the reciprocal, $\frac{a}{b}$.

Turn to page 316 to follow the College Readiness Benchmark Learning Path questions covering Rational Expressions.

RADICAL EXPRESSIONS

In the previous chapter, we covered the rules for simplifying radicals. As a quick review, try solving the following practice questions.

Examples:

Simplify the following arithmetic expressions involving radicals:

1. $(3\sqrt{5})^2=$ ____________

2. $(4+\sqrt{3})(5-\sqrt{3})=$ ____________

TIP

The exponent rules you learned in Chapter 6 also apply to algebraic expressions!

Solutions:

1. $\left(3\sqrt{5}\right)^2 = 3^2 \bullet \left(\sqrt{5}\right)^2 = 9 \bullet 5 = 45$
2. $(4+\sqrt{3})(5-\sqrt{3}) = 4\bullet 5 - 4\bullet\sqrt{3} + 5\bullet\sqrt{3} - \left(\sqrt{3}\right)\left(\sqrt{3}\right) = 20+\sqrt{3}-3 = 17+\sqrt{3}$

The same rules used in the previous questions can also be used to simplify more complicated algebraic expressions involving radicals.

Try your hand at the next three examples:

Examples:

1. Suppose that *x*, *y*, and *z* are positive real numbers. Simplify the following radical expression:

   $\sqrt{8x^8y^2z^3} =$ ________________

2. Suppose that x, y, and z are positive real numbers. Simplify the following radical expression:

   $\dfrac{\sqrt{64x^3y^5}}{xy\sqrt{y}} =$ ________________

3. Simplify the following algebraic expressions involving radicals:

   a) $\left(2-\sqrt{x}\right)\left(x+3\sqrt{x}\right) =$ ____________________

   b) $2\sqrt{a^5b^3c} \bullet \sqrt{abc^2} =$ ________________

Solutions:

1. Two properties are at play here, namely $\sqrt{a \bullet b} = \sqrt{a} \bullet \sqrt{b}$ and $\sqrt{a^2} = a$ whenever $a > 0$.

   The idea is to express the radicand as a product of squared terms and everything that is left over.

   Employing that strategy, we see that:

$$\begin{aligned}\sqrt{8x^8y^2z^3} &= \sqrt{2}\bullet\sqrt{4}\bullet\sqrt{\left(x^4\right)^2}\bullet\sqrt{y^2}\bullet\sqrt{z^2}\bullet\sqrt{z}\\ &= \sqrt{2}\bullet 2\bullet\left(x^4\right)\bullet y\bullet z\bullet\sqrt{z}\\ &= 2\bullet x^4\bullet y\bullet z\bullet\sqrt{2}\bullet\sqrt{z}\\ &= 2\bullet x^4\bullet y\bullet z\bullet\sqrt{2z}\end{aligned}$$

2. This problem is similar to the previous example, but now we need to simplify a rational expression. Indeed, we have:

$$\begin{aligned}\frac{\sqrt{64x^3y^5}}{xy\sqrt{y}} &= \frac{\sqrt{8^2x^2\bullet x\bullet y^4\bullet y}}{xy\sqrt{y}}\\ &= \frac{8x\bullet y^2\bullet\sqrt{xy}}{x\bullet y\bullet\sqrt{y}}\\ &= \frac{8\cancel{x}\bullet y^{\cancel{2}}\sqrt{x}\bullet\cancel{\sqrt{y}}}{\cancel{x}\bullet\cancel{y}\bullet\cancel{\sqrt{y}}}\\ &= 8y\sqrt{x}\end{aligned}$$

3. a) $\left(2-\sqrt{x}\right)\left(x+3\sqrt{x}\right)=2x+6\sqrt{x}-x\sqrt{x}-3\left(\sqrt{x}\right)^2=2x+6\sqrt{x}-x\sqrt{x}-3x=-x+6\sqrt{x}-x\sqrt{x}$

b) $2\sqrt{a^5b^3c}\bullet\sqrt{abc^2}=2\sqrt{\left(a^5b^3c\right)\bullet\left(abc^2\right)}=2\sqrt{a^6b^4c^3}=2a^3b^2c\sqrt{c}$

Turn to page 319 to follow the College Readiness Benchmark Learning Path questions covering Radical Expressions.

COMPLEX NUMBERS

Remember that the square root of a negative real number is *not* a real number. However, it is **imaginary**, meaning that it involves i, where $i^2 = -1$. We can use this to further simplify some radicals. For instance:

$$\sqrt{-36}=\sqrt{-1}\bullet\sqrt{36}=i\bullet 6=6i$$

$$\sqrt{81}-\sqrt{-125}=9-\sqrt{-1}\bullet\sqrt{125}=9-i\bullet 5\sqrt{5}=9-5i\sqrt{5}$$

A **complex number** is a number of the form $a + bi$, where a and b are both real numbers. The number a is called the **real part** and the number b is called the **imaginary part.** The following are the basic rules of arithmetic and some important computations involving complex numbers:

Definition (in Symbols)	Definition (in Words)
Sum $(a + bi) + (c + di) = (a + c) + (b + d)i$	When adding complex numbers, add the real parts and the imaginary parts separately, and form the complex number using those sums.
Difference $(a + bi) + (c + di) = (a + c) + (b + d)i$	When subtracting complex numbers, subtract the real parts and the imaginary parts separately, and form the complex number using those differences.
Product $(a+bi)\bullet(c+di)=(ac+bd)+(bd+ad)i$	To multiply two complex numbers, apply the FOIL technique and use the fact that $i^2 = -1$.
Complex Conjugate The *complex conjugate* of $z = a + bi$ is $a - bi$.	To form the complex conjugate of a complex number, change the sign of the imaginary part, but leave the real part the same.
Quotient $\frac{a+bi}{c+di}=\frac{a+bi}{c+di}\bullet\frac{c-di}{c-di}=\frac{(ac+bd)+(bc-ad)i}{c^2+d^2}$	To divide two complex numbers, multiply top and bottom by the conjugate of the denominator and simplify.

See how these rules can be applied in the next problem.

Which of the following is equivalent to $-\sqrt{-48}+2\sqrt{27}-\sqrt{-75}$?

A. $9\sqrt{3}-6i\sqrt{3}$

B. $6\sqrt{3}+9i\sqrt{3}$

C. $6\sqrt{3}-6i\sqrt{3}$

D. $6\sqrt{3}-9i\sqrt{3}$

E. $9\sqrt{3}+6i\sqrt{3}$

The correct answer is D. Simplify each radical term and then combine those with the same radical part:

$$\begin{aligned}-\sqrt{-48}+2\sqrt{27}-\sqrt{-75} &= -\sqrt{-4^2 \bullet 3}+2\sqrt{3^2 \bullet 3}-\sqrt{-5^2 \bullet 3}\\ &= -4i\sqrt{3}+6\sqrt{3}-5i\sqrt{3}\\ &= (-4-5)i\sqrt{3}+6\sqrt{3}\\ &= 6\sqrt{3}-9i\sqrt{3}\end{aligned}$$

Examples:

Perform the indicated arithmetic operations and express the final answer in the form $a + bi$:

1. $(3 - 2i)(1 - 3i) =$ ________________

2. $\dfrac{2}{4-3i} =$ ________________

Solutions:

1. $(3-2i)(1-3i)=3-2i-9i+6i^2=3-11i-6=-3-11i$

2. $\dfrac{2}{4-3i}\bullet\dfrac{4+3i}{4+3i}=\dfrac{2(4+3i)}{(4-3i)(4+3i)}=\dfrac{8+6i}{16-9i^2}=\dfrac{8+6i}{16+9}=\dfrac{8+6i}{25}=\dfrac{8}{25}+\dfrac{6}{25}i$

Turn to page 321 to follow the College Readiness Benchmark Learning Path questions covering Complex Numbers.

QUADRATIC EQUATIONS AND THE QUADRATIC FORMULA

In the last chapter, we looked at quadratic equations and learned to solve them when the quadratic expression is factorable. But, this is not always the case. When you cannot factor a quadratic expression, the **quadratic formula** comes to the rescue!

The solutions of the equation $ax^2 + bx + c = 0$ can be found by using the quadratic formula:

$$x=\frac{-b\pm\sqrt{b^2-4ac}}{2a}$$

CAUTION

When using the quadratic formula, don't forget to divide *the entire numerator*, not just $-b$, by the denominator $2a$.

Just as when you applied factoring to solve a quadratic equation, you must get all terms to one side before identifying the coefficients a, b, and c in the quadratic formula.

The resulting solutions can be one of three types, depending on the sign of the radicand $b^2 - 4ac$, called the **discriminant**:

$b^2 - 4ac > 0$	Two distinct real solutions
$b^2 - 4ac = 0$	One repeated real solution
$b^2 - 4ac < 0$	Two complex conjugate solutions

Solve the following quadratic equations using the quadratic formula.

Examples:

1. $16x^2 + 9 = -24x$ ________
2. $2x^2 - 5x + 2 = 0$ ________
3. $3x^2 + x + 1 = 0$ ________

Solutions:

1. First, write the equation in standard form by bringing $-24x$ to the left: $16x^2 + 24x + 9 = 0$. Now, identify $a = 16$, $b = 24$, and $c = 9$ and apply the quadratic formula:

$$x = \frac{-24 \pm \sqrt{24^2 - 4(16)(9)}}{2(16)} = \frac{-24 \pm \sqrt{0}}{32} = -\frac{3}{4}$$

This equation has only one real solution.

2. Identify $a = 2$, $b = -5$, and $c = 2$ and apply the quadratic formula:

$$x = \frac{-(-5) \pm \sqrt{(-5)^2 - 4(2)(2)}}{2(2)} = \frac{5 \pm \sqrt{25-16}}{4} = \frac{5 \pm \sqrt{9}}{4} = \frac{5 \pm 3}{4} = -\frac{1}{2}, 2$$

This equation has two distinct real solutions.

3. Identify $a = 3$, $b = 1$, and $c = 1$ and apply the quadratic formula:

$$x = \frac{-(1) \pm \sqrt{(1)^2 - 4(3)(1)}}{2(3)} = \frac{-1 \pm \sqrt{-11}}{6} = \frac{-1 \pm i\sqrt{11}}{6}$$

This equation has two complex conjugate solutions.

Let's take a look at the way this concept would be tested on the ACT.

If the graph of the equation $y = 2(x - 4)^2 + k$ never intersects the x-axis, which of the following could be the value of k?

- **A.** –4
- **B.** –2
- **C.** –1
- **D.** 0
- **E.** 1

The correct answer is E. The number of x-intercepts a parabola has is the same as the number of real roots the corresponding quadratic equation has (found by setting it equal to 0). Since the given parabola never intersects the x-axis, this equation must have no real roots. This occurs when the discriminant, $b^2 - 4ac$, is negative.

To compute the discriminant in this situation, set up the quadratic equation in standard form:

$$2(x-4)^2 + k = 0$$
$$2x^2 - 16x + (32 + k) = 0$$

So the discriminant is
$b^2 - 4ac = (-16)^2 - 4(2)(32 + k) = 256 - 256 - 8k = -8k.$

The only values that make this discriminant negative are positive values of k. So the correct answer must be choice E.

TIP: For exam questions that ask about the nature of solutions of a quadratic equation, the discriminant is often the most efficient tool to use!

Turn to page 324 to follow the College Readiness Benchmark Learning Path questions covering Quadratic Equations and the Quadratic Formula.

LINEAR INEQUALITIES

The same basic strategy used to solve linear equations is also used to solve linear inequalities, with one additional step—the inequality sign must be switched whenever both sides of the inequality are multiplied by a negative real number. Another distinguishing factor of linear inequalities in contrast to linear equations is that the **solution set** of an inequality (that is, the set of real numbers that satisfies the inequality) contains infinitely many values. The solution set is often depicted on a number line, as follows:

Linear Inequality	Picture on Number Line
$x < a$	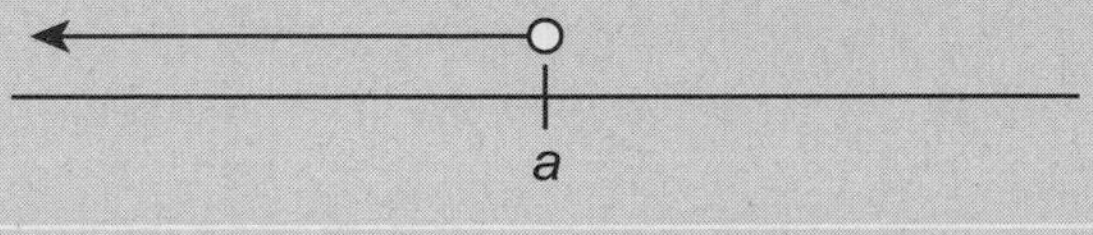
$x \leq a$	
$x > a$	
$x \geq a$	
$a \leq x \leq b$	
$a < x < b$	
$-\infty < x < \infty$	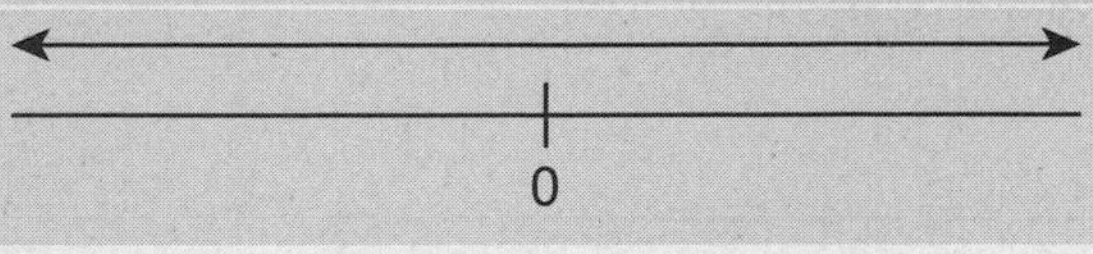

Problems involving inequalities come in different varieties on the ACT exam. The following table gives typical forms in which these questions are frequently asked, along with some suggestions about how to attack them:

Problem Type	Method of Attack
1. Solve a given inequality, where the answer choices are given symbolically (like the left-hand column of the previous table).	Solve the inequality as you would a linear equation, being careful with the inequality sign. The final step will have the variable on one side and a number on the other. This should be one of the choices.
2. Solve a given inequality, where the choices are given graphically on the number line (like the right-hand column of the previous table).	Solve the inequality as you would a linear equation, being careful with the inequality sign. Once you have the variable on one side and a number on the other, match that to the correct picture. Double-check whether each circle over its correct numerical value is open or closed.
3. You are given a ray on the number line and are asked to identify which of the inequalities listed is its solution set.	If the pictured ray has a closed circle at its endpoint, you can discard any of the choices involving a *strict* inequality (that is, one with < or >). Likewise, if there is an open circle on the endpoint of the ray, discard any of the choices involving a ≤ or ≥ sign. To distinguish among the remaining choices, choose an extreme *x*-value (very large or very small) that is in the graphed ray, plug it into the inequalities, and see the one it satisfies. That is the solution.
4. You are given a verbal description whose translation into symbols results in an inequality, and you are asked for the solution set.	Translate the verbal scenario into an inequality, and solve as above.

Consider the following ACT-like problem.

When 2 times a number *x* is decreased by 8, the result is less than 20. Which of the following represents the solution set of this relationship?

F. $x < 2$
G. $x < 6$
H. $x < 14$
J. $x < 20$
K. $x < 28$

The correct answer is H. First, translate the given information into an inequality: $2x - 8 < 20$. Now solve the inequality for *x*:

$$2x - 8 < 20$$
$$2x < 28$$
$$x < 14$$

Sometimes, you will be asked to solve a double inequality, as in the following example. Give it a try.

Example:

Determine the solution set for the double inequality $-4 < 8 - 3x < 20$. __________

Solution:

The strategy behind solving such inequalities is to get the variable *in the middle* by itself. To do that here, simply subtract 8 from all parts of the inequality, and then divide all parts by –3. When you perform this division, make certain to switch *both* signs since you are working with a negative number:

$$-4 < 8 - 3x < 20$$
$$-12 < -3x < 12$$
$$4 > x > -4$$

The last line is the solution set and can be written equivalently as $-4 < x < 4$.

Absolute Value Equations and Inequalities

You should also be comfortable working with linear equations and inequalities involving absolute values. Solve these problems by writing them in equivalent forms involving plain old vanilla linear equations and inequalities *without* absolute values, as follows:

Absolute Value Equation/Inequality	Solution
$\|x\| = a$	$x = a$ or $x = -a$
$\|x\| \geq a$	$x \geq a$ or $x \leq -a$
$\|x\| > a$	$x > a$ or $x < -a$
$\|x\| \leq a$	$-a \leq x \leq a$
$\|x\| < a$	$-a < x < a$

Use these definitions when x is replaced by some linear expression in x, and then solve the resulting equation(s) or inequality in the same manner that you would solve other more standard linear equations and inequalities. Work through the following examples.

Examples:

1. Solve the equation $|4x - 1| = 3$. __________

2. Determine the solution set of the inequality $|2 - 3x| < 7$. __________

Solutions:

1. We must adapt the fact that the solutions of $|x| = a$ are $x = a$ and $x = -a$ to this situation. To do so, we create two equations: $4x - 1 = 3$ and $4x - 1 = -3$. Then, solve each for x.

   For the first equation, $4x = 4$, so $x = 1$. For the second equation, $4x = -2$, so $x = -\frac{1}{2}$.

   Therefore, the solutions of the original equation are 1 and $-\frac{1}{2}$.

2. In this scenario, we must adapt the fact that the solution set of $|x| < a$ is $-a < x < a$. The absolute value inequality can be written equivalently as the double inequality $-7 < 2 - 3x < 7$.

Solve this inequality by subtracting 2 from all parts to get $-9 < -3x < 5$, and then divide all parts by -3, remembering to reverse the signs.

The final solution set is $3 > x > -\frac{5}{3}$. This can be rewritten as $-\frac{5}{3} < x < 3$.

Now see how a question of this type would appear on the ACT.

Which of the following inequalities gives the complete solution set for the inequality $|2x - 3| < 8$?

F. $x < -\frac{5}{2}$ or $x > \frac{11}{2}$

G. $x < \frac{11}{2}$

H. $x > -\frac{5}{2}$

J. $-5 < x < 11$

K. $-\frac{5}{2} < x < \frac{11}{2}$

The correct answer is K. Express the absolute value inequality as the equivalent double inequality $-8 < 2x - 3 < 8$. Then add 3 to all parts of the inequality to get $-5 < 2x < 11$. Finally, divide all parts by 2 to get the solution set $-\frac{5}{2} < x < \frac{11}{2}$.

TIP: If you have to solve an absolute value inequality of the forms $|ax + b| < c$ or $|ax + b| \leq c$, the solution set cannot be a ray (like choices G and H in this problem)! You can discard those answer choices immediately.

Sometimes, absolute value problems sneak in subtly in the form of a word problem, as in this next sample question.

Zane earns an annual salary of Z dollars, and Wendi earns an annual salary of W dollars. If the difference between Zane's and Wendi's average monthly salaries is \$450, which of the following represents the relationship between Z and W?

A. $|Z - W| = 5{,}400$

B. $\left|\frac{Z + W}{2}\right| = 5{,}400$

C. $|Z + W| = 5{,}400$

D. $|Z + W| = 450$

E. $|Z - W| = 450$

The correct answer is A. The difference between Zane's and Wendi's average monthly salaries is \$450, so the difference between their annual salaries is $\$450 \times 12 = \$5{,}400$. We do not know who earns more, but the difference between their annual salaries is $|Z - W|$ dollars. Thus, $|Z - W| = 5{,}400$.

ALERT: Read the problem carefully. Choice E, for instance, is the difference between *monthly* salaries, not *annual* salaries.

Turn to page 325 to follow the College Readiness Benchmark Learning Path questions covering Linear Inequalities.

QUADRATIC INEQUALITIES

A quadratic inequality is an inequality involving a quadratic expression. Here are some examples:

$$x^2 + 6 < 5x,\ 2x^2 \geq 1,\ (3 - x)(4 + x) \leq 0$$

Solving these problems is a little tricky since, unlike linear inequalities, the goal is *not* to get x on one side by itself. Here are the steps used to solve quadratic inequalities:

1) Gather all terms on one side so that you get 0 on one side of the inequality.

2) Factor the resulting quadratic expression, if possible, to determine its roots (that is, where the expression *equals* zero). If you cannot factor it, use the quadratic formula to find the roots.

3) Draw a number line and label the roots. Choose any number in each interval of the number line before, between, or after the roots. Plug this number into the quadratic expression and note its sign.

4) The solution set is those intervals where the sign determined in step 3 satisfies the inequality. If the inequality is *strict* (that is, either < or >), then do NOT include the roots in the solution set; if the inequality includes equals (that is, either ≤ or ≥), DO include the roots in the solution set.

Let's walk through an example together.

Solve the quadratic inequality $x^2 + 6 < 5x$.

Step 1: Write the inequality as $x^2 - 5x + 6 < 0$. (Note: Put the terms in decreasing order according to the exponents on x; this will make it easier to factor.)

Step 2: Factor the left side as $(x - 3)(x - 2) < 0$. The roots of the left side are 2 and 3.

Step 3: Form the following number line:

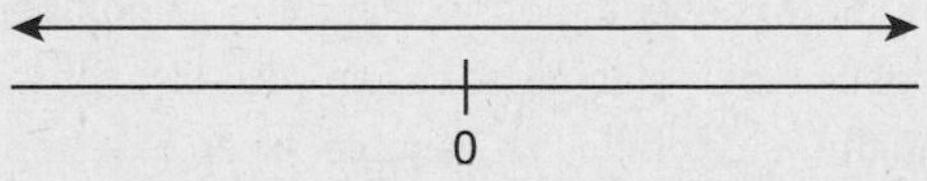

Choose the point 0 in the leftmost interval, 2.5 in the middle interval, and 5 in the rightmost interval, and plug them into the factored expression. The sign shown above each interval is the sign of the quadratic expression on the respective interval.

Step 4: The solution set is the open interval (2, 3).

Now try a couple on your own.

Examples:

Solve these quadratic inequalities.

1. $(3 - x)(x + 6) > 0$ __________

2. $2x^2 + x - 1 \geq 0$ __________

Solutions:

1. $(-6, 3)$

2. $(-\infty, -1] \cup \left[\frac{1}{2}, \infty\right)$

SYSTEMS OF LINEAR EQUATIONS

A **system of linear equations** is a pair of linear equations involving x and y that must be satisfied *at the same time*. Linear equation systems are tested under the category of Preparing for Higher Math. To solve a system means to identify ordered pairs (x, y) that satisfy not just one, but *both* equations.

There are only three possibilities that can occur when trying to find the solution to a system:

Number of Solutions	Geometric Interpretation
0	The graphs of the lines in the system are *parallel*. Hence, there is no point that is on both lines simultaneously.
1	The graphs of the lines in the system intersect in a *single* point. The intersection point is the solution of the system.
Infinitely many	The graphs of the lines in the system are exactly the same. Every point on the line is a solution of the system.

There are two algebraic methods that you can use to solve a system: the **elimination method** and the **substitution method**. Let's look at how to use both methods to solve the same system.

Elimination Method

First, we'll use the elimination method to solve a system.

$$\text{Solve the system: } \begin{cases} 2x+3y=-1 \\ 3x+y=2 \end{cases}$$

The strategy behind this method is to multiply both equations by a number or numbers so that when you add the left sides and the right sides, one of the variables drops out (or is eliminated). Then you solve for that remaining variable and plug the value you get back into either equation to find the value of the first variable. When that step is complete, you have your ordered pair.

For instance, suppose our goal was to eliminate the variable x. One way to do so is to multiply both sides of the first equation by 3 and both sides of the second equation by –2:

$$\begin{cases} 6x+9y=-3 \\ -6x-2y=-4 \end{cases}$$

Now add the left sides and right sides to get the equation $7y = -7$. (Note that the x has indeed been eliminated!) Solving this equation for y yields $y = -1$.

Finally, substitute this value back into either equation in the original system (it does not matter which one!) and solve for x. If we use the second equation, we get $3x + (-1) = 2$. Solving for x yields $3x = 3$, and so $x = 1$. Thus, the solution of the system is $(1, -1)$.

TIP: When it's time to determine the value of the first variable, choose the simpler equation. Doing so will cut down on the arithmetic.

Substitution Method

Now we'll solve the same system again, but this time, let's use the substitution method.

$$\text{Solve the system: } \begin{cases} 2x+3y=-1 \\ 3x+y=2 \end{cases}$$

The strategy behind this method is to solve one of the equations for a variable (either *x* or *y*, whichever is slightly easier to isolate) and *substitute* that expression for the variable into the other equation (doing so results in an equation involving only one variable). Solve that equation and then plug the value you get back into either equation to find the value of the unknown variable. When that step is complete, you have your ordered pair.

Solve the second equation for *y* to get $y = 2 - 3x$. Substitute this expression for *y* in the first equation to obtain $2x + 3(2 - 3x) = -1$. This equation involves only *x*, so you can now solve for *x*, as follows:

> **TIP:** When applying the substitution method, choose the equation in which you can solve for one of the variables easily.

$$\begin{aligned} 2x+3(2-3x) &= -1 \\ 2x+6-9x &= -1 \\ -7x+6 &= -1 \\ -7x &= -7 \\ x &= 1 \end{aligned}$$

Finally, plug this value of *x* back into $y = 2 - 3x$ to get $y = 2 - 3(1) = -1$. Thus, the solution of the system is $(1, -1)$.

What kinds of problems involve solving such systems on the ACT Mathematics test? As usual, there is a variety. You could simply be given two equations and asked which one of the given choices is a solution to the system. In a case like this, it is more efficient to plug the given values into the system to determine which one satisfies both.

ALERT: If you are given a system and asked which of a list of choices is a solution, remember that the ordered pair must satisfy BOTH equations, not just one of them. Among the choices will be points that satisfy one of the equations, but not the other!

It is more likely that the problem involving systems will have a little extra twist to it. For instance, you might be asked to evaluate an expression involving the *x*- and *y*-coordinates of the solution rather than simply identifying the solution itself, as in the following problem.

If $x - 4y = -2$ and $2x + y = 23$, what is the value of $5xy$?

A. 10
B. 13
C. 30
D. 50
E. 150

The correct answer is E. The two methods are equally convenient to use, so let's apply the substitution method. Solve the first equation for *x* to get $x = 4y - 2$ and substitute this in for *x* in the second equation to get $2(4y - 2) + y = 23$. Solving for *y* yields $8y - 4 + y = 23$, which is equivalent to $9y = 27$, so $y = 3$. Plugging this value back into the substitution expression yields $x = 4(3) - 2 = 10$.

The final step here is to evaluate the expression $5xy$ using $x = 10$ and $y = 3$ (since these are the only values of *x* and *y* for which both equations hold simultaneously). Doing so yields $5(10)(3) = 150$.

Another type of problem will ask you to identify the value of a coefficient, such that the nature of the solutions of a given system satisfies some condition. For instance, consider the following problem.

Suppose the system $\begin{cases} x+ky+1=4x \\ -3x=5-2y \end{cases}$ has no solution.

What must be the value of *k*?

F. -2

G. 2

H. $\frac{1}{2}$

J. $-\frac{1}{2}$

K. 4

The correct answer is G. The only way a linear system can have *no solution* is for the two lines to be parallel, which means they have the same slope. So in order to determine the value of *k*, put each of the lines into slope-intercept form and equate the slopes:

$$x+ky+1=4x \Rightarrow ky=3x-1 \Rightarrow y=\frac{3}{k}x-\frac{1}{k}$$

$$-3x=5-2y \Rightarrow -5-3x=-2y \Rightarrow y=\frac{3}{2}k+\frac{5}{2}$$

In this form, the slopes of the lines are $\frac{3}{k}$ and $\frac{3}{2}$. Setting them equal and solving for *k* yields $k = 2$. This is the only value for which these two lines are parallel.

Turn to page 328 to follow the College Readiness Benchmark Learning Path questions covering Systems of Linear Equations.

BASIC COORDINATE GEOMETRY

If you are on the road to taking the ACT exam, you are likely familiar with the (*x*, *y*) coordinate plane and know how to plot points. But you may have forgotten some of the associated terminology and formulas that will probably come up on the exam, the numbering of quadrants, and the distance and midpoint formulas. On the ACT exam, coordinate geometry falls under the category of Preparing for Higher Math.

We'll review the language and application of coordinate geometry concepts in this section.

The (*x*, *y*) coordinate plane is divided into four congruent **quadrants** numbered I, II, III, and IV counterclockwise as shown below. This image is also a good reference for the signs of coordinates that lie in each quadrant.

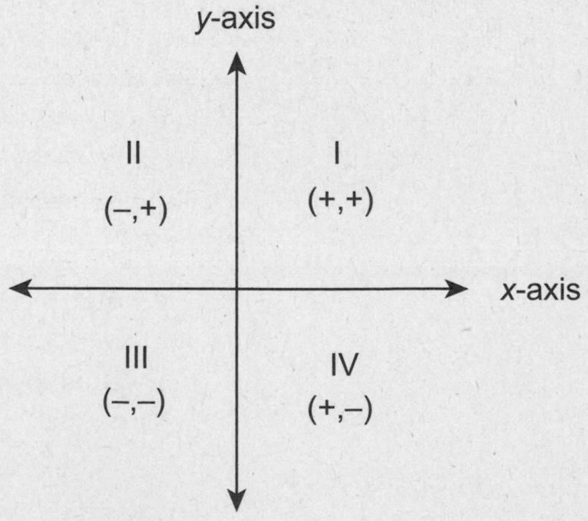

Important Coordinate Geometry Formulas

You can quickly compute the length of any vertical or horizontal line segment by simply subtracting its *y*- or *x*-coordinates, respectively, and taking the absolute value of the result (since length cannot be negative). For diagonal segments, the **distance formula** comes in handy:

The distance between two points $P(x_1, y_1)$ and $Q(x_2, y_2)$ is $\sqrt{(x_2 - x_1)^2 + (y_2 - y_1)^2}$.

Likewise, the midpoint of the line segment with endpoints $P(x_1, y_1)$ and $Q(x_2, y_2)$ is the point with coordinates $\left(\frac{x_1 + x_2}{2}, \frac{y_1 + y_2}{2}\right)$.

Often, the problems on the ACT Mathematics test that involve the distance and midpoint formulas are word problems, such as the following question.

A map is laid out in the standard (*x*, *y*) coordinate plane. How long in units is the path from City A located at (4, 11) to City B located at (8, 9), given that the path is a straight line between the cities?

F. 2 units

G. $\sqrt{6}$ units

H. $2\sqrt{5}$ units

J. 6 units

K. 20 units

The correct answer is H. You can use the distance formula to find the straight-line distance between any two points in the (*x*, *y*) plane.

$$\begin{aligned} d &= \sqrt{(x_1 - x_2)^2 + (y_1 - y_2)^2} \\ &= \sqrt{(4-8)^2 + (11-9)^2} \\ &= \sqrt{-4^2 + 2^2} \\ &= \sqrt{16+4} \\ &= \sqrt{20} \\ &= 2\sqrt{5} \end{aligned}$$

ALERT: Be careful to avoid making these common errors when using the distance formula:

- Forgetting to square the differences inside the radical
- Subtracting the coordinates of a given point rather than subtracting the *x*-coordinates and *y*-coordinates of the two points
- Forgetting to take the square root

These errors are reflected in the distracter choices for these problems.

See how the midpoint formula might be used in an ACT exam question.

Suppose that *P*(–1, 6) is one of the endpoints of a line segment *PQ* and that its midpoint is *M* (4, –5). What is point *Q*?

A. $\left(\frac{3}{2}, \frac{1}{2}\right)$
B. (–5, 11)
C. (5, –11)
D. (9, –16)
E. (–9, 16)

The correct answer is D. Since we do not know the coordinates of *Q*, let's call that point (*x*, *y*); we must determine the values of both *x* and *y*. Using the midpoint formula, we can express the midpoint of *PQ* as $\left(\frac{-1+x}{2}, \frac{6+y}{2}\right)$. Since we are given that the midpoint is (4, –5), we know that $\frac{-1+x}{2} = 4$ and $\frac{6+y}{2} = -5$.

Solving each of these yields *x* = 9 and *y* = –16. Hence, the coordinates of *Q* are (9, –16).

CIRCLES IN THE COORDINATE PLANE

Circles and their graphs appear on the ACT exam occasionally as well. The equation of a circle with center (*h*, *k*) and radius *r*, as pictured below, is $(x - h)^2 + (y - k)^2 = r^2$:

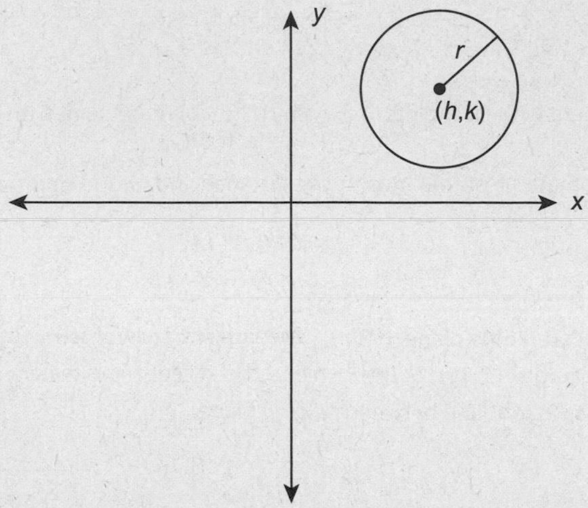

CAUTION Be careful when identifying the coordinates of the center. If the equation of the circle is $(x + 3)^2 + y^2 = 16$, then the center is (–3, 0), not (3, 0)!

The following is a typical ACT mathematics question involving the equation of a circle.

The circle with equation $(x + 2)^2 + (y - 9)^2 = 25$ lies completely inside a square. What is the least possible length of one of the sides of the square?

F. 4
G. 8
H. 10
J. 14
K. 16

The correct answer is H. In order for the circle to lie completely inside the square, the side length of the square must be at least as large as the diameter of the circle. The diameter of a circle is twice its radius. Here, the equation of the circle is in standard form; the right side is the square of the radius. So the radius is 5, which means the diameter is 10 units.

Turn to page 330 to follow the College Readiness Benchmark Learning Path questions covering Basic Coordinate Geometry.

FUNCTIONS

A **function** is a rule that associates a corresponding y-value to each input x. On the ACT exam, functions are tested under the category of Preparing for Higher Math. Commonly, functions are described using algebraic expressions (which can then be illustrated by a graph). Functions are denoted using letters, like f or g. When we want to emphasize the input/output-defining relationship of a function, an expression in the form $y = f(x)$ (read "y equals f of x") is often used.

The **domain** of a function is the set of all values of x that can be substituted into the expression and yield a meaningful output. The **range** of a function is the set of all possible y-values attained at some member of the domain. Try working through these examples.

Examples:

What are the domains of the following functions?

1. $f(x)=2+\frac{3}{x+5}$ __________

2. $g(x)=\sqrt{4-x}$ __________

3. $h(x)=\frac{x+5}{\left(x^2+9\right)(x-4)}$ __________

4. $j(x) = x^3 + x^2 - 5x + 3$ __________

Solutions:

1. The domain is the set of all real numbers *except* –5, because we can substitute any value other than –5 for x and get a well-defined real number as an output.

2. The domain of the function $g(x)=\sqrt{4-x}$ consists of all real numbers x for which the radicand, $4 - x$, is nonnegative—we want the output to be a real number, and we know that the square root of a negative number involves i. As such, we will allow any x that satisfies the inequality $4 - x \geq 0$, which is equivalent to $4 \geq x$, to be an input into the function. So the domain is all real numbers for which $x \leq 4$.

3. All real numbers except 4.

4. All real numbers.

CAUTION

For a rational function like $h(x)$, only the x-values that make the *denominator* equal to zero are excluded from the domain. You do NOT exclude values that make the *numerator* equal to zero.

When working with functions on the ACT exam, you will likely be asked to compute the value $f(x)$ (called the **functional value of *x***) for various inputs. Get some practice with these computations by solving these examples.

Examples:

1. Consider the function $f(x) = 2x^2 - x + 1$. Compute $f(3)$ and $f(a + 2)$. __________

2. How do we compute $f(a + 2)$? __________

3. If $f(x) = -3x^2 + 1$, compute $f(x + 2)$. __________

Solutions:

1. To compute $f(3)$, simply plug in 3 for x to obtain $f(3) = 2(3)^2 - 3 + 1 = 18 - 3 + 1 = 16$.

2. Here, the input happens to be an algebraic expression instead of a number. We must substitute the *entire* quantity within the parentheses for x everywhere it occurs in the formula:

$$\begin{aligned} f(a+2) &= 2(a+2)^2 - (a+2) + 1 \\ &= 2(a^2 + 4a + 4) - (a+2) + 1 \\ &= 2a^2 + 8a + 8 - a - 2 + 1 \\ &= 2a^2 + 7a + 7 \end{aligned}$$

3. $$\begin{aligned} f(x+2) &= -3(x+2)^2 + 1 \\ &= -3(x^2 + 4x + 4) + 1 \\ &= -3x^2 - 12x - 12 + 1 \\ &= -3x^2 - 12x - 11 \end{aligned}$$

CAUTION A common error is to say $f(x + 2) = f(x) + f(2)$. This is wrong! You cannot distribute the function in this manner. You must compute as above.

Functions and Arithmetic

We can define arithmetic operations on functions in the same manner that we perform arithmetic on real numbers. Let f and g be functions. The sum $(f+g)(x)$ is defined to be $f(x) + g(x)$. Likewise, the difference function $(f-g)(x)$ is defined to be $f(x) - g(x)$; the product function $(f \bullet g)(x)$ is defined to be $f(x) \bullet g(x)$; and the quotient function $\left(\frac{f}{g}\right)(x)$ is defined to be $\frac{f(x)}{g(x)}$. Another function that is important is the **composition** of f and g, denoted by $(f \circ g)$. This value is defined by $(f \circ g)(x) = f(g(x))$, as in the example below.

Example:

Let $f(x) = 3x - 2$ and $g(x) = 4x^2 + 1$. Compute $(f \circ g)(x)$ and $(g \circ f)(x)$.

Solution:

$$(f \circ g)(x) = f(g(x)) = f(4x^2+1) = 3(4x^2+1) - 2 = 12x^2 + 1$$

$$(g \circ f)(x) = g(f(x)) = g(3x-2) = 4(3x-2)^2 + 1 = 4(9x^2 - 12x + 4) + 1 = 36x^2 - 48x + 17$$

CAUTION Note that, in general, $(f \circ g) \neq (g \circ f)$. The order in which you compose functions matters!

Graphing Functions

The following are the graphs of some of the most common functions you will encounter on the ACT.

<table>
<tr><th>Function</th><th colspan="3">Typical Graphs</th></tr>
<tr><td>Linear Functions
$f(x) = mx + b$</td><td>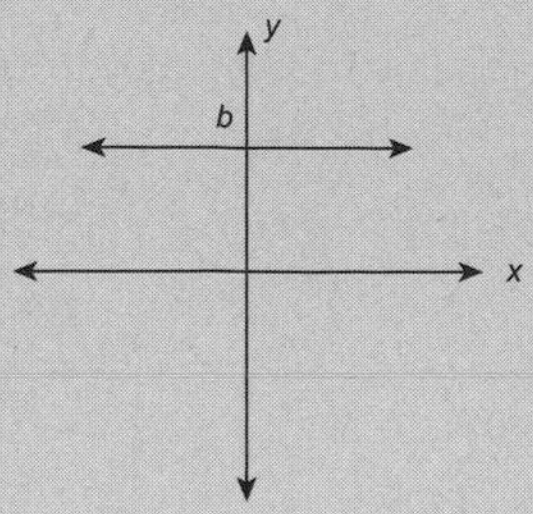
$m = 0$</td><td>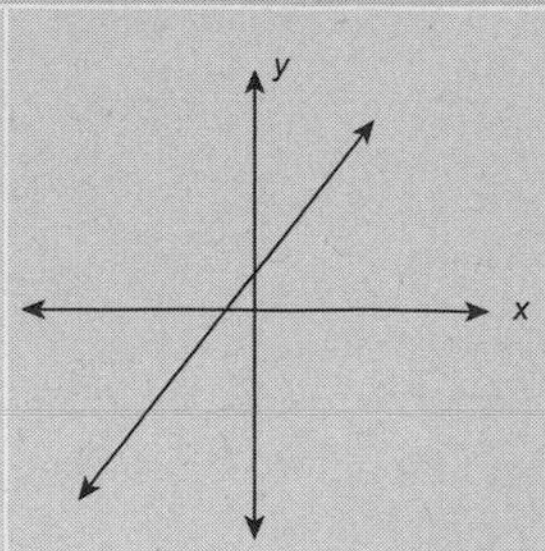
$m > 0$</td><td>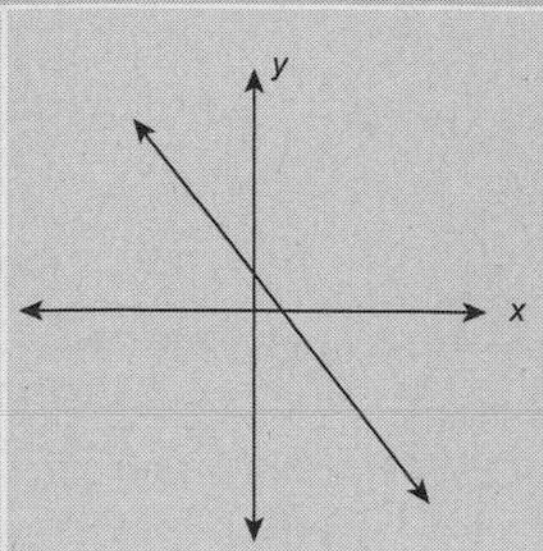
$m < 0$</td></tr>
<tr><td rowspan="2">Quadratic Functions
$f(x) = a(x - h)^2 + k$</td><td>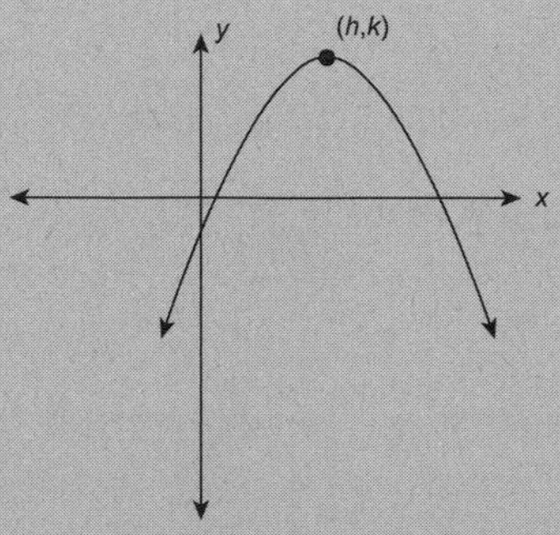
$a < 0$</td><td colspan="2">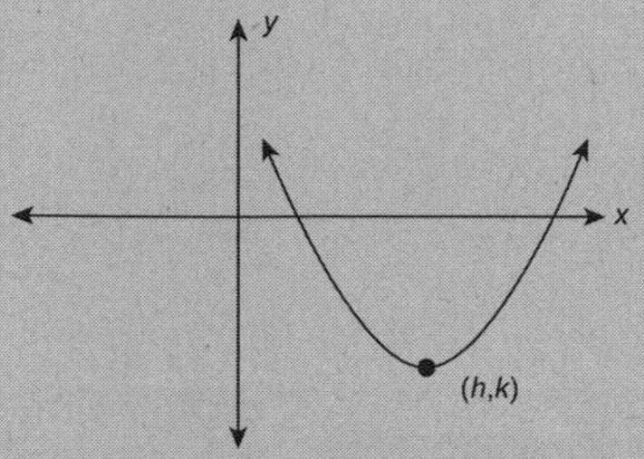
$a > 0$</td></tr>
<tr><td colspan="3">The graph is called a parabola. The vertex is the point (h, k).
Note that the maximum or minimum value of a parabola occurs at the vertex.</td></tr>
<tr><td>Cubic Function
$f(x) = x^3$</td><td colspan="3">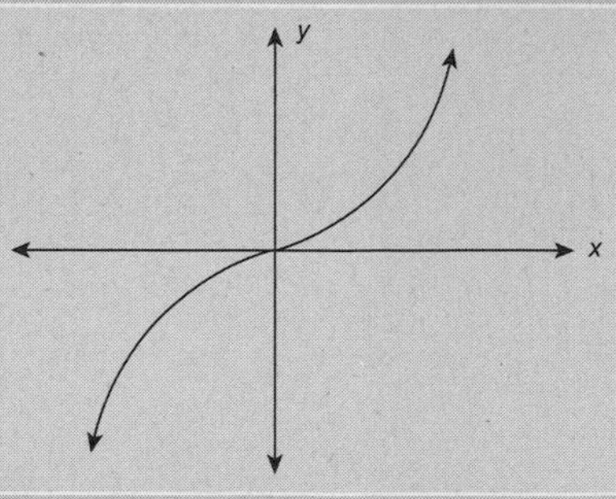</td></tr>
<tr><td>Absolute Value Function
$f(x) = |x|$</td><td colspan="3">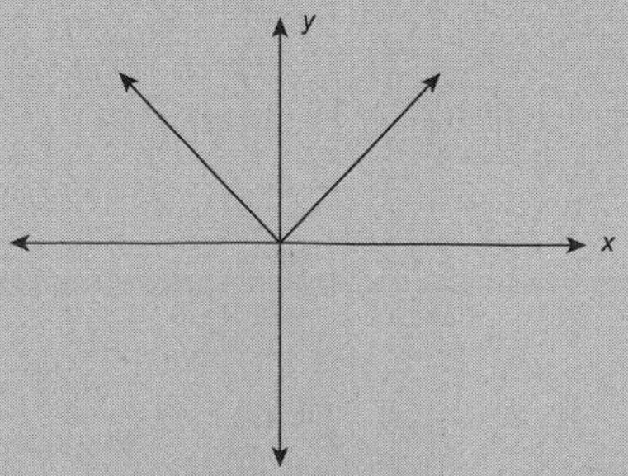
More generally, if h and k are positive numbers, then the graph of $g(x) = |x - h| + k$ is obtained by moving the shown graph to the right h units and up k units.</td></tr>
</table>

Function	Typical Graphs
Square Root Function $f(x)=\sqrt{x}$	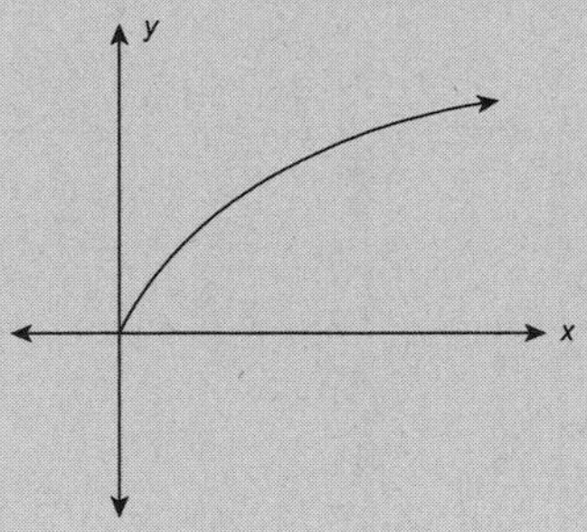

Note that when you have a graph of a function, you can determine if an x-value belongs to the domain of f by simply determining if an ordered pair with that x-value belongs to the graph of f. You should be familiar with the following features of the graph of a function $y = f(x)$:

- The *minimum of f* is the smallest y-value in the range of f; it is the y-value of the lowest point on the graph of f.
- The *maximum of f* is the largest y-value in the range of f; it is the y-value of the highest point on the graph of f.
- f is *decreasing* if its graph falls from left to right as you progress through the interval from left to right.
- f is *increasing* on an interval if its graph rises from left to right as you progress through the interval from left to right.
- An *x-intercept of f* is a point of the form $(x, 0)$. You determine the x-intercepts of a function by solving the equation $f(x) = 0$.
- A *y-intercept of f* is the point $(0, f(0))$.

Let's look at a couple of sample questions.

What is the equation of the parabola graphed below?

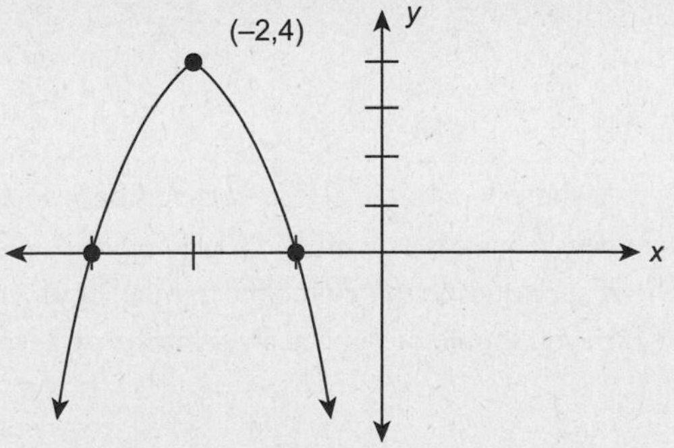

A. $y = -4x^2 - 16x - 12$
B. $y = -x^2 - 2x + 3$
C. $y = -x^2 + 2x - 3$
D. $y = 4x^2 - 16x - 12$
E. $y = 4x^2 + 16x + 12$

The correct answer is A. Factor the expression to get $-4x^2 - 16x - 12 = -4(x^2 + 4x + 3) = -4(x + 3)(x + 1)$.

This equals zero at $x = -3$ and $x = -1$; as shown, the y-intercept is -12; the parabola opens downward because the coefficient of x^2 is negative. So this is the equation of the graph shown. The other choices can be discarded. The graph opens downward, which means that the coefficient of x^2 must be reactive, so you can eliminate choices D and E immediately. The graph also has x-intercepts at -3 and -1. If you factor the expression in choice B, you get $-(x + 3)(x - 1)$, which is zero at 1 and -3, not -1 and -3. So this can be discarded. For a similar reason, you can discard choice C.

Which of the following could be the equation for the graph below?

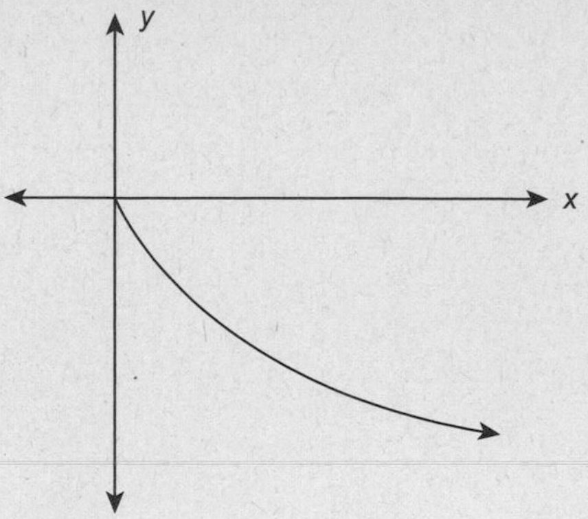

F. $y = Ax$
G. $y = Ax^2$
H. $y = Ax^3$
J. $y = Ax^4$
K. $y = A\sqrt{x}$

The correct answer is K. Even if you didn't immediately recognize that this graph of $y = \sqrt{x}$ reflected over the *x*-axis, you can still answer this question using the process of elimination. Choice F can be immediately eliminated because it is a linear equation, and its graph would therefore be a straight line. Choices G, H, and J can be eliminated because they are defined for *negative* *x*-values, but such values are not used to get the graph shown.

All of these functions can be moved within the coordinate plane using horizontal and vertical **translations** and **reflections**, defined as follows. Here, let *h* and *k* stand for positive real numbers.

New Function	Verbal Description of How to Graph This Function By Translation or Reflecting the Graph of $y = f(x)$
$F(x) = f(x) + k$	Translate the graph of $\mathbf{y = f(x)}$ *k* units vertically upward.
$F(x) = f(x) - k$	Translate the graph of $\mathbf{y = f(x)}$ *k* units vertically downward.
$F(x) = f(x - h)$	Translate the graph of $\mathbf{y = f(x)}$ *h* units to the right.
$F(x) = f(x + h)$	Translate the graph of $\mathbf{y = f(x)}$ *h* units to the left.
$F(x) = -f(x)$	Reflect the graph of $\mathbf{y = f(x)}$ over the *x*-axis.

Polynomials

A polynomial is a function of the form $f(x) = a_n x^n + a_{n-1} x^{n-1} + \ldots + a_1 x + a_0$, where $a_0, a_1, \ldots, a_n$ are real numbers, and *n* is a nonnegative integer. We say the polynomial has **degree *n***. The graphing of polynomials is a bit more difficult to grasp, and you will likely see a question or two about graphing polynomials on the ACT. Often, such questions focus on the terminology involved instead of some obscure property or trick. The three main concepts with which you should be familiar are ***x*-intercept**, **zero**, and **factor**.

Term	Definition
x-intercept	A point $(a, 0)$ on the graph of $y = p(x)$ (In such case, a is a solution of the equation $p(x) = 0$.)
zero (or root)	A real number a such that $p(a) = 0$
factor	An expression of the form $(x - a)$ in which a is a zero of $p(x)$

A high-powered theorem known as the **fundamental theorem of algebra** tells us that a polynomial with degree n has at most n x-intercepts, and these occur at the x-values that make each linear factor equal to zero. Consider the following problem.

In the standard (x, y) coordinate plane, how many roots does the graph of $y = 2(x - 3)(x + 5)(x + 7)$ have?

A. 1
B. 2
C. 3
D. 4
E. 5

The correct answer is C. The graph will have a root at any x-value for which y equals zero, and this occurs when any of its factors equals zero. Set the expression equal to zero and solve for x:

$$0 = 2(x - 3)(x + 5)(x + 7)$$

The right side is zero when x is 3, –5, or –7. This means that the graph has 3 roots.

Turn to page 332 to follow the College Readiness Benchmark Learning Path questions covering Functions.

MODELING

You will encounter all kinds of word problems on the ACT Mathematics test. Some will involve simple arithmetic, while others will require you to set up equations, inequalities, or systems of equations, or to use a trigonometric relationship to identify the value of an unknown. The common link? Your goal is always to first identify the variable(s), and then interpret the information provided into a mathematical expression so that you can make use of all of the rules and methods discussed so far in this chapter. On the test, Modeling is its own subcategory of ACT Math, worth approximately 25% of the overall ACT Math score.

At this point in our review, you have all of the pieces needed to solve the following word problems.

A ball thrown upward from ground level is s feet high after t seconds, where $s = 112t - 16t^2$. At which of the following times will the ball be 96 feet above the ground?

A. 0.25 second
B. 0.5 second
C. 2 seconds
D. 4 seconds
E. 6 seconds

The correct answer is E. You want to know the value of t when $s = 96$. Plugging in $s = 96$ gives you $96 = 112t - 16t^2$. Put this equation into standard quadratic form and solve for t:

$$\begin{aligned} 96 &= 112t - 16t^2 \\ 16t^2 - 112t + 96 &= 0 \\ 16\left(t^2 - 7t + 6\right) &= 0 \\ 16(t-6)(t-1) &= 0 \\ t &= 1, 6 \end{aligned}$$

So the ball is at this height at both 1 and 6 seconds. Since 6 seconds is the only one of the two answers that is listed, it must be the correct answer.

Working together, a standard desktop computer and a supercomputer can complete a data analysis job in 2.5 hours. If it takes the standard desktop computer 6 hours to do the job alone, how many hours would it take the supercomputer to complete the job alone?

F. $\frac{1}{6}$ hour
G. $\frac{2}{5}$ hour
H. 2 hours
J. $4\frac{2}{7}$ hours
K. 5 hours

The correct answer is J. Let x equal the number of hours it takes the supercomputer to complete the job alone. The standard desktop computer can complete the job alone in 6 hours, so every hour it does $\frac{1}{6}$ of the job. That means every hour, the supercomputer does $\frac{1}{x}$ of the job. Working together, the two printers complete the job in 2.5 hours, so each hour they do $\frac{1}{2.5} = \frac{1}{\frac{5}{2}} = \frac{2}{5}$ of the job. The sum of the individual rates equals the rate working together. As such, we have the following equation involving x: $\frac{1}{x} + \frac{1}{6} = \frac{2}{5}$.

Solving this equation yields:

$$\begin{aligned} \frac{1}{x} + \frac{1}{6} &= \frac{2}{5} \\ 30 + 5x &= 12x \\ 30 &= 7x \\ x &= \frac{30}{7} = 4\frac{2}{7} \end{aligned}$$

In which of the following equations is p inversely proportional to the square root of q and directly proportional to the cube of r?

A. $\frac{r^3}{\sqrt{q}} = p$
B. $\frac{\sqrt{p}}{r^3} = q$
C. $\frac{\sqrt{r}}{q^3} = p$
D. $\frac{\sqrt{q}}{p^3} = r$
E. $\frac{\sqrt{q}}{r^3} = p$

The correct answer is A. The equation must contain p, $\sqrt{q}$, and r^3. The only two answer choices that have these are A and E, so immediately eliminate choices B, C, and D. Then, you must remember what both *directly* proportional and *inversely* proportional mean. If a and b are *directly* proportional, there must be a constant k such that $a = kb$, and if they are *inversely* proportional, there must be a constant k such that $a = k \bullet \frac{1}{b}$. Of the two choices, A is the correct one, while E is the two relationships reversed.

While shopping, Dennis finds that one pair of jeans and three T-shirts cost \$140, while two pairs of jeans and one T-shirt cost \$120. If the store charges the same price for all of its T-shirts and the same price for all of its jeans, what is Dennis's cost if he decides to simply buy one pair of jeans and one T-shirt?

- **F.** \$32
- **G.** \$44
- **H.** \$50
- **J.** \$64
- **K.** \$76

The correct answer is K. Let j be the cost of one pair of jeans and t the cost of one T-shirt. The condition, "one pair of jeans and three T-shirts cost \$140" translates to $j + 3t = 140$, and the condition, "two pairs of jeans and one T-shirt cost \$120" translates to $2j + t = 120$. These two equations must be satisfied *simultaneously*, so we must solve a system to determine the cost of one pair of jeans and one T-shirt.

Let's use the elimination method. Multiply both sides of the first equation by –2: $-2j - 6t = -280$. Then add this to the second equation to obtain $-5t = -160$, so that $t = 32$. So we know the price of one T-shirt is \$32.

Now, plug this into the second equation for t and solve for j: $2j + 32 = 120$, so that $2j = 88$ and $j = 44$. So one pair of jeans costs \$44. Finally, to answer the question posed, one pair of jeans and one T-shirt cost \$32 + \$44 = \$76.

Marlene needs an average of 74% on five quizzes in order to get her desired grade in biology. Her first four quiz scores are 64%, 80%, 70%, and 78%. What does she need to score on her fifth quiz to attain her desired average?

- **A.** 74
- **B.** 78
- **C.** 82
- **D.** 86
- **E.** 90

The correct answer is B. Let x represent the fifth quiz score. To compute the average of five numbers, sum them and divide by five. Since we are given percentages for all the scores, as well as the desired average, you can drop the percent sign momentarily and affix it to the final value of x:

$$\frac{64+80+70+78+x}{5}=74$$
$$\frac{292+x}{5}=74$$
$$292+x=370$$
$$x=78$$

So she needs 78% on the fifth quiz to attain the desired average.

Turn to page 334 to follow the College Readiness Benchmark Learning Path questions covering Modeling.

SEQUENCES

Some ACT exam questions will ask you to find the value of an unknown term if given a sequence of terms. There are two special types of sequences for which we can find explicit formulas for the nth term rather easily. These sequence questions fall under the category of Preparing for Higher Math on the ACT exam.

An **arithmetic sequence** is a sequence with terms obtained by adding a fixed constant to the previous term. For instance, the sequence 8, 12, 16, 20, 24, …is an arithmetic sequence because the constant 4 is added to one term to get the next term. Likewise, the sequence 5, 1, –3, –7, –11, …is an arithmetic sequence because the constant –4 is added to one term to get the next term. However, the sequence 3, 6, 10, 15, 21, …is *not* an arithmetic sequence because the *same* constant is not added to each term to get the next. To get the second term, you add 3 to the first one; but, to get the third term, you must add 4 to the second term, and to get the fourth term, you must add 5 to the third one, and so on.

In general, if a sequence is arithmetic (and you add d to a term to get the next term), then the formula for its nth term is given by a_n = (first term) + $(n - 1)d$.

A **geometric sequence** is a sequence with terms obtained by multiplying the previous term by a fixed constant r. For instance, the sequence $\frac{1}{3}, \frac{1}{9}, \frac{1}{27}, \frac{1}{81}, \ldots$ is a geometric sequence because each term is multiplied by $\frac{1}{3}$ to get the next term. However, the sequence 8, 4, 0, –4, –8, ... is *not* geometric because there is no single number by which you can multiply each term to get the next term.

In general, if a sequence is geometric (and you multiply a term by r to get the next term), then the formula for the nth term a_n is given by $a_n = r^{n-1} \times a_1$.

Here's a sequence question problem like you might encounter on the ACT exam.

What is the seventh term of the sequence 6, 12, 18, ...?

F. 24
G. 30
H. 36
J. 42
K. 108

The correct answer is J. To answer this question, we must determine a pattern that the numbers of the sequence follow. Here the pattern is to add 6 to the previous term to get the next one. So the next term in the sequence is 24. But that's not the answer, as that is only the fourth term. We need the seventh term. So we continue to expand, getting 30, 36, and 42. So the seventh term is 42.

Turn to page 336 to follow the College Readiness Benchmark Learning Path questions covering Sequences.

MATRICES

A **matrix** is an array of real numbers. If a matrix **A** has r rows and c columns, we say **A** is an $r \times c$ (read "r by c") matrix. A matrix is written by listing all of its entries in an array, enclosed by brackets. Matrices fall under the ACT category of Preparing for Higher Math. Here are some examples:

$$\underbrace{\begin{bmatrix} a & b \\ c & d \end{bmatrix}}_{2\times2 \text{ matrix}} \quad \underbrace{\begin{bmatrix} 1 & -2 & 3 \\ 1 & 0 & 2 \\ 5 & 2 & 1 \end{bmatrix}}_{3\times3 \text{ matrix}} \quad \underbrace{\begin{bmatrix} 1 \\ 3 \\ 2 \\ 1 \end{bmatrix}}_{4\times1 \text{ matrix}}$$

The basic arithmetic operations involving matrices are performed "component-wise," which means you need to pay attention to each entry's position in a matrix. The following is a list of the basic operations on 2 × 2 matrices that may occur on the ACT Mathematics test, though such questions occur infrequently. (All letters stand for real numbers.)

Term/Operation	Definition
Equality: $\begin{bmatrix} a & b \\ c & d \end{bmatrix} = \begin{bmatrix} e & f \\ g & h \end{bmatrix}$	$\begin{bmatrix} a & b \\ c & d \end{bmatrix} = \begin{bmatrix} e & f \\ g & h \end{bmatrix}$ whenever $\underbrace{a=e,\ b=f,\ c=g,\ d=h}_{\text{corresponding entries are equal}}$
Sum: $\begin{bmatrix} a & b \\ c & d \end{bmatrix} + \begin{bmatrix} e & f \\ g & h \end{bmatrix}$	$\begin{bmatrix} a & b \\ c & d \end{bmatrix} + \begin{bmatrix} e & f \\ g & h \end{bmatrix} = \begin{bmatrix} a+e & b+f \\ c+g & d+h \end{bmatrix}$ In words, add corresponding entries to get the sum.
Difference: $\begin{bmatrix} a & b \\ c & d \end{bmatrix} - \begin{bmatrix} e & f \\ g & h \end{bmatrix}$	$\begin{bmatrix} a & b \\ c & d \end{bmatrix} - \begin{bmatrix} e & f \\ g & h \end{bmatrix} = \begin{bmatrix} a-e & b-f \\ c-g & d-h \end{bmatrix}$ In words, subtract corresponding entries to get the difference.
Scalar Multiplication: $k\begin{bmatrix} a & b \\ c & d \end{bmatrix}$	$k\begin{bmatrix} a & b \\ c & d \end{bmatrix} = \begin{bmatrix} ka & kb \\ kc & kd \end{bmatrix}$ In words, multiply all entries by the constant *k*.

The following is a typical mathematics question on the ACT exam involving matrices.

Determine the value of x that makes the following equation true:

$$3\begin{bmatrix} x & -1 \\ 1 & 1 \end{bmatrix} - \begin{bmatrix} 3 & 1 \\ 0 & -1 \end{bmatrix} = \begin{bmatrix} 9 & -4 \\ 3 & 4 \end{bmatrix}$$

A. –6
B. 3
C. 1
D. 12
E. 4

The correct answer is E. First, simplify the left side of the equation using the rules for multiplying a matrix by a scalar and subtracting matrices. Then, equate corresponding entries to get an equation to solve for x:

$$3\begin{bmatrix} x & -1 \\ 1 & 1 \end{bmatrix} - \begin{bmatrix} 3 & 1 \\ 0 & -1 \end{bmatrix} = \begin{bmatrix} 9 & -4 \\ 3 & 4 \end{bmatrix}$$

$$\begin{bmatrix} 3x & -3 \\ 3 & 3 \end{bmatrix} - \begin{bmatrix} 3 & 1 \\ 0 & -1 \end{bmatrix} = \begin{bmatrix} 9 & -4 \\ 3 & 4 \end{bmatrix}$$

$$\begin{bmatrix} 3x-3 & -4 \\ 3 & 4 \end{bmatrix} = \begin{bmatrix} 9 & -4 \\ 3 & 4 \end{bmatrix}$$

Since two matrices are equal only when their corresponding entries are the same, then $3x - 3$ must equal 9. Solving this equation yields $x = 4$.

Turn to page 338 to follow the College Readiness Benchmark Learning Path questions covering Matrices.

SUMMING IT UP

- The **equation of a line** can come in different forms; the two most common are **standard form**, ($Ax + By = C$), and **slope-intercept form**, ($y = mx + b$).
- The **slope of a line** measures steepness of the line, or the change in y-value per unit change in x-value. If you have two points on a line, say (x_1, y_1) and (x_2, y_2), the slope is the "change in y over the change in x," written as $m = \frac{y_1 - y_2}{x_1 - x_2} = \frac{y_2 - y_1}{x_2 - x_1}$.
- The **point-slope form** for the equation of a line is $y - y_1 = m(x - x_1)$.
- Two lines $y = m_1x + b_1$ and $y = m_2x + b_2$ are **parallel** if the slopes are the same; that is, $m_1 = m_2$. They are **perpendicular** if $m_1 \times m_2 = -1$.
- A **rational expression** is a quotient of polynomials. You can add, subtract, multiply, and divide rational expressions in the same manner as fractions—you're now just combining algebraic expressions.
- The **imaginary number** i satisfies $i^2 = -1$.
- A **complex number** is a number of the form $a + bi$, where a and b are both real numbers. The number a is called the **real part** and the number b is called the **imaginary part**. There are several rules that dictate the arithmetic of complex numbers, and they are very similar to how you perform arithmetic on binomials.
- The **solutions of $ax^2 + bx + c = 0$** are given by the **quadratic formula**: $x = \frac{-b \pm \sqrt{b^2 - 4ac}}{2a}$.
- The **discriminant** of $ax^2 + bx + c = 0$ is $b^2 - 4ac$. The sign of the discriminant determines the number and nature of the quadratic equation's solutions.
- **Linear inequalities** can be solved by using the same basic strategy used to solve linear equations, with the additional step of switching the inequality sign whenever both sides of the inequality are multiplied by a negative real number.
- A **system of linear equations** is a pair of linear equations involving x and y that must be satisfied *at the same time*. To solve a system means to identify ordered pairs (x, y) that satisfy *both* equations—not just one, but both! A linear system can have 0, 1, or infinitely many solutions, which can be determined using the **elimination method** or **substitution method**.
- The **distance between two points** $P(x_1, y_1)$ and $Q(x_2, y_2)$ is $\sqrt{(x_2 - x_1)^2 + (y_2 - y_1)^2}$.
- The **midpoint of the line segment** with endpoints $P(x_1, y_1)$ and $Q(x_2, y_2)$ is the point with coordinates $\left(\frac{x_1 + x_2}{2}, \frac{y_1 + y_2}{2}\right)$.
- The **equation of a circle** with center (h, k) and radius r is $(x - h)^2 + (y - k)^2 = r^2$.
- A **function** is a rule that associates to each input x a corresponding y-value. They are typically named using letters, like f or g. The notation $f(x)$ represents the functional value at x.
  - The **domain** of a function is the set of all values of x that can be substituted into the expression and yield a meaningful output. The **range** of a function is the set of all possible y-values attained at some member of the domain.
  - **The sum $(f+g)(x)$ is defined as $f(x) + g(x)$.** Likewise, the difference function $(f - g)(x)$ is defined as $f(x) - g(x)$, the product function $(f \cdot g)(x)$ is defined as $f(x) \cdot g(x)$, and the quotient function $\left(\frac{f}{g}\right)(x)$ is defined as $\frac{f(x)}{g(x)}$.
- The **composition of f and g**, denoted by $(f \circ g)$, is defined by $(f \circ g)(x) = f(g(x))$. Generally, $(f \circ g) \neq (g \circ f)$.
- The **minimum** of f is the smallest y-value in the range of f; it is the y-value of the lowest point on the graph of f. Likewise, the **maximum** of f is the largest y-value in the range of f; it is the y-value of the highest point on the graph of f.
- f is **decreasing** on an interval if its graph falls from left to right as you progress through the interval from left to right; f is **increasing** on an interval if its graph rises from left to right as you progress through the interval from left to right.

- An ***x*-intercept of *f* is a point of the form (*x*, 0)**. You determine the *x*-intercepts of a function by solving the equation $f(x) = 0$.
- A ***y*-intercept of *f* is the point (0, *f*(0))**.
- A **polynomial** is a function of the form $f(x) = a_n x^n + a_{n-1} x^{n-1} + \ldots + a_1 x + a_0$, where $a_0, a_1, \ldots, a_n$ are real numbers and n is a nonnegative integer. We say the polynomial has *degree n*. Its graph has at most n *x*-intercepts.
- An **arithmetic sequence** is a sequence whose terms are obtained by adding a fixed constant to the previous term. A formula for its nth term is a_n = (first term) + $(n - 1)d$.
- A **geometric sequence** is a sequence whose terms are obtained by multiplying the previous term by a fixed constant r. A formula for the nth term a_n is $a_n = r^{n-1} \times a_1$.
- A **matrix** is an array of real numbers. If a matrix **A** has r rows and c columns, we say **A** is an $r \times c$ matrix. The basic arithmetic operations involving matrices are performed "component-wise."

ONLINE PREP

Want to Know More?

Access more practice questions, lessons, helpful hints, and strategies for the following math topics in *Peterson's Online Course for the ACT® Exam*:

- Rational and Radical Expressions
- 2 Equations, 2 Unknowns
- Inequalities
- Quadratic Formula
- Functions
- Coordinate Geometry

To purchase and access the course, go to **www.petersons.com/testprep/act.**

Directions: The following practice exercises are designed to provide you with more opportunities to familiarize yourself with the content you will encounter on the ACT exam. Read each question carefully and choose the best answer. As you go through the practice set, review each solution and follow the expanded explanations provided to help strengthen your skills in working with Intermediate Algebra and Coordinate Geometry topics.

RATIONAL EXPRESSIONS

1. Suppose a and b are nonzero real numbers. Simplify $\frac{a}{ax-b} - \frac{b}{bx+a}$.

SHOW YOUR WORK HERE

A. $\frac{ax-b}{(ax-b)(bx+a)}$

B. $\frac{a-b}{(a-b)x-(b+a)}$

C. $\frac{1}{(x-1)(x+1)}$

D. $\frac{(a^2-b^2)x-2ab}{(ax-b)(bx+a)}$

E. $\frac{a^2+b^2}{(ax-b)(bx+a)}$

The correct answer is E. All choices are written as single rational expressions, which suggests that to simplify the given expression, you must start by getting a least common denominator, which is $(ax - b)(bx + a)$. If you simply subtract numerators and denominators rather than getting a least common denominator, you will get choice B.

Rewrite each fraction as an equivalent one with this denominator, then subtract:

$$\frac{a}{ax-b} - \frac{b}{bx+a} = \frac{a}{ax-b} \bullet \frac{bx+a}{bx+a} - \frac{b}{bx+a} \bullet \frac{ax-b}{ax-b}$$
$$= \frac{a(bx+a)-b(ax-b)}{(ax-b)(bx+a)}$$

Remember, you multiply the top and bottom of a fraction by the portion of the least common denominator that is NOT already present; if you multiply by the portion that is there, you will get choice D.

Next, simplify the numerator using the distributive property; if you misapply this property and only multiply the first term within the parentheses by the one outside, you will get choice A. Then, combine like terms:

$$\frac{a(bx+a)-b(ax-b)}{(ax-b)(bx+a)} = \frac{abx+a^2-bax+b^2}{(ax-b)(bx+a)} = \frac{\cancel{abx}+a^2-\cancel{bax}+b^2}{(ax-b)(bx+a)} = \frac{a^2+b^2}{(ax-b)(bx+a)}$$

You cannot cancel the *a* and *b* in this expression since they are not factors; doing so will yield choice C.

2. Divide and simplify: $\dfrac{4x^2-12x+9}{3x^2-2x} \div \dfrac{3x-2x^2}{9x^2-12x+4}$

SHOW YOUR WORK HERE

F. $-\left(\dfrac{2x-3}{3x-2}\right)^3$

G. $\dfrac{4x^2-12x+9}{9x^2-12x+4}$

H. $\dfrac{6x^2-13x+6}{-x^2}$

J. $(2x-3)(3-2x)$

K. $12-13x$

The correct answer is H. When faced with the division or multiplication of rational expressions, your first step should be to factor the numerators and denominators as much as possible. Doing so here yields the following:

$$\frac{4x^2-12x+9}{3x^2-2x} \div \frac{3x-2x^2}{9x^2-12x+4} = \frac{(2x-3)(2x-3)}{x(3x-2)} \div \frac{x(3-2x)}{(3x-2)(3x-2)}$$

Since this is a division problem, before you cancel *any* factors, rewrite it as an equivalent product by flipping over the rational expression that is after the division sign:

$$\frac{(2x-3)(2x-3)}{x(3x-2)} \div \frac{x(3-2x)}{(3x-2)(3x-2)} = \frac{(2x-3)(2x-3)}{x(3x-2)} \bullet \frac{(3x-2)(3x-2)}{x(3-2x)}$$

If you forget to do so, you will get choice F, assuming you simplify correctly.

Next, cancel any factor that is identical in the numerator and denominator, with emphasis on *identical*. That is especially important here because the factors $(2x-3)$ in the top and $(3-2x)$ in the bottom look *very* similar. However, they are not the same—they are off by a factor of –1. So before you cancel that pair, you must factor out –1 from one of them. Let's try $(3-2x)$:

$$\begin{aligned}\frac{(2x-3)(2x-3)}{x(3x-2)} \bullet \frac{(3x-2)(3x-2)}{x(3-2x)} &= \frac{(2x-3)(2x-3)}{x(3x-2)} \bullet \frac{(3x-2)(3x-2)}{-x(2x-3)} \\ &= \frac{\cancel{(2x-3)}(2x-3)}{x\cancel{(3x-2)}} \bullet \frac{\cancel{(3x-2)}(3x-2)}{-x\cancel{(2x-3)}} \\ &= \frac{(2x-3)(3x-2)}{-x^2}\end{aligned}$$

Amidst the canceling, you must make certain that you are canceling pairs of common factors such that one is in the top and the other is in the bottom; if you mistakenly cancel the x's in the denominators, you will get choice J.

Finally, FOIL the numerator to get $\dfrac{6x^2-13x+6}{-x^2}$. At this point, if you incorrectly cancel the x^2 term, you get choice K.

3. Simplify: $\dfrac{\frac{m}{n}-\frac{n}{m}}{\frac{m}{n}+\frac{n}{m}}$

SHOW YOUR WORK HERE

A. 0

B. $\dfrac{m^2-n^2}{m^2+n^2}$

C. $\dfrac{m^4-n^4}{m^2n^2}$

D. $\dfrac{m-n}{m+n}$

E. $\left(\dfrac{m-n}{m+n}\right)^2$

The correct answer is B. The most common error committed in this type of problem is canceling the two fractions in the top with the same ones in the denominator. However, you cannot do this because they are being subtracted or added, not multiplied! Doing so results in choice A.

The first step is to rewrite the numerator and denominator as single fractions by getting least common denominators, both of which are *mn*. Doing so yields the following:

$$\frac{\frac{m}{n}-\frac{n}{m}}{\frac{m}{n}+\frac{n}{m}}=\frac{\frac{m}{n}\bullet\frac{m}{m}-\frac{n}{m}\bullet\frac{n}{n}}{\frac{m}{n}\bullet\frac{m}{m}+\frac{n}{m}\bullet\frac{n}{n}}=\frac{\frac{m^2-n^2}{mn}}{\frac{m^2+n^2}{mn}}$$

None of the choices are expressions containing fractions within fractions, so you must go further. Using the definition of division of fractions, this is equivalent to the following:

$$\frac{\frac{m^2-n^2}{mn}}{\frac{m^2+n^2}{mn}}=\frac{m^2-n^2}{mn}\div\frac{m^2+n^2}{mn}=\frac{m^2-n^2}{mn}\bullet\frac{mn}{m^2+n^2}$$

If you mistakenly do not flip over the fraction after the division sign, you will get choice C. Now, cancel the common factor of *mn* in the top and bottom to get the final expression $\frac{m^2-n^2}{m^2+n^2}$. If you arrived at choice D, you made a mistake in factoring; the denominator is the *sum* of squares and does not factor.

1. Assume *x*, *y*, and *z* are positive real numbers. Simplify:

SHOW YOUR WORK HERE

$$\sqrt{32x^{-9}y^{16}z^{-4}} \bullet \frac{\sqrt{xz^2}}{y^2}$$

A. $\frac{4y^2\sqrt{2x}}{x^3z}$

B. $\frac{4y^7\sqrt{2}}{x^5z^3}$

C. $\frac{4y^8\sqrt{2}}{x^4z^2\sqrt{x}}$

D. $\frac{4y^6\sqrt{2}}{x^4z}$

E. $\frac{4x^4z\sqrt{2}}{y^6}$

The correct answer is D. This is a combination of an exponent rule problem and a radical problem. First, take care of the negative exponents inside the first radical:

$$\sqrt{32x^{-9}y^{16}z^{-4}} \bullet \frac{\sqrt{xz^2}}{y^2} = \sqrt{\frac{32y^{16}}{x^9z^4}} \bullet \frac{\sqrt{xz^2}}{y^2}$$

Next, use the radical properties $\sqrt{\frac{a}{b}} = \frac{\sqrt{a}}{\sqrt{b}}$ and $\sqrt{ab} = \sqrt{a}\sqrt{b}$ to simplify:

$$\sqrt{\frac{32y^{16}}{x^9z^4}} \bullet \frac{\sqrt{xz^2}}{y^2} = \frac{\sqrt{32}\sqrt{y^{16}}}{\sqrt{x^9}\sqrt{z^4}} \bullet \frac{\sqrt{x}\sqrt{z^2}}{y^2}$$

Use the fact that if a > 0, then $\sqrt{a^2} = a$ to further simplify the individual radicals. For instance:

$$\sqrt{y^{16}} = \sqrt{\left(y^8\right)^2} = y^8$$

$$\sqrt{x^9} = \sqrt{x^8 \bullet x} = \sqrt{\left(x^4\right)^2 \bullet x} = \sqrt{\left(x^4\right)^2} \bullet \sqrt{x} = x^4\sqrt{x}$$

Doing this for all the radical terms yields the following:

$$\frac{\sqrt{32}\sqrt{y^{16}}}{\sqrt{x^9}\sqrt{z^4}} \bullet \frac{\sqrt{x}\sqrt{z^2}}{y^2} = \frac{4\sqrt{2} \bullet y^8}{x^4 \bullet z^2\sqrt{x}} \bullet \frac{z\sqrt{x}}{y^2}$$

Finally, cancel pair of factors common to the top and bottom of the product to get the final expression:

$$\frac{4\sqrt{2} \bullet y^8}{x^4 \bullet z^2\sqrt{x}} \bullet \frac{z\sqrt{x}}{y^2} = \frac{4\sqrt{2} \bullet y^6 \bullet \cancel{y^2}}{x^4 \bullet z \bullet \cancel{z}\cancel{\sqrt{x}}} \bullet \frac{\cancel{z}\cancel{\sqrt{x}}}{\cancel{y^2}} = \frac{4y^6\sqrt{2}}{x^4z}$$

The incorrect answer choices are the results of misapplying exponent and radical rules. Choice A is the result of saying $\sqrt{x^n} = x^{\sqrt{n}}$. Choices B and E arise by incorrectly simplifying negative powers; remember, if a term has a negative exponent, you take it to the opposite position in the fraction, meaning that if it is in the numerator, take it to the denominator, and vice versa. Choice C is simply the result of forgetting the second term of the original product.

2. Assume that $x > 1$. Simplify: $\left(\sqrt{x}-\sqrt{x-1}\right)^2$

SHOW YOUR WORK HERE

F. $2x-1-2\sqrt{x^2-x}$

G. 1

H. $1-2\sqrt{x^2-x}$

J. $2x-\sqrt{x^2-x}-1$

K. $2x-1-\sqrt{2x^2-2x}$

The correct answer is F. The most typical error here is to distribute the exponent to the two terms to get $\left(\sqrt{x}\right)^2-\left(\sqrt{x-1}\right)^2=x-(x-1)=1$ (choice G). However, you cannot do this. Rather, you must FOIL:

$$\begin{aligned}\left(\sqrt{x}-\sqrt{x-1}\right)^2&=\left(\sqrt{x}-\sqrt{x-1}\right)\bullet\left(\sqrt{x}-\sqrt{x-1}\right)\\&=\left(\sqrt{x}\right)^2-2\sqrt{x}\bullet\sqrt{x-1}+\left(\sqrt{x-1}\right)^2\\&=x-2\sqrt{x}\bullet\sqrt{x-1}+(x-1)\end{aligned}$$

Choice H is the result of getting $-\left(\sqrt{x-1}\right)^2$ instead of $+\left(\sqrt{x-1}\right)^2$. Choice J is the result of not doubling the middle term; that is, using $-\sqrt{x}\bullet\sqrt{x-1}$ instead of $-2\sqrt{x}\bullet\sqrt{x-1}$.

Finally, use the fact that $\sqrt{ab}=\sqrt{a}\sqrt{b}$ to write $2\sqrt{x}\bullet\sqrt{x-1}$ as $2\sqrt{x(x-1)}=2\sqrt{x^2-x}$. This yields the final expression $2x-1-2\sqrt{x^2-x}$. Choice K is the result of bringing the 2 in $2\sqrt{x^2-x}$ inside the radical incorrectly.

3. Assume a and b are positive real numbers. If $x=3\sqrt{ab}$ and $y=b\sqrt{3a}$, then which of these expressions is equivalent to x^4y^{-2}?

SHOW YOUR WORK HERE

A. $\frac{a}{b^2}$

B. $27a$

C. $\frac{6}{\sqrt{3b}}$

D. $\frac{1}{27a}$

E. $243a^3b^4$

The correct answer is A. Substitute the expressions for x and y into x^4y^{-2} to get the following:

$$x^4y^{-2}=\left(3\sqrt{ab}\right)^4\bullet\left(b\sqrt{3a}\right)^{-2}$$

Then get rid of the negative power as follows:

$$\left(3\sqrt{ab}\right)^4\bullet\left(b\sqrt{3a}\right)^{-2}=\left(3\sqrt{ab}\right)^4\bullet\frac{1}{\left(b\sqrt{3a}\right)^2}=\frac{\left(3\sqrt{ab}\right)^4}{\left(b\sqrt{3a}\right)^2}$$

Choice E is the result of ignoring the negative in the power –2.

Next, use the fact that $(c \bullet d)^m = c^m \bullet d^m$ to obtain the following:

$$\frac{\left(3\sqrt{ab}\right)^4}{\left(b\sqrt{3a}\right)^2} = \frac{3^4 \bullet \left(\sqrt{ab}\right)^4}{b^2 \bullet \left(\sqrt{3a}\right)^2}$$

Use the facts that $\sqrt{c} = c^{\frac{1}{2}}$ and $\left(c^m\right)^n = c^{m \bullet n}$ to further simplify:

$$\frac{3^4 \bullet \left(\sqrt{ab}\right)^4}{b^2 \bullet \left(\sqrt{3a}\right)^2} = \frac{3^4 \bullet \left((ab)^{\frac{1}{2}}\right)^4}{b^2 \bullet \left((3a)^{\frac{1}{2}}\right)^2} = \frac{3^4 \bullet (ab)^2}{b^2 \bullet (3a)} = \frac{81a^2b^2}{3ab^2}$$

Finally, cancel pairs of factors common to the numerator and denominator:

$$\frac{81a^2b^2}{3ab^2} = \frac{\cancel{3} \bullet 27 \bullet a \bullet \cancel{a \bullet b^2}}{\cancel{3} \bullet \cancel{a \bullet b^2}} = 27a$$

The incorrect answer choices are standard errors that arise when computing with exponents. Choice C is the result of multiplying the base times the exponent. Choice D represents a misunderstanding of when you take a term in a fraction to an opposite position; this choice is equivalent to $x^{-4}y^2$.

Complex Numbers

1. Assume a is a positive real number. What is the real part of $\left(\frac{1}{a-i}\right)^2$?

SHOW YOUR WORK HERE

A. $\frac{2a}{\left(a^2+1\right)^2}$

B. $\frac{a^2-1}{\left(a^2+1\right)^2}$

C. $\frac{1}{a^2+1}$

D. $\frac{1}{a^2}$

E. $\frac{a}{a^2+1}$

The correct answer is B. Before squaring the given expression, it is helpful to get the i out of the denominator. To do this, multiply inside by 1 in the form of $\frac{a+i}{a+i}$; here, $a + i$ is the conjugate of the denominator. Multiplying by this expression generates a difference of squares in reverse which amounts to squaring the a and the i and not leaving a middle term.

And since $i^2 = -1$, this gets rid of the i in the bottom:

$$\frac{1}{a-i} = \frac{1}{a-i} \bullet \frac{a+i}{a+i} = \frac{a+i}{a^2 - i^2} = \frac{a+i}{a^2+1}$$

If you incorrectly assume that $i^2 = 1$, you will get choice C. If you stopped here and did not square the expression, the real part corresponds to choice E.

Now, square the expression by squaring the top and bottom separately:

$$\left(\frac{1}{a-i}\right)^2 = \left(\frac{a+i}{a^2+1}\right)^2 = \frac{(a+i)^2}{\left(a^2+1\right)^2} = \frac{a^2+2ai+i^2}{\left(a^2+1\right)^2} = \frac{\left(a^2-1\right)+2ai}{\left(a^2+1\right)^2}$$

When squaring the numerator, remember to FOIL. Separate this into two parts:

$$\frac{\left(a^2-1\right)+2ai}{\left(a^2+1\right)^2} = \frac{a^2-1}{\left(a^2+1\right)^2} + \left(\frac{2a}{\left(a^2+1\right)^2}\right)i$$

The real part is the portion *not* multiplied by i, namely $\frac{a^2-1}{\left(a^2+1\right)^2}$. Choice A is the imaginary part.

2. Compute: $\frac{i}{1+3i} - \frac{3}{1-3i}$

SHOW YOUR WORK HERE

F. i

G. $i-3$

H. $\frac{8i}{6i-1}$

J. $-\frac{4}{5}i$

K. $\frac{i-3}{10}$

The correct answer is J. Treat this as you would any difference of fractions. Find the least common denominator, which is $(1+3i)(1-3i)$. If you simply subtract numerators and denominators, you will get choice G.

$$\frac{i}{1+3i} - \frac{3}{1-3i} = \frac{i}{1+3i} \bullet \frac{1-3i}{1-3i} - \frac{3}{1-3i} \bullet \frac{1+3i}{1+3i} = \frac{i(1-3i)-3(1+3i)}{(1+3i)(1-3i)}$$

Simplify the numerator using the distributive property and FOILing the denominator and then combining like terms:

$$\frac{i(1-3i)-3(1+3i)}{(1+3i)(1-3i)} = \frac{i-3i^2-3-9i}{1-9i^2} = \frac{-3(-1)-3-8i}{1-9(-1)} = \frac{3-3-8i}{1+9} = \frac{-8i}{10} = -\frac{4}{5}i$$

If you do not use the distributive property correctly, you will get choice K. Simplifying the denominator incorrectly yields choices F and H.

3. Assume that a and b are positive real numbers. What is the imaginary part of $\frac{bi}{a} - \frac{a}{bi}$?

SHOW YOUR WORK HERE

A. 0

B. $-\frac{a^2+b^2}{ab}$

C. $\frac{b^2-a^2}{ab}$

D. $a+b$

E. $\frac{a^2+b^2}{ab}$

The correct answer is E. The goal is to rewrite this expression in the form of A + B*i*, where A and B are real numbers (that will be in terms of a and b). Doing this requires that you first combine the fractions into a single fraction with the least common denominator abi. Once you do this, simplify the numerator using the fact that $i^2 = -1$:

$$\frac{bi}{a} - \frac{a}{bi} = \frac{bi}{a} \bullet \frac{bi}{bi} - \frac{a}{bi} \bullet \frac{a}{a}$$
$$= \frac{b^2i^2 - a^2}{abi}$$
$$= \frac{b^2(-1) - a^2}{abi}$$
$$= -\frac{a^2+b^2}{abi}$$

A common error here is to identify the imaginary part at this point as $-\frac{a^2+b^2}{ab}$, but you cannot do this because the i is in the denominator. You must first multiply the top and bottom of the fraction by i to get the following:

$$-\frac{a^2+b^2}{abi} = -\frac{a^2+b^2}{abi} \bullet \frac{i}{i} = \left(-\frac{a^2+b^2}{abi^2}\right)i = \left(-\frac{a^2+b^2}{ab(-1)}\right)i = \left(\frac{a^2+b^2}{ab}\right)i$$

So the imaginary part is $\frac{a^2+b^2}{ab}$.

Choice A is the real part, and choices B and C are the results of making an error involving i^2. Choice D is the result of bad cancelation; specifically, you cannot cancel pairs of a's and b's in the expression $\frac{a^2+b^2}{ab}$ because they are terms, not factors.

1. Assume that $a < 0$. The graph of which of the following parabolas does NOT cross the x-axis?

SHOW YOUR WORK HERE

A. $y = (x - a)^2$

B. $y = x(x + a)$

C. $y = x^2 + a$

D. $y = a - x^2$

E. $y = x^2 - a^2$

The correct answer is D. The key here is to understand that the graph of a parabola has an x-intercept at an x-value that makes its expression equal to zero. So whichever of the five choices yields a quadratic equation with imaginary solutions is one that does not cross the x-axis.

Choices A, B, and E are the easiest to eliminate. Choice A crosses at $x = a$; choice B crosses at both $x = 0$ and $x = -a$, as seen by factoring the expression; and choice E crosses at $x = a$ and $-a$ because its expression factors using the difference of squares formula.

So it comes down to choices C and D, which look similar. This is where the assumption that $a < 0$ comes into play. Since a is negative, the graph of $y = x^2 + a$ in choice C has its vertex at $(0, a)$, which is below the x-axis. The graph opens upward because the coefficient of the squared term is positive. So its graph must have two x-intercepts. As such, choice D must be the graph that has no x-intercepts.

2. Assume $a > 0$. What are the solutions of the equation $a^2x^2 + ax - 1 = 0$?

SHOW YOUR WORK HERE

F. $\frac{-1 \pm i\sqrt{3}}{2a}$

G. $\frac{-a \pm \sqrt{a^2 + 4a}}{2a^2}$

H. $\frac{-1 \pm \sqrt{5}}{2a}$

J. $\frac{-1 \pm \sqrt{a^2 + 4a}}{2a}$

K. $-a \pm \frac{\sqrt{5}}{2a}$

The correct answer is H. Use the quadratic formula to find the solutions to this equation and then simplify the result:

$$x = \frac{-a \pm \sqrt{a^2 - 4(a^2)(-1)}}{2(a^2)} = \frac{-a \pm \sqrt{a^2 + 4a^2}}{2a^2} = \frac{-a \pm \sqrt{5a^2}}{2a^2} = \frac{-a \pm a\sqrt{5}}{2a^2} = \frac{\not{a}(-1 \pm \sqrt{5})}{2a \bullet \not{a}} = \frac{-1 \pm \sqrt{5}}{2a}$$

The errors typically made when using the quadratic formula are misidentifying the parameters to use in the formula (choices G and J), and getting the formula wrong by not dividing the entire numerator by the denominator (choice K). Other errors are usually related to arithmetic problems, usually involving signs (choice F).

3. Assume $m > 0$. Which of the following conditions on m guaranteesthattheequation $2mx^2 - \sqrt{m}\,x + (m-1) = 0$ has two imaginary solutions?

SHOW YOUR WORK HERE

A. $m > 1$

B. $m > \frac{9}{8}$

C. $m < \frac{9}{8}$

D. $-8m^2 - 1 < 0$

E. $m < \frac{7}{8}$

The correct answer is B. The sign of the discriminant, or the radicand of the radical part of the quadratic formula, is all you need to determine the nature of the solutions of a quadratic equation. The discriminant for a quadratic equation of the form $ax^2 + bx + c = 0$ is $b^2 - 4ac$.

Applying this to the given equation yields the expression and simplifying yields:

$$\left(-\sqrt{m}\right)^2 - 4(2m)(m-1) = m - 8m(m-1) = m - 8m^2 + 8m = -8m^2 + 9m.$$

Choices A, D, and E are all results of making errors by not identifying the discriminant formula correctly, or not applying the distributive property when simplifying.

If the discriminant is negative, then the equation has imaginary solutions. This yields the condition $-8m^2 + 9m = m(9 - 8m) < 0$.

Since m is assumed to be positive, this expression will be negative only if the other factor, $9 - 8m$, is negative. That is, $9 - 8m < 0$, which is equivalent to $m > \frac{9}{8}$.

Choice C will guarantee two distinct real solutions.

Linear Inequalities

1. For which of these inequalities is this the solution set?

SHOW YOUR WORK HERE

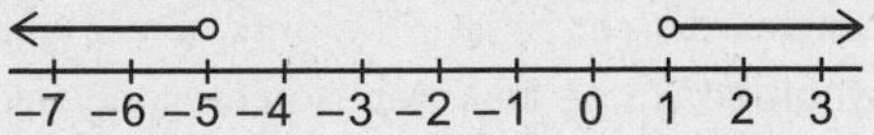

A. $|x-2| > 3$

B. $|x+2| < 3$

C. $|x-3| \geq 2$

D. $|x-2| \geq 3$

E. $|x+2| > 3$

The correct answer is E. One approach would be to choose a solution value from the graph. Selecting a value from the greater than 1 ray, like 2, can be substituted into the equation in each of the distractor choices. In this case, it is true only in choice E. Be careful with this method. In other problems, more than one equation could be true and you would have to choose another solution to check.

You could also solve each of the inequalities to determine its solution set to find the correct solution (assuming you made no errors along the way), but this method is not the most efficient way to approach this type of problem. Rather, it is much better to understand a bit about the nature of absolute value inequalities.

Since the solution set consists of two rays rather than a finite segment between two endpoints, and the ends of the rays are not included in the solution, the absolute value inequality to which this is the solution set must be of the form $|x-a|>b$, for some real numbers a and b. So you can eliminate choices B, C, and D.

This leaves choices A and E. Here, it is helpful to analyze the inequality geometrically. The solution set of $|x-a|>b$ consists of all real number x that are at least b units away from a on either side. So a serves as a center, and b serves as a radius, of sorts. The center for the inequality in choice A would be 2, which is inside the ray extending to the right, while the center for the inequality in choice E is –2, which is halfway between the two ray endpoints. The latter is the correct choice.

2. Determine the solution set for the inequality $\frac{2}{3}\left(6x-\frac{1}{2}\right)-2(2-x)\le-\frac{1}{3}$.

SHOW YOUR WORK HERE

F.
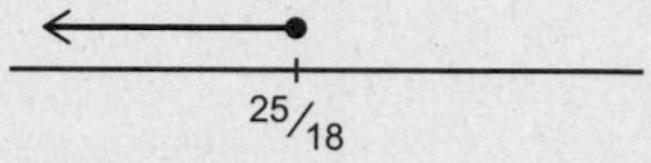

G.
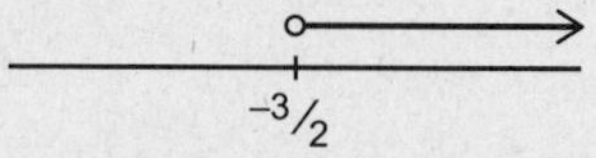

H.
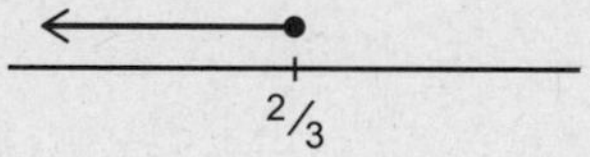

J.
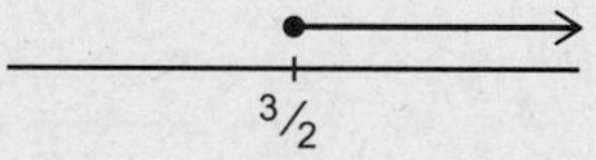

K.
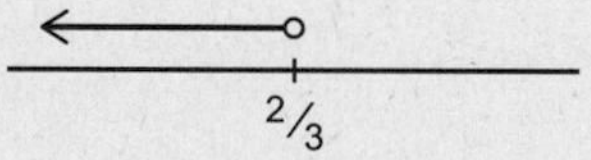

The correct answer is H. You solve a linear inequality just as you would an equation. The only caveat is that if you multiply or divide both sides of the inequality by a negative number in the final step, you must reverse the inequality sign.

To solve this inequality, first apply the distributive property to simplify the left side. Then, isolate the x-terms to the left side:

$$\frac{2}{3}\left(6x-\frac{1}{2}\right)-2(2-x)\le-\frac{1}{3}$$
$$4x-\frac{1}{3}-4+2x\le-\frac{1}{3}$$
$$6x-\frac{13}{3}\le-\frac{1}{3}$$
$$6x\le4$$
$$x\le\frac{4}{6}$$
$$x\le\frac{2}{3}$$

All real numbers to the left of and including $\frac{2}{3}$ are in the solution set (choice H). If you did not include the endpoint in the solution set, you will get choice K.

If you did not use the distributive property when simplifying the left side of the inequality, you will get choice F. Choices G and J are the result of dividing both sides of the inequality by the constant term rather than the coefficient of x in the last step of the solution. Choice G also has the ray extending in the wrong direction.

3. Assume a is a natural number. Which of these is the solution set of the quadratic inequality $3x^2 - 2ax - a^2 \geq 0$?

SHOW YOUR WORK HERE

A. 

B. 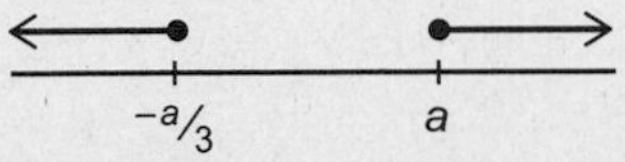

C. 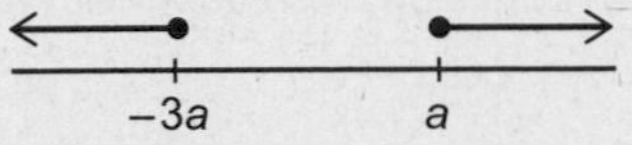

D. 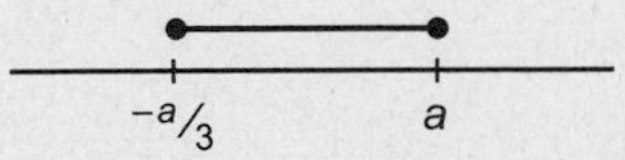

E. 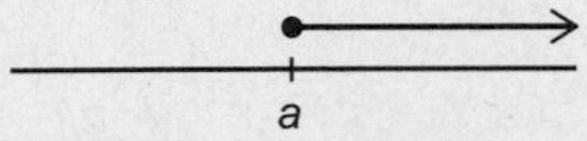

The correct answer is B. First thing—do not panic when you see letters as coefficients! The left side factors as it would if there were just numbers as coefficients. Indeed, it is equivalent to $(3x + a)(x - a) \geq 0$.

The next step is to determine the values of x that make the left side equal to zero. Set each factor equal to zero and solve for x to get $x = a$ and $x = -\frac{a}{3}$.

Since a is a natural number, it is positive. You can see that $-\frac{a}{3}$ is negative; thus, it lies to the left of a on the number line, as shown:

Next, choose a value in each interval to assess the sign of the left side of the inequality; these are called *test points*. But since the zeros are in terms of letters, how exactly do you do this?

The easiest interval is the middle one since one of the endpoints is negative and the other is positive; just use 0 as the test point. For the left ray, note that $-a < -\frac{a}{3}$, so use $-a$. Similarly, for the right ray, note that $2a > a$, so use $2a$.

Plug these values in for x in the factored form of the left side. Use the fact that the product of two negative real numbers is positive and the product of one negative real number and one positive real number is negative to get the following:

Test Points	Sign of 3x + a	Sign of x − a	Sign of left-side of inequality
−a	$-3a + a = -2a < 0$	$-a - a = -2a < 0$	Positive
0	$a > 0$	$-a < 0$	Negative
2a	$3(2a) + a = 7a > 0$	$2a - a = a > 0$	Positive

Summarizing, we have

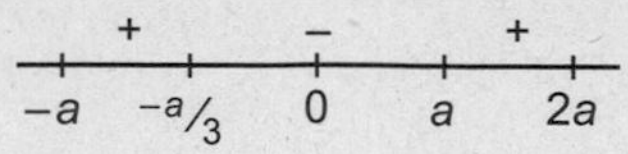

Thus, the solution set is given by choice B:

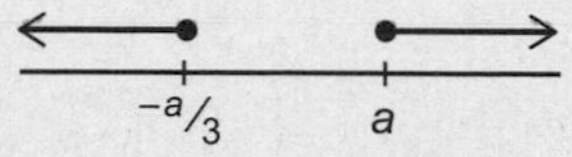

Choice D is the solution set for the reverse inequality, while choice E shows only half of the solution set. Choices A and C are the results of bad factoring.

Systems of Linear Equations

1. If (x, y) satisfies the following system, what is the value of x^y?

SHOW YOUR WORK HERE

$$\begin{cases} x - 2y = -1 \\ y - 2x = 5 \end{cases}$$

A. −1

B. 6

C. $-\frac{1}{3}$

D. 3

E. $\frac{1}{9}$

The correct answer is A. When solving a linear system, you often have your choice of method to use. Whenever at least one of the equations has a variable with coefficient 1, a good strategy is to solve that equation for the variable and substitute it into the other equation. That is the method we will proceed with to solve this system.

Solve the first equation for x to get $x = 2y - 1$. Then, substitute this expression in for x in the second equation to get the following equation involving only y: $y - 2(2y - 1) = 5$.

Solve this equation for y:

$$\begin{aligned} y - 2(2y - 1) &= 5 \\ y - 4y + 2 &= 5 \\ -3y + 2 &= 5 \\ -3y &= 3 \\ y &= -1 \end{aligned}$$

Be careful to use the distributive property when solving the linear equation, otherwise you will get choice E.

Plug –1 in for y in your initial substitution to get the corresponding value of x:

$$x = 2(-1) - 1 = -2 - 1 = -3.$$

Finally, the value of $x^y = (-3)^{-1} = \frac{1}{-3} = -\frac{1}{3}$.

Be careful when computing the quantity once you have solved the system. This is often where errors are made! Choice A is the result of computing y^x, and choice D is the result of computing the product xy. If you also fail to use the distributive property and simplify as in choice D, you will get choice B.

2. For what real numbers a, if any, does the following system have no solution?

$$\begin{cases} \frac{x}{3} = ay \\ \frac{y}{a} = 3x \end{cases}$$

SHOW YOUR WORK HERE

F. $-\frac{1}{3}$ and $\frac{1}{3}$

G. –3 and 3

H. –1 and 1

J. 0 only

K. There is no such value of a

The correct answer is F. Without knowing how to attack the problem, choice J can be eliminated off the bat because the second equation is not defined when $a = 0$.

The key to this problem is knowing that two lines that are parallel do not intersect; so a linear system comprised of such lines has no solution. And, lines are parallel if they have the same slope.

Using these facts, the strategy is to write the two equations in the form $y = mx$. Then, equate the slopes and solve for a.

The equations in this system can be written as follows:

$$\frac{x}{3} = ay \Rightarrow x = 3ay \Rightarrow y = \left(\frac{1}{3a}\right)x$$

$$\frac{y}{a} = 3x \Rightarrow y = (3a)x$$

Equating the slopes yields the equation $\frac{1}{3a} = 3a$. Solve for a, as follows:

$$\frac{1}{3a} = 3a$$

$$9a^2 = 1$$

$$a^2 = \frac{1}{9}$$

$$a = \pm\sqrt{\frac{1}{9}}$$

$$a = \pm\frac{1}{3}$$

So $-\frac{1}{3}$ and $\frac{1}{3}$ (choice F) is the correct answer. Choices G and H are the results of not solving this equation correctly.

3. For what real number a, if any, does the following system have infinitely many solutions?

SHOW YOUR WORK HERE

$$\begin{cases} a(x+y)=3 \\ y+x=-2 \end{cases}$$

A. There is no such value of a.

B. –2

C. 1

D. $-\frac{2}{3}$

E. $a=-\frac{3}{2}$

The correct answer is E. For a linear system to have infinitely many solutions, the equations must be multiples of each other. Dividing both sides of the first equation by a yields the equivalent system:

$$\begin{cases} x+y=\frac{3}{a} \\ y+x=-2 \end{cases}$$

Since the left sides are identical, the only way these two equations are multiples of each other is if the right sides are equal. That is, $\frac{3}{a}=-2$. Solving for a yields $a=-\frac{3}{2}$ (choice E). Be careful when solving this equation for a. It's easy to mix up the 3 and –2, as is the case for choice D.

Choices B and C would give two lines that are parallel, so these systems have no solution.

Basic Coordinate Geometry

1. Suppose $m<n<0$. Which of these ordered pairs cannot be in Quadrant III of the xy-plane?

SHOW YOUR WORK HERE

A. $(n, m+n)$

B. $(m-n, m-n)$

C. $(n, m-1)$+

D. (n^{-1}, m^{-1})

E. $\left(\frac{m}{n}, m\right)$

The correct answer is E. To be in Quadrant III, both the x- and y-coordinates must be negative. In choice E, $\frac{m}{n}$ is positive because it is the quotient of two negative real numbers. Since $m<0$, the points are always in Quadrant IV.

The other points are in Quadrant III for the following reasons:

- In choice A, $n<0$ and $m+n<0$ because the sum of negative real numbers is negative.
- In choice B, $m-n<0$ because m is to the left of n.
- In choice C, $m-1<0$ because $m<0$.
- In choice D, $n^{-1}=\frac{1}{n}$, which is negative because $n<0$. Similarly, $m^{-1}<0$.

2. Assume $a > 0$. Which of these expressions represents the distance between the points $P(-a, 2a)$ and $Q(-3a, -2a)$?

SHOW YOUR WORK HERE

F. $2a$ units

G. $a\sqrt{2}$ units

H. $2a\sqrt{5}$ units

J. $2a^2$ units

K. $20a^2$ units

The correct answer is H. There is no getting around knowing the distance formula for this one. Many of the distractors will be the results of either forgetting part of the formula (like the radical sign, as in choice K), subtracting the wrong coordinates (as in choice G), or making a combination of those errors (as in choice J).

Applying the formula and simplifying yields the following:

$$\begin{aligned}\sqrt{(-a-(-3a))^2+(2a-(-2a))^2} &= \sqrt{(-a+3a)^2+(2a+2a)^2}\\ &= \sqrt{(2a)^2+(4a)^2}\\ &= \sqrt{4a^2+16a^2}\\ &= \sqrt{20a^2}\\ &= 2a\sqrt{5}\end{aligned}$$

Choice F is the result of a typical error involving arithmetic involving negative numbers, namely $2a - (-2a) = 2a + 2a$, not $2a - 2a$.

3. What is the equation of the circle that has a diameter with endpoints (–4, 1) and (–2, 3)?

SHOW YOUR WORK HERE

A. $(x + 3)^2 + (y - 2)^2 = 8$

B. $(x + 3)^2 + (y - 2)^2 = 2$

C. $(x - 3)^2 + (y + 2)^2 = 8$

D. $(x - 3)^2 + (y - 2)^2 = 8$

E. $(x+1)^2+(y+1)^2=\sqrt{2}$

The correct answer is B. The standard form for the equation of a circle with center (h, k) and radius r is $(x - h)^2 + (y - k)^2 = r^2$. So you must find these two pieces of information to determine the equation of the circle.

The radius is half the length of the diameter. Using the distance formula, find the length of the diameter:

$$\sqrt{(-4-(-2))^2+(1-3)^2}=\sqrt{(-4+2)^2+(1-3)^2}=\sqrt{(-2)^2+(-2)^2}=\sqrt{8}=2\sqrt{2}.$$

The radius is $\frac{1}{2}\left(2\sqrt{2}\right)=\sqrt{2}$ units.

The center is the midpoint of the diameter. Using the midpoint formula yields the coordinates $\left(\frac{(-4)+(-2)}{2},\frac{1+3}{2}\right)=(-3,2)$. Thus, the equation is $(x + 3)^2 + (y - 2)^2 = 2$.

Using the diameter instead of the radius and forgetting to square the radius in the equation are typical errors (reflected in choices A and D). Equally as common is getting the signs wrong in the equation, especially when at least one coordinate of the center is negative (choice C).

1. If $f(x) = x^2 - \sqrt{x}$, what is $f(x + 4)$?

SHOW YOUR WORK HERE

A. $x^2 - \sqrt{x} + 4$

B. $x^2 + 16 - \sqrt{x+4}$

C. $x^2 + 8x + 14 - \sqrt{x}$

D. $x^2 + 8x + 16 - \sqrt{x+4}$

E. $x^2 + 14 - \sqrt{x}$

The correct answer is D. Often, students confuse the variable used to define the function, namely *x*, and the expression at which they are to compute the function, namely $x + 4$. To remove this confusion, replace the *x* in the definition of the function by a box (or a place holder). That is, $f(x) = x^2 - \sqrt{x}$ really means:

$$f(\Box) = \Box^2 - \sqrt{\Box}$$

Whatever is inside the parentheses is what goes into each of those boxes. So:

$$f\left(\boxed{x+4}\right) = \boxed{x+4}^2 - \sqrt{\boxed{x+4}}$$

This will help you to avoid the standard error of just "adding 4" to the function as in choice A.

Simplify the expression:

$$\begin{aligned} f(x+4) &= (x+4)^2 - \sqrt{x+4} \\ &= (x+4)(x+4) - \sqrt{x+4} \\ &= x^2 + 8x + 16 - \sqrt{x+4} \end{aligned}$$

Two critical errors that often occur here are (1) not FOILing $(x + 4)^2$, as in choice B, and (2) distributing the radical to both terms of the sum, as in choices C and E.

2. Consider the function $H(x) = \frac{x}{4-x}$, where $x > 0$.
For which pairs of functions f(x) and g(x) does
$H(x) = (f \circ g)(x)$?

SHOW YOUR WORK HERE

F. $f(x) = x$ and $g(x) = \frac{1}{4-x}$

G. $f(x) = \sqrt{\frac{x}{16-x}}$ and $g(x) = x^2$

H. $f(x) = \left(\frac{x}{4-x}\right)^2$ and $g(x) = \sqrt{x}$

J. $f(x) = \frac{x^2}{4-x^2}$ and $g(x) = \sqrt{x}$

K. $f(x) = \sqrt{x}$ and $g(x) = \frac{x^2}{4-x^2}$

The correct answer is J. The most direct approach is to compute $(f \circ g)(x)$, which is $f(g(x))$ for the given pairs to see which one works. Keep in mind that the order of this composition matters!

Using the pairs in choice J yields $\frac{(\sqrt{x})^2}{4-(\sqrt{x})^2}=\frac{x}{4-x}$, as desired.

Choice F is the result of misinterpreting the composition as a product. Choice K is equal to the reverse composition $g(f(x))$. Choices G and H involve errors with computing the radical term; you cannot distribute a radical to the terms of a sum or difference.

3. The graph of which of these functions is as follows:

SHOW YOUR WORK HERE

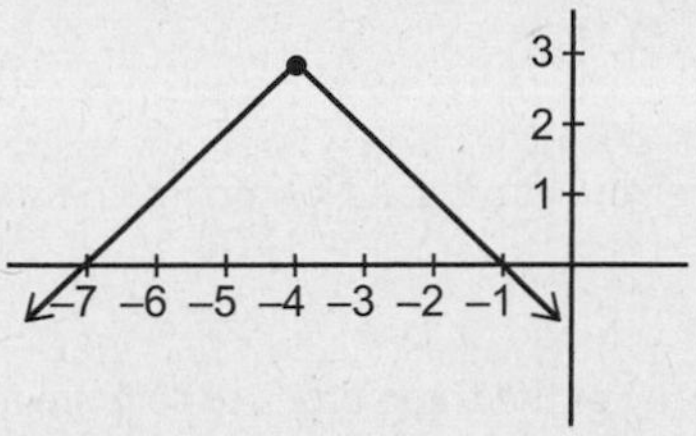

A. $f(x)=3-|x-4|$

B. $f(x)=3+|x+4|$

C. $f(x)=3-|x+4|$

D. $f(x)=|x-4|-3$

E. $f(x)=-|x-4|-3$

The correct answer is C. The idea is to use the translation results with the basic absolute value graph, as follows:

Step	Action	Equation
	Start with basic absolute value graph.	$y=\|x\|$
1	Reflect over the *x*-axis.	$y=-\|x\|$
2	Move the above graph left 4 units	$y=-\|x+4\|$
3	Move the above graph up 3 units	$y=-\|x+4\|+3$

This equation can be written equivalently as $y = 3 - |x + 4|$. All the distractor choices involve sign changes on the constant terms, which change the direction of the translation or if the original graph is reflected over the *x*-axis.

While it is recommended to be familiar with the function translation facts stated above, sometimes the "trial and error" method may be quicker or your only alternative if you forget the facts. In this case, any point on a graph must make the equation true. Choosing either *x* intercept (–7, 0) or (–1, 0) when checked in all five equations is TRUE only for choice C.

1. A collection of nickels, dimes, and quarters is worth \$6.25. There are half as many nickels as dimes and four more quarters than there are dimes. How many coins, in total, comprise the collection?

A. 14

B. 18

C. 25

D. 39

E. 32

SHOW YOUR WORK HERE

The correct answer is D. Do not try to solve this problem by trial and error—it will take far too much time. Rather, set up an equation that can be used to solve it.

First, you must identify the variable x. We do not know how many of any of the three types of coin are in the collection, so the variable could be chosen to be the number of any one of them. That said, note that the number of nickels and the number of quarters are expressed in terms of the number of dimes. So the simplest approach is to let x be the number of dimes.

Then, the number of nickels is $\frac{1}{2}x$ and the number of quarters is $x + 4$.

The equation that you should set up then involves the value each type of coin contributes to the collection. Gather the information as follows:

Type of Coin	Number of This Type of Coin	Value of a Single Coin of this Type	Value This Type of Coin Contributes to the Collection
Dime	x	0.10	$0.10x$
Nickel	$\frac{1}{2}x$	0.05	$0.05\left(\frac{1}{2}x\right)$
Quarter	$x+4$	0.25	$0.25(x+4)$

The value of the collection, \$6.25, is the sum of the expressions in the rightmost column. This gives the following equation that you then solve for x:

$$
\begin{aligned}
0.10x + 0.05\left(\frac{1}{2}x\right) + 0.25(x+4) &= 6.25 \\
10x + 5\left(\frac{1}{2}x\right) + 25(x+4) &= 625 \\
10x + \frac{5}{2}x + 25x + 100 &= 625 \\
37.5x &= 525 \\
x = \frac{625}{37.5} &= 14
\end{aligned}
$$

So there are 14 dimes, 7 nickels, and 18 quarters in the collection. This gives a total of (14 + 7 + 18) = 39 coins.

Pay attention to what you are asked to provide as the final answer in word problems. Here, you were asked for the total number of coins in the collection. The distractors are all different combinations of numbers of coins that are in the collection.

2. Twenty percent of the product of two consecutive even integers is equal to 88. Which of these equations can be used to find these integers?

SHOW YOUR WORK HERE

F. $20x(x+2)=88$

G. $0.20x(x+1)=88$

H. $0.20(x \bullet 2x)=88$

J. $0.20x(x+2)=88$

K. $20(x \bullet 2x)=88$

The correct answer is J. Let x be one of the even integers. A consecutive even integer is two larger than x; that is, it is given by $x + 2$. Adding 1 to x will result in an odd integer, and while multiplying x by 2 does product an even integer, it is not the very next one after x.

The product of these integers is $x(x + 2)$. At this point, you can eliminate choices G, H, and K.

Twenty percent can be written as the decimal 0.20. So 20% of the product is $0.20x(x + 2)$. This is supposed to equal 88, yielding the equation $0.20x(x + 2) = 88$, which is choice J.

3. A plane travels 680 miles from City A to City B with a tailwind in 3.5 hours and makes the return trip along the same route, but against the headwind, in 4.25 hours. Which system can be used to determine the speed of the plane in still air, x, and the speed of the wind, y?

SHOW YOUR WORK HERE

A. $\begin{cases} 3.5x=680 \\ 4.25y=680 \end{cases}$

B. $\begin{cases} 3.5(x+y)=680 \\ 4.25(x-y)=680 \end{cases}$

C. $\begin{cases} \dfrac{x+y}{3.5}=680 \\ \dfrac{x-y}{4.25}=680 \end{cases}$

D. $\begin{cases} \dfrac{680}{x-y}=3.5 \\ \dfrac{680}{x+y}=4.25 \end{cases}$

E. $\begin{cases} 3.5x+y=680 \\ 4.25x-y=680 \end{cases}$

The correct answer is B. The equations represent the trip from City A to City B, and the return trip. The trickiest part is determining the speed of the plane moving with a tailwind and going against a headwind. If the plane is moving with a tailwind, its speed is increased by the speed of the wind, and if the plane is moving against a headwind, its speed is decreased by the speed of the wind.

Gather the information in the following table:

	Distance	Time	Rate
City A to City B	680 miles	3.5 hours	$x+y$
City B to City A	680 miles	3.5 hours	$x-y$

The equations are now obtained using distance equals rate *times* time. This yields the system in choice B.

Choice E contains the correct components in the equations, but the parentheses have been removed. The speeds are not computed correctly in choice A. Choice C is the result of using distance equals rate *divided by* time. Choice D should have the speeds in the two equations interchanged.

Sequences

1. Which of these formulas gives the 58th term of the arithmetic sequence –6, 1, 8, 15, ...?

SHOW YOUR WORK HERE

A. –6 + (58 – 1)(7)

B. –6 + 58(7)

C. –6 + (58 – 1)(–7)

D. –6 + 58(–7)

E. –6(58)

The correct answer is C. You must know the formula for an arithmetic sequence, which is $a_n = a_1 + (n-1)d,\ n \geq 1$, where *d* is the number you add or subtract from a term to get the next term, and a_1 is the first term of the sequence.

Here, $a_1 = -6$ and *d* = 1 – (–6) = 7. Since you want the 58th term, use *n* = 58 with these two values in the formula to get $a_{58} = -6 + (58-1)(7)$.

The incorrect answer choices are variations of mistakes made in the formula itself. For instance, choices B and D do not subtract 1 from the 58, and choices C and D use –7 instead of 7.

2. Which of these formulas gives the 111th term of the geometric series 27, –9, 3, –1, ...?

SHOW YOUR WORK HERE

F. $\left(-\frac{27}{3}\right)^{110}$

G. $-27(3)^{110}$

H. $-27\left(\frac{1}{3}\right)^{110}$

J. $27\left(-\frac{1}{3}\right)^{110}$

K. $27(-3)^{111}$

The correct answer is J. You must know the formula for a geometric sequence, which is $a_n = a_1 \bullet r^{n-1}, n \geq 1$, where r is the number you multiply a term to get the next term and a_1 is the first term of the sequence.

Here, $a_1 = 27$ and $27r = -9$ so that $r = -\frac{1}{3}$. Since you want the 111th term, use $n = 111$ with these two values in the formula to get $a_{111} = 27\left(-\frac{1}{3}\right)^{111-1} = 27\left(-\frac{1}{3}\right)^{110}$.

The incorrect answer choices are variations of mistakes made in the formula itself. For instance, choice F should have the 27 outside the parentheses, while choice H should have the negative sign inside the parentheses. Choices G and K use the wrong value for *r*; this would require the terms to increase in size, and choice K also has the wrong power—it should be reduced by 1.

3. What is the sum of the 45th and 55th terms of the sequence 21, 17, 13, 9, ...?

SHOW YOUR WORK HERE

A. 40

B. –400

C. –358

D. 100

E. –350

The correct answer is E. First, you need to realize that the sequence is arithmetic, so $a_n = a_1 + (n-1)d, n \geq 1$, where d is the number you add or subtract from a term to get the next term and a_1 is the first term of the sequence. Here, $a_1 = 21$ and $d = 17 - 21 = -4$:

$$a_n = 21 + (n-1)(-4) = 21 - 4n + 4 = 25 - 4n, n \geq 1$$

Therefore, the following is true:

$$a_{45} = 25 - 4(45) = -155$$
$$a_{55} = 25 - 4(55) = -195$$

The sum is –155 – 195 = –350.

Choice A is the difference of the two terms. Choices B and C represent mistakes in the formula for the *n*th term of the sequence; choice B does not include the first term in the formula and choice C uses *n* instead of *n* – 1. Choice D is the sum of the indices 45 and 55, not the actual 45th and 55th terms of the sequence.

MATRICES

1. If, $2\begin{bmatrix} x & -1 \\ 0 & y \end{bmatrix} = 4\begin{bmatrix} y & -\frac{1}{2} \\ 0 & x+y+\frac{1}{2} \end{bmatrix}$, what is the value of the expression $\frac{1}{x+y}$?

SHOW YOUR WORK HERE

A. $-\frac{1}{3}$

B. $-\frac{9}{2}$

C. -1

D. $-\frac{2}{3}$

E. $-\frac{1}{9}$

The correct answer is C. Two matrices are equal only when each pair of corresponding entries are equal. Simplifying the matrices yields the equivalent equation $\begin{bmatrix} 2x & -2 \\ 0 & 2y \end{bmatrix} = \begin{bmatrix} 4y & -2 \\ 0 & 4x+4y+2 \end{bmatrix}$.

Equating the upper-left entries and the lower-right entries yields the system $\begin{cases} 2x = 4y \\ 2y = 4x = 4y + 2 \end{cases}$, or more simply (by dividing both sides of both equations by 2), $\begin{cases} x = 2y \\ -1 = 2x - y \end{cases}$.

Using the substitution method, plug in $2y$ for x in the second equation to get the following equation in y that you then solve:

$$\begin{aligned} 2(2y) - y &= -1 \\ 4y - y &= -1 \\ 3y &= -1 \\ y &= -\frac{1}{3} \end{aligned}$$

Substituting this value into the first equation shows that the corresponding value of x is $x = 2\left(-\frac{1}{3}\right) = -\frac{2}{3}$.

Therefore, $\frac{1}{x+y} = \frac{1}{-\frac{2}{3} - \frac{1}{3}} = -1$ (choice C).

Choice A is just the value of y and choice D is just the value of x; just be careful to answer the question posed. Choice B represents a typical error when simplifying a rational expression of this type; you cannot split $\frac{1}{x+y}$ as $\frac{1}{x} + \frac{1}{y}$.

2. Compute: $\frac{1}{3}\begin{bmatrix}-6 & 0 & 3\end{bmatrix} - 2\begin{bmatrix}-\frac{1}{2} & 4 & 0\end{bmatrix}$

SHOW YOUR WORK HERE

F. $\begin{bmatrix}-1 & -4 & 3\end{bmatrix}$

G. $\begin{bmatrix}-3 & 8 & 1\end{bmatrix}$

H. $\begin{bmatrix}-2 & 0 & 1\end{bmatrix}$

J. $\begin{bmatrix}-1 & -8 & 1\end{bmatrix}$

K. $\begin{bmatrix}-3 & -8 & -1\end{bmatrix}$

The correct answer is J. First, perform the scalar multiplication by multiplying each term of a matrix by the constant outside:

$$\frac{1}{3}\begin{bmatrix}-6 & 0 & 3\end{bmatrix} - 2\begin{bmatrix}-\frac{1}{2} & 4 & 0\end{bmatrix} = \begin{bmatrix}-2 & 0 & 1\end{bmatrix} - \begin{bmatrix}-1 & 8 & 0\end{bmatrix}$$

Then, subtract entry-wise to obtain $\begin{bmatrix}-2-(-1) & 0-8 & 1-0\end{bmatrix} = \begin{bmatrix}-1 & -8 & 1\end{bmatrix}$.

Choice F is the result of not multiplying every term of the matrix by the scalar multiple outside. Choice G is the sum of the two matrices, not the difference. Choice H is just the first matrix.

3. For what value(s) of a, if any, is this equation satisfied?

SHOW YOUR WORK HERE

$$a\begin{bmatrix}-1 & a+1 \\ 2 & 4\end{bmatrix} - \begin{bmatrix}a & 0 \\ 2a & 4a\end{bmatrix} = \begin{bmatrix}0 & 0 \\ 0 & 0\end{bmatrix}$$

A. –1 and 0

B. –1 only

C. 0 only

D. 0 and 1

E. There is no such value of a.

The correct answer is C. The strategy is to simplify the expression on the left side first. Then, equate corresponding entries of matrices on both sides of the equation to determine the condition(s) on a that must hold:

$$a\begin{bmatrix}-1 & a+1 \\ 2 & 4\end{bmatrix} - \begin{bmatrix}a & 0 \\ 2a & 4a\end{bmatrix} = \begin{bmatrix}-a & a^2+a \\ 2a & 4a\end{bmatrix} - \begin{bmatrix}a & 0 \\ 2a & 4a\end{bmatrix} = \begin{bmatrix}-a-a & a^2+a \\ 2a-2a & 4a-4a\end{bmatrix} = \begin{bmatrix}-2a & a^2+a \\ 0 & 0\end{bmatrix}$$

Now, equate corresponding entries of the matrices in the equation:

$$\begin{bmatrix}-2a & a^2+a \\ 0 & 0\end{bmatrix} = \begin{bmatrix}0 & 0 \\ 0 & 0\end{bmatrix}$$

This yields the equations $-2a = 0$ and $a^2 + a = 0$. The first equation implies $a = 0$. If this value of a satisfies the second equation, then the two matrices will be equal. Certainly, it satisfies the equation $a^2 + a = 0$. Note that $a = -1$ also satisfies *this* equation, but not the first one. So the lower left entries of the two matrices would not be equal; so it is not a value that satisfies the original matrix equation. Hence, the answer is choice C.

PRACTICE

It's time once again to assess what you have learned with another mathematics practice quiz. When you're finished answering all 20 questions, check the answers and explanations that follow to figure out how well you did and why you may have selected some incorrect answer choices.

SHOW YOUR WORK HERE

1. If line *l* is defined by the equation $2y - x = 8$, which of the following equations could define a line that is parallel to line *l*?

A. $y = -\frac{1}{2}x + 4$

B. $y = \frac{1}{2}x + 5$

C. $y = -x - 8$

D. $y = x + 6$

E. $y = -2x + 1$

2. Which of the following lines is perpendicular to the line graphed below?

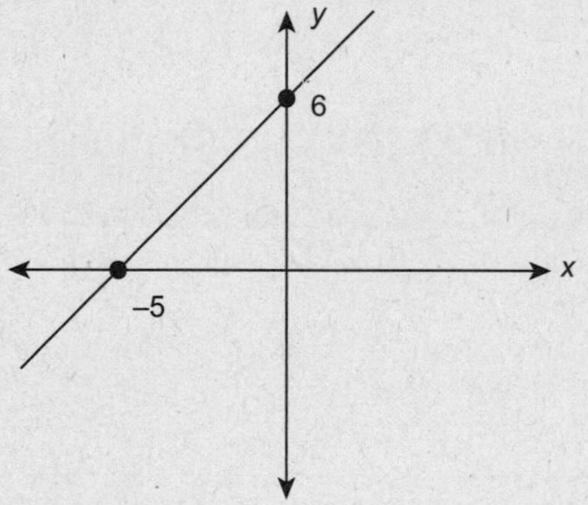

F. $5y = 6x + 2$

G. $5y = -6x + 8$

H. $y = -x + 6$

J. $6y + 5x = -1$

K. $6y - 5x = 0$

3. Which of the following is equal to $\frac{3i}{2i-1}$?

A. $1 - \frac{3}{5}i$

B. 3

C. $-\frac{3}{5}i$

D. $-\frac{3}{5} + \frac{6}{5}i$

E. $\frac{6}{5} - \frac{3}{5}i$

SHOW YOUR WORK HERE

4. If $x^2 - 10x + 4 = 0$, what are the possible values of x?

F. $5 \pm \sqrt{21}$

G. $5 \pm 2\sqrt{21}$

H. $-5 \pm \sqrt{21}$

J. $10 \pm 2\sqrt{21}$

K. $5 \pm i\sqrt{21}$

5. Which of the following represents the solution set to the inequality $-7 - 3x > 2$?

A.
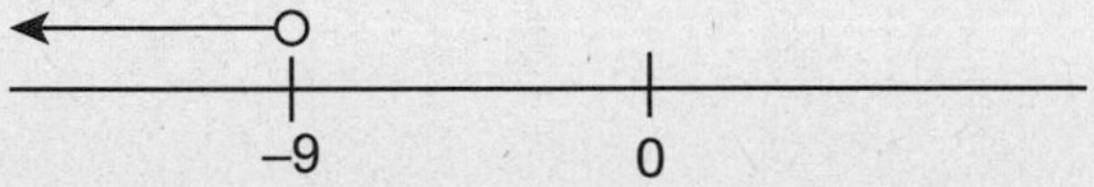

B.
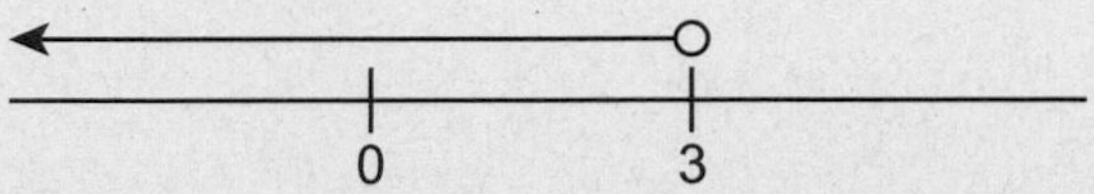

C.
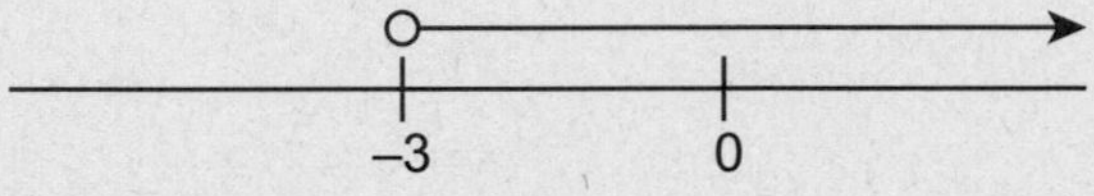

D.
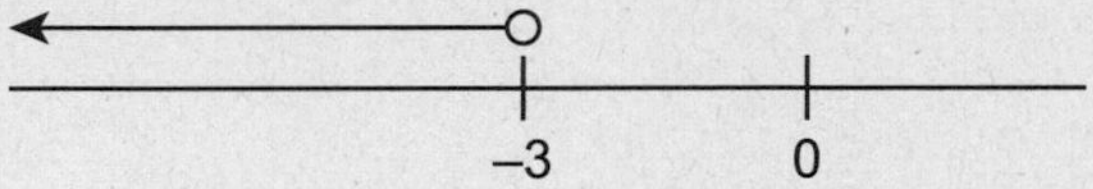

E.

6. What is the solution set for the inequality $|4x+1| < 5$?

F. $x < 1$

G. $-\frac{3}{2} < x < 1$

H. $-1 < x < \frac{3}{2}$

J. $-\frac{3}{2} < x$

K. $-\frac{5}{4} < x < \frac{5}{4}$

7. If $z - w = \frac{1}{4}$ and $w + z = 1$, then what is the value of $\frac{z}{w-z}$?

A. $-\frac{5}{32}$

B. $\frac{5}{8}$

C. $-\frac{2}{5}$

D. $\frac{5}{2}$

E. $-\frac{5}{2}$

8. Which of the following is equivalent to $\frac{24+6x}{42x}$?

SHOW YOUR WORK HERE

F. $\frac{6x+4}{7x}$

G. $\frac{5}{7}$

H. $24\frac{1}{7}$

J. $\frac{x+4}{7x}$

K. $\frac{24+6x}{7x}$

9. If x is a positive real number, which of the following is equal to $\frac{x^2+x}{2x+4} \div \frac{3x}{x+2}$ in simplified form?

A. $\frac{x+1}{6}$

B. $\frac{3x^3+3x}{2x^2+8x+8}$

C. $\frac{6}{x+1}$

D. $x+\frac{1}{6}$

E. $\frac{2x^2+8x+8}{3x^3+3x}$

10. For all nonnegative values of a and b, $\sqrt{5^4y^3z^6} =$

F. $5^8y^6z^{12}$

G. $25y^{\frac{2}{3}}z^{\frac{1}{3}}$

H. $25y^{\frac{3}{2}}z^3$

J. $25y^{-\frac{3}{2}}z^{-3}$

K. $5^4y^3z^6$

11. What is the length of a line segment with endpoints (–3, 2) and (5, –1)?

A. $\sqrt{11}$

B. $\sqrt{61}$

C. 11

D. $\sqrt{73}$

E. 73

12. What is the minimum value of the expression $|x+6|-1$?

SHOW YOUR WORK HERE

F. –6
G. –1
H. 0
J. 1
K. 6

13. The equation of a polynomial is given by $y = 8(2x + 3)(x + 5)(3x - 1)(x - 2)(x + 6)$. How many times does its graph cross the *x*-axis?

A. 6
B. 5
C. 3
D. 2
E. 0

14. Which of the following equations defines a circle in the (*x*, *y*) coordinate plane with a center at *C*(–3, 2) that passes through *P*(5, –4)?

F. $(x - 3)^2 + (y - 2)^2 = 100$
G. $(x + 3)^2 + (y + 2)^2 = 100$
H. $(x + 3)^2 + (y - 2)^2 = 10$
J. $(x + 3)^2 + (y - 2)^2 = 100$
K. $(x + 3)^2 + (y - 2)^2 = 106$

15. For which real values of *x* is $\frac{5^x(x+2)}{(x-6)^3}$ defined?

A. All real numbers
B. All except $x = 6$
C. All except $x = 6$ and $x = -2$
D. All except $x = -6$
E. All except $x = -6$ and $x = -2$

16. If $f(x) = -3x^2 + 4x - 2$, what is the value of $f(-2)$?

F. –22
G. –20
H. –6
J. 18
K. 22

17. If $f(x) = 1 - 2x$ and $g(x) = 3x^2 - x$, what is the value of $f(g(x))$?

A. $1 - 6x^2 - x$
B. $-(6x^2 - 2x - 1)$
C. $12x^2 - 10x + 2$
D. $-(6x^2 + 2x + 1)$
E. $-6x^3 + 5x^2 - x$

18. Snow is falling at a rate of 0.50 inch per hour. At this rate, how many hours would it take for S inches of snow to fall?

F. $\frac{S}{2}$

G. $\frac{1}{2S}$

H. $2S$

J. $S+\frac{1}{2}$

K. $S-\frac{1}{2}$

19. A general contractor calculates that it costs him m dollars per hour in materials costs and l dollars per hour in labor costs to complete a job. Which of the following expressions would provide him with the total cost of a job requiring h hours to complete?

A. ml
B. mlh
C. $m+l$
D. $h(m+l)$
E. $(mh)(lh)$

20. If $M=\begin{bmatrix} 0 & 2 \\ -1 & 3 \end{bmatrix}$ and $N=\begin{bmatrix} -5 & 2 \\ 0 & 1 \end{bmatrix}$ then

$3M-N=$

F. $\begin{bmatrix} 5 & 0 \\ -1 & 2 \end{bmatrix}$

G. $\begin{bmatrix} 15 & 0 \\ -3 & 6 \end{bmatrix}$

H. $\begin{bmatrix} 0 & 6 \\ -3 & 9 \end{bmatrix}$

J. $\begin{bmatrix} -5 & 8 \\ -3 & 10 \end{bmatrix}$

K. $\begin{bmatrix} 5 & 4 \\ -3 & 8 \end{bmatrix}$

SHOW YOUR WORK HERE

Answers and Explanations

1. **The correct answer is B.** First, rewrite the equation for line *l* in slope-intercept form:

$$2y - x = 8$$
$$2y = x + 8$$
$$y = \frac{1}{2}x + 4$$

Now you can see that the line *l* has a slope of $\frac{1}{2}$. The slopes of parallel lines are equal, so the slope of a line parallel to line *l* is also $\frac{1}{2}$. Only choice B satisfies this condition. Choices A, C, D, and E all have different slopes. It is worth noting that the line in choice E is actually perpendicular to *l*: $\frac{1}{2} \times -2 = -1$.

2. **The correct answer is J.** The product of the slopes of perpendicular lines is –1. So first determine the slope of the graphed line and then determine which line listed among the choices has a slope that is its negative reciprocal. Using the slope formula with the points (–5, 0) and (0, 6), we see that the slope of the graphed line is $\frac{6-0}{0-(-5)} = \frac{6}{5}$. So the correct answer will be the line with a slope of $-\frac{5}{6}$. Rewriting the equation in choice J in slope-intercept form yields $y = -\frac{5}{6}x - \frac{1}{6}$.

The line in choice F is parallel to the graphed line since it has the same slope. In choice G, the slope is $-\frac{6}{5}$, not $-\frac{5}{6}$. In choice H, while the lines have the same *y*-intercept, the product of their slopes is not –1, so they cannot be perpendicular. In choice K, the slope is $\frac{5}{6}$, not $-\frac{5}{6}$.

3. **The correct answer is E.** In order to compute this quotient, multiply the numerator and the denominator by the conjugate of the denominator, $2i + 1$. Then, simplify:

$$\frac{3i}{2i-1} = \frac{3i}{2i-1} \bullet \frac{2i+1}{2i+1} = \frac{3i(2i)+3i(1)}{(2i)^2-1^2} = \frac{-6+3i}{-5} = \frac{6}{5} - \frac{3}{5}i$$

Therefore, choice E is the correct answer.

In choice A, the real part is wrong. In choice B, you mistakenly canceled out the *i*'s from the numerator and denominator. In choice C, you forgot to include the real part, which is $\frac{6}{5}$. In choice D, you interchanged the real and imaginary parts.

4. **The correct answer is F.** Use the quadratic formula to complete this problem. Since $x^2 - 10x + 4 = 0$ is in the form $ax^2 + bx + c = 0$, you know that $a = 1$, $b = -10$, and $c = 4$.

$$x = \frac{-b \pm \sqrt{b^2 - 4ac}}{2a}$$
$$= \frac{-(-10) \pm \sqrt{(-10)^2 - 4(1)(4)}}{2(1)}$$
$$= \frac{10 \pm \sqrt{100-16}}{2}$$
$$= \frac{10 \pm \sqrt{84}}{2}$$
$$= \frac{10 \pm 2\sqrt{21}}{2}$$
$$= 5 \pm \sqrt{21}$$

In choice G, you only divided the number before the "±" sign by the denominator, but should have also divided the term after the "±" sign by the denominator. For choice H, –5 should be 5 because in the quadratic formula the first term in the numerator is $-b$, not b. In choice J, you forgot the denominator; in the quadratic formula, you are supposed to divide by $2b$. In choice K, the *i* should not be part of the solution because the radicand was positive, not negative.

5. **The correct answer is D.** Isolate *x* on one side of the inequality, remembering to flip the direction of the inequality sign when you multiply or divide by a negative number:

$$-7 - 3x > 2$$
$$-3x > 9$$
$$x < -3$$

Only choice D properly represents the inequality $x < -3$ on a number line.

In choice A, you forgot to divide both sides by 3. In choice B, the sign of the endpoint of the ray is wrong—it should be –3, not 3. In choice C, you forgot to reverse the inequality sign when dividing both sides by a negative number. In choice E, the endpoint of the ray should be –3, not 3, and it should have an open circle on it instead of a filled circle.

6. **The correct answer is G.** First, rewrite the absolute value inequality as the double inequality $-5 < 4x + 1 < 5$. To solve this inequality, subtract 1 from all parts to get $-6 < 4x < 4$ and then divide all parts by 4 to get $-\frac{3}{2} < x < 1$. This is the solution set.

In choice F, you forgot the left part when converting the absolute value inequality to a double inequality. In choice H, the endpoints of the interval should be reversed and have opposite signs. In choice J, you forgot the right part when converting the absolute value inequality to a double inequality. In choice K, you forgot to subtract 1 from all parts of the double inequality before dividing by 4.

7. **The correct answer is E.** You already have the value for the denominator of the fraction from the first equation (just multiply both sides by –1 to get $w - z = -\frac{1}{4}$). But, we still need to find the value of z. To do so, add the two given equations to get $2z = \frac{5}{4}$, so that $z = \frac{5}{8}$.

Now substitute the values for z and $w - z$ into the expression:

$$\frac{z}{w-z} = \frac{\frac{5}{8}}{-\frac{1}{4}} = \frac{5}{8} \div \left(-\frac{1}{4}\right) = \frac{5}{8} \times (-4) = -\frac{5}{2}$$

You do not need to solve the system to find *both* z and w here, since you already know the value of half of the expression from one the equations. This will save you a little time.

In choice A, you multiplied instead of dividing when computing the value of the given expression. Remember, $\frac{a}{b} \div \frac{c}{d} = \frac{a}{b} \bullet \frac{d}{c}$. Choice B is just the value of z; you did not account for the denominator. Choice C is the reciprocal of the correct answer. Choice D has the opposite sign of the correct answer.

8. **The correct answer is J.** Begin by factoring out the greatest common factor, which is 6, in the numerator. This yields $\frac{24+6x}{42x} = \frac{6(4+x)}{42x}$.

Then cancel the common factor 6 from the numerator and denominator:

$$\frac{24+6x}{42x} = \frac{6(4+x)}{42x} = \frac{4+x}{7x}$$

This is equivalent to $\frac{x+4}{7x}$.

In choice F, you should have canceled the 6 in the $6x$ as well. In choice G, $24 + 6x$ does not equal $(24 + 6)x$; you cannot add coefficients of like terms. In choice H, while you can split up the fractions into a sum of two, the same denominator must be applied to both: $\frac{(24+6x)}{42x} \neq 24 + \frac{6x}{42x}$. In choice K, you should have canceled a 6 in the numerator as well.

9. **The correct answer is A.** Dividing rational expressions is similar to multiplying them, with the exception that the first step is to transform the division problem into a multiplication problem by multiplying the first fraction by the reciprocal of the second fraction. Then, factor whatever you can and cancel common factors in the top and bottom:

$$\begin{aligned}\frac{x^2+1}{2x+4} \div \frac{3x}{x+2} &= \frac{x^2+1}{2x+4} \bullet \frac{x+2}{3x}\\ &= \frac{\cancel{x}(x+1)}{2\cancel{(x+2)}} \bullet \frac{\cancel{x+2}}{3\cancel{x}}\\ &= \frac{x+1}{6}\end{aligned}$$

In choice B, you multiplied instead of divided. In choice C, you flipped the wrong fraction. When converting a quotient of fractions to a product, you take the reciprocal of the fraction *after* the division sign. In choice D, you likely had the correct answer, but then simplified incorrectly. You should have applied the denominator to the x-term as well. In choice E, you multiplied the fractions and *then* took the reciprocal. You should have rewritten the division problem as a multiplication problem by taking the reciprocal of the fraction following the division sign, and *then* multiplied those fractions.

10. **The correct answer is H.** Simplify the expression by taking the square root of each factor separately, as follows:

$$\sqrt{5^4y^3z^6}=\sqrt{5^4}\times\sqrt{y^3}\times\sqrt[3]{z^6}$$
$$=5^2\times y^{\frac{3}{2}}\times z^3=25y^{\frac{3}{2}}z^3$$

In choice F, you squared the expression instead of taking its square root. Choice G is incorrect because $\sqrt{y^3}=y^{\frac{3}{2}}$, not $y^{\frac{2}{3}}$. In choice J, the exponents of *y* and *z* should not be negative. In choice K, you completely ignored the radical sign.

11. **The correct answer is D.** Use the distance formula to find the length:

$$\sqrt{(-3-5)^2+(2-(-1))^2}=\sqrt{(-8)^2+(3)^2}$$
$$=\sqrt{64+9}$$
$$=\sqrt{73}\text{ units}$$

In choice A, you computed the differences of the coordinates of single points rather than the *x*-coordinates of both points and the *y*-coordinates of both points, and you forgot to square these differences. In choice B, you computed the differences of the coordinates of single points rather than the *x*-coordinates of both points and the *y*-coordinates of both points. In choice C, you mistakenly computed $\sqrt{a^2+b^2}=a+b$; remember, you cannot distribute the square root across a sum. In choice E, you forgot to take the square root.

12. **The correct answer is G.** The smallest absolute value of any expression is 0. The absolute value of $x + 6$ equals 0 only when *x* is –6. For this value of *x*, the value of the expression is –1. Choice F is the *x*-value at which the minimum occurs. Choice H is the minimum value of just the absolute value expression—you still need to subtract 1 from it. Choices J and K are incorrect because there are smaller possible values produced by this expression, so they cannot be the minimum value of the expression.

13. **The correct answer is B.** A graph intersects the *x*-axis every time $y = 0$, which occurs whenever one of the factors of the polynomial is equal to 0. Each of the terms inside the parentheses is distinct, so there will be five different values of *x* for which $y = 0$: $-\frac{3}{2},-5,\frac{1}{3}$, 2, and –6. Thus the graph crosses the *x*-axis 5 times.

Choice A is incorrect because while the constant 8 is a factor, it cannot be zero. Choices C and D are incorrect because you must set all factors equal to zero, not just those with a "+" (as in choice C) or those with a "–" (as in choice D). Choice E is way off since each of the five factors equals zero at a different *x*-value, and these are the values at which the graph crosses the *x*-axis.

14. **The correct answer is J.** The general formula for a circle is $(x-h)^2+(y-k)^2=r^2$, where (h, k) is the center of the circle and *r* is the radius. Of the equations given, only $(x+3)^2+(y-2)^2=100$ has a center at (–3, 2) and a radius equal to the distance between *C* and *P*, which is $\sqrt{(-3-5)^2+(2-(-4))^2}=10$.

In choices F and G, the radius is correct, but the center is (–3, 2), not (3, 2) or (–3, –2). In choice H, the right side should be squared. In choice K, the radius is incorrect; you should use the distance formula to compute the distance between *C* and *P*.

15. **The correct answer is B.** A fraction is not defined whenever the denominator equals 0. Set the denominator equal to 0, and note that $(x-6)^3$ will equal 0 only when $x = 6$. Therefore, the fraction is undefined when $x = 6$.

Choice A is incorrect because if $x = 6$, the denominator would equal 0. Choices C and E are incorrect because –2 makes the numerator of the fraction equal to zero, which is permissible—this simply means the fraction itself is equal to zero. For choices D and E, the denominator equals 0 when $x = 6$, not – 6.

16. **The correct answer is F.** To find *f*(–2), plug in –2 for every instance of *x* in the function, and remember to use the order of operations:

$$f(-2)=-3(-2)^2+4(-2)-2$$
$$=-3(4)-8-2$$
$$=-12-8-2$$
$$=-22$$

In choice G, you forgot to include the constant term in the calculation. In choice H, you computed 4(–2) as 8 instead of –8. In choice J, you did not apply the order of operations correctly: the –3 only applies to x^2, not the entire rest of the polynomial. In choice K, you dropped the negative sign off the answer.

17. The correct answer is B. The function $f(g(x))$ is a composition of two functions in which you plug in the expression for $g(x)$, which is $3x^2 - x$, for x in the formula for $f(x)$, which is $1 - 2x$:

$$\begin{aligned} f(g(x)) &= 1-2(3x^2-x) \\ &= 1-6x^2+2x \\ &= -(6x^2-2x-1) \end{aligned}$$

In choice A, after correctly plugging in the expression for $g(x)$ for in the formula for $f(x)$, you did not distribute the –2 to both terms of the binomial. Choice C is the reverse composition, $g(f(x))$. In choice D, you factored out the –1 incorrectly. In choice E, you multiplied $f(x)$ times $g(x)$ instead of solving the composition.

18. The correct answer is H. Set up a proportion equating the ratio of snowfall per hour to the ratio of snowfall per x hours, and cross-multiply to solve for x:

$$\begin{aligned} \frac{1}{0.50} &= \frac{x}{S} \\ S &= 0.50x \\ x &= \frac{S}{0.50} = 2S \end{aligned}$$

Choice F is incorrect because you should divide by 0.50, not multiply by it; you likely inverted half of the proportion to get this answer. Choice G is the reciprocal of the correct expression. Choice J is incorrect because when solving the equation $0.50x = S$, you must divide by 0.50, not add it to both sides. Choice K is incorrect because when solving the equation $0.50x = S$, you must divide by 0.50, not subtract it from both sides.

19. The correct answer is D. The job costs $m + l$ to complete each hour, so if it takes h hours, the expression would be $h(m + l)$. Choices A and B are incorrect because you should be adding m and l, not multiplying them, and then you should multiply the resulting sum by h. Choice C is just the cost per hour; you must multiply by the number of hours, h. Choice E is incorrect because you should be adding mh and lh, not multiplying them.

20. The correct answer is K. First, multiply M by 3 and then subtract the matrices component-wise:

$$\begin{aligned} 3M-N &= 3\begin{bmatrix} 0 & 2 \\ -1 & 3 \end{bmatrix} - \begin{bmatrix} -5 & 2 \\ 0 & 1 \end{bmatrix} \\ &= \begin{bmatrix} 0 & 6 \\ -3 & 9 \end{bmatrix} - \begin{bmatrix} -5 & 2 \\ 0 & 1 \end{bmatrix} \\ &= \begin{bmatrix} 0-(-5) & 6-2 \\ -3-0 & 9-1 \end{bmatrix} \\ &= \begin{bmatrix} 5 & 4 \\ -3 & 8 \end{bmatrix} \end{aligned}$$

Choice F is just $M - N$. Choice G is $3(M - N)$. Choice H is just $3M$. Choice J is $3M + N$.

CHAPTER 8: PLANE GEOMETRY AND TRIGONOMETRY

OVERVIEW

Our final math review chapter will cover two of the most visual portions of the ACT Mathematics test: plane geometry and trigonometry. Our intent in this chapter is to expose you to the visuals, formulas, and terminology that will come up on the ACT exam. We can't say it enough—a huge part of doing well on the ACT Mathematics test is knowing *which* formulas to use *when*. That's why we accompany all of the concepts we explain with sample ACT questions so you can see them in action, rather than just looking at numbers and variables in a table.

The last part of this chapter covers the basic concepts of trigonometry, starting with right triangle trigonometry and then moving to the trigonometric functions and their graphs and trigonometric identities. These are pretty advanced concepts—they're the highest-level math featured on the ACT exam. The good news is that only 5 to 10 percent of mathematics questions might cover these concepts. The better news is that this chapter covers the breadth of what you can expect to see on test day. Review the concepts we give you and practice the questions, and you'll be all set.

Now, on to the final math lesson!

You likely have a general understanding of the terms *point, line, line segment, ray,* and *angle*, so we will not linger there. Rather, let's focus on classifying angles and their relationships—understanding how these smaller elements of geometry relate to one another will be an important factor in your success on the exam. ACT exam questions rarely ask about single components; rather, they want you to figure out how smaller geometry elements fit together.

Mastering the concepts and vocabulary in the first part of this chapter that covers geometry is a big step on the way to excelling with ACT geometry questions—almost all questions will require that you are very familiar with the terms that follow. Let's begin!

COLLEGE READINESS BENCHMARK LEARNING PATH PRACTICE

If you're still finding it tough to know how to approach Plane Geometry and Trigonometry problems, make your way through the College Benchmark Learning Path, starting on page 378. There you will be able to walk through 3 test-like ACT practice questions for each topic—you can see how they'll be presented on the exam, and then walk through each one wlth us step-by-step to see how to approach it in the most efficient way. The goal is to know what to do when you see this problem type on test day—that's where this Benchmark Practice will come in handy.

ANGLES

Angles are classified according to their **measure**. Angle units are expressed in **degrees** (and often **radians** when studying trigonometry), and the notation m $\angle$ (name of angle) is used to denote the measure of a given angle.

These are the various angle characterizations you should know—these terms will likely come up somewhere on the ACT exam:

Term	Illustration	Definition
Acute Angle	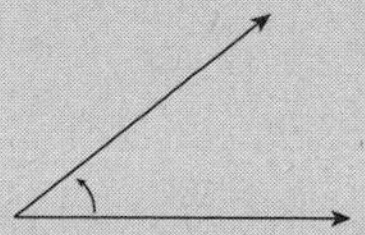	An angle with a measure between 0 and 90 degrees
Right Angle		An angle with a measure of 90 degrees
Obtuse Angle		An angle with a measure between 90 and 180 degrees
Straight Angle		An angle with a measure of 180 degrees
Complementary Angles	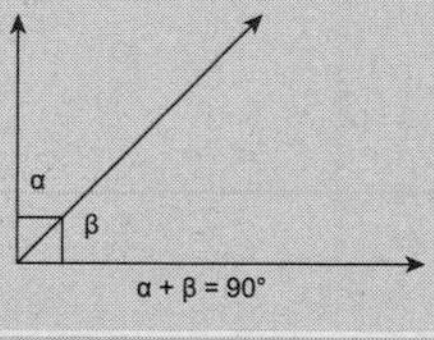	Two angles with measures that sum to 90 degrees
Supplementary Angles	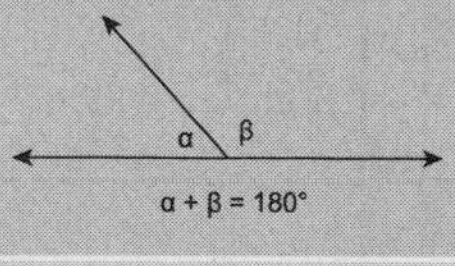	Two angles with measures that sum to 180 degrees
Congruent Angles	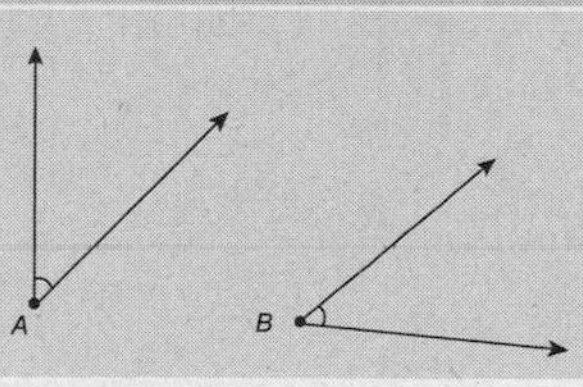	Two angles that have the same measure

It's not only important that you understand individual angle classifications, but also how pairs of angles relate to each other. Knowing these relationships will help you figure out angle values in figures and perform more complex calculations.

Take a look at the following image and the table that follows. You will likely be presented with a figure on the ACT exam that has some angle values filled in, and then be asked to determine missing values in order to solve a problem. We suggest that you review and memorize these angle relationships until they're second nature to you—they are sure to come in handy when you take the test.

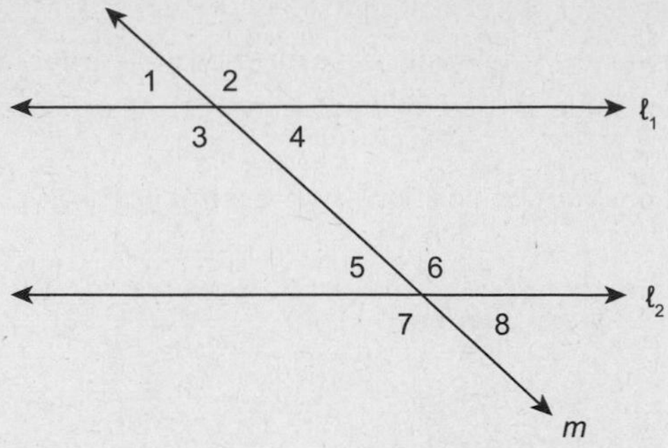

Term	Examples from Diagram
Corresponding Angles	$\angle 1$ and $\angle 5$, $\angle 3$ and $\angle 7$ In a diagram such as the one above, if the lines l_1 and l_2 are parallel, then corresponding angles are congruent.
Adjacent Angles	$\angle 1$ and $\angle 2$, $\angle 5$ and $\angle 7$
Vertical Angles	$\angle 1$ and $\angle 4$, $\angle 6$ and $\angle 7$ Vertical angles are *always* congruent!
Alternate Interior Angles	$\angle 4$ and $\angle 5$, $\angle 3$ and $\angle 6$ In a diagram such as the one above, if the lines l_1 and l_2 are parallel, then alternate interior angles are congruent.

Remember: typically, parallelism is denoted by two vertical hash marks, like $l_1 \parallel l_2$. Congruence is generally denoted by a single hash mark.

CAUTION If two lines cut by a transversal are NOT parallel, then pairs of corresponding angles and pairs of alternate interior angles are *not* necessarily congruent.

Let's look at a sample problem dealing with lines and angles.

Points *A*, *D*, and *E* lie on the same line in the figure below. What is the measure of angle *BEC*?

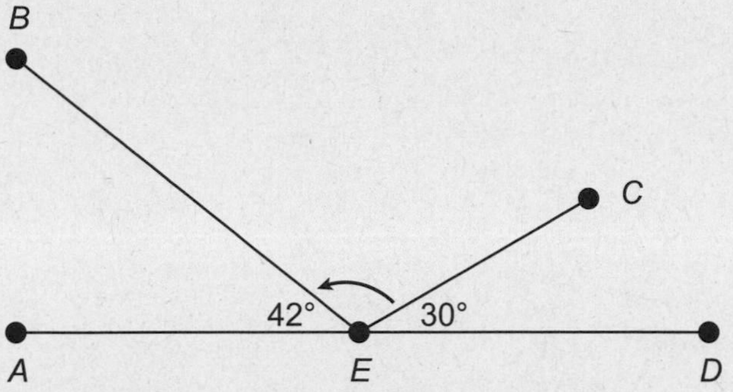

F. 60°
G. 48°
H. 90°
J. 108°
K. 150°

The correct answer is J. In the diagram, the three angles form a straight line and therefore, their measures must sum to 180°.

$$m\angle AEB + m\angle BEC + m\angle CED = 180^\circ$$
$$42^\circ + m\angle BEC + 30^\circ = 180^\circ$$
$$m\angle BEC = 180^\circ - 42^\circ - 30^\circ$$
$$= 108^\circ$$

Turn to page 378 to follow the College Readiness Benchmark Learning Path questions covering Angles.

TRIANGLES

Triangles come in all different sizes and are classified using their angles and sides as follows.

Classified by Angles		
Term	**Definition**	**Illustration**
Right	One of the angles is a right angle (the other two, therefore, must be acute)	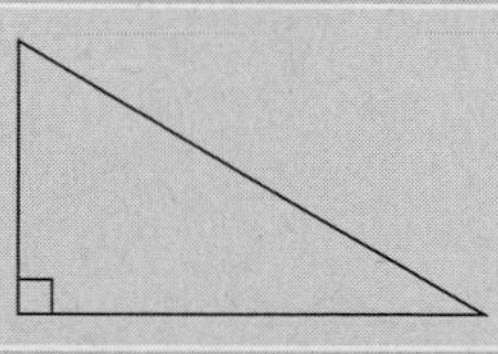
Acute	All three angles are acute	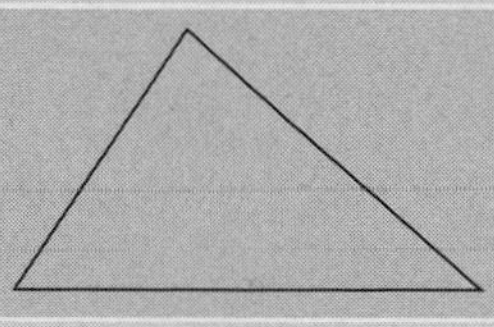
Obtuse	One of the angles is obtuse (the other two, therefore, must be acute)	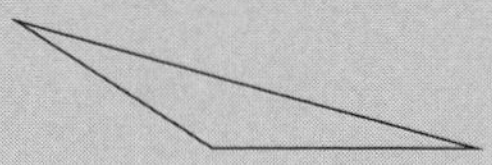

Classified by Sides		
Term	**Definition**	**Illustration**
Equilateral	All three sides have the same length; that is, all three sides are congruent	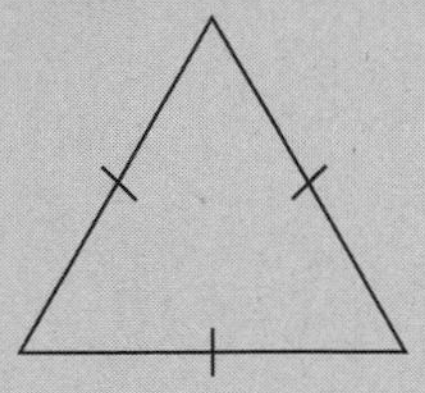
Isosceles	At least two sides have the same length; that is, at least two sides are congruent	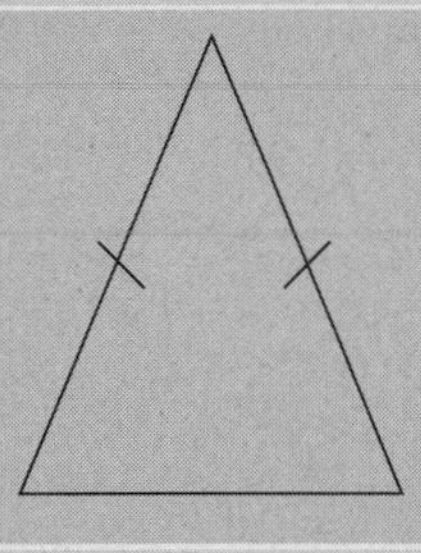
Scalene	All three sides have different lengths	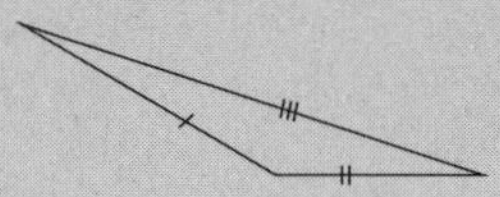

All triangles obey the **triangle sum rule** and the **triangle inequality**. The triangle sum rule says that the sum of the measures of the three angles in any triangle must be 180°. The triangle inequality says that the sum of the lengths of any two sides of a triangle must be strictly larger than the length of the third side.

Let's put some of these rules into practice with this sample problem.

What is the measure of angle *DEF*?

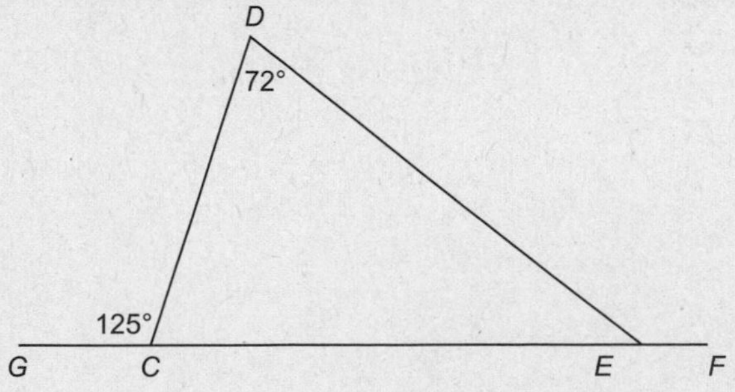

A. 127°
B. 125°
C. 108°
D. 90°
E. 53°

The correct answer is A. Angle *DCE* is supplementary to angle *DCG*, so its measure is 180° – 125° = 55°. The interior angles of a triangle sum to 180°, so the measure of angle *DEC* is 180° – 55° – 72° = 53°. Finally, angle *DEF* is supplementary to angle *DEC*, so its measure is 180° – 53° = 127°.

Right Triangles and the Pythagorean Theorem

The lengths of the sides of right triangles are always related by the **Pythagorean theorem**. Consider the right triangle shown here:

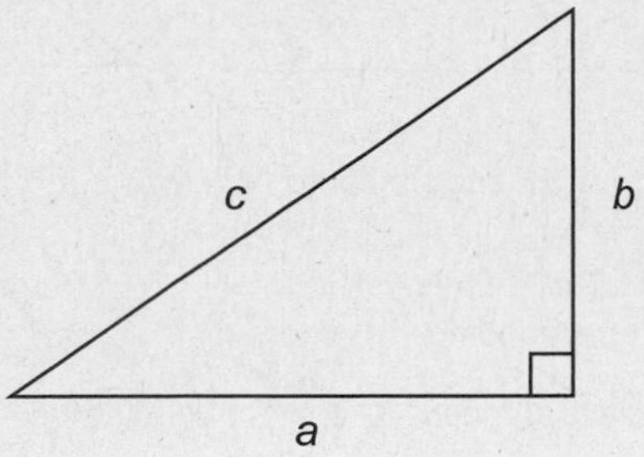

CAUTION The Pythagorean theorem works only for right triangles!

The sides with lengths *a* and *b* are called **legs**, and the side opposite the right angle is the **hypotenuse**. The hypotenuse is the longest side of a right triangle.

Two common right triangles have sides that measure 3-4-5 and 5-12-13, or multiples thereof. Be on the lookout for these **Pythagorean triples**—recognizing them within a problem can make calculating a missing side easier.

The Pythagorean theorem says that $a^2 + b^2 = c^2$.

Two special right triangles are 30-60-90 and 45-45-90 triangles; the numbers indicate the triangles' angle measures. The ratio of the side lengths for these special triangles are given below.

45-45-90 Triangle

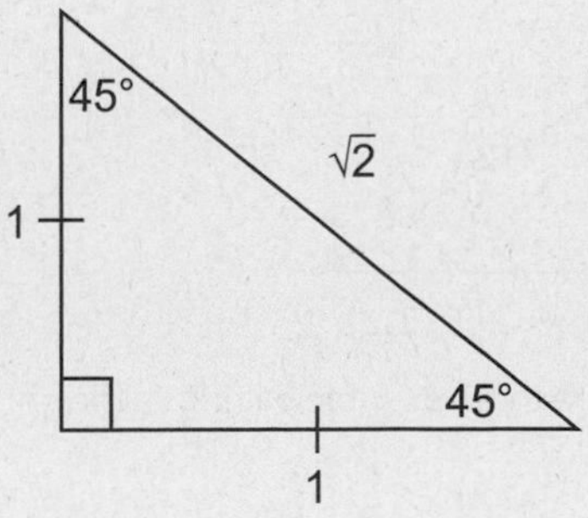

30-60-90 Triangle

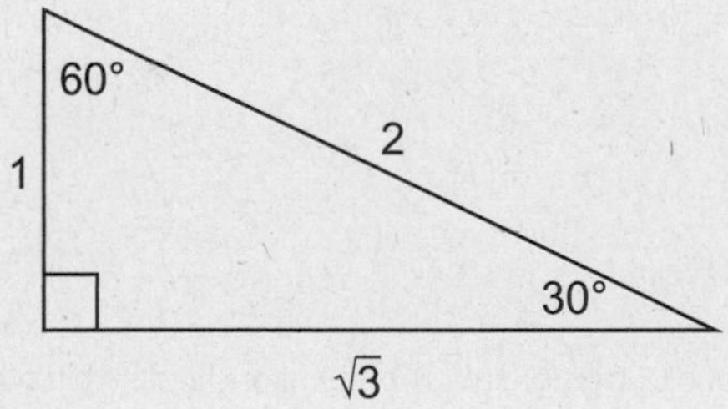

Again, familiarize yourself with these values and be on the lookout for triangles with these angle measures—there is sure to be at least one ACT exam question where knowing them will help you answer quickly and confidently.

Triangles and Measurement

We say two triangles *ABC* and *DEF* are **congruent** if all three corresponding pairs of angles are congruent *and* all three corresponding sides are congruent. Always identify **corresponding** sides of two triangles using the order in which their vertices (i.e., points where two sides meet) are written. As noted here in our description, vertex *A* corresponds to vertex *D*, *B* to *E*, and *C* to *F*.

TIP Congruent triangles have the same perimeter and area.

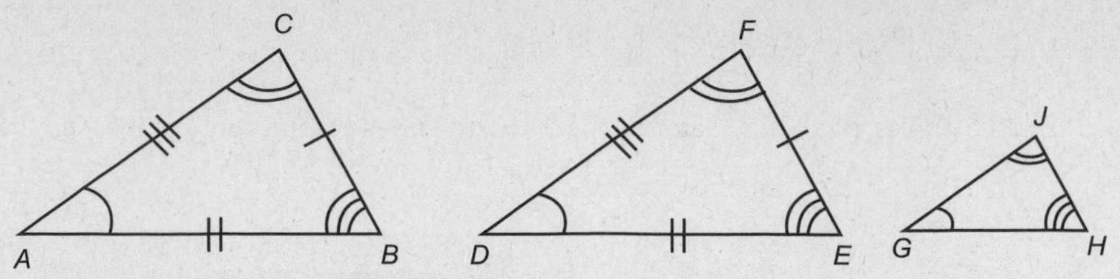

ΔABC is congruent to ΔDEF and similar to ΔGHJ

Two triangles *ABC* and *DEF* that are *not* congruent can still be proportional to each other in the sense that the ratios of the three pairs of corresponding sides are the same—that is, $\frac{AB}{GH} = \frac{BC}{HJ} = \frac{AC}{GJ} = k$, where *k* is a positive number.

TIP: Corresponding angles in two similar triangles must be congruent.

In such cases, we say triangles *ABC* and *GHJ* are **similar**.

The **perimeter** of a closed plane figure is the distance around the figure and is computed by adding the lengths of all segments/sides forming its outer boundary. Some common units used when measuring length are *inches, feet, yards,* etc.; the metric system is also commonly used (*centimeters, meters*, etc.). The perimeter of a triangle is the sum of the lengths of its three sides. Often, a question will require you to compute the perimeter of a right triangle, but you will not explicitly be given the lengths of all the sides. In such a case, do not forget that you have the Pythagorean theorem!

The **area** of a two-dimensional plane figure is the number of **unit squares** needed to cover it. The standard units of measure of area are *square inches, square feet, square yards,* etc.; the metric system is also commonly used (*square centimeters, square meters,* etc.). The area formula for a triangle with base *b* and height *h*, as illustrated below, is $A = \frac{1}{2} b \bullet h$.

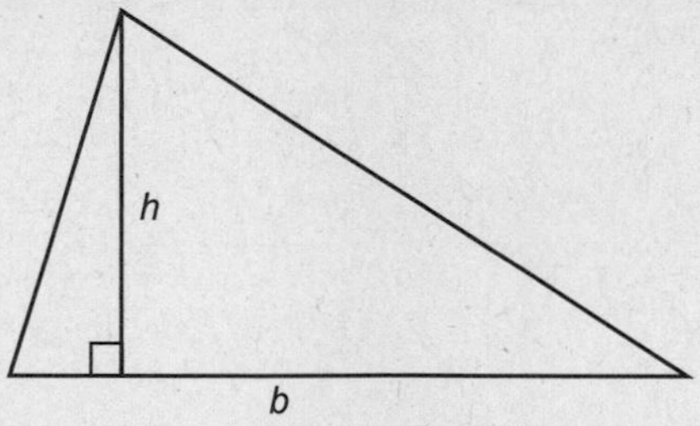

The height of a triangle must be perpendicular to its base. That means there are three possible pairings of heights with bases for any triangle—each base has its own height.

Take a look at a problem like you may see on the ACT exam that deals with the area of a right triangle.

What is the area in square inches of a right triangle with sides of 27 inches, 36 inches, and 45 inches?

F. 972
G. 486
H. 192
J. 96
K. Cannot be determined from the given information

The correct answer is G. This is a multiple of a 3-4-5 right triangle: 3(9) = 27, 4(9) = 36, 5(9) = 45. (We told you they would come up! Whenever you are given three side values of a right triangle, check to see if they are multiples of a Pythagorean triple.) Since it is a right triangle, the legs serve as the base and height. So its area is half the product of its legs: $\frac{1}{2}(27)(36) = 486$ square inches.

ALERT: Be careful with units. Every now and then, all quantities in a problem will NOT be expressed using the same units (some may be in feet and others in inches, for instance). The first thing to do in such case is to convert all quantities to the same units.

Let's look at a couple of problems dealing with measurement.

The open area in front of a museum is a square lawn bordered by footpaths 250 feet long on each side. The museum plans to create a diagonal footpath that would connect the northwest corner of the lawn to the southeast corner of the lawn. Approximately how many feet shorter would the new path be than the shortest possible route on the existing footpaths?

A. 500
B. 354
C. 250
D. 146
E. 125

The correct answer is D. The current paths require a trip of 500 feet (250 feet for each of the two sides one must travel along to get from one corner to the other). A diagonal path would form a 45°–45°–90° isosceles right triangle with the existing paths being its legs. As such, the length of the diagonal path would be $250\sqrt{2}$ feet, or approximately 354 feet. The new path would shorten the route by approximately 500 – 354 = 146 feet.

A certain triangle has sides of lengths 50, 120, and 130 centimeters. If a similar triangle has a perimeter of 1,500 centimeters, what is the length (in centimeters) of the triangle's shortest side?

F. 50
G. 130
H. 250
J. 600
K. 650

The correct answer is H. The two triangles are similar, so their sides are in proportion. The first triangle has a perimeter of 50 + 120 + 130 = 300 centimeters. The second triangle has a perimeter that is 5 times this: 1,500 centimeters. Thus, the sides of the second triangle are exactly 5 times as long as the sides of the first triangle: 250, 600, and 650 centimeters. So the length of the shortest side is 250 centimeters.

Proving Geometric Theorems

The notion of proving theorems in geometry is not tested very often on the ACT exam, but it does come up from time to time, usually in the context of triangles. In this section, we will review congruence and some typical methods of proof used to establish the congruence of two triangles.

Two figures F and G are **congruent** if they have the same size and shape. We denote this fact by writing $F \cong G$. The following two facts are obvious, but very important:

- Two line segments are congruent *if and only if* they have the same length.
- Two angles are congruent *if and only if* they have the same measure.

Two triangles *ABC* and *DEF* are *congruent* if the following conditions hold:

Figures	Segments	Angles
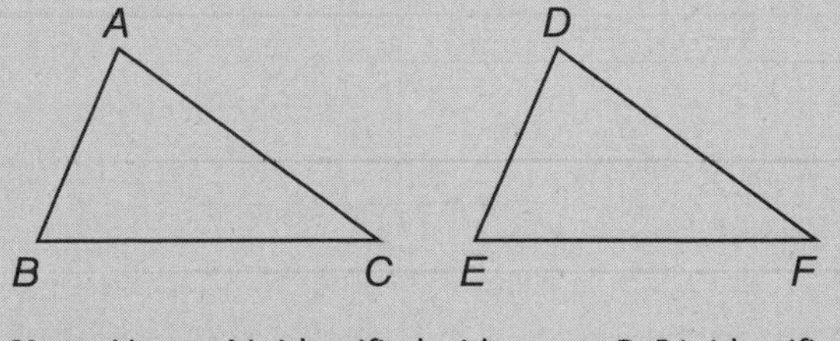	$AC \cong DF$	$m\angle A = m\angle D$
	$AB \cong DE$	$m\angle B = m\angle E$
Note: Vertex *A* is identified with vertex *D*; *B* is identified with *E*; and *C* is identified with *F*.	$BC \cong EF$	$m\angle C = m\angle F$

Although all six conditions must hold in order for the two triangles to be congruent, we do not need to verify all six. Rather, there are different congruence properties that tell us that if we verify certain subsets of these conditions, the others must hold true as a consequence.

Congruence Property	Conditions That Must Be Satisfied
SAS Property	Two pairs of corresponding sides are congruent, and the corresponding angles between them must be congruent.
ASA Property	Two pairs of corresponding angles are congruent, and the included sides between them must be congruent.
SSS Property	All three pairs of corresponding sides are congruent.

Isosceles Triangle Theorem

If the triangle *ABC* is isosceles, then the angles that are opposite the congruent sides (base angles) will also be congruent.

> **TIP** A typical question on the ACT exam that involves proofs consists of a statement and the lines of the proof in scrambled order. The question will ask you to provide the correct order of the statements so that the result constitutes a proof of the statement.

Here is the step-by-step proof:

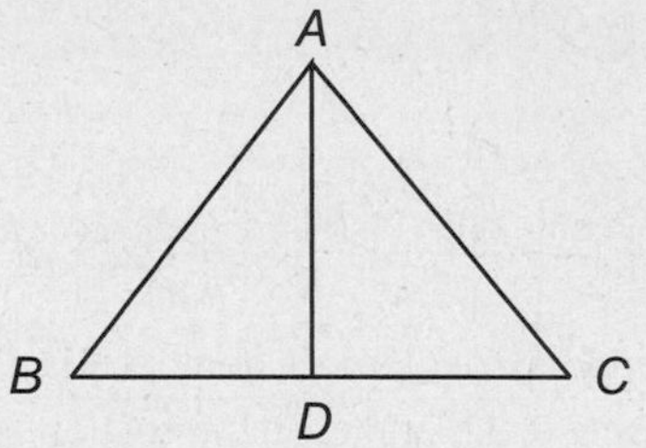

1) Given that triangle *ABC* is isosceles with $AB \cong AC$.
2) Draw angle bisector *AD*, such that $\angle BAD \cong \angle CAD$.
3) $AD \cong AC$ using the reflexive property.
4) Therefore, by the SAS property, $\Delta BAD \cong \Delta CAD$.

Using CPCTC (corresponding parts of congruent triangles are congruent), $\angle B \cong \angle C$.

The proof is complete.

Hypotenuse-Leg (HL) Theorem

If the hypotenuse and one leg of a right triangle are congruent to the corresponding parts of another right triangle, then the two triangles are congruent.

Here is the step-by-step proof:

1) Given triangles *ADB* and *ADC* are right triangles and $AB \cong AC$.
2) *AB* is the hypotenuse of ΔADB and *AC* is the hypotenuse of ΔADC (opposite the right angles).
3) $AD \cong AD$ using the reflexive property.

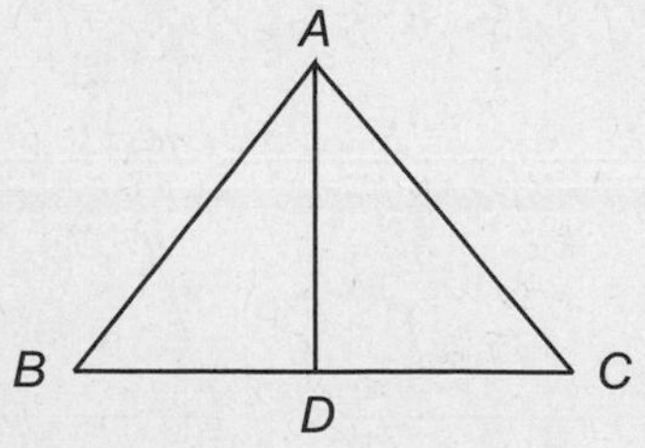

Since the hypotenuse and leg of ΔADB are congruent to the corresponding hypotenuse and leg of ΔADC, the two triangles are congruent using the HL Theorem.

The proof is complete.

Turn to page 380 to follow the College Readiness Benchmark Learning Path questions covering Triangles.

QUADRILATERALS

Quadrilaterals are four-sided plane figures in which each side is a line segment. The following are the most common quadrilaterals you are likely to come across on the ACT exam:

Quadrilateral	Defining Characteristics	Illustration
Square	Two pairs of parallel sides, all four sides congruent, and all four angles congruent (all are right angles)	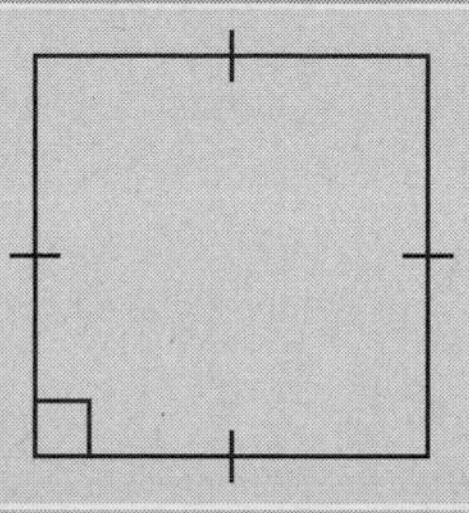
Rectangle	Two congruent pairs of parallel sides and all four angles congruent (all are right angles)	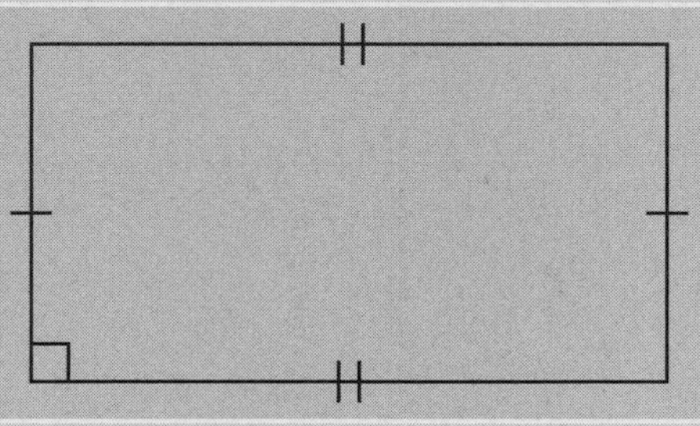
Parallelogram	Two congruent pairs of parallel sides	
Rhombus	Two pairs of parallel sides; all four sides are congruent	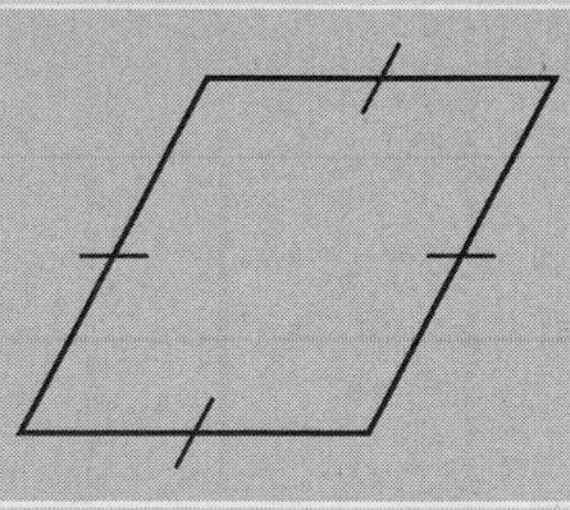
Trapezoid	Exactly one pair of parallel sides	
Isosceles Trapezoid	Exactly one pair of parallel sides; nonparallel sides are congruent	

You have likely learned many facts about the properties of these quadrilaterals in geometry, such as diagonals of a parallelogram bisect each other, and if the parallelogram is a rectangle, the diagonals are perpendicular to each other. Typically, questions involving deeper properties of the quadrilaterals rarely occur on the ACT exam, so we're going to focus more on the formulas and facts you'll need for test questions.

As with triangles, two quadrilaterals of the same type are called **congruent** if all of their corresponding sides are congruent. They are called **similar** if the four ratios of their corresponding sides are equal. You compute the perimeter of any quadrilateral by adding together the lengths of its four sides.

Here are two useful **perimeter formulas** you should know for quadrilaterals:

1. Perimeter of a square with side length s is $P = 4s$.
2. Perimeter of a rectangle with length l and width w is $P = 2l + 2w$.

Likewise, the following are useful **area formulas** for the most common quadrilaterals that surface on the ACT exam:

Square	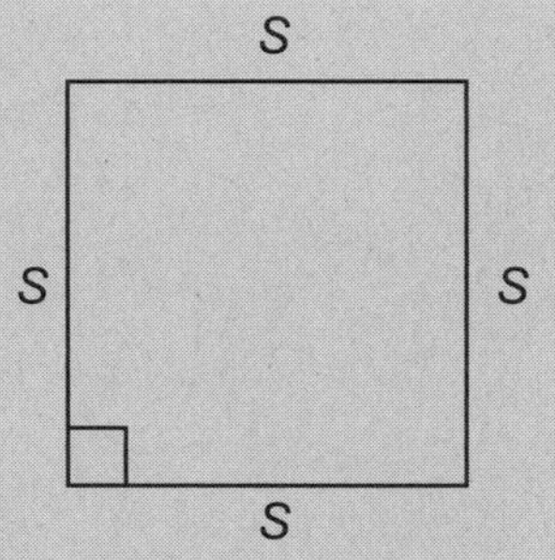	$A = s^2$
Rectangle		$A = l \bullet w$
Parallelogram	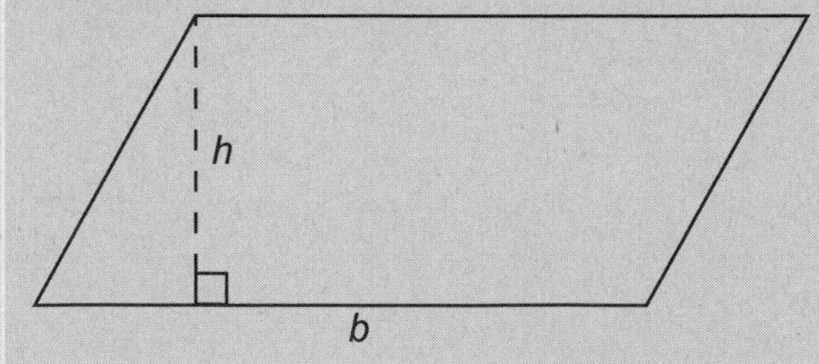	$A = b \bullet h$ **Note:** Do not confuse the height (which must be perpendicular to the base) with the measure of the side adjacent to the base (often referred to as the *width*).

A common mathematics question on the ACT exam will give you the perimeter or area of a square or rectangle and ask you to identify the length of a side. When variables are involved, this requires you to use your algebra skills, as in the problem below.

The area of a rectangle is $4x^2 + 4x - 3$ square units. If its length is $2x + 3$ units, what is its width, in units?

A. $\dfrac{4x^2+4x-3}{2}$

B. $4x + 1$

C. $2x + 1$

D. $x - 1$

E. $2x - 1$

The correct answer is E. The area of a rectangle is equal to lw, where l and w are its length and width, respectively. You are given that the area of the rectangle is $4x^2 + 4x - 3$ square units and that its length is $2x + 3$. You need to find the other factor that, when multiplied by $(2x + 3)$, produces $4x^2 + 4x - 3$. The only factor that works is the one given in choice E.

Other questions may ask you to determine vertices or areas of figures plotted on the standard coordinate (x, y) plane, as in the following samples:

If, in the given figure, the point is the vertex of a square with perimeter of 12 units, which of the following could be another vertex of this square?

F. (3, 2)

G. (7, 2)

H. (–9, 2)

J. (–3, –7)

K. (–5, 5)

The correct answer is K. The perimeter of a square with side length s is given by $P = 4s$. Since the perimeter of this square is 12, s must be 3. The given point has coordinates (–2, 2), so any other vertex of the same square must have an x-coordinate that is either equal to or 3 units away from –2. This means that the x-coordinate can be –5, –2, or 1. The square must have a y-coordinate of –1, 2, or 5. Only choice K, (–5, 5), meets these conditions.

What is the area in square units of the rectangle shown below in the standard (x, y) coordinate plane?

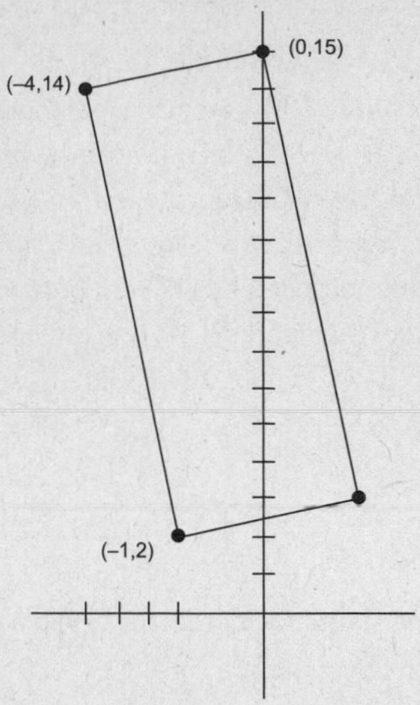

A. 17

B. 51

C. $3\sqrt{17}$

D. 153

E. $8\sqrt{17}$

The correct answer is B. You must first determine the width and length of the rectangle. Recall what we learned in Chapter 7—you can find the lengths when given two points by using the distance formula:

$$w = \sqrt{(-4-(-1))^2 + (14-2)^2} = \sqrt{9+144} = \sqrt{153} = 3\sqrt{17} \text{ units}$$

$$l = \sqrt{(-4-0)^2 + (14-15)^2} = \sqrt{16+1} = \sqrt{17} \text{ units}$$

So the area of the rectangle is $\left(3\sqrt{17}\right)\left(\sqrt{17}\right) = 51$ square units.

Turn to page 383 to follow the College Readiness Benchmark Learning Path questions covering Quadrilaterals.

CIRCLES

The set of all points in the plane that are a given distance *r* from a fixed point *P* is a **circle.** Here is the basic terminology involving circles you should know before you take the ACT exam. Most of these are sure to surface on the exam, so you should absolutely memorize these definitions.

Term	Illustration	Definition
Center	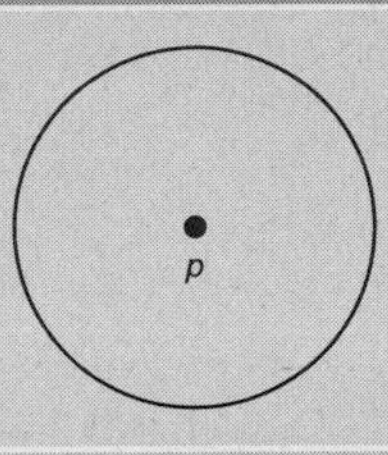	The point *P* equidistant from all points on the circle
Radius	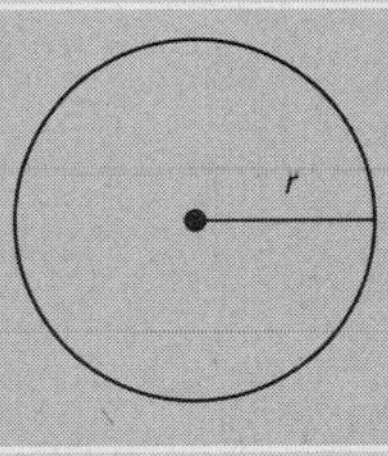	The common distance *r* that points on the circle are from the center
Diameter	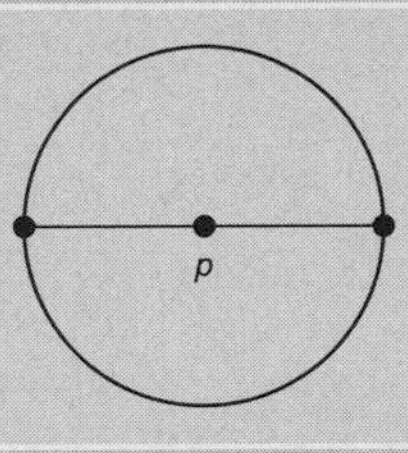	A line segment that passes through the center of the circle and has endpoints on the circle (its length is twice the radius)
Central Angle	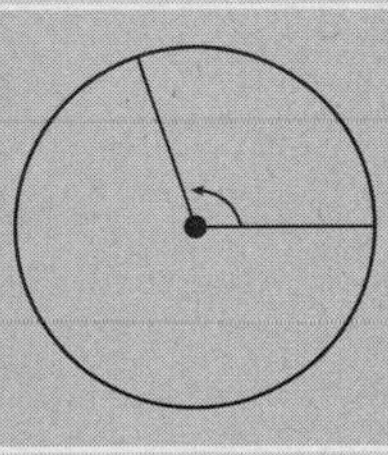	An angle formed between two radial segments
Arc	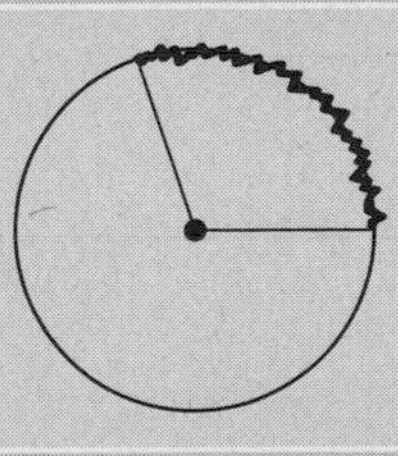	A portion of the circle that lies between two points
Sector	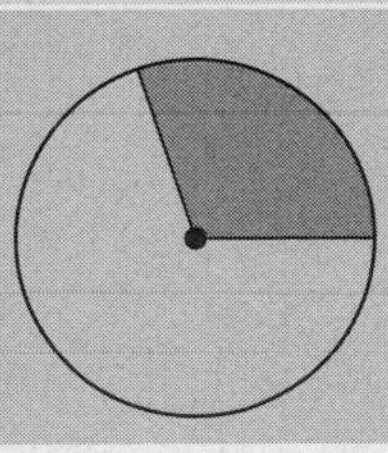	The portion of the inside of a circle that lies between two radial segments

You will use these terms when configuring values of circles, as in the following formulas. Circumference and area of circles are the formulas that come up most frequently on the ACT exam.

Term	Illustration	Definition
Circumference of a Circle	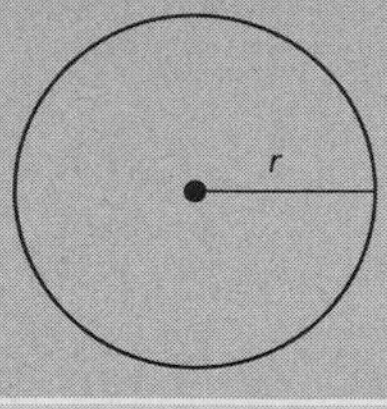	Since the diameter d is $2r$, there are two expressions for this formula: $P = 2\pi r = \pi d$
Length of an Arc of a Circle	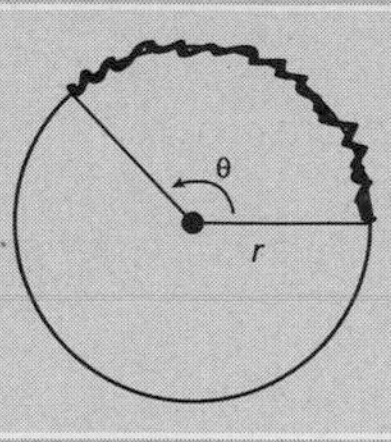	$P = \dfrac{\theta}{180^\circ} \bullet \pi r$
Area of a Circle	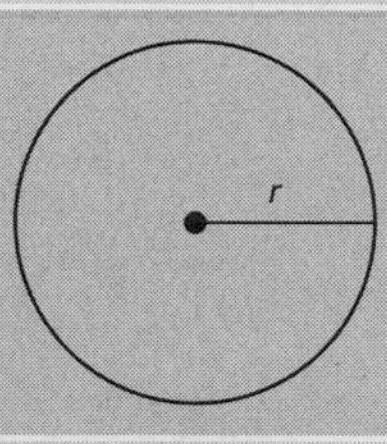	$A = \pi r^2$
Area of a Sector of a Circle	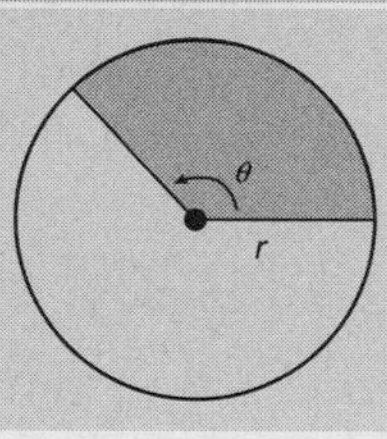	$A = \dfrac{\theta}{360^\circ} \bullet \pi r^2$

Follow along with this sample problem.

The length of the radius of circle A is 4 times as long as the radius of circle B. If the radius of circle B is x units, what is the area (in square units) of circle A?

F. $16x$

G. $\dfrac{x}{16}$

H. $\dfrac{x}{4}$

J. $16\pi x^2$

K. $\dfrac{\pi x^2}{16}$

The correct answer is J. The radius of circle A is $4x$. So its area is $\pi(4x)^2 = 16\pi x^2$.

Problems like these come in different varieties, but they all involve using the same formulas. Sometimes, you will be given a diameter instead of a radius, or you will be given an area or perimeter of a sector and asked to identify the radius or diameter. The key is to be flexible with using the formulas in various ways, depending on what information is provided.

Turn to page 385 to follow the College Readiness Benchmark Learning Path questions covering Circles.

SOLIDS

The solids that show up most frequently on the ACT Mathematics test are cubes, prisms, and cylinders. Let's take a look at formulas (yes, more formulas!) you should know for the test. Understanding the variable parts that make up these formulas well in advance will make it easier for you to translate the words given in ACT geometry problems into values you can calculate.

> **TIP:** You should remember the formulas for the cube and rectangular prism, but the test providers will supply the other formulas. Just be sure you are comfortable using them!

Solid	Illustration	Surface Area Formula	Volume Formula
Cube	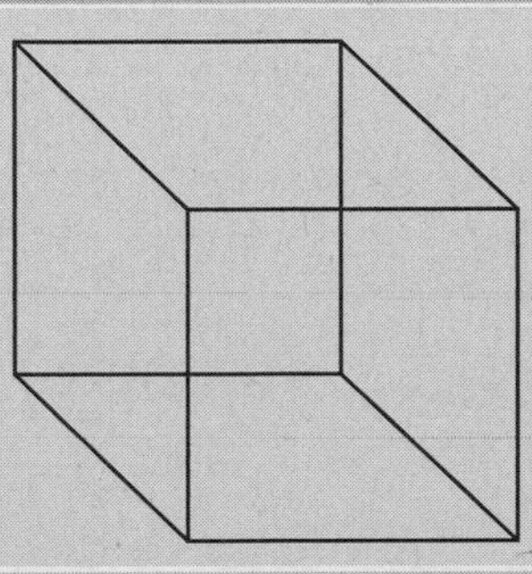	$6A = 6s^2$	$V = s^3$
Rectangular Prism	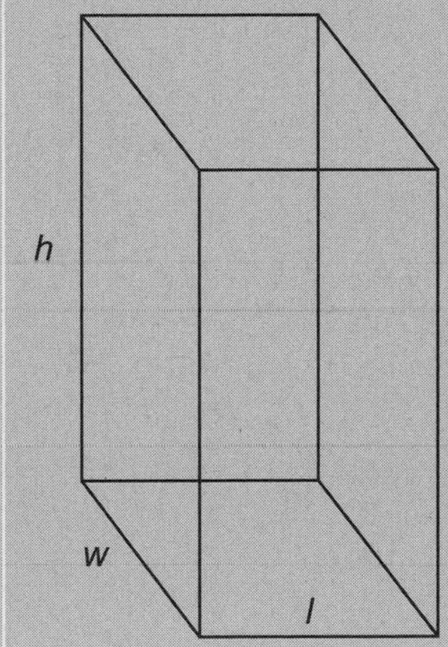	$SA = 2(lw + lh + wh)$	$V = lwh$
Cylinder	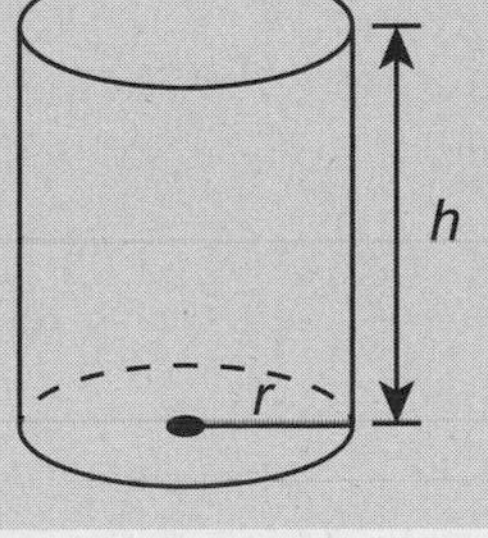	$SA = 2\pi r^2 + 2\pi rh$	$V = \pi r^2 h$

Now try working out some problems on your own.

Examples:

Answer the following computational questions involving these solids.

1. If the volume of a cube is 512 cubic inches, what is the area of one of its faces? ____
2. If the volume of a cylinder is 200π cubic feet and its height is 5 feet, what is the diameter of its base? ____
3. If three distinct sides of a rectangular box have lengths of 4 cm, 10 cm, and 15 cm, what is its surface area? ____

Solutions:

1. Let s represent an edge of the cube. Then, $s^3 = 512$, and $s = 8$ inches. So an area of *one* face is $8^2 = 64$ square inches.

   Again, don't forget to read questions slowly and carefully to make sure you know exactly what value the question is seeking. Then, after you select your answer, check *again*. You don't want to have wasted math done correctly by selecting a value that answers another question.

2. Using the formula $V = \pi r^2 h$, we are given $V = 200\pi$ and $h = 5$. Plug those in and solve for r:

$$200\pi = \pi r^2 \bullet 5$$
$$\frac{200\pi}{5\pi} = r^2$$
$$40 = r^2$$
$$2\sqrt{10} = r$$

   The diameter of the base is $2r$, which is $4\sqrt{10}$ feet.

3. Using the formula $SA = 2(lw + lh + wh)$, simply plug in 4 cm, 10 cm, and 15 cm for l, w, and h—it does not matter which value you associate with which letter:

$$\begin{aligned} SA &= 2(lw + lh + wh) \\ &= 2(4 \bullet 10 + 4 \bullet 15 + 10 \bullet 15) \text{ square centimeters} \\ &= 500 \text{ square centimeters} \end{aligned}$$

Such solids occur within application problems as well. For instance, consider the following example.

Example:

Michael wishes to apply primer to the four walls and the ceiling of a tool shed. The ceiling has dimensions 8 feet by 12 feet, and the height of the shed is 9 feet. If each can of primer is used to seal 200 square feet of wall, how many cans must he purchase? ________

Solution:

First, we must determine the total surface area to be painted. The shed is in the shape of a rectangular prism; its surface area formula is given above. We must account for four walls and a ceiling, but NOT the floor. So the surface area is

$$\underbrace{(8 \bullet 12)}_{\text{Ceiling}} + \underbrace{2(8 \bullet 9) + 2(12 \bullet 9)}_{\text{Walls}} = 456 \text{ square feet.}$$

Since each can coats 200 square feet, he must purchase three cans of primer.

Turn to page 387 to follow the College Readiness Benchmark Learning Path questions covering Solids.

TRANSFORMATIONS

A **transformation** is a sequence of steps that moves a planar figure around in the *xy*-plane without changing its actual size or shape. The result of applying a transformation to a figure creates an **image** of that figure. If *P* is a point on the original figure, then the image of *P* is typically denoted by *P* '.

There are various movements that can be performed to transform figures.

Transformation	Description	Illustration
Translation	All points on a figure are moved in the same direction and distance.	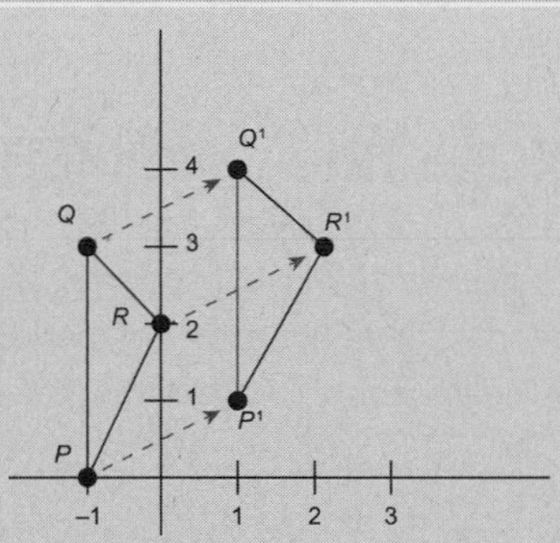 Here, each point on *PQR* was moved two units to the right and one unit up.
Rotation	All points on a figure are connected to a common point (called the **center of rotation**) and are rotated clockwise or counter-clockwise by the same angle.	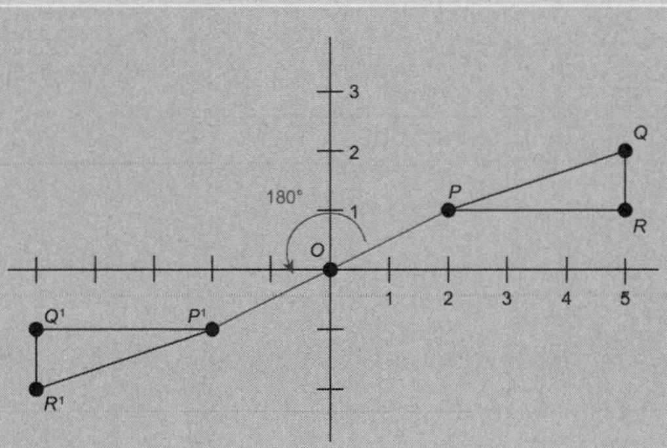 This illustrates a 180-degree rotation counterclockwise of figure *PQR* about the center marked *O*.
Reflection	All points on a figure are reflected over a given line in the plane. To do so, a line segment is drawn from a point on the figure perpendicularly to the line over which it is being reflected. The image of that point is obtained by going the same distance on the opposite side of the reflection line.	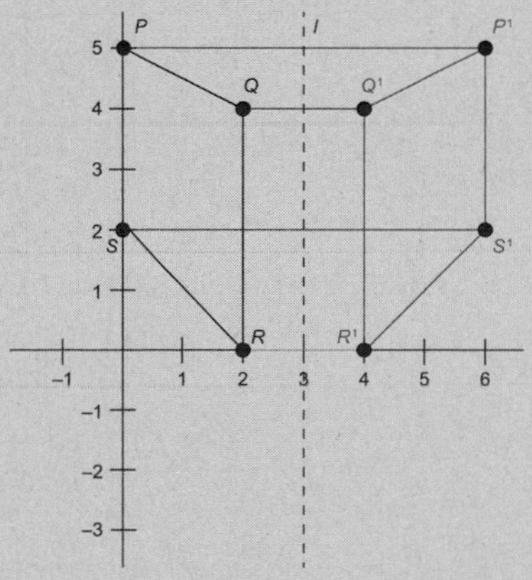 This illustrates quadrilateral *PQRS* being reflected over the line $x = 3$.

Use the information in the table of transformations to solve the following problems.

Examples:

Consider the point P (1, 2) in the plane. Determine the image of this point under the indicated transformation.

1. Translated 5 units up and 2 units left. ___________

2. Reflected over the line $y = 8$. ___________

Solutions:

1. The image P^1 is (–1, 7).

2. The image P^1 is (1, 14).

RIGHT TRIANGLE TRIGONOMETRY

Trigonometric functions were defined, in part, to identify the lengths of sides of a right triangle when one side and one angle (instead of two sides) are known. The names of these six functions, with their abbreviations, are as follows. If given on the ACT exam, you will likely see the abbreviated form of the name. All trigonometry questions fall under the category Preparing for Higher Math.

Trigonometric Function	Abbreviation
Cosine	cos
Sine	sin
Tangent	tan
Secant	sec
Cosecant	csc
Cotangent	cot

Let's explore what these trigonometric functions mean. Consider the following right triangle. In this triangle, θ represents an angle:

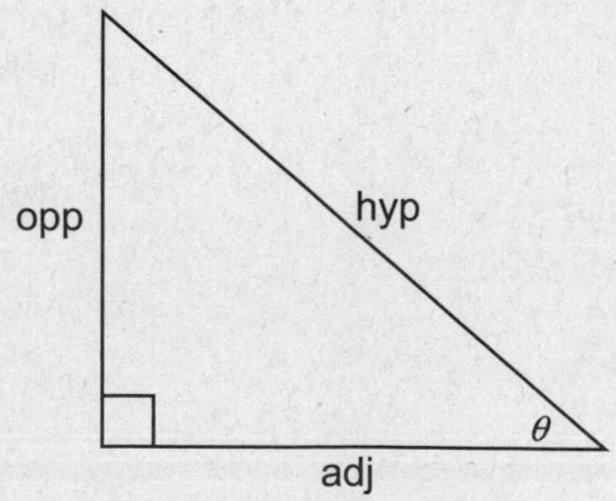

Using this image gives you a visual representation to follow when understanding how trigonometric functions are defined in what we'll call **right triangle trigonometry**. When asked to find the values of these functions on the ACT, you will use the following formulas:

$$\sin\theta = \frac{\text{opposite}}{\text{hypotenuse}}$$

$$\cos\theta = \frac{\text{adjacent}}{\text{hypotenuse}}$$

$$\tan\theta = \frac{\text{opposite}}{\text{adjacent}} = \frac{\sin\theta}{\cos\theta}$$

$$\cot\theta = \frac{\text{adjacent}}{\text{opposite}} = \frac{\cos\theta}{\sin\theta} = \frac{1}{\tan\theta}$$

$$\sec\theta = \frac{\text{hypotenuse}}{\text{adjacent}} = \frac{1}{\cos\theta}$$

$$\csc\theta = \frac{\text{hypotenuse}}{\text{opposite}} = \frac{1}{\sin\theta}$$

The problems related to trigonometry on the ACT Mathematics test come in two main varieties:

1) Compute a trigonometric function or determine a side of a triangle using given information.

2) Solve a word problem that can be modeled using a right triangle.

Let's take a look at a few sample ACT–type trigonometry problems.

In right triangle *ABC*, $\sin A = \frac{1}{2}$. What is the value of cos *A*?

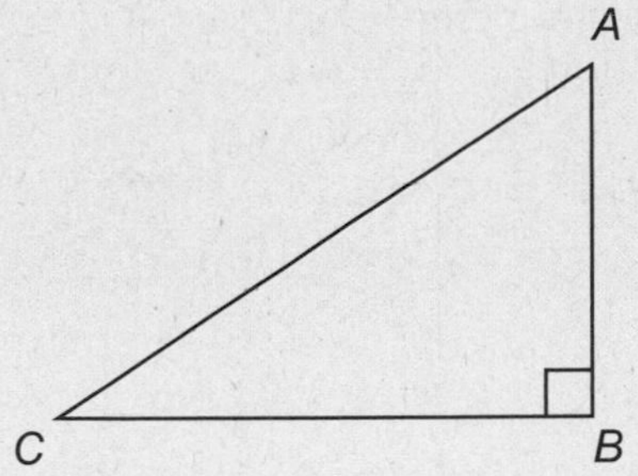

F. $\sqrt{3}$

G. 2

H. $\frac{\sqrt{3}}{3}$

J. $\frac{1}{2}$

K. $\frac{\sqrt{3}}{2}$

The correct answer is K. Remember that sine is $\frac{\text{opposite}}{\text{hypotenuse}}$ and that cosine is $\frac{\text{adjacent}}{\text{hypotenuse}}$. From what is given, $\frac{CB}{AC} = \frac{1}{2}$.

We label the lengths of *CB* and *AC* in the triangle:

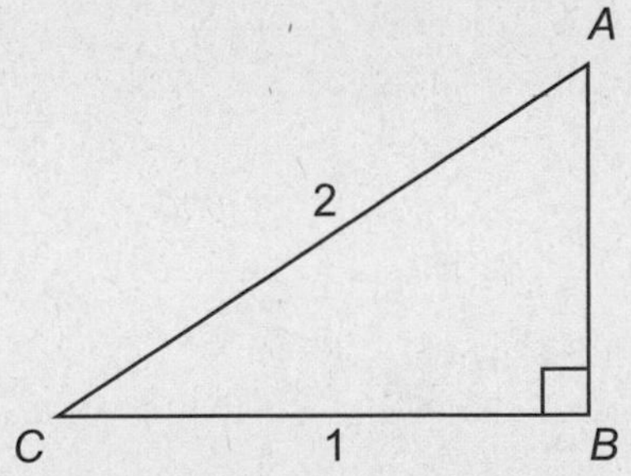

To find the cosine of angle *A*, you need to know the length of the side adjacent to it, namely segment *AB*. Since the length of a leg of this triangle is related to the length of its hypotenuse in the ratio of 1:2, remember from earlier in this chapter that this is a 30-60-90 right triangle, whose three sides are related in the ratio of $1:\sqrt{3}:2$. Therefore, $AB = \sqrt{3}$, so $\cos A = \frac{\sqrt{3}}{2}$.

In the isosceles right triangle below, what is the value of $\sin(z°) + \cos(z°)$?

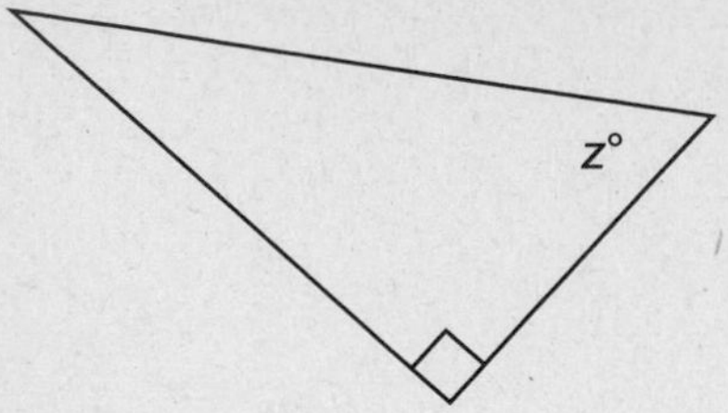

A. $\frac{\sqrt{2}}{2}$

B. 1

C. $\sqrt{2}$

D. $\frac{\sqrt{3}}{2}$

E. $\sqrt{3}$

The correct answer is C. Remember that in an isosceles right triangle, the angles are 45°-45°-90°, the legs have the same length of 1, and the hypotenuse has a length of $\sqrt{2}$. (Familiarizing yourself with all of the charts will really help you out!) So both $\sin(z°)$ and $\cos(z°)$ equal $\frac{1}{\sqrt{2}}$.

Hence, $\sin(z°) + \cos(z°) = \frac{2}{\sqrt{2}} = \sqrt{2}$.

A 95-foot cable attached to the top of a telephone pole is anchored to the ground. If the wire rises at a 64° angle with the ground, how tall is the telephone pole (in feet)?

A. 95 tan 64°

B. 64 cos 95°

C. 95 cos 64°

D. 95 sin 64°

E. 64 sin 95°

The correct answer is D. As shown in the diagram below, the height of the telephone pole, *x*, is opposite a 64° angle, and the hypotenuse of the triangle is 95 feet.

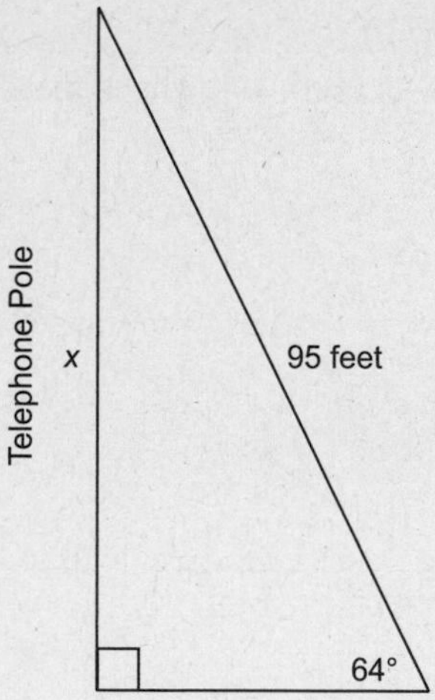

Since sine equals $\frac{\text{opposite}}{\text{hypotenuse}}$, we get the formula

$\frac{x}{95} = \sin 64°; x = 95 \sin 64°$.

Graphs of Trigonometric Functions

In order to graph trigonometric functions, we use a value called **radian measure** instead of degrees to measure angles. To find radian measure, you form the ratio of the arc length of a circle's sector to its radius. Place the vertex of the angle at the center of a circle of radius *r* and denote the length of the arc of the circle formed by the two rays of this angle by *s*:

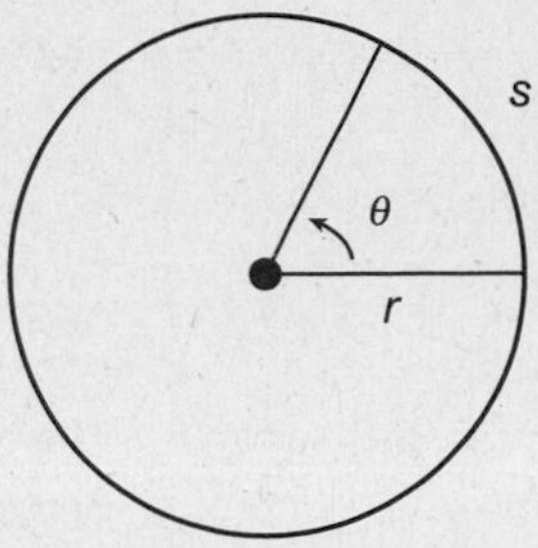

The **radian measure** of the angle θ is given by $\theta = \frac{s}{r}$.

Let's say that $\theta = 90°$. Since the circumference of the entire circle is $2\pi r$, and the central angle of an entire circle is 360°, it follows that an angle with measure $\theta = 90°$ cuts off an arc with a length that is $\frac{1}{4}$ of the entire circle; that is, $s = \frac{1}{4}(2\pi r)$. As such, the measure of angle θ in radians is $\theta = \frac{s}{r} = \frac{\frac{1}{4}(2\pi r)}{r} = \frac{\pi}{2}$ radians.

So $90° = \frac{\pi}{2}$ radians. And that means that an entire 360° circle has a measure of 2π radians. The same type of reasoning works to determine the radian measure corresponding to any degree measure.

The graphs of $f(x) = \sin(x)$ and $g(x) = \cos(x)$ for $0 \le x \le 2\pi$ are as follows:

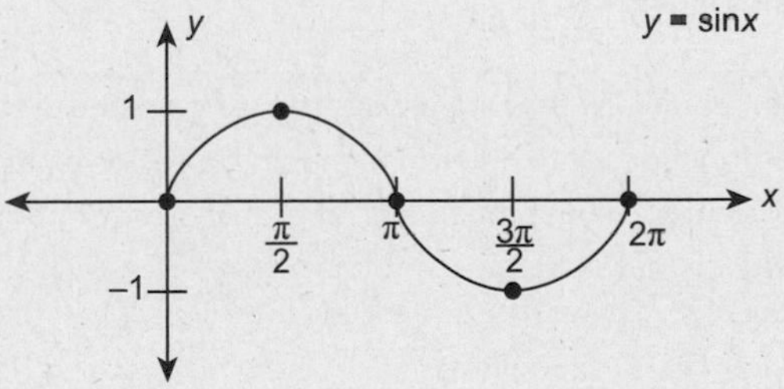

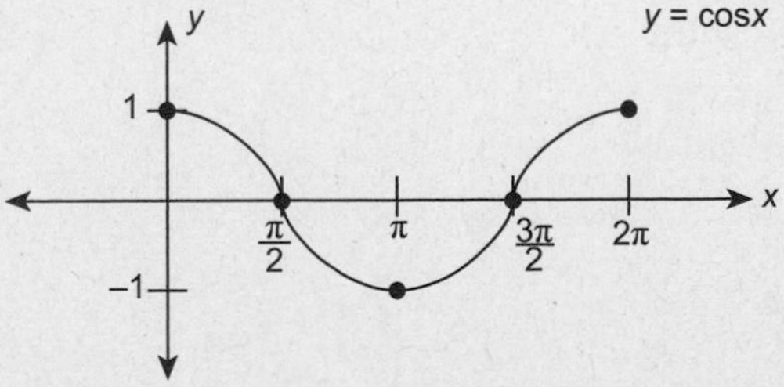

Note: The graphs on the intervals $2\pi \le x \le 4\pi$, $4\pi \le x \le 6\pi$, etc. are identical to the graph above. We say these functions are **periodic.** The **period** is the length of the smallest interval that can be used to produce a graph by replicating what it looks like on that interval on abutting intervals of the same length. Here, the period is 2π—starting after 2π, that exact curve will repeat.

Consider the function $f(x) = \sin(2x)$. As x moves from 0 to π, the angles swept out by $2x$ actually go from 0 to 2π. So an entire period of inputs is swept out by letting x go from only 0 to π in this case. So the period of $f(x) = \sin(2x)$ is $\frac{2\pi}{2} = \pi$.
Similarly, the period of $f(x) = \sin(5x)$ is $\frac{2\pi}{5}$. The same analysis applies for $g(x) = \cos(x)$. In general, the period of $f(x) = \sin(Bx)$ and $g(x) = \cos(Bx)$ is $\frac{2\pi}{B}$.

Now, consider the function $f(x) = 3\sin(x)$. The period is still 2π, but notice the outputs this time go from −3 to 3. If you don't see this, try plotting some points. So multiplying by 3 on the inside to get $\sin(3x)$ changes the period, while multiplying $\sin(x)$ by 3 on the outside to get $3\sin(x)$ changes the maximum and minimum values.

The same goes for the cosine function. We say the **amplitude** of a periodic function equals $\frac{\text{maximum value} - \text{minimum value}}{2}$.

ALERT: $\sin(mx)$ does not equal $m\sin(x)$—you cannot pull out the m!

See if you can solve this cosine function problem.

How many cycles does the function $y = 3\cos(8x)$ complete when $0 \le x \le 2\pi$?

A. $\frac{1}{8}$

B. $\frac{1}{2}$

C. 1

D. 3

E. 8

The correct answer is E. The coefficient of x determines the period of a cosine function, while the coefficient in front (in this case, 3) determines the amplitude and has no effect on the period. Since we know the period of $g(x) = \cos(Bx)$ is $\frac{2\pi}{B}$ and the same is true for $g(x) = A\cos(Bx)$ for any nonzero number A, we conclude that the graph of $y = 3\cos(8x)$ completes 8 full cycles in the interval $0 \le x \le 2\pi$.

Turn to page 389 to follow the College Readiness Benchmark Learning Path questions covering Right Triangle Trigonometry.

TRIGONOMETRIC IDENTITIES

Trigonometric identities are useful equalities that are always true—you can use them on questions that ask you to simplify expressions involving trigonometric functions or to determine the sine or cosine of an angle when the cosine or sine of that angle is known. The following table features just a few of the most commonly used identities you might see on the ACT exam—don't expect anything beyond this to show up on the test.

Name	Identity
Pythagorean Identity	$\cos^2\theta + \sin^2\theta = 1$
Periodicity Identities	$\sin(2n\pi + \theta) = \sin(\theta)$, where n is an integer $\cos(2n\pi + \theta) = \cos(\theta)$, where n is an integer
Symmetry Identities	$\sin(-\theta) = -\sin(\theta)$ $\cos(-\theta) = \cos(\theta)$
Complementary Angle Identities	$\cos \frac{\pi}{2} - \theta = \sin\theta$ $\sin \frac{\pi}{2} - \theta = \cos\theta$
Double-Angle Identities	$\sin(2\theta) = 2\sin\theta\cos\theta$ $\cos(2\theta) = \cos^2\theta - \sin^2\theta$

One term that you might see on the ACT exam is the **terminal side** of an angle. The terminal side of an angle θ swept out from the positive *x*-axis in the counterclockwise direction is the radial segment that forms the angle, along with the positive *x*-axis:

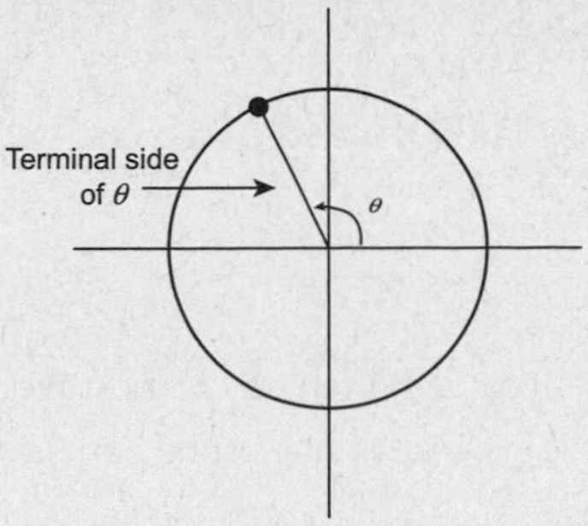

The signs of cos θ and sin θ are determined by the quadrant in which the terminal side lies.

Quadrant in Which the Terminal Side Lies	Illustration	Sign of cos θ	Sign of sin θ
I	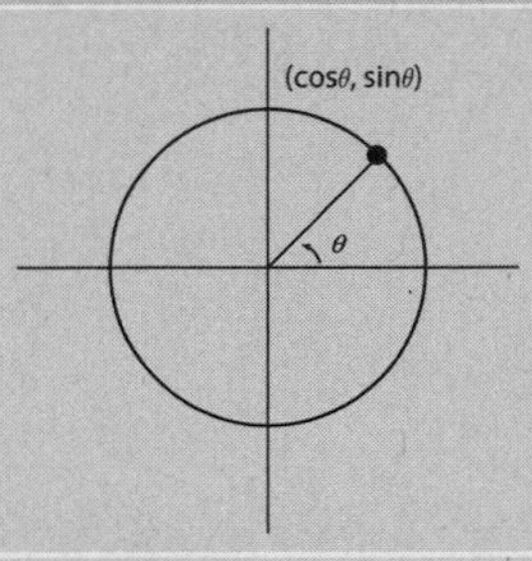	+	+
II	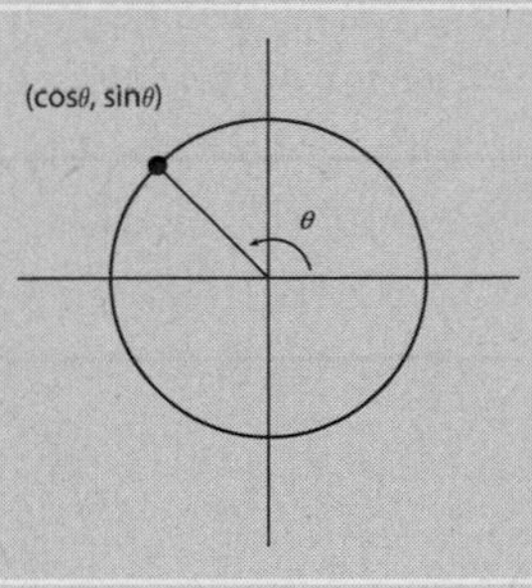	–	+
III	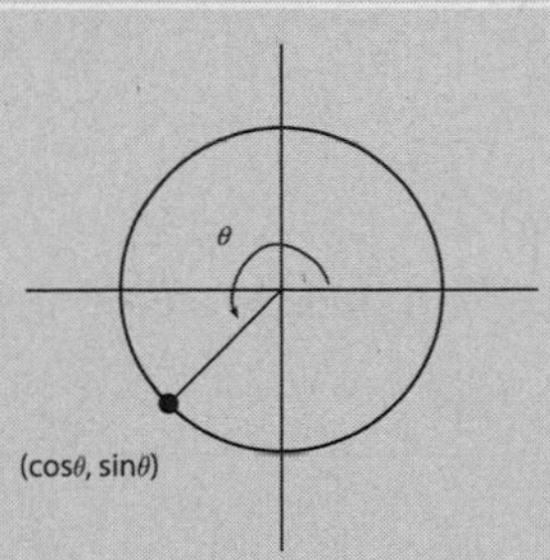	–	–
IV	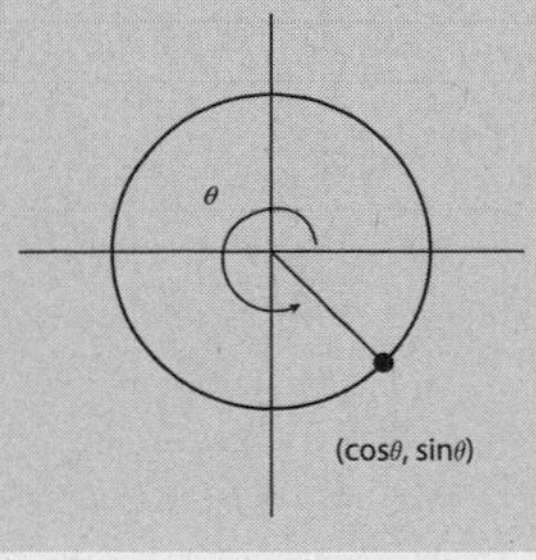	+	–

Now, let's explore how to use these identities to solve an ACT exam problem together.

Example:

Suppose $\cos\theta = -\frac{1}{5}$ and the terminal side of θ intersects the unit circle in Quadrant II. Compute $\sin\theta$.

Solution:

Use the Pythagorean identity $\sin^2\theta + \cos^2\theta = 1$ to find two possible values for $\sin\theta$. Then, use the fact that the sine of an angle whose terminal side is in Quadrant II must be positive to choose the correct value:

$$\sin^2\theta + \cos^2\theta = 1$$
$$\sin^2\theta + \left(-\frac{1}{5}\right)^2 = 1$$
$$\sin^2\theta + \frac{1}{25} = 1$$
$$\sin^2\theta = \frac{24}{25}$$
$$\sin\theta = \pm\frac{\sqrt{24}}{5} = \pm\frac{2\sqrt{6}}{5}$$

Since the terminal side is in Quadrant II, we conclude that the correct value is $\frac{2\sqrt{6}}{5}$.

Now try one on your own.

Suppose that $\sin\theta = \frac{3}{5}$ and that the terminal side of θ is in Quadrant II. Which of the following equals $\cos 2\theta$?

A. $\frac{4}{5}$

B. $-\frac{4}{5}$

C. $\frac{7}{25}$

D. $-\frac{3}{5}$

E. $\frac{9}{5}$

The correct answer is C. First, use the Pythagorean identity $\sin^2\theta + \cos^2\theta = 1$ to find two possible values for $\cos\theta$. Then, use the fact that the cosine of an angle whose terminal side is in Quadrant II must be negative to choose the correct value. Finally, use the double-angle formula $\cos 2\theta = \cos^2\theta - \sin^2\theta$:

$$\sin^2\theta + \cos^2\theta = 1$$
$$\left(\frac{3}{5}\right)^2 + \cos^2\theta = 1$$
$$\cos^2\theta = 1 - \frac{9}{25}$$
$$\cos\theta = \pm\frac{4}{5}$$

Since the terminal side is in Quadrant II, we conclude that $\cos\theta = -\frac{4}{5}$.

Therefore,

$$\cos 2\theta = \cos^2\theta - \sin^2\theta = \left(-\frac{4}{5}\right)^2 - \left(\frac{3}{5}\right)^2 = \frac{16}{25} - \frac{9}{25} = \frac{7}{25}.$$

Turn to page 391 to follow the College Readiness Benchmark Learning Path questions covering Trigonometric Identities.

SOLVING TRIGONOMETRIC EQUATIONS

Just as there are linear equations, quadratic equations, and equations involving radicals of an unknown, there are equations involving the trigonometric functions. The general aim is the same—you need to find values of the input that will make the equation true.

In the case of trigonometric equations, it will be very helpful for you to remember these common values of trigonometric functions. If you can recall these, you will be able to save several steps if faced with a trigonometric equation on the ACT exam. These problems will not turn up frequently on the test—but if they do, there's a good chance that they will include one or more of the values from the following table:

x	$\sin(x)$	$\cos(x)$
0	0	1
$\frac{\pi}{6}$	$\frac{1}{2}$	$\frac{\sqrt{3}}{2}$
$\frac{\pi}{4}$	$\frac{\sqrt{2}}{2}$	$\frac{\sqrt{2}}{2}$
$\frac{\pi}{3}$	$\frac{\sqrt{3}}{2}$	$\frac{1}{2}$
$\frac{\pi}{2}$	1	0
π	0	-1
$\frac{3\pi}{2}$	-1	0
2π	0	1

Let's take a look at how this table can help you on the exam.

Which of the following is a solution of the equation $\cos(3x) = 1$?

A. π

B. $\frac{2\pi}{3}$

C. 2π

D. $\frac{\pi}{6}$

E. $\frac{\pi}{4}$

The correct answer is B. Looking at the table above, you can see any value of x for which $3x = 0$ or 2π is a solution of this equation (it will lead to a value of 1, which is what you are seeking). So $x = 0$ and $x = \frac{2\pi}{3}$ are both solutions. Of these, only the latter is a choice, so the answer is B.

Turn to page 393 to follow the College Readiness Benchmark Learning Path questions covering Trigonometric Equations.

SUMMING IT UP

- Angles are classified according to their "size" or measure; the units in which this is expressed are **degrees** or **radians**.
  - An angle with a measure between 0 and 90 degrees is **acute**.
  - An angle with a measure of 90 degrees is a **right** angle.
  - An angle with a measure between 90 and 180 degrees is **obtuse**.
  - An angle with a measure of 180 degrees is a **straight** angle.
- Two angles with measures that sum to 90 degrees are **complementary**; two angles with measures that sum to 180 degrees are **supplementary**.
- Two angles that have the same measure are **congruent**. Vertical angles are *always* congruent.
- A **right** triangle is one that has a right angle; an **acute** triangle is one in which all three angles are acute; an **obtuse** triangle has one obtuse angle.
- An **equilateral** triangle is one in which all three sides have the same length; an **isosceles** triangle has at least two sides with the same length; a **scalene** triangle has three sides of different lengths.
- The **triangle sum rule** says that the sum of the measures of the three angles in any triangle must be $180°$. The **triangle inequality** says that the sum of the lengths of any two sides of a triangle must be strictly larger than the length of the third side.
- The **Pythagorean theorem** states that for a right triangle with legs a and b and hypotenuse c, $a^2 + b^2 = c^2$.
- Two triangles ΔABC and ΔDEF are **congruent** if all three corresponding pairs of angles are congruent AND all three corresponding sides are congruent. Two triangles ΔABC and ΔDEF are **similar** if the ratios of the three pairs of corresponding sides are the same; that is, $\frac{AB}{DE} = \frac{BC}{EF} = \frac{AC}{DF} = k$, where k is a positive number.
- The **area formula** for a triangle with base b and height h is $A = \frac{1}{2} b \bullet h$.
- Two quadrilaterals of the same type are **congruent** if their corresponding sides are all congruent, and they are called **similar** if the four ratios of their corresponding sides are equal.
- The **perimeter of a square** with side length s is $P = 4s$. The **area of a square** with side length s is $A = s^2$.
- The **perimeter of a rectangle** with length l and width w is $P = 2l + 2w$. The **area of a rectangle** with length l and width w is $A = l \bullet w$.
- The **circumference of a circle** with radius r (or diameter $d = 2r$) is $C = 2\pi r = \pi d$. The **area of a circle** with radius r is $A = \pi r^2$.
- The **volume of a cube** with side length s is $V = s^3$.
- The **volume of a rectangular box** with side lengths l, w, and h is $V = lwh$.
- The **volume of a cylinder** with base radius r and height h is $V = \pi r^2 h$.
- **Trigonometric functions** are used to identify the lengths of sides of a right triangle when one side and one angle (instead of two sides) are known. There are six trigonometric functions: **cosine** (cos), **sine** (sin), **tangent** (tan), **secant** (sec), **cosecant** (csc), and **cotangent** (cot).
- **Trigonometric formulas** are used to find the values of trigonometric functions:

$$\sin\theta = \frac{\text{opposite}}{\text{hypotenuse}} \text{ and } \cos\theta = \frac{\text{adjacent}}{\text{hypotenuse}}$$

$$\tan\theta = \frac{\text{opposite}}{\text{adjacent}} \text{ and } \cot\theta = \frac{\text{adjacent}}{\text{opposite}} = \frac{1}{\tan\theta}$$

$$\sec\theta = \frac{\text{hypotenuse}}{\text{adjacent}} = \frac{1}{\cos\theta} \text{ and } \csc\theta = \frac{\text{hypotenuse}}{\text{opposite}} = \frac{1}{\sin\theta}$$

- **Trigonometric identities** are useful equalities that are always true that can help you to simplify expressions involving trigonometric functions or to determine the sine or cosine of an angle when the cosine or sine of that angle is known. The most commonly used identities are as follows:
    - **Pythagorean identity:** $\cos 2\theta + \sin 2\theta = 1$
    - **Periodicity identities:** $\sin(2n\pi + \theta) = \sin(\theta)$, $\cos(2n\pi + \theta) = \cos(\theta)$, where n is an integer
    - **Symmetry identities:** $\sin(-\theta) = -\sin(\theta)$, $\cos(-\theta) = \cos(\theta)$
    - **Complementary angle identities:** $\cos\left(\frac{\pi}{2} - \theta\right) = \sin\theta$, $\sin \frac{\pi}{2} - \theta = \cos\theta$
    - **Double-angle identities:** $\sin(2\theta) = 2\sin\theta\cos\theta$, $\cos(2\theta) = \cos^2\theta - \sin^2\theta$

ONLINE PREP

Want to Know More?

Access more practice questions, lessons, helpful hints, and strategies for the following science topics in *Peterson's Online Course for the ACT® Exam*:

- Lines and Angles
- Triangles
- Quadrilaterals
- Circles
- Solids
- Multiple Figures
- Trigonometry Functions
- Trigonometry Functions and Identities

To purchase and access the course, go to **www.petersons.com/testprep/act**.

COLLEGE READINESS BENCHMARK LEARNING PATH PRACTICE

Directions: The following practice exercises are designed to provide you with more opportunities to familiarize yourself with the content you will encounter on the ACT exam. Read each question carefully and choose the best answer. As you go through the practice set, review each solution and follow the expanded explanations provided to help strengthen your skills in working with Plane Geometry and Trigonometry topics.

ANGLES

1. The measure of angle *A* is 6 degrees less than twice the measure of angle *B*. If angles *A* and *B* are complementary, what is the measure of angle *A*?

A. 32°

B. 58°

C. 28°

D. 62°

E. 118°

The correct answer is B. Since you are given how two angles are related but do not know the measure of either one, you need to call one of them *x*. Since angle *A* is defined in terms of angle *B*, the better choice is to give the name *x* to the measure of angle *B*. Then, the measure of angle *A* is $2x - 6$.

Being complementary angles, the sum of their measures is 90°. This gives the equation $x+(2x-6)=90$. Solve for *x*, as follows:

$$x+(2x-6)=90$$
$$3x-6=90$$
$$3x=96$$
$$x=32$$

The measure of angle *A* is $2(32) - 6 = 58°$.

Choice A is the measure of angle *B*. Choice C would be the measure of angle *B* if you initially identified the measure of angle *A* as $2x$ (thereby not including the "six less than" portion of the definition). Choice D is the measure of angle *A* if you made the mistake described for choice C. Choice E is the result of assuming angles *A* and *B* are supplementary, not complementary.

2. Assume lines *l* and *m* are parallel in the diagram below. Determine the value of $y + x$.

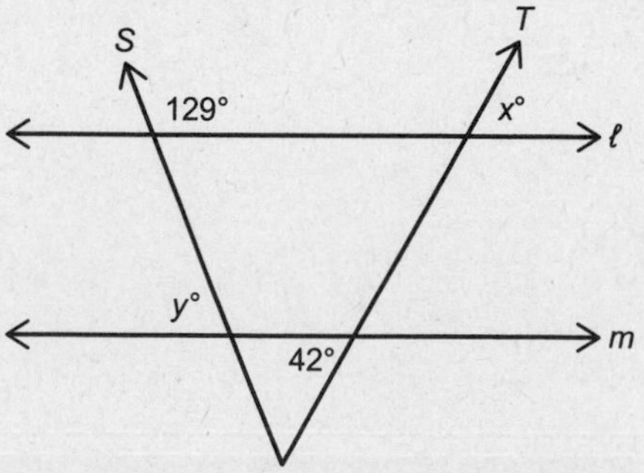

F. 42

G. 51

H. 171

J. 93

K. 189

The correct answer is J. The strategy here is to fill in a bunch of the missing angles using various facts about how corresponding angles and vertical angles are related, as well as supplementary angles. Do so in the order shown in the diagram below, starting with the circled number 1 and proceeding to circled number 4:

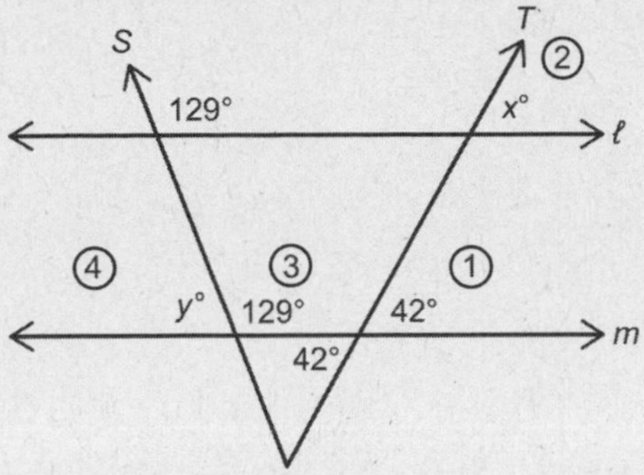

Step 1: Vertical angles are always congruent. So this angle measures 42°.

Step 2: Since lines *l* and *m* are parallel, you can use line *T* as a transversal. Then, corresponding angles are congruent, so that the angle has a measure of 42°.

Step 3: Since lines *l* and *m* are parallel, you can use line *S* as a transversal. Then, corresponding angles are congruent, so that the angle has a measure of 129°.

Step 4: This angle is supplementary to angle 3, so that it measures 180° – 129° = 51°.

Thus, $x = 42$ and $y = 51$. So $x + y = 93$.

Choice F is just the value of *x*, while choice G is just the value of *y*. Choice H is the result of incorrectly using 129 for *y* instead of 51, and choice K is the result of using 138 for *x* instead of 42.

3. If *ABC* is a straight angle in the diagram below, which of the following equations describes the relationship between *x* and *y*?

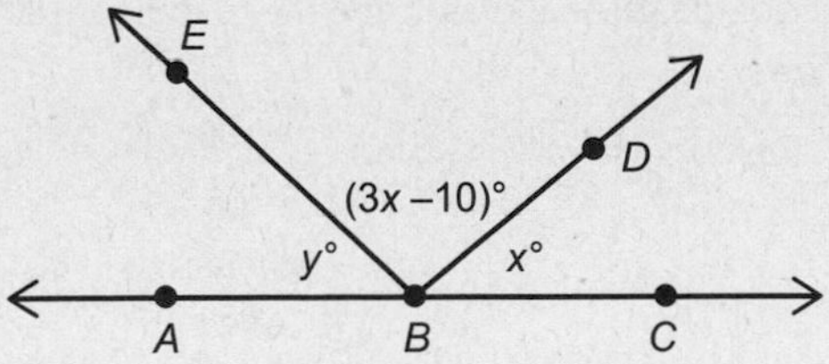

A. $x = 3y$

B. $y + 4x = 190$

C. $y = 4x - 10$

D. $y + x = 90$

E. $4x + y = 100$

The correct answer is B. Since *ABC* is a straight angle, the sum of the measures of angles *ABE*, *EBD*, and *DBC* is 180°. This gives the following equation:

$$y + (3x - 10) + x = 180$$
$$y + 4x - 10 = 180$$
$$y + 4x = 190$$

Choice E is the result of using 90 in place of 180. The other choices are the result of "eyeballing" the angles. Angle *EBD* is not assumed to be a right angle, so you should not assume that its measure is 90°. Likewise, it *looks* like x is about $3y$, but you cannot base your answer on what it looks like. You must use the definitions and assumptions provided to draw your conclusion.

TRIANGLES

1. Consider the following triangle:

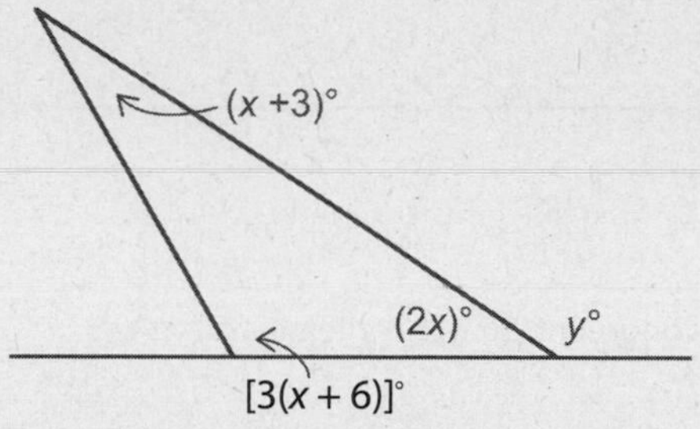

What is the value of $x + y$?

A. 29

B. 122

C. 151

D. 58

E. 180

The correct answer is C. This problem involves two main notions—the triangle sum law and the notion of supplementary angles. It also uses some algebra! This sort of crossover type problem is common on the ACT, so the less you compartmentalize what you learn in algebra, geometry, number systems, etc. and the more capable you are to cross the boundaries of these subjects, the better you will do.

To begin, the sum of the measures of the three angles inside the triangle is 180°. This leads to the equation $(x + 3) + 3(x + 1) + 2x = 180$. Solve for x as follows:

$$\begin{aligned}(x+3)+3(x+1)+2x&=180\\x+3+3x+3+2x&=180\\6x+6&=180\\6x&=174\\x&=29\end{aligned}$$

Next, you need to find y. To do so, note that the adjacent angles with measures $2x$ and y are supplementary. Since $2x = 2(29) = 58$, it follows that $y = 180 - 58 = 122$. Hence, $x + y = 29 + 122 = 151$.

Pay attention to exactly what you are being asked to provide in the problem. Choice A is just the value of x, and choice B is just the value of y. Choice D is $2x$, and choice E is $2x + y$.

2. A family builds three tree houses in the backyard and connects them with bridges, as shown:

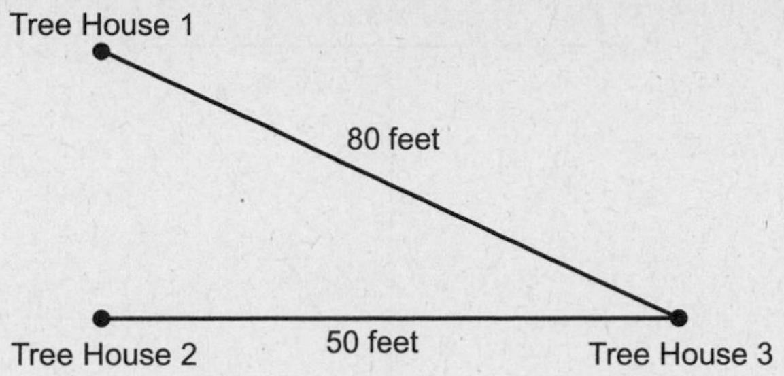

Assuming Tree House 1 is directly across from Tree House 2, which of these expressions represents the length of the bridge connecting these two tree houses?

F. $80^2 - 50^2$ feet

G. 80 – 50 feet

H. $\sqrt{50^2 + 80^2}$ feet

J. 50 + 80 feet

K. $\sqrt{80^2 - 50^2}$ feet

The correct answer is K. First, you should complete the given drawing by connecting Tree House 1 to Tree House 2; this forms a right triangle, as shown:

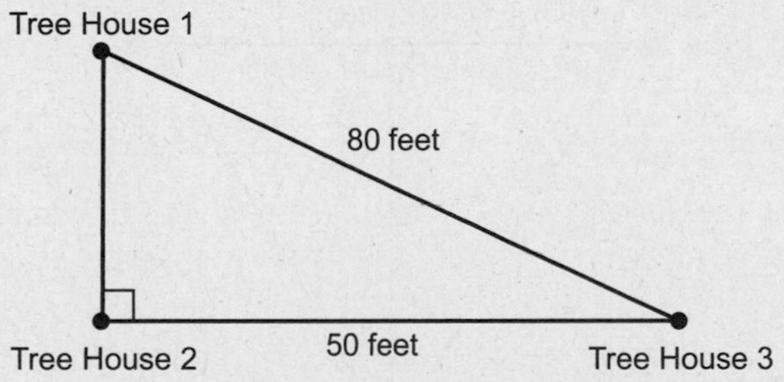

Use the Pythagorean theorem to find its length, *s*. Keep in mind that this side is a leg of the triangle, not the hypotenuse. As such, we see that $s^2 + 50^2 = 80^2$, so that $s = \sqrt{80^2 - 50^2}$ feet.

The incorrect answer choices for problems involving the Pythagorean theorem often involve misidentifying a side as a leg or hypotenuse, misusing the formula, or making an arithmetic error involving radicals. Indeed, choice F is missing the square root sign. Choice H treats the missing side as though it were the hypotenuse, not a leg. Choices G and J involve errors dealing with radicals of sums and differences; specifically, you cannot distribute a radical to the terms of a sum or difference.

3. Which of these expressions represents the height of triangle *ABC*?

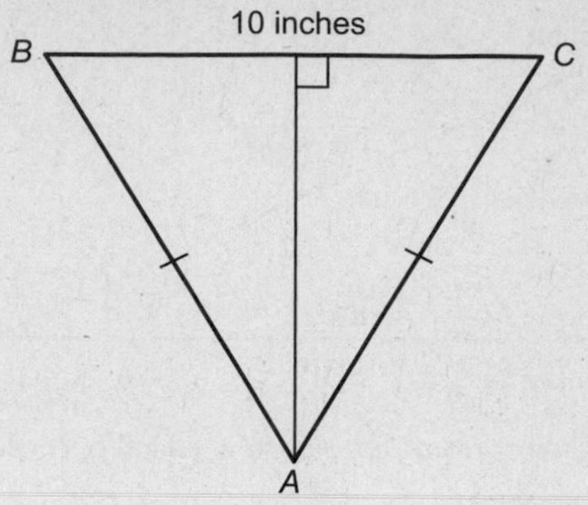

A. $\sqrt{y^2+25}$ inches

B. $\sqrt{y^2-25}$ inches

C. $y+5$ inches

D. y^2+25 inches

E. $y-5$ inches

The correct answer is B. First note that *ABC* is an isosceles triangle. As such, the bisector from vertex *A* to side *BC* must be perpendicular. So we have the following updated diagram:

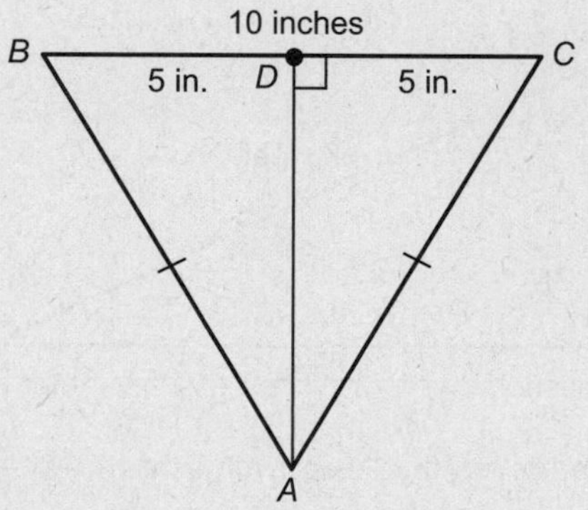

The height of triangle *ABC* is the length of segment *AD*. Use the Pythagorean theorem to find:

$$(AD)^2+5^2=y^2$$
$$(AD)^2=y^2-25$$
$$AD=\sqrt{y^2-25}$$

The nature of the distractor choices is like the previous problem. Choice A treats AC as a leg instead of the hypotenuse. Choice D is missing the radical sign. Choices E and C involve errors dealing with radicals of sums and differences; specifically, you cannot distribute a radical to the terms of a sum or difference.

QUADRILATERALS

1. Which expression represents the length of *CD* in the rectangle *ABCD*?

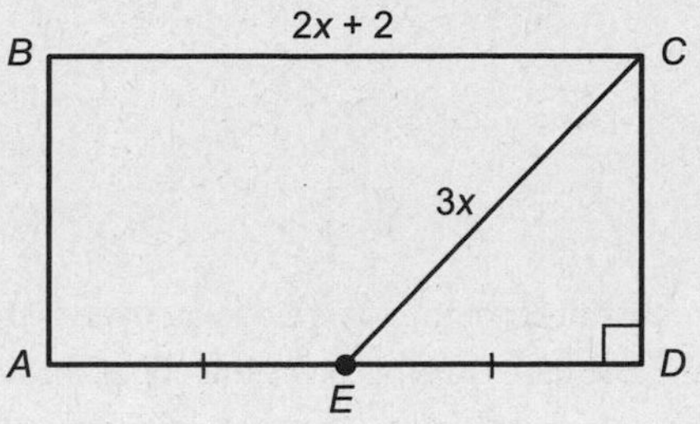

A. $2x - 1$

B. $4x + 1$

C. $8x^2 - 2x - 1$

D. $\sqrt{8x^2 - 2x - 1}$

E. $\sqrt{10x^2 + 2x + 1}$

The correct answer is D. This problem can be intimidating at first glance. But if you break it down into small steps, it is not so difficult. Here is the thought process. If you had the length of *ED*, then you could use the Pythagorean theorem to find *CD*. So can you find the length of *ED*? Well, yes!

Segments *AE* and *ED* have the same number of hash marks, which means they are congruent. Since *ABCD* is a rectangle, *AD* and *BC* are congruent. So *ED* must be half the length of *BC*, or $\frac{1}{2}(2x+2) = x+1$.

Now you can use the Pythagorean theorem to find *ED*:

$$(EC)^2 = (CD)^2 + (ED)^2$$
$$(3x)^2 = (CD)^2 + (x+1)^2$$
$$(CD)^2 = (3x)^2 - (x+1)^2$$
$$(CD)^2 = 9x^2 - (x^2 + 2x + 1)$$
$$(CD)^2 = 8x^2 - 2x - 1$$
$$CD = \sqrt{8x^2 - 2x - 1}$$

Choice A is the result of not squaring any of the sides when applying the Pythagorean theorem. Choice B is just the result of adding *EC* and *ED*. Choice C is missing the radical sign, and choice E treats *EC* as a leg of the right triangle *ECD* rather than as the hypotenuse.

2. The area of a square is 80 square inches. What is its perimeter?

F. $16\sqrt{5}$ inches

G. 400 inches

H. $4\sqrt{10}$ inches

J. $4\sqrt{5}$ inches

K. 160 inches

The correct answer is F. To find the perimeter of the square, all you need is the length of a side, *s*. You are given the area is 80 square inches. Since the area of a square is s^2, this gives the equation $s^2 = 80$. Taking the square root of both sides yields $s = \sqrt{80} = 4\sqrt{5}$ inches. So the perimeter is $4\left(4\sqrt{5}\right) = 16\sqrt{5}$ inches.

Choice G is the result of interchanging the area and perimeter formulas. Choice H is the length of the diagonal of the square, while choice J is the length of just one side. Choice K used the wrong formula for the area; the area of a square is s^2, not $2s$.

3. A rectangle has three vertices, as shown:

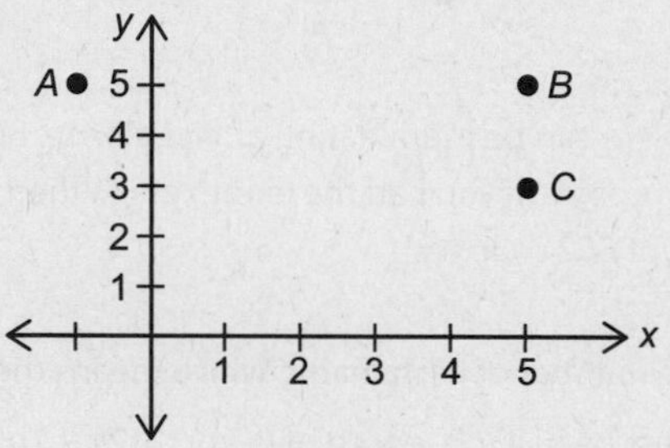

What are the coordinates of the midpoints of segment *BD*, where *D* is the missing vertex?

A. (–3, –1)

B. (2, 4)

C. (3, 1)

D. (–1, 3)

E. (4, 2)

The correct answer is B. First, you must find the coordinates of vertex *D*. This point must be chosen so that *AD* is parallel to *BC* and *AB* is parallel to *DC*. So the coordinates must be (–1, 3).

Now, find the coordinates of the midpoint of *BD*:

$$\left(\frac{-1+5}{2}, \frac{3+5}{2}\right) = (2, 4)$$

Choice D is the vertex *D*. Choice E should have the two coordinates interchanged. Choices A and C involve subtracting the coordinates of *B* and *D* rather than adding them when finding the midpoint.

1. What is the length, *S*, of the arc of the circle corresponding to the shaded sector?

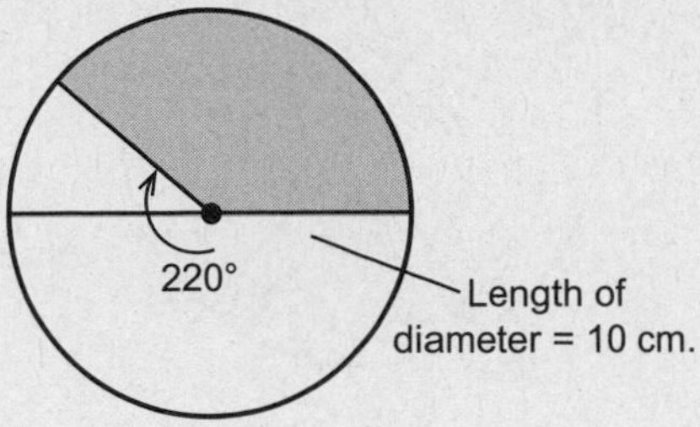

A. $S = \left(\frac{220^\circ}{180^\circ}\right)\pi(5)$ cm.

B. $S = \left(\frac{140^\circ}{180^\circ}\right)\pi(10)$ cm.

C. $S = \left(\frac{220^\circ}{180^\circ}\right)\pi(10)$ cm.

D. $S = \left(\frac{140^\circ}{180^\circ}\right)\pi(5)$ cm.

E. $S = \left(\frac{140^\circ}{360^\circ}\right)\pi(5)$ cm.

The correct answer is D. This problem is basically a "plug-in," but it requires that you know the formula and how to identify the parts. The formula is $S = \left(\frac{\theta^\circ}{180^\circ}\right)\pi(R)$, where θ is the central angle across from the arc and *R* is the radius of the circle.

$$\theta = 360^\circ - 220^\circ = 140^\circ$$

$$R = \frac{1}{2}(10 \text{ cm}) = 5 \text{ cm.}$$

Substituting these into the formula yields $S = \left(\frac{140^\circ}{180^\circ}\right)\pi(5)$ cm.

The distractor choices typically involve using the diameter instead of the radius (choices B and C), using the wrong angle (choices A and C), or making an error in the formula itself (choice E).

2. What is the area of the shaded region?

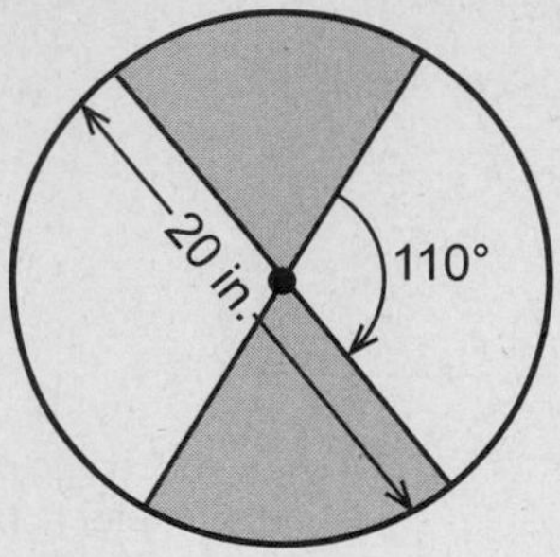

F. $200\pi\left(\frac{70°}{360°}\right)$ square inches

G. $100\pi\left(\frac{70°}{360°}\right)$ square inches

H. $100\pi\left(\frac{110°}{360°}\right)$ square inches

J. $200\pi\left(\frac{110°}{360°}\right)$ square inches

K. $200\pi\left(\frac{70°}{180°}\right)$ square inches

The correct answer is F. The region is comprised of two distinct sectors. Since their central angles are vertical angles, these angles are congruent, so the sectors have the same area. You only need to find the area of one of the sectors and then double it.

To find the area of one of these sectors, you need the radius and the central angle. Notice that the angle corresponding to one of the two congruent unshaded sectors is 110°. Since the combination of one unshaded sector and one shaded sector comprises half the circle, it follows that the central angle for a shaded sector is $180° - 110° = 70°$. Since the diameter is 20 inches, the radius is 10 inches.

The area of one shaded sector is $(10)^2\pi\left(\frac{70°}{360°}\right)$ square inches. Doubling this yields the area of the shaded region as $200\pi\left(\frac{70°}{360°}\right)$ square inches.

Choices G and H represent the area of just one of the shaded sectors. Choices H and J use the wrong angle. Choice K makes an error in the formula itself by using 180° in place of 360°.

3. The circumference of circle *A* is three times the circumference of circle *B*. What is the ratio of the area circle *B* to the area of circle *A*?

A. 1:3

B. 3:1

C. 1:9

D. 1:6

E. 9:1

The correct answer is C. Here again, this problem requires the use of knowledge from two different subjects: number systems and geometry. To begin, you must find the relationship between the radii of the two circles. Use the given information about how the circumferences are related to do so.

The circumference of circle *A* is $2\pi R_A$, and the circumference of circle *B* is $2\pi R_B$. Using the first sentence of the problem yields $2\pi R_A = 3 \bullet 2\pi R_B$. Dividing both sides by 2π shows that $R_A = 3R_B$.

To get the ratio of the areas in the above form, you must express them using multiples of a single radius. To this end, observe the following:

$$\text{Area of circle A} = \pi R_A^2 = \pi(3R_B)^2 = 9\left(\pi R_B^2\right) = 9 \bullet \text{area of circle } B$$

So the ratio of "area of circle *B*" to "area of circle *A*" is 1:9.

Choices A and B give the ratio of the radii or circumferences of the two circles, not their areas. Choice E is written in the wrong order. Choice D is the result of an arithmetic error; 3^2 does not equal 6.

Solids

1. If the surface area of a cube is 150 square inches, what is the length of the diagonal of one of its faces?

A. 5 inches

B. $\sqrt{10}$ inches

C. $2\sqrt{5}$ inches

D. $5\sqrt{2}$ inches

E. 50 inches

The correct answer is D. Think about what a cube looks like and what you are being asked to find. The diagonal of a face of a cube is the hypotenuse of a right triangle whose legs are both edges, *e*, of the cube. So it can be found using the Pythagorean theorem if you know *e*.

You must use the given information about the surface area to find *e*. The surface area of a cube with edge *e* is $6e^2$. Setting that equal to 150 and solving for *e* yields the following:

$$6e^2 = 150$$
$$e^2 = 25$$
$$e = 5$$

So a face of the cube looks like this:

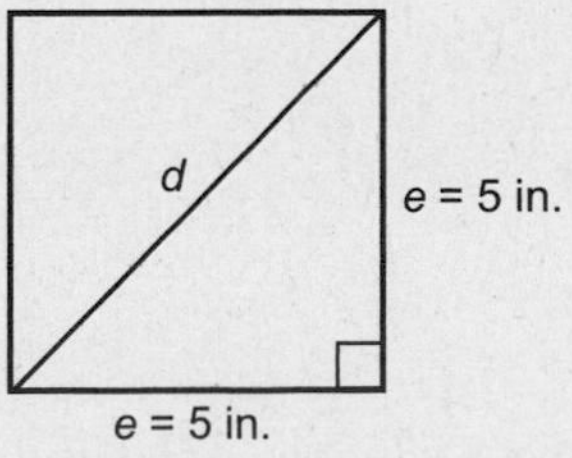

Use the Pythagorean theorem to find *d*:

$$d^2 = 5^2 + 5^2 = 50$$
$$d = \sqrt{50}$$
$$d = 5\sqrt{2}$$

Choice A is the length of an edge, not the diagonal. Choice E is the result of not taking the square root in the Pythagorean theorem, while choice B is the result of not squaring the legs or hypotenuse in the formula. Choice C is a typical simplification error arising when simplifying radicals; here, take the term that is squared outside the radical.

2. The circumference of the base of a right circular cylinder is 10π inches, and the height is 4 times the radius of the base. What is the surface area?

F. 225π square inches

G. $1,000\pi$ square inches

H. 200π square inches

J. 250π square inches

K. 500π square inches

The correct answer is J. The information provided might seem sparse at first, but take a step back and look again. All you need to find are the radius, *R*, and the height, *H*, right? Once you have the radius and the height, you can plug these numbers into the surface area formula.

Use the circumference to find *R*:

$$2\pi R = 10\pi$$
$$2R = 10$$
$$R = 5$$

Since *H* is four times the radius, we know that $H = 4(5) = 20$.

Plug the values for *R* and *H* into the surface area formula:

$$\begin{aligned} S &= 2\pi R^2 + 2\pi RH \\ &= 2\pi(5)^2 + 2\pi(5)(20) \\ &= 50\pi + 200\pi \\ &= 250\pi \end{aligned}$$

Choice F includes the area of only one of the two bases, while choice H includes neither base. Choice G uses the diameter instead of the radius. Choice K uses the volume formula.

3. The diameter of a sphere is $(6x + 2)$ centimeters, where *x* is some positive real number. What is the surface area? (Note: The surface area of a sphere with radius *r* is $4\pi r^2$.)

A. $(36x^2 + 24x + 4)\pi$ square centimeters

B. $(36x^2 + 12x + 4)\pi$ square centimeters

C. $(36x^2 + 4)\pi$ square centimeters

D. $(144x^2 + 16)\pi$ square centimeters

E. $(9x^2 + 6x + 1)\pi$ square centimeters

The correct answer is A. This problem is not hard at all. Simply find the radius, plug it into the formula, and simplify by FOILing two binomials.

The radius is half the diameter: $\frac{1}{2}(6x + 2) = 3x + 1$

So the surface area is $4\pi(3x+1)^2 = 4\pi(3x+1)(3x+1) = 4\pi\left(9x^2+6x+1\right)$, making choice A the correct answer.

Choice B is the result of not using the distributive property when multiplying $6x + 2$ by $\frac{1}{2}$. Choices C and D do not FOIL correctly; the middle term is missing. Choice D also uses the diameter instead of the radius. Choice E is missing a multiple of 4 from the formula.

Right Triangle Trigonometry

1. Let $0 < x < \frac{1}{2}$. Compute sec(B) + csc(C) for the following triangle:

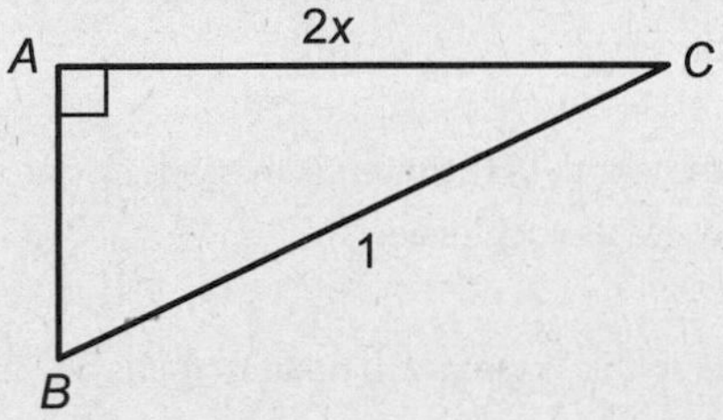

A. $\dfrac{2}{\sqrt{1-4x^2}}$

B. $\dfrac{1}{x}$

C. $\dfrac{1}{2x}+\dfrac{1}{\sqrt{1-4x^2}}$

D. $2\sqrt{1-4x^2}$

E. $2x+\sqrt{1-4x^2}$

The correct answer is A. You need all three sides of the triangle to compute these quantities. Use the Pythagorean theorem to find the missing side:

$$(AB)^2+(AC)^2=(BC)^2$$
$$(AB)^2+(2x)^2=1$$
$$(AB)^2=1-4x^2$$
$$AB=\sqrt{1-4x^2}$$

Now, compute the two quantities in the given expression.

$$\sec B=\frac{1}{\cos B}=\frac{BC}{AB}=\frac{1}{\sqrt{1-4x^2}}$$
$$\csc C=\frac{1}{\sin C}=\frac{BC}{AB}=\frac{1}{\sqrt{1-4x^2}}$$

Then, add the two quantities:

$$\sec B+\csc C=\frac{2}{\sqrt{1-4x^2}}$$

Choice B is the result of interchanging the angles; it equals sec(C) + csc(B). Choice C uses angle B for both expressions. Choice D is cos(B) + sin(C), while choice E is cos(B) + sin(B).

2. What is the minimum value that the graph of $g(x)=\frac{1}{2}\sin(4x)$ achieves?

F. $-\frac{1}{2}$

G. -4

H. -1

J. 0

K. $\frac{1}{2}$

The correct answer is F. Solving this type of problem is simply a matter of knowing the graph of the sine function and how the constants *A* and *B* impact the graph of $y = A\sin(Bx)$.

The value of *B* affects the *period*, or the length of the interval over which one complete cycle of the sine wave is graphed. In particular, this does not affect the *y*-values achieved.

The value of *A* affects the amplitude, so this is what you need to focus on. The low point of the basic sine graph is –1. If you multiply that by $\frac{1}{2}$, the new low point would become $-\frac{1}{2}$.

Choice G uses the wrong number when assessing the amplitude. Choice H is the minimum of the basic sine graph but does not account for the change in amplitude present in *g*(*x*). Choice J ignores the part of the sine graph that extends below the *x*-axis. Choice K is the maximum value achieved.

3. What is the radian measure of the central angle of the shaded sector?

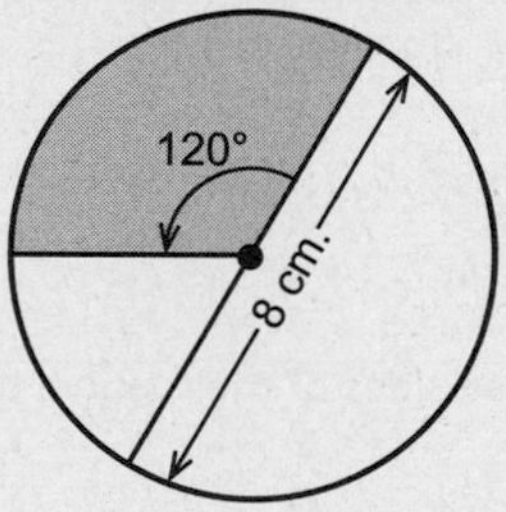

A. $\frac{\pi}{3}$

B. $\frac{5\pi}{6}$

C. $\frac{2\pi}{3}$

D. $\frac{3\pi}{4}$

E. $\frac{3\pi}{4}$

The correct answer is C. The central angle of the shaded sector is 120 degrees. You want the angle units in radians. To convert the degree measure to radians, simply multiply 120 by $\frac{\pi}{180}$ which equals $\frac{2\pi}{3}$. Multiplying by $\frac{\pi}{360}$ would result in choice A. A variety of formula errors would cause choices B, D, or E.

1. Which of the following statements is true for all angles θ?

A. $\sin(-\theta) = \sin(\theta)$

B. $2\sin(\theta) = \sin(2\theta)$

C. $\sin(\pi + \theta) = \sin(\theta)$

D. $\cos\left(\frac{5\pi}{2} - \theta\right) = \sin(\theta)$

E. $\cos(\theta) + \sin(\theta) = 1$

The correct answer is D. Solving this problem is simply a matter of knowing the identities. Choice D is always true because $\cos\left(\frac{5\pi}{2} - \theta\right) = \cos\left(2\pi + \frac{\pi}{2} - \theta\right) = \cos\left(\frac{\pi}{2} - \theta\right) = \sin(\theta)$.

Choice A is missing a multiple of –1 on the right-side, so it is not true. Choice B is missing a multiple of $\cos(\theta)$ on the left-side. You cannot simply factor out a 2 from the input of a trigonometric function like this, so it is not true. Choice C should have a 2π instead of π, so it is not true. Choice E is missing the squares on both terms on the left-side, so it is not true.

In the event you cannot remember all your identities, simply choose an angle/theta (such as $\frac{\pi}{4}$) that you know the sin and cos values of. If you substitute and evaluate into each equation in the choices provided, only one will be true!

2. Suppose $\sin\theta = -\frac{2}{3}$ and that the terminal side of θ intersects the unit circle in Quadrant IV. Compute $\sec\theta$.

F. $\frac{\sqrt{5}}{3}$

G. $-\frac{3}{2}$

H. $\frac{5}{9}$

J. $\frac{3\sqrt{5}}{5}$

K. $-\frac{3\sqrt{5}}{5}$

The correct answer is J. Since $\sec\theta = \frac{1}{\cos\theta}$, you need to find $\cos\theta$ using the given information.

Use the identity $\sin^2\theta + \cos^2\theta = 1$ as follows:

$$\sin^2\theta + \cos^2\theta = 1$$
$$\left(-\frac{2}{3}\right)^2 + \cos^2\theta = 1$$
$$\frac{4}{9} + \cos^2\theta = 1$$
$$\cos^2\theta = \frac{5}{9}$$
$$\cos\theta = \pm\sqrt{\frac{5}{9}} = \pm\frac{\sqrt{5}}{3}$$

In Quadrant IV, the cosine is positive. So use $\cos\theta = \frac{\sqrt{5}}{3}$.

Thus, $\sec\theta = \dfrac{1}{\frac{\sqrt{5}}{3}} = \dfrac{3}{\sqrt{5}} = \dfrac{3\sqrt{5}}{5}$

Choice F is the value of $\cos\theta$, while choice H is its square. Choice G is the value of $\csc\theta$. Choice K used the wrong sign; this value would be in Quadrant III, not IV.

3. Compute $\csc(2\theta)$ for the following triangle:

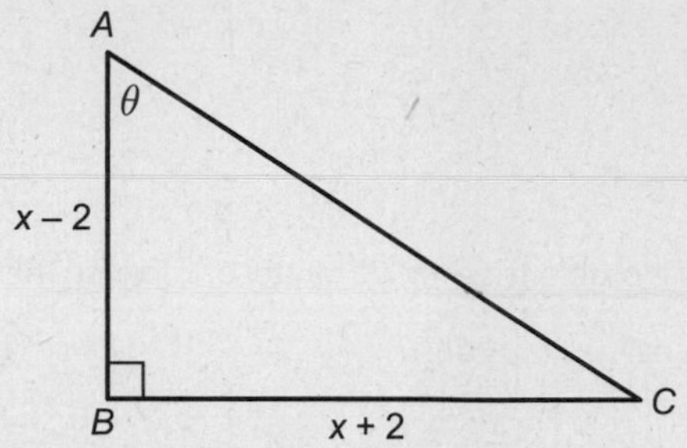

A. -1

B. $\dfrac{2x^2+8}{2x^2-8}$

C. $\dfrac{2\sqrt{x^2+8}}{x+2}$

D. $\dfrac{2x}{x^2-4}$

E. $\dfrac{1}{2x^2-8}$

The correct answer is B. First, write the given expression in terms of $\sin\theta$ and $\cos\theta$:

$$\csc(2\theta) = \frac{1}{\sin(2\theta)} = \frac{1}{2\sin\theta\cos\theta}$$

To compute $\sin\theta$ and $\cos\theta$, you need the hypotenuse of *ABC*. Use the Pythagorean theorem to find it:

$$\begin{aligned}(x-2)^2+(x+2)^2 &= (AC)^2\\ x^2-4x+4+x^2+4x+4 &= (AC)^2\\ 2x^2+8 &= (AC)^2\\ \sqrt{2x^2+8} &= AC\end{aligned}$$

Hence:

$$\sin\theta = \frac{x+2}{\sqrt{2x^2+8}}$$
$$\cos\theta = \frac{x-2}{\sqrt{2x^2+8}}$$

So:

$$\csc(2\theta) = \frac{1}{2\sin\theta\cos\theta}$$
$$= \frac{1}{2} \bullet \frac{1}{\sin\theta} \bullet \frac{1}{\cos\theta}$$
$$= \frac{1}{2} \bullet \frac{\sqrt{2x^2+8}}{x+2} \bullet \frac{\sqrt{2x^2+8}}{x-2}$$
$$= \frac{\left(\sqrt{2x^2+8}\right)^2}{2(x+2)(x-2)}$$
$$= \frac{2x^2+8}{2(x^2-4)}$$
$$= \frac{2x^2+8}{2x^2-8}$$

Choice A is the result of bad cancelation of terms in the last step above; you cannot cancel the $2x^2$s and 8s in the top and bottom! Choice C is the result of saying $\csc(2\theta) = 2\csc(\theta)$. Choice D is what you get If you do not square the legs when using the Pythagorean theorem. And choice E is a result of computing the hypotenuse incorrectly; it is not 1.

Solving Trigonometric Equations

1. Which of the following is the set of all values of θ in the interval $[0, 2\pi]$ for which $\sin^2\theta - \frac{3}{4} = 0$?

A. $\left\{\frac{\pi}{4}, \frac{3\pi}{4}\right\}$

B. $\left\{\frac{\pi}{3}, \frac{2\pi}{3}\right\}$

C. $\left\{\frac{\pi}{6}, \frac{5\pi}{6}\right\}$

D. $\left\{\frac{\pi}{6}, \frac{5\pi}{6}, \frac{7\pi}{6}, \frac{11\pi}{6}\right\}$

E. $\left\{\frac{\pi}{3}, \frac{2\pi}{3}, \frac{4\pi}{3}, \frac{5\pi}{3}\right\}$

The correct answer is E. First, isolate $\sin\theta$ on one side of the equation:

$$\sin^2\theta - \frac{3}{4} = 0$$
$$\sin^2\theta = \frac{3}{4}$$
$$\sin\theta = \pm\sqrt{\frac{3}{4}}$$
$$\sin\theta = \pm\frac{\sqrt{3}}{2}$$

Now, use the known values of $\sin\theta$ to conclude that the solution set is $\left\{\frac{\pi}{3}, \frac{2\pi}{3}, \frac{4\pi}{3}, \frac{5\pi}{3}\right\}$.

Choice B is the result of not putting "$\pm$" when taking the square root of both sides. The other choices simply identify the wrong values of θ.

2. Which of the following is the set of all values of θ in the interval $[0,2\pi]$ for which $\cos\theta = 2\sin\theta\cos\theta$?

F. $\left\{\frac{\pi}{3}, \frac{2\pi}{3}\right\}$

G. $\left\{\frac{\pi}{6}, \frac{5\pi}{6}\right\}$

H. $\left\{0, \frac{\pi}{6}, \frac{5\pi}{6}, \pi, 2\pi\right\}$

J. $\left\{\frac{\pi}{3}, \frac{\pi}{2}, \frac{2\pi}{3}, \frac{3\pi}{2}\right\}$

K. $\left\{\frac{\pi}{6}, \frac{\pi}{2}, \frac{5\pi}{6}, \frac{3\pi}{2}\right\}$

The correct answer is K. First off, do NOT divide both sides by $\cos\theta$! If you do, you will lose the solutions of the equation corresponding to that factor, as in choices F and G. (Think back to your study of algebra—you were told the same thing when asked to solve an equation like $x = 2x(x - 3)$.)

Move all terms to the left-side of the equation, factor out $\cos\theta$, and then set each factor equal to zero.

$$\begin{aligned} \cos\theta &= 2\sin\theta\cos\theta \\ \cos\theta - 2\sin\theta\cos\theta &= 0 \\ \cos\theta(1-2\sin\theta) &= 0 \\ \cos\theta = 0 \quad &\text{or} \quad 1-2\sin\theta = 0 \end{aligned}$$

Note that $\cos\theta = 0$ when $\theta = \frac{\pi}{2}, \frac{3\pi}{2}$ and $1-2\sin\theta = 0$ when $\theta = \frac{\pi}{6}, \frac{5\pi}{6}$. So choice K is the correct answer.

Choices H and J simply identify the wrong values of θ.

3. Which of the following is the set of all values of θ in the interval $[0,2\pi]$ for which $\cot\theta = -1$?

A. $\left\{\frac{\pi}{4}, \frac{5\pi}{4}\right\}$

B. $\left\{\frac{\pi}{2}, \frac{3\pi}{2}\right\}$

C. $\left\{\frac{3\pi}{4}, \frac{7\pi}{4}\right\}$

D. $\left\{\frac{\pi}{4}, \frac{3\pi}{4}, \frac{5\pi}{4}, \frac{7\pi}{4}\right\}$

E. $\{0, \pi, 2\pi\}$

The correct answer is C. Write the equation in terms of $\sin\theta$ and $\cos\theta$:

$$\begin{aligned} \cot\theta &= -1 \\ \frac{\cos\theta}{\sin\theta} &= -1 \\ \cos\theta &= -\sin\theta \end{aligned}$$

The only values of θ for which this is true are $\frac{3\pi}{4}, \frac{7\pi}{4}$.

Choice A is the set of values where $\cot\theta = 1$, while choice B is where it equals 0. Choice D includes the values that make $\cot\theta = 1$ as well. Choice E is the set where $\cot\theta$ is undefined.

PRACTICE

It's time for your final mathematics practice quiz. When you're finished answering all 20 questions, check the answers and explanations that follow to figure out how well you did and why you may have selected some incorrect answer choices.

SHOW YOUR WORK HERE

1. In the figure shown, what is the value of x?

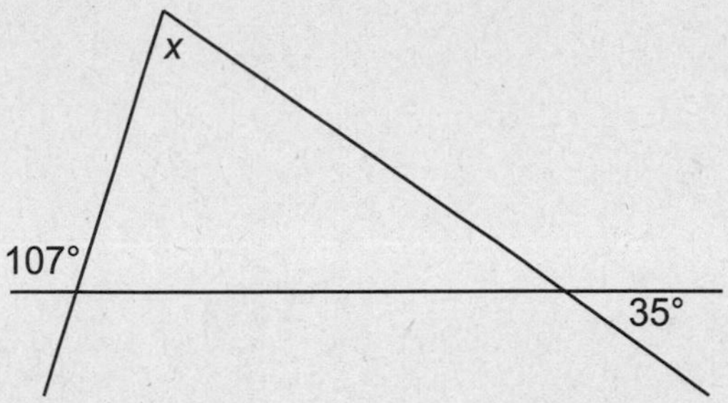

A. 35°
B. 38°
C. 72°
D. 107°
E. 145°

2. Angle Q measures $(180 - x)$ degrees. If angle Q is a positive acute angle, which of the following is true of x?

F. $0 < x < 60$
G. $0 < x < 90$
H. $90 < x < 180$
J. $180 < x < 270$
K. $200 < x < 250$

3. Which of the following sets of triangle side lengths represents a right triangle?

A. 1, 2, 5
B. 2, 3, 4
C. 4, 5, 21
D. 5, 12, 13
E. 6, 9, 11

4. In triangle RST, if $RS = RT = TS$, then which of the following statements is FALSE?

F. All three angles must be acute.
G. The triangle can be a right triangle.
H. There is no obtuse angle.
J. The sum of any two angles in the triangle exceeds 90 degrees.
K. The sides cannot satisfy the Pythagorean theorem.

5. In the following figure, *ABDC* is a square. What is the area of triangle *AFE*?

SHOW YOUR WORK HERE

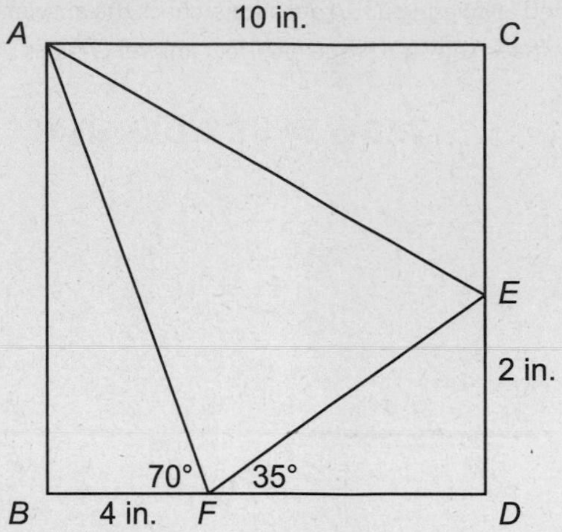

A. 20 square inches
B. 34 square inches
C. 40 square inches
D. 60 square inches
E. 66 square inches

6. In the figure below, triangles *ACB* and *FED* are similar. What is the length of segment *DE*?

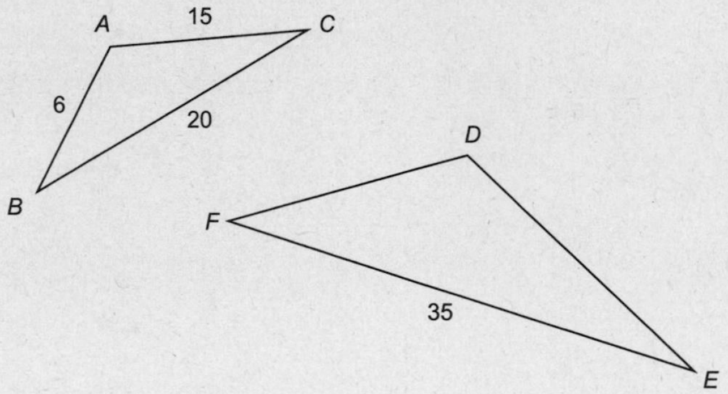

F. 10

G. 21

H. 30

J. $\frac{60}{7}$

K. $\frac{140}{3}$

7. What is the area of an equilateral triangle with a perimeter of 30 feet?

A. $\frac{25}{2}\sqrt{3}$ square feet

B. $100\sqrt{3}$ square feet

C. 10 square feet

D. $50\sqrt{3}$ square feet

E. $25\sqrt{3}$ square feet

8. If the area of triangle *YVZ* is 6 square centimeters and the length of segment *XV* is 12 centimeters, what is the perimeter of parallelogram *WXYZ*?

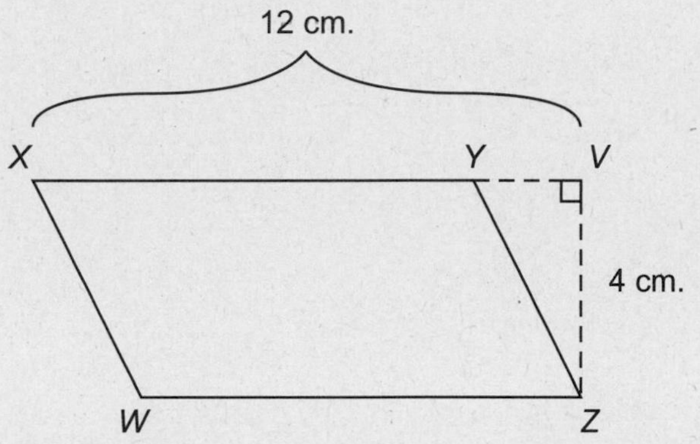

F. 10 centimeters
G. 18 centimeters
H. 24 centimeters
J. 26 centimeters
K. 28 centimeters

9. The length of a narrow rectangular room is 11 yards more than three times its width. If the area of the room is 4 square yards, how many yards long is the room?

A. $\frac{1}{3}$

B. 1

C. 12

D. $24\frac{2}{3}$

E. 36

SHOW YOUR WORK HERE

10. In the given parallelogram, what is the measure of angle *CAB*?

SHOW YOUR WORK HERE

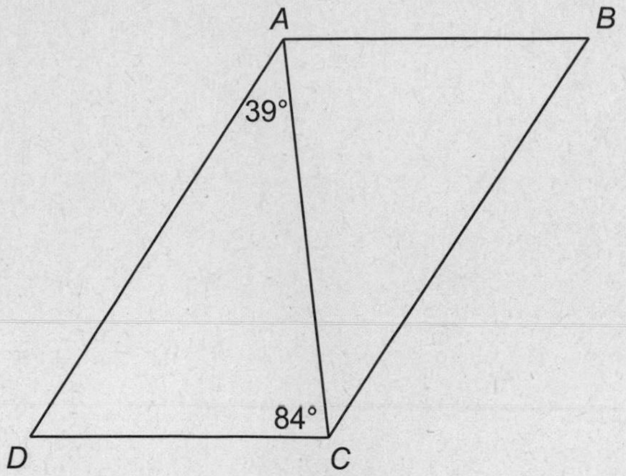

F. 39°
G. 57°
H. 123°
J. 100°
K. 84°

11. In the given figure, a circle is inscribed within a square. If the perimeter of the square is 80 inches, what is the area of the shaded region in square inches?

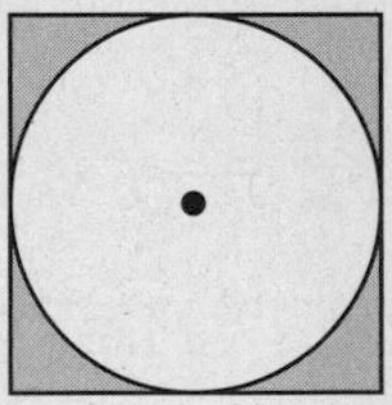

A. $400 - 10\pi$
B. $400 + 100\pi$
C. $80 + 20\pi$
D. $80 - 20\pi$
E. $400 - 100\pi$

12. Points *X*, *W*, and *Y* lie on the circle with center *O*. If the unshaded sectors *XOW* and *XOY* comprise $\frac{1}{10}$ and $\frac{3}{5}$ of the area of the entire circle, respectively, what is the measure of angle *WOY*?

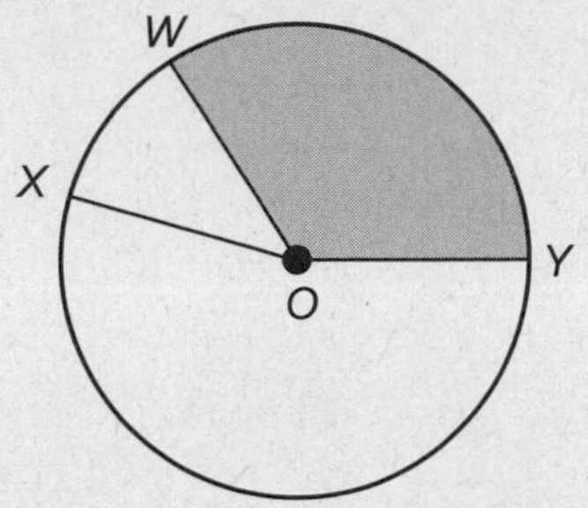

F. 54°
G. 36°
H. 90°
J. 108°
K. 252°

13. What is the surface area of the following solid?

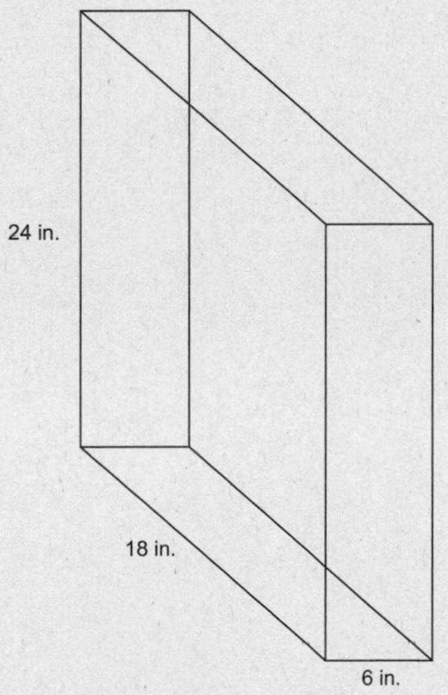

A. 342 square inches
B. 684 square inches
C. 1,368 square inches
D. 2,052 square inches
E. 2,592 square inches

SHOW YOUR WORK HERE

14. A cube has side length *s*. A new cube is formed whose sides are twice as long as the original cube. Which of the following statements is true?

F. The volume of the new cube is twice the volume of the original cube.

G. The volume of the new cube is four times the volume of the original cube.

H. The volume of the new cube is one-half the volume of the original cube.

J. The volume of the new cube is eight times the volume of the original cube.

K. The volume of the new cube is six times the volume of the original cube.

SHOW YOUR WORK HERE

15. Using the following triangle, what is the value of *x*?

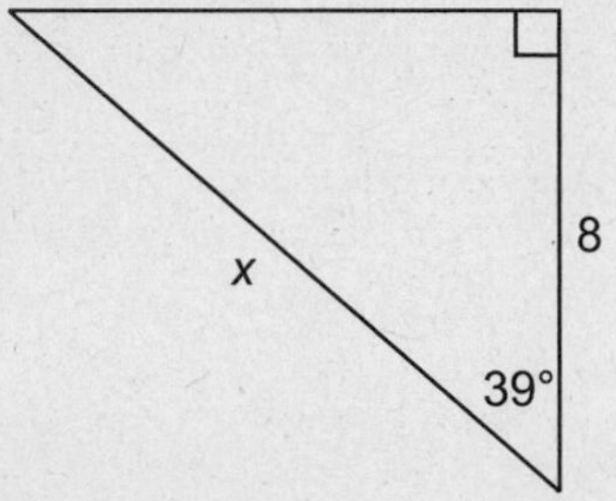

A. $\frac{8}{\cos 39°}$

B. $\frac{8}{\sin 39°}$

C. $\frac{\cos 39°}{8}$

D. $8 \sin 39°$

E. $8 \cos 39°$

16. The ratio of the side lengths of a right triangle is $1:\sqrt{3}:2$. What is the cosine of the largest non-right angle in this triangle?

F. 0

G. $\frac{1}{2}$

H. $\sqrt{3}$

J. $\frac{\sqrt{3}}{2}$

K. 2

17. For $0° < \theta < 90°$, if $\cos\theta = \frac{5}{7}$ then $\cot\theta =$

SHOW YOUR WORK HERE

A. $\frac{5}{24}$

B. $\frac{5\sqrt{6}}{12}$

C. $\frac{2\sqrt{6}}{7}$

D. $\frac{7}{5}$

E. $2\sqrt{6}$

18. Consider rectangle *ABCD* below. What is $\sin\theta$?

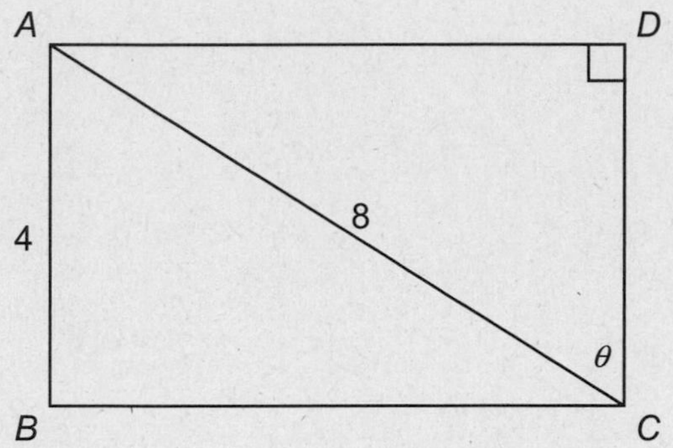

F. $\frac{\sqrt{3}}{2}$

G. 1

H. $\frac{1}{2}$

J. $4\sqrt{3}$

K. $\frac{\sqrt{2}}{2}$

19. What is the period of the graph of $y = 5\cos\frac{x}{2}$?

A. $\frac{\pi}{2}$

B. π

C. $\frac{3\pi}{2}$

D. 2π

E. 4π

20. What is the smallest positive value of x for which $\sin 3x = 0$?

F. 0

G. $\frac{\pi}{6}$

H. $\frac{\pi}{3}$

J. π

K. $\frac{2\pi}{3}$

SHOW YOUR WORK HERE

Answers and Explanations

1. **The correct answer is C.** Use the Triangle Sum Rule to determine x. To do this, you need the values of the other two angles in the triangle. First, the vertical angle to the one marked 35° also has a measure of 35° since vertical angles are congruent. Then, the angle adjacent to the one marked 107° has a measure of 73° because those two angles are supplementary. Therefore, the sum of x, 35°, and 73° is 180°. So solving for x yields:

$$\begin{aligned} x+35^\circ+73^\circ &= 180^\circ \\ x+108^\circ &= 180^\circ \\ x &= 72^\circ \end{aligned}$$

Choice A is the measure of the base angle that is vertical to the one with the same measure, but it does not equal x. In choice B, you mistakenly used 107° as one of the angles in the triangle. Choice D is incorrect because angles on opposite sides of this leg of the triangle are not congruent—they are not alternate interior angles formed by cutting two parallel lines with a transversal. Choice E is the supplementary angle to the one marked 35°, but it is not equal to x.

2. **The correct answer is H.** An acute angle is, by definition, one that measures between 0° and 90°. In order for angle Q to satisfy this definition, its measure of $(180 - x)$ degrees must be between 0 and 90. Algebraically, $0 < 180 - x < 90$. Solving the inequality for x:

$$-180 < -x < -90, \text{ so that } 90 < x < 180$$

Therefore, choice H is correct.

Choices F and G are incorrect because Q would be obtuse. Choices J and K are incorrect because they would make Q acute, but negative.

3. **The correct answer is D.** The sides of any right triangle are related by the Pythagorean theorem, which states that the sum of the squares of the legs is equal to the square of the hypotenuse. This is often written as $a^2 + b^2 + c^2$, where a and b are the legs and c is the hypotenuse (the longest of the three sides). Test each set of sides to see which satisfies the Pythagorean theorem and is therefore a right triangle. In choice D, $\underbrace{5^2+12^2}_{=169}=\underbrace{13^2}_{=169}$. For all other choices, this relationship does not hold.

4. **The correct answer is G.** In any triangle, the angles opposite equal sides are equal to each other. Since all three sides are congruent, it follows that all three angles are congruent. Since the sum of the three angles of a triangle must be 180°, the measure of each angle is 60°. As such, it is not possible for the triangle to be a right triangle.

Choice F cannot be correct because all angles in such a triangle measure 60°, and so they are all acute. Choice H also cannot be correct because all the angles are acute (and measure 60°), so none of them is obtuse. Choice J cannot be correct since the sum of any two angles in such a triangle is 120°. Choice K cannot be correct because only *right* triangles satisfy the Pythagorean theorem, and such a triangle cannot be right because all the angles are acute (and measure 60 degrees).

5. **The correct answer is B.** The strategy is to find the areas of the other three right triangles inside square *ABCD* and then subtract their sum from the area of the square. To do so, you must identify the height and base of each triangle. Since all sides of the square have a length of 10 inches, these are the lengths of other segments:

$CE = 8$ inches, $FD = 6$ inches, $AB = 10$ inches

Using the area formula $A=\frac{1}{2}bh$, where b is the base and h is the height of a triangle, you can calculate the areas:

- Area of triangle $ABF = \frac{1}{2}$(10 in.)(4 in.) = 20 sq. in.
- Area of triangle $EDF = \frac{1}{2}$(6 in.)(2 in.) = 6 sq. in.
- Area of triangle $ACE = \frac{1}{2}$(10 in.)(8 in.) = 40 sq. in.

The area of the square *ABCD* is (10 in.)(10 in.) = 100 sq. in. So the area of triangle *AFE* is $100 - (20 + 6 + 40) = 100 - 66 = 34$ square inches.

Choice A is the area of triangle *ABF*. Choice C is the area of triangle *ACE*. Choice D is the sum of the areas of triangles *ABF* and *ACE*. Choice E is the area of the region inside the square but *outside* triangle *AFE*.

6. **The correct answer is K.** Since the two triangles are similar, the corresponding sides are in proportion: $\frac{AB}{FD}=\frac{AC}{FE}=\frac{BC}{DE}$. Using the second equality, solve for *DE*, as follows:

$$\begin{aligned}\frac{15}{35}&=\frac{20}{DE}\\ 15DE&=20(35)\\ DE&=\frac{20(35)}{15}=\frac{4(35)}{3}=\frac{140}{3}\end{aligned}$$

Choice F is incorrect; since triangle *FED* is larger than triangle *ACB*, the length of its side cannot be less than the length of the corresponding side of *ACB*. In choices G and H, you don't simply subtract the same amount from the length of one side to get another when dealing with similar triangles. Rather, the side lengths are in proportion. In choice J, you set up the proportion incorrectly—one of your fractions needs to be flipped.

7. **The correct answer is E.** All sides of an equilateral triangle have the same length, so an equilateral triangle with a perimeter of 30 feet must have sides with a length of 10 feet. This means that the base of the triangle is 10 feet, and the height is the line that divides the equilateral triangle into two 30-60-90 triangles. Since each of these 30-60-90 triangles has a shorter leg of 5 feet (half the base) and a hypotenuse of 10, the longer leg *h* (the height) must satisfy the Pythagorean theorem: $h^2 + 5^2 = 10^2$ so that $h^2 = 75$; so $h = \sqrt{75} = 5\sqrt{3}$ feet.

Now, substitute these numbers into the area formula:

$$\frac{1}{2}bh=\frac{1}{2}(10)(5\sqrt{3})=25\sqrt{3}\text{ square feet}$$

Choice A is incorrect because the height of the triangle is not 5 feet. In choice B, you multiplied by 2 instead of $\frac{1}{2}$ in the area formula for a triangle. Choice C is incorrect because you cannot use two sides in the area formula since they are not perpendicular to each other and so cannot play the role of the height. In choice D, you forgot to divide by 2; remember that the area of a triangle is $\frac{1}{2}$ times the base times the height.

8. **The correct answer is K.** Since the area of triangle *YVZ* is 6 square centimeters and its height, segment *VZ*, has a length of 4 centimeters, the base, segment *YV*, must have a length of 3 centimeters. As such, using the Pythagorean theorem, segment *YZ* must have a length of 5 centimeters. Given that *XV* has length 12 centimeters, it follows that *XY* has a length of 9 centimeters. As such, since opposite sides of a parallelogram have the same length, it follows that the perimeter is (9 + 9 + 5 + 5) centimeters = 28 centimeters.

In choice F, you only added the lengths of the two shorter sides. In choice G, you only added the lengths of the two longer sides. Choice H is twice the length of *x*, not the perimeter. In choice J, you mistakenly used *VZ* as a side of the parallelogram—you should have used *YZ*.

9. **The correct answer is C.** Start by letting *w* represent the width, and then translate to find the length. "11 yards more than 3 times the width" is the same as $3w + 11$. You're given that the area is 4 square yards, and you have a specific length and width. Substitute them all into the area formula to solve for *w*:

$$\begin{aligned}w(3w+11)&=4\\ 3w^2+11w-4&=0\\ (3w-1)(w+4)&=0\\ w&=\frac{1}{3},\ \cancel{-4}\end{aligned}$$

Solving for *w* yields two possibilities: –4 and $\frac{1}{3}$. However, the width of a rectangle cannot be negative, so *w* must be equal to $\frac{1}{3}$. Thus, the length is $3\times\frac{1}{3}+11=12$ yards.

Choice A is the width of the room. Choice B is the width of the room in feet. Choice D is the perimeter of the room. Choice E is the length of the room in feet, not yards.

10. **The correct answer is K.** Opposite sides of a parallelogram are parallel. This means that $\overline{AD}\parallel\overline{DC}$, and $\overline{AC}$ is a transversal. Alternate interior angles formed by such a transversal are congruent. Therefore, m$\angle CAB = 84°$.

Choice F is the measure of angle *ACB*. Choice G is the measure of angle *ADC*. Choice H is the measure of angle *BCD*. Choice J cannot be correct since alternate interior angles formed by such a transversal are congruent.

11. **The correct answer is E.** The area of the shaded region is the difference between the area of the square and the area of the circle. The perimeter of the square is 80 inches, so each of its sides is $80 \div 4 = 20$ inches. If you draw a diameter through the center of the circle, you will see that it is congruent to a side of the square, so the diameter of the circle is also 20 inches.

Now, find the areas of the large square and the circle. The area of a square is equal to s^2, so the area of this square is $20^2 = 400$ square inches. The area of a circle is equal to πr^2. Since the diameter of the circle is 20 inches, its radius is 10 inches, making its area $\pi(10)^2 = 100\pi$ square inches. Therefore, the area of the shaded region is $400 - 100\pi$ square inches.

In choice A, you forgot to square the radius when computing the area of the circle. Choice B is incorrect because you should be subtracting the area of the circle from the area of the square. Choice C is the sum of the perimeters of the square and circle, not the differences in their areas. In choice D, you subtracted the perimeters of the square and circle, not their areas.

12. **The correct answer is J.** The unshaded sectors *XOW* and *XOY* comprise a total of $\frac{1}{10}+\frac{3}{5}=\frac{7}{10}$ of the circle. This means that the shaded region, sector *WOY*, takes up the remaining $\frac{3}{10}$ of the circle. A circle has 360 total degrees, so set up a proportion to find the measure of angle *WOY*:

$$\frac{3}{10}=\frac{m\angle WOY}{360°}$$
$$10(m\angle WOY)=1080°$$
$$m\angle WOY=108°$$

Choice F is incorrect because a circle has 360 degrees, not 180. Choice G is the measure of the angle *WOX*. Choice H is incorrect because you can't eyeball the sector. Choice K is the measure of 360 – *WOY*, not just *AOC*.

13. **The correct answer is C.** The surface area of a rectangular box is the sum of the areas of the six rectangular faces. The dimensions of the faces are as follows:

24 in. × 18 in.
24 in. × 6 in.
6 in. × 18 in.

There are two faces with each set of dimensions. So find the area of each face, multiply it by 2, and add them:

$$2[24(18) + 24(6) + 6(18)] = 1{,}368 \text{ square inches}$$

In choice A, you took half the area of each face instead of multiplying the areas by 2. Choice B is half the surface area—you must double the area of each face. In choice D, you multiplied the area of each face by 3, not 2. Choice E is the volume, not the surface area.

14. **The correct answer is J.** We need to determine expressions for both cubes and then compare them. The volume of the original cube is $V_{original} = s^3$. The length of a side of the new cube is 2*s*. So the volume of the new cube is $V_{new} = (2s)^3 = 8s^3$. Comparing the two formulas, we see that the volume of the new cube is eight times the volume of the original cube.

Choice F is incorrect because *each* side is doubled, and so the volume increases by a factor larger than 2. Choice G is incorrect because this would be the amount by which the surface area increases, not the volume. Choice H is incorrect because the new cube is larger than the original cube, and so it cannot have a smaller volume than the original cube. Choice K is incorrect because $2^3 = 8$, not 6.

15. **The correct answer is A.** You have the side adjacent to the 39° angle, as well as the hypotenuse. Choose the trig function that uses both of these sides of a right triangle. Note that $\cos 39° = \frac{8}{x}$. If we solve for *x*, we obtain:

$$\cos 39° = \frac{8}{x}$$
$$x\cos 39° = 8$$
$$x = \frac{8}{\cos 39°}$$

In choices B and D, using sin 39° would require you to have the side opposite the 39° angle, which you do not have. Choice C is the reciprocal of the correct answer. In choice E, you should be dividing 8 by cos 39°, not multiplying by it.

16. **The correct answer is G.** Since the sides are in the proportion $1:\sqrt{3}:2$, you can use those as the actual side lengths or any constant multiple of them. For simplicity, assume that the actual lengths are 1, $\sqrt{3}$, and 2. The largest non-right angle in a triangle is opposite the larger of the two legs, so in this triangle, it would be opposite the side of length $\sqrt{3}$. In relation to this angle, the adjacent would be 1 and the hypotenuse would be 2.

Since cosine $= \frac{\text{adjacent}}{\text{hypotenuse}}$, the cosine of this angle would be $\frac{1}{2}$.

Choice F is the cosine of the largest angle—but the largest angle is the right angle, which is not what was asked for. Choice H is the length of the longer of the two legs, not the cosine of the angle across from it. Choice J is cos(30), which is of the smaller of the two non-right angles. Choice K is the reciprocal of the correct answer.

17. **The correct answer is B.** Since $\cos\theta = \frac{5}{7}$, create a right triangle with an adjacent side of 5 and a hypotenuse of 7. Solve for the opposite leg using the Pythagorean theorem:

$$\begin{aligned} 5^2 + b^2 &= 7^2 \\ b^2 &= 49 - 25 \\ b &= \sqrt{24} \\ &= 2\sqrt{6} \end{aligned}$$

Therefore, cot θ is equal to $\frac{1}{\tan\theta} = \frac{\text{adjacent side to } \theta}{\text{opposite side to } \theta'}$ which equals $\frac{5\sqrt{6}}{12}$.

In choice A, you forgot that when using the Pythagorean theorem, you must square both legs and the hypotenuse. Choice C is sine of θ. Choice D is secant of θ. Choice E is the length of the side opposite of θ.

18. **The correct answer is F.** Since opposite sides of a rectangle are congruent, *CD* has length of 4 units. However, you need *AD* and are not given *BC* (the side to which it is congruent). So you must use the Pythagorean theorem to compute its length:

$$\begin{aligned} 4^2 + (BC)^2 &= 8^2 \\ (BC)^2 &= 48 \\ BC &= 4\sqrt{3} \end{aligned}$$

Therefore, *AD* also has length $4\sqrt{3}$.

Since $\sin\theta = \frac{\text{opposite side to } \theta}{\text{hypotenuse}}$, we see that

$\sin\theta = \frac{4\sqrt{3}}{8} = \frac{\sqrt{3}}{2}$.

Choice G is incorrect because it would require the angle θ to be 90°. Choice H is cos θ. Choice J is the length of *BC*. Choice K is incorrect because it would require the angle θ to be 45° and triangle *ABC* would need to be isosceles, but it is not.

19. **The correct answer is E.** The graph of $y = \cos x$ has a period of 2π. However, if you graph $y = 5\cos\frac{x}{2}$, the period doubles in length to 4π. Note that the coefficient of the cosine, 5, affects only the amplitude—not the period. All of the other choices are incorrect because the period for $y = A\cos Bx$ is $\frac{2\pi}{B}$. Each of these choices is the result of not remembering this fact correctly.

20. **The correct answer is H.** First, find the angles with a sine of 0; you will get 0° and 180°, which are equal to 0 and π radians, respectively. Since you want only the positive value of *x*, this means that $3x = \pi$, so that $x = \frac{\pi}{3}$.

Choice F is incorrect because 0 is a solution, but it is not positive. Plugging choice G in for *x* gives $\sin\frac{\pi}{2}$, which is 1, not 0. So this is not a solution. While choices J and K are solutions, neither is the smallest value of *x* that makes the equation true.

PART V: READING STRATEGIES FOR THE ACT® EXAM

Chapter 9: Social Studies and Natural Sciences Passages

Chapter 10: Literary Narrative/Prose Fiction and Humanities Passages

READING STRATEGIES FOR THE ACT® EXAM

While odds are you've been reading for a *while* at this point, reading comprehension for test-taking and assessment purposes is a slightly different ball game. When you read for fun, you generally seek to follow the story and recognize or identify with the characters. You might attempt to understand their motivation, to the extent it clarifies what happens in the narrative, but you probably only read for an appreciative understanding—and even then, only once.

The ACT Reading test wants you to read to . . . answer questions correctly. It's a bonus if you enjoy the passages you read, but your main goal in this test section is to read critically and carefully, so you know for certain the *who*, *what*, *when*, *where*, and (most important) *why* of a passage and the author who wrote it.

The ACT Reading test will contain four excerpts in total. Three of them will be single, longer passages, and one will contain a pair of two shorter passages. Each excerpt represents a different subject category. The subject categories represented in the passages include social studies, natural sciences, literary/narrative prose fiction, and humanities. On test day, you will have 35 minutes to answer 40 multiple-choice questions.

In terms of content, the ACT Reading test is divided into three subcategories: Key Ideas and Details (analyzing main ideas and themes, 55–60% of the ACT Reading score); Craft and Structure (analyzing word choice, perspective, and points of view, 25–30% of the ACT Reading score); and Integration of Knowledge and Ideas (analyzing information presented, 13–18% of the ACT Reading score).

To help you develop your critical reading skills for this section of the ACT, the next two chapters will introduce you to crucial reading strategies, including active and close reading techniques, as well as tools for identifying the main idea, recognizing essential details, making inferences, drawing generalized conclusions, making comparisons, and more. Chapter 9 emphasizes reading techniques, and selected passages come from the Natural Sciences and Social Studies categories; Chapter 10 features passages from the Literary Narrative/Prose Fiction and Humanities categories and teaches you how to recognize and decode question types.

These chapters include sample test passages and practice questions with detailed answer explanations and tips and suggestions for how to effectively read and analyze the passages on test day. At the end of each chapter, you'll find a 20-question practice exam featuring two representative passages, each paired with 10 questions for analysis.

Turn the page to learn more about how to read for ACT exam success!

COLLEGE READINESS BENCHMARK LEARNING PATH PRACTICE

As you make your way through Part V and review all the reading strategies you'll need to score your best on the ACT, you might still find the topic hard to grasp. If that's the case for you, don't worry—just follow our College Readiness Benchmark Learning Path for a whole test's worth of intensive ACT Reading practice, to further familiarize yourself with the passage types and questions you will see on test day. Each question is accompanied by an in-depth answer explanation that addresses every answer option, so you can see why it is correct or incorrect. To access this full-length reading practice test, go to **www.petersons.com/testprep/act**, then select the *Peterson's ACT® Prep Guide Online Companion* and enter the coupon code **ACT2019** at checkout.

This practice test gives you the focused ACT review you need for the topics giving you the most trouble. Follow the College Readiness Benchmark Learning Path to get up to speed on your reading skills!

CHAPTER 9: SOCIAL STUDIES AND NATURAL SCIENCES PASSAGES

OVERVIEW

- Active Reading Techniques
- Key Ideas in Social Studies and Science
- Reading for Key Details
- Craft and Structure in Social Studies and Science
- Summing It Up
- Practice

The ACT Reading test will contain four excerpts (or three longer passages and two shorter passages), each representing a different subject category. This chapter will cover the first two categories, Social Studies and Natural Sciences, and the next chapter will cover the other two, Literary Narrative/Prose Fiction and Humanities. We'll begin with active reading techniques and critical thinking skills that will help you feel prepared to tackle these sections, then we'll take a look at each question type you're likely to see and how to recognize its signal phrases.

The Social Studies category may include passages covering any of the following topics:

- Anthropology, the study of societies around the world
- Archaeology, the study of human activity in the past
- Biography, nonfiction narratives about people's lives
- Business, issues of commerce and corporations
- Economics, the study of production, distribution, and consumption
- Education, the study of the process of imparting knowledge
- Geography, the science of interpreting Earth's topography
- History, the examination of past events
- Political Science, the study of principles and institutions of government
- Psychology, the science of the mind and mental states
- Sociology, the study of how human society functions

The Natural Sciences category includes passages in the following content areas:

- Anatomy, the science of the physical structure of animals and plants
- Astronomy, the science of space outside Earth's atmosphere
- Biology, the science of life in all its forms
- Botany, the science of plants
- Chemistry, the science of composition and properties of substances

- Ecology, the study of organisms and their interactions with their environment
- Geology, the study of the physical history and elements of Earth
- Medicine, the science of diagnosing and treating disease and illness
- Meteorology, the science of atmosphere, weather, and climate
- Microbiology, the science of the structure, function, and existence of microscopic organisms
- Natural History, the earth sciences and study of their origins
- Physiology, the study of organisms and their processes
- Physics, the science of matter, energy, motion, and force
- Technology, the study and use of industrial arts, engineering, and applied sciences
- Zoology, the study of animals

Past passages have included reports, articles, and excerpts from nonfiction books, essays, and textbooks. Of course, you're not going to be familiar with all of the above topics—you probably won't be familiar with most of them! We're going to teach you the best way to approach these passages. In cases where the language is dense or hard to follow, you'll need to be able to stay calm and mine for relevant information.

ALERT: You will *not* need any background or outside experience with these science or history topics in order to answer the reading questions on the ACT. You will be able to derive everything you need to answer the questions from the passage itself.

ACTIVE READING TECHNIQUES

An important key to success when taking the ACT Reading test is to be an active reader. No; that doesn't mean reading while you work out—being an active reader means that you read material with the goal of understanding and evaluating it with a specific purpose in mind. In this case, the purpose is to correctly answer the questions on the ACT exam. The acronym ACTIVE can help you to remember the goals of active reading:

> ACTIVE readers **Ask** questions, make **Connections**, **Track** down important information, **Infer** and predict, **Visualize**, and **Evaluate**, making decisions and discoveries as they explore a text.

We're going to look at a few ways that active reading can help you break down passages so you can determine what's important. Knowing that will help you as you go through the questions associated with each passage.

The most crucial first step to doing well on the ACT Reading test is to read the passage *twice*. The first time, lightly underline any details that seem most essential and use a system of your own devising to indicate questions, key terms, the main idea, and any supporting details. This technique is called **close reading**. Some close reading suggestions: use question marks in the margins for questions, draw big boxes around key terms, draw double lines under main idea or thesis statements, and use wavy lines for supporting details—but you should come up with a system that works for you and practice it often so it becomes a habit by test day.

As you read the passage the second time, think about the probable context of the passage. Word choice, tone, and internal references can give you a sense of *when* the text was written. A text that refers to up-to-date technology is obviously recent; a passage with archaic vocabulary or outdated information could have been chosen for historical significance. Think also about *why* a text was written. Is the author trying to inform? Entertain? Persuade? Disagree with an established context? Synthesize multiple views? Offer a counterargument? Call you to action? Then, try to get inside the test maker's head! Why did they choose *this* text? Because it's a classic? Because it's confusing? Because it has obvious distractions? Because it shows off technical writing abilities?

Let's look at a Social Studies passage on the psychology of advertising. Read this excerpt all the way through once, and then skim the questions that follow.

Advertising is an appeal to the attention, to the memory, to the feeling, to the impulses of the reader. Every printed line of advertisement is thus a lever that is constructed to put some mental mechanism in motion. The science of the mental machinery is psychology, which works on principles with the exact methods of the experiment. It seems unprogressive, indeed, if just this one industry neglects the help that experimental science may furnish. A few slight beginnings, to be sure, have been made, but not by the individuals whose practical interests are involved. They have been made by psychologists who, in these days of carrying psychology into practical life, have pushed the laboratory method into the field of advertising.

The beginnings indicated at once that much of what is sanctioned by the traditions of economic life will have to be fundamentally revised. Psychologists, for instance, examined the memory value of the different parts of the page. Little booklets were arranged in which words were placed in the four quarter pages. The advertiser is accustomed patiently to pay an equal amount for his quarter page, whether it is on the left half or the right, on the lower or on the upper part of the page. The experiment demonstrated that the words on the upper right-hand quarter had about twice the memory value of those on the lower left. The advertiser who is accustomed to spend for his insertion on the lower left the same sum as for that on the upper right throws half his expenditure away. He reaches only half of the customers, or takes only half a grasp of those whom he reaches. This case, which can be easily demonstrated by careful experiments, is typical of the tremendous waste that goes on in the budget of the advertising community. And yet the advertiser would not like to act like the poet who sings his song not caring whose heart he will stir.

According to the second paragraph of the passage, what is one major benefit psychology may have for advertisers?

A. Knowing how best to influence their customers

B. Knowing what mental mechanisms are stirred by print ads

C. Knowing when to hire writers with fresh perspectives

D. Knowing how to strategically place their ads

The passage establishes all of the following EXCEPT:

F. the advertising value of the upper right corner of the page is twice the value of the lower left corner of the page.

G. advertising is a logical field for psychologists to study and influence.

H. the content of an ad is not nearly as important as its placement.

J. many advertising budgets contain wasteful spending.

Here's an example of the passage with close reading annotations. Make use of the margins, underlining, starring, boxing, or note-taking on scrap paper. Keep the questions in mind as you read. These questions ask you for a "major benefit" of advertising and for you to identify significant details that are—and are not—mentioned in the passage.

For this sample close-read, we'll use the following notations:

- Brackets/margin comments to identify big picture ideas
- Underlining to note background information
- Asterisks (*) to help keep track of references to "benefits of advertising"

[Advertising is an appeal to the attention, to the memory, to the feeling, to the impulses of the reader.] Every printed line of advertisement is thus a lever that is constructed to put some

Topic Sentence: We can assume the rest of the passage will be about the science behind advertising.

mental mechanism in motion.* [The science of the mental machinery is psychology, which works on principles with the exact methods of the experiment.] It seems unprogressive, indeed, if just this one industry neglects the help that experimental science may furnish. A few slight beginnings, to be sure, have been made, but not by [the individuals whose practical interests are involved. They have been made by psychologists] who, in these days of carrying psychology into practical life, have pushed the laboratory method into the field of advertising.

This tells us the name for that science is psychology.

Advertisers are not the ones examining the benefits of incorporating psychology—psychologists are.

[The beginnings] indicated at once that much of what is sanctioned by the traditions of economic life will have to be

Refers back to the previous paragraph, in reference to the research findings.

fundamentally revised. [Psychologists, for instance, examined the memory value of the different parts of the page.] Little booklets were arranged in which words were placed in the four quarter pages. The advertiser is accustomed patiently to pay an equal amount for his quarter page, whether it is on the left half or the right, on the lower or on the upper part of the page. [The experiment demonstrated that the words on the upper right-hand quarter had about twice the memory value of those on the lower left.]* The advertiser who is accustomed to spend for his insertion on the lower left the same sum as for that on the upper right throws half his expenditure away. [He reaches only half of the customers or takes only half a grasp of those whom he reaches.] This case, which can be easily demonstrated by careful experiments, is typical of the tremendous waste that goes on in the budget of the advertising community. And yet the advertiser would not like to act like the poet who sings his song not caring whose heart he will stir.

Description of an experiment relevant to advertising.

Results of the experiment.

Conclusion derived from the findings of the experiment.

Now you're ready to close read the questions. You'll notice that the first adopts a more macro (or big-picture) approach, asking for a main idea expressed by the passage. It gives you a specific location within the passage to focus on (the second paragraph) and requires that you make an inference from the evidence presented. Key phrases in the question are in **bold** type so you can start to think like a question maker.

According to the **second paragraph of the passage**, what is **one major benefit** psychology may have for advertisers?

A. Knowing how best to influence their customers

This may be the main idea of the section from which this excerpt is drawn, but it is not the most specific answer supported by this paragraph.

B. Knowing what mental mechanisms are stirred by print ads

Similarly, this is definitely a benefit of psychology implied in the opening sentences of this passage, but the question asks you to focus on the second paragraph and the specific benefit it implies.

C. Knowing when to hire writers with fresh perspectives

While the advertiser may need to hire writers who can play off the insights provided by psychology in their ad copy, this idea is not specifically supported by the passage.

D. Knowing how to strategically place their ads

Most of the discussion in this paragraph is regarding the memory impact of page placement, so it's reasonable to infer the awareness of this tactic would be a major benefit to advertisers. ***This is the correct answer.***

The second question requires you to identify a significant detail; pay careful attention to the *EXCEPT*, which indicates that three of the four answer choices are taken from the passage. The answer choice that is *not* included in the passage is the correct answer to this question. If you zoom past the *except*, you risk selecting the first answer you recognize—a careless mistake that's easy to avoid.

The passage establishes all of the following EXCEPT:

F. the advertising value of the upper right corner of the page is twice the value of the lower left corner of the page.

As covered by the previous question, this IS established by the passage.

G. advertising is a logical field for psychologists to study and influence.

The opening paragraph clearly makes this point.

H. the content of an ad is not nearly as important as its placement.

The passage stops short of implying this, though it refers to advertisers who might think more about the content than the placement. ***This is the correct answer.***

J. many advertising budgets contain wasteful spending.

While you might find this evidence not particularly well-supported, it's presented by the passage as fact.

Another key component of understanding a main idea in a passage is generalizing—thinking outside of what you have read to form an idea that is not explicitly stated. Take a look at this question, which requires you to derive clues from statements within the text.

TIP: Always reread the specific paragraphs, lines, or phrases mentioned in the question or answer choices, even if you're confident. Double-check that you're not misremembering the main idea as described in the question with the main idea you actually read.

The author of this passage would most likely agree with which of the following?

A. In order to keep up with other industries, advertisers need to be more calculated about reaching the most susceptible audience for their message.
B. If their products are good, advertisers can trust that their message will reach their best customers.
C. A picture is worth a thousand words.
D. Advertisers have a lot to learn from poets, who have the broadest reach of all.

The correct answer is A. Based on the last line, "And yet the advertiser would not like to act like the poet who sings his song not caring whose heart he will stir," we can conclude that the author is unlikely to agree that poets have the best targeted marketing plan (so choice D is incorrect). The author refers specifically to "printed words" in the opening paragraph and never mentions images, so choice C is also incorrect. The focus on potential improvements from incorporating psychological insights should suggest to you that the author does *not* think the product is as important as the message, so choice B is incorrect. Choice A is the most reasonable inference based on the sentence in the first paragraph, which says, "It seems unprogressive, indeed, if just this one industry neglects the help that experimental science may furnish." If advertising is "just this one industry" that would be neglecting the help, it implies that every other industry is making use of these innovative techniques.

KEY IDEAS IN SOCIAL STUDIES AND SCIENCE

A **topic** is the general prompt that leads someone to write an essay. The main idea, however, is the **thesis**—the major takeaway an author wants someone to infer after reading his or her work. It might involve the author's feelings about the topic, a crucial piece of information the author wants to highlight, or a realization the author wants the reader to have about the topic. The main idea is usually featured in the first third of an excerpt or is the idea most often referred to or repeated throughout the passage. The rest of the passage is made up of background information, evidence, and supporting details. ACT Reading expects you to be able to identify central ideas, themes, and details, and draw conclusions and make inferences based on that information.

Sometimes questions will ask you outright, "What is the main idea of this passage?" Other times you'll be asked either to refer to explicit information to determine the main idea or to use your critical reasoning abilities to infer it.

Take a look at this archaeology passage from a 1920 guide for travelers in the Middle East.

The hints that it is the object of this volume to convey are not meant for experienced archaeologists. They are rather addressed to those who, while anxious to observe and record the antiquities which they may see on their travels, are likely, owing to lack of training, to miss things that may be of importance, or, having observed them, to bring home an imperfect record. It is hoped also that they may catch the attention of some of those who are not interested in the subject, but, coming into possession of antiquities, may unwittingly do incalculable harm by allowing them to be destroyed or dispersed before any record has been made.

Most, if not all, of the countries with which we are concerned, have their Laws of Antiquities. It cannot be too strongly insisted that those laws, even if they might be better than they are, should be obeyed by the traveller. He should familiarize himself with their main provisions, which are summarized in an Appendix. The traveller who makes it his object to loot a country of its antiquities, smuggling objects out of it and disguising the sources from which they are obtained, does a distinct disservice to archaeological science. Although he may enrich collections, public or private, half or more than half of the scientific value of his acquisitions is destroyed by the fact that their provenance is kept secret or falsely stated. Such action is equivalent to tearing out whole pages from a history and destroying them forever, for each antiquity, whatever it may be, is in its way a part of history, whether of politics, arts, or civilization. For the same reason anything like unauthorized excavation, especially by unskilled hands, is gravely to be deprecated. To dig an ancient site unskillfully or without keeping a proper record is to obliterate part of a manuscript that no one else will ever be able to read. The tendency of recent legislation is to allow more generous terms in the matter of licenses for export to excavators and collectors, and the harsher provisions of some of the existing laws are likely soon to be amended.

Excerpt from "Chapter I, Introductory," by G.F. Hill, from *How To Observe In Archaeology: Suggestions For Travellers In The Near And Middle East.* (1920)

One of the author's main points about traveling in historically significant areas is:

F. undiscovered antiquities are ripe for the taking in remote or unexplored areas.

G. legislation governing the acquisition and use of antiquities is due for an update.

H. visitors have obligations to be respectful and travel with guided tour groups.

J. smuggling objects out of their country of origin has repercussions for history.

The correct answer is J. The stakes of this passage rest on the long-term impact amateur excavations, theft, and looting can have on the legacy of arts and culture. Choice F is incorrect—the author never suggests these artifacts are available to be recovered. While the author does mention laws "might be better than they are," that aside is countered by the final statement, which says the laws are likely to be loosened in the near future. Choice H is incorrect because there is no reference to guided tours; the author might even believe tourism is as bad for the integrity of these sites as the unscrupulous travelers.

Let's examine another passage in search of the main idea, from the Social Studies subcategory of education. The question that follows asks you to refer to information that is explicitly stated in the passage.

The influence of art upon the life of a young child is difficult to measure. It may freely be said, however, that there is little or no danger in exaggerating its influence, and considerable danger in underrating it. It is difficult to measure because the influence is largely an unconscious one. Indeed, it may be questioned whether that form of art which gives him the most conscious and outspoken pleasure is the form that in reality is the most beneficial; for, unquestionably, he will get great satisfaction from circus posters, and the poorly printed, abominably illustrated cheap picture-books afford him undeniable joy. He is far less likely to be expressive of his pleasure in a sun-shiny nursery, whose walls, rugs, white beds, and sun-shiny windows are all well designed and well adapted to his needs. Nevertheless, in the end the influence of this room is likely to be the greater influence and to permanently shape his ideas of the beautiful; while he is entirely certain, if allowed to develop artistically at all, to grow past the circus poster period.

This fact—the fact that the highest influence of art is a secret influence, exercised not only by those decorations and pictures which flaunt themselves for the purpose, but also by those quiet, necessary, everyday things, which nevertheless may most truly express the art spirit—this fact makes it difficult to tell what art and what kind of art is really influencing the child, and whether it is influencing him in the right directions.

Excerpt from "Art and Literature on Child Life," from *Study of Child Life,* by Marion Foster Washburne. (1907) [http://www.gutenberg.org/files/13467/13467-h/13467-h.htm#art]

Which of the following is directly supported by the passage?

A. Elegant decorations are more influential on a child's development than popular, flashy artwork and poorly printed children's books.

B. While it is undeniable that art has an impact on child development, it is difficult to evaluate what elements are most influential.

C. Popular art that a child enjoys is the most significant contributor to artistic development and social maturity.

D. The art we are exposed to as children affects us in specific, measurable ways.

The correct answer is B. The opening and closing sentences of the excerpt directly support this option. Choices A and C are both outright rejected by the passage, which mainly discusses how hard it is to differentiate between specific influences. Similarly, choice D is incorrect because there are no specific, measurable impacts under discussion in the passage.

For this next excerpt, from the Natural Sciences subcategory of botany, you will be asked to *infer* a main idea. This calls for using your reasoning skills to determine implicit meaning—so the main idea may not be directly stated.

In 55 B.C., then-governor Julius Caesar invaded the south of what would later become Great Britain with his nearly 10,000 soldiers, under orders of Emperor Claudius.

It may be safely assumed that, two thousand years ago, before Caesar set foot in southern Britain, the whole countryside visible from the windows of the room in which I write, was in what is called "the state of nature." Except, it may be, by raising a few sepulchral mounds, such as those which still, here and there, break the flowing contours of the downs, man's hands had made no mark upon it; and the thin veil of vegetation which overspread the broad-backed heights and the shelving sides of the coombs was unaffected by his industry. The native grasses and weeds, the scattered patches of gorse, contended with one another for the possession of the scanty surface soil; they fought against the droughts of summer, the frosts of winter, and the furious gales which swept, with unbroken force, now from the Atlantic, and now from the North Sea, at all times of the year; they filled up, as they best might, the gaps made in their ranks by all sorts of underground and overground animal ravagers. One year with another, an average population, the floating balance of the unceasing struggle for existence among the indigenous plants, maintained itself. It is as little to be doubted, that an essentially similar state of nature prevailed, in this region, for many thousand years before the coming of Caesar; and there is no assignable reason for denying that it might continue to exist through an equally prolonged futurity, except for the intervention of man.

Excerpt from "Evolution and Ethics. Prolegomena."[1894], from *Evolution and Ethics and Other Essays*, by Thomas H. Huxley.

From information in the passage, it can be reasonably inferred that:

- **F.** the arrival of Caesar had no effect on the grasses and vegetation of southern Britain.
- **G.** the weather in southern Britain is exceptionally clement and allows for all kinds of growth and plant life.
- **H.** the "state of nature" in southern Britain included a wide variety of animal species.
- **J.** the intervention of humans has destroyed or disrupted the natural ecology of southern Britain.

The correct answer is J. Even though it is never directly stated, the descriptions of Britain prior to the arrival of Caesar and his troops, plus the last line, "it might continue to exist through an equally prolonged futurity, except for the intervention of man," allow for the reasonable assumption that Caesar's invasion had impacts on the natural landscape. Choice F is incorrect because there's no other reason the author would have framed the passage with Caesar's presence in Britain. Choice G is an inaccurate summary of the passage, which describes the British climate as rough and prone to "furious gales." Choice H reflects one supporting point in the passage, but it is not significant enough to qualify as a main idea (nor does it require an inference on the part of the reader).

Finally, we'll revisit drawing generalizations from the main idea of the passage with this passage from the work of Nikola Tesla, an inventor and scientific innovator who lived from 1856 to 1943.

In how far we can understand the world around us is the ultimate thought of every student of nature. The coarseness of our senses prevents us from recognizing the ulterior construction of matter, and astronomy, this grandest and most positive of natural sciences, can only teach us something that happens, as it were, in our immediate neighborhood: of the remoter portions of the boundless universe, with its numberless stars and suns, we know nothing. But far beyond the limit of perception of our senses the spirit still can guide us, and so we may hope that even these unknown worlds—infinitely small and great—may in a measure become known to us. Still, even if this knowledge should reach us, the searching mind will find a barrier, perhaps forever unsurpassable, to the *true* recognition of that which *seems* to be, the mere *appearance* of which is the only and slender basis of all our philosophy.

According to the passage, students of nature should:

- **A.** be guided by the five senses to guide their understanding of the world.
- **B.** stay alert to the distinction between what *is* and what *seems* to be.
- **C.** give up on trying to see beneath the *appearance* of our world.
- **D.** focus on the most recent advancements in technology.

The correct answer is B. Choice A is in direct opposition to the passage, in which Tesla refers to the "coarseness" of our senses. Choice C doesn't seem at all related to Tesla's hope that we will keep searching beyond the surface of the world and its mysteries. Choice D might be a reflection of Tesla's values, but there is nothing in the passage on which to base this inference. Choice B is the best answer—the clue that allows for this inference is the final sentence, "the searching mind will find a barrier, perhaps forever unsurpassable, to the true recognition of that which seems to be, the mere appearance of which is the only and slender basis of all our philosophy." Tesla opened this chapter by addressing himself to all "students of nature"—it's reasonable to generalize that he'd want these students to keep pushing beyond the barrier of appearances.

READING FOR KEY DETAILS

Up to this point, the questions have emphasized extracting main ideas from the passage; we've examined shortened excerpts in order to help you focus. Now we'll look at extended versions of some of the same passages and identify the strategies and techniques that will help you "work micro," i.e., find significant details in the passage to answer questions.

Taking Notes

As we mentioned at the start of the chapter, the most essential technique is taking notes on your own—before you even know what the questions are going to ask, you can make sure you're mining the passage for all its worth.

Let's revisit this archaeology passage. We'll put brackets around the relevant text, make notes in the margins, and then compile the notes at the bottom in a bulleted list.

[The hints which it is the object of this volume to convey are not meant for experienced archaeologists. They are rather addressed to those who, while anxious to observe and record the antiquities which they may see on their travels, are likely, owing to lack of training, to miss things that may be of importance, or, having observed them, to bring home an imperfect record.] It is hoped also that they may catch the attention of some of those who are not interested in the subject, but, coming into possession of antiquities, may unwittingly do incalculable harm by allowing them to be destroyed or dispersed before any record has been made.

The intended audience is not experienced archaeologists, but amateurs.

Most, if not all, of the countries with which we are concerned, have their Laws of Antiquities. It cannot be too strongly insisted that those laws, even if they might be better than they are, should be obeyed by the traveller. He should familiarize himself with their main provisions, which are summarized in an Appendix. The traveller who makes it his object to loot a country of its antiquities, smuggling objects out of it and disguising the sources from which they are obtained, does a distinct disservice to archaeological science. [Although he may enrich collections, public or private, half or more than half of the scientific value of his acquisitions is destroyed by the fact that their provenance is kept secret or falsely stated.] Such action is equivalent to tearing out whole pages from a history and destroying them for ever, for each antiquity, whatever it may be, is in its way a part of history, whether of politics, arts, or civilization. For the same reason anything like unauthorized excavation, especially by unskilled hands, is gravely to be deprecated. [To dig an ancient site unskillfully or without keeping a proper record is to obliterate part of a manuscript which no one else will ever be able to read.] The tendency of recent legislation is to allow more generous terms in the matter of licenses for export to excavators and collectors, and the harsher provisions of some of the existing laws are likely soon to be amended.

Even if a museum pays for a find, the loss of legitimate origin damages its value.

Damaging antiquities has long-term impacts on historical and cultural records.

Before leaving home, the traveller will be well advised to make inquiries at the [museums or at the headquarters of the archaeological societies] which concern themselves specially with the places which he intends to visit. It is hardly necessary to warn him that archaeological training cannot be acquired in a few days, and that he will have to buy his experience in various ways; but the more time he can devote to [working through the collections in this country,] the more useful will be his observations abroad. He will be able to learn what kind of antiquities it is especially desirable to look for, not merely with the object of filling gaps in the public collections, but for the advancement of archaeological knowledge in general.

Resources for travelers.

Travelers can spend time becoming informed about what collections already exist so they have some sense of value of their finds.

[The object of archaeological travel and excavation is not to collect antiquities so that they may be arranged according to the existing catalogues of museums, but to collect fresh information to amplify and correct what we now know, to make our knowledge of the past more complete and useful.]

A mission statement for travelers: Find something new.

On arrival in the country of his choice, he is recommended to continue at the National Museum the study, which we suppose he has already begun in the museums at home, of the kind of antiquities which he is likely to come across. [But he should also take an early opportunity of getting into touch with the local British Archaeological School or other similar institution, where he will receive advice what to look for and where and how to look, and assistance in procuring suitable equipment.] The best

The traveler should consult experts—what does it mean that the author assumes there will be a British school or institution in any place a traveler might wish to go?

maps of the district will also be accessible for examination [(but the traveller is recommended to make inquiries in this respect before leaving England)]; the libraries will provide the literature dealing with the routes he proposes to take; and such a collection as the type–series of pottery and the [Finlay collection of prehistoric sculptures, grave goods, and vases] at the British School at Athens may be useful to supplement his previous studies at museums, and enable him to observe with intelligence [the potsherds, &c.,] that he may find on an ancient site. In return, he will be expected to report his results either to the School or to some other scientific society or museum at home. It should be unnecessary to remind him that the conditions of the law of the land relating to the reporting of discoveries to the competent authorities should be strictly observed. [Such authorities should also be informed of any destruction or removal of monuments which may be noticed.]

The author assumes the reader/traveler is British.

Specific kinds of specimens.

Unfamiliar word "potsherds"; from context: broken shards of pottery? Unfamiliar term "&c."; from context: etc.?

The author appears to sign off on the destruction or removal of less noticeable monuments!

Excerpt from "Chapter I, Introductory," by G.F. Hill, from *How To Observe In Archaeology: Suggestions For Travellers In The Near And Middle East.* (1920)

NOTES

- The intended audience is not experienced archaeologists, but amateurs.
- Even if a museum pays for a find, the loss of legitimate origin decreases its value.
- Damaging antiquities has long-term impacts on historical and cultural records.
- Resources for travelers: museums, archaeological society headquarters
- Travelers can spend time becoming informed about what collections already exist so they have some sense of value of their finds.
- A mission statement for travelers: Find something new.
- The traveler should consult experts—what does it mean that the author assumes there will be a British school or institution in any place a traveler might wish to go?
- The author assumes the reader/traveler is British.
- Specific kinds of specimens: "prehistoric sculptures, grave goods, and vases"
- Unfamiliar word "potsherds"; from context: broken shards of pottery; unfamiliar term "&c."; from context: etc.?
- The author appears to sign off on the destruction or removal of less noticeable monuments!

In this compilation of notes, we've essentially captured what's sometimes called a "reverse outline" of the passage. By recording a main idea from each paragraph, we can document the scope of the excerpt and have a shorter, succinct version to refer back to. We also recorded a question we had about the assumed British presence all around the world. You don't need to be familiar with world politics of 1920 to infer the British had at that time a presence in international societies where prized antiquities exist.

Now, let's see how taking notes can directly lead you to correct answers quickly and efficiently.

What are some examples of the antiquities mentioned in the passage?

I. Rare manuscripts
II. Sculptures
III. Broken pottery
IV. Taxidermy

F. I, III
G. II, IV
H. II, III
J. I, IV

The correct answer is H. Notice how helpful it is to have notes about where specific examples were located! It was easy to return to the bullet points and select the correct combination of answers. Choice I, rare manuscripts, is a figurative reference within the passage. Choice IV, taxidermy, is the skin of a dead animal stuffed to appear lifelike—such items are not usually well preserved in tombs or ancient structures, and moreover, they are not mentioned in the passage.

According to the author in Paragraph 4, the goal of archaeological expeditions is to:

A. renegotiate export licenses, not to contribute new map features.
B. make new discoveries, not to further augment existing collections.
C. give a crash course in excavation, not to prioritize treasure hunting goals.
D. share findings with sponsoring institutions, not to replenish museums' stores of pottery shards.

The correct answer is B. This type of question and its answer choices can be tricky because the answer choices are all paraphrased from the passage—if you rely on mere recognition to point you to the correct answer, you'll be in trouble. Instead, carefully reread your notes. What is the goal of this type of visit? Our shorthand version was, "A mission statement for travelers: Find something new." Which answer choice most nearly reflects that statement? Choice B.

Now it's your turn to practice active note taking. Remember, the goal is to allow you to more easily identify crucial details and answer the questions that check for this up-close kind of understanding.

The influence of art upon the life of a young child is difficult to measure. It may freely be said, however, that there is little or no danger in exaggerating its influence, and considerable danger in underrating it. It is difficult to measure because the influence is largely an unconscious one. Indeed, it may be questioned whether that form of art which gives him the most conscious and outspoken pleasure is the form that in reality is the most beneficial; for, unquestionably, he will get great satisfaction from circus posters, and the poorly printed, abominably illustrated cheap picture-books afford him undeniable joy. He is far less likely to be expressive of his pleasure in a sun-shiny nursery, whose walls, rugs, white beds, and sun-shiny windows are all well designed and well adapted to his needs. Nevertheless, in the end the influence of this room is likely to be the greater influence and to permanently shape his ideas of the beautiful; while he is entirely certain, if allowed to develop artistically at all, to grow past the circus poster period.

This fact—the fact that the highest influence of art is a secret influence, exercised not only by those decorations and pictures which flaunt themselves for the purpose, but also by those quiet, necessary, every-day things, which nevertheless may most truly express the art spirit—this fact makes it difficult to tell what art and what kind of art is really influencing the child, and whether it is influencing him in the right directions.

Color

Until he is three years old, for example, and often until he is past that age, he is unable to distinguish clearly between green, gray, and blue; and hence these cool colors in the decorations around him, or in his pictures, have practically no meaning for him. He has a right, one might suppose, to the gratification of his love for clear reds and yellows, for the sharp, well-defined lines and flat surfaces, whose meaning is plain to his groping little mind. Some of the best illustrators of children's books have seemed to recognize this. For example, Boutet de Monvil in his admirable illustrations of Joan of Arc meets these requirements perfectly, and yet in a manner which must satisfy any adult lover of good art. The Caldecott picture books, and Walter Crane's are also good in this respect, and the Perkins pictures issued by the Prang Educational Co. have gained a just recognition as excellent pictures for hanging on the nursery wall. Many of the illustrations in color in the standard magazines are well worth cutting out, mounting and framing. This is especially true of Howard Pyle's work and that of Elizabeth Shippen Green.

Classic Art

Since photogravures and photographs of the masterpieces can be had in this country very inexpensively, there is no reason why children should not be made acquainted at an early age with the art classics, but there is danger in giving too much space to black and white, especially in the nursery where the children live. Their natural love of color should be appealed to deepen their interest in really good pictures.

Nevertheless, it is a matter of considerable difficulty still to find colored pictures which are inexpensive and yet really good. The Detaille prints, while not yet cheap, are not expensive either, and are excellent for this purpose; but the insipid little pictures of fairies, flowers, and birds may be really harmful, as helping to form in the young child's mind too low an ideal of beauty—of cultivating in him what someone has called "the lust of the eye."

Plastic Art

What holds true of the pictorial art holds equally true of the plastic art. As Prof. Veblin of the University of Chicago has scathingly declared, our ideals of the beautiful are so mingled with worship of expense that few of us can see the genuine beauty in any object apart from its expensiveness. For this reason as well as, perhaps, because of a remnant of barbarism in us, we love gold and glitter, and a great deal of elaboration in our vases, and are far from being over-critical of any piece of statuary which costs a respectable sum.

Excerpt from "Art and Literature on Child Life," from *Study of Child Life*, by Marion Foster Washburne. (1907) [http://www.gutenberg.org/files/13467/13467-h/13467-h.htm#art]

Use this space to record your own notes from this passage—whether you compile your margin comments, reverse outline, record questions, or document main ideas and supporting details, do your own excavating for information so that when you approach the question that follows, you've already begun distilling the passage down into the most useful information.

Now, using only your notes, see if you can identify the correct answer to the question.

According to the passage, what are the first colors a child is able to perceive?

F. Black and white
G. Green, gray, and blue
H. Green, red, and yellow
J. Purple, brown, and orange

The correct answer is F. Although the passage acknowledges yellow and red (given in choice H) as the more clearly visible colors, it indicates children aren't able to "distinguish clearly between green, gray, and blue" until they are at least three years old, eliminating choices G and H. A child's ability to perceive black and white (choice F) is implied in the next paragraph, about classic art, making it the correct answer. There is no mention of purple, brown, or orange in the passage (choice J).

Did you find the answer in your notes? If you discerned that the order in which a child sees colors could be an important point and jotted it down, you saved yourself time by not having to refer back to the passage. You want to be especially aware of managing your time when taking the ACT Reading test. Being an effective active reader will help you with that skill.

Vocabulary in Context

Another purpose of extensive close reading is to help you identify and define key vocabulary or concepts via context. Even if you're unfamiliar with specialized vocabulary—which may be more likely in the sciences or social studies fields—you can derive meaning from the surrounding sentences.

> **TIP:** When you come across a word you don't know, read the sentence, cover the unknown word, and think of a word that you do know that might fit in the sentence. Then, compare your word to the answer choices. Chances are you will find a good fit.

Let's go back to the passage on page 349. Here's a sample question that asks you to practice this technique; pay particular attention to the "most nearly" phrasing to help you distinguish between similar answer choices.

In line 69 the word *barbarism* most nearly means:

- **A.** a quality of being foreign.
- **B.** the practice of hair-cutting techniques.
- **C.** an absence of culture and civilization.
- **D.** extreme cruelty or brutality.

The correct answer is C. If you recognize that barbarism is related to *barbarian* and *barbaric*, you might remember its connotation with cruelty (choice D) and being foreign (choice A). However, in this particular context, *barbarism* is more related to a lack of *taste* than to a lack of compassion or a connection with outsider status, so choice C is the correct answer. You can determine this from nearby references to vases and décor, as well as the topic of the passage as a whole, art and aesthetics. The author is not suggesting our modern ideals lead us to callous or violent behavior, merely that our sense of exalted art objects is diluted by an appreciation for the tacky or gilded.

Cause and Effect

Another kind of detail-oriented question asks you to identify the logical links between ideas in the passage or determine a cause-and-effect relationship. These questions will identify a key concept and then ask you to determine why the author made that point, or how it is supported by information elsewhere in the passage.

Referring back to the passage on page 349, let's take a look at an example of a cause-and-effect question.

The passage suggests that pictures of fairies, flowers, and birds are not appropriate choices for a nursery because:

- **F.** they are too fantastical to encourage a child's understanding of the world.
- **G.** the colorful prints are too expensive for a short-term decorating investment.
- **H.** they are insipid artistic subjects that will warp a child's artistic tastes.
- **J.** they appeal to a child's natural love of color insufficiently.

The correct answer is H. The passage both refers to fairies, flowers, and birds as insipid *and* suggests they may cultivate a "lust of the eye" (which is a whole other interpretive question—you can infer from the context that it is deemed negative by the author, however). Choice F is incorrect because only fairies are actually imagination-based; flowers and birds might be "insipid," but they are factual. Choice G is incorrect; while the passage does consider the expense of finding good prints, it also recommends pages from color magazines, which would certainly be cost-effective. Choice J is incorrect; the passage indicates that fairies, birds, and flowers are an excellent ways to appeal to a child's love of color.

For this next passage, pay attention to which of the questions that follow asks for a big picture "main idea" reading and which one requires a detail-oriented close read.

It may be safely assumed that, two thousand years ago, before Caesar set foot in southern Britain, the whole country-side visible from the windows of the room in which I write, was in what is called "the state of nature." Except, it may be, by raising a few sepulchral mounds, such as those which still, here and there, break the flowing contours of the downs, man's hands had made no mark upon it; and the thin veil of vegetation which overspread the broad-backed heights and the shelving sides of the coombs was unaffected by his industry. The native grasses and weeds, the scattered patches of gorse, contended with one another for the possession of the scanty surface soil; they fought against the droughts of summer, the frosts of winter, and the furious gales which swept, with unbroken force, now from the Atlantic, and now from the North Sea, at all times of the year; they filled up, as they best might, the gaps made in their ranks by all sorts of underground and overground animal ravagers. One year with another, an average population, the floating balance of the unceasing struggle for existence among the indigenous plants, maintained itself. It is as little to be doubted, that an essentially similar state of nature prevailed, in this region, for many thousand years before the coming of Caesar; and there is no assignable reason for denying that it might continue to exist through an equally prolonged futurity, except for the intervention of man.

Reckoned by our customary standards of duration, the native vegetation, like the "everlasting hills" which it clothes, seems a type of permanence. The little Amarella Gentians, which abound in some places to-day, are the descendants of those that were trodden underfoot by the prehistoric residents who have left their flint tools, about, here and there; and they followed ancestors which, in the climate of the glacial epoch, probably flourished better than they do now. Compared with the long past of this humble plant, all the history of civilized men is but an episode.

Yet nothing is more certain than that, measured by the liberal scale of time-keeping of the universe, this present state of nature, however it may seem to have gone and to go on forever, is but a fleeting phase of her infinite variety; merely the last of the series of changes which the earth's surface has undergone in the course of the millions of years of its existence. Turn back a square foot of the thin turf, and the solid foundation of the land, exposed in cliffs of chalk five hundred feet high on the adjacent shore, yields full assurance of a time when the sea covered the site of the "everlasting hills"; and when the vegetation of what land lay nearest, was as different from the present Flora of the Sussex downs, as that of Central Africa now is.

No less certain is it that, between the time during which the chalk was formed and that at which the original turf came into existence, thousands of centuries elapsed, in the course of which, the state of nature of the ages during which the chalk was deposited, passed into that which now is, by changes so slow that, in the coming and going of the generations of men, had such witnessed them, the contemporary conditions would have seemed to be unchanging and unchangeable.

Excerpt from "Evolution and Ethics. Prolegomena."[1894], from *Evolution and Ethics and Other Essays*, by Thomas H. Huxley. [http://www.gutenberg.org/cache/epub/2940/pg2940-images.html]

According to the passage, Paragraph 3 most closely identifies the shift from discussing:

A. botany (the study of plants) to geology (the study of the earth's surface).

B. the geography of Great Britain to the geography of Central Africa.

C. anthropology (the study of humans) to zoology (the study of animals).

D. ancient geology to the modern landscape.

The correct answer is A. This question requires you to pinpoint a shift between two larger ideas, and this answer choice showcases a moment where the author literally moves from the surface to the subterranean features of the landscape when he says, "Turn back a square foot of the thin turf, and the solid foundation of the land, exposed in cliffs of chalk five hundred feet high on the adjacent shore, yields full assurance of a time when the sea covered the site of the 'everlasting hills.'" (lines 44–48). Choice B picks up on a comparison made by the passage, but the paragraph is not actually moving on to a discussion of Central Africa. Choice C is not reflected in the passage. Choice D is a distraction meant to mislead you by referring to the passage of time; while the paragraph does mention "the course of millions of years," it does not signal a shift to discussing the modern landscape.

Which of the following would the author be MOST likely to recommend?

F. Studying the history of the Holy Roman Empire

G. Excavating the burial mounds of early inhabitants of the British Isles

H. Mining the coast of Britain for its chalk and mineral resources

J. Establishing a nature preserve to cultivate southern Britain's original plant life

The correct answer is J. You can make this inference by gauging the author's appreciative tone toward the original flora and fauna of this part of England and his resistance to the arrival of Caesar. Choice F is incorrect because the author's attention is primarily on the natural history of Britain, not the history of the invading populations (who, in any case, would have been unable to properly perceive the shifts in landscape do to their limited lifespans). Choice G is incorrect; the author does not seem particularly interested in the burial mounds of the early inhabitants, nor in exploiting the mineral elements in the region (choice H).

For this next passage, look for the distinction between a question that asks about the sequence of events and a question more focused on cause and effect.

The theory of the origin of sleep that has gained the widest credence is the one that attributes it to anæmia of the brain. It has been shown by Mosso, and many others, that in men with defects of the cranial wall the volume of the brain decreases during sleep. At the same time, the volume of any limb increases as the peripheral parts of the body become turgid with blood. In dogs, the brain has been exposed, and the cortex of that organ has been observed to become anæmic during sleep. It is a matter of ordinary observation that in infants, during sleep, the volume of the brain becomes less, since the fontanelle is found to sink in. It has been supposed, but without sufficient evidence to justify the supposition, that this anæmia of the brain is the cause and not the sequence of sleep. The idea behind this supposition has been that, as the day draws to an end, the circulatory mechanism becomes fatigued, the vasomotor center exhausted, the tone of the blood vessels deficient, and the energy of the heart diminished, and the circulation to the cerebral arteries lessened.

By means of a simple and accurate instrument (the Hill-Barnard sphygmometer), with which the pressure in the arteries of man can be easily reckoned, it has been recently determined that the arterial pressure falls just as greatly during bodily rest as during sleep. The ordinary pressure of the blood in the arteries of young and healthy men averages 110–120 mm. of mercury. In sleep, the pressure may sink to 95–100 mm.; but if the pressure be taken of the same subject lying in bed, and quietly engaged on mental work, it will be found to be no higher. By mental strain or muscular effort, the pressure is, however, immediately raised, and may then reach 130–140 mm. of mercury. It can be seen from considering these facts that the fall of pressure is concomitant with rest, rather than with sleep. As, moreover, it has been determined on strong evidence that the cerebral vessels are not supplied with vasomotor nerves, and that the cerebral circulation passively follows every change in the arterial pressure, it becomes evident that sleep cannot be occasioned by any active change in the cerebral vessels. This conclusion is borne out by the fact that to produce in the dog a condition of coma like to sleep, it is necessary to reduce, by a very great amount, the cerebral circulation.

Thus, both carotids and both vertebral arteries, can be frequently tied at one and the same time without either producing coma or any very marked symptoms. The circulation is, in such a case, maintained through other channels, such as branches from the superior intercostal arteries which enter the anterior spinal artery. While total anæmia of the brain instantaneously abolishes consciousness, partial anæmia is found to raise the excitability of the cortex cerebri. By estimation of the exchange of gases in the blood which enters and leaves the brain, it has been shown that the consumption of oxygen and the production of carbonic acid in that organ is not large. Further, it may be noted that the condition of anæsthesia is not in all cases associated with cerebral anæmia. Thus, while during chloroform anæsthesia the arterial pressure markedly falls, such is not the case during anæsthesia produced by ether or a mixture of nitrous oxide and oxygen.

The arterial pressure of man is not lowered by the ordinary fatigue of daily life. It is only in extreme states of exhaustion that the pressure may be found decreased when the subject is in the standing position. The fall of pressure which does occur during rest or sleep is mainly occasioned by the diminished rate of the heart. The increase in the volume of the limbs is to be ascribed to the cessation of muscular movement and to the diminution in the amplitude of respiration. The duty of the heart is to deliver the blood to the capillaries. From the veins the blood is, for the most part, returned to the heart by the compressive action of the muscles, the constant change of posture and by the respiration acting both as a force and suction pump. All of these factors are at their maximum during bodily activity and at their minimum during rest. On exciting a sleeper by calling his name, or in any way disturbing him, the limbs, it has been recorded, decrease in volume while the brain expands. This is so because the respiration changes in depth, the heart quickens, the muscles alter in tone, as the subject stirs in his sleep in reflex response to external stimuli. Considering all these facts, we must regard the fall of arterial pressure, the depression of the fontanelle, and the turgescence of the vessels of the limbs as phenomena concomitant with bodily rest and warmth, and we have no more right to assign the causation of sleep to cerebral anæmia than to any other alteration in the functions of the body, such as occur during sleep.

We may well here summarize these other changes in function:

- The respiratory movement becomes shallow and thoracic in type.
- The volume of the air inspired per minute is lessened by one-half to two-thirds.
- The output of carbonic acid is diminished by the same amount.
- The bodily temperature falls.
- The acidity of the cortex of the brain disappears.
- Reflex action persists; the knee jerk is diminished, pointing to relaxation in tone of the muscles; consciousness is suspended.

Analyzing more closely the conditions of the central nervous system, it becomes evident that, in sleep, consciousness alone is in abeyance. The nerves and the special senses continue to transmit impulses and to produce reflex movements. If a blanket, sufficiently heavy to impede respiration, be placed upon the face of a sleeping person, we know that it will be immediately pushed away. More than this, complicated movements can be carried out; the postilion can sleep on horseback; the punkah-wallah may work his punkah and at the same time enjoy a slumber; a weary mother may sleep, and yet automatically rock her infant's cradle. Turning to the histories of sleep walkers, we find it recorded that, during sleep, they perform such feats as climbing slanting roofs or walking across dangerous narrow ledges and bridges. The writer knew of the case of a lad who, when locked in his room at night to prevent his wandering in his sleep, climbed a partition eight to ten feet in height which separated his sleeping compartment from the next, and this without waking.

The brain can carry out not only such complicated acts as these, but it has been found to maintain during sleep its normal inhibitory control over the lower reflex centers in the spinal cord.

Excerpt from "Sleep and the Theories of Its Cause"
(*Scientific American Supplement*, Pg. 18768, Vol. XLV., No. 1178, June 25, 1898).
[https://www.gutenberg.org/files/18265/18265-h/18265-h.htm#art16]

According to the passage, the process of falling asleep involves all of the following EXCEPT:

A. lower blood pressure.
B. increase in the blood stored in the limbs.
C. slowed respiration volume.
D. expansion of the brain.

The correct answer is D. The passage states, "On exciting a sleeper by calling his name, or in any way disturbing him, the limbs, it has been recorded, decrease in volume while the brain expands," which implies the brain normally contracts during sleep. Choices A, B, and C are all mentioned specifically in the passage.

The passage indicates that in adults, blood pressure falls during sleep because:

F. the fontanelle sinks in.
G. the muscles stop moving.
H. the heart rate slows down.
J. cerebral vessels contract.

The correct answer is H. The heart is responsible for pumping blood throughout the body, and when it slows, the pressure generated through circulation is reduced as blood stands in the limbs. Choice F is incorrect because the question specifically asks about adults, and the fontanelle is only present in infant skulls. Choice G is incorrect because muscle relaxation is one of the causes of a slowing heart rate—it's a degree removed from the change in blood pressure, and besides, involuntary muscle movement occurs during sleep. Choice J is incorrect—the passage indicates that cerebral blood vessels contract along with the other processes of sleep, as opposed to being their cause.

The next set of questions involves a variety of approaches to reading for implicit and explicit details.

Geology deals with the rocks of the earth's crust. It learns from their composition and structure how the rocks were made and how they have been modified. It ascertains how they have been brought to their present places and wrought to their various topographic forms, such as hills and valleys, plains and mountains. It studies the vestiges which the rocks preserve of ancient organisms which once inhabited our planet.

To obtain a general idea of the nature and method of our science before beginning its study in detail, we may visit some valley on whose sides are rocky ledges. Here the rocks lie in horizontal layers. Although only their edges are exposed, we may infer that these layers run into the upland on either side and underlie the entire district; they are part of the foundation of solid rock which everywhere is found beneath the loose materials of the surface.

The ledges of the valley are of sandstone. Looking closely at the rock we see that it is composed of myriads of grains of sand cemented together. These grains have been worn and rounded. They are sorted also, those of each layer being about of a size. By some means they have been brought hither from some more ancient source. Surely these grains have had a history before they here found a resting place,—a history which we are to learn to read.

The successive layers of the rock suggest that they were built one after another from the bottom upward. We may be as sure that each layer was formed before those above it as that the bottom courses of stone in a wall were laid before the courses which rest upon them.

We have no reason to believe that the lowest layers which we see here were the earliest ever formed. Indeed, some deep boring in the vicinity may prove that the ledges rest upon other layers of rock which extend downward for many hundreds of feet below the valley floor. Nor may we conclude that the highest layers here were the latest ever laid; for elsewhere we may find still later layers lying upon them.

A short search may find in the rock relics of animals, such as the imprints of shells, which lived when it was deposited; and as these are of kinds whose nearest living relatives now have their home in the sea, we infer that it was on the flat sea floor that the sandstone was laid. Its present position hundreds of feet above sea level proves that it has since emerged to form part of the land; while the flatness of the beds shows that the movement was so uniform and gentle as not to break or strongly bend them from their original attitude.

The surface of some of these layers is ripple-marked. Hence the sand must once have been as loose as that of shallow sea bottoms and sea beaches today, which is thrown into similar ripples by movements of the water. In some way the grains have since become cemented into firm rock.

Note that the layers on one side of the valley agree with those on the other, each matching the one opposite at the same level. Once they were continuous across the valley. Where the valley now is was once a continuous upland built of horizontal layers; the layers now show their edges, or outcrop, on the valley sides because they have been cut by the valley trench.

The rock of the ledges is crumbling away. At the foot of each step of rock lie fragments which have fallen. Thus the valley is slowly widening. It has been narrower in the past; it will be wider in the future.

Through the valley runs a stream. The waters of rains which have fallen on the upper parts of the stream's basin are now on their way to the river and the sea. Rock fragments and grains of sand creeping down the valley slopes come within reach of the stream and are washed along by the running water. Here and there they lodge for a time in banks of sand and gravel, but sooner or later they are taken up again and carried on. The grains of sand which were brought from some ancient source to form these rocks are on their way to some new goal. As they are washed along the rocky bed of the stream they slowly rasp and wear it deeper. The valley will be deeper in the future; it has been less deep in the past.

Excerpt from *The Elements of Geology*, by William Harmon Norton.

From information in the passage, it can be reasonably inferred that:

A. the topographical features of a given region are in their permanent state.

B. every geologic survey is recording details that are relatively temporary.

C. the presence of water is the single greatest factor in climate change.

D. fossils occur only in areas with arid, dry climates.

The correct answer is B. The passage consistently discusses that each observation is of a current state: the valley used to be narrower; it will be wider in the future; the valley used to be shallower, it will be deeper in the future. Choice A is incorrect as it directly contradicts the message of the passage. Choice C is incorrect—while water is clearly a vital element of geological transformation, there is no reference to climate change in the passage. Choice D is incorrect—the passage refers to fossils that used to live under water but now reside in the rocks in this valley, which also has water running through the bottom of it.

According to the passage, which of the following most closely identifies the effect of slowly ebbing tides on stone?

- **F.** The rough, jagged texture of crumbling rock
- **G.** The matching heights of the cliffs on either side of the valley
- **H.** The gradual angle of the river bed showing the sand was cemented into rock
- **J.** The presence of embedded fossils

The correct answer is H. The passage indicates that the rippled-texture of the lower walls of the valley suggests "the movement was so uniform and gentle" that it didn't break the rock roughly or abruptly, so choice F is incorrect. Choice G is incorrect because the height of the cliffs doesn't reflect the method of water-based erosion, merely that there was a level plain before the intrusion of a flowing body of water. Choice J is incorrect because fossils are deposited by moving water or the consequence of sediment layers as they contract into rock.

CRAFT AND STRUCTURE IN SOCIAL STUDIES AND SCIENCE

Now we're going to spend time closely reading for clues about the author. What can we find out about intentions, background, or motivations in writing the excerpt? Let's begin with this archaeology-themed excerpt we read earlier in the chapter. (You may recall our notes on it included several questions about the author's intention!)

On arrival in the country of his choice, he is recommended to continue at the National Museum the study, which we suppose he has already begun in the museums at home, of the kind of antiquities which he is likely to come across. But he should also take an early opportunity of getting into touch with the local British Archaeological School or other similar institution, where he will receive advice what to look for and where and how to look, and assistance in procuring suitable equipment. Thus the traveller who starts from Athens or Jerusalem should apply at the British School of Archaeology. He may there be given all possible assistance in obtaining such articles of equipment as are available on the spot. (Photographic supplies and all scientific instruments should be brought out from England.) The best maps of the district will also be accessible for examination (but the traveller is recommended to make inquiries in this respect before leaving England); the libraries will provide the literature dealing with the routes he proposes to take; and such a collection as the type–series of pottery and the Finlay collection of prehistoric antiquities at the British School at Athens may be useful to supplement his previous studies at museums, and enable him to observe with intelligence the potsherds, &c., that he may find on an ancient site. In return, he will be expected to report his results either to the School or to some other scientific society or museum at home. It should be unnecessary to remind him that the conditions of the law of the land relating to the reporting of discoveries to the competent authorities should be strictly observed. Such authorities should also be informed of any destruction or removal of monuments which may be noticed.

What is the author's point of view?

- **A.** An egalitarian attitude that everyone who can travel to historic sites should take advantage of the opportunity
- **B.** An international awareness of the stakes for those who travel abroad to excavate antiquities
- **C.** A British-centric sense of entitlement to the resources of institutions and any undiscovered assets belonging to foreign nations
- **D.** A healthy sense of humility about disturbing the relics of ancient civilizations

The correct answer is C. The author repeatedly refers to British institutions, museums, and materials as the most promising resources for a traveler. The author doesn't encourage anyone to travel to historic sites (choice A), nor does he indicate there are risks to the *travellers* so much as to the antiquities themselves, particularly earlier in the passage (choice B). The author certainly isn't humble about suggesting British explorers help themselves to foreign relics, so long as they notify the authorities.

Read the following excerpt from another passage you've seen before, from *Study of Child Life*, and let's walk through another question together.

The influence of art upon the life of a young child is difficult to measure. It may freely be said, however, that there is little or no danger in exaggerating its influence, and considerable danger in underrating it. It is difficult of measurement because the influence is largely an unconscious one. Indeed, it may be questioned whether that form of art which gives him the most conscious and outspoken pleasure is the form that in reality is the most beneficial; for, unquestionably, he will get great satisfaction from circus posters, and the poorly printed, abominably illustrated cheap picture-books afford him undeniable joy. He is far less likely to be expressive of his pleasure in a sun-shiny nursery, whose walls, rugs, white beds, and sun-shiny windows are all well designed and well adapted to his needs. Nevertheless, in the end the influence of this room is likely to be the greater influence and to permanently shape his ideas of the beautiful; while he is entirely certain, if allowed to develop artistically at all, to grow past the circus poster period.

The author feels that a neutral, bright, and well-lit environment is:

F. the best possible influence on a baby's aesthetic development of taste.

G. only as valuable as the entertaining posters and artwork displayed there.

H. no reason to try to measure the influence of art upon the life of a young child.

J. not something a child will ever notice or enjoy.

The correct answer is F. As indicated by the passage's final sentence, a well-lit room will permanently influence a child's idea of the beautiful. Choice G is incorrect because the author believes a child will outgrow the circus posters or picture books. Choice H is incorrect—the author mentions that it is difficult to measure the influence, but also says it would be dangerous to underrate it, and difficult to overrate. Choice J is incorrect—the author acknowledges it's difficult to determine whether a child is most benefited by what they notice consciously or unconsciously, but can't definitely say that a child *doesn't* notice his or her environment.

Here's another example of how the ACT exam will ask you to get inside the mind of a passage's author to infer what he or she believes. Remember—all you have is the passage in front of you. Leave aside any outside biases, and use only the text you see and the message it has to make assumptions about an author.

There is one industry in the world which may be called, more than any other, a socializing factor in our modern life. The industry of advertising binds men together and tightly knits the members of society into one compact mass. Every one in the big market-place of civilization has his demands and has some supply. But in order to link supply and demand, the offering must be known. The industry which overcomes the isolation of man with his wishes and with his wares lays the real foundation of the social structure. It is not surprising that it has taken gigantic dimensions and that uncounted millions are turning the wheels of the advertising factory. The influence and civilizing power of the means of propaganda go far beyond the help in the direct exchange of goods. The advertiser makes the modern newspaper and magazine possible. These mightiest agencies of public opinion and intellectual culture are supported, and their technical perfection secured, by those who pay their business tax in the form of advertisements.

Surely there is an abundance of clever advertisement writers at work, and great establishments make some careful tests before they throw their millions of circulars before the public. Yet even their so-called tests have in no way scientific character. They are simply based on watching the success in practical life, and the success is gained by instinct. Common sense tells even the most superficial advertiser that a large announcement will pay more than a small one, an advertisement in a paper with a large circulation more than in a paper with a few subscribers, one with a humorous or emotional or exciting text more than one with a tiresome and stale text. He also knows that the cover page in a magazine is worth more than the inner pages, that a picture draws attention, that a repeated insertion helps better than a lonely one. Yet even a score of such rules would not remove the scheme of advertising from the common places of the trade. They still would not show any trace of the fact that the methods of exact measurement and of laboratory research can be applied to such problems of human society.

When the author says, "Surely there is an abundance of clever advertisement writers at work, and great establishments make some careful tests before they throw their millions of circulars before the public. Yet even their so-called tests have in no way scientific character," it is a reflection of his or her belief that:

- **A.** large agencies have a variety of useful tools at their disposal to maximize their influence.
- **B.** brilliant copywriters can accomplish everything that a scientific approach could.
- **C.** psychology will provide more structure and accuracy to the practice of advertising.
- **D.** the tests that advertisers perform add nothing to the strategic impact of their product placement.

The correct answer is C. As you may have remembered from the earlier excerpt from this passage, the author firmly believes in the potential benefits psychological insight can have for the advertising industry. Choice A gets off to the right start, by paraphrasing the author's acknowledgment that advertising companies do have experience-based tests to guide their budgeting choices, but the author doesn't believe these tests are maximizing the advertisers' influence. Choice B is incorrect—the author doesn't think that "clever advertisement writers" have as much to offer as tests with scientific character. Choice D is incorrect because the author acknowledges the "careful tests" the advertisers perform.

Now we're going to look at less familiar passages so you can practice making inferences about the author with much less to go on. Our first example is from a biography of activist Susan B. Anthony (1820–1906), who fought for women's right to vote (or suffrage) as well as legal property rights in the mid- to late-nineteenth century. The temperance movement was a woman-led initiative to ban the production and sale of alcohol in the United States.

Teachers' conventions, however, were only a minor part of her new crusade, plans for which were still simmering in her mind and developing from day to day. Going back to many of the towns where she had held temperance meetings, she found that most of the societies she had organized had disbanded because women lacked the money to engage speakers or to subscribe to temperance papers. If they were married, they had no money of their own and no right to any interest outside their homes, unless their husbands consented.

Discouraged, she wrote in her diary, "As I passed from town to town I was made to feel the great evil of woman's entire dependency upon man for the necessary means to aid on any and every reform movement. Though I had long admitted the wrong, I never until this time so fully took in the grand idea of pecuniary and personal independence. It matters not how overflowing with benevolence toward suffering humanity may be the heart of woman, it avails nothing so long as she possesses not the power to act in accordance with these promptings. Woman must have a purse of her own, and how can this be, so long as the *Wife* is denied the right to her individual and joint earnings. Reflections like these, caused me to see and really feel that there was no true freedom for Woman without the possession of all her property rights, and that these rights could be obtained through legislation only, and so, the sooner the demand was made of the Legislature, the sooner would we be likely to obtain them."

Excerpt from *Susan B. Anthony, Rebel, Crusader, Humanitarian*, by Alma Lutz.

Susan B. Anthony's statement, "Reflections like these, caused me to see and really feel that there was no true freedom for Woman without the possession of all her property rights, and that these rights could be obtained through legislation only" most nearly illustrates:

- **A.** her belief that the key to women's liberation was the temperance movement.
- **B.** her faith in the judicial system to administer women's rights.
- **C.** her passion for women's suffrage.
- **D.** her realization that women's legal empowerment was the key to all the rights that would follow.

The correct answer is D. Her use of "reflections like these, causes me to see and really feel" signals this statement represents a realization, and she clearly identifies property rights as the foundation of women's freedom. Elsewhere in the passage she indicates the temperance movement was in the past, so choice A is incorrect. The quote in the question indicates she was shifting her focus to the legislative branch of government, not the judicial branch, choice B. Choice C is incorrect—even though Anthony was undoubtedly devoted to suffrage, this quote is not the best illustration of that passion.

Of course, scientific papers or journal articles cannot be shown on the ACT exam in their entirety. Sometimes, the test will ask you to infer what later parts of a passage might discuss—ones that you obviously can't see.

We have seen that the usual shape of celestial bodies themselves is spherical. Of what form then are their paths, or *orbits*, as these are called? One might be inclined at a venture to answer "circular," but this is not the case. The orbits of the planets cannot be regarded as true circles. They are ovals, or, to speak in technical language, "ellipses." Their ovalness or "ellipticity" is, however, in each case not by any means of the same degree. Some orbits—for instance, that of Earth—differ only slightly from circles; while others—those of Mars or Mercury, for example—are markedly elliptic. The orbit of the tiny planet Eros is, however, far and away the most elliptic of all, as we shall see when we come to deal with that little planet in detail.

When the author says "The orbit of the tiny planet Eros is, however, far and away the most elliptic of all, as we shall see when we come to deal with that little planet in detail," it is most likely an indication that:

F. the rest of the text will primarily deal with the orbit of Eros.

G. the rest of the text will explore different aspects of the solar system in detail.

H. understanding Eros' orbit is the key to comprehending the rest of the planets.

J. Eros' orbit is not properly an orbit at all.

The correct answer is G. The amount of time spent on other planets and their orbits in the paragraph should tell you the author does not intend to focus only on Eros in the rest of their work. Choices H and J are unsupported by the passage.

SUMMING IT UP

- The **Social Studies and Natural Science** categories feature passages with varying degrees of technical or context-dependent information. You will always be able to answer the questions from the information provided.
- **Active reading can help you to successfully navigate through the ACT Reading test passages.** ACTIVE readers **Ask** questions, make **Connections**, **Track** down important information, **Infer** and predict, **Visualize**, and **Evaluate**, making decisions and discoveries as they explore a text. Master the following before taking the ACT Reading test:
    - **Close reading:** Before beginning to answer questions, take time to read through the passage. Using your own system (or borrowing ours), mark up the text as you read. Underline key concepts, jot down questions in the margins, asterisk supporting details, etc. This will help you focus on the main idea of a passage, and its evidence.
    - **Note taking:** On a separate sheet of paper, or using the margins, reverse outline or take notes paraphrasing/summarizing each paragraph. This will help you retain facts and information for detail-oriented review questions.
    - **Finding the main idea:** The main idea is the "thesis" or major argument you as the reader take away from the passage.
    - **Referring to what is explicitly stated:** These types of questions will ask you cite specific examples from the text.
    - **Reasoning to determine implicit meaning:** These types of questions will ask you to draw conclusions from implications or suggested ideas.
    - **Locating and interpreting significant details:** These types of questions will ask you to use a variety of techniques (read more about them in the next chapter)—you'll be asked to determine the definitions of context-dependent words, select accurate summaries/paraphrases of passage content, understand sequential and cause and effect relationships, and make comparisons within a text.
    - **Analyzing the author's voice and method:** You'll also be asked to read into the author's motivations and intentions using context clues.

ONLINE PREP

WANT TO KNOW MORE?

Access more practice questions, lessons, helpful hints, and strategies for the following reading topics in *Peterson's Online Course for the ACT® Exam*:

- Understanding Social Studies Content
- Understanding Natural Sciences Passages
- Hard Science Passages

To purchase and access the course, go to **www.petersons.com/testprep/act**.

PRACTICE

Now you're ready for a two-passage practice review quiz. In the real ACT, you'll have 35 minutes to answer 40 questions. Here, you will be answering questions based on a Natural Science and a Social Studies passage.

PASSAGE I

NATURAL SCIENCE: This passage is an excerpt from *The Automobilist Abroad* by Francis Miltoun (1907).

In the library of the Patent Office in London the literature of motor road vehicles already fills many shelves. The catalogue is interesting as showing the early hopes that inventors had in connection with steam as a motive power for light road vehicles, and will be of value to all who are interested in the history of the movement or the progress made in motor-car design.

In France, the Bibliothèque of the Touring Club de France contains a hundred entries under the caption "Automobiles," besides complete files of eleven leading journals devoted to that industry. With these two sources of information at hand, and aided by the records of the Automobile Club de France and the Automobile Club of Great Britain and Ireland, the present-day historian of the automobile will find the subject well within his grasp.

There are those who doubt the utility of the automobile, as there have been scoffers at most new things under the sun; and there have been critics who have derided it for its "seven deadly sins," as there have been others who have praised its "Christian graces." The parodist who wrote the following newspaper quatrain was no enemy of the automobile in spite of his cynicism.

"A look of anguish underneath the car,

Another start; a squeak, a grunt, a jar!

The Aspiration pipe is working loose!

The vapour can't get out! And there you are!"

"Strange is it not, that of the myriads who

Have Empty Tanks and know not what to do,

Not one will tell of it when he Returns.

As for Ourselves, why, we deny it, too."

The one perfectly happy man in an automobile is he who drives, steers, or "runs the thing," even though he be merely the hired chauffeur. For proof of this one has only to note how readily others volunteer to "spell him a bit," as the saying goes. Change of scene and the exhilaration of a swift rush through space are all very well for friends in the *tonneau*, but for real "pleasure" one must be the driver. Not even the manifold responsibilities of the post will mar one's enjoyment, and there is always a supreme satisfaction in keeping one's engine running smoothly.

"Nothing to watch but the road," is the general motto for the automobile manufacturer, but the enthusiastic automobilist goes farther, and, for his motto, takes "stick to your post," and, in case of danger, as one has put it, "pull everything you see, and put your foot on everything else."

The vocabulary of the automobile has produced an entirely new "jargon," which is Greek to the multitude, but, oh, so expressive and full of meaning to the initiated.

An automobile is masculine, or feminine, as one likes to think of it, for it has many of the vagaries of both sexes. The French Academy has finally come to the fore and declared the word to be masculine, and so, taking our clue once more from the French (as we have in most things in the automobile world), we must call it *him*, and speak of it as *he*, instead of *her*, or *she*. That other much overworked word in automobilism, *chauffeur*, should be placed once for all. The driver of an automobile is not really a *chauffeur*, neither is he who minds and cares for the engine; he is a *mécanicien* and nothing else—in France and elsewhere. We needed a word for the individual who busies himself with, or drives an automobile, and so we have adapted the word *chauffeur*. Purists may cavil, but nevertheless the word is better than *driver*, or *motor-man* (which is the quintessence of snobbery), or *conductor*.

The word, *chauffeur*, the Paris *Figaro* tells us, was known long before the advent of automobiles or locomotives. History tells that about the year 1795, men strangely accoutered, their faces covered with soot and their eyes carefully disguised, entered, by night, farms and lonely habitations and committed all sorts of depredations. They garroted their victims, demanded information as to the whereabouts of their money and jewels, or dragged them before a great fire where they burned the soles of their feet. Hence they were called *chauffeurs*, a name which frightened our grandfathers as much as the scorching *chauffeur* today frightens our grandchildren.

1. Which of the following statements is supported by the passage?

   A. Early automobile drivers were resentful and fearful of the newly available technology.
   B. Early automobile owners always employed professional drivers to minimize the risks to themselves.
   C. Early automobile drivers enjoyed their vehicles so much they composed poems and essays in their honor.
   D. Early automobile drivers formed clubs to record the development and experience of driving and maintaining cars.

2. One of the author's main points about the literature of motor road vehicles found in the London Patent Office is:

   F. it compiles essential facts and trivia that all drivers should read in order to travel safely and enjoy their time on the road.
   G. it reflects the depth and breadth of interest and knowledge compiled by automobile enthusiasts in Europe.
   H. there's no substitute for the pleasure of being behind the wheel, no matter how entertaining the written materials are.
   J. it ranges from entertaining anecdotes to investigative reports, from descriptions of road trips to the implications of common driving terminology.

3. Based on the context in the passage, it is reasonable to infer the original meaning of the word *chauffeur* (line 32) is:

   A. steering wheel.
   B. driver.
   C. heater.
   D. engine.

4. The slogan "Nothing to watch but the road" used by automobile manufacturers most likely refers to the:

   F. clarity of the new glass windscreens.
   G. absence of the horses that were previously needed to pull carriages.
   H. popularity of long road trips among new car owners.
   J. security of doors that could lock, keeping out vandals.

5. The sentence, "The vocabulary of the automobile has produced an entirely new 'jargon,' which is Greek to the multitude, but, oh, so expressive and full of meaning to the initiated," marks a shift in the passage from:

   A. a broad examining of driving literature to the exploration of the French influence on British driving culture.
   B. an introduction to the history of the automobile to a study of the automobile's gender identity.
   C. the various reactions to the invention of the automobile to the history of vandalism in France.
   D. a discussion of the highlights of automobile enthusiast publications to an examination of specialized terminology relevant to drivers.

6. As used in the passage, *accoutered* (line 65) is most likely defined as:

   F. equipped.
   G. named.
   H. walking.
   J. employed.

7. The passage suggests that you can tell drivers are the happiest person in the car because:

   A. the change of scene and exhilaration of a swift rush are impossible to beat.
   B. the other passengers will offer to take the wheel and drive for a while.
   C. they get to control the radio.
   D. they have a working knowledge of the car's mechanical functions.

8. According to the passage, all of the following are true EXCEPT:

   F. the automobile has been declared masculine by the French Academy.
   G. the "motor-man" is considered arrogant.
   H. the arrival of the automobile was universally celebrated by society.
   J. driving comes with various responsibilities of mechanical ability and operation.

9. Which of the following would the author be LEAST likely to recommend?

   A. The establishment of a monthly road trip society
   B. The adoption of the term *motor-man* for paid drivers
   C. A visit to the British Patent Office
   D. A thorough understanding of the jargon surrounding driving

10. The passage suggests drivers adopted the word *chauffeur* (line 63) because:

F. *mechanic* was taken.

G. they needed a word for the person who tends and drives a car.

H. they wanted to frighten children into practicing automobile safety.

J. the French were very influential in the development of British automobiles.

PASSAGE II

SOCIAL STUDIES: This passage is an excerpt from "The Story of Aaron Burr," from *Famous Affinities of History: The Romance of Devotion, Volumes 1–4, Complete* by Lyndon Orr.

There will come a time when the name of Aaron Burr will be cleared from the prejudice which now surrounds it, when he will stand in the public estimation side by side with Alexander Hamilton, whom he shot in a duel in 1804, but whom in many respects he curiously resembled. When the white light of history shall have searched them both they will appear as two remarkable men, each having his own undoubted faults and at the same time his equally undoubted virtues.

Burr and Hamilton were born within a year of each other—Burr being a grandson of Jonathan Edwards, a famous Calvinist preacher, and Alexander Hamilton being the illegitimate son of a Scottish merchant in the West Indies. Each of them was short in stature, keen of intellect, of great physical endurance, courage, and impressive personality. Each as a young man served on the staff of Washington during the Revolutionary War, and each of them quarreled with him, though in a different way.

On one occasion Burr was quite unjustly suspected by Washington of looking over the latter's shoulder while he was writing.

Washington leaped to his feet with the exclamation:

"How dare you, Colonel Burr?"

Burr's eyes flashed fire at the question, and he retorted, haughtily:

"Colonel Burr DARE do anything."

This, however, was the end of their altercation. The cause of Hamilton's difference with his chief is not known, but it was a much more serious quarrel; so that the young officer left his staff position in a fury and took no part in the war until the end, when he was present at the battle of Yorktown.

Burr, on the other hand, helped Montgomery to storm the heights of Quebec, and nearly reached the upper citadel when his commander was shot dead and the Americans retreated. In all this confusion Burr showed himself a man of mettle. The slain Montgomery was six feet high, but Burr carried his body away with wonderful strength amid a shower of musket-balls and grape-shot.

Hamilton could never obtain an elective office, though Washington's magnanimity and clear-sightedness made Hamilton Secretary of the Treasury. Burr, on the other hand, continued his military service until the war was ended, routing the enemy at Hackensack, enduring the horrors of Valley Forge, commanding a brigade at the battle of Monmouth, and heading the defense of the city of New Haven. He was also attorney-general of New York, was elected to the United States Senate, was tied with Jefferson for the Presidency, and then became Vice-President in 1801.

Both Hamilton and Burr were effective speakers; but, while Hamilton was wordy and diffuse, Burr spoke always to the point, with clear and cogent reasoning. Both were lavish spenders of money, and both were engaged in duels before the fatal one in which Hamilton fell. Both believed in dueling as the only way of settling an affair of honor. Both lost children under tragic circumstances. Neither of them was averse to love affairs, though it may be said that Hamilton sought women, while Burr was rather sought by women. When Secretary of the Treasury, Hamilton was obliged to confess an adulterous amour in order to save himself from the charge of corrupt practices in public office. So long as Burr's first wife Theodosia lived, he was a devoted, faithful husband to her, though she was married when they first became romantically involved. Hamilton confessed his illicit acts while his wife, formerly Miss Elizabeth Schuyler, was living. She spent her later years working to restore Hamilton's legacy, raising funds for the Washington Monument, and establishing the first private orphanage in New York City.

The most extraordinary thing about Aaron Burr was the magnetic quality that was felt by every one who approached him. The roots of this penetrated down into a deep vitality. He was always young, always alert, polished in manner, courageous with that sort of courage which does not even recognize the presence of danger, charming in conversation, and able to adapt it to men or women of any age whatever. His hair was still dark in his eightieth year. His step was still elastic, his motions were still as spontaneous and energetic, as those of a youth.

11. What is a reasonable inference to make about the author's intention in writing this biography?

A. To reveal Burr as the power-mad, resentful politician that he was
B. To rehabilitate Burr's reputation, which is often reduced to his role in the Hamilton duel
C. To introduce readers to key figures in the Revolutionary War
D. To tell the story of Elizabeth Hamilton's orphanage

12. According to the passage, a reader learning about this period in American history should:

F. acknowledge George Washington's flashes of temper.
G. recognize the similarities between Burr and Hamilton.
H. understand the importance of the Battle of Quebec.
J. appreciate Burr's attractiveness in later life.

13. Which of the following statements is NOT a quality that Hamilton and Burr shared?

A. A short stature
B. A great courage
C. A fondness for courting women
D. A restrained oratory style

14. Compared to Burr, Hamilton:

F. worked tirelessly for social change.
G. achieved greater influence without ever being elected to office.
H. was more faithful to his wife.
J. was less appreciated by George Washington.

15. Which quotation from the passage most vividly illustrates Burr's courage?

A. "Colonel Burr DARE do anything." (line 25)
B. "The most extraordinary thing about Aaron Burr was the magnetic quality that was felt by every one who approached him." (lines 67–69)
C. "Burr spoke always to the point, with clear and cogent reasoning." (lines 49–50)
D. "Each as a young man served on the staff of Washington during the Revolutionary War." (lines 14–16)

16. From the mix of personal and political details of Burr's and Hamilton's lives it can be reasonably inferred that:

F. Burr and Hamilton had more uniting them than they had dividing them.
G. they were destined to be enemies due to their conflicting political ambitions.
H. Elizabeth Hamilton's efforts made a major difference in restoring Hamilton's legacy at the expense of Burr's.
J. Burr's strength and clarity would have outlasted Hamilton's diffuse speaking habits and personal frailties, if not for their tragic showdown.

17. When the author mentions "Both were lavish spenders of money, and both were engaged in duels before the fatal one in which Hamilton fell," (lines 50–52) she is most nearly illustrating her main idea that:

A. neither Hamilton nor Burr deserved their illustrious reputations.
B. both had a habit of shooting their mouths off thoughtlessly.
C. Burr was also a flawed individual, though his strengths were considerable.
D. Hamilton had more money than sense.

18. Which of the following most clearly distinguishes between Hamilton's and Burr's quarrels with George Washington?

F. Hamilton's was more drastic; Burr's was a misunderstanding.
G. Burr's was more pivotal in American history; Hamilton's was overrated.
H. Hamilton's was a result of his hot temper; Burr's was attributable to his pride.
J. Burr's made him famous; Hamilton's disgraced him.

19. Which of the following qualities best explains Burr's appeal to his contemporaries?

A. His youthful walk and vitality
B. His polished manners and unselfconscious courage
C. His belief in dueling as the only way of settling an affair of honor
D. His renowned grandfather, Jonathan Edwards

20. Which of the following answer choices reflects the correct chronological arrangement of Hamilton's and Burr's lives?

I. Hamilton is killed in a duel with Burr.
II. Burr becomes Vice-President.
III. The Battle of Yorktown is fought.
IV. Both men join the Revolutionary army.

F. III, IV, I, II
G. IV, III, II, I
H. IV, II, III, I
J. II, IV, I, III

Answers and Explanations

1. **The correct answer is D.** The statement that early automobile drivers formed clubs to record the development and experience of driving and maintaining cars is supported by paragraph 2 where the passage mentions specific clubs that were devoted to the industry. While there is a satirical poem in the passage, it is only one example of its type and insufficient evidence for the conclusion that most or even many early drivers wrote poems or essays about their cars (choice C). Choice A is incorrect because the entire passage is about the joy drivers found behind the wheel; while the passage mentions professional drivers, there's no implication that many or most drivers employed chauffeurs, so choice B is not the best answer.

2. **The correct answer is G.** The opening paragraphs make clear the author has discovered a wide variety of information in the publications of automobile clubs. Choice F is incorrect—there's no indication the author thinks the information he found is crucial to being a safe driver. Choice H is incorrect because the author goes on to discuss other social context issues like the effect on language, which are just as much of interest as being behind the wheel. Choice J is incorrect because there is no discussion of investigative reports.

3. **The correct answer is C.** It is reasonable to infer that the original meaning of the word *chauffeur* is *heater*. The context clues that would help you decode this are in the final paragraph: the masked bandits dragged their victims "before a great fire where they burned the soles of their feet. Hence they were called . . . ." The *hence* is especially helpful because it connects the burning of feet to the meaning of the name.

4. **The correct answer is G.** The rest of the paragraph indicates that drivers were adjusting to the technological demands of driving automobiles, and the reasonable inference is that they were adapting their driving skills from days driving wagons or carriages. The passage does not specifically discuss features like windscreens (choice F), door locks (choice J), or the duration or distance of the driving opportunities available (choice H).

5. **The correct answer is D.** This choice is the best balancing of the specific examples of the first half of the passage and the linguistic close reading of the second half of the passage. In choice A, the second half of the answer is too specific; the passage is not specifically looking at French influence so much as vocabulary, which happens to be French. Choice B is incorrect because the first half is not as broad as an introduction to the entire history of the automobile, nor is a car's gender identity the main focus of the second half. Choice C is incorrect because the second half of the passage is not primarily devoted to vandalism in France.

6. **The correct answer is F.** The context clues that would help you determine this definition were the subsequent descriptions of "faces covered with soot and their eyes carefully disguised." While you might not recognize the root of *accouterments* (accessories), you could determine that *strangely* doesn't refer to the men's names (choice G), walking (choice H), or employment (choice J).

7. **The correct answer is B.** You can rule out choice A with the excerpt, "for real 'pleasure' one must be the driver." Choice C is incorrect—based on the implied time period of this passage, cars do not yet have radios. Choice D is incorrect—while keeping the engine running smoothly is a source of satisfaction, according to the passage, it does not provide the same enjoyment that driving does.

8. **The correct answer is H.** The passage does not mention that the arrival of the automobile was universally celebrated by society. The excerpt directly states choices F, G, and J.

9. **The correct answer is B.** The author indicates his feeling about the term *motor-man* in the second-to-last paragraph when he calls it "the quintessence of snobbery." Based on the passage, it's reasonable to infer that choices A, C, and D would all be supported by the author.

10. **The correct answer is G.** If you speak French you might recognize the reference to *mecanicien* (or mechanic), but even without that outside knowledge, choice G is the only option that reflects a specific quote from the passage. Choices H and J are risky inferences to make based on the information contained in the passage.

11. **The correct answer is B.** The evidence can be found in the opening paragraph, when the author declares Burr's name "will be cleared from the prejudice which now surrounds it" and encourages readers to esteem Burr as highly as they regard Hamilton and his role in establishing the country. The tone of the passage does not support choice A; its content is not sufficiently broad to support choice C, and Elizabeth Hamilton's orphanage is barely mentioned, so it cannot be choice D.

12. **The correct answer is G.** The clue to this inference is the prolonged comparison between the two men. Choices F and H are not given enough attention to be a main idea in the passage; the goal of the passage is not primarily to draw attention to Burr's physical condition (choice J).

13. **The correct answer is D.** The passage distinguishes between Burr's and Hamilton's speaking styles when it says "while Hamilton was wordy and diffuse, Burr spoke always to the point, with clear and cogent reasoning." In the other respects mentioned by answer choices A, B, and C, the two men were similar.

14. **The correct answer is G.** Hamilton's legacy as Treasury Secretary was far more fundamental to the formation of America's financial system than Burr's legacy in any of his elected offices at the state or national levels. Both men worked to effect change throughout their lives; Hamilton was infamously unfaithful to his wife; and Hamilton received political appointments from George Washington, while Burr never received the same recognition from his commander in chief, so choices F, H, and J are incorrect.

15. **The correct answer is A.** In context, it depicts Burr standing up to the pre-eminent American general in history. The question also asks for vividness—choices B, C, and D are descriptive, not illustrative.

16. **The correct answer is J.** Based on the author's stated intent, the emphasis on Burr's achievements was to reshape the reader's perception of this maligned historical figure; this choice would be a reasonable conclusion to reach if you found the evidence persuasive. Choice F is a theme of the passage, but it is not an inference based on the mix of personal and political details, so this choice is incorrect. Choice G is incorrect because there is no discussion of destiny, nor does the dual discussion suggest any fated outcome. Choice H is insufficiently supported by the passage—it's not clear that Elizabeth's work had any effect on Burr's public perception.

17. **The correct answer is C.** The main idea of the passage was to rehabilitate Burr's image; one way to do that is replacing mythology with a more realistic depiction. Referring to Burr's flaws is a compelling example of his humanity. It also humanizes Hamilton by portraying him as someone who believed in participating in duels, but doesn't go so far as to discard the reputations of both men (choice A), dismiss both as hotheads (choice B), or disparage Hamilton's character (choice D).

18. **The correct answer is F.** According to the passage, Burr was "quite unjustly suspected by Washington," while Hamilton's quarrel, whatever the cause, led to his abrupt departure from Washington's service. Choice G is incorrect because Burr's disagreement was not particularly significant in history, at least not as represented in the passage. Choice H is incorrect because we don't have sufficient information to know what triggered Hamilton's argument with Washington. Choice J is incorrect because Burr was not made famous until after his service in the war.

19. **The correct answer is B.** Notice the question asks for what BEST explains Burr's appeal. His personality is a more compelling explanation than his gait and energy level (choice A), his views on dueling (choice C), or his family lineage (choice D).

20. **The correct answer is G.** Hamilton and Burr were both working with George Washington's staff by 1777 (statement IV). The Battle of Yorktown (statement III) occurred in 1781 (which you can also determine from its organization within the passage, and logically—America couldn't have a president or vice-president until after the revolution, and Thomas Jefferson was clearly president after George Washington). Burr became Vice-President in 1801 (statement II), as mentioned in the passage, and shot Hamilton in 1804 (statement I), which is specified in the introductory paragraph.

CHAPTER 10: LITERARY NARRATIVE/ PROSE FICTION AND HUMANITIES PASSAGES

OVERVIEW

- Determine the Key Ideas
- Locate and Interpret Key Details
- Character Description
- Relationships
- Understand Sequences of Events
- Comprehend Cause-and-Effect Relationships
- Make Comparisons
- Determine the Meaning of Context-Dependent Words, Phrases, and Statements
- Draw Generalizations
- Craft and Structure in Literary Narrative, Prose Fiction, and Humanities
- Summing It Up
- Practice

As we learned in the last chapter, when we discussed Social Studies and Natural Science-themed passages, the ACT Reading test is all about inferences—what you can reasonably conclude from having read the passage presented.

Many of the same test-taking strategies apply to the passages we'll cover in this chapter:

- Read the passage carefully and mark up your test booklet with observations and questions, or take notes separately if you're taking the exam online.
- Read the questions carefully, looking out for tricky phrases like "all of the following EXCEPT" or "Which of the following is NOT an example of . . . "
- Consider all the answer choices before you choose the most accurate response (ACT question writers love "most nearly" or "most closely resembles" or "best approximates"—the right answer choice might not perfectly match the answer you came up with on your own, but it should be the closest one to it).
- Refer back to the passage when you answer questions—don't trust your short-term memory! You may be rattled by nerves or unfamiliarity with the text. Always double back and refer to the specific paragraphs, lines, or phrases mentioned in the question or answer choices.

As a reminder, each ACT Reading test will have either a Literary Narrative or a Prose Fiction passage and a Humanities passage. Passages may be anywhere from 350 to 1,000 words long and are likely excerpts from longer works. Some sections will have one long passage; others will have two short passages. In the event there are two shorter passages, some of the questions may ask you to compare and contrast the two texts. Occasionally, you may recognize a passage from elsewhere, but you'll be able to answer all questions based only on the available content, even if you're seeing it for the first time.

Literary Narratives/Prose Fiction

Literary narratives can refer to essays, memoirs, short stories, or novels; prose fiction refers only to short stories or novels. Essays and memoirs are considered nonfiction—i.e., based on fact. The narrator is generally the author, who is most often writing in the first person. Short stories and novels are fictional—although they may be based in reality, the author's imagination is responsible for the plot, characters, and dialogue. The narrator may be omniscient, or a character may be speaking in the first person (Don't confuse the character's point of view with what the author says or believes!). A novel is a long-form piece of writing, so you may be presented with an excerpt from one without a sense of where it falls in the larger plot. Everything you need to answer any question presented will always be in the passage provided to you—you do *not* need to have read the larger work outside of the exam to get every question right.

Humanities

The Humanities category may include passages that talk about a *wide* range of topics: architecture, art, dance, ethics, film, language, literary criticism, music, philosophy, radio, television, theater, memoirs, and personal essays.

- An architecture passage might examine the history of a particular building, landmark, or famous architect's life.
- An art passage may span from a range of artistic periods and include visual art like paintings, or multimedia works like sculptures or installations.
- A film passage might be a portion of a film script or a critical discussion of a scene in a film (television and radio passages would be along the same lines).
- A passage on language might examine the etymology of a word or phrase or a sociological issue related to linguistics.
- A literary criticism passage is the discussion of prose in which its merits and flaws are assessed and evaluated.
- A music-related passage might examine a famous performance, a composer, or a piece of music that an author wishes to interpret.
- A theater passage might look at a play or a critique of a performance.
- A philosophy passage could be an excerpt of a well-known scholar's work, a more recent interpretation of that work, or even a modern exploration of a moral or ethical issue.

A representative sample of these genres will be incorporated for review throughout the chapter and in the end-of-chapter practice.

Now, let's examine the types of questions you're likely to see on the ACT Reading test. For each type, you'll learn to recognize key words and signal phrases that tell you what to look for in the passage. For the purposes of our review, the excerpted passages for each question may be shorter than the versions you'll see on the exam. You'll have a chance to practice with full-length passages at the end of the chapter.

DETERMINE THE KEY IDEAS

The Main Idea question category is the easiest to recognize on the ACT Reading test. You will see questions such as the following:

- *The main idea in this excerpt is . . .*
- *One of the author's main points about [_____] is [____].*
- *Which of the following most closely represents the main idea of the passage?*
- *Which of the following statements is supported by the passage? (main idea/inference)*

When you see questions phrased this way, they're basically asking, "What was the point of this excerpt?" Let's look at an example. Remember, read through the passage once just to get acquainted, then revisit it and read actively. You might underline ideas that are emphasized by repetition or intensity, mark pieces of dialogue that give you hints about character, or take note of other elements that strike you.

The following narrative prose passage is taken from Jane Austen's *Pride and Prejudice*. Read through it and then observe the type of main idea question that you may be asked on the ACT exam.

It is a truth universally acknowledged, that a single man in possession of a good fortune, must be in want of a wife.

However little known the feelings or views of such a man may be on his first entering a neighbourhood, this truth is so well fixed in the minds of the surrounding families, that he is considered the rightful property of some one or other of their daughters.

"My dear Mr. Bennet," said his lady to him one day, "have you heard that Netherfield Park is let at last?"

Mr. Bennet replied that he had not.

"But it is," returned she; "for Mrs. Long has just been here, and she told me all about it."

Mr. Bennet made no answer.

"Do you not want to know who has taken it?" cried his wife impatiently.

"*You* want to tell me, and I have no objection to hearing it."

This was invitation enough.

"Why, my dear, you must know, Mrs. Long says that Netherfield is taken by a young man of large fortune from the north of England; that he came down on Monday in a chaise and four to see the place, and was so much delighted with it, that he agreed with Mr. Morris immediately; that he is to take possession before Michaelmas, and some of his servants are to be in the house by the end of next week."

"What is his name?"

"Bingley."

"Is he married or single?"

"Oh! Single, my dear, to be sure! A single man of large fortune; four or five thousand a year. What a fine thing for our girls!"

"How so? How can it affect them?"

"My dear Mr. Bennet," replied his wife, "how can you be so tiresome! You must know that I am thinking of his marrying one of them."

"Is that his design in settling here?"

"Design! Nonsense, how can you talk so! But it is very likely that he may fall in love with one of them, and therefore you must visit him as soon as he comes."

"I see no occasion for that. You and the girls may go, or you may send them by themselves, which perhaps will be still better, for as you are as handsome as any of them, Mr. Bingley may like you the best of the party."

* * *

"But consider your daughters. Only think what an establishment it would be for one of them. Sir William and Lady Lucas are determined to go, merely on that account, for in general, you know, they visit no newcomers. Indeed you must go, for it will be impossible for us to visit him if you do not."

"You are over-scrupulous, surely. I dare say Mr. Bingley will be very glad to see you; and I will send a few lines by you to assure him of my hearty consent to his marrying whichever he chooses of the girls; though I must throw in a good word for my little Lizzy."

"I desire you will do no such thing. Lizzy is not a bit better than the others; and I am sure she is not half so handsome as Jane, nor half so good-humoured as Lydia. But you are always giving her the preference."

"They have none of them much to recommend them," replied he; "they are all silly and ignorant like other girls; but Lizzy has something more of quickness than her sisters."

"Mr. Bennet, how can you abuse your own children in such a way? You take delight in vexing me. You have no compassion for my poor nerves."

"You mistake me, my dear. I have a high respect for your nerves. They are my old friends. I have heard you mention them with consideration these last twenty years at least."

"Ah, you do not know what I suffer."

"But I hope you will get over it, and live to see many young men of four thousand a year come into the neighbourhood."

"It will be no use to us, if twenty such should come, since you will not visit them."

"Depend upon it, my dear, that when there are twenty, I will visit them all."

TIP: The main idea is often found in the first/topic sentence or in the last few sentences of a passage.

The main point of this excerpt is to:

- **A.** indicate that real estate in this neighborhood is at a premium.
- **B.** establish that marrying off daughters is a high priority.
- **C.** suggest the Bennets are likely to divorce.
- **D.** get the reader invested in Mr. Bingley as a character.

The correct answer is B. You can identify the correct answer to this Main Idea question from the frequency and intensity with which marriage is discussed. In the very opening sentence, Jane Austen signals her readers that the main plot of this novel is going to be the pursuit of marriage. Rather than explaining this explicitly, she then illustrates it with engaging dialogue between two of the novel's more memorable characters.

Notice how insistently Mrs. Bennet invokes marriage to her husband—how in her mind (and apparently, that of her neighbors too), it is the primary reason a wealthy young man would have moved into the neighborhood. There are not enough references to real estate for choice A to be the main idea of the passage. There's no indication the Bennet marriage is in serious trouble (choice C), nor are we given information about Mr. Bingley that might make us care about him as a person (choice D). Instead, this spirited exchange about acting in their daughters' best interests establishes the Bennets' presence in the foreground of the novel.

Variations on this question type might ask you to close read for a particular term or concept in order to make an inference, as in these sample questions.

Based on the passage, the primary purpose of a young single man is to:

- **F.** become a landowning citizen.
- **G.** find a wife.
- **H.** move to the country.
- **J.** have a large family.

The correct answer is G. You can answer this question by taking a look at the passage's opening line. The other answer choices are perfectly fine aspirations—and ones that the characters of *Pride and Prejudice* might support—but they're not the dominant idea of *this* excerpt. Remember—the answers to the questions are right there in the passage in front of you; don't bring in any outside biases.

According to the passage, a young man's best qualification for marriage is a:

- **A.** large fortune.
- **B.** notable family.
- **C.** gift of conversation.
- **D.** willingness to travel.

The correct answer is A. Again, the answer is established in the opening line of the passage. To emphasize the point, recall that Mrs. Bennet knew nothing about Mr. Bingley other than his yearly earnings, but was insistent upon the possibility of a marriage between him and one of her daughters. You should have been able to recognize this point through your earlier close reading.

Another variation of main idea questions asks you to determine which of the answer choices is most *representative* of the passage's main idea. Let's consider this excerpt from *The Atlantic Monthly* magazine article, "Doings of the Sunbeam":

Few of those who seek a photographer's establishment to have their portraits taken know at all into what a vast branch of commerce this business of sun-picturing has grown. We took occasion lately to visit one of the principal establishments in the country, that of Messrs. E & H.T. Anthony, in Broadway, New York. We had made the acquaintance of these gentlemen through the remarkable instantaneous stereoscopic views published by them, and of which we spoke in a former article in terms which some might think extravagant. Our unsolicited commendation of these marvelous pictures insured us a more than polite reception. Every detail of the branches of the photographic business to which they are more especially devoted was freely shown us, and "No Admittance" over the doors of their inmost sanctuaries came to mean for us, "Walk in, you are heartily welcome."

The guests of the neighboring hotels, as they dally with their morning's omelet, little imagine what varied uses come out of the shells which furnished them their anticipatory repast of disappointed chickens. If they had visited Mr. Anthony's upper rooms, they would have seen a row of young women before certain broad, shallow pans filled with the glairy albumen which once enveloped those potential fowls.

The one next takes a large sheet of photographic paper, (a paper made in Europe for this special purpose, very thin, smooth, and compact,) and floats it evenly upon the surface of the albumen. Presently she lifts it very carefully by the turned-up corners and hangs it *bias*, as a seamstress might say, that is, cornerwise, on a string, to dry. This "albumenized" paper is sold most extensively to photographers, who find it cheaper to buy than to prepare it. It keeps for a long time uninjured, and is "sensitized" when wanted, as we shall see by-and-by.

"Doings of the Sunbeam" (*The Atlantic Monthly*, pp. 1–3, Volume 12, No 69, July 1863)

Which of the following statements is supported by the passage?

- **F.** People on vacation never know what's happening around them.
- **G.** People might be surprised at the process required to produce photo paper.
- **H.** There are various uses for chicken eggs and their contents.
- **J.** Photography is a fascinating professional industry.

The correct answer is G. This phrasing requires you either to identify a moment when a key concept is being applied or to make an inference—a reasonable guess based on the evidence at hand—about the main idea of the passage. While the photo process does feature multiple uses for the albumen that fills an egg, "uses for eggs" (choice H) is not the main motivation for the passage, which is to describe how photo paper is produced. Since that's the main idea, and it could easily be new information to most readers, this passage supports choice G. Choice F is a distractor designed to draw your attention to the hotel-dwellers having omelets near the studio. While photography is fascinating, this passage doesn't even get to the process of taking pictures, so choice J can't be the main idea of the passage.

TIP The big realization here is that there are multiple approaches to acquiring the same information and that, once you learn to recognize the cues, finding the main idea is easier than ever.

LOCATE AND INTERPRET KEY DETAILS

Significant Detail questions are designed to assess your ability to distinguish what is significant from what is incidental or unimportant. They also test your ability to use context to understand an unfamiliar word or phrase.

Questions might be phrased like any of the following:

- *This passage establishes all of the following EXCEPT:*
- *According to the passage, which of the following most closely identifies…*
- *Based on the passage, the primary purpose of [______] was to…*
- *According to the passage, use of the word _____ instead of ____ implies which of the following?*
- *When the author does [_____], she is most nearly illustrating her point that:*
- *As used in the passage, the phrase [______] most nearly means:*
- *The [_____] in the passage best symbolizes what?*
- *The sentence [__________________] most closely means:*
- *All of the following are true EXCEPT:*
- *At the time the passage was written, what was most likely true?*

Let's refer again to the *Atlantic Monthly* excerpt to see how this question type might come into play on the ACT exam with the same passage:

Few of those who seek a photographer's establishment to have their portraits taken know at all into what a vast branch of commerce this business of sun-picturing has grown. We took occasion lately to visit one of the principal establishments in the country, that of Messrs. E & H.T. Anthony, in Broadway, New York. We had made the acquaintance of these gentlemen through the remarkable instantaneous stereoscopic views published by them, and of which we spoke in a former article in terms which some might think extravagant. Our unsolicited commendation of these marvelous pictures insured us a more than polite reception. Every detail of the branches of the photographic business to which they are more especially devoted was freely shown us, and "No Admittance" over the doors of their inmost sanctuaries came to mean for us, "Walk in, you are heartily welcome."

The guests of the neighboring hotels, as they dally with their morning's omelet, little imagine what varied uses come out of the shells which furnished them their anticipatory repast of disappointed chickens. If they had visited Mr. Anthony's upper rooms, they would have seen a row of young women before certain broad, shallow pans filled with the glairy albumen which once enveloped those potential fowls.

The one next takes a large sheet of photographic paper, (a paper made in Europe for this special purpose, very thin, smooth, and compact,) and floats it evenly upon the surface of the albumen. Presently she lifts it very carefully by the turned-up corners and hangs it *bias*, as a seamstress might say, that is, cornerwise, on a string, to dry. This "albumenized" paper is sold most extensively to photographers, who find it cheaper to buy than to prepare it. It keeps for a long time uninjured, and is "sensitized" when wanted, as we shall see by-and-by.

"Doings of the Sunbeam" (*The Atlantic Monthly*, pp. 1–3, Volume 12, No 69, July 1863)

Based on the context of the passage, what is *albumen* (line 23)?

A. the white of an egg
B. egg shells
C. a photo-developing fluid
D. egg yolk

The correct answer is A. The author's reference to neighboring hotel guests eating omelets, coming from the "shells which furnished them their anticipatory repast of disappointed chickens" (i.e., the yolks), creates an associative picture of the clear, viscous liquid that fills an egg.

Let's look at another example. This is the first time Jim, the narrator of Robert Louis Stevenson's *Treasure Island*, meets the infamous Long John Silver. Read between the lines to see what Jim is seeing in the moment, and what the author is hinting Jim will understand later.

As I was waiting, a man came out of a side room, and at a glance I was sure he must be Long John. His left leg was cut off close by the hip, and under the left shoulder he carried a crutch, which he managed with wonderful dexterity, hopping about upon it like a bird. He was very tall and strong, with a face as big as a ham—plain and pale, but intelligent and smiling. Indeed, he seemed in the most cheerful spirits, whistling as he moved about among the tables, with a merry word or a slap on the shoulder for the more favoured of his guests.

Now, to tell you the truth, from the very first mention of Long John in Squire Trelawney's letter I had taken a fear in my mind that he might prove to be the very one-legged sailor whom I had watched for so long at the old Benbow. But one look at the man before me was enough. I had seen the captain, and Black Dog, and the blind man, Pew, and I thought I knew what a buccaneer was like—a very different creature, according to me, from this clean and pleasant-tempered landlord.

I plucked up courage at once, crossed the threshold, and walked right up to the man where he stood, propped on his crutch, talking to a customer.

"Mr. Silver, sir?" I asked, holding out the note.

"Yes, my lad," said he; "such is my name, to be sure. And who may you be?" And then as he saw the squire's letter, he seemed to me to give something almost like a start.

"Oh!" said he, quite loud, and offering his hand. "I see. You are our new cabin-boy; pleased I am to see you."

And he took my hand in his large firm grasp.

Just then one of the customers at the far side rose suddenly and made for the door. It was close by him, and he was out in the street in a moment. But his hurry had attracted my notice, and I recognized him at glance. It was the tallow-faced man, wanting two fingers, who had come first to the Admiral Benbow.

"Oh," I cried, "stop him! It's Black Dog!"

"I don't care two coppers who he is," cried Silver. "But he hasn't paid his score. Harry, run and catch him."

One of the others who was nearest the door leaped up and started in pursuit.

"If he were Admiral Hawke he shall pay his score," cried Silver; and then, relinquishing my hand, "Who did you say he was?" he asked. "Black what?"

"Dog, sir," said I. "Has Mr. Trelawney not told you of the buccaneers? He was one of them."

"So?" cried Silver. "In my house! Ben, run and help Harry. One of those swabs, was he? Was that you drinking with him, Morgan? Step up here."

The man whom he called Morgan—an old, grey-haired, mahogany-faced sailor—came forward pretty sheepishly, rolling his quid.

"Now, Morgan," said Long John very sternly, "you never clapped your eyes on that Black—Black Dog before, did you, now?"

"Not I, sir," said Morgan with a salute.

"You didn't know his name, did you?"

"No, sir."

"By the powers, Tom Morgan, it's as good for you!" exclaimed the landlord. "If you had been mixed up with the like of that, you would never have put another foot in my house, you may lay to that. And what was he saying to you?"

"I don't rightly know, sir," answered Morgan.

"Do you call that a head on your shoulders, or a blessed dead-eye?" cried Long John. "Don't rightly know, don't you! Perhaps you don't happen to rightly know who you was speaking to, perhaps? Come, now, what was he jawing—v'yages, cap'ns, ships? Pipe up! What was it?"

"We was a-talkin' of keel-hauling," answered Morgan.

"Keel-hauling, was you? And a mighty suitable thing, too, and you may lay to that. Get back to your place for a lubber, Tom."

And then, as Morgan rolled back to his seat, Silver added to me in a confidential whisper that was very flattering, as I thought, "He's quite an honest man, Tom Morgan, on'y stupid. And now," he ran on again, aloud, "let's see—Black Dog? No, I don't know the name, not I. Yet I kind of think I've—yes, I've seen the swab. He used to come here with a blind beggar, he used."

"That he did, you may be sure," said I. "I knew that blind man too. His name was Pew."

"It was!" cried Silver, now quite excited. "Pew! That were his name for certain. Ah, he looked a shark, he did! If we run down this Black Dog, now, there'll be news for Cap'n Trelawney! Ben's a good runner; few seamen run better than Ben. He should run him down, hand over hand, by the powers! He talked o' keel-hauling, did he? I'LL keel-haul him!"

All the time he was jerking out these phrases he was stumping up and down the tavern on his crutch, slapping tables with his hand, and giving such a show of excitement as would have convinced an Old Bailey judge or a Bow Street runner. My suspicions had been thoroughly reawakened on finding Black Dog at the Spy-glass, and I watched the cook narrowly. But he was too deep, and too ready, and too clever for me, and by the time the two men had come back out of breath and confessed that they had lost the track in a crowd, and been scolded like thieves, I would have gone bail for the innocence of Long John Silver.

Robert Louis Stevenson uses all of the following to describe Long John Silver EXCEPT:

F. plain and pale.
G. clean and pleasant-tempered.
H. intelligent and smiling.
J. trustworthy and innocent.

The correct answer is J. While each of the other choices appears in the description of Long John Silver, it is the narrator, Jim, who is (temporarily) convinced Silver is innocent. The last paragraph, when Jim says "he was too deep, and too ready, and too clever for me" is meant to foreshadow Silver's later misdeeds.

CHARACTER DESCRIPTION

Think about your favorite books or even movies—how do they introduce a character? Do they paint a picture with words from head to toe? How do they communicate crucial information about the character's traits and habits without straight description?

Character description questions on the ACT Reading test might take on the following forms:

- *Based on the passage, [______] could be characterized as:*
- *The passage suggests that [______] could be most nearly described as:*
- *What physical attributes of [character] can be inferred from the passage?*
- *According to the passage, [character] is:*

Take a closer look at a portion of the excerpt from *Treasure Island*. What physical details did Stevenson use to create a picture of Long John Silver?

> As I was waiting, a man came out of a side room, and at a glance I was sure he must be Long John. His left leg was cut off close by the hip, and under the left shoulder he carried a crutch, which he managed with wonderful dexterity, hopping about upon it like a bird. He was very tall and strong, with a face as big as a ham—plain and pale, but intelligent and smiling. Indeed, he seemed in the most cheerful spirits, whistling as he moved about among the tables, with a merry word or a slap on the shoulder for the more favoured of his guests.

Did you find these details?

- *one leg, amputated from the hip*
- *hopping like a bird*
- *plain and pale*
- *tall and strong*
- *big intelligent, smiling face*
- *cheerful demeanor*

When approaching an ACT Reading passage, you can draw clues not only from close reading and identifying significant details, but also from making inferences from the key details an author chooses to include. From the sometimes contradictory description of Silver—plain and pale *and* intelligent and smiling—and Jim's doubt and ensuing decision to trust him, we can infer the author wants us uncertain of his true character.

Let's look at an example from that master of the inference, Sherlock Holmes. This excerpt is taken from Sir Arthur Conan Doyle's *A Study in Scarlet*. As you read, notice how the author creates a sense of Holmes' character. On the ACT Reading test, you will find questions posed like the two examples that follow the passage.

This was a lofty chamber, lined and littered with countless bottles. Broad, low tables were scattered about, which bristled with retorts, test-tubes, and little Bunsen lamps, with their blue flickering flames. There was only one student in the room, who was bending over a distant table absorbed in his work. At the sound of our steps he glanced round and sprang to his feet with a cry of pleasure. "I've found it! I've found it," he shouted to my companion, running towards us with a test-tube in his hand. "I have found a re-agent which is precipitated by haemoglobin, and by nothing else." Had he discovered a gold mine, greater delight could not have shone upon his features.

"Dr. Watson, Mr. Sherlock Holmes," said Stamford, introducing us.

"How are you?" he said cordially, gripping my hand with a strength for which I should hardly have given him credit. "You have been in Afghanistan, I perceive."

"How on earth did you know that?" I asked in astonishment.

"Never mind," said he, chuckling to himself. "The question now is about haemoglobin. No doubt you see the significance of this discovery of mine?"

"It is interesting, chemically, no doubt," I answered, "but practically—"

"Why, man, it is the most practical medico-legal discovery for years. Don't you see that it gives us an infallible test for blood stains? Come over here now!" He seized me by the coat-sleeve in his eagerness, and drew me over to the table at which he had been working. "Let us have some fresh blood," he said, digging a long bodkin into his finger, and drawing off the resulting drop of blood in a chemical pipette. "Now, I add this small quantity of blood to a litre of water. You perceive that the resulting mixture has the appearance of pure water. The proportion of blood cannot be more than one in a million. I have no doubt, however, that we shall be able to obtain the characteristic reaction."

As he spoke, he threw into the vessel a few white crystals, and then added some drops of a transparent fluid. In an instant the contents assumed a dull mahogany colour, and a brownish dust was precipitated to the bottom of the glass jar.

"Ha! ha!" he cried, clapping his hands, and looking as delighted as a child with a new toy. "What do you think of that?"

"It seems to be a very delicate test," I remarked.

"Beautiful! beautiful! The old guaiacum test was very clumsy and uncertain. So is the microscopic examination for blood corpuscles. The latter is valueless if the stains are a few hours old. Now, this appears to act as well whether the blood is old or new. Had this test been invented, there are hundreds of men now walking the earth who would long ago have paid the penalty of their crimes."

"Indeed!" I murmured.

"Criminal cases are continually hinging upon that one point. A man is suspected of a crime months perhaps after it has been committed. His linen or clothes are examined, and brownish stains discovered upon them. Are they blood stains, or mud stains, or rust stains, or fruit stains, or what are they? That is a question which has puzzled many an expert, and why? Because there was no reliable test. Now we have the Sherlock Holmes' test, and there will no longer be any difficulty."

His eyes fairly glittered as he spoke, and he put his hand over his heart and bowed as if to some applauding crowd conjured up by his imagination.

"You are to be congratulated," I remarked, considerably surprised at his enthusiasm.

***

"I have to be careful," remarked Sherlock Holmes, sticking a small piece of plaster over the prick on his finger and turning to me with a smile, "for I dabble with poisons a good deal." He held out his hand as he spoke, and I noticed that it was all mottled over with similar pieces of plaster, and discoloured with strong acids. He seemed delighted at the idea of sharing his rooms with me. "I have my eye on a suite in Baker Street," he said, "which would suit us down to the ground. You don't mind the smell of strong tobacco, I hope?"

"I always smoke 'ship's' myself," I answered.

"That's good enough. I generally have chemicals about, and occasionally do experiments. Would that annoy you?"

"By no means."

"Let me see—what are my other shortcomings? I get in the dumps at times, and don't open my mouth for days on end. You must not think I am sulky when I do that. Just let me alone, and I'll soon be right. What have you to confess now? It's just as well for two fellows to know the worst of one another before they begin to live together."

I laughed at this cross-examination. "I keep a bull pup," I said, "and I object to rows because my nerves are shaken, and I get up at all sorts of ungodly hours, and I am extremely lazy. I have another set of vices when I'm well, but those are the principal ones at present."

"Do you include violin-playing in your category of rows?" he asked, anxiously.

"It depends on the player," I answered. "A well-played violin is a treat for the gods—a badly-played one——."

"Oh, that's all right," he cried, with a merry laugh. "I think we may consider the thing as settled—that is, if the rooms are agreeable to you."

"When shall we see them?"

"Call for me here at noon tomorrow, and we'll go together and settle everything," he answered.

"All right—noon exactly," said I, shaking his hand.

We left him working among his chemicals, and we walked together towards my hotel. "By the way," I asked suddenly, stopping and turning upon Stamford, "how the deuce did he know that I had come from Afghanistan?" My companion smiled an enigmatical smile. "That's just his little peculiarity," he said. "A good many people have wanted to know how he finds things out." "Oh! a mystery is it?" I cried, rubbing my hands.

Compared to Holmes, Watson is more:

A. cautious.
B. arrogant.
C. introverted.
D. elegant.

The correct answer is A. If you pay close attention to Watson's responses to Holmes, you can see he offers diplomatic, deliberate responses after reading Holmes' reaction—while Holmes launches into the discussion of his new process without stopping to consider whether his listeners are interested. It would be difficult to be more arrogant than Holmes (choice B), who congratulates himself on an invention that hasn't proven itself useful yet. Although Watson says he "objects to rows" and mentions having his nerves shaken, he's not more introverted (choice C) than Holmes, who says "I get in the dumps at times, and don't open my mouth for days on end." While Holmes doesn't come across as elegant, with his hands bandaged and burned, Watson's description of himself as lazy, Holmes' assessment that he's fresh from Afghanistan, and the fact that they're each seeking a roommate, proves that neither is particularly elegant (choice D).

Sherlock Holmes observes that Dr. Watson has come from Afghanistan because:

F. he wants to put Watson at ease.
G. it's related to a case he's solving.
H. he wants to show off his mysterious skills.
J. he wants to travel with him.

The correct answer is H. The main clues are the way Holmes refuses to answer when Watson asks how he knows and the joy he takes in his discovery (and general intellectual superiority) elsewhere in the passage. While the men in the excerpt do discuss the applications of Holmes' experiment for unsolved crimes, that discussion is not related to Afghanistan, (choice G). Holmes seems to enjoy confounding Watson, so choice F is incorrect, and although they're planning to become roommates, there's no indication Holmes wants to travel, much less to visit Afghanistan (choice J).

RELATIONSHIPS

Imagine you're a novelist. What tools do you have at your disposal to illustrate a character? Basically, your main ones are straight physical or behavioral description, as we've seen, and expositional backstory. Relationship questions on the ACT exam usually take the following formats:

- *What can be inferred from the passage about [character's relationship with character]?*
- *The [thing] represents what to [character]?*

Or, you might see questions phrased like the next two that follow. Take another look at the excerpt from *Pride and Prejudice* to answer the following examples. Notice how the first question asks you to make an inference based on what a character says.

It is a truth universally acknowledged, that a single man in possession of a good fortune, must be in want of a wife.

However little known the feelings or views of such a man may be on his first entering a neighbourhood, this truth is so well fixed in the minds of the surrounding families, that he is considered the rightful property of some one or other of their daughters.

"My dear Mr. Bennet," said his lady to him one day, "have you heard that Netherfield Park is let at last?"

Mr. Bennet replied that he had not.

"But it is," returned she; "for Mrs. Long has just been here, and she told me all about it."

Mr. Bennet made no answer.

"Do you not want to know who has taken it?" cried his wife impatiently.

"*You* want to tell me, and I have no objection to hearing it."

This was invitation enough.

"Why, my dear, you must know, Mrs. Long says that Netherfield is taken by a young man of large fortune from the north of England; that he came down on Monday in a chaise and four to see the place, and was so much delighted with it, that he agreed with Mr. Morris immediately; that he is to take possession before Michaelmas, and some of his servants are to be in the house by the end of next week."

"What is his name?"

"Bingley."

"Is he married or single?"

"Oh! Single, my dear, to be sure! A single man of large fortune; four or five thousand a year. What a fine thing for our girls!"

"How so? How can it affect them?"

"My dear Mr. Bennet," replied his wife, "how can you be so tiresome! You must know that I am thinking of his marrying one of them."

"Is that his design in settling here?"

"Design! Nonsense, how can you talk so! But it is very likely that he may fall in love with one of them, and therefore you must visit him as soon as he comes."

"I see no occasion for that. You and the girls may go, or you may send them by themselves, which perhaps will be still better, for as you are as handsome as any of them, Mr. Bingley may like you the best of the party."

***

"But consider your daughters. Only think what an establishment it would be for one of them. Sir William and Lady Lucas are determined to go, merely on that account, for in general, you know, they visit no newcomers. Indeed you must go, for it will be impossible for us to visit him if you do not."

"You are over-scrupulous, surely. I dare say Mr. Bingley will be very glad to see you; and I will send a few lines by you to assure him of my hearty consent to his marrying whichever he chooses of the girls; though I must throw in a good word for my little Lizzy."

"I desire you will do no such thing. Lizzy is not a bit better than the others; and I am sure she is not half so handsome as Jane, nor half so good-humoured as Lydia. But you are always giving her the preference."

"They have none of them much to recommend them," replied he; "they are all silly and ignorant like other girls; but Lizzy has something more of quickness than her sisters."

"Mr. Bennet, how can you abuse your own children in such a way? You take delight in vexing me. You have no compassion for my poor nerves."

"You mistake me, my dear. I have a high respect for your nerves. They are my old friends. I have heard you mention them with consideration these last twenty years at least."

"Ah, you do not know what I suffer."

"But I hope you will get over it, and live to see many young men of four thousand a year come into the neighbourhood."

"It will be no use to us, if twenty such should come, since you will not visit them."

"Depend upon it, my dear, that when there are twenty, I will visit them all."

It can reasonably be inferred from the passage that Mr. Bennet:

- **A.** does not care about finding husbands for his daughters.
- **B.** thinks only Lizzy deserves to be married.
- **C.** is eager to assuage Mrs. Bennet's worry over visiting their neighbor.
- **D.** frequently teases Mrs. Bennet about her anxieties.

The correct answer is D. Mr. Bennet's teasing is reflected in lines 64–66 when he comments on his wife's nerves, or in lines 8–17 when he refuses to engage on her favorite topic of conversation. Choice A picks up on his detached attitude, but his teasing tone makes it difficult to conclude that he simply does not care. Choice B refers to his remark that Lizzy has more sense than her sisters, but doesn't support an inference that he doesn't think the rest deserve to be married. Choice C is incorrect because Mr. Bennet clearly has no intention of reassuring his wife.

> *"You take delight in vexing me. You have no compassion for my poor nerves."*
>
> *"You mistake me, my dear. I have a high respect for your nerves. They are my old friends. I have heard you mention them with consideration these last twenty years at least."*

This excerpt most likely suggests what about the Bennets' relationship?

- **F.** They are great friends.
- **G.** They are constantly bickering.
- **H.** Mrs. Bennet doesn't understand her husband's sense of humor.
- **J.** Mr. Bennet is considerate and respectful of his wife's feelings.

The correct answer is H. "You take delight in vexing me" indicates that while Mr. Bennet might be having fun at his wife's expense, she is not in on the joke. The one-sidedness of his teasing should tell you that choice J isn't correct; they might actually be great friends, but this passage doesn't give us any insight into any mutually beneficial aspects of their relationship. Similarly, we can't tell from this snapshot whether they *always* bicker—or indeed, if this is "bickering" or just a moment of pique.

UNDERSTAND SEQUENCES OF EVENTS

Comprehending both humanities and literary texts often involves being able to understand the order in which things happen (a baby step toward understanding cause and consequence reactions, which we'll cover later). Look for questions like:

- *Line [__] marks a shift in the passage from _____ to _____ . . .*
- *What is the first _____ [character] experiences?*
- *Which of the following statements best explains [_____]?*

Let's look at a passage with a sequence to detect and interpret, taken from Louisa May Alcott's *Jo's Boys*:

Things always went by contraries with Jo. Her first book, laboured over for years, and launched full of the high hopes and ambitious dreams of youth, foundered on its voyage, though the wreck continued to float long afterward, to the profit of the publisher at least. The hastily written story, sent away with no thought beyond the few dollars it might bring, sailed with a fair wind and a wise pilot at the helm into public favour, and came home heavily laden with an unexpected cargo of gold and glory.

A more astonished woman probably never existed than Josephine Bhaer when her little ship came into port with flags flying, cannon that had been silent before now booming gaily, and, better than all, many kind faces rejoicing with her, many friendly hands grasping hers with cordial congratul-ations. After that it was plain sailing, and she merely had to load her ships and send them off on prosperous trips, to bring home stores of comfort for all she loved and laboured for.

The fame she never did quite accept; for it takes very little fire to make a great deal of smoke nowadays, and notoriety is not real glory. The fortune she could not doubt, and gratefully received; though it was not half so large a one as a generous world reported it to be. The tide having turned continued to rise, and floated the family comfortably into a snug harbour where the older members could rest secure from storms, and whence the younger ones could launch their boats for the voyage of life.

* * *

This was the sweet and sacred side of the change; but it had its droll and thorny one, as all things have in this curious world of ours. After the first surprise, incredulity, and joy, which came to Jo, with the ingratitude of human nature, she soon tired of renown, and began to resent her loss of liberty. For suddenly the admiring public took possession of her and all her affairs, past, present, and to come. Strangers demanded to look at her, question, advise, warn, congratulate, and drive her out of her wits by well-meant but very wearisome attentions. If she declined to open her heart to them, they reproached her; if she refused to endow pet charities, relieve private wants, or sympathize with every ill and trial known to humanity, she was called hard-hearted, selfish, and haughty; if she found it impossible to answer the piles of letters sent her, she was neglectful of her duty to the admiring public; and if she preferred the privacy of home to the pedestal upon which she was requested to pose, 'the airs of literary people' were freely criticized.

She did her best for the children, they being the public for whom she wrote, and laboured stoutly to supply the demand always in the mouths of voracious youth—'More stories; more right away!' Her family objected to this devotion at their expense, and her health suffered; but for a time she gratefully offered herself up on the altar of juvenile literature, feeling that she owed a good deal to the little friends in whose sight she had found favour after twenty years of effort.

But a time came when her patience gave out; and wearying of being a lion, she became a bear in nature as in name, and returning to her den, growled awfully when ordered out. Her family enjoyed the fun, and had small sympathy with her trials, but Jo came to consider it the worse scrape of her life; for liberty had always been her dearest possession, and it seemed to be fast going from her. Living in a lantern soon loses its charm, and she was too old, too tired, and too busy to like it.

According to the passage, Jo first attained success as an author with:

- **A.** her first book, over which she labored carefully and ambitiously.
- **B.** her second book, which she wrote quickly and with much less thought.
- **C.** a series of articles that she later turned into children's stories.
- **D.** a memoir about a sea voyage that was well received.

The correct answer is B. In the first paragraph, the author describes Jo's first book (choice A) as a wreck that foundered and continues the ship metaphor to describe the unexpected success of her next book. While she later describes her stories as juvenile literature, they did not begin as articles and later become something else (choice C), nor did she ever *actually* go to sea (choice D).

It can be inferred from the last paragraph that Jo:

- **F.** still has a thriving literary career with many admirers.
- **G.** initially appreciated the glowing reception her novels received.
- **H.** tours regularly in support of her latest book.
- **J.** no longer enjoys the celebrity that comes with literary success.

The correct answer is J. The author signals the reader by writing that Jo "considered it the worse scrape of her life" and didn't like "living in a lantern." Choices F and G may be reflected elsewhere in the passage, but they're not the note the author chose to end on. There is no mention of going on a book tour (choice H)—in fact, fans of Jo's work come to her house in search of her!

Now, let's look at sequence of questions accompanying a Humanities passage, excerpted from Vitruvius's *The Ten Books on Architecture*.

Methods of Building Walls

1. There are two styles of walls: *opus reticulatum*, now used by everybody, and the ancient style called *opus incertum*. Of these, the reticulatum looks better, but its construction makes it likely to crack, because its beds and builds spread out in every direction. On the other hand, in the opus incertum, the rubble, lying in courses and imbricated, makes a wall which, though not beautiful, is stronger than the reticulatum.

2. Both kinds should be constructed of the smallest stones, so that the walls, being thoroughly puddled with the mortar, which is made of lime and sand, may hold together longer. Since the stones used are soft and porous, they are apt to suck the moisture out of the mortar and to dry it up. But when there is an abundance of lime and sand, the wall, containing more moisture, will not soon lose its strength, for they will hold it together. But as soon as the moisture is sucked out of the mortar by the porous rubble, and the lime and sand separate and disunite, the rubble can no longer adhere to them, and the wall will in time become a ruin.

3. This we may learn from several monuments in the environs of the city, which are built of marble or dimension stone, but on the inside packed with masonry between the outer walls. In the course of time, the mortar has lost its strength, which has been sucked out of it by the porousness of the rubble; so the monuments are tumbling down and going to pieces, with their joints loosened by the settling of the material that bound them together.

4. He who wishes to avoid such a disaster should leave a cavity behind the facings, and on the inside build walls two feet thick, made of red dimension stone or burnt brick or lava in courses, and then bind them to the fronts by means of iron clamps and lead. For thus his work, being no mere heap of material but regularly laid in courses, will be strong enough to last forever without a flaw, because the beds and builds, all settling equally and bonded at the joints, will not let the work bulge out, nor allow the fall of the face walls which have been tightly fastened together.

5. Consequently, the method of construction employed by the Greeks is not to be despised. They do not use a structure of soft rubble polished on the outside, but whenever they forsake dimension stone, they lay courses of lava or of some hard stone, and, as though building with brick, they bind the upright joints by interchanging the direction of the stones as they lie in the courses. Thus they attain to a perfection that will endure to eternity. These structures are of two kinds. One of them is called *isodomum*, the other *pseudisodomum*.

6. A wall is called isodomum when all the courses are of equal height; pseudisodomum, when the rows of courses do not match but run unequally. Both kinds are strong: first, because the rubble itself is of close texture and solid, unable to suck the moisture out of the mortar, but keeping it in its moist condition for a very long period; secondly, because the beds of the stones, being laid smooth and level to begin with, keep the mortar from falling, and, as they are bonded throughout the entire thickness of the wall, they hold together for a very long period.

The *opus reticulatum* walls tend to crumble and spread out because the:

A. facings are too close to the courses.
B. inner courses weren't spaced far enough apart.
C. joints aren't properly bound by alternating the orientations of the stones.
D. stones absorb moisture from the mortar and it dries out.

The correct answer is D. The answer is located in the first and second steps, where the author examines currently crumbling monuments and detects the shared imperfection in their construction.

COMPREHEND CAUSE-AND-EFFECT RELATIONSHIPS

In literature, authors often seize an opportunity to create outside associations or imply broader meaning by drawing connections between seemingly unrelated events. Often they do this by taking out the middle steps that got their main character from point A to point G. You might be asked to see if you can tell how the author leapt straight from one point to the other. Alternatively, a question might ask for more factual details, to ensure you understand who set a series of events in motion.

Look for questions like these:

- *The passage indicates [______] happened because …*
- *The passage suggests that [character] did [____] in order to …*
- *Based on the excerpt, one reason [______] happened was due to …*
- *According to [______], the main reason for [_____] was:*
- *Which organization is responsible for [______]?*

Let's see a passage that could be accompanied by this type of Reading test question. Read the following, from from *Heroes Every Child Should Know* by Hamilton Wright Mabie.

We do not know anything about Robin Hood, who he was, or where he lived, or what evil deed he had done. Any man might kill him and never pay penalty for it. But, outlaw or not, the poor people loved him and looked on him as their friend, and many a stout fellow came to join him, and led a merry life in the greenwood, with moss and fern for bed, and for meat the King's deer, which it was death to slay. Tillers of the land, yeomen, and some say knights, went on their ways freely, for of them Robin took no toll; but lordly churchmen with money-bags well filled, or proud bishops with their richly dressed followers, trembled as they drew near to Sherwood Forest—who was to know whether behind every tree there did not lurk Robin Hood or one of his men?

One day Robin was walking alone in the wood, and reached a river spanned by a very narrow bridge, over which one man only could pass. In the midst stood a stranger, and Robin bade him go back and let him go over. "I am no man of yours," was all the answer Robin got, and in anger he drew his bow and fitted an arrow to it, "Would you shoot a man who has no arms but a staff?" asked the stranger in scorn; and with shame Robin laid down his bow, and unbuckled an oaken stick at his side. "We will fight till one of us falls into the water," he said; and fight they did, till the stranger planted a blow so well that Robin rolled over into the river.

"You are a brave soul," said he, when he had waded to land, and he blew a blast with his horn which brought fifty good fellows, clad in green, to the little bridge. "Have you fallen into the river that your clothes are wet?" asked one; and Robin made answer, "No, but this stranger, fighting on the bridge, got the better of me, and tumbled me into the stream."

At this the foresters seized the stranger, and would have ducked him had not their leader bade them stop, and begged the stranger to stay with them and make one of themselves. "Here is my hand," replied the stranger, "and my heart with it. My name, if you would know it, is John Little."

"That must be altered," cried Will Scarlett; "we will call a feast, and henceforth, because he is full seven feet tall and round the waist at least an ell, he shall be called Little John." And thus it was done; but at the feast Little John, who always liked to know exactly what work he had to do, put some questions to Robin Hood. "Before I join hands with you, tell me first what sort of life is this you lead? How am I to know whose goods I shall take, and whose I shall leave? Whom I shall beat, and whom I shall refrain from beating?"

And Robin answered: "Look that you harm not any tiller of the ground, nor any yeoman of the greenwood—no knight, no squire, unless you have heard him ill spoken of. But if bishops or archbishops come your way, see that you spoil them, and mark that you always hold in your mind the High Sheriff of Nottingham, the bitterest enemy the foresters have."

According to the passage, why would churchmen and bishops tremble when passing through Sherwood Forest?

- **F.** They had no money to pay Robin Hood's toll.
- **G.** They were scared Robin Hood would turn them in to the king for slaying deer.
- **H.** They carried a lot of money and dressed flashily.
- **J.** They did not want to get lost in the forest.

The correct answer is H. The first and last paragraphs in the passage make it clear that people who work hard and are not wealthy can pass freely through Sherwood Forest. The author specifically sets up a comparison between the hard-working people who come through the forest and the "lordly churchmen" and "proud bishops" who are loaded with money and act rich. This directly contradicts choice F—the churchmen and bishops clearly had money. There's no information in the passage about who, aside from Robin Hood's men, was eating the forbidden deer, so choice G is incorrect. In addition, there is no information given to support the idea that churchmen and bishops would get lost in the forest (choice J). Choice H is correct because it arrives at the conclusion that the churchmen and bishops are afraid because they are unlike the humble tillers and yeomen who can make their way through the forest without paying Robin Hood's toll.

Which of the following best explains why John Little joined Robin Hood's group?

- **A.** Robin Hood was angry and wanted to kidnap the stranger.
- **B.** The High Sheriff of Nottingham sent him to infiltrate the group.
- **C.** By defeating Robin Hood in the fight, he was allowed to replace Robin Hood as head of the group.
- **D.** He earned their respect by fighting fairly.

The correct answer is D. After Robin Hood falls into the water, his response is not anger (choice A). Rather, he compliments John Little by saying, "You are a brave soul." Later, he goes on to stop his men from getting revenge on John Little for pushing Robin Hood into the water. These responses on Robin Hood's part eliminate choice A. The passage shows no information about whether the High Sheriff of Nottingham might be involved, so you can rule out choice B as well. There is also no information to support that John Little replaces Robin Hood (choice C); the passage merely says that he is invited to join them and change his name. Choice D is correct because Robin Hood specifically admits that John Little "got the better of me" after insisting on a fair fight without weapons, and then invites him to become one of the group. Of all the choices, the passage gives the most information to support choice D.

Now, try an example of determining cause and effect in a Humanities passage. The following was excerpted from *Hamlet at the Lyceum*, by Oscar Wilde.

It sometimes happens that at a *première* in London the least enjoyable part of the performance is the play. I have seen many audiences more interesting than the actors, and have often heard better dialogue in the *foyer* than I have on the stage. At the Lyceum, however, this is rarely the case, and when the play is a play of Shakespeare's, and among its exponents are Mr. Irving and Miss Ellen Terry, we turn from the gods in the gallery and from the goddesses in the stalls, to enjoy the charm of the production, and to take delight in the art. The lions are behind the footlights and not in front of them when we have a noble tragedy nobly acted. And I have rarely witnessed such enthusiasm as that which greeted on last Saturday night the two artists I have mentioned. I would like, in fact, to use the word ovation, but a pedantic professor has recently informed us, with the Batavian buoyancy of misapplied learning, that this expression is not to be employed except when a sheep has been sacrificed. At the Lyceum last week I need hardly say nothing so dreadful occurred. The only inartistic incident of the evening was the hurling of a bouquet from a box at Mr. Irving while he was engaged in pourtraying the agony of Hamlet's death, and the pathos of his parting with Horatio. The Dramatic College might take up the education of spectators as well as that of players, and teach people that there is a proper moment for the throwing of flowers as well as a proper method.

As regards Mr. Irving's own performance, it has been already so elaborately criticised and described, from his business with the supposed pictures in the closet scene down to his use of 'peacock' for 'paddock,' that little remains to be said; nor, indeed, does a Lyceum audience require the interposition of the dramatic critic in order to understand or to appreciate the Hamlet of this great actor. I call him a great actor because he brings to the interpretation of a work of art the two qualities which we in this century so much desire, the qualities of personality and of perfection. A few years ago it seemed to many, and perhaps rightly, that the personality overshadowed the art. No such criticism would be fair now. The somewhat harsh angularity of movement and faulty pronunciation have been replaced by exquisite grace of gesture and clear precision of word, where such precision is necessary. For delightful as good elocution is, few things are so depressing as to hear a passionate passage recited instead of being acted. The quality of a fine performance is its life more than its learning, and every word in a play has a musical as well as an intellectual value, and must be made expressive of a certain emotion. So it does not seem to me that in all parts of a play perfect pronunciation is necessarily dramatic.

When the words are 'wild and whirling,' the expression of them must be wild and whirling also. Mr. Irving, I think, manages his voice with singular art; it was impossible to discern a false note or wrong intonation in his dialogue or his soliloquies, and his strong dramatic power, his realistic power as an actor, is as effective as ever. A great critic at the beginning of this century said that Hamlet is the most difficult part to personate on the stage, that it is like the attempt to 'embody a shadow.' I cannot say that I agree with this idea. Hamlet seems to me essentially a good acting part, and in Mr. Irving's performance of it there is that combination of poetic grace with absolute reality which is so eternally delightful. Indeed, if the words easy and difficult have any meaning at all in matters of art, I would be inclined to say that Ophelia is the more difficult part. She has, I mean, less material by which to produce her effects. She is the occasion of the tragedy, but she is neither its heroine nor its chief victim. She is swept away by circumstances, and gives the opportunity for situation, of which she is not herself the climax, and which she does not herself command. And of all the parts which Miss Terry has acted in her brilliant career, there is none in which her infinite powers of pathos and her imaginative and creative faculty are more shown than in her Ophelia.

According to the excerpt, one of the main reasons Wilde thought the production of *Hamlet* was excellent was due to the:

- **F.** fascinating foyer conversation of the audience.
- **G.** actors' fusion of a poetic speaking style with emotional realism.
- **H.** actors' impeccable diction.
- **J.** actors' allowing their personalities to shine through.

The correct answer is G. Wilde found the lead actor and actress' success a result of their "wild and whirling" words and expressiveness. Wilde is very particular about the fact that a play cannot live on actor persona (choice J) or brilliant elocution (choice H) alone, and in the opening paragraph he indicates this was *not* one of those productions where the audience was more interesting than the play.

MAKE COMPARISONS

Along the same lines as cause and effect, making comparisons is a way for readers to come to a deeper understanding of a text. It begins with an observation—for example, one text is portraying mothers sympathetically, while another text takes a dark view of mothers—that you then develop into an argument with textual support, like so: "These texts each use conflict to make a statement about motherhood. Text A reflects the pressure of poverty, while text B shows the benefits of a financially secure family environment."

TIP: Keep an eye out for obvious key words like "compare," and for two shorter excerpts instead of one longer one. As you read, consider what the passages have in common, and what distinguishes them.

Questions with paired passages will look something like these:

- *Which of the following statements provides the most accurate comparison of the tone of each passage?*
- *Compared to the narrator of Passage A, the narrator of Passage B ...*
- *It can reasonably be inferred that compared to [______], the narrator of [______] felt [______].*

Let's practice answering questions that accompany paired passages and ask you to relate one to the other. Passage A comes from Gene Stratton-Porter's *A Girl of the Limberlost*. Passage B is excerpted from Lucy Maud Montgomery's *Rilla of Ingleside*.

Passage A

Elnora looked into her mother's face and smiled. It was a queer sort of a little smile, and would have reached the depths with any normal mother.

"I see you've been bawling," said Mrs. Comstock. "I thought you'd get your fill in a hurry. That's why I wouldn't go to any expense. If we keep out of the poor-house we have to cut the corners close. . ."

Elnora again smiled that pitiful smile.

"Do you think I didn't know that I was funny and would be laughed at?" she asked.

"Funny?" cried Mrs. Comstock hotly.

"Yes, funny! A regular caricature," answered Elnora. "No one else wore calico, not even one other. No one else wore high heavy shoes, not even one. No one else had such a funny little old hat; my hair was not right, my ribbon invisible compared with the others, I did not know where to go, or what to do, and I had no books. What a spectacle I made for them!" Elnora laughed nervously at her own picture. "But there are always two sides! The professor said in the algebra class that he never had a better solution and explanation than mine of the proposition he gave me, which scored one for me in spite of my clothes."

"Well, I'm glad you got enough of it!"

"Oh, but I haven't," hurried in Elnora. "I just got a start. The hardest is over. Tomorrow they won't be surprised. They will know what to expect. . .

I'm willing to bear the hard part to pay for what I'll learn. Already I have selected the ward building in which I shall teach in about four years. I am going to ask for a room with a south exposure so that the flowers and moths I take in from the swamp to show the children will do well."

"You little idiot!" said Mrs. Comstock. "How are you going to pay your expenses?"

"Now that is just what I was going to ask you!" said Elnora. "You see, I have had two startling pieces of news today. I did not know I would need any money. I thought the city furnished the books, and there is an out-of-town tuition, also. I need ten dollars in the morning. Will you please let me have it?"

"Ten dollars!" cried Mrs. Comstock. "Ten dollars! Why don't you say a hundred and be done with it! I could get one as easy as the other. I told you! I told you I couldn't raise a cent. Every year expenses grow bigger and bigger. I told you not to ask for money!"

"I never meant to," replied Elnora. "I thought clothes were all I needed and I could bear them. I never knew about buying books and tuition."

"Well, I did!" said Mrs. Comstock. "I knew what you would run into! But you are so bull-dog stubborn, and so set in your way, I thought I would just let you try the world a little and see how you liked it!"

Elnora pushed back her chair and looked at her mother. "Do you mean to say," she demanded, "that you knew, when you let me go into a city classroom and reveal the fact before all of them that I expected to have my books handed out to me; do you mean to say that you knew I had to pay for them?"

Mrs. Comstock evaded the direct question.

"Anybody but an idiot mooning over a book or wasting time prowling the woods would have known you had to pay. Everybody has to pay for everything. Life is made up of pay, pay, pay! It's always and forever pay! If you don't pay one way you do another! Of course, I knew you had to pay. Of course, I knew you would come home blubbering! But you don't get a penny! I haven't one cent, and can't get one! Have your way if you are determined, but I think you will find the road somewhat rocky."

Passage B

The big living-room at Ingleside was snowed over with drifts of white cotton. Word had come from Red Cross headquarters that sheets and bandages would be required. Nan and Di and Rilla were hard at work. Mrs. Blythe and Susan were upstairs in the boys' room, engaged in a more personal task. With dry, anguished eyes they were packing up Jem's belongings. He must leave for Valcartier the next morning. They had been expecting the word but it was none the less dreadful when it came.

Rilla was basting the hem of a sheet for the first time in her life. When the word had come that Jem must go she had her cry out among the pines in Rainbow Valley and then she had gone to her mother.

"Mother, I want to do something. I'm only a girl—I can't do anything to win the war—but I must do something to help at home."

"The cotton has come up for the sheets," said Mrs. Blythe. "You can help Nan and Di make them up. And Rilla, don't you think you could organize a Junior Red Cross among the young girls? I think they would like it better and do better work by themselves than if mixed up with the older people."

"But, mother—I've never done anything like that."

"We will all have to do a great many things in the months ahead of us that we have never done before, Rilla."

"Well"—Rilla took the plunge—"I'll try, mother—if you'll tell me how to begin. I have been thinking it all over and I have decided that I must be as brave and heroic and unselfish as I can possibly be."

Mrs. Blythe did not smile at Rilla's italics. Perhaps she did not feel like smiling or perhaps she detected a real grain of serious purpose behind Rilla's romantic pose. So here was Rilla hemming sheets and organizing a Junior Red Cross in her thoughts as she hemmed; moreover, she was enjoying it—the organizing that is, not the hemming. It was interesting and Rilla discovered a certain aptitude in herself for it that surprised her. Who would be president? Not she. The older girls would not like that. Irene Howard? No, somehow Irene was not quite as popular as she deserved to be. Marjorie Drew? No, Marjorie hadn't enough backbone. She was too prone to agree with the last speaker. Betty Mead—calm, capable, tactful Betty—the very one! And Una Meredith for treasurer; and, if they were very insistent, they might make her, Rilla, secretary. As for the various committees, they must be chosen after the Juniors were organized, but Rilla knew just who should be put on which. They would meet around—and there must be no eats—Rilla knew she would have a pitched battle with Olive Kirk over that—and everything should be strictly business-like and constitutional. Her minute book should be covered in white with a Red Cross on the cover—and wouldn't it be nice to have some kind of uniform which they could all wear at the concerts they would have to get up to raise money—something simple but smart?

"You have basted the top hem of that sheet on one side and the bottom hem on the other," said Di.

Rilla picked out her stitches and reflected that she hated sewing. Running the Junior Reds would be much more interesting.

Compared to the mother-daughter relationship in Passage B, the mother-daughter relationship dynamic in Passage A could be best described as:

A. more antagonistic.
B. more perfunctory.
C. more distant.
D. more loving.

The correct answer is A. Without knowing more about the book to speculate about Mrs. Comstock's motivations, the moments in the text where she calls her daughter "you little idiot" or where it's clear she deliberately sent Elnora into a humiliating school experience illustrate that Elnora and Mrs. Comstock's relationship is much more hostile and fraught than Rilla and Mrs. Blythe's. When Rilla asks for help, Mrs. Blythe has suggestions for how to help and supports her daughter's efforts to contribute to the war effort. A mother and daughter in a perfunctory relationship would hardly take notice of each other, and Elnora and her mother are at least having this heated conversation.

It can be inferred from both passages that:

F. interpersonal relationships between young women are complicated.
G. Elnora and Rilla are both resilient and resourceful.
H. running a Junior Red Cross is harder than earning money for school.
J. girls have fewer opportunities than boys in both of these societies.

The correct answer is G. While the struggles they face are different, and their degree of family support is highly contrasted, both Elnora and Rilla demonstrate determination and focus as they approach their respective obstacles. While it is undoubtedly true that young women's interpersonal relationships are complicated, that is not the main idea of either passage (choice F). While the implicit stakes for Rilla's Red Cross Society are related to the impending war, Elnora's poverty impedes her ability to get an education, which makes choice H an oversimplification of their individual problems. Though Rilla does say she's "only a girl," that's not sufficient to make choice J correct.

DETERMINE THE MEANING OF CONTEXT-DEPENDENT WORDS, PHRASES, AND STATEMENTS

One of the relatively preferable aspects of the ACT exam is that it doesn't ask you to memorize long lists of vocabulary words or define them in your own words. Instead, you'll be asked to flex the same muscles you strengthened identifying crucial details and use context to determine the meaning of a word. Identifying the meaning of words falls under the ACT subcategory Craft and Structure.

Meaning-in-context questions on the ACT exam will look like this:

- *Which of the following most fully [explains/lists/addresses things considered by the author]?*
- *Which of the following most clearly distinguishes between [key term] and [other key term]?*
- *The passage states that all of the following are [key concept] EXCEPT:*

Looking at one of our earlier examples, let's try a sample question based on the Alcott passage.

Things always went by contraries with Jo. Her first book, laboured over for years, and launched full of the high hopes and ambitious dreams of youth, foundered on its voyage, though the wreck continued to float long afterward, to the profit of the publisher at least. The hastily written story, sent away with no thought beyond the few dollars it might bring, sailed with a fair wind and a wise pilot at the helm into public favour, and came home heavily laden with an unexpected cargo of gold and glory.

A more astonished woman probably never existed than Josephine Bhaer when her little ship came into port with flags flying, cannon that had been silent before now booming gaily, and, better than all, many kind faces rejoicing with her, many friendly hands grasping hers with cordial congratulations. After that it was plain sailing, and she merely had to load her ships and send them off on prosperous trips, to bring home stores of comfort for all she loved and laboured for.

The fame she never did quite accept; for it takes very little fire to make a great deal of smoke nowadays, and notoriety is not real glory. The fortune she could not doubt, and gratefully received; though it was not half so large a one as a generous world reported it to be. The tide having turned continued to rise, and floated the family comfortably into a snug harbour where the older members could rest secure from storms, and whence the younger ones could launch their boats for the voyage of life.

***

This was the sweet and sacred side of the change; but it had its droll and thorny one, as all things have in this curious world of ours. After the first surprise, incredulity, and joy, which came to Jo, with the ingratitude of human nature, she soon tired of renown, and began to resent her loss of liberty. For suddenly the admiring public took possession of her and all her affairs, past, present, and to come. Strangers demanded to look at her, question, advise, warn, congratulate, and drive her out of her wits by well-meant but very wearisome attentions. If she declined to open her heart to them, they reproached her; if she refused to endow pet charities, relieve private wants, or sympathize with every ill and trial known to humanity, she was called hard-hearted, selfish, and haughty; if she found it impossible to answer the piles of letters sent her, she was neglectful of her duty to the admiring public; and if she preferred the privacy of home to the pedestal upon which she was requested to pose, 'the airs of literary people' were freely criticized.

She did her best for the children, they being the public for whom she wrote, and laboured stoutly to supply the demand always in the mouths of voracious youth—'More stories; more right away!' Her family objected to this devotion at their expense, and her health suffered; but for a time she gratefully offered herself up on the altar of juvenile literature, feeling that she owed a good deal to the little friends in whose sight she had found favour after twenty years of effort.

But a time came when her patience gave out; and wearying of being a lion, she became a bear in nature as in name, and returning to her den, growled awfully when ordered out. Her family enjoyed the fun, and had small sympathy with her trials, but Jo came to consider it the worse scrape of her life; for liberty had always been her dearest possession, and it seemed to be fast going from her. Living in a lantern soon loses its charm, and she was too old, too tired, and too busy to like it.

Which of the following most fully explains what Louisa May Alcott meant by "living in a lantern" where she says of Jo, "Living in a lantern soon loses its charm, and she was too old, too tired, and busy to like it." (lines 59–61)?

A. Life so close to the flame of genius is exhausting.

B. Jo considers her surroundings fragile or unstable.

C. Because of her writing, Jo feels isolated from her family.

D. As a famous author, Jo doesn't enjoy the amount of scrutiny she receives.

The correct answer is D. The lantern reference evokes an image of living in a glass house that everyone can see inside. Choice A is not correct because nowhere in the passage does Alcott indicate Jo is tired of being a writer. Choices B and C are incorrect because Jo's family is described as supportive and even as finding her plight humorous.

Now let's see the same question type, but this time with a Humanities passage. The below is from *How to Sing*, by Lilli Lehmann.

What is a vocal register?

A series of tones sung in a certain way, which are produced by a certain position of the vocal organs—larynx, tongue, and palate. Every voice includes three registers—chest, middle, and head. But all are not employed in every class of voice.

Two of them are often found connected to a certain extent in beginners; the third is usually much weaker, or does not exist at all. Only very rarely is a voice found naturally equalized over its whole compass.

Do registers exist by nature? No. It may be said that they are created through long years of speaking in the vocal range that is easiest to the person, or in one adopted by imitation, which then becomes a fixed habit. If this is coupled with a natural and proper working of the muscles of the vocal organs, it may become the accustomed range, strong in comparison with others, and form a register by itself. This fact would naturally be appreciated only by singers.

If, on the other hand, the muscles are wrongly employed in speaking, not only the range of voice generally used, but the whole voice as well, may be made to sound badly. So, in every voice, one or another range may be stronger or weaker; and this is, in fact, almost always the case, since mankind speaks and sings in the pitch easiest or most accustomed, without giving thought to the proper position of the organs in relation to each other; and people are rarely made to pay attention as children to speaking clearly and in an agreeable voice. In the most fortunate instances the range thus practised reaches limits on both sides, not so much those of the person's power, as those set by his lack of skill, or practice. Limitations are put on the voice through taking account only of the easiest and most accustomed thing, without inquiring into the potentialities of the organs or the demands of art.

The author discusses limitations on the voice in order to:

A. discourage amateurs from injuring their voices.

B. introduce the concept of improving through conscious study.

C. explain why not every singer is aware of their register.

D. motivate readers to think of their voice even in speaking.

The correct answer is D. The author introduces the idea of limitations in order to shift the focus onto the demands of art or the voice's potential and to encourage aspiring singers to think beyond the natural limits they've set on their own voices by the way they speak. There are no specific tips given to prevent vocal damage (choice A), and the author does not appear to be urging non-singers to undertake singing lessons (choice B). Choice C is incorrect because the author indicates that singers are the ones most likely to appreciate their individual registers—it's non-singers who lack an understanding of this concept.

Which of the following most clearly distinguishes between the three types of registers?

F. Head comes naturally to everyone; chest and middle are hard to tell apart.

G. Only middle can be improved by rigorous practice.

H. Chest and middle are often found in beginners; head voice needs to be developed.

J. Head voice uses the same muscles as in speech and therefore is the strongest.

The correct answer is H. The answer lies in the third paragraph—your practice at identifying sequences should have come in handy here in helping you match up "first and second" with the registers to which they referred. Choice F is incorrect because head is the hardest register and requires the most practice; chest and middle may be difficult to tell apart for some listeners, but it is not discussed overtly in the passage. Choice G is incorrect because the author is very clear that every speaker can improve his or her register with attentive practice—though only singers may appreciate it. Choice J is incorrect because each person's vocal range is different, so the muscles and their relative strength are specific to the individual speaker or singer.

DRAW GENERALIZATIONS

Where detecting crucial details requires you to zoom in on a text, drawing generalizations asks you to pan out, identify a key concept, and transport it to another context where it can add meaning. A simple example is a friend who owns purple sneakers, purple jeans, a purple phone case—it is reasonable to infer that a purple backpack would make a good gift for her. Some ACT examples will be subtler than others, so learn to recognize key phrases like these question templates:

- *From information in the passage, it can be reasonably inferred that [______].*
- *According to the passage, a [person interacting with key concept] should...*
- *This passage states that in terms of [key concept], [action should be possible]...*
- *In [text] the narrator's description of [thing] suggests she sees [thing] as ultimately...*

The most obvious source of broad generalizations in classic literature is *Aesop's Fables*. Usually featuring animals, these fables end with a practical lesson or moral. For instance, in the fable, "The Fox and the Crane," we read about a fox that invites a crane over for dinner and learn a valuable lesson about hosting—despite the fact that we are neither foxes nor cranes.

Let's work through another example. Read the following fable, "The Man and the Lion," and answer the questions that follow.

A man and a lion traveled together through the forest. They soon began to boast of their respective superiority to each other in strength and prowess. As they were disputing, they passed a statue carved in stone, which represented "a lion strangled by a man." The traveler pointed to it and said: "See there! How strong we are, and how we prevail over even the king of beasts." The lion replied: "This statue was made by one of you men. If we lions knew how to erect statues, you would see the man placed under the paw of the lion."

The author of this fable would most likely agree with which of the following?

A. The one who lives to tell the story has a historical advantage.

B. The powerful have the right to dominate the weak.

C. He who laughs last, laughs longest.

D. There's no point in competing with your friends.

The correct answer is A. This kind of question more overtly asks you to make generalizations—you must draw a conclusion from the passage that allows you to speculate about how an author would interpret a different scenario. Since the lion and the man are ultimately depicted as equals (or at least equally as braggy!) in the fable, it's reasonable to infer Aesop would agree that the individual who gets to tell the story benefits more than the one whose story isn't told. Choice B is not supported by the passage; while choice D might seem true, it doesn't reflect the outcome of the fable. Choice C is the moral to a different fable—neither the lion nor the man is laughing because the stakes of being right are too high.

The moral of this story is most likely:

F. Misfortune tests the sincerity of friends.
G. To the victor go the spoils.
H. One story is good, till another is told.
J. Evil companions bring more hurt than profit.

The correct answer is H. The traveler's evidence is momentarily persuasive, until the lion weighs in with his interpretation of the statue. There is no misfortune depicted in the passage, nor does either partner seem particularly evil, choices F and J. Choice G might be a tempting distractor, but it doesn't refer as directly to the passage in the question.

Let's explore drawing generalizations in a Humanities passage now. The following is from David Hume's *An Enquiry Concerning the Principles of Morals*.

We may observe that, in displaying the praises of any humane, beneficent man, there is one circumstance which never fails to be amply insisted on, namely, the happiness and satisfaction, derived to society from his intercourse and good offices. To his parents, we are apt to say, he endears himself by his pious attachment and duteous care still more than by the connexions of nature. His children never feel his authority, but when employed for their advantage. With him, the ties of love are consolidated by beneficence and friendship. The ties of friendship approach, in a fond observance of each obliging office, to those of love and inclination. His domestics and dependents have in him a sure resource; and no longer dread the power of fortune, but so far as she exercises it over him. From him the hungry receive food, the naked clothing, the ignorant and slothful skill and industry. Like the sun, an inferior minister of providence he cheers, invigorates, and sustains the surrounding world.

As these topics of praise never fail to be employed, and with success, where we would inspire esteem for any one; may it not thence be concluded, that the utility, resulting from the social virtues, forms, at least, a PART of their merit, and is one source of that approbation and regard so universally paid to them?

When we recommend even an animal or a plant as USEFUL and BENEFICIAL, we give it an applause and recommendation suited to its nature. As, on the other hand, reflection on the baneful influence of any of these inferior beings always inspires us with the sentiment of aversion. The eye is pleased with the prospect of corn-fields and loaded vine-yards; horses grazing, and flocks pasturing: but flies the view of briars and brambles, affording shelter to wolves and serpents.

***

In general, what praise is implied in the simple epithet USEFUL! What reproach in the contrary!

With which of the following would David Hume, author of this excerpt, be LEAST likely to agree?

F. The primary purpose of life is to be of use to one's fellows.
G. There is a high value in beauty for its own sake.
H. Utility is a large part of how we estimate value.
J. Humans hate that which is not useful.

The correct answer is G. Choices F, H, and J all summarize parts of Hume's observations about the overlap between virtue and usefulness.

CRAFT AND STRUCTURE IN LITERARY NARRATIVE, PROSE FICTION, AND HUMANITIES

This category is where distinguishing between genres comes in handy. Remember, if it's fiction, the narrator is not necessarily the author—but you can close read to see what the author is doing to convey the character's opinion or perspective. If it's nonfiction (like an essay or memoir), it may be in first-or second person, but the narrator is generally the author—even if the author is thinking of him- or herself as a character. Remember, the Craft and Structure subsection of ACT Reading includes 25–30% of the test, so this type of analysis is crucial to your ACT Reading score.

Look for these kinds of phrases to signal that you should be looking beyond the text into who's doing the talking.

- *What is the point of view (POV)?*
- *Why did the author choose that POV?*
- *What best illustrates that POV?*
- *From the passage, what is a reasonable inference about the narrator's motivation?*
- *Which of these observations can be inferred as something the narrator/author would agree/disagree with?*
- *Which of the following best states the author's response to [______]?*
- *When the author says, "________," she is most likely suggesting ...*
- *Which of the following would the author be LEAST/MOST likely to recommend?*
- *The narrator most nearly suggests [________] because ...*
- *The narrator's statement is most nearly meant to ...*
- *The excerpt indicates that compared to the narrator's expectation about [______], the reality was ...*
- *What do you notice about the author's tone in this passage?*

The following example is an excerpt from the Foreword of Anne Brontë's *The Tenant of Wildfell Hall.*

My object in writing the following pages was not simply to amuse the Reader; neither was it to gratify my own taste, nor yet to ingratiate myself with the Press and the Public: I wished to tell the truth, for truth always conveys its own moral to those who are able to receive it.

But as the priceless treasure too frequently hides at the bottom of a well, it needs some courage to dive for it, especially as he that does so will be likely to incur more scorn and obloquy for the mud and water into which he has ventured to plunge, than thanks for the jewel he procures; as, in like manner, she who undertakes the cleansing of a careless bachelor's apartment will be liable to more abuse for the dust she raises than commendation for the clearance she effects.

Let it not be imagined, however, that I consider myself competent to reform the errors and abuses of society, but only that I would fain contribute my humble quota towards so good an aim; and if I can gain the public ear at all, I would rather whisper a few wholesome truths therein than much soft nonsense.

As the story of 'Agnes Grey' was accused of extravagant over-colouring in those very parts that were carefully copied from the life, with a most scrupulous avoidance of all exaggeration, so, in the present work, I find myself censured for depicting con amore, with 'a morbid love of the coarse, if not of the brutal,' those scenes which, I will venture to say, have not been more painful for the most fastidious of my critics to read than they were for me to describe.

I may have gone too far; in which case I shall be careful not to trouble myself or my readers in the same way again; but when we have to do with vice and vicious characters, I maintain it is better to depict them as they really are than as they would wish to appear. To represent a bad thing in its least offensive light is, doubtless, the most agreeable course for a writer of fiction to pursue; but is it the most honest, or the safest? Is it better to reveal the snares and pitfalls of life to the young and thoughtless traveller, or to cover them with branches and flowers?

Oh, reader! if there were less of this delicate concealment of facts—this whispering, 'Peace, peace,' when there is no peace, there would be less of sin and misery to the young of both sexes who are left to wring their bitter knowledge from experience.

Which of these most accurately reflects the tone of Anne Brontë in this excerpt?

A. Apologetic
B. Defiant
C. Bewildered
D. Hopeful

The correct answer is A. Phrases like "I may have gone too far; in which case I shall be careful not to trouble myself or my readers in the same way again" and her description of writing the scenes in *Agnes Grey* that critics found most difficult indicate that she regrets writing something that readers found troubling. While she is also resolute about continuing to tell the truth as she sees it, she is not defiant (choice B) or bewildered (choice C). You could argue she arrives in a more hopeful tone at the end of the passage (choice D), but that is not the dominant note of the excerpt.

You will also likely be asked to make assumptions about the author's purpose for writing a piece, as in the following.

Based on this excerpt, which of these is the most accurate inference about Brontë's intention in writing this book?

F. To gently introduce readers to the consequences of bad behavior, without upsetting or shocking them
G. To honestly convey the brutal vices and flaws that destroy lives in order to dissuade other young people from making these same mistakes
H. To atone for her previous book by writing in a more lady-like fashion about socially acceptable topics
J. To entertain readers with lurid and graphic stories of dissipation and gossip

The correct answer is G. While Anne Brontë was dismayed to receive such negative reviews for *Agnes Grey*, this introductory essay demonstrates that she thinks writing frankly and honestly is the only way to make negative stories meaningful. Choice F is not correct because Brontë doesn't believe it's helpful to "cover [snares and pitfalls] with branches and flowers." Similarly, choice H is incorrect because Brontë doesn't think writing in a "lady-like" fashion is adequate when lives are in the balance. However, her purpose is not simply to revel in what is "coarse" or "brutal," so choice J is incorrect.

SUMMING IT UP

- Questions in the **Literary Narrative** category are based on passages from short stories, novels, memoirs, and personal essays.
- Questions in the **Prose Fiction** category are based on passages from short stories and novels. Test takers will see either Literary Narrative or Prose Fiction passages on the ACT exam.
- Questions in the **Humanities** category are based on passages in the content areas of architecture, art, dance, ethics, film, language, literary criticism, music, philosophy, radio, television, and theater. Questions may also be based on passages from memoirs and personal essays.
- **ACT Reading test questions** fall into the following types:
    - **Determine main idea:** What is the author getting at? What is the defining idea of the passage? Is there a key concept being introduced or interpreted? Are you meant to be persuaded of something?
    - **Locate and interpret significant details:** This is where you're asked to close-read the passage and identify a specific fact, term, plot point, or key concept.
    - **Character description:** Remember to look not only at what the author *says* about the characters, but also how they behave and how others react to them.
    - **Relationships:** Sometimes relationships are made explicit, other times you have to closely read interactions between characters and infer how they feel about one another.
    - **Understand sequences of events:** Some passages recount events chronologically, others in order of priority—be able to decode this choice and indicate what happened first, second, third, etc.
    - **Comprehend cause-and-effect relationships:** This is another category where the answer may have been made evident by the author or require you to make an inference. Transfer your insights into relationships to this category and understand when one action is responsible for, or the result of, another.
    - **Make comparisons:** Sometimes you'll be asked to compare two elements within the same passage, or more often, to compare two different passages. How are they alike? How are they different? And most important, why does it matter? What is the impact of these differences?
    - **Determine the meaning of context-dependent words, phrases, and statements:** Often, an author's chosen context can change or more precisely identify the meaning of a key term or concept; be able to make a reasonable guess about the author's intention and understand how that might shift a reader's understanding of the passage in question.
    - **Draw generalizations:** Be able to transfer an understanding of one context to other contexts—if an author agrees with X, and X is similar to Y, then it's probable that an author would agree with Y.
    - **Analyze the author or narrator's voice and method:** Approaching these types of questions may vary by genre—be sure you know whether you're reading fiction or nonfiction, and make your inferences about the author/narrator accordingly. Look for literary devices or connotative words that offer insight beyond what is literally being said.
        - **Tone:** Look to features of the text such as word choice, subtext, tense, and pacing to evaluate an author's tone.

ONLINE PREP — Want to Know More?

Access more practice questions, lessons, helpful hints, and strategies for the following reading topics in *Peterson's Online Course for the ACT® Exam*.

- Answering Humanities Questions
- Understanding Difficult Text
- Hard Prose Passages
- Hard Reading Questions
- Advanced Reading Test Strategies

To purchase and access the course, go to **www.petersons.com/testprep/act**.

COLLEGE READINESS BENCHMARK LEARNING PATH PRACTICE

Need more practice? Go to **www.petersons.com/testprep/act** to take the College Readiness Benchmark Learning Path practice test covering Reading Strategies. To access this test, select the *Peterson's ACT® Prep Guide Online Companion* and enter the coupon code **ACT2019** at checkout.

PRACTICE

Now it's time to practice everything we've covered in this chapter. This time, you'll see the passages in full and accompanied by a complete set of questions—the sets will look like the ones you will see on the actual ACT exam. The first 10 questions accompany a Prose Fiction passage, and the second 10 accompany a Humanities passage. After you have completed all 20 questions, you will find detailed answer explanations that walk you through every answer choice.

PASSAGE I

PROSE FICTION: Passage A is an excerpt from a novel, *The Tenant of Wildfell Hall,* by Anne Brontë. Passage B is an excerpt from Charlotte Brontë's debut novel, *Jane Eyre.*

Passage A
by Anne Brontë

I believe it was on that very evening that I ventured on another invasion of Wildfell Hall. From the time of our party, which was upwards of a week ago, I had been making daily efforts to meet its mistress in her walks; and always disappointed (she must have managed it so on purpose), had nightly kept revolving in my mind some pretext for another call.

At length I concluded that the separation could be endured no longer (by this time, you will see, I was pretty far gone); and, taking from the book-case an old volume that I thought she might be interested in, though, from its unsightly and somewhat dilapidated condition, I had not yet ventured to offer it for perusal, I hastened away,—but not without sundry misgivings as to how she would receive me, or how I could summon courage to present myself with so slight an excuse.

But, perhaps, I might see her in the field or the garden, and then there would be no great difficulty: it was the formal knocking at the door, with the prospect of being gravely ushered in by Rachel, to the presence of a surprised, uncordial mistress, that so greatly disturbed me. My wish, however, was not gratified.

Mrs. Graham herself was not to be seen; but there was Arthur playing with his frolicsome little dog in the garden. I looked over the gate and called him to me. He wanted me to come in; but I told him I could not without his mother's leave. "I'll go and ask her," said the child. "No, no, Arthur, you mustn't do that; but if she's not engaged, just ask her to come here a minute. Tell her I want to speak to her." He ran to perform my bidding, and quickly returned with his mother.

How lovely she looked with her dark ringlets streaming in the light summer breeze, her fair cheek slightly flushed, and her countenance radiant with smiles. Dear Arthur! what did I not owe to you for this and every other happy meeting? Through him I was at once delivered from all formality, and terror, and constraint. In love affairs, there is no mediator like a merry, simple-hearted child—ever ready to cement divided hearts, to span the unfriendly gulf of custom, to melt the ice of cold reserve, and overthrow the separating walls of dread formality and pride.

"Well, Mr. Markham, what is it?" said the young mother, accosting me with a pleasant smile.

"I want you to look at this book, and, if you please, to take it, and peruse it at your leisure. I make no apology for calling you out on such a lovely evening, though it be for a matter of no greater importance."

"Tell him to come in, mamma," said Arthur.

"Would you like to come in?" asked the lady.

"Yes; I should like to see your improvements in the garden."

"And how your sister's roots have prospered in my charge," added she, as she opened the gate. And we sauntered through the garden, and talked of the flowers, the trees, and the book, and then of other things.

The evening was kind and genial, and so was my companion. By degrees I waxed more warm and tender than, perhaps, I had ever been before; but still I said nothing tangible, and she attempted no repulse, until, in passing a moss rose-tree that I had brought her some weeks since, in my sister's name, she plucked a beautiful half-open bud and bade me give it to Rose.

"May I not keep it myself?" I asked.

"No; but here is another for you." Instead of taking it quietly, I likewise took the hand that offered it, and looked into her face. She let me hold it for a moment, and I saw a flash of ecstatic brilliance in her eye, a glow of glad excitement on her face—I thought my hour of victory was come—but instantly a painful recollection seemed to flash upon her; a cloud of anguish darkened her brow, a marble paleness blanched her cheek and lip; there seemed a moment of inward conflict, and, with a sudden effort, she withdrew her hand, and retreated a step or two back.

"Now, Mr. Markham," said she, with a kind of desperate calmness, "I must tell you plainly that I cannot do with this. I like your company, because I am alone here, and your conversation pleases me more than that of any other person; but if you cannot be content to regard me as a friend—a plain, cold, motherly, or sisterly friend—I must beg you to leave me now, and let me alone hereafter: in fact, we must be strangers for the future."

"I will, then—be your friend, or brother, or anything you wish, if you will only let me continue to see you; but tell me why I cannot be anything more?" There was a perplexed and thoughtful pause. "Is it in consequence of some rash vow?"

"It is something of the kind," she answered. "Some day I may tell you, but at present you had better leave me; and never, Gilbert, put me to the painful necessity of repeating what I have just now said to you," she earnestly added, giving me her hand in serious kindness.

How sweet, how musical my own name sounded in her mouth!

"I will not," I replied. "But you pardon this offence?"

"On condition that you never repeat it."

"And may I come to see you now and then?"

"Perhaps—occasionally; provided you never abuse the privilege."

"I make no empty promises, but you shall see."

"The moment you do our intimacy is at an end, that's all."

"And will you always call me Gilbert? It sounds more sisterly, and it will serve to remind me of our contract."

She smiled, and once more bid me go; and at length I judged it prudent to obey, and she re-entered the house and I went down the hill.

Passage B

by Charlotte Brontë

The vehemence of emotion, stirred by grief and love within me, was claiming mastery, and struggling for full sway, and asserting a right to predominate, to overcome, to live, rise, and reign at last: yes,—and to speak.

"I grieve to leave Thornfield: I love Thornfield:—I love it, because I have lived in it a full and delightful life,—momentarily at least. I have not been trampled on. I have not been petrified. I have not been buried with inferior minds, and excluded from every glimpse of communion with what is bright and energetic and high. I have talked, face to face, with what I reverence, with what I delight in,—with an original, a vigorous, an expanded mind. I have known you, Mr. Rochester; and it strikes me with terror and anguish to feel I absolutely must be torn from you for ever. I see the necessity of departure; and it is like looking on the necessity of death."

"Where do you see the necessity?" he asked suddenly.

"Where? You, sir, have placed it before me."

"In what shape?"

"In the shape of Miss Ingram; a noble and beautiful woman,—your bride."

"My bride! What bride? I have no bride!"

"But you will have."

"Yes;—I will!—I will!" He set his teeth.

"Then I must go:—you have said it yourself."

"No: you must stay! I swear it—and the oath shall be kept."

"I tell you I must go!" I retorted, roused to something like passion. "Do you think I can stay to become nothing to you? Do you think I am an automaton?—a machine without feelings? and can bear to have my morsel of bread snatched from my lips, and my drop of living water dashed from my cup? Do you think, because I am poor, obscure, plain, and little, I am soulless and heartless? You think wrong!—I have as much soul as you,—and full as much heart! And if God had gifted me with some beauty and much wealth, I should have made it as hard for you to leave me, as it is now for me to leave you. I am not talking to you now through the medium of custom, conventionalities, nor even of mortal flesh;—it is my spirit that addresses your spirit; just as if both had passed through the grave, and we stood at God's feet, equal,—as we are!"

"As we are!" repeated Mr. Rochester—"so," he added, enclosing me in his arms. Gathering me to his breast, pressing his lips on my lips: "so, Jane!"

Questions 1–4 ask about Passage A.

1. The main idea of this passage is:
   - **A.** Gilbert enjoys being neighborly and visiting Mrs. Graham.
   - **B.** Mrs. Graham wants Gilbert to leave her alone.
   - **C.** Gilbert is using her son Arthur to make a good impression on Mrs. Graham.
   - **D.** Gilbert Markham is determined to pursue Mrs. Graham, despite her reticence.

2. Which of the following moments in the passage represents a tonal shift in the dynamic between Gilbert and Mrs. Graham?

   F. When Arthur runs to ask Mrs. Graham to come out and speak to Gilbert
   G. When Gilbert takes Mrs. Graham's hand after she offers him a rose
   H. When Gilbert finally comes up with an excuse to come visit Mrs. Graham
   J. When Mrs. Graham and Gilbert walk in the garden and talk comfortably

3. According to the passage, we can infer that Gilbert is all of the following EXCEPT:

   A. infatuated with Mrs. Graham.
   B. manipulative.
   C. determined.
   D. spontaneous.

4. What is the reader meant to infer from Mrs. Graham's abrupt change in demeanor?

   F. She really doesn't like Gilbert.
   G. She feels awkward about socializing romantically in front of her son.
   H. She is hiding something.
   J. Gilbert has unwittingly offended her.

Questions 5–8 ask about Passage B.

5. Jane confesses her feelings to Rochester because:

   A. she believes he's in love with her.
   B. her passionate nature overcomes her sense of propriety.
   C. she wants to manipulate him into letting her stay.
   D. she wants him to call off his wedding.

6. In line 9, *communion* most nearly means:

   F. a religious ritual.
   G. a collaborative mode of living.
   H. an exchange of intimate feelings.
   J. the recognition of a central authority.

7. Charlotte Brontë may have selected to tell this scene from Jane's point of view for all of the following reasons EXCEPT:

   A. to illustrate the strength of Jane's character.
   B. to maintain the mystery surrounding Rochester's past.
   C. to reveal Jane's insecurities about her position relative to Rochester's.
   D. to instill a sense of magical realism.

8. According to the passage, which of the following would Rochester MOST likely recommend as a successful way to show romantic interest in another person?

   F. Inventing an imaginary romantic partner to make your love interest jealous.
   G. Signing up for the same classes as the object of your affections.
   H. Engineering a meeting outside in a romantic wooded area.
   J. Having a frank and friendly conversation about your feelings.

Questions 9 and 10 ask about both passages.

9. Compared to the first passage, the characters in the second passage are:

   A. more in love than Gilbert and Mrs. Graham are.
   B. less bound by social convention.
   C. not hiding anything from one another.
   D. parodying the romance novel genre.

10. Considering Charlotte and Anne Brontë were living and writing at the same time, what can you conclude about the difference in their respective styles from these two excerpts?

   F. Charlotte's work was more passionately romantic; Anne's work was more grimly realistic.
   G. Anne's novel was more innovative; Charlotte's was more traditional.
   H. Charlotte's work was influenced by real life; Anne's was based solely in her imagination.
   J. Anne's novels were less sensational; Charlotte's were more scandalous.

PASSAGE II

HUMANITIES: This passage is excerpted from the introduction to *The Autobiography of Benjamin Franklin*.

The thing that makes Franklin's *Autobiography* different from every other life story of a great and successful man is the human aspect of the account. Franklin told the story of his life, as he himself says, for the benefit of his posterity. He wanted to help them by the relation of his own rise from obscurity and poverty to eminence and wealth. He is not unmindful of the importance of his public services and their recognition, yet his accounts of these achievements are given only as a part of the story, and the vanity displayed is incidental and in keeping with the honesty of the recital. There is nothing of the impossible in the method and practice of Franklin as he sets them forth. The youth who reads the fascinating story is astonished to find that Franklin in his early years struggled with the same everyday passions and difficulties that he himself experiences, and he loses the sense of discouragement that comes from a realization of his own shortcomings and inability to attain. . . .

The life of Benjamin Franklin is of importance to every American primarily because of the part he played in securing the independence of the United States and in establishing it as a nation. Franklin shares with Washington the honors of the Revolution, and of the events leading to the birth of the new nation. While Washington was the animating spirit of the struggle in the colonies, Franklin was its ablest champion abroad. To Franklin's cogent reasoning and keen satire, we owe the clear and forcible presentation of the American case in England and France; while to his personality and diplomacy as well as to his facile pen, we are indebted for the French alliance and the funds without which Washington's work must have failed. His patience, fortitude, and practical wisdom, coupled with self-sacrificing devotion to the cause of his country, are hardly less noticeable than similar qualities displayed by Washington. In fact, Franklin as a public man was much like Washington, especially in the entire disinterestedness of his public service. . . .

Franklin is a good type of our American manhood. Although not the wealthiest or the most powerful, he is undoubtedly, in the versatility of his genius and achievements, the greatest of our self-made men. The simple yet graphic story in the *Autobiography* of his steady rise from humble boyhood in a tallow-chandler shop, by industry, economy, and perseverance in self-improvement, to eminence, is the most remarkable of all the remarkable histories of our self-made men. It is in itself a wonderful illustration of the results possible to be attained in a land of unequaled opportunity by following Franklin's maxims. . . . Franklin has indeed been aptly called "many-sided." He was eminent in science and public service, in diplomacy and in literature. He was the Edison of his day, turning his scientific discoveries to the benefit of his fellow-men. He perceived the identity of lightning and electricity and set up the lightning rod. He invented the Franklin stove, still widely used, and refused to patent it. He possessed a masterly shrewdness in business and practical affairs. Carlyle called him the father of all the Yankees. He founded a fire company, assisted in founding a hospital, and improved the cleaning and lighting of streets. He developed journalism, established the American Philosophical Society, the public library in Philadelphia, and the University of Pennsylvania. He organized a postal system for the colonies, which was the basis of the present United States Post Office. Bancroft, the eminent historian, called him "the greatest diplomatist of his century." He perfected the Albany Plan of Union for the colonies. He is the only statesman who signed the Declaration of Independence, the Treaty of Alliance with France, the Treaty of Peace with England, and the Constitution. As a writer, he has produced, in his *Autobiography* and in *Poor Richard's Almanac*, two works that are not surpassed by similar writing. He received honorary degrees from Harvard and Yale in the United States, from Oxford and St. Andrews in England, and was made a fellow of the Royal Society, which awarded him the Copley gold medal for improving natural knowledge. He was one of the eight foreign associates of the French Academy of Science. . . .

Franklin's place in literature is hard to determine because he was not primarily a literary man. His aim in his writings as in his life work was to be helpful to his fellow-men. For him writing was never an end in itself, but always a means to an end. Yet his success as a scientist, a statesman, and a diplomat, as well as socially, was in no little part due to his ability as a writer. "His letters charmed all, and made his correspondence eagerly sought. His political arguments were the joy of his party and the dread of his opponents. His scientific discoveries were explained in language at once so simple and so clear that plow-boy and exquisite could follow his thought or his experiment to its conclusion." . . .

. . . Franklin was essentially a journalist. In his swift, terse style, he is most like Daniel Defoe, who in addition to writing *Robinson Crusoe*, was the first great English journalist and master of the newspaper narrative. The style of both writers is marked by homely, vigorous expression, satire, burlesque, repartee. Here the comparison must end. Defoe and his contemporaries were authors. Their vocation was writing and their success rests on the imaginative or creative power they displayed. To authorship Franklin laid no claim. He wrote no work of the imagination. He developed only incidentally a style in many respects as remarkable as that of his English contemporaries. He wrote the best autobiography in existence, one of the most widely known collections of maxims, and an unsurpassed series of political and social satires, because he was a man of unusual scope of power and usefulness, who knew how to tell his fellow-men the secrets of that power and that usefulness.

11. Based on the passage, Ben Franklin was responsible for invention or innovation in all of the following areas EXCEPT:

A. the cleaning and lighting of streets.
B. the implementation of a postal system.
C. the development of a new kitchen stove.
D. the establishment of a national bank.

12. The author characterizes Benjamin Franklin's rise "from obscurity and poverty to eminence and wealth" in order to:

F. diminish his status as a member of early America's elite.
G. encourage young readers who might be struggling with the same issues Franklin did as a young man.
H. dispel the myth that Franklin was born to be a leader.
J. explain why Franklin was so dedicated to spreading knowledge of his discoveries.

13. The phrase, "Although not the . . . the greatest of our self-made men." (lines 37–39) marks a shift in the passage from:

A. a consideration of his impoverished early years to his wealth and consequence in later life.
B. an examination of his long-term contributions to society to the presentation of his smaller reforms and initiatives.
C. a domestic perspective on Franklin to a survey of his international reputation abroad.
D. a discussion of Franklin's patriotic public service to a recounting of his varied literary and scientific discoveries.

14. Benjamin Franklin received honorary degrees from which of the following American universities?

F. Harvard
G. Stanford
H. Oxford
J. King's College

15. One of the author's main points about Benjamin Franklin in this passage is:

A. he was more essential to the American Revolution than George Washington.
B. he is the only statesman who signed the Declaration of Independence, the Treaty of Alliance with France, the Treaty of Peace with England, and the Constitution.
C. his contributions to early America were so varied and significant that everyone should read his autobiography.
D. his autobiography was hugely important at the time of its publication but has little to offer young activists and writers today.

16. According to the author of the passage, Franklin is responsible for the:

F. reconciliation of England and its former colonies.
G. foreign alliance with and funding from France.
H. popularity of autobiography as a genre.
J. invention of satire.

17. From the tone and content of this passage, you can reasonably infer that its purpose was to:

A. elevate Benjamin Franklin to equal status with George Washington.
B. serve as an introduction to Franklin's autobiography.
C. consign Franklin's life and work to its appropriate place in history.
D. reimagine Franklin as a journalist instead of a statesman.

18. Compared to novelist Daniel Defoe, Franklin:

F. was less gifted as a writer.
G. had more imagination and creativity.
H. used writing as a means to an end, rather than as a craft unto itself.
J. was wittier and more prolific.

19. Which of the following best reflects the definition of *exquisite* as used in line 85?

A. Extremely beautiful and, typically, delicate person
B. A person with intense feelings
C. A highly sensitive or discriminating person
D. A man who is affectedly concerned with his clothes and appearance; a dandy

20. "He is not unmindful . . . the honesty of the recital" (lines 6–10) indicates that compared to the author's expectation, Benjamin Franklin's attitude toward his own accomplishments was:

F. vain, self-aggrandizing, and boastful.
G. humble, focused on improving posterity.
H. bemused, as though they happened by accident.
J. resentful, because he was disappointed not to obtain more recognition.

ANSWERS AND EXPLANATIONS

1. **The correct answer is D.** Choice A is incorrect because it does not recognize Gilbert's deliberate intentions (he even says "invasion"!) in selecting a book to loan Mrs. Graham or complimenting her gardens. You might select choice B if you noticed that Mrs. Graham was avoiding Gilbert in the opening paragraph, but she appears to be happy to see him until he starts giving her romantic hints. Similarly, Gilbert certainly *is* using Arthur to get close to Mrs. Graham (choice C), but it is not the main idea of this passage.

2. **The correct answer is G.** To quote Anne Brontë, "She let me hold it for a moment, and I saw a flash of ecstatic brilliance in her eye, a glow of glad excitement on her face—I thought my hour of victory was come—but instantly a painful recollection seemed to flash upon her; a cloud of anguish darkened her brow, a marble paleness blanched her cheek and lip; there seemed a moment of inward conflict, and, with a sudden effort, she withdrew her hand, and retreated a step or two back." Before this moment, they're enjoying one another's company. Afterward, Mrs. Graham is putting Gilbert at arm's length and making him promise to stay there. Choices F, H, and J represent increases in their intimacy, rather than a tonal shift.

3. **The correct answer is D.** Gilbert is frank about having fallen in love with Mrs. Graham, deliberate about his machinations to get close to her, and insistent about maintaining their burgeoning friendship (choices A, B, and C respectively). The fact that he's been seeking opportunities to drop by or meet her by chance suggests he's more scheming than spontaneous.

4. **The correct answer is H.** The "radiant smiles" with which Mrs. Graham greets Gilbert signal that she actually does like him, so choice F is incorrect; Gilbert even notices that having Arthur around helps them both relax and be less formal, so choice G is incorrect as well. She offers him her hand in "serious kindness" even after telling him not to behave romantically, so choice J is not correct either. This is instead a moment of foreshadowing before the reveal of Mrs. Graham's big secret a few chapters later.

5. **The correct answer is B.** In the opening paragraph, Jane describes the warring emotions she's feeling, and in paragraph 12, she defiantly describes their equal status, despite their difference in social status. Choice A is incorrect because there is no evidence she thinks Rochester might reciprocate her feelings. Choice C is incorrect because it is not supported by the passage—Jane is defiantly insisting she will go to Ireland despite her feelings, not trying to convince Rochester to ask her to remain in his employ. Choice D is incorrect for similar reasons—there is no indication Jane expects Rochester to cancel his engagement.

6. **The correct answer is H.** The clues to this answer lie in the context; Jane remarks she has been surrounded by "what is bright and energetic and high" and had the chance to engage with Rochester's "original . . . vigorous . . . and expanded mind." Choice F is incorrect—this may be the most recognizable meaning of *communion*, but given the context, it is not the correct choice. Choice G is incorrect because the idea of communal living is not supported by the passage. Choice J is incorrect because there is no discussion of a higher religious or governing authority.

7. **The correct answer is D.** Presenting the scene from Jane's perspective allows readers to see her determined and passionate character (choice A), and her awareness of the gap of age, wealth, and experience between herself and Rochester. It even successfully keeps Rochester and his intentions mysterious (choice B). However, there is no sense of magical realism in the passage.

8. **The correct answer is F.** Based on his behavior in this passage, Rochester has been pretending he intends to marry someone else in order to provoke Jane into declaring her feelings. He shies away from doing anything direct like talking directly to Jane about his feelings (choice J) or arranging a rendezvous (choice H). Finding out your love interest's schedule (choice G), Rochester might suggest, can backfire if you come across as anything less than favorable.

9. **The correct answer is B.** You can determine this by Jane's description of herself as "poor, obscure, plain, and little" yet spiritually equal to her wealthy noble employer. In contrast, Gilbert and Mrs. Graham are tightly bound by social mores. There is not enough context to determine whether Rochester and Jane are hiding anything from one another (choice C), and there's no way to measure whether they are more in love. The intensity and sincerity of the prose makes it unlikely this is a parody scene (choice D)—nothing is ridiculous or played for laughs at the characters' expense.

10. **The correct answer is F.** Both Charlotte and Anne's work, as represented by these scenes, had innovative elements—the way Charlotte's poor governess is allowed to speak openly to her high-status employer, the way Anne thwarted the typical script for a love scene—as well as traditional components—Mrs. Graham guarding her honor, Mr. Rochester being brooding and vague, so choices G and J are incorrect. There is not enough information in these passages to know which novel was influenced more by the authors' lives.

11. **The correct answer is D.** The passage mentions Franklin's contributions to city street maintenance (choice A), the post office (choice B), and the invention of the Franklin stove (choice C), but while he worked in a chandler's (or candle merchant) shop, there's no mention of his involvement in the establishment of a national bank.

12. **The correct answer is G.** In the opening paragraph, the author writes, "The youth who reads the fascinating story is astonished to find that Franklin in his early years struggled with the same everyday passions and difficulties that he himself experiences, and he loses the sense of discouragement that comes from a realization of his own shortcomings and inability to attain." Choice F is incorrect because based on the amount of praise and appreciation in it, nothing in the passage is intended to diminish Benjamin Franklin. Choice H is incorrect because there is no common wisdom that Franklin was born to power or wealth. Choice J is incorrect because correlation is not causation—being a self-made man may well have factored into Franklin's interest in making his discoveries public, but the passage does not make this conjecture.

13. **The correct answer is D.** The author opens with Franklin's best-known accomplishments during the American Revolution and immediately afterward, then moves to his lesser-known but equally long-lasting achievements. Choice A is incorrect because Franklin's wealth is not the motive for the shift; choice B is incorrect because the author repeatedly makes the point that Franklin's contributions endure across the spectrum and that some of his less-nationalistic works are the most significant. Choice C is incorrect because the passage adopts the opposite approach, moving from Franklin's international influence to his domestic presence.

14. **The correct answer is F.** Read the question carefully—it asks for American universities only. Choices G and J are not mentioned in the passage, and Oxford University (choice H) is in England, so Harvard is the only correct answer.

15. **The correct answer is C.** Choice C reflects the most accurate big-picture summary of the author's attitude toward Benjamin Franklin. Choice A is broad, but not accurate; choice B is accurate but has too narrow a focus. Choice D is not supported by the passage—the author seems to believe the opposite.

16. **The correct answer is G.** The author of the passage says, "while to his personality and diplomacy as well as to his facile pen, we are indebted for the French alliance and the funds without which Washington's work must have failed." Choice F is incorrect; if anything, Franklin's satire and public writing helped make the American colonies' case for independence. Choice H is incorrect—while the passage cites Franklin's autobiography as among the greatest, he does not get credit for its invention; the same goes for his work with satire (choice J).

17. **The correct answer is B.** The passage functions as an overview of the *Autobiography*, with an explicit argument for the work's significance in literature and history. Choice A is incorrect; though the author repeatedly mentions the two together in paragraph 3, it was not the purpose of the passage. Choice C is incorrect because there is no indication the author was trying to diminish or cut Franklin's legacy down to size—on the contrary, he makes every effort to highlight its extraordinary (yet attainable) aspects. Choice D is incorrect because the author repeatedly reflects on the multifaceted nature of Franklin's life and achievements.

18. **The correct answer is H.** The author compares Franklin and Defoe in terms of style and ability, but distinguishes between them on the basis of writing as a tool versus as a vocation. Choice F is incorrect because the author clearly regards them as equal practitioners with different intentions. Choice G is incorrect because the author says, "Defoe and his contemporaries were authors. Their vocation was writing and their success rests on the imaginative or creative power they displayed. To authorship Franklin laid no claim," meaning he used the world around him to inspire his writing, not his imagination. Choice J is incorrect because the author did not compare the sizes of the literary output of the two writers, and clearly both writers are witty.

19. **The correct answer is D.** The context clue is the intended contrast in the comparison with the plow boy—a plow boy could be beautiful (choice A), have intense feelings (choice B), or be sensitive (choice C), but is not generally defined as someone concerned with their appearance or personal style.

20. **The correct answer is G.** The author acknowledges Franklin was aware of the importance of his accomplishments, which rules out choices H and J, but the use of *yet* suggests the author might have expected Franklin to brag about his achievements, when in fact his intention was to provide future generations with tools to succeed.

PART VI: SCIENCE STRATEGIES FOR THE ACT® EXAM

SCIENCE STRATEGIES FOR THE ACT® EXAM

Each section of the ACT exam tests a wide array of knowledge and problem-solving skills, and the Science test is no different. The ACT Science test focuses on your ability to consider science-based questions. You will use your general knowledge of the natural sciences and call upon your reading comprehension, data analysis, and reasoning skills to understand experiments presented to you, interpret and analyze data, and draw logical conclusions. You will be given 35 minutes to complete 40 questions in this section.

The ACT Science test covers a very wide range of material, focusing on the four main natural science disciplines:

- **Biology**, the study of life and living organisms. The field of biology includes a wide range of topics that includes cells, genetics, evolution, taxonomy, anatomy and physiology, and ecology.
- **Chemistry**, the study of matter, including its structure, properties, and reactivity. At its most basic, chemistry examines elements and atoms, which form chemical bonds to create molecules. Both elements and molecules can undergo chemical reactions that change their identities and properties.
- **Physics** is also the study of matter, but physics is more concerned with the relationship between matter and energy. As such, physics includes the study of such topics as mechanics (motion), radiation, and gravity.
- **Earth and space sciences.** Earth science, or geoscience, refers to the study of our home planet, including its composition and atmosphere. Space science, or astronomy, expands this range of knowledge to include the sun and planets of our solar system, along with the universe that exists beyond the boundaries of the Milky Way galaxy.

Together, these four disciplines (biology, chemistry, physics, and earth and space sciences) will provide the content of the ACT Science test, but your ability to reason through topics in these areas will be the main indicator of your success on the test.

While it's true that this section will require some recall of the science you have learned, the fact is that recall is *not* the most important aspect of this test. You won't be expected to have memorized the chemical formula of magnesium tungstate or the name of Saturn's second largest satellite ($MgWO_4$ and Rhea, FYI). As far as information recall goes, you will be responsible only for knowing the basics in each of the four main science disciplines. What is far more important is your ability to *apply* what you know about these disciplines and reason through these applications. For example, you might be asked to interpret a data table that tells you about the phenotypes associated with a number of different genotypes. In order to answer this question, you will need to know the basics about what genes are, and what the words *genotype* and *phenotype* mean.

TIP: It definitely will be helpful to look over books and notes from the natural science classes you have taken throughout high school. Reviewing topics you've studied over the course of your high school career can make these topics seem less scary or imposing if you happen to encounter them on the ACT Science test.

But here's another inside tip: even if you didn't know what these vocabulary words meant, you will be presented with enough information in the passage that you could probably figure it out. The take-home message here is that you can certainly study the various scientific disciplines in order to become familiar again with topics you've studied in the past, but you will not be expected to know everything about every scientific discipline. The most important skills to practice as you prepare for the ACT Science test are your problem-solving and reasoning skills, because most of the questions you'll encounter on this test fall under this category. That's where Part VI of this book comes in handy.

NOTE: There will not be any advanced mathematics on the science test, and you will not be permitted to use a calculator.

So how will the ACT Science test assess your ability to think analytically? There are three types of questions that you will encounter as you make your way through the test:

1) **Data Representation** questions will provide you with tables or graphs that contain scientific data, just like you would find if you were to read a science journal. These questions will require you to examine the data, figure out what information is provided by the data, and draw conclusions based on this information.
2) **Research Summary** questions focus more on experimental design and the results of these experiments. This is where you will come across questions that ask you to think about science procedures and reason through how they can help you answer particular questions. You may also be asked to analyze the results of these experiments.
3) **Conflicting Viewpoints** questions will give you a few different viewpoints or hypotheses that are not consistent. Your job will be to compare these viewpoints and analyze whether or not the viewpoints are valid. Conflicting Viewpoints questions are just like a scientific debate; you get the opportunity to be the judge and determine if the arguments are supported by scientific knowledge or experimental data.

These question types fall into three different ACT Science subcategories:

1) **Interpretation of Data:** This subcategory makes up 45–55% of the test, and asks you to manipulate and analyze scientific data presented in tables, graphs, and diagrams (e.g., recognize trends in data, translate tabular data into graphs, interpolate and extrapolate, and reason mathematically).
2) **Scientific Investigation:** This subcategory makes up 20–30% of the test, and asks you to understand experimental tools, procedures, and design (e.g., identify variables and controls) and compare, extend, and modify experiments.
3) **Evaluation of Models, Inferences, and Experimental Results:** This subcategory makes up 25–35% of the test, and asks you to judge the validity of scientific information, and formulate conclusions and predictions based on that information.

The next three chapters of this book will provide you with an in-depth look at each of these three ACT Science test question types, with each chapter focusing exclusively on one of the three. Each chapter will include a description of what the question type entails and what the passages are like, a walk-through of the concepts tested for the question type and how to handle them, common mistakes made, and examples of how to reason through answers from sample passages. There will also be a practice set at the end of each chapter that will give you the opportunity to practice each question type, and then you can check your answers when you're finished.

THE COLLEGE READINESS BENCHMARK LEARNING PATH

The science questions presented on the ACT exam are tough, and science on a standardized test might not be something you're used to facing. If after you've made your way through a chapter and still feel like you need more work to be your best on test day, it's best to take the College Readiness Benchmark Learning Path.

At the end of chapters 11, 12, and 13, we've created extra practice that really helps you understand what you will see on the ACT Science test. In these Benchmark practice exercises, you will find two science passages and question sets that look like the ones you will see on test day. Following each question is a very detailed answer explanation that walks you not only through the right answer, but also how we got there and why all of the other choices are incorrect.

These College Readiness Benchmark practice exercises really break down each question to explain how you should approach it if you see something similar on the actual ACT exam. They'll give you the deeper understanding you need to interpret scientific information and answer ACT Science questions.

CHAPTER 11: DATA REPRESENTATION

OVERVIEW

- What Information Does the Figure Provide?
- What Conclusions Can I Draw from the Data?
- How Can I Analyze the Data Graphically?
- How Valid Is This Data?
- What Additional Experiments Can Be Done Based on the Data?
- Common Traps in the Science Test
- Summing It Up
- College Readiness Benchmark Learning Path Practice
- Practice

On the ACT Science test, you will be able to recognize Data Representation questions immediately because you will usually see some kind of a graph, scatterplot, figure, or table that you will be required to understand and interpret. Data Representation questions—which comprise 30 to 40 percent of ACT Science test questions—tend to be rather straightforward conceptually, so the key to answering these questions is figuring out what the data actually means and what conclusions can be drawn. This type of material would be covered in Interpretation of Data questions on the exam.

A Data Representation passage always begins with a written introduction that presents the scientific topic covered or question that is being asked, provides some key terminology, and introduces the data you will have to analyze. The introduction paragraph is usually no longer than a few sentences or so; this is because the most important part of a Data Representation passage is the diagram, figure, or chart. In addition to the introduction paragraph, most passages will include an additional written paragraph (or a few paragraphs) to provide details about the experiment and the data.

Each Data Representation passage is usually accompanied by five questions that test you on several key skills in data analysis: understanding the data, drawing conclusions from the data, analyzing graphical figures, assessing the validity of the data, and thinking about future work based on the data. To tackle Data Representation questions, you will have to ask yourself several (or all) of the following questions, each of which is accompanied by a very simple example to give you an idea of how the questions might appear when you're taking the ACT Science test.

TIP: If the written portions of a Data Representation question are confusing, the visuals can usually help you to figure out what is going on in the described scenario.

WHAT INFORMATION DOES THE FIGURE PROVIDE?

This question is the launching point of your data analysis. In order to answer any of the questions in a set, you have to be able to look at the provided figure and determine what it is telling you. Once you are able to read a figure and extract information from it, you can start to draw conclusions and think about the data critically.

When you are attempting to read a figure, the best way to start is to read the introductory and surrounding paragraphs and determine the question the data is supposed to answer; in other words, what is the purpose of the experiment being conducted? Every scientific experiment is performed in order to answer some kind of scientific question—that question will almost always be directly addressed in these paragraphs. The paragraphs may also include a **hypothesis**, which is an educated prediction about the outcome of the experiment. Alternatively, you might be asked to choose a logical hypothesis for the given experiment in the questions themselves.

TIP: It may help to circle key words as you read the introductory and surrounding paragraphs to help you zoom in on the most important concepts.

The introductory and surrounding paragraphs may also provide details about the independent variable and dependent variable in the experiment. The **independent variable** is the condition that the experimenter is altering throughout the experiment, while the **dependent variable** is the condition that the experimenter is measuring throughout the experiment. Any conditions that do not change throughout the experiment, regardless of changes made in the independent variable, are called **constants**. Experiments may also include a **control variable**, which is an experimental trial that minimizes the effect of whatever the independent variable is testing.

For example, say an experiment is testing the effect of five different temperatures on the growth rate of pea plants.

- The independent variable is temperature.
- The dependent variable is the change in pea plant height.
- Constants might include amount of sunlight and amount of water provided because all pea plants receive the same amounts of each.
- A possible control variable could be a pea plant grown under the same conditions as the others, but at standard room temperature.

If you find the introductory and surrounding paragraphs confusing in a Data Representation question, or if you don't understand some of the terminology or vocabulary used, don't worry! Here's a neat insight: the figure itself can tell you all you need to know. If the figure is a diagram or picture, examine it closely, focusing on what is actually happening in the experiment and what is being measured. If the figure is a table, look at the headers along the top of the table to see which variables are being changed or measured. Usually, the headers in a table will include the independent and dependent variables. If the figure is a graph or scatterplot, look at the axes; the *y*-axis (the vertical axis) will usually be the dependent variable, while the *x*-axis (the horizontal axis) will usually be the independent variable. Understanding the passages will definitely help you to understand the specifics of the experiment more easily, but most of the time, you can figure out what is happening in the experiment based on the diagrams and figures alone.

Take a look at the following practice question. We will use the same passage and data throughout the first few examples in this chapter so you can get a sense of the different question types that will come up within a Data Representation set.

Five pea plants were planted in identical pots containing the same amount and type of soil. Each plant was placed in temperature-controlled boxes at different temperatures ranging from 0 to 80°C. Each plant was provided with the same sunlight exposure and volume of water at the same times each day. The height of each plant was measured and recorded at 12 p.m. every eighth day.

Pea Plant Air Temperature (°C)	Pea Plant Height (cm) After *x* Days				
	0	**8**	**16**	**24**	**32**
0°	0	5.2	20.2	26.0	34.3
20°	0	5.3	23.4	28.2	35.0
40°	0	3.2	17.5	22.4	25.7
60°	0	2.7	13.0	15.2	19.0
80°	0	1.2	8.8	12.3	14.2

Which of the following would be an appropriate hypothesis for this experiment?

A. If pea plants tend to favor colder temperatures, then increasing the air temperature will result in faster growth rates.

B. If pea plants tend to favor colder temperatures, then increasing the air temperature will result in slower growth rates.

C. If pea plants tend to favor colder temperatures, then increased water volume will result in faster growth rates.

D. If pea plants tend to favor colder temperatures, then increased water volume will result in slower growth rates.

The correct answer is B. The introduction tells us that the five plants are grown under identical conditions, with the exception of varying temperatures, and that plant height was measured every eight days. That means that the independent variable is temperature, because temperature is the condition that the experimenter is changing. We can also see that the dependent variable is plant height, because this is the variable that the experimenter is measuring. Both of these variables appear in the table; the independent variable is the header of the first column, while the dependent variable is the header of the rest of the columns. So even if we had no idea what the introductory paragraph was discussing, we can determine the scientific question simply by looking at the provided table. Since the experimenter is measuring the changes in height over time, or the growth rates, of pea plants grown at different temperatures, the scientific question might be: *How does temperature affect the growth rate of pea plants?*

The question asks us to choose an appropriate hypothesis. We have to choose a hypothesis that provides a predicted answer to the scientific question we've just asked. If we look at the four possible answer choices, we can immediately rule out both choice C and choice D. These choices both provide predictions that involve changes in water volume, which the passage explicitly states was *not* changed. Choices A and B both relate to temperature. The first part of each hypothesis is "If pea plants tend to favor colder temperatures . . ." The logical prediction would be that if pea plants favor colder temperatures, they will grow more quickly at lower temperatures.

WHAT CONCLUSIONS CAN I DRAW FROM THE DATA?

Once you've successfully read a figure and determined its purpose, you will almost always be asked to use the figure to answer questions or draw conclusions. When examining a data set, you will probably notice patterns and trends. Recognizing these trends will be extremely helpful when you're trying to draw conclusions because the conclusions will usually be based on these observations. Questions that ask you to draw conclusions from the data might ask you to describe a pattern from the data, to predict a result that is not displayed in the figure, or to apply the data to a different but relevant scenario. Patterns and trends in the data will usually be fairly straightforward; for instance, if a few different conditions are tested for a particular independent variable, the results for each condition will be distinctive enough for you to tell them apart and draw conclusions.

If you're a visual thinker, you will probably have an easier time seeing trends and patterns in graphs or scatterplots. These kinds of figures show rather than tell—you will be able to see a line with a positive slope on a graph, or a progressive decrease in magnitude of a variable on a scatterplot. If you're better with numbers, you might prefer tables, on which you can compare values for different conditions. Regardless, you can always convert tables to graphs and vice versa. For example, if you're struggling to understand a scatterplot, you can write up your own small table with numerical estimates of the values from the scatterplot. Or if you're given a table and prefer a graph, you can always sketch a small graphical version of the numbers you've been given.

Once you've figured out the pattern or trend specified in the question, you can apply that trend to answer the question. If a question asks you directly about the trend, choose the answer that most accurately describes the pattern you found. If a question asks you to predict a result that is not given in the figure, you can apply the trend accordingly and predict how the new condition will compare to the conditions provided. If you're asked to apply that trend to a new situation altogether, simply imagine the use of that trend in the new situation and predict how it will apply.

Let's take a look at an example in action.

Five pea plants were planted in identical pots containing the same amount and type of soil. Each plant was placed in temperature-controlled boxes at different temperatures ranging from 0 to 80°C. Each plant was provided with the same sunlight exposure and volume of water at the same times each day. The height of each plant was measured and recorded every eighth day at 12 p.m.

Pea Plant Air Temperature (°C)	Pea Plant Height (cm) After *x* Days				
	0	**8**	**16**	**24**	**32**
0°	0	5.2	20.2	26.0	34.3
20°	0	5.3	23.4	28.2	35.0
40°	0	3.2	17.5	22.4	25.7
60°	0	2.7	13.0	15.2	19.0
80°	0	1.2	8.8	12.3	14.2

If you were to grow a pea plant under the same conditions at 50°C, during which time period would you expect to see the most rapid growth rate?

F. 0–8 days
G. 8–16 days
H. 16–24 days
J. 24–32 days

The correct answer is G. This question asks us to make a prediction about the growth rate of a plant grown at 50°C based on the data provided for these five other temperatures. For each of the five plants described in the table, the most rapid increase in height occurs between 8 days and 16 days. For example, the pea plant grown at 0°C grows 5.2 cm between Day 0 and Day 8, 15.0 cm between Day 8 and Day 16, 5.8 cm between Day 16 and Day 24, and 8.3 cm between Day 24 and 32. The largest difference in height over the course of eight days occurs between Day 8 and Day 16. For confirmation, you could repeat this procedure for the plants at the other temperatures. Since this trend is consistent for all five plants, which includes plants grown at temperatures above and below 50°C, it would be reasonable to predict that a plant grown at 50°C would also experience its most rapid growth rate between Day 8 and Day 16.

HOW CAN I ANALYZE THE DATA GRAPHICALLY?

Graphs are an extremely useful way to convey scientific data. You will almost certainly be asked to graph data or interpret graphs on the ACT Science test, particularly in Interpretation of Data questions. Therefore, it is important to understand the various types of graphs and how they are used.

On a coordinate plane, graphs consist of points that are plotted based on their location along the *x* and *y* axes. (3-D graphs may include a *z*-axis, directed out of the page at you, but you will rarely, if ever, see these on the ACT Science test.)

Graphs that are straight lines indicate **linear functions**, while curved lines represent **exponential functions**. In linear functions, lines that increase from left to right have positive slopes, while lines that decrease from left to right have negative slopes. A perfectly horizontal line has a slope of zero, while a perfectly vertical line is usually described as "undefined" or "infinite." In exponential functions, the line can also increase or decrease; however, in exponential functions, the line is curved, which means that the slope is not constant. In a positive exponential function, the curve approaches zero (or a minimum) to the left and infinity to the right. In a negative exponential function, the curve approaches zero (or a minimum) to the right and infinity to the left.

The key difference between linear and exponential functions is that linear functions have a constant slope, which means that the change in *y* value per *x* value is the *same* for all intervals, while exponential functions have a slope that either increases (positive exponential function) or decreases (negative exponential function) from left to right.

There are other types of graphs, including **parabolas** (*U*-shaped graphs) and **hyperbolas** (curved graphs that approach, but never quite reach, invisible lines called **asymptotes**). However, linear and exponential functions are far and away the most common graphs you'll find on the ACT Science test and are the two types you should focus on when reviewing.

When interpreting a graph, it is important to determine which variable is represented by each axis. If you are given a graph as your figure, this will be quite obvious because the axes will usually be labeled. However, if you are given a table and asked to predict the shape of a graph, it may be a bit trickier. As a general rule, the *x*-axis is usually the independent variable, or the variable that the experimenter alters, while the *y*-axis is usually the dependent variable, or the variable that is being measured in the experiment. Once you recognize which variable is which on a table, converting the values into a graphical form is not so difficult. Questions that ask you to analyze graphs might ask you about graph types and shapes, patterns and trends, or axes and variables.

Five pea plants were planted in identical pots containing the same amount and type of soil. Each plant was placed in temperature-controlled boxes at different temperatures ranging from 0 to 80°C. Each plant was provided with the same sunlight exposure and volume of water at the same times each day. The height of each plant was measured and recorded every eighth day at 12 p.m.

Pea Plant Air Temperature (°C)	Pea Plant Height (cm) After *x* Days				
	0	8	16	24	32
0°	0	5.2	20.2	26.0	34.3
20°	0	5.3	23.4	28.2	35.0
40°	0	3.2	17.5	22.4	25.7
60°	0	2.7	13.0	15.2	19.0
80°	0	1.2	8.8	12.3	14.2

Over the course of the first 16 days of height measurement, the growth rate for the pea plants can best be described as:

- **A.** increasing linearly.
- **B.** decreasing linearly.
- **C.** increasing exponentially.
- **D.** decreasing exponentially.

The correct answer is C. This question asks for a graphical type/shape interpretation based on the numbers provided in a table. You can tell if a graph is linear if the measured dependent variable value increases or decreases by the same amount over the same given independent variable interval.

This particular question asks us to look at the shape over the first 16 days. First, let's take a look at Day 0 through Day 8 for the first plant. The height increases by 5.2 cm. Now let's look at Day 8 through Day 16. The height increases by 15.0 cm. Both of these time intervals are eight days, so if this were a linear trend, the height increases should be the same. They are not the same, however, so this must be an exponential trend. We can therefore rule out choice A and choice B because these answers both refer to linear changes. The difference between choice C and choice D is whether the change in height over time is an increase or decrease. Logically, plants don't decrease in height over time, but as always, we just have to look at the numbers for confirmation. The height of each plant increases over time—therefore, we can rule out choice D.

HOW VALID IS THIS DATA?

When it comes to analyzing scientific data, a scientist must always think critically about his or her work in order to determine whether or not the collected information is valid. One common method for assessing data validity is to use statistics. Specifically, scientists look at accuracy and precision in order to get a sense of whether or not their experiment can be trusted.

Accuracy describes the degree to which a numerical measurement or calculation agrees with a known value or standard. For example, let's say a scientist performs a set of experiments to determine the standard heat of formation for liquid water at 25°C. After she does the experiments, the scientist can compare her final measured value to an actual known value because the standard heat of formation for liquid water is a well-established number that has been determined numerous times in the past.

Let's see what this looks like in real time. Just so you know for this experiment, and in case you happen to come across it again, standard heat of formation for any substance is the change in enthalpy (or heat energy) when one mole of a substance is formed from its pure elements under standard conditions. For liquid water at 25°C, the standard heat of formation is –286 kJ/mol, which means that 286 kJ of energy is released when liquid H_2O forms from its pure elements, gaseous H_2 and O_2.

Accuracy can be described numerically using a percent error calculation:

$$\text{Percent Error} = \left|\frac{\text{Known Value} - \text{Measured Value}}{\text{Known Value}}\right| \times 100\%$$

So in this sample experiment, if the scientist experimentally found that the standard heat of formation for liquid water is –143 kJ/mol, the percent error, using the calculation above, would be calculated like this:

$$\text{Percent Error} = \left|\frac{(-286)-(-143)}{(-286)}\right| \times 100\% = 50\%$$

This value tells us that the scientist's experimental value is half, or 50%, of the actual known value. If multiple trials of the same experiment are performed, the measured value you should use here is the **mean**, or average, value of the trials. For example, if the scientist performs two experimental trials to determine the standard heat of formation of liquid water and gets –144 kJ/mol and –142 kJ/mol, the scientist's measured value would be the average of these two values:

$$\text{Average} = \frac{\text{Sum of Values from All Trials}}{\text{Number of Trials}} = \frac{(-144) + (-142)}{2} = -143 \text{ kJ/mol}$$

Scientific research is aimed at learning new information and discovering the undiscovered. Therefore, known values are not always available. Even though you can't always determine accuracy, you *can* always determine precision when multiple trials of the same experiment are performed.

> **TIP:** In most scientific experiments, you will not know an actual value, so you may not always be able to determine accuracy.

Precision describes how close the measured values are to each other for the same kind of experiment. You can often tell if data is precise simply by looking. If the numbers you measure for several trials of the same experiment are close to one another, your data is probably precise. On the other hand, if the numbers don't agree and are not close to one another at all, the data is probably not precise.

When data is more precise, it means that same experiment, when repeated multiple times, yields consistent numbers. It is important in science to be able to repeat the same experiment and get similar results each time because it helps to confirm that a result is not a fluke. This is why scientists conduct the same experiment repeatedly. Each repeated experiment is called a **trial**. Precision can be measured numerically by calculating **standard deviation**, which indicates how far a set of measured numbers are from their average—in this way, standard deviation describes how precise data is.

> **TIP:** You won't have to calculate standard deviations on the ACT exam; however, it is important to know that a low standard deviation means that the data is generally close to the average and is precise, while a high standard deviation means that the data is less precise.

Data is often considered to be more valid when it is precise, or when the standard deviation is as low as possible. If multiple trials for a particular experiment give precise results, but one trial gives a result that is very different, this data point is called an **outlier**. If you see an outlier for a particular trial, you can usually conclude that an error occurred in this trial because the obtained result was so different from the others.

Remember that you won't have to do any advanced calculations on the ACT Science test. You will usually be able to tell simply by looking at the given values if they are accurate and/or precise. If you come across terms like *mean* and *standard deviation*, you'll be all set if you remember that they refer to accuracy and precision, respectively.

In addition to looking at accuracy and precision, there are other ways to assess data validity. If an experiment is described on the ACT Science test, you might notice a flaw in its design that could cause you to question whether or not the obtained data is valid. For instance, you might notice that the experiment did not control a particular condition while testing another condition, or you might notice that the scientist did not choose the best possible technique to measure a certain value. Observations like these might cause you to question the quality of the results obtained in an experiment.

Another way that the ACT Science test might assess your ability to evaluate data validity is to ask questions about errors that may have occurred during an experiment. For example, you might be asked to suggest an error that would cause the measured value in an experiment to be either too high or too low. Alternatively, you might be asked to predict how a particular error would affect the measured value. For instance, if you are testing the effect of temperature on the growth of a pea plant and you add more water to one plant than to the others, this error could result in a larger height increase for that one plant because it received extra nutrients that the other plants did not receive.

Five pea plants were planted in identical pots containing the same amount and type of soil. Each plant was placed in temperature-controlled boxes at different temperatures ranging from 0 to 80°C. Each plant was provided with the same sunlight exposure and volume of water at the same times each day. The height of each plant was measured and recorded every eighth day at 12 p.m.

Pea Plant Air Temperature (°C)	Pea Plant Height (cm) After *x* Days				
	0	**8**	**16**	**24**	**32**
0°	0	5.2	20.2	26.0	34.3
20°	0	5.3	23.4	28.2	35.0
40°	0	3.2	17.5	22.4	25.7
60°	0	2.7	13.0	15.2	19.0
80°	0	1.2	8.8	12.3	14.2

Because the most drastic change in pea plant height was observed at 20°C, the scientist decides to repeat this experiment two additional times. The following plant heights were obtained:

Pea Plant Air Temperature (°C)	Pea Plant Height (cm) After *x* Days				
	0	**8**	**16**	**24**	**32**
20°	0	5.2	23.8	28.3	35.2
	0	5.3	23.6	28.2	35.0

Based on the additional trials for pea plant growth at 20°C, it can be concluded that the height data over the 32-day range is:

F. accurate.
G. not accurate.
H. precise.
J. not precise.

The correct answer is H. This question asks you to assess the data among the three 20°C trials for accuracy and precision. This particular experiment is measuring pea plant growth over time. No actual or "known" values are provided, so we can't judge accuracy in this experiment. As such, we can rule out choice F and choice G right away. In order to judge precision, we have to look at the height values among the three trials and see if they are close to one another. At all time points, the height values are very close to one another. Therefore, we can conclude that this data is precise. In general, results that are not precise will be very obvious; for example, one plant might not have grown at all. In this example, however, the numbers are close, so we can say that this data is precise.

WHAT ADDITIONAL EXPERIMENTS CAN BE DONE BASED ON THE DATA?

In scientific research, one experiment usually leads to another experiment; when you learn something new from one experiment, you can do additional experiments to learn more about the topic of interest. Additional experiments can be based on what was learned in the original experiment, or they can test a new variable that was not the focus of the original experiment.

Questions that ask you to suggest additional experiments will often state a goal, and you will have to select the response that would most successfully achieve that goal. In order to answer these questions, identifying the independent and dependent variables will be key. Given a particular goal, you can figure out what you are varying and what you are measuring. Once you have identified these variables, you can look at the answer choices and pick the one that uses these variables.

A good strategy for questions like these is process of elimination. You will often be able to rule out answers describing experiments that very obviously vary the wrong conditions or take the wrong measurement. Questions that ask you to suggest further experimentation are more commonly seen in the Research Summaries passages, but you might see them occasionally in Interpretation of Data subcategory questions, so it is best to be prepared!

Five pea plants were planted in identical pots containing the same amount and type of soil. Each plant was placed in temperature-controlled boxes at different temperatures ranging from 0 to 80°C. Each plant was provided with the same sunlight exposure and volume of water at the same times each day. The height of each plant was measured and recorded every eighth day at 12 p.m.

Pea Plant Air Temperature (°C)	Pea Plant Height (cm) After *x* Days				
	0	**8**	**16**	**24**	**32**
0°	0	5.2	20.2	26.0	34.3
20°	0	5.3	23.4	28.2	35.0
40°	0	3.2	17.5	22.4	25.7
60°	0	2.7	13.0	15.2	19.0
80°	0	1.2	8.8	12.3	14.2

The scientist wants to focus on which temperature provides the most rapid germination period of pea plant growth. Germination is the process by which a plant sprouts from a seed. This can best be accomplished by:

A. repeating the experiment at 20°C only, varying the soil type between plants.

B. repeating the experiment at all temperatures, measuring plant heights after much smaller time increments.

C. repeating the experiment at all temperatures, using a variety of plant types.

D. repeating the experiment at all temperatures, extending the eight-day measurements to 40 days rather than 32 days.

The correct answer is B. Remember, with the questions that ask you to suggest additional experiments, it is important to identify the independent and dependent variables right away. This question asks you to suggest an experiment that will measure germination rate, or the rate at which the plant sprouts from the seed, at different temperatures. That means that the independent variable will again be temperature, and that the dependent variable will again be plant height. You can therefore rule out choice A, because if you use only one temperature, you cannot compare germination rates between plants at different temperatures. Choice A does not satisfy the desired independent variable. Based on the question alone, you can also rule out choice C. The goal is to look at germination growth rates in pea plants only, so using different plant types at different temperatures will not help to accomplish this goal.

Choices B and D both have temperature as the independent variable and plant height as the dependent variable, so you must choose the better answer between the two. Since germination refers to the sprouting of a plant from its seed, the new experiment should focus on the earliest stages of pea plant growth. Based on the original data provided, the plants reach heights of 3–5 centimeters after eight days, so the initial germination process is not included in the original experiment. Extending the overall measurement time to 40 days, as described in choice D, will not accomplish the goal of focusing on germination. Choice B, on the other hand, involves measuring after shorter time periods. The experiment described in choice B involves taking more measurements between 0 and 8 days, which will give a much better sense of how quickly each plant at the different temperatures emerges from its seed.

COMMON TRAPS IN THE SCIENCE TEST

Now that we've gone over Data Representation questions and how to tackle the concepts you'll come across in these types of questions, let's talk about some common pitfalls that test takers encounter in these questions and how to avoid them. Discussing common missteps is important—if you're aware in advance of mistakes that others have made in the past, you can avoid them yourself because you will be aware of what you might come across while answering these kinds of questions.

Challenging Terminology

Given the huge range of topics that the ACT Science test can potentially cover, it is likely that you're going to come across a passage describing a subject with which you have little familiarity. Maybe you forgot what mitosis is, or what a double displacement chemical reaction entails. Or you know you've heard the word *capacitance* before but can't quite put your finger on what it means.

First and foremost, it is important that you stay calm and don't assume you won't be able to figure out what an unfamiliar word means. Sometimes the passage will provide you with the definition. In other cases, you will be provided with enough information in the passage to figure out what the word means. In still other cases, you might not even need to determine the definition of the term because it may not be needed to answer the questions. If experimental data provides numbers to show that one liquid has a higher boiling point than another, you don't really need to know what a boiling point is to be able to point out that the boiling point value for Substance A is a higher number than the boiling point value for Substance B.

So if you come across a challenging term in a Data Representation question and have no idea what it means, read the full passage and see if it provides you with any hints about the word's meaning. If it does, proceed with your reading and keep this newly determined definition in mind. If you still don't know what the word means, continue on to the questions and see if you even need to know the precise definition of the word to answer the questions. In the event that you can't figure out a word's definition and you *do* need it to answer a question, make an educated guess about the word's definition given the context. Even if you do come across such a rare word, it is unlikely that more than a question or two will rely on its definition. Enough information will usually be provided in the passage and in the diagrams to help you understand what is going on, so it is unlikely that you will come across a word and have no idea what it describes.

Surface tension is an important property of liquids that is caused by cohesion, the attraction of molecules to one another. A scientist wants to compare the surface tension of water, ethanol, and cyclohexane by measuring the number of drops of each liquid she can fit on a small metal disk, which has a small lip around its edge, before the liquid overflows and spills off of the disk. Using an eyedropper that delivers the same volume of liquid per drop, the scientist obtains the following results:

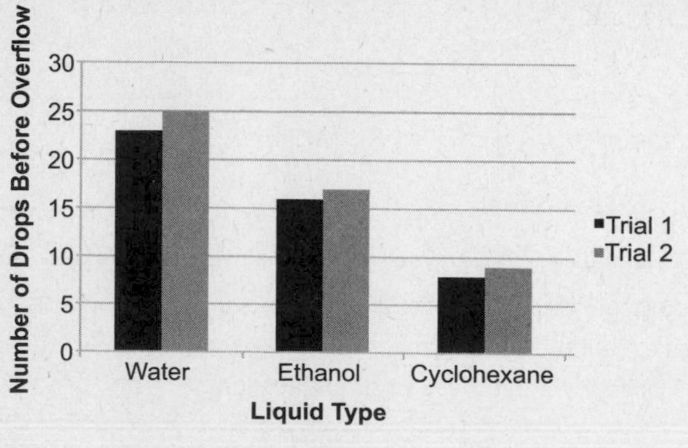

Which of the three tested liquids has the highest surface tension?

F. Water

G. Ethanol

H. Cyclohexane

J. All three liquids have the same surface tension.

The correct answer is F. This passage describes a surface tension experiment, and the question asks you to draw a conclusion based on the provided data. The question requires that you know what surface tension is, and while the passage explains that surface tension is caused by cohesion, it does not specifically provide its definition. Fortunately, you can figure it out based on the information and data provided. If surface tension is caused by cohesion, the attraction of a liquid's molecules to one another, then it would make sense that a liquid that exhibits higher cohesion also exhibits higher surface tension. In this experiment, the scientist is adding drops of liquid to a disk until the liquid overflows. That means that the liquid with the greatest cohesion, and therefore the highest surface tension, will be the liquid for which more drops can fit on the disk, because if more drops can fit on the disk, it means that the liquid molecules have a greater attraction for one another and are able to stick together longer before falling apart and overflowing off of the disk. Based on the data, a graph, more drops of water are able to fit onto the disk than any other liquid. The liquid, of the three tested liquids, with the highest surface tension is therefore water, so the correct answer is choice F. Even without knowing the exact definition of surface tension when starting the question, you can figure out the answer based on the information provided in the passage.

UNNECESSARY INFORMATION

Another common mistake test takers make is getting caught up in extraneous information. Passages might include interesting details about the given topic, or specific tidbits about experimental design. You might find this information interesting, or you might be baffled by its inclusion; either way, if you identify right away that the information is not essential to understanding the passage or the associated questions, cast this information aside for the time being and focus on what is important.

For example, a passage might provide you with some historical information about the discoverer of a particular phenomenon, or a list of properties of a substance. If the provided information does not enhance your understanding of the data provided in the question, then don't spend too much time on this information. Focus on the important information and set the extra details aside. You have 35 minutes to complete 40 questions, and while this is plenty of time to complete the test, it is best to spend your time on the most useful information instead of working through facts you won't actually need to complete the questions.

Max Planck originally proposed the idea of *blackbody radiation* in 1900, suggesting that radiation is quantized. In 1905, Albert Einstein took this concept a step further by describing the *photoelectric effect*, in which radiation is still quantized after absorption by a metal. The photoelectric effect is the observation that when light is shone upon many types of metal, electrons are emitted from the metal. The photoelectric work function is the minimum energy required to eject an electron from the surface of the metal; a photon of light with energy less than the work function will never be able to eject electrons.

An apparatus was set up consisting of an evacuated quartz tube with photosensitive metal plates. The plates were connected separately to negative and positive terminals of a battery, and then they were connected to one another using wires to form a circuit. An ammeter was included in the circuit to measure current. When electrons were ejected by the photosensitive plates, they created a current that was measured by the ammeter. The work functions for three metals, used in the plates, were determined using this setup:

Metal	Work Function (eV)
Aluminum	4.1
Nickel	5.0
Sodium	2.3

If a photon of light of a particular energy strikes the aluminum plate at its work function and creates a current, which of the following must be true?

A. The same light source will eject an electron from the nickel plate only.

B. The same light source will eject an electron from the sodium plate only.

C. The same light source will eject an electron from both the nickel and sodium plates.

D. The same light source will not eject an electron from the nickel or sodium plates.

The correct answer is B. This is a physics question that asks you to look at measured data and apply the definition of a work function to the results. The first two sentences of the first paragraph provide historical context for the photoelectric effect. The first sentence mentions blackbody radiation. While this is an important concept in physics, you will realize as you continue reading that this passage focuses on the photoelectric effect. Blackbody radiation studies were critical studies that contributed to discovery of the photoelectric effect, but you need not focus on this at all because it is unrelated to the data presented. The historical information is interesting, but it too is unnecessary for the analysis of the data. It doesn't matter if you don't know what blackbody radiation is; you can move on because the description of blackbody radiation is simply included to provide historical context for the subject of interest, the photoelectric effect.

In answering the provided question, we can use the definition of "work function" provided in the passage. The passage indicates that the photoelectric work function is the minimum energy required to eject an electron from the surface of the metal, so a photon of light with energy less than the work function will never be able to eject electrons. If a photon of light has the energy of aluminum's work function, this same photon of light will *not* be able to eject electrons from metals with a higher work function, but it *will* be able to eject electrons from metals with a lower work function. The work function of nickel is higher than that of aluminum, while the work function of sodium is lower than that of aluminum. Therefore, the photon will be able to eject an electron from a sodium plate, but not from a nickel plate.

UNEXPECTED RESULTS

It is important to not assume you know a result without looking at the data. Why is this? Science experiments do not always work perfectly. There may be design flaws in the procedure or errors that took place during the experiment, all of which could affect results. A simple experiment could give completely unexpected results, and even if it is clear the results are incorrect, it is important to analyze the data.

For example, experimental data in a passage may indicate that ice is more dense than liquid water, even though liquid water is actually more dense than ice; in this case, make sure that if you are asked to draw conclusions based on the data, you draw your conclusions based on the numbers you see rather than on the results you would expect. For the most part, data included on the ACT Science test will be exactly what you would expect. Still, it is important to pay attention to the numbers and not assume a result without looking closely at the data first.

A student mixes canola oil, ethanol, and pure water, three liquids that are immiscible and form three separate layers without mixing, at room temperature. The student's task is to determine which layer is which within the mixture.

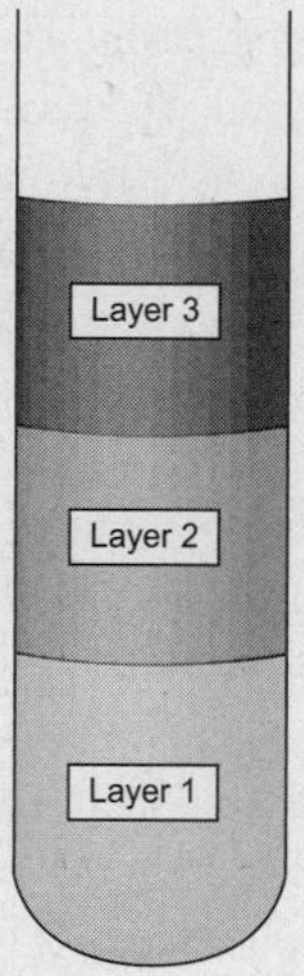

The student decides to use density for this experiment. Density is a measure of mass per unit volume. For each liquid, the student removed a sample from the stock and used a balance to measure the mass of the liquid sample by subtracting the mass of the beaker from the combined mass of the beaker and liquid. The student then used a graduated cylinder to measure the volume of each sample. The results are shown in the table:

Liquid Sample Identity	Mass of Liquid (g)	Volume of Liquid (mL)
Canola Oil	9.00	9.92
Ethanol	7.90	10.00
Water	6.00	4.00

Based on the data, the identity of Layer 2 is:

F. canola oil.
G. ethanol.
H. water.
J. either canola oil or ethanol.

The correct answer is F. In order to answer this question, you must estimate the densities of the three liquids. Based on the data provided, canola oil has a density of just over 0.90 g/mL, ethanol has a density of 0.79 g/mL, and water has a density of 2.0 g/mL. (In reality, water has a density of 1.5 g/mL at room temperature, so this number is actually incorrect, but the question must be answered based on the data. In terms of relative densities, this inaccurate number doesn't actually change the order of liquid densities, but it is important still to base conclusions on the data regardless.) Of the three liquids, water has the highest density, canola oil has the second highest density, and ethanol has the lowest density. Therefore, Layer 1 is water, Layer 2 is canola oil, and Layer 3 is ethanol. The question asks you to determine the identity of the liquid in Layer 2, so the correct answer is canola oil (choice F).

Unusual Data Presentation

Sometimes you will see a graph that is not a simple XY scatter, or a table that is more complicated than a few sets of columns. There is no need to feel flustered if you see data presented in an unusual way.

TIP: As a general rule, the more complicated or strange a data representation may look, the more explanation you will receive in the introductory or surrounding paragraphs.

If the test includes a type of data presentation that you've never seen before, focus on the written introduction, because understanding the kind of data collected will help you to hone in on the most important part of the data table or graph. As always, it will very much help to identify the independent and dependent variables in the experiment. Once you've identified these variables, find where each occurs on the data table or graph. A data figure might include extra information that you may need for some questions but not others; while trying to get a handle on the basics of the data figure, ignore any supplementary information and focus on the independent and dependent variables. Simplifying figures in your mind by blocking out extra information is a solid strategy for understanding the basics of an experiment on a data figure that is new to you.

Protein X is an enzyme that degrades substrate S in humans. The rate at which Protein X degrades S was studied *in vitro* using UV-vis spectroscopy. A number of solutions were made that contained Protein X at the same concentration. Then, S was added to each solution at overall concentrations that ranged from 0 to 1,400 nM. UV-vis spectroscopy was used to observe the initial rate, over the first five seconds of activity, by which Protein X degraded S in each solution. The initial rates of degradation were graphed as a function of the concentrations of S for the various solutions:

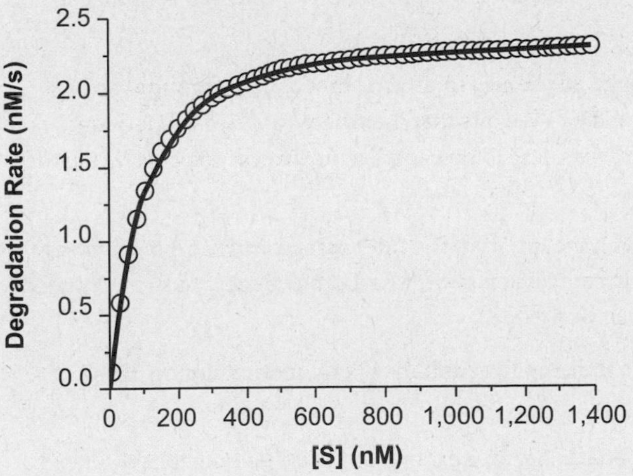

Why does the initial rate of S degradation flatline around 500 nM S?

A. The concentration of Protein X overwhelms the concentration of S at this point, halting the increase in degradation rate.

B. Protein X appears to be inactivated in the presence of 500 nM S, giving a degradation rate of 0 nM/s.

C. The reaction reverses at this point, and S begins to be produced.

D. The concentration of substrate S overwhelms the concentration of Protein X at this point, halting the increase in degradation rate.

The correct answer is D. This passage presents a Michaelis-Menton curve, which is a type of graph used to study the kinetics of protein activity. You've likely never seen a graph like this before, but using the passage and the figure, we can easily determine what is happening here. According to the passage, the independent variable is the substrate concentration, because this is what is different in each sample. This appears on the graph on the *x*-axis. The dependent variable is the initial rate of substrate S degradation, because this is what is being measured. This variable appears on the graph on the *y*-axis. From 0 to 500 nM S, the initial rate of S degradation increases as S concentration increases. From approximately 500 nM S and higher, substrate S is still being degraded, but the rate of degradation is no longer increasing.

Now that you understand the experiment and graph, you can answer the question. The question asks why the graph flatlines around 500 nM S. Remember, the concentration of S is increasing while the concentration of Protein X remains the same. As such, choice A cannot be correct because you are seeing an increase in S, not Protein X, as you move from left to right on the graph. Choice B states that starting at 500 nM S, the degradation rate is 0 nM/s. While the slope of the line here is approximately 0, the *y*-axis is degradation rate, the dependent variable, and at 500 nM and over, the degradation remains fairly constant at around 2.4 nM/s. Choice B, therefore, is incorrect. Choice C indicates that the reaction reverses, and that substrate S starts to be produced rather than degraded. This is definitely not true because the degradation rates are all positive, meaning that at every concentration, we are seeing substrate S being degraded. Choice D indicates that the flat curve is a result of the concentration of substrate S overwhelming that of Protein X. This makes sense because the concentration of S is increasing.

Turn to page 497 to follow the College Readiness Benchmark Learning Path questions covering Data Representation.

SUMMING IT UP

- **Data Representation** passages present you with a graph, table, or figure that describes some kind of scientific experiment or phenomenon.
- **Read the introductory and surrounding paragraphs to determine the questions the data is supposed to answer.** Even if you don't understand the terminology or vocabulary used, the figure itself can usually tell you all you need to know.
- **Recognizing patterns and trends in data sets will be helpful when you're trying to draw conclusions**—questions accompanying data sets will usually ask about these types of observations.
- If you need to change data from a table into a graph, remember that the *x*-axis is usually the **independent variable** (the variable that the experimenter alters), and the *y*-axis is usually the **dependent variable** (the variable being measured in the experiment).
- **Precision** means that the same experiment, when repeated multiple times, will yield consistent numbers—precision can be measured by calculating **standard deviation,** which indicates how far a set of measured numbers are from their average. If the numbers measured for several trials of the same experiment are close to another, the data is probably **precise**; if the numbers don't agree and are not close to one another at all, the data is probably not precise.
- An **outlier** is a result very different from the other multiple and precise results of a trial. An outlier usually means that an error occurred in an experiment.
- **Identifying the dependent and independent variables is key to answering questions that ask you to suggest additional experiments**—you can look at the answer choices and pick the one that uses these variables. A good strategy for these questions is process of elimination. You can rule out answers describing experiments that very obviously vary the wrong conditions or take the wrong measurement.
- **If you come across a challenging term and have no idea what it means, read the full passage and see if it provides you with any hints.** If you still don't know what the word means, continue on to the questions and see if you actually need to know the definition to answer the questions—many times, you won't!
- **Don't spend too much time on information within a passage that does not enhance your understanding of the data provided**—it's likely extraneous and worth casting aside.
- **Don't assume you know a result and skip over looking at the data.** A simple experiment could give completely unexpected results. Even if they are incorrect, the ACT exam questions ask about the exact experiment presented as is. Analyze exactly what you see.
- **A figure might include extra information you don't need to answer the questions.** Simplify figures by blocking out extra information as you answer each question. When in doubt, define and search for the independent and dependent variables.

ONLINE PREP

Want to Know More?

Access more practice questions, lessons, helpful hints, and strategies for the following science topics in *Peterson's Online Course for the ACT® Exam*:

- Data Representation and Research
- Data Representation and Interpretation

To purchase and access the course, go to **www.petersons.com/testprep/act**.

COLLEGE READINESS BENCHMARK LEARNING PATH PRACTICE

Directions: The passages in this practice question set are followed by several questions. Read each passage carefully and choose the best answer to each related question. As you go through the practice set, review each solution and follow the expanded explanations provided to help strengthen your skills in working with Data Representation items.

PASSAGE I

The heat of combustion (H_c) of a substance is the amount of heat released when that substance is burned. It is one way to measure how much energy is contained within the molecule, which can be useful for determining performance of a fuel within a system such as a furnace or motor. Two common classes of fuel molecules are hydrocarbons and alcohols. Hydrocarbons are organic molecules that contain only carbon and hydrogen atoms. Alcohols are similar to hydrocarbons, but also contain an oxygen atom that is covalently bound to one of the carbon atoms and one of the hydrogen atoms. Both hydrocarbons and alcohols can undergo complete combustion in the presence of oxygen to form carbon dioxide (CO_2) and water (H_2O). The balanced reaction for combustion of propane (C_3H_8) is shown below.

$$C_3H_8 + 5O_2 \rightarrow 3CO_2 + 4H_2O + \text{heat}$$

Heats of combustion are generally determined using a **bomb calorimeter**, a constant-volume instrument that measures the amount of heat released during the combustion reaction. Tables 1 and 2 list the heats of combustion of various fuels in terms of energy (kilojoules, kJ) per mole and energy per gram. One mole corresponds to approximately 6.022×10^{23} molecules.

Table 1

Hydrocarbon			H_c	
Chemical	**Formula**	**State at Room Temp**	**kJ/mol**	**kJ/g**
Methane	CH_4	gas	891	55.51
Ethane	C_2H_6	gas	1,561	51.89
Propane	C_3H_8	gas	2,220	50.33
Butane	C_4H_{10}	gas	2,878	49.50
Pentane	C_5H_{12}	liquid	3,509	48.62
Hexane	C_6H_{14}	liquid	4,163	48.31
Octane	C_8H_{18}	liquid	5,470	47.87
Decane	$C_{10}H_{22}$	liquid	6,778	47.63

Table 2

Alcohol			H_c	
Chemical	**Formula**	**State at Room Temp**	**kJ/mol**	**kJ/g**
Methanol	CH_4O	liquid	726	22.65
Ethanol	C_2H_6O	liquid	1,367	29.67
1-Propanol	C_3H_8O	liquid	2,021	33.62
1-Butanol	$C_4H_{10}O$	liquid	2,676	36.09
1-Pentanol	$C_5H_{12}O$	liquid	3,331	37.78
1-Hexanol	$C_6H_{14}O$	liquid	3,984	38.99
1-Octanol	$C_8H_{18}O$	liquid	5,294	40.64
1-Decanol	$C_{10}H_{22}O$	liquid	6,593	41.65

1. Using the information in Table 1, which of the following statements is true about the heat of combustion of hydrocarbons as the number of carbon atoms increases?

A. The energy per mol increases, and the energy per gram decreases.

B. The energy per mol decreases, and the energy per gram increases.

C. Both the energy per mol and energy per gram increase.

D. Both the energy per mol and energy per gram decrease.

The correct answer is A. This question is about trends in the data. The first step is to figure out *which* data are relevant. The question tells you in two ways: (1) it asks about *hydrocarbons* and (2) it gives you the specific table (Table 1). Ignore the other table for this question. The next step is to look at the variables the question is asking about. In this case, you need to look at the heat of combustion and the number of carbon atoms (in *increasing* order).

The heat of combustion is given in two different units, kJ/mol and kJ/g, in the two right-most columns of the table. By looking at the potential answers, you can see that both are needed to answer the question.

The number of carbon atoms might be a little trickier to find—it's in the subscripts of the chemical formulas. The number of carbon atoms is consistently increasing as you go down the table (methane has 1 carbon atom, ethane has 2... decane has 10).

As you go down the table, what happens to the values in the heat of combustion columns? The values in the kJ/mol column get consistently *bigger* (891 for methane, 6,778 for decane). That means you can automatically rule out choices B and D, which say that energy per mol decreases. Also, as you go down the table, values in the kJ/g column get *smaller* (55.51 for methane, 47.63 for decane). That means you can rule out choice C, which says that both increase.

Be careful that you're looking at the columns in the appropriate order. For example, if you switch the kJ/mol and kJ/g trends, choice B would be the correct answer instead of choice A. You will also get the incorrect answer if you look at the other data table (Table 2 with alcohols). In that case, both measures of heat of combustion increase as the number of carbon atoms increases, which would make choice C the correct answer.

2. If three moles of propane are completely combusted within a bomb calorimeter, how many moles of water will be produced?

F. 3

G. 4

H. 9

J. 12

The correct answer is J. This is a stoichiometry question—*stoichiometry* refers to determining the amounts of reactants and products in a chemical reaction. You might not understand how a bomb calorimeter works, but you *don't need to know* how it works in order to answer the question. (It can help to recognize from the passage that a bomb calorimeter is just an instrument that makes a measurement—it doesn't change the results of the chemical reaction).

The first thing you need to solve in a stoichiometry question is a balanced reaction. Fortunately, the balanced reaction for the combustion of propane is provided in the passage:

$$C_3H_8 + 5O_2 \rightarrow 3CO_2 + 4H_2O + \text{heat}$$

Next, you'll need to figure out the relevant stoichiometry numbers—for each propane (reactant) molecule that goes in, how many water (product) molecules come out? In a balanced reaction, those numbers are found *in front* of the corresponding chemical formulas. If there is no written number in front of the chemical formula, the stoichiometry is one. For the combustion of propane,

$$\underline{1}C_3H_8 + 5O_2 \rightarrow 3CO_2 + \underline{4}H_2O + \text{heat}$$

every **one** molecule of propane produces **four** molecules of water. (For reference, the small subscripts within a chemical formula refer to the number of atoms of that element within a molecule; each propane molecule contains three carbon atoms. That is useful for balancing a reaction in the first place but is no longer useful for this question). At this point it becomes a simple algebra problem. The question states that three moles of propane are used, so multiply each side of the reaction by three. 3 moles × 1 (propane molecules) → 3 moles × 4 (water molecules). That gives 12 moles of water (choice J).

The other choices are common distractions. If you assume the stoichiometry is 1→1 (instead of the correct 1→4), you might guess that three moles of propane make three moles of water (choice F). If you remember the correct stoichiometry but forget that *three* moles of propane are used, you might guess that four moles of water are formed. (choice G). And finally, if you look at the wrong product (CO_2 instead of H_2O), you might think that the stoichiometry is 1→3 and get an answer of 9 (choice H).

3. Heptane is a hydrocarbon with the formula C_7H_{16}. What is the *approximate* expected heat of combustion of heptane in kJ/mol?

A. 4,000

B. 5,000

C. 6,000

D. 7,000

The correct answer is B. This is an *interpolation* question. Heptane itself is not found in the tables, but it has 7 carbons, which puts it right between hexane (6) and octane (8) in Table 1. First, make sure that the data have a consistent trend (in this case, they are consistently increasing). If that's true, the expected value for the data in the middle will be *in between* the data on either side. In this case, the value for 7 carbons should be bigger than the value for 6 carbons (hexane, 4,163) so you can rule out choice A. It should be smaller than the value for eight carbons (octane, 5,470), so you can rule out choices C and D. That leaves choice B as the correct answer.

Take a moment to note that the trend is an increase of about 650 kJ/mol per additional carbon atom. For example, notice that the difference between 2-carbon ethane and 3-carbon propane is 2,220 – 1,561 = 659, and the difference between 6-carbon hexane and 5-carbon pentane is 4,163 – 3,509 = 654. You can add that difference onto 6-carbon hexane (4,163 + 650 = 4,813) or subtract it from 8-carbon octane (5,470 – 650 = 4,820)—both answers round to 5,000, which is choice B. In reality, the heat of combustion for heptane is 4,817 kJ/mol.

4. If you plotted the heat of combustion (kJ/g) of alcohols with respect to increasing carbon number, what would the graph look like?

F.

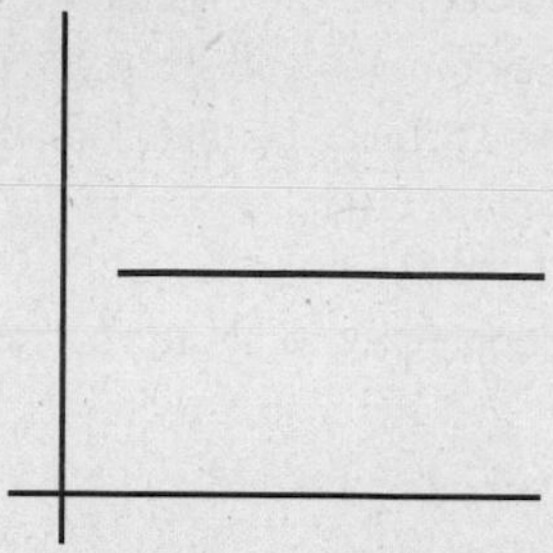

G

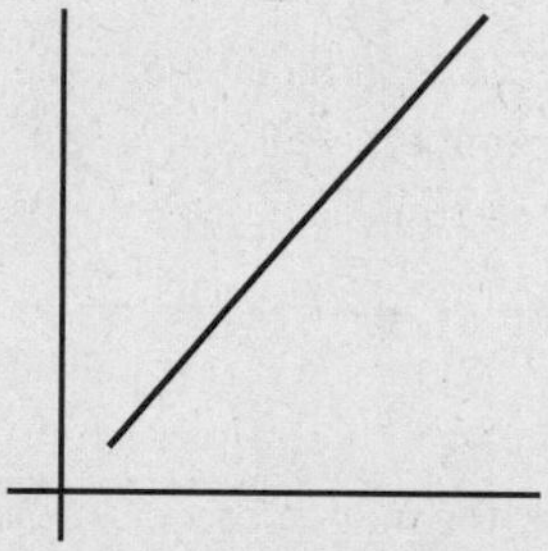

H.

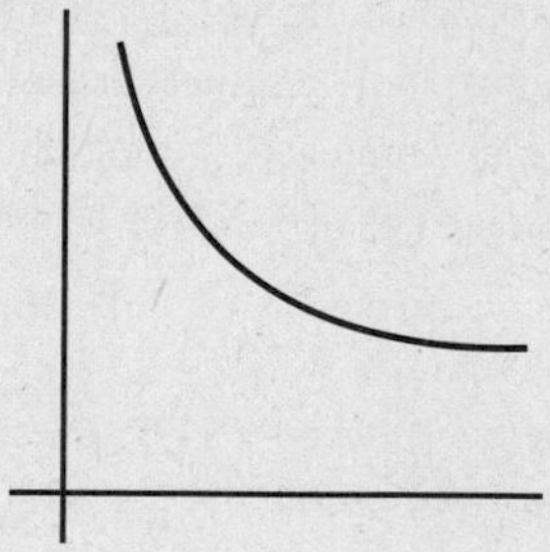

J.

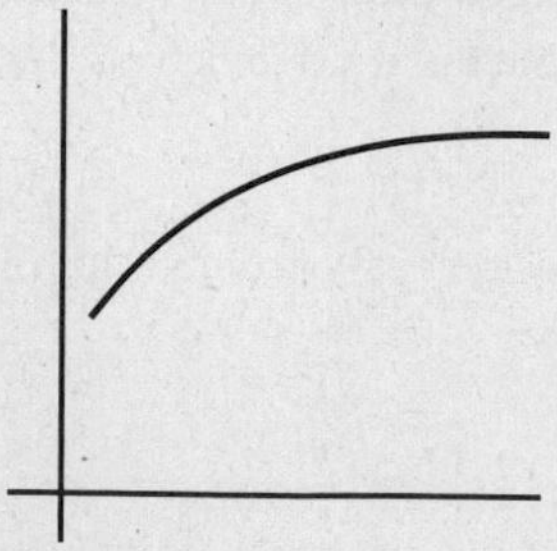

The correct answer is J. This is a question about translating data from a table into a graph. Heat of combustion will be the vertical *y*-axis, and carbon number will be the horizontal *x*-axis. As with question 1, the first (and most important) step is to figure out *which* data are relevant. In this case, the question asks about alcohols, which are in Table 2, and for heats of combustion in kJ/g, the furthest right column. Sometimes it's easy to see what the trend is, but if you're having a hard time, check the choices one by one.

Choice F shows a flat horizontal line, which would fit if there were no change (or no consistent change) in kJ/g as carbon number increases. But if you look at the far-right column in Table 2, the values consistently *increase* as you go down the table. That rules out choice F, and it also rules out choice H. That leaves choice G and choice J—both graphs increase from left to right. Choice G shows a *linear* relationship, which would be the case if there were the same increase in kJ/g with each added carbon. The difference between ethanol and methanol is 29.67 – 22.65 = 7.02. The difference between propanol and ethanol is 33.62 – 29.67 = 3.95. They are not the same, or even close! That rules out choice G and leaves you with choice J.

Again, it's very important to look at the appropriate data set. If you mistakenly look at the values for alcohols in *kJ/mol* (instead of kJ/g), you will see a linear trend like choice G. If you look at the value for *hydrocarbons* in kJ/g (instead of alcohols), you will see a relationship like choice H.

5. A group of students is researching different fuels. For a particular application, they want a fuel with a high energy density that can be easily transported in an unpressurized vessel. Which of the following fuels from this passage would be the best candidate based on the students' criteria?

A. Methane

B. Methanol

C. Decane

D. Decanol

The correct answer is C. This question is asking you to use information from the passage in a new context. One thing that will save you a lot of time in this case is to remember that, while there are a lot of possible fuels in the passage (16, in fact!), there are only four possible choices. Focus in on *only* those choices, even if there is a different fuel that would be a better choice. Next, you want to figure out how those four fuels rank in terms of energy density. Does that mean kJ/mol or kJ/g? In terms of energy density, kJ/g is typically more relevant. But if you don't know, rank them in terms of both units from highest to lowest:

Energy Density				
	Fuel	**In kJ/mol**	**Fuel**	**In kJ/g**
1.	Decane	6,778	Methane	55.51
2.	Decanol	6,593	Decane	47.63
3.	Methane	891	Decanol	41.65
4.	Methanol	726	Methanol	22.65

You can easily rule out methanol (choice B), which ranks last in both cases. Also, in both cases, decane ranks higher than decanol, so you can rule out choice D. That leaves either decane or methane. The other criterium the students had was that the fuel can be transported in an unpressurized vessel. If you look at Table 1, you can see that methane is a gas, while decane is a liquid. Gases have to be pressurized in order to fit a meaningful amount in any container. That leaves decane (choice C) as the best answer.

PASSAGE II

Yellowstone National Park, a nearly 3,500 square mile area in Wyoming, Montana, and Idaho, is the site of a long-running predator reintroduction experiment. Between its establishment in 1872 and 1926, the park deliberately eliminated wolves and cougars, the apex predators, to protect cattle and livestock in the surrounding areas. In subsequent years, park managers saw the local elk population increase substantially. At the same time, they began to recognize other changes in the park, including destruction of the park's aspen, cottonwood, and willow trees, as well as decreases in the populations of songbirds, beavers, and red foxes. In an attempt to remedy these ecological changes, the park began a wolf reintroduction program in 1995, using wolves that had been trapped and relocated from Alberta, Canada. Thirty-one wolves were released over two years, and they and their descendants were counted every year. The annual wolf population in the park is shown in Figure 1. As park managers expected, elk populations declined following wolf reintroduction. Researchers were interested in examining the potential trophic cascade—a domino effect on other species—that might result from reintroduction of this apex predator into the Yellowstone ecosystem. They sampled willow trees from four sites within the park and performed stem sectioning, in which the researchers cut cross sections of willow branches and took measurements of the growth rings. The year and area of each growth ring was determined. Measurements from even-numbered years are shown in Figure 2.

Figure 1

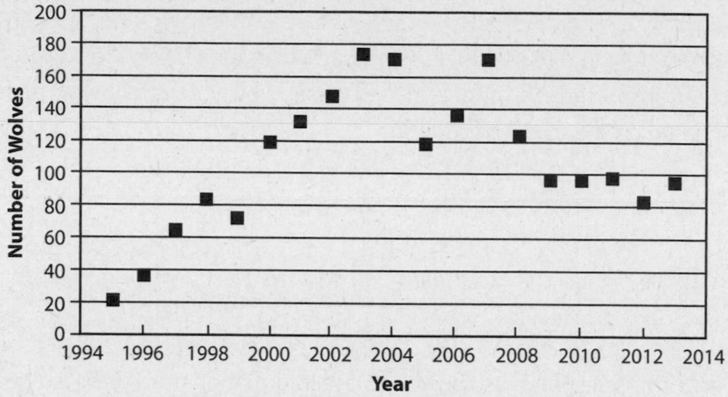

Adapted from Yellowstone NationBenchmark path-credit lineal Park Wolf Project Annual Report 2013

Figure 2
Willow Growth

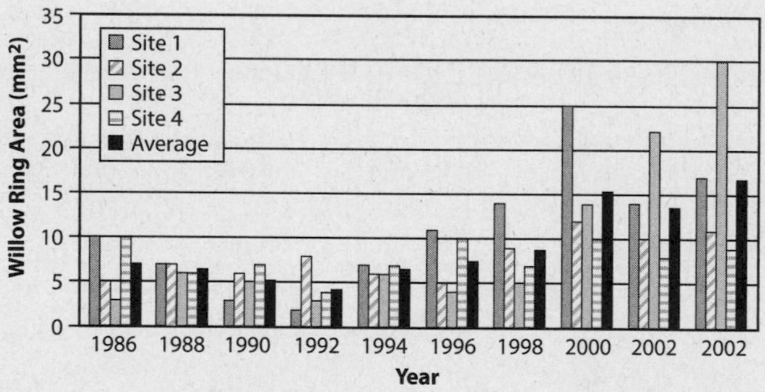

6. Approximately what was the largest wolf population between the years 2000 and 2013?

F. 95

G. 120

H. 175

J. 200

The correct answer is H. This question asks you to interpret data in a graph. Figure 1 shows the wolf population per year, and the highest data point corresponds to the largest number of wolves. Make sure to check the relevant data range—in this case, the question says, "between the years 2000 and 2013," which is a *subset* of the whole graph. In this example, the highest point from 2000–2013 is also the highest point in the entire graph, but that might not always be the case. The highest point (in the year 2003) falls between the horizontal lines that correspond to 160 and 180 wolves, according to the numbers on the vertical *y*-axis. Only choice H falls between those values, so you can figure out the correct answer without determining the exact size of the wolf population.

The other choices are distractors. Choice F (95) is the approximate population in 2013, and choice G (120) is the approximate population in 2000—those are two dates that appear on the graph and might catch your attention. Choice J (200) is the largest number that appears on the vertical axis, but none of the data points are all the way at the top, so that number is not relevant.

7. During which years did the wolf population number over 100 individuals?

A. 1995–1999

B. 2000–2008

C. 2003–2013

D. 2009–2013

The correct answer is B. This question also asks you to interpret data in a graph. To do this, locate the horizontal line in Figure 1 that corresponds to 100 wolves, and find all the points that are above that line. The data points between 2000 and 2008 are all above the 100 line, which corresponds to choice B.

Choice A (1995–1999) can be eliminated because all the data points are *under* the 100 line. Choice D (2009–2013) can also be eliminated because all the data points are under the 100 line, though many of them are close to 100. While choice C (2003–2013) includes some data above the 100 line, it also includes some below the line, making this choice incorrect.

8. Based on the data in Figure 2, the largest increase in the willow ring area was observed at:

F. Site 1 from 1998 to 2000.

G. Site 1 from 2000 to 2002.

H. Site 3 from 1998 to 2000.

J. Site 3 from 2002 to 2004.

The correct answer is F. This question is about interpreting data in a bar graph. Notice that there are horizontal lines at intervals of 5 mm^2—this is very useful for making quick estimates.

Figure 2 has a lot of data, so focus only on the possible options. Start with choice F (site 1 from 1998 to 2000). Site 1 corresponds to the solid gray bars on the left-most side of each grouping. You can quickly see that the Site 1 bar height in 2000 is more than two of the horizontal lines taller than site 1 in 1998. Since the horizontal lines are 5 mm^2 apart, the change is greater than 10 mm^2. (The actual change is from 14 mm^2 to 25 mm^2, an increase of 11.)

Choice G, (site 1 from 2000 to 2002), corresponds to a *decrease*, so immediately eliminate choice G.

Continue to the next choice, H, at Site 3 from 1998 to 2000. Site 3 corresponds to the solid light gray bars in the middle of each clump. Without determining the exact change, you can see that the willow ring area increases less than two horizontal lines between 1998 and 2000 (the exact change is from 5 to 14, a difference of 9). That is less than choice F, so you can eliminate choice H.

Similarly, you can see that Site 3 between 2002 and 2004 increases less than two horizontal lines (the exact change is from 22 to 30, a difference of 8)—eliminate choice J, and you are left with choice F as the correct answer.

It can be tempting to pick choice J because Site 3 in 2004 is the tallest bar in the whole graph. However, the question asks for the largest *increase* (the difference between measurements in the two years) rather than the largest single measurement.

9. Which statement is consistent with the data?

A. The willow ring area at all sites increased to the original levels found before wolves were removed from the park.

B. The willow ring area at all sites decreased during the years when wolf populations were at their peak.

C. The average willow ring area decreased and stabilized over the same years that the wolf population decreased and stabilized.

D. The average willow ring area increased in the nine years following wolf reintroduction.

The correct answer is D. This question is a little more complex because it requires analyzing two sets of data: (1) the wolf populations in Figure 1 and (2) the willow ring area in Figure 2. Tackle the options one at a time. Choice A refers to information that is not provided in the data or passage: "original levels found before wolves were removed from the park." Since wolves were removed in 1926, but the data for the willow ring area only go back to 1986, there's no information about the original levels. You can eliminate choice A.

To evaluate choice B, you need to determine the years at which wolf populations were at their peak. In Figure 1, the highest data points are in the years 2003–2004. In Figure 2, those years correspond to *increases* (not decreases) in willow ring area at all sites, so you can eliminate choice B.

To evaluate choice C, you need to determine years when the wolf population decreased and stabilized. In Figure 1, the data points decrease and level off between the years 2007–2013. However, there are no data in Figure 2 that correspond to those years, so you can eliminate choice C.

To check choice D, you need to know that wolf reintroduction occurred in 1995, which provided in the passage text. The average willow ring area (dark bars on the right side of each grouping) is generally increasing from 1996–2004 compared to the averages from 1986–1994, so choice D is consistent with the data.

10. Which of the following is a weakness of the study that makes it difficult to draw conclusions about the effect of wolf reintroduction on the growth of willow trees?

F. The researchers examined willows at four sites rather than one, leading to greater variability in their data.

G. The researchers included willow measurements both before and after wolf reintroduction, increasing the number of variables that affect willow growth.

H. The researchers did not include data from a similar habitat where wolves were not reintroduced, which could serve as a control.

J. The researchers did not include data from other tree species, which could examine the broader effect of wolf reintroduction on the whole habitat.

The correct answer is H. This is a complex question about the limitations of the experiment, and about conclusions that can be drawn from the data. When you evaluate the options, consider both parts: is this a weakness or a strength of the experiment? Does this aspect affect the stated conclusions?

You might be tempted to pick choice F because it's true in that examining willows at four sites reveals that there is large variability in willow ring area between the sites. However, the strategy of sampling more than one site is typically a *strength* in a scientific study, not a weakness. By averaging data at multiple sites, researchers reduce the probability of artifacts (or coincidences) that can appear to support a particular conclusion. Eliminate choice F.

Choice G might also be tempting because it's true that researchers include willow measurements before and after wolf reintroduction. However, this is also a *strength* of the experiment—the researchers are specifically trying to determine the effect of wolf reintroduction, so it helps to compare willows before and after wolves were reintroduced. Eliminate choice G.

Choice H is true in that researchers only sampled areas within the park where wolves were reintroduced—having a parallel set of sites that did not experience wolf reintroduction would be a control, and controls help evaluate whether a relationship is based on causation or merely correlation. Other factors that have nothing to do with wolf reintroduction (warmer summers, abundant rainfall) might also lead to an increase in willow growth. (In practice, it is probably quite difficult to find an identical habitat that avoids wolf reintroduction.) Keep choice H but continue to check choice J if you have time.

Choice J is true in that the researchers included data only from willows, and it's also true that examining other species would help examine broader impacts from wolf reintroduction. However, the question specifically asked about conclusions about the growth of *willow trees* (not the broader environment), so choice J is incorrect, so choice H is the correct answer.

PRACTICE

Now that we've worked through a series of Data Representation questions together, it's time to try a practice set on your own. When you're finished answering all 20 questions, check the answers and explanations that follow to figure out how well you did and why you may have selected any incorrect answer choices.

PASSAGE I

Rocks are naturally occurring solids composed of one or more kinds of minerals. The outermost solid layer of the earth, the lithosphere is composed of rock. Pumice is a type of volcanic rock that is usually light in color and rough in texture. It is created when very hot, highly pressurized rock is ejected violently from volcanoes. After ejection, the fast rate of cooling and decrease in pressure causes the formation of bubbles on the rock's surface due to lowered internal gas solubility. As a result, pumice is extremely porous. The density of pumice averages around 0.25 g/mL. Granite, on the other hand, is a type of igneous rock that is composed of a wide array of solid chemical compounds. It is very hard, nonporous, and often used for construction. The density of granite averages around 2.75 g/mL.

Your lab group wants to test the absorbency of pumice and granite by examining these rocks' ability to absorb water, with the goal of determining whether rock porosity correlates with the mass of water rock can hold. The masses of three pieces of pumice and three pieces of granite were measured. The six rocks were then submerged completely in water, held down with identical straps. Each hour, the rocks were removed from the water, patted dry, and measured for mass on a balance. This process was repeated over the course of six hours. The rocks were handled carefully throughout the experiment to prevent chipping or loss of rock mass. For each hour mark, the average masses and standard deviations were calculated for each rock type, and the following data was collected, with error bars representing one standard deviation upward and downward:

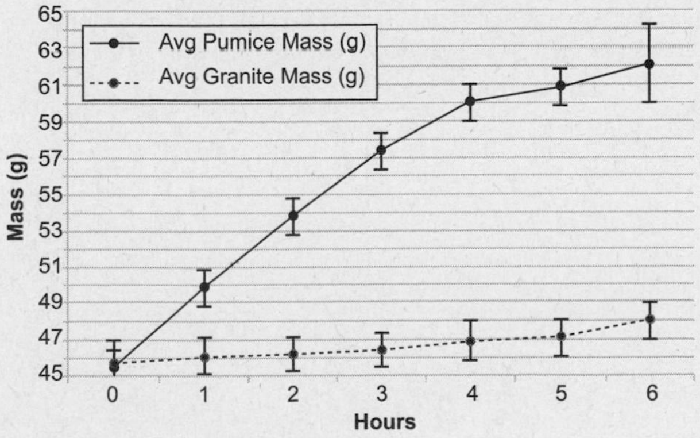

1. Based on the information provided in the passage and the figure, why must the rocks be fastened beneath the water in this and future related experiments?

   A. Pumice is air-sensitive and would corrode upon exposure to oxygen.
   B. Granite is air-sensitive and would corrode upon exposure to oxygen.
   C. Pumice would, based on its density, otherwise float to the surface of the water.
   D. Granite would, based on its density, otherwise float to the surface of the water.

2. What mass of water, on average, did the granite samples absorb after 6 hours?

   F. Slightly less than 1 g of water
   G. Slightly more than 1 g of water
   H. Slightly less than 2 g of water
   J. Slightly more than 2 g of water

3. The least precise set of trials was collected at:

   A. 0 hours for granite.
   B. 0 hours for pumice.
   C. 6 hours for granite.
   D. 6 hours for pumice.

4. Based on the data, which of the following conclusions would appropriately summarize the experimental results?

   F. Regardless of rock type, rocks with larger dry weight absorb more water after 6 hours than rocks with smaller dry weight.
   G. Regardless of rock type, rocks with smaller dry weight absorb more water after 6 hours than rocks with larger dry weight.
   H. As rock porosity increases, the water absorbance capacity of rocks also increases.
   J. As rock porosity increases, the water absorbance capacity of rocks decreases.

5. Which of the following statistical analyses would best account for the fact that all six rocks did not start at exactly the same mass?

A. Graph the average percentage increase in mass rather than the average increase in mass.
B. Calculate the collective average of granite and pumice masses at each time point and graph these values.
C. Subtract the average dry weight of each rock type from each data point.
D. Swap the variables graphed on the *x*- and *y*-axes.

PASSAGE II

To determine the spring constant *k* of a spring found in the laboratory, your lab group decides to apply Hooke's law, which states that the force required to extend or compress a spring by a given distance is proportional to that distance. This can be expressed by the equation $F = -kx$, where F is force, k is the spring constant, and x is the displacement magnitude, a distance.

The spring was hung vertically from a hook. Its resting position was marked as $x = 0$ cm. Various masses were hung at the bottom of the spring, and the spring was allowed to extend as needed. The figure below shows the resting spring and the extended spring with a 40 g weight:

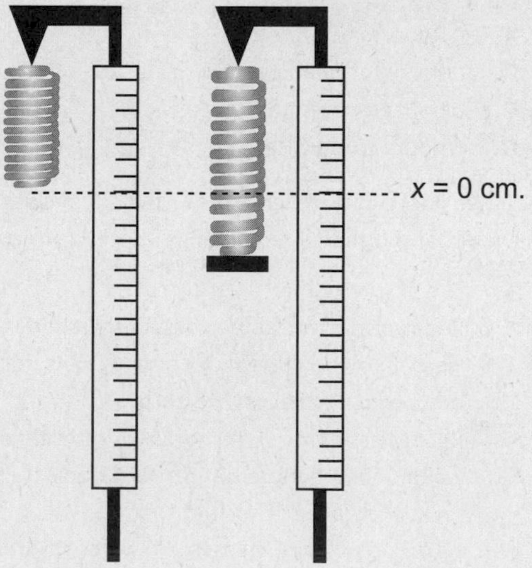

This process was repeated using four different masses, with displacement measured for each mass. Since weight is equivalent to the product of mass and the acceleration of gravity, each mass was converted to a weight in millinewtons. The data is shown below:

Mass Added to Spring (g)	Weight Added to Spring (mN)	Displacement (cm)
51	500	3.5
102	1,000	7.0
153	1,500	10.5
204	2,000	14.0

In order to determine the spring constant, the weight added to the spring was plotted as a function of displacement, and the slope of the line was determined.

6. What displacement magnitude would be expected for a 3,000 mN weight?

F. 1.75 cm
G. 17.5 cm
H. 21.0 cm
J. 28.0 cm

7. The plotted line used to determine the spring constant *k* would most resemble which of the following graphs?

A.

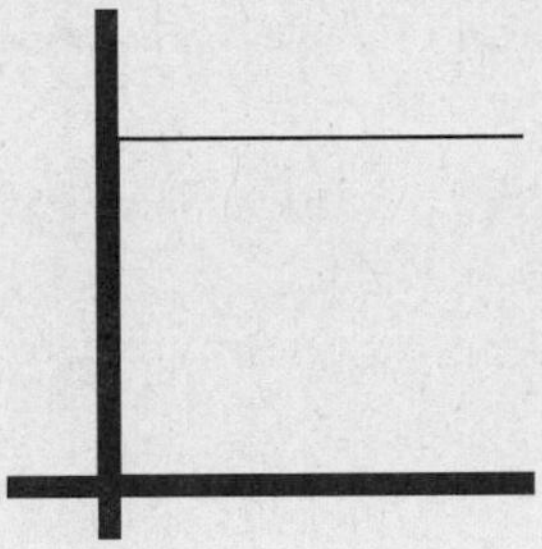

B.

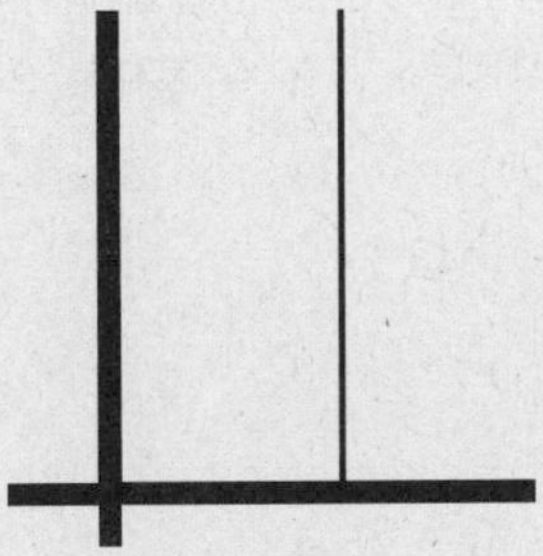

C.

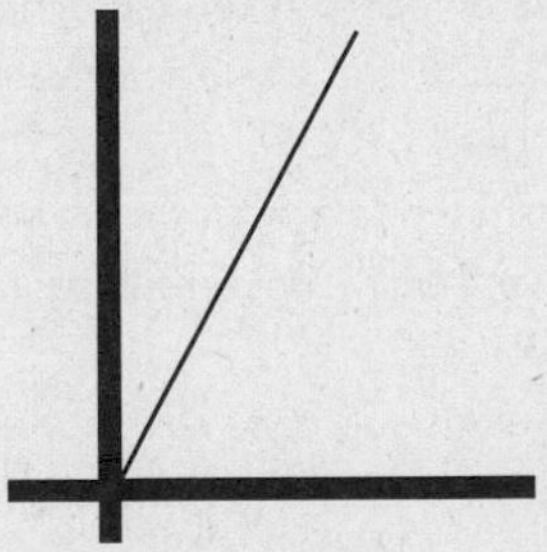

D.

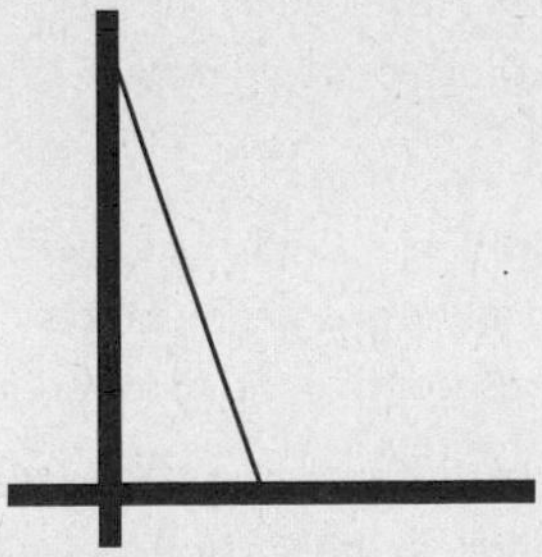

8. Each of the masses was converted to weight for the application of Hooke's law because:

F. mass and force have the same units, but weight does not.

G. weight and force have the same units, but mass does not.

H. mass and force are proportional to one another, but not to weight.

J. weight and force are proportional to one another, but not to mass.

9. How would the spring constant change if this identical experiment were performed on the surface of Mercury, a planet that is much smaller in radius than Earth, assuming similar temperatures?

A. The spring constant would remain the same because the difference in gravitational pull between Earth and Mercury would affect both weight and displacement similarly.

B. The spring constant would remain the same because the difference in gravitational pull between Earth and Mercury is negligible.

C. The spring constant would increase due to the difference in gravitational pull between Earth and Mercury, which would alter the weight on the *y*-axis.

D. The spring constant would decrease due to the difference in gravitational pull between Earth and Mercury, which would alter the weight on the *y*-axis.

10. A mass is applied to the spring displayed in the first figure. The mass is pulled downward slightly and released. This action has turned the setup into:

F. a pulley.

G. a motor.

H. a harmonic oscillator.

J. a torsion spring.

PASSAGE III

Aqueous solutions of hydrochloric acid and sodium sulfide react to form hydrogen sulfide and sodium chloride, according to the following chemical reaction:

$$2HCl(aq)+Na_2S(aq) \rightarrow H_2S(g)+2NaCl(aq)$$

The apparatus displayed in the figure below allows for the reactants to be added, the flask to be sealed, and then the reaction to be mixed; immediately after reactant addition in a flask, a cork containing a syringe is used to seal the reaction flask and collect in the syringe any gas produced by the reaction. The plunger, fully depressed to start, is pushed out as gas fills the syringe. After allowing the reaction to continue to completion, the volume reading on the syringe indicates the amount of hydrogen sulfide gas produced in the reaction.

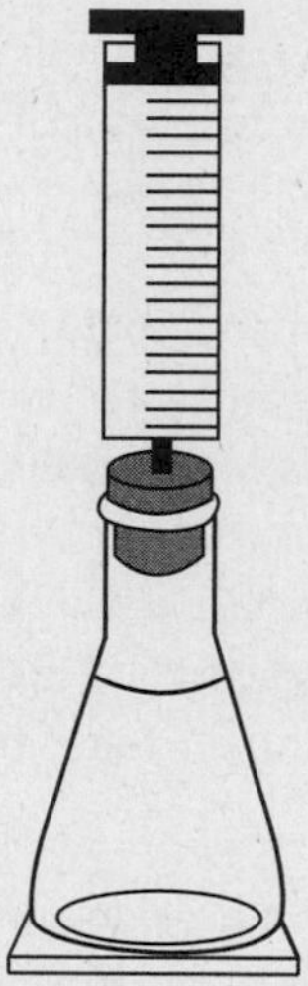

Your lab group has three sodium sulfide solutions (A, B, and C) whose concentrations are 6 M, 10 M, and 14 M; however, you have no idea which is which. To assign the appropriate concentrations to the solutions, a 50 mL sample of each sodium sulfide solution was separately mixed with 50 mL of concentrated hydrochloric acid in identical flask apparatuses like the one above, with the reaction setup ensuring that hydrochloric acid is well in excess. The following volumes of gas were collected when each reaction was allowed to continue to completion:

Solution	Gas Volume Produced (mL)
A	40.0
B	50.7
C	50.7

The experiment was repeated by mixing 5-mL samples of the sodium sulfide solutions with 95 mL of concentrated hydrochloric acid in the apparatuses. The following data was obtained:

Solution	Gas Volume Produced (mL)
A	2.0
B	8.9
C	4.7

11. Based on the data collected, the sodium sulfide solution with the highest concentration (14 M) is:

A. Solution A.
B. Solution B.
C. Solution C.
D. unable to be determined.

12. Lower volumes of gas were produced in the second round of experiments because:

F. the mole ratio of reactivity for hydrochloric acid and sodium sulfide was altered by the volume changes.
G. the reaction shifted to produce more sodium chloride rather than hydrogen sulfide, resulting in a lower gas volume.
H. the sodium sulfide solutions were more diluted in the reaction mixtures and provided less reactant for the reaction.
J. the reaction was reversed by the increased volume of hydrochloric acid relative to sodium sulfide.

13. Why did Solutions B and C produce identical gas volumes in the first round of experiments but different gas volumes in the second round of experiments?

A. Hydrochloric acid was the limiting reagent for Solutions B and C in the first round, while sodium sulfide was limiting for every other experiment.
B. Sodium sulfide was the limiting reagent for Solutions B and C in the first round, while hydrochloric acid was limiting for every other experiment.
C. Solutions B and C must have the same concentration.
D. Human error disrupted the results during the first round.

14. If this experiment is repeated using 5 mL of Solution A and 195 mL of hydrochloric acid, what volume of gas would be produced?

- **F.** 0.0 mL
- **G.** 1.0 mL
- **H.** 2.0 mL
- **J.** 4.0 mL

15. What is another method you could use to identify each of the three sodium sulfide solution concentrations?

- **A.** Paper chromatography
- **B.** Filtration
- **C.** Titration
- **D.** Distillation

PASSAGE IV

The disease hereditary nonpolyposis colorectal cancer (HNPCC) is caused by mutations in human genes that repair errors in DNA. The gene *MLH3* codes for such a DNA repair protein. In an experiment, this gene was modified so that when the protein is expressed, it will be attached to a dye called GFP (green fluorescence protein), which allows for the MLH3 protein to be detected using fluorescence when it is expressed in the cells. The cells were observed using live cell imaging and confocal microscopy, and accumulation of MLH3 was detected at the centrosomes. Centrosomes are the organelles in animal cells where microtubules are organized and which regulate cell division.

Fluorescence recovery after photobleaching (FRAP) is a technique that was used to detect MLH3 at the centrosomes in human cells to determine its stability. An initial burst of light decreases the fluorescence in the centrosomes and when fluorescence is restored in this region, it shows how quickly the protein moves back into the region. Fluorescence measurements were taken over the course of 32 seconds after this initial burst of light. Eight separate trials were performed, and error bars were calculated based on the standard deviations from these trials. The figure shows the two foci, or regions, where the measurements were taken. These foci appear as light-colored dots in the figure. The data is shown below:

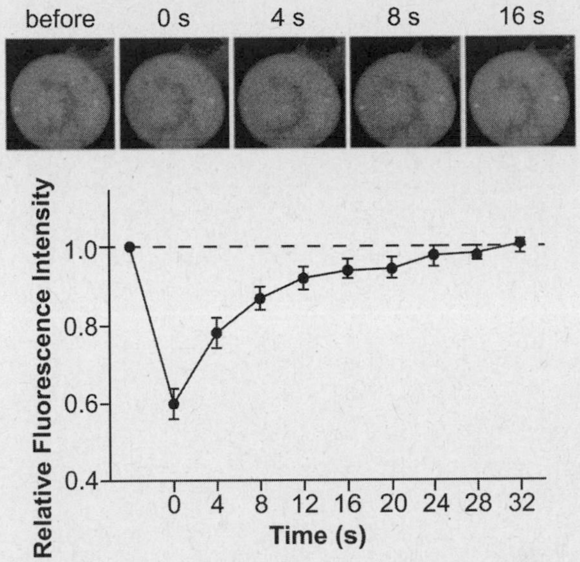

Source: Roesner, Lennart M.; Mielke, Christian; Faehnrich, Silke; Merkhoffer, Yvonne; Dittmar, Kurt E.J.; Drexler, Hans G.; Dirks, Wilhelm G. 2014. "Localization of MLH3 at the Centrosomes." *Int. J. Mol. Sci.* 15, no. 8: 13932–13937.

16. The most rapid rate of fluorescence recovery occurred:

- **F.** before 0 seconds.
- **G.** between 0 and 4 seconds.
- **H.** between 8 and 12 seconds.
- **J.** between 24 and 28 seconds.

17. The advantage of FRAP over live cell imaging alone is the ability to:

- **A.** acquire quantitative data rather than visual data.
- **B.** take advantage of the linked fluorescent protein.
- **C.** collect data without the use of additives.
- **D.** complete the study without harming the cells.

18. The time at which the displayed curve reaches the dotted line indicates:

- **F.** the time required for the foci to photobleach completely.
- **G.** the time required for 100% fluorescence recovery.
- **H.** the time it takes the light burst to decrease fluorescence to its lowest point before recovery begins.
- **J.** the overall time over which all data points were taken throughout the experiment.

19. For time points where multiple independent measurements were taken, which of the following statements is true?

A. Measurement precision increases over time.
B. Measurement precision decreases over time.
C. Measurement accuracy increases over time.
D. Measurement accuracy decreases over time.

20. Based on its organelle association, MLH3 likely plays a key role in successful:

F. apoptosis.
G. phagocytosis.
H. pinocytosis.
J. mitosis.

ANSWERS AND EXPLANATIONS

PASSAGE I

The first passage is an earth sciences topic. The passage describes an experiment to test water absorbency of pumice and granite, two very different types of rock with very different porosities.

1. **The correct answer is C.** This question asks you to think about the specifics of the experimental design, based on the described experiment, for this experiment and any future experiments of the same variety. The passage and figure include no information whatsoever about air sensitivity or corrosiveness; plus, if the rocks are being taken out of the water every hour, it would be disastrous if the rocks were air-sensitive. Therefore, eliminate choices A and B right away. You might already know that the density of water is approximately 1 g/mL at room temperature, but even if you didn't, you can easily figure it out. The passage provides the numerical densities of both pumice and granite. The density of pumice is much less than that of granite, and a less dense rock will be the more likely rock to float in water. This should help you choose choice C as the correct answer. It is true that pumice will get heavier as it absorbs water, but this question is fairly general; granite will never really require the fasteners, but pumice certainly will, particularly at the earliest time points in the experiment.

2. **The correct answer is J.** This question asks you to interpret the graph. If we look at the granite line at 6 hours, the average mass of the rock and water is approximately 48 g. We can find the dry mass of the rock by looking at the granite line at 0 hours. The dry mass is just under 46 g. The difference between these masses, just over 2 g, represents the average mass of water absorbed by the granite.

3. **The correct answer is D.** This question asks you to assess the validity of the data by looking at precision. The passage indicates that the error bars represent standard deviation. The least precise set of trials will be the set of trials with the largest error bar, as a large standard deviation indicates that the individual data points were generally further from the mean. The largest error bar on the graph can be found on the pumice line at 6 hours.

4. **The correct answer is H.** This question asks you to look for trends in the data and draw a conclusion. Choices F and G draw conclusions based on rock dry weight rather than rock type; since the dry weights for all rocks were more or less the same, these answers can be eliminated. Furthermore, the question proposed in the passage was to test porosity, so it wouldn't make sense to draw conclusions that do not address the proposed question. The graph indicates that pumice clearly absorbs much more water than granite. Pumice is much more porous than granite. Therefore, the correct conclusion is that more porous rocks absorb more water, so the answer is choice H.

5. **The correct answer is A.** This question asks you to consider other ways to analyze the data statistically. Choice B is incorrect because it eliminates the distinction between rock types, which is really the basis of the whole proposal. Choice C is incorrect because the graph would look exactly the same, and it does not account for any differences in initial dry mass. Choice D is incorrect because it would just transform the graph without extracting any helpful new information. Using percentage increases rather than mass increases would show how a particular rock absorbs water relative to its own initial mass, thereby eliminating any issues with the fact that all six rocks did not begin at perfectly identical masses.

PASSAGE II

This is a physics passage about springs, Hooke's law, and the calculation of spring constants.

6. **The correct answer is H.** The first question for this passage asks you to use the data to predict a displacement for a weight that has not been tested. Based on the data table, when weight doubles, so does the displacement. It is a linear trend. 3,000 mN is twice the weight of 1,500 mN, which exhibited a displacement of 10.5 cm. Doubling this should give the displacement for 3,000 mN. $10.5 \times 2 = 21.0$ cm., so the correct answer is choice H.

7. **The correct answer is C.** This question asks you to predict what the described graph looks like. The passage indicates that weight was plotted as a function of displacement, and the data shows that as weight increases, displacement also increases. The only graph that shows this positive correlation between these variables is choice C.

8. **The correct answer is G.** This question asks you to think about why the scientists converted mass to weight in order to apply Hooke's law. If you remember that newtons are the correct unit for force, this answer will be obvious, but even if you don't, you can use logic to figure it out. We can immediately rule out choices H and J because the various equations in the passage show that force is proportional to both mass and weight, so neither of these answers can be correct. Now we must decide whether force has the same units as mass or weight. Force can be measured in newtons, just like weight is here, so the correct answer is choice G. If you didn't know that force is measured in newtons, simply think about the process: the scientists took the extra step of converting masses to weights. Why would they do this unless weight had the units necessary to apply Hooke's law? The conversion would be redundant otherwise. This is an example of how you can figure out an answer using logic even if you don't know a particular scientific fact.

9. **The correct answer is A.** This question asks you to predict what would happen if the same experiment were repeated under different conditions. In the situation described in the question, the new condition is lower gravitational pull. If the same experiment is performed on Mercury, the major relevant difference is that the gravitational pull would be significantly lower than on Earth. Gravitational pull comes into play when graphing weight as a function of displacement, but gravity will affect both weight and displacement in the same way. If temperatures are assumed to be similar, decreased gravity-influenced weight on Mercury would be accompanied by a decreased displacement. These variables would change in the same way, resulting in no change in line slope. We can rule out choice B because the reason *k* stays the same is *not* because the gravitational pull between Earth and Mercury is negligible. We can also rule out choices C and D, which indicate that the spring constant would change because only the weight would be affected; these answers do not consider that displacement would also change if the experiment is performed under different gravitational conditions. The answer is therefore choice A. In general, remember that numbers described as "constants" will stay the same under most conditions.

10. **The correct answer is H.** This question asks you to look at the picture of the experimental setup and choose the term that best describes what you would see. This question does require that you have at least some understanding of each of these terms, though really you are all set if you know the term in the correct answer. A pulley is a wheel on an axle that supports movement of a belt and can change direction of motion along its circumference. The figure includes no such setup, so this cannot be a pulley. The answer is not choice F. We can also rule out choice G; a motor, in general, is a machine that converts electrical energy into mechanical energy. The only major energy conversion occurring in the described situation is an interconversion between potential and kinetic energy, so this answer is also incorrect. A torsion spring describes a spring that functions by twisting, which is the definition of *torsion*. No twisting is happening here, so we can rule out choice J. A harmonic oscillator is a system that experiences a restoring force proportional to its displacement when displaced from its equilibrium position. Even if you had no idea what a harmonic oscillator was, you might recognize the root word *oscillate*, which means to vary in magnitude regularly around a central point. When you pull the spring down a bit, the mass will move up and down, above and below the original resting equilibrium position.

PASSAGE III

This is a chemistry passage that describes the use of a gas-collecting apparatus to match three sodium sulfide solutions with their concentrations. This experiment relies on the idea that if the three sodium sulfide solutions are mixed with the same amount of hydrochloric acid, the differences in H_2S gas volume produced will indicate which original sodium sulfide solution contained the greatest concentration of sulfide. As the two rounds of experimentation show, however, this experiment is useful only if hydrochloric acid is in excess; it seems that HCl was in excess in the second round of experimentation, giving useful results there, but not in the first round of experimentation.

11. **The correct answer is B.** This question asks you to interpret the data and draw a conclusion. In order to figure out which sodium sulfide has the highest concentration, you have to determine which solution produced the greatest volume of gas. The first round of experiments will not be

helpful because Solutions B and C both produced the same gas volumes. The second round of experimentation clearly distinguishes among the three solutions, with Solution B producing the most gas. Therefore, the correct answer is choice B.

12. **The correct answer is H.** This question asks you to explain the discrepancies in data between the first and second rounds of experimentation. Looking at the possible answers, we can rule out choice F right away because volume changes will not affect the mole ratio. A chemical equation will not change (unless, in specific cases, environmental conditions change), so F can be ruled out. This same concept helps us to rule out choice G because the reaction will not shift to produce one product over the other. Per stoichiometric concepts, the ratios of reactants and products remain constant for a particular chemical equation. Finally, we can rule out choice J because the reaction is not a reversible reaction; the reaction would have been written with arrows pointing in both directions if it was reversible. The correct answer is choice H because the answer to this question is fairly straightforward; in the first round of experiments, the sodium sulfide solution comprises 50% of the reaction mixture volume, while in the second round of experiments, the sodium sulfide solution comprises 5% of the reaction mixture volume.

13. **The correct answer is A.** This question asks you look at the data and predict why the results were not identical in each round. The key here is that significantly more sodium sulfide was used in the first round of experiments than in the second round. This is important because the reaction will run to completion until the limiting reagent is completely used up. In the first round of experiments, the same amount of HCl was used in every experiment, while the three sodium sulfide solutions had different concentrations. The fact that Solutions B and C yielded the same gas volume indicates that the HCl was limiting in the first round of experiments, when the better experiment for determining relative sodium sulfide concentrations would have HCl in excess. This is exactly what was done in the second round of experiments. The gas volume for Solution B in particular should not be taken at face value, since HCl could potentially still be limiting for that solution, but the second round of experiments clearly confirms that Solutions A and C have lower concentrations than Solution B. Therefore, this discrepancy between rounds is based on limiting reagents, and choice A correctly describes this. Choice B has the solutions backwards and is incorrect. The fact that different gas volumes were measured in the second round of experiments clearly shows that Solutions B and C have different concentrations, so the answer is not choice C. Human error is always a possibility, but it is unlikely that human error would have resulted in Solutions B and C giving exactly the same volume of 50.7 mL.

14. **The correct answer is H.** This question asks you to think about future experimentation. In the described scenario, the sodium sulfide solution volume remains the same as the volume used in the second round of experiments, but the volume of HCl is greatly increased. Since HCl is already the excess reactant in the second round, increasing the amount of HCl will *not* change the amount of gas produced. With sodium sulfide as the limiting reactant, no more H_2S can be produced, regardless of how much extra HCl is added. 5 mL of Solution A reacts with excess HCl to form 2.0 mL of gas, according to the data obtained in the second round of experimentation. This same volume will be obtained under the described conditions, so the correct answer is H.

15. **The correct answer is C.** This question asks you to think of another method for determining which sodium sulfide solution is which. Paper chromatography (choice A), is a method for separating components of a mixture based on affinity for a solid, so this is not relevant for concentration determination. Filtration (choice B) is a method for separating solids from liquids in a mixture, so this answer is not relevant here either. Distillation (choice D) is a method used to separate components of a mixture based on boiling point. With three of the four answers being physical separation techniques, we can use process of elimination to figure out that the correct answer is choice C. If you know what a titration is going in, however, you could pick this answer out as correct right away! A titration is a technique that uses an indicator to allow for determination of the concentration of an unknown solution, and indicators exist that can be used to determine the concentration of a sodium sulfide solution.

PASSAGE IV

This is a biology passage in which a technique called FRAP is described to show the high mobility of the MLH3 protein as it localizes at the centrosomes in a human cell.

16. **The correct answer is G.** This question asks you to read and interpret the provided graph. The most rapid rate of fluorescence recovery occurs where the slope of the line is highest. This occurs between 0 and 4 seconds, so the answer is choice G. Note that a steep slope is also observed before 0 seconds, but this is a negative slope and the direct result of the light burst photobleaching the sample, so this is not part of the fluorescence recovery process.

17. **The correct answer is A.** This question asks you to think about the described techniques and consider why each kind of collected data is useful. FRAP offers a way to quantify MLH3 mobility at the centrosomes, so its advantage is that numerical, or quantitative, data can be collected. Choice B is incorrect because both methods take advantage of fluorescence, and choice D is incorrect because neither method harms the cells; if anything, FRAP is more harmful than live cell imaging because it destroys the fluorescence properties of fluorophores in the cell. Additives do not play a major role in either technique, so choice C can also be ruled out.

18. **The correct answer is G.** This question asks you to interpret the data and explain why the data was presented in the manner in which it was presented. The significance of the dotted line is that it represents 100% fluorescence recovery. Therefore, the time it takes for the fluorescence readings to reach the line indicates the time required for 100% fluorescence recovery (choice G). Choice F is incorrect because photobleaching is the process of *losing* fluorescence, not gaining fluorescence. Choice H is incorrect for the same reason; it refers to the loss, rather than gain, of fluorescence in the region of interest. Choice J is incorrect because data points were taken before time zero, which means that the time at which the data points reach the dotted line will actually be shorter than the total overall time of data point collection over the course of the entire experiment. It is important that you notice that the *x*-axis does not begin with time zero at the far left; otherwise, you might be tempted to choose this answer.

19. **The correct answer is A.** This question asks about the validity of the data by asking you to assess precision and accuracy of the data points. We can rule out choices C and D immediately. Accuracy is determined relative to a known value, and we have no known values here with which to compare the data. Therefore, we cannot assess accuracy. We can assess precision by looking at the error bars, which are based on standard deviation, a statistical measure of precision. Over time, the magnitude of the error bars generally decreases, indicating increased precision.

20. **The correct answer is J.** This question asks you to apply the information in the passage and data with your knowledge of cell biology and processes. The key here is to recognize that centrosomes play a key role in one of these processes but not the others. You might also pick up on the fact that MLH3 is a DNA mismatch repair protein, and DNA is heavily involved in only one of the four listed processes. That process is mitosis. Centrosomes represent the constricted regions of mitotic chromosomes and are the organelle to which spindle fibers attach during mitosis. Apoptosis is programmed cell death, and while it involves a cascade of proteins, maintaining DNA integrity is not so important here, so we can rule out choice F. Phagocytosis mostly occurs in phagocytes and protists, so it is unlikely that MLH3 is important in this process since the passage describes human (animal) cells. Furthermore, DNA is not a key participant in phagocytosis, so there would be no need for a protein like MLH3. The same goes for pinocytosis, so we can rule out choices G and H. That leaves mitosis, which is the part of the cell cycle in which chromosomes in a cell nucleus are split into two identical sets of chromosomes, with each assigned to its own nucleus. This is very much relevant to centrosomes, MLH3, and DNA, so mitosis is the process that makes the most sense here.

CHAPTER 12: RESEARCH SUMMARIES

OVERVIEW

- What to Expect
- What Is the Scientific Question or Purpose of This Experiment?
- What Hypothesis Can Be Proposed to Predict the Outcome of This Experiment?
- How Can the Scientific Question Be Addressed Experimentally?
- How Can the Provided Data Be Analyzed?
- What Conclusions Can Be Drawn Based on the Experiment and Results?
- Common Mistakes to Avoid
- Summing It Up
- College Readiness Benchmark Learning Path Practice
- Practice

Now that we've reviewed Data Representation questions, we will move on to Research Summaries. Research Summaries are the most frequently featured question type on the ACT Science test. Research Summaries questions fall under two different ACT subcategories: Scientific Investigation (which make up 20–30% of the test) and Evaluation of Models, Inferences, and Experimental Results (which make up 25–35% of the test). In the real world of science research, research summaries appear everywhere: in science journals, magazines, newspapers, and even in textbooks for historically important research investigations. Therefore, it makes a lot of sense that such a significant part of the science test focuses on this kind of stimulus passage.

In many ways, questions based on Research Summaries will require a lot of the same skills you used when answering Data Representation questions because both question types require you to analyze data. Furthermore, information from the same natural science disciplines (biology, chemistry, physics, and astronomy/earth sciences) provides the passage source material. The added challenge of Research Summaries passages is that you are often given more background information about the experiment and the thought that went into its design. As such, Research Summaries questions might ask you to identify the purpose of an experiment or to propose a possible hypothesis for the question the experiment is addressing. You might need to identify independent, dependent, or control variables, or suggest methods or alternative techniques that will help answer the question. The similarity to Data Representation questions lies in the fact that you will also be presented with experimental results, which you will be expected to analyze in order to draw conclusions. For questions that involve analyzing data and drawing conclusions, you will certainly be able to apply many of the same skills we've already discussed, but we will still talk about how to use these skills in the context of Research Summaries questions in this chapter.

WHAT TO EXPECT

Research Summaries typically begin with a written introduction that provides background information about a scientific topic before introducing the experiment. Included in this background information may be important vocabulary words, reminders about principles and topics you may have learned about in the past, and specific details about the featured topic.

After the background information is provided, the passage will then give a description of the experiment that was performed. From this information, you should be able to identify the **independent variable, dependent variable,** and **control variables,** which we discussed in Chapter 11. The written parts of Research Summaries will almost certainly be longer and more in-depth than the written parts of Data Representation. The goal of Data Representation passages is to present you with data to analyze, whereas Research Summaries place a far greater emphasis on experimental design and the scientific method in full. Experimental descriptions may include an image to help you visualize the setup described in the passage.

Following the experimental description is data of some kind. This can include a table, a graph, or sometimes a written description of the results obtained. In addition, you may even be provided with a conclusion reached by the scientists who performed the experiment.

Because these passages focus more equally on the experiment and the results (rather than just the results), the questions that accompany Research Summaries cover more ground than the questions that accompany Data Representation questions. As such, there are usually five or six questions that follow each passage of this type, slightly more on average than you might see for Data Representation questions. The questions that follow Research Summaries will test you on a number of important skills: identifying the purpose of a research project, formulating hypotheses to make predictions, proposing experiments or alternative experimental methods, analyzing data, and drawing conclusions based on experimental data. Keep these skills in mind as you read through Research Summaries, because it is very likely you will have to answer relevant questions that test your proficiency in some or all of these areas. In order to give you an idea of how each of these skills may be tested within the context of Research Summaries, consider the following questions, each of which is followed by a sample question so you know what to expect when you come across them on the exam.

> **TIP:** Any provided conclusions should be taken with a grain of salt, because the questions that follow the passage may ask you to support or refute the given conclusion.

WHAT IS THE SCIENTIFIC QUESTION OR PURPOSE OF THIS EXPERIMENT?

Whenever you read about any kind of scientific experiment, the first thing you must do is identify the **scientific question,** mentioned back in Chapter 11. The scientific question is also called the **purpose** of the experiment. Basically, you need to ask yourself:

- Why should anyone bother doing this experiment?
- Why was this particular topic chosen?
- What will this experiment test?
- Why will the results of this experiment be important?

Stating the purpose of an experiment is always the first step of the scientific method because a scientist must establish exactly *why* he or she is performing an experiment before actually performing it. If the purpose of the experiment is not clearly identified, then it will be very difficult to design an experiment because it may not be exactly clear what the scientist is trying to accomplish.

> **TIP:** When you are trying to state the purpose of an experiment, it always helps to identify and include the dependent variable (what is being measured) and the independent variable (what the scientists change) in the statement, which we previously discussed in more depth in Chapter 11.

Almost always, background research is needed to flesh out a scientific question or purpose. Background research helps a scientist to narrow down a general topic to something more specific. For example, if a scientist wants to study the effect of seaweed population on photosynthetic efficiency in a body of water, background research can help the scientist to choose specifically to monitor dissolved oxygen levels in the water as a means of quantifying photosynthesis (since, as you may recall from your biology class, photosynthesis is the process by which plants convert carbon dioxide and water to glucose and oxygen).

As a test taker, you won't have the luxury of being able to do your own background research on a particular topic. Fortunately, Research Summaries save you time by providing you with all the background information you will need to clearly identify the purpose of the experiment of interest! Given the general topic description and background information and then looking ahead at the experimental design (which we will discuss further in a bit), you should be able to determine the purpose for any experiment posed in Research Summaries you come across.

It was important to identify the purpose of an experiment in Data Representation passages so you knew what to look for in the provided data tables or graphs. In Research Summaries, you may be required to delve into this a bit more. For example, you might be asked to choose a relevant scientific question or statement of purpose from four choices, or you could be asked to formulate a different but related question about the topic of interest.

Let's look at a test-style question in action. As in the last chapter, we will use the same passage and data throughout the first few examples in this chapter so you can get a sense of the different question types that will come up within a Research Summary set.

Photosynthesis is a biological process that generates stored energy through the formation of glucose from carbon dioxide and water, according to the following chemical reaction:

$$6\,CO_2 + 6\,H_2O \rightarrow C_6H_{12}O_6 + 6\,O_2$$

Cellular respiration works in opposition, using oxygen to break down the sugar and release that energy to form ATP:

$$C_6H_{12}O_6 + 6\,O_2 \rightarrow 6\,CO_2 + 6\,H_2O$$

Carbon dioxide reacts with water to form carbonic acid. Phenolphthalein is an indicator that remains colorless in acid and turns pink in base. Three drops of phenolphthalein can be added to a small water sample, and the amount of NaOH needed to turn a clear sample pink (its neutralization point) gives an indication of the concentration of carbonic acid in the sample.

Many plants and algae are capable of both photosynthesis and respiration. Among these is an algal species called stonewort, of the genus *Chara*. Stonewort grows well in lime-rich waters, which results in the formation of calcium carbonate deposits on the algae.

A group of students wants to test the rates of photosynthesis and respiration in stonewort in different light conditions. The students acquire two 6.00 g stonewort samples and place each in a beaker containing 250 mL of spring water. One beaker was incubated in the dark at 25°C, while the other beaker was incubated in the light at 25°C. Over the course of one day, two 1 mL water samples were removed from each beaker every six hours. One of each pair of water samples was used to detect dissolved oxygen concentration using an oxygen electrode, which measures O_2 concentration in units of parts per million (ppm). The second water sample per pair was used to test carbon dioxide levels using phenolphthalein and 0.04 M NaOH. Both tests were performed immediately after sample extraction to avoid sample disruption. The following results were obtained:

Stonewort Sample	Measurement	Time (Hours)				
		0	6	12	18	24
Light	Dissolved O_2 (ppm)	2.35	2.81	4.61	5.02	5.30
Light	Volume 0.04 M NaOH (μL)	21.0	18.3	14.0	13.3	12.8
Dark	Dissolved O_2 (ppm)	2.36	2.37	2.01	1.84	1.79
Dark	Volume 0.04 M NaOH (μL)	22.2	23.0	26.1	28.7	30.0

Which of the following questions best summarizes the purpose of this research project?

A. How do the concentrations of O_2 and CO_2 in water affect stonewort survival in dark and light conditions?

B. How do O_2 concentrations impact CO_2 production in stonewort submerged in water?

C. How do light and dark conditions impact net O_2 and CO_2 concentrations in water due to stonewort energy cycles?

D. What is the effect of acidic and basic water conditions on stonewort O_2 and CO_2 production in dark and light conditions?

The correct answer is C. This question requires you to read the passage, recognize precisely what the scientists are trying to discover, and understand the kind of data that was collected. The passage itself gives you most of your answer in one sentence: *A group of students wants to test the rates of photosynthesis and respiration in stonewort in different light conditions.* However, this must be altered to include the kind of data collected. In this experiment, the net production or loss of CO_2 and O_2 was measured in the dark and light as a means of determining whether the rate of photosynthesis surpasses the rate of its reverse, respiration, or vice versa. The only answer choice, among the four provided options, that correctly identifies dark/light conditions as the independent variable and net CO_2/O_2 concentrations as the dependent variable is choice C.

Choice A is incorrect because it indicates that CO_2/O_2 concentrations are the independent variable—as well as dark/light conditions—rather than the dependent variable, and that stonewort survival is the dependent variable, which it is not. Choice B is incorrect because it indicates that O_2 concentration is the independent variable and CO_2 concentration is the dependent variable, without making any mention of light/dark conditions. Choice D is incorrect because it indicates that acidic and basic water conditions were the independent variable, though it does correctly identify O_2/CO_2 concentrations as the dependent variable. While CO_2 does react with water to form an acid, carbonic acid, and while NaOH was indeed used in the phenolphthalein test, the research project is not focused on testing the effects of acidic or basic conditions under light and dark conditions.

WHAT HYPOTHESIS CAN BE PROPOSED TO PREDICT THE OUTCOME OF THIS EXPERIMENT?

A **hypothesis** is an educated prediction about the outcome of a particular experiment. When developing a hypothesis, a scientist must consider cause and effect and rely on both logic and background research. For example, if you had to hypothesize whether a ball will reach a higher speed when dropped from 20 inches or 20 feet, it is perfectly fine to rely on logic. A reasonable prediction might be that the ball dropped from 20 feet will reach a higher speed because it has a longer distance along which to accelerate due to gravitational acceleration.

On the other hand, if you had to predict the effect of different buffers on the stability of a specific protein in solution, you would need more background information about the protein and its amino acid content in order to make a reasonable prediction. In most cases, hypotheses are based on a combination of logic *and* background research. Hypotheses are often framed in the "if–then" format, where the first clause provides the reasoning for your prediction (the cause) and the second clause provides the prediction itself (the predicted effect). An example could be: "If a greater drop distance provides a falling object with more distance over which to accelerate, then the ball dropped from 20 feet will reach a higher maximal speed than the ball dropped from 20 inches." Hypotheses are not absolutely required to take on the "if–then" format, but it is a helpful way to frame predictions and is quite widely used. On the ACT Science test, your ability to develop hypotheses may be tested primarily in two different ways.

1) **Choose a hypothesis.** The most straightforward question type might ask you to select which of the given choices is the most suitable hypothesis for an experiment. In this case, you would have to choose the answer that makes a logical prediction based on the background information you've been given. You should double-check that your answer also satisfies the correct independent and dependent variables described in the passage. For example, if your experiment is measuring the speed of a ball dropped from two different heights, your chosen hypothesis must also relate to speed as the dependent variable. In this example, your hypothesis should not be about, say, which ball will make the most noise or which ball will create the bigger crater when it hits the sand below.

2) **Make a prediction.** Another question type might ask you to make a prediction based on the background information provided. In a question like this, you might be given four choices that are all valid hypotheses for the given experiment—but based on the background information, there may be one choice that makes logical sense where the others do not.

One important thing to remember is that hypotheses are *predictions*, not results. A hypothesis will not always correctly predict the outcome of an experiment. A hypothesis might predict one result, but the experiment might demonstrate something entirely different. This is perfectly fine, and it happens all the time in science. Results of experiments often disprove hypotheses, and this is often how scientists make revolutionary discoveries.

TIP Your hypothesis must always correctly address the appropriate independent and dependent variables.

When a particular experiment consistently gives a result that isn't exactly what you expected, then it opens the door to further experiments to explain why this may be the case. So keep in mind that a hypothesis is still valid even if it is does not correctly predict an experimental result. You may find after performing the experiment that the results do not support your hypothesis, but the hypothesis is simply an attempt to make a prediction and won't always necessarily be correct.

Let's try another question.

Photosynthesis is a biological process that generates stored energy through the formation of glucose from carbon dioxide and water, according to the following chemical reaction:

$$6\,CO_2 + 6\,H_2O \rightarrow C_6H_{12}O_6 + 6\,O_2$$

Cellular respiration works in opposition, using oxygen to break down the sugar and release that energy to form ATP:

$$C_6H_{12}O_6 + 6\,O_2 \rightarrow 6\,CO_2 + 6\,H_2O$$

Carbon dioxide reacts with water to form carbonic acid. Phenolphthalein is an indicator that remains colorless in acid and turns pink in base. Three drops of phenolphthalein can be added to a small water sample, and the amount of NaOH needed to turn a clear sample pink (its neutralization point) gives an indication of the concentration of carbonic acid in the sample.

Many plants and algae are capable of both photosynthesis and respiration. Among these is an algal species called stonewort, of the genus *Chara*. Stonewort grows well in lime-rich waters, which results in the formation of calcium carbonate deposits on the algae.

A group of students wants to test the rates of photosynthesis and respiration in stonewort in different light conditions. The students acquire two 6.00 g stonewort samples and place each in a beaker containing 250 mL of spring water. One beaker was incubated in the dark at 25°C, while the other beaker was incubated in the light at 25°C. Over the course of one day, two 1 mL water samples were removed from each beaker every six hours. One of each pair of water samples was used to detect dissolved oxygen concentration using an oxygen electrode, which measures O_2 concentration in units of parts per million (ppm). The second water sample per pair was used to test carbon dioxide levels using phenolphthalein and 0.04 M NaOH. Both tests were performed immediately after sample extraction to avoid sample disruption. The following results were obtained:

Stonewort Sample	Measurement	Time (Hours)				
		0	6	12	18	24
Light	Dissolved O_2 (ppm)	2.35	2.81	4.61	5.02	5.30
	Volume 0.04 M NaOH (μL)	21.0	18.3	14.0	13.3	12.8
Dark	Dissolved O_2 (ppm)	2.36	2.37	2.01	1.84	1.79
	Volume 0.04 M NaOH (μL)	22.2	23.0	26.1	28.7	30.0

Based on the provided information, which of the following might be a logical hypothesis to predict what will happen in the phenolphthalein/NaOH tests?

F. If light drives photosynthesis but not respiration, then the light samples should exhibit higher O_2 levels than the dark samples over the course of 24 hours.

G. If light drives photosynthesis but not respiration, then the light samples should exhibit lower O_2 levels than the dark samples over the course of 24 hours.

H. If light drives photosynthesis but not respiration, then the light samples should exhibit higher CO_2 levels than the dark samples over the course of 24 hours.

J. If light drives photosynthesis but not respiration, then the light samples should exhibit lower CO_2 levels than the dark samples over the course of 24 hours.

The correct answer is J. This question asks you to choose a valid hypothesis from four choices. All four choices have the same "cause" stem: "If light drives photosynthesis but not respiration..." That means that, based on the background information, we should choose a logical conclusion based on this stem.

We can immediately eliminate choices F and G because the "effect" portions of these hypotheses refer to O_2 levels, and the passage indicates that the phenolphthalein/NaOH test detects CO_2 levels. Now we can hone in on choices H and J. To come up with a reasonable hypothesis, we should focus on the chemical equations for photosynthesis and respiration. According to the passage, the chemical equation for photosynthesis is: $6\ CO_2 + 6\ H_2O \rightarrow C_6H_{12}O_6 + 6\ O_2$. The chemical equation for respiration is: $C_6H_{12}O_6 + 6\ O_2 \rightarrow 6\ CO_2 + 6\ H_2O$. If the "cause" stem of the hypothesis predicts that light will drive photosynthesis but not respiration, then the predictions for CO_2 levels in the light versus dark samples should reflect this. Per this stem, the light samples should promote photosynthesis and decrease CO_2 levels, while respiration should not be affected. Therefore, the light samples should exhibit lower CO_2 levels than the dark samples over 24 hours, based on the "cause" portion of the stem.

HOW CAN THE SCIENTIFIC QUESTION BE ADDRESSED EXPERIMENTALLY?

> **TIP** You may have to apply your science background in order to understand the basics about a particular technique, but there will always be enough content in the passage for you to understand what's happening.

After identifying the purpose of a research project and formulating a hypothesis to predict the outcome, the next section on which you should focus in Research Summaries questions is the experiment. The experiment describes the methods and techniques used in the laboratory to explore the question of interest. Sometimes the experiment will be based on techniques you've seen before, but at other times you'll come across techniques you've never heard of. Fortunately, experimental descriptions in Research Summaries provide enough detail about the experimental design itself, as well as the independent and dependent variables, that you can figure out what's going on. Since Research Summaries will never be pages long, the techniques will not be overly complicated—in many cases, they will be extremely simple and straightforward. But if you do ever come across a technique with which you are unfamiliar, the passage will provide you with the background you need; you won't ever be left completely in the dark about what a particular method does.

When it comes to ACT questions that ask about an experimental design, there are a few different ways you might be tested.

1) **Recognize and identify.** Some questions might simply ask you to recognize the basics: for example, identifying variables and controls, understanding how the technique works based on the information provided, and recognizing how the experiment answers the scientific question posed.

2) **Critique and improve.** You might be asked to critique the experiment and suggest possible improvements.

3) **Provide alternative methods.** You could also come across a few kinds of questions that ask you to think beyond the obvious. For instance, you could be asked to suggest an alternative experimental method. If, for example, a passage describes a study to investigate the rate of a chemical reaction and the scientist measures product formation, an alternative method might be to track reactant disappearance; both are valid ways to acquire data about reaction rate, but they are *different* ways to study the reaction rate.

4) **Consider future experiments.** Another less-than-obvious question type that may be asked about experimental design pertains to future experiments. Questions that ask about future experiments require you to think beyond what is in front of you. Most often, you will be asked to build off what has been provided in order to recommend a logical next step. For example, if an experiment discovers that plants grow better in the light than in the dark, a logical follow-up experiment might be to test optimal light intensity, or optimal duration of light exposure, or some other dependent variable that is related to what was tested in the original described experiment. Again, with this type of question, you won't be expected to know about any specialized techniques off the top of your head; these answers will usually be based on logic, or on some variation of the experiment described in the original passage.

Photosynthesis is a biological process that generates stored energy through the formation of glucose from carbon dioxide and water, according to the following chemical reaction:

$$6\,CO_2 + 6\,H_2O \rightarrow C_6H_{12}O_6 + 6\,O_2$$

Cellular respiration works in opposition, using oxygen to break down the sugar and release that energy to form ATP:

$$C_6H_{12}O_6 + 6\,O_2 \rightarrow 6\,CO_2 + 6\,H_2O$$

Carbon dioxide reacts with water to form carbonic acid. Phenolphthalein is an indicator that remains colorless in acid and turns pink in base. Three drops of phenolphthalein can be added to a small water sample, and the amount of NaOH needed to turn a clear sample pink, its neutralization point, gives an indication of the concentration of carbonic acid in the sample.

Many plants and algae are capable of both photosynthesis and respiration. Among these is an algal species called stonewort, of the genus *Chara*. Stonewort grows well in lime-rich waters, which results in the formation of calcium carbonate deposits on the algae.

A group of students wants to test the rates of photosynthesis and respiration in stonewort in different light conditions. The students acquire two 6.00 g stonewort samples and place each in a beaker containing 250 mL of spring water. One beaker was incubated in the dark at 25°C, while the other beaker was incubated in the light at 25°C. Over the course of one day, two 1 mL water samples were removed from each beaker every six hours. One of each pair of water samples was used to detect dissolved oxygen concentration using an oxygen electrode, which measures O_2 concentration in units of parts per million (ppm). The second water sample per pair was used to test carbon dioxide levels using phenolphthalein and 0.04 M NaOH. Both tests were performed immediately after sample extraction to avoid sample disruption. The following results were obtained:

Stonewort Sample	Measurement	Time (Hours)				
		0	6	12	18	24
Light	Dissolved O_2 (ppm)	2.35	2.81	4.61	5.02	5.30
	Volume 0.04 M NaOH (μL)	21.0	18.3	14.0	13.3	12.8
Dark	Dissolved O_2 (ppm)	2.36	2.37	2.01	1.84	1.79
	Volume 0.04 M NaOH (μL)	22.2	23.0	26.1	28.7	30.0

All of the following steps could significantly improve the reliability of the experiment EXCEPT:

A. using a magnetic stir bar to ensure constant gas composition throughout the beakers.

B. decreasing the concentration of NaOH used in the phenolphthalein test to more efficiently detect acidity.

C. increasing the number of samples taken from each beaker at each time point.

D. decreasing the number of time points over 24 hours to minimize disruption of the beakers.

The correct answer is D. This question asks you to suggest improvements to the experiment to increase the reliability of the results. You must decide which of the given suggestions would be *least likely* to improve the experiment. Choice A provides a method of ensuring that the dissolved gas composition is consistent throughout the beaker, which is something that was not addressed in the original experiment. This is certainly an improvement, so it is not the correct answer here. Choice B suggests decreasing the concentration of NaOH added during the phenolphthalein test. While this would involve adding a greater volume of NaOH to the test sample, this step improves the reliability of the experiment because it allows for smaller concentration increment increases in NaOH base, allowing the students to more closely estimate the solution acidity rather than overshooting it. This is also an improvement. Increasing the number of experimental trials (choice C) is *always* an improvement because increasing the number of trials means you are basing your average numbers on a greater sample size, which improves reliability.

That leaves choice D. While minimizing beaker disruption would be ideal, decreasing the number of time points decreases the number of data points you obtain, and it decreases your chances of seeing more subtle changes. In terms of the data acquired in this particular experiment, there were certain time periods (e.g., 6–12 hours) that experienced more dramatic changes in dissolved gases relative to others, and this would all be missed if the number of time points were decreased.

HOW CAN THE PROVIDED DATA BE ANALYZED?

Beyond analysis of the question, hypothesis, and experiment itself, the rest of the material covered by questions that accompany Research Summaries should look very familiar. That's because we've already discussed data analysis and drawing conclusions in Chapter 11. All of the principles of data analysis that applied to Data Interpretation questions also apply here.

To review, those key skills are as follows:

- Understand the provided data.
- Draw conclusions based on the data.
- Analyze or construct graphs.
- Assess the validity of the data.
- Consider future work based on the data.

> **TIP** Be sure to review Chapter 11 for more detailed information about each of these subcategories of data analysis.

We'll focus on drawing conclusions in the next section, but the rest of these data analysis skills are relevant here. Understanding the data means identifying the variables and controls, and then determining how the data express these variables and controls. Analyzing and constructing graphs becomes essential in data analysis because you have to be able to read data provided in graphical form, but you also might be asked to interpret trends in tabulated data and present that data in graphical form. Finally, considering future work based on data is a bit different than what we just discussed in the previous section, though only slightly. While the previous section focused on the experimental side of considering future work, here the future work is more idea- and data-based. In other words, this aspect of future work is geared more toward building new hypotheses based on data rather than just focusing on experimental variations. Still, the two go hand-in-hand and overlap in many respects.

For our purposes, the following examples fall under the category of considering characteristics of data and possible trends for the future, but in the context of the sample passage we've been working with throughout this chapter.

Which of the following graphs best represents the trend in dissolved oxygen as a function of time for the stonewort grown in the light?

F.

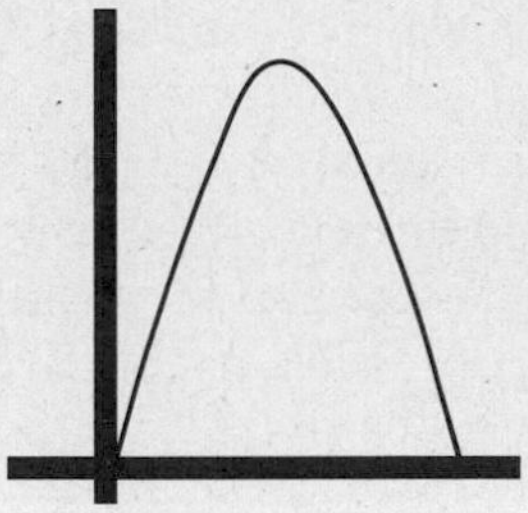

G.

H.

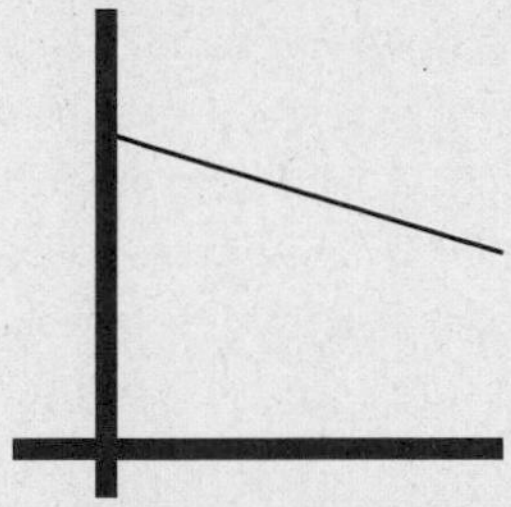

J.

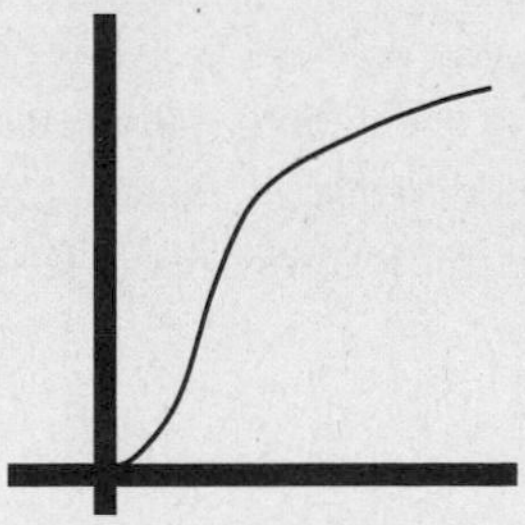

The correct answer is J. This question asks you to construct a chart based on the data provided in the table. Whenever you're asked to construct a graph based on a set of numerical data, the first thing you should do is identify the independent and dependent variables. Based on our data table, as well as the description of the experiment, the independent variable is *time*, and the dependent variable is *the concentration of dissolved oxygen*, as measured by an oxygen electrode.

The next step is to look for the general trend in the numbers—in other words, examine whether the data increase, decrease, or fluctuate throughout the experiment. In this case, we're looking at the dissolved oxygen data for stonewort grown in the light; this would be the first row of data in the data table. As time increases, the concentration of dissolved oxygen also increases. There is never a decrease in oxygen concentration, so we can immediately rule out choices F and H because both exhibit some kind of a decrease in dissolved oxygen concentration over the measured time period. In order to distinguish between choices G and J, we must now determine whether or not the increase in dissolved oxygen is linear. To test this out, check out the increase in dissolved oxygen concentration over a few equivalent time periods; if the increase is the same, the increase is linear.

For this example, let's look at the 0–6 hour and 6–12 hour time periods. From 0 to 6 hours, the dissolved oxygen concentration increases by 0.46 ppm, but from 6 to 12 hours, the dissolved oxygen concentration increases by 1.80 ppm. These are clearly not the same, and if we check out each time point, we can confirm that we are not looking at a linear trend. The answer, then, cannot be choice G. The correct answer, which displays a graph that fits our trend, is choice J.

In this experiment, the more reliable gas measurement is:

A. dissolved oxygen, because it is a direct measurement of gas concentration.

B. carbon dioxide, because it is a direct measurement of gas concentration.

C. dissolved oxygen, because the same trend in concentration is observed in the light and dark.

D. carbon dioxide, because the same trend in concentration is observed in the light and dark.

The correct answer is A. This question asks you to analyze the two types of gas measurements acquired in this experiment and determine which technique is more reliable. We can look at the data to immediately rule out choices C and D; opposite trends are clearly seen in the light and dark conditions, so this reasoning does not work. In the dark, the concentration of CO_2 increases, while in the light, the concentration of CO_2 decreases. In the dark, the concentration of O_2 decreases, while in the light, the concentration of O_2 increases.

The dilemma is now deciding between choices A and B by deciding which technique is more direct. With the CO_2 measurements, CO_2 reacts with water in the presence of phenolphthalein to form acid, which is then measured by adding NaOH. There are a few places where this experiment could give unreliable results; for instance, the experiment relies on a chemical reaction, and not all of the CO_2 may have been converted to acid at the time of detection. Furthermore, a color change is used as a marker of acidity, not even CO_2 concentration specifically. This method is indirect. An oxygen probe, like any probe, directly measures the gas of interest. Therefore, the best answer is choice A.

WHAT CONCLUSIONS CAN BE DRAWN BASED ON THE EXPERIMENT AND RESULTS?

Once you've progressed through the question, hypothesis, experiment, and data, the final feature of Research Summaries on which you'll be tested is your ability to draw conclusions based on the data. Drawing conclusions was a major part of analyzing Data Representation questions, on which we focused heavily in Chapter 11. To review, the goal of drawing conclusions is to answer the posed scientific question by finding trends and patterns in the data. Applying an observed pattern or trend in order to answer a scientific question is really the main point of doing scientific research; performing experiments and gathering data are most beneficial to the scientific community if conclusions can be drawn. The ACT Science test therefore assesses you in this area because drawing conclusions is such an important feature of Research Summaries. If you can look at data, identify trends, and apply these trends in a relevant way to a scientific question, then you have successfully shown your ability to think like a scientist.

Let's see how you might be tested on this skill.

Photosynthesis is a biological process that generates stored energy through the formation of glucose from carbon dioxide and water, according to the following chemical reaction:

$$6\,CO_2 + 6\,H_2O \rightarrow C_6H_{12}O_6 + 6\,O_2$$

Cellular respiration works in opposition, using oxygen to break down the sugar and release that energy to form ATP:

$$C_6H_{12}O_6 + 6\,O_2 \rightarrow 6\,CO_2 + 6\,H_2O$$

Carbon dioxide reacts with water to form carbonic acid. Phenolphthalein is an indicator that remains colorless in acid and turns pink in base. Three drops of phenolphthalein can be added to a small water sample, and the amount of NaOH needed to turn a clear sample pink, its neutralization point, gives an indication of the concentration of carbonic acid in the sample.

Many plants and algae are capable of both photosynthesis and respiration. Among these is an algal species called stonewort, of the genus *Chara*. Stonewort grows well in lime-rich waters, which results in the formation of calcium carbonate deposits on the algae.

A group of students wants to test the rates of photosynthesis and respiration in stonewort in different light conditions. The students acquire two 6.00 g stonewort samples and place each in a beaker containing 250 mL of spring water. One beaker was incubated in the dark at 25°C, while the other beaker was incubated in the light at 25°C. Over the course of one day, two 1 mL water samples were removed from each beaker every six hours. One of each pair of water samples was used to detect dissolved oxygen concentration using an oxygen electrode, which measures O_2 concentration in units of parts per million (ppm). The second water sample per pair was used to test carbon dioxide levels using phenolphthalein and 0.04 M NaOH. Both tests were performed immediately after sample extraction to avoid sample disruption. The following results were obtained:

Stonewort Sample	Measurement	Time (Hours)				
		0	6	12	18	24
Light	Dissolved O_2 (ppm)	2.35	2.81	4.61	5.02	5.30
	Volume 0.04 M NaOH (μL)	21.0	18.3	14.0	13.3	12.8
Dark	Dissolved O_2 (ppm)	2.36	2.37	2.01	1.84	1.79
	Volume 0.04 M NaOH (μL)	22.2	23.0	26.1	28.7	30.0

Based on the data, which of the following conclusions can be drawn about the effect of light and dark conditions on photosynthesis and respiration in stoneworts?

F. The rates of photosynthesis and respiration increase under light conditions relative to dark conditions.

G. The rates of photosynthesis and respiration decrease under light conditions relative to dark conditions.

H. The rate of photosynthesis exceeds the rate of respiration in the light, but the rate of respiration exceeds the rate of photosynthesis in the dark.

J. The rate of respiration exceeds the rate of photosynthesis in the light, but the rate of photosynthesis exceeds the rate of respiration in the dark.

The correct answer is H. This question simply asks you to examine the data and draw a conclusion to answer the scientific question based on the data. The answer choices for this question refer to both photosynthesis and respiration under light and dark conditions, so it is important that we examine the data to include all of these relevant variables.

Based on the data, we can immediately rule out choices F and G, because the trends observed for carbon dioxide and oxygen, respectively, are not the same under light and dark conditions. We must now distinguish between choices H and J. To begin, look at the dissolved oxygen data. Under light conditions, the concentration of oxygen increases over time, but under dark conditions, the concentration of oxygen decreases over time. Oxygen is a product of photosynthesis and a reactant in respiration, so these data indicate that photosynthesis occurs more rapidly than respiration under light conditions and more slowly than respiration under dark conditions. The carbon dioxide data leads us to the same conclusion. Under light conditions, the carbon dioxide concentration decreases, but under dark conditions, the carbon dioxide concentration increases. Carbon dioxide is a reactant in photosynthesis and a product of respiration, so the same conclusion can be drawn from the carbon dioxide data. Based on these trends, the correct answer is choice H. In order to see these net gas increases and decreases, photosynthesis must be stimulated under light conditions, while respiration prevails under dark conditions. If you have any background knowledge of photosynthesis, this conclusion may be obvious, as photosynthesis depends on light absorption.

COMMON MISTAKES TO AVOID

In Chapter 11, some of the common traps we covered for Data Representation questions were challenging terminology, unnecessary information, unexpected results, and unusual data representation. These same pitfalls apply to Research Summaries, so feel free to head back to Chapter 11 to review the relevant explanations and examples again. However, there are a few other common mistakes that test takers make that are more specific to Research Summaries; we'll discuss those here.

Passage Skimming

When you're taking the ACT exam, you will probably experience at least a small amount of stress and urgency. After all, you're being asked to answer quite a few questions in a relatively short period of time. As we've seen already, some of the questions you'll come across will be simple recall and reading comprehension from the passage, while others may require a bit more thinking. Regardless of exactly what kinds of questions you face, you will have plenty of time and should use that time efficiently. Unfortunately, students under stress will often turn to a skimming strategy—they go directly to the questions to see what information they will need, and then they skim through the passage in order to find the specific answers to the questions. While skimming might work sometimes for questions that require simple recall, It Is a flawed strategy and can cause problems if you use it throughout the ACT Science test.

> **TIP** Instead of skimming through a passage after looking at the questions, you should start with the passage itself.

By definition, skimming through a passage involves rapid reading; you look for key words without completely comprehending the meaning of the entire passage. Sure, you might be able to skim the passage to understand what paper chromatography does or to find the equation to calculate a coefficient of friction, but you will miss a lot of important details, too. You could even miss the basic premise of the passage, and this could be devastating for Research Summaries because if you don't understand the scientific question, you will not be clear on the kind of data you need to collect and the kinds of conclusions you should be drawing.

Read through and jot down some notes in the margins of your test. The test booklets are there for you to work out your thoughts, so you might as well use them! As you read, identify the scientific question, and write down some notes about important details you'll want to remember or underline key words you may want to return to later. As you approach the experimental design, jot down the dependent and independent variables, as well as any controls you feel are worth noting. Then, you'll be all set to take on the questions because you've established the basic premise of the passage. This is particularly important because the incorrect answers that follow the questions are often tied very closely to the premise. That means if you simply skim the passage to find the correct answer without actually understanding the passage, you might mistakenly choose a wrong answer simply because it seems closely tied to the topic, when in fact there might be a better answer among the choices.

This question highlights the importance of carefully reading the passage.

Pectinase is an enzyme that breaks down pectin, a polysaccharide found in plant cell walls. Pectin compounds hold together dispersed particles in suspension in fruit juices. As such, pectins increase the viscosity of juice.

A group of students wanted to compare the activities of pectinases from three different plant species (*A*, *B*, and *C*). The students placed 30 mL of applesauce into each of four beakers, labeled 1–4. In beaker 1, 1 mL of distilled water was added. In each of beakers 2–4, 1 mL of pectinase from one of the species *A*, *B*, and *C* was added. The contents of each beaker were thoroughly stirred using separate glass stirring rods, and then the four beakers were allowed to sit at room temperature for 15 minutes. After the 15 minutes, cheesecloth was placed into four separate funnels, each of which was placed onto a 50 mL graduated cylinder. Using the glass stirring rod to move the mixtures along, the contents of each beaker were poured into each of the graduated cylinders, and the filtrate was collected for each. The amount of juice was measured, and the results are shown in the table below:

Beaker (Pectinase Species)	Volume of Filtrate Collected (mL)
1 (Distilled Water)	10.1
2 (Species *A*)	27.5
3 (Species *B*)	22.3
4 (Species *C*)	26.0

The control in this experiment is:

A. the volume of filtrate collected for each sample.
B. the sample to which no pectinase was added.
C. the use of a glass stirring rod for each sample.
D. the applesauce sample containing pectinase.

The correct answer is B. The passage describes an experiment for pectinase activity measurement using applesauce, and at its surface, the question is quite straightforward: identify the control in this experiment. The control is the unaffected sample to which all affected samples are compared. In order to figure out what the control is, we must first determine the variables. The independent variable is the *species from which the different pectinases have been extracted*. The dependent variable is *the volume of juice, or filtrate, acquired after applesauce incubation with pectinase*. Choice A, therefore, describes the dependent variable, not the control, and can be ruled out as a correct answer. The use of a glass stirring rod for each sample (choice C), is a constant, not a control, because it is an experimental feature common to all samples. Thus, choice C can also be eliminated.

In deciding between choices B and D, we are looking for the unaffected sample, which would be the sample to which no pectinase is added. That means that the correct answer is choice B. If you had just skimmed the passage, you might not have been drawn to choice B right away because all four answer choices are directly relevant to the experiment in some way, and two of the distractors (choices A and C) are important variables or constants that are very much relevant to the experiment. If you'd been jotting notes about such variables during your initial reading, you would be able to eliminate these choices right away. So when it comes to Research Summaries, take the time to read carefully and take some notes, because skimming for answers is far from a foolproof strategy.

Information Inference and Assumption

When you read through Research Summaries, it is important to avoid inferring information that is not actually given in the passage. This goes hand in hand with the Unexpected Results trap we discussed in Chapter 11. With unexpected results, the take-home advice was to use the data you're given and base your conclusions on those data, rather than assume you know what *should* happen in an experiment and base conclusions on that. This advice is even more relevant to experimental procedures, which is why it is important to discuss here.

Research Summaries provide fairly in-depth descriptions of experimental procedures and the data obtained from those procedures. Research Summary questions may ask you to suggest an improvement to the experiment or to come up with a way to ensure condition uniformity among your experimental groups. When you're asked questions like these, don't assume the scientists who performed the experiments already made the adjustments. Earlier in the chapter (on page 522), we asked you to choose the one method among the provided choices that would *not* improve the reliability of an experiment. If you look at the three distractors, which in this example are solid ways to improve the reliability of the experiment, you might think that these are obvious steps one would take in this experiment. However, these steps are not explicitly stated in the passage, so you can't assume they were performed, as obvious as they may seem.

The same tip can be applied to the passage as a whole. For instance, if a scientific question is posed and an experiment is performed to test that question, you can't always assume that the results answer the question. Sometimes, the data obtained may not tell you anything new. Other times, you might see unexpected data that answer a different scientific question. The important things to remember are that no science experiment is perfect, and errors or experimental design flaws are always possible. But don't worry about picking up on these on your own—if an experiment contains a major design flaw that you're supposed to notice, there will always be a question that addresses it so you know what to look out for, as in the following example.

Pectinase is an enzyme that breaks down pectin, a polysaccharide found in plant cell walls. Pectin compounds hold together dispersed particles in suspension in fruit juices. As such, pectins increase the viscosity of juice.

A group of students wanted to compare the activities of pectinases from three different plant species (*A*, *B*, and *C*). The students placed 30 mL of applesauce into each of four beakers, labeled 1-4. In beaker 1, 1 mL of distilled water was added. In each of beakers 2-4, 1 mL of pectinase from one of the species *A*, *B*, and *C* was added. The contents of each beaker were thoroughly stirred using separate glass stirring rods, and then the four beakers were allowed to sit at room temperature for fifteen minutes. After the fifteen minutes, cheesecloth was placed into four separate funnels, each of which was placed onto a 50 mL graduated cylinder. Using the glass stirring rod to move the mixtures along, the contents of each beaker were poured into each of the graduated cylinders, and the filtrate was collected for each. The amount of juice was measured, and the results are shown in the table below:

Beaker (Pectinase Species)	Volume of Filtrate Collected (mL)
1 (Distilled Water)	10.1
2 (Species *A*)	27.5
3 (Species *B*)	22.3
4 (Species *C*)	26.0

Which of the following additional constants should be maintained among the samples to allow the different pectinase results to be compared?

F. The organism from which the pectinases are extracted

G. The volume of filtrate collected for each sample

H. The concentration of pectinase in the 1 mL added per sample

J. The use of the same glass stirring rod for all four samples

The correct answer is H. The passage describes a fairly straightforward way to test for pectinase activity by looking at how much juice is collected from applesauce upon the addition of pectinase. This question asks you to choose a variable that should be kept constant for all samples in order to allow for comparison of the activities of the different pectinases. Choice F is incorrect; the passage indicates that the three tested pectinases are from different species, so this answer doesn't make sense. Even if the passage did not specify that the pectinases are from different organisms, the answer makes no logical sense because you can certainly compare the same protein from different organisms—scientists all over the world devote their research to this very cause! Choice G is not correct because it essentially describes the dependent variable of this experiment. If you adjusted your experiment so that all samples collected the same volume of filtrate, then you really wouldn't be accomplishing much, since the filtrate volume is what you're measuring. Choice J is also incorrect. The glass stirring rod is used only for indirect functions, like stirring the solutions or transferring the solutions to the funnels. Using the same glass stirring rod would only increase the likelihood of cross-contamination between samples and would not really improve sample comparability. That leaves choice H, which indicates that the concentration of pectinase added should be the same for all samples. This makes sense; concentration represents the amount of a substance per unit volume, so if you're adding 1 mL of different pectinases at the same concentration to each sample, you ensure you're adding the same amount of enzyme per sample. You can't assume this was done, as it is not stated in the passage, so this is the correct answer.

New Techniques

Because different test takers will have different amounts of exposure to various scientific techniques, this challenge will be more applicable to students who are perhaps less experienced than others. But don't worry if you're not familiar with a particular technique described in the passage—if a more complicated technique is described, you will be provided with enough information in the passage to figure out how it works. In the event that a new technique is presented and you still don't quite understand how it works, you can use clues throughout the passage to figure it out. For example, if a passage describes the separation of components in a mixture using paper chromatography, and you have no idea what paper chromatography is, you can look at the experimental description for hints about how it works and at the data to identify the independent and dependent variables. The independent and dependent variables are almost always included somewhere in any table or graph that contains data, so even if you're not 100 percent sure about how a new technique works, you can still figure out the most important features of the experiment from the given protocol, and you can determine the variables from the experimental description and provided data. Remember, you'll never be expected to know how specific scientific techniques work off the top of your head; you will always be given enough background information to figure out what you need to know about the technique (or set of techniques) discussed in the passage. Let's go back to our sample passage to illustrate.

Pectinase is an enzyme that breaks down pectin, a polysaccharide found in plant cell walls. Pectin compounds hold together dispersed particles in suspension in fruit juices. As such, pectins increase the viscosity of juice.

A group of students wanted to compare the activities of pectinases from three different plant species (*A*, *B*, and *C*). The students placed 30 mL of applesauce into each of four beakers, labeled 1-4. In beaker 1, 1 mL of distilled water was added. In each of beakers 2-4, 1 mL of pectinase from one of the species *A*, *B*, and *C* was added. The contents of each beaker were thoroughly stirred using separate glass stirring rods, and then the four beakers were allowed to sit at room temperature for fifteen minutes. After the fifteen minutes, cheesecloth was placed into four separate funnels, each of which was placed onto a 50 mL graduated cylinder. Using the glass stirring rod to move the mixtures along, the contents of each beaker were poured into each of the graduated cylinders, and the filtrate was collected for each. The amount of juice was measured, and the results are shown in the table below:

Beaker (Pectinase Species)	Volume of Filtrate Collected (mL)
1 (Distilled Water)	10.1
2 (Species *A*)	27.5
3 (Species *B*)	22.3
4 (Species *C*)	26.0

Based on the collected data, which pectinase sample exhibited the highest activity when added to applesauce?

- **A.** Pectinase from Species *A*
- **B.** Pectinase from Species *B*
- **C.** Pectinase from Species *C*
- **D.** All three pectinases exhibited the same level of activity

The correct answer is A. For this question, you are asked to draw a conclusion based on the provided data. But in order to do this, you must understand what is actually happening in the experiment. The passage indicates that pectinase breaks down pectin compounds and that pectin compounds hold particles together in fruit juices, making them more viscous. This means that if you add pectinase to a fruit juice sample, or in this example, applesauce, pectinase will break down the particle clumps in the sample and produce more liquid from the applesauce. This particular experiment uses filtration to separate the liquid from the rest of the applesauce, measuring the volume of filtrate.

If you know what filtration, or filtering, is, you're all set. The more active pectinase will be the sample that produces more juice, or filtrate. If filtration is new to you, you can figure out what it is based on the protocol and data. The protocol describes the use of a funnel and cheesecloth, a porous material that allows liquid through while keeping solid material in the funnel. Another hint about how the technique works is the set of phrases "filtrate was collected" and "amount of juice was measured." These phrases indicate that the juice, a liquid, is what is being collected, and that the juice is therefore the filtrate. The data tell you that the dependent variable is the volume of filtrate, confirming that this technique separates liquid juice from the rest of the applesauce and measures its volume. So even if you don't know what filtration is, or what a filtrate is, you can figure it out from the passage and data. To answer the question, we want to know which pectinase sample was most active, so we want to identify the sample for which the greatest volume of liquid juice, or filtrate, was collected. Based on the data table, the highest volume of juice was collected from the Species *A* pectinase, especially compared to the water control, so the correct answer is choice A.

Turn to page 530 to follow the College Readiness Benchmark Leaning Path questions covering Research Summaries.

SUMMING IT UP

- **Research Summaries pose a scientific question and describe an experiment or set of experiments to answer that question.** They will also include the experimental results obtained, in the form of a table, graph, or chart.
- **Identify the scientific question** or **purpose of the experiment first** whenever you encounter a scientific experiment in an ACT Science passage. Ask yourself why the experiment is being conducted and what it's testing. Research Summaries provide you with all the background information you will need to identify the purpose of the given experiment.
- **Some ACT exam questions might ask you to choose the most suitable hypothesis for an experiment.** Your hypothesis must always correctly address the appropriate independent and dependent variables. Hypotheses are *predictions*, and a hypothesis will not always correctly predict the outcome of an experiment. Results of experiments often disprove hypotheses, which is okay!
- **Some ACT exam questions will ask you to identify variables and controls and recognize why the experiment was designed a certain way and how it answers the scientific question posed.** Research Summaries always provide enough detail so that you can figure out what's going on. The techniques will not be overly complicated—the passage will provide you with the background you need.
- **Drawing conclusions about data presented to you means finding trends and patterns in the data.** When reading over an experiment and its accompanying data, take note of any obvious trends—you are sure to be asked about them and how they relate to the experiment's hypothesis.
- **Don't skim ACT Science passages to simply look for key words you see in the questions—you will miss a lot of important details.** If you don't understand the scientific question, you will not be clear on the data you need to collect and the conclusions you should draw.

- **Avoid making any inferences or assumptions about experiments or data—you should consider *only* what is in front of you in the given passage as true.** If an experiment contains an error or flaw, it's supposed to be there! You will likely see a question asking about it.
- **Don't be daunted by new and unfamiliar scientific techniques you might see in passages.** You are not expected to know about every branch of science off the top of your head! You will always be given enough background information to figure out what you need to know.

ONLINE PREP

Want to Know More?

Access more practice questions, lessons, helpful hints, and strategies for the following science topics in *Peterson's Online Course for the ACT® Exam*:

- Data Interpretation of Experiments
- Research Summaries and Conflicting Viewpoints

To purchase and access the course, go to **www.petersons.com/testprep/act**.

COLLEGE READINESS BENCHMARK LEARNING PATH PRACTICE

Directions: The passages in this practice question set are followed by several questions. Read each passage carefully and choose the best answer to each related question. As you go through the practice set, review each solution and follow the expanded explanations provided to help strengthen your skills in working with Research Summaries items.

PASSAGE I

A group of students was investigating aspects that control the period of a pendulum's swing, or the amount of time it takes a pendulum to complete a full cycle of swinging out and back. The pendulum consisted of a thin rod of adjustable length hanging on a well-greased pivot. On the end of the rod, the students attached a variety of weights with different masses. Using a protractor and a vertical line on the wall, they measured the angle the pendulum made with the vertical before it was released. The students used a stopwatch to measure the amount of time it took the pendulum to complete 10 full swings.

Pendulum Diagram

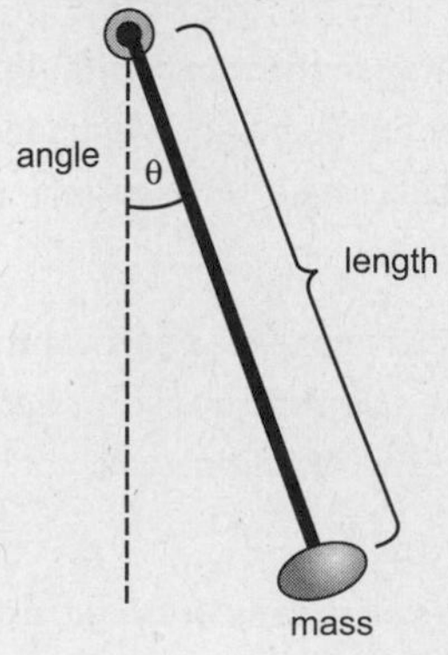

Experiment 1

For the first set of experiments, the students used a pendulum that was 1 meter long and attached one of four different weights on the end. They pulled the pendulum back exactly 15 degrees and released it. The experiment was repeated three times for each pendulum setup. The data is shown in Table 1.

Table 1

	Time for 10 cycles (s)			
Mass (kg)	**Trial 1**	**Trial 2**	**Trial 3**	**Average**
0.25	20.1	20.2	20.5	20.3
0.5	20.3	19.8	20.1	20.1
1	19.9	20.3	20.4	20.2
1.5	20.0	20.3	19.8	20.0

Experiment 2

In the next set of experiments, the students used five different pendulum lengths. They attached a 1-kilogram mass to the end of each pendulum, pulled the pendulum back to the 15-degree mark, and released it. Again, the experiment was repeated three times for each pendulum setup. This data is shown in Table 2.

Table 2

	Time for 10 cycles (s)			
Length (m)	**Trial 1**	**Trial 2**	**Trial 3**	**Average**
0.25	10.1	9.9	10.0	10.0
0.5	14.0	13.7	14.2	14.0
1	20.3	19.8	20.1	20.1
1.5	24.9	24.6	24.5	24.7
2	27.7	28.1	28.5	28.3

Experiment 3

The students chose a pendulum 1 meter long and attached a 1-kilogram mass to the end. Then they pulled it back to at a variety of angles, and once again released it. The experiment was repeated three times for each pendulum setup. This data is shown in Table 3.

Table 3

	Time for 10 cycles (s)			
Angle (°)	**Trial 1**	**Trial 2**	**Trial 3**	**Average**
5	19.7	19.9	20.2	19.9
10	20.3	20.0	20.4	20.2
15	20.5	20.1	20.1	20.2
20	20.7	20.3	19.8	20.2

1. In Experiment 1, what is the independent variable?

A. The length of the pendulum rod

B. The mass on the end of the pendulum

C. The amount of time it takes to complete a full cycle

D. The angle at which the pendulum was pulled to the side

The correct answer is B. For this question (and in general), it's very important to know the definition of an independent variable. The independent variable is the one that experimenters deliberately manipulate, and which is *independent* of the other variables in the experiment. In contrast, the dependent variable is typically the one experimenters measure, which is *dependent* on other aspects of the experiment.

The next thing to check is which experiment the question refers to—the different experiments are testing different things, and so have different variables. For Experiment 1, pendulum length (choice A) and angle (choice D) are constants. The period (choice C) is the dependent variable. The mass on the pendulum (choice B) is the aspect the experimenters are deliberately adjusting and manipulating, so it is the independent variable.

2. What was the average amount of time the students measured for 10 cycles using a pendulum length of 1 meter, a mass of 1.5 kg, and an angle of 15 degrees?

F. 20.0 s

G. 20.1 s

H. 20.2 s

J. 20.3 s

The correct answer is F. This type of question is very straightforward as it is asking you to find an entry in a table. What makes this particular question a little tricky is that you have to figure out which table is relevant, using information in the text. The question states exactly what the experimental conditions are (length of 1 meter, mass of 1.5 kg, and angle of 15 degrees).

Start with checking the length. Experiments 1 and 3 use a constant pendulum length of 1 m, and Experiment 2 uses a variety of pendulum lengths including 1 m. Any of the three tables could be relevant. Next, check the mass. Experiment 1 uses a variety of masses, while Experiments 2 and 3 use a constant mass of 1 kg. The only table with data for 1.5 kg is Table 1. (Note: Checking the angle doesn't help to narrow down the information—Experiments 1 and 2 use a constant angle of 15 degrees, while Experiment 3 uses a variety including 15 degrees).

Now all you need to do is find the mass of 1.5 kg, which is the bottom row, and find the average, which is the right-most column—20.0 s (choice F). The other choices are all distractors that are found in several places in the various tables (for example, all of them are in the averages column of Table 1).

3. In order to double a pendulum's period, the pendulum's length should be

A. halved.

B. doubled.

C. tripled.

D. quadrupled.

The correct answer is D. This question is asking about trends in the data and mathematical relationships. What is the relationship between a pendulum's length and its period? The information that matters is found in Table 2 (where length is varied). Remember that 10 cycles were measured instead of 1, but since that was always the case, it shouldn't affect the answer. If you can't quickly tell the relationship from looking at the data, you can check each of the possible answers.

Choice A can be eliminated quickly, because by looking at the data you can see that longer periods are found as the lengths increase, not as they decrease. The question asks for a doubling of the pendulum's period, so look to see if there are examples where one of the measured periods is twice that of another one. There are two clear examples in Table 2—rows 1 and 3 (10 cycles = approx. 10 s and 20 s) and rows 2 and 5 (10 cycles = approximately 14 s or 28 s). What is the relationship between the corresponding lengths? The difference between 0.25 m (~10 s for 10 cycles) and 1 m (~20 s for 10 cycles) is a factor of 4, or quadruple the length (choice D). The same relationship is found between 0.5 m (~14 s) and 2 m (~28 s).

You may be aware that for a pendulum, $T = 2\pi\sqrt{\frac{L}{g}}$, where T is the period, L is the length of the pendulum, and g is the acceleration from gravity, or about 9.8 m/s^2. Using that equation, in order to double T, you have to quadruple the L under the square root sign. While knowing the equation may be helpful to answer the question, it is not at all *necessary* to correctly answer the question.

4. Which conclusion is supported by the data?

F. A pendulum's period is dependent on the pendulum's length, and not on its mass nor the angle at which it is pulled back.

G. A pendulum's period is dependent on the pendulum's mass, but not on its length nor the angle at which it is pulled back.

H. A pendulum's period is affected by both its mass and its length, but in equal and opposite directions.

J. A pendulum's period is not affected by the angle at which it is pulled back, until that angle becomes very large.

The correct answer is F. This type of question asks you to bring together information from all three data tables, as well as the text describing the experiments. If you look at the three tables, you see that all the entries in Tables 1 and 3 are approximately 20, and if you look at the averages column, there is no clear trend with increasing mass or angle. However, there is a clear dependence in Table 2, which is the pendulum length. Therefore, choice F is correct. Choices G and H are incorrect because the pendulum's period is not dependent on its mass. Choice J is a true statement, but large angles were not tested in these experiments, so it is not supported by the data.

5. Why did the students measure the time it takes for the pendulum to complete 10 cycles, instead of a single cycle?

A. It strengthens the relationship between variables.

B. It acts as a constant in the experiment

C. It increases the variability in the measurement

D. It reduces the amount of error in the measurement.

The correct answer is D. This question asks for reasoning behind an experimental choice and requires some logic. There is always some amount of human error in reaction time for starting/stopping of a stopwatch, and counting 10 cycles per measurement essentially reduces the amount of human error per period. You can also think of it as averaging ten cycles per measurement, which also helps reduce error, so choice D is correct. Choice A may be tempting because determining the relationship between variables is very often the goal of an experiment. However, measuring ten cycles simply multiples the measured value—it doesn't change the relationship. Choice B is true in that ten cycles are always measured, but it would also be consistent if only one cycle were measured. Choice C is incorrect because measuring (and essentially averaging) 10 cycles decreases variability—and in any case, increasing variability is not an obvious benefit for an experiment.

PASSAGE II

Tephra is airborne pyroclastic material produced by volcanic eruptions, including ash particles. Volcanic ash from a single eruption can be deposited over a very large area, up to a 1,500-kilometer radius or more. Over time, the tephra layer produced from a volcanic eruption is buried under more sediment and dirt. When geologists examine the layers of sediment (called **strata**), tephra can act as markers for the time period when the volcano erupted. However, the layers of tephra are not always obvious to the naked eye and require either time-intensive measurements under the microscope by an expert, or chemical analysis that destroys the sample. A group of scientists wanted to test a new, faster method for detecting tephra in strata that does not result in the destruction of the sediment sample. Their technique uses a reflectance spectrometer to analyze different wavelengths of light bouncing off each area of the sediment sample. A special motorized spectrometer was used, which would hang over the sediment sample and take sequential reflectance measurements down the length of the core, with a spatial resolution of 75 micrometers.

Study

A variety of known tephra samples were analyzed using the reflectance spectrometer. The scientists used the data to determine a characteristic pattern for how the tephra reflected different wavelengths of light, which is referred to as the "tephra fingerprint."

Next, a lake sediment core was taken from an ice-free area in Antarctica. The core was sealed in the field with plastic caps and stored at a constant temperature of 4°C while transported to the laboratory. The core was cut in half lengthwise using a thin steel wire to make a flat surface over which the reflectance spectrometer could sit. A representation of the visual colors of the sediment core is shown in column A of Figure 1.

The spectral reflectance was recorded at each point along the length of the core. Using a computer program, each reflectance measurement was compared to the tephra fingerprint and ranked on a scale of 0 to 100 in terms of how much it matched the fingerprint. The reflectance similarity data are shown in column B of Figure 1.

Finally, an expert conducted a detailed analysis of the sediment core under a microscope and identified three bands of tephra based on the presence of characteristic glass shards in the sediment. The location and sizes of the verified tephra bands is shown in column C of Figure 1.

Figure 1

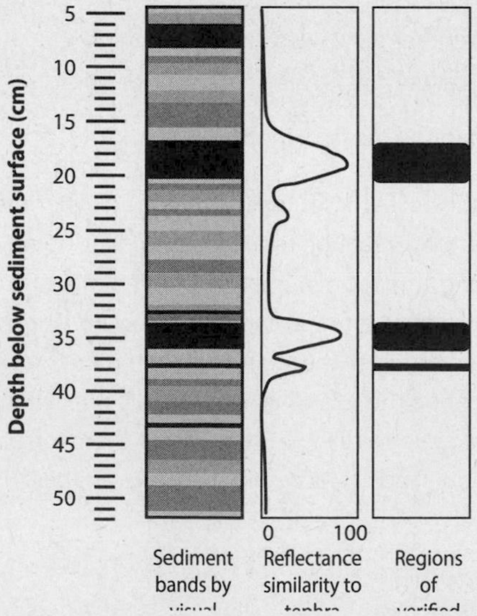

Experiment and figure adapted from: https://journals.plos.org/plosone/article?id=10.1371/journal.pone.0146578

6. Using their new technique, researchers try to determine the location of tephra based on the sediment's

  F. depth.

  G. reflectance.

  H. age.

  J. thickness.

The correct answer is G. This is essentially a reading comprehension question. The passage states that the scientists are using a reflectance spectrometer to measure reflected light. A spectrometer is an instrument that detects electromagnetic radiation (light), but you don't have to remember that in order to answer the question. Choices F, H, and J are distractors that are often associated with layers of sediment.

7. In the sediment core in Figure 1, what is the approximate thickness of the thickest tephra layer?

  A. 1 cm.

  B. 4 cm.

  C. 20 cm.

  D. 37 cm.

The correct answer is B. This question is asking you to interpret data in a figure. Figure 1 isn't a typical scatter plot or bar graph. It has three columns, each of which represents a different type of data. It's important to understand the type of data presented in each column in order to answer the question. Column A represents "sediment bands by visual color", where the vertical axis is the depth from the surface of the sediment. There is no additional information on the horizontal axis. Column B represents the reflectance similarity to a training sample of tephra. Again, the vertical axis is depth from the surface of the sediment, but now the horizontal axis shows how much the reflectance spectrum from each region of the sediment core matches the reflectance spectrum of actual tephra in a training sample. Column C represents the regions of the sediment core that are verified to contain tephra. It has the same vertical axis as the other two columns, and for column C there is no additional information on the horizontal axis.

This question asks you to find the thickest layer of tephra and estimate how thick it is. For that, you want to look at the verified tephra (column C), since the visual color is not relevant, and the accuracy of column B (the test method) is unknown. The thickest band is the one closest to the top, which spans the depth range of about 17 cm to 21 cm.; 21 – 17 = 4, so the thickness is about 4 cm. The other answers are distractors. Choice A is the thickness of the thinnest tephra band. Choice C is the approximate depth of the thickest band. Choice D is the approximate depth of the deepest band.

8. Deeper layers correspond to older sediment layers. What is the depth of the oldest tephra layer in the sediment core in Figure 1?

  F. 7 cm.

  G. 18 cm.

  H. 37 cm.

  J. 52 cm.

The correct answer is H. This question also asks you to interpret data in a figure, using an additional piece of information. Again, you want to look at column C to find the verified locations of tephra. Deeper layers correspond to higher numbers on the vertical axis (shown in cm. below the sediment surface). The deepest band, which also happens to be the thinnest one, is found at about 37 cm. depth (choice H). The other choices are distractors. Choice F (7 cm.) corresponds to the highest black bar in column A, but there is no corresponding tephra layer in column C. Choice G (18 cm.) corresponds to the highest, and thickest, layer of verified tephra (not the deepest). Choice J is the lowest marking on the figure, but there is no corresponding tephra layer at that depth, so it is not relevant.

9. Which of the following is a hypothesis that is being tested in these experiments?

A. Tephra reflects light in a characteristic way that can used to locate tephra layers in a sediment core.

B. Tephra contains glass shards that can be used to locate tephra layers in a sediment core.

C. Tephra layers at the bottom of a sediment core are older than layers at the top of the sediment core.

D. Thicker layers of tephra are easier to detect than thinner layers of tephra.

The correct answer is A. For this question, you need to know how to determine a hypothesis, which is a very important scientific concept. A hypothesis is a testable prediction or explanation for a phenomenon. You can think about it as the question they are trying to answer (or a statement about their best guess for the answer.) The researchers predict that tephra layers can be detected based on reflected light (choice A), and they are conducting the experiment to determine if this is the case. The other statements are distractors that are related to the experiment but are not actually being tested. Choice B is true based on the information in the text, but this is not something that is tested in this experiment, it is a method that is used to test/validate their predictions. Choice C is also typically true of strata, but it is not something tested or measured in the experiment. D is a logical statement but is not being tested.

10. Detection methods sometime result in false positives, in which the method predicts the occurrence of something that is not actually there. In sediment core in Figure 1, a false positive occurs at approximately which depth?

F. 7 cm.

G. 18 cm.

H. 23 cm.

J. 37 cm.

The correct answer is choice H. This question provides some new information (in this case, the definition of the term *false positive*) and asks you to analyze the existing data with this new information. In the sediment core, the first column (A) gives a picture of the sediment bands by eye. The second column (B) gives the similarity index, where horizontal peaks (or bumps that stick out to the right) indicate the reflectance is similar to tephra reflectance in a test case. The third column (C) gives the position of actual tephra layers based on detection of glass shards under a microscope—this verifies the presence of tephra. A false positive would occur if the new method (column B) predicts a band, but there are no corresponding glass shards (column C). That happens at 23 cm depth (choice H), where there is a small but obvious bump in column B but nothing in column C. Choice F (7 cm.) aligns with a dark band in column A, but it is not a false positive because there is no corresponding bump in column B. Choices G and J are true positives (not a false positive) because the bump in column B corresponds with detected tephra in column C.

PRACTICE

Now that you are more familiar with Research Summary questions, it's time to try a practice set on your own. When you're finished answering all 21 questions, check the answers and explanations that follow to figure out how well you did and why you may have selected any incorrect answer choices.

PASSAGE I

Gravitational acceleration is 9.8 m/s^2, and this is the force that pulls an object down an inclined plane. A student is interested in how roller coasters work and wants to test the effect of an angle of an inclined plane on the acceleration of a moving object. To investigate, the student sets up four tracks of the same 1-meter length, *d*, made of the same type of smooth wood. Each track varies in angle, θ, as measured using a protractor and ranging from 5° to 50°.

A marble was released at the top of each inclined plane, and the time, *t*, was recorded that it took for the marble to reach the end of the plane. Two trials were performed for each inclined plane, and the times were averaged. The data was analyzed by calculating the acceleration of the marble at each angle, using the equation $d = \frac{1}{2}at^2$.

Finally, the sine of each angle was calculated, and each acceleration was plotted as a function of sin θ to acquire a linear best-fit line.

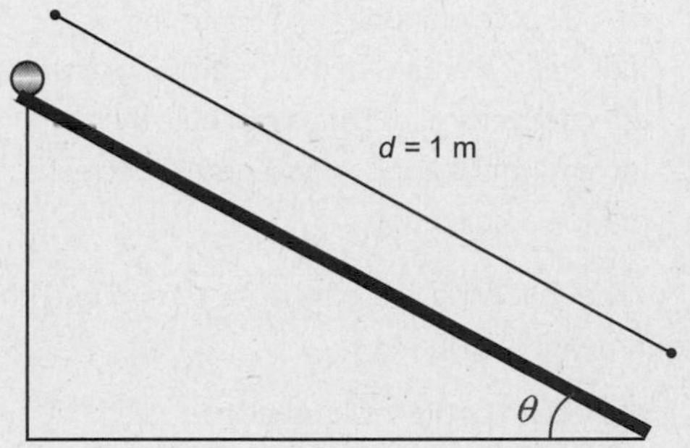

Table 1

Angle of Incline, θ (°)	Average Travel Time (s)	Acceleration (m/s^2)	Sin θ
5	1.56	0.82	0.0872
20	0.748	3.57	0.342
35	0.599	5.57	0.574
50	0.514	7.57	0.766

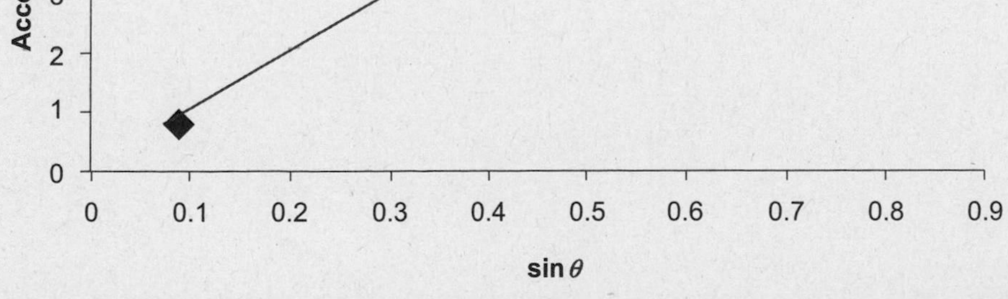

1. Which of the following hypotheses predicts the outcome of this experiment?

   A. If increased angles of incline allow for a greater effect of vertical gravitational pull, then increasing the angle of incline will increase marble acceleration.
   B. If increased angles of incline allow for a greater effect of vertical gravitational pull, then increasing the angle of incline will decrease marble acceleration.
   C. If decreased angles of incline allow for a greater effect of vertical gravitational pull, then increasing the angle of incline will increase marble acceleration.
   D. If decreased angles of incline allow for a greater effect of vertical gravitational pull, then increasing the angle of incline will decrease marble acceleration.

2. All of the following are constants throughout this experiment EXCEPT:

   F. the length of the inclined plane.
   G. the friction of the inclined plane.
   H. the height of the marble from the ground at its starting point.
   J. the height of the marble from the ground at its ending point.

3. The complete equation relating acceleration and time is $d = v_i t + \frac{1}{2}at^2$, where v_i is the initial velocity of the moving object. The student was able to simplify this equation to $d = \frac{1}{2}at^2$ because:

   A. the starting time was 0 seconds for each trial.
   B. the marble's initial velocity was 0 m/s for each trial since it started at rest.
   C. the marble was stopped to a velocity of 0 m/s after reaching the bottom of each inclined plane.
   D. the distance *d* did not vary between each of the trials.

4. The graph of acceleration as a function of sin θ shows that:

   F. there is an exponential relationship between acceleration and sin θ, with the *y*-intercept approximately equal to gravitational acceleration.
   G. there is a linear relationship between acceleration and sin θ, with the *y*-intercept approximately equal to gravitational acceleration.
   H. there is a linear relationship between acceleration and sin θ, with the slope approximately equal to gravitational acceleration.
   J. there is no significant correlation between acceleration and sin θ.

5. If the experiment were repeated using an inclined plane that has a length of 2.0 m, which is twice the length of the plane used in the original experiment, how would the provided graph change?

   A. The slope of the new line would be double that of the original line.
   B. The slope of the new line would be half that of the original line.
   C. The slope of the new line would be the same as that of the original line.
   D. The *y*-intercept of the new line would be double that of the original line.

6. One way to improve this experiment would be to:

   F. use angles of incline up to 90°.
   G. increase the number of trials at each angle of incline.
   H. get the marble rolling in advance and start the time when it is halfway down the inclined plane.
   J. measure the times in minutes rather than seconds.

PASSAGE II

The radioactive decay of uranium produces the noble gas radon. Radon-222 is the most significant isotope of radon, occurring at a much higher concentration than any other radon isotopes, which are barely detectable in the environment. Radon-222 has a relatively long half-life of 3.8 days and appears at measurable levels in the environment. As radon decays, it dissolves into soil pores and fluid, migrating into groundwater, soil gas, and the atmosphere. Many scientists have hypothesized that radon levels might serve as precursors to earthquakes.

A telemetric radon station collected measurements of radon levels, temperature, and air pressure prior to a pair of shallow earthquakes that occurred in Prokopion, Greece, on November 17, 2014. The data are shown in the graphs below, with dates on the *x*-axis formatted as day/month.

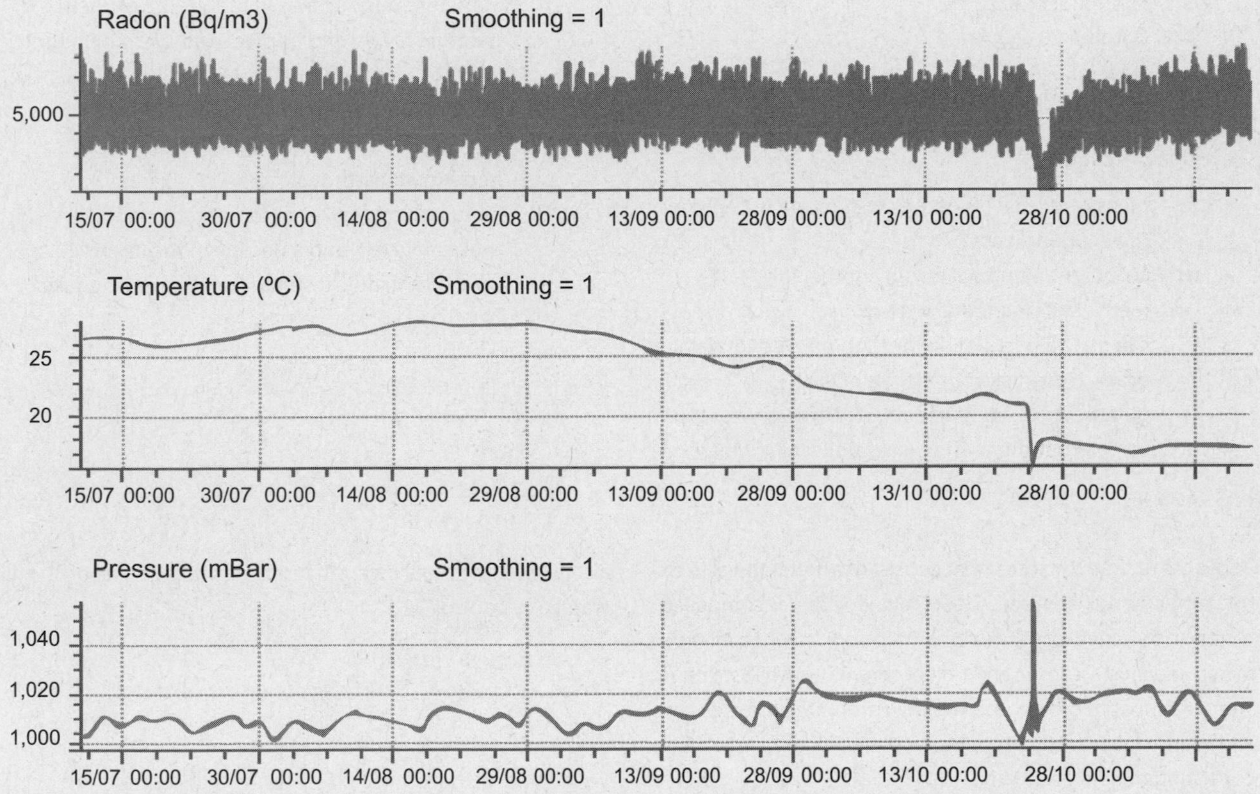

Source: [http://www.omicsonline.org/open-access/longmemory-trends-in-disturbances-of-radon-in-soil-prior-to-the-twin-ml-earthquakes-of-november-greece-2157-7617.1000244.pdf (open access)]

7. Which of the following identifies the scientific question or purpose of the collected data?

   A. How does pressure affect radon levels and temperatures over time?
   B. How do radon levels, temperature, and air pressure vary with altitude?
   C. How do radon levels, temperature, and air pressure change while earthquakes take place?
   D. How might radon levels, temperature, and air pressure be predictive of earthquake occurrence?

8. The date on which the highest air pressure is recorded is:

   F. July 15, 2014.
   G. September 28, 2014.
   H. October 28, 2014.
   J. November 17, 2014.

9. To increase the reliability of the acquired data, investigators could:

   A. measure the levels of the other radon isotopes in the environment.
   B. collect the same data from another local telemetric station for this region.
   C. calculate a best-fit line for all three types of data in order to predict future levels of each.
   D. plot the dependent variables on the same graph, using the same *x*- and *y*-axes units for comparison.

10. A constant among all variables measured in this experiment is the:

   F. regional location of all measurements.
   G. type of instrument or probe used to collect all measurements.
   H. amplitudes of all signals collected.
   J. inclusion of the date of the earthquakes on the *x*-axis.

11. Which of the following conclusions can be drawn based on the collected data?

   A. Simultaneous declines in radon-222, temperature, and air pressure levels might indicate an impending earthquake.
   B. Simultaneous declines in radon-222 and temperature levels, and a spike in air pressure might indicate an impending earthquake.
   C. Simultaneous spikes in radon-222, temperature, and air pressure levels might indicate an impending earthquake.
   D. Simultaneous spikes in temperature and air pressure levels, and a decline in the radon-222 level might indicate an impending earthquake.

PASSAGE III

Alloys are uniform mixtures that consist of a metal and at least one other kind of element. Steel is an alloy that is composed of iron and a variety of other elements; carbon steel is a mixture of iron and mostly carbon and a bit of chromium, while stainless steel is a mixture of iron and mostly chromium. Bronze is an alloy consisting mostly of copper and tin. Electrum is an alloy consisting of gold and silver.

After observing the formation of rust on their cars, several students were interested in testing the reactivity of these four alloys with air. The students hypothesize that the two types of steel will rust because they contain iron, while the other two alloys will not, based on their knowledge that iron reacts with oxygen gas in air to form iron oxide, or rust, which is a solid product of the reaction.

To test their hypothesis, the students weighed 5 g of each solid alloy and fastened it to the bottom of a test tube. They then inverted each test tube and placed it into a beaker containing 30 mL of water. The students took an initial measurement of the distance of the column of air, from the water level in the test tube to the bottom of the inverted test tube. The students also placed an empty inverted test tube into a beaker of 30 mL water as a control.

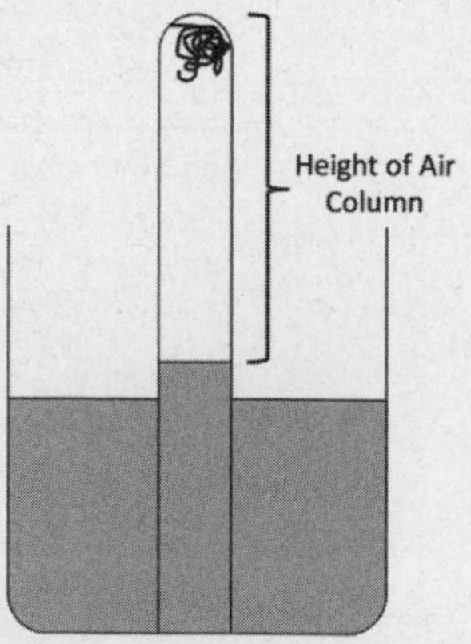

The students measured the height of the air column every three days for 12 days. The control test tube air column remained constant at 19.0 cm throughout the experiment. The alloy results are shown in the following graph.

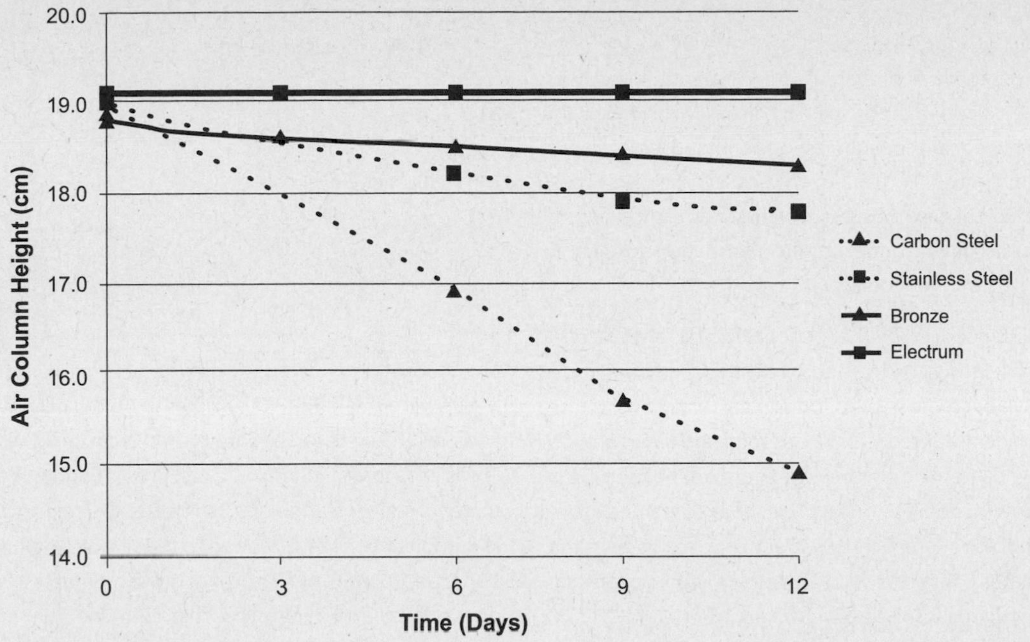

12. Based on their hypothesis, what would the students predict would happen in the bronze and electrum samples?

F. The heights of the air columns will increase significantly.
G. The heights of the air columns will decrease significantly.
H. The heights of the air columns will stay fairly constant.
J. The height of electrum's air column will decrease, while the height of bronze's air column will increase.

13. The dependent variable in this experiment is the:

A. time, in days, at which the measurements were taken.
B. air column heights.
C. types of alloys tested.
D. volumes of water in each beaker.

14. Measuring the mass of the metal in a test tube every three days for 12 days would not be an especially useful alternative method to this experiment because:

F. water is an essential part of the rusting reaction.
G. a key reactant of the rusting reaction is a gas.
H. oxygen is not the predominant gas in air.
J. the key product of the rusting reaction is a solid.

15. Which feature of the collected data most strongly and directly supports the students' hypothesis?

A. The alloys that contain iron exhibit a more significant air column decrease than those that do not contain iron.
B. The alloys that do not contain iron react more extensively with air than the alloys that do contain iron.
C. The minimal decreases in air column volume observed for bronze and electrum are likely due to alternative reactions of the alloys with gases in the air.
D. Bronze exhibited a more significant air column decrease than electrum.

16. A conclusion that can be drawn by comparing the data for carbon steel and stainless steel is:

F. carbon in an alloy may protect iron from rusting.
G. chromium in an alloy may protect iron from rusting.
H. gold in an alloy may promote iron rusting.
J. tin in an alloy may promote iron rusting.

PASSAGE IV

Garlic is a spice that has proven useful in treating a range of ailments, from colds and the flu to heart disease and high blood pressure. The two main substances found in garlic are alliin, a sulfur-rich amino acid, and an enzyme called alliinase. When garlic is crushed, alliinase mixes with alliin to form a compound called allicin. Alliin has no odor, but allicin formation gives garlic its characteristic pungent odor and taste.

A student wanted to test whether or not allicin has antibacterial properties. The student decided to test *Escherichia coli,* a gram-negative bacterial species found in an array of environments. The student wanted to use both solid and liquid growth media to test bacterial growth. First, the student used Luria broth (LB) growth media to make plates that contained kanamycin, an antibiotic to which her strain of *E. coli* is resistant. One set of plates contained solid LB with kanamycin, one set of plates contained LB solidified with kanamycin and 0.3 mM allicin, and one set of plates contained LB solidified with kanamycin and 1.0 mM allicin. There were three plates per set. The plates were grown overnight at 37°C, and the number of colonies was counted for each plate. The average numbers of colonies per plate per set are displayed in the following table:

Plate Content	Average Number of Colonies per Plate
LB + kanamycin	20.7
LB + kanamycin + 0.3 mM allicin	5.3
LB + kanamycin + 1.0 mM allicin	1.3

The student then tested the growth of *E. coli* in liquid medium by growing five different samples in 50 mL of growth media. Samples 1–3 were initially grown in LB with kanamycin. Sample 1 was left alone. In Sample 2, allicin was added to the sample to a final concentration of 0.3 mM after 120 minutes of growth. In Sample 3, allicin was added to the sample to a final concentration of 1.0 mM after 2 hours of growth. Samples 4 and 5 were grown in LB and kanamycin that contained 0.3 and 1.0 mM allicin, respectively, from the start. The cells were grown at 37°C with constant shaking for 6 hours. Each hour, the student measured cell density by removing a sample of the growth and checking its optical density, or absorbance, at a wavelength of 600 nm. The growth curves obtained are shown below:

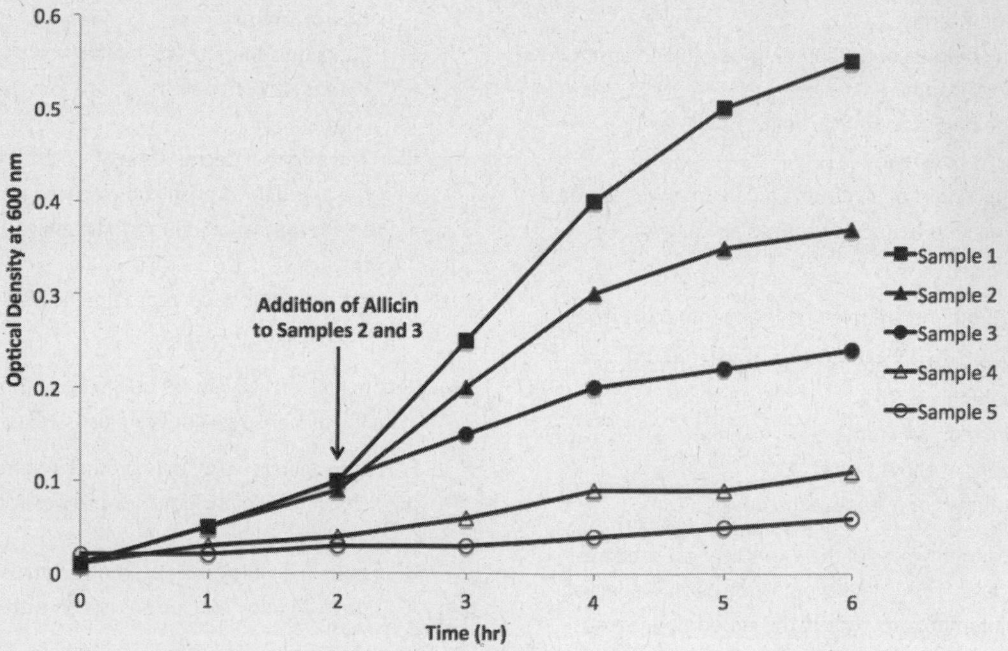

17. These experiments were designed to test the effect of:

A. temperature on *E. coli* bacterial growth.
B. solid and liquid media on allicin concentrations in *E. coli*.
C. cell density on *E. coli* bacterial growth.
D. varying concentrations of allicin on *E. coli* bacterial growth.

18. Based on the graph, what is the optical density for the allicin-free control after 5 hours?

F. 0.2
G. 0.35
H. 0.5
J. 0.55

19. The second set of plates, containing LB, kanamycin, and 0.3 mM allicin, most closely correspond with which liquid growth trial?

A. Sample 1
B. Sample 2
C. Sample 3
D. Sample 4

20. The purpose of adding kanamycin to the growth media for all samples is to:

F. slow *E. coli* growth to make for easier tracking.
G. prevent contamination by other microorganisms.
H. promote any effects of allicin on *E. coli* cells.
J. accelerate *E. coli* growth within the experimental timeframe.

21. Based on the data, which of the following conclusions can be drawn about the effect of allicin on *E. coli* bacterial growth?

A. Increased allicin concentrations promote *E. coli* growth, even when added during the growth process.
B. Increased allicin concentrations promote inhibition of *E. coli* growth, even when added during the growth process.
C. Increased allicin concentrations promote inhibition of *E. coli* growth, but only when included from the beginning of the growth process.
D. Increased allicin concentrations promote *E. coli* growth, but only when included from the beginning of the growth process.

Answers and Explanations

PASSAGE I

The first passage is a physics passage. It describes an experiment that tests the effect of an angle of incline on the acceleration of a marble.

1. **The correct answer is A.** The question asks you to choose the hypothesis that predicts the outcome of the experiment. Of the two hypothesis stems provided in the answer choices, the only one that makes sense and which also corresponds with the observed outcome in the data is, "If increased angles of incline allow for a greater effect of vertical gravitational pull." This allows you to immediately rule out choices C and D. The data show that as the angle of incline increases, the acceleration also increases. This means that you can rule out choice B, which states the opposite.

2. **The correct answer is H.** This question asks you to look at the experimental design and select the answer that is *not* held constant for every trial. The length of the inclined plane is 1 m for every trial, so you can rule out choice F. The friction of the inclined plane is also the same for every trial because the same material was used for all trials, so choice G can also be ruled out. The marble always reaches the ground at its ending point, so you can eliminate choice J. The starting height of the marble differs per trial because the 1-m board is set up at various angles of incline, so the correct answer is choice H.

3. **The correct answer is B.** The only difference between the complete equation and the simplified equation is the term $v_i t$. To eliminate this term, one of the two values must be zero. Since *t* also appears elsewhere in the equation, *t* cannot be zero, so the initial velocity must have been equal to zero. Thus, the correct answer is choice B. The other answers would not affect the equation in any way.

4. **The correct answer is H.** The graph of acceleration as a function of sin θ is provided in the passage. You don't even have to know anything about how to calculate sin θ to determine this answer. You can immediately rule out choice F because the relationship is clearly linear, not exponential. This is confirmed by the passage because it states that a best-fit line was determined for the data set. You can rule out choice J because there is a significant correlation between acceleration and sin θ, as they are related in a linear fashion according to the provided graph. The passage tells you that gravitational acceleration is equal to 9.8 m/s^2. To distinguish between choices G and H, you have to look at the equation given on the graph. The slope, not the *y*-intercept, is about equal to 9.8, so the correct answer is choice H.

5. **The correct answer is C.** This question asks you to think about how the data would look if you doubled the length of the plane. This experiment measures a constant acceleration of a marble rolling down a plane. Doubling the length of the plane will give a different measured time, but the calculated acceleration should be identical. If the angles of incline and the determined accelerations are the same, the graph shouldn't change at all.

6. **The correct answer is G.** This question asks you to suggest an improvement to the experiment. Using angles of incline up to 90° would not improve the experiment because the marble would nearly be in freefall, so the experiment wouldn't really work; you can rule out choice F. Getting the marble rolling in advance before starting time collections would not be an improvement because we cannot assume that the initial velocity of the ball is zero, which means we cannot use the simplified acceleration equation; you can rule out choice H. Measuring the times in minutes rather than seconds wouldn't improve the experiment in any way; it would only give much smaller time values, so you can rule out choice J. Increasing the number of trials is always an improvement because it improves experimental reliability.

PASSAGE II

This passage falls under the earth sciences category. It describes radon, temperature, and air pressure data collected by a telemetric radon station in the months prior to a pair of twin earthquakes in Prokopion, Greece.

7. **The correct answer is D.** This question asks about the scientific question posed by the passage. Technically, the passage measures three dependent variables, radon levels, temperature, and air pressure, so an appropriate scientific question should address all three of these. This fact alone allows you to rule out choice A, which incorrectly uses pressure as the independent variable rather than the dependent variable. You can rule

out choice B because the passage has nothing to do with altitude. You can also rule out choice C because the experiment looks at three measurements *before* the earthquake, not *during* the earthquake (the key incorrect word here is *while*). We know that the earthquake is *not* included because the passage gives the earthquake date (Nov. 17), which does not appear on the *x*-axis in any of the graphs. The hypothesis posed in choice D correctly identifies the three independent variables, as well as the correct pre-earthquake time frame. (Notice the use of the word *predictive,* since the scientists were looking for changes in the levels in the days leading up to the earthquake in order to enhance forecasting.)

8. **The correct answer is H.** This question simply requires you to read the data. Based on the air pressure plot, the highest air pressure occurs on October 28, 2014, and there is a dramatic spike in air pressure on that day.

9. **The correct answer is B.** This question asks you to suggest a way to increase the reliability of the data in the experiment. You can eliminate choice A because the passage states that the other radon isotopes are not abundant enough in the environment to be detected. You can eliminate choice C because, even though it indicates the predictive purpose of the data, it incorrectly suggests using a best-fit line for data points that are clearly not linear. You can rule out choice D because it would not be possible to plot all three dependent variables together with the same axis units because each variable has different units, as displayed on the graphs. Collecting the same kind of data from a different station could confirm the obtained results and increase the reliability.

10. **The correct answer is F.** This question asks you to identify a constant in the experiment. Choice G is incorrect because all measurements require different instruments (e.g., a radon probe measures radon levels, a thermometer measures temperature, and a barometer measures air pressure). Choice H is incorrect because this is essentially the dependent variable and is not a constant among all of the variables. The earthquake date is not included on the *x*-axis, so you can rule out choice J. Choice F is correct; all measurements occur for the same region in Greece.

11. **The correct answer is B.** This question asks you to draw a conclusion based on the collected data. There is a clear anomaly, or deviation from what was expected, for all three tested variables on 10/28/2014. At this point, there is a clear drop in radon-222 and temperature levels, as well as a visible dramatic spike in air pressure. The only answer that correctly describes these patterns as a predictive indicator of an impending earthquake is choice B.

PASSAGE III

This is a chemistry passage that describes an experiment that tests rusting reactions in four alloys, two of which contain iron, by measuring the volume of oxygen that disappears from an inverted test tube over water.

12. **The correct answer is H.** This question asks you to use the students' hypothesis to predict the outcome of the experiment. Since the students predicted that iron-containing alloys would use up oxygen during the rusting process, and since bronze and electrum do not contain iron, the result that would support the students' hypothesis is a decrease in their air column heights, as oxygen from the air is used up.

13. **The correct answer is B.** This question asks you to identify the dependent variable, which is the variable that is being measured in the experiment. The time is an independent variable, so choice A is incorrect. The types of alloys tested are also technically independent variables because they are varied among trials, so choice C is not correct. The volume of water in each beaker is a constant because it is 30 mL for all setups, so choice D is incorrect. The experiment measures the air column heights, so this is the dependent variable.

14. **The correct answer is J.** This question asks you to critique an alternative method, measuring the metal mass rather than oxygen usage. Choice F can be ruled out because the metal never contacts the water, so water is not an essential part of the reaction. You can also rule out choice G; while oxygen is a key reactant in the rusting reaction, it is not a reason why the alternative technique wouldn't work. Choice H is a true statement, but it is also not a reason why the alternative technique wouldn't work. Since rust is a solid, measuring changes in mass would be ineffective because

you really cannot distinguish between the solid reactant and solid product in that way.

15. **The correct answer is A.** This question asks you to determine which data most strongly and directly supports the students' hypothesis that iron-containing alloys will use up more oxygen as they rust. Choice B expresses the opposite of this, so you can rule out this answer. Choice C may be a true statement, but the students did not hypothesize about these alternative side reactions. Choice D is true, but it does not distinguish between alloys that do and do not contain iron. Choice A essentially restates the students' hypothesis as a conclusion supported by the data.

16. **The correct answer is G.** This question asks you to compare the data for the two types of steel used. If carbon protects iron from rusting, then carbon steel should rust more slowly than stainless steel; it does not, so choice F is false and can be ruled out. We can also rule out choices H and J because none of the alloys are a mixture of gold or tin with iron, so there is no data that measures these metals' potential effects on the rate of iron rusting. Stainless steel contains chromium and rusts more slowly than carbon steel; therefore, it seems that chromium could protect iron from rusting.

PASSAGE IV

This is a biology passage that describes an experiment that tests the effect of allicin, a compound from garlic, on the growth of E. coli in solid and liquid LB media.

17. **The correct answer is D.** This question basically asks you to state the purpose of the experiments. Of the answer choices, choice D correctly identifies the experiments measure growth rate (OD per hour) at different allicin concentrations. Choice A incorrectly identifies temperature as the independent variable. Choice B identifies allicin concentration as the dependent variable, when bacterial growth is the dependent variable. Choice C is incorrect because cell density is a means of measuring bacterial growth, so the independent variable is not correctly defined.

18. **The correct answer is H.** This question asks you to read the graph, which displays the data for bacterial growth in liquid media under different allicin concentrations. The allicin-free control is sample 1. If you find 5 hours on the *x*-axis, move vertically until you reach the graph of sample 1, and then move horizontally to the *y*-axis, you can find that the optical density after 5 hours was approximately 0.5.

19. **The correct answer is B.** This question asks you to compare the procedure for the solid and liquid media. The second set of plates contains LB, kanamycin, and 0.3 mM of allicin right from the start, since you can't change any concentrations in solidified media. Sample 1 contains no allicin, so you can eliminate choice A. Sample 3 contains 1 mM of allicin, so you can eliminate choice C. Sample 4 contains the correct allicin concentration, but it is added after 2 hours rather than right from the start, so choice D is incorrect. Sample 2 contains all of the correct chemicals right from the start of the experiment.

20. **The correct answer is G.** This question asks you to reason about the purpose of kanamycin based on the passage. The passage states that kanamycin is an antibiotic, which means that it kills off bacteria, but the passage also states that the *E. coli* used in the experiment is resistant to kanamycin. Therefore, kanamycin will kill off any microorganisms that are not *E. coli*, including unwanted contaminants that could interfere with the optical density measurements.

21. **The correct answer is B.** This question asks you to draw a conclusion about the effect of allicin on *E. coli* growth based on the data. Choice A states that increased allicin concentrations improve *E. coli* growth under all conditions, which is not true according to the data. Choice C states that increased allicin concentrations inhibit *E. coli* growth, except when the allicin is added midway through the growth process; this latter part of the statement is untrue based on Samples 2 and 3. Choice D indicates that allicin promotes *E. coli* growth when included from the beginning of the growth process, which is untrue based on the liquid media results from Samples 4 and 5. Choice B correctly indicates that increased allicin concentrations always inhibit *E. coli* growth, regardless of whether it is added at the beginning of or midway through the growth process.

CHAPTER 13: CONFLICTING VIEWPOINTS

OVERVIEW

- Reading Comprehension, Science Style
- Can You Use Reading Comprehension Skills to Understand Details?
- What Do the Viewpoints Have in Common?
- What Are Key Differences Between the Viewpoints?
- How Can the Viewpoints Be Related or Understood by Inference?
- Common Mistakes to Avoid
- Summing It Up
- College Readiness Benchmark Learning Path Practice
- Practice

Together, the passages in the Data Representation and Research Summaries categories make up the majority of the ACT Science test. The last 15–20 percent of the test that we have not yet discussed consists of Conflicting Viewpoints passages. Even though this is easily the shortest section of the ACT Science test, Conflicting Viewpoints passages are important because they test your ability to read about different views and hypotheses about the same topic and then analyze the pros and cons of each. While the Data Representation and Research Summaries passages have a lot in common with typical research articles in scientific journals, Conflicting Viewpoints passages are more similar to perspective pieces, commentaries, or short communications. These passages briefly convey at least two viewpoints about a particular topic, and it is your job to answer questions based on these views. Conflicting Viewpoints questions can cover all three ACT Science subcategories: Scientific Investigation, Interpretation of Data, and Evaluation of Models, Inferences, and Experimental Results.

READING COMPREHENSION, SCIENCE STYLE

Conflicting Viewpoints passages may seem a bit out of place in the ACT Science test. That's because these passages are extremely similar to reading comprehension passages you might see in the ACT Reading test. Sure, it will absolutely help if you have some background science knowledge in the covered areas, as you may have an easier time wading through the vocabulary or understanding the content. But when it really comes down to it, the ACT Science test is simply a test of reading comprehension in science-based passages. The most common questions you will find accompanying Conflicting Viewpoints passages usually fall under the Interpretation of Data category, since they ask you to analyze the information given and understand each author's point of view.

Conflicting Viewpoints passages will usually pose two or three short descriptions of viewpoints, summaries, or hypotheses about the same science topic or about related science topics. The questions will then test your understanding of the viewpoints as individual pieces and in light of one another. In other words, it will be important to understand each of the viewpoint summaries on its own, but you will then be asked to compare and contrast the summaries or to draw connections between the summaries to show how one might affect the other. Each passage is usually accompanied by seven questions.

As a reminder, a **hypothesis** is an educated guess about the outcome of a particular experiment or scientific phenomenon. Hypotheses are constantly posed to try to explain observations in nature and may be based on collected data, comparisons to similar phenomena, or basic logic, but they are considered hypotheses because they are still predictions rather than well-supported conclusions. A **theory** is often used as a synonym for a hypothesis, but a theory is usually based on a more substantial number of experiments and observations. So a theory is usually less specific but more corroborated than a hypothesis.

Both hypotheses and theories are often based on general principles of a scientific topic that are commonly regarded as correct or true, but they are still considered proposed explanations rather than established fact. When it comes to common viewpoints passages, you will often be presented with two hypotheses or theories that either differ or focus on different features of a particular phenomenon. These explanations are therefore considered to be "viewpoints" in this passage category because they are hypotheses or theories.

> **TIP:** A number of well-known theories include the Big Bang theory, the theory of relativity, and the theory of evolution. These are all considered theories, and not scientific fact, because there is a lot of scientific evidence to support them, but they are still conjectural and subject to experimentation.

However, not all of the passages will be based on well-known scientific theories or hypotheses. You will also see passages in which hypothetical students tackle simpler questions by doing some research and presenting their findings. The practice passages at the end of the chapter will include an example of each type of passage so you know what to expect in each case.

The most basic skill you will need when tackling Conflicting Viewpoints passages is reading comprehension. This skill is really vital to tackling all of the passages and questions in Conflicting Viewpoints clusters (and, in general, to all passages and questions on the Science test), but in addition, there are a few simple steps you can take to make sure you're extracting the appropriate information. Each Conflicting Viewpoints passage will begin with a brief paragraph that introduces the topic of interest.

After identifying the topic of interest, you can move on to the viewpoints themselves. Each viewpoint will be discussed in a paragraph or two and will usually provide supporting data in its explanation. When reading the viewpoints, it is important to figure out the opinions expressed. Underline key words and use the margin to write down the basic theory provided by each viewpoint in a clear and succinct way, so that when you have to start answering questions, you'll know where to look for the correct answers.

> **TIP:** Make sure you clearly identify the topic of interest before proceeding with the rest of the passage. Jot down a note or two in the margins to make sure you don't forget later.

After you've identified the basic hypothesis or theory provided by each scientist, look for the data that support each viewpoint. Feel free to circle the data so you can look at it later. By identifying supporting data for each viewpoint, you can see whether or not the data for one viewpoint might support or refute the other viewpoint, and vice versa. Picking out the key data will also help you to compare and contrast the viewpoints because each piece of data will likely support one theory more strongly than the other; otherwise, the scientist would not bother to include it.

To summarize, the basic strategy to employ when reading Conflicting Viewpoints passages is as follows:

1) Identify the topic.

2) Identify the basic hypotheses or theories of the scientists.

3) Identify the relevant data used to support each of the two viewpoints discussed in the passage.

When you are posed with a set of Conflicting Viewpoints, you will likely be posed with questions that test your ability to understand details, compare the conflicting viewpoints, contrast the conflicting viewpoints, and make inferences either to relate the viewpoints to one another, or to use data (either real or hypothetical) to support or refute the conflicting viewpoints. These are the areas we will focus on in our preparation for these passage types.

CAN YOU USE READING COMPREHENSION SKILLS TO UNDERSTAND DETAILS?

The most straightforward question type you will encounter with Conflicting Viewpoints passages simply asks you to recall details from the passages. Questions may ask you about statements found explicitly in the passages or about implications based on statements found in the passage. For example, if a passage describes the short-term and long-term effects of mutations on human evolution, a question might ask you to choose the event that would most immediately follow a mutation; while all four answer choices may be correct based on the passage, you would have to choose the short-term effect rather than any of the long-term effects based on the use of the word *immediately* in the question. This is an example of why it is important to pay attention to details. When you're reading a question, make sure you understand what you are being asked so that you don't simply choose what appears to be the first correct statement you see, when in fact the question is asking you about something entirely different.

As a general rule, you won't have to bring an abundance of background information to the table when it comes to understanding details in Conflicting Viewpoints passages. Of course, having background knowledge about a particular topic won't hurt; for instance, if you know a lot about deep-sea vents, that background knowledge will certainly be helpful to you if you encounter a Conflicting Viewpoints passage that introduces vocabulary related to deep-sea vents. However, you won't be expected to be an expert on any of the topics presented. Reading comprehension is all about understanding what you read, and the vast majority of information you'll need to answer questions about Conflicting Viewpoints passages can be found in the passages themselves. Occasionally you'll need to figure out a vocabulary definition based on the information provided, but everything you need will be in the passage.

There are usually one to three detail-oriented recall questions per question set for Conflicting Viewpoints questions, and they usually refer to just one viewpoint at a time. You will often see one detail-based reading comprehension question per viewpoint; this setup makes sense because it makes sure you have read both of the passages.

> **TIP:** If you pay attention to details and take notes as you read, you should have no trouble at all identifying the topic and comprehending the details in Conflicting Viewpoints passages.

Let's look at how the ACT Science test will present these questions. As in the other science chapters, we will use one passage and data set for the majority of practice questions in this chapter.

There are numerous theories concerning the origin of life on Earth, focusing on how primitive Earth was able to chemically create biomolecules essential for biological life to arise. Two such ideas are the Theory of Volcanic Origin of Life and the RNA World Hypothesis.

Theory of Volcanic Origin of Life

A widely accepted theory for the origin of life is that lightning and gases from volcanic eruptions may have given rise to the very first life on Earth. The Miller-Urey experiment, performed in 1952, was a chemical experiment that simulated the conditions of primitive Earth. In this experiment, a mixture of gases thought to have been present in the primitive atmosphere (most prominently, H_2O, CH_4, NH_3, and H_2) was stored in a vial connected by a pipe to a heated water tank that simulated the evaporation of the ocean. In that vial, electrodes created a spark, simulating lightning, and reaction products were collected by reliquefying the water vapor. The setup is shown in the illustration:

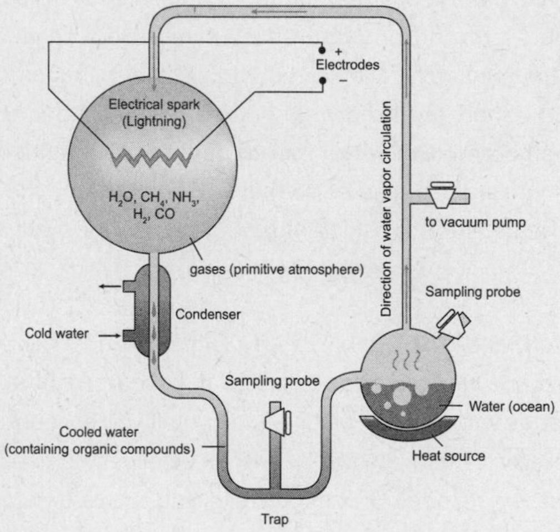

The Miller-Urey experiment showed that simple organic compounds, namely amino acids and various sugars, including ribose, can be produced from the gases in the atmosphere of primitive Earth with the addition of energy.

More recently, scientists performed a similar experiment with CO_2, CO, and N_2, an updated conception of Earth's early atmosphere, and these gases allowed for the production of an even wider array of biomolecules. The addition of volcanic gases like H_2 and CH_4 increased variety and supplied hydrogen, and follow-up experiments have shown that a simple volcanic gas called carbonyl sulfide (COS) helps free-floating amino acids to form peptides, the precursors to proteins, under various conditions, and that metal ions help to intensify this reaction by up to 80 percent. However, since carbonyl sulfide decomposes rather quickly, it is unlikely to be present in large quantities in the atmosphere. Instead, scientists propose that this gas would be most predominant at hydrothermal vents on the seafloor, forming peptide chains that would stick to rocks and continue to lengthen.

RNA World Hypothesis

Francis Crick, among other scientists, first posed the RNA World Hypothesis in the 1960s. RNA has the unique ability to act as both genes and enzymes, which make RNA a sensible first biomolecule in the origin of life. A long-standing weakness of the RNA World Hypothesis had been the inability of prebiotic Earth to form the molecule's nucleotides from its basic ingredients.

Recently, however, lab simulations, have demonstrated that pyrimidine nucleotides cytosine and uracil can form a number of plausible prebiotic molecules under early-Earth conditions, an atmosphere that included H_2O, CH_4, NH_3, and H_2, and that the simplest building blocks of sugars, glycolaldehyde and glyceraldehyde, can be derived from the prebiotic molecule HCN. There is no evidence of formation of the other two nucleotides present in RNA, adenine and guanine, but current research is moving in that direction. *In vitro* experiments under primordial conditions have demonstrated the ability to produce RNA molecules that perform a number of functions, including self-replication and the ability to copy other RNA molecules. These capabilities of RNA make it a very promising "first biomolecule" because RNA is the only biomolecule currently known to be capable of replication, catalysis, and containing genes itself, so RNA could have preceded DNA and proteins in evolution because RNA can self-catalyze to make protein, which can then replicate DNA.

The function of the condenser in the Miller-Urey experiment is to:

A. increase the temperature of the gases for analysis of reaction products.
B. convert the water vapor to liquid for reaction product collection.
C. condense the reacting gases into solid form for product detection.
D. produce RNA from gas precursors capable of self-replication.

The correct answer is B. This passage presents two different views on the origin of life. The first viewpoint describes the theory that atmospheric and volcanic gases, using energy from volcanic lightning, were capable of forming amino acids and simple sugars. The second viewpoint describes the hypothesis that RNA was the first biomolecule because there is some evidence that some of its nucleotides can be formed by the prebiotic atmosphere, and because RNA is genetic, self-replicates, and can act as a catalyst.

The question posed is a recall question that asks you to look back at the viewpoints and use the information to determine the purpose of the condenser in the Miller-Urey experiment. Since the Miller-Urey experiment is exclusively described in the first viewpoint, the answer to the question is found in the first viewpoint. Based on the diagram, there is a cold-water bath around the condenser; a decrease in temperature would promote the conversion of water vapor to liquid water. Even if you didn't catch that, the passage itself indicates that the water vapor was reliquefied for product collection, and in the diagram, the condenser is the link between the simulated atmosphere and the area where cooled water delivers the reaction products. Choice A is incorrect because the cool water won't increase the temperature; it decreases the temperature. Choice C is incorrect because even though the word *condenses* is in the answer, there is no deposition—conversion of a gas to a solid—taking place in this reaction. Choice D is incorrect; while this answer accurately describes one of the experiments mentioned in the second viewpoint, it is unrelated to this particular question.

WHAT DO THE VIEWPOINTS HAVE IN COMMON?

Each passage will present you with two conflicting viewpoints; by definition, *conflicting* seems to indicate that the viewpoints are in opposition to one another. However, in Conflicting Viewpoints passages, this doesn't necessarily mean that the two viewpoints are arguing in favor of opposite ideas; in many cases, the viewpoints are simply arguing in favor of *different* ideas. They are considered to be "conflicting" only because the arguments are not one and the same. In the previous example, both viewpoints could technically be correct, as both ideas seem to be valid based on experiments done thus far. However, they are Conflicting Viewpoints because they are arguing that their theory or hypothesis is the key first step that ignited the development of life on Earth.

When different viewpoints are presented (and even if they are in direct opposition to one another), it is almost always possible to find commonalities between the two. Often, the viewpoints will describe the same effect, but they will propose different causes for that effect. In other cases, viewpoints may be nearly identical, except for a detail or two that leads to a completely different conclusion. In still other situations, two viewpoints may propose entirely different theories about a particular phenomenon, but they could have a feature or two in common. Regardless of the viewpoints you encounter, there will always be some kind of parallel you can draw between them and, more often than not, one of the questions accompanying the passage will draw attention to one of those parallels. The easiest way to identify such parallels is to use the strategy we've already discussed—take notes in the margin to identify the shared topic, viewpoint presented by each author, and supporting data presented in favor of each viewpoint. These notes, however brief, can draw attention to details or data that are relevant to both of the viewpoints. If you come across a question that asks you to compare the conflicting viewpoints, you can use your notes to easily pinpoint where you should focus your efforts when narrowing down your answer choices.

Let's look at this type of question in action.

There are numerous theories concerning the origin of life on Earth, focusing on how primitive Earth was able to chemically create biomolecules essential for biological life to arise. Two such ideas are the Theory of Volcanic Origin of Life and the RNA World Hypothesis.

Theory of Volcanic Origin of Life

A widely accepted theory for the origin of life is that lightning and gases from volcanic eruptions may have given rise to the very first life on Earth. The Miller-Urey experiment, performed in 1952, was a chemical experiment that simulated the conditions of primitive Earth. In this experiment, a mixture of gases thought to have been present in the primitive atmosphere (most prominently, H_2O, CH_4, NH_3, and H_2) was stored in a vial connected by a pipe to a heated water tank that simulated the evaporation of the ocean. In that vial, electrodes created a spark, simulating lightning, and reaction products were collected by reliquefying the water vapor. The setup is shown in the illustration.

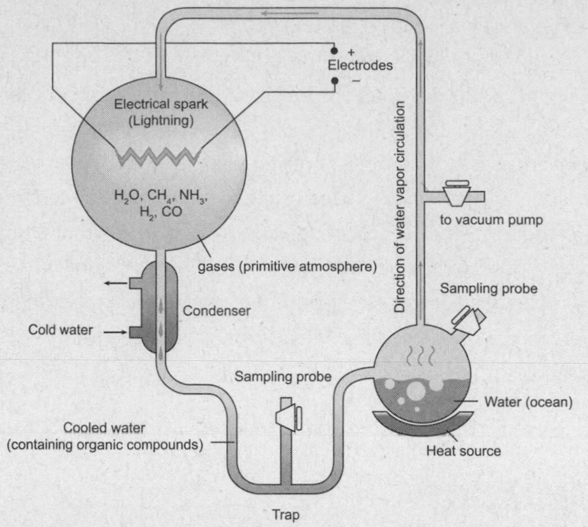

The Miller-Urey experiment showed that simple organic compounds, namely amino acids and various sugars, including ribose, can be produced from the gases in the atmosphere of primitive Earth with the addition of energy.

More recently, scientists performed a similar experiment with CO_2, CO, and N_2, an updated conception of Earth's early atmosphere, and these gases allowed for the production of an even wider array of biomolecules. The addition of volcanic gases like H_2 and CH_4 increased variety and supplied hydrogen, and follow-up experiments have shown that a simple volcanic gas called carbonyl sulfide (COS) helps free-floating amino acids to form peptides, the precursors to proteins, under various conditions, and that metal ions help to intensify this reaction by up to 80 percent. However, since carbonyl sulfide decomposes rather quickly, it is unlikely to be present in large quantities in the atmosphere. Instead, scientists propose that this gas would be most predominant at hydrothermal vents on the seafloor, forming peptide chains that would stick to rocks and continue to lengthen.

RNA World Hypothesis

Francis Crick, among other scientists, first posed the RNA World Hypothesis in the 1960s. RNA has the unique ability to act as both genes and enzymes, which make RNA a sensible first biomolecule in the origin of life. A long-standing weakness of the RNA World Hypothesis had been the inability of prebiotic Earth to form the molecule's nucleotides from its basic ingredients.

Recently, however, lab simulations, have demonstrated that pyrimidine nucleotides cytosine and uracil can form a number of plausible prebiotic molecules under early-Earth conditions, an atmosphere that included H_2O, CH_4, NH_3, and H_2, and that the simplest building blocks of sugars, glycolaldehyde and glyceraldehyde, can be derived from the prebiotic molecule HCN. There is no evidence of formation of the other two nucleotides present in RNA, adenine and guanine, but current research is moving in that direction. *In vitro* experiments under primordial conditions have demonstrated the ability to produce RNA molecules that perform a number of functions, including self-replication and the ability to copy other RNA molecules. These capabilities of RNA make it a very promising "first biomolecule" because RNA is the only biomolecule currently known to be capable of replication, catalysis, and containing genes itself, so RNA could have preceded DNA and proteins in evolution because RNA can self-catalyze to make protein, which can then replicate DNA.

A feature that the two viewpoints have in common is:

F. the type of proposed "first biomolecule" that led to the development of life.

G. the predicted gas content of the earth's prebiotic atmosphere.

H. the argument that proteins are required for any kind of catalysis to occur.

J. the formation of the "first biomolecule" near deep-sea vents.

The correct answer is G. This question asks you to find a feature that the two viewpoints have in common with one another. Since the question stem itself does not specify a particular feature of the viewpoints on which to focus, the easiest way to go about answering this question is to go through each answer choice and decide whether or not it is true.

Choice F indicates that both viewpoints point to the same biomolecule as the "first biomolecule" in the origin of life. This is not the correct answer because the first viewpoint indicates that prebiotic conditions allowed for the production of amino acids and peptides as the "first biomolecule," as well as some sugars, while the second viewpoint argues that RNA was the "first biomolecule." Choice G indicates that both viewpoints agree on the prebiotic atmospheric content. Based on some of the listed gases in the passage, this is definitely a possibility. Choice H indicates that both viewpoints indicate that proteins are required for catalysis. This is not specifically mentioned in the first viewpoint, but a key argument in the second viewpoint is that RNA, which is a nucleic acid and not a protein, is capable of catalysis, so it cannot be correct. Choice J indicates that the viewpoints agree that the formation of the "first biomolecule" occurred in deep-sea vents; this is really only specified in the first viewpoint in reference to carbonyl sulfide, so this cannot be correct. The correct answer, therefore, is choice G.

WHAT ARE KEY DIFFERENCES BETWEEN THE VIEWPOINTS?

If you're going to be asked to compare the viewpoints, it makes sense that you would also be asked to contrast the viewpoints. You can approach the contrast question types in exactly the same way you would approach the comparison questions. If a question asks you to contrast the viewpoints with respect to a particular topic mentioned in the question stem, look through your notes or underlined words and phrases to find that topic within each viewpoint. If a question asks you to find differences between the viewpoints in general, you might need to take the same approach we took with the last example, by going through each answer choice and eliminating incorrect answers until you determine the correct answer.

NOTE: In general, approximately half of the questions that follow a Conflicting Viewpoints passage will ask you to compare and contrast the viewpoints.

When Conflicting Viewpoints differ dramatically in approach to the subject at hand, it may be a little more difficult to pinpoint differences between the viewpoints, but use the questions to your advantage. The ACT Science test consists entirely of multiple-choice questions, and it is a perfectly valid strategy to look at the answers if you aren't sure about exactly what the question is asking you to determine from the viewpoints.

There are numerous theories concerning the origin of life on Earth, focusing on how primitive Earth was able to chemically create biomolecules essential for biological life to arise. Two such ideas are the Theory of Volcanic Origin of Life and the RNA World Hypothesis.

Theory of Volcanic Origin of Life

A widely accepted theory for the origin of life is that lightning and gases from volcanic eruptions may have given rise to the very first life on Earth. The Miller-Urey experiment, performed in 1952, was a chemical experiment that simulated the conditions of primitive Earth. In this experiment, a mixture of gases thought to have been present in the primitive atmosphere (most prominently, H_2O, CH_4, NH_3, and H_2) was stored in a vial connected by a pipe to a heated water tank that simulated the evaporation of the ocean. In that vial, electrodes created a spark, simulating lightning, and reaction products were collected by reliquefying the water vapor. The setup is shown in the illustration.

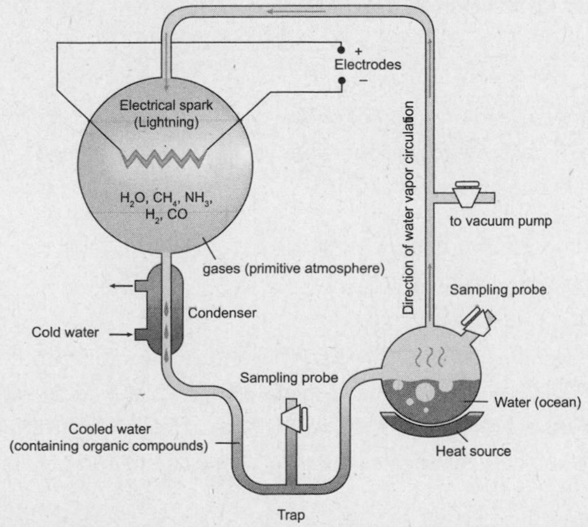

The Miller-Urey experiment showed that simple organic compounds, namely amino acids and various sugars, including ribose, can be produced from the gases in the atmosphere of primitive Earth with the addition of energy.

More recently, scientists performed a similar experiment with CO_2, CO, and N_2, an updated conception of Earth's early atmosphere, and these gases allowed for the production of an even wider array of biomolecules. The addition of volcanic gases like H_2 and CH_4 increased variety and supplied hydrogen, and follow-up experiments have shown that a simple volcanic gas called carbonyl sulfide (COS) helps free-floating amino acids to form peptides, the precursors to proteins, under various conditions, and that metal ions help to intensify this reaction by up to 80 percent. However, since carbonyl sulfide decomposes rather quickly, it is unlikely to be present in large quantities in the atmosphere. Instead, scientists propose that this gas would be most predominant at hydrothermal vents on the seafloor, forming peptide chains that would stick to rocks and continue to lengthen.

RNA World Hypothesis

Francis Crick, among other scientists, first posed the RNA World Hypothesis in the 1960s. RNA has the unique ability to act as both genes and enzymes, which make RNA a sensible first biomolecule in the origin of life. A long-standing weakness of the RNA World Hypothesis had been the inability of prebiotic Earth to form the molecule's nucleotides from its basic ingredients.

Recently, however, lab simulations, have demonstrated that pyrimidine nucleotides cytosine and uracil can form a number of plausible prebiotic molecules under early-Earth conditions, an atmosphere that included H_2O, CH_4, NH_3, and H_2, and that the simplest building blocks of sugars, glycolaldehyde and glyceraldehyde, can be derived from the prebiotic molecule HCN. There is no evidence of formation of the other two nucleotides present in RNA, adenine and guanine, but current research is moving in that direction. *In vitro* experiments under primordial conditions have demonstrated the ability to produce RNA molecules that perform a number of functions, including self-replication and the ability to copy other RNA molecules. These capabilities of RNA make it a very promising "first biomolecule" because RNA is the only biomolecule currently known to be capable of replication, catalysis, and containing genes itself, so RNA could have preceded DNA and proteins in evolution because RNA can self-catalyze to make protein, which can then replicate DNA.

A key difference in biomolecule formation from the atmosphere, as described by these two viewpoints, is:

A. experimental evidence that the prebiotic atmosphere can form the full array of amino acid monomers, but not all of the RNA nucleotide monomers.

B. experimental evidence that the prebiotic atmosphere can form the full array of RNA nucleotide monomers, but not all of the amino acids.

C. experimental evidence that indicates the prebiotic atmosphere directly forms peptides and proteins, bypassing amino acid formation, while RNA nucleotide monomers must be formed first.

D. experimental evidence that indicates the prebiotic atmosphere directly forms RNA, bypassing nucleotide formation, while protein monomers, amino acids, must be formed first.

The correct answer is A. This question asks you to focus on differences in the modes of biomolecule formation. The answer choices are all related to experimental evidence, so if you took the time to underline the experimental data while reading, it would pay off heavily here because that is exactly the topic of focus for this question.

The answer choices are paired answers; choices A and B represent opposite ideas, and choices C and D represent opposite ideas. This means that one of these answer pairs is completely wrong altogether, while the other answer pair contains the correct answer. Choice A states that there is experimental evidence that shows that prebiotic atmosphere can form all of the amino acids, but not all of the nucleotides; this is true, according to the viewpoints, because the first viewpoint indicates that all amino acids have been formed experimentally, while the second passage indicates that only cytosine and uracil have currently been formed experimentally. This evidence indicates that choice A is correct, and that choice B is effectively incorrect.

To confirm our answer, let's check out choices C and D. Choice C indicates that peptide and protein formation bypasses the formation of amino acid monomers, while choice D indicates that RNA formation bypasses the formation of nucleotide monomers. The aforementioned experimental data appears to refute both of these statements, as the experimental evidence shows formation of amino acids and nucleotides rather than direct formation of full-fledged peptides and RNA. This makes sense, as it is much easier to form a smaller subunit of a biomolecule than a more complex one. Therefore, we can rule out choices B, C, and D.

HOW CAN THE VIEWPOINTS BE RELATED OR UNDERSTOOD BY INFERENCE?

So far, the question types we've discussed have been fairly straightforward reading comprehension questions for which you can find the answers simply by reading and understanding the passages. The last category of questions you might encounter will ask you to make inferences or to determine implied information, for one of two purposes:

1) To connect or relate the two viewpoints in some way

2) To introduce real or hypothetical data that might affect one or both of the viewpoints

Inference-based questions are still reading comprehension questions, but they require that you go beyond simply what is written in the text. The first inference question type might ask you to tweak one viewpoint so that it might work in collaboration with the second viewpoint or to indicate whether or not the two viewpoints are mutually exclusive. The second inference question type is much more common because it can be applied to any set of viewpoints, regardless of how similar or different they may be.

On one hand, you may be provided with a particular piece of real or hypothetical data, and you must determine how this new information will impact the two theories. For instance, a new hypothetical discovery might refute one viewpoint and support the other, or it might refute both viewpoints, or it might even be unrelated to either viewpoint. This kind of question requires that you fully understand both viewpoints, because you may have to apply new information to both in order to determine its effect on the two viewpoints.

The other version of this question type works in the reverse, in that you may be asked to choose a particular piece of information that supports or refutes one or both of the viewpoints. This question type may ask you to relate data to both viewpoints or to focus on only one viewpoint; in either case, you'll have to have a thorough understanding of what each viewpoint is conveying so that you know how new data could support or refute it.

The following examples will cover both types of data-based inference questions so you can get a sense of how they work.

There are numerous theories concerning the origin of life on Earth, focusing on how primitive Earth was able to chemically create biomolecules essential for biological life to arise. Two such ideas are the Theory of Volcanic Origin of Life and the RNA World Hypothesis.

Theory of Volcanic Origin of Life

A widely accepted theory for the origin of life is that lightning and gases from volcanic eruptions may have given rise to the very first life on Earth. The Miller-Urey experiment, performed in 1952, was a chemical experiment that simulated the conditions of primitive Earth. In this experiment, a mixture of gases thought to have been present in the primitive atmosphere (most prominently, H_2O, CH_4, NH_3, and H_2) was stored in a vial connected by a pipe to a heated water tank that simulated the evaporation of the ocean. In that vial, electrodes created a spark, simulating lightning, and reaction products were collected by reliquefying the water vapor. The setup is shown in the illustration.

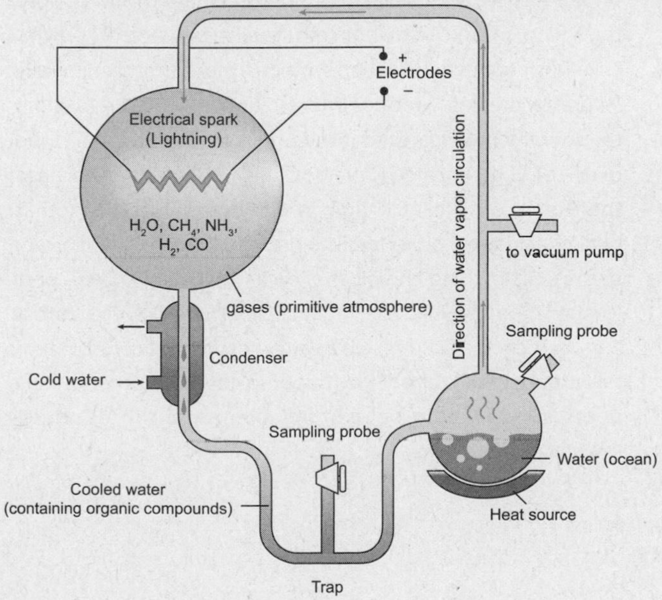

The Miller-Urey experiment showed that simple organic compounds, namely amino acids and various sugars, including ribose, can be produced from the gases in the atmosphere of primitive Earth with the addition of energy.

More recently, scientists performed a similar experiment with CO_2, CO, and N_2, an updated conception of Earth's early atmosphere, and these gases allowed for the production of an even wider array of biomolecules. The addition of volcanic gases like H_2 and CH_4 increased variety and supplied hydrogen, and follow-up experiments have shown that a simple volcanic gas called carbonyl sulfide (COS) helps free-floating amino acids to form peptides, the precursors to proteins, under various conditions, and that metal ions help to intensify this reaction by up to 80 percent. However, since carbonyl sulfide decomposes rather quickly, it is unlikely to be present in large quantities in the atmosphere. Instead, scientists propose that this gas would be most predominant at hydrothermal vents on the seafloor, forming peptide chains that would stick to rocks and continue to lengthen.

RNA World Hypothesis

Francis Crick, among other scientists, first posed the RNA World Hypothesis in the 1960s. RNA has the unique ability to act as both genes and enzymes, which make RNA a sensible first biomolecule in the origin of life. A long-standing weakness of the RNA World Hypothesis had been the inability of prebiotic Earth to form the molecule's nucleotides from its basic Ingredlents.

Recently, however, lab simulations, have demonstrated that pyrimidine nucleotides cytosine and uracil can form a number of plausible prebiotic molecules under early-Earth conditions, an atmosphere that included H_2O, CH_4, NH_3, and H_2, and that the simplest building blocks of sugars, glycolaldehyde and glyceraldehyde, can be derived from the prebiotic molecule

HCN. There is no evidence of formation of the other two nucleotides present in RNA, adenine and guanine, but current research is moving in that direction. *In vitro* experiments under primordial conditions have demonstrated the ability to produce RNA molecules that perform a number of functions, including self-replication and the ability to copy other RNA molecules. These capabilities of RNA make it a very promising "first biomolecule" because RNA is the only biomolecule currently known to be capable of replication, catalysis, and containing genes itself, so RNA could have preceded DNA and proteins in evolution because RNA can self-catalyze to make protein, which can then replicate DNA.

If continued research indicates that the prebiotic atmosphere is unlikely to have been able to synthesize adenine and guanine, which of the following statements is most correct?

F. All described components of the Theory of Volcanic Origin of Life should be regarded as inaccurate.

G. Proteins could be confirmed as the "first biomolecules" per the Theory of Volcanic Origin of Life.

H. All described components of the RNA World Hypothesis should be regarded as inaccurate.

J. RNA may still be a key early biomolecule, but its synthesis requires non-RNA catalysts.

The correct answer is J. This question asks you to use a piece of hypothetical data, the inability of the prebiotic atmosphere to synthesize adenine and guanine, to draw a conclusion about the viewpoints. This piece of hypothetical data seems to clearly impact the RNA World Hypothesis moreso than the Theory of Volcanic Origin of Life, but it is important to make sure by reasoning through each of the answer choices.

Choice F indicates that this new piece of data refutes the entire Theory of Volcanic Origin of Life. This is incorrect because this particular finding would not impact this theory since it does not propose that RNA is the "first biomolecule." Choice G indicates that this piece of data confirms proteins as the "first biomolecule." The need for a new catalyst to make RNA might strongly suggest that proteins are required for its synthesis, but this is a bit of a leap, as nothing about this piece of data specifically confirms that proteins are required for RNA synthesis. Therefore, choice G is incorrect. Choice H indicates that all components of the RNA World Hypothesis can be rejected with the introduction of this piece of data. This is not correct—the RNA World Hypothesis may indicate that RNA was likely the "first biomolecule," which this piece of data seems to reject, but the description of RNA's ability to contain genetic material, self-replicate, and act as a catalyst for propagation are all still very valid points. Therefore, the correct answer is choice J, which indicates that this piece of data rejects RNA as the "first biomolecule," but RNA still performs important functions, particularly in self-propagation, that could make it an important early biomolecule. Therefore, only the "first biomolecule" aspect of the RNA World Hypothesis would be refuted; the rest is still valid.

Which of the following pieces of data would best support the Theory of Volcanic Origin of Life?

A. It is thermodynamically favorable for water to break down peptide chains via hydrolysis reactions.

B. Nucleic acids cannot be converted to proteins without cell machinery already in existence.

C. Pumice, the porous rock that forms when a volcano cools rapidly, can trap gas and nutrients to support microbe growth.

D. There were no metal ions present in the deep sea vent environment.

The correct answer is C. This question asks you to choose a piece of data that best supports one of the two viewpoints; in this case, the question asks you to choose the piece of data that best supports the Theory of Volcanic Origin of Life. To answer this question, we must go through each piece of data in order to determine how it affects the specified theory.

Choice A is incorrect. In fact, this piece of data would oppose the Theory of Volcanic Origin of Life. Since amino acid polymerization requires dehydration synthesis, the thermodynamically favorable breakdown of peptides by water would refute the theory, which indicates that the origin of life occurred at the deep-sea vents, located in water. Choice B is incorrect because the Theory of Volcanic Origin of Life does not indicate that nucleic acids are converted into protein. Choice D is incorrect because, if anything, this piece of data would decrease support for the Theory of Volcanic Origin of Life. Therefore, the correct answer is choice C. Pumice is a volcanic rock that could potentially support microbe life by trapping gas and nutrients in its pores, which would be extremely important in the deep sea environment.

COMMON MISTAKES TO AVOID

In the previous two chapters, we discussed a number of mistakes and pitfalls to avoid during the ACT Science test. Here, we will talk about a few more mistakes test takers sometimes make that are more specific to Conflicting Viewpoints passages. The mistakes we'll discuss are focusing on too many of the details during your first read-through, mixing up the viewpoints, relying on key words in answer choices, and failing to find support for your answers in the text. The previous examples have already highlighted several of these, but we'll go over each again specifically to make sure you don't fall into any traps when you encounter Conflicting Viewpoints passages.

Focusing on Too Many Details During the First Read-Through

When you're reading a set of viewpoints in a Conflicting Viewpoints passage, it is definitely important to pay attention to what you're reading. However, you won't be able to remember absolutely everything. That's why it is so important to take the advice mentioned earlier and take notes. Identifying the overarching topic of the passage, the specific views or theories described by each viewpoint, and any key data will help you to cut out the extraneous information during the first read-through. If a question refers to any of this extra information, you can certainly go back and read through the viewpoints again to find that information. However, during the first read-through, it is essential that you gain a solid understanding of the topic, views, and supporting data, because once you are confident about these three key features of the passage, you will have a much easier time with the questions because you'll know exactly where to look.

There are numerous theories concerning the origin of life on Earth, focusing on how primitive Earth was able to chemically create biomolecules essential for biological life to arise. Two such ideas are the Theory of Volcanic Origin of Life and the RNA World Hypothesis.

Theory of Volcanic Origin of Life

A widely accepted theory for the origin of life is that lightning and gases from volcanic eruptions may have given rise to the very first life on Earth. The Miller-Urey experiment, performed in 1952, was a chemical experiment that simulated the conditions of primitive Earth. In this experiment, a mixture of gases thought to have been present in the primitive atmosphere (most prominently, H_2O, CH_4, NH_3, and H_2) was stored in a vial connected by a pipe to a heated water tank that simulated the evaporation of the ocean. In that vial, electrodes created a spark, simulating lightning, and reaction products were collected by reliquefying the water vapor. The setup is shown in the illustration.

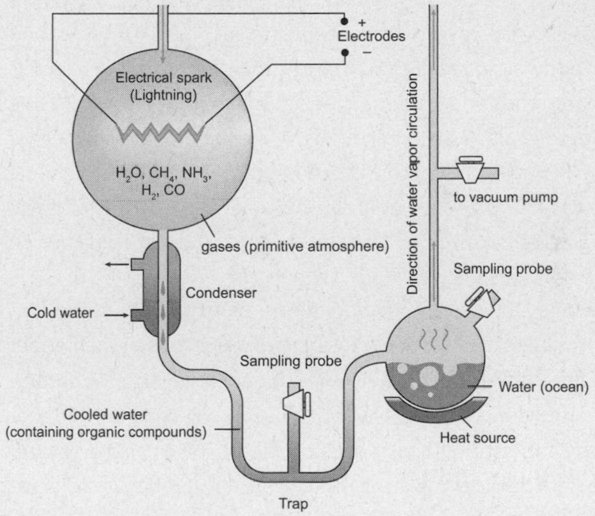

The Miller-Urey experiment showed that simple organic compounds, namely amino acids and various sugars, including ribose, can be produced from the gases in the atmosphere of primitive Earth with the addition of energy.

More recently, scientists performed a similar experiment with CO_2, CO, and N_2, an updated conception of Earth's early atmosphere, and these gases allowed for the production of an even wider array of biomolecules. The addition of volcanic gases like H_2 and CH_4 increased variety and supplied hydrogen, and follow-up experiments have shown that a simple volcanic gas called carbonyl sulfide (COS) helps free-floating amino acids to form peptides, the precursors to proteins, under various conditions, and that metal ions help to intensify this reaction by up to 80 percent. However, since carbonyl sulfide decomposes rather quickly, it is unlikely to be present in large quantities in the atmosphere. Instead, scientists propose that this gas would be most predominant at hydrothermal vents on the seafloor, forming peptide chains that would stick to rocks and continue to lengthen.

RNA World Hypothesis

Francis Crick, among other scientists, first posed the RNA World Hypothesis in the 1960s. RNA has the unique ability to act as both genes and enzymes, which make RNA a sensible first biomolecule in the origin of life. A long-standing weakness of the RNA World Hypothesis had been the inability of prebiotic Earth to form the molecule's nucleotides from its basic ingredients.

Recently, however, lab simulations, have demonstrated that pyrimidine nucleotides cytosine and uracil can form a number of plausible prebiotic molecules under early-Earth conditions, an atmosphere that included H_2O, CH_4, NH_3, and H_2, and that the simplest building blocks of sugars, glycolaldehyde and glyceraldehyde, can be derived from the prebiotic molecule HCN. There is no evidence of formation of the other two nucleotides present in RNA, adenine and guanine, but current research is moving in that direction. *In vitro* experiments under primordial conditions have demonstrated the ability to produce RNA molecules that perform a number of functions, including self-replication and the ability to copy other RNA molecules. These capabilities of RNA make it a very promising "first biomolecule" because RNA is the only biomolecule currently known to be capable of replication, catalysis, and containing genes itself, so RNA could have preceded DNA and proteins in evolution because RNA can self-catalyze to make protein, which can then replicate DNA.

The main topic on which both of the viewpoints focus is the:

F. chemical means by which biomolecules self-replicate.
G. chemical means by which gases formed the first biomolecules.
H. process by which gases can synthesize nucleotides.
J. role of proteins and sugars in the origin of life.

The correct answer is G. This is a comparison question, but it is also a general question that you should answer for every Conflicting Viewpoints passage you encounter. This question basically asks you for the main topic of the entire passage, encompassing both of the viewpoints.

Choice F contains the buzzword *biomolecule*, which appears constantly throughout the passage, but it is not correct because the main topic of the passage is not biomolecule self-replication. Choice G correctly states that the main topic of the passage is the chemical means by which gases formed the first biomolecules; even though each viewpoint offers a different take on how the first biomolecules were created, and importantly, which biomolecule came first, both viewpoints deal with the chemical processes by which the gases in the prebiotic atmosphere could have created biomolecule monomers. Choice H specifies that the topic of the passage is the means by which atmospheric gases form nucleotides, but this is really only the main topic of the second viewpoint, for the RNA World Hypothesis; it is unrelated to the first viewpoint. Choice J indicates that the main topic of the passage is the roles played by proteins and sugars in the origin of life. This is perhaps an indirect summary of the first viewpoint, but it is not especially relevant to the second viewpoint. Therefore, the correct answer is choice G.

If you focused too much on the details in the passage, you might have missed the big picture, and the big picture is exactly what this question focused on. You will likely encounter at least one or two big picture questions per Conflicting Viewpoints passage, so be sure you don't miss the big picture in favor of details that ultimately might not be as important.

Mixing Up the Viewpoints

This potential mistake might seem extremely obvious, but it happens more often than you would think. A question accompanying a passage might ask you about one viewpoint and then include a decoy answer that provides a correct response in relation to the other viewpoint. It may seem like an easy mistake to avoid, but under the pressure of a timed exam, it might also be an easy mistake to make. Read and then reread the questions you encounter to make sure you're looking in the right place for your answer, and then choose the appropriate response. Double-checking is really the only safeguard for this potential error, and careful reading throughout any Conflicting Viewpoints questions will help you to avoid it.

The next question illustrates how extremely important it is to read carefully and avoid mixing up the passages. If a question asks about a particular passage, check and double-check to make sure you are choosing the answer from the correct passage, because there will likely be a decoy answer among the choices that provides a correct answer from the wrong passage.

There are numerous theories concerning the origin of life on Earth, focusing on how primitive Earth was able to chemically create biomolecules essential for biological life to arise. Two such ideas are the Theory of Volcanic Origin of Life and the RNA World Hypothesis.

Theory of Volcanic Origin of Life

A widely accepted theory for the origin of life is that lightning and gases from volcanic eruptions may have given rise to the very first life on Earth. The Miller-Urey experiment, performed in 1952, was a chemical experiment that simulated the conditions of primitive Earth. In this experiment, a mixture of gases thought to have been present in the primitive atmosphere (most prominently, H_2O, CH_4, NH_3, and H_2) was stored in a vial connected by a pipe to a heated water tank that simulated the evaporation of the ocean. In that vial, electrodes created a spark, simulating lightning, and reaction products were collected by reliquefying the water vapor. The setup is shown in the illustration.

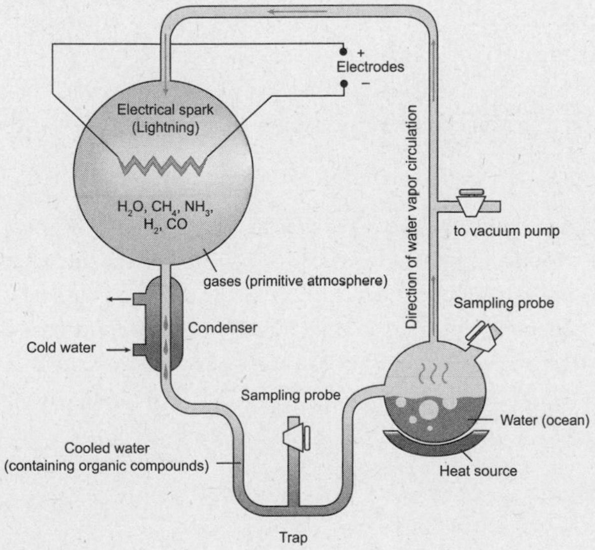

The Miller-Urey experiment showed that simple organic compounds, namely amino acids and various sugars, including ribose, can be produced from the gases in the atmosphere of primitive Earth with the addition of energy.

More recently, scientists performed a similar experiment with CO_2, CO, and N_2, an updated conception of Earth's early atmosphere, and these gases allowed for the production of an even wider array of biomolecules. The addition of volcanic gases like H_2 and CH_4 increased variety and supplied hydrogen, and follow-up experiments have shown that a simple volcanic gas called carbonyl sulfide (COS) helps free-floating amino acids to form peptides, the precursors to proteins, under various conditions, and that metal ions help to intensify this reaction by up to 80 percent. However, since carbonyl sulfide decomposes rather quickly, it is unlikely to be present in large quantities in the atmosphere. Instead, scientists propose that this gas would be most predominant at hydrothermal vents on the seafloor, forming peptide chains that would stick to rocks and continue to lengthen.

RNA World Hypothesis

Francis Crick, among other scientists, first posed the RNA World Hypothesis in the 1960s. RNA has the unique ability to act as both genes and enzymes, which make RNA a sensible first biomolecule in the origin of life. A long-standing weakness of the RNA World Hypothesis had been the inability of prebiotic Earth to form the molecule's nucleotides from its basic ingredients.

Recently, however, lab simulations, have demonstrated that pyrimidine nucleotides cytosine and uracil can form a number of plausible prebiotic molecules under early-Earth conditions, an atmosphere that included H_2O, CH_4, NH_3, and H_2, and that the simplest building blocks of sugars, glycolaldehyde and glyceraldehyde, can be derived from the prebiotic molecule HCN. There is no evidence of formation of the other two nucleotides present in RNA, adenine and guanine, but current research is moving in that direction. *In vitro* experiments under primordial conditions have demonstrated the ability to produce RNA molecules that perform a number of functions, including self-replication and the ability to copy other RNA molecules. These capabilities of RNA make it a very promising "first biomolecule" because RNA is the only biomolecule currently known to be capable of replication, catalysis, and containing genes itself, so RNA could have preceded DNA and proteins in evolution because RNA can self-catalyze to make protein, which can then replicate DNA.

According to the RNA World Hypothesis, the first biopolymer was a:

- **A.** lipid.
- **B.** protein.
- **C.** carbohydrate.
- **D.** nucleic acid.

The correct answer is D. This is a question about details and supporting data from the passage. Previous sample questions have focused on this concept, so the reasoning behind the correct answer shouldn't be a surprise. Choice A is an irrelevant decoy answer. Neither viewpoint refers to lipids, so this is clearly not the correct answer.

You can probably tell choice D is correct simply from the name "RNA World Hypothesis" alone. As the name—and the passage—indicate, the first biopolymer was an RNA molecule. The Theory of Volcanic Origin of Life refers to sugar formation briefly, but its focus is on proteins, which makes choice C incorrect.

However, choice B is the main decoy to watch out for here because if you look at the wrong viewpoint, you might be tempted to choose this answer. The Theory of Volcanic Origin of Life argues in favor of proteins as the first biopolymer, but that theory is not what the question is asking about.

This question demonstrates the importance of keeping the viewpoints straight. Maybe one viewpoint in a set stood out to you because it included a helpful image or diagram, or perhaps one viewpoint in a set was memorable because it was the last one you read. Maybe you just understood one viewpoint better than the other. When it comes to answering a question that refers to a specific viewpoint, you have to make sure you are looking at the right one.

Relying on Key Words in Answer Choices

This potential pitfall may seem a bit tricky at first glance because looking for key words is a common strategy in reading comprehension. Using key words to distinguish between viewpoints, or writing down key words to mark your place while reading passages are perfectly valid strategies, and you should definitely employ them. Where key words can throw you off is in the answer choices for the questions themselves, and this really only becomes an issue if you rely too heavily on key words.

So what exactly does this mean? Let's say you read through a passage that presents three viewpoints about what caused the extinction of dinosaurs, with the three passages attributing the phenomenon to asteroid impact, climate changes, and atmospheric changes. One of the questions might ask you about a detail related to the theory of climate changes. One or more of the decoy answers may relate to asteroid impact or atmospheric changes, so these can be ruled out, but there may be a few answers containing key words related to climate changes. If you simply choose the first answer choice with a climate-related vocabulary word, there are no guarantees that you've chosen the correct answer.

Key vocabulary words can definitely help you to narrow down choices by eliminating incorrect choices related to incorrect passages or by eliminating incorrect choices that are irrelevant to the main topic altogether. However, you have to understand what you're reading, and when several incorrect decoy answers contain key words related to the question stem, you cannot rely solely on these key words. It is important to take notes as you read and understand the viewpoints, rather than choose an answer based solely on key words. Even if you come across an answer that seems correct, make sure you check all of the answers to ensure that there is not a better answer among the rest of the choices.

There are numerous theories concerning the origin of life on Earth, focusing on how primitive Earth was able to chemically create biomolecules essential for biological life to arise. Two such ideas are the Theory of Volcanic Origin of Life and the RNA World Hypothesis.

Theory of Volcanic Origin of Life

A widely accepted theory for the origin of life is that lightning and gases from volcanic eruptions may have given rise to the very first life on Earth. The Miller-Urey experiment, performed in 1952, was a chemical experiment that simulated the conditions of primitive Earth. In this experiment, a mixture of gases thought to have been present in the primitive atmosphere (most prominently, H_2O, CH_4, NH_3, and H_2) was stored in a vial connected by a pipe to a heated water tank that simulated the evaporation of the ocean. In that vial, electrodes created a spark, simulating lightning, and reaction products were collected by reliquefying the water vapor. The setup is shown in the illustration.

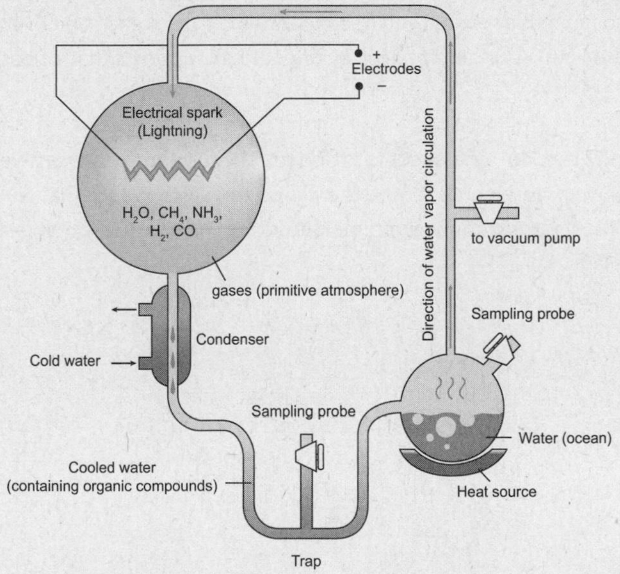

The Miller-Urey experiment showed that simple organic compounds, namely amino acids and various sugars, including ribose, can be produced from the gases in the atmosphere of primitive Earth with the addition of energy.

More recently, scientists performed a similar experiment with CO_2, CO, and N_2, an updated conception of Earth's early atmosphere, and these gases allowed for the production of an even wider array of biomolecules. The addition of volcanic gases like H_2 and CH_4 increased variety and supplied hydrogen, and follow-up experiments have shown that a simple volcanic gas called carbonyl sulfide (COS) helps free-floating amino acids to form peptides, the precursors to proteins, under various conditions, and that metal ions help to intensify this reaction by up to 80 percent. However, since carbonyl sulfide decomposes rather quickly, it is unlikely to be present in large quantities in the atmosphere. Instead, scientists propose that this gas would be most predominant at hydrothermal vents on the seafloor, forming peptide chains that would stick to rocks and continue to lengthen.

RNA World Hypothesis

Francis Crick, among other scientists, first posed the RNA World Hypothesis in the 1960s. RNA has the unique ability to act as both genes and enzymes, which make RNA a sensible first biomolecule in the origin of life. A long-standing weakness of the RNA World Hypothesis had been the inability of prebiotic Earth to form the molecule's nucleotides from its basic ingredients.

Recently, however, lab simulations, have demonstrated that pyrimidine nucleotides cytosine and uracil can form a number of plausible prebiotic molecules under early-Earth conditions, an atmosphere that included H_2O, CH_4, NH_3, and H_2, and that the simplest building blocks of sugars, glycolaldehyde and glyceraldehyde, can be derived from the prebiotic molecule HCN. There is no evidence of formation of the other two nucleotides present in RNA, adenine and guanine, but current research is moving in that direction. *In vitro* experiments under primordial conditions have demonstrated the ability to produce RNA molecules that perform a number of functions, including self-replication and the ability to copy other RNA molecules. These capabilities of RNA make it a very promising "first biomolecule" because RNA is the only biomolecule currently known to be capable of replication, catalysis, and containing genes itself, so RNA could have preceded DNA and proteins in evolution because RNA can self-catalyze to make protein, which can then replicate DNA.

A key piece of evidence from the passage that places the origin of life in the deep sea is:

F. the requirement for metal ions to promote peptide formation.
G. the inability of carbonyl sulfide to tolerate a water-based environment.
H. the derivation of glycolaldehyde and glyceraldehyde from HCN.
J. the instability of carbonyl sulfide in the prebiotic atmosphere.

The correct answer is J. This is a question about details and supporting data from the passage. In particular, this question asks for the evidence that places the physical location for the origin of life at the bottom of the ocean. Since only the Theory of Volcanic Origin of Life refers to deep-sea vents, this question is clearly referring to this viewpoint. If we look through the answers, each answer contains key words that refer back to the passage, but the answers are obviously not all correct.

We can immediately eliminate choice H. This answer contains key words from the passage, but from the wrong passage. The second viewpoint refers to the derivation of glycolaldehyde and glyceraldehyde from HCN, but it is in no way related to the placement of the origin of life in the deep sea. Choice F refers to metal ions, which are discussed in the first viewpoint in the section that describes the deep sea proposal. At first glance, therefore, this might seem like the correct answer based on the key words, but the metal ions are not what caused the proposal for the deep sea location of the origin of life. Choice G contains all of the right key words, particularly "carbonyl sulfide" and the reference to water, but the answer says all of the wrong things. If carbonyl sulfide cannot tolerate a water-based environment, then the origin of life should *not* be pinpointed in the ocean. The correct answer is therefore choice J, which correctly specifies that carbonyl sulfide is not stable and breaks down in the atmosphere, which would be why the origin of life would be more likely to occur in the deep sea.

Failing to Find Support for Your Answers in the Text

At its heart, the analysis of a Conflicting Viewpoint passage is essentially science-based reading comprehension. This means that any answer you choose for a particular question should have some kind of textual support. If an answer choice for a question seems to come out of nowhere and has no textual context based on the passage, it is probably not the correct answer. If you go back and look over all of the examples that have been covered so far in this section, you'll see that this is true of each and every correct answer; you can trace every correct answer back to the passage and find textual evidence that supports that correct answer.

As such, a useful strategy to employ while dealing with Conflicting Viewpoints passages is to find textual support for any answer you've decided on as a correct answer, and if you want to confirm your answer, make sure there is no textual evidence that supports the other answers with respect to the question asked. Think of Conflicting Viewpoints questions like an open-book test, where all of the answers are given to you in some way in the passage.

There are numerous theories concerning the origin of life on Earth, focusing on how primitive Earth was able to chemically create biomolecules essential for biological life to arise. Two such ideas are the Theory of Volcanic Origin of Life and the RNA World Hypothesis.

Theory of Volcanic Origin of Life

A widely accepted theory for the origin of life is that lightning and gases from volcanic eruptions may have given rise to the very first life on Earth. The Miller-Urey experiment, performed in 1952, was a chemical experiment that simulated the conditions of primitive Earth. In this experiment, a mixture of gases thought to have been present in the primitive atmosphere (most prominently, H_2O, CH_4, NH_3, and H_2) was stored in a vial connected by a pipe to a heated water tank that simulated the evaporation of the ocean. In that vial, electrodes created a spark, simulating lightning, and reaction products were collected by reliquefying the water vapor. The setup is shown in the illustration.

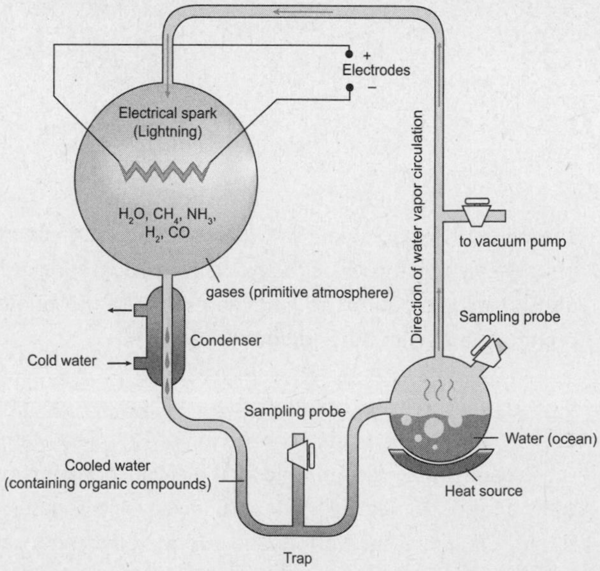

The Miller-Urey experiment showed that simple organic compounds, namely amino acids and various sugars, including ribose, can be produced from the gases in the atmosphere of primitive Earth with the addition of energy.

More recently, scientists performed a similar experiment with CO_2, CO, and N_2, an updated conception of Earth's early atmosphere, and these gases allowed for the production of an even wider array of biomolecules. The addition of volcanic gases like H_2 and CH_4 increased variety and supplied hydrogen, and follow-up experiments have shown that a simple volcanic gas called carbonyl sulfide (COS) helps free-floating amino acids to form peptides, the precursors to proteins, under various conditions, and that metal ions help to intensify this reaction by up to 80 percent. However, since carbonyl sulfide decomposes rather quickly, it is unlikely to be present in large quantities in the atmosphere. Instead, scientists propose that this gas would be most predominant at hydrothermal vents on the seafloor, forming peptide chains that would stick to rocks and continue to lengthen.

RNA World Hypothesis

Francis Crick, among other scientists, first posed the RNA World Hypothesis in the 1960s. RNA has the unique ability to act as both genes and enzymes, which make RNA a sensible first biomolecule in the origin of life. A long-standing weakness of the RNA World Hypothesis had been the inability of prebiotic Earth to form the molecule's nucleotides from its basic ingredients.

Recently, however, lab simulations, have demonstrated that pyrimidine nucleotides cytosine and uracil can form a number of plausible prebiotic molecules under early-Earth conditions, an atmosphere that included H_2O, CH_4, NH_3, and H_2, and that the simplest building blocks of sugars, glycolaldehyde and glyceraldehyde, can be derived from the prebiotic molecule HCN. There is no evidence of formation of the other two nucleotides present in RNA, adenine and guanine but current research is moving in that direction. *In vitro* experiments under primordial conditions have demonstrated the ability to produce RNA molecules that perform a number of functions, including self-replication and the ability to copy other RNA molecules. These capabilities of RNA make it a very promising "first biomolecule" because RNA is the only biomolecule currently known to be capable of replication, catalysis, and containing genes itself, so RNA could have preceded DNA and proteins in evolution because RNA can self-catalyze to make protein, which can then replicate DNA.

Both viewpoints indicate that prebiotic conditions were capable of:

A. converting atmospheric gases into organic amino acids.

B. using carbonyl sulfide as a means of peptide formation.

C. synthesizing lipids from molecules found in the atmosphere and deep sea.

D. forming sugars and sugar precursors from available chemical compounds.

The correct answer is D. This is a comparison question that asks you to find a similarity between the two viewpoints. To answer this question, we can look for textual support from each answer choice in the passage. Choice A indicates that both viewpoints believe that the atmospheric gases were capable of amino acid formation. There is only textual evidence for this in the first viewpoint, but there is no evidence of the sort in the second viewpoint, so this answer is incorrect. Choice B indicates that the passages agree that carbonyl sulfide was likely used for peptide formation. Again, there is only textual evidence for this in the first viewpoint, but there is no evidence for this at all in the second passage. There is no textual evidence anywhere in either viewpoint to support the concept of lipid synthesis, so choice C is incorrect. Choice D indicates that both viewpoints suggest that sugars and sugar precursors could be formed from the available chemical compounds on prebiotic Earth. The first viewpoint states that various sugars can be produced from the gases in the atmosphere of primitive Earth, while the second viewpoint states that the prebiotic molecule HCN is capable of forming glycolaldehyde and glyceraldehyde, which are sugar precursors. There is textual evidence to support this answer for both passages, so it is correct.

Turn to page 565 to follow the College Readiness Benchmark Learning Path questions covering Conflicting Viewpoints.

SUMMING IT UP

- **Conflicting Viewpoints passages provide two (or sometimes three) arguments** that put forth a hypothesis or theory, along with supporting evidence, that are related to a particular common topic.
- **Follow these steps when you encounter a Conflicting Viewpoints passage on the ACT Science test:**
  1) Identify the topic.
  2) Identify the basic hypotheses or theories of the scientists.
  3) Identify the relevant data used to support each of the two viewpoints discussed in the passage.
- **Reading comprehension is all about understanding what you read.** The vast majority of information you'll need to answer questions about Conflicting Viewpoints passages can be found in the passages themselves.
- **Look for commonalities.** There will always be some kind of parallel you can draw, and one of the questions accompanying the passage will draw attention to one of those parallels.
- **Take notes in the margin as you read Conflicting Viewpoints passages.** Doing so will help you to identify the shared topic, viewpoint presented by each author, and supporting data presented in favor of each viewpoint.
- **The ACT Science test is made up entirely of multiple-choice questions.** Use this to your advantage by looking at the answers if you aren't sure about what the question is asking so you can determine it from the viewpoints.
- **Conflicting Viewpoints questions require you to fully understand the ins and outs of each viewpoint.** Understanding the information completely will help you to figure out how new data could support or refute it.
- **When reading through a passage for the first time, identify three components:**
  1) The main topic of the passage
  2) The theories described by each viewpoint
  3) Any data that will help you to cut out the extraneous information
- **Read and reread questions to make sure you're looking in the right passage for your answer.**
- **Take notes as you read to understand the viewpoints presented**. Don't just choose an answer based solely on its inclusion of key words, which is a common trap.

ONLINE PREP

Want to Know More?

Access more practice questions, lessons, helpful hints, and strategies for the following science topics in *Peterson's Online Course for the ACT® Exam*:

- Conflicting Viewpoints
- Hard Science Reasoning Questions
- Time Emergency: Science Test

To purchase and access the course, go to **www.petersons.com/testprep/act**.

Directions: The passages in this practice question set are followed by several questions. Read each passage carefully and choose the best answer to each related question. As you go through the practice set, review each solution and follow the expanded explanations provided to help strengthen your skills in working with Conflicting Viewpoints items.

PASSAGE I

Light emitting diodes (LEDs) are devices that generate light when current is passed through them. There are two main types of LEDs, categorized by the layer of material that generates light. For **inorganic semiconductor-based LEDs** (I-LEDs), the light-emitting layer is built from inorganic (metal-atom containing) films. For **organic-based LEDs** (O-LEDs), the light-emitting layer is made from organic (carbon-based) molecules. Two competing researchers that make LEDs argue the merits of their LED products.

Researcher 1

LEDs are a vast improvement on conventional incandescent and fluorescent lighting. They use far less energy, last longer, and are smaller, making them an efficient way to make traffic lights and exit signs, and light homes and computer and television screens. While the first LEDs were limited to low-intensity red lights, modern LEDs of very high brightness can be found in any color of the visible light spectrum, and can even be made for ultraviolet and infrared wavelengths. Inorganic LEDs are made from cheap metal semiconductors like Gallium phosphide (GaP), Indium gallium nitride (InGaN), aluminum gallium arsenide (AlGaAs), aluminum gallium indium phosphide (AlGaInP), and they avoid the toxic mercury that is used in fluorescent bulbs. Since I-LEDs can be cycled on and off many times, they last 5–40 times longer than incandescent or fluorescent light bulbs. The semiconductor films in I-LEDs are robust and last a long time. Organic LEDs degrade much more quickly, which takes away from a key advantage of LEDs. In particular, blue color OLEDs have shorter lifetimes than corresponding green and red ones, so the color balance of a display will change over time. I-LEDs can operate stably, making bright and focused beams under conditions where O-LEDs start to break down. In addition, O-LEDs are more expensive to make, and haven't been available for purchase long enough to undergo all the testing that I-LEDs have had. I-LEDs will continue to dominate the market for many years to come.

Researcher 2

LEDs have revolutionized the way we light up our electronics, drastically improving energy efficiency. Organic-based LEDs offer the next major advance for building efficient, inexpensive, and scalable lighting for all our needs in the digital age. I-LEDs must be made by depositing potentially-toxic metals on expensive crystal wafers at high temperatures. In contrast, O-LED films can be made much thinner and lighter than I-LEDs, and can simply be printed onto very thin sheets with modern printers. They can be deposited onto glass or plastic—even printed onto rolls of flexible polymers to generate bendable displays. O-LEDs are superior for making displays such as TV and computer screens. While I-LEDs can be made very small, they are not small enough to be used as single pixels – so to make an ILED screen, a liquid crystal display is used in front of the LED back light to selectively dim individual pixel areas. OLEDs can be made small enough that they can be used as individual pixels in a screen—this allows them to turn on and off exactly when and where they are needed, resulting in darker blacks and higher contrast with bright colors. Imagine having a TV or computer monitor that you can roll up and carry around in a backpack, without worrying about cracking it! While O-LEDs are currently more expensive to make, their components and fabrication methods are cheaper, and in the future can be scaled to high yield and throughput, bringing down the cost. O-LEDs will soon become the dominant LEDs on the market.

1. LEDs are referred to as I-LEDs or O-LEDs based on which characteristic?

A. The color of light that they generate

B. The material used in the light-emitting layer

C. The amount of energy that they consume

D. The surface on which they are deposited

The correct answer is B. This is a simple reading comprehension question. LEDs and the two types of LEDs (I-LEDs and O-LEDs) are defined in the first paragraph before the statements of the two Researchers. LEDs are "categorized by the layer of material that generates light." The "I" stands for "inorganic" (inorganic semiconductor film), and the "O" stands for "organic." It's important to remember that while there are quite a few technical words in this passage (semiconductor, diode, polymer), you don't actually have to know any of their definitions in order to answer the questions. Of course, it doesn't hurt if you know what they mean, but it's more important to understand the context in which they are used, and not get distracted by them. Choice A is incorrect because both I-LEDs and O-LEDs can be made to produce light in a wide range of colors. Choice C is incorrect because while LEDs in general consume less energy than fluorescent or incandescent lights, nothing in the passage suggests that I-LEDs and O-LEDs consume different amounts of energy. Choice D might seem correct because I-LEDs must be deposited on crystal wafers while O-LEDs can be deposited on glass or thin polymer films, but it is not the defining characteristic for how they function.

2. Based on the information in this passage, what are two advantages O-LEDs currently have over I-LEDs?

F. Flexibility and size

G. Size and cost

H. Cost and durability

J. Durability and flexibility

The correct answer is F. This question asks you to interpret the information in this passage. In the four choices, there are four characteristics (flexibility, size, cost, and durability), two of which must be advantages that O-LEDs *currently* have. You can either read through the passages to see which ones are an advantage (Researcher 2 favors O-LEDs, so the advantages are most likely to be listed in those arguments) or find those which are disadvantages (Researcher 1 favors I-LEDs, so will most likely list the disadvantages of O-LEDs) and rule out those options. Make sure to read all the words in the question: there are mentions in the text of *future* advantages that O-LEDs might have. For example, Researcher 1 states that O-LEDs are "more expensive to make," and Researcher 2 agrees that "O-LEDs are currently more expensive" but that they might be cheaper in the *future*. Cost is a disadvantage, so you can eliminate choices G and H. Researcher 1 also states that "O-LEDs degrade more quickly," and Researcher 2 says nothing to refute this claim. Therefore, durability is not an advantage, so you can rule out choices H and J. That leaves option F. To confirm choice F: Researcher 2 states that I-LEDs "must be printed on crystal wafers" but O-LEDs "can be printed on flexible polymers to make bendable displays." Researcher 1 says nothing to refute this, so flexibility is an advantage of O-LEDs. Researcher 2 also says that O-LEDs can be made small enough to act as single pixels, while I-LEDs cannot, and Researcher 1 says nothing to refute this claim. Size and flexibility are the two advantages.

3. Which of the following is an argument made by Researcher 2 and NOT Researcher 1?

A. O-LEDs are more expensive to make than I-LEDs.

B. I-LEDs have been around longer than O-LEDs.

C. O-LEDs are more durable when operated at high brightness.

D. I-LEDs cannot be made as small as O-LEDs.

The correct answer is D. This question asks you to differentiate between the arguments of the two researchers, and correctly identify the ones that are associated with Researcher 2. From a quick read of the passage, you should be able to identify the main viewpoints—Researcher 1 is in favor of I-LEDs and Researcher 2 is in favor of O-LEDs. If you look through the answer choices, choices C and D appear to be advantages of O-LEDs (so are more likely to be made by Researcher 2), while choices A and B are disadvantages of O-LEDs. In fact, a closer reading of the text shows that *both* researchers admit that O-LEDs are more expensive (it is a stronger argument for Researcher 1), eliminating choice A. Choice B is stated by Researcher 1 ("O-LEDs haven't been available as long"), and alluded to by Researcher 2 ("O-LEDs are the next major advance"), which also eliminates choice B. As a next step you can look back through the paragraph of Researcher 2's argument. It states that "I-LEDs… are not small enough to use as individual pixels," while O-LEDs *are* small enough (choice D). There is nothing about durability at high brightness, so you can eliminate choice C. To be more confident that choice D is correct, you can read carefully through Researcher 1's paragraph. Researcher 1 does talk about durability at high brightness but asserts that O-LEDs are *not* durable at high brightness (choice C is untrue in addition to being an incorrect choice). Researcher 1 does not make any statements about the size of I-LEDs or O-LEDs, again confirming that choice D is the correct answer.

4. Which statement is most likely to be made by Researcher 1?

F. Incandescent bulbs produce more natural-looking light than LEDs.

G. The longest lasting automotive headlights are those made with I-LEDs.

H. Both I-LEDs and fluorescent light bulbs contain toxic metal elements.

J. The smartphone screens with the highest resolution are made with O-LEDs.

The correct answer is G. For this question you need to understand Researcher 1's viewpoint and be able to extend that viewpoint as well. None of the choices were directly stated by either researcher, but one of them will be a logical extension based on their arguments. Researcher 1 states that I-LEDs last longer than other types of lighting and that I-LEDs are more stable than O-LEDs in applications with bright, focused beams, such as those needed in a car's headlight. That is consistent with the statement "the longest lasting automotive headlights are those made with I-LEDs" (choice G). Choice F is incorrect because neither researcher talks about advantages of incandescent bulbs, and Researcher 1 states that LEDs can be made in any color. Choices H and J are extensions of the arguments made by Researcher 2 (and choice H is partially false, since some I-LED films contain only nontoxic elements), so it's important to focus on the correct viewpoint (Researcher 1) when answering this question.

5. Which of the following statements is something that both Researchers would agree on?

A. I-LEDs have more practical applications than O-LEDs.

B. O-LEDs will one day be cheaper than I-LEDs.

C. LEDs have been developed to their fullest capabilities.

D. LEDs are an improvement over fluorescent and incandescent lighting.

The correct answer is D. This question asks you to find a similarity between the viewpoints. In this case, choice D can be found as a point of agreement in the first statements made by both researchers "LEDs are a vast improvement on conventional incandescent and fluorescent lighting" (Researcher 1) and "LEDs have revolutionized the way we light up our electronics, drastically improving energy efficiency" (Researcher 2). Choices A and B favor one type of LED over the other, making it unlikely that those choices contain a point of agreement. Researcher 2 mentions a number of practical applications for O-LEDs, and so would disagree with choice A. Choice B is directly in line with statements made by Researcher 2, but is not consistent by any statement from Researcher 1. Choices C and D are general to LEDs. However, choice C is not a logical extension of either researcher's statements, and is in direct contradiction with Researcher 2, who alludes to future developments "Imagine having a TV or computer monitor that you can roll up…" and that O-LEDs "in the future can be scaled to high yield and throughput."

PASSAGE II

The enzyme lactase makes it possible for baby mammals, including human babies, to digest the sugar lactose in their mothers' milk. However, as mammals mature, they lose the ability to produce the enzyme. As a consequence, most humans lose their ability to digest lactose after weaning, resulting in lactose intolerance. If these adults consume dairy products, they can show symptoms such as abdominal pain, bloating, and nausea. However, some individuals have genetic mutations that confer lactase persistence, and produce the enzyme throughout their lives. Figure II-1 shows the incidence of lactase persistence in Africa and Eurasia.

Figure II-1. Incidence of lactase persistence in Africa and Eurasia.

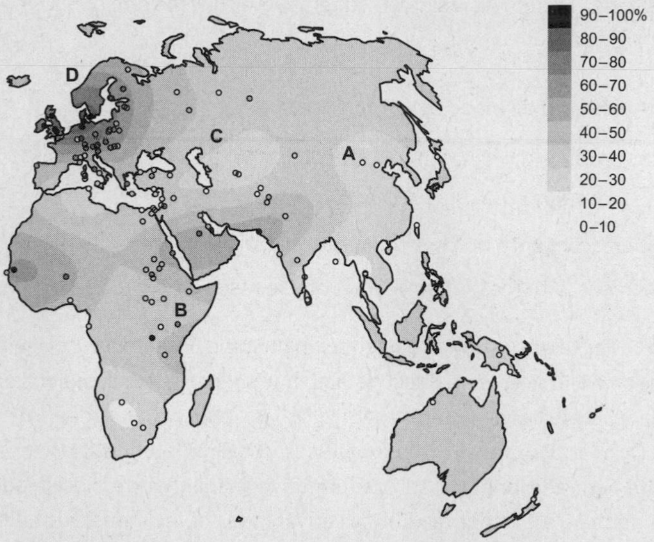

From https://bmcevolbiol.biomedcentral.com/articles/10.1186/1471-2148-10-36

Scientist 1

Humans began domesticating cattle and other milk-producing animals many thousands of years ago. Milk from these animals provided herders with a year-round source of fat, protein, nutrients, and a source of clean hydration, but with unpleasant gastric side effects among adults. This gave a strong evolutionary advantage to individuals with genes for lactase persistence. Those individuals could enjoy the health benefits of milk products without the side effects, and therefore produce more children. Their children who carried the same genes would be more likely to survive into reproductive adulthood. Once a mutation for lactase persistence emerged, it would have quickly spread through nearby populations that practice dairying (consuming milk and producing milk products). For example, the mutation for lactase persistence that is prevalent in Kenya (location B in Figure II-1) is estimated to be 4,000 years old and coincides with the timing of pastoralist migrations from northern Africa. Scientists who have performed genetic analysis on individuals from various countries have found that different mutations for lactase persistence emerged in separate populations of herders throughout the world. This is known as **convergent evolution** and shows how strongly evolutionary pressure favors lactase persistence in herding communities. Today, the percentage of people with lactase persistence in a given area is related to the historical ability to maintain dairy herds. While 65% of adults are lactose intolerant on average, this varies from less than 10% lactose intolerance in northern Europe, to greater than 90% lactose intolerance in some parts of Asia and Africa.

Scientist 2

The emergence of the dairying culture thousands of years ago was a critical step for humans. It provided a rich and reliable source of nutrition and hydration without requiring the slaughter of herd animals. However, since the ability to digest lactose is typically limited to children, adults would have been unable to take advantage of milk without suffering painful side effects. Lactase persistence would be advantageous to select individuals with the appropriate genes, but human ingenuity provided an alternative that could benefit everyone in the herding community—harnessing the ability of microbes. During fermentation, bacteria break down lactose into components that are easier for adult humans to digest. By fermenting milk to produce yogurt, cheese, and a host of other products, people in the dairying culture could produce energy-rich foods with low lactose content. This discovery would have occurred soon after the occurrence of dairying. Researchers have found fragments from 7,000-year-old cheese strainers, which is 2,000 years before the first evidence of lactase persistence. Using chemical techniques to analyze the fragments, they found the characteristic fatty acids and proteins that are present in milk. In modern Mongolia (location A in Figure II-1), traditional herders milk seven kinds of mammals and get up to a third of their yearly calories from milk products including yogurt, cheese, and fermented milk. Clearly, lactase persistence is not essential for humans to benefit from dairying, nor can herding by itself explain the occurrence of lactase persistence.

6. Lactase is a type of

F. fat.

G. sugar.

H. enzyme.

J. bacteria.

The correct answer is H. This is purely a reading comprehension question, and the answer can be found in the first sentence, "The enzyme lactase…". What makes this question potentially tricky is the similarity between two important and related terms in this passage: *lactase*—with an *a*—the enzyme that breaks down milk sugar (choice H), and *lactose*—with an *o*—the sugar found in milk (choice G). The other choices are also terms that are found in the passage. Milk collected by herders provides an important source of dietary fat (choice F). Bacteria (choice J) can break down lactose during fermentation in the production of cheese and yogurt.

7. Based on the map in Figure II-1, which of the following countries is expected to have the highest percentage of people with lactase persistence?

A. Mongolia (location A)

B. Kenya (location B)

C. Kazakhstan (location C)

D. Norway (location D)

The correct answer is D. This question asks you to interpret data presented in a figure. The legend in Figure II-1 shows that darker regions on the map correspond to higher percentages of people with lactase persistence. Of the four marked countries, Norway is colored the darkest—the colors correspond to 50–80% lactase persistence. Scientist 1 also states that the many northern European countries (which include Norway) have low incidences of lactose intolerance, which corresponds to high lactase persistence (many adults continue to make lactase and can digest lactose). All the other regions correspond to lighter colors (and lower lactase persistence). Mongolia (choice A) is specifically referred to by Scientist 2 as having a low incidence of lactase persistence. Kenya (choice B) is mentioned by Scientist 1 as having individuals with lactase persistence, but according to the map, the percentage of those people is lower than in Norway.

8. Which is the main point of disagreement between the two scientists?

F. Whether lactose can be broken down by bacteria

G. Whether lactase persistence is advantageous to people in herding cultures

H. Whether lactose can be digested by children

J. Whether lactase persistence will always occur in herding cultures

The correct answer is J. To answer this question, you must understand the main arguments of both scientists and pick out the aspect in which they differ. Scientist 1 argues that there is a very strong evolutionary pressure for people in herding cultures to have lactase persistence, and populations that have been herding for a long time are very likely to have a high percentage of individuals with the genes for lactase persistence. Scientist 2 argues that humans have multiple ways of making milk products digestible (either lactase persistence or use of bacteria to break down lactose through fermentation) and so lactase persistence does not have to occur in order for herding culture to persist, and may occur for different reasons. Scientist 1 is in favor of the statement in choice J, while Scientist 2 is against it. Therefore, choice J is correct. Choice F is a key component of Scientist 2's argument, but it does not contradict anything said by Scientist 1 (and Scientist 1 does not mention it). Choice G is the main component of Scientist 1's argument, but Scientist 2 also admits it to be true. Choice H is a fact stated in the text and neither scientist argues against it.

9. Archaeology is the study of human activity through the analysis of artifacts, such as tools, pottery, clothing, and jewelry. Which scientist uses archaeological evidence to support their argument?

A. Scientist 1

B. Scientist 2

C. Both

D. Neither

The correct answer is . This question asks you to understand the different types of evidence the scientists use in their arguments. Scientist 2 mentions a 7,000-year-old cheese strainer (pottery, which could also be considered a tool) on which milk proteins have been discovered—that is a type of archaeological evidence, which eliminates choices A and D. Scientist 1 says that the gene for lactase in Kenya is 4,000 years old and aligns with historical migrations but does not cite any material evidence in that argument, eliminating option C.

10. Recently, scientists analyzing 3,000-year-old remains in Mongolia found milk proteins on the teeth. DNA analysis on the same teeth showed that those individuals lacked the ability to produce lactase, and that they are genetically related to modern Mongolians. Which viewpoint does this new evidence support?

F. Scientist 1

G. Scientist 2

H. Both

J. Neither

The correct answer is G. This question provides additional information and asks you how it fits in with the existing arguments. This information is about people who lived in Mongolia, which is most directly related to the viewpoint of Scientist 2 (who specifically refers to Mongolians). Next, it's important to check whether this new data *supports or refutes* the arguments made by Scientist 2. Scientist 2 argues that lactase persistence is not required in order for humans to consume milk products, as long as they use another means to reduce the amount of lactose (fermentation). The new evidence supports the idea that Mongolians have been practicing herding and dairying for a long time, and the fact that neither ancient nor modern Mongolians have lactase persistence supports Scientist 2's arguments that lactase persistence is not an inevitable result of herding. That eliminates choices F and J. Scientist 1 states that "The length of time that a group of people has been herding and dairying… is directly related to the incidence of lactose tolerance," which is the opposite of the new evidence. That eliminates choice H and makes choice G the correct answer.

PRACTICE

You now know the ins and outs of Conflicting Viewpoints questions, so it's time to try a full practice set on your own. When you're finished answering all 20 questions, check the answers that follow to read full explanations of all answer choices.

PASSAGE I

There are a number of theories that have been proposed to explain how the moon was formed. Two of those theories are the Fission Theory and the Giant Impact Theory.

Fission Theory

Many scientists support the Fission Theory of moon formation, which indicates that the moon was spun off from Earth when early Earth was rapidly rotating on its axis. This theory was first proposed by George Darwin in the 1800s. The piece of Earth that separated to form the moon may be from the Pacific Ocean basin. Key evidence that supports Fission Theory is the common composition between Earth's mantle and the moon. Siderophile ("metal-loving") elements, including molybdenum and rhenium, occur in both Earth's mantle and on the moon, though their concentrations in lunar rocks are significantly lower than concentrations found in Earth's mantle. Furthermore, the densities of moon rocks are very similar to those of Earth rocks found just below the crust. Additionally, the core of the moon is largely composed of metallic iron, alloyed with a small amount of sulfur and nickel. A 2010 study of seismic data on deep moonquakes confirmed that the outer core of the moon is iron-rich, and that the solid inner core is made of pure iron. The figure below shows the layers of the moon:

The analysis of the composition of the moon's core is relevant to Fission Theory because it is again very similar to that of Earth, though far smaller in radius. Earth would have to have been spinning extremely rapidly for the mode of moon formation proposed by Fission Theory to be true, but there is currently no evidence to suggest that this was the case.

Giant Impact Theory

The Giant Impact Theory is perhaps the most widely accepted theory for moon formation. According to this theory, an indirect collision between Earth and an astronomical body the size of Mars, called Theia, occurred 4.5 billion years ago; rock aging techniques indicated that Earth and the moon are approximately this same age. In consequence, the impact blasted pieces of Earth and Theia into Earth's orbit. Over time, the debris from the impact then eventually came together to form the mass that is the moon. Moon rocks have exhibited signs of having been molten at some point in the ancient past, which is atypical of Earth rocks, indicating that the moon was formed under very hot conditions. Additionally, Earth has a tilt and ecliptic plane orientation that differs from most other planets in the solar system, a possibly permanent effect of the collision of Earth with a Mars-sized mass. Furthermore, a similar collision was recently observed in 1994 between the gas giant Jupiter and the Shoemaker-Levy comet; despite the small size of the comet, the comet's collision with Jupiter resulted in its breakdown into a number of fragments. Finally, the stable isotope ratios of rocks from Earth and the moon were found to be identical, implying a common origin. These data support the theory that the moon formed as a result of Earth's impact with another sizeable astronomical body, Theia.

1. According to the first viewpoint, how does siderophile composition compare between Earth and the moon?
   - **A.** Earth and the moon contain the same kinds and concentrations of siderophiles.
   - **B.** Earth and the moon contain the same kinds of siderophiles, but the siderophiles are not present in the same concentrations in each.
   - **C.** Earth and the moon contain different kinds of siderophiles, but the concentrations of the siderophiles are very similar.
   - **D.** Earth and the moon contain different kinds of siderophiles that are present in very different concentrations.

2. Which piece of data from the passage indicates that the moon formed under extremely hot conditions?

F. The average temperature of the moon's atmosphere is significantly higher than the average temperature of Earth's atmosphere.
G. Earth has a tilt and ecliptic plane orientation inconsistent with most other planets in the solar system.
H. Siderophiles are present on both Earth and the moon.
J. Moon rocks were found to have been liquefied during the development of the young moon.

3. The moon does not have an overall magnetic field like Earth, but scientists decided to study the magnetic properties of its surface rocks. Which piece of evidence would most support both of the described theories for moon formation?

A. The moon surface rocks show signs of having had a magnetic field early in the moon's history.
B. The moon surface rocks likely had no magnetic field early on, but they have since developed that property.
C. The moon surface rocks proved to be capable of conducting electricity under standard atmospheric conditions.
D. There is no indication that there was ever any magnetic field in the histories of the moon surface rocks.

4. Scientists decided to look at oxygen isotopes because planets and moons have a distinct oxygen fingerprint that indicates the exact environmental conditions in which they were formed. They find that some of the moon rocks contain a slightly *higher* amount (12 ppm more) of the rare isotope oxygen-17 than Earth rocks do. If this difference is considered to be significant, this piece of data would most support:

F. the Fission Theory of moon formation.
G. the Giant Impact Theory of moon formation.
H. both the Fission Theory and the Giant Impact Theory of moon formation.
J. neither the Fission Theory nor the Giant Impact Theory of moon formation.

5. An additional theory of moon formation, the Capture Theory, proposes that the moon was formed somewhere else in the solar system and was later captured by the gravitational field of Earth. Which piece of data from the passage best supports the Fission Theory and Giant Impact Theory and refutes the Capture Theory?

A. Rock aging data indicates that the rocks from Earth and the moon are approximately the same age of 4.5 billion years.
B. The moon has a solid inner core, but its outer core is fluid.
C. The moon's crust is thinner on the side nearest Earth.
D. The Shoemaker-Levy comet fragmented upon collision with Jupiter.

6. With which statement would supporters of the Fission Theory be most likely to agree?

F. The Pacific Ocean basin was created by the impact of an astronomical body.
G. Moon rocks should have formed more recently than Earth rocks.
H. Early Earth was very stable and compact.
J. Moon rocks and Earth rocks should be very similar to one another in terms of their composition.

7. The Giant Impact Theory most deviates from the Fission Theory because it involves:

A. superheating of moon rocks during early development.
B. the existence of an iron core in the moon.
C. the interaction of Earth with another massive object.
D. pieces of Earth contributing to the formation of the moon.

PASSAGE II

Two students became involved in a debate of nature versus nurture, arguing whether human behavior is influenced more by one's genes or by one's upbringing. The students focus on academic success, the ability to do well in school. Each student did some research and wrote a brief argument in favor of either nature or nurture as the predominant force in academic success.

Student 1

One's genes are far more important for academic success than one's upbringing. A study compared identical twins and non-identical twins in their 20s, a reflection on the effect of genetics versus environment because identical twins share 100% of their genes, while non-identical twins share only 50% of their genes. The study found that identical twins performed similarly in tests of English, science, and math, but showed more variation in personality, behavior and health, indicating that genes are more closely linked with academic performance.

In addition, there are a number of single-gene genetic disorders, including dyslexia, and neural disorders, like autism and Down syndrome, that affect cognitive ability, which demonstrates another effect of genes on academic performance. Also, researchers have recently found that genetic variation affects expression of the *NPTN* gene, which encodes an NPTN protein that affects how brain cells communicate and results in a thinner brain cortex in the left cerebral hemisphere. Teenagers with this gene also performed worse on intelligence tests. Similar effects were seen for the same gene in mice. However, this gene only seems to affect 0.5% of total variation in intelligence.

Student 2

A person's environmental upbringing is more important for his or her academic success than genetics. A recent study, based on a pool of over 100,000 people, picked out 69 gene variants linked to educational achievement and cross-checked the list with gene variants found to be related to higher IQ based on cognitive tests taken by 24,000 people. Three gene variants were found to be linked to both educational achievement and high IQ. However, the researchers calculated that each variant contributed to an average of 0.3 points on an IQ test, in which two-thirds of the population normally scores between 85 and 115. This means that a person with all three variants would only score 1.8 points higher on an intelligence test than a person with none of them, which is hardly any effect at all. Furthermore, there are a dozen different single-nucleotide polymorphisms (SNPs) in DNA that correlate with IQ scores in certain humans, but with a statistically significant sample size, none are really linked to intelligence.

Genes aside, however, there are many environmental influences that can affect intelligence and academic performance. Nutrition, stress, and exposure to violence have all been associated with lower school grades and lower IQs. Even a child's position in birth order was found to influence intelligence, with firstborn children generally scoring higher, though these studies did not control for age or family size. Access to education and socioeconomic status can also influence one's performance in school.

8. Based on Student 1's viewpoint, increased expression of the *NPTN* gene would result in:

- **F.** lower levels of *NPTN* protein.
- **G.** a thicker brain cortex in the left cerebral hemisphere.
- **H.** a decreased effect of stress on academic performance.
- **J.** lower scores on intelligence tests.

9. Based on Student 2's viewpoint, which of the following factors would have the most significant negative impact on a teenager's academic performance?

- **A.** Readily available educational resources
- **B.** The expression of the *NPTN* gene
- **C.** A demanding and stressful part-time job
- **D.** The presence of SNPs in the teenager's DNA

10. Students 1 and 2 might agree that:

- **F.** individual genes will not have a significant effect on intelligence across a population.
- **G.** genetic and neural disorders have no effect on academic performance.
- **H.** a child's home life will be the most important determinant of academic success.
- **J.** the effect of hormones outweighs the effects of genes or environment in a student's academic success.

11. A common strategy used by both students to support their arguments is:

- **A.** surveying small samples of people for information on environmental backgrounds.
- **B.** focusing on twin studies in their approaches.
- **C.** finding genetic studies that support their respective views.
- **D.** connecting brain and neuronal development to the academic success of individuals.

12. What is a major weakness of Student 1's argument compared to Student 2's argument?

- **F.** Student 1 fails to focus on environmental effects, while Student 2 uses both environmental and genetic evidence.
- **G.** Student 1 fails to focus on genetic effects, while Student 2 uses both environmental and genetic evidence.
- **H.** Student 1 uses a wide variety of genetic evidence to support his viewpoint.
- **J.** Student 1 uses a wide variety of environmental evidence to support his viewpoint.

13. A new study finds that the presence of a particular gene product significantly decreases one's IQ and intelligence test scores. This result would support the viewpoint of:

A. Student 1.
B. Student 2.
C. both Student 1 and Student 2.
D. neither Student 1 nor Student 2.

14. The twin study described by Student 1 provides strong support for his argument, assuming that:

F. all of the twins express the *NPTN* protein.
G. none of the twins express the *NPTN* protein.
H. their genomes have been fully sequenced.
J. the twins were brought up in similar environments.

PASSAGE III

Two students were interested in investigating the pros and cons of acquiring and burning fossil fuels as an energy source. Fossil fuels are hydrocarbons, mostly oil, coal and natural gas, that form from the remains of decomposed organic matter. The students did some research to support their conflicting views on using fossil fuels as an energy source, and they presented their results here.

Student 1

Burning fossil fuels may be an effective and safe means for acquiring energy at this point, but it will not remain that way for long. Fossil fuels will become increasingly expensive to extract as they become scarcer on the planet. It will also become more dangerous to acquire fuel, as mines must go deeper into the earth, and oil rigs must travel further out to sea. In addition, burning fossil fuels also has negative environmental effects. Pollution from burning fossil fuels contributes to global warming and acid rain, and the means of fuel acquisition increases the risk of oil spillage. Fossil fuels contain high amounts of carbon, and burning these fuels leads to the release of high levels of CO_2 and greenhouse gases that cause damage to the ozone layer. The graph below shows global fossil carbon emissions over the last 200 years.

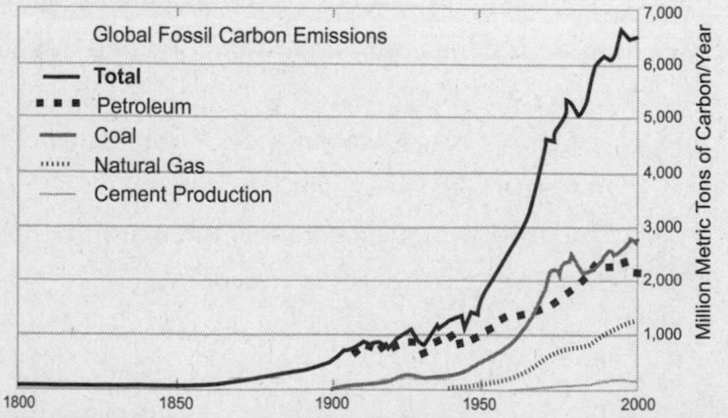

Controlling this pollution requires additional expense, and fuel prices will rise accordingly. Additionally, continued fossil fuel usage is unsustainable and nonrenewable. There are a limited amount of fossil fuels available that could take millions of years to naturally replenish.

Therefore, it is important to look into alternative energy sources, including solar, wind, wave, and water (hydro) power, all of which are renewable and sustainable. Alternative energy sources provide environmental benefits due to low or zero carbon emission, they are sustainable, and they also provide a stable and cost-effective energy supply that could decrease the country's reliance on international supply.

Student 2

It is relatively cheap to burn fossil fuels, and the process is an extremely effective way to acquire energy. Advanced technologies have been developed to ensure safe extraction, at least given the current extraction techniques, and plenty of technology has already been developed for the extraction process, including petrol-driven engines. Fossil fuels are also easily transported and can readily be converted to liquid, solid, or gas forms. Though it is costly, the means of controlling fuel-derived pollution exists, but the fuels also provide a source of income because fuel sales can improve the country's economy. The fossil fuel industry is a stable source of employment too.

There are currently no other energy sources that can replace fossil fuels completely and safely. Fossil fuel usage makes up the majority of US energy acquisition, as the 2011 US energy breakdown below shows.

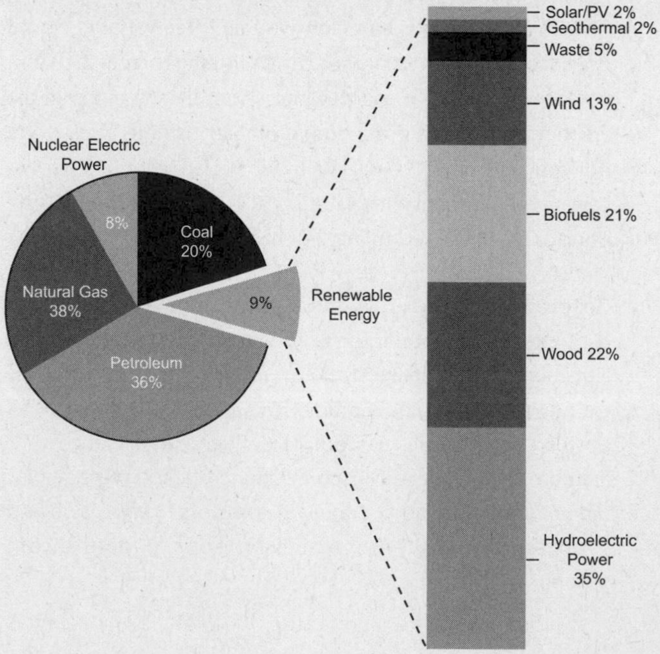

Alternative energy sources tend to be inefficient, and they do not currently have the capability of meeting the required energy demands. Therefore, it does not make sense to try to replace an energy source that is clearly such a significant source of energy in the country.

15. With which of the following statements would Student 1 disagree?

A. The use of fossil fuels is an efficient means of energy acquisition.
B. Alternative energy sources provide a way to decrease carbon emissions into the atmosphere.
C. Fossil fuel usage has increased dramatically over the last few centuries.
D. Fossil fuel renewal is timely enough to ensure resource sustainability.

16. Which of the following statements best summarizes Student 2's view on alternative energy sources?

F. Alternative energy sources currently comprise the majority of the US's energy supply.
G. Alternative energy sources are more costly but more efficient than fossil fuel usage.
H. It will be difficult for alternative energy sources to provide sufficient energy for what is required by the US currently.
J. The burning of fossil fuels is a major contributor to acid rain, global warming, and oil spills.

17. The resource sustainability of fossil fuels is a concern posed by:

A. Student 1.
B. Student 2.
C. both students.
D. neither student.

18. Students 1 and 2 would agree that:

F. the United States should continue to rely on fossil fuels because additional natural energy sources will always be found.
G. fossil fuels are currently the most efficient source of energy in the United States.
H. carbon emissions are not a major concern in the 21st century.
J. alternative energy sources are sufficient and sustainable enough to replace fossil fuels in the near future.

19. Concern for the economy is expressed specifically by:

A. Student 1.
B. Student 2.
C. both students.
D. neither student.

20. Which of the following hypothetical new technologies would best satisfy the main concern of Student 2 regarding the use of fossil fuels and alternative energy sources?

F. The development of a process to efficiently absorb and use carbon byproducts from fossil fuel burning
G. The creation of a new mode of transport for fossil fuels
H. The discovery of a new, highly efficient natural alternative energy source
J. Increased safety features with regard to fossil fuel technology

Answers and Explanations

The first passage is an earth sciences/astronomy passage that provides two theories for how Earth's moon was formed.

1. **The correct answer is B.** This question is a detail question that asks you to use the first viewpoint to compare the siderophile concentration between Earth and the moon. The first viewpoint indicates that same types of siderophiles are present on Earth and the moon, but that the moon has lower concentrations of these same siderophiles. The answer choice that best describes this relationship is choice B.

2. **The correct answer is J.** This question is also a detail question. The reference to the hot conditions that existed when the moon was formed occurs in the second viewpoint. Choice F has no textual support and is incorrect. Choice G is a true statement that occurs near the discussion of the hot moon formation in the second viewpoint, but it is irrelevant to the question. Choice H is also a true statement, but it is from the first passage and is also irrelevant to the question. Therefore, the correct answer is choice J. The second viewpoint describes the moon rocks as having been "molten" early on, which indicates that the rocks were probably in liquid form during the development of the moon.

3. **The correct answer is A.** This question requires both comparison and inference, as it involves new hypothetical information that pertains to both passages. Both theories posit that a significant portion of the moon's rocks came from Earth, so if Earth rocks are magnetic, it is likely that moon rocks were at least magnetic initially when they were derived from Earth. The correct answer, therefore, is choice A. Choice B states the opposite, choice C is irrelevant to the question, and choice D does not really support either theory.

4. **The correct answer is G.** This is an inference question. If the oxygen fingerprint gives a sense of rock origin, the newly presented piece of data suggests that some of the moon rocks are not derived from Earth since they have different oxygen fingerprints. These moon rocks may have been derived from Theia, the non-Earth astronomical body that may have collided with Earth and contributed to the rock composition of the moon, so this piece of data only supports the Giant Impact Theory because the Fission Theory indicates that the moon rocks were only derived from Earth.

5. **The correct answer is A.** This is an inference question that asks you to select the piece of data that supports the two posed theories, but refutes the newly introduced Capture Theory, which proposes that the moon was formed elsewhere in the solar system and was captured by Earth's gravitational field. Choice A indicates that the earth and moon rocks are approximately the same age, as this indicates that the rocks have the same origin and are likely not from some other source elsewhere in the solar system. Choice B is irrelevant to the question; choice C is a true statement that is not mentioned in either viewpoint; and choice D, though true, does not particularly refute the Capture Theory.

6. **The correct answer is J.** This is an inference and detail question. Supporters of the Fission Theory would not agree that the Pacific Ocean basin was created by the impact of an astronomical body; while they would indicate that this it the source of moon rock, it would not be due to any impact, so the answer is not choice F. The answer is not choice G, as Fission Theory supporters would expect the earth and moon rocks to have the same age. The answer is also not choice H; if early Earth was extremely stable and compact, then pieces of rock would not be flying off to form the moon due to high-velocity spinning. The answer, therefore, is choice J, as similar composition between moon and Earth rocks indicates common origin.

7. **The correct answer is C.** This question asks you to contrast the two theories. The key difference between the theories is the involvement of impact, which occurs in the Giant Impact Theory but not in Fission Theory, so the correct answer is choice C. Choices A and B are not especially relevant to the question, and choice D is a similarity, not a difference, between the theories.

The second passage is a biology passage that uses the format in which two students debate a topic after researching their respective viewpoints. In this passage, the students are debating the classic nature versus nurture question with respect to academic performance.

8. **The correct answer is J.** This question is a detail question. Based on the explanation in the first viewpoint of how the *NPTN* gene works, increased expression of *NPTN* would result in higher levels of *NPTN* protein, a thinner brain cortex in the left cerebral hemisphere, and lower scores on intelligence tests. This means that choices F and G are incorrect and choice J is correct. Choice H brings into the picture a nurture-based effect on intelligence and key vocabulary mentioned in the second viewpoint, but it is not relevant to this question because the question asks about the first viewpoint, not the second viewpoint.

9. **The correct answer is C.** This question is a detail question that asks you to predict which factor would have the most negative effect on a student's academic performance, according to the second viewpoint. The second viewpoint argues in favor of the domination of "nurture" over "nature." Therefore, we can immediately eliminate choices B and D because both are genetic factors discussed in the first viewpoint. Choices A and C both describe nurture-based factors, but logically, choice A should have a positive effect on academic performance, not a negative effect. The answer, therefore, is choice C, which is also mentioned in the second viewpoint as a factor that can affect academic performance due to the key word *stress*.

10. **The correct answer is F.** This question asks you to compare the two viewpoints. While the first viewpoint favors nature over nurture, and the second viewpoint favors nurture over nature, both viewpoints include experimental evidence that individual genes do not significantly affect intelligence across a population. The first passage uses this information to imply that gene systems are more complex than that, while the second passage uses this information in an attempt to dismiss the effect of genes on intelligence. Choices G and H are both mentioned in only one of the viewpoints each, and choice J is mentioned in neither viewpoint.

11. **The correct answer is C.** This question also asks you to compare the viewpoints in terms of strategies each student used to make his or her argument. Choice A is incorrect because large sample sizes were used, and because the second viewpoint focused on environmental backgrounds, though it is implied that the first student inquired about environmental backgrounds in the twin studies. Choice B is incorrect because only Student 1 employed this strategy. Student 1 alluded to brain and neuronal development in the discussion of the *NPTN* protein, but there was no mention of this topic in Student 2's argument. Both students referred to genetic studies, so the correct answer is choice C.

12. **The correct answer is F.** This question asks you to compare and contrast the two viewpoints. We can immediately eliminate choices H and J because using a wide variety of genetic evidence would be a strength, not a weakness. Between choices F and G, the correct answer is choice F because Student 1 does not explicitly explore environmental effects, while Student 2 explores both genetic and environmental effects to show why environment effects might predominate over genetic effects.

13. **The correct answer is A.** This is an inference question. If new hypothetical data finds that a gene significantly affects intelligence and academic performance, it would clearly strengthen the argument posed by Student 1, who is arguing in favor of nature (genetics) over nurture (environment and upbringing).

14. **The correct answer is J.** This is an inference question that asks you to consider implied information. The conclusions drawn by Student 1 from the twin studies can be considered valid only if the twins are considered to have been brought up in similar environments; that way, genetics would be the only thing causing a difference between the two. Because the twins exhibited different personality traits but similar academic performances, the student's argument is strengthened because it indicates that twins with the same genes perform similarly academically, even though their personalities are not identical. In fact, the difference in personalities might be considered a difference in "nurture," so if twins perform similarly academically, it would seem that the genes, and not the personality differences, correlate with the academic performance.

The final passage is a chemistry passage, with some biological implications. The conflicting viewpoints explore the pros and cons of using fossil fuels as an energy source.

15. **The correct answer is D.** This is a detail question. Even though the first student is arguing against the use of fossil fuels, the student still acknowledges that fossil fuels are an efficient mode of energy acquisition, so the answer is not choice A. Choice B essentially sums up the student's argument, and choice C supports the data the student provides, so neither of these answers is correct. The student indicates that fossil fuel turnover is not rapid enough to sustain the resource, so the student would disagree with choice D.

16. **The correct answer is H.** This is a detail question. Choice F is not true according to either viewpoint, nor is choice G, so these answers can be ruled out. Choice J is a true statement discussed by Student 1, but it is not relevant to this question. Choice H correctly sums up Student 2's view on alternative energy sources: that these sources will have a tough time providing enough energy for US demand.

17. **The correct answer is A.** This is a detail question, though it might also be considered a compare/contrast question. The question asks you to determine which student or students addressed resource sustainability of fossil fuels. Only Student 1 does this, so the correct answer is choice A.

18. **The correct answer is G.** This question asks you to compare the viewpoints. Choice F is incorrect because Student 1 specifically argues against the use of fossil fuels, while Student 2 would disagree with the implication that natural energy sources are infinite and plentiful. Choice H is incorrect because the data provided by Student 1 specifically show that carbon emissions are very much a concern today, and the student notes several negative effects caused by carbon emissions. Choice J is incorrect because Student 2 indicates that alternative energy sources are not sufficient or sustainable enough to replace fossil fuels. The correct answer is choice G, as both students acknowledge that fossil fuels are currently the most efficient energy source in the United States, even though Student 1 is more concerned with the negative effects of the use of fossil fuels as an energy source.

19. **The correct answer is C.** This is a detail and compare/contrast question. The question asks you to choose which student or students expressed economic concerns in each viewpoint. Student 1 discusses the increased cost of finding increasingly scarce fossil fuels as the current stock is depleted, as well as the expense of pollution control. Student 2 discusses the economic benefits of fossil fuels on an international scale and as a source of employment. Therefore, both students express economic concerns.

20. **The correct answer is H.** This is an inference question. This question asks you to choose the hypothetical technology that would most satisfy the key concern of Student 2 regarding fossil fuels and alternative energy sources. Student 2 was not so concerned with environmental impacts, so we can rule out choice F. Student 2 was also satisfied with the current mode of fossil fuel transport, so this was not a concern in the student's viewpoint. Student 2 also referred to fossil fuel extraction technology practices as "safe," so safety was not the student's main concern either. The answer is not choice J. Student 2 was not in favor of eliminating fossil fuels because there is not efficient replacement natural alternative energy source, so the development of such an energy source would address this concern. Such a technology would likely also get Students 1 and 2 on the same page because, as long as this new natural alternative energy source is safe, all of the arguments Student 2 makes in favor of fossil fuels could also be made in favor of the new energy source, minus the environmental concerns discussed by Student 1.

PART VII: WRITING STRATEGIES FOR THE ACT® EXAM

Chapter 14: Mastering the ACT® Writing Test

WRITING STRATEGIES FOR THE ACT® EXAM

Doing well on every section of the ACT—including the Writing test—is a great way for you to stand out from the crowd of college applicants and will increase your chances of getting into the college of your choice. If you've purchased this book and have decided to take preparing for the ACT exam *seriously*, you've already taken a great step forward toward achieving your goals.

This chapter provides you with everything you need to know to do your best on the ACT Writing test—including an overview of the test, what to expect on test day, how the Writing test is scored, and what the official test readers are looking for in a high-scoring essay—as well as how to avoid getting a low score. You'll also find plenty of advice and strategies for building your writing skills, tackling essay prompts, and using your time effectively to plan and construct a great essay on test day. Then you'll be able to sharpen your skills with effective practice and review using sample prompts and model essays to compare your work against.

Use the information in this chapter to help you do your best on the writing section of the ACT exam, impress the official ACT essay readers, and get a great score.

Chapter 14: Mastering the ACT® Writing Test

OVERVIEW

The ACT Writing test is one of five test sections on the ACT exam, but it is the only test section of the ACT that is *optional*—which means that you get to decide whether or not taking the writing test is the right decision for you.

SHOULD YOU TAKE THE ACT® WRITING TEST?

Whether or not the colleges that you're applying to require you to submit an ACT Writing test score should help guide your decision to take this optional test. Requirements vary by school, so make sure you check with your target schools well in advance. You have a few options:

- Look up the information on the school's website.
- Ask your high school counselor for assistance.
- Contact the schools directly.

> **ACT Writing Test: It's Your Call**
>
> Your decision to take—or not take—the ACT Writing test will not impact your scores on the other ACT subject area tests or your overall composite score. However, the *only* way to receive an English Language Arts (ELA) test score is by taking the ACT Writing test.

Even if your target colleges don't *require* an ACT Writing test score, you can still take the test and submit your score. If you're a confident writer and feel that you'll get a great score on test day and you'd like to include it as part of your college applications, you have the option of doing so—it could really help college admissions personnel make a decision regarding acceptance, as well as help guide later decisions regarding course placement.

TEST OVERVIEW

The ACT Writing test is a 40-minute essay-writing exam designed to do the following:

- Measure your English-language writing capabilities
- Test your ability to focus thoughtfully on a provided topic
- Assess your analytical ability
- Gauge your ability to develop ideas using logical reasoning

You'll use your experience and breadth of knowledge from English classes and writing projects throughout your academic career to create an argumentative essay that responds to a provided essay prompt.

The best test preparation for the ACT Writing test is—you guessed it—writing practice. We've got you covered. You'll get to practice writing using essay prompts that are similar to what you might see on the ACT later on in this chapter. You'll also get to see sample essays at each score level to help you evaluate your own writing and determine what you need to work on to get a great score on test day!

The ACT Writing test can be taken on all six of the official national test dates (which includes the United States, US territories, Canada, and Puerto Rico), as well as the five official international test dates and special or arranged test dates.

The test is taken using a pencil (remember to bring a few sharpened, non-mechanical No. 2 pencils with you on test day), and you'll write your essay in an answer folder provided to you by the test administrator. If you require specific test accommodations, please visit the official ACT website for additional information.

ACT® Writing Test Features

The ACT Writing test is just what the name implies—a test of your writing abilities. Here are some of its features:

- **Guidance and structure for essay planning:** The test features prewriting guidance for structuring and crafting a written response. We'll cover the essay information you'll receive on test day later on in this chapter.
- **Wide range of subjects:** Essay prompts will draw from a wide array of engaging subjects and topical issues.
- **Broad topic perspectives provided:** Test takers will get three diverse perspectives on the issue provided in the essay prompt, allowing for a multifaceted analytical engagement.
- **Reflective of real-world topic discussion:** Student responses are built alongside, and in dialogue with, varying perspectives.
- **Comprehensive scoring:** The ACT Writing test provides test takers with scoring in four specific writing proficiency domains: **Ideas and Analysis, Development and Support, Organization,** and **Language Use and Conventions**. You'll also receive a writing score and an English Language Arts (ELA) score (ranging from 1–36, similar to the other test sections on the ACT). Additional scoring information appears later in this chapter.

How the ACT® Writing Test Is Scored

The ACT Writing test is designed to provide a comprehensive assessment of your abilities across a range of fundamental writing proficiency domains. You'll have the opportunity to respond to a writing prompt based on a carefully chosen topic, which will be presented alongside three distinct perspectives, each of which will be suggestive of a certain way of thinking about the issue.

During the essay writing process, you'll be tasked as follows:

- Analyze and evaluate the perspectives given
- State and develop your own perspective on the issue
- Explain the relationship between your perspective and those given

As you plan and structure your written response, your unique perspective on the issue can agree with any of the three perspectives provided, agree partially, or be completely distinct. Really, your opinion doesn't matter, as long as you have one! And as long as you *have* an opinion and develop it, you're on the right track. Regardless of your perspective, you'll need to develop and support your essay using careful analysis, solid reasoning, sound ideas, and compelling examples.

As previously mentioned, your essay will be scored by two separate (and highly experienced) certified ACT essay readers in four specific writing proficiency domains.

1) Ideas and Analysis

This grading area measures how well you can organize critical analysis toward a provided prompt and perspectives on a given topic, and then develop effective ideas to build your own perspective. A high-scoring essay will demonstrate a solid understanding of the topic and provide a compelling, relevant argument in support of a clear perspective.

2) Development and Support

This grading area measures your ability to generate an effective written argument with sound ideas, solid reasoning, a clear rationale, and thoughtful support. A high-scoring essay will demonstrate a clear flow of thoughts alongside a solid stance on the issue provided in the prompt and strong support in defense of your perspective, creating a clear, convincing piece of argumentative writing.

3) Organization

This grading area measures your ability to carefully and thoughtfully organize your ideas to create a convincing, coherent essay. A high-scoring essay will be a clear, on target, and purposeful piece of writing that demonstrates a solid understanding of essay structure and an effective flow of ideas, from introduction to conclusion.

4) Language Use and Conventions

This grading area measures your ability to effectively utilize English-language writing principles such as spelling, vocabulary, grammar, syntax, and language mechanics. A high-scoring essay will be a clear, polished, and effective piece of writing that demonstrates a solid understanding of language use and conventions.

TIP

If you need a refresher on grammar, language mechanics, and sentence structure, you're in luck! Part III of this book offers comprehensive coverage of how to recognize proper usage, mechanics, and rhetoric for the ACT English test; applying the rules and tips to your writing will help you create a strong ACT essay! We strongly suggest you review Chapters 4 and 5 if you need a confidence boost with language use and conventions.

You will receive five scores for your ACT Writing section:

- Four separate domain scores (Ideas and Analysis, Development and Support, Organization, and Language Use and Conventions)
- An overall subject-level score ranging from 2–12

Two readers will score your essay, with each providing a score from 1–6 in each of the four domains. Your total domain score for each of the four areas will be the sum of the two scores and will range from 2–12. (If the scores of the two readers in any domain area differ by more than one point, a third reader will be used to resolve the discrepancy.) You will also receive a fifth score for your essay overall, a single subject-level writing score reported on a range of 2-12. This score is the average of your four domain scores.

Your domain scores will reflect the essay readers' impressions of your abilities as follows:

Score 6: Your essay demonstrates a highly effective skill level in this domain area.
Score 5: Your essay demonstrates a well-developed skill level in this domain area.
Score 4: Your essay demonstrates an adequate skill level in this domain area.
Score 3: Your essay demonstrates some developing ability in this domain area.
Score 2: Your essay demonstrates a weak or inconsistent skill level in this domain area.
Score 1: Your essay demonstrates a deficient skill level in this domain area.

The test readers will calculate your individual domain scores based on the following ACT scoring rubric:

Score Level	Ideas and Analysis	Development and Support	Organization	Language Use and Conventions
Score 6	**Essay demonstrates:** • Effective critical engagement with perspectives • Nuance and purpose-driven precision • Excellent depth and contextual insight on the topic • Thoughtful analysis of the prompt issue(s) and implications of the writer's perspective	**Essay demonstrates:** • A deep and insightful level of effective idea development to promote understanding • Skilled reasoning and use of relevant and varied support to strengthen a perspective	**Essay demonstrates:** • A skilled ability to capably organize ideas into a cogent piece of writing • An effective and insightful central narrative theme that unifies the text • A thorough understanding of standard essay structure and flow, including effective transitions between sentences and thoughts	**Essay demonstrates:** • Skillful deployment of standard English language principles • Excellent use of varied and engaging vocabulary and sentence structures • A clear, authoritative, and effective voice and tone • Few or no errors in grammar, mechanics, and syntax
Score 5	**Essay demonstrates:** • Productive critical engagement with perspectives • Purpose-driven precision • Depth and contextual insight on the topic • Commendable analysis of the prompt issue(s) and acknowledgment of the implications of the writer's perspective	**Essay demonstrates:** • A commendable level of idea development to deepen understanding • Solid reasoning and use of relevant and varied support to strengthen a perspective	**Essay demonstrates:** • A solid ability to capably organize ideas into a cogent piece of writing • A solid central narrative theme that unifies the text • A commendable understanding of standard essay structure and flow, including effective transitions between sentences and thoughts	**Essay demonstrates:** • Commendable deployment of standard English language principles • Strong use of varied and engaging vocabulary and sentence structures • A capable and effective voice and tone • Few or no errors in grammar, mechanics, and syntax

Score Level	Ideas and Analysis	Development and Support	Organization	Language Use and Conventions
Score 4	**Essay demonstrates:** • Critical engagement with perspectives • Noticeable clarity and purpose • Insight on the topic • Analysis of the issue(s) in the essay prompt	**Essay demonstrates:** • A good level of idea development that provides clarity • Good reasoning and use of relevant and varied support to strengthen a perspective	**Essay demonstrates:** • An ability to organize ideas into a coherent piece of writing • A central narrative theme that demonstrates a real effort to unify the text • A good understanding of standard essay structure and flow, including evidence of clear transitions between sentences and thoughts	**Essay demonstrates:** • A good use of standard English language principles • Use of varied and engaging vocabulary and sentence structures • A good attempt to establish voice and tone • Some errors in grammar, mechanics, and syntax, which may occasionally impede meaning
Score 3	**Essay demonstrates:** • A limited engagement with perspectives • Noticeable clarity and purpose • Some dicernible insight on the topic • Some analysis of the issue(s) in the essay prompt	**Essay demonstrates:** • Some general but simplistic idea development • Some evidence of reasoning in an attempt to clarify the argument	**Essay demonstrates:** • An attempt to organize ideas into a piece of writing with a basic structure • A grouping of ideas in some logical order • An attempt to provide a structure and flow between sentences and thoughts that the reader can follow	**Essay demonstrates:** • Attempt to deploy standard English language principles, with occasional errors • Attempt to display some varied range of vocabulary and sentence structures, though errors are present • A discernible voice and tone, though largely hard to discern • Noticeable errors in grammar, mechanics, and syntax that impede meaning

Score Level	Ideas and Analysis	Development and Support	Organization	Language Use and Conventions
Score 2	**Essay demonstrates:** • A weak engagement with perspectives • Limited clarity and purpose • Deficient insight on the topic • Poor analysis of the issue(s) in the essay prompt	**Essay demonstrates:** • Weak or deficient idea development • An effort to offer reasoning in an attempt to clarify the argument, though largely ineffective or off target	**Essay demonstrates:** • A weak organi-zation of ideas and deficient structure • Ideas are weakly ordered, adversely affecting comprehensibility • A largely inef-fective attempt at providing sound structure and flow between sentences and thoughts	**Essay demonstrates:** • A deficient attempt to deploy standard English language principles, with several noticeable errors • A weak or deficient vocabulary range and basic, often flawed, sentence structures • A weak, ineffective voice and tone, largely hard to discern • Several obvious errors in grammar, mechanics, and syntax that strongly impede meaning
Score 1	**Essay demonstrates:** • No engagement with perspectives • Lack of clarity and purpose • No insight on the topic • Lack of analysis of the issue(s) in the essay prompt	**Essay demonstrates:** • An absence of appropriate idea development • No appropriate or discernible effort to offer reasoning in an attempt to clarify the argument	**Essay demonstrates:** • No organization of ideas and a lack of basic structure • A lack of thoughtful order of ideas, severely affecting comprehensibility • An absent attempt at providing sound structure and flow between sentences and thoughts	**Essay demonstrates:** • No attempt to deploy standard English language principles, with serious errors • A very basic and often erroneous use of vocabulary, and many serious errors in sentence structure • A largely absent or indistinct voice and tone • Serious and widespread errors in grammar, mechanics, and syntax that profoundly impact meaning and comprehension

Like your domain scores, your overall subject-level writing score will be an average of your domain scores, and reported on a scale of 2–12. If you decide to take the ACT Writing test, your score reports will be released approximately five to eight weeks after your test date. The colleges to which you decide to release your ACT score report will also be able to view your complete ACT Writing test essay.

Now that you know what to expect on test day, you're ready to take a closer look at what the ACT Writing test essay will look like, so you can take your preparation to the next level.

At some point, after making it through the ACT exam registration and preparation processes, and completing the required four ACT tests, you'll find yourself sitting at a desk with a pencil and paper, poised to write an essay that will hopefully dazzle the test readers and earn you a great score that will impress your target colleges. The best way to make this happen is by looking at what an actual ACT essay prompt might look like, as well as sample essays at each scoring level—so you'll have a better idea of what the essay readers might be looking for on test day. Let's get started!

THE ESSAY PROMPT

On test day, you'll be given a prompt from which you'll craft a thoughtfully constructed, well-written, and compelling essay that will reflect your perspective on the issue(s) provided. The essay prompt can be based on a myriad of topics, so the best way to prepare is to be prepared for anything.

It's a good idea to read the essay prompt *at least* twice.

- Your first read-through should focus solely on the information provided. Make sure you know exactly what the issue being presented is and what questions and ideas you are being asked to address in your essay response. Don't rush into furiously writing your essay without first knowing what it should cover!
- Your second read-through should confirm that you are clear on the essay task at hand and should also be an opportunity to start preliminary brainstorming ideas that you plan to include in your essay.

Don't race off into writing your own essay after your second read-through just yet. A major component of your essay will be to take into account the three perspectives provided alongside the essay prompt and task.

Here's a sample essay prompt, in the format you'll encounter on test day:

The Focus of Education: STEM versus STEAM

In recent years, there has been a concerted effort by some educational policy makers to reposition the focus of academic curricula to a STEM model (Science, Technology, Engineering, and Math), instead of a STEAM model (Science, Technology, Engineering, Arts, and Math). Given the limited educational resources available and America's desire to reassert its commitment to education so that its citizens are prepared to tackle the challenges of the twenty-first century and succeed on a global scale, it is worth examining the debate regarding educational models, as well as exploring additional ideas for shaping policy in this area.

Make sure you carefully read, analyze, and consider the entire essay prompt. Notice that the prompt includes conflicting viewpoints, designed to help stimulate your thinking on the issue provided. You'll likely find a format similar to this in your test day prompt. This prompt serves as the foundation for the perspectives you will encounter next, and it should get you thinking about your own opinion on the topic.

The ACT® Writing Test: The Best Way to Prepare? Stay Aware!

It's important to stay aware of what's going on in the world and in the news—it's your best chance at preparing yourself to tackle any essay topic on test day. Make it a habit to stay aware of the issues and current events that people are talking about—online, in magazines and newspapers, on TV, and in debates and conversations that are taking place around you. Get involved in these conversations as often as possible. Getting comfortable arguing your perspective on a range of issues is valuable practice. One of these issues just might be the foundation for your essay prompt when you take the ACT Writing Test.

After reading the prompt, you shouldn't go into full essay planning mode just yet, but feel free to start taking a few notes at this point if something important crosses your mind that would fit well into your essay.

Now you're ready to move on to the three perspective snapshots provided.

THE ESSAY PERSPECTIVES

Along with the sample essay prompt, you'll be given three varying perspectives on the general issue described in the prompt. You'll be asked to carefully consider each of these three perspectives as you begin to plan—and eventually construct—your essay.

For your own essay, you should read and consider the stated issue and each of the three perspectives, state your own perspective on the issue, and analyze the relationship between your perspective and at least one of the given perspectives. And remember: the perspective you take on the issue won't affect your score. The important part is that you express and support *an* opinion—any opinion.

As you read the three perspectives, think about how they fit or contrast with *your* thoughts on the issue. As with your second read-through of the essay prompt, use the ideas provided to help you begin to structure and refine your own perspective.

This is a great opportunity to do some additional brainstorming. Feel free to take notes—whether on paper or in your head—in whatever way has worked for you in your previous writing experiences. These notes will help you outline the core structure of your essay when you move fully into the planning phase.

The following are three perspectives on "The Focus of Education: STEM versus STEAM":

Read and carefully consider these perspectives. Each suggests a particular way of thinking about the notion of instituting a STEM- or STEAM-based curriculum model.

Perspective One

Schools nationwide, and at every grade level, should strictly follow a STEM curriculum model. The direction that the twenty-first century is taking has become quite clear in its early decades—the primacy of science and technology in every facet of society is apparent—and education programs should be able to shift and pivot to accurately reflect society. However, educational institutions are forced to deal with severe limitations in money, time, and resources. Making sure that the limited resources that are available are used in the wisest and most beneficial areas, those that will most benefit students as they become the workers and innovators of the future—locally, nationally, and globally—is the best way to position the United States for future success.

Perspective Two

A collective failure to acknowledge the importance of the arts in education is both tragic and dangerous—for future generations and society at large. Providing students with a deep and comprehensive education in science, technology, engineering, and mathematics is important to prepare them for success beyond the classroom, but there is clearly both room and importance for tempering this model with an education in the liberal arts. It isn't wise to assume that there won't be a need or place for the arts in the future, and demonstrating or advocating a collective "devaluing" of the arts, or history, or music doesn't bode well for society. In order to create a future that allows individuals to fully flourish, express themselves, and grow and live in a world where there's room for wonderful innovations in technology and the arts, a STEAM model is the wisest approach.

Perspective Three

Mandating a rigid educational model for every student, at every level, is confining at best—and potentially stifling. A "one size fits all" approach to life is rarely beneficial to the individuals who make up the "all," and this is true in education as well. While it's true that there are benefits to both STEM and STEAM models, a truly progressive society that's eager to refocus education for the future should allow students to individually tailor their academic experiences to match their unique interests and goals. In recent years, there has been a growing concern over the general lack of focus and attention students give to school; perhaps if they had a greater opportunity to create learning programs that engage them, they'd be more inclined to give school the attention it deserves—and all facets of society will benefit as a result.

Read these perspectives carefully, and think about how each point of view might complement—or not complement—your own perspective on the issue of utilizing a STEM versus STEAM education model.

Read each perspective *critically*, analyzing how each tackles the issues provided in the essay prompt. As you move forward, continue thinking about the issues, brainstorming ideas, and formulating your essay's plan of attack.

Before you start actually drafting your essay, *make sure* you review the essay task provided. You want to be 100 percent positive you are planning to take a stance on the exact issue(s) raised by the prompt. Don't waste your time and energy creating an essay that does not address what the test wants you to address!

TIP: Remember—a great piece of writing that fails to fully address the essay prompt and task will not earn you great scores on test day.

THE ESSAY TASK

Now that you've fully digested the essay prompt and carefully considered each of the three perspectives provided and how they fit with your specific perspective, you'll be given a specific essay task. Be sure to read this *carefully*—the test readers will be checking to make sure your essay capably addresses the task provided, and it will factor into your final scores.

Read the following essay task for "The Focus of Education: STEM versus STEAM":

Write a cohesive, logical essay in which you consider multiple perspectives on the STEM versus STEAM education model. In your essay, be sure to:

- examine and assess the perspectives given
- declare and explain your own perspective on the issue
- discuss the relationship between your perspective and those given

Your perspective may be in full or partial agreement, or in total disagreement, with any of the others. Whatever the case, support your ideas with logical reasoning and detailed, persuasive examples.

> **NOTE:** The wording on the actual ACT task is slightly different, but the task remains the same: form an opinion about the given topic, read and evaluate the perspectives, and present your opinion while relating the perspectives to your own.

Okay—you've read the essay prompt, considered your take on the issue alongside the three perspectives provided, and you're fully aware of the essay task at hand. The next step is to move forward and structure your essay!

PLANNING YOUR ESSAY

The first thing to acknowledge about essay planning is that there's no single, proven method that works for everyone. Just as everyone has a different way and style of writing, everyone has a unique way to prepare. At this point in your academic career, you've written lots of essays—perhaps some more successful than others. Do you like to write an outline or plan in your head? How do you like to brainstorm ideas?

Although your essay will be unique and reflect your distinct perspective on the issue provided in the prompt, an effective piece of argumentative writing should follow a basic structure.

Introduction

Use your essay opening to introduce your thoughts on the topic and explain why you think it's an important issue worth exploration. Also be sure to begin to discuss—or fully assert—the central idea or thesis of your essay. This should directly address the topic in the prompt and make your perspective on the issue quite clear for readers.

Body

The body paragraphs of your essay should bolster the claims made in your central thesis, through thoughtful analysis, effective idea development, and strong support. Make sure your essay considers all three perspectives provided alongside the essay prompt. A high-scoring essay will be an in-depth, complex piece of writing that covers all possible viewpoints (including opposing ones!) while strengthening your central thesis.

CONCLUSION

Here's where you'll wrap up your essay, tying up all of the ideas you've provided in your essay while reasserting your position. Relevant, insightful ideas for further exploration and consideration can also be included here. It's always a good idea to end your work on a powerful concluding note—always remember, a great closing will leave a positive and lasting impression on your readers.

TAKING NOTES

One suggestion we like is to make a quick list of ideas you want to include in each structural element of your essay: introduction, body paragraphs, and conclusion. Your ideas can include any questions you'd like to ask yourself (and eventually answer!) while you write. When you read the prompt, perspectives, and task, what major questions arose in your mind? Jotting these down will eventually help you analyze all sides of the essay prompt in greater depth and will lead to a more comprehensive written response.

Don't waste time making these into grammatically perfect, well-constructed sentences—this should simply be a rough collection of thoughts that you'll soon develop into the polished, carefully organized, and compelling sentences that will make up your essay.

Let's take a look at a sample brainstorming list for this essay task:

Introduction Ideas

- STEAM is a better educational model
- Discuss power of education to highlight issue importance (give quote?)
- Why so important at this moment in history?
- Discuss local, national, global implications, for present and future

Body Paragraph Ideas

- Why is STEAM a better model than STEM?
- Advantages of liberal arts education
    - More well-rounded students
    - Culture and arts to feed our souls and enhance society
    - Provide richness and meaning to life
- Acknowledge importance of STEM learning for future innovation, etc.
- Discuss "real" educational problem—lack of sufficient money and resources
    - How should this be addressed?
    - How should policy change or should it stay the same?

Conclusion Ideas

- Advantages/disadvantages/realistic limitations regarding education/focus
- Supplement school learning with home learning—"H" in STEAM?
- Reiterate importance of this issue, for current and future generations

As you can see, by using this method, your essay is already starting to take shape! Don't be surprised if the act of writing your ideas down in a list helps to stimulate new ideas as you move forward.

Feel free to refer back to your brainstorming list as you write your essay. It will help keep you on track and can act as a checklist to make sure you include all of your ideas and thoughts in your final work.

Take *no more than 10 minutes* to plan your essay before you start writing your first draft. Again, this is where practice before test day comes in handy! Use the practice essay at the end of this chapter to see if the 10 minutes of preplanning/30 minutes of writing and editing approach works for you, and don't be afraid to tweak it if necessary!

> **TIP:** The best strategy for essay planning—and writing—is to use the strategies that have worked well for you in the past. If you're one of those lucky people who can jot down a plan in 3 minutes and head straight into writing, go for it. The main takeaway from this chapter: find the method that works for *you*, practice it, and stick with it.

After you've taken about 10 minutes to develop a solid plan or outline for your essay, take a deep breath and pick up your pencil, because you're ready to start writing your first draft!

WRITING YOUR ESSAY

When you're ready, find a quiet place to work, get a pencil and some paper, set a timer for 40 minutes, and get started.

Take the first 10 minutes to think about the issue and the information provided, and use the worksheet on the next page to brainstorm ideas that will help you construct your final work.

The ACT® Writing Test: Use Your Time Wisely

Use this guide to make the most of your time on test day:

Total test time: 40 minutes
Brainstorming: 10 minutes
Essay writing: 20–25 minutes
Editing and revising: 5–10 minutes

Brainstorming Ideas for:
"The Focus of Education: STEM versus STEAM"

Introduction

Body Paragraphs

Conclusion

Okay, you've used your first 10 minutes to brainstorm and construct a solid list of ideas, thoughts, and questions, which will help form the core of your essay—consider this time well spent!

Now it's time to begin crafting your essay on "The Focus of Education: STEM versus STEAM." Remember that although your essay will be unique and reflect your distinct perspective on the issue provided in the prompt, an effective piece of argumentative writing should follow a basic structure of an introduction, then supporting body paragraphs, and finally a conclusion.

Remember, your essay should:

- Thoroughly address the prompt
- Include your own perspective
- Connect your perspective to at least one of the given perspectives
- Include core structural elements (introduction, supporting body paragraphs, conclusion)

TIP: Try to save 5–10 minutes after writing to review and edit your work, making sure it's polished and free of errors.

Once you've planned your essay, use the time you have left (which should be around 30 minutes) to write the essay.

After you've written and edited your essay and your total 40 minutes are up, take some time to review the following sample essays—there's one at each score level. Use them to help you figure out at what level you're writing and what you need to do between now and test day to prepare for success.

Write Your Essay

You'll also find sample scoring explanations for each of the four tested writing domains for the highest and lowest scoring essays. Use these to determine the level of your writing and the areas of strength and weakness and to help you structure your preparation plan between now and test day.

SAMPLE ESSAYS

Sample Essay—Score 1

Ideas and Analysis:	Score = 1
Development and Support:	Score = 1
Organization:	Score = 1
Language Use and Conventions:	Score = 1

Each person shuld be able to decide if go to school why should someone else tell people what to do with their time or even what they should be studied about. Some people like some classes what does bother most people is when they have to get up too late so this way they can sleep later and go to classes when they wake up? Some classes too long and students cant think about what teacher is talking about or saying, so can some of the classes be shorter even please.

School is expensive and people should pay what they can to make it happen if they get into colleges they aplly to. Students should spend more time on computers and learning on technologee like phones cause thats how people learn and communicate these days so schools should know that and teachers should know that too. Why shuld someone else tell students what to study and which classes they should even care about. Let everybody tell everyone which classes they want to go to and then they should get the chance to go and learn more.

Scoring Explanation

Ideas and Analysis: Score = 1

This essay attempt fails to provide a discernible level of insight or analysis into the issue of utilizing a STEM versus STEAM education model. The essay quickly falls off target and fails to establish a relevant perspective or appropriate unifying theme that addresses the prompt; as a result, we have no idea what the writer's thoughts on this issue are. The purpose and intent of the writer's essay is tangential at best ("Students should spend more time on computers and learning on technologee like phones"), and it reflects a poor level of analysis of the topic.

Development and Support: Score = 1

This essay response demonstrates a serious lack of idea development, and a complete lack of relevant support to bolster the writer's perspective on the merits of STEM versus STEAM. Rather, it seems as if the writer failed to fully digest the essay topic and task, and instead simply provided a brief and scattered response that loosely discusses his or her college plans ("Each person should be able to decide if go to school why should someone else tell people what to do with their time or even what they should be studied about"); the end result is an unsuccessful essay that completely misses the mark.

Organization: Score = 1

This essay is a rough, disjointed piece of writing that greatly suffers from a serious lack of cohesive organization and structure. Rather than provide a relevant, engaging, and thoughtful perspective that effectively addresses the prompt and task, the essay offers an incoherent series of jumbled ideas on taking college classes ("Let everybody tell everyone which classes they want to go to") and how class decisions should be made ("Some classes too long and students cant think about what teacher is talking about or saying, so can some of the classes be shorter even please"). The essay is hard to follow, and the writer's intent is confusing and murky at best.

Language Use and Conventions: Score = 1

There are serious errors in language use and conventions throughout this essay, which seriously impact its overall effectiveness. Errors in word choice and vocabulary ("aplly," "technologee"), grammar (run-ons, punctuation), and usage ("or even what they should be studied about") demonstrate both a profound weakness in writing skills and a failure to appropriately review and edit the finished work.

Sample Essay— Score 2

Ideas and Analysis:	Score = 2
Development and Support:	Score = 2
Organization:	Score = 2
Language Use and Conventions:	Score = 2

Technology is important and that what students learn in the classroom should show that they think its good. Students should give time learning about science and math and these things for the future, so they can be ready when they graduate and get good jobs. This is important for them and everyone.

Art and English and history, and classes like that are important, and that students that are interested in things like this should be able to learning more about them. Studnets that aren't interested can use more time learning about computers and science and hopefuly they can be the ones who make all the great new inventions in the future when they finish with school.

Students would like to go to a school where the students did get to decide what classes they take. Its important that students know something about all kinds of different subjects but they should be able to spend most of their time in class lerning about the things that they want to focus on when they get jobs after school. Getting students ready to get good jobs is important.

Sample Essay—Score 3

Ideas and Analysis:	Score = 3
Development and Support:	Score = 3
Organization:	Score = 3
Language Use and Conventions:	Score = 3

It's clear that technology is the wave of the future. Every day the news reports about some great new invention that's designed to help make lives a little easier, to improve and advance our society. All of these great thinkers, and inventors, and innovators have who help shape our world one thing in common. They all sat in classrooms during their early years, where their brains were stimulated and challenged with new conceps.

Who knows how many great ideas started behind desks while listen to teachers speak? Schools are definitely important, and what happens in classrooms can help build young minds and shape the future. Therefore, what type of model that schools follow couldn't be more importent.

Since technology is so important to our future, the classes that students should have to take should be science and technology based. The classes mentioned in the essay instructions, science, technology, engineering, and math should be the class model that schools use. If students learn a lot about these subjects they will be ready to get really great jobs and help our society advance and improve. They will be the ones who make computers and cell phones better and invent new things for example, and medecines and make all of lives better.

In conclusion, everyone can see how important these subjects are to the world, and to keep the world moving forward, so the time that students spend in classrooms, and learning, should be spent in these areas. There's no better way to ensure that society has the best futures possible than by giving students the education and knowledge they need to be succesful.

Sample Essay—Score 4

Ideas and Analysis:	Score = 4
Development and Support:	Score = 4
Organization:	Score = 4
Language Use and Conventions:	Score = 4

There's no better way to ensure our nation's prosperity than to make sure that those who will be responsible for carrying society into the future—the young learners who now sit in classrooms but who will soon inherit the future—are well-equipped to do so. They'll require the knowledge and skills to lead and innovate, to make sure that the country continues to remain at the forefront of advancement and achievement.

The crucial first steps, and perhaps the most important steps, will occur in our nation's classrooms. The guidance, direction, support, and mental fuel that students receive in school will directly contribute to America's ongoing success. Therefore, this question, about what curriculum model the nation should follow, couldn't be more important. A STEM model would best allow the United States to use and focus its resources to educate its students for ongoing success on a global scale.

Making the firm and clear decision to focus educational resources on the classes and programs that really matter for the future, which includes science, technology, engineering, and mathematics, is a bold but necessary step. These are the fields in which great societal advancements will likely be made—in science, and computer technology, and medicine, among others—and instilling an interest and yearning to learn and explore these fields in the nation's fertile young minds is critical.

There will likely be some people who feel that the STEAM model offers some advantages, that students will be better off learning about the arts as well as the other science and technology classes. It's ok to learn about these subjects, but people can learn about them outside of the classroom and on their own time. Students spend too much time these days doing unimportant things. They can learn STEM classes in the classroom and after school they can explore the arts and other things they're interested in.

There have been quite a lot of disturbing stories in the news about the poor state that our country's educational system is currently in. If the United States is going to be serious about using its resources wisely, and wants to fix the problems that plague education today, then policymakers will have to rethink and refocus the model schools use to teach students, which should reflect the subjects that are most important. The STEM model is America's best shot at ensuring that students lead society bravely and boldly through this century and beyond.

SAMPLE ESSAY—SCORE 5

Ideas and Analysis:	Score = 5
Development and Support:	Score = 5
Organization:	Score = 5
Language Use and Conventions:	Score = 5

The United States is at a pivotal moment in its development. Throughout the rapid industrialization that characterized twentieth century global expansion and progression, the America was positioned at the vanguard of innovation and the bold exploration of new ideas. However, significant segments of the developed world—including the United States—have entered into the "technological era" that has characterized the dawning and early years of the twenty-first century thus far. And it's no longer clear that America stands at the forefront of this exciting time, or that its doing everything it can to best position itself to lead and inspire the world through the technological era, and what lies ahead. However, there is a way forward.

Any great structure is only as good as its foundation, and the cornerstone of America's foundation is a living thing that's capable of change—it's the boundless minds and imaginations of the people, and they're inspired to grow, create, and soar when properly nurtured behind the desks of its classrooms.

The resources available for education in America are certainly abundant compared to many other nations, but they aren't limitless. Therefore, policymakers need to allocate precious and finite funds in the most beneficial areas. Utilizing a STEM-focused educational model represents the collective best interests of the nation. Beyond a wise allocation of limited resources, it will hopefully send a clear and inspiring signal to hungry and eager student minds—and to the entire world—that the United States recognizes the role that science, technology, engineering, and math will play in building a better tomorrow and brighter future, and that it has made a serious commitment and investment towards making sure that today's students become tomorrow's skilled and trained leaders.

Beyond financial resources, the attention and focus of today's students are more atomized than ever before, and harder than ever to grab a hold of. With endless pervasive media outlets and technological gadgets vying for student's attention, educational policymakers need to acknowledge that opportunities to effectively engage with students are limited, and that the most important classes, which fall under the STEM umbrella, should take clear and established primacy.

The consequences of adopting a STEM-centric educational model would be that certain liberal arts classes would receive less, or little, attention. However, it's foolhardy to eradicate them completely, or to fear that individuals would lose their interest in the arts if they weren't taught as extensively—or at all—in the classroom. Students at all grade levels should have opportunities to supplement a core STEM education with elective coursework in classes they're interested in. These electives don't have to be liberal arts based, but the option should exist. Beyond the classroom, interest in the liberal arts can flourish in other ways—through extracurricular activities, on weekends and at home after class, and alongside friends and family.

It isn't too late—in fact it never will be—to change our present in the service of our future. All it will ever take is for enough people to recognize a need for change and the will to follow through until it happens. This includes the focus and direction of the nation's educational system. Making a change this large wouldn't be easy. Change is rarely easy, but some things in life are worth the effort.

Sample Essay—Score 6

Ideas and Analysis:	Score = 6
Development and Support:	Score = 6
Organization:	Score = 6
Language Use and Conventions:	Score = 6

Nelson Mandela once said, "Education is the most powerful weapon which you can use to change the world." Throughout history, the progressive march of nations worldwide has been fueled by improved access to education, and continued refinement to educational models and processes, which makes instinctual sense; as a nation evolves, so should its method and model for educating it's people. The 21st century, thus far a heady mix of rapid technological and social progression, has left the United States at a true inflection point. The entrenched educational models utilized to stimulate and expand the minds of future leaders and innovators feel outdated, and out of step with the pace of our current technological era. To make a complicated issue even more challenging, resources for system-wide educational overhaul remain woefully limited. Regardless, great nations become great in times of adversity, when challenges are met and overcome, with real forward progress as lasting proof of wise decisions having been made precisely when decisions were needed.

The best education has no walls beyond those in the classroom. The hungry minds of America should be nourished with the full range of "fruits" that this great nation has to offer. In this regard, a STEAM-based model offers the best of both worlds: a solid education in science, technology, engineering, and math—the fields that will continue to drive progress and innovation through this century and beyond; and the arts—the fields that allow citizens to learn from a society's collective and individual experiences and histories, celebrate life and distinct, varied cultures, and feed souls through creative expression in art, writing, music, film, and more. If a STEM education allows individuals to build their houses, the "A" in STEAM allows people to make them homes, to bring richness and meaning to living. Who could argue that a model that's missing any of these is a step forward?

The true issue at the heart of America's "educational problem" is the fact that a choice has to be made in the first place. A truly progressive nation should place a higher value on education, and find a way to provide the resources needed to ensure that it doesn't have to choose one or the other. Educational policy should be among a nation's highest priorities. Furthermore, funds given to education should not be looked at as an expense but rather as an investment in the future.

Until this happens, educational policymakers need to make the most of available, albeit limited, resources. This means that hard choices need to be made; a focus on STEM-centric model with time allocated for core liberal arts curricula—in history, English, and elective programs that engage students by letting them pursue the areas they're most interested in—is a wise approach given the circumstances.

However, an additional letter should be added to the acronym—an "H" for home. Educational administrators and policymakers need to do a better job of spreading the message that learning doesn't just happen in the classroom. Teachers need to work with families and parents to spread the message that learning at school can, and should, be supplemented by learning at home. This way, no subject gets shortchanged. In sum, if part of our educational focus is to spread the message that learning is an ongoing, lifelong process that occurs in all of the rooms that we find ourselves in throughout our lives, not just the classroom, we'll all be better off—and the pace of progress in all areas of life will be more of a confident march than a tentative stroll.

Scoring Explanation

Ideas and Analysis: Score = 6

This essay offers an engaging, nuanced, and thoughtful analysis of the issue of STEM versus STEAM and takes it a step further—the writer expands on the issue and provides ideas on what he or she perceives to be core problems regarding the direction and focus of education today ("A truly progressive nation should place a higher value on education, and find a way to provide the resources needed to ensure that it doesn't have to choose one or the other"); the idea to add a greater focus on learning outside of the classroom was a particularly insightful addition. The overall result is an in-depth, multifaceted, and carefully considered argument.

Development and Support: Score = 6

The writer of this essay provides an exceptional level of development and support to bolster his or her argument—from the opening quote from Nelson Mandela regarding the transformative power of education to the stirring salvo at the conclusion highlighting the role learning plays in dictating the pace of global progress. The writer establishes his preference for an all-inclusive educational model and develops a stirring case for why it's a wise choice. The overall level of sophistication and depth in the writing greatly supports the writer's perspective and leads to a persuasive argument.

Organization: Score = 6

It's clear the writer of this essay has a strong command of the basic principles of essay structure, and was able to effectively deploy them in service of his or her position on the essay prompt. A strong introduction, well-reasoned review of both sides of the prompt, additional insight on the core issues facing education, and holistic approach to idea generation results in a very successful essay.

Language Use and Conventions: Score = 6

An impressive display of vocabulary and varied word choice throughout the piece, use of engaging analogies (i.e., comparing STEM versus STEAM to a house versus a home), and sophisticated sentences and transitions clearly indicate a high level of writing proficiency. The writer was able to infuse a great deal of passion into his or her essay and to capture the reader's attention from beginning to end. The essay is largely free from errors, resulting in a highly polished and provocative piece.

At the end of the chapter, you'll also have the opportunity to practice writing another essay and review your work against some high- and low-scoring samples. Hopefully, as you continue to practice writing essays, you'll notice that your work is continually improving!

SUMMING IT UP

- **Understand the prompt material.** Read the instructions, the essay prompt, the perspectives, and the essay task *carefully*. Be sure you understand the issue and know *exactly* what you're being asked to write before you write it. Use the perspectives provided to help shape your work.
- **Use what you know.** The essay prompt that you'll encounter on test day can be based on a wide array of topics. Since you won't know your topic, the best way to prepare is to be ready to draw upon your wealth of experience to help you develop a well-rounded essay with sufficient real-world support—including your academic and life experiences. Stay aware of the issues and current events taking place around you.
- **Use your time wisely.** You'll have 40 minutes to plan and write your essay. Use this time efficiently. Practice planning and writing essays in the time provided—it'll help you find a comfortable writing pace and put you in great shape to impress the readers on test day.
- **Plan carefully.** When you feel the pressure and clock ticking on test day, your first instinct may be to pick up your pencil as quickly as possible and write furiously, to get as much down on the pages before the end of the test. Resist this urge. Instead, take a few minutes to analyze and think critically about the issue and the perspectives presented and plan your written response, creating an outline that will help you properly structure your essay. It will be time well spent.
- **Write purposefully.** Use the writing techniques and strategies that you've learned throughout your academic career as you craft your essay. Establish a clear perspective and focus for the reader and craft compelling, well-structured sentences that support your argument and address the essay prompt and perspectives provided, as well as the implications and potential consequences of your ideas.
- **Edit your work.** Do your best to leave a few minutes to review and edit your work after writing your essay. Think about the four writing domains that your essay will be judged on as you review your work:
    - Does your essay present a wealth of compelling ideas and nuanced analysis that responds to the prompt and fulfills the writing task?
    - Are the ideas in your essay fully developed, and do they contain sufficient support to bolster your perspective?
    - Is your essay well-structured and organized?
    - Do you effectively utilize English language principles and mechanics in your essay?
    - Polishing your first draft—checking for errors, proper word choice, grammar, sense, and sentence usage—is a great way to ensure that your final work is as good as it can possibly be.
- **Practice makes perfect.** Use the time you have between now and test day to practice writing essays on a variety of subjects. Choose a topic that's getting a lot of news attention or, better still, work with a writing partner who'll help you choose writing topics and who'll also review your work. Your partner may also be able to provide you with different perspectives to work with. If you can find a practice reader who's capable of reviewing your work along the four ACT test domains and providing you helpful critical feedback, that's even better!

ONLINE PREP

Want to Know More?

Access more practice questions, lessons, helpful hints, and strategies for the following writing topics in *Peterson's Online Course for the ACT® Exam*:

- Introduction to Writing
- Essay Writing Method
- Organize and Develop Ideas
- Effective Style in Essays
- Avoid Common Errors
- Putting It All Together

To purchase and access the course, go to **www.petersons.com/testprep/act**.

PRACTICE

As previously stated, there's no better way to build your writing skills than by practicing. In the following section, we have provided six practice essay opportunities to help you get your writing into test-conquering shape. Use everything that you've learned in this chapter to help you craft high-scoring essays that effectively respond to the prompts and perspectives. Choose from any of the topics listed below to get started. Be sure to review the model high-scoring and low-scoring essays that follow to gauge how well you did.

- **The Price of Higher Education Versus Value**
- **Solar Energy of the Future**
- **Frankenfoods or Friendly Foods?**
- **Bike Lanes**
- **The Internet: Neutral Zone or Open Marketplace?**
- **School Vouchers**

Plan Your Essay

Write Your Essay

The Price of Higher Education Versus Value

The expense of obtaining a college education has steadily increased in recent decades—some would argue to an alarming degree—leading many politicians, legislators, and educational policy makers to wonder if the cost of higher education has reached a point where it's unclear if the potential benefits justify the daunting expense.

Some people strongly feel that the cost of a college degree is out of control, and real system-wide reform is urgently needed before an entire generation of students gets stuck with the financial burdens of overpriced educations and sizable loans to help finance their academic endeavors. Others feel that the value of a college degree justifies the price—including data that highlights the enhanced earning potential and greater professional fulfillment and options of college graduates compared to nongraduates.

Given the increased attention on the rising costs of obtaining a college degree, as well as questions regarding its relative value in a changing employment landscape, it is worth examining the debate regarding this issue, as well as how policy should be affected moving forward.

Read and carefully consider these perspectives. Each suggests a particular way of thinking about the cost of college and what should be done about it.

Perspective One

The cost of college has certainly become too expensive, and it has finally reached the point where the potential benefits of obtaining a diploma need to be seriously weighed against the alarmingly bloated expense. There needs to be a serious overhaul of both the cost of college and the student loan industry, which is reaping tremendous profits from students and their families. Educational policymakers should seriously commit to exploring alternative measures. Schools should work toward finding ways to trim their expenses so they can operate effectively without having to charge enormous tuition sums. Improved financial aid packages should be implemented. If something isn't done regarding this issue, one thing is clear—generations of students will continue to buckle and fold under the crushing financial burden of a college education.

Perspective Two

It's true that school is expensive, but it's a realistic expense, considering both the costs of operating an institution of higher education and the return value of a college diploma. It's a wise investment in one's future—there's no denying that, on average, college graduates earn more money over their lifetimes and experience greater professional fulfillment, happiness, and success. There are financial aid tools in place that are designed to help students at all financial levels afford the cost of college, including scholarships, work-study programs, and student loans. Furthermore, there are a wide variety of schools, with widely varying tuitions, from community colleges to public and private universities. Every potential student's financial background is different, and there are schools and aid programs to help all qualified students cover the expenses.

Perspective Three

It's tricky to make a general, blanket statement such as "college is too expensive"; the truth is, college is a big expense for *some*, but not so much for others who possess the financial means to handle the expense. It's also challenging to quantify the return on such an investment, so it's tough to determine whether or not it's a worthwhile investment over the long term. Instead of racing to the conclusion that the cost of higher education is objectively "out of control," a wiser use of time and resources would be to consider each student and his or her financial means individually, and make an effort to make school affordable for each of them. Perhaps implementing a realistic sliding scale cost program, so families can pay what they truly can afford, would be a worthwhile endeavor.

Essay Task

Write a cohesive, logical essay in which you consider multiple perspectives on the cost of college. In your essay, be sure to:

- examine and assess the perspectives given
- declare and explain your own perspective on the issue
- discuss the relationship between your perspective and those given

Your perspective may be in full agreement with any of the others, in partial agreement, or wholly different. Whatever the case, support your ideas with logical reasoning and detailed, persuasive examples.

Plan and Write Your Essay

Use the first two pages of the Writing test answer sheet (located before the essay prompt) to generate ideas and plan your essay. Then use the following four pages to write your essay.

Consider the following as you compose your essay:

What are the strengths and weaknesses of the three perspectives provided?

- Identify the insights they present and what they fail to consider.
- Ascertain why a given perspective might persuade or fail to persuade.

How can you apply your own experience, knowledge, and values?

- Express your perspective on the issue, identifying the perspective's strengths and weaknesses.
- Formulate a plan to support your perspective in your essay.

PLAN YOUR ESSAY

Write Your Essay

Solar Energy of the Future

As the United States looks for alternative energies to oil and coal, solar energy has become a leading candidate to be the "new" energy. As of 2015, solar energy accounted for only 0.6 percent of net utility-scale electricity generated in the United States, putting it behind other renewable sources like hydroelectric (mechanical energy created from harnessing water), biomass (energy converted by natural plant processes like photosynthesis), and wind energy. However, the amount of solar electricity capacity in the United States has increased in recent years, increasing from 334 megawatts in 1997 to 13,406 megawatts in 2015, setting the stage for potential growth. As solar energy companies emerge and work to make solar the go-to sustainable energy in the United States, it's important to consider the implications of putting resources into solar energy.

Read and carefully consider these perspectives. Each suggests a particular way of thinking about solar energy.

Perspective One

Solar energy is the wave of the future. It's renewable, abundant, and sustainable, because the sun is a constant resource. Although setup can be expensive, the long-term costs are comparable (and in many states, even less) than we spend on other sources of energy. It makes sense to prioritize solar energy as our main renewable energy plan moving forward.

Perspective Two

Solar energy is problematic. It lags behind hydroelectric, biomass, and wind energy because it can be expensive to install the necessary equipment and to store on a large scale, and it can be weaker in areas that receive less sun exposure. Solar energy is too expensive and unpredictable to prioritize over other energy resources.

Perspective Three

Solar energy has potential, but is less proven than energy sources we currently have, like nuclear energy, natural gas, and oil-based energy. Our resources should be spent maximizing proven methods and finding ways to make them sustainable.

ESSAY TASK

Write a cohesive, logical essay in which you consider multiple perspectives on whether solar energy is truly the energy source of the future.

In your essay, be sure to:

- examine and assess the perspectives given
- declare and explain your own perspective on the issue
- discuss the relationship between your perspective and those given

Your perspective may be in full or partial agreement, or in total disagreement, with any of the others. Whatever the case, support your ideas with logical reasoning and detailed, persuasive examples.

Plan and Write Your Essay

Use the first two pages of the Writing test answer sheet (located before the essay prompt) to generate ideas and plan your essay. Then use the following four pages to write your essay.

Consider the following as you compose your essay:

What are the strengths and weaknesses of the three perspectives provided?

- Identify the insights they present and what they fail to consider.
- Ascertain why a given perspective might persuade or fail to persuade.

How can you apply your own experience, knowledge, and values?

- Express your perspective on the issue, identifying the perspective's strengths and weaknesses.
- Formulate a plan to support your perspective in your essay.

SAMPLE ESSAY—SCORE 1

Ideas and Analysis:	Score = 1
Development and Support:	Score = 1
Organization:	Score = 1
Language Use and Conventions:	Score = 1

So solar energy . . . Its a good option, who doesn't like the sun? It's a concern that global warming can increase temperatures, so why not take that increased heat and make it into some solar? Sollar panels are expensive which I know because my uncle had them installed last year and was very surprised by how much his bill was. But its an expense that is necessary if we want to improove our energy. Critics don't agree with that but I really think it's the way we need to go energywise.

Scoring Explanation

Ideas and Analysis: Score = 1

This essay reads like a dialogue the writer is having in his head. There's no depth of analysis or evidence of a coherent argument.

Development and Support: Score = 1

There's an anecdote that could, in theory, support a point about solar energy (the expense of the panels, as experienced by the writer's family), but the information is just placed there, with no cohesive connection to the topic at hand, or to what the writer is trying to say.

Organization: Score = 1

This essay is certainly not structured like an essay. There is no introduction, no obvious conclusion, and very few supporting details. It meanders without any real control or forethought.

Language Use and Conventions: Score = 1

There are obvious spelling errors (including solar, which is spelled out many times in the prompt) and odd sentence construction that make this essay difficult to read. Language doesn't have to be perfect in an ACT essay (nobody's perfect and you're under a time crunch), but whatever you write, make sure it's as clear and clean as possible.

Sample Essay—Score 2

Ideas and Analysis:	Score = 2
Development and Support:	Score = 2
Organization:	Score = 2
Language Use and Conventions:	Score = 2

Do we need solar energy? Some people believe so, and so do I, for three reasons. Solar is the wave of the future. It's the green energy resuorce we need to invest in, starting now.

One: The son will be there forever. Even when it's raining, you know the sun will be back out, providing solar energy. That alone is an argument for picking Solar Energy.

Two: Is it expensive to take and use solar energy? Probably. Solar panels don't come cheap, especially if you need to buy them for your entire city. But what does that cost matter when you're talking about a source of green energy that can provide energy forever? We need to look past those costs and understand that the long term costs will be less than other forms of energy.

Three: We do have other energy methods, like nuclear and oil. However, those are relics of the past, and are draining the world's resources. Solar is an energy source that will keep going, leaving those other methods behind.

In conclusion, solar energy is the one which that we should invest in.

Sample Essay—Score 3

Ideas and Analysis:	Score = 3
Development and Support:	Score = 3
Organization:	Score = 3
Language Use and Conventions:	Score = 3

As solar energy grows as a more prominent energy option here in the United States, it has it's strengths and its drawbacks. The sun is a very strong resource that will never go away, but critics also say that solar energy will be too expensive, and is not proven compared to other forms of energy.

First, solar energy is a dependable energy for the future. It is renewable, because the sun is a very stable power source. It is also sustainable, because of that stability. We can keep renewing that energy, for as long as the solar panels are working. It's important to have a sustainable energy resource that we can pass on to our children and their children someday.

Second, there are many costs associated with solar energy. Panels are expensive, and require a big investment by people who want to install the panels on their homes, or governments who want to make solar energy the default energy for their communities. For some, this is an investment in the future. For others, the big initial investment is too risky, when we have other options that we already know are reliable, like hydroelectric or nuclear energy.

Third, as I mentioned, we already have energy resources that work well. My town uses nuclear energy, and it's a method that works. There's also oil and natural gas, for which we already have systems in place. When we have reliable options already, why spend the money on newer methods when we could put that money into improving the ones we already have?

In conclusion, solar energy has it's benefits, but also problems that are not necessarily outweighed by those benefits.

Sample Essay—Score 4

Ideas and Analysis:	Score = 4
Development and Support:	Score = 4
Organization:	Score = 4
Language Use and Conventions:	Score = 4

Solar energy is the prince of "green" energy right now. It is an eternally renewable resource (as long as the sun rises every day), which makes it an appealing option to make our country more energy independent. And while it can be expensive to set up the panels for homes and cities, these are costs that balance out over the years as we pay less for day-to-day energy. With the right commitment and investment now, we can turn solar energy from that prince into the king of sustainable energy in the United States.

First, there is the dependability of solar. The sun is as regular as it gets (you can literally set your watch by It!), which means that any energy based on it is something that will stay consistent. Critics argue that some places get more sun that others, making solar inconsistent. However, with planning and adaptation, this can be overcome by improving storage methods to compensate for times when the weather doesn't allow for a lot of sunshine, or shortened winter days leave less time for solar energy gathering. This kind of planning requires commitment and development, but the dependable base is there.

Despite an initial investment, expenses of solar are likely not as daunting as they may seem. Sure, solar panels, installation, and equipment can be expensive. However, once those are installed, the main costs are based on maintaining on those, and this is less than the big initial expense. Ideally, solar panels can last for years (or even decades), so this investment is one that is increasingly beneficial as time passes and the energy user saves money by not buying oil or gas to heat their homes every month. The benefits of being able to have your own house generate energy balance out some of those costs.

Making the commitment to solar energy lets us focus our energies on improving our methods of harnessing and using solar energy in the most efficient ways. Right now, we split our energy, so to speak, between too many different kinds of resources: nuclear, wind, solar, fossil fuels, etc. If we pick a lane and can focus on it, we will be able to make that energy form into a better version of itself. If our top researchers and companies are working on better solar panels instead of solar panels plus wind turbines plus hydroelectric grids, we can make it into an even better resource in the near future.

Solar energy is growing in popularity for a reason: it is a renewable, sustainable energy resource that will let us build and grow for the future. No energy form is perfect, but if you look at the long term picture, solar offers benefits (decreased energy costs overall, a power source that will not be going away, and scientific advancements to make it more efficient) that make it the best option moving forward.

Sample Essay—Score 5

Ideas and Analysis:	Score = 5
Development and Support:	Score = 5
Organization:	Score = 5
Language Use and Conventions:	Score = 5

Solar energy seems like a great option on paper: it's renewable, it's growing, and it's dependable. However, things are not always as they seem. Because of drawbacks like expense and being untested on a large scale, it is too risky to make solar our energy priority.

Solar energy has a lot of hidden expenses associated with it that make it a less-than-ideal commitment for the U.S. Panels (for the home or for large solar energy farms) are very expensive. It can be less expensive for consumers themselves, due to government incentives and subsidies. These incentives and subsidies are passed on to taxpayers, so the costs are not really decreased, just shuffled around. It is still an expensive investment for local, state, and federal governments.

Space is also a concern for solar energy investment. Large panels are necessary, especially if they're intended to provide energy on a community level. Space is a challenging commodity in this country, especially for cities and the communities that require the most energy. In rural areas, setting aside space for solar panel farms is much less of an issue. Finding miles of space in the middle of New York City, however, is a much different issue. If you've ever been to Times Square, you know that there is barely space for all the people and cars, let alone acres of solar panels. Without large available spaces to put solar panels, some communities will need to find other ways to install solar panels.

Even though solar energy is growing, it still accounts for a very small percentage of American energy resources. The fact is that even when solar energy works on a smaller scale, it is still relatively unknown as an energy resource for entire communities and states. Going down the solar path, at the expense of other options like hydroelectric and wind energy, is a big gamble to make. If we roll the dice with solar and it proves to be too challenging to implament on a broader basis, we run the risk of having to start over with other energy sources, after having spent all the time and energy on solar.

At this point, the risks of committing to solar energy outweigh the benefits. Solar energy might not be the one-size-fits-all solution to our need for a renewable energy investment. The initial price tags of getting solar energy systems up and running, coupled with the many unknowns of making it a primary energy source (without our current oil and gas reserves to fall back on), are too risky for us to commit to solar as our Next Big Thing at this time.

Sample Essay—Score 6

Ideas and Analysis:	Score = 6
Development and Support:	Score = 6
Organization:	Score = 6
Language Use and Conventions:	Score = 6

As our world grows and changes so quickly, it's essential that we find new and sustainable ways to meet the energy demands of the population. Here in the United States, where we have more than 300 million people, it is also essential that we find energy resources that help make us less dependent on oil produced by other countries. Although it may not be the perfect energy resource, solar energy may very well be our best bet for the future, economically and environmentally.

Costs have been one of the main sources of debate for solar energy. Solar panels, especially ones installed on a large scale to make energy accessible to entire communities, can be very expensive. It is a significant commitment, either for the homeowner installing panels on his roof or the state seeking to expand solar energy throughout its cities and towns. However, sticker shock shouldn't be a reason to discount solar energy. Think of it as a marathon, rather than as a sprint: investing in solar energy equipment and infrastructure now will mean fewer expenses as time goes on, and we are no longer importing oil (at the mercy of the market) or funding expensive nuclear energy programs.

Solar energy also has the benefit of relying on our world's most dependable resource: the sun. Temperatures may change across the globe, and water is scarce in many parts of the world—but the sun comes up day after day. This is not without challenges; some places do receive more direct sunlight than others. Solar energy may not be a practical option in far northern regions that experience long periods of darkness. However, in places like the United States, access to the sun is consistent enough that communities could plan solar storage around weather events and seasons with shorter days. Other energy sources, like biomass and hydroelectric, are subject to issues like droughts that are unpredictable.

Not only is solar energy abundant, it is also sustainable. "Green" energy, or sustainable energy, needs to meet current needs without putting future generations at a disadvantage. Solar energy meets (and exceeds) that expectation. Again, because the sun is a consistent factor, there is no concern that it will run out for our grandchildren. If we invest resources in developing new ways to harness and store this energy, we will be leaving these future generations the tools they need to keep building on the solar base we create.

Committing to solar energy doesn't need to be a perfect decision—it needs to be the one that works best for us right now, with assurances of growth in the future. As we try to take our energy future into our own hands and out of the hands of other countries and market forces beyond our control, it makes the most sense to go with a resource we know we can depend on (the sun) and make the infrastructure investments we need to make so that we can develop that resource into a dependable, sustainable energy source for generations to come.

Scoring Explanation

Ideas and Analysis: Score = 6

This essay offers a nuanced, thoughtful perspective on solar energy. The writer has clearly looked at all three of the perspectives, and the pros and cons of each one. She clearly agrees with Perspective One, but takes the time to point out the merits of the other perspectives, while explaining why solar energy is a good bet for commitment. This is particularly clear in the analysis of how solar energy may be expensive to start, but would be less expensive as time goes on.

Development and Support: Score = 6

The writer uses concepts and examples that aren't necessarily found in the prompt or the perspectives, like referring to the political desire for energy independence in the United States, and examples of places where solar energy might not work as well. She adds a population stat as well, for effect. The writer also scores well with comparisons, such as comparing the commitment to solar energy to a race (marathon vs. sprint).

Organization: Score = 6

The essay is very clearly laid out. The writer sets out the main idea in the first paragraph, and indicates that he or she is going to talk about the economic and environmental implications of committing to solar energy. Each supporting paragraph tackles one of these implications, and the conclusion summarizes that information, while also acknowledging the different perspectives on the issue.

Language Use and Conventions: Score = 6

The writer uses very sophisticated sentence structure, with varied punctuation and advanced vocabulary. The style is not overly formal (she uses contractions occasionally), but the tone and perspective are consistent throughout.

Plan Your Essay

Write Your Essay

Frankenfoods or Friendly Foods?

When most people think of "genetic engineering," they probably think of laboratories and extreme experiments, removed from our everyday lives. In reality, genetic engineering is as close as our dinner plates, as more and more food producers turn to "genetically modified organisms" (GMOs), or crops that have been genetically manipulated to be resistant to pests and diseases. Scientific and government consensus says that foods containing GMOs pose no more of a health risk than foods without. However, with more GMOs entering our food supply than ever before, this has become an area of concern for many people, one that calls for more analysis of the implications of adding unnatural elements to our food.

Read and carefully consider these perspectives. Each suggests a particular way of thinking about genetically modified organisms (GMOs).

Perspective One

GMO crops and food additives pose no risk to public health, and in fact can improve the quality of food entering our food supply. We should embrace them as a way to modernize our food production and improve the quality of food that reaches consumers.

Perspective Two

GMOs are untrustworthy, as are the corporations and conglomerates who change our food behind the scenes without our knowledge. GMOs are an unknown quantity, and shouldn't be trusted as a driving force on our farms and in manufacturing.

Perspective Three

GMOs are an important tool for farmers and food producers to have. They cut down on the pesticides and chemicals needed for crops, and can save money on farming and production, which ultimately passes savings on to consumers.

ESSAY TASK

Write a cohesive, logical essay in which you consider multiple perspectives on whether GMOs are acceptable additions to our food supply.

In your essay, be sure to:

- examine and assess the perspectives given
- declare and explain your own perspective on the issue
- discuss the relationship between your perspective and those given

Your perspective may be in full or partial agreement, or in total disagreement, with any of the others. Whatever the case, support your ideas with logical reasoning and detailed, persuasive examples.

Plan and Write Your Essay

Use the first two pages of the Writing test answer sheet (located before the essay prompt) to generate ideas and plan your essay. Then use the following four pages to write your essay.

Consider the following as you compose your essay:

What are the strengths and weaknesses of the three perspectives provided?

- Identify the insights they present and what they fail to consider.
- Ascertain why a given perspective might persuade or fail to persuade.

How can you apply your own experience, knowledge, and values?

- Express your perspective on the issue, identifying the perspective's strengths and weaknesses.
- Formulate a plan to support your perspective in your essay.

Sample Essay—Score 1

Ideas and Analysis:	Score = 1
Development and Support:	Score = 1
Organization:	Score = 1
Language Use and Conventions:	Score = 1

The name "frankenfoods" tells you everything you need to know about GOMs like why they are too scary to include in our food chain. It's a proven fact that GMOs are poison and why would you want to feed your kids poison and ruin their futures. I'd rather have unpoisoned natural foods and I think most people would agree with me that no one wants fake food for dinner. The government is not always honest with Americans and I dont think we should blindly trust that fake food is okay for us.

Scoring Explanation

Ideas and Analysis: Score = 1

This essay doesn't present any concrete arguments or show that the writer has thought much about the topic or any of the perspectives. She seems to have picked a lane (that GMOs are bad) and just riffs on that, without really considering what the different perspectives say on the matter. She also introduces an idea that isn't included in the prompt or any of the perspectives (that GMOs are "poison") without providing any support for that claim.

Development and Support: Score = 1

None of the writer's points are supported in a real way. Although the writer does have a point of view (GMOs are bad), there is nothing offered to support that idea in an insightful or meaningful way.

Organization: Score = 1

The essay is short and jumbled and has no clear organization. There's no introduction, no conclusion, and no coherent transitions to make the essay flow.

Language Use and Conventions: Score = 1

Even though it is very short, the essay contains a large number of spelling and grammatical mistakes. Mistakes happen, especially when you're writing on the spot, but when there are this many, it shows that the writer took very little care in expressing herself.

SAMPLE ESSAY—SCORE 2

Ideas and Analysis:	Score = 2
Development and Support:	Score = 2
Organization:	Score = 2
Language Use and Conventions:	Score = 2

GMOs are controversial, with benefits and drawbacks. However, the bottom line is that they are safe, and we should not be afraid to embrace them.

GMOs make food better, because they improve the quality and farming process for our fruits and vegetables. Shouldn't our main concern be whether our food is safe? Too much attention is being paid to the idea that we don't know what's going into our food. Groups have signed off on what's going into our food, so we know enough.

Another issue is cost. The money saved on pesticides and crops killed from natural events is nothing to sneeze at, and we should think about how this effects our economy. The economy is bad, and needs improvement.

In conclusion, the benefits of GMOs are more important than the drawbacks.

SAMPLE ESSAY—SCORE 3

Ideas and Analysis:	Score = 3
Development and Support:	Score = 3
Organization:	Score = 3
Language Use and Conventions:	Score = 3

If the old saying is true and you are what you eat, what does it say about you if you consume foods that have been artificially enhanced? GMOs have become an asset to the food industry, improving the growing process and making crops less susseptible to things like pests. Yet those advances should be taken with a grain of salt.

For starters, although they say these GMOs are safe to eat, it is unclear what the long term effects are, given that these GMOs have been in place for a pretty short time. They do pose no risk to public health, supposedly, and can improve the quality of food. But have they been tested for affects ten, twenty, thirty years down the line?

There's also the fact that GMOs are used by big companies that are making these changes behind the scenes. We don't like it when Big Brother is watching us through digital surveillance, so I don't think we should necessarily accept what Big Brother is doing to our food behind the scenes.

But it is also important to consider the farmers. They are part of the food production process too, and stand to benefit from crops that are easier to grow and need less pesticides. They often embrace GMOs as a way to improve their product and bottom line, but like with the companies, what's best for the bottom line may not be best for us, the consumers of this food.

In conclusion, we just do not know enough about GMOs to embrace them wholeheartedly. Until we know more about how they affect us and the environment on a more long term basis, we shouldn't just accept that GMOs are a part of our food supply now.

SAMPLE ESSAY—SCORE 4

Ideas and Analysis:	Score = 4
Development and Support:	Score = 4
Organization:	Score = 4
Language Use and Conventions:	Score = 4

The idea of creating magically enhanced foods that improve upon the originals sounds like a good one, like something you'd see in a futuristic movie. But rather than be carried away with the Hollywood version where futuristic people eat a single tablet that contains a meal's worth of nutrition, we should pay more attention to the changes that are going on in our food supply right now. Specifically, that means taking a closer look at what changes are being made to our foods before they ever get to our house.

Genetically modified organisms are a very hot topic right now. If you've ever tried to read a food label, you know that what you think is in your food, versus what's actually in it, can be two different things. Strange, chemical-sounding ingredients tell you very little about what is in your food, or how it was processed. Theoretically, these ingredients are tested and safe by agencies like the FDA. But just because something is "safe" in the short term, how comfortable are we that it will be safe in the long term? Every day we hear new information about what causes cancer or other health problems, meaning that our current version of "safe" is not necessarily tomorrow's version of "safe." Until we know more about the long term effects of these modified crops and growing processes, we should be hesitant to use them widely throughout our food supply.

There is also the fact that even though these changed crops and processes work well for farmers and companies' bottom lines, that does not necessarily guarantee that these producers have the consumers' best interests at heart. More transparency about how these products are grown and processed could help consumers make more informed decisions about what they're buying and ultimately putting in their own bodies. We shouldn't take it for granted that all benefits and no drawbacks are being passed along to consumers.

Although GMOs may seem like the fast route to that future where all of our dietary needs are addressed by food that has been "improved" into an unrecognizable format, we should be weary of taking that route without examining it too closely. Without knowing more of the long-term implications of using GMO crops and ingredients, this is not a path we should blindly take.

Sample Essay—Score 5

Ideas and Analysis:	Score = 5
Development and Support:	Score = 5
Organization:	Score = 5
Language Use and Conventions:	Score = 5

Genetically modified organisms (GMO) foods are often casually known by the catchy nickname of "frankenfoods," but in reality they are not as scary as some make them out to be. In fact, GMOs represent advancements in science and nutrition which show great promise. As the world population grows and resources grow more scarce, it will be more important than ever to find ways to make those resources go even further.

There are legitimate concerns about GMOs, with the most frequently expressed one that large scale farms and companies may not have the public's best interests at heart. The image of an enterprising American farmer sending good, healthy food right to your plate is an appealing one; the image of a faceless corporate drone deciding what ends up on your plate is not. Yet the GMOs currently in our food supply have been vetted by agencies like the FDA, and determined to be safe for us to eat. Studies have shown that there is no real difference between crops that have GMO elements vs. crops that are grown as they always have been. That kind of continued oversight can help overcome the idea that we're about to be victims of a company willing to poison the public in the interest of saving and making money.

That argument against GMOs also glosses over a potential benefit to the public. When food production is more cost-effective and efficient, those cost savings are passed on to the consumer as well. The power may still be in the hands of those faceless corporations, but this is an advantage that is passed along as food production improves. If the benefits of improved nutrition and potential savings could be made clearer to the public, it might help to overcome the hesitation that people have toward GMOs in their food.

After all, food can be an infinite resource, if we plan and evolve along with the changing needs of a growing population. In the United States in particular, we've been moving away from an agricultural economy, which means we need to find smarter, not necessarily more, ways to feed the public. GMOS offer a way to start future proofing our food supply against possible population and climate changes, and will let us be more flexible as we move into the future. It's important that we learn to embrace these changes, rather than fear them.

SAMPLE ESSAY—SCORE 6

Ideas and Analysis:	Score = 6
Development and Support:	Score = 6
Organization:	Score = 6
Language Use and Conventions:	Score = 6

It sounds like a plot from a horror movie: monsters invading your home, through something as innocuous as a grocery bag. The terror is coming from inside the house! That is the kind of stigma that has been coming up around genetically modified food products (GMOs), and it can be a challenging image to overcome. However, these "scary" GMOs are nothing more than scientific and technological improvements that help us make our foods better, safer, and more efficient.

One of the biggest concerns with having GMOs in our crops and our food supply is the safety factor. How can an "enhanced" tomato be as healthy and natural as one that grew through the same reproduction and growth process tomatoes have followed for many thousands of years? The fact is that "natural" or slightly modified, that tomato can be used in a BLT sandwich. These GMO crops have been evaluated by scientific and government safety groups, and have been found to be entirely safe for human consumption. Giving in to the "what if" scenarios indulges a speculative kind of pseudoscience, when actual science already tells us that these foods are safe for us to eat.

In fact, the benefits from these GMOs outweigh the phantom risks of consuming these products. By modifying crops to be able to grow in climates they may not have been able to grow before, or by increasing the nutritional value, these foods could have a transformational effect in areas of the world hit hard by droughts, shortages, and famine. Imagine villages in central Africa that could grow crops using less precious water, or nutrient-dense vegetables that could be distributed where they're needed the most. We owe it to the world to make improvements to food and food production that have the potential to solve longstanding problems around the globe.

Yet in order to move forward with these advances, we need to do a better job of overcoming the stigma attached to "frankenfoods." Right now, GMOs are shrouded in a kind of corporate secrecy, with these developments happening and being implemented behind the scenes. This lack of transparency leads to distrust that companies are doing the right thing. One way to build confidence about the safety of these crops and processes is to make sure there's stronger oversight, to ensure that farms and companies are following best practices, and that these modifications continue to be safe for the population. The best way to take the fear of the unknown is to make sure it's familiar.

It would be a shame to lose the progress we've seen with genetically modified crops that resist disease and damage, merely because we have a fear of the unknown factors lurking in our refrigerators. These advancements have the potential to improve the way we eat all over the globe, if only we could get past the fear factor and embrace the benefits and growth opportunities.

Scoring Explanation

Ideas and Analysis: Score = 6

This essay takes a strong stance on the subject: that GMOs are something to be embraced, and that opposition to it is based on fear. However, the writer is careful to acknowledge the "anti" perspective in the response. A great ACT essay doesn't need to embrace all sides, but it does need to acknowledge them and determine how the perspectives are related.

Development and Support: Score = 6

The student includes specific examples throughout to support her points, like the tomato analogy that establishes that a modified food is still a familiar food. The mention of Africa also serves to underline her point about the global benefits of GMOs. The writer also uses a common theme (fear, "phantom risks") to unify her ideas throughout the essay.

Organization: Score = 6

The essay has a clear beginning, middle, and end, with transitions throughout that make the essay feel like a conversation. There are no leaps or gaps between the paragraphs, and it flows well from one end to the other.

Language Use and Conventions: Score = 6

The sentences are varied and complex, with very strong vocabulary words used throughout the essay (*pseudoscience*, *transparency*, and the like) that illustrate sophisticated concepts. Again, the use of the thread of fear throughout the essay helps to elevate the difficulty level and sophistication of the writing. There may be a stray spelling, punctuation, or grammar error, but this is largely a very clean, precise essay.

Plan Your Essay

Write Your Essay

Bike Lanes

A recent government study revealed that nearly half of American adults have access to a bicycle, and that more than half of those with access had ridden their bike recently. From 2000–2013, the number of people commuting on bikes grew in major metropolitan areas by more than 100 percent across the country. As this trend continues to grow, it's important to consider the implications of our changing commutes and the resources necessary to support these trends. These resources include bike-friendly roads (like dedicated bike lanes) and traffic management and enforcement policies that work for bicyclists as well as traditional drivers.

Read and carefully consider these perspectives. Each suggests a particular way of thinking about bike lanes.

Perspective One

Bike lanes are an essential infrastructure need for communities as people look for healthier, more sustainable ways to get from point A to point B. Cities and towns should be prioritizing bike lanes as a necessary part of their infrastructure.

Perspective Two

Bike lanes divert attention and resources from roads, and negatively affect traffic flow. On busy roads and streets, they take up valuable space that could ease traffic congestion. Not only that, they're expensive to create and enforce, when the vast majority of people on the road are drivers, not bicyclists.

Perspective Three

From a safety perspective, bike lanes are a necessity. Without them, bicyclists are left unprotected from the hazards of driving a bike while all other vehicles around are massive and potentially deadly machines.

ESSAY TASK

Write a cohesive, logical essay in which you consider multiple perspectives on whether bike lanes are a transportation necessity.

In your essay, be sure to:

- examine and assess the perspectives given
- declare and explain your own perspective on the issue
- discuss the relationship between your perspective and those given

Your perspective may be in full or partial agreement, or in total disagreement, with any of the others. Whatever the case, support your ideas with logical reasoning and detailed, persuasive examples.

Plan and Write Your Essay

Use the first two pages of the Writing test answer sheet (located before the essay prompt) to generate ideas and plan your essay. Then use the following four pages to write your essay.

Consider the following as you compose your essay:

What are the strengths and weaknesses of the three perspectives provided?

- Identify the insights they present and what they fail to consider.
- Ascertain why a given perspective might persuade or fail to persuade.

How can you apply your own experience, knowledge, and values?

- Express your perspective on the issue, identifying the perspective's strengths and weaknesses.
- Formulate a plan to support your perspective in your essay.

Sample Essay—Score 1

Ideas and Analysis:	Score = 1
Development and Support:	Score = 1
Organization:	Score = 1
Language Use and Conventions:	Score = 1

I see bike lanes in my town, but no one using them. The stats say that more and more people are using bikes to get around but I don't see evidence of that because no one uses the one's we already have. Some disagree, they say that bike lanes are necessary for safety of bike riders. But I think their is not enough evidence yet to say that we need bike lanes everywhere by demand. Until that information comes out I don't think we should make changes to our streets.

Scoring Explanation

Ideas and Analysis: Score = 1

The good part of this essay: the writer expresses an opinion. The bad news: he doesn't take that opinion and engage in any meaningful way with the information presented in the prompt or the perspectives. The writer makes a series of statements without offering any analysis on the topic.

Development and Support: Score = 1

The writer's main support of his points is the phrase "I think." There are no supporting details that flesh out his perspective, or provide context. Having opinions on the prompt and expressing them is exactly what you should do in your ACT essay, but you need to make sure that for every argument or point you make, there is information that supports it.

Organization: Score = 1

This essay has no organizational structure; it reads like a short series of stream-of-consciousness opinions as the writer thinks of them.

Language Use and Conventions: Score = 1

The essay is full of run-on sentences and grammatical errors like *their* for *there*. Again, this reads like the writer is writing things down as he thinks of them. Your essay prep time should include some notes and organizing thoughts, so that you're not doing it on the fly while you try to write your actual essay. Take those 10 minutes to think carefully about what you want to say in your essay, and how you want to say it.

Sample Essay—Score 2

Ideas and Analysis:	Score = 2
Development and Support:	Score = 2
Organization:	Score = 2
Language Use and Conventions:	Score = 2

More then half of the country rides bikes, according to a study conducted by the govt. As this number grows, we need to consider the implications of how and why we create bike lanes.

Some believe bike lanes are a good thing. They can improve safety for people riding bikes instead of driving, and let people make the healthy choice of riding your bike instead of driving and causing pollution.

Others believe that bike lanes are a problem. They cause problems for traffic, like taking away driving lanes or parking spots. Also we are a nation of drivers, not bicyclists. Bike lanes can be expensive to build and they are not an easy fix for problems on our roads.

In conclusion, I can see both sides of the issue. If you ride a bike, you are likely to want to see bike lanes set up in your town but if you're a driver you are likely to want to see more improvements in that driving experience. Until we know more about how many people actually need and want bike lanes, we shouldn't just install them everywhere.

Sample Essay—Score 3

Ideas and Analysis:	Score = 3
Development and Support:	Score = 3
Organization:	Score = 3
Language Use and Conventions:	Score = 3

If you ever rode a bike on a busy street, you know how nerve racking it can be. You can feel small and vulnerable up against all those cars and trucks. You need to be super aware of your surroundings or you risk getting seriously injured...or even killed! Bike lanes are a good way to help you feel more safe as you ride your bike on the street.

Taking bikes out of the main traffic flow and putting them in they're own lane will work wonders for bicyclist safety. Cars will know what is in their lanes and be able to watch for issues, and bicyclists will have their own space where they don't have to worry about cars coming up behind them cutting them off. Everyone can concentrate on their own safe driving.

Sure, bike lanes are expensive, and require cities to spend money to get them up and running. But is public safety not worth that investment? If installing bike lanes saves even one life, most people would agree that it is a worthwhile measure. We are spending money on maintaining streets and roads anyway, so this should be seen as another expense in that existing area.

Changing traffic may be a problem for people who are already used to having several driving lanes and/or more space for their driving and parking, but taking bikes out of traffic and putting them in their own lane is important to support a growing number of people who want to bike instead of drive. The population is changing and our expecatations of traffic should change too.

In conclusion, bike lanes are a good thing, and if we have to adjust our thinking (and our budgets!) to make this happen, then this is a necessary cost of improving road safety for everyone.

Sample Essay—Score 4

Ideas and Analysis:	Score = 4
Development and Support:	Score = 4
Organization:	Score = 4
Language Use and Conventions:	Score = 4

As studies point out that the number of people who have and use bicycles is growing, it is also important to consider that public transportation is not an all-or-nothing issue. We can acknowledge the growth of bicycling as a valid transportation alternative, but we also don't need to make blanket statements about how bike lanes are essential everywhere. It is more important to make a community-by-community decision about what the local needs are, rather than make one size fits all decisions.

Bike lanes are an expensive investment. City and town budgets, which may already be feeling the pinches of cuts and shortfalls, may not have much room for public street improvements. Even if it is a one-time expense, not every town has the ability to prioritize bicyclists over other potential (and just as necessary) street improvements. What needs to be clearer is how much of the community is affected by bike lanes? In large cities, where transportation is difficult and expensive, it makes sense that bike lanes would help alleviate that. However, in communities like my smaller city, you rarely see bicyclists sharing the road with the cars, and the city council has been vocal about putting more resources toward maintaining sidewalks and roadways for heavier vehicle and pedestrian traffic.

In addition to the costs associated with installing bike lanes on a bassis big enough to make an impact, there is the question of whether or not bicyclists will even use them safely. In my town alone, there were several accidents in the past year where bicyclists were not following traffic rules, and were hit by passing vehicles. Unless the bike lanes are coupled with stronger traffic enforcement for the bicyclists (on par with drivers being pulled over for speeding or running red lights), the lanes themselves might not do much to improve safety for anyone on the road, let alone bicyclists.

Another area that should give us pause is the fact that less than a quarter of the population is currently interested in regular biking, if the studies are accurate. We should be hesitant to make large, impactful decisions about our roads when the stats say that people might be moving toward a more bike-friendly perspective. Each town and city should be conducting more thorough research to see what the actual impact is on there streets, rather than allocate resources based on vague national statistics.

In conclusion, bike lanes can be a great help in places where bicyclists see direct hazards on the street, or where driving and public transportation are not appealing alternatives. However, we should be wary of saying that bike lanes are the solution for all communities without doing further do diligence about what the needs of our communities are, and what resources we have available to accommodate them.

SAMPLE ESSAY—SCORE 5

Ideas and Analysis:	Score = 5
Development and Support:	Score = 5
Organization:	Score = 5
Language Use and Conventions:	Score = 5

As one of the growing numbers of Americans who use a bicycle to get around town, I know that it can be a challenging method of transportation. In traffic, you are made to compete with cars, trucks, and other vehicles that can do great damage to you and your bike if something goes wrong, someone isn't paying attention, etc. Weaving in and out of traffic is not an ideal way to travel—it requires constant vigilance and care to make sure that not only are you driving well, but everyone around you is too. This is a fundamental reason why bike lanes are a necessary investment for communities, despite the potential traffic and cost implications.

With nearly 25% of Americans riding bicycles regularly, this is a segment of the population that demands more care and attention. Our roads and highways were designed in the 1950s with one form of transportation in mind: cars, and lots of them. The great American open road, free to anyone with four wheels and a full tank of gas. As our thinking modernizes and people look for ways to get around outside of that traditional model, we need to rethink these roads and how they meet our needs. We may still be a car-centric population, but as that grows into more of a car + bike mindset, we need to start adapting our infrastructure accordingly.

Bike lanes are a significant part of that conversation. They're controversial because they necessarily subtract from space originally devoted entirely to cars; you can't create a new bike lane out of nowhere. Making these changes requires either widening existing road ways, or taking space (and potentially lanes) away from cars. In large cities, this is especially a problem, as the streets are already too crowded and often too gridlocked. However, a commitment needs to be made to make these roads safer for everyone (drivers, pedestrians, and bicyclists) and not just convenient for drivers. Cyclists and pedestrians may not be as visible in the traffic flow as vehicles are, but accommodations need to be made. Think of bike lanes as an extension of crosswalks: modifications to roads that make things much safer for people to pass through. After all, you never hear someone saying things like, "these crosswalks are just too much of a hassle." They are an accepted part of street safety, and bike lanes should reach that level as well.

Strained city budgets are often used as another weapon in the fight against creating dedicated bike lanes. Many cities barely have the funds to maintain roads and streets at the existing level. The idea of taking already-precious funds and diverting them away from standard road maintenance can be a tough sell. Yet if you approach this from an investment perspective, the numbers seem less scary. Once the heavy work of refining roads to allow for a bike lane on the side, that's it—you don't need to hire people to oversee the bike lanes on a daily basis, or have people out there maintaining the lanes every week. Once they're up, they're up—and the costs spread out into general street maintenance, which would be budgeted anyway.

Implementing bike lanes on a large scale is not necessarily the easy decision, but it's the right one. The safety of bicyclists matters just as much as the safety of drivers, so supportive measures like bike lanes should receive the same level of consideration.

Sample Essay—Score 6

Ideas and Analysis:	Score = 6
Development and Support:	Score = 6
Organization:	Score = 6
Language Use and Conventions:	Score = 6

Last July, I was biking to my summer job when I was hit by a delivery truck that made an illegal right turn, without regard for anyone around it. I was not seriously hurt, but my bike was totaled—and I remember the truck driver saying that he never even saw me. I was very lucky that day, but ever since, I've been struck by the thought that if there had been a dedicated bike lane and better awareness of non-car drivers on the road in my town, the accident might never have happened. As more and more people around the country turn to bikes as a convenient, environmentally sustainable way to get around, it's more important than ever for our cities and towns to devote resources to creating bike lanes and supporting bicyclists.

According to studies, the number of bicyclists is growing. Biking offers a great way to get exercise and get around—a little extra cardio while you commute to work or school. It's also a very environmentally friendly option, with no gasoline necessary, and zero pollution. Collectively, Americans tend to say they want to do a better job as stewards of the environment, and make sustainable choices. Like recycling and conserving water, bicycling instead of driving is a small personal decision that can have big impacts, the more people get on board. Right now, however, the challenge is that this is not an easy decision to make; cars are a more convenient option for many people. Bicycling requires more of a trust that while you will be responsibly following the rules of the road, other drivers will as well. The exact scenario that happened to me is a fear for anyone who's riding a several-pound bike among several-ton vehicles. This is where the resources come in. If cities and towns put more money and energy into creating safe space for bikes to travel (bike lanes), this can help remove fear from the equation for many people who would otherwise choose the more sustainable option of bicycling instead of driving.

Furthermore, installing bike lanes signals a community commitment to alternative transportation. It serves as a statement that cars are not the kings of the road—that safety for non-drivers is a transportation priority. With the number of bicyclists increasing more than 100 percent in metropolitan areas over the past decade, this shows a seismic shift in how people are approaching transportation. Deterred by heavy traffic and public transportation systems that may not be any better, people want alternatives. It is in the best interest of these cities and towns to put resources against the most popular alternatives—and right now, that is bicycling.

For those critics who believe that the expense of installing bike lanes on existing roads is too much of a burden on communities, I would counterargue that these costs should be seen as more of an investment than a burden. Outside of the costs of re-engineering streets slightly to accommodate space for bike lanes and amending signage, this is not an ongoing financial burden to cities and towns. There are few upkeep needs for bike lanes; they don't need to be tended or refreshed once they exist. And in fact, they may save these cities more money in the long run: fewer drivers decreases wear and tear on the streets themselves, and helps reduce the unmistakable pollution related to cars and trucks.

As we learn to think differently about how we move from one place to another, it is essential that our infrastructure keep up. Bike lanes are an effective way to commit to bicycling as a valid alternative transportation for people who want to commute sustainably, or who just don't have access to cars. These segments shouldn't be left to just deal with the roads as they are—their decision should be supported every bit as much as the drivers who hit the road as well.

Scoring Explanation

Ideas and Analysis: Score = 6

This essay offers a detailed analysis of why the writer thinks bike lanes are a necessity. He is able to connect the topic to a personal experience (his bike accident), and coherently extrapolate that to show why better road resources for bicyclists is a must. The writer shows an understanding of the different perspectives, and what is involved in allocating more funds and energy toward improving bike lanes and life for bicyclists.

Development and Support: Score = 6

The student makes sure to use examples throughout that support his points about why supporting bike lanes is the better option: the stats on the growing bicyclist population, the specific details about re-engineering roads, etc. These supporting details are woven throughout the essay so that they don't feel like a basic point + supporting detail formula.

Organization: Score = 6

The writer has clearly put thought into the flow of this essay. Not only is there a clear introduction, body, and conclusion, but by starting with a personal anecdote and moving into a more general argument mode, he pulls the reader into his argument.

Language Use and Conventions: Score = 6

Throughout the essay, the writer uses a mix of complex and simple sentences, with strong vocabulary words used correctly in context. While sophistication is a necessary part of the ACT essay, you should be careful to make sure that you're using words and phrases that you know you're using correctly. A fancy word may sound good, but if the meaning is off, it can confuse the reader and the points you are trying to make.

Plan Your Essay

Write Your Essay

The Internet: Neutral Zone or Open Marketplace?

The internet can feel like the Wild West sometimes: no one owns it outright, but everyone wants to hold a piece of it. While the internet started as an entity that was not attached to any particular company or country, internet service providers own the ways we access it in our homes, workplaces, and schools. As such, these service providers are seeking to take more control over our internet access, offering tiered systems where people who pay more get better data plans and faster access. This doesn't necessarily affect content on the Internet itself, but rather how it's accessed, and by whom.

Critics contend that this is a disaster for the open nature of the internet, which has been an equalizing force where everyone can get access to the same resources at more or less the same speed. It has become a political debate between two major ideas: that the internet is a commodity like anything else, and should be monetized by companies who find themselves in a position to do that as part of a free and open market; and that the internet should be equally open to all, regardless of one's ability to pay more for better access.

Read and carefully consider these perspectives. Each suggests a particular way of thinking about Internet access, (or Net neutrality).

Perspective One

Internet service providers should be regulated against offering this exclusive access for higher-paying customers. The government should take action to keep the companies from taking advantage of the public, and putting people with less money at a disadvantage.

Perspective Two

Internet access is a service, to be provided by companies as they see fit, with the charges they see fit. If companies abuse this privilege, people will simply take their business elsewhere, because this is an open market.

Perspective Three

There needs to be a balance between keeping the internet equally available to people while still allowing companies to develop their businesses and make profits. Companies should have to offer a basic, affordable, and effective level of access to all customers, while maintaining the option to offer faster connection speeds or special extra content to premium subscribers.

ESSAY TASK

Write a cohesive, logical essay in which you consider multiple perspectives on whether internet service providers should adhere to net neutrality.

In your essay, be sure to:

- examine and assess the perspectives given
- declare and explain your own perspective on the issue
- discuss the relationship between your perspective and those given

Your perspective may be in full or partial agreement, or in total disagreement, with any of the others. Whatever the case, support your ideas with logical reasoning and detailed, persuasive examples.

PLAN AND WRITE YOUR ESSAY

Use the first two pages of the Writing test answer sheet (located before the essay prompt) to generate ideas and plan your essay. Then use the following four pages to write your essay.

Consider the following as you compose your essay:

What are the strengths and weaknesses of the three perspectives provided?

- Identify the insights they present and what they fail to consider.
- Ascertain why a given perspective might persuade or fail to persuade.

How can you apply your own experience, knowledge, and values?

- Express your perspective on the issue, identifying the perspective's strengths and weaknesses.
- Formulate a plan to support your perspective in your essay.

Sample Essay—Score 1

Ideas and Analysis:	Score = 1
Development and Support:	Score = 1
Organization:	Score = 1
Language Use and Conventions:	Score = 1

Net neutrality is a problem because people don't want to pay more for more websites. Websites go out of business if they don't get traffic. So I don't support NET NEUTRALITY. The companies all support net neutrality because they want to get more money out of us the American public. Its a fact. I don't want to pay more for less internet access. So I am totally against net neutrality letting companies do that.

Scoring Explanation

Ideas and Analysis: Score = 1

The writer's point here isn't very clear. He seems to have mixed up who's for net neutrality (people who don't want there to be tiered access) and who's against net neutrality (the companies that want to be able to charge more for higher quality internet access), so the argument starts off on a very confused footing. It's important to read the prompt and the perspectives carefully, so that you can analyze what the prompt is asking you to evaluate, and how your perspective and the given perspectives compare and contrast.

Development and Support: Score = 1

There's no real support in this essay. The writer is stating a confused series of opinions, but is not offering any details that could support whatever argument he is trying to make. Stating "it's a fact" does not support a statement.

Organization: Score = 1

There's no discernible structure here. It's clear the writer did not take the time to carefully consider the prompt or the perspectives, and instead just dived right in with his own opinions.

Language Use and Conventions: Score = 1

Random capitalizations and punctuation problems are all throughout this essay. The essay is also a confusing mess of run-on sentences and short sentences that seem cut off. There is no indication in this essay that the writer has a grasp of general grammar rules.

Sample Essay—Score 2

Ideas and Analysis:	Score = 2
Development and Support:	Score = 2
Organization:	Score = 2
Language Use and Conventions:	Score = 2

If you provide internet access, you shouldn't get to decide what I view online. Net neutrality means that these companies will control the internet, and this is a bad thing. America is about freedom, and not limiting what people want to do.

If companies are allowed to decide access, that means they control what you can and can't search for on the internet. Internet access is a service, as they say but as a service it should be what we want it to be.

Second, offering better internet for more money is unpatriotic. As the land of the free, it's essential that companies don't get to step in and tell us what we can and can't do on the internet. They have that kind of censorship in China, and that is just very wrong. We don't want to fall behind the rest of the world in what our people can and cannot do online.

In conclusion, more money should determine your ability to access and enjoy the internet…not! The internet is for everyone and should stay that way.

Sample Essay—Score 3

Ideas and Analysis:	Score = 3
Development and Support:	Score = 3
Organization:	Score = 3
Language Use and Conventions:	Score = 3

The United States was built on the principal that everyone is free to pursue a better life. I don't know if Thomas Jefferson thought about large corporations when he talked about that freedom to pursue, but in modern times, with the economy we've built, that means that people who own companies are free to do whatever they can to make their lives better. That applies to the internet as well. The government should not step in and stop internet providers from setting whatever fees and standards they want to set for people who use them to access the internet.

The internet doesn't belong to anyone. It belongs to all of us. Some would argue that this means that the big companies should not swoop in and set different prices for different levels of internet access. However that can also be turned to show that the government doesn't own the internet either, and has no place stepping in to regulate what the companies can or can't do.

People are also free not to be customers of the service providers who set pricing they don't like. In the American economy, there are almost always alternatives. If a company can be successful offering the same internet access at the same price for all of its customers, then that will chase the other companies out of business. If it turns out that the company offering the same internet access at the same price for all of its customers isn't successful, then that reinforces the companies that charged more for better and faster access. The free market should decide this, not the government.

In conclusion, the internet is about freedom. If I provide access, I am free to set whatever boundaries I want. You are free to find someone else to provide your internet access that is more to your liking. The government should not be interfering in any of these freedoms.

Sample Essay—Score 4

Ideas and Analysis:	Score = 4
Development and Support:	Score = 4
Organization:	Score = 4
Language Use and Conventions:	Score = 4

The internet has been built on the idea that it is accessible by all. That idea continues to this day, and an entire e-commerce economy has developed around the idea that information or goods posted online will reach any person in the world who wants it. That idea is what makes the concept of net neutrality so controversial. As internet companies move to offer special premium access to people who pay more, this threatens the best parts about the internet: that everyone can access the same information at any time.

It is very clear that being able to charge more for better, faster internet access benefits the service provider companies. If the cable companies can get even more money out of your monthly bill, they will. They're companies, and that's what they do: try to improve their bottom lines. However, I don't think we can trust companies to do the right thing on their own, especially if those profit margins are endangered.

As Americans, we value the idea that anyone can rise from any lot in life, and achieve what they want to achieve. That very idea is threatened when there's a fast lane for rich people, and a slow barely moving line for everyone else who can't afford to get in that fast lane. Make no mistake: that is what the service providers are trying to do. They want everyone to pay extra to get in that fast lane. That runs contrary to the way we view ourselves as Americans. As critics of net nutrality believe, there is a certain amount of freedom that companies should have to pursue all the profits they can, but that should not come at the expense of our strongest American ideals. The only real solution to this issue is to keep the service provider companies in check. That means ensuring that the playing field should stay level for everyone. It means that you can offer internet acess for whatever price you want, but you cannot offer "better" service for people just because they can afford to pay more. There should be strict government regulation around these companies to ensure that the very American ideals of life, liberty, and the pursuit of happiness continue to apply to the internet.

Sample Essay—Score 5

Ideas and Analysis:	Score = 5
Development and Support:	Score = 5
Organization:	Score = 5
Language Use and Conventions:	Score = 5

It can be hard to believe, but the internet has only been around for a few decades. In the grand scheme of things, this is relatively new—and as a result, we find ourselves grappling with how to handle issues like internet access now that virtually the entire world is online. This is not an issue that our grandparents had to face, so we have no real playbook here. What we have is a conflict between the gatekeepers of the internet (the service provider companies) and the people who want and need to access it easily. And what we need is a compromise between the two: a way to let the companies do their thing as part of a free and open economy, while making sure that no one is left out.

The rules in an open, capitalistic economy like ours are pretty clear: as long as you're not hurting anyone or breaking laws, you're free to conduct business as you see fit. That means offering goods and services at a price point that people will pay, but that also benefits your own bottom line. This means companies have an incentive to work with customers to find that balance—but it also means that the companies are welcome to take advantage of any way they can improve those profits without input from the general public. The drive to create a tiered internet access system, where people who pay more get better speeds and portals to connect to the internet, is understandable from the corporate perspective. People want to get online. The companies have ways for people to get online. Why not get as much money as they can from people willing and able to pay?

However, the other side of the issue is understandable as well. People don't necessarily want to pay significantly more for a service they have had all along, or risk having that service impeded if they can't pay exorbitant fees. Basically, they want what they've had ever since the internet became a common factor. From this perspective, the service providers' plans to create levels of access is a kind of threat.

That both sides have a valid point to make is why a compromise is so essential. Letting companies have free reign to charge customers whatever they want can be dangerous. After all, that kind of freedom is why we have labor laws restricting child labor, and regulations about what can be put into food products. Some base standards are necessary to make sure that no one is harming others in the name of wringing profits out of goods and services. To that end, the government should be able to regulate on a very basic level, mandating that the internet service providers offer a reasonable internet access level to all customers. If the company wants to go on and then offer premium content for customers willing to pay a little more, then they should have the ability to offer those additional services.

Without compromises from both sides, it is unlikely that there will be any significant progress made. The decisions we make now can help decide how the internet evolves in its next phases, and it is most important that all sides have a say.

SAMPLE ESSAY—SCORE 6

Ideas and Analysis:	Score = 6
Development and Support:	Score = 6
Organization:	Score = 6
Language Use and Conventions:	Score = 6

The internet is incredibly prevalent in our everyday lives. We track our activities with small devices, let people on social media know what we ate for breakfast and what we think about political candidates, and can look up even the most obscure information with the swipe of a finger. The internet is also a great equalizing force: as long as you and I both have basic access, we can get to the same massive wealth of information, regardless of where we are in the world, who we are, or what our circumstances are. That equalizing access to the internet is in danger, thanks to companies that want total control over the whats and the hows of getting online, and this is unacceptable.

It is understandable that internet service providers want to find ways to manufacture more profits out of internet access. Companies are necessarily profit-driven, especially in a capitalistic economy like the United States'. However, this becomes an issue when they chase this profit at the expense of consumers. The "haves" would have no problem absorbing higher costs to get online, and would likely enjoy the perks of that privileged access. The "have nots," on the other hand—people who may already just be scraping by, unable to afford expensive equipment or high monthly fees for internet access—will be put at a major disadvantage. These are the people who would be left out by the profit-driven business decisions made by internet providers.

In fact, the divide between the haves and the have-nots will be made even deeper, going beyond the basic issue of internet access. The VIP section vs. the out-of-luck section doesn't just create a cultural difference. Rather, it can lead to educational and quality of life divisions as well. For example, last year the educational children's show Sesame Street, which had run for decades on PBS, would be moving to a new home on premium cable channel HBO, where paid subscribers would have first access to new shows and content. A show that once prided itself on providing the same educational building blocks to all kids, regardless of family income or social status, will now be reaching higher-income families first. It stands to reason that the advantages of the internet (information access to all comers) would follow a similar pattern, if the service providers got their way: premium access leads to better information and better education.

The way to avoid this conflict between people who can afford premium access and those who cannot is to make sure that the internet stays equally available to all. This requires checks and balances on the companies themselves, particularly in the form of regulations. As the advocate for all people who live and work here, the government owes it to its citizens to make sure that one of the biggest achievements of the past hundred years—the living digital archive of the internet—remains as open to a poor person as it is to a rich one. Sitting out this fight is not an option for the government. The internet is a utility much like electricity or water, and the government has strong regulations in place to make sure provider companies are not taking undue advantage of customers.

As a resource, the internet is a remarkable one, and made even more so for its ability to reach everyone in the same way. It is a shared experience, but if the internet service providers have their way, it will be a tiered experience, a golden gateway for some while others are forced to go through the doggie door. The fight to protect equal access for all is an important and worthy one.

Scoring Explanation

Ideas and Analysis: Score = 6

The student takes a rather passionate stance on this issue, coming down firmly on the side of regulating internet service providers to ensure they can't privilege some customers over others. By tying the main topic (net neutrality) to broader social issues like inequality, the writer is able to open up her analysis and create room for her argument.

Development and Support: Score = 6

The essay includes very specific examples (*Sesame Street*, comparing internet access to doors) that help illustrate her stance on the issue. Throughout the essay, it expands her connection of the topic to the larger social implications, but always sticks fairly close to the topic at hand.

Organization: Score = 6

The essay has a clear and logical introduction, supporting paragraphs that develop her thesis, and a conclusion that makes sure that the points about society in general are still tied to the very specific topic at hand (internet access). The writer has clearly thought through the points she wanted to make, and made sure she was aligning that with a functional structure.

Language Use and Conventions: Score = 6

The student uses a good mix of long, sophisticated sentences and shorter ones for exposition or emphasis. There are very few errors throughout, and she has chosen strong, precise words like *equalizing* to support her points.

Plan Your Essay

Write Your Essay

School Vouchers

Education policy in the United States is often controversial, but few issues have been so controversial as school vouchers. The American school system has long been segmented into public schools (free for all students) and private schools (typically requiring paid tuition). The idea behind school vouchers is that families with school-age students would receive government "vouchers" that could be applied to any school in a particular area, meaning that the government would pay tuition to ensure that students aren't limited to public school by financial considerations. Given the importance of education in every child's life, the implication of whether vouchers divert resources away from public schools is worth exploring.

Read and carefully consider these perspectives. Each suggests a particular way of thinking about school vouchers.

Perspective One

Vouchers do a disservice to students, their families, and their communities. If people run away from public schools, that endangers the public schools' ability to get funding and resources necessary to improve the schools and educational outcomes. The money that would be spent on vouchers should be used to improve our existing public schools.

Perspective Two

Students shouldn't be herded into public schools by default. It should be a choice that lets families make the best decisions for their children, regardless of the family's ability to pay tuition. Vouchers allow parents to take this decision into their own hands.

Perspective Three

The school system is broken, and charter schools (which are privately operated and publicly funded) are the way to go. Resources should be spent instead on developing charter schools that combine the private school experience with public funding. No vouchers would be necessary; children would simply apply for these tuition-free schools.

ESSAY TASK

Write a cohesive, logical essay in which you consider multiple perspectives on whether educational resources should be channeled into public schools, private school vouchers, or a third option (for example, charter schools).

In your essay, be sure to:

- examine and assess the perspectives given
- declare and explain your own perspective on the issue
- discuss the relationship between your perspective and those given

Your perspective may be in full or partial agreement, or in total disagreement, with any of the others. Whatever the case, support your ideas with logical reasoning and detailed, persuasive examples.

Plan and Write Your Essay

Use the first two pages of the Writing test answer sheet (located before the essay prompt) to generate ideas and plan your essay. Then use the following four pages to write your essay.

Consider the following as you compose your essay:

What are the strengths and weaknesses of the three perspectives provided?

- Identify the insights they present and what they fail to consider.
- Ascertain why a given perspective might persuade or fail to persuade.

How can you apply your own experience, knowledge, and values?

- Express your perspective on the issue, identifying the perspective's strengths and weaknesses.
- Formulate a plan to support your perspective in your essay.

Sample Essay—Score 1

Ideas and Analysis:	Score = 1
Development and Support:	Score = 1
Organization:	Score = 1
Language Use and Conventions:	Score = 1

If I had the choice I would never be at the school I'm at now. Choice is important, but not as important as a good education. If I had the choice to make and a voucher I would choose to go to school in another town. My parents would probably want me to go to parokeal school, but I woul'dnt want that for myself. Charter schools seem cool I wish there was one in my town. There's not, tho, so I can't say whether that would be the best option available. It's important to know about all choices before you make your choice, so that's why vouchers are probably the best option here.

Scoring Explanation

Ideas and Analysis: Score = 1

From this essay, it's not clear that the writer even read the full prompt or any of the perspectives. There are some key words that may have been skimmed from the prompt, like "choice" and "charter schools," but there's no cohesive argument presented here.

Development and Support: Score = 1

The writer goes off on a tangent about her own school and what she would want to do, but provides very little evidence or support. It's fine to share personal experiences in your ACT essay, but you should always make sure they're appropriate, and that they relate directly to the points you're trying to make.

Organization: Score = 1

Again, it's unlikely that the writer paid much attention to the prompt or the perspectives, or the task at hand. There is no clear introduction, body, or conclusion here—it's all a big mashup of the writer's personal musings and opinions.

Language Use and Conventions: Score = 1

This essay is made very difficult to read by the numerous spelling, punctuation, and sentence errors. When writing your essay on test day, pay special attention to your sentences and the words you use, in order to make sure that you're conveying the information you want to convey, and that you're not hiding it in unclear or distracting language.

Sample Essay—Score 2

Ideas and Analysis:	Score = 2
Development and Support:	Score = 2
Organization:	Score = 2
Language Use and Conventions:	Score = 2

The Constitution says that we have freedom of choice. That should expend to our education choices as well. Public schools are not up to snuff any more. Common core has basically destroyed public school education, which I can personally vouch for. Private schools are not subject to common core, so that is the best option.

Common core sets national standards that do not allow schools to meet their students individual needs. It means we're all learning the same things to take the same tests. We are students and individuals, not cookies that come from the same mold. Now that Common core is the law of the land, I think education resources should be put into helping students get away from that failing system.

Private schools mean we have choices. The vouchers would be for any school that we want to go to, and the government would have to pay for it no matter whether or not our families can afford the tution. The vouchers are a ticket out of a failing system but let's us have input into our educational destiny.

Whether or not schools should offer vouchers is a complicated issue, and I believe we should have as much choice as possible.

Sample Essay—Score 3

Ideas and Analysis:	Score = 3
Development and Support:	Score = 3
Organization:	Score = 3
Language Use and Conventions:	Score = 3

School choice is a very difficult issue. Do we try to focus in the system we have (public schools)? Or should we let everyone decide where they want to go (vouchers)? Or do we ignore both of those options and put our resources in schools that are like a hybrid of public and private schools (charter schools)? The issue is complicated but the answer is clear: charter schools.

Public schools are basically failing. I read an article that says that they are basically indocktrinating students to particular points of view, which is a problem since they receive public taxpayer funds. I also know that test scores are down all across the state, which means that our public schools are not very healthy. This makes public schools a poor option in the school choice debate.

However, I am not convinced that private schools are the best option either. There is only one private school in my town. If everyone had a voucher to go where they wanted to (out of public schools), where would all the students go? Private schools have their own problems as well: if a school is religious but a student is not, that could cause some issues. Besides, if the government is willing to spend money to send students to private schools, that money could probably be better spent on improving the schools we already have.

This is why charter schools are the best comparison. As stated, they are publicly funded like public schools, but are run by private companies that are presumably experts in education. You get the welcoming of public schools, but with the educational focus of a private one.

To sum up, both public schools and private schools are not the best options for students who want the best education. Families should have the choice of sending their kids to schools, but to schools that are better than what we have now (charter schools).

Sample Essay—Score 4

Ideas and Analysis:	Score = 4
Development and Support:	Score = 4
Organization:	Score = 4
Language Use and Conventions:	Score = 4

Freedom to choose is one of the strongest American principles we have: the freedom to speak freely, the freedom to live our lives as we see fit, the freedom to be whoever we want to be, etc. There is no reason this freedom should not extend to our educational options. With such freedom to choose, it is cruel to limit children's education to whatever school is nearby, regardless of how good (or bad) that school is. For families who can't afford to pull their kids out and send them to more expensive private schools, that removes freedom completely. Government-funded vouchers, available to children who might otherwise be limited to failing schools that can't support their needs, restores that freedom.

As a student in a crowded urban school, I understand firsthand what it's like to struggle for attention and resources in a public school that is spread too thin. Class sizes are huge, and teachers do their best, but can only do so much with classes of 30 kids or more. If you're struggling, you might get extra help, or if you're an elite honors student, there are programs. But for many of us, we get the "good enough," one size fits all resources. If I and my parents had the opportunity to send me to a private school without regard to being able to pay tens of thousands of dollars in tuition, we might well have taken it. We never had that choice, and so I've done the best I can in the school I was dealt. Yet the "what if?" questions might always linger.

If we took the money that would be spent on vouchers and instead sent it to public school budgets, there is little guarantee that things would improve. Public schools are already receiving millions in public funds, and yet the educational atmosphere is more challenging than ever. If public schools are forced to compete with private schools for students and resources, that may very well prompt a more focused overhaul that would improve the schools beyond what we see when there is very little competition.

Education should not be reduced to a default option—and that is what it has become for so many students and their families who are stuck in schools that they would not have chosen on their own. Kids deserve schools that match their needs and their goals. The only way to achieve that in the short term is to create a system that puts freedom of choice back into the hands of students and their parents.

Sample Essay—Score 5

Ideas and Analysis:	Score = 5
Development and Support:	Score = 5
Organization:	Score = 5
Language Use and Conventions:	Score = 5

In an ideal world, every person would have exactly the education he or she wants, without regard to local resources, or ability to pay for it. Since we don't live in and ideal world, we often find ourselves struggling with the concept of how to ensure that we are offering education as close to that ideal as possible, but within real-world constraints like budgets, population changes, and personal finances. Public schools have been the gold standard for decades in this country, but more and more as schools struggle with large class sizes and strained resources, that gold feels tarnished. The idea of school vouchers, where families can choose whether to send their kids to public or private schools of their choice, can seem like an easy out. However, vouchers are not a practical long term solution. Putting more energy and resources into restoring our public schools is the far better option.

Vouchers are an escape hatch for families looking for improved educational opportunities for their children. The smaller size of private schools and the focused curricula are appealing, especially for students caught in underperforming public schools. However, having the government spend money on voucher tuition at the private schools diverts public funds that could be better spent investing in the public schools for more teachers and more programs.

Diverting funds from public schools to pay for students' private schooling will create a vicious cycle. Underfunded schools will continue to be underfunded, leaving them little room to improve and offer better education to diverse groups of students who rely on public schools. Eventually, these schools will not be viable options at all, leaving fewer schools in general where students can go.

Also, it seems that pro-voucher proponents have not considered what happens when too many people decide to take the plunge and use their vouchers elsewhere. Families typically want their children to go to school nearby. If a town has, say, two private schools and six public schools, where will the students go after the two private schools are full? This calls for a method that fixes the root problem rather than fixing the symptoms currently plaguing public schools. Increasing resources to the public school system helps work on those underlying problems rather than shifting the problems somewhere else.

If something is broken, you have two options: try to fix it, or move on completely and buy a replacement. Vouchers let people move on without a second thought and replace the broken item. But taking that same money you would have spent, and working to fix what's worth saving means you will have a durable product that can be enjoyed for a long time to come.

Sample Essay—Score 6

Ideas and Analysis:	Score = 6
Development and Support:	Score = 6
Organization:	Score = 6
Language Use and Conventions:	Score = 6

Few issues are as personal or important for families as their kids' futures. Education is a significant part of that, because it is such a crucial building block for a child's success later in life; without the best foundation possible, students could be missing out on essential skills and opportunities. This makes debates like the one over school vouchers fraught and emotional, so it is more important than ever to take a reasonable approach to the issue that accounts for the concerns of both sides. This means finding a compromise—in this case, that compromise is the charter school.

Charter schools take the best of both worlds when it comes to education. They are structured like private schools, with specialized curriculum and operated by non-government entities. However, they are free for students to attend, because they are publicly funded. For parents who find their local schools unsatisfactory, but are unable or unwilling to pay tuition for local private schools, it can be a fantastic option.

Walking away from the public school model can feel like a kind of failure. After all, the United States's public school system was founded on the ideal that people should have equal access to an education that would allow them to pursue whatever life they want to pursue. Rich children, poor children, all could have access to the "three Rs," as the old saying goes (Reading, wRiting, aRithmetic). Admitting that the public schools may not be good enough anymore can feel unpatriotic, or a little disloyal to those ideals. This is part of why charter schools are so effective: they are not exclusive like some of the more elite private schools, and so are available to virtually any student; but they also don't come with the same financial and social price tags.

Similarly, private school vouchers can feel constraining as well. Even with a scholarship, private school costs may be difficult for some families to manage. There are also social factors to consider, as many private schools are also parochial, or religious ones. Sending one's child there also means agreeing to specific kinds of instruction that may be mandated by the private school's social or religious mission. Plus, as privately owned institutions, these schools may not be subject to the same non-discrimination regulations that public schools are. Like public schools, charter schools are not committed to particular points of view, as they're publicly funded.

Charter schools combine the best of both worlds: the active choice of attending private schools, with the resources available to private school students; and the ease of attending public schools, where inclusivity is the norm. These schools are the way to channel public resources into a more rigorous educational experience than many public schools offer these days, without the obligations of a private school.

Scoring Explanation

Ideas and Analysis: Score = 6

This essay focuses mostly on the third perspective, but the writer finds ways to draw in elements of perspectives one and two while fleshing out her opinion that the third option—neither public schools nor private schools—is the best possible compromise on the issue.

Development and Support: Score = 6

The writer builds on the drawbacks of both public and private schools, by intuiting things that may give parents pause about each (religious and social implications of private schools that aren't subject to non-discrimination laws, or the hectic, oversized classes in some public schools). The writer does a good job showing how perspectives one and two are constraining, while the third is a more open and fruitful option.

Organization: Score = 6

This essay is organized pretty clearly; the writer wants to achieve three things: showing why public schools are problematic, showing why private schools are problematic, and explaining why charter schools are the best possible compromise to a sticky issue. She starts with a fairly broad introduction, but dives into these specific perspectives and makes concrete transitions throughout to keep the flow moving.

Language Use and Conventions: Score = 6

The student creates strong imagery that both public schools and vouchers are unappealing by using very specific words (*mandated*, *unpatriotic*) to set her tone. The sentences she uses are complex, but also clear. In the ACT essay, you shouldn't be complicated just for the sake of it, but should make sure that your points are coming across clearly no matter what.

PART VIII: PRACTICE TESTS FOR THE ACT® EXAM

Chapter 15: Practice Tests for the ACT® Exam

Chapter 16: Scoring Your Practice Tests

PRACTICE TESTS FOR THE ACT® EXAM

No matter where you are in your preparation process, taking a full-length practice test is the best way to test your skills, assess your strengths and weaknesses, and determine where you should focus your study plan in the time leading up to test day. The first of the final two chapters of this guide, Chapter 15, contains four full-length practice tests that mirror the ones you will see when you take the actual ACT exam. The last chapter, Chapter 16, contains the information you need to score your exams to give you a good idea of the results you would get on the official score report.

CHAPTER 15: PRACTICE TESTS FOR THE ACT® EXAM

OVERVIEW

It's practice test time—time to see how much you've learned and how close you are to being ready to take the ACT exam. Before you start taking your practice tests, consider the following reminders and suggestions.

When you take each test, do your best to simulate the most test-like conditions possible. Be sure to get your answer sheets ready—you can either cut them out of the book or photocopy them. Set aside a 3-hour and 30-minute chunk of time, and find a quiet spot free from distractions. Yes, it's hard to find hours of free time to devote to taking a practice test, but the end result is worth it—by the time you sit down to take the actual ACT exam, you will be used to the exact format, length, and process.

Test Day Preparation: Simulate the Silence

Even if you feel you work best with noise in the background, you won't have that option on test day. It's best to work under the same conditions you will have when taking your actual exam. Don't have a television on in the background or music blaring in your earbuds. Most importantly, switch all of your electronic devices to silent (or turn them off!)—as much as you think you can resist the temptation of checking a new text or email, you probably can't.

After you take each practice test, you should: 1) calculate your scores using the information and charts in Chapter 16, and 2) review your answers with the detailed explanations given at the end of each test. Calculating your score will assign a numerical value to each test you take, so you can get a sense of where you started and how you improve throughout your study plan. You can also get a sense of which sections are giving you the most trouble, so you can focus your review on a specific test section (or even a specific subsection) before you take your next practice test. The answer explanations in this book are extremely helpful, as they not only explain why the correct answer is right, but they also go into detail about why each incorrect answer is wrong. You will see the mistakes you tend to repeat, which will help you avoid them in the future.

At this point, you're ahead of the game—you've dedicated yourself to preparation and practice, which is a huge step in the direction of ACT success. So don't get too discouraged if the results to your first few practice tests aren't exactly at your goal score. If you put in the time and focus, assess your test results, and tailor your study plan to hit the areas where you need help, you will reach the results you want by test day.

GOOD LUCK!

English Test

1. Ⓐ Ⓑ Ⓒ Ⓓ	16. Ⓕ Ⓖ Ⓗ Ⓙ	31. Ⓐ Ⓑ Ⓒ Ⓓ	46. Ⓕ Ⓖ Ⓗ Ⓙ	61. Ⓐ Ⓑ Ⓒ Ⓓ
2. Ⓕ Ⓖ Ⓗ Ⓙ	17. Ⓐ Ⓑ Ⓒ Ⓓ	32. Ⓕ Ⓖ Ⓗ Ⓙ	47. Ⓐ Ⓑ Ⓒ Ⓓ	62. Ⓕ Ⓖ Ⓗ Ⓙ
3. Ⓐ Ⓑ Ⓒ Ⓓ	18. Ⓕ Ⓖ Ⓗ Ⓙ	33. Ⓐ Ⓑ Ⓒ Ⓓ	48. Ⓕ Ⓖ Ⓗ Ⓙ	63. Ⓐ Ⓑ Ⓒ Ⓓ
4. Ⓕ Ⓖ Ⓗ Ⓙ	19. Ⓐ Ⓑ Ⓒ Ⓓ	34. Ⓕ Ⓖ Ⓗ Ⓙ	49. Ⓐ Ⓑ Ⓒ Ⓓ	64. Ⓕ Ⓖ Ⓗ Ⓙ
5. Ⓐ Ⓑ Ⓒ Ⓓ	20. Ⓕ Ⓖ Ⓗ Ⓙ	35. Ⓐ Ⓑ Ⓒ Ⓓ	50. Ⓕ Ⓖ Ⓗ Ⓙ	65. Ⓐ Ⓑ Ⓒ Ⓓ
6. Ⓕ Ⓖ Ⓗ Ⓙ	21. Ⓐ Ⓑ Ⓒ Ⓓ	36. Ⓕ Ⓖ Ⓗ Ⓙ	51. Ⓐ Ⓑ Ⓒ Ⓓ	66. Ⓕ Ⓖ Ⓗ Ⓙ
7. Ⓐ Ⓑ Ⓒ Ⓓ	22. Ⓕ Ⓖ Ⓗ Ⓙ	37. Ⓐ Ⓑ Ⓒ Ⓓ	52. Ⓕ Ⓖ Ⓗ Ⓙ	67. Ⓐ Ⓑ Ⓒ Ⓓ
8. Ⓕ Ⓖ Ⓗ Ⓙ	23. Ⓐ Ⓑ Ⓒ Ⓓ	38. Ⓕ Ⓖ Ⓗ Ⓙ	53. Ⓐ Ⓑ Ⓒ Ⓓ	68. Ⓕ Ⓖ Ⓗ Ⓙ
9. Ⓐ Ⓑ Ⓒ Ⓓ	24. Ⓕ Ⓖ Ⓗ Ⓙ	39. Ⓐ Ⓑ Ⓒ Ⓓ	54. Ⓕ Ⓖ Ⓗ Ⓙ	69. Ⓐ Ⓑ Ⓒ Ⓓ
10. Ⓕ Ⓖ Ⓗ Ⓙ	25. Ⓐ Ⓑ Ⓒ Ⓓ	40. Ⓕ Ⓖ Ⓗ Ⓙ	55. Ⓐ Ⓑ Ⓒ Ⓓ	70. Ⓕ Ⓖ Ⓗ Ⓙ
11. Ⓐ Ⓑ Ⓒ Ⓓ	26. Ⓕ Ⓖ Ⓗ Ⓙ	41. Ⓐ Ⓑ Ⓒ Ⓓ	56. Ⓕ Ⓖ Ⓗ Ⓙ	71. Ⓐ Ⓑ Ⓒ Ⓓ
12. Ⓕ Ⓖ Ⓗ Ⓙ	27. Ⓐ Ⓑ Ⓒ Ⓓ	42. Ⓕ Ⓖ Ⓗ Ⓙ	57. Ⓐ Ⓑ Ⓒ Ⓓ	72. Ⓕ Ⓖ Ⓗ Ⓙ
13. Ⓐ Ⓑ Ⓒ Ⓓ	28. Ⓕ Ⓖ Ⓗ Ⓙ	43. Ⓐ Ⓑ Ⓒ Ⓓ	58. Ⓕ Ⓖ Ⓗ Ⓙ	73. Ⓐ Ⓑ Ⓒ Ⓓ
14. Ⓕ Ⓖ Ⓗ Ⓙ	29. Ⓐ Ⓑ Ⓒ Ⓓ	44. Ⓕ Ⓖ Ⓗ Ⓙ	59. Ⓐ Ⓑ Ⓒ Ⓓ	74. Ⓕ Ⓖ Ⓗ Ⓙ
15. Ⓐ Ⓑ Ⓒ Ⓓ	30. Ⓕ Ⓖ Ⓗ Ⓙ	45. Ⓐ Ⓑ Ⓒ Ⓓ	60. Ⓕ Ⓖ Ⓗ Ⓙ	75. Ⓐ Ⓑ Ⓒ Ⓓ

Mathematics Test

1. Ⓐ Ⓑ Ⓒ Ⓓ Ⓔ	16. Ⓕ Ⓖ Ⓗ Ⓙ Ⓚ	31. Ⓐ Ⓑ Ⓒ Ⓓ Ⓔ	46. Ⓕ Ⓖ Ⓗ Ⓙ Ⓚ
2. Ⓕ Ⓖ Ⓗ Ⓙ Ⓚ	17. Ⓐ Ⓑ Ⓒ Ⓓ Ⓔ	32. Ⓕ Ⓖ Ⓗ Ⓙ Ⓚ	47. Ⓐ Ⓑ Ⓒ Ⓓ Ⓔ
3. Ⓐ Ⓑ Ⓒ Ⓓ Ⓔ	18. Ⓕ Ⓖ Ⓗ Ⓙ Ⓚ	33. Ⓐ Ⓑ Ⓒ Ⓓ Ⓔ	48. Ⓕ Ⓖ Ⓗ Ⓙ Ⓚ
4. Ⓕ Ⓖ Ⓗ Ⓙ Ⓚ	19. Ⓐ Ⓑ Ⓒ Ⓓ Ⓔ	34. Ⓕ Ⓖ Ⓗ Ⓙ Ⓚ	49. Ⓐ Ⓑ Ⓒ Ⓓ Ⓔ
5. Ⓐ Ⓑ Ⓒ Ⓓ Ⓔ	20. Ⓕ Ⓖ Ⓗ Ⓙ Ⓚ	35. Ⓐ Ⓑ Ⓒ Ⓓ Ⓔ	50. Ⓕ Ⓖ Ⓗ Ⓙ Ⓚ
6. Ⓕ Ⓖ Ⓗ Ⓙ Ⓚ	21. Ⓐ Ⓑ Ⓒ Ⓓ Ⓔ	36. Ⓕ Ⓖ Ⓗ Ⓙ Ⓚ	51. Ⓐ Ⓑ Ⓒ Ⓓ Ⓔ
7. Ⓐ Ⓑ Ⓒ Ⓓ Ⓔ	22. Ⓕ Ⓖ Ⓗ Ⓙ Ⓚ	37. Ⓐ Ⓑ Ⓒ Ⓓ Ⓔ	52. Ⓕ Ⓖ Ⓗ Ⓙ Ⓚ
8. Ⓕ Ⓖ Ⓗ Ⓙ Ⓚ	23. Ⓐ Ⓑ Ⓒ Ⓓ Ⓔ	38. Ⓕ Ⓖ Ⓗ Ⓙ Ⓚ	53. Ⓐ Ⓑ Ⓒ Ⓓ Ⓔ
9. Ⓐ Ⓑ Ⓒ Ⓓ Ⓔ	24. Ⓕ Ⓖ Ⓗ Ⓙ Ⓚ	39. Ⓐ Ⓑ Ⓒ Ⓓ Ⓔ	54. Ⓕ Ⓖ Ⓗ Ⓙ Ⓚ
10. Ⓕ Ⓖ Ⓗ Ⓙ Ⓚ	25. Ⓐ Ⓑ Ⓒ Ⓓ Ⓔ	40. Ⓕ Ⓖ Ⓗ Ⓙ Ⓚ	55. Ⓐ Ⓑ Ⓒ Ⓓ Ⓔ
11. Ⓐ Ⓑ Ⓒ Ⓓ Ⓔ	26. Ⓕ Ⓖ Ⓗ Ⓙ Ⓚ	41. Ⓐ Ⓑ Ⓒ Ⓓ Ⓔ	56. Ⓕ Ⓖ Ⓗ Ⓙ Ⓚ
12. Ⓕ Ⓖ Ⓗ Ⓙ Ⓚ	27. Ⓐ Ⓑ Ⓒ Ⓓ Ⓔ	42. Ⓕ Ⓖ Ⓗ Ⓙ Ⓚ	57. Ⓐ Ⓑ Ⓒ Ⓓ Ⓔ
13. Ⓐ Ⓑ Ⓒ Ⓓ Ⓔ	28. Ⓕ Ⓖ Ⓗ Ⓙ Ⓚ	43. Ⓐ Ⓑ Ⓒ Ⓓ Ⓔ	58. Ⓕ Ⓖ Ⓗ Ⓙ Ⓚ
14. Ⓕ Ⓖ Ⓗ Ⓙ Ⓚ	29. Ⓐ Ⓑ Ⓒ Ⓓ Ⓔ	44. Ⓕ Ⓖ Ⓗ Ⓙ Ⓚ	59. Ⓐ Ⓑ Ⓒ Ⓓ Ⓔ
15. Ⓐ Ⓑ Ⓒ Ⓓ Ⓔ	30. Ⓕ Ⓖ Ⓗ Ⓙ Ⓚ	45. Ⓐ Ⓑ Ⓒ Ⓓ Ⓔ	60. Ⓕ Ⓖ Ⓗ Ⓙ Ⓚ

Reading Test

1. Ⓐ Ⓑ Ⓒ Ⓓ	11. Ⓐ Ⓑ Ⓒ Ⓓ	21. Ⓐ Ⓑ Ⓒ Ⓓ	31. Ⓐ Ⓑ Ⓒ Ⓓ
2. Ⓕ Ⓖ Ⓗ Ⓙ	12. Ⓕ Ⓖ Ⓗ Ⓙ	22. Ⓕ Ⓖ Ⓗ Ⓙ	32. Ⓕ Ⓖ Ⓗ Ⓙ
3. Ⓐ Ⓑ Ⓒ Ⓓ	13. Ⓐ Ⓑ Ⓒ Ⓓ	23. Ⓐ Ⓑ Ⓒ Ⓓ	33. Ⓐ Ⓑ Ⓒ Ⓓ
4. Ⓕ Ⓖ Ⓗ Ⓙ	14. Ⓕ Ⓖ Ⓗ Ⓙ	24. Ⓕ Ⓖ Ⓗ Ⓙ	34. Ⓕ Ⓖ Ⓗ Ⓙ
5. Ⓐ Ⓑ Ⓒ Ⓓ	15. Ⓐ Ⓑ Ⓒ Ⓓ	25. Ⓐ Ⓑ Ⓒ Ⓓ	35. Ⓐ Ⓑ Ⓒ Ⓓ
6. Ⓕ Ⓖ Ⓗ Ⓙ	16. Ⓕ Ⓖ Ⓗ Ⓙ	26. Ⓕ Ⓖ Ⓗ Ⓙ	36. Ⓕ Ⓖ Ⓗ Ⓙ
7. Ⓐ Ⓑ Ⓒ Ⓓ	17. Ⓐ Ⓑ Ⓒ Ⓓ	27. Ⓐ Ⓑ Ⓒ Ⓓ	37. Ⓐ Ⓑ Ⓒ Ⓓ
8. Ⓕ Ⓖ Ⓗ Ⓙ	18. Ⓕ Ⓖ Ⓗ Ⓙ	28. Ⓕ Ⓖ Ⓗ Ⓙ	38. Ⓕ Ⓖ Ⓗ Ⓙ
9. Ⓐ Ⓑ Ⓒ Ⓓ	19. Ⓐ Ⓑ Ⓒ Ⓓ	29. Ⓐ Ⓑ Ⓒ Ⓓ	39. Ⓐ Ⓑ Ⓒ Ⓓ
10. Ⓕ Ⓖ Ⓗ Ⓙ	20. Ⓕ Ⓖ Ⓗ Ⓙ	30. Ⓕ Ⓖ Ⓗ Ⓙ	40. Ⓕ Ⓖ Ⓗ Ⓙ

Science Test

1. Ⓐ Ⓑ Ⓒ Ⓓ	11. Ⓐ Ⓑ Ⓒ Ⓓ	21. Ⓐ Ⓑ Ⓒ Ⓓ	31. Ⓐ Ⓑ Ⓒ Ⓓ
2. Ⓕ Ⓖ Ⓗ Ⓙ	12. Ⓕ Ⓖ Ⓗ Ⓙ	22. Ⓕ Ⓖ Ⓗ Ⓙ	32. Ⓕ Ⓖ Ⓗ Ⓙ
3. Ⓐ Ⓑ Ⓒ Ⓓ	13. Ⓐ Ⓑ Ⓒ Ⓓ	23. Ⓐ Ⓑ Ⓒ Ⓓ	33. Ⓐ Ⓑ Ⓒ Ⓓ
4. Ⓕ Ⓖ Ⓗ Ⓙ	14. Ⓕ Ⓖ Ⓗ Ⓙ	24. Ⓕ Ⓖ Ⓗ Ⓙ	34. Ⓕ Ⓖ Ⓗ Ⓙ
5. Ⓐ Ⓑ Ⓒ Ⓓ	15. Ⓐ Ⓑ Ⓒ Ⓓ	25. Ⓐ Ⓑ Ⓒ Ⓓ	35. Ⓐ Ⓑ Ⓒ Ⓓ
6. Ⓕ Ⓖ Ⓗ Ⓙ	16. Ⓕ Ⓖ Ⓗ Ⓙ	26. Ⓕ Ⓖ Ⓗ Ⓙ	36. Ⓕ Ⓖ Ⓗ Ⓙ
7. Ⓐ Ⓑ Ⓒ Ⓓ	17. Ⓐ Ⓑ Ⓒ Ⓓ	27. Ⓐ Ⓑ Ⓒ Ⓓ	37. Ⓐ Ⓑ Ⓒ Ⓓ
8. Ⓕ Ⓖ Ⓗ Ⓙ	18. Ⓕ Ⓖ Ⓗ Ⓙ	28. Ⓕ Ⓖ Ⓗ Ⓙ	38. Ⓕ Ⓖ Ⓗ Ⓙ
9. Ⓐ Ⓑ Ⓒ Ⓓ	19. Ⓐ Ⓑ Ⓒ Ⓓ	29. Ⓐ Ⓑ Ⓒ Ⓓ	39. Ⓐ Ⓑ Ⓒ Ⓓ
10. Ⓕ Ⓖ Ⓗ Ⓙ	20. Ⓕ Ⓖ Ⓗ Ⓙ	30. Ⓕ Ⓖ Ⓗ Ⓙ	40. Ⓕ Ⓖ Ⓗ Ⓙ

WRITING TEST

PLAN YOUR ESSAY

Write Your Essay

ENGLISH TEST

45 Minutes—75 Questions

DIRECTIONS: In this section, you will see passages with words and phrases that are underlined and numbered. In the right-hand column you will see a question corresponding to each number that provides alternatives to the underlined part. In most of the items, you are to choose the best alternative. If no change is needed, choose NO CHANGE.

In other items, there will be either a question about an underlined portion of the passage, or a question about a section of the passage, or about the passage as a whole. This question type will correspond to a number or numbers in a box.

For each question, choose the best alternative or answer and fill in the corresponding circle on the answer sheet.

PASSAGE I

Fossey's Quest

[1]

Dian Fossey was a <u>researcher, a visionary and a pioneer</u> [1] in the field of animal conservation. More specifically, Fossey dedicated her life to preserving the endangered mountain gorilla in Africa.

[2]

<u>She was born in San Francisco, Fossey made her first trip to Africa in 1963.</u> [2] At the time, she was 31 years old. In the course of her trip, she met <u>Dr. Louis Leakey. A prominent</u> [3] archaeologist and anthropologist. Dr. Leakey believed in the importance of research on large apes, and he <u>encourages</u> [4] Fossey to undertake it. Fossey took up the <u>challenge. Deciding</u> [5] to study mountain gorillas.

1. A. NO CHANGE
   B. a researcher a, visionary and a, pioneer
   C. a researcher, a visionary, and a pioneer
   D. a researcher a visionary, and a pioneer

2. F. NO CHANGE
   G. Fossey, was born in San Francisco, made her first trip to Africa in 1963.
   H. Fossey was born in San Francisco and made her first trip to Africa in 1963.
   J. Born in San Francisco, in 1963 Fossey made her first trip, to Africa.

3. A. NO CHANGE
   B. Dr. Louis Leakey. Who was a prominent
   C. Dr. Louis Leakey a prominent
   D. Dr. Louis Leakey, a prominent

4. F. NO CHANGE
   G. was encouraging
   H. will encourage
   J. encouraged

5. A. NO CHANGE
   B. challenge; deciding
   C. challenge deciding
   D. challenge, deciding

CONTINUE

[3]

Fossey began her work in the African country of Zaire, but was forced to leaf (6) because of political unrest. She moved to another African country, Rwanda, where she established a research camp in a national park. There, she spent thousands of hours observing the behavior of gorillas. Her steadfast patience won the trust of the animals, and they began to accept (7) her presence among them. As a result, she was able to observe gorillas' behavior that had previously never been seen by humans.

[4]

Spending so much time to observe the gorillas, (8) Fossey naturally distinguished (9) among them and had particular favorites. One of these favorites, was a young male gorilla name (10) Digit. Still, (11) Digit was killed by a poacher, an illegal hunter of protected animals. Fossey was stunned and saddened. She began a public campaign to raise awareness of the problem of gorilla poaching, a practice that threatened the continued existence of mountain gorillas. The rhinoceros, too, from poaching has faced grave danger. (12) Fossey's campaign earned worldwide attention and support, and she continued to live and work in Africa for many years thereafter.

[5]

In 1980, Fossey took a teaching position at Cornell University and wrote a book, *Gorillas in the Mist*, that brought further

6.
- **F.** NO CHANGE
- **G.** leave
- **H.** relieve
- **J.** reprieve

7.
- **A.** NO CHANGE
- **B.** began to accept and also tolerate
- **C.** began to show an acceptance, even, and also a tolerance
- **D.** began to show that they accepted

8.
- **F.** NO CHANGE
- **G.** Because she spent so much time observing the gorillas
- **H.** Spending much time in observation of the gorillas
- **J.** Being very sure to observe the gorillas

9.
- **A.** NO CHANGE
- **B.** Fossey naturally distinguishing
- **C.** the naturally distinguished Fossey
- **D.** Fossey was naturally distinguished

10.
- **F.** NO CHANGE
- **G.** named
- **H.** naming
- **J.** nameable

11.
- **A.** NO CHANGE
- **B.** Unfortunately
- **C.** In fact
- **D.** Because

12.
- **F.** NO CHANGE
- **G.** The rhinoceros, too, has faced grave danger from poaching.
- **H.** From poaching as well, has the rhinoceros faced grave danger.
- **J.** OMIT the underlined portion.

attention to the crisis of diminishing numbers of mountain gorillas. Afterward, Fossey returned to Rwanda and spent the rest of her life working to protect the mountain gorilla. <u>She continues working even after her death.</u> (13) [14]

[6]

Today, the population of mountain gorillas in Rwanda is rising, thanks to the legacy of Dian Fossey.

13. A. NO CHANGE
B. She worked even after her death continues.
C. Even after her death, she continues working.
D. Her work continues even after her death.

14. Which of the following sentences, when inserted after the second sentence in Paragraph 5, would provide a concrete example of a statement made by the author?
F. She loved gorillas very much.
G. She remains well-known among conservationists.
H. Her efforts included organizing patrols to protect gorillas from poachers.
J. Another primate conservationist who was influenced by Louis Leakey was Jane Goodall.

Question 15 asks about the passage as a whole.

15. Suppose the author of this passage had been assigned to write an essay that discussed whether Fossey's goals justified her very controversial methods. Would this essay successfully address that topic?
A. Yes, because the author details the controversy Fossey inspired.
B. Yes, because the author describes Fossey's important legacy in the field of conservation.
C. No, because the author never offers an opinion as to whether Fossey's work was of any benefit to the mountain gorilla.
D. No, because the author does not mention that any of Fossey's methods were controversial.

PASSAGE II

The Smoke That Thunders

[1]

The <u>Zambezi river</u> (16) rushes along which the border of the African countries of Zambia and Zimbabwe. This is no ordinary river; it is home to one of the most stunning achievements of nature: a spectacular waterfall that is <u>bigger and twice as large</u> (17)

16. F. NO CHANGE
G. zambezi River
H. zambezi river
J. Zambezi River

17. A. NO CHANGE
B. twice as large and bigger
C. twice as large
D. smaller but twice as large

CONTINUE

as North America's Niagara Falls. The Kololo tribe, who lived in the area in the 1800s, called the falls "Mosi-oa-Tunya," or "The Smoke That Thunders." Around the same time, British explorers who saw the falls (18) for the first time dubbed them "The Victoria Falls," after their queen.

[2]

The waterfall, which is composed of five actually separate falls, (19) is considered to be one of the seven wonders of the natural world—and for good reason. (20) Visitors to the falls can spot columns of spray from up to 25 miles away, as millions of cubic meters of water per minute plunge 100 meters over a cliff. Anyone observing who witnesses (21) this wonder will understand the name "Smoke That Thunders." The roaring, crashing fall's (22) send up soaking billows of spray. Imagine (23) —a rushing, two-kilometer-wide river makes a sudden plunge downward for over 100 meters, slamming into the gorge below.

[3]

Opposite the cliff, across the gorge, stands a spectacular stretch of rain forest? (24) This forest provides another perspective on the grandiosity (25) of the falls.

18.
- **F.** NO CHANGE
- **G.** who will see the falls
- **H.** who will saw the falls
- **J.** who will have been seeing

19.
- **A.** NO CHANGE
- **B.** which of five separate falls actually is composed
- **C.** which is actually composed of five separate falls
- **D.** it is actually composed of five separate falls

20.
- **F.** NO CHANGE
- **G.** one of the others is the Grand Canyon
- **H.** some people don't think it's that spectacular
- **J.** Africa contains many wonders

21.
- **A.** NO CHANGE
- **B.** who witnesses
- **C.** who looks to see
- **D.** observing to see

22.
- **F.** NO CHANGE
- **G.** crashing's falls
- **H.** crashing falls'
- **J.** crashing falls

23.
- **A.** NO CHANGE
- **B.** spray, imagine
- **C.** spray. To imagine
- **D.** spray imagining

24.
- **F.** NO CHANGE
- **G.** rain forest
- **H.** rain forest.
- **J.** rain forest,

25.
- **A.** NO CHANGE
- **B.** generosity
- **C.** fruitfulness
- **D.** peacefulness

Visitors can enjoy, a walk along a path through the lush forest and a breathtaking, spray-soaked vision of the falls. The Knife Edge Bridge provides a particularly spectacular view of the falls and of the Boiling Pot, a dramatic turn in the river. As some would say, "a watched pot never boils." Many visitors choose to view the sights from above, taking advantage of the services of pilots who fly small planes filled with tourists over the falls.

(Underlined: "enjoy, a" = 26; "As some would say, "a watched pot never boils."" = 27)

[4]

While the waterfall is the attention-grabbing attraction of the area, the surrounding Mosi-oa-Tunya National Park is full of wonders as well. The natural beauty of the local wildlife is to be admired by visitors. Among the animals who make their homes at the Mosi-oa-Tunya National Park are zebras, giraffes, several species of antelope, wildebeests, a dazzling array of birds, and rare white rhinos.

(Underlined: "The natural beauty of the local wildlife is to be admired by visitors." = 28)

[5]

Whichever attractions visitors choose to view during their time at the Mosi-oa-Tunya National Park, they will surely never forget the striking power and beauty of the falls. The image of the massive wall of water is one that lasts a lifetime.

26. **F.** NO CHANGE
G. enjoy, a,
H. enjoy a
J. be enjoying, a

27. **A.** NO CHANGE
B. Some say a watched pot never boils.
C. Never watch a pot that you're waiting to boil.
D. OMIT the underlined portion.

28. **F.** NO CHANGE
G. Visitors can admire the natural beauty of the local wildlife.
H. By visitors can the natural beauty of the local wildlife be admired.
J. OMIT the underlined portion.

Questions 29 and 30 ask about the passage as a whole.

29. Suppose the author had been asked to write an essay describing why it is more worthwhile to see Victoria Falls than the other six wonders of the natural world. Would this essay meet the assignment?

A. Yes, because it describes in detail how marvelous Victoria Falls is.
B. Yes, because it does not mention most of the other wonders of the natural world.
C. No, because it does not attempt to compare Victoria Falls to any other attractions.
D. No, because the author does not seem to think that Victoria Falls is a very interesting place to visit.

30. The writer wishes to insert a paragraph about a place where visitors can buy locally made crafts. This paragraph would most logically be inserted:

F. between Paragraph 1 and Paragraph 2.
G. between Paragraph 2 and Paragraph 3.
H. between Paragraph 3 and Paragraph 4.
J. between Paragraph 4 and Paragraph 5.

CONTINUE

PASSAGE III

The Real Value of Money

[1]

[31] Although I always considered myself a relatively responsible person, I can honestly say that I didn't understand the real value of money until the winter of my senior year in high school. During [32] which I learned valuable lessons—about money and the value of friendship.

31. The author would like to add an introductory sentence to this passage. Which of the following would be the most effective?
    - **A.** Are you a fan of adventure stories and comic books?
    - **B.** Do you know the real value of money in your life?
    - **C.** How did you earn money when you were in high school?
    - **D.** How much do you know about your best friend?

32.
    - **F.** NO CHANGE
    - **G.** . School during
    - **H.** school, during
    - **J.** school during.

[2]

I've always been a somewhat bookish kid, and ever since I could read, I had my face buried in one book after another. The tons of family photos that show me sitting and reading will contest [33] to this fact. In truth, I haven't found a genre that I don't like, but my favorite is adventure. Tales of bravery and daring in the face of seemingly certain danger in exotic locations have captured and held my imagination for as long as I can remember.

33.
    - **A.** NO CHANGE
    - **B.** attest
    - **C.** regress
    - **D.** egress

[3]

My earliest exposure to adventure stories was from my dad, who read me classic tales like treasure island [34] and *The Count of Monte Cristo*, one chapter at a time, while I lay in bed each night before falling asleep.

34.
    - **F.** NO CHANGE
    - **G.** Treasure Island
    - **H.** *Treasure Island*
    - **J.** Treasure island

[4]

It was late in the middle of my final year in junior high school that I discovered my latest obsession—comic books—and I've been hooked ever since. Having amazing illustrations alongside stories of action and adventure with characters with fantastic powers and abilities <u>was like catnip to me and really attracted me</u>[35]. Everything about them, from the smell of the paper to the bold and colorful artwork and the fantastical tales, <u>kidnapped</u>[36] my imagination and attention, along with any spare money I had.

35. A. NO CHANGE
B. was like attractive catnip to me
C. was both attractive as well as like catnip to me
D. was like catnip to me

36. F. NO CHANGE
G. captured
H. hijacked
J. attacked

[5]

It's fair to say that building a respectable comic book collection was the early major initiative of my adolescence. I spent countless hours—and whatever meager savings <u>we could</u>[37] cobble together—to gather together as many of the comic books I wanted as possible.

37. A. NO CHANGE
B. they could
C. she could
D. I could

[6]

My favorite character was, and still is, Spider-Man—the notion of a socially awkward and bookish young adult suddenly having these incredible super powers and struggling with how to use them responsibly while finding his way in the world really resonated <u>with me?</u>[38] Ever since I discovered my arachnid-like role model, <u>it was, as I possibly could acquire, as many Spider Man comics as I could—my mission.</u>[39]

38. F. NO CHANGE
G. with me;
H. with me.
J. with me,

39. A. NO CHANGE
B. it was my mission to acquire as many Spider-Man comics as I possibly could.
C. Spider-Man comics, to acquire as many, it was my mission as I possibly could.
D. as I possibly could, as many it was my mission to acquire Spider-Man comics.

CONTINUE

[7]

My parents always said that <u>when I set my mind on something,</u> 40 there was absolutely no stopping me, and that notion certain applied to my comic collecting passion. Every extra dollar I received—from birthdays and holidays to the money I made during my first summer job, <u>making pizza boxes cleaning tables and washing dishes</u> 41 at the pizzeria a few blocks from my house, went to buying comic books. Gino, my boss at the pizzeria, jokingly asked me if he should just send my paycheck to the comic book store to save me the trouble. I actually considered his offer, believe it or not.

40. **F.** NO CHANGE
G. when I mix my mind with something
H. when I put my mind on top of something
J. when I remove my mind to combine it with something

41. **A.** NO CHANGE
B. making pizza boxes, cleaning tables, and washing dishes
C. making pizza boxes; cleaning tables, and washing dishes
D. making pizza, boxes cleaning, tables and washing, dishes

[8]

A few years passed and my collection grew. And so did my friendship with Simon, my next-door neighbor and classmate. He shared my love of comics, and it really became something we bonded over, although his favorite character was Batman (<u>there's no accounting for taste</u>) 42. We spent countless hours in the tree house at the northeast corner of my family's yard reading, discussing, and trading comic books. We even created a small comic book club, which we affectionately dubbed "The Adventurers' Realm," where other like-minded kids in the neighborhood could join and share in our love of comic books. Life was great—until everything changed, seemingly overnight.

42. **F.** NO CHANGE
G. there's no accounting for taste
H. ; there's no accounting for taste;
J. *there's no accounting for taste*

[9]

I remember being in the tree house one afternoon when Simon came over. He didn't look like himself. His face was pale and he looked sullen beyond belief—I knew something was wrong, and I asked him if everything was ok.

[10]

"I just spoke to my parents," he said. He just lost it—he started crying, and I knew that whatever he told me next was going to be serious. "My dad...he has cancer."

[11]

The new reality of his <u>dads illness</u> (43) was hard on him and his whole family, and I did my best to support my friend after that, in any way that I could. Our high school did what it could as well, and even decided to hold a silent raffle to help raise money for Simon's dad's medical bills. When I heard that this raffle was happening, I knew what I had to do.

[12]

I thought about the things that I owned that I could donate to the raffle. But the truth is, I knew what I was going to do already. I was prepared to say goodbye to my comic book collection, and I never once second-guessed my decision. Why? Because there are things more important than money or the possessions we own and cherish—and they are the connections we have and nurture with our families, friends, and loved ones.

43. **A.** NO CHANGE
B. dads' illness
C. dad's illness
D. dad's illness's

Questions 44 and 45 ask about the passage as a whole.

44. The author of this essay is thinking of submitting his work to a school contest, which is calling for writing about learning a lesson in adolescence. Does the essay fulfill this requirement?

F. No, because the essay is mainly about comic book collecting.
G. No, because the essay was written when the author was an adult.
H. Yes, because the author discusses learning the value of money and friendship.
J. Yes, because the author tells a heartwarming story that we all could relate to.

45. The author would like to add a concluding sentence to this passage. Which of the following would be the most effective?

A. As I learned that winter, those bonds beat any adventure story I've ever come across, and ever will.
B. I eventually lost interest in comic books after high school, and really got into skateboarding.
C. My friend Simon and I both went to different colleges, but we still kept in close contact.
D. After graduating from college, I bought the pizzeria that I worked in as a youth.

CONTINUE

PASSAGE IV

Conserving a Natural Resource

[1]

The Great Smoky Mountains National Park is created of [46] over half a million acres of the Appalachian Mountains, straddling the border between Tennessee and North Carolina. It attracts more visitors each year than any other national park. This may be in large part to its central location—it is within a day's drive for more than half of the American population—but surely most wouldn't make the trip if the mountains were not so majestic. The blue mist that gives the mountains their name rise above [47] its peaks. The mountains are rich with streams, waterfalls, vegetation, and wildlife. Hikers choose among many trails, ranging from a brisk, uphill walk, a truly [48] challenging three-hour hike to the dramatic view from a mountain peak. However, it's likely that many of the visitors who enjoy the scenery are unaware of how this stunning stretch of land came to be preserved as a national park.

[2]

The idea of establishing a national park in the mountains of the Southeastern United States first emerged in the 1880s, when conservationists wished to protect the vast acres of forest area. The decision was a politically tricky one that required balancing logging interests with conservation concerns. Recognizing that trying to ban logging was unrealistic, [49] conservationists suggested that in a national park area, the government could

46.
- **F.** NO CHANGE
- **G.** is owned by
- **H.** consists of
- **J.** establishes

47.
- **A.** NO CHANGE
- **B.** rising above
- **C.** rises above
- **D.** rose above

48.
- **F.** NO CHANGE
- **G.** walk to a truly
- **H.** walk for a truly
- **J.** walk, then toward a

49.
- **A.** NO CHANGE
- **B.** unrealistically
- **C.** unreal
- **D.** not real

regulate the logging that, unchecked; threatened to destroy the entire forest. [51]

50. F. NO CHANGE
G. that unchecked
H. that, unchecked
J. that, unchecked,

51. The purpose of Paragraph 2, as it relates to the rest of the essay, is primarily to:
A. give us a feeling for the motives behind the establishment of the park.
B. encourage us to conserve endangered land by creating more national parks.
C. argue that logging is a threat to America's national parks.
D. provide background for further discussion of the conflict between environmentalists and loggers.

[3]

[1] In 1926, Congress approved the idea of a national park in the Southeast. [2] Next, it had to determine what the location of this park would be. [3] This was no easy task; initially, about sixty different sites were proposed for the park. [4] After the decision was made, the United States Geological Survey an organization that explored and mapped land in the United States, created a topographical chart of a proposed park stretching from western North Carolina to eastern Tennessee. [53]

52. F. NO CHANGE
G. Survey, an organization
H. Surveyed an organization
J. Survey, having an organization

53. Suppose the writer wanted to add the following sentence to Paragraph 3:
After much debate, the Smoky Mountains region emerged as the winner.
This sentence would most logically be added:
A. before Sentence 1.
B. between Sentence 1 and Sentence 2.
C. between Sentence 3 and Sentence 4.
D. after Sentence 4.

[4]

To make this plan become a reality, it would be no easy task. Unlike the vast stretches of land in the American West that had been preserved as national parks, much of the designated land

54. F. NO CHANGE
G. It would not be, making this plan a reality, an easy task.
H. No easy task would it be, making this plan become a reality.
J. Making this plan a reality would be no easy task.

CONTINUE

was owned in privacy. It would have to be purchased and then deeded to the federal government. This, of course, meant that
55

55. **A.** NO CHANGE
B. privately owned
C. owned as a private
D. owned in a private manner

an enormous amount of dollars would have to be raised to
56

56. **F.** NO CHANGE
G. amount of money
H. number of monies
J. dollar

purchase land from private owners and lumber companies, some of whom recognized their leverage and hiked their prices. [57]

57. The writer's description of the landowners who hiked their prices makes the acquisition of the land seem even more:

A. challenging.
B. heroic.
C. foolish.
D. immoral.

[5]

Fundraisers in North Carolina and Tennessee collected over two million dollars from private citizens. Each of the two states' legislatures provided over a million dollars, and—just as the park's supporters feared—they had fallen short; they hadn't raised enough money. Just as it appeared that the conservationists had failed, the Rockefeller family rushed to the rescue by donating an additional five million dollars. The federal government provided the final one and a half million dollars needed to complete the purchase. On June 15, 1934, over 800 majestic square miles of forested peaks were designated a national park.
58

58. **F.** NO CHANGE
G. short—they hadn't raised enough money.
H. short: they hadn't raised enough money.
J. short.

Questions 59 and 60 ask about the passage as a whole.

59. Suppose the writer wanted to more closely examine the conflict between loggers and environmentalists. In order to expand upon material already present, this information would most logically be added to Paragraph:

A. 1.
B. 2.
C. 3.
D. 4.

60. Suppose that the writer had been asked to write an essay detailing the attractions that tourists can enjoy when they visit the Great Smoky Mountains National Park. Would this essay successfully fulfill that assignment?

F. Yes, because it describes the park's beauty.
G. Yes, because it mentions the park's popularity with visitors.
H. No, because it concentrates on how the park was established.
J. No, because it does not describe the park as being someplace that tourists would want to visit.

PASSAGE V

A Mayan Worldview

[1]

The ancient Mayans inhabited the area that now consists of Mexico, Guatemala, Belize, Honduras, and El Salvador. Their rich civilization flourished (61) from the third through the ninth centuries. Plus (62) the many notable achievements of this society was the Mayan understanding of astronomy, which was manifest not only in Mayan science but in every aspect of the culture.

[2]

Ancient Mayans kept meticulous records of the movements of the sun and moon, the planets, and the stars that were visible to the naked eye. Based on the solar year, they created a calendar which they used to keep track of time. So were astute (63) the Mayans' observations that they could predict such events as solar and lunar eclipses, and the movement of the planets.

61. A. NO CHANGE
B. civilization flourished and it was rich
C. civilization richly flourished
D. civilization was rich, flourished

62. F. NO CHANGE
G. Despite
H. Among
J. Between

63. A. NO CHANGE
B. (Place before *were*)
C. (Place before *So*)
D. (Place before *Mayans'*)

CONTINUE

[3]

For the ancient Mayans, astronomy was <u>not just</u> 64 a science; it was a combination of science, religion, and philosophy that <u>was found</u> 65 into many aspects of their lives, including architecture. Mayan ceremonial buildings, for example, were aligned <u>exact</u> 66 with compass points, so that at the fall and spring equinoxes, light would flood the interior of the building. These buildings were designed and built as acts of worship to the <u>Mayan gods:</u> 67 science, architecture, and religion, then, were all intricately and beautifully blended. [68]

64. **F.** NO CHANGE
G. merely
H. just
J. not

65. **A.** NO CHANGE
B. had to find
C. found its way
D. could be found

66. **F.** NO CHANGE
G. exactly
H. to be exact
J. exacting

67. **A.** NO CHANGE
B. Mayan gods,
C. Mayan gods;
D. Mayan gods

68. Which of the following words best expresses the writer's tone in this paragraph?

F. Gleeful
G. Indifferent
H. Resentful
J. Admiring

[4]

Government, too, was inextricably linked with astronomy. The beginning and ending of the reigns of Mayan leaders appear to have been timed to coincide with astronomical events. Ancient Mayan <u>artwork, carvings and murals—show</u> 69 royalty wearing symbols relating to the sun, moon, and sky. The Mayans believed that the sun and moon were guided across the sky by benevolent gods, and that these gods needed human help to thwart the evil

69. **A.** NO CHANGE
B. artwork, carvings, and murals, show
C. artwork, including carvings and murals—shows
D. artwork shows

gods <u>and wanted</u> [70] to stop them. Human intervention took the form of different rituals, including sacrifice. It was considered an honor to die for this cause, and those who were sacrificed were believed <u>to have</u> [71] gained eternal life.

[5]

The planet Venus, which can often be seen by the unaided eye, played a large role in Mayan life. <u>Mayans appeared to Venus</u> [72] in the sky as a means of timing when they attacked enemies. The night sky, then, among its other duties, served as a call to war.

[6]

<u>In short, the</u> [73] ancient Mayans, in looking to the night sky for <u>guidance; discovered</u> [74] a natural order around which they were able to base a rich and textured civilization. [75]

70. **F.** NO CHANGE
G. who wanted
H. which are wanting
J. they want

71. **A.** NO CHANGE
B. and felt they
C. that they would soon have
D. one day they would have

72. **F.** NO CHANGE
G. Venus, to all appearances,
H. The Mayans used the appearance of Venus
J. Venus appeared to be to the Mayans

73. **A.** NO CHANGE
B. Shortly, the
C. To sum up the
D. Lastly, the

74. **F.** NO CHANGE
G. guidance, discovered
H. guidance discovering
J. guidance: discovered

75. Suppose the writer were to add the following sentence at the end of the last paragraph:

The ancient Babylonians, too, were astronomers of remarkable accomplishment.

This change would have which of the following effects on the last paragraph?

A. It would make the paragraph into a more effective conclusion.
B. It would make the paragraph serve as a transition to another topic.
C. It would provide an illustrative detail.
D. It would contradict the information in the rest of the passage.

STOP

MATHEMATICS TEST

60 Minutes—60 Questions

DIRECTIONS: For each of the following items, solve each problem, choose the correct answer, and then fill in the corresponding circle on the answer sheet. If you encounter problems that take too much time to solve, move on. Solve as many problems as you can, then return to the others in the time remaining for the test.

You may use a calculator on this test for any problems you choose, but some of the problems may best be solved without the use of a calculator.

SHOW YOUR WORK HERE

Note: Unless otherwise stated, assume the following:

1. Illustrative figures are NOT necessarily drawn to scale.
2. Geometric figures lie in a plane.
3. The word *line* indicates a straight line.
4. The word *average* indicates arithmetic mean.

1. It takes an athlete 7 minutes 20 seconds to complete a segment of a workout. This is 20% less time than it took her to complete the same segment one month ago. What was her original time one month ago?

A. 1 minute, 28 seconds
B. 3 minutes, 40 seconds
C. 5 minutes, 52 seconds
D. 9 minutes, 10 seconds
E. 36 minutes, 40 seconds

2. If $a = 5$, what value of b solves the proportion below?

$$\frac{a}{6} = \frac{b}{15}$$

F. 14
G. $12\frac{1}{2}$
H. 10
J. $2\frac{1}{2}$
K. 2

CONTINUE

Practice Test 1 — MATHEMATICS

3. In the figure below, points X, Y, and Z lie on the same line. What is the measure of $\angle WYZ$?

SHOW YOUR WORK HERE

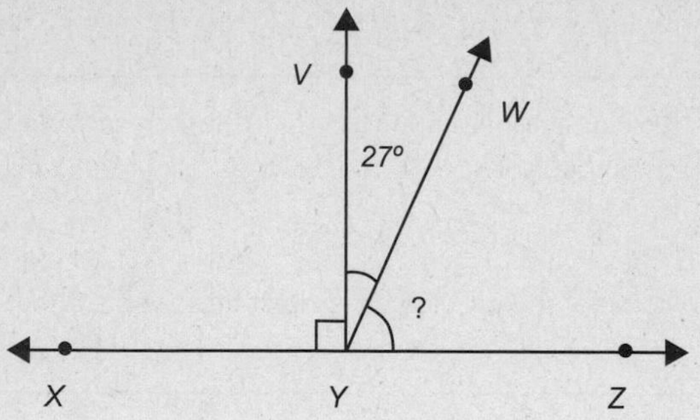

A. 63°
B. 73°
C. 90°
D. 117°
E. 153°

4. Determine the fifth term of the sequence $\frac{3}{4}, \frac{4}{9}, \frac{5}{16}, \ldots$

F. $\frac{4}{25}$
G. $\frac{6}{25}$
H. $\frac{7}{36}$
J. $\frac{8}{49}$
K. $\frac{7}{37}$

5. Martha cuts four pieces of ribbon, each 1.5 feet long, from a spool of ribbon. If 27.5 feet of ribbon are now left on the spool, how many feet of ribbon did it originally contain?

A. 21.5
B. 26
C. 29
D. 33.5
E. 39.5

6. Let $f(x) = \begin{cases} \sqrt{2x-3} - x, & x > 5 \\ 1-2x, & x \leq 5 \end{cases}$. Compute $f(6)$.

F. –11
G. –6
H. –3
J. 3
K. 9

7. If $\sqrt{w}$ is greater than 8, which of the following could be the value of w?

A. 9
B. 16
C. 49
D. 64
E. 81

8. Line segment $\overline{AB}$ in the coordinate plane has endpoint A located at (3, –2). If the midpoint of the line segment is (–3, –1), what are the coordinates of endpoint B?

F. (0, –1.5)
G. (9, –3)
H. (–9, 0)
J. (–15, 1)
K. (–3, 0)

9. Which of these does NOT describe y as a function of x?

A. $y = 6$

B.

x	1	2	3	8	9	10
y	–2	1	–2	0	–2	3

C.

x	15	10	5	0	–5	–10
y	3	3	3	3	3	3

D. $f(x) = x(1 - 2x)(3x + 1)$

E.

x	–3	2	1	5	–1	2
y	0	2	4	6	8	10

10. A bag contains only red, blue, and green marbles. There are a total of 20 marbles in the bag, and the probability of NOT selecting a blue marble is $\frac{1}{4}$. How many blue marbles are in the bag?

F. 4
G. 5
H. 8
J. 10
K. 15

11. Which of the following pairs of lines are parallel?

A. $3y = 2x - 1$ and $y = -\frac{3}{2}x + 1$
B. $y = 2x + 1$ and $y = 1 - 2x$
C. $\frac{1}{2}x - y = 2$ and $2y = x - 1$
D. $2y = 5x$ and $5y = 2x$
E. $x = 3$ and $y = 1$

SHOW YOUR WORK HERE

CONTINUE

12. A nutritionist prescribes two supplements, vitamin D and a turmeric blend, to a patient in a ratio of 4:3. If $2\frac{1}{4}$ teaspoons of the turmeric blend is the prescribed dose, what is the dose of vitamin D?

SHOW YOUR WORK HERE

F. $2\frac{3}{4}$ teaspoons

G. 3 teaspoons

H. $3\frac{3}{4}$ teaspoons

J. 4 teaspoons

K. 9 teaspoons

13. Data collected in an experiment strongly supports the conclusion that as the percentage of nutrient solution applied to lima bean seeds increases, the number of hours needed for the seed to germinate decreases. Which of these scatterplots could represent this data?

A.

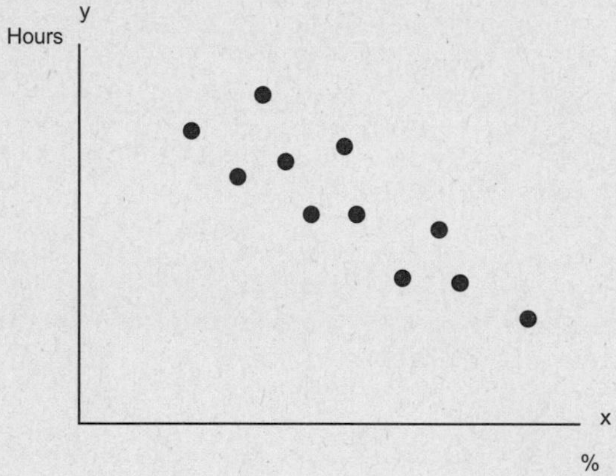

B.

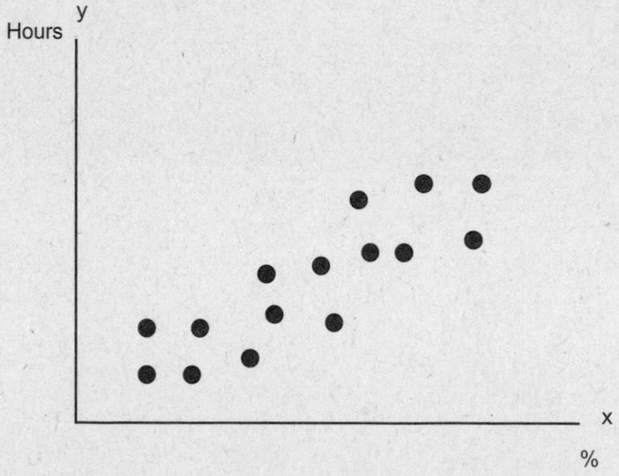

C.

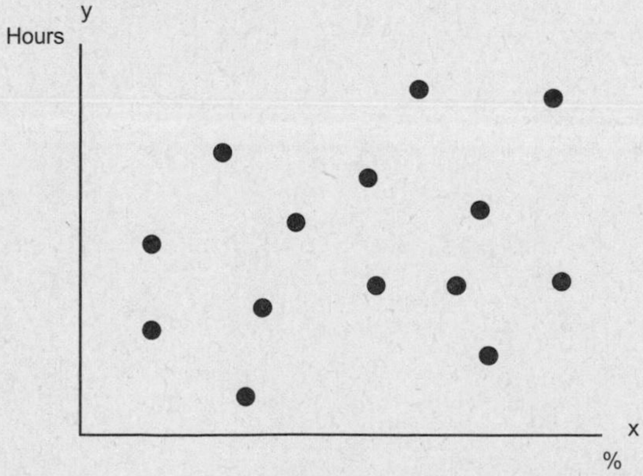

D.

E.

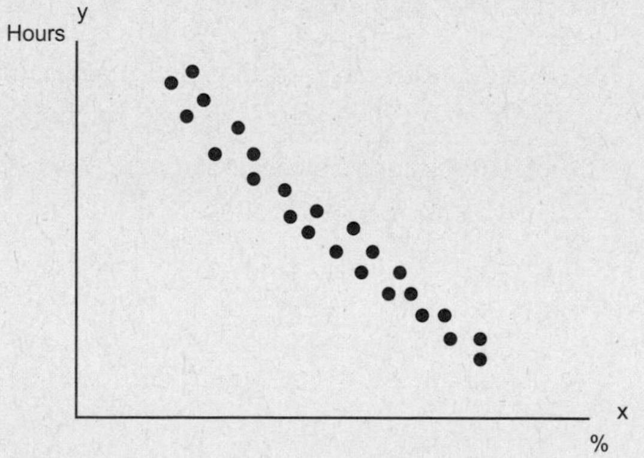

14. Michelle posted a dining room set for sale for \$800 using an online auction store. Following weeks of receiving no bids on the set, she reduced the price by 15%. What is the new asking price for the dining room set?

F. \$120
G. \$680
H. \$785
J. \$815
K. \$920

15. For all m and n, $-m(n-m)+n(m-n)=$

A. m^2+n^2
B. $(m-n)^2$
C. $(m+n)^2$
D. n^2-m^2
E. m^2-n^2

16. Which number is a root of the equation $5(x-4)(x+2)=0$?

F. –4
G. –2
H. 0
J. 2
K. 5

17. In the diagram below, what is the measure of angle *BCD*?

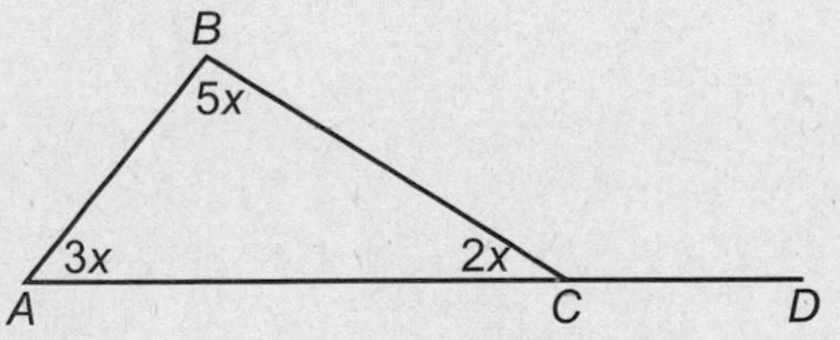

A. 18°
B. 36°
C. 90°
D. 126°
E. 144°

18. A jacket that normally sells for \$75 is on sale for \$50. By what percent is the original price discounted for this sale?

F. 20%
G. 25%
H. $33\frac{1}{3}\%$
J. 50%
K. 75%

SHOW YOUR WORK HERE

CONTINUE

SHOW YOUR WORK HERE

19. If the point (–3, 2) is on the graph of $y = F(x)$, what is the corresponding point on the graph of $g(x) = F(x + 1) – 4$?

A. (–7, 1)
B. (–4, 6)
C. (–2, 6)
D. (–4, –2)
E. (–2, –2)

20. If an inch of wire costs $0.20, how much will 5.25 feet of wire cost?

F. $1.05
G. $2.40
H. $12.60
J. $63
K. $315

21. $\frac{1}{3x-1} - \frac{2-9x}{1-3x} =$

A. –3

B. 0

C. $\frac{9x-1}{6x-2}$

D. $-\frac{9x+1}{6x-2}$

E. Undefined

22. A rectangle has a length of 8 inches and a width of 3 inches. What is the width, in inches, of a rectangle whose length and width are in the same proportion and whose perimeter is 44 inches?

F. 6
G. 11
H. 12
J. 16
K. 22

23. An online used book store vendor charges a flat fee of $8.50 per shipment plus $2.25 for each book. If a customer orders *b* books, what is the cost of her order?

A. 2.25*b* dollars
B. 2.25 + 8.50*b* dollars
C. 8.50 + 2.25*b* dollars
D. (2.25 + 8.50)*b* dollars
E. 8.50 + 2.25 + *b* dollars

24. The garden in the figure below was created by adding equal semicircles to the four faces of a square. If the perimeter of this garden is 16π feet, what is its area in square feet?

F. $64 + 8\pi$
G. $64 + 32\pi$
H. $64 + 64\pi$
J. $256 + 32\pi$
K. $256 + 64\pi$

25. Which of the following best describes the graph on the number line below?

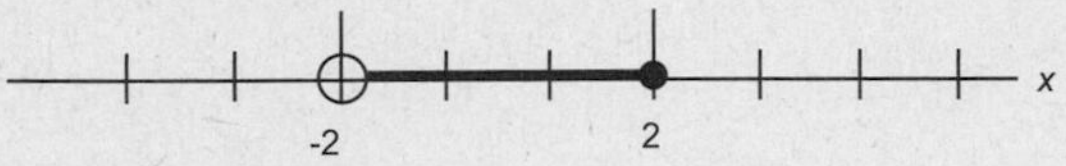

A. $-2 \le x < 2$
B. $-2 < x \le 2$
C. $-2 \le x \le 2$
D. $-2 < x < 2$
E. $x > 2$

26. Suppose n is an odd integer. Which of the following must be an odd integer?

F. $n + 3$
G. $2n$
H. $n - 1$
J. n^2
K. $\frac{1}{3}n$

27. If the area of a square is 144 square inches, what is the length of a diagonal of this square?

A. $2\sqrt{12}$ inches
B. $2\sqrt{6}$ inches
C. 12 inches
D. $12\sqrt{2}$ inches
E. 24 inches

SHOW YOUR WORK HERE

CONTINUE

28. The graph of $g(x)$ on the interval $[-5, 5]$ is shown below:

SHOW YOUR WORK HERE

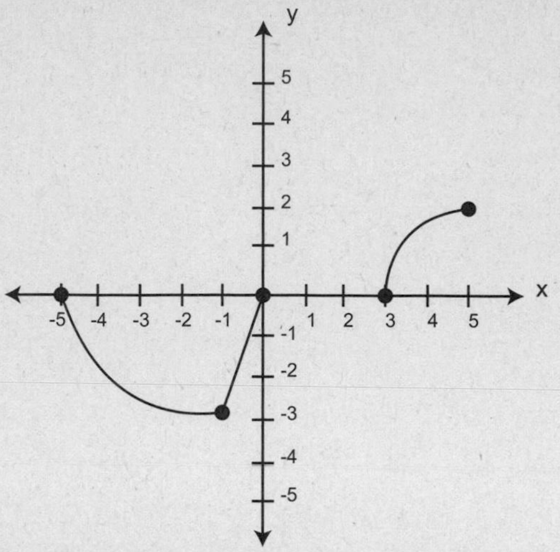

On what interval(s) is the graph of $g(x)$ decreasing?

F. $(-3, 0)$

G. $(-5, -1)$

H. $(-1,0)\cup(3,5)$

J. $(-1, 3)$

K. It is never decreasing.

29. Two sides of a triangle have lengths 7 and 2. Which of the following could be the perimeter of this triangle?

A. 9

B. 11

C. 14

D. 16

E. 18

30. Consider the circle whose equation is $(x-1)^2+(y-1)^2=4$. Which of these lines intersects the circle at exactly one point?

F. $x=-1$

G. $y=x$

H. $y=-x$

J. $y=3-x$

K. $y=3$

31. An athlete tracks the number of times various exercises or movements appears in the daily X-Fit workouts over a period. The data he compiles is illustrated below.

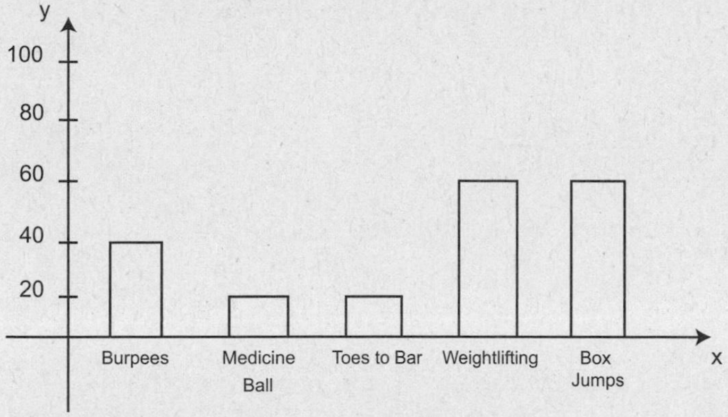

Based on this data, what is the probability that a workout contains either box jumps or weightlifting?

A. 0.12
B. 0.30
C. 0.40
D. 0.60
E. 0.70

32. In right triangle *TRI*, $TR = 8$ and $RI = 6$. What is the length of line segment *IT*?

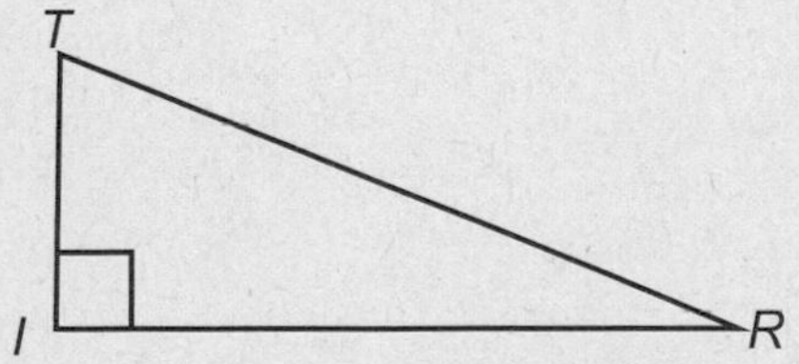

F. 10
G. $2\sqrt{7}$
H. 28
J. $\sqrt{2}$
K. Cannot be determined from the given information

33. The length of a square is increased by 5, and its width is decreased by 2 to create a rectangle. If the perimeter of the square is $4s$, what is the area of the rectangle, in terms of s?

A. $4s + 6$
B. $2s + 3$
C. $s^2 - 10$
D. $s^2 + 3s - 10$
E. $s^2 + 7s + 10$

SHOW YOUR WORK HERE

CONTINUE

SHOW YOUR WORK HERE

34. In the right triangle *XYZ* below, $\cos\angle YXZ = \frac{4}{5}$.

What is the value of tan $\angle ZYX$?

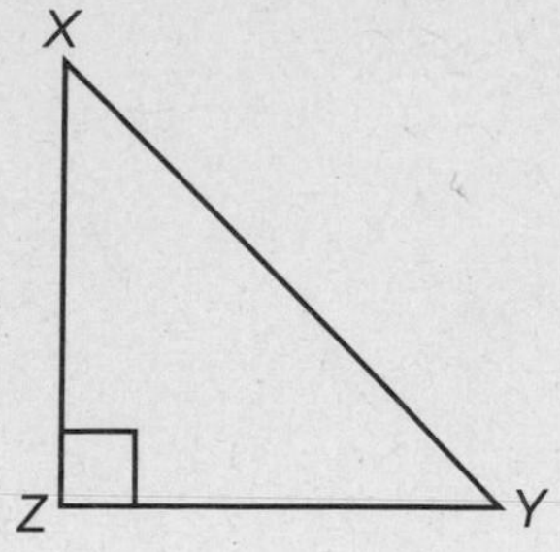

F. $\frac{4}{5}$

G. $\frac{5}{4}$

H. $\frac{3}{5}$

J. $\frac{3}{4}$

K. $\frac{4}{3}$

35. There are twice as many boys as girls in Mr. Botti's math class. The class's average grade on a recent test was 84. If the girls' average grade was 91, what was the boys' average grade?

A. 70
B. 77
C. 80.5
D. 87.5
E. 98

36. Which of the following is the graph of the solution set of $3x - 9 \leq 15$?

F.

G.

H.

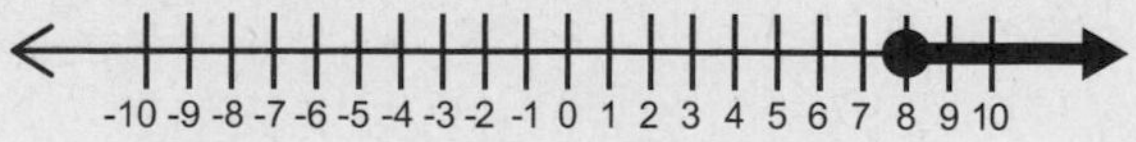

J.

K.

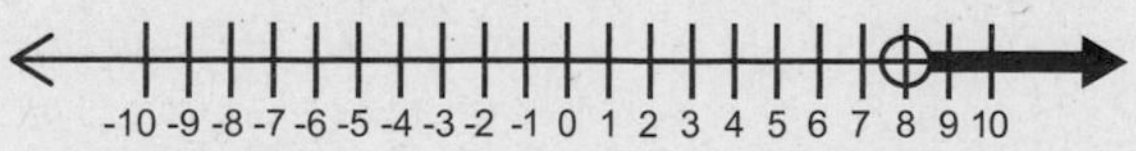

37. The figure below was formed by combining two equal squares, such that a vertex of one square is at the center of the other square. The area of the shaded region is x. In terms of x, what is the area of the unshaded region?

SHOW YOUR WORK HERE

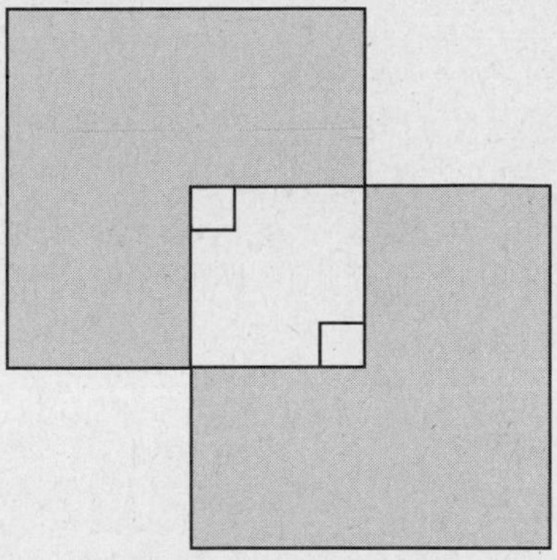

A. $\frac{6x}{7}$

B. $\frac{3x}{4}$

C. $\frac{x}{6}$

D. $\frac{x}{7}$

E. $\frac{x}{8}$

38. The average of three different positive integers is 99. What is the greatest possible value for one of these integers?

F. 33
G. 96
H. 294
J. 295
K. 296

39. In right triangle *ABC*, what is the measure of angle *BCA*?

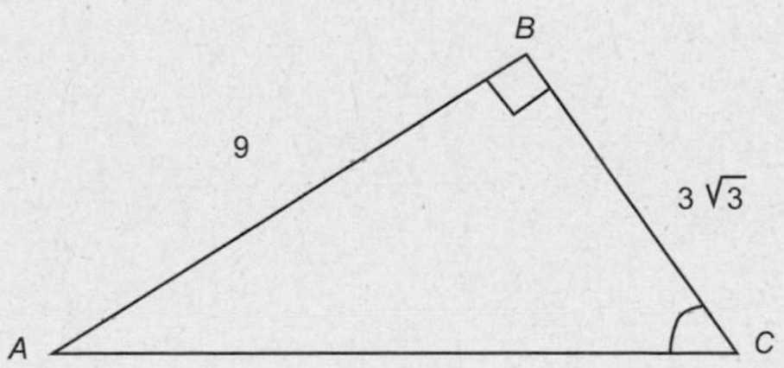

A. 90°
B. 60°
C. 45°
D. 30°
E. Cannot be determined from the given information

CONTINUE

40. Suppose (–1, 2) and (3, –*x*) are points on a line with slope $-\frac{1}{4}$. What is the value of $\frac{1}{2}x$?

SHOW YOUR WORK HERE

F. –1

G. $-\frac{1}{2}$

H. $\frac{1}{2}$

J. 1

K. 2

41. In the figure below, lines l_1 and l_2 are parallel. What is the value of *n*?

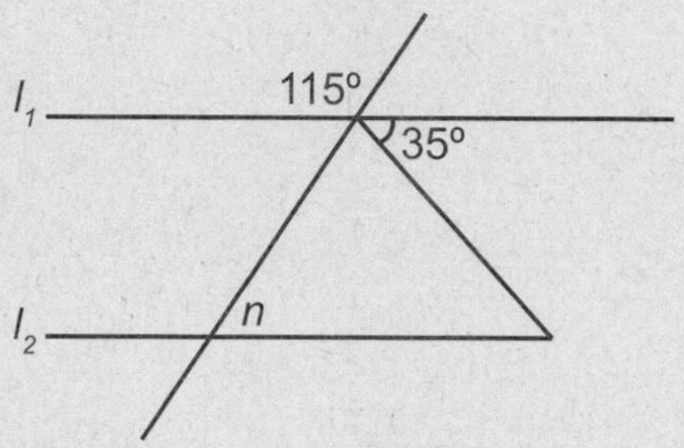

A. 35°
B. 65°
C. 80°
D. 100°
E. 115°

42. What is the slope of the line perpendicular to the line whose equation is $3x = 4y - 1$?

F. –4
G. $-\frac{4}{3}$
H. $\frac{3}{4}$
J. 3
K. 4

43. Which of the following numbers is closest to 0.000000301 on a number line?

A. 3.16×10^{6}
B. 3.21×10^{-6}
C. 3.01×10^{-7}
D. 2.01×10^{-8}
E. 2.99×10^{-9}

44. In triangle *XYZ* below, what is the length of segment *XZ*?

SHOW YOUR WORK HERE

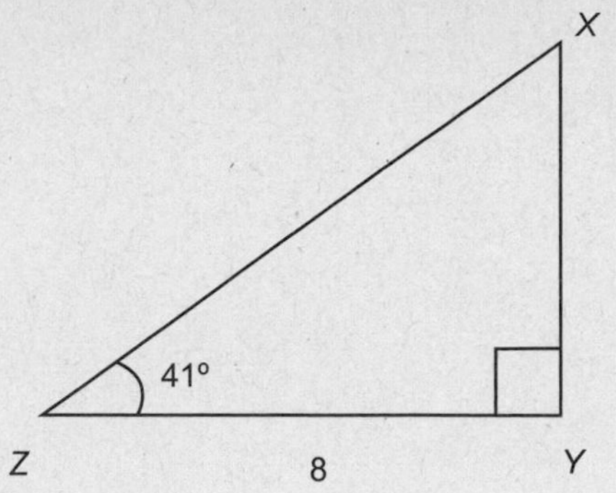

F. $8 \cos 41°$

G. $8 \sin 41°$

H. $\frac{8}{\cos 41°}$

J. $\frac{8}{\sin 41°}$

K. $8 \tan(41)$

45. If $f(x)=\frac{x}{2x-1}$ and $g(x)=\frac{2}{x}$, what is $(f \circ g)(x)$?

A. 1

B. $\frac{4x-2}{x}$

C. $\frac{2}{2x-1}$

D. $\frac{2}{x(2x-1)}$

E. $\frac{2}{4-x}$

46. A student has a 20-section spinner. She is going to color each section red, yellow, or blue. She wants the probability of landing on a blue section to be $\frac{1}{4}$, and she wants the probability of landing on a yellow section to be $\frac{1}{4}$ of the probability of landing on a red section.

How many sections should she color red?

F. 3

G. 4

H. 5

J. 8

K. 12

CONTINUE

SHOW YOUR WORK HERE

47. Of the 24 guests who attended a barbecue, 8 guests ate hot dogs and 12 guests ate chicken. If 4 people ate both hot dogs and chicken, what fraction of the guests ate neither?

A. $\frac{2}{3}$

B. $\frac{1}{2}$

C. $\frac{1}{3}$

D. $\frac{1}{5}$

E. $\frac{1}{6}$

48. For all nonzero values of a and b, $\dfrac{\frac{1}{a}-\frac{1}{b}}{\frac{1}{a}+\frac{1}{b}} =$

F. 0

G. $b^2 - a^2$

H. $\dfrac{a+b}{a-b}$

J. $\dfrac{b-a}{b+a}$

K. $\dfrac{a-b}{a+b}$

49. In a right triangle *ABC*, the measure of angle *C* is 30°. If the length of *BC* is 4 meters, what is the length of the leg *AB*?

A. $\frac{4\sqrt{3}}{3}$ meters

B. $4\sqrt{3}$ meters

C. 4 meters

D. 2 meters

E. 8 meters

50. $\dfrac{(\sin x-\cos x)^2}{(\sin x+\cos x)^2} =$

F. $\sin^2 x - \cos^2 x$

G. $(\sin x - \cos x)^2$

H. $\dfrac{1-\sin 2x}{1+\sin 2x}$

J. $1-\sin 2x$

K. -1

51. If $m(x) = -2x(1 - x)$ and $n(x) = x^3$, compute $(n \circ m)(-1)$.

SHOW YOUR WORK HERE

A. 0
B. 4
C. 16
D. 36
E. 64

52. A drawer contains 7 black socks, 5 white socks, and 4 green socks. If 1 black sock is removed from the drawer, what is the probability that the next sock removed at random will NOT be black?

F. $\frac{1}{15}$

G. $\frac{3}{8}$

H. $\frac{2}{5}$

J. $\frac{9}{16}$

K. $\frac{3}{5}$

53. If line 1 is defined by the equation $2y + x = 4$, and line 2 is defined by the equation $3y + 6x = 6$, then which of the following statements must be true?

A. Line 1 is parallel to line 2.
B. Line 1 is perpendicular to line 2.
C. Line 1 and line 2 both have positive slopes.
D. Line 1 and line 2 both pass through the origin.
E. Line 1 and line 2 intersect at (0, 2).

CONTINUE

54. Science fiction fans are asked to indicate (1) if they prefer reading science fiction novels or watching science fiction movies/television programs, and (2) their preferred subgenre: alien invasion, alternate history, cyberpunk, or time travel. The summary of the data is summarized below:

	Alien Invasion	Alternate History	Cyberpunk	Time Travel
Prefers reading novels	50	20	65	30
Prefers watching movies/TV	25	15	40	55

Based on this data, what is the probability that a science fiction fan who prefers to read novels identifies cyberpunk as her preferred subgenre?

SHOW YOUR WORK HERE

F. $\frac{13}{60}$

G. $\frac{8}{21}$

H. $\frac{13}{33}$

J. $\frac{27}{60}$

K. $\frac{13}{21}$

55. Suppose $a < b$ and that a and b are not equal to zero. Which of the following must be true?

A. $\frac{1}{a} > \frac{1}{b}$

B. $a^2 < b^2$

C. $a \bullet c < b \bullet d$ for any nonzero real numbers c and d

D. $\frac{1}{a} < \frac{1}{b}$

E. $a - c < b - c$, for any real number c

56. Janey goes to the movies with 5 friends. They decide to sit in a row that contains exactly 7 seats. In how many different ways can they arrange themselves if Janey insists on sitting in the middle seat?

F. 24

G. 35

H. 120

J. 720

K. 5,040

57. The dimensions of a rectangular solid are in the ratio 2:4:8. If the volume of the solid is 512 cubic meters, what is the length of the longest edge of the solid?

A. 2 meters
B. 4 meters
C. 8 meters
D. 16 meters
E. 64 meters

SHOW YOUR WORK HERE

58. Greg buys a stock on Monday. The price of the stock holds steady on Monday, remaining at the price Greg paid for it. On Tuesday the price of the stock increases by 20%. On Wednesday, the price of the stock falls by 25%. By what percentage must the stock price rise on Thursday to regain the original price Greg paid for it on Monday?

F. 45%
G. $22\frac{2}{9}\%$
H. $11\frac{1}{9}\%$
J. 10%
K. 5%

59. Square *WXYZ* is inscribed within circle *O* as shown in the figure below.

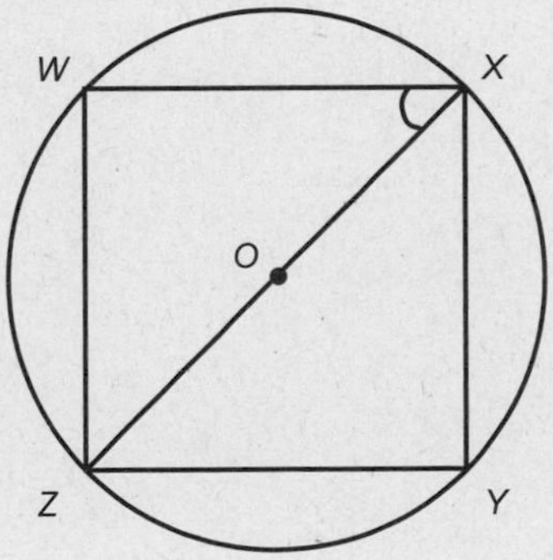

If the sine of $\angle WXZ = \frac{a}{b}$, which of the following represents the area of the circle?

A. $a^2\pi$
B. $b^2\pi$
C. $b\pi$
D. $\frac{b^2\pi}{4}$
E. $\frac{b\pi}{2}$

60. What is the units digit of 338^{340}?

F. 8
G. 6
H. 4
J. 2
K. 0

STOP

READING TEST

35 MINUTES—40 QUESTIONS

DIRECTIONS: There are several passages in this test. Each passage is followed by several questions. Read each passage, choose the best answer, and fill in the corresponding circle on the answer sheet. You may refer back to the passages at any time.

PASSAGE I

PROSE FICTION: Passage A is an excerpt from the novel *House of Mirth* by Edith Wharton. Passage B is an excerpt from the novel *Emma* by Jane Austen.

Passage A
by Edith Wharton

Selden paused in surprise. In the afternoon rush of the Grand Central Station his eyes had been refreshed by the sight of Miss Lily Bart.

It was a Monday in early September, and he was returning to his work from a hurried dip into the country; but what was Miss Bart doing in town at that season? If she had appeared to be catching a train, he might have inferred that he had come on her in the act of transition between one and another of the country-houses which disputed her presence after the close of the Newport season; but her desultory air perplexed him. She stood apart from the crowd, letting it drift by her to the platform or the street, and wearing an air of irresolution which might, as he surmised, be the mask of a very definite purpose. It struck him at once that she was waiting for some one, but he hardly knew why the idea arrested him. There was nothing new about Lily Bart, yet he could never see her without a faint movement of interest: it was characteristic of her that she always roused speculation, that her simplest acts seemed the result of far-reaching intentions.

An impulse of curiosity made him turn out of his direct line to the door, and stroll past her. He knew that if she did not wish to be seen she would contrive to elude him; and it amused him to think of putting her skill to the test.

"Mr. Selden—what good luck!"

She came forward smiling, eager almost, in her resolve to intercept him. One or two persons, in brushing past them, lingered to look; for Miss Bart was a figure to arrest even the suburban traveller rushing to his last train.

Selden had never seen her more radiant. Her vivid head, relieved against the dull tints of the crowd, made her more conspicuous than in a ball-room, and under her dark hat and veil she regained the girlish smoothness, the purity of tint, that she was beginning to lose after eleven years of late hours and indefatigable dancing. Was it really eleven years, Selden found himself wondering, and had she indeed reached the nine-and-twentieth birthday with which her rivals credited her?

"What luck!" she repeated. "How nice of you to come to my rescue!"

Passage B
by Jane Austen

Sixteen years had Miss Taylor been in Mr. Woodhouse's family, less as a governess than a friend, very fond of both daughters, but particularly of Emma. Between them it was more the intimacy of sisters. Even before Miss Taylor had ceased to hold the nominal office of governess, the mildness of her temper had hardly allowed her to impose any restraint; and the shadow of authority being now long passed away, they had been living together as friend and friend very mutually attached, and Emma doing just what she liked; highly esteeming Miss Taylor's judgment, but directed chiefly by her own.

The real evils, indeed, of Emma's situation were the power of having rather too much her own way, and a disposition to think a little too well of herself; these were the disadvantages which threatened her many enjoyments. The danger, however, was at present so unperceived, that they did not by any means rank as misfortunes with her.

Sorrow came—a gentle sorrow—but not at all in the shape of any disagreeable consciousness—Miss Taylor married. It was Miss Taylor's loss which first brought grief. It was on the wedding-day of this beloved friend that Emma first sat in mournful thought of any continuance. The wedding over, and the bride-people gone, her father and herself were left to dine together, with no prospect of a third to cheer a long evening.

CONTINUE

Her father composed himself to sleep after dinner, as usual, and she had then only to sit and think of what she had lost.

The event had every promise of happiness for her friend. Mr. Weston was a man of unexceptionable character, easy fortune, suitable age, and pleasant manners; and there was some satisfaction in considering with what self-denying, generous friendship she had always wished and promoted the match; but it was a black morning's work for her. The want of Miss Taylor would be felt every hour of every day. She recalled her past kindness—the kindness, the affection of sixteen years—how she had taught and how she had played with her from five years old—how she had devoted all her powers to attach and amuse her in health—and how nursed her through the various illnesses of childhood. A large debt of gratitude was owing here…the equal footing and perfect unreserve which had soon followed Isabella's marriage, on their being left to each other, was yet a dearer, tenderer recollection.

She had been a friend and companion such as few possessed: intelligent, well-informed, useful, gentle, knowing all the ways of the family, interested in all its concerns, and peculiarly interested in herself, in every pleasure, every scheme of hers—one to whom she could speak every thought as it arose, and who had such an affection for her as could never find fault.

How was she to bear the change?—It was true that her friend was going only half a mile from them; but Emma was aware that great must be the difference between a Mrs. Weston, only half a mile from them, and a Miss Taylor in the house; and with all her advantages, natural and domestic, she was now in great danger of suffering from intellectual solitude. She dearly loved her father, but he was no companion for her. He could not meet her in conversation, rational or playful.

Questions 1–3 ask about Passage A.

1. Miss Lily Bart's behavior suggests that she:

A. is late for a train she desperately needs to catch.
B. is more interested in meeting someone than catching a train.
C. is not very fond of Mr. Selden and wants to avoid him.
D. is deciding whether or not to move back to town.

2. Miss Lily Bart's behavior toward Mr. Selden can best be described as:

F. affectionate.
G. mysterious.
H. desperate.
J. friendly.

3. Mr. Selden believes that Miss Lily Bart might:

A. be older than people say she is.
B. think he is being too forward.
C. not want to talk to him.
D. not remember who he is.

Questions 4–6 ask about Passage B.

4. As it is used in line 23, the word *cheer* most nearly means:

F. encouragement.
G. joy.
H. applaud.
J. brighten.

5. In the passage, Emma thinks about Miss Taylor's marriage:

A. right before the wedding.
B. while talking to Mr. Weston.
C. after having dinner with her father.
D. after getting into bed.

6. Mr. Weston's qualities include:

I. pleasant manners.
II. unexceptional character.
III. high self-regard.

F. I only
G. I and II only
H. II and III only
J. I, II, and III

Questions 7–10 ask about both passages.

7. Both Miss Lily Bart in Passage A and Emma in Passage B:

A. begin their respective passages without a companion.
B. lose companions over the course of their respective passages.
C. reminisce about companions they have lost.
D. meet new companions.

8. One can infer from the passages that Miss Lily Bart and Emma:

F. love to go dancing.
G. both want to meet someone.
H. have a tendency to get depressed.
J. would not get along with each other.

9. Both passages are about:

A. ways to get along without companionship.
B. relationships that come to abrupt endings.
C. the excitement of forming a new friendship.
D. the need for human interaction.

10. According to the passages, Miss Lily Bart and Emma are both:

F. at least in their twenties.
G. city dwellers.
H. waiting for trains.
J. going to attend weddings.

PASSAGE II

SOCIAL SCIENCE: The following passage is excerpted from a history of advertising in the United Kingdom originally published in 1874.

The first newspaper supposed to have been published in England appeared in the reign of Queen Elizabeth during the Spanish Armada panic. This journal was called the *English Mercurie*, and was by authority "imprinted at London by Christopher Barker, Her Highnesses printer, 1583." This paper was said to be started for the prevention of the fulmination of false reports, but it was more like a succession of extraordinary gazettes, and had by no means the appearance of a regular journal, as we understand the term … Periodicals and papers really first came into general use during the civil wars in the reign of Charles I, and in the time of the Commonwealth; in fact, each party had its organs, to disseminate sentiments of loyalty, or to foster a spirit of resistance against the inroads of power. The country was accordingly overflowed with tracts of every size and of various denominations, many of them displaying great courage, and being written with uncommon ability. *Mercury* was the prevailing title, generally qualified with some epithet; and the quaintness peculiar to the age is curiously exemplified in the names of some of the news-books, as they were called: the *Dutch Spye*, the *Scots Dove*, the *Parliament Kite*, the *Screech Owle*, and the *Parliamentary Screech Owle*, being instances in point. The list of *Mercuries* is almost too full for publication. There was *Mercurius Acheronticus*, which brought tidings weekly from the infernal regions; there was *Mercurius Democritus*, whose information was supposed to be derived from the moon; and among other *Mercuries* there was the *Mercurius Mastix*, whose mission was to criticize all its namesakes. It was not, however, until the reign of Queen Anne that a daily paper existed in London—this was the *Daily Courant*, which occupied the field alone for a long period, but which ultimately found two rivals in the *Daily Post* and the *Daily Journal*, the three being simultaneously published in 1724. This state of things continued with very little change during the reign of George I, but publications of every kind increased abundantly during the reign of his successor. The number of newspapers annually sold in England, according to an average of three years ending with 1753, was 7,411,757; in 1760 it amounted to 9,464,790; in 1767 it rose to 11,300,980; in 1790 it was as high as 14,035,636; and in 1792 it amounted to 15,005,760. All this time advertising was a growing art, and advertisements were beginning to make themselves manifest as the main support and chief source of profit of newspapers, as well as the most natural channel of communication between the buyers and sellers, the needing and supplying members of a vast community…

The victories of Cromwell gave Scotland her first newspaper. This was called the *Mercurius Politicus*, and appeared at Leith in October 1653; but it was in November 1654 transferred to Edinburgh, where it was continued until the 11th April 1660, when it was rechristened, and appeared as the *Mercurius Publicus*. This paper was but a reprint, for the information of the English soldiers, of a London publication. But a newspaper of native manufacture, we are told by a contemporary writer, soon made its appearance under the title of *Mercurius Caledonius*. The first number of this was published at Edinburgh on the 31st December 1660, and comprised, as its title sets forth, "the affairs in agitation in Scotland, with a summary of foreign intelligence." The publication, however, extended to no more than ten numbers, which, it is said by Chambers, "were very loyal, very illiterate, and very affected." After the Revolution the custom was still to reprint in Scotland the papers published in London, an economic way of doing business … In February 1699 the *Edinburgh Gazette*, the first original Scotch newspaper or periodical, was published by James Watson, author of a "History of Printing;" but he, after producing forty numbers, transferred it to a Mr John Reid, whose son continued to print the paper till even after the Union. In February 1705, Watson, who seems to have been what would now be called a promoter of newspapers, established the *Edinburgh Courant*, but relinquished it after the publication of fifty-five numbers, and in September 1706 commenced the *Scots Courant*, with which he remained connected until about 1718. To these papers were added in October 1708 the *Edinburgh Flying Post*; in August 1709 the *Scots Postman*, "printed by David Fearne for John Moncur;" and in March 1710 the *North Tatler*, "printed by John Reid for Samuel Colvil." In 1715 the foundation was laid of the present splendid Glasgow press by the establishment of the *Courant*, but this did not in any way affect the publications in the then far more important town of Edinburgh. In March 1714 Robert Brown commenced the *Edinburgh Gazette* or *Scots Postman*, which was published twice a week; and in December 1718 the Town Council gave an exclusive privilege to James M'Ewen to publish three times a week the *Edinburgh Evening Courant*, upon condition, however, that before publication "the said James should give ane coppie of his print to the magistrates." This journal is still published, and it is but fair to assume that the original stipulation is yet complied with. The *Caledonian Mercury* followed the *Courant* on the 28th of April 1720, and was, like its

CONTINUE

forerunner, a tri-weekly organ. In these, as well as in those we have mentioned, advertisements slowly but gradually and surely began to make their appearance, and, as the sequel proves, to show their value.

11. Based on the information in the passage, one can infer that the first newspapers in the United Kingdom:

A. were completely biased.
B. were intended to convey facts.
C. were not successful.
D. started for political reasons.

12. The first paragraph (lines 1–43) implies that the titles of the first UK newspapers:

F. displayed a lack of originality.
G. were utterly absurd.
H. reflected modern times.
J. indicated the philosophy of each newspaper.

13. The author explains that, compared with *Mercurius Publicus, Mercurius Caledonius:*

A. contained news relevant to Scotland.
B. was a reprint of an English newspaper.
C. was produced in Scotland.
D. was always widely circulated.

14. According to the first paragraph (lines 1–43), British newspapers published before the reign of Queen Anne included the:

I. *Daily Courant.*
II. *Scots Dove.*
III. *Mercurius Acheronticus.*

F. I only
G. II only
H. III only
J. II and III only

15. Information in the first paragraph (lines 1–43) supports which of these statements?

A. 1792 was the most successful year for newspaper sales in the history of the United Kingdom.
B. Newspaper circulation in the UK grew steadily during the second half of the eighteenth century.
C. George I was responsible for the lack of change in the UK newspaper industry during his reign.
D. The first Scottish newspaper was the result of Cromwell's victories.

16. In the second paragraph (lines 44–89), the author includes the circulation of the *Mercurius Caledonius* to support the idea that:

F. readers of the *Mercurius Caledonius* were very illiterate.
G. readers of the *Mercurius Caledonius* were exceptionally loyal.
H. the *Mercurius Caledonius* was an instant and substantial success.
J. Scotland did not yet have a strong desire for a newspaper published at home.

17. The passage as a whole can primarily be characterized as the author's:

A. explanation of why the history of newspapers in the United Kingdom is important.
B. argument that newspapers in the United Kingdom dramatically improved over time.
C. description of significant events in the early history of newspapers in the United Kingdom.
D. concerns that newspapers in the United Kingdom are no longer as effective as they once were.

18. In the second paragraph (lines 44–89), the main idea is that Scottish newspapers:

F. took some time to mature but eventually resulted in some successful publications.
G. failed to sell as well as newspapers produced in England.
H. were required to be given to Scottish magistrates free of cost.
J. included such titles as *Mercurius Caledonius*, *Scots Courant*, and *Edinburgh Gazette*.

19. As it is used in line 11, the word *party* most nearly means:

A. political faction.
B. social gathering.
C. group with a common purpose.
D. to enjoy without restraint.

20. Before 1699, Scotland mostly reprinted British newspapers because:

F. nobody purchased Scottish newspapers.
G. British newspapers were known for their excellence.
H. most news affecting the UK occurred in England.
J. it was less costly than producing homegrown newspapers.

PASSAGE III

HUMANITIES: The following biography is adapted from a philosophical history of vegetarianism by Howard Williams.

The most renowned of all the prose writers of antiquity may be said to have been almost the lineal descendant, in philosophy, of the teacher of Samos. He belonged to the aristocratic families of Athens—"the eye of Greece"—then and for long afterwards the centre of art and science. His original name was Aristocles, which he might well have retained. Like another equally famous leader in literature, François Marie Arouet, he abandoned his birth-name, and he assumed or acquired the name by which he is immortalized, to characterize, as it is said, either the breadth of his brow or the extensiveness of his mental powers. In very early youth he seems to have displayed his literary aptitude and tastes in the various kinds of poetry—epic, tragic, and lyric—as well as to have distinguished himself as an athlete in the great national contests or "games," as they were called, the grand object of ambition of every Greek. He was instructed in the chief and necessary parts of a liberal Greek education by the most able professors of the time. He devoted himself with ardor to the pursuit of knowledge, and sedulously studied the systems of philosophy which then divided the literary world.

In his twentieth year he attached himself to Socrates, who was then at the height of his reputation as a moralist and dialectician. After the judicial murder of his master, he withdrew from his native city, which, with a theological intolerance extremely rare in pagan antiquity, had already been disgraced by the previous persecution of another eminent teacher—Anaxagoras—the instructor of Euripides and of Pericles. Plato then resided for some time at Megara, at a very short distance from Athens, and afterwards set out, according to the custom of the eager searchers after knowledge of that age, on a course of travels.

He traversed the countries which had been visited by Pythagoras, but his alleged visit to the further East is as traditional as that of his predecessor. The most interesting fact or tradition in his first travels is his alleged intimacy with the Greek prince of Syracuse, the elder Dionysius, and his invitation to the western capital of the Hellenic world. The story that he was given up by his perfidious host to the Spartan envoy, and by him sold into slavery, though not disprovable, may be merely an exaggerated account of the ill-treatment which he actually received.

His grand purpose in going to Italy was, without doubt, the desire to become personally known to the eminent Pythagoreans whose headquarters were in the southern part of the Peninsula, and to secure the best opportunities of making himself thoroughly acquainted with their philosophic tenets. At that time the most eminent representative of the school was the celebrated Archytas, one of the most extraordinary mathematical geniuses and mechanicians of any age. Upon his return to Athens, at about the age of forty, he established his ever-memorable school in the suburban groves or "gardens"... All the most eminent Athenians, present and future, attended his lectures, and among them was Aristotle, who was destined to rival the fame of his master. From about 388 to 347, the date of his death, he continued to lecture in the Academy and to compose his Dialogues.

In the intervals of his literary and didactic labors he twice visited Sicily; the first time at the invitation of his friend Dion, the relative and minister of the two Dionysii, the younger of whom had succeeded to his father's throne, and whom Dion hoped to win to justice and moderation by the eloquent wisdom of the Athenian sage. Such hopes were doomed to bitter disappointment. His second visit to Syracuse was undertaken at the urgent entreaties of his Pythagorean friends, of whose tenets and dietetic principles he always remained an ardent admirer. For whatever reason, it proved unsuccessful. Dion was driven into exile, and Plato himself escaped only by the interposition of Archytas. Thus the only chance of attempting the realization of his ideal of a communistic commonwealth—if he ever actually entertained the hope of realizing it—was frustrated. Almost the only source of the biographies of Plato are the *Letters* ascribed to him, commonly held to be fictitious, but maintained to be genuine by Grote. . . .

The characteristic of the purely speculative portion of Platonism is the theory of *ideas* (used by the author in the new sense of *unities*, the original meaning being *forms* and *figures*), of which it may be said that its merit depends upon its poetic fancy rather than upon its scientific value. Divesting it of the verbiage of the commentators, who have not succeeded in making it more intelligible, all that need be said of this abstruse and fantastic notion is, that by it he intended to convey that all sensible objects which, according to him, are but the shadows and phantoms of things unseen, are ultimately referable to certain abstract conceptions or ideas, which he termed *unities*, that can only be reached by pure thinking. Hence he asserted that "not being in a condition to grasp the idea of the Good with full distinctness, we are able to approximate to it only so far as we elevate the power of thinking to its proper purity."

CONTINUE

21. In the first paragraph of the passage (lines 1-19), the author describes Plato in a manner that:

A. emphasizes Plato's reliance on his prestigious family.
B. highlights Plato's lifelong pursuit of knowledge.
C. exaggerates Plato's intelligence and achievements.
D. showcases Plato's tendency to surpass his instructors.

22. According to the passage, the tenets of Platonism might include which of the following concepts?

I. The theory of ideas
II. The rejection of abstract ideas
III. Pure thinking

F. I only
G. I and II only
H. I and III only
J. I, II, and III

23. Plato is described as similar to François Marie Arouet in that they both:

A. were prominent philosophers.
B. became interested in literature at young ages.
C. belonged to aristocratic families.
D. changed their names.

24. The passage explains that Plato traveled to Italy to:

F. explore the Peninsula.
G. meet Archytas.
H. learn from the Pythagoreans.
J. give a series of lectures.

25. Which of these statements is supported by information from the first paragraph (lines 1–19)?

A. Athleticism was very important to Greeks during Plato's time.
B. Athens is located at the very center of Greece.
C. Plato had to travel the world because he there were no good teachers in Athens.
D. Plato studied with the philosopher Socrates.

26. As it is used in line 1, the word *renowned* most nearly means:

F. infamous.
G. crafty.
H. curious.
J. celebrated

27. The passage states that Plato traveled a lot during his studies because:

A. he wanted to escape from persecution.
B. it was what scholars tended to do during Plato's time.
C. he wanted to escape a death sentence.
D. it was the only way to obtain a rich education.

28. The main point of the final paragraph (lines 70–84) is that Platonism is:

F. confusing and difficult to explain.
G. among the most influential philosophies.
H. poetic yet scientific.
J. an example of pure thinking.

29. It can be inferred from the passage that Plato's ideas were most likely shaped by is:

A. François Marie Arouet.
B. Archytas.
C. Socrates.
D. Aristotle.

30. The author suggests that the Letters ascribed to Plato are "commonly held to be fictitious" (line 68) to:

F. admit that his own biography is completely false.
G. imply that Plato might not have actually existed.
H. call attention to the fact that all biographies contain false information.
J. imply that what is known about Plato might not actually be true.

PASSAGE IV

NATURAL SCIENCE: The following is adapted from Peter Mere Latham's article about diseases that affect the human heart published in the *Monthly Journal of Foreign Medicine* in 1828.

The membrane which lines the cavities of the heart is very liable to disease, but not equally so in every part. Where it is thin and transparent, and admits the color and character of the muscular structure upon which it is spread to be seen through it, it is seldom found diseased; but where it is of a denser texture, either in itself or from an admixture of other structures, whether cellular or fibrous, with its own, it is frequently, and often exclusively diseased. This latter character of a denser texture belongs to it where it forms the tough white circles which surround the apertures of communication between the auricles and ventricles; also where it is reflected upon itself, and forms the loose duplicatures of membrane, which are given off, as it were, from the internal surface of the heart, either at the fibrous circles intermediate between the auricles and ventricles, constituting the tricuspid and the mitral valves, or at the commencement of the pulmonary artery and aorta, constituting the semilunar valves.

It is remarkable how curiously disease is apt to limit itself to the spaces just pointed out. Of the fibrous circle between the auricle and ventricle, of the valves which originate from it, and of the tendinous cords which connect the valves with the carneæ columnæ, there will not be the smallest space free from disease; but the disease will abruptly stop where the tendinous cords cease and the carneæ columnæ begin.

The membrane, however, where it covers the fleshy columns of the heart, is not exempt from the possibility of disease: but when disease actually affects it, it has seldom originated there, but has generally spread from other parts of the same membrane, although (as we have just remarked) it is apt to stop short before it reaches this.

Of the two sides of the heart, the membrane which lines the left is unquestionably the more liable to disease. But my own observation would never have led me to conclude that the membrane of the right side was so far exempt as it is commonly thought to be. Speaking from the best recollection I have of the specimens which have fallen under my examination, I should say that, in one-third of the cases where disease has been found on the left side, it has existed on the right side also, and been essentially of the same character. But there has been a remarkable difference in the extent to which it has proceeded on each side respectively: while on the left it has gone so far as to be the undoubted cause of death, on the right, although essentially of the same character, it has been only just beginning.

It very seldom happens that disease appertains to the lining of the right cavities of the heart exclusively; and, where it affects both, the disease in the right cavities is very seldom found in advance of that in the left.

It should seem, indeed, according to the ordinary course of things, that disease does not begin in the lining of the right cavities of the heart, until it has already advanced to an extreme degree in the left.

The internal lining of the heart, as well as of the arteries, is often found to have become of a red color. This redness, so well-known to all who are accustomed to examine dead bodies, used to be regarded as a mere stain imparted to it by the coloring matter of the blood after death. Yet a due consideration of various circumstances connected with it will hardly warrant this conclusion.

It has been found whether the heart or artery be full or empty of blood; and if blood be present it has been found, whether it is liquid or clotted; and if it be clotted, whether it does or does not retain its coloring matter. External temperature, and length of time between the death of the patient and the dissection of his body, have not made any difference in the frequency with which this peculiar appearance occurs. Lastly, no artificial methods, such as washing of any kind, can get rid of it; nor will inclosing blood within an artery for any period produce it. This simple redness is sometimes seen universally in both sides of the heart and throughout the whole arterial system, and sometimes in patches only, of greater or less extent, whether in the arteries or in the heart.

Now, when all these circumstances are considered, although in some instances it may be a mere stain imparted by the coloring matter of the blood after death, it is plainly impossible that it should be of that nature in any large proportion of the numerous instances in which it is found.

But if the appearance in question implies (as I believe it generally does) a morbid condition, of what kind is that condition? There are the same objections to considering mere redness as equivalent to inflammation here as in the pericardium, or in any other part of the body: here, as elsewhere, in one case it may be the condition out of which inflammation is to spring; while in another it may not be destined to give origin to any change in the structure of the part beyond itself, and may itself constitute the whole disease.

It appears to me, that this mere redness of the internal lining of the heart and arteries has become a matter of undue perplexity to pathologists, because they have labored to infer from it more than the simple fact itself will authorize. All I wish to establish concerning it is, first, that it is not always (probably very seldom) a mere stain imparted by the coloring matter of the blood after death; secondly, that it alone does not constitute inflammation.

31. The passage suggests that the two sides of the heart are similar because:

A. they are both susceptible to disease.
B. infection of both sides always leads to death.
C. diseases begins in both sides at the same time.
D. they are equally likely to become diseased.

CONTINUE

32. The passage states that the thin, transparent area of the heart membrane:

F. is particularly vulnerable to disease.
G. forms loose duplicatures.
H. rarely becomes diseased.
J. is found between the auricle and ventricle.

33. As it is used in line 3, the word *admits* most likely means:

A. acknowledges.
B. allows.
C. confesses.
D. reveals.

34. According to the first paragraph (lines 1–17), the loose duplicatures of membrane that extend from the pulmonary artery and aorta are the:

F. tricuspid valves.
G. semilunar valves.
H. mitral valves.
J. auricles.

35. One purpose of the last paragraph is to suggest that the author:

A. does not have much faith in the scientific community.
B. thinks that pathologists are the least reliable medical professionals.
C. believes that contemporary medical science can be extremely perplexing.
D. has a unique perspective on the topic of the passage.

36. As defined by the passage, the internal lining of the heart is red if:

I. the heart is full of blood.
II. the heart is emptied ofbloods.
III. the heart is clotted.

F. II only
G. I and II only
H. I and III only
J. II and III only

37. The final five paragraphs mainly cover the:

A. author's theory that the heart's redness is a morbid condition.
B. circumstances under which the heart is found to be red.
C. differences between how disease affects the right and left sides of the heart.
D. possible reasons the heart appears to be red in color.

38. According to the passage, the author has found disease in both the left and right sides of the heart in:

F. all of the cases he has studied.
G. half of the cases he has studied.
H. one-third of the cases he has studied.
J. one-fourth of the cases he has studied.

39. The passage mentions that "inclosing" blood within an artery:

A. cannot eliminate redness from the heart.
B. does not cause the heart to turn red.
C. does not cause a heart to become diseased.
D. alters the frequency with which hearts appear to be red.

40. The author concludes that the red coloring of the heart:

F. is neither a blood stain nor does it constitute inflammation.
G. is evidence of the area from which inflammation originated.
H. constitutes the entire diseased area of the heart.
J. is not as perplexing as most scientists believe it to be.

STOP

SCIENCE TEST

35 Minutes—40 Questions

DIRECTIONS: There are seven passages in this test. Each passage is followed by several questions. Read each passage, choose the best answer, and fill in the corresponding circle on the answer sheet. You may refer back to the passages at any time.

Remember, you are NOT allowed to use a calculator on this test.

PASSAGE I

Diabetes, a disease in which the body does not produce or properly use insulin to convert sugar into usable energy, is marked by elevated blood sugar levels. A *glycated hemoglobin* test reveals a person's average blood sugar level for the past three months. A result of 5% or more is considered high. A glycated hemoglobin reading above 7% is a strong indicator of diabetes.

Table 1 indicates the breakdown of glycated hemoglobin levels among 100 non-diabetics tested.

Table 1

Glycated Hemoglobin Reading	Number of Test Subjects
3%	12
4%	21
5%	19
6%	29
7%	17
8%	2
9%	0

Scientists estimated the risk of developing cardiovascular disease associated with various glycated hemoglobin levels, first among a group of non-diabetics, and then among a group of diabetics. The results are represented in Figure 1.

FIGURE 1

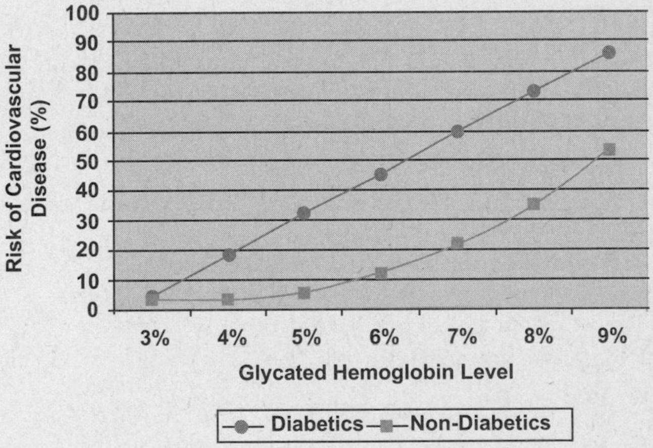

1. According to the data in Figure 1, as glycated hemoglobin levels increase, the risk of cardiovascular disease generally increases for:

   A. diabetics but not for non-diabetics.
   B. non-diabetics but not for diabetics.
   C. both diabetics and non-diabetics.
   D. neither diabetics nor non-diabetics.

Practice Test 1 — SCIENCE

CONTINUE

2. Based on the data in Figure 1, is the risk of cardiovascular disease ever the same for both diabetics and non-diabetics?

   F. No, the lines representing risk of cardiovascular disease for the two groups do not intersect.
   G. No, the risk of cardiovascular disease for diabetics is always higher for each glycated hemoglobin level measured.
   H. Yes, the lines representing risk of cardiovascular disease for the two groups will eventually intersect at a 10% glycated hemoglobin level.
   J. Yes, the risk of cardiovascular disease is the same for both groups at the lowest glycated hemoglobin level measured.

3. If the data in Table 1 is representative of non-diabetics in general, what can be concluded about non-diabetics compared to diabetics?

   A. More than 90% of non-diabetics have less than a 50% risk of developing cardiovascular disease.
   B. Around 30% of non-diabetics have the same risk of developing cardiovascular disease as diabetics.
   C. Around 20% of non-diabetics have glycated hemoglobin levels indicative of diabetes.
   D. Fewer than 5% of non-diabetics have the same risk as diabetics of developing cardiovascular disease.

4. Figure 1 indicates that the change in the risk of cardiovascular disease associated with each 1% increase in glycated hemoglobin level is

   F. always greater for non-diabetics than for diabetics.
   G. more consistent for diabetics than for non-diabetics.
   H. positive for diabetics and negative for non-diabetics.
   J. most similar for diabetics and non-diabetics at the 6% glycated hemoglobin level and below.

5. The information in Table 1 suggests that:

   A. non-diabetics are at a lower risk for cardiovascular disease than are diabetics.
   B. a glycated hemoglobin test is not a perfectly reliable predictor of diabetes.
   C. none of the subjects tested has a risk of developing diabetes in the near future.
   D. cardiovascular disease has a positive correlation with glycated hemoglobin levels.

PASSAGE II

At the end of the Cretaceous Period 66 million years ago, all dinosaurs except birds went extinct. Dinosaurs were not the only organisms that died out—more than half of all plant and animal species on Earth, both on land and in the oceans, went extinct at that time as well. The two most likely hypotheses for the cause of this catastrophic mass extinction are described below.

Asteroid Impact Hypothesis

Around 66 million years ago, a huge asteroid struck Earth just off the coast of what is now Mexico. The impact would have superheated the atmosphere, generated an earthquake 1 million times stronger than the strongest ever recorded, blasted 5,000 cubic miles of dust into the atmosphere, and released huge amounts of carbon dioxide (CO_2) into the air. Over the next few months, dust would blot out the sun, causing freezing temperatures and complete darkness. Highly acidic rain, formed from reactions in the heated atmosphere, would have fallen into the seas, killing marine organisms. After the dust cleared, the released CO_2 would have caused extreme global warming for as long as tens of thousands of years. All of these environmental effects could have caused organisms to go extinct relatively quickly in geological terms, over thousands of years.

Volcanic Eruption Hypothesis

Between 68 to 65 million years ago, about 480,000 cubic miles of molten lava seeped out of cracks in the earth's crust in present-day India. The lava erupted in many separate episodes, each lasting from a few days to a year or more, and each expelling tremendous amounts of ash and toxic gases into the air. In the short term, the ash would decrease the amount of sunlight reaching the earth's surface, decreasing temperatures, inhibiting photosynthesis, and disrupting the food chain. Sulfur dioxide (SO_2) gas from the eruptions would form super-acid rain that would poison marine organisms. In the long term, after the ash settled, the carbon dioxide (CO_2) released would cause global warming. These continuing environmental stresses would have caused a gradual extinction of organisms lasting from tens to hundreds of thousands of years.

6. The main difference between the Asteroid Impact and Volcanic Eruption hypotheses is:

   F. the way that carbon dioxide affects the climate.
   G. the length of time it takes for extinction to occur.
   H. the effect of highly acidic rain on marine organisms.
   J. the effect of dust or ash on sunlight.

7. According to the passage, which statement would be accepted by proponents of both the Asteroid Impact and Volcanic Eruption hypotheses?

A. Long-term effects on global temperatures were caused by carbon dioxide.
B. Carbon dioxide caused a short-term decrease in the amount of sunlight reaching Earth's surface.
C. The extinction-triggering event happened in an instant.
D. Environmental stresses occurred over hundreds of thousands of years.

8. Which of the following pieces of evidence would help support the Asteroid Impact Hypothesis but not the Volcanic Eruption Hypothesis?

F. Isotope data from rock layers at the end of the Cretaceous show warmer temperatures than earlier in the Cretaceous.
G. Large amounts of volcanic ash are found in rock layers that are 68 to 65 million years old.
H. Shells of marine organisms from the end of the Cretaceous show acid damage.
J. Fossils of Cretaceous organisms disappear quickly over a few thousand years just before the end of the Cretaceous.

9. According to the Volcanic Eruption hypothesis, what substance in the atmosphere caused super-acid rain to fall at the end of the Cretaceous?

A. Carbon dioxide gas
B. Sulfur dioxide gas
C. Volcanic ash
D. Dust

10. The Asteroid Impact Hypothesis proposes that which event occurred at the moment of asteroid impact?

F. Freezing temperatures over all of Earth
G. An exceptionally powerful earthquake
H. Extreme global warming over all of Earth
J. Highly acidic rain falling into the oceans

11. With which of the following statements would proponents of both the Asteroid Impact and Volcanic Eruption hypotheses agree?

The mass extinction at the end of the Cretaceous was caused by:

A. an object from outer space.
B. lava flows that buried organisms.
C. strong earthquakes.
D. environmental stresses.

12. Mount Tambora, in what is now Indonesia, exploded in a massive volcanic eruption in 1815. The following year, 1816, has been called "The Year without a Summer," as average global temperatures fell by about 0.5°C (1.0°F) that year. What part of the volcanic eruption hypothesis does "The Year without a Summer" support?

F. Short-term effects of SO_2
G. Long-term effects of CO_2
H. Short-term effects of ash
J. Long-term effects of acid rain

PASSAGE III

Heart rate, a measure of the number of heart beats per minute, rises as the body strives to meet the demands of physical activity. Fitness generally increases as one's resting heart rate decreases and as the degree of change in heart rate during exercise increases. *Recovery rate* is the decrease in the number of beats per minute calculated for each minute following the cessation of physical activity, until heart rate returns to normal resting levels. Greater fitness correlates with higher recovery rates.

CONTINUE

Scientists conducted three studies to investigate how heart rate fluctuates during and after two kinds of physical activity.

Study 1

A high school swimmer and a high school basketball player participated for 10 continuous minutes in their respective sports, while an electronic device measured their heart rates in beats per minute (bpm) over the course of their exertions. Both began with their heart rate at normal resting levels. Both athletes ceased physical activity after 10 minutes, whereupon the devices continued to monitor their heart rates during 5 minutes of subsequent inactivity. The results are indicated in Figure 1.

FIGURE 1

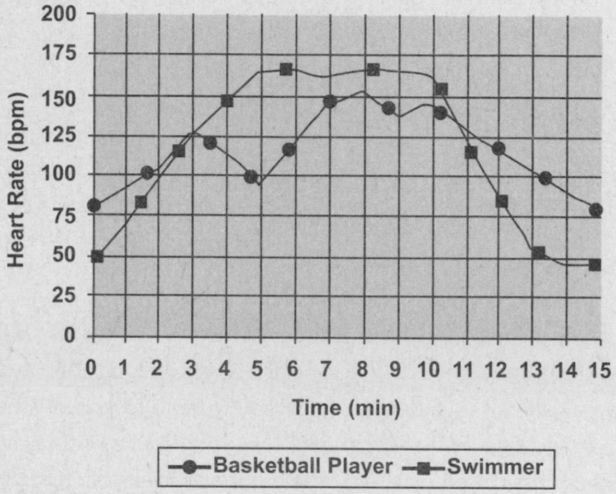

Study 2

Next, researchers analyzed a videotape of the basketball player's recorded activities during Study 1 and classified his movements into the following categories: walking, jogging, sprinting, shuffling (slight intense movements back and forth or side to side), and jumping. Figure 2 shows the percentage of time that the basketball player performed each kind of movement.

FIGURE 2

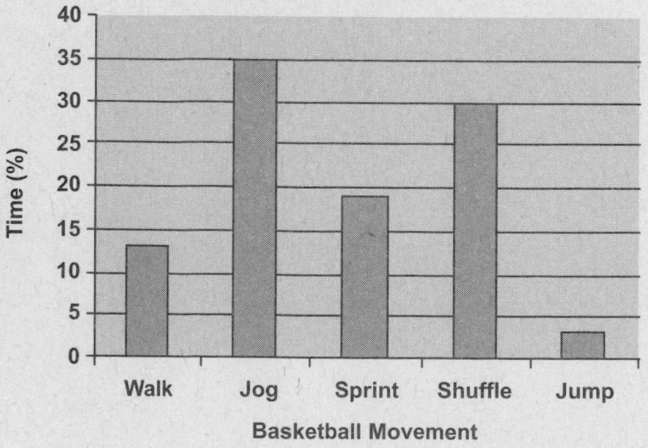

Study 3

Researchers then instructed the athletes to repeat the exercise according to the same parameters observed in Study 1, except this time with the swimmer playing basketball and the basketball player swimming. The athletes' heart rates after 10 minutes, and the decreases in their heart rates during the 5 minutes following that, are recorded in Table 1.

Table 1

	Basketball Player Swimming	Swimmer Playing Basketball
Heart rate after 10 minutes	145	150
Decrease in heart rate between 10 and 11 minutes	15	40
Decrease in heart rate between 11 and 12 minutes	15	35
Decrease in heart rate between 12 and 13 minutes	11	30
Decrease in heart rate between 13 and 14 minutes	10	0
Decrease in heart rate between 14 and 15 minutes	10	0

13. Based on the results of Study 2, what can the researchers conclude about Figure 1?

A. The highest heart rates on the graph correspond to the times that the basketball player was jogging.

B. The lowest heart rates on the graph correspond to the times that the basketball player was jumping.

C. The heart rate of the basketball player fluctuates based on the type of movement performed.

D. The basketball player first jumped, then walked, then sprinted, then shuffled, and finally jogged.

14. The results of Study 1 suggest that:

F. the swimmer is more fit than the basketball player.

G. the basketball player is more fit than the swimmer.

H. swimming is a more strenuous activity than basketball.

J. basketball is a more strenuous activity than swimming.

15. The researchers most likely designed Study 3 to investigate whether:

A. swimmers are generally more fit than basketball players.

B. swimmers are better at basketball than basketball players are at swimming.

C. recovery rates are influenced by the type of physical activity in which one engages.

D. the degree of change in heart rate during exercise is related to overall fitness.

16. After he stopped swimming, the swimmer's heart rate first returned to normal resting levels:

F. by minute 12.

G. 5 minutes after he stopped swimming.

H. after the basketball player's heart rate returned to normal resting levels.

J. before the basketball player's heart rate returned to normal resting levels.

17. The zeros in Table 1 indicate that the:

A. swimmer is in worse physical condition than the basketball player.

B. swimmer's heart stopped three minutes after he had stopped playing basketball.

C. swimmer disobeyed instructions and played basketball for 13 minutes instead of 10 minutes.

D. swimmer's heart rate had returned to normal resting levels by 3 minutes after he finished playing basketball.

18. The breathing rate, or number of breaths taken per minute (bpm), is another way to gauge the demands placed on the heart by physical activity. If breathing rate was also measured during Study 1, which of the following graphs best shows the breathing rate for the swimmer over the time of Study 1?

F.

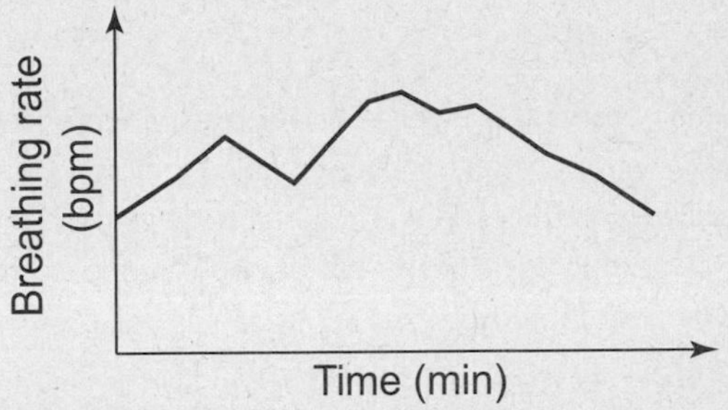

G.

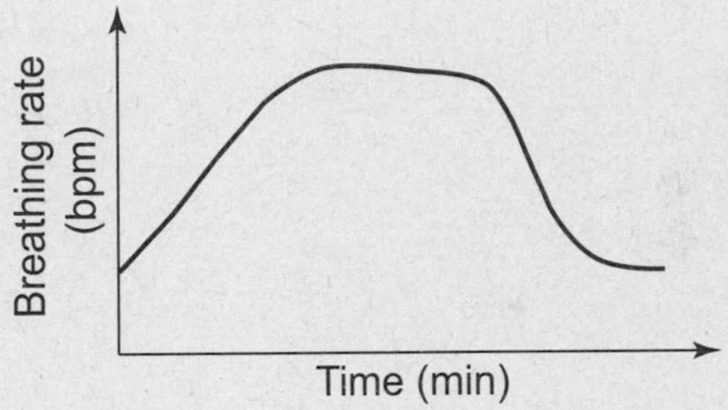

H.

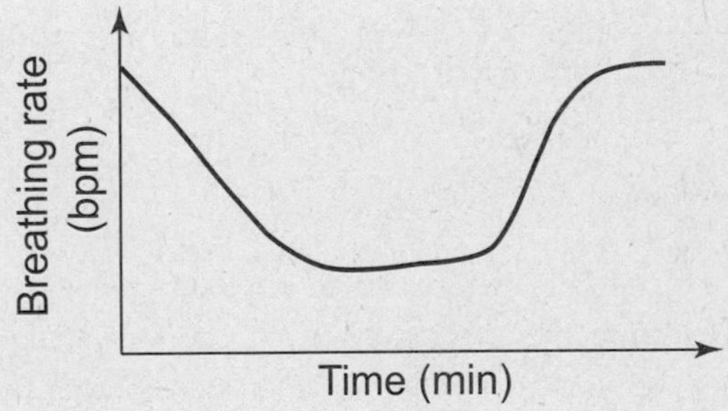

J.

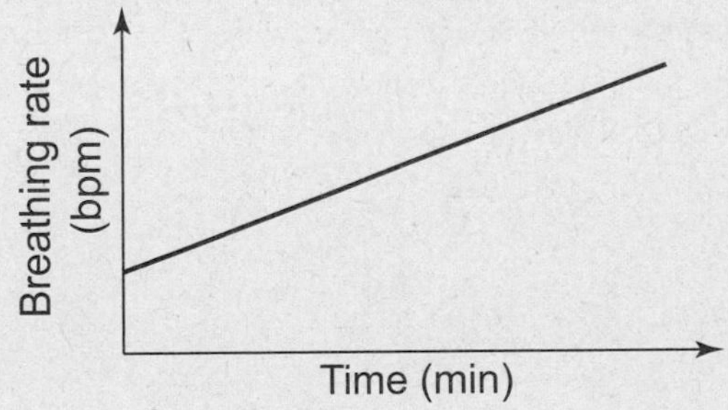

CONTINUE

PASSAGE IV

Mitochondria are the source of energy within every living cell. Scientists conducted studies on a wasp species known as the European beewolf to investigate the mitochondria's role in species survival.

Study 1

Upon observing beewolf behavior, researchers noted that beewolves attack larger honeybees, which they sting, paralyze, and then feed to their young. The researchers tracked the breeding and hunting activities of six beewolves and compiled their findings in Table 1.

Table 1

Beewolf	Number of Offspring	Average number of honeybees fed to each offspring
A	22	3
B	7	1
C	35	4
D	12	2
E	5	1
F	29	4

Study 2

The researchers then calculated, for 100 beewolves, the density of folded membranes inside the mitochondria of flight muscles. They were able to establish a general relationship between the density of these membranes and mitochondrial energy output (see Figure 1).

FIGURE 1

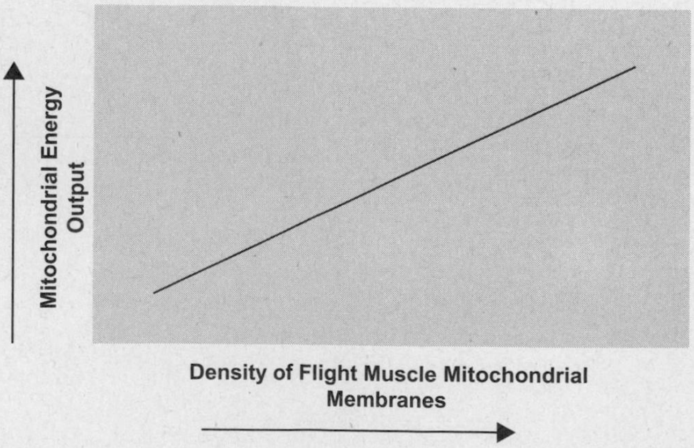

Study 3

Next the researchers measured the density of flight muscle mitochondrial membranes, expressed in folds per cubic centimeter (f/cc), of the original six beewolves observed in Study 1. The results are depicted in Table 2.

Table 2

Beewolf	Density of Flight Muscle Mitochondrial Membranes (f/cc)
A	78
B	9
C	168
D	30
E	6
F	140

19. Based on the data from Study 1, an observed trend is that:

A. beewolves with more offspring tend to provide fewer honeybees to each.
B. beewolves with more offspring tend to provide more honeybees to each.
C. the output of mitochondrial energy tends to correlate positively with the density of flight muscle mitochondrial membranes.
D. the output of mitochondrial energy tends to correlate negatively with the density of flight muscle mitochondrial membranes.

20. The results of the studies suggest that mitochondrial energy output is directly related to:

F. the honeybee-hunting proficiency of beewolves.
G. the number of flight muscles a beewolf possesses.
H. a beewolf's risk of being killed by a honeybee.
J. the mortality rate of beewolf offspring.

21. Scientists tracked the hunting and breeding activities of an additional four beewolves, G, H, I, and J. Which beewolf's activities do NOT follow the trends of the beewolves in Study 1?

A. Beewolf G: 18 offspring, 2 honeybees fed to each offspring
B. Beewolf H: 6 offspring, 4 honeybees fed to each offspring
C. Beewolf I: 31 offspring, 4 honeybees fed to each offspring
D. Beewolf J: 8 offspring, 1 honeybee fed to each offspring

22. Using only the data from Studies 1 and 3, and without the data from Study 2, the scientists would only be able to directly observe the relationship between which two variables?

F. Mitochondrial energy output and density of flight muscle mitochondrial membranes
G. Average number of honeybees fed to each offspring and mitochondrial energy output
H. Density of flight muscle mitochondrial membranes and average number of honeybees fed to each offspring
J. Total number of honeybees killed and mitochondrial energy output

23. If the researchers conclude from the studies' results that mitochondrial energy output is directly related to species survival, this conclusion would be most strengthened by a further study showing that:

A. the density of flight muscle mitochondrial membranes is directly related to mitochondrial energy output.
B. beewolf species survival is enhanced in proportion to the volume and nourishment of offspring.
C. the density of honeybee mitochondrial membranes is equal to or greater than that of beewolves.
D. beewolves with higher mitochondrial energy output tend to have fewer offspring than beewolves with lower mitochondrial energy output.

24. Another beewolf, Beewolf K, is found to have a flight muscle mitochondrial membrane density of 92 f/cc. If Beewolf K is consistent with the other beewolves in this study, it is likely that:

F. its mitochondrial energy output is greater than that of Beewolf F.
G. it fed fewer than 60 honeybees total to its offspring.
H. its mitochondrial energy output is less than that of Beewolf D.
J. it fed more than 60 honeybees total to its offspring.

PASSAGE V

A mineral is a naturally occurring inorganic solid with a definite chemical composition and an ordered atomic arrangement. Minerals with the same chemical composition but different atomic arrangements can form under different temperature and pressure conditions. These minerals are called polymorphs. There are three polymorphs with the formula Al_2SiO_5: andalusite, kyanite, and sillimanite. Scientists have experimentally determined the conditions under which these three polymorphs form, and their results are shown in Figure 1. Figure 1 is a phase diagram in which each shaded area includes all the temperature and pressures under which the labeled polymorph forms. Pressures are shown in gigapascals (GPa); one billion pascals (Pa) = one GPa. The average pressure at Earth's surface is about 100,000 Pa, or only 0.0001 GPa. Temperatures are shown in degrees Celsius.

FIGURE 1

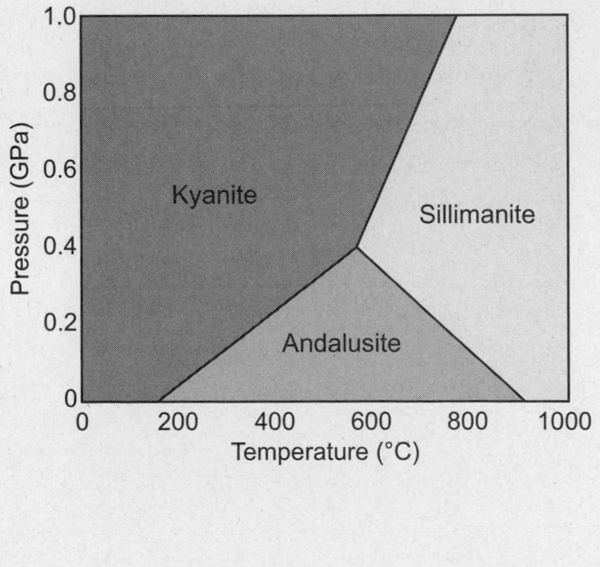

CONTINUE

Scientists have also studied the temperature and pressure conditions in different geologic settings around the earth, including those at different depths in the earth's interior. Figure 2 shows the range of temperature and pressure conditions in different geologic settings. Each shaded triangle includes the temperature, pressure, and depth range of its geologic setting.

FIGURE 2

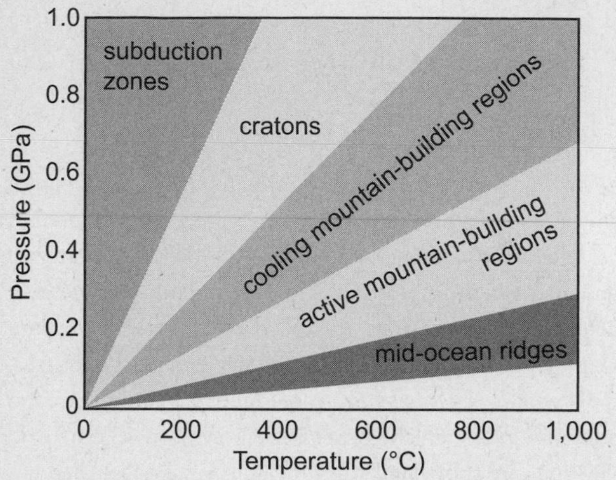

25. The lines between the shaded areas in Figure 1 represent conditions where two polymorphs are in equilibrium. One can conclude along these lines that:

A. the two polymorphs can transform into the third polymorph.
B. only the more stable polymorph can exist.
C. the two polymorphs can both exist.
D. the temperature and pressure stay the same.

26. Based on the information in Figures 1 and 2, sillimanite is most likely to form in:

F. the lowest-pressure part (0–0.05 GPa) of a mid-ocean ridge.
G. the hottest part (800–1,000°C) of a mountain-building region.
H. cratons.
J. subduction zones.

27. According to Figure 1, which mineral(s) are most likely to form on the earth's surface, where temperatures and pressures are low?

A. Kyanite
B. Andalusite
C. Sillimanite
D. Both kyanite and sillimanite

28. A subduction zone is a region where one tectonic plate is pushed underneath another and sinks deep into the earth. From the subduction zone portion of Figure 2, what can one conclude about the relationship between pressure and depth inside the earth?

F. Pressure increases with depth only where temperatures are high.
G. Pressure decreases with depth only where temperatures are low.
H. Pressure increases as depth increases.
J. Pressure decreases as depth increases.

29. According to Figure 2, a rock from the hottest part (800–1,000°C) of an active mountain-building region would most likely contain:

A. andalusite only.
B. both kyanite and andalusite.
C. both andalusite and sillimanite.
D. sillimanite only.

PASSAGE VI

The rubbing between solid objects is called *friction*, while the rubbing between a solid object and a liquid or gas is called *drag*. Each produces a resistance force, measured in newtons (N), that works against the momentum of moving objects subjected to these forces. Both friction and drag produce heat. Researchers performed the following experiments to investigate the various properties of and relationships between these phenomena.

Experiment 1

A 20 kg box was placed on top of a long, inclined ramp and released such that it slid down the ramp, ranging in velocity from 0 km/hr. at the top of the ramp to 30 km/hr. at the bottom. A monitoring device was positioned to record the friction resistance force slowing the box's descent at five different velocities during five different trials. A boat on a river also accelerated from 0 km/hr to 30 km/hr., and the drag resistance force impeding its progress was measred during the course of five trials at the same five velocities at which the box friction was measured. The results are depicted in Figure 1.

FIGURE 1

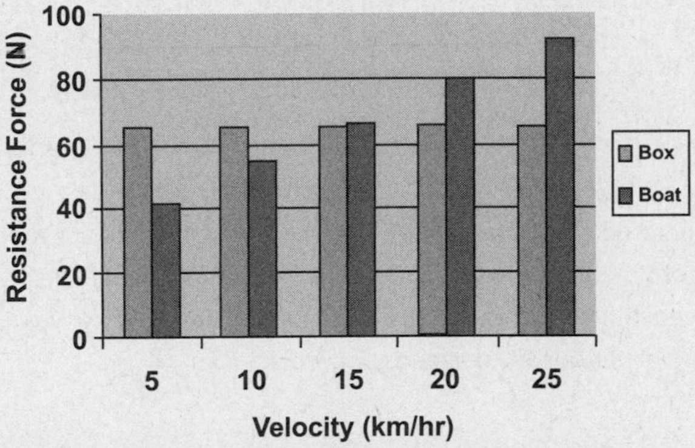

Experiment 2

Researchers repeated the ramp and box experiment, replacing the original box with a 10 kg box, a 30 kg box, and a 40 kg box. The friction resistance force working against each box was recorded at the point each attained a velocity of 20 km/hr. Moreover, the level of heat generated at that point was measured. The results are noted in Table 1.

Table 1

Box	Friction Resistance Force	Heat Generated
10 kg	55 N	3.5°C
30 kg	75 N	10.5°C
40 kg	85 N	14°C

Experiment 3

The ramp used in Experiment 1 was coated with a layer of sand and the original 20 kg box was released from the same spot, reaching a velocity of 18 km/hr. at the bottom of the ramp. The sand was then fully cleared away and running water was sprayed down the ramp as the same box was again released from the same spot, this time achieving a velocity of 39 km/hr. at the bottom.

30. Based on the results of Experiment 1, approximately what friction resistance force would you expect the 20 kg box to experience when it reached 30 km/hr. at the bottom of the ramp?

F. 40 N
G. 65 N
H. 90 N
J. 105 N

31. Experiment 2 demonstrates a positive correlation between:

A. velocity and drag.
B. weight and drag.
C. heat and weight.
D. friction and velocity.

32. It can be concluded from the investigation that friction differs from drag in that friction:

F. produces a resistance force.
G. produces heat.
H. varies with weight.
J. does not vary with velocity.

33. The results of Experiment 3 are best explained by the hypothesis that:

A. both water and sand decrease the resistance force between the ramp and the box.
B. both water and sand increase the resistance force between the ramp and the box.
C. sand decreases the resistance force between the ramp and the box, while water increases it.
D. water decreases the resistance force between the ramp and the box, while sand increases it.

CONTINUE

34. When the 20 kg box was released down the ramp that was coated with sand in Experiment 3, what can you conclude about the heat that was generated by the block at the bottom of the ramp?

F. It is lower than the heat generated by a 10 kg box sliding down the original ramp in Experiment 1.
G. It is higher than the heat generated by the same box sliding down the original ramp in Experiment 1.
H. It is lower than the heat generated by the same box sliding down the ramp when it was sprayed with running water.
J. It is higher than the heat generated by a 30 kg box sliding down the sand-coated ramp.

35. The best way for researchers to build on the results of Experiment 1 to test the effects of different fluids on drag resistance force is to measure the drag resistance force while they:

A. accelerate the boat from Experiment 1 through different bodies of water.
B. accelerate a heavier and lighter boat than the original boat from Experiment 1 through the same river.
C. accelerate the boat from Experiment 1 through the same river while towing different-sized loads.
D. accelerate a heavier and lighter boat than the original boat from Experiment 1 through different bodies of water.

PASSAGE VII

Wind speed is influenced by the obstacles the wind confronts on Earth's surface. Scientists have classified various types of Earth's terrain into roughness classes: the higher the roughness class, the rougher the terrain. Roughness Class 0 represents water surfaces, roughness Class 2 represents sparsely populated agricultural land, and roughness Class 4 represents very large cities with tall buildings.

Table 1 shows mean wind speeds observed at three different heights above Earth's surface, in three different roughness classes. Observation heights are represented in meters (m), and wind speed is represented in meters per second (m/s).

Table 1

Height Above Ground (m)	Roughness Class	Wind Speed (m/s)
50	0	13.73
50	2	10.7
50	4	8.1
100	0	14.4
100	2	11.7
100	4	9.39
150	0	14.8
150	2	12.29
150	4	10.14

Wind turbines convert wind power into electricity. The power generated from wind is expressed in watts per square meter, according to the formula $W/m^2 = (0.5)(1.225)(v^3)$, where v is wind speed in meters per second. Table 2 indicates the power of the wind at various wind speeds.

Table 2

Wind Speed (m/s)	Wind Power (W/m²)	Wind Speed (m/s)	Wind Power (W/m²)
0	0	8	313.6
1	0.6	9	446.5
2	4.9	10	612.5
3	16.5	11	815.2
4	39.2	12	1,058.4
5	76.2	13	1,345.7
6	132.3	14	1,680.7
7	210.1	15	2,067.2

36. For a given height above the ground, the data indicates that as the roughness of the terrain increases, wind speed:

F. decreases.
G. decreases, then increases.
H. increases.
J. increases, then decreases.

37. Table 1 indicates that as the height above the ground decreases, wind speed:

A. increases more rapidly in rougher terrain.
B. declines more rapidly in rougher terrain.
C. increases more rapidly in smoother terrain.
D. declines more rapidly in smoother terrain.

38. A wind turbine 100 m tall is built at the edge of a farm field to provide electricity for the farm. Using the data in Tables 1 and 2, what is the expected power generation of this turbine?

F. 446 W/m^2
G. 815 W/m^2
H. 1050 W/m^2
J. 1680 W/m^2

39. Based on the information in Table 1, which of the following locations exhibits the greatest mean wind speed?

A. 50 meters above sparsely populated agricultural land
B. 150 meters above a very large city with tall buildings
C. 50 meters above a very large city with tall buildings
D. 100 meters above sparsely populated agricultural land

40. A large coastal city wants to at least triple the power generation of its 50 m wind turbine, which is currently located in the city center. Which of the following changes would provide the necessary boost in power generation?

F. Double the height of the turbine to 100 m.
G. Triple the height of the turbine to 150 m.
H. Move the turbine to a farm field on the outskirts of the city.
J. Move the turbine offshore onto the ocean.

STOP

WRITING TEST

40 MINUTES

DIRECTIONS: This is a test of your writing skills. You have forty (40) minutes to write an essay in English. Be sure to carefully read the issue and three perspectives presented before planning and writing your essay so you understand clearly the task you are being asked to do. Your essay will be graded on the evidence it provides of your ability to analyze the issue; evaluate and analyze the perspectives; state and develop a personal perspective; and describe the relationship between the given perspectives and your own, while effectively using organization, logic, and language according to the conventions of standard written English.

ARE 3D PRINTERS DANGEROUS?

As humankind marches bravely through the current era of rapid technological innovation, we continue to create wondrous new inventions that help us live easier, work faster, and enhance our collective and individual experiences. A curious new gadget that has arisen in recent years is the 3D printer, which allows users to "print" solid three-dimensional objects through a complex shaping and molding process. 3D printing technology, which will continue to evolve and improve over time and become more accessible to the average consumer, also brings with it a growing concern—that 3D printers will be used to create potentially dangerous weapons, like guns, for criminal use, or for counterfeiting objects. With that in mind, some feel that the sale of such technology should be subject to government oversight and regulation.

Read and carefully consider these perspectives. Each suggests a particular way of thinking about how to address the potential dangers of 3D printers.

PERSPECTIVE ONE

The potential dangers of 3D printers use are too great to allow private citizens to be able to own this new technology. They may at first seem to be a fascinating innovation and a great way to be creative, but as they continue to evolve and become more sophisticated, they come with the real potential for misuse. Imagine a world in which anyone with a 3D printer can create untraceable weapons and use them to commit crimes. It's hard enough for the government to deal with the volume of dangerous and illegal weapons now; how would it handle a society where we can create them at will from our own homes? To market and sell 3D printers to the general population would be irresponsible and not in the best interest of society.

PERSPECTIVE TWO

People should be allowed to freely use 3D printers. It isn't rational to automatically assume that they will be routinely misused for nefarious purposes, like creating plastic guns or other weapons. Just because something has the potential for danger doesn't mean that it needs to be automatically stripped from the hands of the public. Anyone can freely buy a set of kitchen knives, or a baseball bat, and both have the potential to cause harm—should they be taken off the market? Then, why should access to 3D printers be handled differently? These printers are exciting new outlets for creative thinking and future innovation, and banning them out of fear would be a sad and tragic move.

Perspective Three

While it is true that 3D printers carry the potential risk of abuse, they also have the potential to be amazing outlets for creative expression and technological innovation. We can't discard this intriguing new technology just because of a possible risk for misuse. Granted, it would be unwise to just let individuals "run free" and use 3D printers however they see fit. However, systems and rigid guidelines are already in place for handling the sale and purchase of other potentially dangerous items, such as handguns. These rules could easily be extended to include 3D printers; guidelines for sellers and purchasers and registration can be decided on at a state or national level. Careful and pragmatic product regulation is not a new concept; extending it to 3D printers would help ensure that they are used responsibly.

Essay Task

Write a cohesive, logical essay in which you consider multiple perspectives addressing the concerns about 3D printing technology. In your essay, be sure to:

- examine and assess the perspectives given
- declare and explain your own perspective on the issue
- discuss the relationship between your perspective and those given

Your perspective may be in full or partial agreement, or in total disagreement, with any of the others. Whatever the case, support your ideas with logical reasoning and detailed, persuasive examples.

Plan and Write Your Essay

Use the first two pages of the Writing test answer sheet (found at the beginning of the test) to generate ideas and plan your essay. Then use the following four pages to write your essay. Consider the following as you compose your essay:

What are the strengths and weaknesses of the three perspectives provided?

- Identify the insights they present and what they fail to consider.
- Ascertain why a given perspective might persuade or fail to persuade.

How can you apply your own experience, knowledge, and values?

- Express your perspective on the issue, identifying the perspective's strengths and weaknesses.
- Formulate a plan to support your perspective in your essay.

1.	C	**20.**	F	**39.**	B	**58.**	J
2.	H	**21.**	B	**40.**	F	**59.**	B
3.	D	**22.**	J	**41.**	B	**60.**	H
4.	J	**23.**	A	**42.**	F	**61.**	A
5.	D	**24.**	H	**43.**	C	**62.**	H
6.	G	**25.**	A	**44.**	H	**63.**	B
7.	A	**26.**	H	**45.**	A	**64.**	F
8.	G	**27.**	D	**46.**	H	**65.**	C
9.	A	**28.**	G	**47.**	C	**66.**	G
10.	G	**29.**	C	**48.**	G	**67.**	C
11.	B	**30.**	J	**49.**	A	**68.**	J
12.	J	**31.**	B	**50.**	J	**69.**	D
13.	D	**32.**	H	**51.**	A	**70.**	G
14.	H	**33.**	B	**52.**	G	**71.**	A
15.	D	**34.**	H	**53.**	C	**72.**	H
16.	J	**35.**	D	**54.**	J	**73.**	A
17.	C	**36.**	G	**55.**	B	**74.**	G
18.	F	**37.**	D	**56.**	G	**75.**	B
19.	C	**38.**	H	**57.**	A		

1. **The correct answer is C.** Items in a list, like those in this sentence, should be separated by commas. As written, the items are not correctly separated by commas. Choices B and D also fail to correctly separate the items in the list by commas. Choice C effectively inserts commas into the list in this sentence.

2. **The correct answer is H.** As it appears in the passage, this sentence is confusing and contains a comma splice (a comma separating two complete sentences). Choice G is incorrect because the first comma stands between the subject (*Fossey*) and the verb (*was*), and because the second comma should precede a conjunction (such as *and*). Choice J is incorrect because the comma placed after *trip* gives the impression that it was her first trip ever, instead of her first trip to Africa. Choice H correctly separates the two parts of the sentence with a conjunction, and it is the most logical and straightforward of all of the choices.

3. **The correct answer is D.** As it appears in the passage, "A prominent archaeologist and anthropologist" is a sentence fragment because it contains no verb. Choice B also leaves the second sentence a fragment. Choice C is incorrect because it lacks a comma before the descriptive phrase about Dr. Leakey and merges the two phrases into a run-on sentence. Choice D is correct because it connects the two phrases together into a complete sentence, with a comma between "Dr. Louis Leakey" and the descriptive phrase that follows.

4. **The correct answer is J.** This is a verb tense question. The sentence describes something that happened in the past (Dr. Fossey met Dr. Leakey, and because of his influence, she decided to study the apes), so you need the past tense form of *encourage*. The correct answer is *encouraged*. As originally written, the verb is in the present tense, so choice F is incorrect. Choice G is in the past continuous tense, and choice H is in the future tense.

5. **The correct answer is D.** As written, we have a sentence fragment that needs to be fixed. Choice D correctly fixes the challenge, joining the independent clause (*Fossey took up the challenge*) and the dependent clause (*Deciding to study mountain gorillas*) with a comma. Choice B incorrectly uses a semicolon, which should only be used to join two independent clauses. Choice C removes the punctuation and creates a run-on sentence.

6. **The correct answer is G.** Here, we must determine the correct word choice given the context of the sentence. Fossey is facing political unrest in Zaire, and although she began her work here she must leave in order to maintain her safety, so choice G is correct. The other word choices are inappropriate given the context.

7. **The correct answer is A.** The sentence is correct as it is written. Choice B is redundant because *tolerate*, in this sentence, means approximately the same thing as *accept*. Choice C features the same problem but is even more verbose. Choice D, "began to show that they accepted," is not significantly different from the existing phrase, but it is wordy. In this case, the simplest option is the best one.

8. **The correct answer is G.** "Spending so much time to observe the gorillas" is incorrect because the infinitival form "to observe" does not agree with the rest of the sentence; the proper verb form is *observing*. This becomes clearer if you cut the "spending so much time" modifier: saying "To observe the gorillas, Fossey naturally distinguished among them" would imply that Fossey distinguished among the gorillas *in order to* observe them, not that she distinguished among them *by* observing them. The only option that contains the correct verb form is choice G. Choice H would be too wordy in any context. Choice J would be correct if the sentence took place in the present, but it is incorrect in this context.

9. **The correct answer is A.** The sentence is correct as it is written in the passage. The past tense fits well with the rest of the passage, which discusses Fossey's actions while she was studying the gorillas in Rwanda. Choices B and C create fragments, and choice D changes the meaning of the sentence.

10. **The correct answer is G.** As written, the form of "to name" is incorrect. As the gorilla was already named in the past, *named* is the correct choice here. The other choices contain incorrect forms given the context of the sentence.

11. **The correct answer is B.** This question asks you to pick the best introductory phrase for the sentence. Since the sentence describes an unhappy turn of events, *Unfortunately* is the best choice. *Still* (choice A) would be a good choice if the sentence set up a contrast to the one before it—as in "Still, despite all of Fossey's efforts, Digit was killed"—but Fossey, prior to this point, had not engaged in any efforts to save gorillas from poachers. "In fact" (choice C) would be a good choice only if the sentence provided support or an example for the sentence before it. *Because* (choice D) generally would not stand alone as an introductory phrase, though if it were part of such a phrase, it would signal cause and effect, which is inappropriate here.

12. **The correct answer is J.** This awkward sentence should be eliminated rather than rewritten, because there is no reason to include information about the rhinoceros in a passage that is about Dian Fossey's life, research, and conservation efforts among mountain gorillas in Africa. Choice G does not improve upon this problem in the original sentence, and choice H introduces the additional problem of confusing syntax.

13. **The correct answer is D.** Here we can see that subtle shifts in word placement and use can drastically alter meaning. As written, the sentence implies that Fossey continued working after her death, which is impossible. Choices B and C fail to fix this incorrect notion. Only choice D correctly fixes this error.

14. **The correct answer is H.** The author says that Fossey spent the rest of her life "working to protect the mountain gorilla." A concrete example would be a specific description of some sort of action she took to protect the mountain gorilla, which is provided by choice H. Choices F and G provide opinions about Fossey but no description of her work, while choice J concerns another prominent anthropologist and thus can't serve as an example of a specific step that Fossey took.

15. **The correct answer is D.** The author of this essay does not discuss any controversy surrounding Fossey, so eliminate choice A. Eliminate choice B as well, because while the author does describe Fossey's important legacy in the field of conservation, this has nothing to do with whether the author fulfilled the assignment of writing an essay about Fossey's controversial methods. The author clearly states that Fossey's work was of benefit to the mountain gorilla, so eliminate choice C. The author simply does not discuss the controversial nature of Fossey's methods and, therefore, would not successfully meet the assignment described in the question, so the best choice is D.

16. **The correct answer is J.** Proper nouns, like Zambezi River, should always be capitalized. Choices F, G, and H fail to correctly capitalize this proper noun.

17. **The correct answer is C.** As written, this sentence contains a redundancy—the phrase "twice as large" implies that the waterfall is bigger, so it doesn't need to be repeated. Choice C fixes this redundancy. Choice B

fails to fix the error, and choice D creates an internal error in logic—something can't be both "smaller" and "twice as large."

18. **The correct answer is F.** In this question, we're seeking to determine the appropriate verb form of *to see*. The sentence is correct as written; the British explorers who named the falls most likely have already seen it, so the past tense is correct. The other answer choices contain incorrect verb forms.

19. **The correct answer is C.** The sentence as written seems to emphasize how separate the five falls are from each other, as though readers already understand that there are five of them. The sentence *should* emphasize that rather than being one waterfall, Victoria Falls is a collection of five separate falls. Choice C does the best job at clarifying this. Choice B is awkwardly written, and choice D makes matters worse by inserting a standalone sentence.

20. **The correct answer is F.** The underlined phrase should be a bridge into the description of why Victoria Falls is considered one of the seven wonders of the natural world. Of all the answer choices, choice F provides the best transition from the fact that the falls is one of the seven wonders of the natural world to the reasons why it is on this list. The others introduce separate subjects—the Grand Canyon (choice G), people's differing opinions (choice H), the other wonders of Africa (choice J)—that are not directly relevant to why the waterfall is considered one of the world's natural wonders.

21. **The correct answer is B.** *Observing* and *witnessing* are describing the same action, so you need to choose an option that eliminates one of these words as redundant. Choice B is the correct one. The others express some redundancy, with choice C using the redundant words *looks* and *see* and choice D using *observing* and *see*.

22. **The correct answer is J.** As written, *falls* is in its possessive form and is incorrect, as there is no possession indicated in this sentence. Choice J fixes this error. Choice G incorrectly sets *crashing* in possessive form. Choice H incorrectly sets *falls* in a plural possessive form.

23. **The correct answer is A.** The sentences are correctly separated. Choices B and D would create run-on sentences. In the second sentence, *Imagine* is a command to the reader and does not need the *to* added in choice C.

24. **The correct answer is H.** In this question we need to determine the correct end punctuation for the sentence. The sentence is incorrect as written, as it is not a question. This declarative sentence should end in a period, so choice H is correct. Choice G incorrectly omits the end punctuation, leaving this sentence dangling unfinished. Choice J incorrectly adds internal punctuation to the end of this sentence.

25. **The correct answer is A.** This word choice question asks you to understand the point that the author is trying to make about the falls. Contextual clues indicate that what the author is trying to describe is the size and splendor of the falls. In that case, neither *generosity* (choice B) nor *fruitfulness* (choice C) fits the description. Likewise, *peacefulness* (choice D) is a bad fit with the rest of the passage: words such as *crashing* and *roaring* in the previous paragraph do not imply that the falls are particularly peaceful. *Grandiosity*, however, is certainly in keeping with earlier descriptions of the falls as *spectacular* and "twice as large as…Niagara Falls."

26. **The correct answer is H.** The phrase "enjoy a walk" should not be split by any commas to indicate a pause, which eliminates choices F, G, and J. Only choice H deletes the unnecessary comma without adding any new ones.

27. **The correct answer is D.** Other than echoing the words *pot* and *boil* from the previous sentence, this sentence has no relevance to the passage and should be eliminated. Rewording the sentence does not make it any more relevant, so choices B and C are not correct.

28. **The correct answer is G.** The subject matter of this sentence fits into the rest of the paragraph, which is about the additional natural attractions of the park. It should not be eliminated (choice J), just rewritten with the active voice—"is to be admired by" (choice F) is an example of the passive voice, which typically adds a phrase like "can be" or "will be" to a verb that should stand on its own. Choice H uses the passive voice and is lengthy and awkward.

29. **The correct answer is C.** Choice A can be eliminated; the essay does describe how marvelous Victoria Falls is, but that alone does not make it fulfill an assignment to describe why the falls are more worthwhile than other attractions. In order to do so, it would have to specifically describe the other six wonders of the natural world and give specific reasons why Victoria Falls is superior, so choice B is incorrect and choice C is correct. The writer does think Victoria Falls is interesting, so choice D misidentifies the reason the essay would fail to meet the assignment.

30. **The correct answer is J.** A paragraph about buying locally made crafts would have to come after the introduction of the idea that there are other, non-falls attractions in the park. Since that idea is introduced in Paragraph 4, a paragraph about crafts would most logically come between Paragraphs 4 and 5. Choices F, G, and H would all place it too early in the essay, which would disrupt its logical flow.

31. **The correct answer is B.** An introductory sentence grabs a reader's attention and introduces the topic of the piece. Choice B most effectively performs these tasks. Choices A, C, and D reference minor details of the essay and would not serve as appropriate introductory sentences.

32. **The correct answer is H.** As written, the final sentence of the paragraph is a fragment, and it needs to be combined with the previous independent clause. Choice H correctly combines the two clauses with a comma. Choices G and J incorrectly create two sentence fragments by adding periods inappropriately.

33. **The correct answer is B.** Context is the most important tool in determining appropriate word choice in a sentence. Here, *attest*, which means "to serve as clear evidence of," is the correct word choice; the family photos of the author reading serve as evidence of him being a bookworm. As written, *contest*, which means "to dispute," has the opposite meaning of what's intended. *Regress* (choice C) means "to return to a former state," and isn't appropriate here. *Egress* (choice D) means "to leave," and is inappropriate here.

34. **The correct answer is H.** Book titles need to be both capitalized and italicized, which choice H correctly does. Choices F, G, and J either incorrectly capitalize or fail to italicize the title, or both.

35. **The correct answer is D.** Understanding word economy is an important skill to acquire when building effective writing skills. As written, the sentence contains an awkward redundancy—the phrase "like catnip" implies that the thing being discussed is attractive, so both need not be mentioned in the same sentence. Choice D correctly fixes the redundancy. Choices B and C simply shift the words in the redundancy around and fail to eliminate it.

36. **The correct answer is G.** In order to figure out the correct word choice, an understanding of common language usage and context is essential. Here, *captured* is the most recognized and appropriate word choice. Choices F, H, and J utilize words that aren't appropriate given the context, and are less effective choices.

37. **The correct answer is D.** In order to determine the correct pronoun choice here, we need to examine the antecedent. The pronoun here must replace the author, who refers to himself in the first person; therefore, *I* is the correct choice. Choices A, B, and C use incorrect pronoun choices to replace the antecedent.

38. **The correct answer is H.** The correct punctuation to end this declarative sentence is a period, so choice H is correct. Choice F is incorrect, as this is not a question. Choices G and J incorrectly deploy internal punctuation at the end of a sentence.

39. **The correct answer is B.** A strong knowledge of the English language will help you determine the correct flow of words and ideas within sentences. As written, the word flow is awkward and confusing. Choice B fixes the error and provides a logical flow of thoughts. Choices C and D simply shuffle around the words in the sentence without repairing the confusion or awkwardness.

40. **The correct answer is F.** Understanding the appropriateness of commonly used phrases in the English language is critical for comprehension and understanding. "When I set my mind on something" may sound strange if you're unfamiliar with the phrase and take it literally, but it is a commonly accepted idiom, so the sentence is correct as written. Choices G, H, and J provide incorrect variations of the phrase and would only add confusion to the sentence.

41. **The correct answer is B.** Items in a simple list, like the ones presented in this sentence, should be separated by commas, so choice B is correct. As written, the sentence is a run-on. The other answer choices make incorrect use of commas and semicolons.

42. **The correct answer is F.** Additional information that is relevant to the ideas expressed in a sentence but which could potentially interrupt the sentence flow are typically set in parentheses, as written here. Without parentheses (choice G), the sentence becomes an awkward run-on. Semicolons and asterisks (choices H and J) are incorrect here.

43. **The correct answer is C.** Apostrophes are used to create possessive word forms, to show ownership. As written, *dads* is in the plural form, not possessive, which is incorrect here. Choice C correctly shows that it is the *dad's* illness. (That is, the illness that belongs to or is part of the dad.) Choice B is in the plural possessive form,

which is incorrect here. Choice D incorrectly places *illness* in the possessive form. Choices A and B would be used only if the narrator was not discussing a group of children to which he or she belonged.

44. **The correct answer is H.** We are trying to determine if the essay effectively achieves a particular goal; here, it is whether the essay is suitable for a contest that's calling for writing about learning a lesson in adolescence. After a careful, holistic analysis of the essay we can say that choice H is correct—the author discusses learning the value of money and friendship in the essay, so it is appropriate for the contest.

45. **The correct answer is A.** An effective concluding sentence ties up the key themes of the piece; choice A most effectively achieves this goal. Choices B, C, and D contain information and assumptions that are not supported by the information in the passage.

46. **The correct answer is H.** Based on the rest of the sentence, the underlined word or words should mean something like "is made up of," as in "over half a million acres make up the Great Smoky Mountains National Park." "Is created of" (choice F) is awkward because the verb *create* generally does not take a modifier such as *of*. *Consists*, on the other hand, is frequently paired with *of* and communicates the same meaning as "is made up of," so choice H is correct. Mountains cannot own anything, so choice G makes no sense. Similarly, a park cannot establish mountains, which eliminates choice J.

47. **The correct answer is C.** The sentence as written is incorrect, because the verb phrase "rise above" should have a plural subject. In this sentence, however, the subject is "the blue mist," not "the mountains." Choice C uses the appropriate singular form, "rises above." Choice B creates a sentence fragment, and choice D creates a sentence that uses both present and past tenses.

48. **The correct answer is G.** This is a complex sentence that lists several options for the hiker. Since the sentence begins by saying that hikers can choose walks "ranging from a brisk, uphill walk…," you can predict that the rest of the sentence will tell you the other end of the range of choices: "ranging *from* a brisk, uphill walk *to* a truly challenging three-hour hike." The *from… to* construction is common in a sentence that tries to provide a brief sketch of different extremes; that is exactly what this sentence attempts to do, and choice G is the only answer that fits the demand. Choice F contains a comma splice, while choices H and J simply fail to complete the *from … to* construction.

49. **The correct answer is A.** *Unrealistic* is the adjective that conveys that conservationists knew a ban on logging was not likely to happen. This is the author's meaning in the context. Slightly rephrased, the author is trying to say that because the conservationists knew that a full ban on logging was not likely to be effective, they suggested a compromise. *Unrealistic* implies that they recognized that a ban was unlikely and is thus the correct adjective. Choice B converts *unrealistic* to its adverb form, so it does not modify anything. Choices C and D make it seem as though an attempt to ban logging was something that could not happen.

50. **The correct answer is J.** In this sentence, *unchecked* is extra information that needs to be set off by commas. In other words, you could eliminate *unchecked* and the sentence would have a similar meaning, but *unchecked* helps make the author's meaning clearer. A semicolon is used only to separate two independent clauses, so it isn't a good choice here. Therefore, choice F is incorrect. Choice G is missing all necessary commas, while choice H is missing one.

51. **The correct answer is A.** This question asks you what function the second paragraph serves in the passage. The essay as a whole is about the establishment of the Great Smoky Mountains National Park, so this paragraph should further that point. Paragraph 2 describes the initial reason for the establishment of the park—it was a compromise struck by conservationists and loggers. This idea is best described by choice A. The essay does not go on to describe further conflict between loggers and conservationists; nor is this an important part of the essay's topic. Therefore, choice D is incorrect. As a historical account of the events leading up to the establishment of the park, it may have a viewpoint but does not argue for one particular political or social viewpoint over another, so eliminate choices B and C.

52. **The correct answer is G.** A phrase that contains extra information about the subject, in this case "an organization that explored and mapped land in the United States," must be set off by commas. The phrase modifies "United States Geological Survey," so the comma comes between *Survey* and "an organization… ." As originally written, the phrase lacks the necessary comma. Choice H turns a word in an organization's title into a verb. Choice J would result in an awkward and illogically constructed sentence.

53. **The correct answer is C.** The sentence in the question needs to be placed logically in a series of events. Logically, a sentence saying that the Smoky Mountains region emerged as a winner would have to come after a sentence explaining what the competition was, but before a sentence detailing what happened next. Sentences 2 and 3 explain the competition: the location of the park had to be determined, and there were sixty proposed sites. The logical place to describe the decision would come next, right before Sentence 4 begins, "After the decision was made. . . ." The sentence is clearly the continuation of a previous idea, which makes it a poor introductory statement, so choice A is incorrect. Choice B places it too early in the passage, which would disrupt its logical flow. Choice D places it too late.

54. **The correct answer is J.** As it is written, the sentence contains an unnecessary pronoun, *it*. Since you already know that the object in this sentence is the *plan*, there is no need for the additional *it* to clarify matters. The option that uses the smallest number of words and eliminates redundancy is usually your best bet, and that is choice J. Both choices G and H add extra words and commas and lack clear syntax.

55. **The correct answer is B.** All of these choices have different shades of meaning. *Privacy* (choice A) means "seclusion or lack of exposure," implying that the ownership carries a certain secrecy; this is different from "private ownership," which indicates that something is not common or public property. "Privately owned" conveys the meaning: that this land would be difficult to acquire because it belonged to many private individuals. *Private*, not *privacy*, should modify the verb, and choice B is the most concise answer. Choice C is incorrect because use of the noun form of *private* (the lowest rank in the military) makes no sense in the context of the sentence. Choice D is an awkward rewording of the correct answer.

56. **The correct answer is G.** This question tests the fine distinction between *amount* and *number*. The underlined phrase, "amount of dollars," tries to describe countable items (dollars) with an indefinite quantifier (amount). *Amount* describes things that cannot be individuated (e.g., the *amount of rain* that fell), whereas *number* describes things that can be specifically counted (e.g., the *number of inches* that fell). What is needed here, therefore, is either "number of dollars," which is not listed, or "amount of money" (choice G). While "number of monies" (choice H) is slightly more correct than the original, it is awkward and generally not an accepted phrasing. Choice J distorts the meaning of the sentence, implying that the park's founders sought paper currency that was physically much larger than standard monetary bills.

57. **The correct answer is A.** The detail about the landowners hiking their prices is intended to show the reader that purchasing the land was a challenging task. *Heroic* (choice B) might provide an alternative, since the author clearly approves of the purchasing of the land, but *challenging* is the better choice because the author is trying to give a straightforward account of the difficulties of establishing the park. *Heroic* does not necessarily imply difficulty, just as difficulty does not necessary imply heroism. The fact that the author approves of the purchasing of the land eliminates the negative descriptions *foolish* (choice C) and *immoral* (choice D).

58. **The correct answer is J.** "They had fallen short" is the same thing as "they hadn't raised enough money." To write both is redundant, so you should omit the phrase "they hadn't raised enough money" entirely. Choices F, G, and H fail to eliminate this redundancy.

59. **The correct answer is B.** This question requires you to go back to the passage and find a paragraph that already contains material about the conflict between loggers and conservationists; Paragraph 2 discusses how compromises between conservation interests and logging interests led to the founding of the park, so this would be the best place to add this information. Paragraph 1 (choice A) is about how visitors are attracted to the Great Smoky Mountains National Park's location. Paragraph 3 (choice C) is about Congress' approval of the park. Paragraph 4 (choice D) is about the purchase of the park.

60. **The correct answer is H.** While the first paragraph does mention a few of the park's attractions, it serves only as an introduction to an essay about the establishment of the park. Because only a small fraction of the essay discusses this theme, and someone who would want to know more about visiting the park would probably prefer knowing about the park's features rather than its history, the passage would not successfully respond to the assignment. Therefore, choice H is correct, and choices F and G can be eliminated. Choice J misidentifies the reason the essay would not fulfill the assignment; the essay does describe the park as a place tourists like to visit.

61. **The correct answer is A.** In this sentence, the simplest version works best, so the phrase does not need to be

changed. Choice B has the same meaning, but it is unnecessarily awkward. Choice C changes the meaning of the sentence by using *richly* as an adverb to describe *flourished*. Choice D is missing a conjunction.

62. **The correct answer is H.** *Among* is the correct choice because it indicates that the Mayan understanding of astronomy was one of many notable achievements. *Plus* (choice F) doesn't make sense because it means "in addition to"—in other words, in addition to "notable achievements," the Mayans had a profound understanding of astronomy. Astronomy is *one* of these notable achievements, so the word choice needs to acknowledge this. *Despite* (choice G) means "in spite of," which would contradict the meaning of the sentence, and *between* (choice J) works only when there are exactly two achievements, not many.

63. **The correct answer is B.** The description *astute* must appear before the verb *were* because *astute* functions as an adjective, describing the observations that will follow the verb. Choices A, C, and D all result in poor syntax.

64. **The correct answer is F.** The underlined words are correct as written. The sentence intends to convey that astronomy is more than a science. *Merely* (choice G) and *just* (choice H) make the sentence mean that astronomy is nothing more than a science; this is not the author's argument. Choice J claims that astronomy is not a science at all, which clearly contradicts what follows the semicolon.

65. **The correct answer is C.** *Found* (or *find*) and *into* as a combination of words doesn't work, because it's impossible to *find* something *into* many aspects, so choice A is incorrect. By realizing that *found* must have an object paired with it, you can choose the one option that pairs *found* with an object. "Found its way" provides this pairing. Something cannot "find" (choice B) or "found" (choice D) into something else.

66. **The correct answer is G.** Because *exact* modifies the verb *aligned*, it must be an adverb. Choices F, H, and J do not use the adverb form of *exact*. Most adverbs end with *-ly*, making choice G the correct answer.

67. **The correct answer is C.** A semicolon connects two related clauses that could stand on their own as sentences. A colon, on the other hand, indicates that the author is about to make a list without a subject. Since *were* is the verb in the second part of the sentence, a semicolon is a better choice, despite the list that appears at the beginning of the clause. Therefore, choice A is incorrect and choice C is correct. Choice B uses a comma where a semicolon is needed, and choice D fails to use any punctuation at all.

68. **The correct answer is J.** The author's tone is one of praise, which is most apparent in the reference to the "notable achievements" of the Mayans in the first paragraph. There is an evident admiration of the civilization's accomplishments, so choice J is the best answer. While *gleeful* (choice F) is a positive word, it does not capture the author's tone as well as *admiring* does. *Indifferent* (choice G) and *resentful* (choice H) are both negative words.

69. **The correct answer is D.** On the ACT, the choice that makes the sentence the simplest is usually the correct choice. Carvings and murals are examples of artwork, so choice D simplifies the sentence by eliminating redundancy. Choices A, B, and C retain the redundant words *carvings* and *murals*. They all contain unnecessary punctuation between *murals* and *shows* too.

70. **The correct answer is G.** The pronoun *who* is generally used when referring to people (or even gods with human characteristics). *Which* (choice H) refers to non-human subjects. A relative pronoun is needed in this case to make clear that it is the evil gods who wanted to stop the benevolent gods, and *they* (choice J) is a personal pronoun. As the sentence reads in the original, the verb appears to refer to the benevolent gods, which does not fit the context of the sentence. The evil gods, not the benevolent gods, are the ones attempting to stop the progress of the sun and moon.

71. **The correct answer is A.** Again, the simplest form is usually correct. "Believed to have gained" correctly indicates that those who died were believed by the Mayans to have gained eternal life. "And felt they" (choice B) makes the sentence redundant because *believed* and *felt* mean approximately the same thing in the context. While "they soon would have" (choice C) and "one day they would have" (choice D) express similar ideas, they do so awkwardly and with more words.

72. **The correct answer is H.** Word order is very important here. To determine it, you need to look at the context. The Mayans did not appear in the sky; Venus did. Therefore, you can eliminate the original sentence. The Mayans were using Venus to make a decision; choice H is the only choice that indicates this fact, so it is the correct answer. Choices G and J use awkward, grammatically incorrect wording.

73. The correct answer is A. The phrase "In short" accurately indicates that this paragraph will serve as a summary for the rest of the passage. *Shortly*, however, because it is an adverb, would have to modify the closest verb. "Shortly, in looking to the night sky for guidance" is not the author's meaning, so choice B is incorrect. The phrase "to sum up the," (choice C) implies that everything about ancient Mayan culture is encapsulated by this passage, which is certainly an exaggeration. *Lastly* indicates the final item in a list, and since that is not what the final sentence in the essay is, choice D is incorrect.

74. The correct answer is G. The phrase "in looking to the night sky for guidance" is extra information that should be set off by commas. The two halves of the sentence cannot stand on their own as sentences, so the punctuation mark cannot be a semicolon. Therefore choice F is incorrect. A colon is not the correct punctuation either, so choice J is incorrect too. Choice H fails to use any punctuation at all.

75. The correct answer is B. Since the passage is not about the ancient Babylonians, mentioning them would signal a transition to another topic. A new topic or supporting detail would not be introduced as part of a conclusion, which is meant to summarize the information already presented, so choice A is incorrect. The sentence does not illustrate (choice C) or contradict (choice D) any of the passage's information either.

1.	D	**16.**	G	**31.**	D	**46.**	K
2.	G	**17.**	E	**32.**	G	**47.**	C
3.	A	**18.**	H	**33.**	D	**48.**	J
4.	H	**19.**	D	**34.**	K	**49.**	A
5.	D	**20.**	H	**35.**	C	**50.**	H
6.	H	**21.**	A	**36.**	G	**51.**	E
7.	E	**22.**	F	**37.**	C	**52.**	K
8.	H	**23.**	C	**38.**	H	**53.**	E
9.	E	**24.**	G	**39.**	B	**54.**	H
10.	K	**25.**	B	**40.**	G	**55.**	E
11.	C	**26.**	J	**41.**	B	**56.**	J
12.	G	**27.**	D	**42.**	G	**57.**	D
13.	E	**28.**	G	**43.**	C	**58.**	H
14.	G	**29.**	D	**44.**	H	**59.**	D
15.	E	**30.**	K	**45.**	E	**60.**	G

1. **The correct answer is D.** Using 1 minute = 60 seconds, convert the total time to seconds: 7 minutes 20 seconds = 7(60) + 20 seconds = 440 seconds.

Let x be the number of seconds it took to complete the original workout. Then, $0.80x = 440$. Dividing by 0.80 yields $x = \frac{440}{0.80} = 550$ seconds. Now, convert back to minutes by dividing by 60. This yields 9 minutes, 10 seconds. Choice A is incorrect because it computes 20% of the given time. Choice B is incorrect because it computes 50% of the given time. Choice C is incorrect because it computes 80% of the given time. In choice E, you incorrectly divided the given time by 0.2, not 0.8.

2. **The correct answer is G.** Plugging in $a = 5$ gives you $\frac{5}{6} = \frac{b}{15}$. Cross-multiply to solve for b:

$$\begin{aligned}(5)(15) &= 6b\\ 75 &= 6b\\ b &= \frac{75}{6}\\ &= 12\frac{1}{2}\end{aligned}$$

To get choice F, you subtracted 1 from the denominator to get a new fraction, which does not yield an equivalent fraction to the other side of the proportion. For choice H, you multiplied the numerator and denominator of a single fraction and divided that product by 15; you must cross-multiply in the proportion instead. To get choice J, you divided 15 by 6, but this does not yield b; you must cross-multiply in the proportion instead. For choice K, the resulting fraction on the right side of the proportion would be much smaller than the one on the left.

3. **The correct answer is A.** Since $\overleftrightarrow{XYZ}$ is a straight line, angles VYX, VYW, and WYZ must total 180°. Therefore:

$$\begin{aligned}90° + 27° + \angle WYZ &= 180°\\ \angle WYZ &= 180° - 90° - 27°\\ &= 63°\end{aligned}$$

Choice B is likely an arithmetic error, since angles *VYW* and *WYZ* should sum to 90 degrees. Choice C is the value of either *VYZ* or *VYX*, but not *WYZ*. Choice D is supplementary to the correct value of *WYZ*. Choice E is incorrect because *VYW* and *WYZ* are complementary, not supplementary.

4. **The correct answer is H.** The pattern is to add 1 to the numerator and to add 1 and square the denominator. Doing so yields the fourth term as $\frac{6}{5^2} = \frac{6}{25}$ and the fifth term as $\frac{7}{6^2} = \frac{7}{36}$. Choice F is an attempt at computing the fourth term but subtracting 1 in the numerator instead of adding 1. Choice G is the fourth term. Choice J is the sixth term. Choice K is incorrect because once you squared the denominator, you added 1.

5. **The correct answer is D.** Martha cuts 4(1.5 feet) = 6 feet of ribbon from the spool. If 27.5 feet remain, then originally there were 6 + 27.5 = 33.5 feet of ribbon. For choice A, you subtracted 6 from 27.5 instead of adding. To get choice B, you subtracted the length of 1 piece of ribbon from 27.5, but you should have *added* 4 lengths to 27.5. For choice C, you added the length of 1 piece of ribbon, but you should have added the lengths of *4* pieces. To get choice E, you added 8 pieces of ribbon, not 4.

6. **The correct answer is H.**

$$f(6)=\sqrt{2(6)-3}-6=\sqrt{12-3}-6=\sqrt{9}-6=3-6=-3$$

Choice F is incorrect because you used the wrong portion of the function to compute *f*(6). Choice G is incorrect because you used the wrong portion of the function to compute *f*(6), and you did not use the order of operations correctly: 1 – 2(–6) does not equal (1 – 2)(6). Choice J is incorrect because you ignored the radical sign. Choice K is incorrect because you computed $\sqrt{2(6)-3}+6$, not $\sqrt{2(6)-3}-6$.

7. **The correct answer is E.** Squaring both sides of the inequality $\sqrt{w}>8$ yields $w > 64$. The only choice that satisfies this inequality is 81.

8. **The correct answer is H.** Find the changes in the *x* and *y* coordinates between endpoint *A* and the midpoint, then repeat those changes starting at the midpoint to find endpoint *B*. Moving from *A* (3, –2) to the midpoint (–3, –1), *x* decreases by 6, and *y* increases by 1. Therefore, the coordinates of *B* are (–3 – 6, –1 + 1) = (–9, 0). Choice F is the midpoint of the two points given in the question. Choice G results from using *A* as the midpoint, rather than an endpoint. Choice J is twice as far from the midpoint as endpoint *A*. Choice K is the result of a calculation error in computing the coordinates of the unknown endpoint.

9. **The correct answer is E.** The input 2 has two different *y*-values associated with it. Choice A is incorrect because this represents a horizontal line, which is the graph of a function. Choice B is incorrect because no input is associated with more than one output. An output can be the same for different inputs. Choice C is incorrect because no input is associated with more than one output. An output can be the same for different inputs. Choice D is incorrect because this is a polynomial function.

10. **The correct answer is K.** If the probability of NOT selecting a blue marble is $\frac{1}{4}$, then the probability of selecting a blue marble is $\frac{3}{4}$: $\frac{3}{4}(20)=15$; therefore, there are 15 blue marbles in the bag. Choice F represents $\frac{1}{5}$ of the bag, not $\frac{3}{4}$. Choice G represents how many marbles in the bag are NOT blue. Choice H represents $\frac{2}{5}$ of the bag, and choice J represents $\frac{1}{2}$ of the bag.

11. **The correct answer is C.** Convert both lines to slope-intercept form: $\frac{1}{2}x-y=2$ is equivalent to $\frac{1}{2}x-2=y$, and $2y = x - 1$ is equivalent to $y=\frac{1}{2}x-\frac{1}{2}$. Since the lines have the same slope, they are parallel. Choices A and E have two perpendicular lines. Choices B and D have two lines that are neither parallel nor perpendicular.

12. **The correct answer is G.** Let *x* be the dose of vitamin D (in teaspoons). Set up and solve the following proportion:

$$\frac{4}{3}=\frac{x}{2\frac{1}{4}}$$
$$4\left(2\frac{1}{4}\right)=3x$$
$$4\left(\frac{9}{4}\right)=3x$$
$$9=3x$$
$$3=x$$

Choices F and H are the results of arithmetic errors involving mixed numbers. Choice J is incorrect because you did not set up the proportion correctly. Choice K is incorrect because when solving the proportion for the unknown, you did not divide both sides of the equation by the coefficient of the variable in the last step.

13. **The correct answer is E.** The points fall from left to right and are tightly packed. This represents the fact that the number of hours decreases as the percentage of nutrient solution increases, and that this conclusion is strong. Choice A is incorrect because while the points do fall from left to right, they are not packed tightly together, suggesting the conclusion is not strong. Choice B is incorrect because the points should fall from left to right to illustrate the fact that the number of hours decreases as the percentage of nutrient solution increases. Choice C is incorrect because the scattering of the points in this manner suggests no association between hours it takes for germination and percentage

of nutrient solution applied to the seeds. Choice D is incorrect because this suggests that the number of hours it takes for germination to occur is unaffected by the percentage of nutrient solution added.

14. **The correct answer is G.** The reduced price is $800 – 0.15($800) = $800 – $120 = $680. Choice F is the amount by which the price is reduced. Choices H and J are the resulting of equating 15% with $15. Choice K is the result of increasing the price by 15%.

15. **The correct answer is E.** Use the distributive property and combine like terms:

$$-m(n-m)+n(m-n)=-mn+m^2+nm-n^2=m^2-n^2$$

Choice A adds the terms when they should be subtracted. Choices B and C involve various sign errors. Choice D is the difference in the wrong order.

16. **The correct answer is G.** Since the right side of the equation is 0, the zero product property tells us that at least one factor on the left side must equal 0. So either $5 = 0$, $x - 4 = 0$, or $x + 2 = 0$. We know that 5 cannot be 0, so either $x - 4 = 0$ or $x + 2 = 0$. Therefore, x must be either 4 or –2.

Choices F, H, J, and K are all numbers in the equation. None of these values make a factor of the left side of the equation equal 0.

17. **The correct answer is E.** The interior angles of a triangle add up to 180°. Therefore:

$$\begin{aligned} 2x+3x+5x&=180 \\ 10x&=180 \\ x&=18 \end{aligned}$$

The measure of angle *ACB* is $2x$, so plugging in $x =$ 18 gives you 2(18) = 36. Since angle *BCD* is supplementary to angle *ACB*, their measures add up to 180°. Therefore, the measure of angle *BCD* is 180° – 36° = 144°. Choice A is the value of x. Choice B is the measure of angle *ACB*. Choice C is the measure of angle *B*. Choice D is $7x$, the sum of the measures of angles *B* and *C*.

18. **The correct answer is H.** The jacket is discounted by $75 – $50 = $25. Percent $= \dfrac{\text{part}}{\text{whole}} \times 100\%$ (keep in mind that the whole must be the original price of $75), so this is a discount of $\dfrac{\$25}{\$75} \times 100\% = \dfrac{1}{3} \times 100\% = 33\dfrac{1}{3}\%$.

The percentage in choice F is too low—the discount would need to be $15 for it to be true. For choice G, while the jacket is discounted by $25, $25 does not mean 25%. To get choice J, you used $50 as the whole instead of $75. For choice K, $75 does not mean 75%.

19. **The correct answer is D.** Shift the point 1 unit to the left by subtracting 1 from the x-coordinate and shift the point 4 units downward by subtracting 4 from the y-coordinate. This yields the point (–3 – 1, 2 – 4) = (–4, –2). Choice A is incorrect because you applied the shifting by 1 unit and 4 units to the wrong coordinates. Choice B is incorrect because you moved the point up 4 units instead of down. Choice C is incorrect because you moved the point right 1 unit and up 4 units but should have moved it left 1 unit and down 4 units. Choice E is incorrect because you moved the point right 1 unit instead of left.

20. **The correct answer is H.** If 1 inch of wire costs $0.20, 1 foot costs 12($0.20) = $2.40. Therefore, 5.25 feet of wire cost ($2.40)(5.25) = $12.60. In choice F, you calculated the price of 5.25 inches, not feet, of wire. Choice G is the cost of 1 foot of wire, not 5.25 feet. In choice J, you multiplied the correct answer by 5. Choice K is the correct answer multiplied by 25. These latter two errors are the likely result of unit conversion problems.

21. **The correct answer is A.** The least common denominator of these two fractions is $3x - 1$. Convert the second fraction to an equivalent one with this denominator, then add:

$$\begin{aligned} \frac{1}{3x-1}-\frac{2-9x}{1-3x}&=\frac{1}{3x-1}+\frac{2-9x}{3x-1} \\ &=\frac{3-9x}{3x-1} \\ &=\frac{-3\cancel{(3x-1)}}{\cancel{3x-1}} \\ &=-3 \end{aligned}$$

Choice B is the result of canceling terms, not factors, common to the numerator and denominator. Choices C and D are incorrect because the numerators and denominators were both subtracted, which is not how you subtract fractions. Choice E is incorrect because you likely added the numerators and denominators and got zero in the denominator. This is not how you add fractions.

22. **The correct answer is F.** The lengths of the sides of the two rectangles are proportional. The perimeter of a rectangle is $2(l + w)$, where l and w are the length and width, respectively. Therefore, the perimeter of the original rectangle is 2(8 + 3) = 2(11) = 22. The perimeter of the similar figure is 44, so each of its dimensions must be twice that of the original rectangle. Since the width of the original rectangle is 3, the width of the similar rectangle must be 2(3) = 6. Choice G is the sum of the width and length of the given rectangle, not the width of the proportionally larger rectangle. Choice H is twice the width of the proportionally larger rectangle. Choice J is the length of the proportionally larger rectangle, not its width. Choice K is the perimeter of the given rectangle.

23. The correct answer is C. The cost of b books is $2.25b$ dollars. Adding the flat fee to this yields the cost $8.50 + 2.25b$ dollars. Choice A does not include the flat fee. Choice B multiplies b by the wrong value. Choice D incorrectly multiplies both 2.25 and 8.50 by b books; the flat fee does not depend on the number of books in the shipment. Choice E adds b to 2.25 instead of multiplying by it.

24. The correct answer is G. The perimeter is composed of four equal semicircles, so each must have a circumference of $16\pi \div 4 = 4\pi$. That means that the circumference of an entire circle would be 8π, and its diameter would be 8. Since the diameter of each semicircle lies on a face of the center square, each side of the square is also 8. The area of a square is equal to a side length squared, or 64 square feet. Since the diameter of each semicircle is 8, its radius is 4. The area of a circle is πr^2, where r is a radius of a circle, so the area of an entire circle is 16π. This makes the area of each semicircle 8π, so the combined area of all four semicircles is 32π. Therefore, the area in square feet of the entire garden is $64 + 32\pi$. Choice F accounts only for one of the four congruent semicircles. Choice H accounts for four congruent *circles*, not semicircles. In choice J, the area of the square is 64 square units, not 256; the diameter here is doubled. In choice K, the area of the square is not 256 units, and you accounted for four congruent circles, not semicircles.

25. The correct answer is B. The closed circle at 2 indicates that the solution set to the inequality includes 2; eliminate choices A, D, and E since they do not include 2. The open circle at –2 indicates that the solution set does not include –2; eliminate choice C since it includes –2. This leaves only choice B, which says that x is greater than –2 and less than or equal to 2.

26. The correct answer is J. Note that $n^2 = n \bullet n$. The product of two odd integers is always an odd integer. So n^2 is an odd integer. Choice F can be even, as seen by taking $n = 3$. Choices G and H are always even. Choice K might not even be an integer, as seen by taking $n = 5$.

27. The correct answer is D. Let x be the length of a side of the square. Then, the area formula yields the equation $x^2 = 144$. So $x = 12$. The diagonal of a square can be viewed as the hypotenuse of a right triangle with two adjacent legs having lengths 12 inches. Using the Pythagorean theorem then yields the length of the diagonal, d, as satisfying the equation $12^2 + 12^2 = d^2$. This is equivalent to $d^2 = 2 \bullet 12^2$, so that $d = 12\sqrt{2}$ inches. Choice A is incorrect because the 2 and 12 should be interchanged. Choice B is incorrect because you did not square the legs when applying the Pythagorean theorem. Choice C is the length of a side of the square, not its diagonal. Choice E is incorrect because $\sqrt{a+b} \neq \sqrt{a} + \sqrt{b}$.

28. The correct answer is G. The graph falls from left to right on this interval, so it is decreasing here. Choice F is incorrect because this is the y-value, not the x-value. Choice H is incorrect because the graph is increasing on this interval. Choice J is incorrect because the graph is constant on this interval. Choice K is incorrect because there is an interval on which the graph falls from left to right.

29. The correct answer is D. The third side of a triangle must be greater than the positive difference of its other two sides, and less than their sum. In this triangle:

$$(7-2) < \text{third side} < (7+2)$$
$$5 < \text{third side} < 9$$

If the third side must be between 5 and 9, then:

$$(7+2+5) < \text{perimeter} < (7+2+9)$$
$$14 < \text{perimeter} < 18$$

The only choice within this range is 16, so choice D must be correct. Choices A, B, and C are too small, and choice E is too big.

30. The correct answer is K. The center of the circle is (1, 1), and its radius is 2. The topmost point of the circle occurs when $x = 1$ and $y = 3$. The horizontal line $y = 3$, therefore, intersects the circle in exactly one point. Choices F and H do not intersect the circle. Choice G and J intersect the circle in two points.

31. The correct answer is D. First, compute the total frequency by adding the heights of the bars: 40 + 20 + 20 + 60 + 60 = 200. Now, the probability of a workout containing either box jumps or weight lifting is $\frac{60+60}{200} = \frac{120}{200} = 0.6$. Choice A is incorrect because, while the number of workouts out of 200 that satisfy the condition is 120, you must divide this by 200, not 100. Choice B is incorrect because this is either the probability of box jumps occurring in a workout, or the probability that weight lifting occurs in a workout. Choice C is incorrect because this is the probability that a workout does NOT contain box jumps or weight lifting. Choice E is incorrect because this is the probability that a workout contains anything except weight lifting.

32. **The correct answer is G.** Apply the Pythagorean theorem. Note that *TR* is the hypotenuse, so $c = 8$.

$$a^2+b^2=c^2$$
$$a^2+6^2=8^2$$
$$a=\sqrt{64-36}$$
$$a=\sqrt{28}$$
$$a=2\sqrt{7}$$

Choice F would be the length of the hypotenuse if 6 and 8 were the lengths of the legs. Choice H is the square of the unknown side. Choice J is the square root of the difference of the given side lengths, rather than the square root of the difference of their squares.

33. **The correct answer is D.** A square has four equal sides, so each side of the square has a length of $4s \div 4 = s$. Adding 5 makes its length $s + 5$; subtracting 2 makes its width $s - 2$. The area of a rectangle is equal to length times width, or $(s + 5)(s - 2)$. Using FOIL, you find that the area of this rectangle is $s^2 - 2s + 5s - 10 = s^2 + 3s - 10$. Choice A is the perimeter of the new rectangle, not its area, and choice B is half the perimeter of the rectangle. In choice C, you forgot the middle term when squaring the binomial. For choice E, the width is $s - 2$, not $s + 2$.

34. **The correct answer is K.** Use the information provided to label the side lengths of the triangle. Since the cosine of $\angle YXZ$ is $\frac{4}{5}$, the leg adjacent to that angle, *XZ*, is 4, and the hypotenuse is 5. Note that these are not the exact lengths, but that the *ratios* between side lengths are what matters here. With a leg of length 4 and a hypotenuse of 5, this is a 3-4-5 right triangle, so *ZY* has a side length of 3. Now we can find the tangent of *ZYX*: $\tan = \frac{\text{opposite}}{\text{adjacent}}$, so $\tan \angle ZYX = \frac{4}{3}$. Choice F is the sine of $\angle ZYX$. Choice G is the cosecant of $\angle ZYX$. Choice H is the cosine of $\angle ZYX$. Choice J is the cotangent of $\angle ZYX$ and the tangent of $\angle YXZ$.

35. **The correct answer is C.** There are twice as many boys as girls in the class, so let *x* equal the number of girls and 2*x* equal the number of boys. This means that there are 3*x* total students in the class. Given a class average of 84, calculate the total of all students' grades:

$$\text{average} = \frac{\text{sum of values}}{\text{number of values}}$$
$$\text{sum of grades} = \text{average grade} \times \text{number of students}$$
$$=84(3x)$$
$$=252x$$

You're also given that the girls' average is 91, so:

$$\text{sum of girls' grades} = \text{average grade} \times \text{number of girls}$$
$$=91x$$

If the total score for the class is 252*x* and the girls' total score is 91*x*, then the boys' total score must be their difference, 161*x*. Therefore, the boys' average is $\frac{161x}{2x} = 80.5$. You could also have started off by saying that the ratio of boys to girls is 2:1, which means that the average is weighted 2 to 1 in favor of boys. Given that the girls' average, 91, is higher than the class average, 84, by 7 points, it follows that the boys' average must be *lower* than the class average (eliminate choices D and E right away) by exactly *half* of this difference: $84 - 3.5 = 80.5$.

36. **The correct answer is G.** Solve the inequality as you would solve an equation:

$$\begin{aligned} 3x-9 &\le 15 \\ +9 \quad &+9 \\ \hline 3x &\le 24 \\ x &\le 8 \end{aligned}$$

The graph of the solution set of the inequality should include 8 and all values less than 8. Choice G is correct because the point on 8 is shaded, as are all the values less than 8.

Choice F is the graph of the solution set of $x \le 2$, which results from subtracting 9 from both sides of the inequality, rather than adding it. Choice H is the graph of $x \ge 8$, which may be the result of incorrectly reversing the inequality sign when solving. Choice J is the graph of $x < 8$, which does not include the endpoint 8. Choice K is the graph of $x > 8$, which does not include the endpoint and results from incorrectly reversing the inequality sign when solving.

37. **The correct answer is C.** Based on the given description and figure, the unshaded square is exactly one fourth of either larger square, so within one of the

larger squares the ratio of shaded area to unshaded area is 3:1. However, there is a second square that has an identical shaded region but no additional unshaded region, so over both squares the ratio of shaded area to unshaded area becomes 6:1. Therefore, if the shaded area is *x*, the unshaded area must be $\frac{x}{6}$. Choice A is the portion of the overall region (formed using the two overlapping squares) that is shaded, but *x* represents the area of just the shaded region, not including the unshaded square in the middle. For choice B, it is true that 3 of 4 congruent small squares are shaded within a single larger square, but $\frac{3}{4}$ is not the correct proportion of the entire shaded area that describes the unshaded region. For choice D, you included the unshaded region as part of the region whose area is *x*. For choice E, you included the unshaded region *twice* in the region whose area is *x*.

38. The correct answer is H.

Since $\text{average} = \frac{\text{sum of terms}}{\text{number of terms}}$, it follows that the sum of terms is equal to the product of the average and the number of terms. Therefore, the sum of these three positive integers is 3(99) = 297. You can find the greatest possible value for one number by setting the other two numbers equal to their smallest possible values. Since each term is a different positive integer, the smallest integer is 1, and the next smallest is 2. That makes the greatest possible value for one of the numbers 297 – 1 – 2 = 294.

Choice F is $\frac{99}{3}$, so it cannot be one of the biggest integers of three total that average to 99. Choice G is also way too small; you can make one of the integers very large as long as you make the others very small. Choice J is too big, since the smallest the other two integers can be is 1 and 2, and the average of 1, 2, and 295 exceeds 99. Choice K can be eliminated for the same reason as choice J.

39. The correct answer is B. The key to this question is recognizing that triangle *ABC* is a 30-60-90 right triangle. In such a triangle the sides are related in a ratio of $1:\sqrt{3}:2$. Since $BC = 3\sqrt{3}$, it follows that $AB = (\sqrt{3})(3\sqrt{3}) = 9$. Therefore, angle *BCA*, the angle opposite segment *AB*, must measure 60°. Choice A is impossible because the sum of all three angles in a triangle is 180 degrees. Choice C uses the wrong proportions; this is a 30-60-90 triangle, not a 45-45-90 triangle. Choice D is the measure of angle *BAC*. Choice E is not true because you can use the Pythagorean theorem with the proportions of a 30-60-90 triangle.

40. The correct answer is G. Use the slope formula to obtain the equation:

$$\frac{2-(-x)}{-1-3} = -\frac{1}{4}$$
$$\frac{2+x}{-4} = -\frac{1}{4}$$
$$4(2+x) = (-1)(-4)$$
$$2+x = 1$$
$$x = -1$$

So the value of $\frac{1}{2}x$ is $\frac{1}{2}(-1) = -\frac{1}{2}$. Choice F is the value of *x*. Choices H and K dropped the negative, and Choice K is also the reciprocal of the correct value. Choice J is the result of a sign error when solving for *x*.

41. The correct answer is B. You may use angle relationships in many ways to find the measures of all the angles in the diagram, including supplementary angles and the relationships between angles formed by parallel lines and a transversal. Note that the base of the triangle in the diagram is part of l_2, and is therefore parallel to l_1. Therefore the other two sides of the triangle are both transversals.

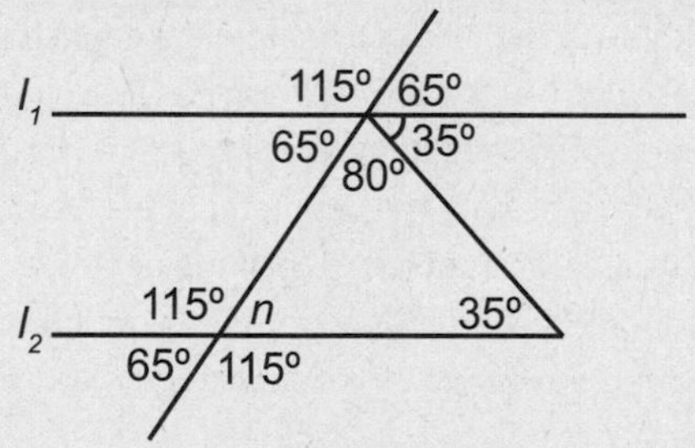

Choices A, C, and E are all angles that occur in the diagram (see above). Choice D is the supplement of 80°, or the sum of 65° and 35°.

42. The correct answer is G. The slope-intercept of the line $3x = 4y - 1$ is $y = \frac{3}{4}x + \frac{1}{4}$. So its slope is $\frac{3}{4}$. Thus, any line perpendicular to it must have slope $-\frac{4}{3}$. Choice F is the result of using the *y*-intercept instead of the slope. Choice H is parallel to the line. Choices J and K are the result of using the coefficients of *x* or *y* without first converting the line to slope-intercept form.

43. **The correct answer is C.** Each choice represents a number in scientific notation by raising a numerical value between 1 and 10 to a power of 10. Rewriting the given value of 0.000000301 in this way yields 3.01×10^{-7}. Since changing the power of 10 would most significantly change the overall value, the answer choice with the *same* power of 10 (choice C) will be closest.

All other choices are off by at least a factor of 10 and are obtained by making an error when converting to scientific notation.

44. **The correct answer is H.** You're given the side of the triangle adjacent to the angle marked 41° and asked about its hypotenuse. The cosine of an angle is equal to $\frac{\text{adjacent side}}{\text{hypotenuse}}$, so:

$$\cos 41^\circ = \frac{8}{XZ}$$
$$(XZ)(\cos 41^\circ) = 8$$
$$XZ = \frac{8}{\cos 41^\circ}$$

In choice F, you solved the cosine equation incorrectly. In choice G, you used the sine function and solved the equation incorrectly. Choice J is incorrect because you must use cos(41) instead of sin(41) since you are given the adjacent side to that angle and you want to find the hypotenuse. Choice K is incorrect because it is the length of *XY*, not *XZ*.

45. **The correct answer is E.** Compute the composition as follows:

$$\begin{aligned}(f \circ g)(x) &= f(g(x)) \\ &= \frac{\frac{2}{x}}{2\left(\frac{2}{x}\right)-1} \\ &= \frac{\frac{2}{x}}{\frac{4}{x}-1} \\ &= \frac{\frac{2}{x}}{\frac{4-x}{x}} \\ &= \frac{2}{4-x}\end{aligned}$$

Choice A is incorrect because $\frac{\cancel{a}}{\cancel{a}+b} \neq \frac{1}{b}$. Choice B is $(g \circ f)(x)$. Choice C is the product, not the composition. Choice D is the result of not substituting *g*(*x*) into both *values of x* in the formula for *f*(*x*).

46. **The correct answer is K.** In order for the probability of landing on a blue section to be $\frac{1}{4}$, there must be 5 blue sections, since $\frac{5}{20} = \frac{1}{4}$. That leaves 15 sections to divide between red and yellow. If yellow will be $\frac{1}{4}$ as likely as red, then red must be 4 times as likely as yellow, so we need two numbers that add up to 15 where one of the numbers is 4 times the other number: 3 and 12. Therefore, there must be 12 red sections.

Choice F is the number of yellow sections. Choice G is incorrect and may be the result of assuming that there will be only 1 yellow section. Choice H is the number of blue sections. Choice J is incorrect and may be the result of assuming that there will be 2 yellow sections.

47. **The correct answer is C.** Create a Venn diagram showing what the guests ate:

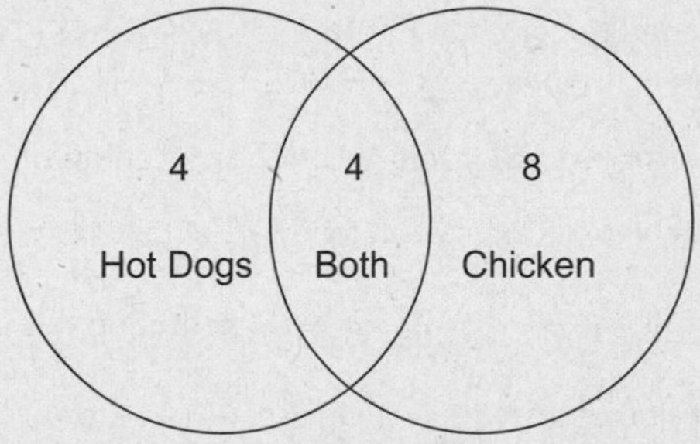

Now you can see that the number of people who ate hot dogs, chicken, or both is $4 + 4 + 8 = 16$. That means that $24 - 16 = 8$ guests ate neither, which is $\frac{8}{24} = \frac{1}{3}$ of the guests. Choice A is the fraction who ate either hot dogs, chicken, or both. Choice B is the fraction who ate chicken. Choice D is too small, and note that $\frac{1}{5}$ of 24 would not produce an integer. Choice E is the fraction who ate both, not neither.

48. The correct answer is J. Get a common denominator in the numerator and denominator of the complex fraction. Then, simplify:

$$\frac{\frac{1}{a}-\frac{1}{b}}{\frac{1}{a}+\frac{1}{b}}=\frac{\frac{b}{ab}-\frac{a}{ab}}{\frac{b}{ab}+\frac{a}{ab}}$$
$$=\frac{\frac{b-a}{ab}}{\frac{b+a}{ab}}$$
$$=\frac{b-a}{ab}\div\frac{b+a}{ab}$$
$$=\frac{b-a}{\cancel{ab}}\bullet\frac{\cancel{ab}}{b+a}$$
$$=\frac{b-a}{b+a}$$

Choice F is the result of canceling terms, not factors, common to the numerator and denominator. Choice G is the result of multiplying $(b - a)$ by $(b + a)$ instead of dividing by it. Choice H is the result of adding the fractions incorrectly. Choice K is the negative of the correct answer.

49. The correct answer is A. Let x be the length of AB. From the given information, it follows that $\tan 30^\circ = \frac{x}{4}$. Also, $\tan 30^\circ = \frac{\sin 30^\circ}{\cos 30^\circ} = \frac{\frac{1}{2}}{\frac{\sqrt{3}}{2}} = \frac{1}{\sqrt{3}}$. Substituting this into the left side of the equation yields $\frac{1}{\sqrt{3}} = \frac{x}{4}$. Cross-multiplying yields $4 = \sqrt{3}\,x$, so that $x = \frac{4}{\sqrt{3}} = \frac{4\sqrt{3}}{3}$ m. Choice B used the reciprocal of tan 30°, which arises from interchanging the values of sin 30° and cos 30°. Choice C is the result of computing tan 45°, which arises from using the wrong values of sin 30° and cos 30°. Choice D is incorrect because $\tan 30^\circ \neq \frac{1}{2}$. Choice E is incorrect because $\tan 30^\circ \neq 2$.

50. The correct answer is H. FOIL the numerator and denominator and then simplify using the identities $\sin^2\theta + \cos^2\theta = 1$ and $\sin 2\theta = 2\sin\theta\cos\theta$:

$$\frac{(\sin x-\cos x)^2}{(\sin x+\cos x)^2}=\frac{\sin^2 x-2\sin x\cos x+\cos^2 x}{\sin^2 x+2\sin x\cos x+\cos^2 x}$$
$$=\frac{(\sin^2 x+\cos^2 x)-2\sin x\cos x}{(\sin^2 x+\cos^2 x)+2\sin x\cos x}$$
$$=\frac{1-\sin 2x}{1+\sin 2x}$$

Choice F is incorrect because $(a + b)^2 \neq a^2 + b^2$. Choices G and J are incorrect because $\sin x + \cos x \neq 1$; which should not be confused with the identity $\sin^2 x + \cos^2 x = 1$. Choice K is the result of canceling terms, not factors.

51. The correct answer is E. First, observe the following:

$$(n\circ m)(x) = n(m(x)) = [-2x(1-x)]^3$$
$$= (-2)^3x^3(1-x)^3$$
$$= -8x^3(1-x)^3.$$

So $(n\circ m)(-1) = n(m(-1))$
$$= -8(-1)^3(1-(-1))^3$$
$$= -8(-1)(2)^3$$
$$= -8(-1)(8) = 64.$$

Choice A is incorrect because $1 - (-1) = 2$, not 0. Choice B is incorrect because this is $(m\circ n)(-1)$. Choice C is incorrect because you did not cube –2 when computing $(n\circ m)(x)$. Choice D is incorrect because $(-2)^3 = -8$, not –6. Don't multiply base times exponent when computing a power.

52. The correct answer is K. After 1 black sock is removed, there are 6 black, 5 white, and 4 green socks, for a total of 15 socks. The probability of NOT selecting a black sock is equal to the probability of selecting a white or green sock, or $\frac{5+4}{15} = \frac{9}{15} = \frac{3}{5}$. Choice F is the probability of a single sock (irrespective of color) of being selected from the drawer. In choice G, you kept the sample size as 16 instead of changing it to 15. Choice H is the probability of the complement of the event. For choice J, you included the removed black sock among those in the drawer for the second selection.

53. The correct answer is E. Putting both equations into slope-intercept form will make them easier to work with:

$$2y + x = 4 \qquad 3y + 6x = 6$$
$$2y = -x + 4 \qquad 3y = -6x + 6$$
$$y = -\frac{1}{2}x + 2 \qquad y = -2x + 2$$

When a line is in slope intercept form, $y = mx + b$, its slope is m and its y-intercept is b. Lines 1 and 2 both have y-intercepts of 2, which means that they both pass through point (0, 2), so choice E is correct. Because the slopes of the lines are $-\frac{1}{2}$ and –2, choice C cannot be correct. If the lines were parallel, their slopes would be equal, so choice A cannot be correct either. If the lines were perpendicular, their slopes would be negative reciprocals, so choice B can also be eliminated. If both lines passed through the origin, the coordinates (0, 0) would satisfy both equations; however, if you plug (0, 0) into the equations, it satisfies neither equation, eliminating choice D as well.

54. **The correct answer is H.** Restrict your attention to the first row for the new sample space. Of these 165, 65 indicate a preference for the cyberpunk subgenre. So the desired probability is $\frac{65}{165}=\frac{13}{33}$. Choice F is incorrect because you divided 65 by 300 instead of 165. This is a conditional probability since you are given information that is known to be true; this enables you to restrict your attention to the first row of the table. Choice G is incorrect because this is the probability that a fan does not prefer reading given that he or she indicates cyberpunk as the preferred subgenre. Choice J is incorrect because this is the probablIlty that a fan prefers watching movies/television. Choice K is incorrect because you did not use the given information correctly in that you divided 65 by105 instead of 165.

55. **The correct answer is E.** Subtracting the same number from both sides of an inequality always results in an inequality in the same direction. Choices A, B, C, and D need not be true if *a* and *b* have opposite signs.

56. **The correct answer is J.** Janey must sit in the middle, so one of the 7 seats is taken. This leaves 6 choices for the first friend, then 5 choices for the second friend, 4 choices for the third friend, 3 choices for the fourth friend, and 2 choices for the fifth friend. So the total number of possible arrangements of the 6 people is $1 \times 6 \times 5 \times 4 \times 3 \times 2 = 720$. Choice F is the number of ways of arranging four seats, not six. In choice G, you multiplied the two numbers in the problem, but this is not the way to compute the number of arrangements. Choice H is the number of ways of arranging five friends in five seats, not six seats. Choice K is the number of ways to arrange six people in seven seats, but Janey's seat is fixed. So you must arrange five friends in six seats.

57. **The correct answer is D.** Let $2x$ be the length of the shortest edge. Then, the other two edges have lengths $4x$ and $8x$. So the volume is $(2x)(4x)(8x) = 512$. This is equivalent to $64x^3 = 512$, so that $x^3 = 8$. So $x = 2$. Therefore, the three edges have lengths 4m, 8m, and 16m. So the longest edge has length 16m. Choice A is half the length of the shortest edge. Choice B is the length of the shortest edge. Choice C is the length of the middle edge. Choice E is the product of the ratios of the lengths of the three edges.

58. **The correct answer is H.** Pick a number for the original price of the stock. Choose 100, since it's the easiest number to use with percentages. On Tuesday, the price increases by 20%, so the price increases to $100 + $20 = $120. On Wednesday, the price falls by 25%; 25% of 120 is 30, so the price drops to $120 – $30 = $90. The original price was $100, so the price of the stock must increase by $10. As a percent of the stock price, this is:

$$\frac{10}{90}\times 100\% = \frac{1}{9}\times 100\% = \frac{100\%}{9} = 11\frac{1}{9}\%$$

Choice F is the result of adding the percentages together instead of applying them to specific amounts. Choice G is double the correct percentage. In choice J, the dollar increase in the stock is $10, not 10%. Choice K is incorrect because you cannot subtract percentages like this; they must each be applied to specific values.

59. **The correct answer is D.** The sine of an angle is $\frac{\text{opposite side}}{\text{hypotenuse}}$. Since the sine of $\angle WXZ = \frac{a}{b}$, $WZ = a$ and $XZ = b$.

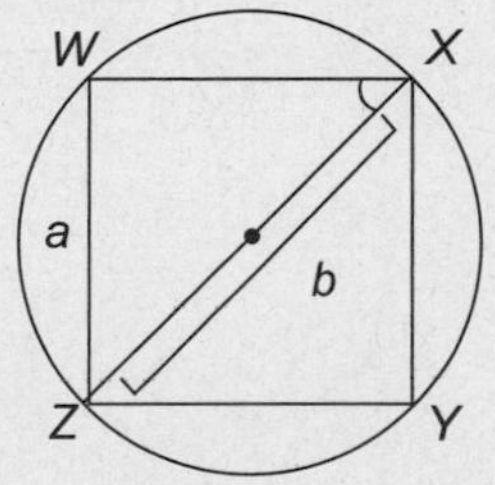

Since segment *XZ* passes through the center of the circle, it is a diameter of the circle. The area of a circle is equal to πr^2, where *r* is a radius of the circle. The diameter of the circle is *b*, so its radius is half of this, or $\frac{b}{2}$. Plugging this into the area formula gives you:

$$\pi\left(\frac{b}{2}\right)^2 = \pi \times \frac{b^2}{4}$$
$$= \frac{b^2\pi}{4}$$

Choice A is incorrect because *a* is not the radius of the circle. Choice B is incorrect because *b* is the diameter, not the radius. Choice C is the circumference of the circle, not its area. Choice E is incorrect because you must square the radius when computing the area.

60. **The correct answer is G.** Since the units digit of 338 is 8, the units digits of its powers will follow the pattern of powers of 8. You can use your calculator to figure the first few powers of 8 and find this pattern:

$8^1 = \underline{\mathbf{8}}$	$8^5 = 32{,}76\underline{\mathbf{8}}$
$8^2 = 6\underline{\mathbf{4}}$	$8^6 = 262{,}14\underline{\mathbf{4}}$
$8^3 = 51\underline{\mathbf{2}}$	etc.
$8^4 = 4{,}09\underline{\mathbf{6}}$	

The pattern here is 8, 4, 2, 6. That means that every fourth power of 8 (and, in turn, of 338) will have a units digit of 6. In this question, the number is raised to the 340th power; since 340 is evenly divisible by 4 with no remainder, the 340th power corresponds to the 4th term in the pattern, 6. Choices F, H, J, and K are all possible digits that arise, but none is the units digit for the specified power.

Reading

1.	B	11.	D	21.	B	31.	A
2.	J	12.	F	22.	H	32.	H
3.	C	13.	C	23.	D	33.	D
4.	J	14.	J	24.	H	34.	G
5.	C	15.	B	25.	A	35.	D
6.	G	16.	J	26.	J	36.	G
7.	A	17.	C	27.	B	37.	D
8.	G	18.	F	28.	F	38.	H
9.	D	19.	A	29.	C	39.	B
10.	F	20.	J	30.	J	40.	F

1. **The correct answer is B.** If Miss Lily Bart was late for a train, she probably would be more concerned with getting on it than chatting with Mr. Selden, so choice A is not likely. If she were not fond of him, she probably would not go out of her way to chat with him in the first place, so you can eliminate choice C too. While Mr. Selden wonders what Miss Lily Bart is doing in town at this time of year, there is no reason to conclude that she is deciding whether or not to move back to town, so choice D is not the best answer. The best answer is choice B, since Miss Lily Bart seems like she has come to a place where there are a lot of people so she can meet someone, and she does go out of her way to meet Mr. Selden, who has already reached this conclusion.

2. **The correct answer is J.** Miss Lily Bart is not physical with Mr. Selden, so *affectionate* (choice F) does not describe her behavior accurately. Although Mr. Selden believes there is an air of mystery to Miss Lily Bart, her behavior toward him is hardly mysterious (choice G). Her comment that Mr. Selden has come to her rescue is meant jokingly and not literally, so choice H is not the best answer. The best answer is choice J, since Miss Lily Bart is merely being friendly with Mr. Selden.

3. **The correct answer is C.** Mr. Selden imagines that Miss Lily Bart may try to "elude" him, which suggests that she might not want to talk to him, so choice C is the best answer. At the end of the passage, Mr. Selden wonders if Miss Lily Bart has reached the birthday "with which her rivals credited her," which suggests the opposite of choice A. He never expresses concern that she might think he is being too forward (choice B) or that she might not remember who he is (choice D).

4. **The correct answer is J.** *Cheer* is used as a verb in line 23. Since *encouragement* and *joy* are both nouns, choices F and G can be eliminated. *Applaud* (choice H) is a verb, but it does not make much sense to applaud a long evening. However, it does make sense to brighten an evening, so choice J is the best explanation of how *cheer* is used in the context of the sentence.

5. **The correct answer is C.** This is a detail question. The last sentence of Paragraph 3 reveals that Emma has just finished having dinner with her father, and the next paragraph finds her thinking about Miss Taylor's marriage. So choice C is the correct answer. The wedding has already taken place before this passage begins, so choice A is incorrect. Emma never speaks to Mr. Weston in this passage, so choice B cannot be correct. It is Emma's father who goes to bed after dinner, not Emma, so choice D is not correct.

6. **The correct answer is G.** Paragraph 4 confirms that Mr. Weston has "pleasant manners" and "unexceptional character." However, there is no indication that he has "high self-regard," though Paragraph 2 does mention that Emma thinks "a little too well of herself." Since that quality does not apply to Mr. Weston, any answer choice that includes Statement III can be eliminated, which means choices H and J. Choice F makes the mistake of failing to acknowledge the fact that Mr. Weston had unexceptional character. Only choice G includes the qualities mentioned in the passage without including the quality that is not mentioned.

7. **The correct answer is A.** As each passage begins, the two characters are without companions, though Miss Lily Bart may have made a new one by the end of Passage A. In Passage B, Emma has lost a companion, but this happened before the passage even began, so choice B is true of neither her nor Miss Lily Bart. Only Emma reminisces about a companion she has lost, so choice C is not the best answer, and only Miss Lily Bart

may have met a new companion, so choice D is incorrect too.

8. **The correct answer is G.** Miss Lily Bart goes out of her way to meet Mr. Selden in Passage A, and Emma laments the fact that she does not have a companion in Passage B, so choice G is the best answer. However, only Miss Lily Bart is described as a dancer, so choice F is not the best answer. Emma seems a bit depressed in Passage B, but Miss Lily Bart does not in Passage A, so choice H is unlikely. There is no reason to conclude that these two characters would or would not get along, so you can eliminate choice J.

9. **The correct answer is D.** In Passage A, two people make an effort to interact with each other and in Passage B a woman misses the fact that she no longer has a governess to interact with, so choice D is the best answer and choice A can be eliminated. Only Emma's relationship with her governess has ended, so choice B is not the best description of the passages' main ideas. Only Miss Lily Bart seems to have formed a new friendship, so choice C does not describe both passages either.

10. **The correct answer is F.** According to Passage A, Miss Lily Bart "has reached the nine-and-twentieth birthday," which means she is 29 years old or older. Passage B states that Emma was five years old when she first came to know Miss Taylor and it is now sixteen years later, which means that Emma is at least twenty-one years old. Therefore, choice F is true. There are no details about whether or not they live in cities (choice G). Only Miss Lily Bart is at a train station, and she may not actually be waiting for a train, so choice H is incorrect. Only Emma has attended a wedding, which is over before Passage B even begins, so choice J is incorrect.

11. **The correct answer is D.** In the first paragraph, the author's statement that the first newspapers in the UK were ". . . organs, to disseminate sentiments of loyalty, or to foster a spirit of resistance against the inroads of power . . ." heavily implies that they were started for political reasons (choice D). While that purpose may imply bias, there is no support for that extreme conclusion in choice A. Similarly, the papers' political purpose implies that the conclusion in choice B is incorrect. Since the writer implies nothing about the success of these newspapers, choice C is not a strong answer.

12. **The correct answer is F.** The author mentions a number of newspapers with birds in their titles and explains that "The list of *Mercuries* is almost too full for publication." The reliance on the same ideas over and over displays a lack of originality (choice F). Choice G reaches an extreme conclusion that the passage does not support. The author's reference to the quaintness of these titles contradicts the conclusion in choice H, since *quaint* is the opposite of *modern*. Since these titles do not reveal any particular philosophy, choice J is not a strong answer.

13. **The correct answer is C.** In the second paragraph, the author explains that the Scottish newspaper *Mercurius Publicus* was actually "but a reprint" of an English newspaper, while *Mercurius Caledonius* was the first newspaper actually manufactured in Scotland, so choice C is the best answer. Even though it was not manufactured in Scotland, *Mercurius Publicus* might still have contained news relevant to that country, so choice A is not the best answer. Choice B mixes up the two newspapers. The author notes that the *Mercurius Caledonius* "extended to no more than ten numbers," which contradicts the conclusion in choice D.

14. **The correct answer is J.** In the first paragraph, the author counts the *Scots Dove* and the *Mercurius Acheronticus* among the earliest British newspapers but states that the *Daily Courant* did not exist until later during the reign of Queen Anne. So the best answer will eliminate statement I and include both statements II and II. Only choice J does this. Choice F only includes the wrong publication. Choices G and H each fail to include one of the necessary publications.

15. **The correct answer is B.** Statistics in the first paragraph for newspaper sales from 1753 to 1792 support the conclusion in choice B. According to the first paragraph, 1792 was certainly the most successful year for newspaper sales in the UK yet, but it is unlikely that it was the most successful year of all time, as choice A suggests. Choice C assumes a false cause/effect relationship; just because the newspaper industry failed to change much during George I's reign does not mean that George I was directly responsible for that lack of change. Choice D reflects an idea in the second paragraph, not the first one.

16. **The correct answer is J.** The author states that the first newspaper manufactured in Scotland, and another home-grown newspaper "extended to no more than ten numbers," so choice J is the most logical answer. While the author does include a quotation about how readers of the *Mercurius Caledonius* were illiterate (choice F) and loyal (choice G), the circulation of the paper does not really support either of those assessments. That poor circulation contradicts the idea in choice H.

17. **The correct answer is C.** While the author does imply some personal opinions throughout this passage, it is mainly an informative piece of writing that describes significant events in the early history of newspapers in the United Kingdom. Choices A and B suggest that the author is particularly concerned with convincing the reader of sharing a particular personal opinion, which is not the case in this passage. Choice D also implies that this informative passage is mainly argumentative, while also suggesting that the author is comparing the newspapers he discusses in the passage with contemporary newspapers, yet he never even mentions contemporary newspapers in this passage.

18. **The correct answer is F.** Choice F summarizes the overall arc of the second paragraph well. Choice G focuses only on the first part of the arc, so it is not as strong an answer as choice F. Choice H describes only one particular Sottish newspaper— the *Edinburgh Evening Courant*—not all of the Scottish newspapers discussed in the second paragraph, so it is inadequate as a main idea statement. Choice J merely lists the names of newspapers; it fails to capture the most important idea of the paragraph as a whole.

19. **The correct answer is A.** Each answer choice can be used as a synonym for *party*, but in this particular context, choice A makes the most sense, since references to the Commonwealth, loyalty, and power imply political factions. These words certainly do not imply anything social (choice B). Choice C is not the best answer, since it is not as specific as choice A. The word *party* is used as a noun in line 11, but choice D implies that it is used as a verb.

20. **The correct answer is J.** The author's description of reprinting English newspapers in Scotland as an economic way of doing business supports choice J. While few people bought the first homegrown Scottish newspaper, this is not the reason the author gives, so choice F is both incorrect and too extreme. There is no support for choices G or H in the passage.

21. **The correct answer is B.** The opening paragraph indicates that Plato began pursuing knowledge at a young age and goes on to describe the various ways he continued to pursue knowledge, so choice B is the best answer. Plato's prestigious family is mentioned only in passing, so choice A is not the best answer. The author presents the information in Paragraph 1 in a straightforward, informative manner, and there is no indication that any of the information is exaggerated, so choice C is not a strong answer. The author never implies in the first paragraph that Plato tended to surpass his instructors, so choice D does not make much sense.

22. **The correct answer is H.** The final paragraph of the passage identifies Platonism as the theory of ideas (statement I) and Plato is quoted as having said that his philosophy involves elevating "the power of thinking to its proper purity" (statement III). However, his assertion that all things "are ultimately referable to certain abstract conceptions or ideas" contradicts statement II. Therefore, the correct answer must include statements I and III and eliminate statement II, and only choice H accomplishes this. Choice F fails to include one of the true statements. Choice G contains a true and false statement. Choice J includes the two true statements, but it also includes the one false statement.

23. **The correct answer is D.** In the first paragraph, the author writes that, "Like another equally famous leader in literature, François Marie Arouet, [Plato] abandoned his birth-name," which supports choice D. Since this is the only information about François Marie Arouet that the author provides, the reader cannot conclude that Arouet was a philosopher (choice A), became interested in literature at a young age (choice B), or belonged to an aristocratic family (choice C).

24. **The correct answer is H.** The fourth paragraph explicitly states that Plato's ". . . grand purpose in going to Italy was, without doubt, the desire to become personally known to the eminent Pythagoreans . . ." and to secure the best opportunities of making himself thoroughly acquainted with their philosophic tenets, so choice H is the best answer. While the Pythagoreans were located on the Peninsula, merely exploring that area (choice F) was not Plato's main reason for visiting it. Archytas was one of the Pythagoreans, and Plato did want to meet the Pythagoreans, but there is no suggestion that he knew whom Archytas was before traveling to Italy, and choice G simply is not as thorough an answer as choice H is. Plato did not give his lectures until returning to Athens, so choice J is incorrect.

25. **The correct answer is A.** According to the first paragraph, Plato ". . . distinguished himself as an athlete in the great national contests or 'games,' as they were called, the grand object of ambition of every Greek . . .," which supports the conclusion in choice A. While the paragraph describes Athens as the "eye of Greece," this does not necessarily mean that the city was located in the very center of the country (choice B). Although Plato did travel far to study, the first paragraph states that he also ". . . was instructed in the chief and necessary parts

of a liberal Greek education by the most able professors of the time," so choice C is not a strong answer. Choice D contains information from the second paragraph, not the first paragraph.

26. **The correct answer is J.** Only *celebrated* makes complete sense if used in place of *renowned* in line 1, especially since *celebrated* and *famous* are synonyms and Plato is described as *famous* in line 6. *Infamous* (choice F) means "famous for negative reasons," so it is not the best answer. *Crafty* (choice G) has similarly negative connotations. Plato's thirst for knowledge may qualify him as curious, but his fame is a more significant thing to mention in the passage's introductory line than his curiosity, so choice H is not the best answer.

27. **The correct answer is B.** According to the second paragraph, Plato went traveling because it was the "custom of the eager searchers after knowledge of that age," which supports choice B. While scholars were persecuted during his time, choice A was not the reason the author gives for Plato's travels. Plato's teacher, Socrates, had received the death sentence; Plato had not, so choice C is incorrect. While traveling was a good way to obtain a strong education, choice D is too extreme because it suggests that traveling was the *only* way to obtain a rich education.

28. **The correct answer is F.** In the final paragraph, the author describes Platonism as unintelligible, abstruse, and fantastic, all of which support the idea that the author thinks it is a confusing and difficult to explain philosophy (choice F). The influence of Platonism is not discussed at all in the paragraph, so there is no support for choice G. While the author suggests that Platonism is poetic, he also says that it is not scientific, so choice H is only half correct. The quotation at the end of the paragraph indicates that Plato believed in "pure thinking" (choice J), but the confusing nature of his philosophy means that the author probably would not agree that it is an example of such pure and clear thought.

29. **The correct answer is C.** According to the passage, Plato studied under Socrates, whom the author describes as Plato's "master" and, since one's ideas are often shaped by teachers, choice C is the best answer. François Marie Arouet shared only a superficial similarity to Plato, so choice A is not a strong answer. The passage states only that Archytas helped Plato flee from Syracuse—there is no suggestion that Archytas shaped Plato's ideas, so choice B is not a strong answer either. The author indicates that Plato shaped Aristotle's ideas more than Aristotle shaped Plato's, so choice D can be eliminated.

30. **The correct answer is J.** The author states that all biographies of Plato are based on his Letters, which many believe to be fictitious, and this supports the conclusion that what is known about Plato might not actually be true (choice J). However, this is just one theory, so there is not enough support for the conclusion in choice F, and choice G reaches an even more extreme and unlikely conclusion. The author's statement specifically pertains to Plato's biographies, not all biographies, so choice H is not the best answer.

31. **The correct answer is A.** In the fourth paragraph, the author refutes notions that only one side of the heart is susceptible to disease by saying that they are both susceptible (choice A). However, the author also states that death more commonly occurs when disease affects the left side of the heart, which contradicts the extreme statement in choice B. The author also states that disease in the right cavities is very seldom found "in advance of that in the left," which contradicts choice C. Since only one third of cases of heart disease affect the right side of the heart, and the author explicitly states that "the left is unquestionably the more liable to disease," choice D is incorrect.

32. **The correct answer is H.** In the first paragraph, the author identifies the thin, transparent heart membrane as the area least likely to become diseased. This supports the conclusion in choice H and contradicts the one in choice F. Choices G and J both describe the thicker membrane, which is more likely to become diseased.

33. **The correct answer is D.** Each answer choice can be used as a synonym for *admits*, but only *reveals* (choice D), makes sense in this particular context. Since it is the membrane that lines the heart's cavities that does the admitting in this context, it would not make sense to indicate that such a membrane *acknowledges* (choice A) anything, since acknowledging is something a sentient being, not an unthinking membrane, would do. "Allows a view" would be a strong answer to this question, but *allows* (choice B) on its own is too vague to provide a definition of how the author uses *admits* in this context. Confessing is another act performed by a sentient being and not an unthinking membrane, so choice C does not make sense.

34. The correct answer is G. The first paragraph states that the loose duplicatures of membrane that extend from the pulmonary artery and aorta are the semilunar valves. The same paragraph indicates that the tricuspid (choice F) and mitral (choice H) valves both extend at the fibrous circles intermediate between the auricles and ventricles. The fact that auricles are not identified as loose duplicatures of membrane eliminates choice J.

35. The correct answer is D. The phrase "It appears to me" implies a personal perspective, while the author's simple explanation of something that perplexes pathologists implies that this perspective is a unique one. Therefore, choice D is the best answer. While the author clearly believes that he has knowledge most others do not possess, choice A is too extreme a conclusion to reach based on the information in the last paragraph of the passage. Choice B is both too extreme and too specific. The author's confidence in his own conclusions contradicts choice C.

36. The correct answer is G. According to the eighth paragraph, the internal lining of the heart is red regardless of whether the heart is full or emptied of blood or whether the blood inside the heart is clotted or not. Therefore, the correct answer must include all three statements, since they are all true. Only choice G does this. Choice F leaves out two of the true statements. Choices H and J each leave out one true statement.

37. The correct answer is D. In general, the final four paragraphs mainly cover the possible reasons the heart appears to be red in color (choice D). Choice A is only an idea in the very last paragraph. Choice B describes the eighth paragraph only. Choice C does not describe any of the final four paragraphs; it describes the first half of the passage.

38. The correct answer is H. The author explicitly states the answer to this question in the fourth paragraph when he writes, ". . . in one-third of the cases where disease has been found on the left side, it has existed on the right side also, and been essentially of the same character." Therefore, choice H is correct and there is no support for choices F, G, or J.

39. The correct answer is B. The answer to this question appears in the eighth paragraph, where the author states that "inclosing blood within an artery for any period" will not produce redness in the heart. Choices A and C may be essentially true, but neither are mentioned in the passage, and this question asks you to find the information the author specifically mentions in the passage. Choice D neither appears in the passage, nor is it true in any case.

40. The correct answer is F. In the final sentence of the passage, the author concludes that the heart's redness, " … is not always (probably very seldom) a mere stain imparted by the coloring matter of the blood after death and that it alone does not constitute inflammation." Therefore, choice F is the best answer. In the previous paragraph, the author explains that the redness is only evidence of the inflammation's origin (choice G) or constitutes the entire diseased area (choice H) in *some* cases. While the author makes an assertive statement about what he believes is not the nature of the heart's redness, he does not explain what it is, so it is likely that he would admit that the redness is perplexing, which eliminates choice J.

1.	C	**11.**	D	**21.**	B	**31.**	C
2.	J	**12.**	H	**22.**	H	**32.**	J
3.	A	**13.**	C	**23.**	B	**33.**	D
4.	G	**14.**	F	**24.**	J	**34.**	G
5.	B	**15.**	C	**25.**	C	**35.**	A
6.	G	**16.**	J	**26.**	G	**36.**	F
7.	A	**17.**	D	**27.**	A	**37.**	B
8.	J	**18.**	G	**28.**	H	**38.**	H
9.	B	**19.**	B	**29.**	D	**39.**	D
10.	G	**20.**	F	**30.**	G	**40.**	J

1. The correct answer is C. While the risk of cardiovascular disease increases at a generally steeper and more consistent pace for diabetics than for non-diabetics, it nonetheless increases for both groups as glycated hemoglobin levels increase. The upward slope of both lines attests to this fact. Choices A, B, and D all claim one or both groups do not show an increase.

2. The correct answer is J. In Figure 1, the lines representing the risk of cardiovascular disease intersect at a glycated hemoglobin level of 3%, the lowest level measured, indicating that both diabetics and non-diabetics have the same risk of cardiovascular disease with a 3% glycated hemoglobin level. Thus, choices F and G are incorrect because the lines do intersect and the risk for diabetics is not always higher. Choice H is incorrect because Figure 1 does not show the risk for glycated hemoglobin levels above 9%.

3. The correct answer is A. Based on the data in Figure 1, a 50% chance of developing cardiovascular disease does not occur for non-diabetics until glycated hemoglobin levels reach 9%. According to Table 1, none of the non-diabetics has a glycated hemoglobin level above 8%, so it is true that more than 90% of non-diabetics have less than a 50% risk of developing cardiovascular disease. Non-diabetics and diabetics have the same risk of developing cardiovascular disease when both have a glycated hemoglobin level of 3%. According to Table 1, 12% of non-diabetics have a glycated hemoglobin level of 3%, so choices B and D are incorrect. A glycated hemoglobin reading above 7% is a strong indicator of diabetes, but only 2% of non-diabetics have a reading above 7% in Table 1, so choice C is incorrect.

4. The correct answer is G. Choice G can be arrived at by noticing the difference in the shapes of the two upward lines on the graph. The diabetics' line is very nearly straight, indicating a steady and consistent rise in cardiovascular disease risk for each 1% increase in glycated hemoglobin. The non-diabetics' line, however, does not increase at all between 3% and 4% glycated hemoglobin and barely increases between 4% and 5%. The rise in risk for each 1% increase gets larger and larger until by the end, between 8% and 9%, it approximates the risk increase for diabetics. The risk associated with each 1% increase in glycated hemoglobin level is much more consistent across the graph for diabetics than for non-diabetics. Choice F is incorrect, as evidenced by the fact that there appears to be no increase at all in risk for non-diabetics between the 3% and 4% hemoglobin levels, while diabetic risk increases significantly at this level. Choice H is incorrect because there is no decrease in risk for non-diabetics indicated anywhere in the graph. As glycated hemoglobin levels rise, the increase in cardiovascular risk appears to be 0 between 3% and 4% and then is positive from there on. Choice J is incorrect, for at 6% and below, the two lines in the graph are most dissimilar. The lines appear to better resemble one another between the 6% and 9% levels.

5. The correct answer is B. Choice B can be deduced from a combination of the table figures and information provided in the passage's introduction. We're told that a glycated hemoglobin reading above 7% is a strong indicator of diabetes. Yet Table 1 indicates two non-diabetics with a glycated hemoglobin level of 8%. Knowing that these people do not have diabetes allows us to conclude that one cannot infallibly predict diabetes via a glycated hemoglobin test, since a person with a reading that might normally point toward the existence of the disease may not, in fact, have diabetes. Choices A and D are incorrect because Table 1 provides no information on diabetics or the risk of cardiovascular disease. Moreover, the correlation referred to in choice D is suggested in Figure 1, not Table 1. Choice C is incorrect, as the table provides no information regarding what may happen in the future. All we know for sure is that the 100 individuals did not have diabetes at the time they were tested.

6. **The correct answer is G.** The Asteroid Impact and Volcanic Eruption Hypotheses are fairly similar in how the environmental effects they cause would make life difficult for organisms on Earth, causing the extinction of over half of Earth's species. The main difference is how long the triggering event takes and thus how long it would take for that event to cause extinction. In the case of asteroid impact, the impact is an instantaneous one-time event; an asteroid can only hit Earth once and then it breaks apart. Its effects take place right after the impact, and so it took only a few thousand years for extinction to take place. In the case of volcanic eruptions, lava was erupting in many separate episodes over 3 million years, causing continued environmental stresses that would have caused a gradual extinction over tens to hundreds of thousands of years. Choice F is incorrect because in both hypotheses, carbon dioxide causes long-term global warming. Choice H is incorrect because in both hypotheses, highly acidic rain would kill marine organisms. Choice J is incorrect because in both hypotheses, dust or ash would block sunlight in the short term.

7. **The correct answer is A.** In the Asteroid Impact Hypothesis, large amounts of carbon dioxide (CO_2) were blasted into the atmosphere by the impact. In the Volcanic Eruption Hypothesis, large amounts of CO_2 were released by repeated eruptions. In both hypotheses, the CO_2 caused long-term global warming, or a long-term global temperature increase. Choice B is incorrect because dust (Asteroid Impact Hypothesis) or ash (Volcanic Eruption Hypothesis), not CO_2, caused a short-term decrease in the amount of sunlight reaching Earth's surface. Choice C is incorrect because an extinction-triggering event that happened in an instant applies only to the Asteroid Impact Hypothesis. Choice D is incorrect because environmental stresses occurring over hundreds of thousands of years applies only to the Volcanic Eruption Hypothesis.

8. **The correct answer is J.** According to the Asteroid Impact Hypothesis, extinction occurred relatively quickly, over a few thousand years at the end of the Cretaceous. Therefore fossil evidence of Cretaceous organisms disappearing over only a few thousand years just before the end of the Cretaceous would support the Asteroid Impact Hypothesis. Choice F is incorrect because both the Asteroid Impact and Volcanic Eruption hypotheses predict higher temperatures at the end of the Cretaceous, due to increased levels of carbon dioxide. Isotopic evidence for higher temperatures would support both hypotheses. Choice G is incorrect because large amounts of volcanic ash in Late Cretaceous rock layers would provide evidence for abundant volcanic eruptions. This would support the Volcanic Eruption Hypothesis but not the Asteroid Impact Hypothesis. Choice H is incorrect because both the Asteroid Impact and Volcanic Eruption hypotheses propose that super-acid rain would have fallen into the oceans, killing marine organisms. Acid damage to marine organism shells provides evidence for the presence of highly acidic conditions in the oceans, and would support both hypotheses.

9. **The correct answer is B.** According to the passage, sulfur dioxide gas expelled by each volcanic eruption would form super-acid rain. Choice A is incorrect because carbon dioxide gas would cause long-term global warming in the Volcanic Eruption Hypothesis. Choice C is incorrect because volcanic ash would cause short-term global cooling as it blocked sunlight from reaching the earth's surface. Choice D is incorrect because dust would be generated by an asteroid impact, not volcanic eruptions. In addition, dust would play a similar role as volcanic ash and cause short-term cooling, not create acid rain.

10. **The correct answer is G.** From the information in the passage, at the moment of asteroid impact, an earthquake 1 million times stronger than the strongest ever recorded was generated. In addition, the atmosphere was superheated, 5,000 cubic miles of dust was blasted into the atmosphere, and huge amounts of carbon dioxide (CO_2) were released into the air at the moment of impact. Choice F is incorrect because freezing temperatures occurred after impact, when the dust blown into the atmosphere by the impact blocked sunlight from reaching Earth's surface. This occurred in the first few months after the impact. Choice H is incorrect because global warming was a long-term effect of the CO_2 released into the air by the asteroid impact, happening after the dust settled and

continuing for as long as tens of thousands of years after the impact. Choice J is incorrect because it occurred after the impact, when gases in the heated atmosphere reacted to produce acid rain.

11. **The correct answer is D.** In the passage, the last sentence of each hypothesis' description states that environmental effects or stresses caused the extinction of organisms. The only difference between the two hypotheses is the length of time it took for the extinctions to occur. Therefore proponents of both hypotheses would agree that environmental stresses caused the mass extinction at the end of the Cretaceous. Choice A is incorrect because only proponents of the Asteroid Impact Hypothesis would agree that the mass extinction was caused by an object from outer space. Choice B is incorrect because lava flows did not cause extinction by burying organisms; it was the environmental effects of the ash and gases released by the lava flows that caused extinction. In addition, lava flows would be associated with the Volcanic Eruption Hypothesis rather than with the Asteroid Impact Hypothesis. Choice C is incorrect because while a strong earthquake did occur with the asteroid impact and might have caused local extinction of populations, it was not responsible for the mass extinction of over half of Earth's species at the end of the Cretaceous. In addition, the earthquake would be associated with the Asteroid Impact Hypothesis rather than with the Volcanic Eruption Hypothesis.

12. **The correct answer is H.** According to the passage, the short-term effect of a volcanic eruption is decreased temperatures as volcanic ash decreases the amount of sunlight reaching Earth's surface. The decreased global temperatures in the year after the massive eruption of Mount Tambora would be a short-term effect that supports the short-term effects of ash proposed by the Volcanic Eruption Hypothesis. Choice F is incorrect because the short-term effect of sulfur dioxide is highly acidic rain, the presence of which cannot be determined from decreased temperatures. Choice G is incorrect because the long-term effects of carbon dioxide are increased temperatures, not decreased temperatures. Choice J is incorrect because the long-term effects of acid rain are the extinction of marine organisms, the occurrence of which cannot be determined from decreased temperatures.

13. **The correct answer is C.** While swimming is inferably a fairly constant activity, Figure 2 indicates that basketball is a sport consisting of numerous types of physical motions, some very strenuous (e.g., sprinting), some not (e.g., walking). This helps explain why the heart rate curve of the basketball player depicted in Figure 1 shows sudden and dramatic dips, while the swimmer's curve does not. However, Figure 2 does not indicate which of these movements is most strenuous (leading to the highest heart rate) or least strenuous (leading to the lowest heart rate), nor does it provide information about when each of these movements was performed. Figure 2 only provides information about what percentage of time each type of movement was performed, so heart rate cannot be matched to any specific movement at any specific time. Therefore, choices A, B, and D are incorrect.

14. **The correct answer is F.** The passage's introduction indicates that, as a general rule, increasing fitness correlates with lower resting heart rates, a greater degree of change in heart rate during exercise, and greater recovery rates. The swimmer wins on all three counts. The swimmer's resting heart rate is under 50, while the basketball player's is over 75. His heart rate increases faster during exercise than does the basketball player's (note the swimmer's steeper curve as his heart rate shoots from under 50 to around 160 at the 5-minute mark). Finally, the swimmer's steep downward curve from 10 to around 13 minutes when his heart rate is back to normal indicates a higher recovery rate than that of the basketball player. All of these clues allow us to deduce that the swimmer is fitter, which both confirms choice F and eliminates choice G. Choices H and J are incorrect because Study 1 provides data only on the heart rates of these two individuals. That, by itself, is not enough to state that one sport is more demanding overall. Observing a single individual participating in both sports might shed light on this issue, but Study 1 alone is insufficient to do so.

15. **The correct answer is C.** Study 3 deals exclusively with minutes 10–15, which constitute the resting period following the end of physical activity. This study was, therefore, designed to explore some aspect of recovery rates. Having the athletes switch activities allows one to compare the recovery rates observed in Study 3 with those observed in Study 1 and, thus, to hypothesize whether the kind of activity one engages in changes one's recovery rate. Choice A is incorrect, because a study focusing on only two athletes cannot yield enough information to allow one to compare the overall fitness level of swimmers with that of basketball players. Choice B is incorrect, because the relative quality of the swimming and basketball playing is not an issue in the studies, which are concerned only with how heart rate is

affected by these activities. Study 3 was not constructed to determine which athlete is better at the other's sport. Choice D is incorrect, because it merely restates an accepted fact given in the passage's introduction. Scientists already know that the degree of change in heart rate during exercise correlates with overall fitness; they don't need to design another study to discover this.

16. **The correct answer is J.** Study 1 is the only one that measures the swimmer's heart rate before and after swimming, so we need to refer to Figure 1 to answer this question. According to the introduction, each athlete began Study 1 with their heart rate at normal resting levels, so the heart rate at 0 minutes is each athlete's resting heart rate. The swimmer's heart rate first returned to normal resting levels at minute 13, not minute 12, so choice F is incorrect. The basketball player's heart rate first returned to normal resting levels at minute 15, so the heart rate of the swimmer returned to normal resting levels before that of the basketball player, which is why choice J is correct and choice H is incorrect. Choice G is incorrect because it only took 3 minutes after ceasing swimming for the swimmer's heart rate to return to normal resting levels.

17. **The correct answer is D.** The numbers in Table 1 represent the decrease in heart rate at each 1-minute interval following the end of activity. The fact that the swimmer who had just played basketball has zeros as his final two entries shows that his heart rate is no longer decreasing following the 13-minute mark. This indicates that his heart rate has returned to normal resting levels 3 minutes after he has stopped playing. Choice A is incorrect, as the zeros actually represent the opposite. The swimmer's heart rate has returned to normal faster than the basketball player's heart rate, which is still decreasing 3 to 5 minutes after he finished swimming. The faster recovery indicated in the table suggests that the swimmer is in better shape. Choice B is incorrect, as the numbers in the table represent *decreases* in heart rate, not heart rate itself. A heart rate of zero would presumably suggest cardiac arrest, but in this case the zeros simply mean that the swimmer's heart rate is back to normal and is no longer descending from an elevated level. Choice C is incorrect, as nothing supports the hypothesis that the swimmer kept playing after he was told to stop. In fact, the large decreases in the swimmer's heart rate, as indicated in the first three rows of the table, suggest that he did indeed stop playing at the appointed time.

18. **The correct answer is G.** If breathing rate is also a way to judge the demands on the heart during physical activity, then it should show a pattern similar to heart rate, which is another way to judge the demands on the heart. The swimmer shows a steady increase in heart rate to a more or less steady level, followed by a steady decrease in heart rate. Breathing rate should follow the same pattern, which is seen in choice G. Choice F shows the expected pattern in breathing rate for the basketball player, which has a fluctuating heart rate and would therefore also have a fluctuating breathing rate. Choice H shows the opposite pattern of what is expected; breathing rate is directly proportional to heart rate, not inversely proportional. Choice J shows a breathing rate that steadily increases without decreasing, which is not consistent with Study 1. In Study 1, the swimmer stops swimming after 10 minutes, so breathing rate should eventually decrease.

19. **The correct answer is B.** The three beewolves with significantly more offspring fed a larger average number of honeybees to their offspring, while the opposite was true for the two beewolves with significantly fewer offspring. Choice A is incorrect because it describes the opposite trend. Choice C is incorrect because it describes the trend in the data collected in Study 2. Choice D is incorrect because it provides an incorrect analysis of the data collected in Study 2.

20. **The correct answer is F.** Study 2 shows that the denser the flight muscle mitochondrial membranes, the more energy is produced by the mitochondria. Bringing Studies 1 and 3 into the equation, we see that the beewolves with the highest density of flight muscle mitochondrial membranes (and, therefore, the highest mitochondrial energy output) are the same ones with the highest honeybee kill rates noted in Study 1. So it is reasonable to infer that mitochondrial energy output is directly related to beewolves' skill at procuring honeybees for their young. This reasoning contradicts choice J, as we'd expect beewolf mortality rate to decrease as mitochondrial energy output increases. Choice G is incorrect because Study 3 concerns the density of certain membranes within beewolf flight muscles, not the number of flight muscles a beewolf possesses overall. Choice H distorts the investigation, which focuses on beewolves killing honeybees, not the other way around. If anything, the results suggest the opposite of choice H—that the more mitochondrial energy a beewolf possesses, the more success it will have in killing honeybees.

21. **The correct answer is B.** In Study 1, beewolves that have a high number of offspring (greater than 20) also feed a relatively high number of honeybees to each offspring (3 or 4). Conversely, beewolves with a low number of offspring (fewer than 20) also feed a relatively low number of honeybees to each offspring (1 or 2). Beewolf H does not follow this trend, having a low number of offspring but feeding a high number of honeybees to each offspring. Beewolves G and J have a low number of offspring and feed a low number of honeybees to each one, following the trends seen in Study 1, and so choices A and D are incorrect. Beewolf I has a high number of offspring and feeds a high number of honeybees to each one, also following the trends seen in Study 1, so choice C is also incorrect.

22. **The correct answer is H.** The introduction states that the scientists wanted to investigate the mitochondria's role in species survival. Study 1 measured the number of offspring and average number of honeybees fed to each offspring for six beewolves, from which total number of honeybees killed can be calculated (by multiplying the number of offspring and average number of honeybees fed). Study 3 measured the density of flight muscle mitochondrial membranes of the same beewolves. So without Study 2, the scientists can only directly observe the relationship between the four variables just mentioned: number of offspring, average number of honeybees fed to each offspring, total number of honeybees killed, and density of flight muscle mitochondrial membranes. Choice H is correct because it is the only choice that includes two of the variables from this list. Mitochondrial energy output was only measured in Study 2, so any choice that includes this variable cannot be correct. Choices F, G, and J are thus incorrect.

23. **The correct answer is B.** The three studies, taken together, seem to imply that the higher the mitochondrial energy output of an individual beewolf, the more offspring it has and the more food it provides to each. Comparing the numbers in Study 3 with the results of Study 1, one finds a positive linear correlation to that effect, taking into account Study 2's indication that greater flight muscle mitochondrial density means more mitochondrial energy output. However, even with this implicit correlation in place, we still haven't gotten to the original point of the study—that is, to connect mitochondrial energy output with *species survival*. The way to do this would be to find a connection between species survival and the thing we have found correlated with mitochondrial energy output—namely, the volume of beewolf offspring and their nourishment. If beewolf species survival is enhanced in proportion to these things—a reasonable inference, but *one never stated anywhere in the passage*—then the conclusion that mitochondrial energy output is related to species survival would be more tenable. Choice B fills in this missing link, connecting the implications of the studies to the investigation's original speculation. No further study is needed to indicate the correlation in choice A, since Study 2 provides this already. The density of honeybee membranes (choice C) is irrelevant to the investigation and provides no further link between the study results and species survival. The study result cited in choice D contradicts the implication of the three studies described in the passage, so this result does not support the original speculation regarding species survival.

24. **The correct answer is J.** Beewolf K has a higher mitochondrial membrane density than Beewolves A, B, D, and E, which, according to the results of Study 2, means that it has a higher mitochondrial energy output than these beewolves as well. Thus, choice H is incorrect. Beewolf K has a lower mitochondrial membrane density and lower mitochondrial energy output than Beewolves C and F, so choice F is incorrect. Beewolf A fed a total of 66 honeybees to its offspring, so we can use Beewolf A as a rough guide to the mitochondrial membrane density expected for a beewolf that can kill 60 honeybees. Beewolf A has a flight muscle mitochondrial membrane density of 78 f/cc, while Beewolf K has a density of 92 f/cc, so we can predict that it can kill more than 60 honeybees. Thus, choice G is incorrect and choice J is correct.

25. **The correct answer is C.** In a phase diagram like Figure 1, the lines between shaded areas represent conditions in which the two substances on either side of the line are in equilibrium. This means that both substances can exist under these conditions, and the rate of formation of one substance equals the rate of formation of the other substance. Even if you did not remember the exact definition of equilibrium, by looking at Figure 1 you could reason that on the boundary between two polymorphs' areas, both polymorphs would be able to exist because both areas make up that boundary—they intersect at that line and so those points are part of both shaded areas. Choice A is incorrect because the third polymorph does not touch the boundary between the other two polymorphs except at a single point. The question asks what can be concluded for the entire boundary line, not just a single point. The point where

all three polymorphs can exist is called the triple point, and for Figure 1 it is located at approximately 600°C and 0.4 GPa. Choice B is incorrect because both polymorphs can exist along the boundary because both are equally stable. Choice D is incorrect because you can see in Figure 1 that the lines between the shaded regions pass through a range of different temperatures and pressures.

26. **The correct answer is G.** Based on Figure 1, sillimanite is most likely to form at high temperatures and a range of pressures. The hottest parts of both cooling and active mountain-building regions, between 800–1,000°C, are both squarely in the sillimanite area of Figure 1, so sillimanite will form here. Choice F is incorrect because the lowest-pressure part of a mid-ocean ridge, between 0–0.05 GPa, is also at low temperatures. Below 200°C and 0.05 GPa, kyanite will form; between 200–500°C, andalusite will form. Choices H and J are incorrect because both the craton and subduction zone regions in Figure 2 fall entirely within the kyanite area in Figure 1. Thus, only kyanite will form in these geologic settings.

27. **The correct answer is A.** You can estimate the temperature of Earth's surface by thinking about familiar temperatures, such as the boiling point of water, which is 100°C. You can reason that it is too cool on Earth's surface for water to spontaneously boil, so it is safe to assume that Earth's surface temperature is always below 100°C. (The hottest temperature ever recorded on Earth's surface is actually only 54°C.) The introduction tells you that Earth's surface pressure is about 0.0001 GPa. The scale of the pressure axis in Figure 2 is so large that you can just estimate the surface pressure to be around 0 GPa on the figure. So below 100°C and around 0 GPa on Figure 1, kyanite is the only mineral that forms. Choice B is incorrect because andalusite only forms around 200–900°C at surface pressures. Choice C is incorrect because sillimanite only forms around 900–1,000°C at surface pressures. Choice D is incorrect because only kyanite forms.

28. **The correct answer is H.** From Figure 2, you can see that the shaded area for a subduction zone extends all the way from 0 to 1.0 GPa, while temperatures stay relatively cool, not going above 400°C. The question stem tells you that in a subduction zone, a tectonic plate sinks deep into the earth. You know from the introduction that surface pressures are close to 0 GPa, so the higher pressures in the subduction zone must be occurring deeper within the earth. Therefore, you can conclude that pressure increases as depth increases.

Choice F is incorrect because there are high pressures at all the temperatures in the subduction zone shaded area. If choice F were true, there would be an unshaded area at low temperatures and high pressures. Choices G and J are incorrect because pressure increases, rather than decreases, with depth.

29. **The correct answer is D.** According to Figure 2, the hottest part of an active mountain-building region, from 800–1,000°C, is between about 0.2–0.6 GPa. On Figure 1, this falls completely within the sillimanite area, so only sillimanite will form in the hottest part of an active mountain-building region. Choice A is incorrect because andalusite forms in the intermediate-temperature parts (300–800°C) of active mountain-building regions. Choice B is incorrect because kyanite forms in the coolest parts (below 300°C) of active mountain-building regions, and we've already seen that andalusite forms in the intermediate-temperate parts only. Choice C is incorrect because only sillimanite forms in the hottest parts of active mountain-building regions.

30. **The correct answer is G.** The results of Experiment 1, graphed in Figure 1, show that friction resistance force does *not* change for the 20 kg box as its velocity changes. The friction resistance force stays constant at about 65 N for all five velocities measured. Thus, at a different velocity than the ones shown, such as 30 km/hr, the friction resistance force can be predicted to remain at 65 N. Choice J is the drag resistance force that can be estimated for the boat at 30 km/hr, not the box. Figure 1 shows that the drag resistance force increases by around 12 N for every 5 km/hr increase in velocity, so at 30 km/hr, the drag resistance force would be 92 N + 12 N = 104 N ≈ 105 N. Choices F and H are the drag resistance forces for the boat at 5 km/hr and 25 km/hr, respectively, so they are also incorrect.

31. **The correct answer is C.** The table indicates that as the weight of the boxes observed increases from 10 to 30 to 40 kg, the heat generated at the point the box reaches a speed of 20 km/hr. increases as well. That constitutes a positive correlation between weight and heat. Choice A is incorrect, because the correlation between velocity and drag is evident in Experiment 1, not Experiment 2. Drag, in fact, is not part of Experiment 2 at all—the resistance created between the ramp and box is friction—so choice B must also be incorrect. Choice D suggests another relationship involving velocity, but Experiment 2 is arranged such that velocity is kept constant.

32. The correct answer is J. The bars in Figure 1 representing the friction between the box and the ramp are constant at every velocity, roughly 65 N. In contrast, the drag on the boat increases at every velocity listed. These results indicate that unlike drag, friction does not vary with velocity. Choices F and G contradict the passage's introduction, which states that both friction and drag produce a resistance force and heat. These choices, therefore, do not represent a point of differentiation. Choice H is incorrect, because nothing in any of the experiments suggests that drag is unaffected by weight. While we know from Experiment 2 that friction does indeed vary with weight, we cannot conclude from the information given that drag does not.

33. The correct answer is D. In Experiment 1, the original 20-kg box reached a velocity of 30 km/hr. at the bottom of the untreated ramp. Experiment 3 shows that the same box on a sandy ramp hits the bottom of the ramp at 18 km/hr., while on a wet ramp, the box reaches the bottom moving at 39 km/hr. This means that the box moves slower than normal on a ramp covered with sand and faster than normal on a ramp covered with water. The most logical explanation is that sand provides greater resistance to the box's movement and water provides less resistance, making all the other choices incorrect.

34. The correct answer is G. In Table 1, we can see that there is a positive correlation between weight and heat, but we can also see a positive correlation between friction resistance force and heat. The higher the friction resistance force, the more heat generated. From Experiment 3, we see that sand increases the resistance force between the box and the ramp, while water decreases the resistance force. So since the resistance force between the box and the ramp is greater when there is sand on the ramp, the heat generated by the box will be greater on a sand-covered ramp than on the original ramp. Choice F is incorrect because a lighter box will already generate less heat than a heavier box, and will generate even less heat on a clean ramp. Choice H is incorrect because there is less resistance between the water-sprayed ramp and the box than between the sand-covered ramp and the box, so there is less heat generated on the water-sprayed ramp. Choice J is incorrect because a heavier box will generate more heat than a lighter box on the same type of surface.

35. The correct answer is A. To build on the results of Experiment 1 to test the effects of different fluids on drag resistance force, the researchers should try to keep one of the variables the same and only change the variable they are interested in studying. Studying the effects of different fluids on drag resistance force is similar to what the researchers did in Experiment 3, in which they studied the effects of different surfaces on friction resistance force. In that case, they kept the box the same and changed the surfaces. Similarly, to study the effect of fluid on drag, the researchers should keep the boat the same and change the fluids through which it accelerates. Choice B is incorrect because by changing the weight of the boat but keeping the fluid the same (i.e., by staying in the same river), the researchers will be testing the effect of boat weight on drag resistance force. Choice C is incorrect because by adding different loads to the boat but keeping the fluid the same, the researchers are just studying the effect of boat weight on drag in a different way. Choice D is incorrect because the researchers are changing two variables at the same time. By changing both the weight of the boat and the fluid, the researchers will not know which variable is causing any changes in drag.

36. The correct answer is F. At all three heights listed in Table 1, as roughness increases from 0 to 2 to 4, wind speed decreases. Using 50 meters above ground as an example, the wind speed at roughness Class 0 is 13.73, at Class 2 is 10.7, and at Class 4 is 8.1. The figures corresponding to 100 and 150 meters above ground exhibit the same pattern of consistently decreasing wind speeds as roughness increases. Since there is this constant decrease, all the other choices are incorrect.

37. The correct answer is B. There are two important things to notice that help answer this question. First, we're asked to notice something about what happens when height above the ground decreases, and we're looking to compare the magnitude of wind speed changes in various kinds of terrain. In all three terrains, wind speed decreases as height above the ground decreases. For example, follow the numbers for Class 4 at 150 meters, then 100 meters, then 50 meters; you'll see that the wind speeds decrease. That observation eliminates choices A and C from consideration. The issue is now the rate of the decrease—do the numbers drop more quickly in rougher terrain or in smoother terrain? Let's use the figures in the table to determine this.

In the roughest terrain, Class 4, wind speed drops from 10.14 at 150 meters above ground to 9.39 at 100 meters and 8.1 at 50 meters. This is a drop of approximately 0.7 and 1.3, respectively. In a less rough terrain, Class 2, the corresponding decrease is from 12.29 to 11.7 to 10.7, which represents a drop of roughly 0.6 and 1.0. This drop is less dramatic, and the decrease in roughness Class 0 even less so—from 14.8 to 14.4 (a drop of 0.4) to 13.73 (a drop of 0.67). Therefore, the drop-off in wind speed as height above ground decreases is more rapid in rougher terrains.

38. **The correct answer is H.** A farm field is an example of sparsely populated agricultural land and thus represents roughness Class 2. According to Table 1, wind speed 100 m above the ground over land of roughness Class 2 is 11.7 m/s, or just under 12 m/s. Looking at Table 2, a wind speed of 12 m/s will generate 1058.4 W/m^2 of wind power, or just over 1050 W/m^2. Choice F is the power generated at wind speeds of 9 m/s, or the wind speed 100 m above the ground over land of roughness Class 4, not 2. Choice G is the power generated at wind speeds of 11 m/s, or for 50 m above the ground, not 100 m, over land of roughness Class 2. Choice J is the power generated at wind speeds of 14 m/s, or the wind speed 100 m above the ground over land of roughness Class 0, not 2.

39. **The correct answer is D.** Table 1 indicates that 100 meters above ground at roughness Class 2, the level that corresponds to sparsely populated agricultural land, the mean wind speed is 11.7 m/s. The corresponding values for the locations listed in choices A, B, and C are 10.7 m/s, 10.14 m/s, and 8.1 m/s, respectively.

40. **The correct answer is J.** Based on the information in Tables 1 and 2, wind speed in a large city, a roughness class of 4, at 50 m above the ground is about 8 m/s, which will generate around 314 W/m^2 of wind power. Triple that amount is 942 W/m^2. Looking at Table 2, wind speeds of 11 m/s will generate 815 W/m^2 of wind power, while speeds of 12 m/s will generate 1058 W/m^2 of wind power. So to get 942 W/m^2 of power, any change must lead to the turbine experiencing wind speeds of around 11.5 m/s or more. Choice F is incorrect because doubling the height of the turbine to 100 m will expose it to wind speeds of only 9 m/s. Choice G is incorrect because even tripling the height of the turbine to 150 m will expose it to wind speeds of only 10 m/s. Choice H is incorrect because although moving the turbine to a farm field will improve roughness Class to 2, a 50 m turbine will only experience wind speeds of 11 m/s. Choice J is the only successful change because the ocean has a roughness Class of 0, and a 50 m turbine will experience wind speeds of almost 14 m/s.

Sample Essay: Score 1

Ideas and Analysis:	Score = 1
Development and Support:	Score = 1
Organization:	Score = 1
Language Use and Conventions:	Score = 1

I never saw no 3D printer what am I supposed to do with it I can buy the things I need at any store or online so why bother whith this thing. I cant imagine anything you pretend to create will be as good as real as the real thing so its not gonna fool anybody or make people think that we don't need stores or place to buy things anymore. how does it even work I don't understand does it just work like a printer at the library where you make copies of books or papers and they just come out? What makes this better than the prinders we already have to use, if someone can convince me that I need a new printer Ill think of ways to use and do things with it but I don't think anyone should be worried or think that people are gonna do bad things with it so that's what I think about it.

Scoring Explanation

Ideas and Analysis: Score = 1

The writer of this essay does not address the questions provided; instead, he or she provides a weak, peripheral set of random ideas on the value of 3D printers ("I cant imagine anything you pretend to create will be as good as real as the real thing") and barely mentions the notion that they may be dangerous or used improperly ("I don't think anyone should be worried or think that people are gonna do bad things with it"). This off-task response is ultimately an unsuccessful and confusing piece of writing.

Development and Support: Score = 1

A few scattered, poorly developed thoughts that largely veer off topic ("I cant imagine anything you pretend to create will be as good as real as the real thing so its not gonna fool anybody or make people think that we don't need stores or place to buy things anymore.") make up this essay response. The writer's perspective on the potential dangers of 3D printers is barely mentioned and thoughts on government regulation are completely absent, resulting in a wholly ineffective essay.

Organization: Score = 1

This essay demonstrates a complete lack of careful forethought toward creating an effective, well-structured essay. Instead of crafting a persuasive argument to convince readers of the author's perspective regarding the concerns of 3D printers, we are given a confusing response that invites more off-target questions than answers ("how does it even work I don't understand does it just work like a printer at the library"). There is no clear introduction, thesis statement, body, or conclusion, and it is not evident that the writer has a firm grasp on the fundamentals of essay structure.

Language Use and Conventions: Score = 1

This essay is hampered by an abundance of errors in spelling ("whith," "prinders"), grammar (run-ons), and punctuation (missing question marks, etc.). Sentences are weak, simplistic, and poorly developed, and the level of word choice is relatively basic. This response seems hastily written and in need of serious revision.

Sample Essay: Score 6

Ideas and Analysis:	Score = 6
Development and Support:	Score = 6
Organization:	Score = 6
Language Use and Conventions:	Score = 6

In our current era of technological innovation, we have been fortunate enough to witness an explosion of new ideas, gadgets, and processes, which are reshaping how we work, live, and interact. Many of these technological marvels have ushered in dramatic, lasting, and positive impacts (imagine going back to a world without smartphones). Others have, thus far, shown themselves to be little more than opportunities to show off the creativity and skill of their creators (sorry, Segway). There's also another category of innovation that deserves our attention—those that come with an unexpected social cost, namely the potential for serious misuse and abuse. It can be argued that 3D printers have earned this dubious distinction. However, that doesn't mean that we should try and stuff this exciting new technology back into Pandora's Box. It is worth our collective time to explore the potential societal hazards and benefits of the 3D printer and make a carefully considered, responsible decision regarding its use.

Although still in its relative technological infancy, 3D printing offers a great deal of exciting promise in nearly every field of endeavor—art, medicine, and architecture are just a few examples. Imagine a world in which advanced 3D printers create artificial limbs or braces, produce amazing and creative sculptures, and even help reduce the costs and labor involved in new construction projects. Like all new technology, the best way to refine it, improve it, and make it evolve is by putting it in the hands of the people. As a society, and as individuals, we think of fantastic new ways to enhance gadgets and ideas by using them. Taking 3D printers out of the hands of average citizens would be a big mistake and would not be in the best interests of the technology or society as a whole.

However, as previously stated, 3D printers do possess the potential for misuse. They can be used to create dangerous, untraceable weapons, and even make counterfeit items. And, unfortunately, as the technology evolves, the ability to misuse it will expand and improve as well. This wouldn't be the first innovation with a negative social cost. Nuclear technology and automobiles can be added to this list—both of these have led to unfortunate accidents and deaths, but as the technology improves and we better understand and adopt new ways to use them responsibly, the social benefits clearly begin to outweigh the costs.

The evolution of 3D printing technology can follow a similar trajectory—exploring new safety features and allowing responsible levels of government regulation and oversight—all designed to protect users and society at large as we enjoy and make the most of this new innovation. An avenue of research regarding 3D printing should be to explore ways that possible template or molding limits can be implemented for certain dangerous objects like guns, as well as items where there's a counterfeiting concern. Perhaps we can adjust 3D printing technology so that all items created in each machine is marked with the appropriate registration number, which can be traced to the owner.

There should be a mandatory registration process for individuals who purchase 3D printers, which can be done quickly online or through an application process. Having people register or even obtain licensure in order to purchase potentially dangerous items is not a new concept, and its purpose is a noble one—to make us all safer. Furthermore, the way we approach, react, and respond to a new invention often evolves alongside the technology; as we gain increased exposure to 3D printers, and learn more about them and how they're used, our strategies for ensuring their responsible use will continue to become refined. Societies and cultures often follow a trajectory similar to new products—forward, sometimes in leaps and bounds and other times in small, cautious steps, occasionally with fits and starts through trial and error, but confidently and assuredly heading in a positive direction. When we're bolstered and supported by creative new ideas and wondrous, innovative marvels like 3D printing, we're truly putting our best foot forward.

Scoring Explanation

Ideas and Analysis: Score = 6

This essay response contains a wealth of ideas on how we could address the potential dangers of 3D printing ("exploring new safety features and allowing responsible levels of government regulation and oversight"), as well as how to react to the potential for misuse that many new innovations bring ("I think that the way we approach, react, and respond to a new invention often evolves alongside the technology"). Ideas are deeply explored and responsibly weighed, both for this instance as well as the larger social context ("as the technology improves and we better understand and adopt new ways to use them responsibility, the social benefits clearly begin to outweigh the costs"). The end result is a carefully considered and multi-faceted response to the essay task, with a confident, clear, and convincing perspective.

Development and Support: Score = 6

The writer of this essay clearly gave careful thought to the topic, and developed a compelling response that serves his or her perspective quite well. He or she provides a clear point of view ("taking 3D printers out of the hands of average citizens would be a big mistake, and would not be in the best interests of the technology or society as a whole," while acknowledging the need to find "new ways to use them responsibly"), took the time to consider the perils of restrictive use of technology, and wisely offers other innovations for comparison (automobiles and nuclear technology) to bolster the position. The essay concludes with a stirring call for an acceptance of the risky yet potentially wonderful outcomes that can result from bold and innovative technological exploration and discovery.

Organization: Score = 6

From its engaging introduction to its memorable conclusion, this essay is a strong example of persuasive, impassioned writing, all of which supports a central unifying notion ("I feel that it is worth our collective time to explore the potential societal hazards and benefits of the 3D printer, and make a carefully considered, responsible decision regarding its use"). Although verbose, the writing is crisp, on target, and well organized, and the writer delivers a successful argument.

Language Use and Conventions: Score = 6

The author of this essay has a strong command of English language conventions and deploys them effectively throughout this piece of writing. The piece is largely free from errors in grammar and spelling, and a rich and varied word choice is on display, as are well-developed and interesting sentences and transitions. The result is a compelling essay that successfully responds to the task provided.

English Test

1. Ⓐ Ⓑ Ⓒ Ⓓ	16. Ⓕ Ⓖ Ⓗ Ⓙ	31. Ⓐ Ⓑ Ⓒ Ⓓ	46. Ⓕ Ⓖ Ⓗ Ⓙ	61. Ⓐ Ⓑ Ⓒ Ⓓ
2. Ⓕ Ⓖ Ⓗ Ⓙ	17. Ⓐ Ⓑ Ⓒ Ⓓ	32. Ⓕ Ⓖ Ⓗ Ⓙ	47. Ⓐ Ⓑ Ⓒ Ⓓ	62. Ⓕ Ⓖ Ⓗ Ⓙ
3. Ⓐ Ⓑ Ⓒ Ⓓ	18. Ⓕ Ⓖ Ⓗ Ⓙ	33. Ⓐ Ⓑ Ⓒ Ⓓ	48. Ⓕ Ⓖ Ⓗ Ⓙ	63. Ⓐ Ⓑ Ⓒ Ⓓ
4. Ⓕ Ⓖ Ⓗ Ⓙ	19. Ⓐ Ⓑ Ⓒ Ⓓ	34. Ⓕ Ⓖ Ⓗ Ⓙ	49. Ⓐ Ⓑ Ⓒ Ⓓ	64. Ⓕ Ⓖ Ⓗ Ⓙ
5. Ⓐ Ⓑ Ⓒ Ⓓ	20. Ⓕ Ⓖ Ⓗ Ⓙ	35. Ⓐ Ⓑ Ⓒ Ⓓ	50. Ⓕ Ⓖ Ⓗ Ⓙ	65. Ⓐ Ⓑ Ⓒ Ⓓ
6. Ⓕ Ⓖ Ⓗ Ⓙ	21. Ⓐ Ⓑ Ⓒ Ⓓ	36. Ⓕ Ⓖ Ⓗ Ⓙ	51. Ⓐ Ⓑ Ⓒ Ⓓ	66. Ⓕ Ⓖ Ⓗ Ⓙ
7. Ⓐ Ⓑ Ⓒ Ⓓ	22. Ⓕ Ⓖ Ⓗ Ⓙ	37. Ⓐ Ⓑ Ⓒ Ⓓ	52. Ⓕ Ⓖ Ⓗ Ⓙ	67. Ⓐ Ⓑ Ⓒ Ⓓ
8. Ⓕ Ⓖ Ⓗ Ⓙ	23. Ⓐ Ⓑ Ⓒ Ⓓ	38. Ⓕ Ⓖ Ⓗ Ⓙ	53. Ⓐ Ⓑ Ⓒ Ⓓ	68. Ⓕ Ⓖ Ⓗ Ⓙ
9. Ⓐ Ⓑ Ⓒ Ⓓ	24. Ⓕ Ⓖ Ⓗ Ⓙ	39. Ⓐ Ⓑ Ⓒ Ⓓ	54. Ⓕ Ⓖ Ⓗ Ⓙ	69. Ⓐ Ⓑ Ⓒ Ⓓ
10. Ⓕ Ⓖ Ⓗ Ⓙ	25. Ⓐ Ⓑ Ⓒ Ⓓ	40. Ⓕ Ⓖ Ⓗ Ⓙ	55. Ⓐ Ⓑ Ⓒ Ⓓ	70. Ⓕ Ⓖ Ⓗ Ⓙ
11. Ⓐ Ⓑ Ⓒ Ⓓ	26. Ⓕ Ⓖ Ⓗ Ⓙ	41. Ⓐ Ⓑ Ⓒ Ⓓ	56. Ⓕ Ⓖ Ⓗ Ⓙ	71. Ⓐ Ⓑ Ⓒ Ⓓ
12. Ⓕ Ⓖ Ⓗ Ⓙ	27. Ⓐ Ⓑ Ⓒ Ⓓ	42. Ⓕ Ⓖ Ⓗ Ⓙ	57. Ⓐ Ⓑ Ⓒ Ⓓ	72. Ⓕ Ⓖ Ⓗ Ⓙ
13. Ⓐ Ⓑ Ⓒ Ⓓ	28. Ⓕ Ⓖ Ⓗ Ⓙ	43. Ⓐ Ⓑ Ⓒ Ⓓ	58. Ⓕ Ⓖ Ⓗ Ⓙ	73. Ⓐ Ⓑ Ⓒ Ⓓ
14. Ⓕ Ⓖ Ⓗ Ⓙ	29. Ⓐ Ⓑ Ⓒ Ⓓ	44. Ⓕ Ⓖ Ⓗ Ⓙ	59. Ⓐ Ⓑ Ⓒ Ⓓ	74. Ⓕ Ⓖ Ⓗ Ⓙ
15. Ⓐ Ⓑ Ⓒ Ⓓ	30. Ⓕ Ⓖ Ⓗ Ⓙ	45. Ⓐ Ⓑ Ⓒ Ⓓ	60. Ⓕ Ⓖ Ⓗ Ⓙ	75. Ⓐ Ⓑ Ⓒ Ⓓ

Mathematics Test

1. Ⓐ Ⓑ Ⓒ Ⓓ Ⓔ	16. Ⓕ Ⓖ Ⓗ Ⓙ Ⓚ	31. Ⓐ Ⓑ Ⓒ Ⓓ Ⓔ	46. Ⓕ Ⓖ Ⓗ Ⓙ Ⓚ
2. Ⓕ Ⓖ Ⓗ Ⓙ Ⓚ	17. Ⓐ Ⓑ Ⓒ Ⓓ Ⓔ	32. Ⓕ Ⓖ Ⓗ Ⓙ Ⓚ	47. Ⓐ Ⓑ Ⓒ Ⓓ Ⓔ
3. Ⓐ Ⓑ Ⓒ Ⓓ Ⓔ	18. Ⓕ Ⓖ Ⓗ Ⓙ Ⓚ	33. Ⓐ Ⓑ Ⓒ Ⓓ Ⓔ	48. Ⓕ Ⓖ Ⓗ Ⓙ Ⓚ
4. Ⓕ Ⓖ Ⓗ Ⓙ Ⓚ	19. Ⓐ Ⓑ Ⓒ Ⓓ Ⓔ	34. Ⓕ Ⓖ Ⓗ Ⓙ Ⓚ	49. Ⓐ Ⓑ Ⓒ Ⓓ Ⓔ
5. Ⓐ Ⓑ Ⓒ Ⓓ Ⓔ	20. Ⓕ Ⓖ Ⓗ Ⓙ Ⓚ	35. Ⓐ Ⓑ Ⓒ Ⓓ Ⓔ	50. Ⓕ Ⓖ Ⓗ Ⓙ Ⓚ
6. Ⓕ Ⓖ Ⓗ Ⓙ Ⓚ	21. Ⓐ Ⓑ Ⓒ Ⓓ Ⓔ	36. Ⓕ Ⓖ Ⓗ Ⓙ Ⓚ	51. Ⓐ Ⓑ Ⓒ Ⓓ Ⓔ
7. Ⓐ Ⓑ Ⓒ Ⓓ Ⓔ	22. Ⓕ Ⓖ Ⓗ Ⓙ Ⓚ	37. Ⓐ Ⓑ Ⓒ Ⓓ Ⓔ	52. Ⓕ Ⓖ Ⓗ Ⓙ Ⓚ
8. Ⓕ Ⓖ Ⓗ Ⓙ Ⓚ	23. Ⓐ Ⓑ Ⓒ Ⓓ Ⓔ	38. Ⓕ Ⓖ Ⓗ Ⓙ Ⓚ	53. Ⓐ Ⓑ Ⓒ Ⓓ Ⓔ
9. Ⓐ Ⓑ Ⓒ Ⓓ Ⓔ	24. Ⓕ Ⓖ Ⓗ Ⓙ Ⓚ	39. Ⓐ Ⓑ Ⓒ Ⓓ Ⓔ	54. Ⓕ Ⓖ Ⓗ Ⓙ Ⓚ
10. Ⓕ Ⓖ Ⓗ Ⓙ Ⓚ	25. Ⓐ Ⓑ Ⓒ Ⓓ Ⓔ	40. Ⓕ Ⓖ Ⓗ Ⓙ Ⓚ	55. Ⓐ Ⓑ Ⓒ Ⓓ Ⓔ
11. Ⓐ Ⓑ Ⓒ Ⓓ Ⓔ	26. Ⓕ Ⓖ Ⓗ Ⓙ Ⓚ	41. Ⓐ Ⓑ Ⓒ Ⓓ Ⓔ	56. Ⓕ Ⓖ Ⓗ Ⓙ Ⓚ
12. Ⓕ Ⓖ Ⓗ Ⓙ Ⓚ	27. Ⓐ Ⓑ Ⓒ Ⓓ Ⓔ	42. Ⓕ Ⓖ Ⓗ Ⓙ Ⓚ	57. Ⓐ Ⓑ Ⓒ Ⓓ Ⓔ
13. Ⓐ Ⓑ Ⓒ Ⓓ Ⓔ	28. Ⓕ Ⓖ Ⓗ Ⓙ Ⓚ	43. Ⓐ Ⓑ Ⓒ Ⓓ Ⓔ	58. Ⓕ Ⓖ Ⓗ Ⓙ Ⓚ
14. Ⓕ Ⓖ Ⓗ Ⓙ Ⓚ	29. Ⓐ Ⓑ Ⓒ Ⓓ Ⓔ	44. Ⓕ Ⓖ Ⓗ Ⓙ Ⓚ	59. Ⓐ Ⓑ Ⓒ Ⓓ Ⓔ
15. Ⓐ Ⓑ Ⓒ Ⓓ Ⓔ	30. Ⓕ Ⓖ Ⓗ Ⓙ Ⓚ	45. Ⓐ Ⓑ Ⓒ Ⓓ Ⓔ	60. Ⓕ Ⓖ Ⓗ Ⓙ Ⓚ

Reading Test

1. Ⓐ Ⓑ Ⓒ Ⓓ	11. Ⓐ Ⓑ Ⓒ Ⓓ	21. Ⓐ Ⓑ Ⓒ Ⓓ	31. Ⓐ Ⓑ Ⓒ Ⓓ
2. Ⓕ Ⓖ Ⓗ Ⓙ	12. Ⓕ Ⓖ Ⓗ Ⓙ	22. Ⓕ Ⓖ Ⓗ Ⓙ	32. Ⓕ Ⓖ Ⓗ Ⓙ
3. Ⓐ Ⓑ Ⓒ Ⓓ	13. Ⓐ Ⓑ Ⓒ Ⓓ	23. Ⓐ Ⓑ Ⓒ Ⓓ	33. Ⓐ Ⓑ Ⓒ Ⓓ
4. Ⓕ Ⓖ Ⓗ Ⓙ	14. Ⓕ Ⓖ Ⓗ Ⓙ	24. Ⓕ Ⓖ Ⓗ Ⓙ	34. Ⓕ Ⓖ Ⓗ Ⓙ
5. Ⓐ Ⓑ Ⓒ Ⓓ	15. Ⓐ Ⓑ Ⓒ Ⓓ	25. Ⓐ Ⓑ Ⓒ Ⓓ	35. Ⓐ Ⓑ Ⓒ Ⓓ
6. Ⓕ Ⓖ Ⓗ Ⓙ	16. Ⓕ Ⓖ Ⓗ Ⓙ	26. Ⓕ Ⓖ Ⓗ Ⓙ	36. Ⓕ Ⓖ Ⓗ Ⓙ
7. Ⓐ Ⓑ Ⓒ Ⓓ	17. Ⓐ Ⓑ Ⓒ Ⓓ	27. Ⓐ Ⓑ Ⓒ Ⓓ	37. Ⓐ Ⓑ Ⓒ Ⓓ
8. Ⓕ Ⓖ Ⓗ Ⓙ	18. Ⓕ Ⓖ Ⓗ Ⓙ	28. Ⓕ Ⓖ Ⓗ Ⓙ	38. Ⓕ Ⓖ Ⓗ Ⓙ
9. Ⓐ Ⓑ Ⓒ Ⓓ	19. Ⓐ Ⓑ Ⓒ Ⓓ	29. Ⓐ Ⓑ Ⓒ Ⓓ	39. Ⓐ Ⓑ Ⓒ Ⓓ
10. Ⓕ Ⓖ Ⓗ Ⓙ	20. Ⓕ Ⓖ Ⓗ Ⓙ	30. Ⓕ Ⓖ Ⓗ Ⓙ	40. Ⓕ Ⓖ Ⓗ Ⓙ

Science Test

1. Ⓐ Ⓑ Ⓒ Ⓓ	11. Ⓐ Ⓑ Ⓒ Ⓓ	21. Ⓐ Ⓑ Ⓒ Ⓓ	31. Ⓐ Ⓑ Ⓒ Ⓓ
2. Ⓕ Ⓖ Ⓗ Ⓙ	12. Ⓕ Ⓖ Ⓗ Ⓙ	22. Ⓕ Ⓖ Ⓗ Ⓙ	32. Ⓕ Ⓖ Ⓗ Ⓙ
3. Ⓐ Ⓑ Ⓒ Ⓓ	13. Ⓐ Ⓑ Ⓒ Ⓓ	23. Ⓐ Ⓑ Ⓒ Ⓓ	33. Ⓐ Ⓑ Ⓒ Ⓓ
4. Ⓕ Ⓖ Ⓗ Ⓙ	14. Ⓕ Ⓖ Ⓗ Ⓙ	24. Ⓕ Ⓖ Ⓗ Ⓙ	34. Ⓕ Ⓖ Ⓗ Ⓙ
5. Ⓐ Ⓑ Ⓒ Ⓓ	15. Ⓐ Ⓑ Ⓒ Ⓓ	25. Ⓐ Ⓑ Ⓒ Ⓓ	35. Ⓐ Ⓑ Ⓒ Ⓓ
6. Ⓕ Ⓖ Ⓗ Ⓙ	16. Ⓕ Ⓖ Ⓗ Ⓙ	26. Ⓕ Ⓖ Ⓗ Ⓙ	36. Ⓕ Ⓖ Ⓗ Ⓙ
7. Ⓐ Ⓑ Ⓒ Ⓓ	17. Ⓐ Ⓑ Ⓒ Ⓓ	27. Ⓐ Ⓑ Ⓒ Ⓓ	37. Ⓐ Ⓑ Ⓒ Ⓓ
8. Ⓕ Ⓖ Ⓗ Ⓙ	18. Ⓕ Ⓖ Ⓗ Ⓙ	28. Ⓕ Ⓖ Ⓗ Ⓙ	38. Ⓕ Ⓖ Ⓗ Ⓙ
9. Ⓐ Ⓑ Ⓒ Ⓓ	19. Ⓐ Ⓑ Ⓒ Ⓓ	29. Ⓐ Ⓑ Ⓒ Ⓓ	39. Ⓐ Ⓑ Ⓒ Ⓓ
10. Ⓕ Ⓖ Ⓗ Ⓙ	20. Ⓕ Ⓖ Ⓗ Ⓙ	30. Ⓕ Ⓖ Ⓗ Ⓙ	40. Ⓕ Ⓖ Ⓗ Ⓙ

WRITING TEST

Plan Your Essay

Write Your Essay

ENGLISH TEST

45 MINUTES—75 QUESTIONS

DIRECTIONS: In this section, you will see passages with words and phrases that are underlined and numbered. In the right-hand column you will see a question corresponding to each number that provides alternatives to the underlined part. In most of the items, you are to choose the best alternative. If no change is needed, choose NO CHANGE.

In other items, there will be either a question about an underlined portion of the passage, or a question about a section of the passage, or about the passage as a whole. This question type will correspond to a number or numbers in a box.

For each question, choose the best alternative or answer and fill in the corresponding circle on the answer sheet.

PASSAGE I

A Bad Omen

[1]

Helen Thayer threw herself a birthday party, only it's being (1) held at the South Pole and she was the only one invited. Helen walked part of the way, ski (2) over longer distances, and pulled her own sled loaded with the gear and food she needed to survive. Why would a mature woman want to journey to a bleak, nearly

1. **A.** NO CHANGE
   B. but it was
   C. yet its being
   D. the kind to be

2. **F.** NO CHANGE
   G. skier
   H. skied
   J. skiing

Practice Test 2 — ENGLISH

CONTINUE

featureless landscape of unbroken white and ice, lit only by a never-setting sun to visit a place that doesn't exist! [3] [4]

3. A. NO CHANGE
B. exist?
C. exist.
D. exist;

4. Which of the following sentences, if added here, would best conclude and support the main idea of the first paragraph?
F. To know Helen Thayer, one would have to explore the mind of an explorer and ask the ultimate question of why one climbs a mountain just because it is there.
G. The answer, it seems, lies in the fact that Helen and her husband, Bill, once decided to live in many different countries and keep themselves in superb athletic shape.
H. While part of her motivation was obviously the quest for adventure, she was also drawn to the Pole—which is not a physical location, but a point defined by scientists to describe Earth's magnetic field.
J. And why would she have flown to Punta Arenas, a city in Chile, and boarded a Hercules aircraft intending to begin a challenge with another challenge in itself—a safe landing in hostile conditions?

[2]

Helen's journey began along the Antarctic coastline, at a place called Hercules Inlet. In what may later have seemed to be a bad omen, her boot buckle snapped off before she took her first step. Helen commented later in her email messages [5] that she was discouraged but decided to make repairs and start fresh the next day. Soon after getting underway, she faced miles of *sastrugi*, a type of ice formation marked by hard mounds and jagged ridges of frozen water that formed a nearly indefatigable [6] barrier to the pole.

5. A. NO CHANGE
B. (place after *Helen*)
C. (place after *discouraged*)
D. (place after *fresh*)

6. F. NO CHANGE
G. illegitimate
H. incomprehensible
J. insurmountable

Overwhelmed by frustration, [7] Helen trusted her compass and global positioning system to guide her through.

7. The writer intends here to provide readers a description of the type of personality Helen Thayer possessed that allowed her to survive this challenge. Assuming all are true, which alternative best accomplishes this?
A. NO CHANGE
B. Fighting off frustration and relying on patience,
C. Knowing that she'd face these conditions for some time,
D. OMIT the underlined portion.

[3]

The problem of high and sustained winds turned out to be a more daunting challenge than the danger of falling into ice <u>crevasses and open cracks.</u> (8) Helen had to lash a line around her waist and place an ice screw into a massive wall of ice to keep from being blown away. [9]

<u>After the winds passed, total whiteout followed, Helen had to go slowly, any step could be into a crevasse.</u> (10) [11]

8. F. NO CHANGE
   G. open cracks and crevasses.
   H. crevasses.
   J. open crevasses and cracks.

9. Assuming all are true, which of the following sentences, if added here, would best contribute to the narration of events in this paragraph?
   A. The seasonal storm called El Niño was roaring through the Antarctic, causing these high winds.
   B. Huddled against the roar of 100-mile-per-hour winds, she felt like she was inside a jet engine, hanging on for her very life.
   C. She was passing through one of the most lifeless areas on the planet.
   D. Some of the crevasses could be as wide as twenty feet and required extensive detours around them.

10. F. NO CHANGE
    G. After the winds passed, total whiteout followed. Helen had to go slowly; any step could be into a crevasse.
    H. After the winds passed; total whiteout followed; Helen had to go slowly; any step could be into a crevasse.
    J. After the winds passed. Total whiteout followed. Helen had to go slowly; any step could be into a crevasse.

11. Which of the following best introduces a secondary element to the article's focus and provides an appropriate transition between paragraphs?
    A. NO CHANGE
    B. She next climbed a high ridge to scout for upcoming dangers in the form of the black lines of crevasses.
    C. As she carefully made her way, Helen thought of her first adventure to the North Pole years earlier and remembered how even in fine weather, things can go wrong—and soon they did.
    D. The next day, Helen celebrated her birthday with a frozen cupcake that she had carried in her pack.

CONTINUE

[4]

[1] A few days later, in an area that seemed safe, Helen plunged into a crevasse, finding herself in a most troublesome (12) predicament few sixty-year-old women ever face. [2] As she fell, her ski's tips scraped against the wall and flipped her. [3] Its length was wider than the crevasse and had bridged the gap above, saving her. [4] Helen found herself hanging from her sleds pull ropes (13). [5] Through some fancy maneuvering, she eventually was able to get herself back on solid ground. [14]

[5]

Helen Thayer never made it to the South Pole. Not long after the crevasse incident, she was badly injured in another fall. She considered braving her difficulties and continuing her journey in pain. But in the end, she gave herself and her many friends a birthday present by radioing for help.

12.
- **F.** NO CHANGE
- **G.** more troublesome
- **H.** most dangerous
- **J.** OMIT the underlined portion.

13.
- **A.** NO CHANGE
- **B.** sled's pull ropes
- **C.** sleds pull rope's
- **D.** sled's pull's ropes

14. For the sake of logic and coherence, Sentence 3 should be placed:
- **F.** where it is now.
- **G.** before Sentence 1.
- **H.** before Sentence 2.
- **J.** after Sentence 4.

Question 15 asks about the passage as a whole.

15. Suppose the writer had been assigned to write an essay about the personal challenges faced by Helen Thayer. Would this passage successfully fulfill the assignment?
- **A.** No, because the writer has failed to provide details of Helen's thinking when she was injured or alone or doubting herself.
- **B.** No, because the reader learns little about her motivations and how she supported this expensive adventure.
- **C.** Yes, because the reader can sense what the ordeal was like after reading this account of her trip.
- **D.** Yes, because the basic physical challenges she faced have been outlined and covered.

PASSAGE II

Yakutsk

[1]

[16] At one point or another in your life, you've probably complained about the treacherous cold you've experienced in the heart of the <u>winter month's</u> (17), but chances are if you knew how cold it could *really* get, you wouldn't complain quite so much. Spend a winter in Yakutsk, and you might completely rethink how bad winters get where you live!

[2]

Yakutsk, a Russian city located less than 300 miles south of the Arctic Circle, is among the world's northernmost and coldest cities. In fact, it is often given the dubious distinction of being the coldest <u>Major City</u> (18) in the world. Here's a chilly bit of trivia that might make you want to put on another layer of warm clothing: the average temperature during the winter in Yakutsk is a freezing –30°F (or –34°C). At that temperature, nearly everything <u>accelerates from</u> (19) a brisk pace to a frigid crawl and the fight

16. The author of this passage would like to add an introductory sentence to the piece. Which of the following would make the most appropriate introductory sentence?

F. Have you ever wondered what life is like in a cold city?
G. Have you ever had the opportunity to travel abroad?
H. What cultural attractions are there in your city?
J. Does your city have a booming mining industry?

17. **A.** NO CHANGE
B. winter months
C. winter's month's
D. winter months'

18. **F.** NO CHANGE
G. major City
H. Major city
J. major city

19. **A.** NO CHANGE
B. slows from
C. remains steady from
D. darkens from

CONTINUE

for survival against the bitter natural elements becomes very real. [20]

20. The author would like to add an additional fact about Yakutsk to Paragraph 2. Which of the following would be the most appropriate addition to this paragraph?

- **F.** The record low temperature in Yakutsk
- **G.** The size of the largest diamond ever mined in Yakutsk
- **H.** An example of when Yakutsk served as a military fort
- **J.** The name of a Siberian town that early settlers arrived from

[3]

Despite the totally messed up (21) temperature, many people have managed to create a life for themselves and their families in Yakutsk, which is the official capital city of the Sakha Republic. Current estimates set the population of Yakutsk at around 270,000 people; (22)

21.
- **A.** NO CHANGE
- **B.** extreme
- **C.** ridiculous
- **D.** moderate

22.
- **F.** NO CHANGE
- **G.** around 270,000 people!
- **H.** around 270,000 people.
- **J.** around 270,000 people?

[4]

Where did all of these people come from, and how have they managed to survive living in this frigid locale? The earliest settlers of Yakutsk arrived from neighboring Siberian towns and villages in the thirteenth century, so they were certainly no strangers to the cold. They were in search of new lands to populate and settle upon. Over the next several hundred years, settlers from all over Siberia began to trickle into (23) Yakutsk, which was "officially" founded in 1632.

23.
- **A.** NO CHANGE
- **B.** stumble into
- **C.** flee from
- **D.** evade with

[5]

In it's (24) early years, Yakutsk—which is approximately 50 square miles in area, making it smaller than every American state, including the District of Columbia—was a port city and military fort. Life was certainly not easy for its residents, who relied on hunting, fishing, and gathering to survive.

24.
- **F.** NO CHANGE
- **G.** its
- **H.** its'
- **J.** it was its

[6]

As the years went on, it was discovered that Yakutsk has a rich supply of minerals and valuable resources beneath the *permafrost*, a geological term used to describe a layer of rock and soil that has been frozen for at least two consecutive years, upon which the city is built. Iron ore, coal, natural gas, and tin are among the <u>redundant</u> [25] reserves that have spurred a booming mining industry in Yakutsk. But perhaps the greatest discoveries made beneath the city's frost are gold and diamonds—vast supplies of these precious items have helped the city grow and develop. Currently, Yakutsk is one of the world's key suppliers of diamonds.

25. A. NO CHANGE
B. redacted
C. abeyance
D. abundant

[7]

[26] Residents are also employed in the tanning and construction material development industries, and citizens have several cultural activities to take advantage of, including museums, theaters, festivals, and cathedrals. The city also possesses a <u>bourgeoning and quickly developing</u> [27] infrastructure, with transportation, education, research, healthcare systems, and an airport.

26. The author of this passage would like to add a sentence to the beginning of Paragraph 7 that effectively transitions from Paragraph 6. Which of the following sentences most effectively achieves this?
F. Yakutsk isn't the only cold city in Russia.
G. Yakutsk does have a much warmer summer climate, however.
H. The distance between Yakutsk and Moscow is approximately 5,197 miles.
J. However, there's more to life in Yakutsk than ice and mining.

27. A. NO CHANGE
B. bourgeoning and quickly shrinking
C. bourgeoning
D. dwindling and quickly diminishing

CONTINUE

[8]

Despite what you may be thinking, it isn't *always* frigid in Yakutsk—average monthly temperatures in the summer actually exceed 65°F. [28]

28. The author of this passage would like to add a concluding sentence to the paragraph. Which of the following would make the most appropriate concluding sentence?

F. The next time you have some free time from school or work, consider taking a trip to a new city, town, or village that you've never seen before!

G. So if you're ever curious about what life is like there and have a taste for travel, the summer might be the best time to visit Yakutsk!

H. Most cities have some type of industry that they specialize in, as does Yakutsk.

J. Most cities have a wide temperature variance based on the time of year and season.

Questions 29 and 30 ask about the entire passage.

29. The author would like to add the following sentence to the passage:

Residents of Yakutsk fish for salmon and hunt for wild elk and moose.

Into which paragraph would this sentence most logically fit?

A. Paragraph 3

B. Paragraph 4

C. Paragraph 5

D. Paragraph 6

30. Into what type of publication would this passage most logically fit?

F. A current events website

G. A travel website

H. A women's fashion magazine

J. A scientific journal

PASSAGE III

A Park Under the Sea

[1]

Someday it will be Smokers International Park or the Atlantis Massif Preserve. You and other nature lovers will journey to the middle of the ocean to see wonders rivaling Old Faithful or the Grand Canyon. <u>In addition to that, you</u> (31) also will have to board a deep-sea submersible to travel thousands of feet below the waves to visit underwater hot springs. [32]

[2]

Powerful spotlights <u>nearly will illuminate all of the</u> (33) black depths, revealing odd formations. Two monstrous mineral towers resembling ragged chimneys spew what looks like black smoke, yet <u>neither of these towers have</u> (34) a fire inside.

31. **A.** NO CHANGE
B. Additionally, you
C. However, you
D. You

32. Would it contribute to the understanding of the passage to define the term *submersible* at this point?
F. No, because it would distract from the introduction of the passage.
G. Yes, because it may be confused with a word most readers know, *submarine*.
H. Yes, because there will be many technical words in a science passage and the reader can become overwhelmed.
J. No, because the word is implicitly defined in the first sentence of the next paragraph.

33. **A.** NO CHANGE
B. will nearly illuminate all of the
C. will illuminate nearly all of the
D. will illuminate all of the nearly

34. **F.** NO CHANGE
G. neither of these towers had
H. neither tower have
J. neither of these towers has

CONTINUE

The clouds are tiny metallic sulfide particles, the enormous heat and pressure cause the particles to precipitate, the minerals settle out, they build up quickly (over a meter a day) into towers, shelves, and icicles. (35) Hot water collects under the shelves into upside down reflecting pools. [36]

35.
A. NO CHANGE
B. The clouds are tiny metallic sulfide particles. The enormous heat and pressure cause the particles to precipitate. The minerals settle out; they build up quickly into towers, shelves, and icicles.
C. The clouds are tiny metallic sulfide particles; the enormous heat and pressure cause the particles to precipitate; the minerals settle out; they build up quickly into towers, shelves, and icicles.
D. The clouds are tiny metallic sulfide particles: the enormous heat and pressure cause the particles to precipitate. The minerals settle out; they build up quickly into towers, shelves, and icicles.

36. In Paragraph 2, should the final sentence be omitted?
F. No, because it adds a vivid image to the description.
G. No, because it adds an element of mystery to the surroundings and will keep the reader interested in the narrative.
H. Yes, because it is confusing and it introduces an element that would need further description to be clear.
J. Yes, because it incorrectly describes what you might see.

[3]

Turning, you see "snowblowers," (37) churning plumes of white powder that shoot out from the ocean bottom. Of course, it isn't snow in this seawater that is three times hotter than (38) boiling, but is rather the byproducts of bacteria living inside vents under the ocean bottom. Life abounds in this otherwise lifeless world. [39] You have entered the realm of chemosynthesis.

37.
A. NO CHANGE
B. "snowblowers"
C. "snowblowers";
D. snowblowers, being

38.
F. NO CHANGE
G. three times more hot than
H. the hottest water next to
J. triple hot

39. At this point, the writer wants to emphasize the main theme of the passage. Assuming all are true, adding which sentence best accomplishes this?
A. NO CHANGE
B. Volcanic activity under the seafloor brings heat and chemicals to these unique environments.
C. At this great depth, there is little food or shelter for organisms.
D. Technology will someday allow the average vacationer the opportunity to journey to this type of extreme habitat.

The animals down here depend not on sunlight but on chemical reactions. [40]

40. Which of these choices most effectively shortens the length of Paragraph 3 while preserving the author's original meaning?

- **F.** NO CHANGE
- **G.** Place a paragraph break before the previous sentence.
- **H.** Place a paragraph break after the next sentence.
- **J.** Place a paragraph break at this spot.

The reason microbes thrive <u>is because</u> (41) they create energy by metabolizing hydrogen sulfide in the water. They grow in enormous white mats that cover <u>everything and over</u> (42) 300 different species feed on them <u>directly, including</u> (43) blind shrimp, giant mussels, amphipods, limpets the size of small bullets, octopuses, and bright red tube worms, which can grow to twelve feet in length.

41.
- **A.** NO CHANGE
- **B.** is when
- **C.** because
- **D.** is that

42.
- **F.** NO CHANGE
- **G.** everything over
- **H.** everything, and over
- **J.** everything. Over

43.
- **A.** NO CHANGE
- **B.** directly. These will include:
- **C.** directly, including,
- **D.** directly, including;

[4]

[44] This place is more like the frozen oceans of Jupiter's moon Europa or the Martian ice caps than anywhere above water on Earth. Indeed, scientists wonder whether life on Earth began under oceans and spread upward to land. Some speculate that life in outer space hides in an equally bizarre environment, beyond our detection—for now.

44. Given that all are true, which of the following sentences, if added here, would best enhance the author's method of bringing the reader to this hostile environment and introduce the last paragraph?

- **F.** Have you ever visited outer space and experienced its hostility?
- **G.** As your time on the bottom draws to a close, you may feel that you've been on another planet.
- **H.** What can live in a hostile world of 400°F water chilled to 36°F an inch or so from the vents under extremes of pressure reaching 6,000 pounds per square inch?
- **J.** The concentration of chemicals in the water here is so corrosive that it leaches minerals out of stone and would kill ordinary sea life.

CONTINUE

Question 45 asks about the passage as a whole.

45. If this passage were revised to include a paragraph on how various life forms have come to these underwater hot springs, the new paragraph would most logically follow Paragraph:

A. 1
B. 2.
C. 3.
D. 4.

PASSAGE IV

Dialogues with the Dead

[1]

In sub-Saharan Africa, the living provide their deceased ancestors with a functional role in <u>everyday aliveness</u>.[46] Western anthropologists have described <u>it</u>[47] as an ancestor cult or worship: more properly, the role of elders, both living and deceased, functions as a controlling factor among kinsmen. The living elders of the Suku <u>as protectors</u>[48] from southeastern Kinshasa go to the graves of the dead to appeal to them during times of illness or misfortune. A monologue with the dead ensues, often following a traditional form and in normal <u>conversational tones!</u>[49] "Your junior is sick. Are you angry? Have you been offended?

46. **F.** NO CHANGE
G. everyday living
H. alive everyday
J. everyday being alive

47. **A.** NO CHANGE
B. them
C. these roles
D. this phenomenon

48. **F.** NO CHANGE
G. (move to after *elders*)
H. (move to after *dead*)
J. (move to after *them*)

49. **A.** NO CHANGE
B. conversational tones.
C. conversational tones?
D. conversational tones;

Other lineages are doing fine. Why do you not look after us?" [50]

50. The writer wishes to close Paragraph 1 with a sentence that will define the topic and sharpen the focus on the particular subject of this essay. Assuming all are true, which of the following would most effectively accomplish this?

F. The dead are expected to be as much a part of generational authority as the living.
G. The ancestors are also expected to lend assistance for other affairs of the lineage, such as marriage proposals and the success of a newborn.
H. The Suku go to any grave of any ancestor who was older than them to make these appeals.
J. This is a generalized pattern for most African ancestor cults with some local variations to be expected.

[2]

[1] The Suku do not even have a word for *ancestor,* <u>while they do have a term for *grave* and *long ago*</u> (51). [2] The role of the dead is <u>much the same as it was when they were living which is that they</u> (52) are merely on another level in the rigid structure of elder relationships within the lineage. [3] A <u>Suku, of any age, calls himself, Kusu, the name of his lineage</u> (53), until someone senior to him arrives and is then called Kusu. [4] Appeals for <u>authority, help, and advice</u> (54) are made only to the immediately previous generation of elders, never skipping a generation.

51. Which choice most effectively and appropriately expands the idea introduced in the sentence?

A. NO CHANGE
B. but they have a term for *grave* and *long ago,* which signifies their acknowledgment of the dead
C. while they have many terms that relate to elders and lines of authority
D. yet the single term *mbuta* refers to all elders without distinguishing between the living and the dead

52. **F.** NO CHANGE
G. much the same as it was when they were living; they
H. the same as when they were living and they
J. that they

53. **A.** NO CHANGE
B. Suku of any age calls himself Kusu, the name of his lineage
C. Suku, of any age, calls himself Kusu the name of his lineage
D. Suku of any age calls himself, "Kusu," the name of his lineage

54. **F.** NO CHANGE
G. authority help and advice
H. authority help, and advice
J. authority; help and advice

CONTINUE

[5] As such, the last living elders turn to their elders even if they are deceased. [6] Authority is fluid any (55) man is an elder until an older Suku appears. [56]

55. A. NO CHANGE
B. fluid; any
C. fluid, any
D. fluid—any

56. Which of the following provides the most logical ordering of the sentences in Paragraph 2?
F. NO CHANGE
G. 1, 3, 2, 4, 5, 6
H. 1, 2, 4, 5, 3, 6
J. 1, 2, 4, 5, 6, 3

[3]

Elders intervene in the lives of their juniors due to the fact that the dead are expected to affect the lives of the living. The powers of the elders derive from the powers of her (57) ancestors.

57. A. NO CHANGE
B. their
C. its
D. his

The Suku worship both dead or living elders, (58) believing that each male in the lineage is an elder, even if he happens to be dead. [59]

58. F. NO CHANGE
G. dead if living elders
H. dead but living elders
J. dead and living elders

59. The writer wishes to add another relevant example to Paragraph 3 in order to show how the Suku honor the dead like the living. Which of the following sentences would best further the writer's purpose?
A. A sheep sacrifice to an elder is not a prayer offering but a tribute or gift the elder would have received if alive.
B. The oldest of the living Suku elders will go to a grave or crossroads at night and bury food the ancestor enjoyed in life.
C. The place of the dead in Suku lineage is paralleled by the European custom of leaving an empty chair at the table to signify a missing elder.
D. Other tribes, like the Songye, transfer attention from the dead to the living by believing the ancestors are reincarnated in the grandchildren and thus honor newborns.

Question 60 asks about the essay as a whole.

60. Which of the following statements most effectively summarizes the essay as a whole?

F. The ancestors of the Suku are worshiped because they exercise authority over all the elders and owe protection to the entire lineage.
G. The Suku have arranged their society into complex levels of eldership, each determined by age or death.
H. The Suku give tribute to their elders for their authority, advice, and assistance, whether those elders are alive or dead.
J. The ancestors of the Suku are not dead in a Western sense, because their powers are not supernatural but are the same powers the living elders possess.

PASSAGE V

Departures

[1]

One of my more favorite destinations in my youth (61) was the airport, even though I never went anywhere. Departure wasn't even part of my realm of possibilities in those days (62) because cherished relatives came from afar to visit my family and my (63) parents always taked (64) me along on their drives back to the airport when my relatives would abandon me until the next visit. The

61. A. NO CHANGE
B. my favorite destinations when I was young
C. my favoritest destinations in my youth
D. my most youthful favorite destinations

62. F. NO CHANGE
G. (move to after *Departure*)
H. (move to after *even*)
J. (move to after *afar*)

63. A. NO CHANGE
B. family; my
C. family. My
D. family because my

64. F. NO CHANGE
G. had always taked
H. always taken
J. always took

CONTINUE

glorious flying machines—so shiny and aerodynamic—taxied imperiously before picture windows the size of movie screens. (65)

It was like Tinsel-town—like one of the Saturday matinees I so loved to attend. (66) Who wouldn't delight in soaring through the clouds in these sleek missiles?

[2]

On my first flight, I was filled with unadulterated joy and wonder. Having (67) never been thousands of feet up in the air before. I was enjoying a vacation, caring little about life's problems, and that flying was less mystifying than I expected. (68) However, my next experience in an airport transformed my attitude towards the place (and forever ruined the innocence of comings and goings.) (69) My father was offered a job overseas and would not return for a

65. The writer intends here to emphasize how unfamiliar, mysterious, and alluring the planes and the idea of travel were to him. Given that all of the statements are true, which choice would best accomplish the writer's goal?

- **A.** NO CHANGE
- **B.** identical except in size to my toy models back home
- **C.** promising adventures I had yet to experience
- **D.** terrifying with their whirling blades and screaming engines

66.
- **F.** NO CHANGE
- **G.** It was like Tinsel-town—I could almost taste the popcorn.
- **H.** It was like Tinsel-town—movies were the only way I had ever seen air travel before.
- **J.** OMIT the underlined portion.

67.
- **A.** NO CHANGE
- **B.** wonder, having
- **C.** wonder having
- **D.** was wonderful having

68.
- **F.** NO CHANGE
- **G.** that I had expected flying to be more mystifying than it was.
- **H.** to be flying, which I had expected to be mystifying.
- **J.** flying through the air with the greatest of ease.

69.
- **A.** NO CHANGE
- **B.** place. And forever ruined the innocence of comings and goings.
- **C.** place and forever ruined the innocence of comings and goings.
- **D.** place; and forever ruined the innocence of comings and goings.

year. Standing in the waiting area by the gate, I sensed the loneliness, the loss, the unhappy good-byes all around me. [70]

70. The writer wishes to add another sentence to the end of this paragraph that would emphasize his theme of how the connotations of a place can change. Which of the following sentences does that best?

F. The brand new plastic smell of airplanes brought back memories of the magic found here.
G. He had been offered an excellent salary and a great promotion, and he couldn't say no.
H. Other businessmen boarded the plane without a wave, but airports to them were all business, nothing more.
J. The gate area had changed little since I was a child, only now I noticed that it could use a paint job.

[3]

Before too many years had passed, I would be on the other end of that boarding <u>ramp, the part that connects to the hatch door on the airplane itself</u> (71). After receiving a scholarship to a distant university, I found myself blowing kisses to tear-stained faces, trembling chins, and stiff upper lips. I had to be their <u>brave, unwavering, football, player</u> (72) who wouldn't let family and friends feel left behind.

71. A. NO CHANGE
B. ramp, which is the bridge-like structure that connects the airplane hatch to the gate
C. ramp, walking down the part that connects to the hatch door on the airplane itself
D. ramp

72. F. NO CHANGE
G. brave unwavering football player
H. brave, unwavering, and football player
J. brave, unwavering football player

[4]

Today, when my family and I pick up loved ones at the airport, my children are as excited <u>as me</u> (73).

73. A. NO CHANGE
B. as I used to be
C. as we all are
D. as I am

CONTINUE

But unfortunately, as I dance with ghosts, awash in lost moments, the rushing, the lost bags, the missed connections, the never coming home again. They can close all of the airports down as far as I'm concerned. I'll go by rail. I'm not effected one way or the other by train stations.

74. **F.** NO CHANGE
G. But unfortunately, as I dance with ghosts, awash in lost moments, the rushing, the lost bags, the missed connections are the never coming home again.
H. But unfortunately, as I dance with ghosts, awash in lost moments, airports will forever be to me the rushing, the lost bags, the missed connections, the never coming home again.
J. But unfortunately, as I dance with ghosts, awash in lost moments, there is the rushing, the lost bags, the missed connections, and the never coming home again.

75. **A.** NO CHANGE
B. I show no affects
C. I am not effected
D. I'm not affected

STOP

MATHEMATICS TEST

60 MINUTES—60 QUESTIONS

DIRECTIONS: For each question, solve each problem, select the correct answer, and fill in the corresponding circle on the answer sheet.

Do not spend too much time on problems that you cannot solve quickly. Answer as many questions as you can; then return to the others in the time remaining for this test.

You are allowed to use a calculator on this test. Although you may use your calculator for any problem on this test, keep in mind that some of the problems may be solved more efficiently without using a calculator.

SHOW YOUR WORK HERE

Note: Unless otherwise stated, assume the following:

1. Illustrative figures are NOT necessarily drawn to scale.
2. Geometric figures lie in a plane.
3. The word *line* indicates a straight line.
4. The word *average* indicates arithmetic mean.

1. A cat food company conducted a poll of people who bought its product. When the marketing director asked 400 people to select one of three colors for new packaging, 150 people chose blue, 200 people chose red, and the rest chose green. Of the people questioned, what percentage chose green?

A. 12.5%
B. 25%
C. 37.5%
D. 50%
E. 87.5%

2. A *hand* is a unit of length equivalent to 4 inches. If the height of a horse's back is 57 inches, what is the height of the horse's back in hands?

F. 10
G. 14.25
H. 53
J. 142.5
K. 228

3. In a certain parking lot, $\frac{1}{8}$ of the cars are convertibles and $\frac{3}{4}$ of the convertibles are red. If there are 22 convertibles in the lot that are NOT red, what is the total number of cars parked in the lot?

A. 88
B. 176
C. 526
D. 616
E. 704

CONTINUE

4. What value of z makes the following proportion true?

SHOW YOUR WORK HERE

$$\frac{15}{3z}=\frac{10}{4}$$

F. 2

G. $2\frac{1}{2}$

H. 5

J. 6

K. 30

5. Airplane A travels at a constant speed of 540 miles per hour for 3 hours. Airplane B travels at a constant speed of 400 miles per hour for 3 hours and 30 minutes. What is the total number of miles traveled by the two airplanes?

A. 1,400

B. 1,620

C. 3,020

D. 3,090

E. 6,110

6. The upload speed offered by an internet provider is x megabits per second. If running several Wi-Fi™ devices in a house decreases this speed by 12%, what is the upload speed in such case?

F. $0.12x$

G. $x - 0.12$

H. $0.88 + x$

J. $0.88x$

K. $\frac{12x}{88}$

7. What is the value of $-a^2(1 - 3a)$ when $a = -2$?

A. −28

B. −20

C. −16

D. 20

E. 28

8. If $f(x) = 2x^2 - 3x + 6$, what is the value of $f(3)$?

F. 5

G. 6

H. 9

J. 15

K. 33

9. Suppose the point $M(-3,1)$ is the midpoint of the line segment $\overline{AB}$, where A has coordinates $(7, -9)$. What are the coordinates of the other endpoint B?

A. (11, −13)
B. (1, −7)
C. (−7, 1)
D. (−13, 11)
E. (2, −4)

SHOW YOUR WORK HERE

10. For $i = \sqrt{-1}$, compute $-i(2 - 5i)^2$.

F. $20 - 21i$
G. $-20 + 21i$
H. $-20 + 29i$
J. $-21 - 20i$
K. $-29i$

11. A student listened to a radio station for eight separate half-hour sessions. He counted the number of songs played during each session and listed the results in the table below.

Number of songs	6	8	9	12
Number of sessions	1	3	2	2

What is the average number of songs played per half-hour?

A. 4.375
B. 8.5
C. 8.75
D. 9
E. 18

12. If $(m + 4)(m - 2) = 0$, which of the following is a possible value of m?

F. 0
G. 2
H. 4
J. 6
K. 8

13. What is the value of $|7| + |-9|$?

A. −63
B. −2
C. 2
D. 16
E. 63

CONTINUE

14. In the figure below, $\overline{UV}$ is perpendicular to both $\overline{PQ}$ and $\overline{ST}$. What is the measure of angle *VRW*?

SHOW YOUR WORK HERE

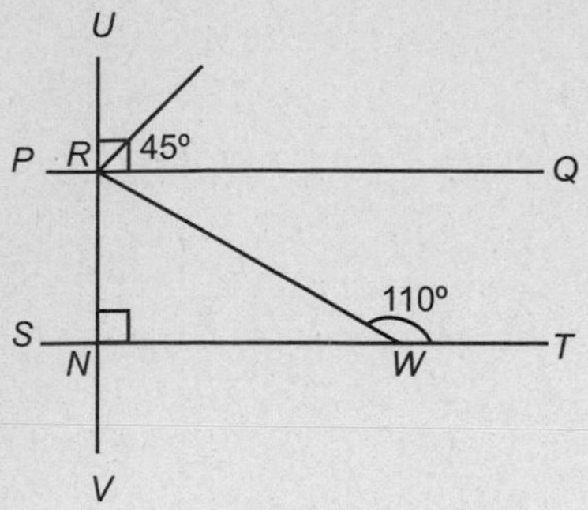

F. 20°

G. 45°

H. 70°

J. 90°

K. 110°

15. A solution of the equation $x^2 = 155$ lies between which two consecutive negative integers?

A. –14 and –15

B. –15 and –16

C. –12 and –13

D. –13 and –14

E. –11 and –12

16. What is the least common multiple for the set of whole numbers 12, 18, 24?

F. 2

G. 6

H. 48

J. 72

K. 144

17. How many times does the graph of $y = x^2 + 4x - 21$ intersect the *x*-axis?

A. 0

B. 1

C. 2

D. 3

E. 4

18. If rectangle *ABCD* is rotated 180°, centered at point *A*, what are the new coordinates of point *C*?

SHOW YOUR WORK HERE

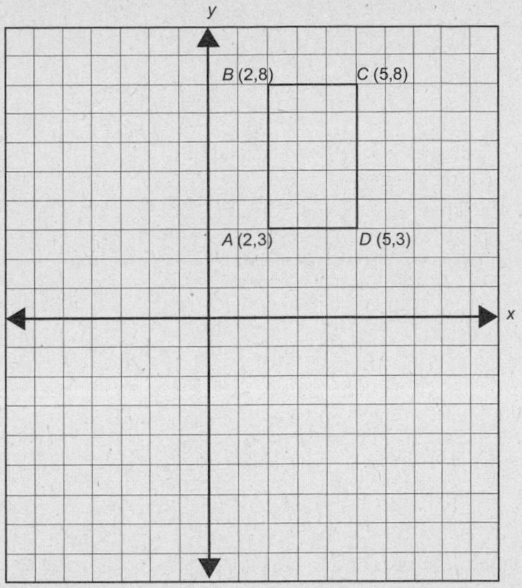

F. (7, 0)
G. (–3, 6)
H. (2, –2)
J. (–1, 3)
K. (–1, –2)

19. A farmer uses baskets to deliver apples to the local fruit stand. Each basket can hold 20 apples. Which equation represents the relationship between the number of apples, *a*, and the number of baskets, *b*?

A. $b = \frac{a}{20}$

B. $a = \frac{b}{20}$

C. $b = \frac{20}{a}$

D. $20 = \frac{b}{a}$

E. $b = 20a$

20. What is the equation of the line passing through the points (4, –4) and (–4, 8)?

F. $3x + 2y = 4$
G. $-3x + 2y = 4$
H. $2x + 3y = -4$
J. $2x - 3y = 4$
K. $3x + 2y = -8$

21. Which number is NOT a factor of 96?

A. 2
B. 3
C. 16
D. 18
E. 24

CONTINUE

22. The sale price of an ultra HD television is \$2,250. If this is the price after a 15% discount has been applied, which expression represents the original price of the television?

SHOW YOUR WORK HERE

F. 0.85(2,250) dollars

G. 2,250 + 0.85 dollars

H. $\frac{2,250}{1.15}$ dollars

J. 1.15(2,250) dollars

K. $\frac{2,250}{0.85}$ dollars

23. If $4x^2 - 25 = 0$ and $x > 0$, what is the value of x?

A. $-\frac{5}{2}$

B. $\frac{2}{5}$

C. $\frac{5}{4}$

D. $\frac{5}{2}$

E. $\frac{25}{4}$

24. In a group of 40 students, each student is asked to identify math, history, or art as his or her favorite class. The probability that a student chosen randomly from this group did NOT say math is his or her favorite is $\frac{1}{5}$.

How many students said math is their favorite?

F. 8

G. 10

H. 20

J. 32

K. 36

25. What is the y-intercept, if one exists, of the function $k(x) = -2\sqrt{25-5x}$?

A. no y-intercept

B. (0, 5)

C. (0, –10)

D. (0, –50)

E. (5, 0)

26. There are 8 fluid ounces in a cup. If 9 cups of imported olive oil cost $23.04, what is the cost per fluid ounce?

F. $0.24
G. $0.32
H. $1.36
J. $2.56
K. $2.88

27. The length of a rectangle is 6 inches greater than the width. If the perimeter of the rectangle is 44 inches, what is the area of the rectangle, in square inches?

A. 55
B. 112
C. 121
D. 187
E. 475

28. What is the *x*-intercept of the line whose equation is $2y = 1 - 4x$?

F. $\frac{1}{4}$
G. $\frac{1}{2}$
H. 2
J. 4
K. 8

29. A broadcasting network shows 5 commercial segments during a 30-minute sit-com. The lengths of four of these segments are 85 seconds, 125 seconds, 95 seconds, and 145 seconds. For the average length of the five segments to be 130 seconds, what must be the length of the fifth segment?

A. 70 seconds
B. 100 seconds
C. 130 seconds
D. 200 seconds
E. 650 seconds

SHOW YOUR WORK HERE

CONTINUE

30. In triangle *PQR* below, what is the cosine of angle *P*?

SHOW YOUR WORK HERE

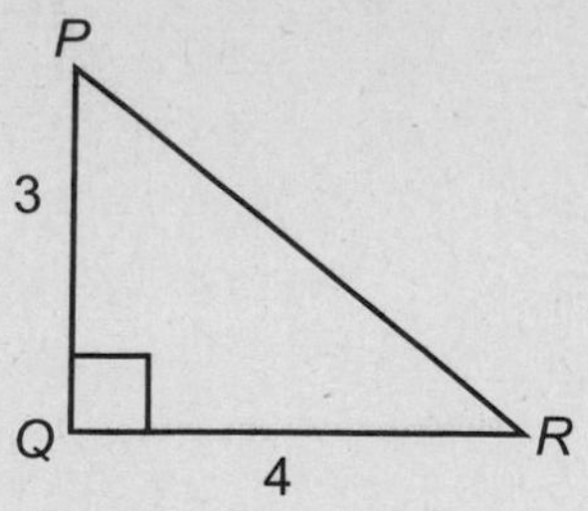

F. $\frac{3}{4}$

G. $\frac{3}{5}$

H. $\frac{4}{3}$

J. $\frac{4}{5}$

K. $\frac{5}{4}$

31. Maria bought music CDs for her club. She bought 2 single CDs and 1 double CD, all on sale for 30% off. The single CDs regularly cost \$16 each, and the double CDs regularly cost \$24. Assuming no sales tax, how much in total did Maria pay for her CDs?

A. \$16.80
B. \$28
C. \$39.20
D. \$46.40
E. \$48.80

32. The average of a set of 7 integers is 13. When an eighth number is included in the set, the average of the set decreases to 12. What is the eighth number?

F. 4
G. 5
H. 8
J. 13
K. 25

33. For all nonzero values of a, b, and c,

$$\frac{-a^4\left(b^2\right)^4 c^6}{(-a)^3 b^3 c^8} = \underline{\hspace{2cm}}.$$

SHOW YOUR WORK HERE

A. $-\frac{ab^3}{c^2}$

B. $a^7b^{11}c^{14}$

C. $-a^{12}b^{24}c^{48}$

D. $\frac{ab^3}{c^2}$

E. $\frac{ab^5}{c^2}$

34. A small pump can remove water from a pool at the rate of 8.25 gallons per minute. How many minutes would it take to remove g gallons at this rate?

F. $8.25g$

G. $8.25 + g$

H. $\frac{8.25}{g}$

J. $g - 8.25$

K. $\frac{g}{8.25}$

35. If a square has perimeter 22 cm, what is its area?

A. 5.5 square centimeters

B. 11 square centimeters

C. 30.25 square centimeters

D. 44 square centimeters

E. 121 square centimeters

36. If $A = \begin{bmatrix} -2 & -3 \\ 1 & -1 \end{bmatrix}$ and $B = \begin{bmatrix} 4 & -2 \\ -3 & -1 \end{bmatrix}$, what is $2B - 3A$?

F. $\begin{bmatrix} 14 & 1 \\ -4 & 0 \end{bmatrix}$

G. $\begin{bmatrix} 2 & -13 \\ -3 & -5 \end{bmatrix}$

H. $\begin{bmatrix} 8 & -4 \\ -6 & -2 \end{bmatrix}$

J. $\begin{bmatrix} 14 & 5 \\ -9 & 1 \end{bmatrix}$

K. $\begin{bmatrix} -6 & -9 \\ 3 & -3 \end{bmatrix}$

CONTINUE

SHOW YOUR WORK HERE

37. How many x-intercepts does the graph of $f(x) = x(x^2 - 4)(x^2 + 9)$ have in the standard xy-plane?

A. 1
B. 2
C. 3
D. 5
E. 6

38. If $\log_3\left(\frac{1}{81}\right) = y$, what is y?

F. –27
G. –4
H. $\frac{1}{243}$
J. $\frac{1}{27}$
K. 4

39. If the graph of $g(x) = (x + 3)^2 - 2$ is translated 2 units to the right, what is the range of the resulting function?

A. $(-\infty,\infty)$
B. $(-\infty,-1]$
C. $[-2,\infty)$
D. $[-1,\infty)$
E. $(-\infty,-2]$

40. In the diagram below, a circle is inscribed in a square. If the radius of the circle is 3 units, what is the area of the square, in square units?

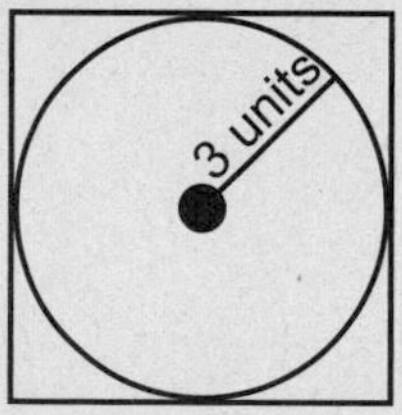

F. 9
G. 24
H. 28
J. 36
K. 113

SHOW YOUR WORK HERE

41. For real numbers a, b, and c, $a > b$ and $c < 0$. Which of the following inequalities must be true?

A. $ab > 0$

B. $ac < 0$

C. $\frac{a}{b} > \frac{c}{b}$

D. $\frac{a}{c} > \frac{b}{c}$

E. $\frac{a}{c} < \frac{b}{c}$

42. The rectangular picture shown below has a shaded frame that is 2 inches wide. What is the area, in square inches, of the frame?

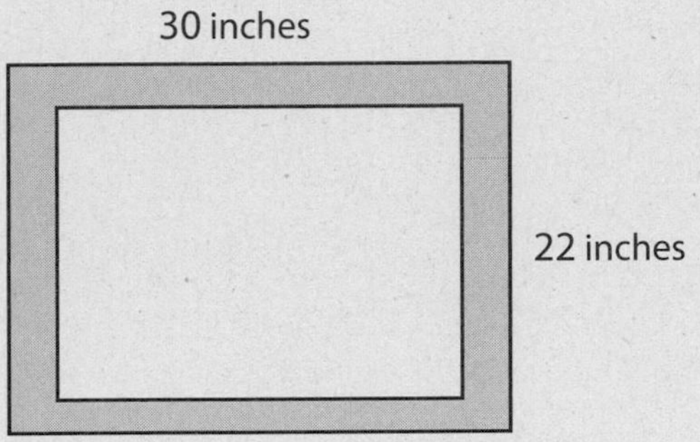

F. 468
G. 192
H. 132
J. 96
K. 48

43. If m is a negative integer and n is a positive integer, which of the following must be true?

A. $|m-n| = |m| - |n|$

B. $|m-n| = |m+n|$

C. $|m-n| \leq |m| - |n|$

D. $|m-n| = -|m+n|$

E. $|m-n| \neq 0$

44. For what value of a, if any, does the system $\begin{cases} y = 5x - 1 \\ x = ay - 1 \end{cases}$ have infinitely many solutions?

F. –5

G. $-\frac{1}{5}$

H. $\frac{1}{5}$

J. 5

K. No such value of a

CONTINUE

45. What is the equation of the line passing through the point (–2, –1) that is parallel to the line whose equation is $x = -\frac{1}{3}y + 4$?

A. $3x - y + 5 = 0$

B. $3x + y = 1 = 0$

C. $3x - y - 1 = 0$

D. $x + 3y + 5 = 0$

E. $3x + y + 7 = 0$

SHOW YOUR WORK HERE

46. A right triangle has a hypotenuse of 17 and a leg of 15. What is the length of the other leg?

F. 4

G. $\sqrt{32}$

H. 8

J. $\sqrt{514}$

K. 64

47. Suppose (a, –b) and (b, –a) are points in the *xy*-plane. Which of these expressions represents the distance between these two points?

A. $2a$

B. $\sqrt{2}\,|a - b|$

C. $\sqrt{2}\,|a| + \sqrt{2}\,|b|$

D. $\sqrt{2(a^2 + b^2)}$

E. $2(a - b)^2$

48. The temperature at 9 a.m. is –15.5°C. The temperature at 10 a.m. is –13.0°C. If the temperature changes by the same amount each hour, what will the temperature be at 1 p.m.?

F. –20.5°C

G. –8.0°C

H. –5.5°C

J. 2.5°C

K. 7.5°C

SHOW YOUR WORK HERE

49. A line passes through the points $\left(-\frac{4}{5}, \frac{1}{2}\right)$ and $\left(\frac{3}{10}, -\frac{5}{6}\right)$. What is the slope of a line perpendicular to this line?

A. $-\frac{40}{33}$

B. $-\frac{33}{40}$

C. $\frac{40}{33}$

D. $\frac{33}{40}$

E. $-\frac{22}{15}$

50. From the top of an airport control tower, the angle between a horizontal line and an approaching airplane is 27°, as shown below. If the distance between the control tower and the airplane is 35,000 meters, what is the difference, in meters, between the altitude of the plane and the top of the control tower?

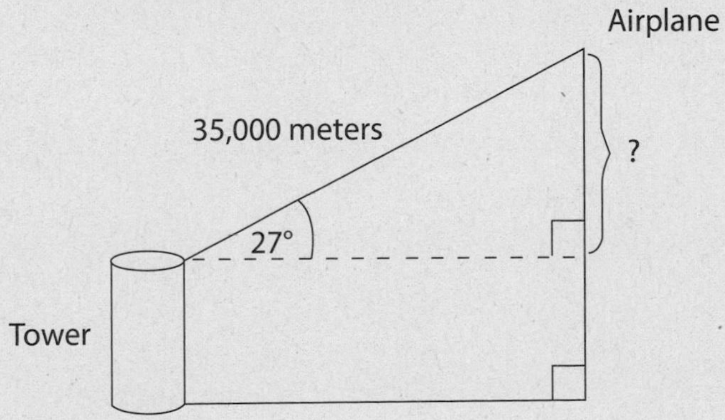

F. $35{,}000 \times \sin 63°$

G. $35{,}000 \times \sin 27°$

H. $35{,}000 \times \cos 27°$

J. $\frac{35{,}000}{\sin 27°}$

K. $\frac{35{,}000}{\cos 27°}$

51. The length of the floor of a rectangular storage closet is four feet more than twice the width. If the perimeter is 62 feet, what is the area of the floor of the closet?

A. 9 square feet

B. 22 square feet

C. 81 square feet

D. 124 square feet

E. 198 square feet

CONTINUE

SHOW YOUR WORK HERE

52. A balanced six-sided die with faces 1, 2, 3, 4, 5, 6 is rolled twice. What is the probability of getting one 5 and one 6?

F. $\frac{1}{3}$

G. $\frac{17}{18}$

H. $\frac{1}{18}$

J. $\frac{5}{9}$

K. $\frac{1}{6}$

53. During the winter months, the thermostat in a sunroom is programmed to increase the temperature by 25% at 6 a.m. to warm it up. Once it reaches this temperature, it decreases the temperature by 10% and keeps it there for the duration of the day. If the starting temperature in the sunroom is 60˚F, what is the final temperature?

A. 62.5˚F
B. 65˚F
C. 67.5˚F
D. 75˚F
E. 76.5˚F

54. If W and Z represent the solutions of the equation $2x(4x - 3) = 3(3 - 4x)$, what is the value of $W \bullet Z$?

F. $-\frac{9}{8}$

G. $-\frac{3}{4}$

H. $-\frac{8}{9}$

J. $\frac{8}{9}$

K. $\frac{9}{8}$

55. A bucket contains 10 red balls, 5 blue balls, 3 green balls, and 2 yellow balls. What is the probability of randomly selecting a ball that is neither blue nor yellow?

A. 0.25
B. 0.35
C. 0.65
D. 0.75
E. 0.90

56. If $f(x)=\dfrac{1}{x+2}$ and $g(x)=\dfrac{3}{2x}$, compute $(f\circ g)(-4)$.

SHOW YOUR WORK HERE

F. -3

G. $-\dfrac{3}{8}$

H. $-\dfrac{1}{2}$

J. $\dfrac{3}{16}$

K. $\dfrac{8}{13}$

57. Jane can row 300 meters in 80 seconds. If she maintained this pace, how many kilometers would she row in one hour?

A. 9.6
B. 10.8
C. 13.5
D. 18
E. 45

58. The formula for the volume of a right circular cone is $V=\dfrac{1}{3}\pi r^2 h$, where r is the radius of the base and h is the height. If the radius is tripled and the height is doubled, by what factor is the volume increased?

F. 2
G. 3
H. 6
J. 9
K. 18

59. What is the maximum value of $y = 4\sin(3x) - 1$?

A. 0
B. 1
C. 3
D. 4
E. 5

60. For every point on a certain line in the standard (x, y) coordinate plane, two times the x-coordinate plus three times the y-coordinate is equal to 12. What is the slope of this line?

F. $-\dfrac{3}{2}$

G. $-\dfrac{2}{3}$

H. $\dfrac{1}{6}$

J. $\dfrac{2}{3}$

K. 4

STOP

READING TEST

35 Minutes—40 Questions

DIRECTIONS: There are four passages in this test. Each passage is followed by several questions. Read each passage, select the best answer to each related question, and fill in the corresponding circle on the answer sheet. You may look back at the passages as often as you need.

PASSAGE I

PROSE FICTION: Passage A is an excerpt from *The Time Machine* by H.G. Wells. Passage B is an excerpt from *Twenty Thousand Leagues Under the Sea* by Jules Verne.

Passage A

by H.G. Wells

The thing the Time Traveller held in his hand was a glittering metallic framework, scarcely larger than a small clock, and very delicately made. There was ivory in it, and some transparent crystalline substance. And now I must be explicit, for this that follows—unless his explanation is to be accepted—is an absolutely unaccountable thing. He took one of the small octagonal tables that were scattered about the room, and set it in front of the fire, with two legs on the hearthrug. On this table he placed the mechanism. Then he drew up a chair, and sat down. The only other object on the table was a small shaded lamp, the bright light of which fell upon the model. There were also perhaps a dozen candles about, two in brass candlesticks upon the mantel and several in sconces, so that the room was brilliantly illuminated. I sat in a low arm-chair nearest the fire, and I drew this forward so as to be almost between the Time Traveller and the fireplace. Filby sat behind him, looking over his shoulder. The Medical Man and the Provincial Mayor watched him in profile from the right, the Psychologist from the left. The Very Young Man stood behind the Psychologist. We were all on the alert. It appears incredible to me that any kind of trick, however subtly conceived and however adroitly done, could have been played upon us under these conditions.

The Time Traveller looked at us, and then at the mechanism. 'Well?' said the Psychologist.

'This little affair,' said the Time Traveller, resting his elbows upon the table and pressing his hands together above the apparatus, 'is only a model. It is my plan for a machine to travel through time. You will notice that it looks singularly askew, and that there is an odd twinkling appearance about this bar, as though it was in some way unreal.' He pointed to the part with his finger. 'Also, here is one little white lever, and here is another.'

The Medical Man got up out of his chair and peered into the thing. 'It's beautifully made,' he said.

'It took two years to make,' retorted the Time Traveller. Then, when we had all imitated the action of the Medical Man, he said: 'Now I want you clearly to understand that this lever, being pressed over, sends the machine gliding into the future, and this other reverses the motion. This saddle represents the seat of a time traveller. Presently I am going to press the lever, and off the machine will go. It will vanish, pass into future Time, and disappear. Have a good look at the thing. Look at the table too, and satisfy yourselves there is no trickery. I don't want to waste this model, and then be told I'm a quack.'

Passage B

by Jules Verne

Clearly we could do nothing but submit, and afterwards Captain Nemo showed me his wondrous craft … It was indeed a thing of marvels; for, besides the dining-room, it contained a large library of twelve thousand volumes, a drawing-room measuring thirty feet by eighteen, and fifteen high. The walls of this apartment were adorned with masterpieces of the great painters, and beautiful marbles and bronzes. A large piano-organ stood in one corner, and there were glass cases containing the rarest marine curiosities which a naturalist could wish to see. A collection of enormous pearls in a cabinet must have been worth millions, and Captain Nemo told me he had rifled every sea to find them.

The room assigned to me was fitted up with every luxury, yet the captain's own apartment was as simply furnished as a monastic cell, but in it were contained all the ingenious instruments that controlled the movements of the *Nautilus*, as his submarine was named. The electricity was manufactured by a process of extracting chloride of sodium from the sea-water, but the fresh air necessary for the life of the crew could only be obtained by rising to the surface. The engine-room was sixty-five feet long, and in it was the machinery for producing electricity as well as that for applying the power to the propeller.

The *Nautilus*, Captain Nemo explained, was capable of a speed of fifty miles an hour, and could be made to sink or rise

CONTINUE

with precision by flooding or emptying a reservoir. In a box, raised somewhat above the hull and fitted with glass ten inches thick, the steersman had his place, and a powerful electric reflector behind him illumined the sea for half a mile in front.

The submarine also carried a small torpedo-like boat, fitted in a groove along the top, so that it could be entered from the *Nautilus* by opening a panel, and, after that was closed, the boat could be detached from the submarine, and would then bob upwards to the surface like a cork. The importance of this and its bearing on my story will appear in due time.

It was on a desert island that Captain Nemo had carried out the building of the *Nautilus*, and from many different places he had secured the various parts of the hull and machinery, in order to maintain secrecy.

Deeply interested as I was in every detail of this extraordinary vessel, and excited beyond measure at the wonders which awaited me in exploring the world beneath the waves, I had still the feeling of a prisoner who dared scarcely hope that liberty might some day be obtained. But when the metal plates which covered the windows of the saloon were rolled back as we sailed under the water, and on each hand I could see a thronging army of many-coloured aquatic creatures swimming around us, attracted by our light, I was in an ecstasy of wonder and delight.

Questions 1–3 ask about Passage A.

1. According to the first paragraph (lines 1–22), the model of the time travelling apparatus contains:

A. glitter.
B. crystal.
C. ivory.
D. wax.

2. It can be reasonably inferred from the passage that the Time Traveller is:

F. worried his time travelling apparatus will not work.
G. not concerned about what people think of him.
H. trying to make fools of his colleagues.
J. proud of his time travelling apparatus.

3. As depicted in the passage, the Medical Man's feelings toward the model of the time travelling apparatus can best be described as:

A. amused.
B. ambivalent.
C. fearful.
D. admiring.

Questions 4–6 ask about Passage B.

4. It can be inferred that Captain Nemo:

F. values extravagance.
G. has specific goals.
H. avoids people.
J. values function over comfort.

5. The passage suggests that the narrator feels:

A. completely honored to have access to the *Nautilus*.
B. both amazed and uneasy in the *Nautilus*.
C. like a co-owner of the *Nautilus*.
D. terrified being underwater in the *Nautilus*.

6. As it is used in line 1, the word *submit* most nearly means:

F. surrender.
G. quit.
H. humor.
J. send.

Questions 7–10 ask about both passages.

7. Both the Time Traveller and Captain Nemo:

A. invite people into their machines.
B. build dangerous weapons.
C. build unusual machines.
D. explore the oceans.

8. Which of the following is known about the *Nautilus* but NOT known about the time machine?

F. How long it took to build
G. Where it was built
H. Who built it
J. How it looks

9. It can be inferred from the passages that the Time Traveller and Captain Nemo are both:

A. tiresome eccentrics.
B. plotting something evil.
C. original thinkers.
D. wary of danger.

10. Which of the following is something Captain Nemo needs that the Time Traveller DOES NOT?

F. Secrecy
G. Credibility
H. Music
J. Adventure

PASSAGE II

SOCIAL SCIENCE: The following passage is adapted from a book that called for the equal treatment of women and men written in 1792.

To do every thing in an orderly manner is a most important precept, which women, who, generally speaking, receive only a disorderly kind of education, seldom attend to with that degree of exactness that men, who from their infancy are broken into method, observe. This negligent kind of guesswork, for what other epithet can be used to point out the random exertions of a sort of instinctive common sense, never brought to the test of reason prevents their generalizing matters of fact, so they do today, what they did yesterday, merely because they did it yesterday.

This contempt of the understanding in early life has more baneful consequences than is commonly supposed for the little knowledge which women of strong minds attain is, from various circumstances, of a more desultory kind than the knowledge of men, and it is acquired more by sheer observations on real life, than from comparing what has been individually observed with the results of experience generalized by speculation. Led by their dependent situation and domestic employments more into society, what they learn is rather by snatches, and as learning is with them, in general, only a secondary thing, they do not pursue any one branch with that persevering ardor necessary to give vigor to the faculties and clearness to the judgment. In the present state of society, a little learning is required to support the character of a gentleman, and boys are obliged to submit to a few years of discipline. But in the education of women, the cultivation of the understanding is always subordinate to the acquirement of some corporeal accomplishment; even while enervated by confinement and false notions of modesty, the body is prevented from attaining that grace and beauty which relaxed half-formed limbs never exhibit. Besides, in youth their faculties are not brought forward by emulation, and having no serious scientific study, if they have natural sagacity it is turned too soon on life and manners. They dwell on effects and modifications without tracing them back to causes, and complicated rules to adjust behavior are a weak substitute for simple principles.

As a proof that education gives this appearance of weakness to females, we may instance the example of military men, who are, like them, sent into the world before their minds have been stored with knowledge or fortified by principles. The consequences are similar: soldiers acquire a little superficial knowledge snatched from the muddy current of conversation, and from continually mixing with society, they gain what is termed a knowledge of the world, and this acquaintance with manners and customs has frequently been confounded with a knowledge of the human heart. But can the crude fruit of casual observation, never brought to the test of judgment, formed by comparing speculation and experience, deserve such a distinction? Soldiers, as well as women, practice the minor virtues with punctilious politeness. Where is then the sexual difference when the education has been the same; all the difference that I can discern arises from the superior advantage of liberty which enables the former to see more of life.

It is wandering from my present subject, perhaps, to make a political remark, but as it was produced naturally by the train of my reflections, I shall not pass it silently over.

Standing armies can never consist of resolute, robust men; they may be well-disciplined machines, but they will seldom contain men under the influence of strong passions or with very vigorous faculties. And as for any depth of understanding, I will venture to affirm, that it is as rarely to be found in the army as amongst women, and the cause, I maintain, is the same. It may be further observed that officers are also particularly attentive to their persons, fond of dancing, crowded rooms, adventures, and ridicule. Like the FAIR sex, the business of their lives is gallantry. They were taught to please, and they only live to please. Yet they do not lose their rank in the distinction of sexes for they are still reckoned superior to women, though in what their superiority consists, beyond what I have just mentioned, it is difficult to discover.

The great misfortune is that they both acquire manners before morals, and a knowledge of life before they have from reflection, any acquaintance with the grand ideal outline of human nature. The consequence is natural: satisfied with common nature, they become a prey to prejudices, and taking all their opinions on credit, they blindly submit to authority. So that if they have any sense, it is a kind of instinctive glance, that catches proportions, and decides with respect to manners; but fails when arguments are to be pursued below the surface, or opinions analyzed.

CONTINUE

11. From the statement "This negligent kind of guesswork, for what other epithet can be used to point out the random exertions of a sort of instinctive common sense, never brought to the test of reason prevents their generalizing matters of fact" (lines 5–8), it can be inferred that:

A. common sense is no substitute for a formal education.
B. guessing is an important aspect of any education.
C. no one is educated without learning to have common sense.
D. events tend to be random and can only be understood with common sense.

12. What is the main idea of the fifth paragraph (lines 56–69)?

F. Both women and soldiers are taught to please others rather than be well educated.
G. Society considers military men to be superior to women because military men risk their lives.
H. Soldiers are often considered to be superior to women even though they both follow orders.
J. The military discourages soldiers from being passionate or vigorously intellectual.

13. The passage mentions that women and soldiers tend to receive educations that begin with the acquisition of:

A. morals.
B. grace.
C. gallantry.
D. virtuousness.

14. The author describes soldiers as:

I. men with vigorous faculties.
II. resolute, robust men.
III. well-disciplined machines.

F. I only
G. II only
H. III only
J. I, II, and III

15. According to the second paragraph (lines 11–35), women are expected to learn more by observation than by:

A. contempt.
B. experience.
C. knowledge.
D. comparison.

16. The author's statement, "But in the education of women, the cultivation of the understanding is always subordinate to the acquirement of some corporeal accomplishment" (lines 25–27) means that:

F. society tends to be more concerned with the way women appear than with how women think.
G. women cannot cultivate understanding if they are concerned with how they appear.
H. women should receive a much better education and society needs to change the way it treats women.
J. women need to adjust to the needs of society rather than society needing to change for the sake of women.

17. As it is used in line 42, the word *mixing* most nearly means:

A. combining.
B. stirring.
C. switching.
D. interacting.

18. According to this passage, society mainly expects women to:

F. receive formal educations.
G. perform domestic tasks.
H. be extremely observant.
J. join the military.

19. The author mentions that military officers tend to be fond of:

A. ridicule.
B. fighting.
C. studying.
D. politeness.

20. The passage as a whole can primarily be characterized as the narrator's:

F. explanation of why schooling is extremely flawed.
G. description of the ways that women are educated.
H. argument for allowing more women in the military.
J. concerns about inferior educational opportunities for women.

PASSAGE III

HUMANITIES: The following passage is adapted from *The Problems of Philosophy* in which philosopher Bertrand Russell discusses the problems with his chosen field.

Is there any knowledge in the world which is so certain that no reasonable man could doubt it? This question, which at first sight might not seem difficult, is really one of the most difficult that can be asked. When we have realized the obstacles in the way of a straightforward and confident answer, we shall be well launched on the study of philosophy—for philosophy is merely the attempt to answer such ultimate questions, not carelessly and dogmatically, as we do in ordinary life and even in the sciences, but critically, after exploring all that makes such questions puzzling, and after realizing all the vagueness and confusion that underlie our ordinary ideas.

In daily life, we assume as certain many things which, on a closer scrutiny, are found to be so full of apparent contradictions that only a great amount of thought enables us to know what it is that we really may believe. In the search for certainty, it is natural to begin with our present experiences, and in some sense, no doubt, knowledge is to be derived from them. But any statement as to what it is that our immediate experiences make us know is very likely to be wrong. It seems to me that I am now sitting in a chair, at a table of a certain shape, on which I see sheets of paper with writing or print. By turning my head I see out of the window buildings and clouds and the sun. I believe that the sun is about ninety-three million miles from the earth; that it is a hot globe many times bigger than the earth; that, owing to the earth's rotation, it rises every morning, and will continue to do so for an indefinite time in the future. I believe that, if any other normal person comes into my room, he will see the same chairs and tables and books and papers as I see, and that the table which I see is the same as the table which I feel pressing against my arm. All this seems to be so evident as to be hardly worth stating, except in answer to a man who doubts whether I know anything. Yet all this may be reasonably doubted, and all of it requires much careful discussion before we can be sure that we have stated it in a form that is wholly true.

To make our difficulties plain, let us concentrate attention on the table. To the eye it is oblong, brown and shiny, to the touch it is smooth and cool and hard; when I tap it, it gives out a wooden sound. Any one else who sees and feels and hears the table will agree with this description, so that it might seem as if no difficulty would arise; but as soon as we try to be more precise our troubles begin. Although I believe that the table is 'really' of the same color all over, the parts that reflect the light look much brighter than the other parts, and some parts look white because of reflected light. I know that, if I move, the parts that reflect the light will be different, so that the apparent distribution of colors on the table will change. It follows that if several people are looking at the table at the same moment, no two of them will see exactly the same distribution of colors, because no two can see it from exactly the same point of view, and any change in the point of view makes some change in the way the light is reflected.

For most practical purposes these differences are unimportant, but to the painter they are all-important: the painter has to unlearn the habit of thinking that things seem to have the color which common sense says they 'really' have, and to learn the habit of seeing things as they appear. Here we have already the beginning of one of the distinctions that cause most trouble in philosophy—the distinction between 'appearance' and 'reality', between what things seem to be and what they are. The painter wants to know what things seem to be, the practical man and the philosopher want to know what they are; but the philosopher's wish to know this is stronger than the practical man's, and is more troubled by knowledge as to the difficulties of answering the question.

21. As it is used in line 5, the word *straightforward* most nearly means:

A. complex.
B. rapid.
C. honest.
D. uncomplicated.

22. It can be inferred from the passage that understanding:

F. is shared in the exact same way by all people.
G. may depend a great deal on personal perspectives.
H. can only be gained from years of study.
J. is something nobody can ever truly have.

23. In suggesting that basic conclusions about the world seem "to be so evident as to be hardly worth stating" (lines 30–31), the author means that:

A. people tend to take for granted the possibility that everyone does not share the same understanding of the world.
B. our shared understanding of the world is so clear that there is no point in even discussing it.
C. our shared understanding of the world is too confusing to ever be understood meaningfully.
D. people should spend more time enjoying their lives than trying to understand the world around them.

CONTINUE

24. The author explains that appearances can be affected by:

F. problems with eyesight.
G. changes in light.
H. shapes that shift.
J. the observer's attitude.

25. The main point of the third paragraph (lines 35–51) is that:

A. a table only *seems* to have a certain color, texture, shape, and temperature.
B. a particular object will always appear the same way to anyone who is observing it.
C. inanimate objects are capable of tricking people into perceiving them the wrong way.
D. there are many factors that affect the way an individual perceives a particular thing.

26. Which of the following statements is supported by the fourth paragraph (lines 52–64)?

F. Painters must unlearn the habit of thinking that things have a certain color.
G. Painters are troubled by the difficulties of answering questions about reality.
H. Painters are more practical than other people.
J. Painters are more concerned with appearances than reality.

27. The passage explains that the process of understanding begins with examining:

A. one's present experiences.
B. what is normal.
C. intense concentration.
D. a chair.

28. According to the passage, the philosopher's desire to understand reality:

F. relieves anything troubling about that desire.
G. is not as strong as the painter's desire to know what things seem to be.
H. is stronger than that of the practical man's.
J. is a pointless desire that must be avoided.

29. The author suggests that for most people, the differences in how objects appear:

A. can be extremely frustrating.
B. do not matter in any meaningful way.
C. can affect how those people work.
D. are more important than how those objects really are.

30. As it is used in line 13, the word *scrutiny* most likely means:

F. listening.
G. calling.
H. reading.
J. examination.

PASSAGE IV

NATURAL SCIENCE: The following passage is adapted from an article about ways that spiders protect themselves.

There are, among spiders, two forms of protective modification: the first, including all cases of protective resemblance to vegetable and inorganic things—that is, all modifications of color or of color and form that tend to make them inconspicuous in their natural relations—I shall call direct protection. The second form, which I shall call indirect protection, includes two classes: the spiders which are specially protected themselves and those which mimic other creatures which are specially protected.

Spiders are specially protected when they become inedible through the acquisition of hard plates and sharp spines. The modification of form is frequently accompanied by conspicuous colors, which warn their enemies that they belong to an unpalatable class.

The second class of indirectly protected spiders—those that mimic specially protected creatures—presents some difficulties, since it is not always easy to determine whether the purpose of mimicry is protection or the capture of prey. The resemblance may, as is frequently the case in direct protection, serve both purposes.

In looking for instances of protective form and color among spiders we encounter one difficulty at the outset. The meaning of a protective peculiarity can be determined only when the animal is seen in its natural home. The number of strangely modified forms depicted in descriptive works on spiders is enormous. Bodies are twisted, elongated, inflated, flattened, truncated, covered with tubercles or spines, enclosed within chitinous plates, colored like bark, like lichens, like flowers of every imaginable hue, like bird droppings, like sand or stones, and in every one of these modifications there is doubtless an adaptation of the spider to its surroundings which, when it is studied out of its natural relations, we can only guess at.

It has been well said that in these protective resemblances those features of the portrait are most attended to by nature which produce the most effective deception when seen in nature; the faithfulness of the resemblance being much less striking when seen in the cabinet. . . .

As a general rule the forms and colors of spiders are adapted to render them inconspicuous in their natural homes. Bright colored spiders. . . either keep hidden away or are found upon flowers whose tints harmonize with their own. This rule, while it has numerous exceptions, is borne out by the great majority of cases. A good illustration is found in the genus *Uloborus*, of which the members bear a deceptive resemblance to small pieces of bark or to such bits of rubbish as commonly become entangled in old deserted webs. The only species in our neighborhood is *Uloborus plumipes*, which I have almost invariably found building in dead branches, where its disguise is more effective than it would be among fresh leaves. The spider is always found in the middle of the web, with its legs extended in a line with the body. There has been, in this species, a development along several lines, resulting in a disguise of considerable complexity. Its form and color make it like a scrap of bark, its body being truncated and diversified with small humps, while its first legs are very uneven, bearing heavy fringes of hair on the tibia and having the terminal joints slender. Its color is a soft wood-brown or gray, mottled with white. It has the habit of hanging motionless in the web for hours at a time, swaying in the wind like an inanimate object. The strands of its web are rough and inelastic, so that they are frequently broken; this gives it the appearance of one of those dilapidated and deserted webs in which bits of wind-blown rubbish are frequently entangled. . .

Out of seven examples of the species taken during one summer, five were found in dead tamarack branches, one on a dead bush, and the seventh, an interesting variety, under the eaves of a porch. My eye was caught by what seemed to be a string of eleven cocoons (it is not common to see more than four in a web). On attempting to take them down, I was surprised to see one of the supposed cocoons begin to shake the web violently. Ten were what they seemed to be, but the eleventh was the mother spider, whose color and general appearance was exactly like that of the little cases that she had made for her eggs....

We come now to a large and interesting class in genus *Epeira*. I refer to those species, mostly nocturnal, which are protected during the day, not by hiding in crevices, nor in any way actually getting out of sight, but by the close resemblance which they bear to the bark of the trees to which they cling. This resemblance is brought about in two ways: through their color, which is like that of wood or lichens, and through their tuberculated and rugose forms, which resemble rough bark.

One of the most remarkable of these forms is *C. mitralis*, a Madagascar species, which, looked at in profile, probably resembles a woody knot. The abdomen is divided into two divergent cones. The entire upper surface of the body is covered with conical elevations, which render it rough and uneven; the sides of the abdomen are made up of several layers, which form stages, one above another, like the ridges of bark on a woody excrescence. The legs, formed of wide, flattened plates, make the base. The color of the spider is yellowish-gray, varied with white and dark reddish-brown. It has the habit of perching on a

CONTINUE

branch and clasping it like a bird, so that the elaborate modification of form, which would be useless if the spider hung exposed in the web, is made as effective as possible.

31. In the eighth paragraph (lines 73–80), the author claims that a class in genus *Epeira* is interesting because the spiders:

A. are protected during the day.
B. hide in crevices.
C. use camouflage for protection.
D. are mostly nocturnal.

32. The passage defines *C. mitralis* as a:

F. species of spider from Madagascar.
G. nocturnal species of spider.
H. spider found in tamarack branches.
J. spider that resembles bark or rubbish.

33. The passage explains that *Uloborus plumipes:*

I. lives in dead branches.
II. has a mottled appearance.
III. resembles fresh leaves.

A. I and II only
B. I and III only
C. II and III only
D. I, II, and III

34. One can tell by reading the passage that spiders:

F. are easiest to study in laboratories.
G. never use mimicry for both protection and hunting.
H. can resemble different things for different reasons.
J. always have certain colors to hide from predators.

35. As it is used in line 6, the word *classes* most likely means:

A. lessons.
B. programs.
C. schoolrooms.
D. categories.

36. The passage states that modifications of different spiders include bodies that are:

I. covered with tubercles.
II. enclosed within chitinous plates.
III. colored like lichens.

F. I only
G. I and III only
H. II and III only
J. I, II, and III

37. According to the second paragraph (lines 10–14), animals cannot eat certain spiders if those spiders are:

A. venomous.
B. covered with plates and spines.
C. adapted to their surroundings.
D. able to blend in with their environment.

38. The passage claims that some spiders use coloring to:

F. protect their young.
G. frighten away predators.
H. show predators that they taste bad.
J. reveal that they belong to the genus *Uloborus*.

39. The faithfulness of protective resemblances are not striking when a spider appears in a cabinet because:

A. there is not enough light in a cabinet for the spider to be seen clearly.
B. certain spiders are adapted to blend in with cabinets.
C. spiders tend to run away too quickly to be seen when hiding in cabinets.
D. spiders are not adapted to resemble human-made objects.

40. What is the main idea of the final paragraph (lines 81–92)?

F. The entire upper surface of *C. mitralis'* body is covered with conical elevations.
G. Every feature of *C. mitralis* helps it resemble a woody knot.
H. *C. mitralis* is one of the most remarkable spiders in genus *Epeira*.
J. *C. mitralis* has the habit of perching on a branch and clasping it like a bird.

STOP

SCIENCE TEST

35 MINUTES—40 QUESTIONS

DIRECTIONS: There are seven passages in this test. Each passage is followed by several questions. Read each passage, select the best answer to each related question, and fill in the corresponding circle on the answer sheet. You may look back at the passages as often as you need.

You are NOT allowed to use a calculator on this test.

PASSAGE I

According to quantum theory, light consists of individual particles called *photons*. When photons with enough energy strike a bare metal surface, they can eject negatively charged electrons from that surface. The energy of a single photon is transferred to a single electron, called a *photoelectron*, in a phenomenon known as the *photoelectric effect*.

The photoelectric effect, one of the first important tests of quantum theory, can be observed with the use of an apparatus similar to the one shown in Figure 1. A metal plate and a small electrode are placed within a glass tube called a *photocell*. The photocell is connected to a circuit through which electric current can flow. The circuit contains an ammeter, a device that measures electric current. When the photocell is in the dark, the ammeter shows a reading of zero; when light shines on the photocell, the ammeter indicates a current flowing in the circuit. This current is produced by the photoelectrons emitted from the metal plate.

FIGURE 1

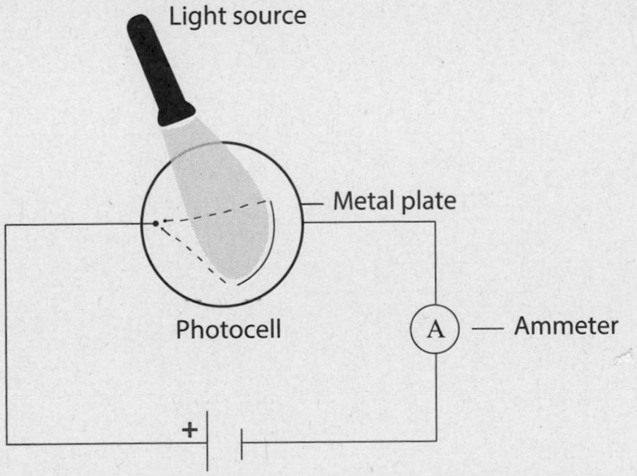

In 1986, at a physics workshop in Boulder, Colorado, a group of high school teachers studied the photoelectric effect in a two-part experiment.

Study 1

In the first part of the experiment, the teachers placed a light source at different distances from the photocell and measured the *photocurrent*, which is proportional to the number of photoelectrons being ejected from the surface. The experiment was conducted with two different color filters, blue and green, as different colors of light have different wavelengths. A filter transmits only one wavelength of light—a green filter, for example, allows only green light to pass through it. The results of this part of the experiment are shown in Table 1. (Current is being measured in microamperes, μA.)

Table 1

Distance to light source with green filter (m)	Photocurrent in μA (a)	Distance to light source with blue light filter (m)	Photocurrent in μA (a)
0.10	430	0.10	350
0.20	100	0.20	90
0.30	50	0.30	45
0.40	25	0.40	20

Practice Test 2 — SCIENCE

CONTINUE

Study 2

A voltage can be applied to a circuit to either speed up or stop the flow of photoelectrons. The voltage required to stop the flow of photoelectrons is known as the *stopping potential.*

In the second part of the experiment, the teachers measured the stopping potential. Four different color filters were used, and the stopping voltage was measured three times for each color filter as well as for no filter at all. The distance to the light source was held constant. Table 2 is a summary of the data from this part of the experiment.

Table 2: Stopping Potential (Volts)

Color of filter	Trial 1	Trial 2	Trial 3
Red	0.0	0.0	0.0
Yellow	0.4	0.4	0.4
Green	0.65	0.65	0.65
Blue	1.0	1.1	1.1
No filter (white)	1.2	1.1	1.0

1. Which of the following graphs best represents the relationship between light source distance (m) and photocurrent (a) in Study 1?

A.

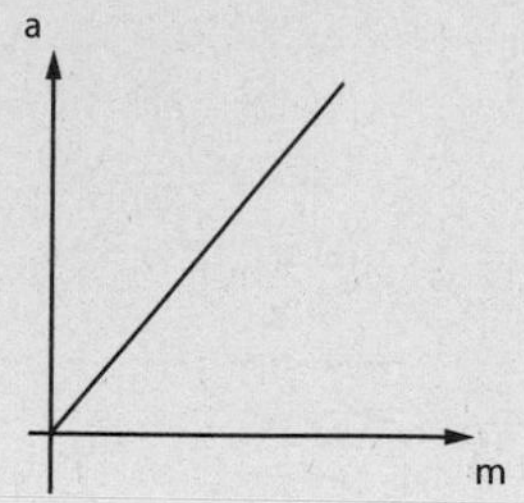

B.

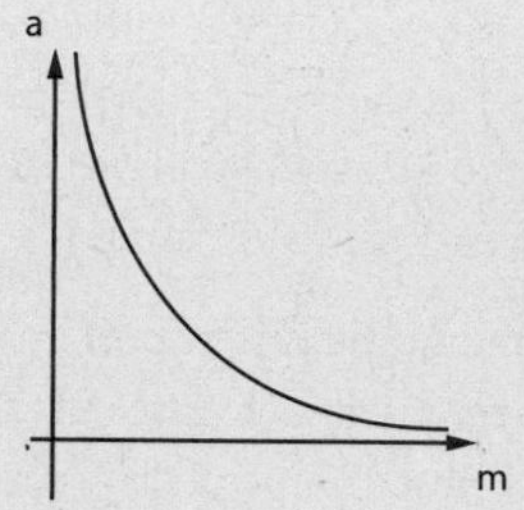

C.

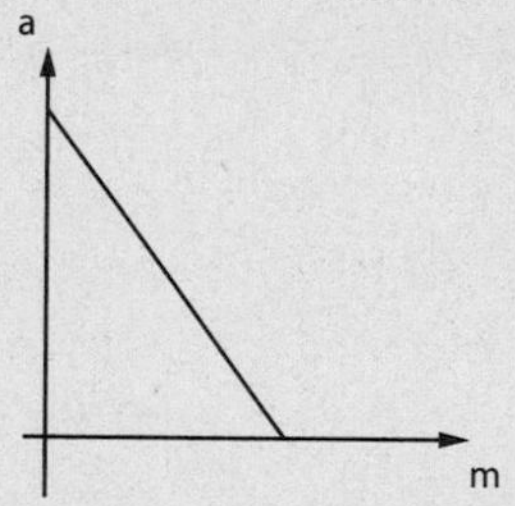

D.

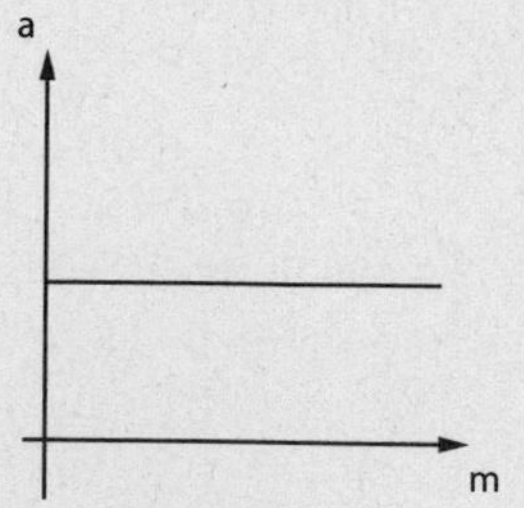

2. The data in Table 2 suggests that stopping potential:

   F. depends on the intensity of light.
   G. depends on the wavelength of light.
   H. depends on the characteristics of the metal plate.
   J. is constant for all wavelength of light.

3. Light intensity obeys an inverse square law, meaning that if the distance is halved, the light intensity is increased by a factor of 4. What conclusion can be drawn from the first part of the experiment?

   A. The greater the light intensity, the greater the number of photoelectrons ejected from the metal plate.
   B. The greater the light intensity, the smaller the number of photoelectrons ejected from the metal plate.
   C. Photoelectrons are not emitted from the metal plate until the light intensity reaches a threshold level.
   D. The number of photoelectrons ejected from the metal plate is independent of light intensity.

4. Of the wavelengths of light used in Study 2, red light has the longest wavelength, while blue light has the shortest. From the results of Study 2, what can one conclude about the relationship between the wavelength of light and its energy?

   F. Energy increases as wavelength increases.
   G. Energy decreases as wavelength increases.
   H. Energy is the same for all wavelengths.
   J. Energy depends on both wavelength and distance.

5. Which of the following was an independent variable in both Study 1 and Study 2?

   A. Distance to light source
   B. Photocurrent magnitude
   C. Stopping potential
   D. Filter color

6. Suppose the teachers were to use an orange filter in Study 2. One would expect the stopping potential with this filter to be:

   F. between 0 and 0.4 volts.
   G. between 0.4 and 0.65 volts.
   H. between 0.65 and 1.1 volts.
   J. greater than 1.1 volts.

PASSAGE II

Although different regions of Earth's surface are assigned specific names, it is dominated by a single ocean that covers about 70 percent of the surface. The continents and oceans are not evenly distributed around Earth. If you look at Earth from a viewpoint in the South Pacific, as shown in Figure 1, you can see that almost one-half of the planet has no land masses larger than small islands. In fact, in the Southern Hemisphere, between the latitudes of 50°S and 65°S, there are essentially no land masses at all.

FIGURE 1

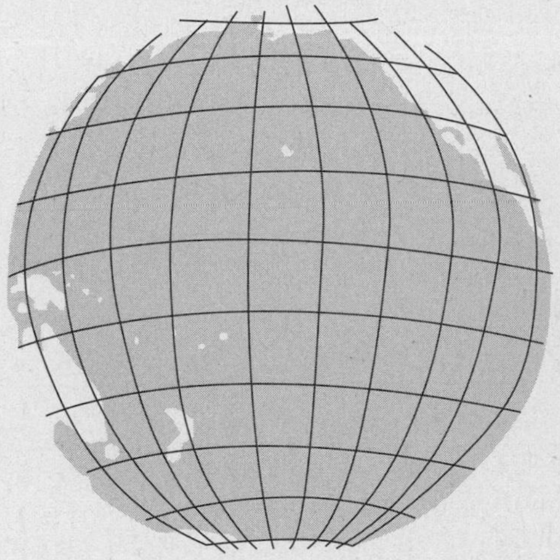

Figure 2 considers various elevations and depths and indicates the percentage of Earth's surface that lies at each level.

FIGURE 2

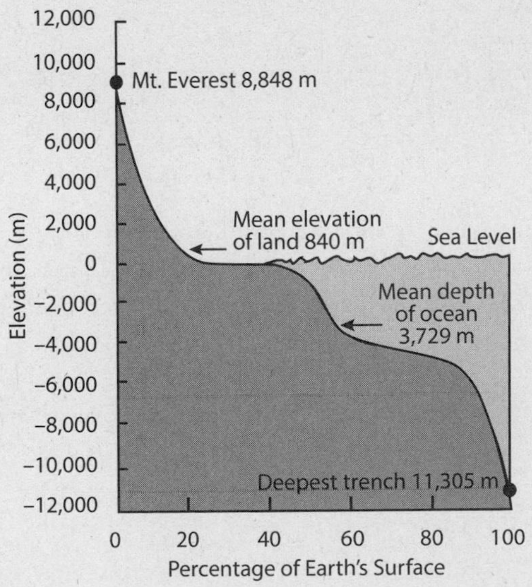

CONTINUE

Ocean water is saltwater, which means that the water contains dissolved salts and other minerals. The most abundant salt found in ocean water is sodium chloride. Sodium chloride is the most soluble of all the common minerals, so it dissolves readily out of rocks and soil and washes into the ocean.

The amount of dissolved salts and minerals in ocean water contributes to its density. The *density* of a substance is the mass of the substance per unit of volume. The greater the amount of dissolved salts, the greater the density. The percentage of dissolved salts is known as *salinity*.

Density is also affected by temperature. Pure water, which freezes at 0°C, reaches its maximum density at around 4°C. Adding salt and other minerals to water lowers both the freezing point and the temperature at which maximum density occurs. Figure 3 shows the relationship among the salinity of water, its freezing point, and temperature of maximum density.

FIGURE 3

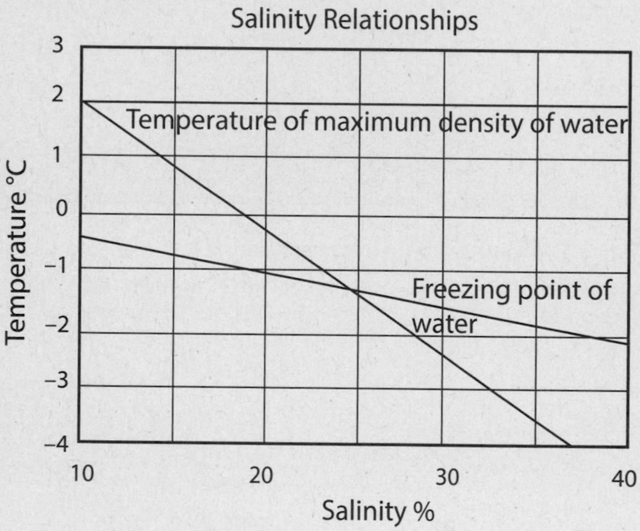

7. Based on the information in Figure 2, what is the approximate median elevation of Earth's surface (the midpoint between the highest and lowest elevations on Earth's surface)?

A. 4,500 m
B. 0 m
C. −1,000 m
D. −5,500 m

8. Oceans moderate weather. One would expect to find less extreme weather in the:

F. Northern Hemisphere, because of the presence of large land masses.
G. Southern Hemisphere, because of the presence of large oceans.
H. Northern Hemisphere, because of the presence of large oceans.
J. Southern Hemisphere, because of the presence of large land masses.

9. According to Figure 2, about what percentage of Earth's surface lies above the mean land elevation of 840 m?

A. 10%
B. 20%
C. 30%
D. 40%

10. In Figure 3, at what salinity does the temperature of maximum density drop below the freezing point?

F. 15%
G. 20%
H. 25%
J. 30%

11. Assuming that the relationship between temperature of maximum density and salinity is constant, what would be the expected temperature of maximum density for ocean water with 40% salinity?

A. 4°C
B. −2.1°C
C. −4°C
D. −4.8°C

PASSAGE III

Bone loss in astronauts is a serious concern during long-term spaceflights. The gravity on a space station is much less than the gravity on Earth, a condition called microgravity. In microgravity, astronauts' bones do not support the weight that they normally do on Earth, so they begin to lose mass because they are not being worked as hard. Weight-bearing bones experience the greatest change in weight load in space, so they experience the greatest bone loss. To counteract bone loss, astronauts exercise all parts of the body on specially designed resistance machines that simulate the weights that their bones support on Earth.

To test the effectiveness of different types of exercise machines on preventing bone loss, researchers measured the bone mineral density (BMD) of astronauts before and after they spent several months on the Mir space station or the International Space Station

(ISS). The astronauts on the Mir did not have specially designed resistance machines, only aerobic exercise and muscular endurance machines. Some ISS astronauts used a resistance machine called an interim resistive exercise device (iRED) that could simulate weights up to 297 pounds. Other ISS astronauts used a newer resistance machine called the Advanced Resistive Exercise Device (ARED) that could simulate weights up to 600 pounds. Astronauts exercised for the same amount of time per day on these different machines. The typical change in BMD for the pelvis and average change in BMD for the whole body of these astronauts is shown in Figure 1.

FIGURE 1

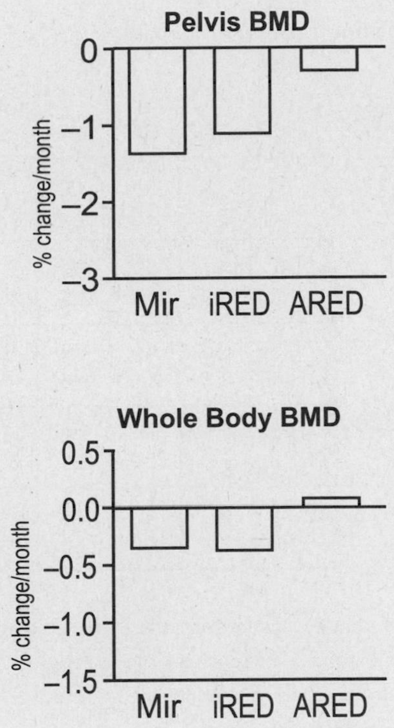

Researchers also tested whether diet could help prevent bone loss. Astronauts on the ISS logged how much protein they ate every day, and the average number of grams of protein they ate per kilogram of their body weight was calculated. Their bone mineral content (BMC) was measured before and after their time on the ISS. These results are shown in Figure 2.

FIGURE 2

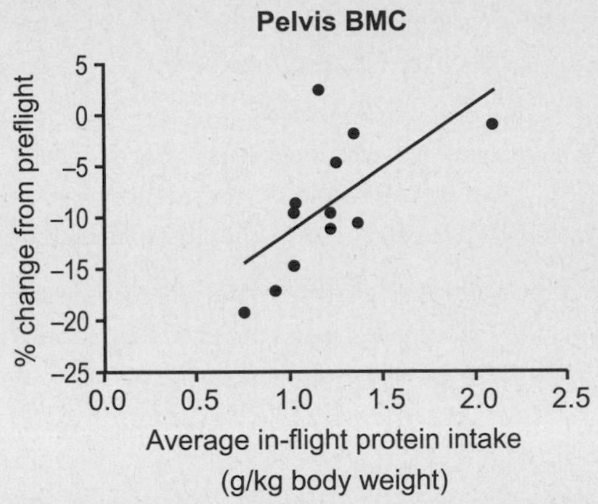

12. Based on the data from Figure 1, which type of exercise machine is most effective in preventing bone loss?

F. ARED
G. iRED
H. Aerobic exercise machine
J. Muscular endurance machine

13. Based on the information in the passage, which of the following best explains why the change in BMD for the pelvis is different from that for the whole body?

A. The astronauts exercise only certain parts of their bodies on the exercise machines.
B. The weight-bearing parts of the body like the pelvis will have greater bone loss than the average bone loss for the entire body.
C. The pelvis is a non-weight-bearing part of the body, so it experiences less bone loss than the average bone loss for the entire body.
D. The different types of exercise machines result in different degrees of bone loss.

14. According to the trend line in Figure 2, in order to maintain BMC at preflight levels, an astronaut should eat approximately how many grams of protein per kilogram of body weight?

F. 0.5
G. 1.0
H. 1.5
J. 2.0

CONTINUE

15. Based on the results shown in Figures 1 and 2, the researchers would most likely recommend which regimen to keep bone loss in astronauts as low as possible?

A. Low-protein diet and low-resistance exercise
B. High-protein diet and low-resistance exercise
C. Low-protein diet and high-resistance exercise
D. High-protein diet and high-resistance exercise

16. According to Figure 1, what is the difference in the change in BMD in the pelvis between the astronauts using ARED and the astronauts on the Mir space station?

F. Mir astronauts lost 0.2% less BMD than ARED-using astronauts.
G. Mir astronauts lost 0.2% more BMD than ARED-using astronauts.
H. Mir astronauts lost 1.0% more BMD than ARED-using astronauts.
J. Mir astronauts lost 1.4% more BMD than ARED-using astronauts.

17. The researchers also measured the percent change in BMD for the humerus (upper arm bone) for the astronauts using iRED. Which of the following graphs best shows the result you would expect from the information in the passage?

A.

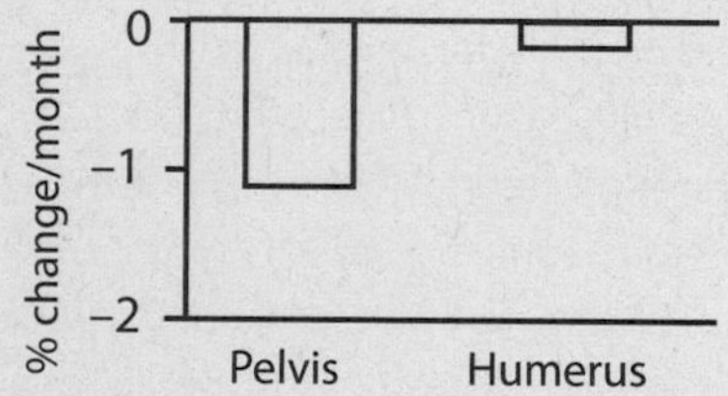

B.

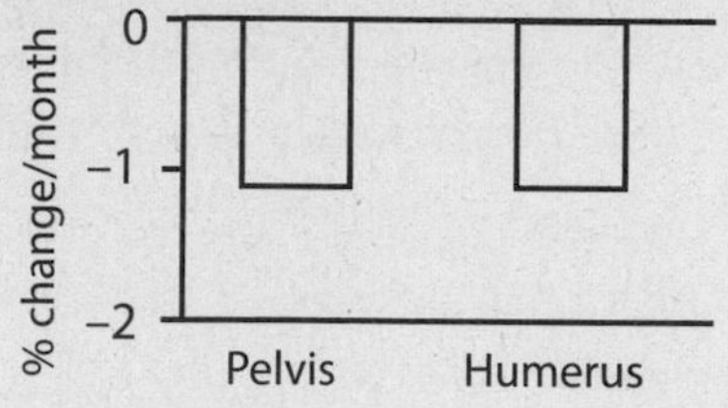

C.

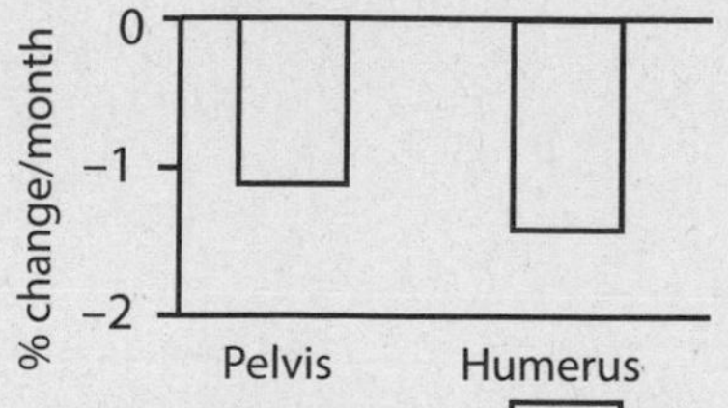

D.

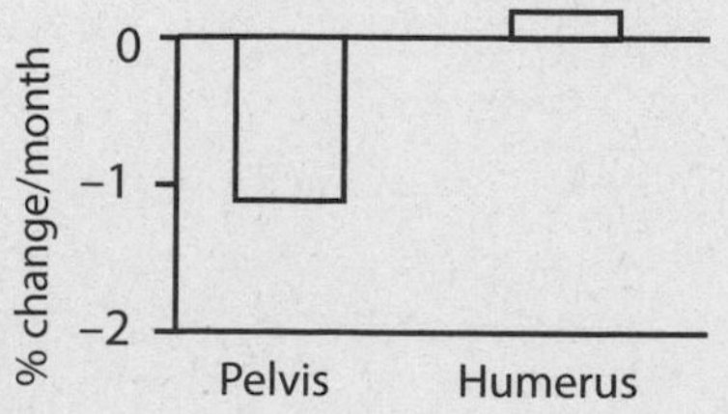

PASSAGE IV

All matter is composed of atoms. An *atom* consists of a positively charged nucleus surrounded by negatively charged particles called *electrons*. Some atoms join, or bond, together by transferring or sharing electrons.

The nature of the electron bonds between two atoms is largely determined by the *electronegativity* of each atom. Electronegativity is the ability of an atom to attract the electrons of other atoms. A greater electronegativity value signifies a superior ability to attract electrons. Figure 1 shows the electronegativities of selected groups of elements in the periodic table.

FIGURE 1

Electronegativities of Groups 1A–7A

1A	2A	3A	4A	5A	6A	7A
H 2.2						
Li 1.0	Be 1.6	B 1.8	C 2.5	N 3.0	O 3.4	F 4.0
Na 0.93	Mg 1.3	Al 1.6	Si 1.9	P 2.2	S 2.6	Cl 3.2
K 0.82	Ca 1.0	Ga 1.8	Ge 2.0	As 2.2	Se 2.6	Br
Rb 0.82	Sr 0.9	In 1.8	Sn 1.8	Sb 2.0	Te 2.1	I 2.7
Cs 0.79	Ba 0.9	Tl 2.0	Pb 2.3	Bi 2.0	Po 2.0	At 2.2

Atoms with very similar electronegativities form molecules that are *nonpolar*. The electrons of these atoms are shared equally, and their molecules are said to be electrically symmetrical. The electron bond is equidistant between the nuclei of each atom.

Atoms with moderately different electronegativities form *polar covalent bonds*. In this case, one atom attracts electrons more than the other atom does; these molecules are said to be electrically asymmetrical. The electron bond between such atoms is closer to the more electronegative atom. Molecules that contain such atoms have a relative concentration of negativity at the end that is closer to the more electronegative atom.

The greater the difference in electronegativity, the more polar the molecule is.

18. In Figure 1, elements are arranged in vertical columns called *groups*, or *families*, and in horizontal rows called *periods*. Based on the patterns of electronegativity values among the families and periods, one would predict that the approximate electronegativity of bromine (Br) is:

F. 2.6.
G. 3.0.
H. 3.6.
J. 4.0.

19. Which element has the least ability to attract electrons?

A. Li (Lithium)
B. Na (Sodium)
C. Al (Aluminum)
D. Ti (Titanium)

20. Which of the following molecules is most likely to be nonpolar?

F. NaCl
G. MgO
H. Cl_2
J. HCl

21. Which of the following bonds is likely to be the most polar?

A. K–Cl
B. Ba–Se
C. Na–S
D. Be–O

22. Based on Figure 1, what is the most highly polar bond that can be generated from the presented elements?

F. O-F
G. H-At
H. Cs-F
J. K-Cl

PASSAGE V

In 2001, members of a national health foundation who were interested in examining possible links between cigarette smoking and cancer in the United States gathered relevant data from ten selected states.

First, they surveyed residents in each state to determine what percentage of the state's residents were cigarette smokers. For the purpose of consistency, smokers were defined as those who smoked every day or most days and who had smoked at least 100 cigarettes in their lifetime. Smokers were further asked whether they had ever attempted to quit smoking. For the purpose of consistency, a quit attempt was defined as having gone one day or longer without a cigarette in a deliberate effort to stop smoking. In both cases, percentages were weighted to reflect population characteristics.

The foundation's members then collected information from medical facilities, disease control centers, and other health organizations to reflect numbers of cancer-related deaths. They compared these numbers with the population figures in each state.

The members separated each state's data by gender and reported their findings. Table 1 summarizes the data.

Table 1

State	Cigarette Smoking Rate		Number of Cancer Deaths per 100,000 Population		Percent of Smokers Who Attempt to Quit	
	Females	Males	Females	Males	Females	Males
California	13.3%	19.6%	156.7	212.8	63.6%	62.9%
Colorado	19.4%	21.4%	150.7	200.4	57.7%	52.7%
Florida	20.6%	23.4%	155.3	229.8	55.3%	48.4%
Indiana	25.7%	29.7%	172.9	271.9	61.0%	51.6%
Kentucky	30.3%	34.7%	182.0	297.6	53.6%	42.9%
Maine	21.0%	26.4%	170.5	262.7	62.2%	60.2%
Ohio	25.0%	28.3%	173.5	261.4	53.8%	49.5%
Rhode Island	20.9%	24.0%	167.7	253.9	64.4%	66.6%
Utah	11.4%	14.1%	117.2	181.0	72.1%	64.6%
West Virginia	27.2%	29.7%	186.0	267.9	48.9%	47.3%

CONTINUE

Figure 1 plots these same ten states' cancer mortality rates against the percentage of their residents who smoke. Data in this graph is not separated by gender.

FIGURE 1

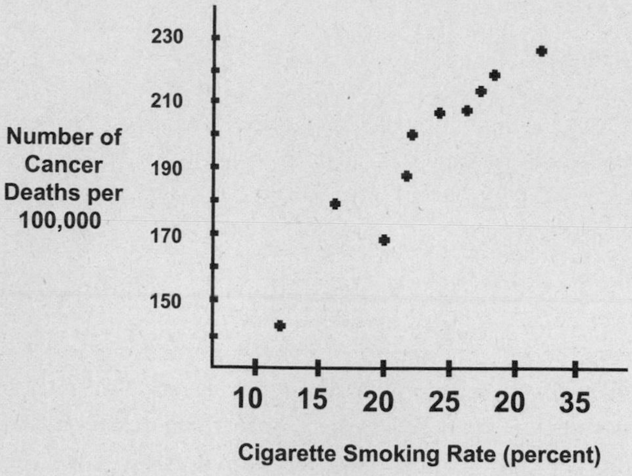

23. In Figure 1, approximately what happens to the cancer death rate for every 5% increase in the number of people who smoke?

A. The rate increases by 10 per 100,000.
B. The rate increases by 18 per 100,000.
C. The rate increases by 40 per 100,000.
D. The rate decreases by 10 per 100,000.

24. Which of the following statements is NOT supported by Table 1?

F. Kentucky has a higher percentage of smokers than any other listed state.
G. Within each listed state, the percentage of males who smoke is higher than the percentage of females who smoke.
H. Rhode Island has the highest listed percentage of males who attempt to quit smoking.
J. Within each listed state, the percentage of females who attempt to quit smoking is higher than the percentage of males who attempt to quit smoking.

25. Taken together, the data indicates that there is a relationship between higher rates of smoking and increased risk of death from cancer. What could the researchers do to try and prove that smoking increases death rates in the study region?

A. Limit the study to those cancers known to be associated with smoking.
B. Add more states that have even higher rates of smoking.
C. Examine cancer rates in those who successfully quit smoking.
D. Find a comparison population made up only of non-smokers.

26. In New Jersey, nearly 177 out of every 100,000 females died from cancer in 2001. Based on the information in Table 1, out of every 100,000 males in New Jersey in 2001, a likely estimate of the number who died from cancer would be:

F. 246.
G. 177.
H. 150.
J. 118.

27. A separate study of social networks in these states determined that women in every state but Rhode Island have an average of 2.4 more social connections then men. Which is a plausible statement based on that information and Table 1?

A. Most smoking occurs in social settings.
B. Friendships help patients survive cancer.
C. Friends encourage each other to quit smoking.
D. Friends encourage each other to start smoking.

PASSAGE VI

One hallmark of the modern world is the ease of travel for both people and goods. For most of human history, people didn't move around very much. Except for certain seafaring peoples, until the invention of sailing ships, moving between continents was virtually impossible. Sailing ships made travel across the oceans possible, but still slow and not that widespread.

But as technology improved, travel and shipping got easier. Steamships could cross the oceans in weeks or days, and ships grew larger, carrying greater and greater loads between more and more places. Air travel eased connections between far-flung areas even more. And it isn't only people taking advantage of greater connectivity between places: plants, animals, and marine life are moving around as well. Plants or animals from Asia or Europe that previously would have been confined to their native range can now easily establish populations in the Americas. When a species settles in a place far from its native range, it is said to be introduced. Examples include house sparrows, zebra mussels, and rats.

Frequently, when a species from one area ends up in another, it does well. These species often flourish in their new habitat, reproducing rapidly and spreading out into the new habitat. They can be especially damaging in isolated areas or areas with low species diversity, where local species are more specialized and less likely to have encountered new risks.

Perspective 1

The mere presence of an introduced species is an invasion, a disruptive change caused by humans. The ecosystems and species already present, called natives, cannot compete with the newcomers. The new species are threats, killing or replacing native species and permanently destroying unique environments. They may also present an economic nuisance. The newcomers often have an edge over native species, as the natives are not familiar with the newcomers. These species often have few or no predators or parasites, and the natives have no defense against them. Introduced species can be fish, snakes, mammals, plants, insects, aquatic invertebrates, or even diseases. Native forests get replaced with invasive trees, invasive grasses replace native grasslands, and soon the original native environment is unrecognizable.

Managers must do everything in their power to eradicate introduced species. It's especially important to find and eradicate new infestations before a new species can take hold, but otherwise all steps must be taken to fight the spread of new species and remove or kill them where they are established. Introduced species must be removed even if some damage occurs to native species in the process. Otherwise unique native ecosystems will be destroyed or forever changed.

Perspective 2

Some ecologists have a different view of introduced species. Some of these species can now be considered to be part of the new environment. In this view, restoring or preserving the "original" ecosystem is impossible because after hundreds of years of human impact nobody knows for sure what the original ecosystem is, and that's assuming introduced species can even be removed, given that removal is not always successful. Many introduced species become established in new territories and experience rapid population growth, but it is not always clear if they are actually harming native species or simply coexisting alongside the natives. Some introduced species provide food or habitat for native species, even rare or important native species. Introduced species are part of a global ecosystem and introduced populations are simply another population. There may even be economic benefits if an invasive species can be commercially exploited.

Perspective 2 acknowledges that there may be harmful impacts from introduced species, but there may also be no impact or benefits, depending on the situation. It is not always worth making intensive efforts to fight against introduced species and remove them wherever they are found.

Perspective 3

A third point of view acknowledges that while some introduced species are an immediate threat to native ecosystems, most problems are temporary. In this view, most introduced species follow a pattern of initial population growth and ecosystem disruption, followed by a decline in the introduced population. Eventually, native and introduced species adjust to one another, and the populations of both native and introduced species stabilize at an acceptable level. Monitoring of introduced populations is required.

28. Given the information about each, what would be appropriate names for Perspective 1 and Perspective 2, respectively?

- **F.** The introduction perspective and the acceptance perspective
- **G.** The eradication perspective and the invasion perspective
- **H.** The unacceptable perspective and the beneficial perspective
- **J.** The invasion perspective and the assessment perspective

CONTINUE

29. A population of wattle-necked turtles from Asia has been found in the Hawaiian island of Kauai. Which statement is most likely true about this situation?

A. Perspective 1 would support leaving the turtles alone.
B. Perspective 2 would support eradicating the turtles.
C. Perspective 2 would leave the turtles alone if they were endangered in their native range.
D. Perspective 1 would wait to assess the turtles' impact before recommending removal.

30. The resources available for conservation work are limited. This would factor into:

F. only Perspective 2, because funds need to be reserved only for harmful species.
G. only Perspective 1, because eradicating species is more expensive then acting on a case-by-case basis.
H. only Perspective 2, because resources should be used exclusively for other purposes besides introduced species.
J. both Perspectives 1 and 2, since there is not enough money to eradicate everything, regardless of whether it is desirable to do so.

31. Rats are a species that have been introduced all over the world. Based on the passage, in which area are they likely to disrupt the local ecosystem the most?

A. A small, isolated island
B. A large rainforest
C. A different continent
D. A coastal island

32. What is the one point that is common to all three perspectives?

F. Introduced species should be managed according to the actual risk.
G. Some introduced species are very harmful.
H. Introduced species become less harmful over time.
J. All species introductions present a risk.

33. Which of the following is a strategy for managing introduced species on which all three perspectives would most likely agree?

A. Divert all resources to eradicating introduced species.
B. Wait a few years, then eradicate all non-helpful species.
C. Eliminate harmful species and ignore the others.
D. Prevent species from hitchhiking on planes and ships.

34. What would a graph of introduced and native species populations over time look like according to Perspective 3?

F.

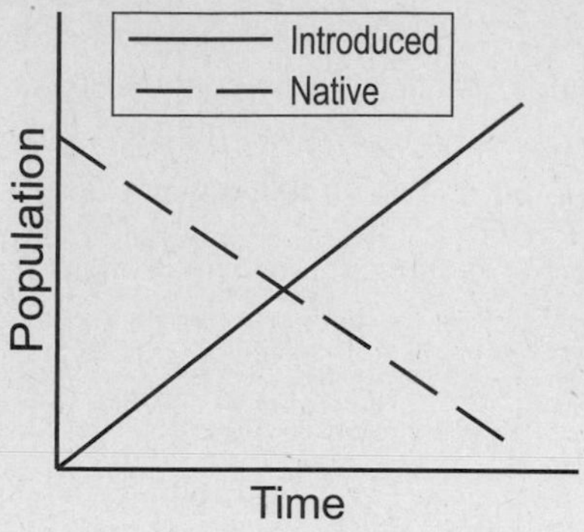

G.

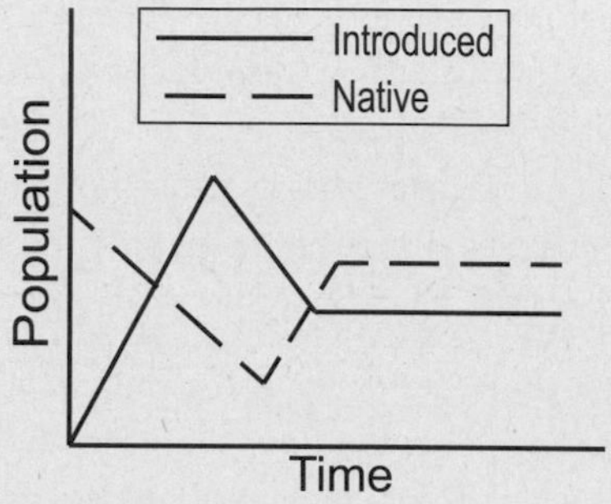

H.

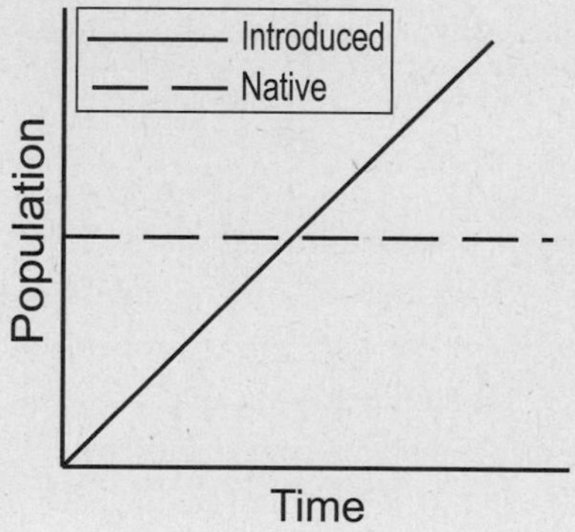

J.

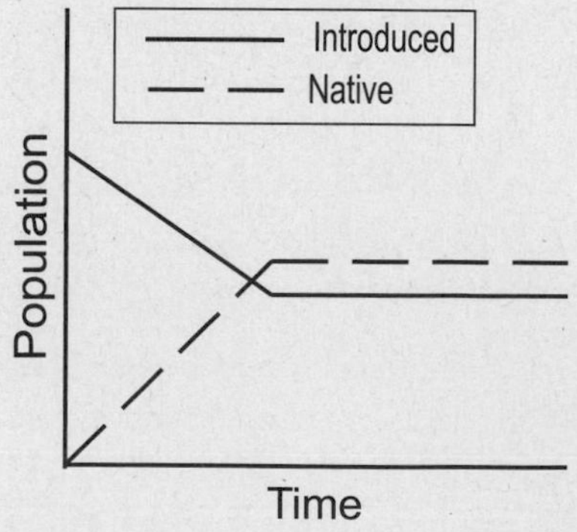

PASSAGE VII

Researchers have discovered that rattlesnakes have a number of sensory organs. These include eyes, heat sensors in two pits located beneath the eyes, and odor sensors on the roof of the mouth. In addition, rattlers are equipped with venom glands located on each side of the head. When a rattler strikes its prey, venom is delivered into the prey through a pair of hollow fangs. Typically, the rattler then releases the prey, which subsequently runs off. After a few minutes, the prey dies as a result of the venom. By this time, the prey is some distance from the rattler. The rattler can no longer see the prey or sense the prey's body heat—yet the snake invariably finds the prey. How does the rattlesnake accomplish this extraordinary tracking feat? Intrigued researchers performed the three experiments described here in an attempt to answer this question.

Experiment 1

Scientists exposed a rattlesnake to a live mouse. The rattlesnake observed the mouse. It then struck the mouse. During this sequence of events, the scientists observed the activity of the snake's tongue. The table below summarizes this data.

Rattlesnake Behavior

Time (minutes)	Tongue Flicks
1	2
2	1
3	2
4*	2
5	76
6	80
7	74
8	79

** Rattlesnake strikes mouse*

Experiment 2

The scientists placed a live mouse out of reach of the rattlesnake. They again observed the activity of the snake's tongue. The table below summarizes this data.

Rattlesnake Behavior

Time (minutes)	Tongue Flicks
1	2
2	1
3	3
4	2
5	1
6	3
7	2
8	1

Experiment 3

The scientists exposed a rattlesnake to two different dead mice. One had been killed by rattlesnake venom; the other had been killed in a humane, nonpoisonous manner by the scientists. The snake flicked its tongue more frequently at the poisoned mouse.

35. If the snake in Experiment 2 had been allowed to strike the mouse at 8 minutes, a likely number of tongue flicks during the ninth minute would be:

A. 1.
B. 3.
C. 40.
D. 76.

36. A fourth experiment is performed in which a rattlesnake is exposed to but unable to reach first a living mouse and then a fresh dead one. In both cases, the number of tongue flicks remains constant, but the snake turns toward the living mouse and moves towards it while ignoring the dead mouse. This information suggests that:

F. snakes hunt by tracking odors.
G. snakes hunt using temperature stimuli.
H. snakes are only interested in prey when they strike.
J. snakes find prey by chance.

CONTINUE

37. Based on all the information in the study, what is the likely purpose of tongue flicking?

A. To provide the snake's sense of smell
B. To help snakes detect the location of heat sources
C. To help snakes detect the location of odors
D. To improve the accuracy of the snake's strike

38. Sometimes a rattlesnake will deliver a "dry bite," or a bite where no venom is injected. Dry bites are meant to warn off a threat, not kill. Which result regarding dry bites is consistent with the rest of the experiment?

F. The snake increases tongue flicks after a dry bite.
G. Tongue flicks remain constant before and after a dry bite.
H. Tongue flicks decrease after a dry bite.
J. The snake will ignore a dry-bitten animal.

39. Which of the following graphs most accurately describes the relationship between time (*t*) and number of tongue flicks (*f*) in Experiment 2?

A.
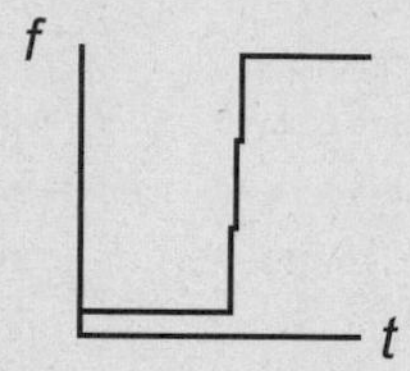

B.
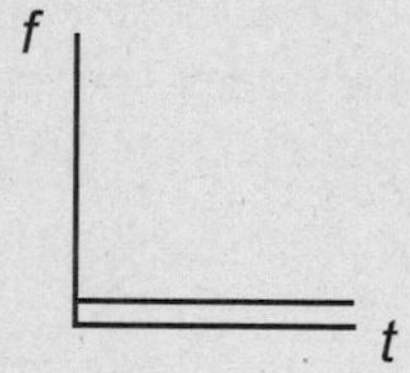

C.
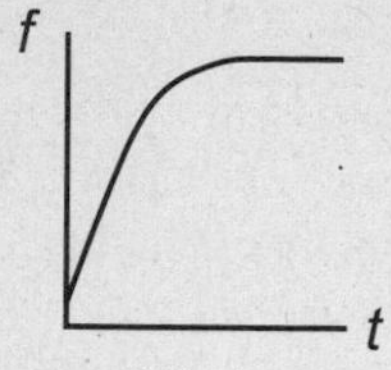

D.
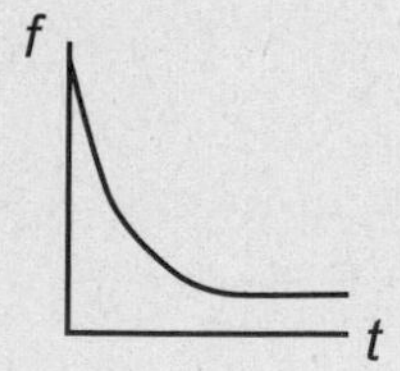

40. How would you test a hypothesis suggesting that a rattlesnake follows the scent of its own venom?

F. Remove the rattlesnake's tongue and observe the behavior of the snake.
G. Make a trail with a dead mouse that has NOT been bitten by a rattlesnake and observe the behavior of the snake.
H. Make a trail with rattlesnake venom and observe the behavior of the snake.
J. Make a trail with a live mouse that has NOT been bitten by a rattlesnake and observe the behavior of the snake.

STOP

WRITING TEST

40 MINUTES

DIRECTIONS: This is a test of your writing skills. You have forty (40) minutes to write an essay in English. Be sure to carefully read the issue and three perspectives presented before planning and writing your essay so you understand clearly the task you are being asked to do. Your essay will be graded on the evidence it provides of your ability to analyze the issue; evaluate and analyze the perspectives; state and develop a personal perspective; and describe the relationship between the given perspectives and your own, while effectively using organization, logic, and language according to the conventions of Standard Written English.

LOOK WHO'S WATCHING

Have you ever heard the phrase, "Big Brother is watching"? It refers to the way governments and other institutions with power and influence can enact invasive surveillance measures upon groups of people. Although it's a line from a fictional story, some people feel that the massive increase in camera surveillance in public and private spaces comes close—or reaches—the eerie promise that we are constantly being watched and have lost our rights to privacy, immersed in a "culture of surveillance." Others feel that this is an acceptable infringement, as surveillance provides us a record of events to help settle disputes and also helps to deter and solve crimes. Whether we applaud the advantages or decry the disadvantages of increased surveillance in public and private spheres, we all must acknowledge the role of surveillance as technology rapidly evolves and continues to become a part of every aspect of our lives.

Read and carefully consider these perspectives. Each suggests a particular way of thinking about the increase in surveillance.

PERSPECTIVE ONE

Institutions with power and influence, such as governments and corporations, have littered the skies with surveillance equipment that has become so advanced and powerful that we must now live with the notion that very little of our lives are lived in private. The surveillance culture has even trickled down to the level of small businesses and homeowners. Not only is Big Brother watching, Little Brother and Sister are watching too. We must reverse this trend before it gets any worse.

PERSPECTIVE TWO

Although it's true that increased surveillance has affected our lives and impacted our privacy, its overall effect has been a positive one on society, and is well worth any perceived social costs. Surveillance helps deter and solve crimes, settle all manner of disputes by providing a tangible record, and protects business and property owners. In an increasingly complex society, we need increasingly sophisticated methods for protecting citizens. Surveillance technology provides the necessary means for doing this, and its value more than outweighs any perceived detriment.

PERSPECTIVE THREE

Surveillance is a potentially helpful tool in a wide variety of situations, but its use should not be impulsive or flippant; instead, it should be carefully considered in each instance. There are places where surveillance technology can be beneficial, such as in areas with traditionally high crime rates or valuable items. But if surveillance technology is used to watch us walk down the street, have private conversations, and record people who come into our homes, then we've gone too far. We've reached the point where we need to make more judicious use of a tool that can easily—and quickly—be misused. The next step should be open conversations about ways that we can ensure the responsible use of surveillance technology.

Essay Task

Write a cohesive, logical essay in which you consider multiple perspectives on the rise of surveillance. In your essay, be sure to:

- examine and assess the perspectives given
- declare and explain your own perspective on the issue
- discuss the relationship between your perspective and those given

Your perspective may be in full or partial agreement, or in total disagreement, with any of the others. Whatever the case, support your ideas with logical reasoning and detailed, persuasive examples.

Plan and Write Your Essay

Use the first two pages of the Writing test answer sheet (found at the beginning of the test) to generate ideas and plan your essay. Then use the following four pages to write your essay. Consider the following as you compose your essay:

What are the strengths and weaknesses of the three perspectives provided?

- Identify the insights they present and what they fail to consider.
- Ascertain why a given perspective might persuade or fail to persuade.

How can you apply your own experience, knowledge, and values?

- Express your perspective on the issue, identifying the perspective's strengths and weaknesses.
- Formulate a plan to support your perspective in your essay.

English

1.	B	**20.**	F	**39.**	B	**58.**	J
2.	H	**21.**	B	**40.**	G	**59.**	A
3.	B	**22.**	H	**41.**	D	**60.**	H
4.	H	**23.**	A	**42.**	J	**61.**	B
5.	A	**24.**	G	**43.**	A	**62.**	F
6.	J	**25.**	D	**44.**	G	**63.**	C
7.	B	**26.**	J	**45.**	C	**64.**	J
8.	H	**27.**	C	**46.**	G	**65.**	C
9.	B	**28.**	G	**47.**	D	**66.**	J
10.	G	**29.**	C	**48.**	J	**67.**	B
11.	C	**30.**	G	**49.**	B	**68.**	J
12.	J	**31.**	D	**50.**	F	**69.**	C
13.	B	**32.**	F	**51.**	D	**70.**	H
14.	J	**33.**	C	**52.**	G	**71.**	D
15.	A	**34.**	J	**53.**	B	**72.**	J
16.	F	**35.**	B	**54.**	F	**73.**	B
17.	B	**36.**	H	**55.**	B	**74.**	H
18.	J	**37.**	A	**56.**	J	**75.**	D
19.	B	**38.**	F	**57.**	B		

1. **The correct answer is B.** This birthday party was something out of the ordinary, so the author is taking note of its difference. *Only* suggests this exception; however, "it's being" is in the present tense, while the story takes place in the past, so choice A is incorrect. *But* (choice B) uses the correct tense and retains the meaning of the original. You might choose *yet* because it is another contrast word, but *its* is a possessive pronoun, and there is no need to indicate that the party owned anything, so choice C is incorrect. Choice D indicates that there is a well-known kind of birthday party that is held at the South Pole, which is not true.

2. **The correct answer is H.** An important aspect of making sure a sentence is grammatically correct is ensuring that it is in appropriate parallel form. The verbs *walked*, *ski*, and *pulled* are not in parallel form, so the sentence is incorrect as written. Here, the action of the sentence occurred in the past, so the verbs should all be in the past tense, and *skied* (choice H) is correct. The other choices are inappropriate given the context of the sentence.

3. **The correct answer is B.** In this question, we're seeking to determine the appropriate end punctuation for a sentence. The sentence begins with a common question word, *why*, so we know that we're dealing with a question and a question mark is appropriate to end the sentence with.

4. **The correct answer is H.** Choice H achieves the dual purpose proposed by the question. It concludes the paragraph by answering the previous question, while echoing the first sentence by addressing why Helen decided to spend her birthday alone in a far-off place. It also explains the reference to "a place that doesn't exist." Choice J asks another question and causes us to continue wondering what motivated Helen. There are references to Helen's motivations in choices F and G, yet choice G would make us wonder more about these additional elements in Helen's character rather than keep us focused on the trip that is the topic of this selection. Choice F is vague—it doesn't answer any questions. Because this question might require you to reread the first paragraph, you may want to delay answering it until you have finished the rest of the passage.

5. **The correct answer is A.** This phrase produces different meanings depending upon where it is placed in the sentence. Choice A is correct because it puts the modifier "in her email messages" close to the word being modified, *commented*. Choices C

and D both create misplaced modifiers. Helen was discouraged in life, not in her email messages (choice C). She is starting fresh on the journey, not in her email messages (choice D). Choice B, though not incorrect, is awkward compared with choice A.

6. **The correct answer is J.** Here, we're looking to determine the appropriate word choice given the meaning of the sentence. What sort of barrier would be formed by an "ice formation marked by hard mounds and jagged ridges of frozen water"? The most appropriate word choice here among the answer choices is *insurmountable*, which means nearly impossible to get around. The words in the other choices don't fit given the sentence in its entirety.

7. **The correct answer is B.** We want the correct choice to give us a sense of Helen's character by showing how she handled this particular obstacle. The original sentence doesn't tell us enough about how she deals with her frustration; if anything, the sentence gives the impression that she was likely to give in. Choice B offers an example of her coping strategy and how it helps her to survive, making it the best answer. Choice C doesn't reveal much more to us than facts. Eliminating the phrase, as choice D suggests, would not tell the reader anything about Helen and thus not accomplish the writer's purpose.

8. **The correct answer is H.** As written, this sentence is excessively wordy, as there is a redundancy—*crevasses* are *open cracks*, so there is no need to repeat it. Choice H fixes the redundancy. Choice G simply reverses the two redundant phrases and is incorrect. Choice J does not fix the redundancy either.

9. **The correct answer is B.** The correct answer is choice B because it adds to Helen's story of using an ice screw as an anchor against the wind. It further describes the experience of the wind and helps the reader envision what Helen had to endure. Choice A introduces causes for the wind but it distracts from the description of the effects of this wind. Neither of the facts added in choice C, that the area was lifeless, nor choice D, that the crevasses were huge, builds on the main idea of the paragraph, which is how Helen dealt with the winds.

10. **The correct answer is G.** The original sentence doesn't seem to know where to end or how to link ideas—it's a run-on sentence. Choice H replaces all the commas in the original with semicolons and still doesn't order and link the different ideas properly. Choice J places a period after the first subordinate clause, creating a fragment. Choice G correctly divides separate ideas with a period, keeps the comma after the opening subordinate clause in the first sentence, and then links related but independent ideas with a semicolon in the second sentence.

11. **The correct answer is C.** The correct answer should introduce us to ideas we haven't encountered up to this point. Choice C does this by referring to past experiences and then leading right into events that will soon follow in the next paragraph. A birthday cupcake (choice D) is also a new idea, but it fails to connect this paragraph with the next. Choice B is linked to the adventure in the crevasse but introduces no additional element to the story; it also doesn't make sense, as she couldn't scout in a whiteout. Choice A doesn't introduce a secondary element.

12. **The correct answer is J.** Any predicament is by definition a fair bit of trouble, so "most troublesome" is redundant and wordy. There is no point in changing *most* to *more* (choice G), as *more* is used when two things are being compared, and there is no comparison here. Changing *troublesome* to *dangerous* (choice H), retains the same problem of redundancy and wordiness as seen in choice F. The best choice is to omit the underlined portion entirely.

13. **The correct answer is B.** This question tests your ability to utilize appropriate possessive word forms given the context of the sentence. Here, we are focusing on the pull ropes that are part of the sled, so the correct word choice is *sled's pull ropes*. The other choices don't properly utilize the possessive word forms given the context of the sentence.

14. **The correct answer is J.** As the paragraph is written, it's not clear what *Its* refers to at the start of Sentence 3, and there's a problem with the order of events. Putting Sentence 3 before Sentence 1 or 2 (choices G and H), doesn't solve either problem; in fact, doing so makes the paragraph more confusing. Choice J is the only choice that gives *Its* a proper antecedent and orders the events and facts so they make sense.

15. **The correct answer is A.** The assignment proposed to this writer was to create an intimate portrayal of personal challenges. The article would have had to provide us with her thinking and feelings and evidence of how she personally dealt with the ups and downs of the trip. Choice B introduces the idea of motivation, which would be part of an intimate portrayal, but also brings in financial support, which wouldn't necessarily be included in an intimate account of personal challenges. You may sense what the trip was like (choice C), but it's not a clear account of her feelings and emotions

while she experienced these trials. And you do find out the basics of her trip (choice D), but not intimate details. Choice A is correct because, during the events narrated, we aren't informed in any great detail about how Helen felt.

16. **The correct answer is F.** An opening sentence should serve to intrigue readers and hold their attention, in addition to introducing the topic of the essay. Choice F is the most effective option among the answer choices. The other choices aren't as on-target as this choice in terms of capturing the topic of the essay—life in Yakutsk, a cold city.

17. **The correct answer is B.** There are no items that need their possession established here, so we don't need the possessive forms of these words. Choices A, C, and D utilize inappropriate possessive forms of the underlined words. As shown in choice B, *winter months* is correct.

18. **The correct answer is J.** There is no need to capitalize the common nouns *major* and *city* when inside of a sentence, so choice J is correct. Choices F, G, and H each utilize incorrect capitalization of these nouns.

19. **The correct answer is B.** In order to determine the appropriate word choice here, we need to determine the context. Here, we're taking about movement from "a brisk pace to a frigid crawl," so clearly, we are talking about a slowing down, and choice B is the best fit. Choice A provides the opposite of the intended meaning. Choice C does not describe the slowdown being discussed here. Choice D is out of context, and is thus incorrect.

20. **The correct answer is F.** In order to determine the appropriate information to add to this paragraph we need to first determine the paragraph's purpose. After carefully reading Paragraph 2, we can determine that it is focused on the weather conditions in Yakutsk, specifically the cold temperatures there. Therefore, choice F would be the most appropriate choice. Choice G would fit best in Paragraph 6, which discusses diamond mining in Yakutsk. Choice H would best fit in Paragraph 5, which mentions that Yakutsk once served as a military fort. Choice J would best fit in Paragraph 4, which discusses early settlers of Yakutsk.

21. **The correct answer is B.** Making appropriate word choices includes making sure that the tone of a piece is consistent throughout. As written, the underlined portion of the sentence is too casual given the tone of the piece. Choice B corrects this problem and supports the notion that the temperatures in Yakutsk are punishing. Choice C also presents the same problem in tone and is incorrect. Choice D provides the opposite of the intended meaning and is also incorrect.

22. **The correct answer is H.** This is a simple declarative sentence that should end in a period, not a semicolon as written. Choice H shows the correct punctuation.

23. **The correct answer is A.** Here, we are seeking to determine whether the underlined portion of the sentence reflects appropriate word choices given the context of the entire sentence. The passage refers to settlers coming into Yakutsk from other parts of Siberia prior to its official founding, so *trickle into* is correct. Choices B, C, and D don't make sense here given the context of the sentence and paragraph.

24. **The correct answer is G.** The various forms of *its* are often misused. Here, since *it is* does not fit in the sentence, the contraction *it's* is incorrect. Choice G fixes this error and is the correct word choice. Choices H and J don't fit within the context of the sentence.

25. **The correct answer is D.** In this question, we're seeking to determine the appropriate word choice for the underlined portion of the sentence. Here, we are looking at resources native to Yakutsk that *spurred* its booming mining industry. Therefore, the word choice that makes the most sense here would be *abundant*, which means *plentiful*. The other choices don't fit, given the context of the sentence.

26. **The correct answer is J.** Since we're looking for a transition sentence between paragraphs 6 and 7, we should first make sure we know the primary purpose of each paragraph. Paragraph 6 focuses on ice and mining in Yakutsk, and Paragraph 7 turns to cultural aspects of the city. The sentence that best serves as a transition between these two concepts is choice J: *However, there's more to life in Yakutsk than ice and mining.* The other choices don't bridge the primary concepts of paragraphs 6 and 7 as effectively as this choice does.

27. **The correct answer is C.** As written, this sentence contains a redundancy—*bourgeoning* means "quickly developing," so there's no need to say it twice. Choice C fixes this redundancy and is correct. Choice B creates an internal error in logic—something can't be both "bourgeoning" and "quickly shrinking." Choice D fails to fix the error and reverses the intended meaning of the sentence.

28. The correct answer is G. In order to determine the most effective concluding sentence, we should first determine the focus of the passage and paragraph in which it will appear. Here, the fact that Yakutsk has a warmer summer climate is being discussed within a passage that talks all about what life is like there. The most appropriate concluding sentence among the answer choices would be choice G: *So if you're ever curious about what life is like there and have a taste for travel, the summer might be the best time to visit Yakutsk!* The other choices are more off-target and would not be as effective as concluding sentences.

29. The correct answer is C. In order to determine the proper placement of this sentence, we need to scan the passage for where animals and/or hunting are discussed. Paragraph 5 states the following: "Life was certainly not easy for its residents, who relied on hunting, fishing, and gathering to survive." The additional sentence would fit well after this sentence, so choice C is correct. The paragraphs in choices A, B, and D don't discuss hunting or animals in Yakutsk.

30. The correct answer is G. This passage takes a look at what life is like in an exotic city and would best fit in a travel website, as this information might be of interest to someone looking to travel to a new place. The passage would not really work well in any of the other publication types mentioned in the other answer choices.

31. The correct answer is D. The word *also* in the sentence makes choices A and B unnecessary and redundant. The use of *However* in choice C suggests the introduction of an opposing thought, but no opposing thought is being presented—just an additional step that you will need to take to reach the park under the sea. Choice D, which leaves out the modifier, is correct.

32. The correct answer is F. The term is not defined in the next paragraph (choice J) so you might consider having it defined here. However, pausing to define a term just as the passage is being introduced is rather jarring. Choice G states that the word's similarity to *submarine* may confuse readers, but, in fact, that similarity is more likely to help readers guess the correct definition. *Submersible* (choice H) is not a technical term. Since its meaning is easy to determine from the context clues in the sentence ("travel thousands of feet below the waves"), choice F is correct.

33. The correct answer is C. To determine the correct version of this sentence, ask yourself to what the word *nearly* is referring. The spotlights are showing you "nearly all" of the depths, so choice C is correct. The only variation among other answer choices is the placement of the word *nearly*, and choices A, B, and D do not use it in the appropriate place.

34. The correct answer is J. The subject of the sentence is *neither*, not *towers*, so the verb must be the singular *has*, to match *neither*. Choice F uses the plural *have*. Changing the verb to a past form *had* (choice G) is incorrect because the narrative of this paragraph is told in the present tense. "Neither tower have" (choice H), also fails to eliminate the mismatched state of the subject and predicate, and it sounds awkward.

35. The correct answer is B. Choice B takes a cluster of statements and imposes order upon them through proper punctuation. Each new sentence has a subject and a verb. The third sentence pairs the two thoughts (the settling out of the minerals and their building up into towers, shelves, and icicles) that belong together because of their similar subject. Placing a colon between the first two statements, choice D makes the second a definition of the first, which it isn't. Placing semicolons (choice C) or commas (choice A), after every sentence does not define places where there need to be periods to signify the ends of complete thoughts.

36. The correct answer is H. You may have noticed that the reasons offered in each of these choices help to define the value of this sentence. It does offer an image (choice F) but it is a somewhat confusing visual that is jarring at this point before we know much about how these smokers function. We may be intrigued about the image (choice G), but it will take a longer explanation to help us understand why hot water rises in super-cold depths, and the purpose of the article is not to mystify the reader. We have no way of judging the accuracy of the image based on the passage (choice J), so that really isn't a good reason to eliminate it.

37. The correct answer is A. *Snowblowers* is in quotes because it is being used as a term with a slightly different meaning than it most often has. The author is not referring to real snowblowers, so the quotation marks are needed to set it off. A comma is needed after the term (choice A) to set it off from the appositive phrase that follows and defines the term, so choice B is not correct. Adding a semicolon (choice C), turns what follows it into a sentence fragment. Adding *being* (choice D) is an awkward means of explaining the term.

38. The correct answer is F. It is enough to say this water is "three times hotter than boiling" (choice F). *Hotter* is the correct comparative form, and "more hot" (choice G) is awkward. *Hottest* (choice H) is superlative and shouldn't be used to compare two items. "Triple hot" (choice J) is neither idiomatic nor clear. What is *triple hot*? If the writer never explains it, you shouldn't choose this option.

39. **The correct answer is B.** Because the author's overall idea may not yet have become evident, this may be a good question to set aside and come back to later. The futuristic angle of visiting these extreme environments (choice D), is only part of the author's method and is not the main theme of the passage. The author has just begun to introduce the idea of life in this place, so replacing one mention of living things with another (choice C) won't necessarily lead to the main theme. Also, many readers won't make the connection that bacteria are organisms in need of food and shelter, a fact that subsequent sentences explain. Left as is (choice A), the passage lacks the scientific explanation for why this place exists. Choice B is correct because it explains how life can be found in unexpected places.

40. **The correct answer is G.** Choice F allows a rather unwieldy paragraph to remain. In order to consider how it should be broken up, the idea strands have to be sorted. The paragraph begins with snowblowers, brings in other life and chemosynthesis, and then provides examples of living things. It's best to break somewhere in the middle of this chain when chemosynthesis has been introduced but before it's expanded upon further, as suggested by choice G. Placing a break after the sentence that follows (choice H) breaks up the discussion of microbes by separating two closely related sentences that should not be separated. That change also creates a too-short paragraph consisting of one sentence. Choice J leaves the paragraph hanging without much of a conclusion or promise of anything noteworthy to come.

41. **The correct answer is D.** The existing construction—"the reason...is because..."—is redundant, as *reason* already implies a cause. The appropriate construction is "the reason...is that..." as seen in choice D. "When" (choice B) is awkward and inappropriate. Choice C lacks a verb.

42. **The correct answer is J.** Choice G doesn't work because the preposition *over* could cause us to think *over* goes with *cover* instead of with *300*. As written, the compound sentence is too long and confusing and is missing the necessary comma before *and*. However, even adding a comma, as in choice H, still leaves us with the problem of a compound sentence that's too long and confusing. Choice J breaks the compound sentence into two separate sentences that are much clearer to read and understand.

43. **The correct answer is A.** You may want to break up what appears to be a rather long sentence, as choice B suggests, but you have already broken up this sentence in the previous question choice. Therefore, it makes the sentence read smoothly to leave it as it is (choice A). Neither a semicolon (choice D) nor a comma (choice C) would be necessary or appropriate here, when the sentence does not require further division.

44. **The correct answer is G.** Read each of the choices in the position indicated by the question. You'll notice that choices H and J both provide important information that could be added here, but they don't refer to the reader or lead into the subject of the last paragraph. The author's earlier method of taking you on a tour (choice G) is effectively echoed in this last paragraph. Choice F asks an absurd question and compromises what credibility the passage has gained so far.

45. **The correct answer is C.** The migration of life is discussed in the last paragraph (choice D); however, it is a brief mention and is part of the conclusion of the passage. Choice C is more appropriate because Paragraph 3's discussion of life forms that exist now at these vents is enhanced by knowing how life came to these remote areas. Bringing in these ideas at the very start (choice A), would interfere with the opening, and the reader wouldn't be ready to consider the implications. The second paragraph (choice B) is concerned more with the smoker towers, not with life forms.

46. **The correct answer is G.** As written, the sentence is awkward—the underlined portion is not a common phrase used in the English language. Choice G fixes the awkwardness with a more commonly accepted usage.

47. **The correct answer is D.** Choice D is correct because it properly defines the reference being made to an element of the previous sentence. *It* (choice A) lacks a proper antecedent and is vague. *Them* (choice B) seems to refer to cults or anthropologists, which is confusing. "These roles" (choice C) is specific but obscures the meaning of the sentence. The reference is to the act of endowing by the living. "This phenomenon" is exactly what the passage is describing.

48. **The correct answer is J.** The underlined phrase is referring to the dead, not the "elders" or the "graves." It must be placed beside the word it is modifying, which is *them* (choice J). Placed after *elders* (choice G) it seems to say they are the protectors, when they're appealing to the dead for protection from illness or misfortune. Placed after *dead* (choice H) it actually modifies *graves* because *dead* is only telling us whose graves are being visited. If the sentence isn't changed (choice F), the elders again seem to be the protectors.

49. **The correct answer is B.** Here, we are tasked with determining the appropriate end punctuation for a sentence. This is a straightforward, declarative sentence and should end in a period, so choice B is correct. Choice A incorrectly uses an exclamation point, which should only be used for sentences that are surprises or exclamations. Choice C incorrectly uses a question mark, as this is not a question. Choice D incorrectly uses a semicolon, which is not appropriate end of sentence punctuation.

50. **The correct answer is F.** This added sentence should both summarize the main theme of the passage and direct the reader's attention to larger issues that will be covered throughout the passage. Choice F is best because it reiterates the role of the dead in light of the responsibilities of the living. It confirms what we have just read and points to the rest of the passage. Mentioning other details the ancestors tend to (choice G) fails to provide the broader picture for the remainder of the passage. Describing which grave is selected (choice H) is another less important detail and lacks an overall focus. Discussing a generalized pattern (choice J) would provide a significant fact but would not restate the theme of the passage.

51. **The correct answer is D.** The sentence as it is written (choice A) provides irrelevant details about words that are not crucial to this discussion. Choice D is correct because it offers another word that further delineates how the Suku see the dead and the living. It is a contribution to the ideas introduced earlier in the sentence. Further explanation of the irrelevant terms (choice B) does not make them relevant. The additional information about lines of authority (choice C) is notable, but not in this context.

52. **The correct answer is G.** This awkward sentence structure can really be adjusted only by removing unnecessary words and creating two sentences, as suggested by choice G. The other fixes either lose ideas or mash them together into unwieldy linkage. Leaving the sentence as it is (choice F) has too many connections that blur meaning. Removing *much* from "the same" (choice H) changes the meaning. The addition of *and* also forces an awkward transition between two thoughts. Chopping down the verbiage, as choice J does, may read more smoothly, but the concept of the unchanging role of the dead is lost.

53. **The correct answer is B.** Commas are used to set off an appositive that defines an unfamiliar term or a person's name and role. *Suku* may be a proper name, but "of any age" does not define who or what a Suku is. Therefore, choices that keep this construction, such as choices A and C, are misusing the commas. *Kusu* is an unfamiliar term that needs to be defined. The description should be set off with commas, as in choices B and D. However, *Kusu* is not a direct quote but a term of reference, so it does not need to be set off by quotation marks and commas, as in choice D.

54. **The correct answer is F.** The sentence is correct as written. Choice G omits all punctuation and is thus incorrect, while choice H is missing a comma. Choice J inserts a semicolon, which should only be used in complex lists or to separate independent clauses.

55. **The correct answer is B.** Related ideas can be included as independent clauses within a single sentence or can stand alone as separate sentences. The choice is a matter of effect and clarity of meaning. The original construction creates a run-on sentence, offers no connection between these ideas, and blurs the meaning. Adding a comma (choice C) doesn't help; we still have a run-on sentence. Inserting a dash (choice D) does, would be an effective way to offer a thought that is relevant but incomplete, which this second sentence isn't. It is related but needs to stand alone, as in choice B, to give full weight to its contribution.

56. **The correct answer is J.** Sentence 3 is out of place. Leaving it where it is (choice F) makes it unrelated to its surrounding sentences. Switching it with the previous sentence (choice G) merely breaks the connection between Sentences 1 and 2. Moving it before Sentence 6 (choice H) deprives it of the thought that sets up its meaning. It flows properly after Sentence 6 as a demonstration of the fluid nature of authority in the Suku, so choice J is the best answer.

57. **The correct answer is B.** The pronoun being used in the underlined portion of this sentence should match the antecedent, *elders*. Since this is a plural noun, the pronoun also needs to be plural, and choice B is correct. The other answer choices use incorrect pronouns, given the context of this sentence.

58. **The correct answer is J.** As written, the sentence contains an internal error in logic, as the Suku can't

worship both dead or living elders. Choice J corrects this problem by using *and* instead of *or*. Choices G and H fail to fix the error in the sentence.

59. The correct answer is A. Each of these additions can be judged by how well it meets the criteria established in the question. Here, we need to find ideas that show how the dead are honored. Choice A works best because it explains how a sacrifice functions both as a tribute to the dead and an identical offering to the living elders, which is the theme of the paragraph and the passage. The mention of burying food (choice B) does show one way the dead are honored but fails to serve as a relevant detail because it doesn't echo the themes stressed throughout the passage. The reference to European customs (choice C) introduces another element of tribute but tells us little about the Suku and even less about how this relates to the entire passage. The introduction of other tribes' beliefs (choice D) makes an interesting side note about other ways the dead are honored like the living, but the topic isn't relevant to the themes of this paragraph or of the passage as a whole.

60. The correct answer is H. The role of the dead for the Suku has been stressed throughout the passage, so any summary must reiterate how ancestor worship is actually a continuation of the elder relationships that were present in life. Choice H is correct because it cites specific examples of these relationships and notes this continuation. The role of the ancestors as authority figures (choice F) fails to effectively explain their role both before and after death. Focusing on the levels of eldership (choice G) reveals only one side of what is, in fact, a rather simple arrangement of authority between generations that extends beyond death. The introduction of additional ideas about Western conceptions of death (choice J) fails to explain how the dead and the living share authority for the Suku people.

61. The correct answer is B. The phrase "more favorite," which appears in the original sentence, is awkward and also incorrectly implies comparison between two destinations. If *favorite* were to take a modifier, it would be the superlative *most*, but since the word *favorite* already means "preferred above all others," the word alone is sufficient and choice B is correct. *Favoritest* in choice C might be tempting, but no such word exists. The word *most* in choice D accompanies *youthful* instead of *favorite* and thus distorts the meaning.

62. The correct answer is F. Moving this prepositional phrase after *departure* (choice G) limits the meaning of the sentence. It seems to refer only to "departure" as being different back then from now; that's not the author's intention. Choice F is correct because the phrase modifies the idea that needs to be placed in a time context. The author's "realm of possibilities" is what has changed over time. When he or she was young, this scheme was different, and, presumably, now it has changed. Placing the phrase after *even* (choice H) could work, but the sentence is awkward. Placing the phrase after *afar* (choice J) suggests that the relatives come from shorter distances these days, which may or may not be true.

63. The correct answer is C. Choice C is correct because it breaks up a long, convoluted sentence whose meaning is unclear without some separation of ideas. A period best accomplishes this separation. A semicolon (choice B) should be used to create a compound sentence only when the ideas in the separate independent clauses are closely related. The substitution of *because* (choice D) links the ideas as a cause and effect, which they are not.

64. The correct answer is J. This sentence requires the past tense of the verb *take*. The correct past tense is *took*, and choice J is the only answer containing *took*. Choices F and G both use a nonexistent word (*taked*). Choice H contains the past participle *taken*, which creates the wrong verb tense; it fails further because it's missing the required auxiliary verb, *has* or *had*.

65. The correct answer is C. Choice C is correct because it gives the reader a sense of how the author lacks any real connection to these mysterious machines, which are essential to travel. Having never experienced them, he finds them unreal. Describing them as "identical" to his own toy airplanes (choice B) makes them seem more familiar and less mysterious. Referring to them as "shiny" (choice A) creates only a visual image. Considering them as "terrifying" (choice D) is contradictory to the idea that they're alluring.

66. The correct answer is J. The author's use of the movie metaphor is overdone in the original (choice F). Mentioning popcorn (choice G) is equally redundant and adds little to the sentence. The third mention of the movie connection (choice H) is both wordy and repetitive. Eliminating this unnecessary element (choice J) is the wisest option.

67. The correct answer is B. The second part of the original (choice A) is a sentence fragment. It must be joined to the previous sentence, which choice B does correctly with a comma. Not using any punctuation or connection (choice C) is also confusing. Creating a different, seemingly parallel phrase (choice D) changes the meaning of the sentence and produces a construction that doesn't make sense.

68. **The correct answer is J.** You might be able to make sense of the original (choice F), but it lacks parallel construction, which would give the sentence consistent form and clearer meaning. Choice J is correct because it provides a form *flying*, which matches the other verb forms in this list, *enjoying* and *caring*. The original is a noun clause, and it is repeated in a different form (choice G) which fails to make it smoother. Changing it into a prepositional phrase (choice H) also defies parallel construction.

69. **The correct answer is C.** The important decision to make here is whether the parenthetical phrase indeed needs to be set off from the rest of the sentence. The use of parentheses, as in choice A, is reserved for ideas that have no essential relation to the rest of the sentence, such as an explanation, figures, data, or examples. The phrase here is very strongly related, however, so it should not be tucked away in parentheses. Choice C is correct because it properly joins the second part of the predicate to the rest of the sentence. Choices B and D, by adding either a period or semicolon, cause the second part of the sentence to stand alone as a fragment.

70. **The correct answer is H.** The author's additional sentence must amplify the ideas of the previous sentence without repeating them. The author's view of other businessmen in similar surroundings points to the change occurring within the author's mind. Airports will soon be different places for him. The loss and separation of that moment will become an accepted part of the airport experience from now on. The smell of airplanes (choice F) may have come from his youth, but it fails to pinpoint the changing connotations. Details about the father's job (choice G) do little to advance the author's theme. Observations about the physical condition of the gate area (choice J) may be a telling detail but the author's noticing wear and tear is not indicative of his feelings.

71. **The correct answer is D.** It's highly doubtful that the author needs to describe which part of the airport is being mentioned. The coming sentences make it clear that he is the one leaving, not the one being left behind. Eliminating these irrelevant details (choice D) will improve the sentence and the paragraph. The other choices merely add more irrelevant detail. Further explaining the structure's shape (choice B) or adding a verb (choice C) do not tell the reader anything important.

72. **The correct answer is J.** Choice J is correct because the relationship between the adjectives in a series governs the use of commas to separate them. The term *football player* has to stay together as it is a word group whose meaning is defined by being united. The original (choice F) places a comma between *football* and *player*, which upsets the meaning. Having no commas, as in choice G, blurs all the adjectives together. The word *and* can't be placed between *unwavering* and *football player*, as in choice H, because *unwavering* describes the compound noun *football player*. There is no comma between the last adjective in a series and the noun being described. Therefore, choice J is correct in placing a comma only between *brave* and *unwavering*.

73. **The correct answer is B.** The original sentence uses the objective pronoun form *me*. To properly complete the parallel construction, a subject is needed, as in "they are as excited as I am/was." Choice C is confusing, because it is unclear to whom *we* refers. Choice D might seem to make better sense until we remember that the writer has revealed that airports are no longer exciting places for him. We are left with choice B, which is grammatically correct and makes sense in the context of the essay.

74. **The correct answer is H.** The original sentence (choice F) is a fragment—it lacks a predicate. Choice G is a complete sentence saying that the "rushing, lost bags, and missed connections" *are* the "never coming home again." The sentence doesn't make sense. Choice J is a complete sentence and makes sense, so we should consider it. However, choice H is a better option. It more clearly and completely explains the contrast between the children's excitement and the writer's adult feelings about airports.

75. **The correct answer is D.** Choice D is correct because the word the author intends to use is the verb *affected*, meaning "emotionally stirred or moved" or "influenced by." *Effect* is usually a noun, although in its occasional verb form, it means "to bring about," which is inappropriate in the context of the original sentence (choice A). Used as a noun in choice B, the word *affects* means "feelings or emotions," but to say, " I feel no affects…by train stations" makes no sense grammatically. Changing the contraction *I'm* to *I am*, as in choice C, doesn't alter the misuse of *effected* as a verb.

1.	A	16.	J	31.	C	46.	H
2.	G	17.	C	32.	G	47.	B
3.	E	18.	K	33.	E	48.	H
4.	F	19.	A	34.	K	49.	D
5.	C	20.	F	35.	C	50.	G
6.	J	21.	D	36.	J	51.	E
7.	A	22.	K	37.	C	52.	H
8.	J	23.	D	38.	G	53.	C
9.	D	24.	J	39.	C	54.	F
10.	G	25.	C	40.	J	55.	C
11.	D	26.	G	41.	E	56.	K
12.	G	27.	B	42.	G	57.	C
13.	D	28.	F	43.	E	58.	K
14.	F	29.	D	44.	K	59.	C
15.	C	30.	G	45.	E	60.	G

1. **The correct answer is A.** To figure out what percentage chose green, first determine *how many* chose green. Out of 400 total people, 150 chose blue and 200 chose red, leaving 400 – (150 + 200) = 50 people. So 50 out of 400 chose green. Now calculate the percentage:

$$\text{Percent} = \frac{\text{part}}{\text{whole}}$$
$$\frac{x}{100} = \frac{50}{400}$$
$$400x = 5{,}000$$
$$x = \frac{50}{4} = 12.5$$

Choices B and C are incorrect due to arithmetic errors. For choice D, while 50 out of 400 chose green, this does not amount to 50%. Choice E is the percentage who did not choose green.

2. **The correct answer is G.** You're given that 1 hand equals 4 inches, and you want to find out how many hands are in 57 inches. This can be best solved by setting up a proportion:

$$\frac{1}{4} = \frac{x}{57}$$
$$4x = 57$$
$$x = \frac{57}{4} = 14.25$$

Choice F is too low; you must divide 57 by 4 and make certain not to approximate the answer. For choice H, when solving the equation $4x = 57$, you subtracted 4 from both sides, but you should have divided both sides by 4. In choice J, the decimal point is off by one place. For choice K, when solving the equation $4x = 57$, you multiplied both sides by 4 instead of dividing by it.

3. **The correct answer is E.** If $\frac{3}{4}$ of the convertibles are red, then $\frac{1}{4}$ of the convertibles are NOT red.

We're told that 22 convertibles are NOT red, so there must be a total of 4(22) = 88 convertibles. Since we're also told that $\frac{1}{8}$ of the cars are convertibles, it follows that there are a total of 8(88) = 704 cars.

Choice A represents the number of convertibles. Choice B is twice the number of convertibles, but not the number of cars in the lot. Choice C is $\frac{3}{4}$ of the number of cars; you likely misinterpreted the quantity to which $\frac{3}{4}$ is to be applied. Choice D is the number of cars minus the number of convertibles.

4. **The correct answer is F.** You're already given the properly laid out proportion, so cross-multiply to solve for z:

$$\frac{15}{3z} = \frac{10}{4}$$
$$30z = 60$$
$$z = 2$$

Beware of choice J (6), which is a partial answer. This value satisfies 3z, the unknown denominator, but doesn't correctly answer the question.

If you plug the values of z in choices G, H, and J into the proportion, you do not get equality.

5. **The correct answer is C.** To find the total number of miles traveled by the two airplanes, first find the distance traveled by each, remembering that distance = rate × time.

For Airplane A:
distance = (540 mph)(3 hours) = 1,620 miles.

For Airplane B:
distance = (400 mph)(3.5 hours) = 1,400 miles.

The total distance, therefore, is 1,620 miles + 1,400 miles = 3,020 miles.

Choice A is the number of miles Airplane B has traveled. Choice B is the number of miles Airplane A has traveled. For choice D, you multiplied the rate of Airplane B times the time for Airplane A, and vice versa. For choice E, you added the rates and times for both planes and multiplied those quantities.

6. **The correct answer is J.** Twelve percent of x is 0.12x. Reducing the speed by this amount is represented by subtracting it from x: $x - 0.12x = 0.88x$.

7. **The correct answer is A.** Substitute $a = -2$ into the expression and simplify:

$$-(-2)^2(1-3(-2)) = -4(1+6) = -4(7) = -28$$

Choices B and D are the result of sign errors. Choice C is the result of not applying the order of operations to simplify the expression. Choice E is the opposite of the correct answer.

8. **The correct answer is J.** To find $f(3)$, plug in 3 for every instance of x in the function and remember to follow PEMDAS.

$$\begin{aligned} f(3) &= 2(3)^2 - 3(3) + 6 \\ &= 18 - 9 + 6 \\ &= 15 \end{aligned}$$

Choice F is $f(1)$, and choice G is $f(0)$. In choice H, note that $3^2 = 9$, not 6. For choice K, you have ignored the negative sign in the expression $-3x$.

9. **The correct answer is D.** Call the coordinates of B (x, y). Using the midpoint formula yields:

$$(-3,1) = \left(\frac{x+7}{2}, \frac{y-9}{2}\right)$$

Therefore,

$$\begin{aligned} \frac{x+7}{2} &= -3 & \frac{y-9}{2} &= 1 \\ x+7 &= -6 & y-9 &= 2 \\ x &= -13 & y &= 11 \end{aligned}$$

B has coordinates (–13, 11). In choice A, the coordinates are reversed. Choices B and C are incorrect because you average the coordinates of the endpoints of a line segment to find the midpoint, not take half of the difference. Choice E is the midpoint of the segment $\overline{AM}$.

10. **The correct answer is G.** FOIL the squared binomial, then distribute the $-i$ and simplify:

$$\begin{aligned} -i(2-5i)^2 &= -i(2-5i)(2-5i) \\ &= -i(4-20i+25i^2) \\ &= -i(4-20i-25) \\ &= -i(-21-20i) \\ &= 21i+20i^2 \\ &= 21i-20 \\ &= -20+21i \end{aligned}$$

Choice F is the negative of the correct answer. Choice H is incorrect because $i^2 = -1$. Choice J is just the squared portion; you forgot to multiply by $-i$. Choice K is incorrect because $(a-b)^2 \neq a^2 - b^2$.

11. **The correct answer is D.** To find the average, divide the total number of songs played by the number of half-hour sessions. To find the total number of songs played, add up all the numbers of songs and divide by 8. Remember that some of the numbers of songs occur more than once, as indicated in the bottom row of the table:

$$\frac{6+8+8+8+9+9+12+12}{8} = \frac{72}{8} = 9$$

Therefore, the average was 9 songs per half-hour session.

Choice A is the result of dividing the sum of the first row by the sum of the second row. This does not account for the fact that some of the numbers of songs occur more than once, namely 8 occurs 3 times, while 9 and 12 both occur twice. Choice B is the *median* number of songs played per half-hour session, not the mean or average. Choice C is the average of the four numbers of songs that occurred: $\frac{6+8+9+12}{4} = 8.75$, which does not account for some song numbers occurring multiple times or for a total of 8 sessions. Choice E divides the total number of songs by 4, rather than 8. This is the average number of songs played per *hour*, not per half-hour.

12. **The correct answer is G.** If the product of two expressions is zero, then one of those expressions must equal zero. So either $m + 4 = 0$ or $m - 2 = 0$.

$$m+4=0 \quad \text{or} \quad m-2=0$$
$$m=-4 \qquad\qquad m=2$$

Only 2 is among the answer choices, so it must be correct. If you substitute any of the values in choices F, H, and K in for *m*, you do not get zero.

13. **The correct answer is D.** This expression is read as "the absolute value of 7 plus the absolute value of –9." Remember that absolute value is always the positive distance from zero on a number line, so the sum of two absolute values can never be negative. Eliminate choices A and B.

The absolute value of a number is basically the number without a positive or negative sign, so:

$$|7|+|-9|=7+9=16$$

In choice A, the absolute value signs are ignored and the numbers are multiplied; in choice B, the absolute value signs are ignored and the numbers are added. In choice C, $|7 + (-9)|$ is computed, not the given sum. In choice E, the numbers are multiplied instead of added.

14. **The correct answer is F.** There are multiple ways to find this solution using angle properties. One possibility is as follows. The measure of angle *RWS* is 70° because it is supplementary to angle *RWT*. The angle measures in triangle *RNW* must add up to 180°, so 180° – 70° – 90° = 20°. Another method is to consider that angles *PRW* and *RWT* are alternate interior angles between parallel lines, and therefore have the same measure. Since *PRV* is a right angle, the measure of angle *VRW* is 110° – 90° = 20°. The measures of all angles are shown in the figure below.

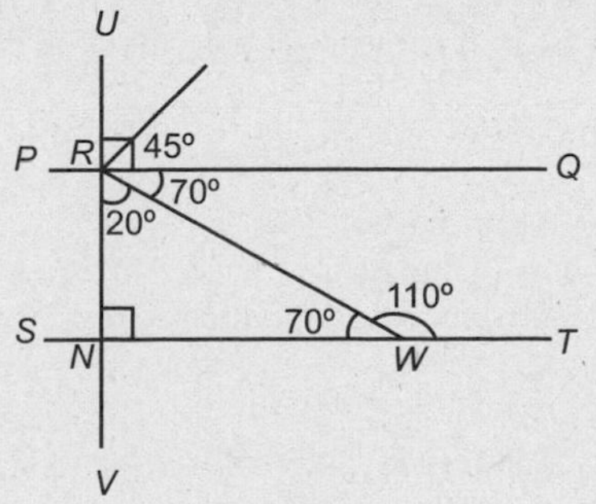

Choices G, H, J, and K are all measures of angles in the figure, but not the measure of angle *VRW*.

15. **The correct answer is C.** The two nearest consecutive perfect squares between which 155 lies are 144 and 169; that is, 144 < 155 < 169. Taking the square root of all terms of the inequality yields $12 < \sqrt{155} < 13$. Multiplying by –1 then gives $-13 < -\sqrt{155} < -12$. All other choices have pairs of integers for which 155 does not lie between their squares.

16. **The correct answer is J.** Compute the least common multiple of 12, 18, and 24 as follows:

$$\begin{array}{r|rrr} 6 & 12 & 18 & 24 \\ \hline 2 & 2 & 3 & 4 \\ \hline & 1 & 3 & 2 \end{array}$$

So the least common multiple is $6 \bullet 2 \bullet 3 \bullet 2 = 72$. Choice F is a common factor, but not the least common multiple. Choice G is the greatest common factor. Choice H is incorrect because 48 is not a multiple of 18. Choice K is a common multiple of these numbers, but not the *least* common multiple.

17. **The correct answer is C.** You should recognize that $y = x^2 + 4x - 21$ is the equation of a parabola that opens upward. One of the characteristics of such a parabola is that it will always intersect the *x*-axis 0, 1, or 2 times, but never more. This means that you can eliminate choices D and E right away.

Remember that the graph will intersect the *x*-axis only when *y* equals zero. To find the number of *x*-intercepts of a quadratic equation, $ax^2 + bx + c = 0$, evaluate the discriminant, $b^2 - 4ac$. If the discriminant is positive, there are two *x*-intercepts; if it's zero, there is one *x*-intercept; if it's negative, there are none. In this case:

$$\begin{aligned} b^2-4ac &= (4)^2-4(1)(-21) \\ &= 16-(-84) \\ &= 100 \end{aligned}$$

Since this is a positive discriminant, the graph will cross the *x*-axis exactly twice. Hence, choices A and B cannot be correct.

18. **The correct answer is K.** The final rectangle after a 180° rotation, centered at *A*, is shown below.

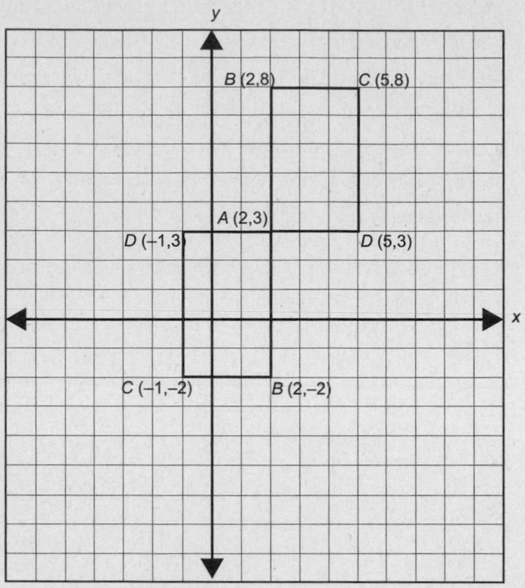

The final position of point *C* is (–1, –2).

Choice F is the final location of point *C* after rotating 90° clockwise, centered at *A*. Choice G is the final location of point *C* after rotating 90° counterclockwise, centered at *A*. Choice H is the final location of point *B*. Choice J is the final location of point *D*.

19. **The correct answer is A.** Since each basket holds 20 apples, the number of apples must be divided by 20 to find the number of baskets that will be needed.

Choices B, D, and E are all equivalent equations that reverse the relationship between *a* and *b*—that is, they assume that the number of baskets is 20 times the number of apples. Choice C also misrepresents the relationship between *a* and *b*, in this case by assuming that the number of baskets is 20 divided by the number of apples, rather than the inverse.

20. **The correct answer is F.** The slope of the line containing these two points is $m=\frac{8-(-4)}{-4-4}=\frac{12}{-8}=-\frac{3}{2}$. Using the point-slope form of the equation of a line with the point (4, –4) and then simplifying yields the following:

$$y+4=-\frac{3}{2}(x-4)$$
$$y+4=-\frac{3}{2}x+6$$
$$y=-\frac{3}{2}x+2$$
$$2y=-3x+4$$
$$3x+2y=4$$

Choice G is incorrect because the sign of the slope is wrong. Choice H is incorrect because this line has the reciprocal of the correct slope. Choice J is incorrect because this line has the negative reciprocal of the correct slope. In choice K, you did not apply the distributive property correctly when simplifying the point-slope form for the equation of the line.

21. **The correct answer is D.** $18\times5=90$ and $18\times6=108$, so there is no whole number that can be multiplied by 18 to get a product of 96.

Choices A, B, C, and E are all factors of 96:

$$96\div2=48$$
$$96\div3=32$$
$$96\div16=6$$
$$96\div24=4$$

22. **The correct answer is K.** Let *x* be the original price. Then, $0.85x=\$2{,}250$. So $x=\frac{\$2{,}250}{0.85}$. Choice F represents an 85% discount off the price $2,250. Choices G and J are the result of not applying the 85% correctly. Choice H would make the sale price higher than the original price.

23. **The correct answer is D.** Factor the quadratic expression, which is a difference of squares, then use the zero product property to find the solutions:

$$4x^2-25=0$$
$$(2x+5)(2x-5)=0$$
$$(2x+5)=0 \text{ or } (2x-5)=0$$
$$x=-\frac{5}{2} \text{ or } x=\frac{5}{2}$$

Since $x>0$, $x=\frac{5}{2}$ is the only acceptable solution.

Choice A is a solution to the equation, but does not satisfy $x>0$. Choices B, C, and E are incorrect because they do not result in a true statement when substituted for *x* in the original equation. These choices may result from one of several factoring errors.

24. **The correct answer is J.** If the probability of NOT saying math is the favorite is $\frac{1}{5}$, then the probability of saying math IS the favorite is $1-\frac{1}{5}=\frac{4}{5}$. Therefore, we have the following proportion:

$$\frac{4}{5}=\frac{\text{number of students who say math is their favorite}}{40}$$

Cross-multiplying yields $4(40)=5\times$ number of students who say math is their favorite, and then dividing both sides by 5 yields that the number of students who say math is their favorite is 32. Choice F is the number of students who do NOT say math is their favorite. Choice G would mean $\frac{1}{4}$, not $\frac{1}{5}$, of students who say math is NOT their favorite.

Choice H would mean $\frac{1}{2}$ of the sample did NOT say math is their favorite, which is not the case. Choice K would mean $\frac{1}{10}$ of the sample did NOT say math is their favorite, which is not the case.

25. The correct answer is C. Calculate as follows: $k(0) = -2\sqrt{25-5(0)} = -2\sqrt{25} = -2(5) = -10$. Choice A is incorrect because $k(0)$ is a real number, and so the graph of $y = k(x)$ does have a y-intercept. Choice B is incorrect because this is the x-intercept but written backwards. Choice D is incorrect because you need to take the square root of 25. Choice E is incorrect because this is the x-intercept.

26. The correct answer is G. You're given the number of fluid ounces in a cup and the cost of 9 cups, and you're asked to find the cost per fluid ounce. First, convert 9 cups into fluid ounces by setting up a proportion:

$$\frac{9 \text{ cups}}{x \text{ fl. oz.}} = \frac{1 \text{ cup}}{8 \text{ fl. oz.}}$$
$$x = 72$$

So you know that 72 fluid ounces cost \$23.04. Use another proportion to find the cost of one fluid ounce:

$$\frac{72}{\$23.04} = \frac{1}{x}$$
$$72x = \$23.04$$
$$x = \frac{\$23.04}{72} = \$0.32$$

Choice F is calculated assuming 12 cups, not 9 cups. For choice H, you've added 8 fluid ounces and 9 cups without converting the units; you should have multiplied these quantities. For both choices J and K, you did not multiply the number of cups by 8 fluid ounces before dividing.

27. The correct answer is B. The perimeter of a rectangle is $P = 2(l + w)$. Since the length is 6 inches greater than the width, we can substitute $l = w + 6$ and $P = 44$ and solve:

$$P = 2(l + w)$$
$$44 = 2[(w+6)+w]$$
$$22 = (w+6)+w$$
$$22 = 2w+6$$
$$16 = 2w$$
$$8 = w$$

Since the width is 8 inches, the length is $8 + 6 = 14$ inches, and the area is $A = l \times w = 8 \times 14 = 112$.

Choice A results from dividing the perimeter by 4 to find the length, then subtracting 6 to find the width: $11 \times 5 = 55$. Choice C assumes that the rectangle is a square and that both the length and width are 11 inches. Choice D results from dividing the perimeter by 4 to find the width, then adding 6 to find the length: $17 \times 11 = 187$. Choice E results from subtracting 6 from the perimeter, then dividing by 2 to find the width and adding 6 to find the length: $19 \times 25 = 475$.

28. The correct answer is F. Set $y = 0$ in $2y = 1 - 4x$ and solve for x:

$$1 - 4x = 0$$
$$1 = 4x$$
$$x = \frac{1}{4}$$

Choice G is the y-intercept. Choice H is an attempt at computing the y-intercept. Choice J is the reciprocal of the correct answer. Choice K is the result of an arithmetic error.

29. The correct answer is D. Let x be the length of the fifth commercial segment. For the average to be 130 seconds, x must satisfy the equation $\frac{85+125+95+145+x}{5} = 130$. Solving for x yields the following:

$$\frac{85+125+95+145+x}{5} = 130$$
$$\frac{450+x}{5} = 130$$
$$450 + x = 650$$
$$x = 200$$

Choice A is incorrect because you divided the sum of the five commercial segments by 4 when computing the average. Choice B is the result of an arithmetic error. Choice C is incorrect because this would necessitate the average of the given four commercial segment lengths to be 130 seconds, which is not the case. Choice E is incorrect because you need to subtract 450; this is the result of not solving the linear equation used to compute the average correctly.

30. **The correct answer is G.** In a right triangle, $\text{cosine} = \frac{\text{adjacent}}{\text{hypotenuse}}$, so first you need to find *PR*, the length of the hypotenuse. You may use the Pythagorean theorem or simply recognize a 3-4-5 right triangle. Since 3 is the side adjacent to *P* and 5 is the length of the hypotenuse, the cosine of *P* is $\frac{3}{5}$. Choice F is cot(*P*). Choice H is tan(*P*). Choice J is sin(*P*). Choice K is csc(*P*).

31. **The correct answer is C.** The total price for the CDs at regular price is \$16 + \$16 + \$24 = \$56.

To find the discounted price, you can find 30% of the total price and subtract it from \$56, or find 70% of \$56, since Maria paid 70% of the regular price (100% – 30% = 70%):

$$70\% \text{ of } \$56 = \frac{70}{100} \times \$56 = \$39.20$$

Choice A is the amount of the discount, or 30% of the regular price. Choice B accounts for only one of the single CDs. Choice D applies the discount to only the single CDs, not the double CD. Choice E applies the discount to only the double CD, not the single CDs.

32. **The correct answer is G.** Since average is equal to $\frac{\text{sum of values}}{\text{number of values}}$, the sum is the product of the average and the number of values.

The average of the first 7 integers is 13, so their sum is 7 × 13 = 91. The average of all 8 integers is 12, so their sum is 8 × 12 = 96. The value of the eighth number must be equal to the difference between the two sums: 96 – 91 = 5. Choice F is too small; the resulting average would be less than 12. Choice H would not reduce the average by 1. Choice J would result in the same average, 13, not a decreased average. Choice K would increase the average if added as an eighth number.

33. **The correct answer is E.** Use the exponent rules to simplify the expression:

$$\frac{-a^4\left(b^2\right)^4c^6}{(-a)^3b^3c^8} = \frac{-a^4b^8c^6}{-a^3b^3c^8} = \frac{a^{4-3}b^{8-3}}{c^{8-6}} = \frac{ab^5}{c^2}$$

Choice A is incorrect because it should not have a factor of –1 and $\left(b^2\right)^4 = b^{2\,\bullet\,4}$, not b^{2+4}. Choices B and C are incorrect because when dividing powers of the same base, you subtract the exponents. Choice D is incorrect because when raising a power of a number to another power, you multiply the powers.

34. **The correct answer is K.** To compute the time, divide the total number of gallons to be removed by the rate at which the pump can remove them. Doing so yields the following:

$$\frac{g \text{ gallons}}{8.25 \text{ gallons/minute}} = \frac{g}{8.25} \text{ minutes}$$

Choice F is incorrect because the resulting units are not minutes, so this cannot be the correct quantity. Gallons must cancel, leaving only minutes. Choice G is incorrect because you cannot add these two quantities because they have different units. Choice H is incorrect because this is the reciprocal of the correct answer. Choice J is incorrect because you cannot subtract these two quantities because they have different units.

35. **The correct answer is C.** Let *s* be the length of a side of the square. Using the perimeter formula yields 4*s* = 22, so that $s = \frac{22}{4} = 5.5$ cm. So the area of the square is $(5.5 \text{ cm})^2 = 30.25$ square centimeters. Choice A is the length of a side of the square. Choice B is incorrect because you square the length of a side to get the area of a square, not multiply it by 2. Choice D is incorrect because the area of a square is not equal to twice the perimeter. Choice E is incorrect because the perimeter of a square is 4 times the length of a side, not 2 times the length of a side.

36. **The correct answer is J.** Since $2B = \begin{bmatrix} 8 & -4 \\ -6 & -2 \end{bmatrix}$ and $3A = \begin{bmatrix} -6 & -9 \\ 3 & -3 \end{bmatrix}$, it follows that

$$2B - 3A = \begin{bmatrix} 8-(-6) & -4-(-9) \\ -6-3 & -2-(-3) \end{bmatrix} = \begin{bmatrix} 14 & 5 \\ -9 & 1 \end{bmatrix}.$$

Choice F is incorrect because you only multiplied the top left corner by the scalar each time when computing

2*B* and 3*A*. Choice G is the sum of 2*B* + 3*A*. Choice H is 2*B*. Choice K is 3*A*.

37. **The correct answer is C.** Factor the expression as $f(x) = x(x - 2)(x + 2)(x^2 + 9)$. The x-intercepts of a function are the real x-values for which the function equals 0. This only occurs when $x = -2$, 0 and 2. The other two values that make $x^2 + 9 = 0$ are imaginary ($3i$ and $-3i$); a graph does not have an x-intercept at an imaginary value. So there are three x-intercepts. Choices A and B are incorrect because there are three distinct factors that can be zero. Choice D is incorrect because imaginary solutions, like those of the equation $x^2 + 9 = 0$, are not x-intercepts. Choice E is incorrect because a fifth degree polynomial can have at most 5 x-intercepts.

38. **The correct answer is G.** Rewrite the equation in exponential form: $3^y = \frac{1}{81}$. Since $81 = 3^4$, it follows that $\frac{1}{81} = \frac{1}{3^4} = 3^{-4}$. So $y = -4$. Choice F is incorrect because you do not multiply base times exponent to compute a power. Choice H is incorrect because you do not solve the equivalent exponential equation $3^y = \frac{1}{81}$ by dividing both sides by 3. Choice J is incorrect because you do not solve the equivalent exponential equation $3^y = \frac{1}{81}$ by multiplying both sides by 3. Choice K is incorrect because $3^4 = 81$, not $\frac{1}{81}$.

39. **The correct answer is C.** The translation of $g(x)$ two units to the right is given by $g(x - 2)$. Computing this yields $g(x - 2) = (x - 2 + 3)^2 - 2 = (x + 1)^2 - 2$. This is a parabola opening upward with vertex $(-1, -2)$. So the range is $[-2, \infty)$. Choice A is incorrect because it is the domain. Choice B is incorrect because this is the part of the domain to the left of the vertex. Choice D is incorrect because this is the part of the domain to the right of the vertex. Choice E is incorrect because this would be the range had the parabola opened downward instead of upward.

40. **The correct answer is J.** If the radius of the circle is 3, then the diameter is 6. Since a diameter of the circle is congruent to one side of the square, as shown below, the side length of the square is 6 units, and the area of the square is $6 \times 6 = 36$ square units.

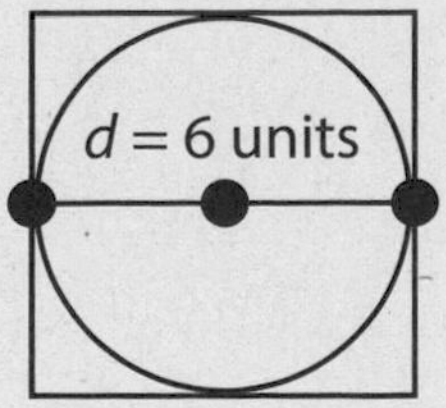

Choice F assumes that the radius is equal in length to one side of the square. Choice G gives the perimeter of the square, 24 units. Choice H is an approximation of the area of the circle, $3^2 \times \pi \approx 28$. Choice K is an approximation of 36π, which is π times the diameter of the circle squared.

41. **The correct answer is E.** Plug in numbers to solve this problem. Let $a = 0$, because this will quickly get rid of answer choices that might otherwise remain with "easier" numbers. Since $b < a$, we can use -3 to replace b. And since $c < 0$, let's pick -1. So $a = 0$, $b = -3$, and $c = -1$.

If you plug these numbers into each answer choice, you'll see that only choice E yields a valid result:

$$\frac{a}{c} < \frac{b}{c}$$
$$\frac{0}{-1} < \frac{-3}{-1}$$
$$0 < 3$$

Choice A is incorrect—use sample values like $a = 1$ and $b = -2$ to see that this need not be true. For choice B, use $a = -1$ and $c = -2$ to see that this need not be true. For choices C and D, use $a = -1$, $b = -2$, and $c = -2$ to see that this need not be true.

42. **The correct answer is G.** To find the area of the shaded frame, calculate the area of the entire picture (including frame) and then subtract the unshaded region (the picture alone).

The entire rectangle is 30 inches by 22 inches, so it has an area of $(30)(22) = 660$ square inches.

For the unshaded region, remember that the picture is surrounded by a 2-inch border on all four sides. So its length is $30 - 2 - 2 = 26$ inches, and its width is $22 - 2 - 2 = 18$ inches. This makes its area $(26)(18) = 468$ square inches.

Therefore, the area of the shaded frame is $660 - 468 = 192$ square inches.

Choice F is the area of the picture portion of the entire frame, not the shaded portion. In choice H, you likely made an arithmetic error. Choice J only accounts for half of the frame. Choice K is just one-fourth of the shaded portion.

43. **The correct answer is E.** The only way $|m - n|$ could equal zero is for m to equal n. But, m and n have opposite signs and so cannot be equal. Choices A and C are incorrect because the statements are false if $m = -2$ and $n = 3$. Choice B is incorrect because the statement is false if $m = -2$ and $n = 2$. Choice D is never true because the right side is always negative, and an absolute value expression is always nonnegative.

44. The correct answer is K. Solve both equations for y and equate the resulting expressions. The second equation can be written as $y = \frac{1}{a}x + \frac{1}{a}$. Equating the expressions yields the equation $5x - 1 = \frac{1}{a}x + \frac{1}{a}$. Solve for x, as follows:

$$\begin{aligned} 5x - 1 &= \frac{1}{a}x + \frac{1}{a} \\ 5x - \frac{1}{a}x &= 1 + \frac{1}{a} \\ \left(5 - \frac{1}{a}\right)x &= 1 + \frac{1}{a} \end{aligned}$$

If $a = \frac{1}{5}$, then this equation becomes $0 = 6$, which means there is no solution. Otherwise, there is a unique solution: $x = \dfrac{1 + \frac{1}{a}}{5 - \frac{1}{a}}$

In no case are there infinitely many solutions.

45. The correct answer is E. The line $x = -\frac{1}{3}y + 4$ can be written equivalently as $y = -3x + 12$. So its slope is -3. Using the point-slope form of a line with slope -3 and the point $(-2,-1)$ gives the following equation:

$$\begin{aligned} y + 1 &= -3(x + 2) \\ y + 1 &= -3x - 6 \\ y &= -3x - 7 \end{aligned}$$

46. The correct answer is H. Use the Pythagorean theorem to solve for the missing length:

$$\begin{aligned} a^2 + b^2 &= c^2 \\ 15^2 + b^2 &= 17^2 \\ b &= \sqrt{17^2 - 15^2} \\ &= \sqrt{289 - 225} \\ &= \sqrt{64} \\ &= 8 \end{aligned}$$

Choice F is incorrect because the correct expression is $\sqrt{17^2 - 15^2}$, not $(17 - 15)^2$. For choice G, you treated the hypotenuse like a leg in the Pythagorean theorem and forgot to square each of the legs. For choice J, you treated the hypotenuse like a leg in the Pythagorean theorem. For choice K, you forgot to take the square root.

47. The correct answer is B. Use the distance formula:

$$\begin{aligned} \sqrt{(a-b)^2 + (-b-(-a))^2} &= \sqrt{(a-b)^2 + (-b+a)^2} \\ &= \sqrt{(a-b)^2 + (a-b)^2} \\ &= \sqrt{2(a-b)^2} \\ &= \sqrt{2}\,|a-b| \end{aligned}$$

Choice A is incorrect because $\sqrt{a^2 + b^2} \neq a + b$. Choice C is incorrect because $|a-b| \neq |a| + |b|$. Choice D is incorrect because you subtracted the y-coordinates incorrectly. Choice E is missing the radical sign.

48. The correct answer is H. The temperature at 9 a.m. is $-15.5°$, and at 10 a.m., it is $-13.0°$. This is a difference of $-13.0° - (-15.5°) = 2.5°$. If the temperature increases by 2.5° each hour, then 3 hours later at 1 p.m., it will be $-13.0° + 3(2.5°) = -13.0° + 7.5° = -5.5°$.

For choice F, you assumed the temperature was decreasing by 2.5 degrees Celsius per hour, but it is increasing at this rate. Choice G is the temperature after two hours of such an increase, not three hours. Choice J is the amount by which the temperature increases, and choice K is the total amount by which the temperature increases.

49. The correct answer is D. The slope of the line passing through these two points is

$$\frac{\frac{1}{2} - \left(-\frac{5}{6}\right)}{-\frac{4}{5} - \frac{3}{10}} = \frac{\frac{3}{6} + \frac{5}{6}}{-\frac{8}{10} - \frac{3}{10}} = \frac{\frac{8}{6}}{-\frac{11}{10}} = \frac{8}{6} \bullet \left(-\frac{10}{11}\right) = -\frac{40}{33}.$$

So a line perpendicular to this line must have slope $\frac{33}{40}$. Choice A is the slope of a line parallel to the given line. Choice B must be multiplied by -1. Choice C must also take the reciprocal. Choice E is the result of dividing fractions incorrectly.

50. The correct answer is G. The distances in the diagram form a right triangle. To find the height difference, h, between the altitude of the plane and the top of the control tower, use the sine function:

$$\begin{aligned} \text{sine} &= \frac{\text{opposite}}{\text{hypotenuse}} \\ \sin 27^\circ &= \frac{h}{35{,}000} \\ h &= 35{,}000 \times \sin 27^\circ \end{aligned}$$

Choices F and H are incorrect; both these answers equal the length of the base of the triangle. For choice J, you did not multiply the numerator and denominator. For choice K, you should be using either sin(27) or cos(63) in place of cos(27), and you should be multiplying the numerator by it, not dividing these quantities.

51. **The correct answer is E.** Let x be the width of the closet floor. The length is then $2x + 4$. Using the perimeter formula yields the equation $2x + 2(2x + 4) = 62$. Simplifying yields $6x + 8 = 62$, so $6x = 54$. Thus, $x = 9$ so the width is 9 feet and length is $2(9) + 4 = 22$ feet. Thus, the area is $9(22) = 198$ square feet. Choice A is the width of the floor. Choice B is the length of the floor. Choice C is the result of computing the area, assuming the width and length are equal. Choice D is incorrect because the area does not equal twice the perimeter.

52. **The correct answer is H.** Rolling a fair six-sided die twice gives $6^2 = 36$ outcomes. You must determine how many of these outcomes yield one 5 and one 6. The only rolls that can result in this scenario are (5, 6) or (6, 5). Since all rolls are equally likely, the probability of this occurring is $\frac{2}{36} = \frac{1}{18}$. Choice F is the probability of getting either a 5 or a 6 in one roll. Choice G is the probability of the complement of the event "getting one 5 and one 6." Choice J is the probability of getting at least one 5 or one 6 in two rolls. Choice K is the probability of getting a 5 in one roll.

53. **The correct answer is C.** The initial 25% increase is given by $60^\circ + 0.25(60^\circ) = 75^\circ$. The subsequent 10% decrease is then given by $75^\circ - 0.10(75^\circ) = 67.5^\circ$. Choice A is the result of an arithmetic error. Choice B is incorrect because you should subtract 10% of 75, not simply 10, from 75 to get the 10% decrease. Choice D is incorrect because you need to now reduce this by 10%. Choice E is incorrect because the initial increase in temperature should be 25% of 60, not 25.

54. **The correct answer is F.** Distribute terms on both sides and take all terms of the left and factor, as follows:

$$\begin{aligned} 2x(4x - 3) &= 3(3 - 4x) \\ 8x^2 - 6x &= 9 - 12x \\ 8x^2 + 6x - 9 &= 0 \\ (4x - 3)(2x + 3) &= 0 \\ x &= \frac{3}{4}, -\frac{3}{2} \end{aligned}$$

So the product of the solutions is $\left(\frac{3}{4}\right)\left(-\frac{3}{2}\right) = -\frac{9}{8}$.

Choice G is the sum of the solutions. Choice H is the reciprocal of the solution. Choice J is the negative reciprocal of the solution. Choice K is the negative of the solution.

55. **The correct answer is C.** All balls are equally likely to be chosen. So the probability of selecting a red ball or a green ball is $\frac{10+3}{20} = \frac{13}{20} = 0.65$. Choice A is incorrect because this is the probability of selecting a blue ball. Choice B is incorrect because this is the probability of selecting either a blue or yellow ball. Choice D is incorrect because this is the probability of not selecting a blue ball. Choice E is incorrect because this is the probability of not selecting a yellow ball.

56. **The correct answer is K.** First, $g(-4) = \frac{3}{2(-4)} = -\frac{3}{8}$. Compute as follows:

$$\begin{aligned} (f \circ g)(-4) &= f(g(-4)) \\ &= f\left(-\frac{3}{8}\right) \\ &= \frac{1}{-\frac{3}{8} + 2} \\ &= \frac{1}{\frac{13}{8}} \\ &= \frac{8}{13} \end{aligned}$$

Choice F is $g(f(-4))$. Choice G is $g(-4)$. Choice H is $f(-4)$. Choice J is the product of $f(-4)$ and $g(-4)$.

57. **The correct answer is C.** Since 1 hour = 60 minutes and 1 minute = 60 seconds, it follows that 1 hour = 3,600 seconds. Also, 300 m = 0.3 km. Let x be the number of kilometers rowed in one hour. Set up and solve the following proportion:

$$\begin{aligned} \frac{0.3\text{ km}}{80\text{ sec}} &= \frac{x\text{ km}}{3{,}600\text{ sec}} \\ (3{,}600)(0.3) &= 80x \\ x &= \frac{3{,}600(0.3)}{80} = 13.5\text{ km} \end{aligned}$$

Choice A is incorrect because you set up the proportion incorrectly. Choice B is incorrect because you should have divided 1,080 by 80, not 100. Choice D is the result of an arithmetic error. Choice E is incorrect because you must multiply by 0.3.

58. **The correct answer is K.** Substitute $3r$ in for the radius and $2h$ in for the height in the volume formula to get $V=\frac{1}{3}\pi(3r)^2(2h)=18\bullet\left(\frac{1}{3}\pi r^2h\right)$. So the volume increases by a factor of 18. Choice F is the factor by which the height is increased only. Choice G is the factor by which the radius is increased only. Choice H is incorrect because you did not square the 3 when replacing the radius by $3r$ in the volume formula. Choice J is incorrect because you did not double the height in the volume formula.

59. **The correct answer is C.** The maximum value of $y = 4\sin(3x)$ is 4. Subtracting 1 from this shifts the entire graph down 1 unit. So the new maximum is 3. Choice A is incorrect because it does not account for the amplitude of 4. Choice B is incorrect because this is just the maximum of $y = \sin(3x)$. Choice D is incorrect because the graph was not shifted down 1 unit. Choice E is incorrect because the graph was translated up 1 unit instead of down 1 unit.

60. **The correct answer is G.** To find the slope of the line, we must first find the equation of the line. Translate the given information into algebra: "two times the x-coordinate plus three times the y-coordinate is equal to 12" means that $2x + 3y = 12$. Now put this equation into slope-intercept form, $y = mx + b$:

$$2x+3y=12$$
$$3y=-2x+12$$
$$y=-\frac{2}{3}x+4$$

Since m represents slope, the slope of this line is $-\frac{2}{3}$.

Choice F is the reciprocal of the correct slope. For choice H, you divided both sides by 12 and used the coefficient of x; instead, you should have divided both sides by the coefficient of y. For choice J, you have left out the negative sign. Choice K is the y-intercept, not the slope.

1.	C	**11.**	A	**21.**	D	**31.**	C
2.	J	**12.**	F	**22.**	G	**32.**	F
3.	D	**13.**	C	**23.**	A	**33.**	A
4.	F	**14.**	H	**24.**	G	**34.**	H
5.	B	**15.**	D	**25.**	D	**35.**	D
6.	F	**16.**	F	**26.**	J	**36.**	J
7.	C	**17.**	D	**27.**	A	**37.**	B
8.	G	**18.**	G	**28.**	H	**38.**	H
9.	C	**19.**	A	**29.**	B	**39.**	D
10.	F	**20.**	J	**30.**	J	**40.**	G

1. **The correct answer is C.** This is a detail question, and the only substance in the apparatus the narrator identifies specifically is ivory (choice C). While the framework of the apparatus glittered, it did not necessarily contain glitter (choice A). The narrator also identifies a crystalline substance in the apparatus, but this merely means it contained a substance resembling crystal, not necessarily actual crystal, so choice B is not correct. Candles surrounded the apparatus after the Time Traveller laid it on a table, but the apparatus itself did not contain wax (choice D).

2. **The correct answer is J.** This is an inference question about the Time Traveller, and considering how he has gathered his colleagues together to examine the model of his time travelling apparatus, how he keeps pointing out its details, and how he boasts about how long it took him to make, it is clear he is proud of it. Therefore, choice J is the best answer. The fact that he has gathered his colleagues together also indicates that he does care about what they think, so choice G is incorrect. The Time Traveller's pride and confidence make choice F an unlikely correct answer. Since the Time Traveller specifically says that he is not trying to trick his colleagues, and there is no evidence that he is lying, choice H is not the best answer.

3. **The correct answer is D.** The Medical Man says only that the model of the time travelling apparatus is "beautifully made," so you can infer only that he sincerely admires it. That means choice D is correct and choice B can be eliminated. There is no evidence that he finds the model amusing (choice A) or frightening (choice C).

4. **The correct answer is F.** Captain Nemo filled his submarine with extravagances such as fine art, a huge organ, enormous pearls, and large, opulent rooms. He clearly values extravagance even though his own apartment is simplistic, which confirms choice F and eliminates choice J. However, we never learn what his goals for the *Nautilus* are in the passage, so choice G is not the best answer. The fact that he brings people into the *Nautilus* also proves he does not avoid them, which eliminates choice H.

5. **The correct answer is B.** While the narrator marvels at all the wonderments inside the *Nautilus*, he also says he feels like "a prisoner who dared scarcely hope that liberty might some day be obtained." Choice B sums up those conflicting feelings well. Choice A only hints at the narrator's positive feelings about the *Nautilus* while not indicating his negative ones. Choice D only exaggerates those negative feelings. There is no indication that he feels like a co-owner of the *Nautilus* (choice C).

6. **The correct answer is F.** Considering that there are hints Captain Nemo has taken the narrator on the *Nautilus* against his will, *surrender* is the likeliest definition of *submit* in this context. While *submit* can also mean *quit* (choice G), *humor* (choice H), or *send* (choice J), none of those words makes sense in the context of line 1.

7. **The correct answer is C.** Passage A specifies that the Time Traveller built his time machine and Passage B specifies that Captain Nemo built his luxurious submarine, both of which are very unusual machines. However, only Captain Nemo invites someone into his machine; the Time Traveller is merely showing off a model of his creation. Therefore, choice A is incorrect. The *Nautilus* submarine has a boat that looks like a torpedo, but there is no evidence in Passage B that it contains an actual weapon. Nothing about the Time Traveller's machine is weaponlike at all. Therefore, choice B is incorrect. Only Captain Nemo explores the oceans, so choice D is also incorrect.

8. **The correct answer is G.** The answer to this detail question is at the beginning of the fifth paragraph of Passage B: "It was on a desert island that Captain Nemo had carried out the building of the *Nautilus* . . . ." Passage A contains no information about where the Time Traveller built his time machine. However, the Time Traveller does mention that it took him two years to build his machine, while we do not know how long it took Captain Nemo to build the *Nautilus*, so choice F is incorrect. Considering that the reader knows the Time Traveller built his time machine and Nemo built his *Nautilus* submarine, choice H can be eliminated. The appearances of both machines are described in their respective passages, so choice J is incorrect.

9. **The correct answer is C.** To solve this inference question, think about what the Time Traveller and Captain Nemo do in their respective passages: the Time Traveller builds a time machine and Nemo builds a submarine full of opulent rooms, strange machinery, and a gigantic organ. Clearly, they are both original thinkers, so choice C is the best answer. While such originality of thought may also signal eccentricity, the genuinely interested reactions of their colleagues indicate they are not tiresome, which eliminates choice A. While there is some indication that Captain Nemo has taken the narrator of Passage B prisoner, there is no evidence that the Time Traveller is plotting something evil (choice B), and their desire to travel through time and explore the ocean proves they are not wary of danger (choice D).

10. **The correct answer is F.** While the Time Traveller is very open about how his time machine works, Captain Nemo built his *Nautilus* on a desert island and secured its parts "from many different places . . . in order to maintain secrecy," according to the fifth paragraph of Passage B. This supports choice F. The Time Traveller says he does not want his colleagues to think he is a "quack," which indicates that he is concerned about his credibility, so choice G is incorrect. Although Captain Nemo's inclusion of an organ in the *Nautilus* makes it clear that he needs music, there is nothing in Passage A that indicates that the Time Traveller does not need music, so choice H is not the best answer. Both characters clearly need adventure, so choice J is incorrect.

11. **The correct answer is A.** In the statement, the author is criticizing an education based only on the kind of guesswork that comes with common sense, so choice A is the best answer. That interpretation of the statement contradicts the inferences in choices B and C. The author is not suggesting that the events of life are random (choice D); she is accusing a common sense-based education of being based on random ideas.

12. **The correct answer is F.** The question is asking for the main idea of the paragraph as a whole, and only choice F captures all of the most important ideas in the paragraph. Choice G is never implied in the paragraph at all. Choice H is the conclusion of the paragraph rather than its main idea. Choice J cannot be correct because it fails to account for the important role of women in the paragraph.

13. **The correct answer is C.** The author states the answer to this question explicitly in the first line of the sixth paragraph, when she writes that women and soldiers "both acquire manners before morals." Therefore, choice C is the best answer. This statement contradicts choice A. Choice B is incorrect because grace is only mentioned as something that is not learned from a common sense-based education. While the author does state that both soldiers and women are expected to learn the "minor virtues," she does not imply that either education begins with the acquisition of virtuousness (choice D).

14. **The correct answer is H.** The answer to this question can be found in the first sentence of the fifth paragraph, which states, "Standing armies can never consist of resolute, robust men (which eliminates statement II); they may be well-disciplined machines (which validates statement III), but they will seldom contain men under the influence of strong passions or with very vigorous faculties (which eliminates statement I)." Therefore, the correct answer must only include statement III, and only choice H does that. Choices F and G can be eliminated because each only accounts for one false statement. Choice J can be eliminated because it includes the two false statements as well as the one true one.

15. **The correct answer is D.** In the second paragraph, the author charges that for women, education ". . . is acquired more by sheer observations on real life, than from comparing what has been individually observed with the results of experience generalized by speculation." This statement confirms choice D as the correct answer. The author only refers to a general contempt for women receiving a proper education by their society; she does not imply that women learn more by observation than by contempt (choice A). The author implies that observation and experience are similar, so choice B

is not the best answer. Knowledge is learning, so choice C does not make much sense.

16. **The correct answer is F.** The word *corporeal* refers to the body, so choice F is the best interpretation of the statement in lines 25–27. Choice G is not true because it implies that one cannot receive a particular education if she is concerned with appearing a certain way, which is not what the author is suggesting in lines 25–27. Choice H is an accurate summary of the author's overall idea in the passage, but it fails to interpret the particular idea in lines 25–27. Choice J is both the opposite of the author's overall idea and an incorrect interpretation of lines 25–27.

17. **The correct answer is D.** Each answer choice can be used as a synonym of the word *mixing*, but only *interacting* (choice D) makes sense in this particular context. If you were to replace the word *mixing* in line 42 with *combining* (choice A), *stirring* (choice B), or *switching* (choice C), the line would not make much sense.

18. **The correct answer is G.** In line 18, the author refers to the commonness of women having *domestic employments*, which supports choice G. Throughout the passage, the author charges that society denies women formal educations, so choice F cannot be correct. While the author explains that women are expected to learn through observation, she does not exactly suggest that society expects women to be *extremely observant*, so choice H is incorrect. The author discusses the similarity between women and men in the military at great length in the passage, but she never implies that women are actually expected to join the military (choice J).

19. **The correct answer is A.** The author gives the answer to this question when she states that "... officers are also particularly attentive to their persons, fond of dancing, crowded rooms, adventures, and ridicule" (choice A). While military officers may be expected to fight (choice B), the author never implies that they are fond of fighting. The author criticizes the fact that soldiers are deprived of a formal education, so choice C does not make much sense. The author states that military officers are expected to be polite, but she does not suggest that they are fond of being polite (choice D).

20. **The correct answer is J.** Throughout the passage, the author expresses concerns about the poor educational opportunities available to women during her time, so choice J is the best answer. The author is specifically concerned with women's education, and since choice F just refers to education in general without specifying gender, it is not the best answer. The author also has a greater purpose than merely describing how women are educated, so choice G is not the best answer either. While the author discusses both men in the military and women, she is not making an argument for allowing more women in the military (choice H).

21. **The correct answer is D.** *Uncomplicated*, would make the most sense if used in place of *straightforward* in line 5. *Complex* (choice A) is the opposite of *straightforward*. While the word *straightforward* seems to imply something moving forward rapidly, *rapid* (choice B) would not make more sense than *uncomplicated* if used in place of *straightforward* in line 5. The word *honest* (choice C) can be a synonym of *straightforward*, but *honest* does not make as much sense as *uncomplicated* in this particular context.

22. **The correct answer is G.** Throughout the passage, the author explains that the way each person understands the world may depend on her or his personal perspective of the world, so choice G is the best answer, and choice F can be eliminated because it is the opposite of that answer. The author never implies that study affects understanding, so choice H is not a strong answer. The author suggests that each person may have her or his own particular understanding, not that nobody can ever gain any understanding at all, so choice J is not the best answer.

23. **The correct answer is A.** In this statement, the author means that people tend to take the possibility that everyone does not share the same understanding of the world for granted (choice A), which supports the overall idea of the passage. Choice B contradicts that idea; if our shared understanding of the world were not worth discussing, why would the author spend this entire passage discussing it? While the author might agree that it might be difficult to reach any firm conclusions about our shared understanding of the world, choice C reaches an extreme conclusion for which there is no firm evidence in this passage. The author never implies that we should spend more time enjoying the world and less time trying to understand it (choice D).

24. **The correct answer is G.** Each answer choice may make sense, but only choice G has actual specific support in the passage, particularly in the third paragraph. The author never discusses eyesight problems (choice F), shapes that shift (choice H), or the observer's attitude (choice J), in this particular passage.

25. **The correct answer is D.** Throughout the paragraph, the author explains different factors that may cause one

to observe a table in different ways, which supports choice D. Choice A is too focused on the table, which is only the object the author uses to make a more general point about all objects. Choice B reaches the opposite conclusion of the main point the author makes with the third paragraph. Choice C implies that inanimate objects are capable of actively trying to trick people, which is neither the author's intention nor realistic.

26. **The correct answer is J.** The fourth paragraph mainly focuses on the idea that painters are more concerned with appearances than reality (choice J). Choice F is just one detail in the fourth paragraph and fails to capture the main idea of the paragraph as a whole. Choice G refers to something the author says about philosophers, not painters. The author never implies that painters are more practical than other people (choice H) in the fourth paragraph.

27. **The correct answer is A.** Lines 15–17 supports choice A. The author does not really discuss the concept of what is or isn't normal in the passage, so choice B lacks support. The author implies that intense concentration (choice C) may come later in the process of understanding, but does not state that this is how the process tends to begin. The author uses a chair (choice D) only as an example of something that can be perceived, not as the starting point of the entire process of understanding.

28. **The correct answer is H.** In the fourth paragraph, the author states, "... the practical man and the philosopher want to know what they are; but the philosopher's wish to know this is stronger than the practical man's ...," which supports choice H. The author acknowledges that this desire troubles the philosopher, which contradicts choice F. The author never makes any comparison between the strength of the desire for understanding between the painter and the philosopher, so choice G lacks support. The author does not make any judgments about the philosopher's desires, so choice J also lacks support.

29. **The correct answer is B.** At the beginning of the fourth paragraph, the author states, "For most practical purposes these differences are unimportant ...," which supports the conclusion in choice B. Something that does not matter is not normally frustrating, so choice A is not a strong answer. According to the passage, differences in appearance may affect the way painters work, but there is no evidence that they affect the work of most other people, so choice C is a weak answer. Choice D is the opposite of what the author states about the concerns of "the practical man" in the fourth paragraph.

30. **The correct answer is J.** *Examination* makes the most sense if used in place of *scrutiny* in line 13. While *listening* (choice F), *calling* (choice G), and *reading* (choice H) may be part of the process of *scrutinizing* something, they do not make sense in this particular instance, since one would not listen to, call, or read some of the examples the author uses. Therefore, a more general term such as *examination* is the best answer.

31. **The correct answer is C.** Immediately after describing these spiders as interesting, the author points the ways the spiders do not protect themselves, which implies that such ways are too common to be interesting before pointing out how they do protect themselves, which implies that the fact that they look like bark as a form of camouflage is what makes them interesting. Therefore, choice C is the best answer. Choices A and D may be true in themselves, but the author does not suggest that these details make the spiders in question interesting. Choice B is the opposite of what the author says in the eighth paragraph.

32. **The correct answer is F.** In the ninth paragraph, the author defines *C. mitralis* as a Madagascar species (choice F). Choice G would better define the class of *Epeira* described in the previous paragraph. Choices H and J better define *Uloborus* spiders.

33. **The correct answer is A.** The answer to this question can be found in the sixth paragraph, in which the author explains that she has invariably found *Uloborus plumipes* "building in dead branches" (statement I) and that its "color is a soft wood-brown or gray, mottled with white" (statement II). She also suggests that these spiders' disguise would not be effective "among fresh leaves," which implies that the spiders do not resemble fresh leaves (statement III). Therefore, the correct answer must include the two true statements—I and II—and eliminate the false statement—statement III. Only choice A accomplishes this. Choices B and C each include one true statement and one false one. Choice D includes both true statements and the one false statement.

34. **The correct answer is H.** The third paragraph discusses the problem of determining "whether the purpose of mimicry is protection or the capture of prey," which implies that spiders use mimicry for both reasons, which supports choice H. The final sentence of the paragraph contradicts choice G. The first sentence of the fourth

paragraph contradicts choice F. The second sentence of the second paragraph states that some spiders are brightly colored to warn predators that they are unpalatable, which contradicts the extreme statement in choice J.

35. **The correct answer is D.** While each of the answer choices can be used as a synonym for *classes*, only choice D makes sense in this particular context, because the author is discussing two categories of spiders. Choices A, B, and C all indicate that *classes* refers to schooling in some way, which does not make sense in relation to spiders.

36. **The correct answer is J.** In the fourth paragraph, the author explains, "The number of strangely modified forms depicted in descriptive works on spiders is enormous. Bodies are twisted, elongated, inflated, flattened, truncated, covered with tubercles (statement I) or spines, enclosed within chitinous plates (statement II), colored like bark, like lichens (statement III) . . . ." Therefore, the correct answer must include all three statements, since they are all true. Only choice J accomplishes this. Choice F leaves out two of the true statements. Choices G and H each leave out one of the true statements.

37. **The correct answer is B.** The second paragraph supports the conclusion in choice B since *inedible* means "unable to be eaten." Venomous spiders are never mentioned in the passage, so choice A cannot be correct. While being adapted to their surroundings (choice B) or able to blend in with their environment (choice D) might make certain spiders more difficult to catch and therefore less *likely* to be eaten, these qualities do not actually make them inedible.

38. **The correct answer is H.** While the author does state that most spiders use coloring to hide, some are also ". . . accompanied by conspicuous colors, which warn their enemies that they belong to an unpalatable class . . .," which supports choice H. While the author describes a spider resembling a cocoon when hiding among her young, the author does not say that this actually protects the young, so choice F lacks support. Appearing unpalatable is not the same thing as appearing frightening, so choice G does not really have support either. There is no reason to believe a spider would be concerned with revealing its particular genus, so choice J does not make sense.

39. **The correct answer is D.** In the fifth paragraph, the author uses the cabinet as an example of the kind of human-made object to which spiders are not specifically adapted to resemble, so choice D is the best answer. The author provides no support for the conclusions in choice A, B, or C.

40. **The correct answer is G.** The final paragraph of the passage consists almost entirely of details about *C. mitralis'* body and behavior that show how it resembles a woody knot, so choice G is the best answer. Choices F and J are just individual details that support the main idea. Choice H is too general a statement to effectively capture the paragraph's main idea.

1.	B	**11.**	D	**21.**	A	**31.**	A
2.	G	**12.**	F	**22.**	H	**32.**	G
3.	A	**13.**	B	**23.**	B	**33.**	D
4.	G	**14.**	J	**24.**	J	**34.**	G
5.	D	**15.**	D	**25.**	A	**35.**	D
6.	F	**16.**	H	**26.**	F	**36.**	G
7.	C	**17.**	A	**27.**	C	**37.**	C
8.	G	**18.**	G	**28.**	J	**38.**	G
9.	B	**19.**	B	**29.**	C	**39.**	B
10.	H	**20.**	H	**30.**	J	**40.**	H

1. **The correct answer is B.** Both sets of data in Table 1 show inverse relationships between distance to light source (m) and the photocurrent in μA (a), meaning that they change in opposite directions. The change, however, is not linear; they do not necessarily change by the same amount. Choice B is the best choice because it depicts nonlinear, inverse variation. Choice A is incorrect because the graph is linear and varies directly, not inversely. Choice C is incorrect because the graph is linear, even if its inverse variation is appropriate. The data here do not have a linear relation. Choice D cannot be correct because it represents constant photocurrent, when the data clearly indicate changing values.

2. **The correct answer is G.** According to Table 2, the stopping potential varies with the color of light. The color of light is determined by its wavelength. Therefore, the stopping potential must depend on the wavelength. Choice F is incorrect because Study 2 did not vary the light intensity. Choice H is not correct because Study 2 did not vary the metal used. Choice J is not correct because the stopping potential changes for different colors of light. If it were constant, Table 2 would show the same value for all colors of light.

3. **The correct answer is A.** The fact that light intensity increases as distance decreases means that changing the distance to the light source is one way to change the light intensity. According to Table 1, the photocurrent increases as the distance to the light source decreases. The photocurrent depends on the number of photoelectrons emitted from the metal plate. Therefore, the photocurrent increases as the light intensity increases. Choice B is incorrect because it states that the photocurrent decreases with increasing light intensity, an assertion that is the opposite of what the data show. Choice C is incorrect because there is nothing in Study 1 that tests for a threshold level. This conclusion cannot be reached based on the data provided. Choice D is incorrect because there is indeed a relationship between light intensity and photocurrent.

4. **The correct answer is G.** According to the introduction to the passage, energy is required to eject photoelectrons from the metal plate. The stopping potential measured in Study 2 must reflect the amount of energy in the flow of photoelectrons because it is the energy required to stop the flow of photoelectrons. From Table 2, it takes the least amount of energy to stop the flow of photoelectrons generated by red light, while the greatest amount of energy is required to increase the flow of photoelectrons generated by blue light. Therefore, red light must have the least amount of energy, while blue light has the most. From the question stem, we know that red light has the longest wavelength while blue light has the shortest. Thus, longer wavelengths of light must have lower energy than shorter wavelengths of light. To put it another way, energy decreases as wavelength increases. Choice F is incorrect because it is the opposite of the correct relationship. Choice H is incorrect because you can see in Table 2 that stopping potential changes as wavelength changes. Choice J is incorrect because the distance of the light source was held constant in Table 2, so you cannot determine the relationship between distance and energy from this study.

5. **The correct answer is D.** The question is asking you which independent variable is common to both studies. An independent variable is one that the researchers control and can change as they wish. In Study 1, the researchers changed the color of the filter and the distance to the light source. In Study 2,

the researchers changed the color of the filter. Thus, the only independent variable that the two studies have in common is the filter color. Don't be fooled by choice A; while the distance to the light source was an independent variable in Study 1, it was held constant in Study 2. So in Study 2, distance to the light source was *not* a variable. Choice B is incorrect because photocurrent magnitude was the dependent variable—the experimental variable not controlled by the researchers—in Study 1. Choice C is incorrect because stopping potential was the dependent variable in Study 2.

6. **The correct answer is F.** Orange is a color between red and yellow, so use the stopping potential values from Table 2 to interpolate the approximate stopping potential of an orange filter. Since the three red trials yielded 0.0 volts and the three yellow trials yielded 0.4 volts, you can assume that a typical trial with an orange filter would yield a stopping potential between 0.0 and 0.4 volts. Choice G gives a stopping potential between those of yellow and green. Choice H gives one between those of green and blue. Choice J gives one greater than that of blue, which suggests a color closer to violet or white.

7. **The correct answer is C.** The median elevation of Earth's surface, because it is the midpoint between the highest and lowest elevations on that surface, will be the elevation that 50% of Earth's surface lies above. So you do not have to make any calculations to find the answer—you can just read the graph. Going up from 50% on the horizontal axis to the curve, and then going across to the vertical axis, we see that the corresponding elevation is about –1,000 m. So 50% of Earth's surface is above (or below) –1,000 m, the median elevation. If you did not figure out that you could just read the graph to find the median elevation, you can also calculate it. We can estimate the highest elevation on Earth to be about 9,000 m (≈ 8,848 m, the elevation of Mt. Everest) and the lowest elevation to be about –11,000 m (≈ –11,305 m, the elevation of the deepest trench). So the total range of elevation on Earth is 9,000 m – (–11,000 m) ≈ 9,000 m + 11,000 m = 20,000 m. The midpoint of this range is half of the range either added to the lowest point or subtracted from the highest point: (20,000 m ÷ 2) + (–11,000 m) = 10,000 m – 11,000m = –1,000 m. Choice A is too high; this is the midpoint between sea level (0 m) and the highest point on Earth's surface. Choice B is too high; this is sea level, which is not the median elevation on Earth's surface. Choice D is too low; this is the midpoint between sea level and the lowest point on Earth's surface.

8. **The correct answer is G.** If oceans moderate weather, one would expect to find the mildest or least extreme weather in areas dominated by oceans. According to the passage, the Southern Hemisphere is dominated by oceans, so one would expect less extreme weather in the Southern Hemisphere. Choice F has the information reversed. The Northern Hemisphere is dominated by the continents, but that makes weather in the Northern Hemisphere generally more extreme than in the Southern Hemisphere. Choice H confuses the hemispheres. The Northern Hemisphere is dominated by land masses, not by oceans. Choice J also confuses the hemispheres. The Southern Hemisphere is dominated by oceans, not by land masses.

9. **The correct answer is B.** On Figure 2, read down from the arrow pointing to the mean elevation of land at 840 m to the horizontal axis to find the percentage of land above this elevation. The value on the horizontal axis associated with 840 m is approximately 20%. Choice A is incorrect because it is too low (10% of land is above 4,000 m). Choice C is incorrect because 30% is the amount of land above sea level, not the mean land elevation. Choice D is incorrect because it is too high (40% of land is above the shallowest part of the ocean, around –100 m).

10. **The correct answer is H.** Look for the point at which the lines representing the temperature of maximum density and the freezing point of water intersect. This happens at the point corresponding to 25 percent on the horizontal axis, so above 25 percent salinity, the temperature of maximum density of water is below the freezing point of water, as opposed to below 25 percent salinity, where it is above the freezing point. For choices F and G, the freezing point of water is below the temperature of maximum density. For choice J, the freezing point of water has already been above the temperature of maximum density.

11. **The correct answer is D.** Looking at Figure 3, the temperature of maximum density drops by about 2.3°C for every 10% increase in salinity. Using this estimate, since the temperature of maximum density at 30% salinity is about –2.5°C, then at 40% salinity it should be 2.3°C less, or about –4.8°C. If you trace the line for temperature of maximum density to 40% salinity, extend the temperature axis down to –5°C, and reading across, you will see that this estimate is correct. Choice A is incorrect because 4°C is the temperature of

maximum density for pure water, which has a salinity of 0%, as stated in the passage. Choice B is incorrect because this is the freezing point of water, not the temperature of maximum density, at 40% salinity. Choice C is incorrect because –4°C is just where the line for the temperature of maximum density is cut off in Figure 3; this is the temperature of maximum density for ocean water with a salinity of about 37%.

12. **The correct answer is F.** From Figure 1, you can see that bone loss is the least with the ARED, in both the pelvis and the whole body. With the ARED, you even get a slight average gain in bone density for the whole body. Be careful when reading the graphs in Figure 1 because the *x*-axis is at or near the top of the *y*-axis rather than at the bottom, so a larger bar below the *x*-axis means a greater negative change, or greater loss of bone density. A bar above the *x*-axis indicates a gain in bone density. Choice G is incorrect because loss of bone density is in the middle with the iRED, for both the pelvis and whole body. Choices H and J are incorrect because aerobic exercise and muscular endurance machines were the only machines available on the Mir. Bone loss was greatest for astronauts on the Mir, so these machines were least effective in preventing bone loss. Since astronauts were using both of these machines on the Mir, it is not clear if one might have been better than the other.

13. **The correct answer is B.** In the introduction to the passage, it is explained that bone loss occurs in space because bones do not have to bear as much weight as usual. From Figure 1, for all exercise machines, the pelvis experiences more bone loss than the whole body average. It is also stated in the introduction that bones that bear the most weight will experience the largest change in weight load and so experience the largest change in bone density. The pelvis is a weight-bearing part of the body, as it supports the upper body and anchors the legs. Choice A is incorrect because the introduction states that astronauts exercise their entire bodies on the exercise machines. Choice C is incorrect because the data in Figure 1 show that the pelvis experiences more bone loss than the whole body average. Choice D is incorrect because although the different types of exercise machines do result in different degrees of bone loss, this does not explain why one body part (the pelvis) has a degree of bone loss different than the whole-body average.

14. **The correct answer is J.** The question asks about maintaining BMC at preflight levels, which means that you are looking for the protein intake that causes no change in BMC. Be sure to use the trend line in Figure 2 rather than trying to find an individual point with a *y*-value of 0%. If you find the point on the trend line where *y* equals 0% change from preflight and read down, the approximate protein intake required to maintain BMC is 2.0 g/kg body weight. Choice F is incorrect because a protein intake of 0.5 g/kg body weight (BW) is too low to maintain preflight BMC. None of the astronauts went below a protein intake of about 0.7 g/kg BW, but if we extend the trend line, we can see that a protein intake of 0.5 g/kg BW would lead to a 20% loss of BMC. Choice G is also too low. A protein intake of 1.0 g/kg BW would lead to a 12% loss of BMC. Choice H is too low as well. A protein intake of 1.5 g/kg BW would lead to a 5% loss of BMC.

15. **The correct answer is D.** To minimize bone loss, researchers should recommend the most effective methods of reducing bone loss. In Figure 1, exercising on ARED leads to the least amount of bone loss. The passage states that ARED offers the highest resistance of all the exercise machines, up to 600 pounds, so high-resistance exercise should be one of the recommendations. In Figure 2, the higher the protein intake, the lower the amount of bone loss. Therefore, a high-protein diet should be the other recommendation. Choice A is incorrect because a low-protein diet and low-resistance exercise would lead to the most bone loss of all the choices listed. As seen in Figure 2, a low-protein diet would lead to a large degree of bone loss. The machines available on Mir did not provide any resistance and led to the most bone loss, as seen in Figure 1. Choice B is incorrect because while a high-protein diet would help prevent bone loss, low-resistance exercise leads to greater bone loss. Choice C is incorrect because while high-resistance exercise is the best way to prevent bone loss through exercise, a low-protein diet would lead to higher bone loss.

16. **The correct answer is H.** In Figure 1, the change in BMD in the pelvis for an astronaut on the Mir is about –1.4%, while for an astronaut exercising with ARED the loss is about –0.4%. The difference between these two values is –1.4% – (–0.4%) = –1.4% + 0.4% = –1.0%. Thus, Mir astronauts lost 1.0% more BMD than ARED-using astronauts. Choice F is incorrect because Mir astronauts lost the most BMD of all the astronauts studied, so they would not have lost less BMD than the ARED-using astronauts. Choice G is incorrect because 0.2% is the difference between Mir astronauts and iRED-using astronauts. Astronauts using iRED had a change in BMD of about –1.2%, so the difference between them and the

Mir astronauts is –1.4% – (–1.2%) = –0.2%. Choice J, Mir astronauts losing 1.4% more BMD than ARED-using astronauts, is too high and may have been chosen if you just looked at the change in BMD for Mir astronauts.

17. **The correct answer is A.** In the introduction, it is stated that bone loss will be greater for weight-bearing bones. For bones like the humerus, the upper arm bone, that do not typically support much weight on Earth, bone loss will be less than for the pelvis, which supports a lot of weight on Earth. Thus, a graph showing the change in BMD per month for the pelvis and humerus should show a smaller negative change for the humerus (less loss of BMD) than for the pelvis. Choice B is incorrect because the change in BMD will not be the same for the weight-bearing pelvis and the non-weight-bearing humerus. Choice C is incorrect because it shows the opposite of what will occur; the humerus will not show a greater loss of BMD than the pelvis. Choice D is incorrect because while the humerus does have less loss of BMD than the pelvis, it is very unlikely to have gained BMD. In Figure 1, the whole body average change in BMD for astronauts using iRED is negative, so it is unlikely that any parts of the body gained bone mass.

18. **The correct answer is G.** Notice that electronegativity increases from left to right in a given period, and it decreases from top to bottom in a given family. Therefore, the electronegativity of Br should be greater than that of Se (2.6) and between that of Cl (3.2) and I (2.7). In other words, it should be in the range of 2.8 – 3.1. Choices F, H, and J do not fall in this range.

19. **The correct answer is B.** Higher electronegativity means a greater ability to attract electrons, so an atom with higher electronegativity attracts electrons more easily. The element with the lowest electronegativity will have the lowest ability to attract electrons. Of the choices, the lowest electronegativity rating belongs to Na, sodium, at 0.93. This is lower than lithium (choice A) by a small amount, and aluminum (choice C) by a larger margin. Titanium (choice D) is a very unreactive element, but it still has a relatively high electronegativity, compared to sodium.

20. **The correct answer is H.** The polarity of a molecule is determined by the difference in electronegativity between its atoms. A smaller difference in electronegativity means less polarity. In a nonpolar molecule, therefore, if you subtract the value of the smaller electronegativity from that of the larger electronegativity, you should get a result near zero. Since two atoms of the same element, such as Cl_2, have identical values for electronegativity, the result of subtracting one electronegativity from the other is exactly 0, making the molecule nonpolar. In choice F, the electronegativity values for Cl (3.2) and Na (0.93) yield a difference of: 3.2 – 0.93 = 2.27. This is greater than the value for Cl_2, so choice F should be eliminated. In choice G, the difference in electronegativity values for O (3.4) and Mg (1.3) is: 3.4 – 1.3 = 2.1. Thus, MgO is more polar than Cl_2. You can also eliminate choice J, since subtracting the value for Be (1.6) from that of O (3.4) yields 1.8, which is much greater than the value for Cl_2.

21. **The correct answer is A.** In this case, use the reverse reasoning from that used to find the answer to Question 20. Look for the *greatest* difference between the electronegativities of the bonded atoms. The difference for K–Cl (choice A) is 2.38, and none of the other differences are as great. The difference is 1.7 for Ba–Se (choice B), 1.67 for Na–S (choice C), and 1.8 for Be–O (choice D). The question asks you to identify the electron bond that is *most* polar, so you can eliminate choices B, C, and D.

22. **The correct answer is H.** The most highly polar bond would be generated from a bond between the element with the highest polarity and the element with the lowest polarity, which would be F and Cs, respectively. The other options involve bonds with smaller differences in electronegativity.

23. **The correct answer is B.** The recorded range of smoking rates in the study population is 10% on the low end and 35% on the highest end. That is 5 increments of 5% over the entire range of the study. As the smoking rate increases from 10% to 35%, the rate increases from about 140 deaths per 100,000 people when 10% of the population smokes to 230 deaths per 100,000 people when 35% of the population smokes, a difference of 90 deaths per 100,000 people. Over the range of the study there is some variation from point to point, but overall 90 deaths per 100,000 people divided by 5 increments of 5% gives approximately 18 more deaths per 100,000 people per 5% increase in the smoking rate. Choices A, C, and D are all changes that occur between particular data points in the study, but only choice B reflects the entire range of smoking rates examined.

24. **The correct answer is J.** This is an EXCEPT question, meaning that three of the four answer choices will be supported by Table 1. The correct answer will be the one that is *false*. Choices F, G, and H are all supported by the numbers in the table. Choice J, however, is *not* supported by the data, because the percentage of Rhode

Island females who attempt to quit smoking is actually lower than the percentage of Rhode Island males.

25. **The correct answer is A.** The study is examining all cancer mortality, but cancer has a variety of causes. Some cancers are not associated with smoking and may be affiliated with other health or environmental problems in the study area. The study would be much stronger if cancers not caused by smoking were eliminated from the findings. Choice B in theory would simply extend the trend shown in Figure 1; higher smoking rates and more cancer. It would strengthen the evidence of the relationship between smoking and cancer but would not add any evidence regarding cause. Quitting smoking (choice C) might help show that quitting smoking reduces risk, but the results really only apply to the quitters, not to the population at large. There Is no way to know what would happen to those individuals if they didn't quit. Similarly, it would be impossible to find a population of non-smokers representative of the entire population of several states.

26. **The correct answer is F.** This question relates to the second data group in Table 1, number of cancer deaths. In all ten listed states, the number of males who died from cancer was significantly higher than the number of females who died from cancer. Having only these data to consult, it's reasonable to conclude that New Jersey would be likely to have a similar result. The only answer greater than 177, the number of females, is 246 (choice F). Choices G, H, and J are too small to make sense.

27. **The correct answer is C.** In every state but Rhode Island, women are more likely to attempt to quit smoking than men are; that is the only major difference between Rhode Island and the rest of the study. Without any other additional information, it is conceivable that the larger social networks mean women have more people to support them as they try to quit. Choice A has no information to back it up; the nature of smoking is not discussed, only how often it occurs. Choice B might possibly be true but the study does not provide any information about people who have cancer but survive. Choice D is unlikely to be correct as in every state women smoke at lower rates than men do.

28. **The correct answer is J.** Perspective 1 is very focused on the negative aspects of introduced species, viewing these introductions as unwelcome invasions. Perspective 2 takes a more nuanced view, assessing what the actual impact of an introduced species is and how the introduction fits into the global conservation picture. Choice F is not a good choice, for Perspective 1 goes beyond viewing new species as merely introduced and Perspective 2 does not automatically accept all introduced species (nor always considers them beneficial, choice H). Choice G offers a good name for Perspective 1, eradication, but invasion is too exclusively negative for Perspective 2.

29. **The correct answer is C.** Advocates of Perspective 2 regard introduced members of a species as part of the global population of that species. If a species is endangered, and if an introduced population elsewhere can help the species as a whole survive, then this point of view would support letting the turtles establish their new population. Choices A and D are not likely true since Perspective 1 advocates fighting introduced species at all costs, regardless of their status in their native range or their actual impact in their new environment. Choice B is incorrect because Perspective 2 does not support the automatic removal of an introduced species.

30. **The correct answer is J.** Limited resources will play a role in both perspectives. Perspective 1 aims to eliminate all introduced species, but without unlimited resources it is impossible to tackle them all. In practice, biologists can only work to eradicate some introduced species and even then it's very difficult to eradicate all of them everywhere. In Perspective 2, limited resources help justify this point of view. Since there aren't enough resources to fight every introduced species, it only makes sense to spend resources on the ones causing the most harm. Choice F is true about Perspective 2, but ignores the effects on Perspective 1. It is also true that removing species is usually more expensive than leaving them be, but resource limits are also a factor for Perspective 2. Choice H is not true; Perspective 2 does not suggest that all introduced species should be ignored.

31. **The correct answer is A.** The passage states that introduced species are most harmful in isolated or low-diversity areas. A small, remote island is definitely isolated, and small areas usually have lower diversity since there is not enough space for more species. Introduced species such as rats have in fact done tremendous damage on isolated islands where the native species are highly specialized. Choice B is incorrect, since a large rainforest is not isolated and rainforests are typically very high diversity. A new continent (choice C) is also not nearly as isolated as an island. A coastal barrier island (choice D) is not as isolated as a more remote island. A lot of species can

cross smaller stretches of water but fewer can cross large expanses of open ocean.

32. **The correct answer is G.** While each view of introduced species disagrees in part about how to manage introduced populations and the degree of risk they pose, all three perspectives agree that some species introductions really do pose a serious risk to native ecosystems. All three perspectives agree that if at all possible, some of these introductions must be eliminated. Choice F is really unique to Perspective 2, and choice H is a major part of Perspective 3. Choice J, that all introductions present a risk, is closer to Perspective 1 and not really a part of Perspectives 2 and 3.

33. **The correct answer is D.** All three perspectives differ on the degree of risk and how to handle introduced species, but none of the perspectives fully embraces introduced species as a benefit. All three perspectives involve costs, no matter how serious they consider the threat of invasive species to be, and those costs will be minimized if species are never introduced in the first place. Choice A would be favored by Perspective 1, but not the other two. Choices B and C are both more in line with Perspectives 2 and 3 than with Perspective 1.

34. **The correct answer is G.** According to Perspective 3, the population of an introduced species typically increases at first, then decreases, and then the populations of both introduced and native species stabilize. Only choice G shows the initial population increase and decrease prior to stabilization for introduced species. Choice F is a graph of the worst fears of Perspective 1, where an introduced species simply replaces a native species. Choice H represents a scenario where an introduced species population continues to increase while a native population remains stable. Choice J is a similar situation to Perspective 3 but without the initial increase and decrease of the introduced population.

35. **The correct answer is D.** Table 1 shows that the rate of tongue flicking increases to 76 flicks per minute at a time 1 minute after the snake strikes. Therefore, in Experiment 2, one would expect a similar response 1 minute after a hypothetical strike at minute 8. Choice A is incorrect because the results of Experiment 1 indicate that a dramatic increase in tongue flicking follows a strike. Choice B is incorrect, too. If you chose this as the answer, you may have focused on the repeating pattern in Table 2. If this pattern were followed, a rate of 3 flicks per minute would be expected at minute 9. However, the pattern in Table 2 was generated in an experiment in which the snake did NOT strike. This question relates to a snake striking, which is reflected in the data for Experiment 1. Choice C is incorrect but is closer to the correct answer.

36. **The correct answer is G.** The main difference between a live mouse and a fresh dead one is that live mice are warm. The snake's behavior indicates a clear interest in the live mouse (eliminating choice J) and an awareness that it is there. The snake can find the live mouse and is either unable or uninterested in finding the dead one. A fresh dead mouse has similar odor to a live one, so choice F is unlikely. There are none of the behavior changes exhibited by the snake in Experiment 1, but the snake can still detect the live prey (choice H).

37. **The correct answer is C.** Tongue flicking occurs constantly, so clearly it has an important sensory function. However, tongue flicking really ramps up only after the snake has struck and needs to track down its prey so it can eat; at that point the location of the prey, based on odor, is of tantamount importance, so helping pinpoint odors is the best answer. Choice A cannot be correct since the passage states that the snakes have odor detectors in their mouths. For this same reason, choice B is likely incorrect; the tongue is in the mouth and thus better positioned to work in concert with the odor detectors. The heat sensors are underneath the eyes and less convenient to the tongue. Choice D is less likely, since to guide a strike, tongue flicking would need to occur during a strike. This is both impractical and not discussed in any of the results.

38. **The correct answer is G.** Experiment 1 suggests that tongue flicking increases after a strike, while Experiment 3 suggests that the snakes are specifically increasing the rate of tongue flicks in reaction to their venom. A dry bite has no venom, so it would follow that the snake will not react in the same way for a dry bite as it will for a bite where venom is injected (eliminating choice F as a possible answer). Tongue flicks ought to stay the same before and after a bite. Choice H is unlikely, as no part of this study suggests that tongue flicks ever decrease in number; according to Experiment 2, they tend to be fairly constant. Choice H is not a good choice since tongue flicks might not increase but there is no reason to assume that the snake will ignore the dry-bitten target.

39. **The correct answer is B.** The data from Experiment 2 are summarized in Table 2, which shows the number of tongue flicks remaining relatively constant as time passes. The graph that describes this relationship should, therefore, resemble a horizontal line. Choice A is incorrect because it actually represents the data from Experiment 1, with the number of tongue flicks jumping from a low constant to a high constant halfway across the graph. Choice C is incorrect because it depicts a steady increase in tongue flicking during the first several minutes, which results in a constant high level. This is inaccurate even for Experiment 1. Choice D completely misses the mark by showing a steady decrease during the first several minutes, followed by a constant low level. This is vastly different from anything indicated by either table.

40. **The correct answer is H.** This experiment would eliminate all variables except rattlesnake venom. If the snake does not follow the trail of the venom, then the hypothesis will not be supported. If the snake does follow the trail of the venom, then the hypothesis will be supported. Choice F is not correct. Carefully reread the question and the opening paragraph. Snakes do use their tongues to sense odors, but depriving a snake of this sense cannot support or refute the hypothesis that a rattlesnake follows the scent of its own venom; under those conditions, it cannot follow the scent of anything. Choices G and J can be eliminated for the same reason. Neither answer can be correct because the question asks whether a snake follows the scent of its own venom; there is no way of answering the question if there is no venom in the experiment.

Sample Essay: Score 1

Ideas and Analysis:	Score = 1
Development and Support:	Score = 1
Organization:	Score = 1
Language Use and Conventions:	Score = 1

I don't care if noone or anyone is watching me cause I'm not doing anything wrong or will be so why should I care? I see cameras wherever I go the movies and the mall and restaurants and they don't hurt me and I don't do anything that's worth being bothered about. Why should you care, are you doing illegal things? Cameras are used to make movies and TV shows and I watch a ton of videos so do you want people to stop making things on Youtube or put things on Instagram? I got a camera on my phone and I take pictures of things all the time, so should I stop doing that? I like that every time I buy a new phone that cameras get better and the pictures I can take wherever I go get much better, so I don't want to change that. You shouldn't want that either, so people should be able to make cameras better and use them too.

Scoring Explanation

Ideas and Analysis: Score = 1

The writer of this argument provides minimal ideas or insight that relates to the topic at hand; instead of offering an analysis of the advantages and disadvantages of surveillance, the essay quickly veers off on a tangent with scattered thoughts regarding phone cameras and making YouTube videos. The end result is an argument that widely misses the mark and fails to address the essay task.

Development and Support: Score = 1

There is little or no evidence of thoughtful idea development in this essay. The resulting essay is a loose collection of thoughts that fail to offer a cogent perspective on the benefits or dangers of the rise of so-called surveillance culture. There is also no support offered to bolster the writer's thoughts, and little provided to compel the reader into agreeing with his or her murky viewpoint.

Organization: Score = 1

The ideas presented in this argument are largely disconnected from a central unifying theme that addresses the specific essay task. There is no assertion of a clear position regarding surveillance and a lack of well-organized ideas to lend credence and support; instead, what's offered is a loose amalgam of disorganized thoughts on marginally related subjects.

Language Use and Conventions: Score = 1

The response provided shows a lack of basic grammar skills mastery and a deficiency in effective language mechanics. The weaknesses and errors demonstrated throughout the essay ultimately lead to an ineffective argument that fails to address the given task.

Sample Essay: Score 6

Ideas and Analysis:	Score = 6
Development and Support:	Score = 6
Organization:	Score = 6
Language Use and Conventions:	Score = 6

Perhaps Big Brother *is* watching—surveillance is a part of the world and time in which we live, a time when increasingly sophisticated forms of technology exist not only to watch us, but also to heal us, to connect us, and to make our lives easier.

Is the rise of the so-called "surveillance culture" an unfortunate symptom of the expanding technological era? No. Surveillance equipment, like *most* technological advancements, is a benefit, providing tools whose purpose is to make our society better.

The assertion that expansive surveillance provides a benefit to society is not an abstract one. Two years ago, my aunt was walking to her car in a multi-level parking garage after a day of shopping. It was mid-afternoon, and out of nowhere she was attacked. She was knocked to the ground, her bags and purse were stolen—but that wasn't the worst of it. She also lost a sense of comfort and ease that day, and she became afraid to go into unattended public places. Around every corner and in every shady area she felt a real potential for danger. Worse still, the burglar had her identification and address. These feelings persisted long after the incident, and the *only* thing that made her feel better was when the person that robbed her was caught. How did they catch him? They reviewed surveillance footage of the incident and matched the image of the criminal to existing mug shots. Without surveillance, they may never have caught him, and the peace of mind that he stole from my aunt along with her things may have been lost forever. What better way to see the benefits of a technology than through a clear example of its success?

The purpose of surveillance technology is to keep a watchful eye on things and make people safer. Why should we limit that? Those who race to label us a "culture of surveillance" are merely referring to the increased use of a technology that has proven itself to be beneficial. Do we live in a "culture of penicillin" because of its increased use?

Some bemoan the notion that surveillance has gone too far, and has reached the point to where we've lost the right to expect some measure of personal privacy, but in reality that notion is an exaggeration. There are certainly places where we are not being watched, and any misuse of surveillance technology should not count as a strike against its very existence.

Besides, history is full of examples of technological advances that have improved society but have also included a social cost. Should doctors and hospitals get rid of X-rays because of the radiation they emit? Some argue that the Internet has created a generation of self-involved people with limited attention spans and an inability to make meaningful connections. Should we abandon all of the great things the Internet has provided? It often takes time to figure out how to responsibly use new technologies in their relative infancies. But as a society we learn and progress, often through trial and error. It's true, there is some measure of privacy that is traded away when surveillance technology is employed. But would you rather be safe or unwatched?

Scoring Explanation

Ideas and Analysis: Score = 6

This essay demonstrates a thoughtful, carefully considered analysis of the role surveillance should have in our society and the culture at large. The ideas are well integrated and support a clear, nuanced perspective on the issue—including insightful social commentary (i.e., "culture of penicillin," inherent trade-offs in historical technological advances) and a powerful personal angle (the writer's aunt's mugger getting caught thanks to surveillance footage). The end result is a compelling and convincing argument that capably frames the issue—from a personal perspective to its larger social relevancy.

Development and Support: Score = 6

From the writer's provocative opening notion ("Perhaps Big Brother *is* watching") to the thought-provoking conclusion ("would you rather be safe or unwatched?"), the writer galvanizes a well-stocked toolkit of capably developed ideas in support of the notion that surveillance is largely a benefit to society. This assertion is examined from various levels (impact on an individual; impact on society; impact on culture), with an impressive degree of development and deft deployment of support. The examination of quick cultural labels and their impact is particularly deft, and the writer's willingness to concede that surveillance may indeed contain a social cost demonstrates a confidence and willingness to examine the essay task from more than just a narrow lens.

Organization: Score = 6

This argument demonstrates an impressive mastery of structure and organization. The writer delivers a compelling piece of writing with clear focus, from its attention-grabbing opening and thoughtful, multi-faceted analysis to its memorable closing. Rather than simply offering a straightforward defense of one closed perspective on the value of surveillance technology, the writer capably weaves in micro and macro level thoughts, and an examination of hasty cultural labels and society's responsibility to learn how to best use new technology (often through trial and error).

Language Use and Conventions: Score = 6

The writer of this argument exhibits a commendable use of varied language and a skilled hand at writing conventions for crafting effective essays. The word choices made by the writer are rich, thoughtful, and varied without being dry or academic, and sentences are well-constructed, resulting in an impressive essay that's both enjoyable to read and convincing.

English Test

1. Ⓐ Ⓑ Ⓒ Ⓓ	16. Ⓕ Ⓖ Ⓗ Ⓙ	31. Ⓐ Ⓑ Ⓒ Ⓓ	46. Ⓕ Ⓖ Ⓗ Ⓙ	61. Ⓐ Ⓑ Ⓒ Ⓓ
2. Ⓕ Ⓖ Ⓗ Ⓙ	17. Ⓐ Ⓑ Ⓒ Ⓓ	32. Ⓕ Ⓖ Ⓗ Ⓙ	47. Ⓐ Ⓑ Ⓒ Ⓓ	62. Ⓕ Ⓖ Ⓗ Ⓙ
3. Ⓐ Ⓑ Ⓒ Ⓓ	18. Ⓕ Ⓖ Ⓗ Ⓙ	33. Ⓐ Ⓑ Ⓒ Ⓓ	48. Ⓕ Ⓖ Ⓗ Ⓙ	63. Ⓐ Ⓑ Ⓒ Ⓓ
4. Ⓕ Ⓖ Ⓗ Ⓙ	19. Ⓐ Ⓑ Ⓒ Ⓓ	34. Ⓕ Ⓖ Ⓗ Ⓙ	49. Ⓐ Ⓑ Ⓒ Ⓓ	64. Ⓕ Ⓖ Ⓗ Ⓙ
5. Ⓐ Ⓑ Ⓒ Ⓓ	20. Ⓕ Ⓖ Ⓗ Ⓙ	35. Ⓐ Ⓑ Ⓒ Ⓓ	50. Ⓕ Ⓖ Ⓗ Ⓙ	65. Ⓐ Ⓑ Ⓒ Ⓓ
6. Ⓕ Ⓖ Ⓗ Ⓙ	21. Ⓐ Ⓑ Ⓒ Ⓓ	36. Ⓕ Ⓖ Ⓗ Ⓙ	51. Ⓐ Ⓑ Ⓒ Ⓓ	66. Ⓕ Ⓖ Ⓗ Ⓙ
7. Ⓐ Ⓑ Ⓒ Ⓓ	22. Ⓕ Ⓖ Ⓗ Ⓙ	37. Ⓐ Ⓑ Ⓒ Ⓓ	52. Ⓕ Ⓖ Ⓗ Ⓙ	67. Ⓐ Ⓑ Ⓒ Ⓓ
8. Ⓕ Ⓖ Ⓗ Ⓙ	23. Ⓐ Ⓑ Ⓒ Ⓓ	38. Ⓕ Ⓖ Ⓗ Ⓙ	53. Ⓐ Ⓑ Ⓒ Ⓓ	68. Ⓕ Ⓖ Ⓗ Ⓙ
9. Ⓐ Ⓑ Ⓒ Ⓓ	24. Ⓕ Ⓖ Ⓗ Ⓙ	39. Ⓐ Ⓑ Ⓒ Ⓓ	54. Ⓕ Ⓖ Ⓗ Ⓙ	69. Ⓐ Ⓑ Ⓒ Ⓓ
10. Ⓕ Ⓖ Ⓗ Ⓙ	25. Ⓐ Ⓑ Ⓒ Ⓓ	40. Ⓕ Ⓖ Ⓗ Ⓙ	55. Ⓐ Ⓑ Ⓒ Ⓓ	70. Ⓕ Ⓖ Ⓗ Ⓙ
11. Ⓐ Ⓑ Ⓒ Ⓓ	26. Ⓕ Ⓖ Ⓗ Ⓙ	41. Ⓐ Ⓑ Ⓒ Ⓓ	56. Ⓕ Ⓖ Ⓗ Ⓙ	71. Ⓐ Ⓑ Ⓒ Ⓓ
12. Ⓕ Ⓖ Ⓗ Ⓙ	27. Ⓐ Ⓑ Ⓒ Ⓓ	42. Ⓕ Ⓖ Ⓗ Ⓙ	57. Ⓐ Ⓑ Ⓒ Ⓓ	72. Ⓕ Ⓖ Ⓗ Ⓙ
13. Ⓐ Ⓑ Ⓒ Ⓓ	28. Ⓕ Ⓖ Ⓗ Ⓙ	43. Ⓐ Ⓑ Ⓒ Ⓓ	58. Ⓕ Ⓖ Ⓗ Ⓙ	73. Ⓐ Ⓑ Ⓒ Ⓓ
14. Ⓕ Ⓖ Ⓗ Ⓙ	29. Ⓐ Ⓑ Ⓒ Ⓓ	44. Ⓕ Ⓖ Ⓗ Ⓙ	59. Ⓐ Ⓑ Ⓒ Ⓓ	74. Ⓕ Ⓖ Ⓗ Ⓙ
15. Ⓐ Ⓑ Ⓒ Ⓓ	30. Ⓕ Ⓖ Ⓗ Ⓙ	45. Ⓐ Ⓑ Ⓒ Ⓓ	60. Ⓕ Ⓖ Ⓗ Ⓙ	75. Ⓐ Ⓑ Ⓒ Ⓓ

Mathematics Test

1. Ⓐ Ⓑ Ⓒ Ⓓ Ⓔ	16. Ⓕ Ⓖ Ⓗ Ⓙ Ⓚ	31. Ⓐ Ⓑ Ⓒ Ⓓ Ⓔ	46. Ⓕ Ⓖ Ⓗ Ⓙ Ⓚ
2. Ⓕ Ⓖ Ⓗ Ⓙ Ⓚ	17. Ⓐ Ⓑ Ⓒ Ⓓ Ⓔ	32. Ⓕ Ⓖ Ⓗ Ⓙ Ⓚ	47. Ⓐ Ⓑ Ⓒ Ⓓ Ⓔ
3. Ⓐ Ⓑ Ⓒ Ⓓ Ⓔ	18. Ⓕ Ⓖ Ⓗ Ⓙ Ⓚ	33. Ⓐ Ⓑ Ⓒ Ⓓ Ⓔ	48. Ⓕ Ⓖ Ⓗ Ⓙ Ⓚ
4. Ⓕ Ⓖ Ⓗ Ⓙ Ⓚ	19. Ⓐ Ⓑ Ⓒ Ⓓ Ⓔ	34. Ⓕ Ⓖ Ⓗ Ⓙ Ⓚ	49. Ⓐ Ⓑ Ⓒ Ⓓ Ⓔ
5. Ⓐ Ⓑ Ⓒ Ⓓ Ⓔ	20. Ⓕ Ⓖ Ⓗ Ⓙ Ⓚ	35. Ⓐ Ⓑ Ⓒ Ⓓ Ⓔ	50. Ⓕ Ⓖ Ⓗ Ⓙ Ⓚ
6. Ⓕ Ⓖ Ⓗ Ⓙ Ⓚ	21. Ⓐ Ⓑ Ⓒ Ⓓ Ⓔ	36. Ⓕ Ⓖ Ⓗ Ⓙ Ⓚ	51. Ⓐ Ⓑ Ⓒ Ⓓ Ⓔ
7. Ⓐ Ⓑ Ⓒ Ⓓ Ⓔ	22. Ⓕ Ⓖ Ⓗ Ⓙ Ⓚ	37. Ⓐ Ⓑ Ⓒ Ⓓ Ⓔ	52. Ⓕ Ⓖ Ⓗ Ⓙ Ⓚ
8. Ⓕ Ⓖ Ⓗ Ⓙ Ⓚ	23. Ⓐ Ⓑ Ⓒ Ⓓ Ⓔ	38. Ⓕ Ⓖ Ⓗ Ⓙ Ⓚ	53. Ⓐ Ⓑ Ⓒ Ⓓ Ⓔ
9. Ⓐ Ⓑ Ⓒ Ⓓ Ⓔ	24. Ⓕ Ⓖ Ⓗ Ⓙ Ⓚ	39. Ⓐ Ⓑ Ⓒ Ⓓ Ⓔ	54. Ⓕ Ⓖ Ⓗ Ⓙ Ⓚ
10. Ⓕ Ⓖ Ⓗ Ⓙ Ⓚ	25. Ⓐ Ⓑ Ⓒ Ⓓ Ⓔ	40. Ⓕ Ⓖ Ⓗ Ⓙ Ⓚ	55. Ⓐ Ⓑ Ⓒ Ⓓ Ⓔ
11. Ⓐ Ⓑ Ⓒ Ⓓ Ⓔ	26. Ⓕ Ⓖ Ⓗ Ⓙ Ⓚ	41. Ⓐ Ⓑ Ⓒ Ⓓ Ⓔ	56. Ⓕ Ⓖ Ⓗ Ⓙ Ⓚ
12. Ⓕ Ⓖ Ⓗ Ⓙ Ⓚ	27. Ⓐ Ⓑ Ⓒ Ⓓ Ⓔ	42. Ⓕ Ⓖ Ⓗ Ⓙ Ⓚ	57. Ⓐ Ⓑ Ⓒ Ⓓ Ⓔ
13. Ⓐ Ⓑ Ⓒ Ⓓ Ⓔ	28. Ⓕ Ⓖ Ⓗ Ⓙ Ⓚ	43. Ⓐ Ⓑ Ⓒ Ⓓ Ⓔ	58. Ⓕ Ⓖ Ⓗ Ⓙ Ⓚ
14. Ⓕ Ⓖ Ⓗ Ⓙ Ⓚ	29. Ⓐ Ⓑ Ⓒ Ⓓ Ⓔ	44. Ⓕ Ⓖ Ⓗ Ⓙ Ⓚ	59. Ⓐ Ⓑ Ⓒ Ⓓ Ⓔ
15. Ⓐ Ⓑ Ⓒ Ⓓ Ⓔ	30. Ⓕ Ⓖ Ⓗ Ⓙ Ⓚ	45. Ⓐ Ⓑ Ⓒ Ⓓ Ⓔ	60. Ⓕ Ⓖ Ⓗ Ⓙ Ⓚ

Reading Test

1. Ⓐ Ⓑ Ⓒ Ⓓ	11. Ⓐ Ⓑ Ⓒ Ⓓ	21. Ⓐ Ⓑ Ⓒ Ⓓ	31. Ⓐ Ⓑ Ⓒ Ⓓ
2. Ⓕ Ⓖ Ⓗ Ⓙ	12. Ⓕ Ⓖ Ⓗ Ⓙ	22. Ⓕ Ⓖ Ⓗ Ⓙ	32. Ⓕ Ⓖ Ⓗ Ⓙ
3. Ⓐ Ⓑ Ⓒ Ⓓ	13. Ⓐ Ⓑ Ⓒ Ⓓ	23. Ⓐ Ⓑ Ⓒ Ⓓ	33. Ⓐ Ⓑ Ⓒ Ⓓ
4. Ⓕ Ⓖ Ⓗ Ⓙ	14. Ⓕ Ⓖ Ⓗ Ⓙ	24. Ⓕ Ⓖ Ⓗ Ⓙ	34. Ⓕ Ⓖ Ⓗ Ⓙ
5. Ⓐ Ⓑ Ⓒ Ⓓ	15. Ⓐ Ⓑ Ⓒ Ⓓ	25. Ⓐ Ⓑ Ⓒ Ⓓ	35. Ⓐ Ⓑ Ⓒ Ⓓ
6. Ⓕ Ⓖ Ⓗ Ⓙ	16. Ⓕ Ⓖ Ⓗ Ⓙ	26. Ⓕ Ⓖ Ⓗ Ⓙ	36. Ⓕ Ⓖ Ⓗ Ⓙ
7. Ⓐ Ⓑ Ⓒ Ⓓ	17. Ⓐ Ⓑ Ⓒ Ⓓ	27. Ⓐ Ⓑ Ⓒ Ⓓ	37. Ⓐ Ⓑ Ⓒ Ⓓ
8. Ⓕ Ⓖ Ⓗ Ⓙ	18. Ⓕ Ⓖ Ⓗ Ⓙ	28. Ⓕ Ⓖ Ⓗ Ⓙ	38. Ⓕ Ⓖ Ⓗ Ⓙ
9. Ⓐ Ⓑ Ⓒ Ⓓ	19. Ⓐ Ⓑ Ⓒ Ⓓ	29. Ⓐ Ⓑ Ⓒ Ⓓ	39. Ⓐ Ⓑ Ⓒ Ⓓ
10. Ⓕ Ⓖ Ⓗ Ⓙ	20. Ⓕ Ⓖ Ⓗ Ⓙ	30. Ⓕ Ⓖ Ⓗ Ⓙ	40. Ⓕ Ⓖ Ⓗ Ⓙ

Science Test

1. Ⓐ Ⓑ Ⓒ Ⓓ	11. Ⓐ Ⓑ Ⓒ Ⓓ	21. Ⓐ Ⓑ Ⓒ Ⓓ	31. Ⓐ Ⓑ Ⓒ Ⓓ
2. Ⓕ Ⓖ Ⓗ Ⓙ	12. Ⓕ Ⓖ Ⓗ Ⓙ	22. Ⓕ Ⓖ Ⓗ Ⓙ	32. Ⓕ Ⓖ Ⓗ Ⓙ
3. Ⓐ Ⓑ Ⓒ Ⓓ	13. Ⓐ Ⓑ Ⓒ Ⓓ	23. Ⓐ Ⓑ Ⓒ Ⓓ	33. Ⓐ Ⓑ Ⓒ Ⓓ
4. Ⓕ Ⓖ Ⓗ Ⓙ	14. Ⓕ Ⓖ Ⓗ Ⓙ	24. Ⓕ Ⓖ Ⓗ Ⓙ	34. Ⓕ Ⓖ Ⓗ Ⓙ
5. Ⓐ Ⓑ Ⓒ Ⓓ	15. Ⓐ Ⓑ Ⓒ Ⓓ	25. Ⓐ Ⓑ Ⓒ Ⓓ	35. Ⓐ Ⓑ Ⓒ Ⓓ
6. Ⓕ Ⓖ Ⓗ Ⓙ	16. Ⓕ Ⓖ Ⓗ Ⓙ	26. Ⓕ Ⓖ Ⓗ Ⓙ	36. Ⓕ Ⓖ Ⓗ Ⓙ
7. Ⓐ Ⓑ Ⓒ Ⓓ	17. Ⓐ Ⓑ Ⓒ Ⓓ	27. Ⓐ Ⓑ Ⓒ Ⓓ	37. Ⓐ Ⓑ Ⓒ Ⓓ
8. Ⓕ Ⓖ Ⓗ Ⓙ	18. Ⓕ Ⓖ Ⓗ Ⓙ	28. Ⓕ Ⓖ Ⓗ Ⓙ	38. Ⓕ Ⓖ Ⓗ Ⓙ
9. Ⓐ Ⓑ Ⓒ Ⓓ	19. Ⓐ Ⓑ Ⓒ Ⓓ	29. Ⓐ Ⓑ Ⓒ Ⓓ	39. Ⓐ Ⓑ Ⓒ Ⓓ
10. Ⓕ Ⓖ Ⓗ Ⓙ	20. Ⓕ Ⓖ Ⓗ Ⓙ	30. Ⓕ Ⓖ Ⓗ Ⓙ	40. Ⓕ Ⓖ Ⓗ Ⓙ

WRITING TEST

Plan Your Essay

WRITE YOUR ESSAY

ENGLISH TEST

45 Minutes—75 Questions

DIRECTIONS: In this section, you will see passages with words and phrases that are underlined and numbered. In the right-hand column you will see a question corresponding to each number that provides alternatives to the underlined part. In most of the items, you are to choose the best alternative. If no change is needed, choose NO CHANGE.

In other items, there will be either a question about an underlined portion of the passage, or a question about a section of the passage, or about the passage as a whole. This question type will correspond to a number or numbers in a box.

For each question, choose the best alternative or answer and fill in the corresponding circle on the answer sheet.

Practice Test 3 — ENGLISH

PASSAGE I

The Names of Flowers

[1]

I look and staring (1) at the first green shoots sprouting up through the dead leaves. The sight sets me trembling with anticipation (2), and I kneel toward the earth to make sure I'd seen (3) correctly. Yes, the daffodils have already begun (4) pushing toward the sun. Like in a fever, I forget my work and wander about the garden inspecting the mulched beds. Winter is almost over, I (5) can taste the coming delirium of flowers.

[2]

Gardening is something new to me, a delight this city boy never imagined. As a child growing up in an apartment in New York, it seems (6) enough to know that there were flowers and trees.

1. **A.** NO CHANGE
   B. look and stare
   C. looking and staring
   D. looking and stare

2. **F.** NO CHANGE
   G. to anticipate
   H. and anticipating
   J. OMIT the underlined portion.

3. **A.** NO CHANGE
   B. I've seen
   C. I can see
   D. I will see

4. **F.** NO CHANGE
   G. have beginning
   H. will soon began
   J. soon beginning to

5. **A.** NO CHANGE
   B. over and I
   C. over, and I
   D. over, yet I

6. **F.** NO CHANGE
   G. does seem
   H. did seem
   J. seemed

CONTINUE

Culture marked even more than the seasons were by nature. [7] Autumn was when we played football in the street, or when I was older, tried to pick the peak foliage weekend to go camping. We were familiar with the highlights that marked each season, though not the subtle particulars, the gradual way one transformed into another. [8] Such intimacy was reserved for buildings, crowds, and subway trains. [9]

7. A. NO CHANGE
B. Even culture was marked more than the seasons than nature.
C. Even the seasons were marked more by culture than by nature.
D. Seasons were marked more even by culture than by nature.

8. If the writer were to delete the underlined portion, the paragraph would primarily lose:
F. proof that the author did not understand the seasons.
G. an example of a particular with which the author was not familiar.
H. a poetic turn of phrase that makes the essay more appealing to read.
J. a key transition between two different yet related ideas.

9. The purpose of Paragraph 2 as it relates to the remainder of the essay is primarily to:
A. provide background that helps to explain the significance of the garden to the writer.
B. provide background that explains why the writer feels lucky to have escaped the city.
C. portray the writer's childhood as vividly as the writer's garden.
D. establish the writer's sensitive personality and ability to appreciate flowers.

[3]

Now the twilight of summer is marked for me by budding chrysanthemums spilling over the retaining wall at the side of the house. In too seasons, [10] they've grown huge and sprawling. At the height of autumn, they are as bright yellow and red and purple [11] as any foliage, and the season ends when they turn brown and the last rose buds on the climbers leaning up the porch fail to open.

10. F. NO CHANGE
G. too season's
H. to seasons
J. two seasons

11. A. NO CHANGE
B. bright yellow red and purple
C. bright, yellow, and red, and purple
D. bright yellow, and red, and purple

[4]

Daffodils along the front walk mark [12] the beginning of a long Missouri spring that unfolds with crocuses and tulips, irises and peonies under my study window, and forsythia and spirea around the edges of the lawn. Summer means daisies swaying on the hill, and later, black-eyed susans jostling along the fence.

12. F. NO CHANGE
G. have marked
H. marks
J. marked

[5]

At thirty-five, I'm beginning to learn the names of flowers, and more than just the names. Names are our entry into the world, and I feel a fresh side of myself come alive as i become familiar with the words standing for all those vivid scents and colors springing from the ground. It's nice to know that one can keep on <u>growing. finding</u> enough space inside for gardens and
13
for subway trains.

13. **A.** NO CHANGE
B. growing finding
C. growing, finding
D. growing Finding

Questions 14 and 15 ask about the passage as a whole.

14. Suppose the writer's primary purpose had been to provide a basic explanation of the timeline of a chrysanthemum's life. Would this essay accomplish that purpose?

F. Yes, because it describes how chrysanthemums look at different points in their life cycle.
G. Yes, because it explains when to plant chrysanthemums, when they bloom, and when they die.
H. No, because the author is more concerned with explaining personal experiences than gardening tips.
J. Yes, because it uses the changing times of season as a way to describe when chrysanthemums bud, when they bloom, and when they die.

15. The writer wishes to insert the following detail into the essay:

I could tell you there were pines, but not distinguish them from cedar.

The sentence would most logically be inserted into Paragraph:

A. 1.
B. 2.
C. 3.
D. 4.

CONTINUE

PASSAGE II

Pasta and Tomatoes

[1]

As trade goes, so also goes the world. In these days of global markets where people and goods crisscross the world, the idea that a development in Asia can have a major affect on America is taken for granted. Less widely understood was the fact that exchange has always been a major force in world affairs.

16. F. NO CHANGE
G. so therefore,
H. also
J. so

17. A. NO CHANGE
B. effect on
C. effect over
D. affect over

18. F. NO CHANGE
G. is
H. had been
J. could be

[2]

[19] Agricultural techniques developed in the Near East spread deeper into Asia, as well as Europe and Africa, evolving form as they went. Goods, religion, knowledge, all of these things have moved about through the ages, adopted here by one people, forced on another people there, and every wealth of interchange also witnessed a wealth of transformation.

19. Which of the following sentences, if inserted at this point, would provide the most effective transition to the second paragraph?
A. Throughout history, agriculture has always played a major role in the development of civilizations.
B. Throughout history, the movement of people and goods has been a major factor in changing human societies.
C. Many examples of this can be found by studying the history of trade over the past 100 years.
D. However, this phenomenon was never as important as it is in the modern world.

20. F. NO CHANGE
G. Goods, religion, knowledge: all of these things have moved
H. Movement has occurred in goods, religion, and knowledge
J. Goods, religion, and knowledge have all moved

[3]

That is why Herodotus could marvel at the different practices he found upon his tour, of the ancient Mediterranean, and why

21. A. NO CHANGE
B. tour—of
C. tour; of
D. tour of

too his impressions <u>had been</u> 22 passed on to generations born two millennia later. In fact, the ancient Greeks, <u>whom</u> 23 were well aware of the influences of Egypt on their civilization, did not pass their wealth of knowledge directly on to the rest of Europe, which claims Greece as its root. Greek thought was kept alive by Arab scholars at the height of Islam's <u>power and Greek</u> 24 texts had to be translated from Arabic into Latin before the likes of Thomas Aquinas could open the intellectual door to the European Renaissance.

[4]

But perhaps the clearest examples of this exchange and transformation lay in a realm less heady and much closer to the stomach. <u>How would modern Italy be</u> 25 without pasta and tomatoes? <u>Imagine</u> 26 Switzerland without chocolate or Ireland and Eastern Europe without potatoes. [27]

22. **F.** NO CHANGE
G. have been
H. are
J. will be

23. **A.** NO CHANGE
B. that
C. who
D. which

24. **F.** NO CHANGE
G. power, and Greek
H. power, but Greek
J. power, therefore Greek

25. **A.** NO CHANGE
B. What would modern Italy be like
C. Where would modern Italy be
D. Would modern Italy be

26. **F.** NO CHANGE
G. Can you imagine
H. It's like imagining
J. Isn't it strange to imagine

27. Which of the alternatives provides the most logical conclusion for Paragraph 4?

A. Yet none of these familiar staples was known in the Europe of the Middle Ages.
B. These staples have become part of the very identity of these nations.
C. They would not be the same countries that they are today.
D. Cuisine is an important element of every culture.

CONTINUE

[5]

Marco Polo brought pasta back to Europe from China. Tomatoes, potatoes, and <u>cacao, they</u> (28) were all brought back from the Americas and transformed into something else. <u>Therefore,</u> (29) while neither tomatoes nor pasta is originally Italian, <u>one cannot think of pasta and tomato sauce in all their glorious forms without thinking of Italy.</u> (30)

28. **F.** NO CHANGE
G. cacao,
H. cacao
J. cacao, which

29. **A.** NO CHANGE
B. Because
C. Since
D. For

30. Which of the alternatives would conclude this sentence so that it supports the writer's point about culture?
F. NO CHANGE
G. they have been adapted by Italians.
H. they are now important in Italian cooking.
J. one cannot forget that they were once unknown in Italy.

PASSAGE III

The Life of Aspirin

[1]

There are so many innovations and inventions in our lives that we take for <u>granted there</u> (31) are even things that are a part of our daily lives that we have little or no idea about, including where they came from or how they developed, although we're happy that they exist and that we have access to them. [32]

31. **A.** NO CHANGE
B. granted; there
C. granted there;
D. . Granted there

32. The author of this passage would like to add a sentence to the end of Paragraph 1, which would help transition to Paragraph 2. Which of the following sentences would best serve that purpose?
F. Take, for instance, aspirin.
G. Perhaps that means we're ignorant.
H. The truth is, some things are better unknown.
J. The Internet is a good place to research new things.

[2]

Little serious thought is <u>given; to</u> (33) these humble, unassuming little pills by the average person, although billions are bought and sold each year and you'd be hard pressed to find someone

33. **A.** NO CHANGE
B. given to
C. given, to
D. given. To

who doesn't have some in his or her house. These simple-looking little discs have been responsible for easing <u>countless and innumerable</u> [34] headaches, aches, and pains around the world, yet most of us don't know much more about <u>it</u> [35] beyond the fact that there's likely a bottle full of them somewhere in our medicine cabinets. Let's give aspirin the respect its due by taking a <u>closer—look!</u> [36]

34. F. NO CHANGE
G. countless
H. innumerable or countless
J. many and several

35. A. NO CHANGE
B. him
C. us
D. them

36. F. NO CHANGE
G. closer—look.
H. closer; look.
J. closer look.

[3]

Aspirin has taken on different forms over its long and illustrious history, dating back over 2,400 years to salicin extracts from the bark of the <u>Willow Tree</u> [37], which are metabolized by the human body into salicylic acid <u>an active ingredient of aspirin</u> [38]. Evidence of this has been recorded in ancient Egyptian, Assyrian, and Sumerian texts.

37. A. NO CHANGE
B. Willow tree
C. willow tree
D. willow Tree

38. F. NO CHANGE
G. (an active ingredient of aspirin)
H. <u>an active ingredient of aspirin</u>
J. "an active ingredient of aspirin"

[4]

Through the centuries that followed, chemists sought to improve the effectiveness of salicylic acid, reduce its side effects, and make it easier to mass produce as a medicine for widespread public use. In the late nineteenth century, acetylsalicylic acid was studied as a possible replacement for salicylic acid and, in 1899, the modern aspirin was born and named by the pharmaceutical company Bayer.

CONTINUE

[5]

Today, aspirin is perhaps the most widely used medicine on the planet, and <u>exceeds 50 billion pills estimates the consumption, globally and annually</u>.(39) This nonsteroidal anti-inflammatory drug (NSAID) is used to treat a wide array of symptoms, inflammatory conditions, and illnesses. These include fevers, blood clots, headaches, rheumatoid arthritis, and everyday aches and pains. In specific low doses, aspirin has also been suggested as a preventative medicine to reduce the risk of strokes and certain types of cancer.

[6]

Despite its impressive array of beneficial effects, over the years <u>weve learned</u>(40), largely through <u>trail and error</u>(41), that there are some common unwanted side effects connected with aspirin consumption. These include stomach pain and bleeding, worsening of asthma symptoms, and ulcers. Aspirin can also be hazardous for women who are pregnant or those who drink excessive amounts of alcohol. [42]

[7]

Here's an interesting bit of aspirin trivia: Humans aren't the only creatures who benefit from the medicinal effects of aspirin. Veterinarians sometimes administer aspirin to a wide array of

39. **A.** NO CHANGE
B. 50 billion estimates the globe—annual consumption of excess pills
C. the globe annually consumes 50 billion estimated pill excess
D. estimates of global annual consumption exceed 50 billion pills

40. **F.** NO CHANGE
G. weave learned
H. we've learned
J. we've leaned

41. **A.** NO CHANGE
B. trial and error
C. trail and era
D. tryer and error

42. In Paragraph 6, should the final sentence be omitted?
F. Yes, because it repeats information stated earlier in the paragraph.
G. Yes, because the paragraph has already provided sufficient evidence that aspirin can have dangerous side effects.
H. No, because it is the paragraph's most convincing evidence that aspirin can be dangerous.
J. No, because it adds relevant information.

animals, including dogs and horses, as an anticoagulant and pain reliever. [43] [44]

43. The author of this passage has just discovered that aspirin, when taken at regular low doses, can help reduce the risk of heart attacks. To which of the following paragraphs should the author add this information?

A. Paragraph 3
B. Paragraph 4
C. Paragraph 5
D. Paragraph 6

44. The author of this passage has decided to add a concluding sentence to this passage. Which of the following would be the most effective choice?

F. The next time you reach for an aspirin, remember that you're about to have a tiny bit of medicinal history and innovation!
G. There are lots of other things you can take if you're feeling ill; aspirin is not your only option!
H. Aspirin is among the most easy-to-purchase medicines, and you'll find it in most small grocery stores, supermarkets, and pharmacies!
J. Can you think of any other significant medical innovations that have changed our daily lives?

Question 45 asks about the passage as a whole.

45. The author of this essay was recently given an assignment to research the history of medicines in the ancient world. Does this essay fulfill this requirement?

A. Yes, because this essay discusses a medicine that has existed for a long time.
B. Yes, because aspirin was used by the ancient Egyptians, Assyrians, and Sumerians.
C. No, because this essay isn't comprehensive enough to fulfill the scope of the assignment.
D. No, because aspirin wasn't invented until the twentieth century.

PASSAGE IV

A Professional Lesson

[1]

When I first began working as a journalist in the 1970s, <u>there are few women in the field who are taken seriously.</u> (46) I had no

46. F. NO CHANGE
G. there are few women in the field who is taken seriously.
H. there were few women in the field who are taken seriously.
J. there were few women in the field who were taken seriously.

CONTINUE

illusions, I would have to prove, 47 myself again and again.

47. **A.** NO CHANGE
B. prove
C. prove;
D. prove—

[2]

Editors were surprised when my work turned out to be first rate. It took me a long time to understand that the reason had to do with the way I carried myself, not to mention the fact that I was making no attempt with which to conceal my anxieties. 48 I had not yet learned to put on a professional face.

48. **F.** NO CHANGE
G. not to mention the fact that I made no attempt to conceal my anxieties
H. with the fact that I made no attempt to conceal my anxieties
J. I made no attempt to conceal my anxieties

[3]

Editors who would try to hand me the softer stories, 49 or the stories with a "woman angle." "Maybe you could do a piece on the charity work of 50 the First Lady." I was undaunted by these incidents, and by the inevitable sexist jokes and innuendoes. After all, I had chosen a career that meant not breaking ground in 51 a traditional male bastion. Determination and a thick skin were mandatory.

49. **A.** NO CHANGE
B. Editors would try to hand me the softer stories,
C. The softer stories were the ones editors would try to hand me,
D. Editors who tried to hand me the softer stories,

50. **F.** NO CHANGE
G. could do the charity work of
H. could be doing it on the charity work of
J. could do a piece on charity work for

51. **A.** NO CHANGE
B. breaking ground in
C. it broke ground in
D. broken ground in

[4]

There was, however, an aspect of professional life for whom 52 many of us were not prepared. I remember that when I will be working 53 on a difficult assignment and I checked in with the editor, I would tell him about my worries, describe the obstacles I had yet to surmount, or sometimes even complain about the minor frustrations that had made for a bad day. I thought of it as communication, being honest in my work. I never doubted that I would get past these problems. They merely represented

52. **F.** NO CHANGE
G. for which
H. for what
J. for why

53. **A.** NO CHANGE
B. I was working
C. I will have worked
D. I will work

the moment-to-moment process of doing my job. After all, life was like that too—full of difficulties that I discussed with friends as a way of getting through them. [54]

[5]

I noticed, therefore, that when my male colleagues spoke to editors, no matter what doubts they had, they always said that everything was under control. It seemed like lying. What were these men <u>afraid of,</u> (55) I didn't realize that <u>by behaving the way in which I'd been acting,</u> (56) my honesty was creating a negative impression with my editors. Editors assumed that if I was speaking about my difficulties, then I must really be in trouble. Like all managers, they wanted to know that everything was under control. By <u>sharing the struggles</u> (57) that are part of the process of all work, I made my editors worry and at the same time reinforced all those stereotypes about women who can't stand the pressure.

54. Would it add to the effectiveness of the essay if the writer inserted a paragraph at this point describing the way in which she discussed problems with a close friend?

- **F.** No, because the writer's description of how she interacted with her editor is already clear.
- **G.** No, because such a description belongs just before this paragraph.
- **H.** Yes, because the writer needs to more fully illustrate how she interacts with other people.
- **J.** Yes, because the writer needs to show why she wanted the "softer stories" she was assigned.

55.
- **A.** NO CHANGE
- **B.** afraid of
- **C.** afraid of?
- **D.** afraid of—

56.
- **F.** NO CHANGE
- **G.** my behavior and
- **H.** my behaving in that way and
- **J.** OMIT the underlined portion.

57.
- **A.** NO CHANGE
- **B.** share the struggles
- **C.** shared the struggles
- **D.** will share the struggle

Questions 58–60 ask about the passage as a whole.

58. For the sake of unity and coherence, Paragraph 2 should be placed:

- **F.** where it is now.
- **G.** before Paragraph 1.
- **H.** after Paragraph 4.
- **J.** after Paragraph 5.

59. The writer is considering eliminating Paragraph 4. If the writer removed this paragraph, the essay would primarily lose:

- **A.** relevant details about the mistakes the writer made that led to her ultimate realization.
- **B.** historical information regarding women in the workplace.
- **C.** relevant details regarding the writer's male colleagues' behavior.
- **D.** a revealing anecdote about the writer's experience with her friends.

CONTINUE

60. Which of the following assignments would this essay most clearly fulfill?

- **F.** Write a persuasive essay about the benefits of holding a job.
- **G.** Write an essay comparing current and past business environments for women.
- **H.** Write an essay about a lesson you learned from a professional experience.
- **J.** Write an essay about an experience in which your personal integrity was challenged.

PASSAGE V

Edwidge Danticat, A Born Writer

[1]

Those who live in countries where a large proportion of the population <u>is illegible</u> (61) share their stories orally. In Haiti, <u>one of the world's smaller countries</u>, (62) when someone has a tale to tell, he or she will call out *Krik?* <u>Neighbors:</u> (63) friends, and relatives will then gather around with an answering call of *Krak!*, signaling <u>there</u> (64) willingness to listen.

61.
- **A.** NO CHANGE
- **B.** are ineligible
- **C.** is illiterate
- **D.** are illiterate

62.
- **F.** NO CHANGE
- **G.** a small country
- **H.** a particularly small country
- **J.** DELETE the underlined portion

63.
- **A.** NO CHANGE
- **B.** Neighbors;
- **C.** Neighbors
- **D.** Neighbors,

64.
- **F.** NO CHANGE
- **G.** they're
- **H.** their
- **J.** they are

[2]

The Haitian-born writer Edwidge Danticat would have been (65) only twenty-six when she took these two words and made them the title for her collection of stories. The nine stories in *Krik?Krak!* focus on the hardships of living under a dictatorship. [66]

65. A. NO CHANGE
B. having been
C. was being
D. was

66. For the sake of the logic and coherence of this paragraph, Sentence 2 should be placed:
F. where it is now.
G. before Sentence 1.
H. after Sentence 3.
J. after Sentence 4.

Families are forced to flee Haiti and seek new lives, in (67) the United States.

67. A. NO CHANGE
B. lives' in
C. lives in
D. life in

The book received much critical (68) acclaim and even became a finalist for the National Book Award.

68. F. NO CHANGE
G. many critically
H. too critical
J. much criticism

[3]

Born in Port-au-Prince in 1969, her family moved to New York City when Danticat was twelve (69). She spoke little as a new immigrant, because when she did speak, other children made fun of her heavily accented English. [70] Her thesis in graduate school later became the novel *Breath,Eyes, Memory*. That

69. A. NO CHANGE
B. Danticat moved to New York City when she was twelve
C. New York City is where Danticat moved when she was twelve
D. when she was twelve Danticat moved to New York City

70. Which of the following sentences, if added here, would best provide a transition from the description of Danticat as a young girl to that of Danticat as an author?
F. Danticat refrained from criticizing them in return, however, and was successful in the end.
G. Most Haitians speak Creole, and the language is quite different from American English.
H. Many writers have had difficult childhoods.
J. Although she was silent much of the time, Danticat watched and remembered, as if already thinking like a writer.

CONTINUE

novel, which was subsequently chosen by Oprah Winfrey for her book club, featured a heroine who, like the author [71], moved from Haiti to New York City at the age of twelve. Danticat's third book, *The Farming of Bones*, is also set in Haiti.

[4]

This young authors [72] chosen subject matter, as well as the Creole-accented language she uses to tell her stories, demonstrate that while Danticat has left Haiti for her adopted country of America, she hasn't forgotten both the land of her birth and its [73] brave people.

71.
- **A.** NO CHANGE
- **B.** not unlike the author
- **C.** just as the author did
- **D.** in much the same manner as the author

72.
- **F.** NO CHANGE
- **G.** authors'
- **H.** author's
- **J.** author

73.
- **A.** NO CHANGE
- **B.** either the land of her birth or its
- **C.** neither the land of her birth or its
- **D.** neither the land of her birth nor its

Questions 74 and 75 ask about the passage as a whole.

74. The writer wishes to open the essay with a sentence that will set the theme and tone of the essay. Which of the following would most effectively accomplish this?

- **F.** Whether or not they can read, people all over the world love stories.
- **G.** One of my favorite books is a collection of stories set in Haiti.
- **H.** The problem of illiteracy results in a variety of consequences for people all over the world.
- **J.** Have you ever wondered what it feels like not to be able to read?

75. Suppose the writer's goal had been to provide a detailed history of the hardships the people of Haiti have endured. Would this essay accomplish that goal?

- **A.** Yes, because the essay mentions that the plot of *Krik? Krak!* involves such hardships.
- **B.** Yes, because the essay is about Edwidge Danticat, who fled Haiti because of the hardships she endured while living there.
- **C.** No, because the essay does not provide nearly enough information about Haiti to serve as a detailed history.
- **D.** No, because the essay does not imply that the people of Haiti ever suffered hardships.

STOP

MATHEMATICS TEST

60 Minutes—60 Questions

DIRECTIONS: For each of the following items, solve each problem, choose the correct answer, and then fill in the corresponding circle on the answer sheet. If you encounter problems that take too much time to solve, move on. Solve as many problems as you can; then return to the others in the time remaining for the test.

You may use a calculator on this test for any problems you choose, but some of the problems may best be solved without the use of a calculator.

SHOW YOUR WORK HERE

Note: Unless otherwise stated, assume the following:

1. Illustrative figures are NOT necessarily drawn to scale.
2. Geometric figures lie in a plane.
3. The word *line* indicates a straight line.
4. The word *average* indicates arithmetic mean.

1. Of the 80 children at a daycare center, 32 missed at least 1 day because of illness in January. What percent of the children at the center missed at least 1 day due to illness in January?

A. 4%
B. 16%
C. 24%
D. 32%
E. 40%

2. Three lines intersect to form the triangle below. What is the value of x?

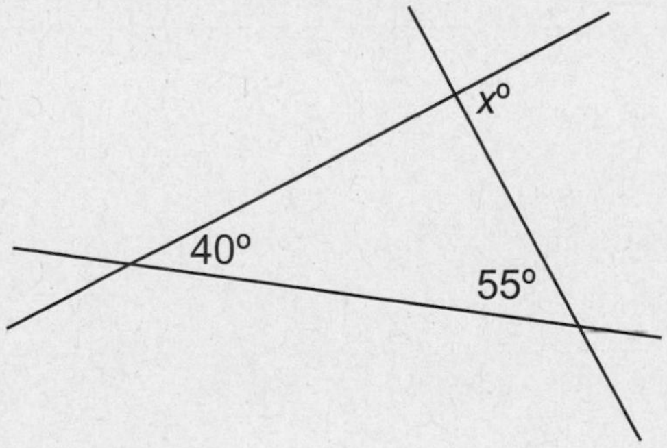

F. 55°
G. 75°
H. 85°
J. 95°
K. 105°

CONTINUE

SHOW YOUR WORK HERE

3. A businessperson calculates that it costs her *p* dollars per hour in parts costs and *l* dollars per hour in labor costs to operate a certain piece of machinery. Which of the following expressions would provide her with the total cost of operating this machine for *x* hours?

A. plx

B. $(px)(lx)$

C. $x(p + l)$

D. pl

E. $p + l$

4. Which of the following is the graph of $j(x) = 3^x - 2$?

F.

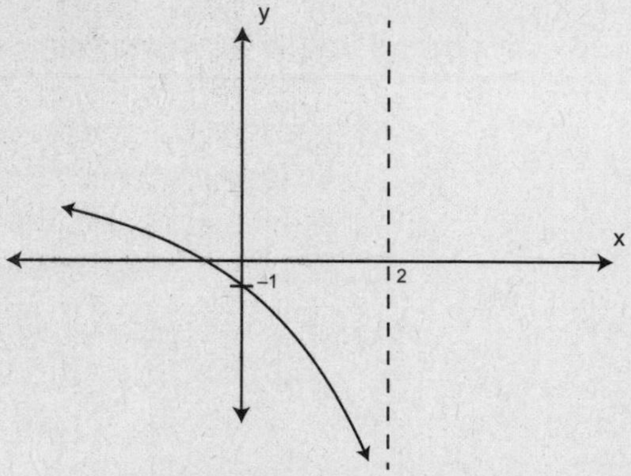

G.

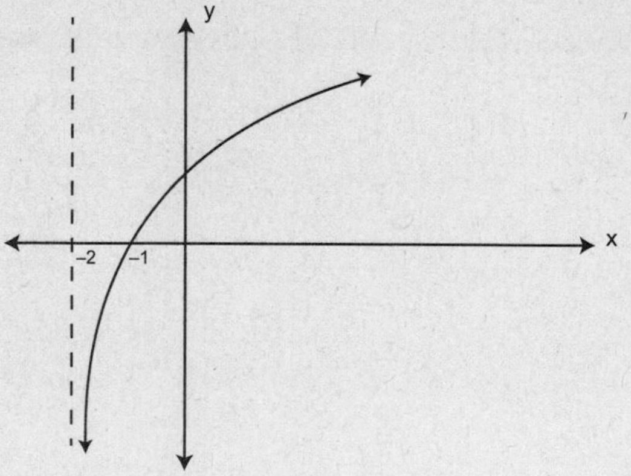

H.

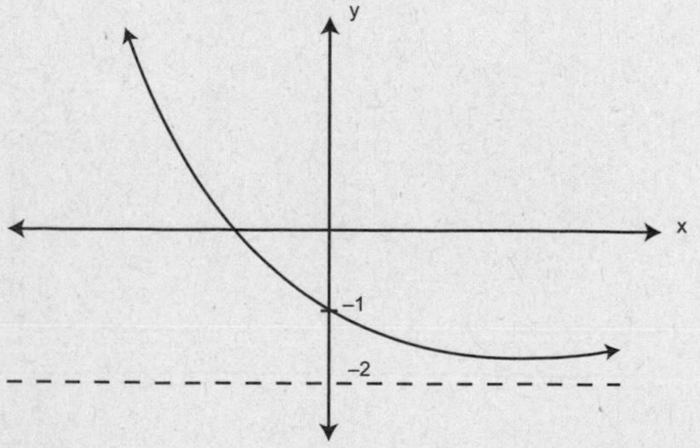

J.

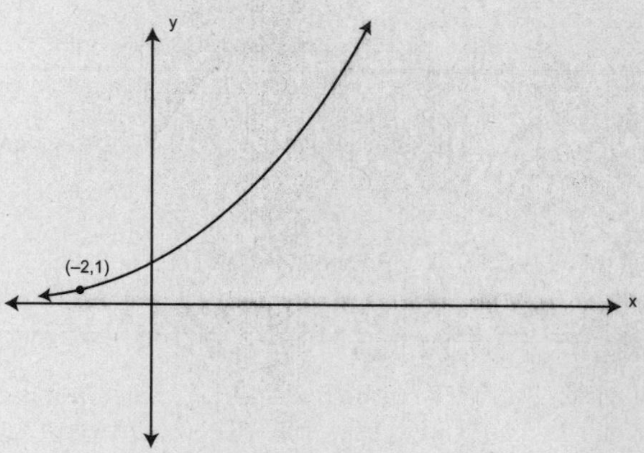

K.

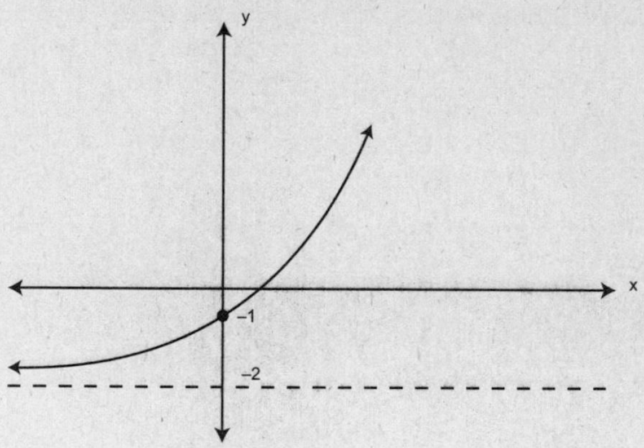

SHOW YOUR WORK HERE

5. A phone company charges \$1 for a calling card, plus 25 cents per minute for the length of a call. If Jacob uses a calling card to make 7 calls, each of which lasts 3 minutes, what is his total cost for the calls?

A. \$1.75
B. \$2.75
C. \$5.25
D. \$5.50
E. \$6.25

6. An amateur artist bought a painting at a yard sale for \$85. She restored the painting and sold it via an online auction for \$125. What percent profit did she earn if she had to pay 3% in fees to the manager of the auction site?

F. $\frac{36.25}{85} \times 100\%$
G. $\frac{36.25}{125} \times 100\%$
H. 40%
J. $\frac{40}{85} \times 100\%$
K. 36.25%

7. Which of the following is equal to the sum of $\frac{2}{5}$, $\frac{1}{8}$, and 0.177?

A. 0.525
B. 0.577
C. 0.602
D. 0.692
E. 0.702

8. In the figure below, $BC = 2$ and $BD = 10$. If the area of triangle ABC is 5 square inches, what is the area, in square inches, of triangle ACD?

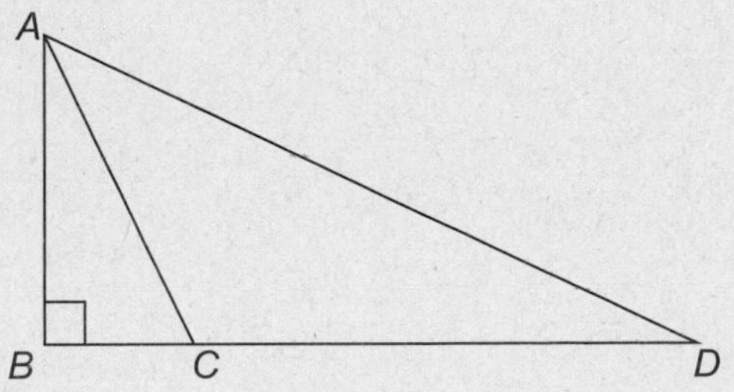

F. 8
G. 15
H. 20
J. 25
K. 30

CONTINUE

SHOW YOUR WORK HERE

9. If $w = \frac{2}{3}$ and $z = -\frac{1}{9}$, what is the value of $\frac{w+z}{2(w-z)}$?

A. $-\frac{1}{3}$

B. $-\frac{5}{14}$

C. $\frac{5}{14}$

D. $\frac{1}{2}$

E. $\frac{14}{5}$

10. What is the asymptote for the graph of $F(x) = 5 - \log(x + 4)$?

F. $x = -4$
G. $y = 5$
H. $y = -4$
J. $x = 4$
K. $x = 5$

11. What is the inverse of the function $g(x) = \frac{2x}{x-1}$?

A. $g^{-1}(x) = \frac{x-1}{2x}$

B. $g^{-1}(x) = \frac{1}{x-2}$

C. $g^{-1}(x) = \frac{x-2}{x}$

D. $g^{-1}(x) = \frac{x}{x-2}$

E. $g^{-1}(x) = \frac{x(x-1)}{2}$

12. Suppose p, q, and r are prime numbers. What is the least common multiple of the whole numbers p^2qr^3, pq^3r^3, and p^3r^4?

F. pqr^3
G. $p^2q^3r^3$
H. $p^3q^3r^4$
J. pqr
K. $p^6q^4r^{10}$

13. Colin earns an annual salary of *C* dollars, and Daryl earns an annual salary of *D* dollars. If the difference between Colin's and Daryl's average monthly salary is $500, which of the following represents the relationship between *C* and *D*?

A. $|C-D|=500$

B. $|C+D|=500$

C. $\left|\frac{C+D}{2}\right|=6{,}000$

D. $|C-D|=6{,}000$

E. $|C+D|=6{,}000$

14. A 1980s-style arcade charges customers an admission fee of $8.50, and it costs just $0.25 per game. Mike and Stan, together, spent $35. If Stan played three fewer than twice the number of games Mike played, how many games did they play, total?

F. 18
G. 25
H. 47
J. 72
K. 75

15. In the figure below, segments *AD* and *BC* intersect at point *E*, and $\overline{AB} \parallel \overline{CD}$. What is the measure of $\angle CED$?

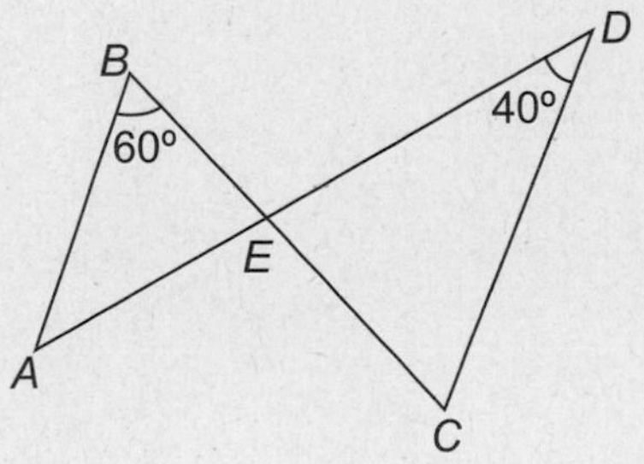

A. 40°
B. 60°
C. 80°
D. 100°
E. Cannot be determined from the given information

SHOW YOUR WORK HERE

CONTINUE

16. Two eight-sided dice are used in a board game. One is red with faces labeled as A, B, C, D, E, F, G, and H, while the other is blue with faces labeled as 0, 10, 20, 50, 100, 500, 1,000, and 5,000. If the result of rolling both dice is recorded, how many possible outcomes are there?

F. 8
G. 16
H. 32
J. 64
K. 128

SHOW YOUR WORK HERE

17. What is the slope of a line perpendicular to the line whose equation is $2x - 5y - 1 = 0$?

A. $-\frac{5}{2}$
B. $-\frac{1}{2}$
C. $\frac{2}{5}$
D. $\frac{1}{2}$
E. 2

18. A painter calculates that one gallon of paint can cover a 400 square foot wall with no paint left over. A house has four walls that are 20 feet tall. Two of the walls are 30 feet long, and two of the walls are 40 feet long. How many gallons of paint will the painter need to cover all four walls?

F. $3\frac{1}{2}$
G. $5\frac{1}{2}$
H. 6
J. 7
K. 30

19. What value of w makes the proportion true?

$$\frac{2w+1}{3} = \frac{5}{6}$$

A. $\frac{3}{4}$
B. $\frac{4}{3}$
C. $\frac{7}{6}$
D. 9
E. 15

SHOW YOUR WORK HERE

20. In the figure below, triangles *BCA* and *DEF* are similar. What is the length of segment *EF*?

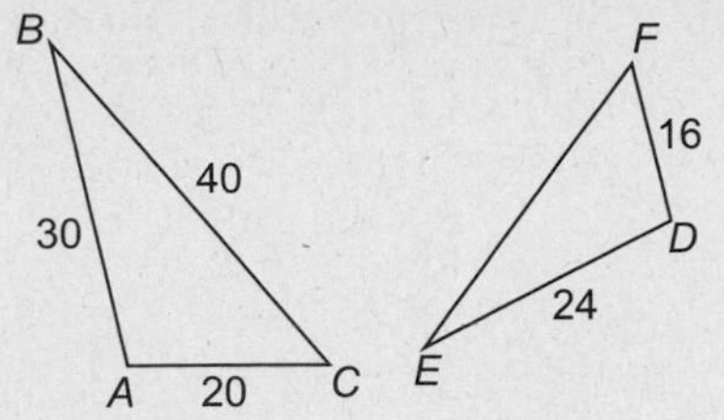

F. 28
G. 30
H. 32
J. 36
K. 40

21. For all nonnegative values of *x* and *y*, to which expression is $\sqrt{\dfrac{4^3x^7y}{3^2x^4y^3}}$ equal?

A. $\frac{8}{3}x^{14}y^{\frac{3}{2}}$

B. $\dfrac{4x^{\frac{2}{3}}}{3y}$

C. $\dfrac{8x^{\frac{3}{2}}}{3y}$

D. $\frac{8}{3}x^{\frac{1}{2}}y^2$

E. $\dfrac{8x^{\sqrt{3}}}{3y^{\sqrt{2}}}$

22. The average of six test scores is 80. When two more tests are included, the average for all eight tests is 85. What is the average score of the two added tests?

F. 70
G. 85
H. 90
J. 95
K. 100

CONTINUE

23. What is the area of right triangle *ABC* below, in square centimeters?

SHOW YOUR WORK HERE

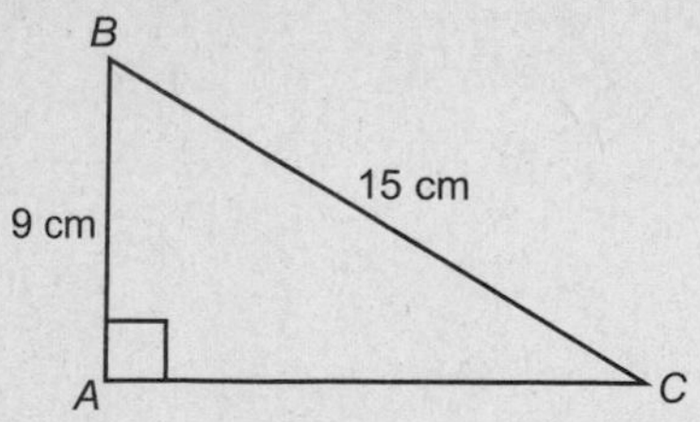

A. 12
B. 36
C. 54
D. 108
E. 135

24. It took Renee exactly 4 minutes and 26 seconds to download a file from the internet to her computer. At that same rate, how long would it take Renee to download a file that is $2\frac{1}{2}$ times as large as the first file?

F. 10 minutes and 5 seconds
G. 10 minutes and 26 seconds
H. 10 minutes and 52 seconds
J. 11 minutes and 5 seconds
K. 11 minutes and 15 seconds

25. A college campus's central green is a square lawn bordered by footpaths 100 feet long on each side. The college plans to create a diagonal footpath that would connect the southwest corner of the green to the northeast corner of the green. Approximately how many feet shorter would the new path be than the shortest possible route on the existing footpaths?

A. 40
B. 50
C. 60
D. 140
E. 150

26. Nick sold his riding mower for \$5,400. If this is 30% less than what he originally paid, how much did the mower originally cost?

F. $\frac{5{,}400}{0.7}$ dollars
G. 0.7(5,400) dollars
H. 0.3(5,400) dollars
J. 5,400 + 0.7 dollars
K. $\frac{5{,}400}{0.3}$ dollars

27. Ben has won the bid to repaint the local high school football stadium. If one gallon of paint covers an area of 150 square feet, what is the minimum number of gallons he will need to paint two rectangular walls that are 100 yards long and 15 yards high?

A. 20
B. 60
C. 90
D. 150
E. 180

SHOW YOUR WORK HERE

28. In the figure below, *WXYZ* is a square. Points are chosen on each pair of adjacent sides of *WXYZ* to form four congruent right triangles, as shown below. Each of the triangles has one leg that is three times longer than the other leg. What is the ratio of the area of the four triangles to the area of the shaded region?

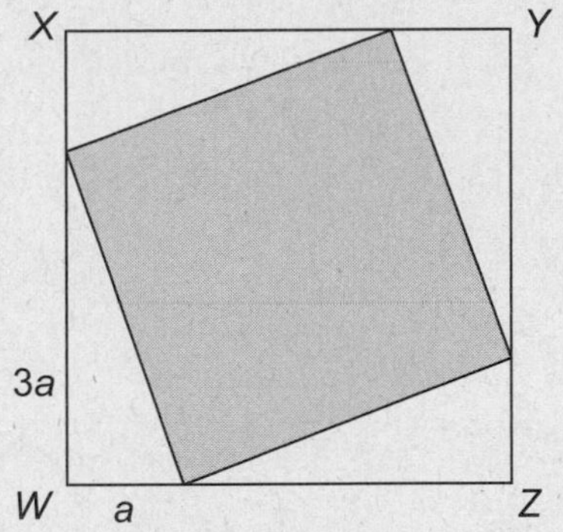

F. $\frac{3}{8}$

G. $\frac{2}{5}$

H. $\frac{1}{2}$

J. $\frac{3}{5}$

K. $\frac{3}{4}$

CONTINUE

SHOW YOUR WORK HERE

29. $\dfrac{\frac{1}{10}-\frac{1}{100}}{\frac{1}{5}-\frac{1}{25}}=$

A. $\dfrac{9}{625}$

B. $\dfrac{1}{4}$

C. $\dfrac{9}{16}$

D. $\dfrac{16}{9}$

E. $\dfrac{625}{9}$

30. What is the equation of the linear function shown in the graph below?

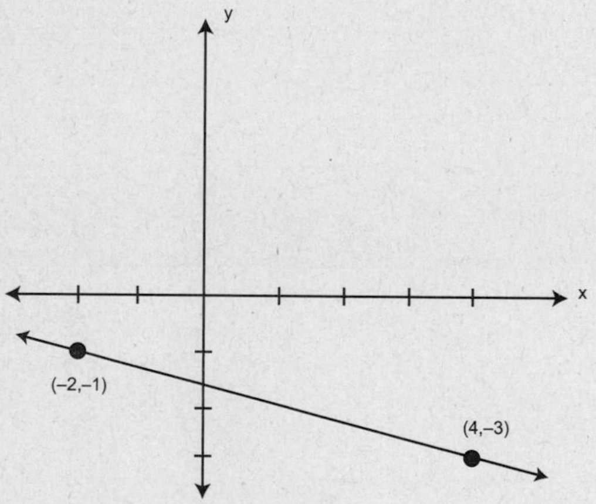

F. $f(x)=-3x-7$

G. $f(x)=-\frac{1}{3}x-\frac{5}{3}$

H. $f(x)=-3x-2$

J. $f(x)=-\frac{1}{3}x-2$

K. $f(x)=\frac{1}{3}x+\frac{5}{3}$

31. At a township meeting, thirty residents are asked how many robocalls they received, on average, in a typical evening during election season. They responded as follows:

5	1	0	8	5	4
2	4	1	8	0	5
2	1	0	0	7	8
1	5	1	2	7	1
1	4	4	1	3	1

What is the relationship between the mean, median, and mode of this data set?

A. mean < median < mode
B. mean < mode < median
C. mode < median < mean
D. median < mean < mode
E. mode < mean < median

32. For $90^\circ < \theta < 180^\circ$, if $\sin\theta = \frac{2}{3}$, then $\cot\theta =$

F. $-\frac{\sqrt{5}}{2}$
G. $-2\sqrt{5}$
H. $-\frac{\sqrt{5}}{3}$
J. $\frac{\sqrt{5}}{3}$
K. $-\frac{2\sqrt{5}}{9}$

33. The average of x numbers is 15. If two of the numbers are each increased by y, the new average will be increased by how much?

A. $2y$
B. y
C. $\frac{x}{2y}$
D. $\frac{y}{x}$
E. $\frac{2y}{x}$

SHOW YOUR WORK HERE

CONTINUE

34. Points *A*, *B*, and *C* below lie on the circumference of a circle with center *O*. If the unshaded sectors *AOB* and *BOC* comprise $\frac{2}{5}$ and $\frac{1}{3}$ of the area of the circle, respectively, what is the measure of $\angle AOC$?

SHOW YOUR WORK HERE

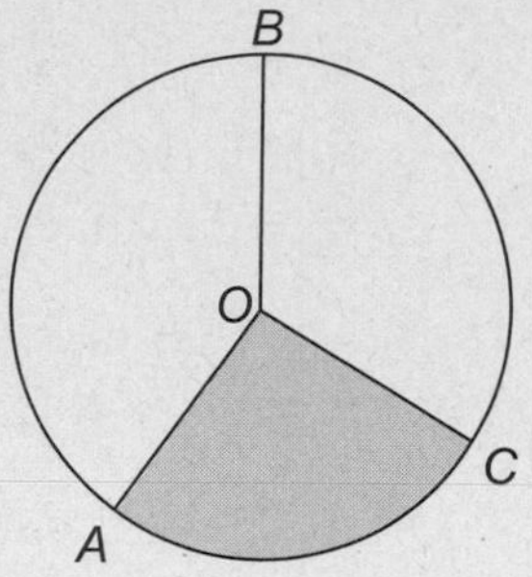

F. 48°
G. 90°
H. 92°
J. 96°
K. 264°

35. A 12-foot ladder is propped against a 10-foot house as shown below. Approximately how many feet is the base of the ladder from the wall of the house?

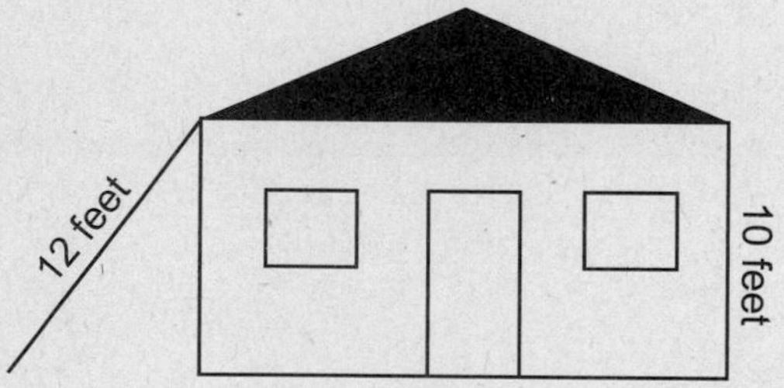

A. 2.0
B. 4.0
C. 6.6
D. 15.6
E. 44

36. What is the area of a circle with a diameter of 12 yards?

F. $36\pi^2$ square yards
G. 144 square yards
H. 12π square yards
J. 36π square yards
K. 144π square yards

37. There are 3 teaspoons in 1 tablespoon. A bottle of cough medicine contains 24 tablespoon-sized servings and costs $4.50. What is the approximate cost per teaspoon?

A. $0.06
B. $0.15
C. $0.19
D. $0.60
E. $1.50

SHOW YOUR WORK HERE

38. A line passing through the point (–1, 4) is perpendicular to the line passing through (–3, 2) and (–3, –5). What is the equation of this line?

F. $y = x + 5$
G. $y = 4$
H. $9x + 2y = 5$
J. $x = -1$
K. $y = -x - 5$

39. A right triangle has hypotenuse with length 5 yards and one leg has length 2 yards. What is the area of this triangle?

A. 3 square yards
B. $\sqrt{29}$ square yards
C. 5 square yards
D. $\sqrt{21}$ square yards
E. $\frac{5}{2}\sqrt{21}$ square yards

40. Let $h(x) = 1 - \frac{2}{3x}$. Compute $h\left(-\frac{4}{x}\right)$.

F. x
G. $\frac{x+24}{x}$
H. $\frac{2x+1}{12}$
J. $\frac{8-12x}{3x^2}$
K. $\frac{x+6}{6}$

41. What is the *y*-intercept, if one exists, of the following piecewise-defined function?

$$F(x) = \begin{cases} \sqrt{x+1}+5, & x \leq -2 \\ 4+3x, & -2 < x \leq 1 \\ -x^2+1, & x > 1 \end{cases}$$

A. No *y*-intercept
B. $-\frac{4}{3}$
C. 1
D. 4
E. 6

CONTINUE

42. What is the least possible value for the product xy, if $x + y = 24$ and x and y are both prime numbers?

SHOW YOUR WORK HERE

F. 23
G. 44
H. 95
J. 119
K. 143

43. The center of a circle is (–4, 3). If the point (2, –2) lies on this circle, what is the equation of this circle?

A. $(x - 4)^2 + (y + 3)^3 = 61$
B. $(x - 4)^2 + (y + 3)^3 = \sqrt{61}$
C. $(x + 4)^2 + (y - 3)^3 = 11$
D. $(x - 2)^2 + (y + 2)^2 = \sqrt{61}$
E. $(x + 4)^2 + (y - 3)^2 = 61$

44. If $0.3z - 0.24 = 1.2(0.3 - z)$, what is the value of $z \bullet 10^{-3}$?

F. 0.0004
G. 0.004
H. 0.4
J. 400
K. 4,000

45. In the isosceles right triangle below, what is the value of $\tan x°$?

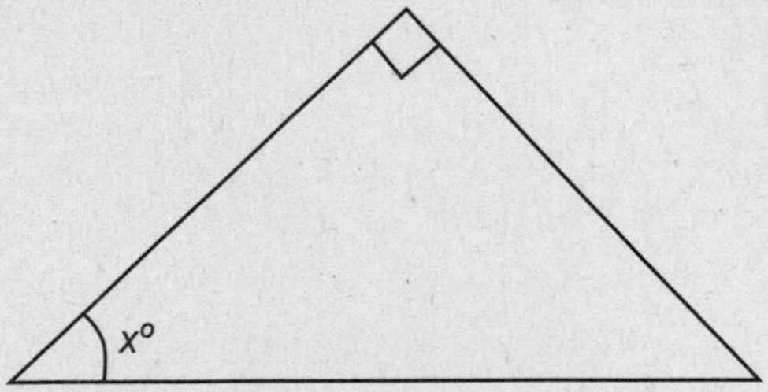

A. $\frac{\sqrt{2}}{2}$
B. 1
C. $\sqrt{2}$
D. $\frac{\sqrt{3}}{2}$
E. $\sqrt{3}$

46. What is the area of the rectangle shown below in the standard (x, y) coordinate plane?

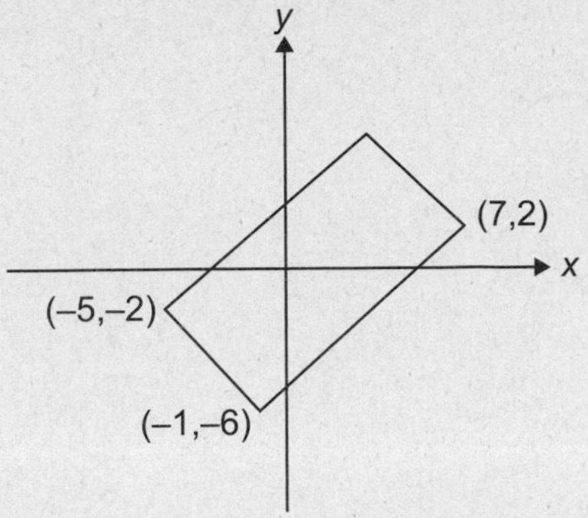

F. $32\sqrt{2}$

G. 64

H. $24\sqrt{2}$

J. 128

K. 144

47. If $\frac{x^3y^2}{z}$ is positive, then which of the following could be true?

I. x and z are both negative

II. x is negative and z is positive

III. x is zero

A. I only

B. II only

C. I and II

D. II and III

E. I, II, and III

48. What is the value of $\log_5\left(\frac{1}{625}\right)$?

F. –4

G. –3

H. $\frac{1}{4}$

J. 4

K. 125

SHOW YOUR WORK HERE

CONTINUE

SHOW YOUR WORK HERE

49. If x is inversely related to y and y is directly related to z, which of the following expressions gives one possibility for y in terms of x and z?

A. $y = \frac{x}{z}$

B. $y = \frac{z}{x}$

C. $y = zx$

D. $y = x^z$

E. $y = z^x$

50. Mary is weatherproofing her rain gutters for the winter. To prevent freezing, she needs to install heat tape along the gutters. The local hardware store charges $8.10 per 3-foot segment. What is the cost for 114 feet of heat tape if 5% sales tax is added to the cost?

F. $292.41

G. $307.80

H. $323.19

J. $923.40

K. $969.57

51. If $\frac{3(1-2y)}{4} - \frac{2-4y}{3} = y$, what is y^{-1}?

A. -16

B. $-\frac{1}{5}$

C. $-\frac{1}{16}$

D. 5

E. 16

52. What is the period of the graph of $y = 4\cos\left(3x - \frac{\pi}{2}\right) + 1$?

F. $\frac{\pi}{6}$

G. $\frac{2\pi}{3}$

H. 3

J. 4

K. 2π

53. The length of a diagonal of a square is 8 inches long. What is the perimeter of the square?

A. $4\sqrt{2}$ inches

B. $8\sqrt{2}$ inches

C. 16

D. $16\sqrt{2}$ inches

E. 32 inches

54. A positive number x is increased by 20 percent, and the result is then decreased by 30 percent. The final result is equal to which of the following?

F. x decreased by 50 percent
G. x decreased by 16 percent
H. x decreased by 10 percent
J. x increased by 10 percent
K. x increased by 24 percent

55. A 50-foot wire is attached to the top of an electric pole and is anchored on the ground. If the wire rises in a straight line at a 70° angle from the ground, how many feet tall is the pole?

A. $50 \sin 70^\circ$
B. $50 \cos 70^\circ$
C. $50 \tan 70^\circ$
D. $\frac{\cos 70^\circ}{50}$
E. $\frac{50}{\cos 70^\circ}$

56. What is the complete solution set of the inequality $2|3x + 1| > 8$?

F. $\{x: x > 5\}$
G. $\{x: x < -\frac{5}{3}\}$
H. $\{x: x > 1 \text{ or } x < -\frac{5}{3}\}$
J. $\{x: x > 5 \text{ or } x < -\frac{17}{5}\}$
K. $\{x: x > 1\}$

57. For what values of c do the lines $2x - cy = 1$ and $8cx - 2 = y$ never intersect in the standard xy-plane?

A. $c = 0$
B. $c = -\frac{1}{2}, c = \frac{1}{2}$
C. $c = -2, c = 2$
D. $c = -4, c = 4$
E. $c = -\frac{1}{16}, c = \frac{1}{16}$

SHOW YOUR WORK HERE

CONTINUE

58. Lines *m* and *n* are perpendicular in the standard (x, y) coordinate plane below. Which of the following is the equation for line *n*?

SHOW YOUR WORK HERE

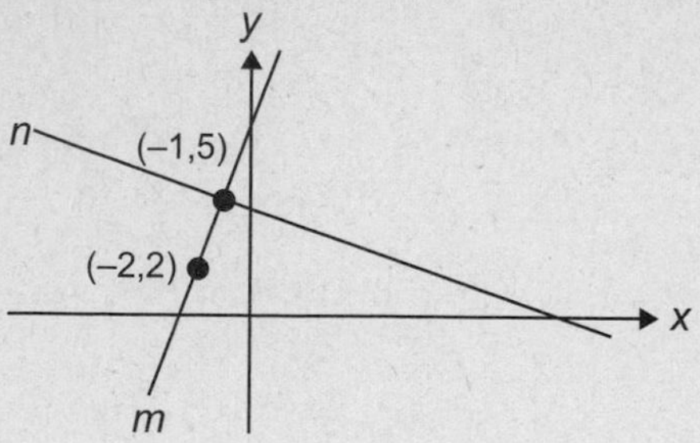

F. $y = -x + 5$

G. $y = -2x + 3$

H. $2y = -x - 4$

J. $3y = -x + 14$

K. $3y = x + 16$

59. Equally sized cards numbered from 1 to 30 are placed in a box. If one card is selected at random, what is the probability that the number on the card is either odd or divisible by 5?

A. 0.18

B. 0.40

C. 0.50

D. 0.60

E. 0.70

60. While shopping at a clothing store, Ben finds that a shirt and two ties cost \$105, while two shirts and one tie cost \$135. If the store charges the same price for all of its shirts and the same price for all of its ties, what is Ben's cost if he wants to buy just one tie?

F. \$15

G. \$25

H. \$30

J. \$50

K. \$55

READING TEST

35 Minutes—40 Questions

DIRECTIONS: There are four passages in this test. Each passage is followed by several questions. Read each passage, select the best answer to each related question, and fill in the corresponding circle on the answer sheet. You may look back at the passages as often as you need.

PASSAGE I

PROSE FICTION: Passage A is an excerpt from *Pride and Prejudice* by Jane Austen. Passage B is an excerpt from *Middlemarch* by George Eliot.

Passage A
by Jane Austen

Mr. Bennet was among the earliest of those who waited on Mr. Bingley. He had always intended to visit him, though to the last always assuring his wife that he should not go; and till the evening after the visit was paid she had no knowledge of it. It was then disclosed in the following manner. Observing his second daughter employed in trimming a hat, he suddenly addressed her with:

"I hope Mr. Bingley will like it, Lizzy."

"We are not in a way to know what Mr. Bingley likes," said her mother resentfully, "since we are not to visit."

"But you forget, mamma," said Elizabeth, "that we shall meet him at the assemblies, and that Mrs. Long promised to introduce him."

"I do not believe Mrs. Long will do any such thing. She has two nieces of her own. She is a selfish, hypocritical woman, and I have no opinion of her."

"No more have I," said Mr. Bennet; "and I am glad to find that you do not depend on her serving you."

Mrs. Bennet deigned not to make any reply, but, unable to contain herself, began scolding one of her daughters.

"Don't keep coughing so, Kitty, for Heaven's sake! Have a little compassion on my nerves. You tear them to pieces."

"Kitty has no discretion in her coughs," said her father; "she times them ill."

"I do not cough for my own amusement," replied Kitty fretfully. "When is your next ball to be, Lizzy?"

"Tomorrow fortnight."

"Aye, so it is," cried her mother, "and Mrs. Long does not come back till the day before; so it will be impossible for her to introduce him, for she will not know him herself."

"Then, my dear, you may have the advantage of your friend, and introduce Mr. Bingley to her."

"Impossible, Mr. Bennet, impossible, when I am not acquainted with him myself; how can you be so teasing?"

"I honour your circumspection. A fortnight's acquaintance is certainly very little. One cannot know what a man really is by the end of a fortnight. But if we do not venture somebody else will; and after all, Mrs. Long and her daughters must stand their chance; and, therefore, as she will think it an act of kindness, if you decline the office, I will take it on myself."

The girls stared at their father. Mrs. Bennet said only, "Nonsense, nonsense!"

"What can be the meaning of that emphatic exclamation?" cried he. "Do you consider the forms of introduction, and the stress that is laid on them, as nonsense? I cannot quite agree with you there. What say you, Mary? For you are a young lady of deep reflection, I know, and read great books and make extracts."

Mary wished to say something sensible, but knew not how.

Passage B
by George Eliot

Celia thought privately, "Dorothea quite despises Sir James Chettam; I believe she would not accept him." Celia felt that this was a pity. She had never been deceived as to the object of the baronet's interest. Sometimes, indeed, she had reflected that Dodo would perhaps not make a husband happy who had not her way of looking at things; and stifled in the depths of her heart was the feeling that her sister was too religious for family comfort. Notions and scruples were like spilt needles, making one afraid of treading, or sitting down, or even eating.

When Miss Brooke was at the tea-table, Sir James came to sit down by her, not having felt her mode of answering him

CONTINUE

at all offensive. Why should he? He thought it probable that Miss Brooke liked him, and manners must be very marked indeed before they cease to be interpreted by preconceptions either confident or distrustful. She was thoroughly charming to him, but of course he theorized a little about his attachment. He was made of excellent human dough, and had the rare merit of knowing that his talents, even if let loose, would not set the smallest stream in the county on fire: hence he liked the prospect of a wife to whom he could say, "What shall we do?" about this or that; who could help her husband out with reasons, and would also have the property qualification for doing so.

As to the excessive religiousness alleged against Miss Brooke, he had a very indefinite notion of what it consisted in, and thought that it would die out with marriage. In short, he felt himself to be in love in the right place, and was ready to endure a great deal of predominance, which, after all, a man could always put down when he liked. Sir James had no idea that he should ever like to put down the predominance of this handsome girl, in whose cleverness he delighted. Why not? A man's mind—what there is of it—has always the advantage of being masculine,—as the smallest birch-tree is of a higher kind than the most soaring palm,—and even his ignorance is of a sounder quality. Sir James might not have originated this estimate; but a kind Providence furnishes the limpest personality with a little gunk or starch in the form of tradition.

"Let me hope that you will rescind that resolution about the horse, Miss Brooke," said the persevering admirer. "I assure you, riding is the most healthy of exercises."

"I am aware of it," said Dorothea, coldly. "I think it would do Celia good—if she would take to it."

"But you are such a perfect horsewoman."

"Excuse me; I have had very little practice, and I should be easily thrown."

"Then that is a reason for more practice. Every lady ought to be a perfect horsewoman, that she may accompany her husband."

"You see how widely we differ, Sir James. I have made up my mind that I ought not to be a perfect horsewoman, and so I should never correspond to your pattern of a lady." Dorothea looked straight before her, and spoke with cold brusquerie, very much with the air of a handsome boy, in amusing contrast with the solicitous amiability of her admirer.

Questions 1–3 ask about Passage A.

1. Lizzy is described in the passage as the Bennets':

A. youngest daughter.
B. oldest daughter.
C. sensible daughter.
D. second daughter.

2. As it is used in line 22, the phrase "You tear them to pieces" most likely means:

F. "you are extremely destructive."
G. "you have a tendency toward violence."
H. "you are making me upset."
J. "you are making me physically ill."

3. When Mr. Bennet tells his wife that she should introduce Mr. Bingley to Lizzy, she feels that Mr. Bennet:

A. has lost his mind.
B. is breaching etiquette.
C. does not understand his wife.
D. does not love his wife.

Questions 4–6 ask about Passage B.

4. According to the passage, people seem to think that Miss Brooke is:

F. too rude.
G. too religious.
H. too happy.
J. too unscrupulous.

5. In the context of the passage, the primary function of lines 28–30 is to:

A. quote something Sir James said about Miss Brooke.
B. reveal Sir James's true feelings about Miss Brooke.
C. contradict the idea that Sir James was charming.
D. list examples of why Sir James loved Miss Brooke.

6. As it is used in line 3, the word *pity* most nearly means:

F. sorry.
G. compassion.
H. sympathy.
J. shame.

Questions 7–10 ask about both passages.

7. Given the way they are presented in each passage, Mrs. Bennet and Miss Brooke are best described as:

A. demure.
B. disgusted.
C. short-tempered.
D. amusing.

8. In what way is Kitty in Passage A DIFFERENT from Miss Brooke in Passage B?

   F. Kitty is concerned about how others interpret her behavior.
   G. Kitty does not care about what is expected of women.
   H. Kitty uses hostility to mask her romantic feelings.
   J. Kitty is extremely selfish and hypocritical.

9. The narrators of Passage A and Passage B reveal the inner thoughts of which characters from each passage?

   A. Kitty and Celia
   B. Elizabeth and Miss Brooke
   C. Mr. Bingley and Sir James
   D. Mary and Celia

10. It can be inferred that Mr. Bingley in Passage A and Sir James in Passage B are both:

   F. extremely charming.
   G. uninterested in etiquette.
   H. unmarried men.
   J. in love with the women they meet.

PASSAGE II

SOCIAL SCIENCE: The following passage is excerpted from a biography of social reformer and activist Susan B. Anthony, who worked to ensure that women have the right to vote in the United States.

Susan preached militancy to women throughout the presidential campaign of 1872, urging them to claim their rights under the Fourteenth and Fifteenth Amendments by registering and voting in every state in the Union.

Even before Francis Minor had called her attention to the possibilities offered by these amendments, she had followed with great interest a similar effort by Englishwomen who, in 1867 and 1868, had attempted to prove that the "ancient legal rights of females" were still valid and entitled women property holders to vote for representatives in Parliament, and who claimed that the word "man" in Parliamentary statutes should be interpreted to include women. In the case of the 5,346 householders of Manchester, the court held that "every woman is personally incapable" in a legal sense. This legal contest had been fully reported in *The Revolution*, and disappointing as the verdict was, Susan looked upon this attempt to establish justice as an indication of a great awakening and uprising among women.

There had also been heartening signs in her own country, which she hoped were the preparation for more successful militancy to come. She had exulted in *The Revolution* in 1868 over the attempt of women to vote in Vineland, New Jersey. Encouraged by the enfranchisement of women in Wyoming in 1869, Mary Olney Brown and Charlotte Olney French had cast their votes in Washington Territory. A young widow, Marilla Ricker, had registered and voted in New Hampshire in 1870, claiming this right as a property holder, but her vote was refused. In 1871, Nannette B. Gardner and Catherine Stebbins in Detroit, Catherine V. White in Illinois, Ellen R. Van Valkenburg in Santa Cruz, California, and Carrie S. Burnham in Philadelphia registered and attempted to vote. Only Mrs. Gardner's vote was accepted. That same year, Sarah Andrews Spencer, Sarah E. Webster, and seventy other women marched to the polls to register and vote in the District of Columbia. Their ballots refused, they brought suit against the Board of Election Inspectors, carrying the case unsuccessfully to the Supreme Court of the United States. Another test case based on the Fourteenth Amendment had also been carried to the Supreme Court by Myra Bradwell, one of the first women lawyers, who had been denied admission to the Illinois bar because she was a woman.

With the spotlight turned on the Fourteenth Amendment by these women, lawyers here and there throughout the country were discussing the legal points involved, many admitting that women had a good case. Even the press was friendly.

Susan had looked forward to claiming her rights under the Fourteenth and Fifteenth Amendments and was ready to act. She had spent the thirty days required of voters in Rochester with her family and as she glanced through the morning paper of November 1, 1872, she read these challenging words, "Now Register … If you were not permitted to vote you would fight for the right, undergo all privations for it, face death for it…."

This was all the reminder she needed. She would fight for this right. She put on her bonnet and coat, telling her three sisters what she intended to do, asked them to join her, and with them walked briskly to the barber shop where the voters of her ward were registering. Boldly entering this stronghold of men, she asked to be registered. The inspector in charge, Beverly W. Jones, tried to convince her that this was impossible under the laws of New York. She told him she claimed her right to vote not under the New York constitution but under the Fourteenth Amendment, and she read him its pertinent lines. Other election inspectors now joined in the argument, but she persisted until two of them, Beverly W. Jones and Edwin F. Marsh, both Republicans, finally consented to register the four women.

CONTINUE

This mission accomplished, Susan rounded up twelve more women willing to register. The evening papers spread the sensational news, and by the end of the registration period, fifty Rochester women had joined the ranks of the militants.

On election day, November 5, 1872, Susan gleefully wrote Elizabeth Stanton, "Well, I have gone and done it!!—positively voted the Republican ticket—Strait—this a.m. at 7 o'clock—& swore my vote in at that.... All my three sisters voted—Rhoda deGarmo too—Amy Post was rejected & she will immediately bring action against the registrars.... Not a jeer not a word—not a look—disrespectful has met a single woman.... I hope the mornings telegrams will tell of many women all over the country trying to vote.... I hope you voted too."

Election day did not bring the general uprising of women for which Susan had hoped. In Michigan, Missouri, Ohio, and Connecticut, as in Rochester, a few women tried to vote. In New York City, Lillie Devereux Blake and in Fayetteville, New York, Matilda Joslyn Gage had courageously gone to the polls only to be turned away. Elizabeth Stanton did not vote on November 5, 1872, and her lack of enthusiasm about a test case in the courts was very disappointing to Susan.

However, the fact that Susan B. Anthony had voted won immediate response from the press in all parts of the country. Newspapers in general were friendly, the *New York Times* boldly declaring, "The act of Susan B. Anthony should have a place in history," and the *Chicago Tribune* venturing to suggest that she ought to hold public office. The cartoonists, however, reveling in a new and tempting subject, caricatured her unmercifully, the New York Graphic setting the tone. Some Democratic papers condemned her, following the line of the Rochester *Union and Advertiser* which flaunted the headline, "Female Lawlessness," and declared that Miss Anthony's lawlessness had proved women unfit for the ballot.

11. The passage specifies that when more than seventy women were refused the right to vote in the District of Columbia in 1871 they:

A. tried to vote anyway, but only the vote of Nannette B. Gardner was accepted.
B. sued the Board of Election Inspectors in a case heard by the US Supreme Court.
C. organized a march on Washington, D.C., to protest such unfair treatment.
D. traveled to Washington Territory to vote there instead.

12. Based on information in the passage, Susan B. Anthony would most likely promote which of the following methods to secure one's civil rights?

F. Conduct a violent revolution.
G. Complain to the press.
H. Vote for sympathetic politicians.
J. Invoke the US constitution.

13. The efforts described in the third paragraph are presented in order to illustrate the idea that:

A. a militant effort to secure women the right to vote was in full force.
B. Susan B. Anthony was not alone in her efforts to secure women the right to vote.
C. every woman in the United States was angered that they did not have the right to vote.
D. activists would use the Supreme Court as their main tool for securing equal rights.

14. The author of the passage appears to feel that the question "What does it take to enact social change?" is best answered by the assertion that it takes:

F. the dedicated work of a single visionary.
G. an effort to vote out the politicians currently in charge.
H. a unified effort by many dedicated individuals.
J. a lawsuit brought in front of the US Supreme Court.

15. The author states in paragraph 6 that Beverly W. Jones and Edwin F. Marsh "finally consented to register the four women" because:

A. Susan B. Anthony's argument was so persistent.
B. Susan B. Anthony read lines from the Fourteenth Amendment.
C. Susan B. Anthony turned election inspectors against each other.
D. Susan B. Anthony rounded up twelve more women willing to register.

16. As it is used in line 61, the word *pertinent* most nearly means:

F. relevant.
G. interesting.
H. persistent.
J. remorseful.

17. According to the passage, the news media reported on the registration of women voters in Rochester after:

A. fifty women had joined the ranks of the militants.
B. Anthony wrote a gleeful letter to Elizabeth Stanton.
C. Amy Post sued the registrars who would not allow her to vote.
D. Anthony had successfully gotten sixteen women to register to vote.

18. In the third paragraph (lines 19–40), the author discusses Myra Bradwell in a manner that:

F. emphasizes how Myra Bradwell was not qualified for the Illinois bar.
G. exaggerates the difficulties of being a woman during Susan B. Anthony's time.
H. highlights the challenges women faced during Susan B. Anthony's time.
J. showcases the brightest women who lived during Susan B. Anthony's time.

19. According to the ninth paragraph, Susan B. Anthony was NOT criticized by:

A. the *New York Graphic*.
B. the Rochester *Union and Advertiser*.
C. many editorial cartoonists.
D. the *Chicago Tribune*.

20. One of the main points made in the eighth paragraph is that although Anthony brought a great deal of attention to the movement to win women the right to vote in the United States, her initial efforts:

F. inspired women such as Lillie Devereux Blake and Matilda Joslyn Gage to vote.
G. were heavily criticized by Elizabeth Stanton.
H. failed to inspire many other women to fight for that right.
J. were ruthlessly mocked in all news media outlets.

PASSAGE III

HUMANITIES: The following passage is adapted from a history of French Impressionist painters originally published in 1903.

Now I must speak at some length of a painter who, together with the luminous and sparkling landscapist Félix Ziem, was the most direct initiator of Impressionist technique. Monticelli is one of those singular men of genius who are not connected with any school, and whose work is an inexhaustible source of applications. He lived at Marseilles, where he was born, made a short appearance at the Salons, and then returned to his native town, where he died poor, ignored, paralyzed and mad. In order to live he sold his small pictures at the cafés, where they fetched ten or twenty francs at the most. Today they sell for considerable prices, although the government has not yet acquired any work by Monticelli for the public galleries. The mysterious power alone of these paintings secures him a fame which is, alas! posthumous. Many Monticellis have been sold by dealers as Diaz's; now they are more eagerly looked for than Diaz, and collectors have made fortunes with these small canvases bought formerly, to use a colloquial expression which is here only too literally true, "for a piece of bread."

Monticelli painted landscapes, romantic scenes, "fêtes galantes" in the spirit of Watteau, and still-life pictures: one could not imagine a more inspired sense of color than shown by these works which seem to be painted with crushed jewels, with powerful harmony, and beyond all with an unheard-of delicacy in the perception of fine shades. There are tones which nobody had ever invented yet, a richness, a profusion, a subtlety which almost vie with the resources of music. The fairyland atmosphere of these works surrounds a very firm design of charming style, but, to use the words of the artist himself, "in these canvases the objects are the decoration, the touches are the scales, and the light is the tenor." Monticelli has created for himself an entirely personal technique which can only be compared with that of Turner; he painted with a brush so full, fat and rich, that some of the details are often truly modeled in relief, in a substance as precious as enamels, jewels, ceramics—a substance which is a delight in itself. Every picture by Monticelli provokes astonishment; constructed upon one color as upon a musical theme, it rises to intensities, which one would have thought impossible. His pictures are magnificent bouquets, bursts of joy and color, where nothing is ever crude, and where everything is ruled by a supreme sense of harmony.

Claude Lorrain, Watteau, Turner and Monticelli constitute really the descent of a landscapist like Claude Monet. In all matters concerning technique, they form the direct chain of Impressionism. As regards design, subject, realism, the study of modern life, the conception of beauty and the portrait, the Impressionist movement is based upon the old French masters, principally upon Chardin, Watteau, Latour, Largillière, Fragonard, Debucourt, Saint-Aubin, Moreau, and Eisen. It has resolutely held aloof from mythology, academic allegory, historical painting, and from the neo-Greek elements of Classicism as well as from the German and Spanish elements of Romanticism. This reactionary movement is therefore entirely French, and surely if it deserves reproach, the one least deserved is that leveled upon it by the official painters: disobedience to the national spirit. Impressionism is an art which does not give

CONTINUE

much scope to intellectuality, an art whose followers admit scarcely anything but immediate vision, rejecting philosophy and symbols and occupying themselves only with the consideration of light, picturesqueness, keen and clever observation, and antipathy to abstraction, as the innate qualities of French art. We shall see later on, when considering separately its principal masters, that each of them has based his art upon some masters of pure French blood.

Impressionism has, then, hitherto been very badly judged. It is contained in two chief points: search after a new technique, and expression of modern reality. Its birth has not been a spontaneous phenomenon. Manet, who, by his spirit and by the chance of his friendships, grouped around him the principal members, commenced by being classed in the ranks of the Realists of the second Romanticism by the side of Courbet; and during the whole first period of his work he only endeavored to describe contemporary scenes, at a time when the laws of the new technique were already dawning upon Claude Monet. Gradually the grouping of the Impressionists took place. Claude Monet is really the first initiator: in a parallel line with his ideas and his works Manet passed into the second period of his artistic life, and with him Renoir, Degas and Pissarro. But Manet had already during his first period been the topic of far-echoing polemics, caused by his realism and by the marked influence of the Spaniards and of Hals upon his style; his temperament, too, was that of the head of a school; and for these reasons legend has attached to his name the title of head of the Impressionist school, but this legend is incorrect.

21. As it is used in line 21, the word *inspired* most likely means:

A. animated.
B. encouraged.
C. exceptional.
D. educated.

22. The author of the passage would most likely agree with which of the following statements?

F. The use of symbols is not necessarily an integral element of good art.
G. Romantic and Classical art is worthless.
H. The finest art depicts imagery from mythology.
J. The Impressionists were the most technically advanced artists.

23. The image in lines 35–40 functions figuratively to suggest that:

A. music had a direct influence on Monticelli's paintings.
B. Monticelli never used more than one color in his paintings.
C. Monticelli was a great musical composer as well as a great artist.
D. the basic elements in Monticelli's paintings have great emotional impact.

24. According to the third paragraph, Impressionistic art involves:

I. abstract imagery.
II. the consideration of light.
III. picturesqueness.

F. I only
G. III only
H. II and III only
J. I, II, and III

25. It can be inferred from the second paragraph that:

A. Impressionistic art can provoke strong emotions.
B. no artist can be compared to Monticelli.
C. landscape art was too mundane for the Impressionists.
D. Monticelli was not appreciated during his lifetime.

26. The passage suggests that Manet was considered a Realist because:

F. of his peculiar temperament.
G. he tended to paint contemporary scenes.
H. he was friends with many Realists.
J. he was often confused with Monet.

27. The main idea of the passage is that:

A. Monticelli is one of the key artists of Impressionism, though his work was not appreciated until after his death.
B. Impressionism is an exciting art form that took some time to develop and it has often been unfairly judged.
C. in terms of subject, realism, modernity, beauty, and portraiture, Impressionism is based on the old French masters.
D. Manet was often considered the head of the Impressionist school, but this is inaccurate.

28. According to Paragraph 2, Monticelli:

I. used a thick brush.
II. often painted jewels.
III. was influenced by music.

F. I only
G. I and II only
H. II and III only
J. I, II, and III

29. Based on the information in the passage, which of the following is a fact rather than an opinion?

A. Monticelli's use of color was inspired.
B. Monticelli's style was entirely personal.
C. All of Monticelli's pictures provoke astonishment.
D. Monticelli painted landscapes and "fêtes galantes."

30. The phrase "an art whose followers admit scarcely anything but immediate vision" in Paragraph 3 implies that:

F. the Impressionists refuse to discuss their work.
G. spontaneity is the main quality of Impressionist art.
H. the Impressionists are not honest about their work processes.
J. the Impressionists are only influenced by artists of pure French blood.

PASSAGE IV

NATURAL SCIENCE: The following passage is excerpted from a book about the principles of geology.

Geology is the science which investigates the successive changes that have taken place in the organic and inorganic kingdoms of nature; it inquires into the causes of these changes, and the influence which they have exerted in modifying the surface and external structure of our planet.

By these researches into the state of the earth and its inhabitants at former periods, we acquire a more perfect knowledge of its present condition, and more comprehensive views concerning the laws now governing its animate and inanimate productions. When we study history, we obtain a more profound insight into human nature, by instituting a comparison between the present and former states of society. We trace the long series of events which have gradually led to the actual posture of affairs; and by connecting effects with their causes, we are enabled to classify and retain in the memory a multitude of complicated relations—the various peculiarities of national character—the different degrees of moral and intellectual refinement, and numerous other circumstances, which, without historical associations, would be uninteresting or imperfectly understood. As the present condition of nations is the result of many antecedent changes, some extremely remote, and others recent, some gradual, others sudden and violent; so the state, of the natural world is the result of a long succession of events; and if we would enlarge our experience of the present economy of nature, we must investigate the effects of her operations in former epochs.

We often discover with surprise, on looking back into the chronicles of nations, how the fortune of some battle has influenced the fate of millions of our contemporaries, when it has long been forgotten by the mass of the population. With this remote event we may find inseparably connected the geographical boundaries of a great state, the language now spoken by the inhabitants, their peculiar manners, laws, and religious opinions. But far more astonishing and unexpected are the connections brought to light, when we carry back our researches into the history of nature. The form of a coast, the configuration of the interior of a country, the existence and extent of lakes, valleys, and mountains, can often be traced to the former prevalence of earthquakes and volcanoes in regions which have long been undisturbed. To these remote convulsions the present fertility of some districts, the sterile character of others, the elevation of land above the sea, the climate, and various peculiarities, may be distinctly referred. On the other hand, many distinguishing features of the surface may often be ascribed to the operation, at a remote era, of slow and tranquil causes—to the gradual deposition of sediment in a lake or in the ocean, or to the prolific increase of testacea and corals...

Geology is intimately related to almost all the physical sciences, as history is to the moral. An historian should, if possible, be at once profoundly acquainted with ethics, politics, jurisprudence, the military art, theology; in a word, with all branches of knowledge by which any insight into human affairs, or into the moral and intellectual nature of man, can be obtained. It would be no less desirable that a geologist should be well versed in chemistry, natural philosophy, mineralogy, zoology, comparative anatomy, botany; in short, in every science relating to organic and inorganic nature. With these accomplishments, the historian and geologist would rarely fail to draw correct and philosophical conclusions from the various monuments transmitted to them of former occurrences. They would know to what combination of causes analogous effects were referable, and they would often be enabled to supply, by inference, information concerning many events unrecorded in the defective archives of former ages. But as such extensive acquisitions are

CONTINUE

scarcely within the reach of any individual, it is necessary that men who have devoted their lives to different departments should unite their efforts; and as the historian receives assistance from the antiquary, and from those who have cultivated different branches of moral and political science, so the geologist should avail himself of the aid of many naturalists, and particularly of those who have studied the fossil remains of lost species of animals and plants.

The analogy, however, of the monuments consulted in geology, and those available in history, extends no farther than to one class of historical monuments—those which may be said to be undesignedly commemorative of former events. The canoes, for example, and stone hatchets found in our peat bogs, afford an insight into the rude arts and manners of the earliest inhabitants of our island; the buried coin fixes the date of the reign of some Roman emperor; the ancient encampment indicates the districts once occupied by invading armies, and the former method of constructing military defenses; the Egyptian mummies throw light on the art of embalming, the rites of sepulture, or the average stature of the human race in ancient Egypt. This class of memorials yields to no other in authenticity, but it constitutes a small part only of the resources on which the historian relies, whereas in geology it forms the only kind of evidence which is at our command. For this reason we must not expect to obtain a full and connected account of any series of events beyond the reach of history. But the testimony of geological monuments, if frequently imperfect, possesses at least the advantage of being free from all intentional misrepresentation. We may be deceived in the inferences which we draw, in the same manner as we often mistake the nature and import of phenomena observed in the daily course of nature; but our liability to err is confined to the interpretation, and, if this be correct, our information is certain.

It was long before the distinct nature and legitimate objects of geology were fully recognized, and it was at first confounded with many other branches of inquiry, just as the limits of history, poetry, and mythology were ill-defined in the infancy of civilization. Even in Werner's time, or at the close of the eighteenth century, geology appears to have been regarded as little other than a subordinate department of mineralogy; and Desmarest included it under the head of Physical Geography. But the most common and serious source of confusion arose from the notion, that it was the business of geology to discover the mode in which the earth originated, or, as some imagined, to study the effects of those cosmological causes which were employed by the Author of Nature to bring this planet out of a nascent and chaotic state into a more perfect and habitable condition. Hutton was the first who endeavored to draw a strong line of demarcation between his favorite science and cosmogony, for he declared that geology was in nowise concerned "with questions as to the origin of things."

31. The passage mentions that features of Earth may be the results of:

A. undisturbed areas of land.
B. land elevation.
C. ancient cataclysms.
D. natural erosion.

32. According to the passage, the geologist should also have a background in:

I. botany.
II. anatomy.
III. chemistry.

F. I only
G. I and II only
H. II and III only
J. I, II, and III

33. The passage suggests that geology was considered a branch of mineralogy as recently as:

A. the late 1600s.
B. the early 1700s.
C. the late 1700s.
D. the late 1800s.

34. It can reasonably be inferred from the passage that geology is all of the following EXCEPT:

F. a study of how Earth originated.
G. an area of study similar to the study of history.
H. an area of study dependent on all the physical sciences.
J. a means to explain Earth's present condition.

35. As it is used in line 12, the word *trace* most likely means:

A. outline the shape.
B. make a sketch.
C. a very small amount.
D. locate and follow.

36. The reason that geologists depend on naturalists is due to the:

F. difficulty of excavating the rocks, minerals, and other materials that geologists study.
G. reluctance of geologists to share their discoveries with each other.
H. fact that geologists must often study the things that naturalists have discovered.
J. importance of understanding different branches of moral and political science.

37. According to the passage, an increase in coral may:

A. alter Earth's surface features.
B. impede the understanding of a geological feature.
C. cause an increase of *Testacea*.
D. increase the tranquility of Earth.

38. The passage states that historians may study mummies in order to:

F. learn the dates in which rulers lived.
G. find out the areas that armies occupied.
H. gain knowledge about the human form.
J. know how ancient physicians treated the ill.

39. Based on information from the passage, historians have all of the following characteristics EXCEPT:

A. knowledge of ethics and politics.
B. working relationships with other academics.
C. insight into human affairs.
D. understanding of natural philosophy.

40. Which of the following would be the best example of violent "antecedent changes" that might affect "the present condition of nations"?

F. The eruptions of volcanoes
G. Nineteenth-century political revolutions
H. Current wars
J. Presidential elections with unfortunate outcomes

STOP

SCIENCE TEST

35 Minutes—40 Questions

DIRECTIONS: There are seven passages in this test. Each passage is followed by several questions. Read each passage, select the best answer to each related question, and fill in the corresponding circle on the answer sheet. You may look back at the passages as often as you need.

You are NOT allowed to use a calculator on this test.

PASSAGE I

As power is supplied to a circuit, current flows through the circuit. An ammeter is the device used to measure the current, and many ammeters measure current in milliamperes (mA). The voltage responsible for the current can be measured by a voltmeter and is measured in volts. When a resistor is placed in a circuit, it dampens the current flowing through a circuit at a given voltage.

If there is a linear relationship between current and voltage when a resistor is placed in the circuit, the resistor is considered an *ohmic* device. If the temperature of the resistor changes, then it is not considered an ohmic device. Some resistors are sensitive to small external temperature changes and will show a change in resistance as a result of these temperature changes. These resistors are called *thermistors*. The change in resistance exhibited by a thermistor can be detected by a change in the observed current at a given voltage.

The following procedure was performed to investigate whether different resistors acted as ohmic devices in a circuit. The circuit was constructed as shown in Figure 1.

FIGURE 1

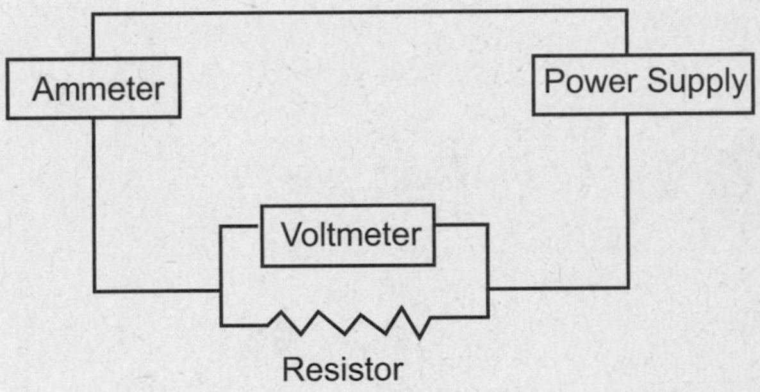

After each resistor was connected to the circuit, the resistor was submerged in water to detect any changes in temperature as well as its sensitivity to different beginning temperatures. The power source was turned on and the voltages of the power source and the resulting current were recorded. The voltage was changed several times, and the corresponding current was noted.

CONTINUE

Table 1 summarizes the results when three different resistors were tested at two different temperatures. In all cases, no change in water temperature was observed.

Table 1

Voltage (V)	Current (mA)	Current (mA)
Resistor A		
	23°C	**25°C**
0.25	25	25
0.50	50	50
1.00	100	100
2.00	200	200
3.00	300	300
4.00	400	400
4.50	450	450
5.00	500	500
Resistor B		
	23°C	**25°C**
0.25	150	150
0.50	195	195
1.00	230	230
2.00	295	295
3.00	345	345
4.00	405	405
4.50	420	420
5.00	445	445
Resistor C		
	23°C	**25°C**
0.25	5	4.5
0.50	10	9.0
1.00	20	18.0
2.00	40	36.0
3.00	60	54.0
4.00	80	72.0
4.50	90	81.0
5.00	100	90.0

1. When the temperature is 25°C and the voltage is 4.5 volts, what is the current of the circuit when Resistor B is used?

A. 81 mA
B. 90 mA
C. 420 mA
D. 450 mA

2. If 3.5 volts were used with Resistor A at 27°C, approximately what would the current have read?

F. 63 mA
G. 70 mA
H. 350 mA
J. 375 mA

3. According to the data in Table 1, which of the following resistors respond linearly to a change in voltage?

I. Resistor A
II. Resistor B
III. Resistor C

A. I only
B. II only
C. II and III
D. I and III

4. Resistor B does NOT appear to be a thermistor because:

F. at low voltages, Resistor B produces higher currents than either of the other resistors.
G. at higher temperatures, Resistor B produces lower currents than either of the other resistors.
H. there is a change in resistance at different voltages.
J. there is no change in resistance at different temperatures.

5. What additional information would be necessary to conclude whether Resistor C is a thermistor?

A. The current-voltage response of Resistor C at a third temperature
B. The temperature of Resistor C at various voltages
C. Whether the current of Resistor C responds linearly with temperature
D. There is enough information to determine whether Resistor C is a thermistor.

6. Which of the following hypotheses would be disproved if there had been a noted temperature change in the water for all six trials?

   F. Resistor A is an ohmic device because of its linear relationship between voltage and current.
   G. Resistor B is affected by different starting temperatures.
   H. Resistor C is not an ohmic device because it does not have a linear relationship between voltage and current.
   J. Resistor C is not affected by different starting temperatures.

PASSAGE II

Seagrasses are plants that grow along the coasts of warm, shallow seas. They form underwater meadows that improve water quality, help prevent erosion of sand and sediment during storms, and provide shelter and food for fish and other aquatic animals. Ecologists have discovered that they also store a large amount of carbon and other nutrients in the sediment. The ecologists were interested in how much.

Ecologists selected an area that was undergoing restoration after the original seagrass meadow was wiped out during a severe hurricane. Seagrass had been seeded onto two separate meadows; one meadow had been reseeded four years ago, and the other had been reseeded ten years ago. From each meadow, the ecologists took four 20-cm deep, 10-cm diameter sediment cores. They also took four similar cores from the unplanted sediment immediately around each of the meadows. They removed shells, rocks, and large roots from the sediment, weighed them wet and again after drying to determine bulk density, and determined the percentages of organic matter, carbon, and nitrogen in the sediment. The averages of their results are summarized in Table 1.

Table 1

Site	Meadow Age (years)	Seagrass Density (shoots /m²)	% Carbon	% Nitrogen	% Organic Matter	Bulk Density (g/cm³)
Site 1	0	0	0.4	0.2	1.6	1.53
Site 1	4	123	0.39	0.2	1.6	1.44
Site 2	0	0	0.36	0.86	1.4	1.61
Site 2	10	429	0.52	3.75	1.9	1.30

CONTINUE

After examining nutrient accumulation, the ecologists wanted to determine which physical characteristics of the seagrass meadow are most helpful in stabilizing sediment to prevent erosion. They placed four sediment traps within the 10-year old meadow, and recorded the characteristics of the seagrass around the sediment trap: the shoot density (in shoots/m^2 of seabed), leaf mass (grams of seagrass leaves/ m^2 of seabed), seagrass height (cm), and leaf surface area (m^2 leaf surface/m^2 of seabed). After each day, they weighed the amount of sediment collected in each sediment trap (g/m^2 of trap area, per day). They compared the average of six days of sediment results with each of the seagrass characteristics in Table 2.

Table 2

Trapped Sediment Weight (g/m^2/day)	Seagrass Density (shoots/m^2)	Seagrass Mass (g/m^2)	Seagrass Surface Area (m^2/m^2)	Seagrass Height
3.3	200	6.0	1.8	29
3.8	170	10.2	2.8	56
4.1	260	6.8	3.0	33
4.8	230	10.0	4.1	52

7. According to the data in Table 1, the greatest difference in sediment bulk density was found between:

A. years 0 and 4 at Site 1.
B. years 0 and 10 at Site 2.
C. the two sites without seagrass.
D. the two sites with seagrass.

8. According to the data, the biggest relative change between 0 and 10 years was found in:

F. % carbon.
G. % nitrogen.
H. % organic matter.
J. bulk density.

9. Which of the following best explains why the scientists collected sediment from an unplanted area at each site?

A. To control for differences in original sediment composition between the two sites
B. To control for differences in water depth between the two sites
C. To determine the most effective seagrass density for nutrient sequestration
D. To determine the rate of nutrient loss in unvegetated seabeds

10. Which hypothesis is supported by the data in Table 2?

F. Taller seagrass plants reduce turbulence in a larger portion of the water column, resulting in greater sediment deposition.
G. More densely planted seagrass meadows prevent sand from settling to the seabed, resulting in reduced sediment deposition.
H. Greater seagrass mass increases turbulence in the water column, resulting in reduced sediment deposition.
J. Greater seagrass surface area more effectively dissipates the energy of ocean currents, resulting in greater sediment deposition.

11. A local company wants to dredge a nearby seagrass meadow to collect sand for a public beach. To decrease the negative impacts of the dredging, they would like to replant seagrass afterwards. What is the most likely outcome of replanting?

A. After 10 years, the replanted seagrass meadow would have a higher shoot density than the original one.
B. The percentage of organic matter found in the sediment would be unchanged by dredging and replanting.
C. There would be immediate storage of carbon and nitrogen in the sediment, similar to that in the original meadow.
D. There would be a lag of more than four years before carbon and nitrogen storage reached that of the original meadow.

12. Scientists have measured atmospheric carbon dioxide (CO_2) levels that are higher now than they have been in any measured year and estimated to be higher than any time in the last 400,000 years. If ecologists want to increase the amount by which seagrass meadows take up CO_2 and store it in the sediment, what action is most likely to be effective?

    F. Protect and expand existing seagrass meadows.
    G. Allow increased fertilizer runoff into coastal waterways.
    H. Harvest and replant seagrass meadows every 10 years.
    J. Plant native plants along the shore near seagrass meadows.

PASSAGE III

Elements are organized into a periodic table to help understand their similarities and differences. They are arranged by the number of protons (positively charged particles) in the nucleus, which increases along each row of the periodic table. In its neutral state, each element has an equal number of protons and electrons—negatively charged particles that orbit the nucleus in different energy levels called orbitals. Elements in each column of the periodic table share the same number of electrons in the highest (outermost) energy level. Elements in the rightmost column, the noble gases, have a completely filled outermost energy level and are relatively stable and unreactive elements. They are gases at room temperature and pressure and have slightly different characteristics.

Table 1 contains data for the noble gases, including atomic number, atomic weight (in atomic mass units, amu) atomic radius (in picometers, pm), density, and boiling point.

Table 1

Element	Atomic Number	Atomic Weight (amu)	Atomic Radius (pm)	Density (g/L)	Boiling Point (°C)
Helium	2	4.0	31	0.18	–269
Neon	10	20.2	38	0.9	–246
Argon	18	39.9	71	0.86	–186
Krypton	36	83.8	88	3.75	–153
Xenon	54	131.3	108	5.9	–108
Radon	86	222	120	9.73	–62

13. The element with atomic radius of 88 pm has a boiling point of:

    A. –62°C.
    B. –108°C.
    C. –153°C.
    D. –246°C.

14. According to the table, which element has an atomic weight approximately four times that of neon?

    F. Helium
    G. Krypton
    H. Xenon
    J. Radon

CONTINUE

15. Data in the table indicates that as the atomic number increases, the boiling point:

A. increases.
B. decreases.
C. remains constant.
D. does not vary systematically.

16. One hypothesis is that as atomic weight increases, density will increase as well. Which pair of elements supports this hypothesis?

I. Neon and argon
II. Krypton and xenon
III. Helium and radon

F. I and II
G. II and III
H. II only
J. III only

17. A new element, oganesson, with atomic number 118 has been discovered to lie in the same periodic column as the noble gases. Based on the information in this passage, what would be the best prediction for oganesson's atomic radius and boiling point?

A. Greater than 120 pm and greater than –62°C
B. Less than 120 pm and less than –62°C
C. Greater than 120 pm and less than –62°C
D. Less than 120 pm and greater than –62°C

PASSAGE IV

Sedimentary rocks are formed when sediment—sand, dirt, minerals, and organic particles—settle into place and are gradually compressed and cemented together. The relatively mild conditions of this rock-forming process make it ideal for the preservation of fossils. Geologists can use sedimentary rocks to determine an area's geologic history, including the different environments that an area experienced over time. Figure 1 shows different layers of sedimentary rock exposed at the edge of a canyon. The composition of rock, approximate age, thickness, and depth of each layer are listed in Table 1.

FIGURE 1

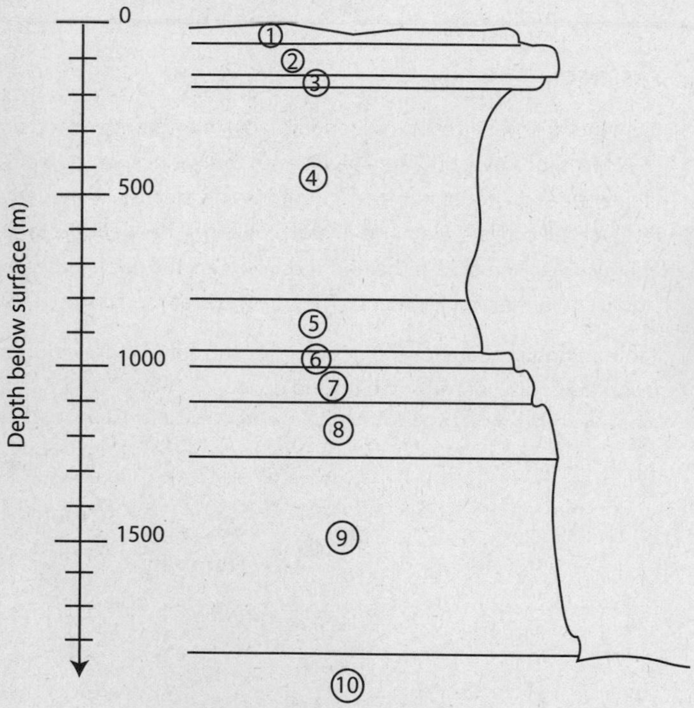

18. What is the relationship between thickness and depth of the rock layers?

F. Thicker layers are typically found at greater depths.
G. Thicker layers are typically found at shallower depths.
H. Rock layers less than 50 m thick are only found at depths of less than 500 m.
J. There is no relationship between thickness and depth of rock layers.

Table 1

Layer	Rock/Layer Composition	Age (Mill yrs)	Thickness (m)	Depth (m)
1	Conglomerate, Sandstone	100	30	10.0
2	Limestone, Mudstone, Sandstone, Gypsum	130	80	0–30
3	Sandstone	160	30	30–110
4	Sandstone	170	670	110–140
5	Siltstone, Sandstone, Mudstone	180	150	140–810
6	Sandstone, Freshwater Fish Fossils	190	40	810–960
7	Siltstone, Sandstone, Mudstone, Shale	200	110	960–1,000
8	Shale, Conglomerate, Gypsum, Limestone, Sandstone, Quartz, Petrified Wood	220	160	1,110–1,270
9	Shale, Sandstone, Limestone, Siltstone, Mudstone, Gypsum	230	550	1,270–1,820
10	Limestone, Chert	260	*	1,820

* There is no thickness listed for Layer 10 because the thickness cannot be measured without excavating.

19. Limestone is composed mainly of compressed skeletal fragments from sea organisms such as coral, forams, and mollusks. It is high in calcium carbonate-containing minerals like calcite and aragonite. During which of the following time periods is it most likely that the region of the canyon was covered by a shallow sea?

A. 60 million years ago
B. 100 million years ago
C. 130 million years ago
D. 200 million years ago

20. Which measurement is shown on the vertical axis of Figure 1?

F. Temperature
G. Age of rock
H. Depth below the canyon surface
J. Thickness of rock layers

21. Carnotite is a bright greenish-yellow mineral found around petrified wood. It is a uranium ore and is radioactive. Assuming the sedimentary rock layers are uniform as they extend away from the canyon, approximately how deep would miners have to excavate in the surrounding area in order to obtain uranium?

A. 160 m
B. 500 m
C. 1,200 m
D. 2,000 m

22. Which conclusion is NOT supported in the data?

F. The age of the rock layers increases with depth.
G. The most common rock type in the canyon is sandstone.
H. Thicker rock layers correspond to longer time periods.
J. Gypsum is only found in layers that also contain limestone.

CONTINUE

23. Geologists have found small remnants of a rock called welded tuff exposed at the surface (above layer 1) near the canyon. Welded tuff forms when rock and dust is exposed to temperatures over 1,000°C, hot enough that the rock welds together. What does this suggest about the area near the canyon?

- **A.** The area experienced a hot, tropical climate around 100 million years ago.
- **B.** A volcano erupted in the area less than 100 million years ago.
- **C.** The area was covered by sea at least twice in the last 260 million years.
- **D.** A volcano erupted in the area more than 260 million years ago and then went extinct.

PASSAGE V

The apparent bird-dinosaur evolutionary connection has been a source of considerable debate among paleontologists during the second half of the twentieth century. This association was proposed on the basis of numerous anatomical similarities and has been supported by the discovery of fossils of a small number of seeming transitional forms uncovered in Europe and Asia. Yet scientists differ in their interpretation of the significance of these similarities and the nature of the fossil evidence as well.

Paleontologist A

The discovery of fossil reptiles equipped with feathers, wings, and beak-like snouts may be significant but more likely provides only limited support for the dinosaurs-into-birds hypothesis. Convergent evolution often provides animals of very distant lineages with similar appendages—witness, for example, the similarities in the body shape and presence of fins in fish and cetaceans such as whales and dolphins. We would never put forth the idea that orcas evolved from sharks based on the morphological similarities of these creatures; it would be immediately deemed absurd.

It is more likely the case that birds and dinosaurs share a very distant common ancestor, perhaps from among the thecodonts. These prototypical reptiles of the late Permian survived the largest mass extinction recorded in the planet's history to bring forth many more recent lines; crocodiles, dinosaurs, pterosaurs, and birds are the most notable among these.

Paleontologist B

In our studies of numerous dinosaur fossils, it has become obvious that the lifestyles of dinosaurs were amazingly varied. No longer is it acceptable to view dinosaurs only as lumbering, cold-blooded monsters; indeed, the most frightening dinosaurs did not lumber at all. They were agile, swift, and deadly predators who could run, leap, kick, and shred to pieces an animal they were intent upon consuming. Lightweight muscular body structure would be crucial to the success of this type of predator.

Based upon this observation, along with a number of obvious physical similarities and evidence from the fossil record, we are convinced that birds evolved from small, carnivorous dinosaurs called theropods. A mere examination of the forelimb, hindlimb, and feet of a theropod fossil, and a comparison to one of the five available specimens of *Archaeopteryx**, will bear this out. In addition, more recent discoveries of fossil dinosaurs with bird-like traits and habits, particularly the finds uncovered in the Liaoning province of China, lend further credible support for our position that birds are for all intents and purposes actual members of the lineage Dinosauria living and thriving in our midst.

**Archaeopteryx was a feathered reptile of the late Jurassic Era thought to represent an intermediate form between dinosaurs and birds.*

24. According to Paleontologist A, similarities in the body forms of dinosaurs and birds:

- **F.** represent a failed experiment of evolution.
- **G.** are the products of convergent evolution.
- **H.** are completely without significance.
- **J.** helped both types of organism survive a large mass extinction.

25. Which of the following types of evidence, if found, would lend strong support to the position of Paleontologist A?

- **A.** Discovery of thecodont fossils with characteristics of modern birds and existing dinosaur fossils
- **B.** Discovery of another possible intermediate form between dinosaurs and birds from the Jurassic Era
- **C.** Discovery of an avian prototype dating back to before the beginning of the era of dinosaur dominance
- **D.** A careful examination of several sets of theropod fossil remains

26. Which of the following is a criticism that Paleontologist A would make of the avian evolutionary hypothesis of Paleontologist B?

- **F.** It ignores the possibility of the existence of transitional forms.
- **G.** It ignores the impact of a very large mass extinction.
- **H.** It assumes that morphological similarities are a result of a direct lineage.
- **J.** It proposes that dinosaurs and birds arose from distant lineages.

27. Which of the following perspectives would be consistent with the views of Paleontologist B?

A. Convergent evolution produces similar forms in diverse lineages.
B. Dinosaurs and birds may be related via a common ancestor.
C. Birds and dinosaurs arose from completely separate lineages.
D. Birds arose from a lineage of dinosaurs.

28. If genetic evidence were established to date the avian lineage 85 million years prior to the rise of *Archaeopteryx*, this finding would tend to:

F. support the theory of Paleontologist A.
G. support the theory of Paleontologist B.
H. support the theories of both paleontologists.
J. refute the theories of both paleontologists.

29. If Paleontologist B could confirm that birds appeared much later in evolutionary history than any dinosaurs, which of the following statements would reconcile this fact with the theory of Paleontologist A?

A. The ancestors of birds and the ancestors of dinosaurs were exposed to specific environmental conditions at the same time, and this caused the development of similar characteristics.
B. The ancestors of birds and the ancestors of dinosaurs were exposed to specific environmental conditions that caused the development of similar characteristics, but the dinosaur ancestors were exposed to these environmental conditions later than the bird ancestors were.
C. The rate of evolutionary change from the thecodont ancestor was much slower for the lineage that resulted in birds than for the lineage that resulted in dinosaurs.
D. The rate of evolutionary change from the thecodont ancestor was much faster for the lineage that resulted in birds than for the lineage that resulted in dinosaurs.

PASSAGE VI

Ecology graduate students wished to experiment with levels of diversity in a simple community to observe the relationship between increasing complexity and stability of populations. In particular, they were interested in the impact of changing certain conditions in a community on populations of two species of *Paramecium*, a common ciliated protozoan.

A *trophic* level is the number of steps a species is away from the producer species in a community. Producers are organisms that synthesize energy out of chemical products into nutrients. Table 1 shows the trophic level occupied by each type of organism involved in the experiments and the number of species that would be used on each level.

Table 1

Trophic Level	Organism	Number of Species Studied
First	Bacteria	3
Second	Paramecia	2
Third	Amoebae (predator of protozoa)	2

Experiment 1

The graduate students wished to study the relationship between one species of *Paramecium* and the number of species of bacteria available for consumption in the community. They created 300 "microcosms"—100 cultures each populated with communities of one, two, or three species of bacteria and one of the *Paramecium* species. After 20 days, they examined the cultures individually. The results are displayed in Table 2.

Table 2

Number of Bacterium Species	Number of Cultures in Which Paramecia Survived
1	32/100
2	61/100
3	70/100

CONTINUE

Experiment 2

The students then decided to study how two species of *Paramecium* would be affected when different combinations of *Paramecium* and bacteria were mixed in the cultures. They created 100 dishes each of six separate types of communities—600 cultures with different combinations of the *Paramecium* and the three bacteria species. After 20 days, they examined the cultures and recorded their results. These results are reproduced in Table 3.

Table 3

Number of Bacterium/ *Paramecium* Species	Number of Cultures in Which Paramecia Survived
1/1	35/100
2/1	58/100
3/1	65/100
1/2	20/100
2/2	26/100
3/2	31/100

Experiment 3

The last condition that the graduate students studied was the addition of a third trophic level to their microcosms. They introduced two different species of *Amoebae* that feed on *Paramecium*. They decided to use five different versions in 100 culture dishes each, creating 500 communities for this last experiment. They allowed them to grow undisturbed for 20 days, and then examined the cultures and recorded their results in Table 4 displayed below.

Table 4

Number of Bacterium/ *Paramecium*/ Amoeba Species	Number of Cultures in Which Paramecia Survived
1/1/1	22/100
2/1/1	15/100
2/2/1	8/100
2/2/2	6/100
3/2/2	2/100

30. What was the dependent variable in Experiment 2?

F. The number of species of bacteria
G. The number of species of *Paramecium*
H. The length of time after which cultures were examined
J. The number of cultures with surviving *Paramecium*

31. According to the results of Experiments 1 and 2, increasing the number of bacteria species present in the community:

A. decreased the survival rates of the paramecia in the community.
B. increased the survival rates of the paramecia in the community.
C. had no effect on any species in the community.
D. decreased the survival rates of one type of bacteria in the community.

32. According to the results of Experiment 2, increasing the number of *Paramecium* species in the community was related to:

F. decreased survival rates for the paramecia, depending on the number of bacteria species present in the community.
G. decreased survival rates for all species present in the community.
H. decreased survival rates for the paramecia, independent of the number of bacteria species present in the community.
J. increased survival rates for the *Paramecium*, depending on the number of bacteria species present in the community.

33. What new factor was introduced in Experiment 3?

A. An additional species of bacteria
B. A longer time for incubation of the experimental cultures
C. A new method for culturing the experimental microbes
D. An additional trophic level

34. After examining the results of Experiment 3, it would be reasonable to conclude that increased diversity in the experimental communities:

F. was beneficial to all species present in the communities.
G. had no effect on any species in the communities.
H. had a detrimental effect on the survival rate of one species of *Amoeba* only.
J. had a detrimental effect on the survival rates of both species of *Paramecium* under study.

PASSAGE VII

Classification of planets in our solar system has been a controversial issue, especially in the last decade. Advanced telescopes have allowed scientists to see more celestial objects in space, so scientists have observed characteristics among the objects that have caused them to reconsider whether certain planets should retain their "planet" status. Some of the characteristics that make these objects distinct include size, mass, and shape, as well as orbital characteristics. Two orbital characteristics of planets often compared by astronomers are orbital inclination and orbital eccentricity. Orbital inclination is the amount an object's orbit is tilted with respect to the plane of the solar system. Orbital eccentricity refers to the amount that an object's orbit deviates from a circular orbit.

In 2006, the International Astronomical Union (IAU) officially defined what a planet is and established a system of classification for celestial bodies other than satellites (moons). According to the definition, a planet is a celestial body that orbits the sun, has sufficient mass to be rounded in shape by its own gravity, and has cleared out other large rocks and bodies from its orbital path. The other classifications established were *dwarf planets* and *small solar system bodies*. Based on these new definitions, Pluto was reclassified from a planet to a dwarf planet.

The table below summarizes many of the qualities of the eight planets in our solar system.

Table 1

	Inner Planets				Outer Planets			
Celestial Body	**Mercury**	**Venus**	**Earth**	**Mars**	**Jupiter**	**Saturn**	**Uranus**	**Neptune**
Mass (kg)	3.3×10^{23}	4.9×10^{24}	6.0×10^{24}	6.4×10^{23}	1.9×10^{27}	5.7×10^{26}	8.7×10^{25}	1.0×10^{26}
Mean Density (kg/m^3)	5,427	5,204	5,520	3,933	1,326	687	1,318	1,638
Black-body Temp. (°K)	442.5	238.9	247.3	216.6	90.6	63.9	35.9	33.2
Orbital Inclination (°)	7.000	3.390	0.000	1.850	1.305	2.484	0.770	1.769
Orbital Eccentricity (°)	0.2056	0.0068	0.0167	0.0934	0.0484	0.0542	0.0472	0.0086
Rotation Period (hrs.)	1,407.60	5,832.50	23.93	24.62	9.93	10.50	17.24	16.11

35. Uranus has a mass greater than which of the following planets?

    A. Mars, Jupiter, and Saturn
    B. Neptune, Mercury, and Earth
    C. Venus, Mars, and Saturn
    D. Mercury, Earth, and Mars

36. Black-body temperature is the temperature that would result from a planet absorbing all received electromagnetic radiation without reflection. If black-body temperatures are higher for objects closer to the sun, which of the following would be considered farthest from the sun based on the data presented?

    F. Mercury
    G. Uranus
    H. Jupiter
    J. Neptune

CONTINUE

37. If an astronomer proposed that a celestial body does not qualify as a planet based solely on having an orbital inclination greater than 5 degrees and orbital eccentricity greater than 0.2, how many of the current planets would lose their planet classification?

A. four
B. three
C. two
D. one

38. The orbital eccentricity of a celestial body refers to the amount that its orbit deviates from a perfectly circular orbit. A value of 0 is a circular orbit. The higher the eccentricity value, the more distorted the orbit, which can result in objects displaying elliptical, parabolic, and hyperbolic orbits.

Which pair lists the planet with an orbit that deviates the least from a perfect circle and the one that deviates the most?

F. Earth; Mercury
G. Mercury; Neptune
H. Venus; Mercury
J. Neptune; Venus

39. It was hypothesized that Jupiter, Saturn, Neptune, and Uranus were gaseous planets, whereas the others were composed of solid material. Which of the following statements best supports this hypothesis?

A. Jupiter, Saturn, Neptune, and Uranus have lower temperatures than most of the other planets.
B. Jupiter, Saturn, Neptune, and Uranus have densities much smaller than the densities of the other planets.
C. Jupiter, Saturn, Neptune, and Uranus have greater masses than the other planets.
D. Jupiter, Saturn, Neptune, and Uranus have rotation periods that are much shorter than the other planets.

40. Which of the following statements is supported by the data?

F. Rotational period increases as mass increases.
G. The two planets with the highest mass also have the lowest densities.
H. The two planets closest in mass are also closest in rotational period.
J. The planet with the lowest mass has the highest orbital eccentricity.

STOP

WRITING TEST

40 Minutes

DIRECTIONS: This is a test of your writing skills. You have forty (40) minutes to write an essay in English. Be sure to carefully read the issue and three perspectives presented before planning and writing your essay so you understand clearly the task you are being asked to do. Your essay will be graded on the evidence it provides of your ability to analyze the issue; evaluate and analyze the perspectives; state and develop a personal perspective; and describe the relationship between the given perspectives and your own, while effectively using organization, logic, and language according to the conventions of standard written English.

Alternative Energy

The United States—and the entire world—is at a crossroads when it comes to our sources of energy. Traditional fossil fuels, including coal, petroleum, and natural gas, are our primary fuel sources, and are responsible for everything from powering our vehicles to warming our homes and providing electricity for our favorite gadgets. However, fossil fuels are also responsible for emitting carbon dioxide into the atmosphere, which most climate scientists feel adversely impacts the environment and contributes to global warming. As a result, some have called for increased exploration and investment in renewable, non-fossil sources of energy, including hydroelectric, solar, nuclear, and wind power, which are better for the environment and would also help reduce our dependence on foreign oil supplies. Efforts to find new, more efficient, and more cost-effective methods for harnessing the power of these alternative energy sources is already underway. As we continue to march through the twenty-first century, what are your thoughts on the advantages and disadvantages of alternative energy exploration and use? What roles should we play regarding strategies, investment, and incentives for alternative energy use?

Read and carefully consider these perspectives. Each suggests a particular way of thinking about if and how alternative energies should be used to meet the needs of the country.

Perspective One

The United States has sufficient fuel from coal, oil, and gas, and we should continue to use these fossil fuels for all of our energy needs. The media exaggerate their negative effects and the science isn't definitive. Our nation has thrived through the twentieth century thanks to these abundant and effective sources of power, and the government shouldn't waste time, energy, and resources on alternative energies, which are expensive, inefficient, and unable to fully meet the needs of the country.

Perspective Two

A serious and committed investment in alternative energy is not only needed right now, it's long overdue. Our reliance on fossil fuels has kept us dependent on energy sources that are destroying our planet. We cannot afford any further apathy, or to put off figuring out how to free ourselves from fossil fuels—even if it's expensive and difficult. We need to end our reliance on fossil fuels immediately. Our planet is worth the effort.

Perspective Three

A decision as large and important as the direction of energy sourcing in the United States should not be made impulsively. Available scientific evidence indicates that a continued long-term reliance on fossil fuels as our primary energy sources might not be the most responsible approach. However, quitting fossil fuels "cold turkey" or without a clear plan isn't realistic either. Our nation needs to develop a long-term plan that includes a tapering off from fossil fuels and an increased use of alternative, renewable energy sources. Furthermore, we need to work with other responsible countries around the world on decreasing fossil fuel reliance; only a worldwide effort will help us tackle this issue.

Essay Task

Write a unified, coherent essay in which you evaluate multiple perspectives on alternative energy. In your essay, be sure to:

- examine and assess the perspectives given
- declare and explain your own perspective on the issue
- discuss the relationship between your perspective and those given

Your perspective may be in full or partial agreement, or in total disagreement, with any of the others. Whatever the case, support your ideas with logical reasoning and detailed, persuasive examples.

Plan and Write Your Essay

Use the first two lined pages of the Writing test answer sheet (found at the beginning of the test) to generate ideas and plan your essay. Then use the following four pages to write your essay. Consider the following as you compose your essay:

What are the strengths and weaknesses of the three perspectives provided?

- Identify the insights they present and what they fail to consider.
- Ascertain why a given perspective might persuade or fail to persuade.

How can you apply your own experience, knowledge, and values?

- Express your perspective on the issue, identifying the perspective's strengths and weaknesses.
- Formulate a plan to support your perspective in your essay.

ENGLISH

1.	B	**20.**	J	**39.**	D	**58.**	J
2.	F	**21.**	D	**40.**	H	**59.**	A
3.	B	**22.**	G	**41.**	B	**60.**	H
4.	F	**23.**	C	**42.**	J	**61.**	C
5.	C	**24.**	G	**43.**	C	**62.**	J
6.	J	**25.**	B	**44.**	F	**63.**	D
7.	C	**26.**	F	**45.**	C	**64.**	H
8.	G	**27.**	A	**46.**	J	**65.**	D
9.	A	**28.**	H	**47.**	B	**66.**	F
10.	J	**29.**	D	**48.**	H	**67.**	C
11.	A	**30.**	F	**49.**	B	**68.**	F
12.	F	**31.**	B	**50.**	F	**69.**	B
13.	C	**32.**	F	**51.**	B	**70.**	J
14.	G	**33.**	B	**52.**	G	**71.**	A
15.	B	**34.**	G	**53.**	B	**72.**	H
16.	J	**35.**	D	**54.**	F	**73.**	D
17.	B	**36.**	J	**55.**	C	**74.**	F
18.	G	**37.**	C	**56.**	J	**75.**	C
19.	B	**38.**	G	**57.**	A		

1. **The correct answer is B.** As written, the verbs in the sentence are not in proper parallel form. Both of the verbs in the underlined portion of the sentence need to be in the present tense. The other answer choices have *to look* and *to stare* in inappropriate tenses for this sentence.

2. **The correct answer is F.** *With* is the appropriate preposition in this common phrase. Choice G introduces a grammatical error, and choice H changes the meaning of the sentence. The phrase should not be omitted because it explains the writer's trembling, so choice J is incorrect.

3. **The correct answer is B.** The verb here refers to an action (staring at the green shoots) that began in the immediate past and continues into the present; therefore, the present perfect tense is appropriate. The original sentence mistakenly uses the past perfect tense, so choice A is incorrect. Choice C would be used only if the sentence were written in the simple present tense, and choice D would be used if it was written in the simple future tense.

4. **The correct answer is F.** The verb tense of the underlined portion of this sentence is correct as written. The other answer choices contain incorrect verb forms for this sentence.

5. **The correct answer is C.** The conjunction *and* is needed to correct the comma splice in the original sentence, which is the incorrect use of just a comma to connect two independent clauses. A comma before the *and* is also needed, because this conjunction is being used to coordinate two independent clauses with two separate subjects, so choice B is incorrect. The conjunction *yet* (choice D) is inappropriate, because there is no change in direction between the two clauses.

6. **The correct answer is J.** The past tense is appropriate because the writer is describing his childhood. Choices F, G, and H are all written in the present tense.

7. **The correct answer is C.** This option clearly states the writer's point that in New York, culture was the dominating element, even when it came to marking the passage of the seasons. Choices A, B, and D are all worded confusingly.

8. **The correct answer is G.** In the sentence, the phrase *the gradual way one transformed into another* primarily functions as an example of one of the particulars with which the author was not familiar. The phrase is merely an example of one particular that eluded the author; it is not proof that he did not understand the seasons, so choice F is not the best

answer. The phrase is not particularly poetic and serves a more important function than merely making the essay more appealing to read, so choice H is not the best answer, either. The phrase does not serve as a transition between two different yet related ideas, so choice J is incorrect.

9. **The correct answer is A.** Paragraph 2 tells us that the writer grew up knowing little about nature. This fact is essential to understanding the garden's effect on the writer. The writer's current environment is quite different from a city, but he never suggests the city was something he felt lucky to have escaped, so choice B is incorrect. Paragraph 2 may be a vivid recollection (choice C) or an indication of the writer's sensitivity (choice D), but neither of these describes the paragraph's main purpose.

10. **The correct answer is J.** As written, the underlined portion of the sentence contains an incorrect, commonly confused word—*too*. Its homonym, *two*, is the appropriate word choice here, so choice J is correct. Choice G contains the incorrect too and an inappropriate possessive form of season. Choice H contains another incorrect homonym, *to*.

11. **The correct answer is A.** No comma should be used before yellow because *bright* modifies yellow and all the other colors. No commas are needed to separate the colors because the writer has chosen to link them with the conjunction *and*. Therefore, choices C and D are incorrect. Choice B fails to link *yellow* and *red* with either a comma or *and*, so it is incorrect.

12. **The correct answer is F.** The present tense is appropriate for a general situation that is repeated year after year. The plural, *Daffodils*, demands the third-person plural form of the verb. Choices G and J are in the past tense. Choice H is a singular verb when a plural one is required.

13. **The correct answer is C.** As written, this sentence creates a sentence fragment. There is a need for internal sentence punctuation here, so choices B and D are incorrect. Choice C correctly uses a comma to separate the underlined words.

14. **The correct answer is G.** In the third paragraph, the author uses colorful detail to describe when chrysanthemums bud, when they bloom, and when they die, while relating the timeline to the change of seasons, so choice G is the best answer. Choice F is not the best answer, since it provides no details about planting chrysanthemums. Choice H is true in itself, but it does not answer this particular question. Choice J is simply wrong; there is specific information about the life cycle of chrysanthemums in the third paragraph.

15. **The correct answer is B.** This detail is an example of how little the writer knew about nature; therefore, it belongs in the paragraph that discusses growing up in New York. Paragraphs 1 (choice A), 3 (choice C), and 4 (choice D) all take place in the present.

16. **The correct answer is J.** The idiomatic expression is: *as x goes, so goes y,* so choice J is correct. Choices F and G add unnecessary words. Choice H is simply awkward.

17. **The correct answer is B.** As these words are most commonly used, *affect* is the proper verb form, while *effect* is the noun form. Here the word is a noun, so the proper word to use is *effect*, which means you can eliminate choices A and D. The preposition that properly follows *effect* is *on*, so choice B is correct and choice C is incorrect.

18. **The correct answer is G.** The writer is speaking about our present understanding of trade in the past, so you can eliminate choices F and H, which are in the past tense. It is an assertion without any sense of the conditional, so choice J is incorrect.

19. **The correct answer is B.** This is the only sentence that stresses the historical importance of exchange and thereby links the previous paragraph to the examples of this phenomenon presented in Paragraph 2. Choice A is inappropriate, since agriculture is merely one detail in Paragraph 2 and not its main idea. Choice C would be a more fitting concluding sentence for Paragraph 1 than an introductory sentence for Paragraph 2, since a phrase such as "Many examples of this…" should continue a previous idea directly. Choice D introduces that same organizational error and focuses on the modern world, while Paragraph 2 focuses on the historical importance of exchange.

20. **The correct answer is J.** The clearest construction lists the subjects and proceeds directly to the verb without punctuation or unnecessary words. As originally written, the list lacks the conjunction *and* between the last two items in the list and misuses a comma to separate the list from the rest of the sentence. In choice G, a colon is correctly used instead of a comma, but the conjunction *and* is still missing. Choice H changes the meaning of the sentence.

21. **The correct answer is D.** No punctuation should separate the noun from the prepositional phrase that identifies it. Choices A, B, and C all contain unnecessary punctuation.

22. **The correct answer is G.** The present perfect tense indicates the connection between the past and the present, between antiquity and today. Choices F, H, and J are all in the wrong tense.

23. **The correct answer is C.** *Greeks* is the subject of the relative clause, so the relative pronoun *who* is appropriate. *Whom* is a personal pronoun, so the original sentence is incorrect. Choices B and D are inappropriate because they refer to non-human subjects.

24. **The correct answer is G.** A comma is required before a coordinating conjunction when linking two independent clauses. *And* is the best choice because it indicates the non-contrasting relationship between the clauses, so choices F and H are incorrect. *Therefore* also expresses this relationship but cannot be used to link two independent clauses with only a comma; a semicolon would be required instead, so you can eliminate choice J.

25. **The correct answer is B.** This phrasing properly indicates that the question is about the character of modern Italy. Choices A, C, and D ask different questions.

26. **The correct answer is F.** The imperative form avoids unnecessary words and maintains the authoritative tone of the essay. Choices G and J ask questions and would be appropriate only if the sentence ended with a question mark. Choice H changes the meaning of the sentence.

27. **The correct answer is A.** This sentence makes the point that these foods are not indigenous to the nations that rely on them, and this point is crucial to the main idea of the essay. Choice C makes this point awkwardly, while choices B and D do not make this point at all.

28. **The correct answer is H.** The sentence begins with a series of subjects and should proceed to the verb without punctuation (choices F, G, and J) or unnecessary words (choices F and J).

29. **The correct answer is D.** *For* creates a smooth transition from the previous sentence without changing the meaning. *Therefore* (choice A) wrongly indicates that the way we think of Italy is a direct consequence of the transformation of exchanged goods. Choices B and C do not make grammatical sense in the context of this sentence.

30. **The correct answer is F.** This option emphasizes the creative transformation of tomatoes and pasta by Italian cooking. Choices G, H, and J do not express this crucial idea effectively.

31. **The correct answer is B.** As written, the sentence is a run-on and needs to be fixed. Choice B correctly combines the two independent clauses while eliminating the run-on sentence. Choice C places the semicolon in the wrong place in the sentence. Choice D incorrectly creates a fragment by inserting a period.

32. **The correct answer is F.** Paragraph 1 discusses everyday innovations that we take for granted; Paragraph 2 jumps into discussing aspirins. Choice F would make an effective transition sentence from Paragraph 1 to Paragraph 2. The other choices are off-target and would not serve as effective transitions.

33. **The correct answer is B.** No punctuation is required at this position in the sentence, so choice B is correct. The other answer choices create sentence fragments and are therefore incorrect.

34. **The correct answer is G.** Since *countless* and *innumerable* have the same meaning, including both words in this sentence is redundant. Choice G eliminates the redundancy. Choice H simply reverses the words and does nothing to eliminate the redundancy. Choice J substitutes in two other redundant words and fails to eliminate the problem.

35. **The correct answer is D.** A plural pronoun is required to replace the antecedent *discs*, so *them* (choice D) is correct. Choice B is singular and gender-specific and is therefore incorrect here. Choice C is a plural pronoun reserved for animate nouns, so would be incorrect here.

36. **The correct answer is J.** This simple declarative statement should end in a period, and no internal punctuation is needed between *closer* and *look*.

37. **The correct answer is C.** *Willow tree* is a common noun that should not be capitalized unless it appears at the beginning of a sentence, so choice C is correct.

38. **The correct answer is G.** The underlined portion of the sentence contains an aside regarding salicylic acid and belongs in parentheses. The other answer choices are inappropriate treatments for this information.

39. **The correct answer is D.** As written, the flow of information in the underlined portion of the sentence is confusing and awkward. Choice D avoids the confusion by adjusting the word flow and is the correct answer. Choices B and C fail to eliminate the awkwardness and confusion and are incorrect.

40. **The correct answer is H.** As written, the contraction *we've* is missing an apostrophe. Choice H correctly fixes the error. Choice G replaces *we've* with *weave*, which is a homonym and an inappropriate word choice here. Choice J incorrectly replaces *learned* with *leaned*, which is an inappropriate word choice here.

41. **The correct answer is B.** Recognizing commonly used phrases is a helpful skill to have for effective reading comprehension. The correct phrase for this sentence is *trial and error*; the other choices sound similar, but are not appropriate phrases or word combinations for this sentence.

42. **The correct answer is J.** The final sentence adds relevant additional evidence supporting the paragraph's topic that aspirin can have dangerous side effects, so choice J is the best answer. The sentence provides additional evidence; it does not repeat evidence already provided earlier in the paragraph as choice F suggests. While the paragraph has already provided some evidence that aspirin can have dangerous side effects, additional evidence just strengthens the paragraph's thesis, so choice G is not the best answer. However, the fact that aspirin can be hazardous to pregnant women or those who drink excessive amounts of alcohol is not necessarily more convincing evidence than any evidence previously given in the paragraph, so choice H is not as strong an answer as choice J is.

43. **The correct answer is C.** Adding information about aspirin reducing the risk of heart attacks would best fit in Paragraph 5, which covers the wide array of symptoms, inflammatory conditions, and illnesses that aspirins are used to help treat.

44. **The correct answer is F.** An effective concluding sentence ties up the ideas presented in the written piece. The passage is about how aspirin, an everyday object often taken for granted, is actually an interesting bit of medicinal history and innovation, and choice F effectively captures this notion. Choices G and J take the focus off aspirin, and are incorrect. Choice H focuses on a minor detail, and is too narrow in scope for a concluding sentence.

45. **The correct answer is C.** This essay focuses solely on aspirin and no other medicines, so it isn't comprehensive enough fulfill the requirements of an assignment to research the history of medicines in the ancient world.

46. **The correct answer is J.** The phrase refers to the past, so the verbs must be in the past tense. Choices F and G are in the present tense and choice G contains a singular verb (*is*) that does not agree with its plural antecenent (*women*). Choice H combines the present and past tenses.

47. **The correct answer is B.** As written, punctuation in the underlined portion of the sentence creates an awkward pause and is incorrect. Choice B correctly fixes the sentence. Choices C and D also contain incorrect internal sentence punctuation.

48. **The correct answer is H.** This option maintains the parallel structure set up by the preposition *with*, thus indicating that the two factors mentioned are sides of the same problem. As originally written, the phrase "not to mention the fact" suggests an incidental piece of information and not the explanatory information that actually follows the phrase. Choices G and J are phrased awkwardly.

49. **The correct answer is B.** As written, the underlined portion is a fragment, which eliminates choices A and D. Choice B turns the fragment into a complete sentence and avoids the needless use of the passive voice in choice C.

50. **The correct answer is F.** This option makes it clear that the writer is being asked to write a piece about the First Lady's charity work. Choices G and J change the sentence's meaning. Choice H is unnecessarily wordy.

51. **The correct answer is B.** The gerund phrase acts as a noun—in this case the object of the verb *meant*, creating a correct sentence. The verbs in choices C and D are in the wrong form. The form should be positive because the essay makes it clear that the author did break ground. As originally written, the sentence contradicts its own meaning by including the word *not*.

52. **The correct answer is G.** As written, the sentence contains an incorrect word choice; the pronoun *whom* does not fit into the sentence as written. Choice G corrects the sentence: *There was, however, an aspect of professional life for which many of us were not prepared.*

53. **The correct answer is B.** The words "I remember" signal us that the action in the sentence is a memory of something that has already happened, so the past tense should be used in the underlined portion of the sentence. Therefore, choice B is the correct answer. Choices C and D use the incorrect verb tenses.

54. **The correct answer is F.** The suggested paragraph would add unnecessary details and distract from the writer's point. Since that suggested paragraph does not belong at any point in this essay, choices G, H, and J can all be eliminated.

55. **The correct answer is C.** This sentence is a question and should end in a question mark; the question word

what at the beginning of the sentence serves as a clue. Therefore, choice C is correct. Choice B incorrectly neglects to include end-of-sentence punctuation and is incorrect. Choice D incorrectly uses an em-dash, which is not appropriate end-of-sentence punctuation.

56. The correct answer is J. This option avoids unnecessary wording and correctly conveys the writer's feeling that her complete honesty was inappropriate for her workplace. Choices F, G, and H would all leave the sentence wordy and unclear.

57. The correct answer is A. The sentence is correct as written and utilizes the correct form of the verb *to share*. The other answer choices utilize incorrect verb forms, given the context of the sentence.

58. The correct answer is J. The opening sentence of the paragraph indicates that the writer has set up some kind of expectation that her work will not be first rate. Therefore, in order for this paragraph to be most effective, it should come at the end of the passage, after the writer has shown us what she has done to set up such an expectation. In addition, the last line of the paragraph serves to point out the lesson that has been learned, concluding the essay. The paragraph would disrupt the flow of the essay if placed anywhere else, so choices F, G, and H are incorrect.

59. The correct answer is A. In Paragraph 4, the writer sets up important, relevant information regarding her behavior that ultimately helped her to understand why she needed to put on a professional face. Choice B is incorrect because there are no historical details about women in the workplace in the paragraph. The paragraph mentions nothing about the writer's male colleagues (choice C) or friends (choice D) either.

60. The correct answer is H. The writer is conveying an experience she had in her professional life that led to a personal revelation. The paragraph is a personal essay, not a persuasive (choice F) or comparative (choice G) one. The writer's personal integrity is not challenged in the essay, so choice J does not make sense.

61. The correct answer is C. *Illiterate* means unable to read, and *population* is a singular noun, so choice C is the correct answer and choice D, which uses the plural verb *are*, can be eliminated. The original sentence is incorrect because *illegible* means *unreadable*. Choice B uses the wrong verb form and the wrong word; *ineligible* means "not entitled."

62. The correct answer is J. The size of Haiti is completely irrelevant to the topic being discussed, so this underlined information should be deleted. Therefore, choice J is correct and choice F can be eliminated. Choices G and H merely reword the irrelevant underlined phrase, so both of those answer choices can be eliminated as well.

63. The correct answer is D. The word *Neighbors* is part of a list and should be separated from the next item by a comma. Choices A and B use incorrect punctuation, and choice C uses no punctuation at all.

64. The correct answer is H. The *willingness* refers to that of the neighbors, friends, and relatives, so the possessive pronoun *their* is appropriate. Choices F and G both use homonyms mistakenly: *there* means a particular spot, and *they're* is a contraction of *they* and *are*. Since *they are* does not make sense in this context under any circumstances, choice J is incorrect.

65. The correct answer is D. The sentence describes the age of the author at the specified time, requiring the simple past tense of the verb *to be*. Choice A would be used only if the subject did not get a chance to be something, which is not the case in this essay. Choice B is a perfect gerund that indicates a state of being no longer in effect, and it is not the clearest form to use in this sentence. Choice C indicates an ongoing action that occurred in the past.

66. The correct answer is F. Because it logically follows the first sentence, the second sentence would not be as effective if moved elsewhere in the paragraph. It does not make sense to discuss the plot of *Krik? Krak!* before the book is introduced in the first sentence, so choice G is incorrect. It also does not make sense to introduce the role of hardships in the plot *after* an example of such a hardship, so choice H does not make sense. Choice J would split up the sentences that discuss the plot, so it can be eliminated.

67. The correct answer is C. No punctuation is needed before the prepositional phrase that begins with *in*, so choice C is correct and choice A can be eliminated. The sentence discusses plural *families*, so they must be seeking new *lives*, which eliminates choice D. An apostrophe is used to show possession, yet the *lives* possess nothing in this sentence. Therefore, choice B is incorrect.

68. The correct answer is F. Since *acclaim* is a noun, it should be modified by the adjective *critical*, not the adverb *critically* (choice G) or the noun *criticism* (choice J). Adding *too* in front of this adjective changes the connotation, so choice H is not as strong an answer as choice F.

69. The correct answer is B. The first word that follows the comma should be the subject of the modifying phrase *born in Port-au-Prince in 1969*. That would be *Danticat*, which is not the first word in choices A, C, or D. Choice C is also too wordy.

70. The correct answer is J. This option links Danticat's childhood behavior with her development as a writer. Choices F and G do not create such a link. Choice H is too vague.

71. The correct answer is A. This option notes the similarity between Danticat and the heroine in the clearest language. *Like* is the appropriate preposition to use when comparing nouns. The wordiness of choices B and D leaves the sentence unclear. Choice C suggests a comparison between actions, not people.

72. The correct answer is H. Only one author is being discussed, and the possessive form is used to indicate that the subject matter belongs to the author. Choices F and G indicate more than one author. Choice J lacks the elements needed to show possession.

73. The correct answer is D. This option is the most logical, given the author's subject matter. The proper negative construction is *neither . . . nor*. The constructions in choices A and B create sentences that contradict their own intended meanings. Choice C disrupts the proper negative construction by following *neither* with *or*.

74. The correct answer is F. This option introduces the informative, impersonal tone of the essay and provides an introduction to the theme of storytelling. Choice G is too personal. Choice H is too vague. Choice J is too informal and suggests the main theme of the essay is illiteracy, not storytelling.

75. The correct answer is C. The essay does not provide nearly enough information about Haiti to serve as a detailed history, so choice C is the best answer. Choices A and B may be true in themselves, but neither makes a convincing argument that this essay could serve as a detailed history of the hardships the people of Haiti have endured. Choice D is simply untrue.

MATHEMATICS

1.	E	**16.**	J	**31.**	C	**46.**	G
2.	J	**17.**	A	**32.**	F	**47.**	A
3.	C	**18.**	J	**33.**	E	**48.**	F
4.	K	**19.**	A	**34.**	J	**49.**	B
5.	E	**20.**	H	**35.**	C	**50.**	H
6.	F	**21.**	C	**36.**	J	**51.**	D
7.	E	**22.**	K	**37.**	A	**52.**	G
8.	H	**23.**	C	**38.**	G	**53.**	D
9.	C	**24.**	J	**39.**	D	**54.**	G
10.	F	**25.**	C	**40.**	K	**55.**	A
11.	D	**26.**	F	**41.**	D	**56.**	H
12.	H	**27.**	E	**42.**	H	**57.**	B
13.	D	**28.**	J	**43.**	E	**58.**	J
14.	J	**29.**	C	**44.**	F	**59.**	D
15.	C	**30.**	G	**45.**	B	**60.**	G

1. **The correct answer is E.** Plug the given numbers into the percent formula, where 32 is the part, 80 is the whole, and x is the unknown percent:

$$\frac{32}{80}=\frac{x}{100}$$
$$80x=3{,}200$$
$$x=40$$

Choice A is the result of an arithmetic error; you are off by a multiple of 10. Choices B and C are incorrect because when taken out of 100, both 16 and 24 give a number less than $\frac{32}{80}$, so these percentages cannot be correct. Choice D would imply that the whole part being used is 100, but it is actually 80.

2. **The correct answer is J.** The sum measure of a triangle's interior angles is 180°, so the missing interior angle measures 180° – 40° – 55° = 85°. Since this angle is supplementary to the angle measuring $x°$, $x = 180 - 85 = 95$.

Choice F is incorrect because the angles labeled x and 55 in the diagram are not congruent alternate interior angles. Choices G and K are the likely result of an arithmetic error; you should be computing 180 – 85. Choice H is the measure of the third angle in the triangle, not the one labeled x.

3. **The correct answer is C.** The machine costs $p + l$ to operate each hour, so if it operates for x hours, the expression would be $x(p + l)$.

Choice A is incorrect because you should be adding p and l, not multiplying them. In choice B, you should be adding px and lx, not multiplying them. Choice D is incorrect because you should be adding p and l, not multiplying them, and you should multiply the resulting sum by x. Choice E is just the cost per hour—you must multiply by the number of hours, x.

4. **The correct answer is K.** This is the graph of $y = 3^x$ shifted down 2 units. The shape remains the same and the horizontal asymptote goes from $y = 0$ to $y = -2$. This results in the graph of choice K. Choice F is incorrect because this is the graph of a log function; exponential functions do not have vertical asymptotes. Choice G is incorrect because this is the graph of a log function; exponential functions do not have vertical asymptotes. Choice H is incorrect because the graph should increase from left to right. Choice J is incorrect because the horizontal asymptote should be $y = -2$.

5. **The correct answer is E.** Jacob uses a total of 7 × 3 = 21 minutes, at a cost of \$0.25 per minute, and has to pay \$1.00 for the card. 21 × 0.25 = \$5.25, so the total cost is \$5.25 + \$1.00 = \$6.25.

Choice A only includes 1 of the 7 calls. Choice B would be the cost if each call were 1 minute long. Choice C does not include the \$1 for the calling card. Choice D results from adding the \$1 to 21 before multiplying by 0.25.

6. The correct answer is F. The profit before fees is \$125 – \$85 = \$40. The fee charged by the merchant is 0.03(\$125) = \$3.75. So the total profit is \$40 – \$3.75 = \$36.25. Thus, the percent profit earned is $\frac{36.25}{85}\times 100\%$. Choice G is incorrect because you should divide by 85, not 125. Choice H is incorrect because while the profit earned before the fee is applied is \$40, this does not represent the percent profit. Choice J is incorrect because you did not subtract the fee. Choice K is incorrect because while the actual profit earned is \$36.25, this does not represent the percent profit.

7. The correct answer is E. Convert the fractions to decimals: $\frac{2}{5}=0.4$ and $\frac{1}{8}=0.125$. Now add the three decimals: 0.4 + 0.125 + 0.177 = 0.702.

In choice A, you dropped 0.177 from the sum. In choice B, you dropped $\frac{1}{8}$ from the sum. To get choice C, you forgot to carry one to the tenths place when adding. For choice D, you neglected to carry one to the hundredths place when adding.

8. The correct answer is H. The area of triangle *ABC* is 5 square inches. Plug this area and the length of the base, $\overline{BC}$, into the area formula to solve for the height, $\overline{AB}$:

$$A=\frac{1}{2}bh$$
$$5=\frac{1}{2}(2)(AB)$$
$$AB=5$$

Triangle *ACD* has the same height as triangle *ABC*. To find the length of its base, $\overline{CD}$, subtract *BC* from *BD*: 10 – 2 = 8. Therefore, the area of triangle *ACD* is $\frac{1}{2}(8)(5)=20$. Choice F is the length of *CD*, not the area. In choice G, you used 8 in place of 10 as the length of the base *ABD*. Choice J is the area of triangle *ABD*. In choice K, you should have subtracted the area of triangle *ABC* from the area of triangle *ABD*, not added it.

9. The correct answer is C. Substitute the values for *w* and *z* into the expression and simplify:

$$\frac{\frac{2}{3}-\frac{1}{9}}{2\left(\frac{2}{3}+\frac{1}{9}\right)}=\frac{\frac{6}{9}-\frac{1}{9}}{2\left(\frac{6}{9}+\frac{1}{9}\right)}=\frac{\frac{5}{9}}{2\left(\frac{7}{9}\right)}$$
$$=\frac{\frac{5}{9}}{\frac{14}{9}}=\frac{5}{9}\div\frac{14}{9}=\frac{5}{\not 9}\bullet\frac{\not 9}{14}=\frac{5}{14}$$

In choice A, you added fractions incorrectly; you must first get a common denominator. Choice B has the wrong sign. In choice D, you canceled terms, not factors, common to the numerator and denominator. Choice E is the reciprocal of the correct answer; when converting a quotient of fractions to a product, flip the fraction *after* the division sign.

10. The correct answer is F. The asymptote for such a logarithmic function occurs at the value of *x* that makes the input of the logarithm equal to zero. Here, that is $x = -4$. Choice G is incorrect because this is a horizontal line, and logarithmic functions do not have horizontal asymptotes. Choice H is incorrect because this is a horizontal line, and logarithmic functions do not have horizontal asymptotes. Choice J is incorrect because this value of *x* does not make the input of the logarithm equal to zero. Choice K is incorrect because this value of *x* does not make the input of the logarithm equal to zero.

11. The correct answer is D. Write *g*(*x*) as $y=\frac{2x}{x-1}$. To find the inverse, switch the *x* and *y* and solve for *y*:

$$y=\frac{2x}{x-1}$$
$$x=\frac{2y}{y-1}$$
$$x(y-1)=2y$$
$$xy-x=2y$$
$$xy-2y=x$$
$$y(x-2)=x$$
$$y=\frac{x}{x-2}$$

So $g^{-1}(x)=\frac{x}{x-2}$.

12. The correct answer is H. When whole numbers are written as products of powers of prime numbers as is the case here—the least common multiple (LCM) is formed by using the highest power of each prime number that occurs in any of the numbers. Applying that principle here gives the LCM of $p^3q^3r^4$. Choice F is the greatest common factor. In choice G, you did not account for the third whole number in the list. Choice J is a common factor of all three whole numbers, but not a common multiple. Choice K is a common multiple of all three whole numbers, but not the *least* common multiple.

13. The correct answer is D. The difference between Colin's and Daryl's average monthly salary is \$500, so the difference between their annual salaries is \$500 × 12 = \$6,000. We don't know who earns more, but the difference between their annual salaries is $|C - D|$ dollars. Thus, $|C - D| = 6{,}000$.

Choice A is the difference of *monthly* salaries, not the *annual* salaries. Choice B is incorrect because you should be subtracting salaries, not adding them—even so, the right side would represent the difference of *monthly* salaries, not annual salaries. In choice C, the average of the annual salaries is 6,000, which is not given in the problem. In choice E, you should be subtracting, not adding salaries.

14. The correct answer is J. Let x be the number of games Mike played. Then, Stan played $2x - 3$ games. Together, they played $x + (2x - 3) = 3x - 3$ games. The cost of playing this number of games is $0.25(3x - 3)$. Adding the admission fee of 2(\$8.50) = \$17, we get the equation $0.25(3x - 3) + 17 = 35$. Solve for x:

$$\begin{aligned} 0.25(3x-3)+17&=35\\ 3x-3+68&=140\\ 3x+65&=140\\ 3x&=75\\ x&=25 \end{aligned}$$

The total number of games played is 3(25) – 3 = 72.

Choice F is incorrect because you did not multiply the total number of games played by 0.25, the cost per game. Choice G is incorrect because this is the number of games Mike played. Choice H is incorrect because this is the number of games Stan played. Choice K is incorrect because this would imply that Stan played exactly twice the number of games that Mike did, which is not the case.

15. The correct answer is C. When parallel lines are cut by a transversal, the alternate interior angles are equal. Therefore, $\angle DCE$ measures 60°. Since the measures of the angles in a triangle add up to 180°, $\angle CED$ measures $180° - 40° - 60° = 80°$.

Choice A is incorrect because $\angle CED$ is neither corresponding nor alternate interior to $\angle CDE$, and so it is not congruent to it in this scenario. In choice B, $\angle CED$ is neither corresponding nor alternate interior to $\angle ABE$, and so it is not congruent to it in this scenario. For choice D, you must subtract this sum from 180 degrees to get the desired angle. Choice E is not true since you can use the various relationships among angles formed by two parallel lines cut by a transversal.

16. The correct answer is J. There are 8 different faces on which the red die can land. For each of these faces, there are 8 faces on which the blue die can come to a rest. Multiplying yields 8(8) = 64 different outcomes for the faces on which both die can come to rest in a single roll. Choice F is incorrect because it is the number of different outcomes for a single die. Choice G is incorrect because you should multiply the number of outcomes for each die, not add them. Choice H is incorrect because it is half the correct number. Choice K is incorrect because the order in which the dice are arranged does not affect the faces on which they come to rest. So the correct number should be one-half this.

17. The correct answer is A. Rewrite the equation in slope-intercept form:

$$\begin{aligned} 2x-5y-1&=0\\ 2x-1&=5y\\ y&=\frac{2}{5}x-\frac{1}{5} \end{aligned}$$

$$y=\frac{2}{5}x-\frac{1}{5}$$

The slope of the given line is $\frac{2}{5}$. So a line perpendicular to it must have slope $-\frac{5}{2}$. Choices B, D, and E represent various errors based on using 2 as the slope of the given line; you must first solve for y before identifying the coefficient of x as the slope. Choice C would be the slope of a line parallel to the given line.

18. The correct answer is J. Each of the larger walls has an area of 20 × 40 = 800 square feet, which requires 2 gallons of paint. Each of the smaller walls has an area of 20 × 30 = 600 square feet, which requires $1\frac{1}{2}$ gallons of paint. The total area is 2,800 square feet, and the total number of gallons is $2+2+1\frac{1}{2}+1\frac{1}{2}=7$.

Choice F is half of the correct answer, which may be the result of only counting one of the smaller walls and one of the larger walls. Choice G results from incorrectly calculating that each of the smaller walls requires $\frac{3}{4}$ of a gallon of paint. Choice H may result from a calculation error. Choice K is the number of gallons that would be needed if the total area were 24,000 square feet; 24,000 is the volume of the house, in cubic feet.

19. **The correct answer is A.** Cross-multiply and then solve for *w*:

$$\frac{2w+1}{3}=\frac{5}{6}$$
$$(2w+1)(6)=5(3)$$
$$12w+6=15$$
$$12w=9$$
$$w=\frac{9}{12}=\frac{3}{4}$$

Choice B is incorrect because this is the reciprocal of the correct value of *w*. Choice C is incorrect because after cross-multiplying you did not apply the distributive property. Choice D is incorrect because you need to divide by 12, the coefficient of *w*, in the final step of the solution. Choice E is incorrect because this is just the right side of the equation once you cross-multiplied.

20. **The correct answer is H.** Set up a proportion between similar sides:

$$\frac{24}{30}=\frac{x}{40}$$
$$30x=960$$
$$x=32$$

None of the values in choices F, G, J, and K retain the proportionality.

21. **The correct answer is C.** Use the exponent rules:

$$\sqrt{\frac{4^3x^7y}{3^2x^4y^3}}=\sqrt{\frac{4^2 \bullet 4 \bullet x^3}{3^2 \bullet y^2}}$$
$$=\frac{\sqrt{4^2} \bullet \sqrt{4} \bullet \sqrt{x^3}}{\sqrt{3^2} \bullet \sqrt{y^2}}$$
$$=\frac{4 \bullet 2 \bullet x^{\frac{3}{2}}}{3 \bullet y}=\frac{8x^{\frac{3}{2}}}{3y}$$

In choices A and D, you did not apply the correct rule for simplifying quotients of powers of the same base; the exponents should be subtracted, not multiplied or added. Choice B is incorrect because $\sqrt{x^3}=x^{\frac{3}{2}}$, not $x^{\frac{2}{3}}$. In choice E, you did not compute the square root of a power correctly: $\sqrt{x^3}=x^{\frac{3}{2}}$, not $x^{\sqrt{3}}$.

22. **The correct answer is K.** The total of the 6 original scores is (6)(80) = 480 points. The total of all 8 tests is (8)(85) = 680 points. Since the total of the 2 added tests must be 680 – 480 = 200, the average of these 2 tests is 200 ÷ 2 = 100. The values listed in choices F, G, H, and J will all result in an average lower than 85.

23. **The correct answer is C.** The area of a triangle is $\frac{1}{2}bh$. We already know the height of the triangle, 9 centimeters. To find the base, use the Pythagorean theorem, or recognize this as similar to a 3-4-5 right triangle:

$$9^2+AC^2=15^2$$
$$81+AC^2=225$$
$$AC^2=144$$
$$AC=12$$

Since the base of the triangle is 12, the area of the triangle is $\frac{1}{2}(12)(9)=54$ square centimeters.

Choice A is the length of the unknown side, in centimeters. Choice B is the perimeter of the triangle, in centimeters. Choice D is double the area, which may result from forgetting the $\frac{1}{2}$ in the area formula. Choice E is the product of the two known sides, which is not the area because side *BC* is neither the base nor the height of the triangle.

24. **The correct answer is J.** Since the second file is $2\frac{1}{2}$ times as large as the first, multiply the amount of time needed for the first file by $2\frac{1}{2}$. You can do this either by converting 4 minutes and 26 seconds to seconds, then converting back to minutes, or by multiplying both the minutes and seconds by $2\frac{1}{2}$, then combining the results:

$$4 \text{ minutes} \times 2\frac{1}{2} = 10 \text{ minutes}$$
$$26 \text{ seconds} \times 2\frac{1}{2} = 65 \text{ seconds}$$

10 minutes and 65 seconds = 11 minutes and 5 seconds

Choice F results from replacing 65 seconds with 5 seconds, ignoring the additional minute. Choice G results from only multiplying the minutes by $2\frac{1}{2}$, not the seconds. Choice H results from multiplying the minutes by $2\frac{1}{2}$ and the seconds by 2. Choice K is likely the result of an arithmetic error when converting between seconds and minutes.

25. The correct answer is C. The current paths require a trip of 200 feet. A diagonal path would form an isosceles right triangle with the existing paths. By the rules of 45°-45°-90° triangles, the length of the path would be $100\sqrt{2}$ feet, or approximately 140 feet. The new path would shorten the route by about 200 – 140 = 60 feet.

Choice A is likely the result of an arithmetic error. For choice B, you used the wrong triangle relationship; this is a 45-45-90 triangle, not a 30-60-90 triangle. Choice D is the approximate length of the path. For choice E, you used the wrong triangle relationship; this is a 45-45-90 triangle, not a 30-60-90 triangle, and this would be the length of the path.

26. The correct answer is F. Let x be the original price. Then, $0.70x = 5{,}400$, so that $x = \frac{5{,}400}{0.70}$ dollars. Choice G is incorrect because you should divide by 0.7, not multiply by it. This represents 70% of 5,400. Choice H is incorrect because this is 30% of 5,400. Choice J is incorrect because you do not apply percentages by adding the percent to a quantity. Choice K is incorrect because the denominator should be 0.7.

27. The correct answer is E. Each wall is 100 yards long and 15 yards high. Convert these yards to feet, since the paint coverage is measured in square feet. There are 3 feet in a yard, so each wall measures 300 feet by 45 feet, and the total square footage is 2 × 300 × 45 = 27,000 square feet. One gallon of paint covers an area of 150 square feet, so calculate the number of gallons needed for this job:

$$27{,}000 \text{ square feet} \times \frac{1 \text{ gallon}}{150 \text{ square feet}} = 180$$

In choice A, you did not convert to feet when computing square footage. In choice B, you did not convert 100 yards to feet. In choice C, you did not account for the fact that there are two walls. Choice D is the information given to you; you must determine total square footage and then divide by 150.

28. The correct answer is J. First calculate the area of the four triangles. Since the area of a triangle is $\frac{1}{2}bh$, each triangle has an area of $\frac{1}{2}(a)(3a) = \frac{3}{2}a^2$. Thus, the total area of all four triangles is $4 \times \frac{3}{2}a^2 = 6a^2$. The easiest way to calculate the area of the shaded region is to subtract the area of the four triangles from the area of square *WXYZ*, each side of which has a length of $a + 3a = 4a$. The area of square *WXYZ* is $(4a)^2 = 16a^2$, so the area of the shaded region is $16a^2 - 6a^2 = 10a^2$. Therefore, the ratio of the area of the 4 triangles to the area of the shaded region is:

$$\frac{6a^2}{10a^2} = \frac{3}{5}$$

In choice F, you compared the area of four triangles to the area of the square *WXYZ*, not the shaded region. Choice G is incorrect because the area of the four triangles is $6a^2$, not $4a^2$. Choice H is incorrect because the area of the four triangles is $6a^2$, not $5a^2$. In choice K, the area of the shaded region is $10a^2$, not $8a^2$.

29. The correct answer is C. Get a common denominator in the top and bottom separately; then, divide the resulting fractions:

$$\frac{\frac{1}{10} - \frac{1}{100}}{\frac{1}{5} - \frac{1}{25}} = \frac{\frac{10}{100} - \frac{1}{100}}{\frac{5}{25} - \frac{1}{25}} = \frac{\frac{9}{100}}{\frac{4}{25}}$$

$$= \frac{9}{100} \div \frac{4}{25} = \frac{9}{4\cancel{100}} \bullet \frac{\cancel{25}}{4} = \frac{9}{16}$$

Choice A is the result of multiplying the numerator and denominator of the complex fraction instead of dividing them. In choice B you canceled terms, not factors, common to the numerator and denominator. Choice D is the reciprocal of the correct answer. Choice E is the result of flipping the fraction *before* the division sign when converting the quotient of two fractions to a product.

30. The correct answer is G. Use the two labeled points to determine the slope of the line:

$$m = \frac{-3-(-1)}{4-(-2)} = -\frac{2}{6} = -\frac{1}{3}$$

Using point-slope form with the point (–2, –1) yields the equation

$$y-(-1) = -\frac{1}{3}(x+2)$$

$$y+1 = -\frac{1}{3}x - \frac{2}{3}$$

$$y = -\frac{1}{3}x - \frac{5}{3}$$

Choice F is incorrect because the slope is the change in *y* divided by the change in *x*. Choice H is incorrect because the slope is the change in *y* divided by the change in *x*, and you seemed to have eyeballed the *y*-intercept. Choice J is incorrect because you seemed to have eyeballed the *y*-intercept. Choice K is incorrect because the sign of the constant term should be negative.

31. **The correct answer is C.** Construct a frequency table:

Data value	Frequency
0	3
1	9
2	3
3	1
4	4
5	5
6	0
7	2
8	3

The mode is the most frequently occurring data value, which is 1. The median is the average of the 15th and 16th data value, namely $\frac{2+2}{2}=2$. The mean is the average of all the data values:

$$\frac{0(3)+1(9)+2(3)+3(1)+4(4)+5(5)+6(0)+7(2)+8(3)}{30}$$
$$=\frac{97}{30}=3\frac{7}{30}.$$

Mode < median < mean.

32. **The correct answer is F.** First, find $\cos\theta$ using the identity $\sin^2\theta+\cos^2\theta=1$:

$$\sin^2\theta+\cos^2\theta=1$$
$$\left(\frac{2}{3}\right)^2+\cos^2\theta=1$$
$$\frac{4}{9}+\cos^2\theta=1$$
$$\cos^2\theta=\frac{5}{9}$$
$$\cos\theta=\pm\sqrt{\frac{5}{9}}=\pm\frac{\sqrt{5}}{3}$$

Since the terminal side of θ is in the second quadrant, use $\cos\theta=-\frac{\sqrt{5}}{3}$. Now, $\cot\theta=\frac{\cos\theta}{\sin\theta}=\frac{-\frac{\sqrt{5}}{3}}{\frac{2}{3}}=-\frac{\sqrt{5}}{2}$.

33. **The correct answer is E.** If the average of *x* numbers is 15, then the total of these numbers is 15*x*. When two numbers are increased by *y*, 2*y* will be added to this total. The value of *x* does not change, so the new average will be $\frac{15x+2y}{x}=15+\frac{2y}{x}$. This is an increase of $\frac{2y}{x}$ over the original average.

Choice A is the amount added to the overall total before averaging. Choice B is just the amount by which each of the two numbers increased, not the amount by which the average increases. Choice C is the reciprocal of the correct answer. The value given in choice D should be doubled, since *two* numbers were increased by *y*.

34. **The correct answer is J.** The unshaded sectors *AOB* and *BOC* comprise a total of $\frac{2}{5}+\frac{1}{3}=\frac{11}{15}$ of the circle. This means that the shaded region, sector *AOC*, takes up the remaining $\frac{4}{15}$ of the circle. A circle has 360 total degrees, so set up a proportion to find the measure of $\angle AOC$:

$$\frac{4}{15}=\frac{m\angle AOC}{360°}$$
$$15(m\angle AOC)=1{,}440°$$
$$m\angle AOC=96°$$

Choice F is incorrect because the number of degrees in a circle is 360, not 180. In choice G, you seem to have mistakenly said that the shaded region is $\frac{1}{4}$ of the circle—don't eyeball it! Choice H is close, but is likely the result of eyeballing the region rather than using the information provided in the problem. Choice K is the measure of 360 – $\angle AOC$, not just $\angle AOC$.

35. **The correct answer is C.** The ladder forms a right triangle with the house and the ground, so use the Pythagorean theorem to solve for the distance:

$$10^2+b^2=12^2$$
$$b^2=144-100$$
$$b=\sqrt{44}$$
$$\approx 6.6$$

In choice A, when using the Pythagorean theorem, you forgot to square the legs and hypotenuse. For choice B, you computed the squares of the legs and hypotenuse incorrectly; note that a^2 does not equal $2a$. For choice D, you treated the hypotenuse as a leg in the Pythagorean theorem. For choice E, you forgot to take the square root.

36. **The correct answer is J.** Since the diameter of the circle is 12 yards, the radius must be 6 yards. So the area of the circle is $6^2\pi = 36\pi$ square yards. In choice F, you incorrectly squared π when computing the area. In choice G, you used the wrong formula for area; it should be πr^2, where r is the radius. Choice H is the circumference of the circle. In choice K, you used the diameter instead of the radius when computing the area.

37. **The correct answer is A.** There are 3(24) = 72 teaspoons in the jar of cough medicine. Divide the total cost by 72 to get the cost per teaspoon: $\frac{\$4.50}{72} \approx \$0.06$.

Choice B is incorrect because you divided by 30 instead of 72, the number of teaspoons in the jar. Choice C is incorrect because you divided by 24; this is the cost per tablespoon, not teaspoon. Choice D is incorrect because you are off by a factor of 10. Choice E is incorrect because you divided by 3, not 3(24).

38. **The correct answer is G.** The given line is vertical since it passes through two points having the same x-coordinate. So the desired line must be horizontal. Since it passes through the point (–1, 4), its equation must be $y = 4$. In choices F, H, and K, you used the point (–1, 4) when computing the slope of the given line, but it does not pass through this point. Choice J is parallel to the given line.

39. **The correct answer is D.** Let x be the missing leg of the triangle. Using the Pythagorean theorem yields $2^2 + x^2 = 5^2$, so that $x^2 = 21$. Thus, $x = \sqrt{21}$. The area of the triangle is therefore $\frac{1}{2}(2)(\sqrt{21}) = \sqrt{21}$ square yards. In choice A, you did not square the lengths of the sides when applying the Pythagorean theorem. In choices B and C, you applied the Pythagorean theorem treating the hypotenuse as a leg. In choice E, you used the hypotenuse when computing the area, but you should use both legs.

40. **The correct answer is K.** Calculate as follows:

$$h\left(-\frac{4}{x}\right) = 1 - \frac{2}{3\left(-\frac{4}{x}\right)}$$
$$= 1 - \frac{2}{-\frac{12}{x}} = 1 + 2\left(\frac{x}{12}\right)$$
$$= 1 + \frac{x}{6} = \frac{6+x}{6} = \frac{x+6}{6}$$

Choice F is incorrect because $\frac{x+6}{6} \neq \frac{x+\cancel{6}}{\cancel{6}}$. Choice G is incorrect because you did not simplify the complex fraction correctly. Choice H is incorrect because $\frac{2x}{12} + 1 \neq \frac{2x+1}{12}$; you must first get a common denominator. Choice J is incorrect because it is the product of $h(x)$ and $-\frac{4}{x}$.

41. **The correct answer is D.** Use the second portion of the function since that is the interval to which $x = 0$ belongs. Doing so yields $F(0) = 4$. Choice A is incorrect because the portion of the function corresponding to the interval containing zero is, in fact, defined at 0; so the y-intercept does exist. Choice B is incorrect because this is the x-intercept. Choice C is incorrect because you used the wrong portion of the function; 0 does not belong to the interval for which the function is defined by the third expression. Choice E is incorrect because you used the wrong portion of the function; 0 does not belong to the interval for which the function is defined by the first expression.

42. **The correct answer is H.** Three pairs of prime numbers add to 24: 5 + 19, 7 + 17, and 11 + 13. The smallest resulting product is 5 × 19 = 95, so 95 is the least possible value of xy.

Choice F gives you a prime, so it cannot be a product of prime numbers. You get choice G from the choice 2 + 22, but 22 is not prime. You get choice J from 7 and 17 and choice K from 11 and 13, but neither one yields the least product.

43. **The correct answer is E.** The radius is the length of the segment connecting the two given points:

$\sqrt{(2-(-4))^2+(-2-3)^2}=\sqrt{6^2+5^2}=\sqrt{36+25}=\sqrt{61}.$

Using the center $(h, k) = (-4, 3)$ and radius $r = \sqrt{61}$ in the standard form for the equation of a circle $(x - h)^2 + (y - k)^2 = r^2$ yields the equation $(x-(-4))^2+(y-3)^2=\left(\sqrt{61}\right)^2$, which simplifies to $(x+4)^2+(y-3)^2=61$. Choices A and B have the signs of the center wrong, and the right side in choice B should be squared. In choice C, you did not square the differences in the *x*- and *y*-coordinates when computing the distance between the given points. In choice D, you used the wrong point for the center and should square the right side.

44. **The correct answer is F.** Solve for *z*:

$$\begin{aligned}0.3z-0.24&=1.2(0.3-z)\\0.3z-0.24&=0.36-1.2z\\1.5z&=0.60\\z&=\frac{0.60}{1.5}=0.4\\z&=\frac{0.60}{1.5}=0.4\end{aligned}$$

So $z \bullet 10^{-3}=(0.4)\bullet 10^{-3}=0.0004$. All other choices are off by various powers of 10.

45. **The correct answer is B.** Tangent equals opposite divided by adjacent. In an isosceles right triangle, the legs are equal. In this case, that means the opposite and adjacent sides are equal, so $\tan x° = 1$. Choice A is either sine or cosine of 45 degrees. Choice C is either the secant or cosecant of 45 degrees. For choices D and E, you used the wrong triangle relationships—this is a 45-45-90 triangle, not a 30-60-90 triangle.

46. **The correct answer is G.** Solve for the width and length of the rectangle using the distance formula:

$$\begin{aligned}w&=\sqrt{(-5-(-1))^2+(-2-(-6))^2}\\&=\sqrt{16+16}\\&=\sqrt{32}\\&=4\sqrt{2}\end{aligned}$$

$$\begin{aligned}l&=\sqrt{(-1-7)^2+(-6-2)^2}\\&=\sqrt{64+64}\\&=\sqrt{128}\\&=8\sqrt{2}\end{aligned}$$

The area of the rectangle is $\left(4\sqrt{2}\right)\left(8\sqrt{2}\right)=64.$

For choice F, note that $\sqrt{2}\bullet\sqrt{2}=2$, not $\sqrt{2}$.

Choice H is the perimeter, not the area. Choice J is the square of the length of a side of the rectangle. For choice K, you seem to have assumed the rectangle was a square with side 12. You must use the distance formula to find a side length.

47. **The correct answer is A.** In order for the expression to be positive, *x* and *z* must either both be negative or both be positive. Choice B would produce a quotient involving an odd number of negative signs, which must be odd. Choice C is incorrect because option II is false—this would produce a quotient involving an odd number of negative signs, which must be odd. Choices D and E are incorrect because options II and III are false. Option II is false because this would produce a quotient involving an odd number of negative signs; option III is false because if $x = 0$, then the quotient is 0.

48. **The correct answer is F.** Since $\frac{1}{625}=\frac{1}{5^4}=5^{-4}$, it follows that $\log_5\left(\frac{1}{625}\right)=\log_5\left(5^{-4}\right)=-4$. Choice G is incorrect because $5^{-3}=\frac{1}{125}$. In choice H, you applied the power in the wrong way:, but $625^{\frac{1}{4}}=5$. Choice J has the wrong sign. In choice K, you incorrectly multiplied the base times the power.

49. **The correct answer is B.** For *x* to have an inverse relationship with *y*, it must be in the denominator of the right side. For *z* to have a direct relationship with *y*, it must be in the numerator of the right side. Only the equation $y=\frac{z}{x}$ does this.

Choice A is incorrect because the right side should be the reciprocal of what is listed here. Choice C is incorrect because it means *y* is inversely proportional to both *z* and *x*. For choice D, applying the logarithm rules, this would make log(*y*) inversely proportional to *z* and proportional to log(*x*). For choice E, applying the logarithm rules would make log(*y*) inversely proportional to *x* and proportional to log(*z*).

50. The correct answer is H. Divide 114 feet into 3-foot segments to see that there are 38 such segments. The cost, before tax, is therefore 38($8.10) = $307.80. The 5% sales tax on this amount is 0.05($307.80) = $15.39. So the total cost is $307.80 + $15.39 = $323.19.
Choice F is incorrect because you subtracted 5% of the pre-tax cost instead of adding it to it. Choice G is incorrect because you did not include the 5% tax. Choice J is incorrect because you used $8.10 as the cost per foot, not per 3-foot segment, and did not include the 5% tax. Choice K is incorrect because you used $8.10 as the cost per foot, not per 3-foot segment.

51. The correct answer is D. Solve for *y*:

$$\frac{3(1-2y)}{4}-\frac{2-4y}{3}=y$$
$$12(1-2y)-4(2-4y)=12y$$
$$12-24y-8+16y=12y$$
$$4-8y=12y$$
$$4=20y$$
$$y=\frac{1}{5}$$

So, $y^{-1}=\left(\frac{1}{5}\right)^{-1}=5$. In choices A, C, and E, you solved an equation of the form $ay=b$ incorrectly (you should divide both sides by a) and computed y^{-1} incorrectly. In choice B, you multiplied the base and exponent when computing y^{-1}.

52. The correct answer is G. The period of a graph of the form $y=A\cos(Bx+C)+D$ is $\frac{2\pi}{B}$. So the period of the graph of $y=4\cos\left(3x-\frac{\pi}{2}\right)+1$ is $\frac{2\pi}{3}$. Choice F is the phase shift. In choice H, you incorrectly identified the coefficient of *x* as the period. Choice J is the amplitude. In choice K, you did not divide by the coefficient of *x*.

53. The correct answer is D. Let *s* be a side of the square. Two adjacent sides and the corresponding diagonal form a right triangle. So using the Pythagorean theorem yields $s^2+s^2=8^2$, or equivalently, $2s^2=64$. So $s^2=32$ and hence, $s=4\sqrt{2}$ inches. Therefore, the perimeter is $4\left(4\sqrt{2}\right)=16\sqrt{2}$ inches. Choice A is the length of a side of the square. Choice B is one-half the perimeter. In choice C you did not use the Pythagorean theorem correctly to find the length of a side of the square. Choice E is the area of the square.

54. The correct answer is G. Begin by plugging in 100 for *x*. If 100 is increased by 20 percent, the result is 120. This number is then decreased by 30 percent. Thirty percent of 120 is 36, so the final result is 120 – 36 = 84. This is the same as decreasing 100 by 16 percent. Choice F is incorrect because the percentages are actually acting in different directions, so you cannot simply add them in this manner. Choices H and J are incorrect because you cannot just add percentages; they must be applied to a whole. For choice K, you assumed that *x* was initially decreased by 20% and then applied 30% to 0.80*x*.

55. The correct answer is A. As shown in the diagram below, the height of the pole, *x*, is opposite a 70° angle, and the hypotenuse of the triangle is 50.

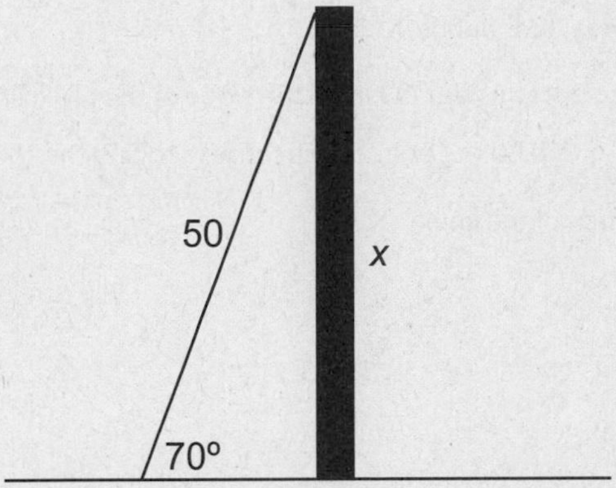

Sine equals opposite divided by hypotenuse:

$$\frac{x}{50}=\sin 70^\circ$$
$$x=50\sin 70^\circ$$

Choice B is the length of the unlabeled leg of the triangle. In choice C, you used an incorrect definition of tangent. In choices D and E, you used an incorrect definition of cosine.

56. The correct answer is H. The inequality $2|3x+1|>8$ is equivalent to $|3x+1|>4$. This implies that either $3x+1>4$ or $3x+1<-4$. Solving the first inequality yields $x>1$ and solving the second one yields $x<-\frac{5}{3}$. So the solution set is $\{x: x>1 \text{ or } x<-\frac{5}{3}\}$. In choices F and J, you multiplied both sides of the original inequality by 2 instead of dividing by 2. Choices F, G, and K only provide one of the two rays that comprise the solution set.

57. **The correct answer is B.** For the lines to never intersect, they must be parallel. So they must have the same slope. The equation $2x - cy = 1$ can be written equivalently as $y = \frac{2}{c}x - \frac{1}{c}$. So its slope is $\frac{2}{c}$. The slope of the second line is $8c$. Equating the slopes yields the equation $\frac{2}{c} = 8c$. This is equivalent to $2 = 8c^2$, so that $c^2 = \frac{1}{4}$. Solving for c gives $c = -\frac{1}{2}, c = \frac{1}{2}$. Choice A would produce lines that are perpendicular. Choice C shows the reciprocals of the correct values of c. Choice D is the result of solving an equation of the form $ax = b$ incorrectly; you should divide both sides by a, not multiply both sides by it. In choice E, you squared both sides when attempting to solve $c^2 = \frac{1}{4}$ instead of taking the square root of both sides.

58. **The correct answer is J.** Find the slope of the given line. $\frac{5-2}{-1+2} = 3$. Use the point-slope formula to find the equation of the line.

$$y - y_1 = m(x - x_1)$$
$$y - 5 = 3(x + 1)$$
$$y - 5 = 3x + 3$$
$$y = 3x + 8$$

The equation for line m is $y = 3x + 8$. Since line n is perpendicular to line m, it must have a slope of $-\frac{1}{3}$. By putting the given equations in slope-intercept form, you can see that only the line represented by $3y = -x + 14$ has a slope of $-\frac{1}{3}$: $y = -\frac{1}{3}x + \frac{14}{3}$. The slopes of the lines in choices F, G, and H are not $-\frac{1}{3}$. Remember, the product of the slopes of perpendicular lines must be -1. Choice K is incorrect because the slope of line m is 3. Since the product of the slopes of perpendicular lines must be -1, this cannot be the equation of line n.

59. **The correct answer is D.** The outcomes that satisfy the given criteria are as follows:

1 3 5 7 9 11 13 15 17 19 21 23 25 27 29 and 10 20 30

So 18 of the possible 30 outcomes satisfy the condition. Thus, the probability is $\frac{18}{30} = 0.60$. Choice A is incorrect because while 18 outcomes satisfy the condition, you must divide this by the number of outcomes possible, not by 100. Choice B is the probability of NOT selecting such a card. Choice C does not account for the cards 10, 20, or 30. In choice E, you double counted the outcomes 5, 15, and 25.

60. **The correct answer is G.** A shirt and two ties cost \$105, which translates to $s + 2t = 105$. Two shirts and one tie cost \$135, which translates to $2s + t = 135$. Multiply both sides of the first equation by 2: $2s + 4t = 210$. Then subtract the second equation from the first equation to solve for t, the price of one tie:

$$\begin{aligned} 2s + 4t &= 210 \\ \underline{-(2s + t} &\underline{= 135)} \\ 3t &= 75 \\ t &= 25 \end{aligned}$$

In choice F, when solving the system you added the t-terms but should have subtracted them. In choice H, you likely made an arithmetic error. In choice J, you have the cost of two ties, not one. In choice K, you calculated the cost of one shirt.

1.	D	**11.**	B	**21.**	C	**31.**	C
2.	H	**12.**	J	**22.**	F	**32.**	J
3.	B	**13.**	B	**23.**	D	**33.**	C
4.	G	**14.**	H	**24.**	H	**34.**	F
5.	B	**15.**	A	**25.**	A	**35.**	D
6.	J	**16.**	F	**26.**	H	**36.**	H
7.	C	**17.**	D	**27.**	C	**37.**	A
8.	F	**18.**	H	**28.**	F	**38.**	H
9.	D	**19.**	D	**29.**	D	**39.**	D
10.	H	**20.**	H	**30.**	G	**40.**	G

1. **The correct answer is D.** Paragraph 1 states that Mr. Bennet addressed his second daughter, and the following line finds him addressing Lizzy, so choice D is correct and choice B can be eliminated. A second daughter could be the youngest one if there are only two daughters, but we know based on this passage that there are at least three daughters in the Bennet family (Lizzy, Kitty, and Mary), so choice A is not the correct answer. The only mention of anyone being sensible in this passage refers to Mary, not Lizzy, and she fails in her attempt to do so, so choice C is not the correct answer.

2. **The correct answer is H.** Mrs. Bennet uses this figurative phrase in reference to her nerves and to indicate that Kitty's coughing is making her upset, so choice H is the best answer. While physically tearing up something is destructive, and perhaps even violent, Kitty is not literally tearing up Mrs. Bennet's nerves, so choices F and G are not correct. Mrs. Bennet's issue is emotional, not physical, so choice J is not the best answer.

3. **The correct answer is B.** After Mr. Bennet makes the suggestion, Mrs. Bennet dismisses it as a breach of etiquette, which is apparently very important in this story. According to etiquette, Mrs. Bennet cannot make the introduction when she does not know Mr. Bingley personally. Although Mrs. Bennet believes Mr. Bennet has made a poor suggestion, it is extreme to conclude that she thinks he has lost his mind (choice A), he does not understand her (choice C), or he does not love her (choice D).

4. **The correct answer is G.** Although Miss Brooke's behavior toward Sir James may be interpreted as rude, no one in the passage ever says she is too rude, so choice F is not the best answer. Although the words *happy* and *scruples* are used in the first paragraph, neither word is used to describe Miss Brooke, so you can eliminate choices H and J. However, both Celia and Sir James are familiar with the notion that Miss Brooke is too religious, so choice G is the best answer.

5. **The correct answer is B.** The main purpose of lines 28–30 is to reveal Sir James' inner thoughts about Miss Brooke, so choice B is the best answer. This is not a quotation, though, so choice A cannot be correct. The information in lines 28–30 does not contradict the idea that Sir James is charming, so choice C is incorrect. While lines 28–30 do reveal some of Miss Brooke's qualities that Sir James loved, the lines' main purpose is not structured as a list.

6. **The correct answer is J.** The sentence reads: "Celia felt that this was a *pity*." It is clear from this sentence that the word *pity* is a noun, so you can eliminate choice F since *sorry* can be used only as an adjective. *Compassion* (choice G) and *sympathy* (choice H) have the same meaning, so they most likely cancel each other out. They also would not make sense if used in place of *pity* in the original sentence. The only answer choice that would is *shame*.

7. **The correct answer is C.** In Passage A, Mrs. Bennet has little patience for her daughters' comments, and Miss Brooke is abrupt and cold with Sir James, so the answer that best describes both women is *short-tempered* (choice C). *Demure* means *shy,* and neither woman has any reservations about expressing her opinions, so choice A does not make sense. *Disgusted* may describe Miss Brooke since she may "despise" Sir James, but it is too harsh a word to describe Mrs. Bennet, so choice B is not the best answer. The narrator of Passage B describes

Miss Brooke's behavior as an amusing contrast to Sir James's solicitous amiability, but that word does not really describe her in general, and it does not really describe Mrs. Bennet either, so choice D is not the best answer.

8. **The correct answer is F.** This is an inference question. Kitty becomes fretful when her parents interpret her coughing as impudence. This implies that she is concerned about how others interpret her behavior. However, Miss Brooke says exactly what is on her mind no matter how others might interpret her words. So choice F describes a difference between the two characters. Choice G describes how Miss Brooke is different from Kitty, not the other way around. Choice H is Sir James's interpretation of Miss Brooke's behavior; it is not anyone's interpretation of Kitty's. Mrs. Bennet describes Ms. Long as selfish and hypocritical; no one describes Kitty this way, so choice J is incorrect.

9. **The correct answer is D.** At the end of Passage A, the narrator reveals Mary's unspoken wish "to say something sensible." The first paragraph of Passage B reveals Celia's private thoughts. Choice D is the best answer. Kitty's inner thoughts are never revealed in Passage A, so choice A is incorrect. Neither Elizabeth nor Miss Brooke's inner thoughts are known in these passages, so choice B is also incorrect. Mr. Bingley never even appears in Passage A, so choice C cannot be correct.

10. **The correct answer is H.** In Passage A, the Bennets intend to introduce their daughter Lizzy to Mr. Bingley in the hope that there will be a romantic connection between them. In Passage B, Sir James expresses romantic interest in Miss Brooke. Therefore, you can infer that both men are unmarried. The other answer choices are difficult to confirm. Mr. Bingley does not actually appear in Passage A, so it is not possible to know whether or not he is extremely charming (choice F), uninterested in etiquette (choice G), or if he even meets Lizzy (choice J).

11. **The correct answer is B.** The answer to this question can be found in the second paragraph, which states, "Sarah Andrews Spencer, Sarah E. Webster, and seventy other women marched to the polls to register and vote in the District of Columbia. Their ballots refused, they brought suit against the Board of Election Inspectors, carrying the case unsuccessfully to the Supreme Court of the United States." This supports choice B. Choice A confuses the situation in the District of Columbia with one in Detroit. While the passage states that the women marched to the polls to register and vote, it does not say that organized a protest march (choice C). While at least two women had voted successfully in the Washington Territory, there is no implication that the women in question were able to vote in that area after being refused in the District of Columbia, so choice D is incorrect.

12. **The correct answer is J.** In this passage, Susan B. Anthony first successfully secures the right to vote by invoking the Fourteenth Amendment of the US Constitution, so choice J is the best answer. While Anthony read a publication called *The Revolution* and hoped for more militancy among women, such matters do not necessarily support the conclusion in choice F, since the passage never indicates Anthony took violent measures to secure voting rights for women. While Anthony did take her issue to the press, this was not the action that was most successful for her cause, so choice G is not as strong of an answer as choice J. Her actions described in this passage are to secure the right to vote, but voting, itself, is not one of those actions, so choice H is not as strong of an answer as choice J.

13. **The correct answer is B.** The third paragraph describes numerous other women who attempted to vote or secure the right to vote in Susan B. Anthony's time, so choice B is the best answer. The beginning of the paragraph specifically states that the actions it describes only gave Anthony hope that more successful militancy was to come, which suggests that a militant effort to secure women the right to vote was not yet in full force. Therefore, choice A can be eliminated. The paragraph refers to several specific women who were working to secure the right to vote, but it does not support the extreme statement in choice C. The paragraph also refers to the fact that some women took their cases to the Supreme Court, but it does not quite support the conclusion in choice D, since those cases were unsuccessful.

14. **The correct answer is H.** While Susan B. Anthony is the main focus of this passage, the passage describes the actions of many people who worked toward enacting social change, so choice H is the best answer. Choice F would have been correct if the passage discussed only Anthony. The passage focuses on securing the right to vote, but using voting as a tool to enact social change is not discussed in the passage, so there is no support for choice G. Choice J is too specific, since taking cases to the Supreme Court was just one of the numerous methods for affecting change discussed in the passage.

15. **The correct answer is A.** The author indicates that it was Susan B. Anthony's persistence that caused Jones and Marsh to consent to allowing the women to vote. While she did read lines from the Fourteenth Amendment, the author does not imply that this is what inspired Jones and Marsh to consent. There is a suggestion that Anthony stirred up an argument and that Jones and Marsh broke from their colleagues when they decided to consent to allowing Anthony and the other women, but there is not enough evidence to support the very specific conclusion in choice C. Anthony only rounded up more women to vote after Jones and Marsh allowed them the right to vote, so choice D is incorrect.

16. **The correct answer is F.** The word *relevant* (choice F) would make the most sense if used in place of the word *pertinent* in line 61. While *interesting* (choice G) would make sense, it does not fit the specific meaning of line 61 as well as choice F. *Persistent* (choice H) may be spelled similarly to *pertinent*, but the two words have very different meanings. Choice J seems to confuse *pertinent* for *penitent*, the latter of which means "sorry or remorseful."

17. **The correct answer is D.** According to the seventh paragraph, the news media reported on the registration of women voters in Rochester after Susan B. Anthony had successfully gotten sixteen women to register to vote (choice D). Choice A describes something that most likely happened after the news media reported Anthony's accomplishment. Choice B describes something that definitely happened after it. Choice C describes something that Anthony only says will happen in the future in this passage, so the passage does not even make clear whether Post went through with her plans to sue the registrars.

18. **The correct answer is H.** While the passage is not specifically about the difficulties women faced in becoming lawyers during Susan B. Anthony's time, it is about difficulties women faced during that period, and the details about Myra Bradwell are relevant to that particular theme, so choice H is the best answer. Myra Bradwell was denied admission to the Illinois bar because she was a woman, not because she was unqualified, so choice F is incorrect. There is no exaggeration in this passage; women really did face major challenges during Susan B. Anthony's time, so choice G is a weak answer. While it is likely that Myra Bradwell was bright, choice J does not explain why the author discusses her difficulties in the third paragraph.

19. **The correct answer is D.** According to the ninth paragraph, the *Chicago Tribune* suggested that Anthony should hold public office, which indicates that the paper supported her, rather than criticized her. Therefore, choice D is the best answer. The *New York Graphic* (choice A), however, contained editorial cartoons that "caricatured her unmercifully." And since the paragraph points out that such critical cartoons were very common, choice C is not the best answer either. The Rochester *Union and Advertiser* criticized Anthony as lawless and charged that her actions ". . . proved women unfit for the ballot."

20. **The correct answer is H.** The first line of the eighth paragraph states that "Election day did not bring the general uprising of women for which Susan had hoped," which supports the conclusion in choice H. Choice F is not the best answer, since Lillie Devereux Blake and Matilda Joslyn Gage only *tried* to vote; they did not do so successfully. Choice G is not a strong answer either, since Stanton only seemed to lack motivation; there is no evidence in this passage that she actually criticized Anthony. Choice J is incorrect because it is too extreme; while some news media outlets did mock Anthony, the ninth paragraph proves that not all news media outlets mocked her.

21. **The correct answer is C.** Each answer choice can be used as a synonym for *inspired*, but choice C makes the most sense in this particular context. A single painted canvass cannot really be animated, so choice A does not make much sense. *Encouraged* does not make sense in this context either, so choice B can also be eliminated. There is no real indication that education is what inspired Monticelli to use color in a particular way, so choice D is not the best answer.

22. **The correct answer is F.** The author clearly appreciates Impressionism, and in the third paragraph, he writes that Impressionism rejects symbols. Therefore, choice F is a logical conclusion. The author indicates that Impressionism is different from Romanticism and Classicism, but that does not mean he would necessarily agree with the statement in choice G. The author states that Impressionistic art is "aloof from mythology," which implies the opposite of choice H. The author implies that Impressionists were technically advanced, but nothing he writes really supports the extreme conclusion in choice J.

23. **The correct answer is D.** The author compares Monticelli's use of color to a musical theme to indicate that such basic elements of art and music can still have

great emotional impact, so choice D is the best answer. Choices A and C take the comparison between Monticelli's use of color and musical themes too literally. There is no evidence that Monticelli actually used music as an inspiration for his art (choice A) or that he actually composed music (choice C). Choice B is too extreme; while Monticelli may have emphasized one particular color in each of his paintings, there is no evidence that he never used more than one color in his paintings.

24. **The correct answer is H.** In the third paragraph, the author writes that the Impressionists occupy themselves with consideration of light (statement II) and picturesqueness (statement III), but have an antipathy to abstraction, which means that they rejected abstract imagery (statement I). Therefore, the correct answer must include statements II and II and eliminate statement I, and that is what choice H does. Choice F only includes the false statement. Choice G includes only one of the two true statements. Choice J includes both the false statement and the two true ones.

25. **The correct answer is A.** The author's use of strong, emotional words such as *delight*, *astonishment*, and *joy* support the inference in choice A. While the author states that Monticelli has an entirely personal technique, he immediately follows this by stating that Monitcelli's work can be "compared with that of Turner," so choice B is not the best answer. The author explains in the paragraph that Monticelli painted landscapes, so choice C is incorrect. Choice D is a conclusion that can be reached after reading the first paragraph, not the second one.

26. **The correct answer is H.** In the fourth paragraph, the author writes, "Manet, who, by his spirit and by the chance of his friendships, grouped around him the principal members, commenced by being classed in the ranks of the Realists . . .," which supports choice H. The author does not offer choice F as an explanation and never implies that Impressionist art does not depict contemporary scenes, so choice G is incorrect. While their names are similar, the author never implies that Manet and Monet were confused with each other, nor does the author imply that Monet was a Realist. Therefore, choice J is incorrect.

27. **The correct answer is C.** The first three paragraphs deal with the gradual development of Impressionism, while the fourth paragraph deals with how it has been unfairly judged. The author's own descriptions of Impressionist art indicates that it is an exciting form. So there is sufficient support for choice C. Choice A only describes the first two paragraphs, so it is not a very complete explanation of the primary purpose of the passage as a whole. Choices B and D each reflect specific details in the passage and both fail to capture the purpose of the entire passage.

28. **The correct answer is F.** The author describes Monticelli's brush as "full, fat and rich," which supports statement I. However, the author only compares Monticelli's reliefs to jewels and his construction of color to musical themes; he does not actually suggest that Monticelli painted jewels (statement II) or was directly influenced by music (statement III). Therefore, the best answer should include statement I and eliminate statements II and II, and only choice F accomplishes this. Choice G includes one true statement and one false one. Choice H includes only the two false statements. Choice J includes the one true statement as well as the two false ones.

29. **The correct answer is D.** A fact is a statement with which no one can argue, and this can be said only of choice D. The author states choice A in the second paragraph, but it is only an opinion, since not everyone may agree that Monticelli's use of color was inspired. Choice B is not a fact, since the author compares Monticelli to both Watteau and Turner, which implies that Monticelli's style was not actually *entirely* personal. Not everyone may agree with the author's statement that "Every picture by Monticelli provokes astonishment," so choice C is incorrect.

30. **The correct answer is G.** Choice G is the best interpretation of this line, especially since the author emphasizes the role of spontaneity in creating Impressionistic art. While the phrase does imply that Impressionists were reluctant to discuss their art, it does not support the extreme conclusion in choice F. Since the author discusses the role of spontaneity in impressionism, choice H is not true. Choice J is a statement the author makes in the paragraph, but it has nothing to do with the phrase in question.

31. **The correct answer is C.** In the third paragraph, the author explains that "The form of a coast, the configuration of the interior of a country, the existence and extent of lakes, valleys, and mountains, can often be traced to the former prevalence of earthquakes and volcanoes," which supports choice C. The author states only that such cataclysms may have occurred in areas that are currently undisturbed, not that such undisturbed areas are the direct causes of Earth's features, so choice A is not the best answer. The author mentions

land elevation in the paragraph, but does not indicate that it is the cause of Earth's features, so choice B is incorrect. Choice D may be true, but it is not something the author discusses in the passage, so it cannot be the correct answer.

32. **The correct answer is J.** In the fourth paragraph, the author writes that "... a geologist should be well versed in chemistry [statement III], natural philosophy, mineralogy, zoology, comparative anatomy (statement II) [and] botany (statement I) ...." Therefore, the correct answer should include all three statements, which is what choice J does. Choice F only accounts for one of the three true statements. Choices G and H each only account for two of them.

33. **The correct answer is C.** In the sixth paragraph, the author writes, "... at the close of the eighteenth century, geology appears to have been regarded as little other than a subordinate department of mineralogy," which supports choice C. Therefore, choices A and B cannot be true. Choice D seems to assume that the eighteenth century and 1800s are the same period.

34. **The correct answer is F.** The final sentence of the passage specifies that "geology was in nowise concerned 'with questions as to the origin of things,'" so choice F is the best answer. The author draws many comparisons between geology and history throughout the passage, so choice G is not the best answer. At the beginning of the fourth paragraph, the author writes, "Geology is intimately related to almost all the physical sciences," which eliminates choice H. At the beginning of the second paragraph, the author writes that by studying geology, "... we acquire a more perfect knowledge of its present condition ...," which eliminates choice J.

35. **The correct answer is D.** Each answer choice can be used as a synonym for *trace*, but choice D makes the most sense in this particular context, because the author is discussing finding and following a series of events. Choices A and B refer to creating a drawing, not tracking events. The author uses *trace* as a verb, but choice C suggests a noun.

36. **The correct answer is H.** In the fourth paragraph, the author writes, " ... as such extensive acquisitions are scarcely within the reach of any individual, it is necessary that men who have devoted their lives to different departments should unite their efforts; and as the historian receives assistance from the antiquary, and from those who have cultivated different branches of moral and political science, so the geologist should avail himself of the aid of many naturalists ...," which supports the conclusion in choice H. There is nothing about the difficulty of excavation in the passage, so choice F is incorrect. The passage does not imply that geologists withhold information from each other either, so choice G similarly lacks support. Choice J refers to historians, not geologists.

37. **The correct answer is A.** At the end of the third paragraph, the author writes that "... many distinguishing features of the surface may often be ascribed to the operation, at a remote era, of slow and tranquil causes—to the gradual deposition of sediment in a lake or in the ocean, or to the prolific increase of *Testacea* and corals," which supports choice A. This contradicts choice B. Increases in *Testacea* and coral are just examples of events that may alter Earth's surface, and there is no implication that one affects the other, so choice C is incorrect. The author merely uses an increase in coral as an example of a tranquil cause of Earth's features and does not imply that such a thing would make the Earth a more tranquil place (choice D).

38. **The correct answer is H.** In the fifth paragraph, the author explains that "... the Egyptian mummies throw light on the art of embalming, the rites of sepulture, or the average stature of the human race in ancient Egypt ...," which supports the conclusion in choice H. The author uses the study of coins, not mummies, as an example of ways to learn about rulers (choice F). The author uses the study of ancient encampments, not mummies, as an example of way to discover the districts once occupied by armies (choice G). Choice J is not implied in the passage; generally, mummification is a way to preserve the dead, not cure the living.

39. **The correct answer is D.** The author states that geologists, not historians, should have an understanding of natural philosophy, so choice D is the best answer. The author states that historians need knowledge of ethics and politics (choice A) in Paragraph 4. In that same paragraph, the author explains that historians often rely on antiquaries, which implies that historians must have working relationships with other academics. He says they need insight into human affairs (choice C) in Paragraph 4.

40. **The correct answer is G.** In the second paragraph, the author refers to such antecedent changes—violent past events that affect the nations of today. Therefore, choice G is the best example. Choice F can be eliminated because it refers to geology rather than history. Choice H is incorrect because current wars are not past events. Choice J is incorrect because an unfortunate presidential election is not as inherently violent as a revolution.

1.	C	**11.**	D	**21.**	C	**31.**	B
2.	H	**12.**	F	**22.**	H	**32.**	F
3.	D	**13.**	C	**23.**	B	**33.**	D
4.	J	**14.**	G	**24.**	G	**34.**	J
5.	D	**15.**	A	**25.**	A	**35.**	D
6.	F	**16.**	G	**26.**	H	**36.**	J
7.	B	**17.**	A	**27.**	D	**37.**	D
8.	G	**18.**	J	**28.**	F	**38.**	H
9.	A	**19.**	C	**29.**	C	**39.**	B
10.	J	**20.**	H	**30.**	J	**40.**	J

1. **The correct answer is C.** From the table, at 4.5 V the current for Resistor B is 420 mA at either temperature. Choice A is the current of Resistor C at the same temperature and voltage. Choice B is Resistor C at 23°C. Choice D is the current for Resistor A.

2. **The correct answer is H.** Resistor A does not appear to be affected by external temperature. While 27°C is not within the tested temperatures, it is a small change, and it's reasonable to assume that Resistor A would show a similar current compared to the other tested temperatures. The current of Resistor A is linear with response to voltage, with 100 mA/volt. Therefore, 350 mA is the expected current at 3.5 V. Choice F is the expected current of Resistor C at 23°C and 3.5 V. Choice G is the expected current of Resistor C at 25°C and 3.5 V. Choice J is the approximate expected current of Resistor B at 3.5 V.

3. **The correct answer is D.** Both Resistor A and C behave linearly, while Resistor B does not. The amount to which the current of Resistor C depends on voltage is different at different temperatures, but in a linear fashion in both cases. Therefore, choice A is insufficient, and choices B and C are incorrect.

4. **The correct answer is J.** At a given applied voltage, a thermistor produces different currents at different external temperatures. Choices F and H do not address temperature at all. Choice G is incorrect because the definition of a thermistor does not depend on absolute currents produced, nor on comparison to other resistors.

5. **The correct answer is D.** For a thermistor, a change in current is observed when external temperature is changed. At a given voltage with Resistor C, the observed current at 25°C is lower than that at 23°C. Choices A, B, and C are incorrect because no additional information is necessary to conclude that Resistor C is a thermistor.

6. **The correct answer is F.** Resistor A seems to be an ohmic device because there is a linear relationship between voltage and current. If Resistor A released heat into the water, it would not be considered an ohmic device. Choice G is incorrect because according to the table, Resistor B is not affected by temperature change. Choice H is incorrect because temperature change would not affect this outcome. Choice J is incorrect because according to the table, temperature does affect the current of Resistor C.

7. **The correct answer is B.** The difference in sediment bulk density between years 0 and 10 at Site 2 is 0.31 g/cm^3. Choice A (between years 0 and 4 at Site 1) is a difference of only 0.09 g/cm^3. Choice C (between the two unplanted sites) is a difference of only 0.08 g/cm^3. Choice D (between the two planted sites) is a difference of only 0.17 g/cm^3.

8. **The correct answer is G.** The % nitrogen at the 10-year mark is more than 4 times greater than what was measured in the seagrass-free control. The greatest change in Table 1 between years 0 and 10 is the seagrass density; however that is not one of the choices. Choice F (% carbon) is less than twice as high at the 10-year measurement. Choice H (% organic matter) is less than 1.5 times as high at the 10 year measurement. Choice J (bulk density) decreases by approximately 20% at the 10-year measurement.

9. **The correct answer is A.** The ecologists cannot go back in time to test the original sediment composition before seagrass planting, nor can they go back to test the sediment of each replanted

meadow over time. The original sediment composition under each of the two meadows may have been different, so it is important to collect a separate "year zero" for each of the meadows. Choice B is incorrect because nothing in the passage indicates how sediment composition changes with water depth. Choice C is incorrect because the ecologists have not experimentally controlled seagrass density in their experiments. Choice D is incorrect because the ecologists have not conducted multiple measurements in unplanted seabeds over time.

10. **The correct answer is J.** Larger amounts of trapped sediment were found in areas with greater seagrass surface area. The ecologists did not experimentally change one physical characteristic at a time, so Table 2 looks at correlations, not causations. For the data to support each hypothesis, there should be a clear trend between increasing sediment weight and an increase or decrease of the seagrass characteristic. Choice F would be correct if seagrass height increased consistently down the table; however, there is no clear trend. Choice G would be correct if seagrass density decreased down the column; however, there is no clear trend. Choice H would be correct if seagrass mass decreased down the column; however there is no clear trend.

11. **The correct answer is D.** The data in Table 1 shows little or no change in % carbon and % nitrogen between 0 and 4 years, followed by significant change by 10 years. Choice A is incorrect because the passage has no record of the original seagrass density, nor how the replanted areas compare. Choice B is similarly incorrect because there is no record of % organic matter in the original meadow before seagrass removal. Choice C is incorrect because Table 1 shows little or no change in % carbon and % nitrogen between years 0 and 4.

12. **The correct answer is F.** The data in this passage indicates that older seagrass meadows are more productive at storing carbon in the sediment than younger meadows, at least up to (and perhaps beyond) 10 years. Choice G could be correct if there was a demonstrated connection between added nutrients and seagrass uptake and storage of atmospheric CO_2—however, none of that is demonstrated in this passage. Choice H is incorrect, since the data in Table 1 indicates that meadows 4 years or younger are less effective at storing carbon than those at least 10 years old. Choice J is incorrect—while planting native plants along the shore may help overall ecosystem health, there is no indication in the passage of how the presence or absence of shore plants changes carbon storage by the seagrass meadows.

13. **The correct answer is C.** The element with an atomic radius of 88 pm is krypton, which has a boiling point of −153°C. Choice A is the boiling point of radon. Choice B is the boiling point of xenon. Choice D is the boiling point of neon.

14. **The correct answer is G.** Neon has an atomic weight of 20.2 amu. Four times that weight is 80.8 amu, which is close to the atomic weight of krypton: 83.8 amu. Helium (choice F) has an atomic weight of 4 amu, which is approximately one fifth that of neon. Xenon (choice H) has an atomic weight of 131.3 amu, more than six times that of neon. Radon (choice J) has an atomic weight of approximately 222 amu, which is more than ten times that of neon.

15. **The correct answer is A.** As the atomic number increases from 2 to 86 down the column, the boiling point increases from −269 to−62°C. All boiling points in the table are below 0°C, but they approach zero as the atomic number increases.

16. **The correct answer is G.** The only pair of elements in the table that does not support the hypothesis is neon and argon (option I). All of the other pairs, including both options II and III, support the hypothesis.

17. **The correct answer is A.** As the elements progress down the column, atomic number, atomic radius, and boiling point all increase. With an atomic number of 118, oganesson lies below radon and therefore is expected to have both a greater atomic radius and a greater boiling point than those of radon.

18. **The correct answer is J.** There is no systematic relationship between thickness and depth of rock layers—the thickest layer (4) is found at less than 800 m, and one of the thinnest layers (6) is below that. Based on this information, you can eliminate choices F and G. Choice H is incorrect because layer 6 is 40 m thick, at depths of 960–1,000 m.

19. **The correct answer is C.** Limestone is formed in marine environments, so the layers containing limestone give the age at which the region of the canyon was covered by sea. The time periods 130 million years and 220–260 million years contain limestone, but the latter time period is not one of the choices. Choice A is incorrect because there is no layer corresponding to 60 million years ago. Choices B and D are incorrect because they do not contain limestone.

20. **The correct answer is H.** Choice F is incorrect because temperature is not listed at all in Figure 1. Choice G (age of rock) is related to depth (the vertical axis), but that is not the measurement shown on the figure. Choice J

(thickness of rock layers) can be inferred from the figure, but it is not the vertical axis.

21. **The correct answer is C.** The uranium ore (carnotite) is found around petrified wood, which is found in layer 8. That is at a depth of 1,110–1,270 m, which includes 1,200 m. Choice A is incorrect because it refers to the thickness of layer 8, not the depth. Choice B is incorrect because layer 4 (500 m) does not contain petrified wood. Choice D is incorrect because there is no information for rock composition at 2,000 m.

22. **The correct answer is H.** The data does not show what range of ages are found in each layer, only the approximate age difference between the different layers. The thickest layer (4) occurs between a separation of less than 20 million years, while one of the thinnest ones (3) occurs between a separation of 40 million years. In reality, the thickness of a layer depends on a number of factors, including the rate of sedimentation, the length of time the region experienced a particular environment, and the amount of weathering the rock layer experienced before being covered by a new layer.

23. **The correct answer is B.** Layers found at the top of the canyon are youngest, so rocks at the surface were deposited there less than the age of the highest layer—100 million years. The extreme temperatures necessary to form welded tuff are indicative of a volcano. Choice A could be true, but a tropical climate is not hot enough by itself to produce welded tuff. Choice C is true based on the data in Table 1, but is not related to the existence of welded tuff. Choice D would be correct if the welded tuff was found at the lowest layer of the canyon, not the very surface.

24. **The correct answer is G.** Paleontologist A believes that morphological (body) similarities can just as reasonably be assumed to represent the effects of convergent evolution on distant lineages inhabiting similar environments. Choice F is incorrect—this paleontologist does not mention a failed experiment of evolution. Choice H is incorrect because even though the paleontologist does not think birds evolved directly from dinosaurs, a connection is acknowledged. Choice J is incorrect—there is no discussion of what caused the thecodonts to survive extinction.

25. **The correct answer is A.** Paleontologist A believes that dinosaurs and birds share a common ancestor. A fossil find from before the age of the dinosaurs with common features would support this view. An intermediate form between dinosaurs and birds (choice B) or an avian prototype before dinosaur dominance (choice C) would not directly support the position of a common ancestor. Examining theropod remains (choice D) does not relate to Paleontologist A's theory—he or she talks about thecodonts.

26. **The correct answer is H.** Paleontologist B assumes that the body similarities between dinosaurs and early birds must be evidence that birds came forth from the dinosaur lineage. This view does subscribe to the idea of transitional forms. Mass extinction is not relevant to this view. Choice F is incorrect because Paleontologist B directly discusses transitional forms—shared features from immediate ancestors. Choice G is incorrect because extinction is not a main feature of Paleontologist A's argument. Choice J is incorrect—neither paleontologist thinks the lineages are distant.

27. **The correct answer is D.** Paleontologist B believes that birds arose from a lineage of dinosaurs, which makes choice C incorrect. Choice A is incorrect—Paleontologist B does not believe in convergent evolution. Choice B is the view of Paleontologist A.

28. **The correct answer is F.** This contradicts the theory of Paleontologist B, who suggests that birds arose from dinosaurs (making choices G and H incorrect). Paleontologist A suggests that the two arose from an extremely distant ancestor, and the theory of convergent evolution is not inconsistent with birds appearing before dinosaurs. Paleontologist A's view is present, so choice J is incorrect.

29. **The correct answer is C.** Paleontologist A postulates the existence of a very distant common ancestor for birds and dinosaurs. The development of birds much later than that of dinosaurs might seem to refute this argument. However, the rate of evolutionary change is not constant across different lineages. Dinosaurs may have developed relatively rapidly from thecodonts, for example, whereas birds did not evolve until much later. Choice D is the opposite of this correct answer. Choices A and B are unrelated to the timing of the appearance of birds and dinosaurs.

30. **The correct answer is J.** The dependent variable is the condition the experimenter is measuring throughout the experiment—in this case, that is the number of cultures with surviving paramecia. Choice F (the number of species of bacteria) and choice G (the number of species of *Paramecium*) were both independent variables in this experiment. Choice H (the length of time) could have been another independent variable if the researchers had examined the cultures at

multiple points in time; since they were examined only once, the length of time is a constant.

31. The correct answer is B. Examining the results in Tables 2 and 3 shows that increasing the number of species of their food sources, the bacteria, did produce a relative increase in the survival rate of paramecia. Choice A states the opposite, so it is incorrect. Choice C is incorrect because there is a definite increase. Choice D is incorrect—the only variable being observed is paramecia, which increased.

32. The correct answer is F. Looking at Tables 2 and 3, it appears that increasing the number of species of *Paramecium* from one to two was most detrimental to their overall survival. The number decreased, making choice J incorrect. Choice G is incorrect because it cannot be confirmed—the only variable being observed is paramecia. Choice H is incorrect—according to Table 3, the number of species did have an effect on paramecia survival.

33. The correct answer is D. Experiment 3 added a predator of paramecia. Choices A, B, and C are incorrect; the number of bacteria species remained at 3, and we have no information that the time or the culture method was changed.

34. The correct answer is J. The results of this experiment suggest that increasing diversity in terms of trophic levels was ultimately harmful to the survival of the *Paramecium* species under study. Choices F and G are incorrect; it was not beneficial to all species because of the decreasing survival rates for the paramecia, and it definitely had an effect on paramecia. Choice H is incorrect, as we do not know the effect the experiment had on *Amoebae*.

35. The correct answer is D. At 8.7×10^{25} kg, Uranus has the fourth greatest mass of the planets in the solar system. Jupiter, Saturn, and Neptune all have greater masses; therefore, choices A, B, and C are incorrect. It is important to note the size of the exponent; otherwise, any of the choices could appear correct.

36. The correct answer is J. Neptune has the lowest temperature; based on that measure, it would seem to be the farthest from the sun. Mercury (choice F), Uranus (choice G), and Jupiter (choice H) all have higher black-body temperatures and so are closer to the sun.

37. The correct answer is D. Mercury has an orbital inclination of 7.000 degrees and an orbital eccentricity of 0.2056. Therefore, Mercury would be reclassified. Choices A, B, and C are incorrect because none of these planets have an orbital inclination greater than 5 or an orbital eccentricity greater than 0.2.

38. The correct answer is H. The orbital eccentricity of Venus is 0.0068; its orbit is the most circular in the solar system. Mercury has an orbital eccentricity of 0.2056; its egg-shaped orbit exhibits the greatest eccentricity in the solar system and thus deviates the most from a circular orbit. Choice F is incorrect—there is a planet with an orbital eccentricity closer to 0 than Earth. Choice G is incorrect—there is a planet with an orbital eccentricity closer to 0 than Neptune. Choice J is incorrect—there is a planet with an orbital eccentricity further from 0 than Neptune.

39. The correct answer is B. The gaseous planets would be expected to be less dense than the ones made of solid material. Choices A and D are incorrect—temperature and rotation period should not be affected whether a planet is a solid or a gas. Choice C is incorrect because these planets do not have greater masses than the others.

40. The correct answer is J. Mercury has the lowest mass (3.3×10^{23} kg) and the highest orbital eccentricity (0.2056°). The trend described in choice F is the opposite of what is observed; while not a perfect trend, more massive planets typically have shorter rotation periods. Choice G is incorrect, because the two planets with the highest mass (Jupiter and Saturn) are not the two planets with the lowest densities (Saturn and Uranus). Choice H would appear to be correct if the exponent in the mass term is ignored, since Earth and Mars have the closest rotational period, less than an hour different. The two planets with the closest relative mass (Uranus and Neptune) have rotational periods that differ by more than an hour.

Sample Essay: Score 1

Ideas and Analysis:	Score = 1
Development and Support:	Score = 1
Organization:	Score = 1
Language Use and Conventions:	Score = 1

I'm not sure I don't use fossils for anything not something I care about even. I only plug in the stuff I used my phone and my laptop and I think my TV they're all plugged into the wall and I don't bother anybody with them. Keep the sound down low especially when its late and its late at night my parents say, so I do that and I know how to take care of my stuff! If anybody wants to use anything they want to make theyre stuff work and as long as theyre not hurting anybody its ok with me. If thyre hurting everybody they should stop and be nice people and use just the wall to plug theyre stuff in, it is safe and I use it all the time and noone gets hurt so everybody should do that.

Scoring Explanation

Ideas and Analysis: Score = 1

This essay reflects a poor grasp of the essay task and a weak understanding of the role of fossil fuels and available energy sources. As a result, ideas are scattered and confusing, the writer's argument fails to address the questions provided, and the argument veers off in a largely unrelated direction regarding his or her use of electricity and favorite electronic devices.

Development and Support: Score = 1

This argument suffers from a significant lack of development and support for a discernible perspective regarding the use of alternative energy versus fossil fuels. This lack of idea development hinders comprehension and results in a disjointed essay that does not address the essay task at hand.

Organization: Score = 1

The writer provides a disjointed set of loosely connected thoughts with little or no thought given to effective essay construction or organization. There is no assertion of a clear perspective regarding the essay task, and the ideas provided don't follow a natural and coherent flow or support a unifying essay theme. The end result is a confusing piece of writing that falls off topic.

Language Use and Conventions: Score = 1

This essay demonstrates poor use of fundamental grammar and a deficient understanding of core English language rules. As a result, this piece of writing, which is full of errors in usage and mechanics, fails to competently address the given essay task.

Sample Essay: Score 6

Ideas and Analysis:	Score = 6
Development and Support:	Score = 6
Organization:	Score = 6
Language Use and Conventions:	Score = 6

Let's be honest. It's nice to be able to drive to the beach on a warm summer day. It's a wonderful luxury to have air conditioning in our homes, heat during the winter, and enough electricity to power all of the electronic gadgets that make our lives more comfortable. But is it worth any cost? Is it worth the destruction of our environment, the safety and well-being of future generations who have not yet had the opportunity to enjoy the natural wonders of our world, the very future of our planet? Each of us can pretend that our use of energy doesn't matter much, that it doesn't have a huge impact on the Earth, but this is the sort of apathetic mindset that keeps us from meaningful change.

The hard truth is that fossil fuels power our planet and are weaved into our social fabric; extricating ourselves from such a complex intertwining won't be easy. But that doesn't mean it's an issue we should avoid, or push off onto future generations. However, calls for an immediate, rash, or unrealistic abatement of fossil fuel usage are unrealistic and prevent us from intelligently addressing the challenge at hand.

What might a realistic, considered approach look like? There needs to be vastly increased incentives for individuals and businesses of all sizes that are both utilizing renewable energy sources and working on innovative green energy solutions for society, including tax breaks, monetary compensation, and government support. Towns, cities, and states need to galvanize and energize their citizens, adopt greater alternative energy programs, and execute expanded information campaigns. Local and state governments need to offer realistic strategies for reduced fossil fuel consumption and increased use of alternative energy that are not cost prohibitive. Local, state, and federal budgets need to shift towards greater investment in this effort or we will surely stall before we make any further progress.

Our country needs to keep energy consumption change at the forefront of our list of challenges to overcome. How can each of us help make this happen? The power of the vote is a great place. We need to demand that our elected officials at all levels tackle these issues—if they want to stay in office. Our collective concern can continue to be made known to our elected officials through social media campaigns, petitions, and voting patterns. Nations around the world work together all the time and tackle tough issues. Worldwide collaboration to effect positive climate change and reduce carbon emissions have already begin, but it needs to move beyond its careful early steps and into larger and more audacious strategies. It's too important an issue to not face it bravely and boldly.

Here's the bottom line: we need to figure out a realistic approach for decreasing fossil fuel reliance at every level—individuals, towns, cities, states, countries, and nations working in unison can reduce non-renewable fuel consumption, advocate for and invest in alternative fuel use, and—perhaps most importantly—acknowledge that we're *all* responsible for the welfare of our planet. Until we decide to make the hard decisions to effect positive change we're placing our world in peril. Will it be easy? Certainly not. But, the cost of continued complacency is much larger and more onerous—for each of us, for our children, and for future generations.

Scoring Explanation

Ideas and Analysis: Score = 6

The writer of this essay provides a well-reasoned, insightful argument in support of a realistic, unilateral approach to reducing fossil fuel dependency and increasing investment, exploration, and use of alternative sources of fuel. The ideas are carefully considered and represent a confident perspective on the issue. Progressive ideas for taking bolder steps are provided at every level—from individuals to countries and political entities in-between, resulting in a cohesive, thoughtful piece of writing that clearly tackles this issue with the seriousness it deserves.

Development and Support: Score = 6

This argument is a capably structured response to a challenging essay task, one that touches on hot-button social and political issues and requires the writer to think on both micro and macro scales, which this response does quite well. From the provocative opening question about fossil fuels (is it worth any cost?), through the detailed exploration of possible strategies for reducing our non-renewable energy reliance and concluding plea for future generations, this essay demonstrates an impressive ability to develop and support a clear perspective.

Organization: Score = 6

This argument is a well-organized, cogent piece of writing that serves the writer's thoughts on the issue of alternative energy quite well. It contains a clear perspective and sharp focus, from the mature and realistic introduction to the thought-provoking conclusion. It does an especially admirable job of outlining what" a realistic, considered approach" aligned with the writer's thoughts on tapering off from fossil fuels might look like.

Language Use and Conventions: Score = 6

This essay demonstrates an impressive command of standard language use and conventions, especially pertaining to argumentative writing. The grammar and mechanics are strong throughout, and a wide array of engaging sentences and transitions are displayed. The varied, thoughtful word choices and careful construction all lead to a thorough and effective essay that more than meets the task at hand.

English Test

1. A B C D	16. F G H J	31. A B C D	46. F G H J	61. A B C D
2. F G H J	17. A B C D	32. F G H J	47. A B C D	62. F G H J
3. A B C D	18. F G H J	33. A B C D	48. F G H J	63. A B C D
4. F G H J	19. A B C D	34. F G H J	49. A B C D	64. F G H J
5. A B C D	20. F G H J	35. A B C D	50. F G H J	65. A B C D
6. F G H J	21. A B C D	36. F G H J	51. A B C D	66. F G H J
7. A B C D	22. F G H J	37. A B C D	52. F G H J	67. A B C D
8. F G H J	23. A B C D	38. F G H J	53. A B C D	68. F G H J
9. A B C D	24. F G H J	39. A B C D	54. F G H J	69. A B C D
10. F G H J	25. A B C D	40. F G H J	55. A B C D	70. F G H J
11. A B C D	26. F G H J	41. A B C D	56. F G H J	71. A B C D
12. F G H J	27. A B C D	42. F G H J	57. A B C D	72. F G H J
13. A B C D	28. F G H J	43. A B C D	58. F G H J	73. A B C D
14. F G H J	29. A B C D	44. F G H J	59. A B C D	74. F G H J
15. A B C D	30. F G H J	45. A B C D	60. F G H J	75. A B C D

Mathematics Test

1. A B C D E	16. F G H J K	31. A B C D E	46. F G H J K
2. F G H J K	17. A B C D E	32. F G H J K	47. A B C D E
3. A B C D E	18. F G H J K	33. A B C D E	48. F G H J K
4. F G H J K	19. A B C D E	34. F G H J K	49. A B C D E
5. A B C D E	20. F G H J K	35. A B C D E	50. F G H J K
6. F G H J K	21. A B C D E	36. F G H J K	51. A B C D E
7. A B C D E	22. F G H J K	37. A B C D E	52. F G H J K
8. F G H J K	23. A B C D E	38. F G H J K	53. A B C D E
9. A B C D E	24. F G H J K	39. A B C D E	54. F G H J K
10. F G H J K	25. A B C D E	40. F G H J K	55. A B C D E
11. A B C D E	26. F G H J K	41. A B C D E	56. F G H J K
12. F G H J K	27. A B C D E	42. F G H J K	57. A B C D E
13. A B C D E	28. F G H J K	43. A B C D E	58. F G H J K
14. F G H J K	29. A B C D E	44. F G H J K	59. A B C D E
15. A B C D E	30. F G H J K	45. A B C D E	60. F G H J K

Reading Test

1. Ⓐ Ⓑ Ⓒ Ⓓ	11. Ⓐ Ⓑ Ⓒ Ⓓ	21. Ⓐ Ⓑ Ⓒ Ⓓ	31. Ⓐ Ⓑ Ⓒ Ⓓ
2. Ⓕ Ⓖ Ⓗ Ⓙ	12. Ⓕ Ⓖ Ⓗ Ⓙ	22. Ⓕ Ⓖ Ⓗ Ⓙ	32. Ⓕ Ⓖ Ⓗ Ⓙ
3. Ⓐ Ⓑ Ⓒ Ⓓ	13. Ⓐ Ⓑ Ⓒ Ⓓ	23. Ⓐ Ⓑ Ⓒ Ⓓ	33. Ⓐ Ⓑ Ⓒ Ⓓ
4. Ⓕ Ⓖ Ⓗ Ⓙ	14. Ⓕ Ⓖ Ⓗ Ⓙ	24. Ⓕ Ⓖ Ⓗ Ⓙ	34. Ⓕ Ⓖ Ⓗ Ⓙ
5. Ⓐ Ⓑ Ⓒ Ⓓ	15. Ⓐ Ⓑ Ⓒ Ⓓ	25. Ⓐ Ⓑ Ⓒ Ⓓ	35. Ⓐ Ⓑ Ⓒ Ⓓ
6. Ⓕ Ⓖ Ⓗ Ⓙ	16. Ⓕ Ⓖ Ⓗ Ⓙ	26. Ⓕ Ⓖ Ⓗ Ⓙ	36. Ⓕ Ⓖ Ⓗ Ⓙ
7. Ⓐ Ⓑ Ⓒ Ⓓ	17. Ⓐ Ⓑ Ⓒ Ⓓ	27. Ⓐ Ⓑ Ⓒ Ⓓ	37. Ⓐ Ⓑ Ⓒ Ⓓ
8. Ⓕ Ⓖ Ⓗ Ⓙ	18. Ⓕ Ⓖ Ⓗ Ⓙ	28. Ⓕ Ⓖ Ⓗ Ⓙ	38. Ⓕ Ⓖ Ⓗ Ⓙ
9. Ⓐ Ⓑ Ⓒ Ⓓ	19. Ⓐ Ⓑ Ⓒ Ⓓ	29. Ⓐ Ⓑ Ⓒ Ⓓ	39. Ⓐ Ⓑ Ⓒ Ⓓ
10. Ⓕ Ⓖ Ⓗ Ⓙ	20. Ⓕ Ⓖ Ⓗ Ⓙ	30. Ⓕ Ⓖ Ⓗ Ⓙ	40. Ⓕ Ⓖ Ⓗ Ⓙ

Science Test

1. Ⓐ Ⓑ Ⓒ Ⓓ	11. Ⓐ Ⓑ Ⓒ Ⓓ	21. Ⓐ Ⓑ Ⓒ Ⓓ	31. Ⓐ Ⓑ Ⓒ Ⓓ
2. Ⓕ Ⓖ Ⓗ Ⓙ	12. Ⓕ Ⓖ Ⓗ Ⓙ	22. Ⓕ Ⓖ Ⓗ Ⓙ	32. Ⓕ Ⓖ Ⓗ Ⓙ
3. Ⓐ Ⓑ Ⓒ Ⓓ	13. Ⓐ Ⓑ Ⓒ Ⓓ	23. Ⓐ Ⓑ Ⓒ Ⓓ	33. Ⓐ Ⓑ Ⓒ Ⓓ
4. Ⓕ Ⓖ Ⓗ Ⓙ	14. Ⓕ Ⓖ Ⓗ Ⓙ	24. Ⓕ Ⓖ Ⓗ Ⓙ	34. Ⓕ Ⓖ Ⓗ Ⓙ
5. Ⓐ Ⓑ Ⓒ Ⓓ	15. Ⓐ Ⓑ Ⓒ Ⓓ	25. Ⓐ Ⓑ Ⓒ Ⓓ	35. Ⓐ Ⓑ Ⓒ Ⓓ
6. Ⓕ Ⓖ Ⓗ Ⓙ	16. Ⓕ Ⓖ Ⓗ Ⓙ	26. Ⓕ Ⓖ Ⓗ Ⓙ	36. Ⓕ Ⓖ Ⓗ Ⓙ
7. Ⓐ Ⓑ Ⓒ Ⓓ	17. Ⓐ Ⓑ Ⓒ Ⓓ	27. Ⓐ Ⓑ Ⓒ Ⓓ	37. Ⓐ Ⓑ Ⓒ Ⓓ
8. Ⓕ Ⓖ Ⓗ Ⓙ	18. Ⓕ Ⓖ Ⓗ Ⓙ	28. Ⓕ Ⓖ Ⓗ Ⓙ	38. Ⓕ Ⓖ Ⓗ Ⓙ
9. Ⓐ Ⓑ Ⓒ Ⓓ	19. Ⓐ Ⓑ Ⓒ Ⓓ	29. Ⓐ Ⓑ Ⓒ Ⓓ	39. Ⓐ Ⓑ Ⓒ Ⓓ
10. Ⓕ Ⓖ Ⓗ Ⓙ	20. Ⓕ Ⓖ Ⓗ Ⓙ	30. Ⓕ Ⓖ Ⓗ Ⓙ	40. Ⓕ Ⓖ Ⓗ Ⓙ

WRITING TEST

Plan Your Essay

Write Your Essay

ENGLISH TEST

45 Minutes—75 Questions

DIRECTIONS: In this section, you will see passages with words and phrases that are underlined and numbered. In the right-hand column you will see a question corresponding to each number that provides alternatives to the underlined part. In most of the items, you are to choose the best alternative. If no change is needed, choose NO CHANGE.

In other items, there will be either a question about an underlined portion of the passage, or a question about a section of the passage, or about the passage as a whole. This question type will correspond to a number or numbers in a box.

For each question, choose the best alternative or answer and fill in the corresponding circle on the answer sheet.

PASSAGE I

Vaudeville

[1]

Ask people if they have ever heard of vaudeville, and most of them will have no idea what the word even means. However, around 100 years ago, vaudeville was the, most popular form, of [1] entertainment in the United States. Between the years 1875 and 1932, it was vaudeville bringing laughter and joy throughout the country to millions of people. [2]

[2]

The fact that vaudeville had something for everyone led to its wonderful a peel. [3]

Each show featured jugglers horseback riders; musicians and puppeteers [4] to entertain the crowd.

1. A. NO CHANGE
   B. the most popular form of
   C. the most, popular, form of
   D. the most. Popular form of

2. F. NO CHANGE
   G. vaudeville brought laughter and joy to millions of people throughout the country.
   H. it was vaudeville that brought laughter and joy throughout the country to millions of people.
   J. vaudeville was bringing laughter and joy to people throughout the country in the millions.

3. A. NO CHANGE
   B. a pile
   C. appeal
   D. apple

4. F. NO CHANGE
   G. jugglers horseback; riders musicians; and puppeteers
   H. jugglers, horseback riders, musicians, and puppeteers
   J. jugglers, horseback; riders; musicians, and puppeteers

CONTINUE

The audience would laugh at the clowns and comedians, joining the singers in song, and in amazement of the magic tricks and acrobats. [5] Since acts like magic, mime, and dancing required little

5. **A.** NO CHANGE
B. The audience would laugh at the clowns and comedians, join the singers in song, and watch the magic tricks and acrobats in amazement.
C. The audience would laugh at the clowns and comedians, join the singers in song, and being amazed by the magic tricks and acrobats.
D. The audience would have laughed at the clowns and comedians, joining the singers in song, and be amazed by the magic tricks and acrobats.

to no verbal communication or speaking, [6] many of the new immigrants to this country did not need to speak English to join in the fun. In addition, tickets to vaudeville shows were relatively

6. **F.** NO CHANGE
G. verbal communication, or speaking
H. verbal communication or speech,
J. verbal communication,

inexpensive. Making [7] it possible for people with limited means

7. **A.** NO CHANGE
B. inexpensive, this made
C. inexpensive, making
D. inexpensive, yet making

to purchase them. Another reason for vaudeville's popularity will be [8] the family-oriented nature of the acts. Vulgarity was not

8. **F.** NO CHANGE
G. was
H. is
J. will never be

allowed, so when parents took their children, we could [9] enjoy the show without worrying about exposing them to improper language or behavior.

9. **A.** NO CHANGE
B. he or she could
C. they could
D. one could

[3]

[10] The word *vaudeville* comes from the French phrase *voix de ville*, or "voices of the town." In France, people would gather in the valleys to amuse each other with song and dance. Gradually, vaudeville spread to America, into the saloons of the wild west.

10. Which of the following sentences offers the best introduction to Paragraph 3?
F. The French language has given us many words commonly used in English.
G. People have always enjoyed singing and dancing.
H. The origins of vaudeville can be traced to Europe.
J. Historians have different theories about the origins of vaudeville.

There, performers delighted the audience with acts like singing and rope spinning. As the acts became mostly creative [11] and

11. **A.** NO CHANGE
B. mostly creative
C. more creative
D. overly creative

diverse, they attracted a wider audience (12) and businesspeople began opening theaters all over the country. Rapidly growing in popularity, businesspeople began opening theaters all over the country. When vaudeville reached its peak in the 1920s, there were over 600 theaters showcasing 60,000 acts.

[4]

[1] W. C. Fields, Ethel Merman, and Will Rogers are just a few examples of performers who achieved celebrity status. [2] Some performers gained fame and stardom on the vaudeville stage. [3] Other famous vaudevillians include the Marx Brothers and Sarah Bernhardt. [13]

[5]

Despite its immense success, vaudeville would not last forever. The Great Depression as well as technological advances like the radio and movies contributed to the demise of a great form of entertainment.

12. If the writer were to delete the underlined portion, the sentence would primarily lose:

F. an explanation of who was attending the vaudeville shows.

G. an explanation of why businesspeople began opening more vaudeville theaters.

H. an explanation of why the vaudeville shows were attracting wider audiences.

J. an explanation of how much the audience for vaudeville shows grew.

13. Which of the following sequences of sentences makes Paragraph 4 most logical?

A. NO CHANGE

B. 3, 1, 2

C. 2, 3, 1

D. 2, 1, 3

Questions 14 and 15 ask about the essay as a whole.

14. For the sake of the unity and coherence of this essay, Paragraph 3 should be placed:

F. where it is now.

G. after Paragraph 4.

H. before Paragraph 1.

J. after Paragraph 1.

15. Suppose the author wanted to write an essay to convince readers that modern movie theaters should be replaced by vaudeville theaters. Which paragraph in the essay would offer the best support for his argument? Follow the original order of the paragraphs.

A. Paragraph 1

B. Paragraph 2

C. Paragraph 3

D. Paragraph 4

CONTINUE

PASSAGE II

The Huang He Flood

[1]

Rivers are an essential natural resource to human life. [16] They provide fish, water for drinking and farming, and a means of transportation. Unfortunately, rivers can also be a source of destruction. The Huang He, which flows through China [17] has brought both life and death to the people of the region.

[2]

The Huang He cuts a meandering path across the North China Plain. Also known as the Yellow River, it gets its [18] name from the yellow mud that coats the riverbed. For centuries it is being [19] a vital part of Chinese life. [20] The Huang He has an unfortunate propensity for flooding, bursting its banks an average of two years in every three and washing away entire villages with their [21] raging floodwaters. The flood in the summer of 1935 was

16. **F.** NO CHANGE
G. Rivers are to human life an essential natural resource.
H. Rivers are an essential resource natural to human life.
J. Rivers are a natural resource essential to human life.

17. **A.** NO CHANGE
B. Huang He which flows through China,
C. Huang He that flows through China
D. Huang He, which flows through China,

18. **F.** NO CHANGE
G. get's it's
H. get's its
J. gets it's

19. **A.** NO CHANGE
B. it be
C. it has been
D. it is

20. At this point, the writer would like to add a sentence to Paragraph 2. Which of the following choices would provide the best transition between these two sentences?

F. It has helped to sustain the people, but it has demanded a heavy price.
G. The river deposits fertile mud each time it floods the nearby lowlands.
H. It has been a valuable natural resource for the Chinese people.
J. It is about 3,000 miles long, and its receding floodwaters have caused it to change course numerous times in the last few thousand years.

21. **A.** NO CHANGE
B. they're
C. them
D. its

devastating, which caused enormous suffering for the villagers flooded out of their homes.
22

[3]

In that tragic summer, the villagers and farmers who resided along the river had endured a long drought. Their crops, which included sweet potatoes, corn, wheat, and cucumbers, were in serious need of rain. With their crops and lives in jeopardy, they were content when the long-awaited rain finally arrived. However, the rain turned into a torrential downpour. Some areas received 20 inches of rain in two days, more than some parts of the world receive for the period of an entire year. The river swelled to dangerously high levels, threatening to overflow the dikes along the riverbank.
23 24 25

[4]

The villagers working desperately to raise the dikes, the farms and houses in the fields below were on the verge of disaster.
26

They reinforced the dikes with rocks and kaoling stalks. Sadly, this did not prevent the Huang He from bursting its banks and
27

22. **F.** NO CHANGE
G. devastating and caused
H. devastating that caused
J. devastating, and which caused

23. **A.** NO CHANGE
B. whom
C. which
D. whose

24. **F.** NO CHANGE
G. satisfied
H. pleased
J. elated

25. **A.** NO CHANGE
B. the duration of
C. the length of
D. OMIT the underlined portion.

26. **F.** NO CHANGE
G. The villagers were working desperately to raise the dikes, the farms and houses in the fields below were on the verge of disaster.
H. The villagers worked desperately to raise the dikes and save the farms and houses in the fields below.
J. The villagers worked desperately to raise the dikes and the farms and houses in the fields below.

27. Kaoling is a plant similar to sugarcane. Would it be good strategy for the writer to define this word in the passage?
A. Yes, because the writer defines other unfamiliar words in the passage.
B. Yes, because defining a word unfamiliar to most readers would enhance the readers' understanding of the sentence.
C. No, because this passage is not about kaoling or sugarcane.
D. No, because most readers will know what *kaoling* means.

CONTINUE

rushing down in explosive and deadly power. The valley below was washed away in floodwaters that like Niagara Falls swelled to six times the volume. (28) The river flooded 6,000 square miles of land. The results were disastrous.

[5]

Thousands of people drowned. Some were lucky and were able to flee in small boats. Others managed to climb to the roofs of the more stable buildings and wait for possible rescue. They suffered great hunger and thirst. Surrounded by floodwater, they were unable to drink from it because it contained sewage and the corpses of people who had been unable to escape. The situation turned even more tragic, as hundreds of thousands died from the famine that followed. The villagers were also beset by outbreaks of cholera and the bubonic plague. An earlier catastrophic flood occurred when the Huang He burst its banks in 1887, resulting in the deaths of possibly a million people. [29]

[6]

It is little wonder that the Huang He has earned the nickname "China's Sorrow." It is a river of life, but it is also a river of tears.

28.
- **F.** NO CHANGE
- **G.** floodwaters, which like Niagara Falls swelled to six times the volume.
- **H.** floodwaters that swelled to six times the volume of Niagara Falls.
- **J.** floodwaters that swelled to six times the volume, like Niagara Falls.

29. In Paragraph 5, should the final sentence be kept or eliminated?
- **A.** Kept, because the passage is about floods.
- **B.** Kept, because it is an interesting detail.
- **C.** Eliminated, because the flood of 1887 is not a focus of this paragraph or the passage.
- **D.** Eliminated, because it happened too long ago to be historically important or relevant.

Question 30 asks about the passage as a whole.

30. Which of the following statements most effectively summarizes the passage as a whole?
- **F.** The Huang He floods the river valley along its banks every two out of three years.
- **G.** The Huang He Flood of 1935 caused massive devastation throughout the river valley.
- **H.** The villagers' failure to build stronger dikes left them vulnerable to the disastrous flood of 1935.
- **J.** The Huang He has brought both life and death to villagers of the river valley.

PASSAGE III

Buyer Beware

[1]

The items that we purchase can be placed into different categories. Some items we buy are *insignificant*, and these are (31) the things we need to have, like groceríe's (32) or clothing. Other items we buy are *indulgences*, like movie tickets or hot fudge sundaes. There are also things that we buy that can be classified as *investments*; stocks-bonds-and precious metals (33) can be placed in this category.

[2]

Then there's the other category of purchases that I recently had an experience with, one that I have affectionately dubbed *mistakes*—if yore lucky (34), you'll have little or no experience with throwing your money away in this category, although if you do, make sure it's a real learning experience for you!

[3]

[35] I was lying in bed and just couldn't seem to fall asleep for some reason, despite being tired, which, in retrospect, might have led to my lapse in judgment and poor decision making. I thought that watching a little television might make me sleepy, so I turned it on and started flipping through the channels.

31. **A.** NO CHANGE
B. essential
C. inconsequential
D. delicious

32. **F.** NO CHANGE
G. grocery
H. groceries
J. grocerys

33. **A.** NO CHANGE
B. (stocks bonds and precious metals)
C. stocks*bonds*and precious metals
D. stocks, bonds, and precious metals

34. **F.** NO CHANGE
G. you're lucky
H. your lucky
J. youre lucky

35. The author of the passage would like to add an introductory sentence to Paragraph 3. Which of the following sentences would serve as an effective introductory sentence here?

A. I quickly fell into a blissful sleep.
B. I had horrible nightmares that I couldn't forget.
C. I remember the night clearly.
D. I prefer to sleep with a window open.

CONTINUE

[4]

Attention my, one channel in particular got caught[36]—it showed a lively fellow with a distinctive English accent talking enthusiastically about a new miracle product that I've never heard of—and couldn't believe existed. It was called Confidence in a Can, and it was being touted as an easy and effective way to build your personal confidence with just a few quick sprays. Amazing!

36. **F.** NO CHANGE
G. My attention was caught by one channel in particular
H. One channel—my attention—got in particular caught
J. In particular, one my channel got caught on attention

[5]

Admittedly, at first I was a bit skeptical, but the charisma and energy of the guy selling it was hard to resist. And like I said earlier, I was tired and my resolve was already weak. I was curious to hear more, so I kept watching. Before long, a parade of happy and satisfied customers began endorsing[37] Confidence in a Can, with stories of how the product completely changed their lives for the better. Who could argue with that?

37. **A.** NO CHANGE
B. entering
C. enraging
D. enveloping

[6]

After everything I heard and saw, I was interested, but still hadn't decided whether or not I was going to make a purchase. Of course, I was interested in boosting my confidence and knew that if this can actually worked, it would help me be more successful at work and in my relationships with the people in my life. Who wouldn't want that? And then, when the host said that if I called the toll-free number right now I could have not one but *two* full cans of Confidence in a Can for one low discount price—that was all I'm needing (38) to hear! [39]

[7]

I tore off the packaging as fast as I could and wrapped my eager hands around one of the cans. It felt cool and light, and I read the instructions.

[8]

The next several days for me was just a waiting game until my new canned confidence arrived in the mail. Each day when I got home from work I raced to the mailbox to see if it had finally arrived. Eventually, after several days of anxious nail biting, the package arrived, and I couldn't be more excited.

[9]

"Hold 6 inches away from your body and spray liberally for 5 seconds." I happily complied.

[10]

Admittedly, it smelled strange, and not in a good way, but I didn't care—as long as it worked! I let the spray set in for 10 minutes, as the directions suggested, and raced out of my front door, eager to share my newfound confidence with the world. I went to buy a coffee at the shop near my house. I didn't notice an immediate effect, but maybe it needed more time. However, (40) I went to my friend Jackie's house for a visit. But not only did I

38. **F.** NO CHANGE
G. I need
H. I will be needing
J. I needed

39. Which of the following true statements would provide the best transition from the preceding paragraph to this paragraph?

A. I was impressed by how convincing the host was
B. The whole concept of Confidence in a Can seemed ridiculous.
C. I pulled out my phone and made an order.
D. The offer could only have been better if it was for three cans.

40. **F.** NO CHANGE
G. So
H. Nevertheless
J. In other words

CONTINUE

not feel more confident, my friend Jackie said (You're acting weird and you smell terrible!) [41] [42]

[11]

I thought I'd give it one more try at work tomorrow, but when my boss called me into his office and said that he heard many people mention that I was acting odd and emitted an odd aroma, I knew that I made a bad purchase. My Confidence in a Can quickly became trash and I learned a valuable lesson. [43]

41. **A.** NO CHANGE
B. *You're acting weird and you smell terrible!*
C. You're acting weird and you smell terrible!
D. "You're acting weird and you smell terrible!"

42. For essay clarity, the most effective organizational flow for paragraphs 7, 8, 9, and 10 should be which of the following?

F. 7, 8, 9, 10
G. 8, 7, 9, 10
H. 9, 8, 7, 10
J. 10, 9, 8, 7

43. The author would like to add a final sentence to this essay that captures what he's learned from this experience. Based on the information provided in the passage, which of the following would be the most effective concluding sentence?

A. You should never make any risky purchasing decisions when you're tired!
B. Nothing that's sold in a can ever works!
C. You should never rely too much on confidence to help you achieve your goals!
D. Some products take more than just a few days to start working properly!

Questions 44 and 45 ask about the passage as a whole.

44. The author of the passage is thinking of deleting the first paragraph in an effort to make the piece shorter and meet his assignment guidelines. Do you recommend this approach?

F. No, because the first paragraph contains information essential for following the story.
G. No, because paragraph 3 would be a better choice to cut from the passage.
H. Yes, because the passage is definitely too long as it currently is.
J. Yes, because readers don't need the information presented in this paragraph.

45. What writing genre does this passage best fit into?

A. Humor
B. Mystery
C. Current events
D. Business

PASSAGE IV

The Sport of Rowing

[1]

Have you ever wondered what it would be like to glide silently across the water, using only your muscles but not an engine or sail to power your travel 46? Thousands, in fact millions, of rowers worldwide experience this feeling every day as they train on their local rivers. Rowing is such a popular sport that there are now clubs in cities and towns across the globe. 47

46. **F.** NO CHANGE
G. using only your muscles, not an engine or sail, to power your travel
H. using only your muscles, and not an engine or sail to power your travel
J. using only your muscles, but not an engine, or sail to power your travel

47. **A.** NO CHANGE
B. Rowing is such a popular sport, because there are now clubs in countless cities and towns across the globe.
C. Rowing is such a popular sport, that there are now, rowing clubs in cities and towns across the globe.
D. Rowing is such a popular sport. There are now rowing clubs in cities and towns across the globe.

[2]

Its not as effortless is 48 it looks. The best athletes make it look easy, but in reality it takes an intense coordinated effort of body and mind 49 to propel a rowing shell over the surface of the water. When rowing in a team boat, the athletes must mimic 50 the exact movements of their teammates, right down to their breathing at times. If they become unsynchronized, you see, even for a moment 51, the boat will lose crucial speed necessary to thrust the boat through the water.

48. **F.** NO CHANGE
G. of
H. as
J. or

49. **A.** NO CHANGE
B. body of mind
C. body but mind
D. body and mind

50. **F.** NO CHANGE
G. When rowing together in a team boat; rowers must mimic
H. When rowing together in a team boat. Rowers must mimic
J. When rowing together in a team boat and rowers must mimic

51. **A.** NO CHANGE
B. If they become unsynchronized, consequently, even for a moment
C. If they become unsynchronized, just a bit, even for a moment
D. If they become unsynchronized, even for a moment

CONTINUE

[3]

Lost speed is not something rowers want to happen to their boat (52), especially when racing. Sometimes, (53) races are won or lost by thousandths of a second, which can be devastating for a team that trains as hard as elite rowers usually do. They often train on the water two times a day (morning and night) and spend hours in the weight room additionally (54) the time they spend on the water.

[4]

Races, which are usually 2,000 meters in length, only last for about 6 to 8 minutes, depending on the size of the boat and wind conditions. Often rowers will train thousands of hours a year for one inconsequential (55) race, such as the World Championships. These are (56) a lot of training for such a short race! [57] Dedicated rowers, however, will tell you that the sacrifice is well worth having the chance to win a national or even Olympic medal one day.

52. **F.** NO CHANGE
G. Losing speed is not something rowers want happening to their boat
H. Losing speed (is not something rowers want) happening to their boat
J. To lose speed is not something that should have happened to their boat

53. **A.** NO CHANGE
B. Conversely,
C. Instead,
D. However,

54. **F.** NO CHANGE
G. in addition to
H. because of
J. since

55. **A.** NO CHANGE
B. important
C. imperfect
D. illegitimate

56. **F.** NO CHANGE
G. That
H. That been
J. That is

57. At this point in the essay, the author is considering the addition of the following sentence:

There are a few long-distance races that measure approximately 3.5 miles and are raced in a "chase" fashion with each boat starting in 10-second intervals.

Would this be a logical and relevant addition to the essay?

A. Yes, because it serves to further explain the types of races in which rowers participate.
B. Yes, because it serves to establish the main point of this paragraph.
C. No, because this paragraph is discussing only the World Championships for which rowers train many hours.
D. No, because it does not serve to emphasize the difference in the amount of training relative to the length of the races.

[5]

You may be watching a past, present, or future Olympian. Or perhaps you will see someone who just loves to spend his or her morning on the river, enjoying the sport of rowing.

58. How can the author best combine these two sentences?
   - F. future Olympian, or perhaps
   - G. future Olympian: or perhaps
   - H. future Olympian and perhaps
   - J. future Olympian so perhaps

Questions 59 and 60 ask about the passage as a whole.

59. The writer wants to add the following sentence to the essay:

   The next time you travel near a river, be sure to notice any long, skinny boats skimming lightly atop the water, silently propelled by these well-trained athletes.

   The sentence would most logically be placed at the beginning of:
   - A. Paragraph 1.
   - B. Paragraph 2.
   - C. Paragraph 3.
   - D. Paragraph 5.

60. Suppose the author had been assigned to write a brief essay detailing the technical aspects of the training and performance of elite rowers. Would this essay successfully fulfill the requirement?
   - F. No, because the essay does not discuss any training or performance techniques in detail.
   - G. No, because the essay suggests that rowing is not a sport that requires much training or technique.
   - H. Yes, because the essay describes the length and time of rowing races.
   - J. Yes, because the essay tells us in great detail-about the weight-room training schedule of elite rowers.

PASSAGE V

A New Link Between Saturated Fats and Alzheimer's Disease

[1]

Recent studies seem to indicate that (61) a diet high in fat is somehow linked to the onset of Alzheimer's disease and dementia.

61. A. NO CHANGE
   B. for
   C. in
   D. how

A recent article in the *Archives of Neurology* cite (62) experiments that show how sticking to a diet rich in "good fats"—fats found in

62. F. NO CHANGE
   G. citation
   H. citing
   J. cites

CONTINUE

nuts, fatty fish, and vegetable oils—seems to lower the risk of mental disease. "Bad fats," otherwise known as saturated fats, seem to increase the risk. It was interesting that, the (63) new studies point out that antioxidant vitamins, once touted as possessing curative effects for Alzheimer's and dementia, now seem to be ineffective.

63. A. NO CHANGE
B. In a bit of interest, the
C. Interestingly enough, the
D. Enough to be interesting, the

[2]

The new studies seem to make a profound discovery saturated fats and cholesterol (64) are detrimental to overall brain functions. In one study, scientists assembled a group of 815 senior citizens who reported no signs of deteriorated mental condition.

64. F. NO CHANGE
G. a profound discovery: saturated fats and cholesterol
H. a profound discovery with saturated fats and cholesterol
J. a profound discovery saturating fats and cholesterol

Each member of the group was asked to list the foods it (65) ate regularly. Two years later, each was asked again to list the foods

65. A. NO CHANGE
B. he or she
C. that they
D. that was

eaten on a regular basis. Then, for a period of four years followed the second (66) test, the research team tracked the health of each member of the group. By the end of the observation period, 131 seniors had developed Alzheimer's.

66. F. NO CHANGE
G. that following the second
H. following the second
J. follow did the second

[3]

The data collected from this experiment showed that the seniors who had reported eating more saturated and hydrogenated fats from foods such as (67) red meat, fried foods, and packaged

67. A. NO CHANGE
B. like
C. with
D. because

goods such as cookies, chips, and cakes were more than double (68) as likely to develop Alzheimer's. Those who had recorded salmon, tuna, fruits, avocados, nuts, and grains as their favorite foods carried less of a risk for dementia. These foods are rich in polyunsaturated and monounsaturated fats.

68. F. NO CHANGE
G. over double
H. more than twice
J. plus more than twice

[4]

A second experiment attacks a very popular and long-upheld medical theory. Many researchers have gone on record in supporting the notion that unstable compounds in the bloodstream, called "free radicals," are responsible for damaging nerve cells and causing the onset of dementia. Traditionally, vitamins such as C, E, and beta carotene has been singled out as agents that can reduce the risk of free-radical damage within the human system.

(Underlined: "attacks" = 69; "in supporting the notion that" = 70; "has" = 71)

[5]

[1] During that time, 242 people developed Alzheimer's. [2] Researchers tracked the eating habits of 980 elderly people —none of whom displayed dementia symptoms—for four years. [3] Lead researcher Jose A. Luchsinger, an associate at Columbia University in New York City, wrote: "Neither dietary, supplemental, nor intake of carotenes and vitamins C and E was associated with a decreased risk." [4] No link could be found between the afflicted people's dietary supplement intake and the prevention of disease. [73]

(Underlined: "Researchers tracked the eating habits of 980 elderly people —none of whom displayed dementia symptoms—for four years." = 72)

69.
- **A.** NO CHANGE
- **B.** does an attack on
- **C.** will attack
- **D.** did attack

70.
- **F.** NO CHANGE
- **G.** to supporting the notion that
- **H.** to support the notion that
- **J.** with support for the notion which

71.
- **A.** NO CHANGE
- **B.** have
- **C.** are
- **D.** will be

72. In the sentence, the clause "none of whom displayed dementia symptoms" primarily serves to indicate:
- **F.** a consequential detail about the people in the study.
- **G.** why researchers were concerned about the people in the study.
- **H.** how dementia develops in people with no previous symptoms.
- **J.** when it is important to begin treatment for dementia.

73. Which of the following ordering of the sentences will make Paragraph 5 most logical?
- **A.** NO CHANGE
- **B.** 3, 4, 1, 2
- **C.** 1, 2, 4, 3
- **D.** 2, 1, 4, 3

CONTINUE

Questions 74 and 75 ask about the passage as a whole.

74. The writer wrote this piece in response to a school assignment. The assignment was to provide the reader with an overview of a recent scientific discovery. Was this objective accomplished?

F. No, because the author does not offer valuable details concerning food sources for antioxidant vitamins.
G. Yes, because the author outlines the findings of two new experiments, providing illustrations and details only as needed.
H. No, because the author makes no attempt to provide counterpoints to the information supposedly gleaned by the experiments.
J. Yes, because the author wisely references the work of Jose A. Luchsinger, a researcher from Columbia University.

75. After reading this article, readers should infer that in order to reduce their own risk of contracting Alzheimer's disease or dementia, they should:

A. increase their dosage of antioxidant vitamins.
B. maintain a diet rich in saturated fats rather than polyunsaturated and monounsaturated fats.
C. maintain a diet rich in polyunsaturated and monounsaturated fats rather than saturated fats.
D. remove antioxidant vitamins from their diet.

STOP

MATHEMATICS TEST

60 Minutes—60 Questions

DIRECTIONS: For each of the following items, solve each problem, choose the correct answer, and then fill in the corresponding circle on the answer sheet. If you encounter problems that take too much time to solve, move on. Solve as many problems as you can; then return to the others in the time remaining for the test.

You may use a calculator on this test for any problems you choose, but some of the problems may best be solved without the use of a calculator.

Note: Unless otherwise stated, assume the following:

1. Illustrative figures are NOT necessarily drawn to scale.
2. Geometric figures lie in a plane.
3. The word *line* indicates a straight line.
4. The word *average* indicates arithmetic mean.

SHOW YOUR WORK HERE

1. On the final project in Juan's art class, 14 students earned a grade of B. Those 14 students were exactly 20% of the total number of students in the class. How many students were in the class?

A. 28
B. 34
C. 56
D. 70
E. 84

2. Determine the x-intercept(s), if any, of the function $g(x)=4-|2x-16|$.

F. No x-intercepts
G. (8, 0)
H. (0, −12)
J. (10, 0)
K. (6, 0) and (10, 0)

3. If $1-\frac{3x}{2}=\frac{x+1}{6}$, what is the value of x^3?

A. $\frac{1}{8}$
B. $\frac{1}{2}$
C. $\frac{3}{2}$
D. 2
E. 8

CONTINUE

4. In the figure below, points G, H, and I are on the same line. What is the measure of $\angle GHK$?

SHOW YOUR WORK HERE

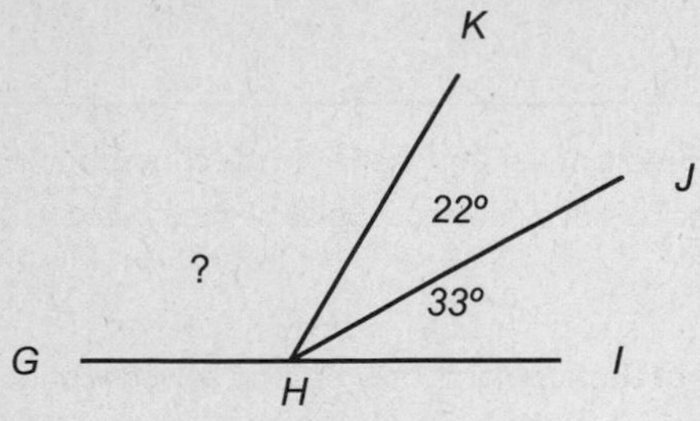

F. 35°
G. 55°
H. 75°
J. 125°
K. 147°

5. If $f(x) = 1 - 2^x$, which of the following equals $f(2x + 3)$?

A. $-5 - 4^x$
B. $1-8 \bullet 4^x$
C. $1 - 16^{2x}$
D. $1 - 32^x$
E. $-4^x - 9$

6. At a certain construction site, there is a pile containing 55 tons of sand. Four trucks, each of which holds 11.4 tons of sand, are filled from this pile. How many tons of sand remain in the pile?

F. 9.4
G. 20.8
H. 22.8
J. 43.6
K. 45.6

7. If $x = \frac{2}{3}$ and $y = \frac{1}{6}$, what is the value of $\frac{1}{\sqrt{x \bullet y}}$?

A. $\frac{1}{9}$
B. $\frac{1}{3}$
C. $\frac{1}{2}$
D. 3
E. 9

8. What is the value of $-3^2\left|-6-(-4)\right|$?

F. −90
G. −18
H. −12
J. 18
K. 90

9. Which of the following is the graph of $f(x) = 2 + (x + 3)^2$?

A.

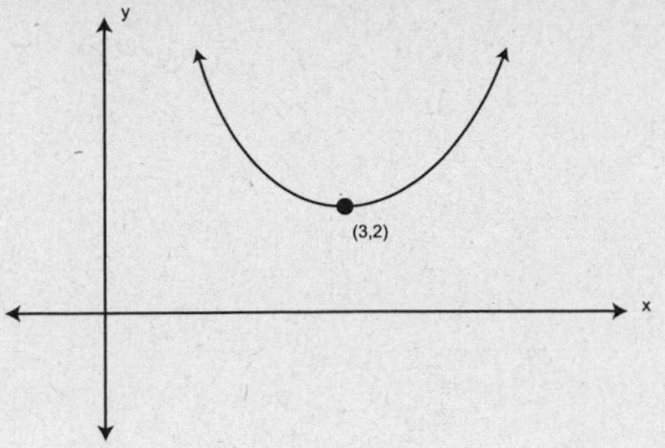

B.

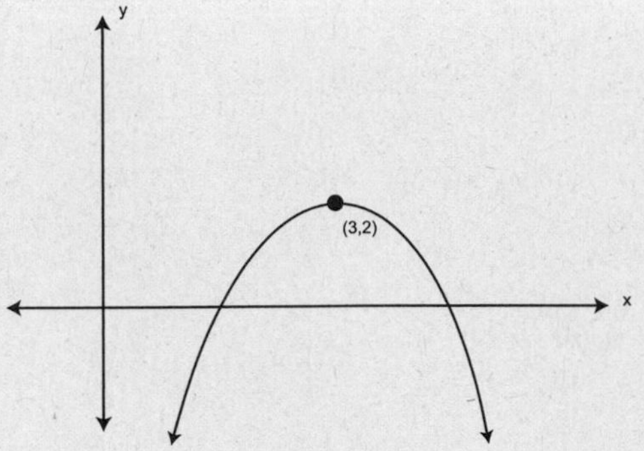

C.

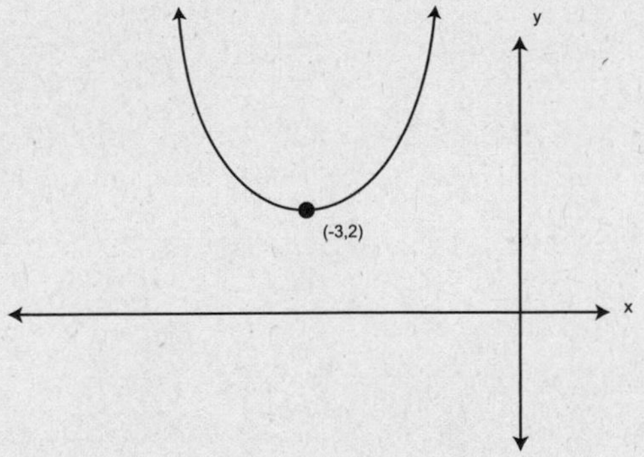

D.

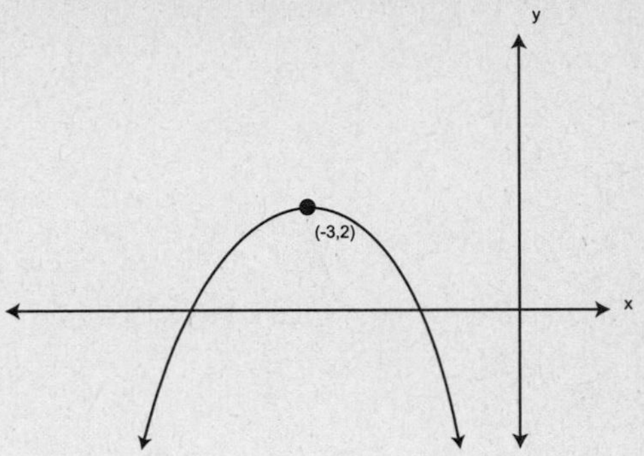

E.

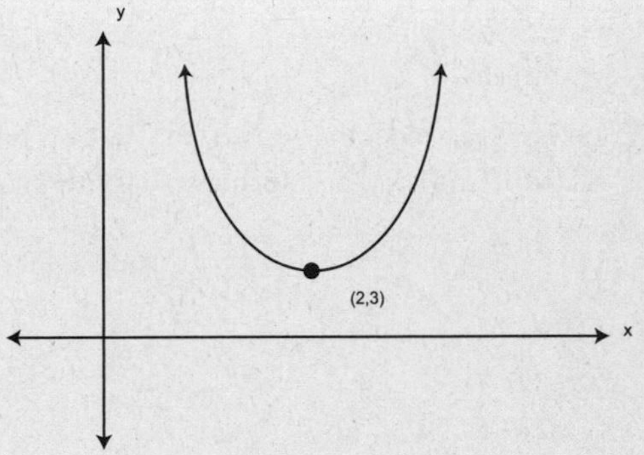

CONTINUE

10. If x is a real number such that $x^3 = 80$, between which two consecutive integers does x lie on the number line?

SHOW YOUR WORK HERE

- **F.** 2 and 3
- **G.** 3 and 4
- **H.** 4 and 5
- **J.** 5 and 6
- **K.** 6 and 7

11. If $2a - 38 = -26$, then what is the value of $3a$?

- **A.** −96
- **B.** −18
- **C.** 6
- **D.** 18
- **E.** 72

12. Joel is 8 years older than Karen, and Karen is twice as old as Lina. If Lina is x years old, how old is Joel in terms of x?

- **F.** $x + 8$
- **G.** $2x$
- **H.** $x - 8$
- **J.** $-2x$
- **K.** $2x + 8$

13. A rectangle is graphed in the standard (x, y) coordinate plane. Three of the rectangle's corners have coordinates (−4, 5), (2, 5), and (−4, −2). What are the coordinates of the fourth corner?

- **A.** (−5, 2)
- **B.** (4, −2)
- **C.** (−2, 2)
- **D.** (−4, 5)
- **E.** (2, −2)

14. To which of the following expressions is $2(4y - 3z) - 4(2z - 3y)$ equal?

- **F.** $5y - 11z$
- **G.** $20y - 14z$
- **H.** $6yz$
- **J.** $25yz$
- **K.** $-4y - 14z$

15. In the parallelogram below, what is the measure of $\angle WZY$?

SHOW YOUR WORK HERE

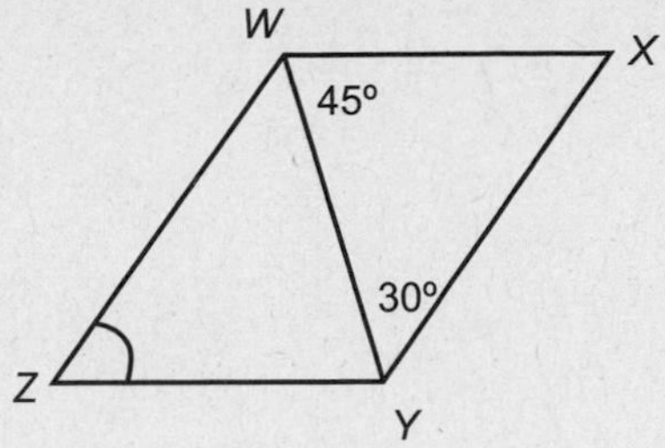

A. 55°
B. 75°
C. 90°
D. 105°
E. 115°

16. What is the x-intercept of the line $4y + 3x = 12$?

F. 3
G. 4
H. 9
J. 12
K. 15

17. What are the solutions of the equation $(3x + 1)^2 + 9 = 0$?

A. $x = -\frac{4}{3}$

B. $x = -\frac{4}{3}, x = \frac{2}{3}$

C. $x = -\frac{\sqrt{10}}{3}, x = \frac{\sqrt{10}}{3}$

D. $x = -\frac{1}{3} - i, x = -\frac{1}{3} + i$

E. $x = -\frac{i\sqrt{10}}{3}, x = \frac{i\sqrt{10}}{3}$

18. The perimeter of a rectangle is 60 units. If the width of the rectangle is 12 units, what is the area of the rectangle, in square units?

F. 18
G. 34
H. 216
J. 432
K. 576

CONTINUE

19. The discounted price of a framed print of a lunar landscape is $75.50. If this is a 30% reduction of the original price, what was the original price?

A. $\frac{75.50}{0.70}$ dollars

B. $\frac{75.50}{0.30}$ dollars

C. 0.70(75.50) dollars

D. 75.50 – 0.30(75.50) dollars

E. 75.50 + 0.70 dollars

20. Which of the following is equal to $(p^2q - 2pq^3)^2$?

F. $p^4q^2 + 4p^2q^6$

G. $p^4q^2 - 2p^3q^4 + 4p^2q^6$

H. $p^4q - 4p^2q^3 + 4pq^9$

J. $p^4q^2 - 4p^2q^6$

K. $p^4q^2 - 4p^3q^4 + 4p^2q^6$

21. If $x = 2y - 1$ and $y = 2x - 1$, what is the value of 3^{x+y}?

A. 1

B. 2

C. 6

D. 8

E. 9

22. At a certain store, a 7.5-pound bag of rice costs $4.80. What is the cost per ounce of rice? (There are 16 ounces in a pound.)

F. $0.02

G. $0.03

H. $0.04

J. $0.05

K. $0.15

23. On a certain farm, workers earn $23 per day, plus $0.74 per bushel filled. If a worker works 6 days and fills x bushels, which expression can be used to calculate the worker's total earnings?

A. $138x + 0.74x$

B. $138 + 0.74x$

C. $6(23 + 0.74x)$

D. $x(138 + 0.74)$

E. $138 + 4.44x$

SHOW YOUR WORK HERE

24. A garden needs to be covered with grass sod. The garden has the dimensions shown below. How many square feet of sod are required to cover the garden?

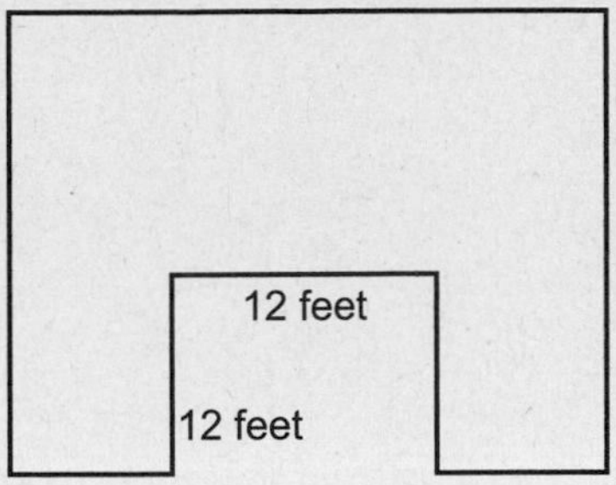

F. 656
G. 912
H. 984
J. 1,056
K. 1,200

25. If $f(x) = 2x - 6$, what is $f^{-1}\left(\frac{1}{2}\right)$?

A. -5

B. $-\frac{1}{5}$

C. $\frac{7}{2}$

D. $\frac{13}{4}$

E. $\frac{25}{4}$

26. Which of the following has the largest value?

F. $\sqrt{2}$
G. 36^0
H. 1^{200}
J. 3^{-2}
K. $\left(\frac{1}{4}\right)^3$

27. A right triangle has sides of length 15, 20, and 25 meters. What is the area of the triangle in square meters?

A. 60
B. 150
C. 250
D. 625
E. 7,500

SHOW YOUR WORK HERE

CONTINUE

28. A store displays all the AA batteries it has in a display case on a wall. The batteries can be displayed in three columns of equal height. The batteries can also be displayed in four, five, or six columns of equal height. What is the smallest number of batteries that the store can have?

F. 15

G. 30

H. 60

J. 180

K. 360

SHOW YOUR WORK HERE

29. Which of the following triples cannot be the lengths of the sides of a triangle?

A. 4, 4, 3

B. 3, 4, 5

C. 1, 1, 2

D. 5, 12, 14

E. 7, 8, 9

30. For all real numbers a and b for which $b \neq 0$, to which of the following is $\frac{a}{b} - \frac{a}{b^2}$ equal?

F. $-\frac{a}{b}$

G. $\frac{a(b-1)}{b^2}$

H. $\frac{ab^2 - a}{b^2}$

J. $-\frac{a^2}{b^3}$

K. 0

31. An amateur bowler keeps track of the number of times per game (in a series of 10 games) she makes a spare (that is, she clears all 10 pins in two rolls of the ball). Here is the data:

Table 1

Game	Number of Spares
1	2
2	4
3	0
4	2
5	1
6	1
7	0
8	4
9	4
10	3

What is the median number of spares that she made?

A. 1
B. 2
C. 2.1
D. 2.5
E. 4

32. The width and length of a rectangle are w yards and l yards long, respectively. If the width is increased by 30% and the length is decreased by 25%, what is the perimeter of the resulting rectangle?

F. $2l + 2w$ yards
G. $2l + 2w + 0.05$ yards
H. $2.6w + 1.5l$ yards
J. $60w + 50l$ yards
K. $1.30w + 0.75l$ yards

33. Suppose $\sin\theta = -\frac{\sqrt{3}}{2}$ and $\cos\theta = -\frac{1}{2}$. What is $\cot\theta$?

A. $-\frac{2\sqrt{3}}{3}$
B. -2
C. $\sqrt{3}$
D. $-\sqrt{3}$
E. $\frac{\sqrt{3}}{3}$

SHOW YOUR WORK HERE

CONTINUE

34. Which of the answer choices best describes the graph on the number line below?

SHOW YOUR WORK HERE

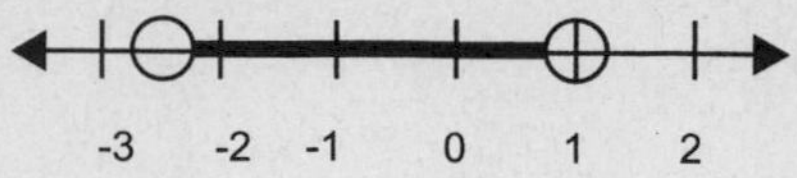

F. $1 > x > -2.5$
G. $1 < x < -2.5$
H. $-1 < x < 2.5$
J. $1 > |x| > -2.5$
K. $1 < |x| < -2.5$

35. A large group of food tasters was asked to sample and rate a new cheesecake recipe. They were to use a scale of 1 to 5. 10% of the tasters gave the recipe a rating of 4. 15% gave a rating of 3. Half the tasters, 50%, gave the recipe a rating of 2. And 25% gave the recipe a rating of 1. What was the average rating for the cheesecake recipe, rounded to the nearest tenth?

A. 2.0
B. 2.1
C. 2.2
D. 2.3
E. 2.4

36. *ABC* is an isosceles triangle. What is the measure of $\angle A$?

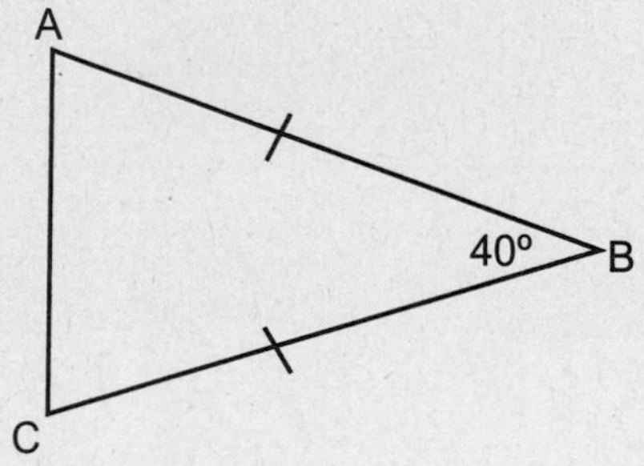

F. 40°
G. 60°
H. 70°
J. 100°
K. 140°

37. What is the smallest possible sum of 2 positive integers whose product is 36?

A. 9
B. 10
C. 12
D. 13
E. 15

38. In the figure below, lines *a* and *b* are parallel to each other, and lines *c* and *d* are parallel to each other. If the two angles have measures of 40° and 115°, as shown, what is the measure of angle *x*?

SHOW YOUR WORK HERE

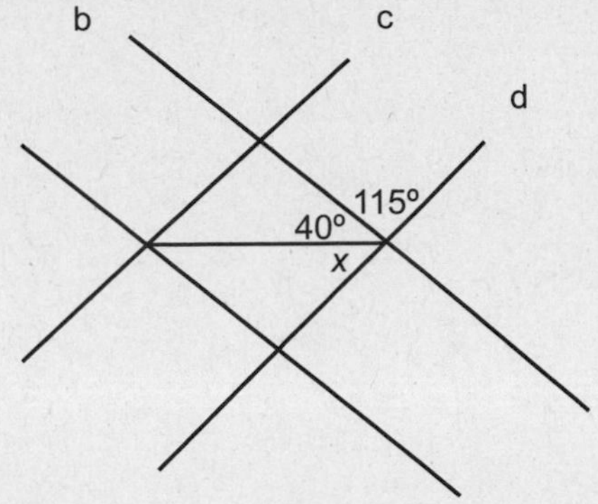

F. 25°
G. 35°
H. 50°
J. 65°
K. 75°

39. What is the slope of the line $3(2y - 4x) = 1$?

A. –12
B. –4
C. 2
D. 6
E. 12

40. Among the points on the number line below, which is closest to $\sqrt{6}$?

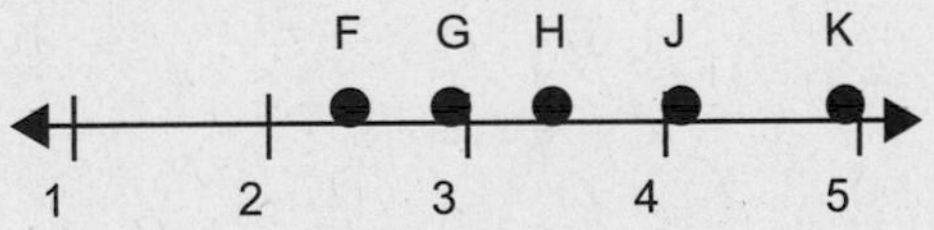

F. F
G. G
H. H
J. J
K. K

41. Angle *H* measures (180 – *x*) degrees. If angle *H* is an obtuse angle, which of the following is true of *x*?

A. $0 < x < 60$
B. $0 < x < 90$
C. $90 < x < 180$
D. $180 < x < 270$
E. $135 < x < 180$

CONTINUE

SHOW YOUR WORK HERE

42. To which of these expressions is $\frac{-x}{2-\frac{1}{2x}}$ equal?

F. $-2x^2$

G. $-\frac{2x}{3}$

H. $2x^2-\frac{x}{2}$

J. $\frac{2x^2}{1-4x}$

K. $-(4x-1)$

43. Let $f(x) = (2x + 1)^2 + 1$ and $g(x)=\sqrt{x-5}$. What are the x-intercept(s), if any, of $(g \circ f)(x)$?

A. $\left(-\frac{3}{2},0\right)$ and $\left(\frac{5}{2},0\right)$, $\left(\frac{3}{2},0\right)$

B. (5, 0)

C. (0, 2)

D. $\left(\frac{1}{2},0\right)$ and $\left(-\frac{3}{2},0\right)$

E. No x-intercepts

44. Starting at the point (3, –1), another point on a line can be obtained by going up 4 units and to the left 5 units. What is the y-intercept of the resulting line?

F. $-\frac{17}{5}$

G. $-\frac{4}{5}$

H. $\frac{7}{5}$

J. $\frac{7}{4}$

K. $\frac{12}{5}$

45. Two numbers have a greatest common factor of 6 and a least common multiple of 36. Which of the following could be the pair of numbers?

A. 6 and 12

B. 6 and 18

C. 12 and 18

D. 12 and 24

E. 18 and 24

46. The diameter of a circle is x inches. What is the area of a circle with triple the radius?

F. $3\pi x$ square inches

G. $\frac{9\pi}{4}x^2$ square inches

H. $\frac{3\pi}{4}x^2$ square inches

J. $9\pi x^2$ square inches

K. $\frac{\pi}{4}x^2$ square inches

SHOW YOUR WORK HERE

47. What is the slope of the line having x-intercept (–3, 0) and y-intercept (0, 5)?

A. –3

B. $-\frac{5}{3}$

C. $\frac{3}{5}$

D. $\frac{5}{3}$

E. 5

48. What is the area of the shaded region below, if the radius of the inner circle is 2.5 inches and the radius of the outer circle is 5 inches?

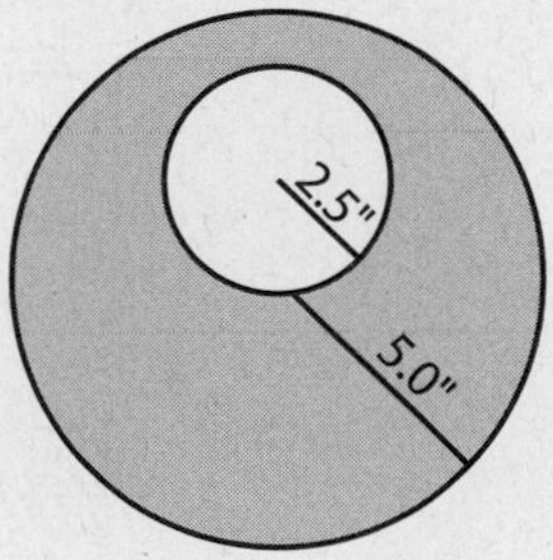

F. 1.5625π

G. 6.25π

H. 7.5π

J. 12.5π

K. 18.75π

CONTINUE

SHOW YOUR WORK HERE

49. Which of these is a solution of the system

$$\begin{cases} 2x-3y=1 \\ -6x+7=3y \end{cases}?$$

A. $x=3,\ y=\frac{5}{3}$

B. $x=1,\ y=\frac{1}{3}$

C. $x=4,\ y=-\frac{17}{3}$

D. $x=5, y=3$

E. $x=\frac{7}{6}, y=0$

50. Consider the graphs of $f(x)$ and $g(x)$ shown below:

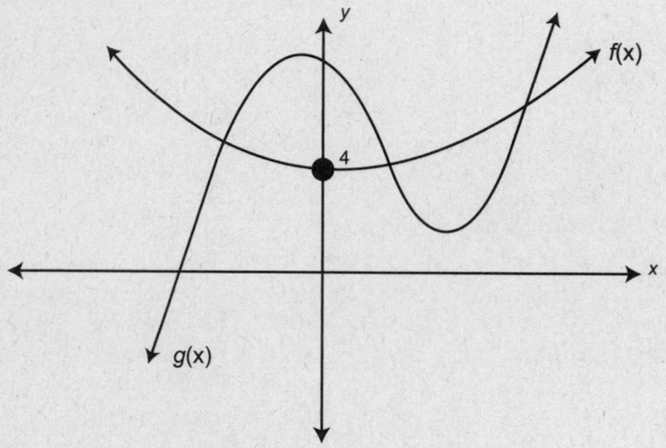

Which of the following statements is true?

F. The solution set of the inequality $f(x) - g(x) > 0$ is the empty set.

G. The solution set of the inequality $g(x) - f(x) > 0$ is the empty set.

H. The solution set of the inequality $f(x) > 4$ is the set of all real numbers.

J. The equation $f(x) - g(x) = 0$ has three solutions.

K. The equation $g(x) = -2$ has no solution.

51. What is the value of $\left(\frac{2x+1}{2x-1}\right)^{-2}$ if $x=\frac{2}{3}$?

A. -14

B. $\frac{14}{9}$

C. $\frac{1}{49}$

D. $\frac{81}{49}$

E. 49

52. The graph of the function $H(x)$ is shown below:

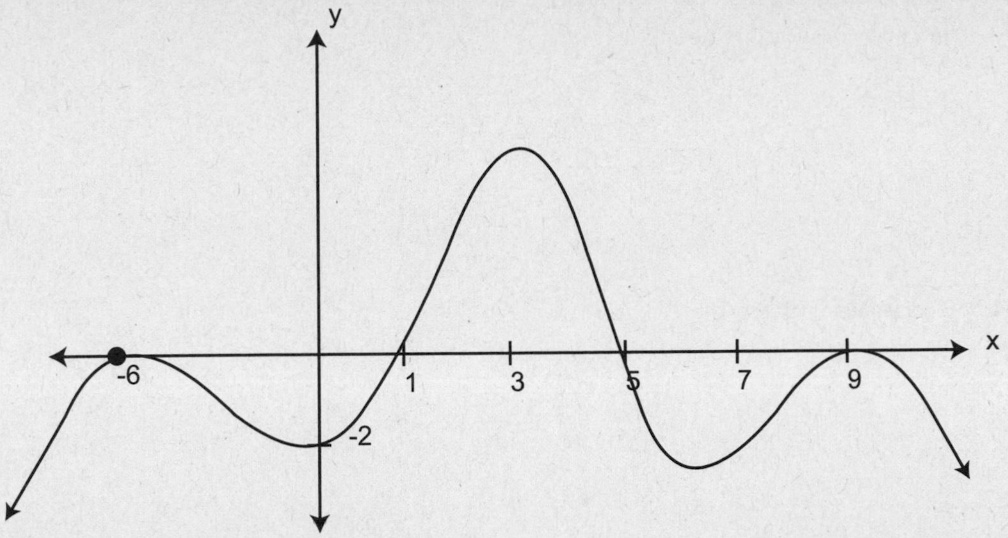

On what interval(s), if any, is $H(x)$ positive?

SHOW YOUR WORK HERE

F. $(-\infty,-6)\cup(0,3)\cup(7,9)$

G. $(-\infty,-6)\cup(-6,1)\cup(5,9)\cup(9,\infty)$

H. $(-6,0)\cup(3,7)\cup(9,\infty)$

J. $(1, 5)$

K. no such interval

53. A rectangle of length $(w + 6)$ inches and width $(w - 1)$ inches is shaded, except for a square region of side length $(w - 3)$ inches. What is the area of the shaded region, in terms of w?

A. $w^2 + 5w - 6$

B. $w^2 + 4w - 9$

C. $2w^2 + 11w + 3$

D. $11w - 15$

E. $-w - 7$

CONTINUE

54. If three jazz CDs are added to a box of only classical CDs, the probability of randomly drawing a classical CD from the box becomes $\frac{4}{5}$. How many classical CDs are in the box?

SHOW YOUR WORK HERE

F. 6
G. 9
H. 12
J. 15
K. 18

55. How many different integer values of x satisfy the inequality $\frac{1}{12} < \frac{2}{x} < \frac{1}{8}$?

A. 3
B. 4
C. 5
D. 6
E. 7

56. If a is a positive real number, what is the distance between the points $\left(\frac{1}{2}a, -\frac{1}{4}a\right)$ and $\left(-\frac{1}{4}a, -\frac{1}{2}a\right)$?

F. $\frac{\sqrt{10}}{4}a$

G. $\frac{\sqrt{2}}{2}a$

H. $\frac{5}{8}a^2$

J. $\frac{\sqrt{5}}{4}a$

K. $\sqrt{2}\,a$

57. What are the final coordinates of point P after a 180° rotation centered at point C?

SHOW YOUR WORK HERE

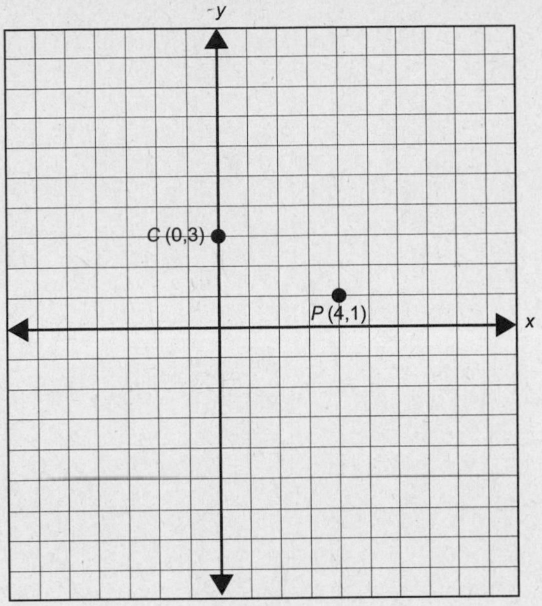

A. (–4, –1)
B. (2, 7)
C. (–2, –1)
D. (–4, 3)
E. (–4, 5)

58. A tin of candy contains three flavors. There are twice as many grape candies in a tin as there are cherry candies. There are three times as many lemon candies as grape candies. If a number of apple candies, equal to the number of cherry candies already in the tin, is added to the tin, what is the probability of randomly selecting a lemon candy from the tin?

F. $\frac{1}{20}$

G. $\frac{1}{10}$

H. $\frac{1}{5}$

J. $\frac{3}{5}$

K. $\frac{2}{3}$

CONTINUE

59. In order to set up loudspeakers for a conference room, the following amounts of wire are needed for each speaker:

2 wires at 15 feet each
4 wires at 3.5 feet each
2 wires at 8 inches each

If the room requires 9 speakers, and wire costs $0.031 per inch, approximately how much will it cost to set up the speakers for the room?

A. $112
B. $152
C. $168
D. $360
E. $544

SHOW YOUR WORK HERE

60. In tossing a fair coin three consecutive times, what is the probability of getting heads on two consecutive tosses but NOT on three consecutive tosses? (A fair coin has an equal likelihood of a heads or tails outcome.)

F. $\frac{1}{4}$

G. $\frac{3}{8}$

H. $\frac{1}{8}$

J. $\frac{1}{2}$

K. $\frac{3}{4}$

STOP

READING TEST

35 Minutes—40 Questions

DIRECTIONS: There are four passages in this test. Each passage is followed by several questions. Read each passage, select the best answer to each related question, and fill in the corresponding circle on the answer sheet. You may look back at the passages as often as you need.

PASSAGE I

PROSE FICTION: Passage A is an excerpt from "Bartleby the Scrivener: A Story of Wall Street" by Herman Melville. Passage B is an excerpt from *The Adventures of Tom Sawyer* by Mark Twain.

Passage A

by Herman Melville

At first Bartleby did an extraordinary quantity of writing. As if long famishing for something to copy, he seemed to gorge himself on my documents. There was no pause for digestion. He ran a day and night line, copying by sun-light and by candle-light. I should have been quite delighted with his application, had he been cheerfully industrious. But he wrote on silently, palely, mechanically…

Now and then, in the haste of business, it had been my habit to assist in comparing some brief document myself, calling Turkey or Nippers for this purpose. One object I had in placing Bartleby so handy to me behind the screen, was to avail myself of his services on such trivial occasions. It was on the third day, I think, of his being with me, and before any necessity had arisen for having his own writing examined, that, being much hurried to complete a small affair I had in hand, I abruptly called to Bartleby. In my haste and natural expectancy of instant compliance, I sat with my head bent over the original on my desk, and my right hand sideways, and somewhat nervously extended with the copy, so that immediately upon emerging from his retreat, Bartleby might snatch it and proceed to business without the least delay.

In this very attitude did I sit when I called to him, rapidly stating what it was I wanted him to do—namely, to examine a small paper with me. Imagine my surprise, nay, my consternation, when without moving from his privacy, Bartleby in a singularly mild, firm voice, replied, "I would prefer not to."

I sat awhile in perfect silence, rallying my stunned faculties. Immediately it occurred to me that my ears had deceived me, or Bartleby had entirely misunderstood my meaning. I repeated my request in the clearest tone I could assume. But in quite as clear a one came the previous reply, "I would prefer not to."

"Prefer not to," echoed I, rising in high excitement, and crossing the room with a stride. "What do you mean? Are you moon-struck? I want you to help me compare this sheet here—take it," and I thrust it towards him.

"I would prefer not to," said he.

I looked at him steadfastly. His face was leanly composed; his gray eye dimly calm. Not a wrinkle of agitation rippled him. Had there been the least uneasiness, anger, impatience or impertinence in his manner; in other words, had there been any thing ordinarily human about him, doubtless I should have violently dismissed him from the premises. But as it was, I should have as soon thought of turning my pale plaster-of-paris bust of Cicero out of doors. I stood gazing at him awhile, as he went on with his own writing, and then reseated myself at my desk. This is very strange, thought I. What had one best do? But my business hurried me. I concluded to forget the matter for the present, reserving it for my future leisure.

Passage B

by Mark Twain

Monday morning found Tom Sawyer miserable. Monday morning always found him so—because it began another week's slow suffering in school. He generally began that day with wishing he had had no intervening holiday, it made the going into captivity and fetters again so much more odious.

Tom lay thinking. Presently it occurred to him that he wished he was sick; then he could stay home from school. Here was a vague possibility. He canvassed his system. No ailment was found, and he investigated again. This time he thought he could detect colicky symptoms, and he began to encourage them with considerable hope. But they soon grew feeble, and presently died wholly away. He reflected further. Suddenly he discovered something. One of his upper front teeth was loose. This was lucky; he was about to begin to groan, as a "starter," as he called it, when it occurred to him that if he came into court with that argument, his aunt would pull it out, and

CONTINUE

that would hurt. So he thought he would hold the tooth in reserve for the present, and seek further.

Nothing offered for some little time, and then he remembered hearing the doctor tell about a certain thing that laid up a patient for two or three weeks and threatened to make him lose a finger. So the boy eagerly drew his sore toe from under the sheet and held it up for inspection. But now he did not know the necessary symptoms. However, it seemed well worth while to chance it, so he fell to groaning with considerable spirit…

Sid said: "Tom! Say, Tom!" [No response.] "Here, Tom! Tom! What is the matter, Tom?" And he shook him and looked in his face anxiously.

Tom moaned out: "Oh, don't, Sid. Don't joggle me."

"Why, what's the matter, Tom? I must call auntie…"

Sid flew down-stairs and said:

"Oh, Aunt Polly, come! Tom's dying!"

"Dying!"

"Yes'm. Don't wait—come quick!"

"Rubbage! I don't believe it!"

But she fled up-stairs, nevertheless, with Sid and Mary at her heels. And her face grew white, too, and her lip trembled. When she reached the bed-side she gasped out:

"You, Tom! Tom, what's the matter with you?"

"Oh, auntie, I'm—"

"What's the matter with you—what is the matter with you, child?"

"Oh, auntie, my sore toe's mortified!"

The old lady sank down into a chair and laughed a little, then cried a little, then did both together. This restored her and she said:

"Tom, what a turn you did give me. Now you shut up that nonsense and climb out of this."

The groans ceased and the pain vanished from the toe. The boy felt a little foolish, and he said:

"Aunt Polly, it *seemed* mortified, and it hurt so I never minded my tooth at all."

"Your tooth, indeed! What's the matter with your tooth?"

"One of them's loose, and it aches perfectly awful."

"There, there, now, don't begin that groaning again. Open your mouth. Well—your tooth is loose, but you're not going to die about that. Mary, get me a silk thread, and a chunk of fire out of the kitchen."

Tom said:

"Oh, please, auntie, don't pull it out. It don't hurt any more. I wish I may never stir if it does. Please don't, auntie. I don't want to stay home from school."

"Oh, you don't, don't you? So all this row was because you thought you'd get to stay home from school and go a-fishing? Tom, Tom, I love you so, and you seem to try every way you can to break my old heart with your outrageousness."

Questions 1–3 ask about Passage A.

1. As it is used in line 10, the word *object* means:

A. thing.
B. item.
C. protest.
D. purpose.

2. Why exactly doesn't Bartleby want to compare the sheet?

F. He does not say.
G. He thinks it is unworthy of his skills.
H. He is in the middle of doing his own work.
J. He wants to make his boss angry.

3. The boss stops insisting Bartleby compare the sheet:

A. on Bartleby's first day working in the office.
B. before Bartleby has a chance to say whether or not he will do the task.
C. while Bartleby is in the middle of doing another task.
D. after Bartleby says he would prefer not to do it for the third time.

Questions 4–6 ask about Passage B.

4. Aunt Polly reacts to Tom Sawyer's antics with:

F. complete intolerance.
G. terrifying scorn.
H. loving exasperation.
J. incredible boredom.

5. It is reasonable to infer from the passage that the author mentions that Tom Sawyer did not want to go into "captivity and fetters" (line 5) because:

A. he thinks school is like a jail.
B. he has committed a crime.
C. he is claustrophobic.
D. he lives in constant fear.

6. Which of the following most accurately describes how Sid feels about Tom Sawyer?

   F. Sid does not trust Tom.
   G. Sid is afraid to disobey Tom.
   H. Sid delights in assisting Tom's deceitfulness.
   J. Sid feels genuine concern for Tom.

Questions 7–10 ask about both passages.

7. Both passages are mainly about characters who:

   A. work in an office.
   B. do not want to do something.
   C. are trying to fool a relative.
   D. confuse all the people around them.

8. In what way are Bartleby in Passage A and Tom Sawyer in Passage B DIFFERENT?

   F. Bartleby is lazy and sloppy, and Tom Sawyer is hard-working but feeling sick.
   G. Bartleby gets what he wants by stating his position, and Tom Sawyer tries to get what he wants by being underhanded.
   H. Bartleby refuses to speak his mind, and Tom Sawyer cannot control his constant babbling.
   J. Bartleby regrets being defiant, but Tom Sawyer is proud of his ability to devise elaborate schemes.

9. Considering how Bartleby is portrayed in Passage A and Tom Sawyer is portrayed in Passage B, they would both most accurately be described as:

   A. lawbreakers.
   B. followers.
   C. nonconformists.
   D. geniuses.

10. In what way are Bartleby's boss in Passage A and Aunt Polly in Passage B DIFFERENT?

   F. Bartleby's boss is bothered by Bartleby's behavior, yet Aunt Polly is not bothered by Tom's behavior.
   G. Bartleby's boss conducts himself in a very professional manner, yet Aunt Polly is completely unprofessional.
   H. Bartleby's boss is surprised by Bartleby's behavior, yet Aunt Polly expects Tom to act as he does.
   J. Bartleby's boss is firm and controlling, yet Aunt Polly is meek and easygoing.

PASSAGE II

SOCIAL SCIENCE: The following passage is adapted from a history of England written in 1890.

The origin of towns

As in the case of the manor, which was the Norman name for the Saxon "townships," the town, in the modern sense of the word, had its origin from the primitive settlement known as the mark. The only difference between a town and a manor originally lay in the number of its population, and in the fact that the town was a more defensible place than the "township," or rural manor, probably having a mound or moat surrounding it, instead of the hedges which ran round the villages. In itself it was merely a manor or group of manors; as Professor Freeman puts it, "one part of the district where men lived closer together than elsewhere." The town had at first a constitution like that of a primitive village in the mark, but its inhabitants had gradually gained certain rights and functions of a special nature. These rights and privileges had been received from the lord of the manor on which the town had grown up; for towns, especially provincial towns, were at first only dependent manors, which gained safety and solidity under the protection of some great noble, prelate, or the king himself, who finally would grant the town thus formed a charter.

Rise of towns in England

Towns first became important in England towards the end of the Saxon period. Saxon England had never been a settlement of towns, but of villages and townships, or manors. But gradually towns did grow up, though differing widely in the circumstances and manner of their rise. Some grew up in the fortified camps of the invaders themselves, as being in a secure position; some arose from a later occupation of the once sacked and deserted Roman towns. Many grew silently in the shadow of a great abbey or monastery. Of this class was Oxford, which first came into being round the monasteries of St Frideswide and Osney. Others clustered round the country houses of some Saxon king or earl. Several important boroughs owed their rise to the convenience of their site as a port or a trading center. This was the origin of the growth of Bristol, whose rise resulted directly from trade; and London of course had always been a port of high commercial rank. A few other towns, like Scarborough and Grimsby, were at first small havens for fishermen. But all the English towns were far less flourishing before the arrival of the Normans than they afterwards became.

CONTINUE

Towns in Domesday: London

If, now, we once more go back to our great authority, the survey made by William the Norman, we find that the status of these towns or boroughs is clearly recognized, though they are regarded as held by the lord of the manor "in demesne," or in default of a lord, as part of the king's demesne. Thus Northampton at that time was a town in the king's demesne; Beverley was held in demesne by the Archbishop of York. It was possible, too, that one town might belong to several lords, because it spread over, or was an aggregate of, several manors or townships. Thus Leicester seems to have included four manors, which were thus held in demesne by four lords—one by the king, another by the Bishop of Lincoln, another by a noble, Simon de Senlis, and the fourth by Ivo of Grantmesnil, the sheriff. In later times it was held under one lord, Count Robert of Meulan.

Now, in the Domesday Book there is mention made of forty-one provincial cities or boroughs, most of them being the county towns of the present day. There are also ten fortified towns of greater importance than the others. They are Canterbury, York, Nottingham, Oxford, Hereford, Leicester, Lincoln, Stafford, Chester, and Colchester. London was a town apart, as it had always been, and was the only town which had a civic constitution, being regulated by a port-reeve and a bishop, and having a kind of charter, though afterwards the privileges of this charter were much increased. London was of course a great port and trading centre, and had many foreign merchants in it. It was then, as well as in subsequent centuries, the centre of English national life, and the voice of its citizens counted for something in national affairs. The other great ports of England at that time were Bristol, Southampton, and Norwich, and as trade grew and prospered, many other ports rose into prominence.

Special privileges of towns

Even at the time of the Conquest most towns, though small, were of sufficient importance to have a certain status of their own, with definite privileges. The most important of these was the right of composition for taxation, *i.e.* the right of paying a fixed sum, or rent, to the Crown, instead of the various tallages, taxes, and imposts that might be required of other places. This fixed sum, or composition, was called the *firma burgi*, and by the time of the Conquest was nearly always paid in money. Previously it had been paid both in money and kind, for we find Oxford paying to Edward the Confessor six sectaries of honey as well as £20 in coin; while to William the Norman it paid £60 as an inclusive lump sum. By the end of the Norman period all the towns had secured the *firma burgi*, and the right of assessing it themselves, instead of being assessed by the sheriff; they had the right also of choosing a mayor of their own, instead of the king's bailiff or *reeve*. They had, moreover, their own tribunals, a charter for their customs, and special rules of local administration, and, generally speaking, gained entire judicial and commercial freedom.

11. According to the passage, which of the following does NOT accurately describe a manor?

A. A rural township
B. A less defensible place than a town
C. A human settlement named by Normans
D. A group of townships

12. The author explains that towns in England arose:

I. in the camps of invaders.
II. near shops and stores.
III. around the homes of royalty.

F. I only
G. II only
H. III only
J. I and III only

13. According to the passage, anyone who holds a town "in demesne":

A. rules the town but does not own it.
B. understands that the town really belongs to the king.
C. is the owner of that town.
D. shares the town with other lords.

14. The primary purpose of the passage is to:

F. compare life in English towns to life in manors.
G. provide a history of the development of English towns.
H. prove that the English town evolved from the mark.
J. describe the qualities that define a town.

15. The passage implies that living in a town affords:

A. access to imports.
B. the right of assessing it themselves.
C. more space than rural living.
D. The ability to have the king's bailiff select a mayor.

16. As it is used in line 7, the word *mound* refers to a:

F. human-made body of water.
G. protective wall.
H. small heap of dirt.
J. scenic hill.

17. The author would most likely agree with which of the following statements regarding London?

A. London was flourishing even before the Normans arrived there.

B. Most people know of London's status as a great port and trading center.

C. People are too cramped and crammed together to be comfortable in London.

D. Living in London is preferable to rural living because of the privileges town life affords.

18. The passage implies that all of the following are valuable sources for information about English towns EXCEPT:

F. The Domesday Book

G. William the Norman's survey

H. The writings of Professor Freeman

J. Town charters

19. In terms of a town's influence on national matters, which of the following seems to play the most important role?

A. The town's success as a trading center

B. The town's ability to draw in people from other areas

C. The influence of the town's civic constitution

D. The town's ability to distinguish itself from other towns

20. Towns paid the king a form of rent called:

F. tallages.

G. imposts.

H. the reeve.

J. the firma burgi.

PASSAGE III

HUMANITIES: The following passage is adapted from a book about artistic design.

It is an article of faith that to design entails the possession of the creative faculty, which may be taken for granted with the proviso, that the creative faculty is concerned rather with the association of elements common to all than with invention pure and simple.

Human Limitations

To be more explicit, the human imagination is limited to personal or acquired experience. At no period has any form been created that is not traceable to some process of production, or natural suggestion; for instance, the artistic conception of an angel is merely a combination of human and bird form, and is in no sense an original creation.

The term originality is indeed generally misunderstood, and for the reasons already advanced it is impossible to be original. The real interest in artistic production of any kind is the expression of personality, in other words, the individual point of view of the artist; which is more or less interesting, as it is more or less personal in idea and expression.

In the training of the designer it is essential that the imagination be carefully cultivated and trained to accept suggestion from any possible source.

Design is distinct from any phase of realistic expression inasmuch as the subject does not exist in any concrete form, but has to be mentally visualized.

"Inspiration"

Too much importance is attached to what is believed to be inspiration, but obviously if inspired, design is rather in the nature of an accident than of the deliberate intention it should be and cannot be credited to the individual exponent. What at first sight suggests inspired thought may be accounted for by sub-consciousness, which is really responsible for the evolution of an idea or the solution of some problem.

It would be beneficial to reject once and for all the idea of inspiration with its tendency to encourage the "artistic temperament" in the belief that it "does not feel like it."

The designer must be ready to respond at any time, and this implies a logical and balanced mind, capable of grasping essentials, and conditions, and of evolving some desirable solution.

Another superstition is that a design is a drawing, and it only requires a facility in this form of expression to produce a design. This is a fallacy, as though many designs are for convenience expressed through this medium, any such drawing must be made with a knowledge of the technical details of the final method of production, to be a practical design.

Process and Material

Design is therefore inseparable from consideration of material and process, with which the designer must be acquainted; without this technical knowledge it is impossible to take full advantage of the method of production either in the direction of economy or effect.

Other considerations are utilitarian and aesthetic, the former having regard to purpose, the latter to appearance.

That mere utility is not in itself sufficient is evident; the common enameled saucepan and the medicine bottle are certainly utilitarian, but no one would assert that they are satisfying from the aesthetic point of view.

CONTINUE

An important consideration in design is the "market" which is governed by popular or individual demand.

Those who pay the piper call the tune, and the designer has often to work to prescribed conditions.

This apparently implies restriction of individuality, but the designer who refuses to conform will probably find the market even more restricted.

It also implies that he must be well versed in the various styles or historic tradition, so that his work, if desirable, may be in harmony with existing environment; but in these circumstances it is quite possible to produce work that is individual and distinctive.

Designers, craftsmen and manufacturers are all dependent upon public demand, which must be taken into account, and their business is as far as possible to raise the general standard of taste, by producing of their best. Any attempt on their part to insist on what shall or shall not be done would undoubtedly result in failure.

To sum up, the designer must not only be an accomplished draughtsman well versed in traditional ornament and style, but it is necessary that he should cultivate the imaginative and perceptive faculties; and, in addition, the commercial qualities of promptness and business insight.

21. According to the passage, which qualities must a designer possess?

I. Quick responses
II. Logic
III. Originality

A. I only
B. I and II only
C. II and III only
D. I, II, and III

22. As it is used in line 58, the phrase "those who pay the piper call the tune" most likely means:

F. musicians rarely perform without getting paid.
G. true artists must be paid for their work.
H. workers must follow the instructions of their employers.
J. designers must follow their own instincts when creating.

23. According to the information in the seventeenth and eighteenth paragraphs, the author of this passage would most likely describe which of the following as being a concern of designers?

A. How an object with his or her design is manufactured
B. The commerciality of an image
C. Creating art that fits contemporary tastes
D. Delivering work that is inexpensive to produce

24. According to the passage, it is important for designers to be familiar with the materials available to them because:

F. their materials should always be utilitarian, if nothing else.
G. they might be able to change public tastes by using new materials.
H. certain materials are less expensive than others.
J. choosing the right materials helps them create economical and effective work.

25. As it is used in line 40, the word *fallacy* most nearly means:

A. a popular notion.
B. a factual statement.
C. an untrue belief.
D. a common law.

26. According to the passage, the author suggests that inspiration is:

I. similar to an accident.
II. an essential element in the artistic process.
III. something for which deliberate thought is often mistaken.

F. I only
G. II and III only
H. I and III only
J. I, II, and III

27. Which of the following quotations best expresses the main point of the passage?

A. "It is an article of faith that to design entails the possession of the creative faculty, which may be taken for granted with the proviso, that the creative faculty is concerned rather with the association of elements common to all than with invention pure and simple."

B. "At no period has any form been created that is not traceable to some process of production, or natural suggestion; for instance, the artistic conception of an angel is merely a combination of human and bird form, and is in no sense an original creation."

C. "That mere utility is not in itself sufficient is evident; the common enameled saucepan and the medicine bottle are certainly utilitarian, but no one would assert that they are satisfying from the aesthetic point of view."

D. " ... the designer must not only be an accomplished draughtsman well versed in traditional ornament and style, but it is necessary that he should cultivate the imaginative and perceptive faculties; and, in addition, the commercial qualities of promptness and business insight."

28. Which of the following descriptions most accurately and completely represents this passage?

F. A comprehensive history of design

G. A brief description of the evolution of design

H. An explanation of how commercial designers work

J. An analysis of what makes up effective design

29. As it is defined in the passage, the "market" is determined by:

I. the current economy.
II. popular demand.
III. the availability of materials.

A. I only

B. II only

C. II and II only

D. I, II, and III

30. Based on the information in the passage, the author rejects the concept of "artistic temperament" because it:

F. undermines the designer's readiness.

G. is a lazy excuse used by untalented designers.

H. implies that art is created in anger.

J. is an obsolete concept.

PASSAGE IV

NATURAL SCIENCE: The following passage is adapted from a book about a special natural ability of butterflies published in 1915.

Mimicry is a special branch of the study of adaptation. The term has sometimes been used loosely to include cases where an animal, most frequently an insect, bears a strong and often most remarkable resemblance to some feature of its inanimate surroundings. Many butterflies with wings closed are wonderfully like dead leaves; certain spiders when at rest on a leaf look exactly like bird-droppings; "looper" caterpillars simulate small twigs; the names of the "stick-" and "leaf-" insects are in themselves an indication of their appearance. Such cases as these, in which the creature exhibits a resemblance to some part of its natural surroundings, should be classified as cases of "protective resemblance" in contradistinction to mimicry proper. Striking examples of protective resemblance are abundant, and though we possess little critical knowledge of the acuity of perception in birds and other insect feeders it is plausible to regard the resemblances as being of definite advantage in the struggle for existence. However, it is with mimicry and not with protective coloration in general that we are here directly concerned, and the nature of the phenomenon may perhaps best be made clear by a brief account of the facts which led to the statement of the theory.

In the middle of last century the distinguished naturalist, H. W. Bates, was engaged in making collections in parts of the Amazon region. He paid much attention to butterflies, in which group he discovered a remarkably interesting phenomenon. Among the species which he took were a large number belonging to the group *Ithomiinae*, small butterflies of peculiar appearance with long slender bodies and narrow wings bearing in most cases a conspicuous pattern. When Bates came to examine his catch more closely he discovered that among the many *Ithomiines* were a few specimens very like them in general shape, color, and markings, but differing in certain anatomical features by which the *Pierinae*, or "whites," are separated from other groups. Most *Pierines* are very different from *Ithomiines*. It is the group to which our common cabbage butterfly belongs and the ground color is generally white. The shape of the body and also of the wings is in general quite distinct from what it is in the *Ithomiines*. Nevertheless in these particular districts certain of the species of *Pierines* had departed widely from what is usually regarded as their ancestral pattern and had come to resemble very closely the far more abundant *Ithomiines* among whom they habitually flew. To use Bates' term they "mimicked" the *Ithomiines*, and he set to work to devise an explanation of

CONTINUE

how this could have come about. The *Origin of Species* had just appeared and it was natural that Bates should seek to interpret this peculiar phenomenon on the lines there laid down. How was it that these *Pierines* had come to depart so widely from the general form of the great bulk of their relations, and to mimic so closely in appearance species belonging to an entirely different group, while at the same time conserving the more deeply seated anatomical features of their own family? If the change was to be regarded as having come about through the agency of natural selection it must clearly be of advantage to the mimicking forms; otherwise natural selection could not come into operation. What advantage then have the *Ithomiines* over the majority of butterflies in those parts? They are small insects, rather flimsy in build, with comparatively weak powers of flight, and yet so conspicuously colored that they can hardly be mistaken for anything else. In spite of all this they are little subject to the attacks of enemies such as birds, and Bates attributed this to the fact that the juices of their bodies are unpalatable. According to him their striking and conspicuous pattern is of the nature of a warning coloration, advertising their disagreeable properties to possible enemies. A bird which had once attempted to eat one would find it little to its taste. It would thenceforward associate the conspicuous pattern with a disagreeable flavor and in future leave such butterflies severely alone. The more conspicuous the pattern the more readily would it be noticed by the enemy, and so it would be of advantage to the *Ithomiine* to possess as striking a pattern as possible. Those butterflies showing a tendency to a more conspicuous pattern would be more immune to the attacks of birds and so would have a better chance of leaving progeny than those with a less conspicuous pattern. In this way variations in the direction of greater conspicuousness would be accumulated gradually by natural selection, and so would be built up in the *Ithomiine* the striking warning coloration by which it advertises its disagreeable properties. Such is the first step in the making of a mimicry case—the building up through natural selection of a conspicuous pattern in an unpalatable species by means of which it is enabled to advertise its disagreeable properties effectively and thereby secure immunity from the attacks of enemies which are able to appreciate the advertisement. Such patterns and colors are said to be of a "warning" nature. The existence of an unpalatable model in considerable numbers is the first step in the production of a mimetic resemblance through the agency of natural selection.

31. H. W. Bates asserts that birds do not attack *Ithomiines* because *Ithomiines*:

A. are too fast to capture.
B. fly in unpredictable patterns.
C. do not taste good.
D. are stronger than most birds.

32. This passage states that *Pierines* have striking patterns because those patterns:

F. make *Pierines* more recognizable to predators.
G. serve as camouflage that help hide the *Pierines*.
H. are examples of protective resemblance.
J. are difficult for predators to understand.

33. The main point of the first paragraph is that:

A. many butterflies use mimicry to protect themselves from predators.
B. mimicry and protective resemblance are two ways animals protect themselves from predators.
C. many butterflies look like dead leaves when their wings are closed.
D. some *Pierines* resemble *Ithomiines* as a form of mimicry to protect themselves from predators.

34. The word *contradistinction* in the first paragraph refers to the fact that:

F. protective resemblance is just one branch of mimicry.
G. protective resemblance and mimicry are not quite the same things.
H. protective resemblance and mimicry are completely different things.
J. protective resemblance is the opposite of mimicry.

35. According to the passage, in which order did the following events occur?

I. The *Origin of Species* was published.
II. H. W. Bates caught some *Ithomiines*.
III. H. W. Bates noticed similarities between *Ithomiines* and certain *Pierines*.

A. I, II, III
B. II, III, I
C. III, II, I
D. I, III, II

36. As it is used in line 46, the phrase "the lines there laid down" most likely means:

F. phrases in a book.
G. most convincing argument.
H. available information.
J. straightest shapes.

37. The word *distinguished* in line 22 refers to the fact that H. W. Bates:

A. came up with distinctive theories.
B. was different from any other naturalist.
C. was a respected naturalist.
D. was an extremely charming man.

38. The passage states that most *Pierines* are very different from *Ithomiines* because most *Pierines*:

I. are white.
II. are shaped differently from *Ithomiines*.
III. are bulky.

F. I only
G. I and II only
H. II and III only
J. I, II, and III

39. You could reasonably conclude from lines 5–9 that:

A. looper caterpillars got their names because of their appearances.
B. naturalists give certain insects ridiculous names intentionally.
C. all insects are capable of mimicking plant life.
D. there are insects that resemble sticks and leaves.

40. The passage states that certain *Pierines* most likely came to resemble *Ithomiines:*

F. through a process known as natural selection.
G. as a warning from nature.
H. through the process of protective resemblance.
J. after H.W. Bates first captured some *Ithomiines*.

STOP

SCIENCE TEST

35 MINUTES—40 QUESTIONS

DIRECTIONS: There are seven passages in this test. Each passage is followed by several questions. Read each passage, choose the best answer, and fill in the corresponding circle on the answer sheet. You may refer back to the passages at any time.

Remember, you are NOT allowed to use a calculator on this test.

PASSAGE I

Enzymes are proteins that perform chemical reactions, converting one molecule (called a substrate) into a different molecule (called a product). There are a variety of ways to measure how active an enzyme is under a particular set of conditions. One way is called a fluorimetric enzyme assay. Fluorescence occurs when a molecule absorbs light of one color and emits light of a different color. If an enzyme's product is fluorescent but the substrate is *not* fluorescent, the enzyme's activity is directly related to the amount of fluorescent light that is produced.

An instrument called a fluorimeter is used to measure fluorescence. The fluorimeter shines light of a particular color onto a sample, and then detects light of a second color that is emitted by the sample. It turns this second color of light into an electronic signal, which can be displayed on a computer (Figure 1). The amount of fluorescence produced under different conditions can be plotted on a graph, as in Figure 2.

FIGURE 1

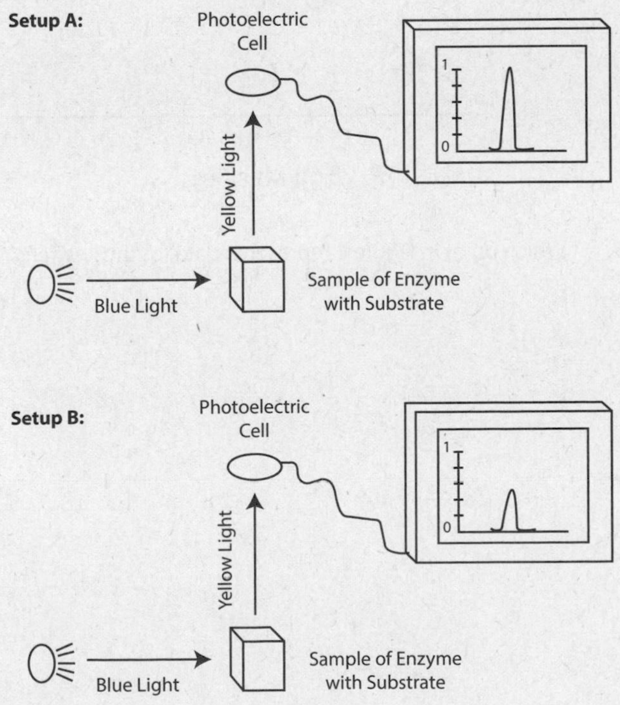

The spectrophotometric data are used to produce a graph, such as the one below, that relates optical density to cell number.

FIGURE 2

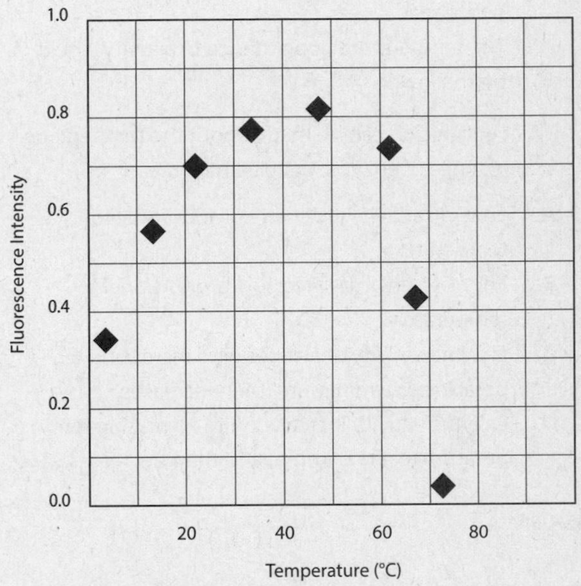

1. In Figure 1, how does the enzyme's activity in Setup A compare with the activity in Setup B?

A. The activity in Setup A is greater.
B. The activity in Setup B is greater.
C. The activity is the same in Setups A and B.
D. Neither setup contains an active enzyme.

2. In Figure 2, assuming that the fluorescence intensity of the product molecule is not affected by temperature, at approximately which temperature is the enzyme most active?

F. 10°C
G. 30°C
H. 50°C
J. 70°C

CONTINUE

3. Based on the graph in Figure 2, the fluorescence intensity at 20°C would be approximately:

   A. 0.50
   B. 0.65
   C. 0.75
   D. 0.80

4. In Figure 1, if the experiment in Setup B were repeated using twice as much enzyme, what would be the expected result?

   F. The fluorescence intensity would be approximately twice as much.
   G. The fluorescence intensity would be approximately half as much.
   H. The temperature dependence of activity would be steeper.
   J. The temperature dependence of activity would be shallower.

5. What conclusion can be made about the temperature dependence of enzyme activity in Figure 2?

   A. Enzyme activity is directly proportional to temperature.
   B. Enzyme activity is inversely proportional to temperature.
   C. Enzyme activity decreases with increasing temperature to a minimum, then increases.
   D. Enzyme activity increases with increasing temperature to a maximum, and then decreases.

PASSAGE II

During incubation, a bird embryo, like a mammal embryo, uses oxygen to satisfy its energy needs. However, unlike a mammal embryo, a bird embryo cannot rely on its mother to supply the necessary oxygen. The oxygen must be supplied directly from the outside environment by *diffusion* through pores in the egg's shell. Diffusion is the movement of substances through a membrane from a region of higher concentration to a region of lower concentration.

Based on this fact, a group of scientists suspected that there might be a relationship between the mass of an egg and its total pore area. A *pore* is a channel through which substances can diffuse from one side of the membrane to the other.

To investigate this concept, the scientists collected the data shown in Table 1 and displayed in the graph of Figure 1.

Table 1

Bird	Average Egg Mass (g)	Average Pore Area (mm^2)
Pigeon	27.0	0.70
Warbler	1.4	0.02
Goose	250.0	15.00
Emu	800.0	55.00
Kestrel	8.5	0.20
Skua	90.0	6.00
Chicken	80.0	4.00
Ostrich	1100.0	250.00
Redwing blackbird	6.0	0.80
Shearwater	60.0	2.00
Rhea	820.0	5.00

FIGURE 1

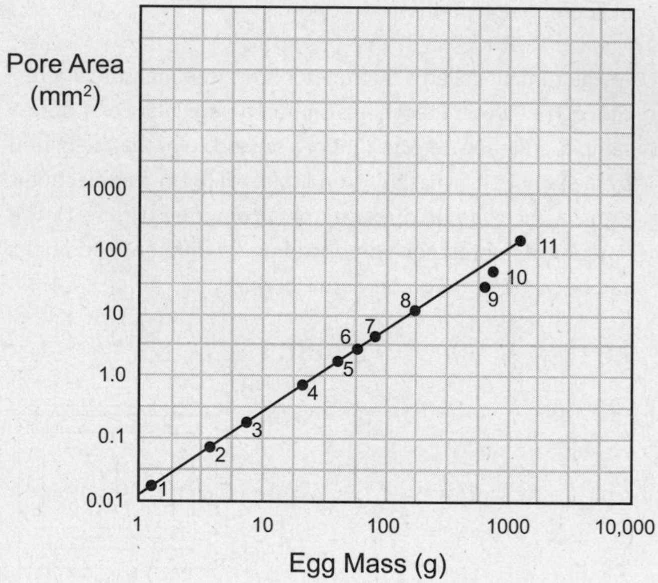

6. Which point in Figure 1 represents data for the kestrel?

   F. 2
   G. 3
   H. 4
   J. 5

7. The elephant bird, which has been extinct since the 17th century, is thought to have weighed about 400 kg (400,000 g), and to have produced an egg that weighed 10 kg (10,000 g). Assuming the trend from Figure 1 holds for the extinct species, approximately what would its egg pore area have been?

A. 0.3 mm^2
B. 30 mm^2
C. 1,200 mm^2
D. 10,000 mm^2

8. Which type of bird egg has the greatest ratio of average egg mass to average pore area?

F. Skua
G. Rhea
H. Warbler
J. Redwing blackbird

9. Which of the following conclusions can be drawn from the data?

A. Egg mass and pore area exhibit an inverse relationship.
B. Egg mass and pore area exhibit a direct relationship.
C. There is no discernable relationship between egg mass and pore area.
D. The larger the bird, the larger the egg it produces.

10. A bird species has a pore area of 15 mm^2 on its eggs. The approximate mass of the egg is:

F. between 1 and 10 g.
G. between 10 and 100 g.
H. between 100 and 1,000 g.
J. between 1,000 and 10,000 g.

PASSAGE III

Plants must be able to change their growth in response to environmental conditions or stimuli in order to find sunlight and nutrients, and avoid predators and damage—this is called *tropism*. For example, plants can detect light and direct the growth of their leaves toward the light source—this is called *phototropism*. Plants also respond to gravity by growing their stems upward and their roots downward—this is called *gravitropism*. Some plants, like the Venus flytrap, can rapidly close some of their leaf structures in response to touch—this is called *thigmotropism*. Plants can also detect airborne chemicals and change their growth patterns in response—this is called *chemotropism*.

The dodder vine is a parasitic plant that cannot grow using energy from sunlight, and instead attaches itself to a host plant and grows by sucking nutrients and energy-rich molecules out of the host. Scientists wanted to examine how the dodder vine determines which direction to grow in order to find a host plant. They set up potted dodder vines with a variety of external stimuli, and examined the direction in which the vines grew. The results of three experiments are depicted in Figure 1.

FIGURE 1

CONTINUE

11. What factor is a constant in all three experiments?

- **A.** The intensity of the light source
- **B.** The airflow around the tomato plant
- **C.** The position of the wheat plant
- **D.** The position of the vine

12. What type of response is being exhibited by the vine in Experiment 1?

- **F.** Phototropism
- **G.** Gravitropism
- **H.** Chemotropism
- **J.** Thigmotropism

13. What conclusion can be drawn from Experiments 2 and 3?

- **A.** The dodder vine is attracted only to tomato plants.
- **B.** The dodder vine is attracted only to wheat plants.
- **C.** The dodder vine prefers tomato plants to wheat plants.
- **D.** The dodder vine prefers wheat plants to tomato plants.

14. What is the dependent variable in all three experiments?

- **F.** The increase in length of the dodder vine
- **G.** The direction of growth of the dodder vine
- **H.** The length of time the dodder vine is allowed to grow
- **J.** The position of the tomato plant with respect to the dodder vine

15. What conclusion can be drawn from all three experiments?

- **A.** The dodder vine senses chemical signals to determine which direction to grow.
- **B.** The dodder vine senses gravity and grows at an angle to the ground.
- **C.** The dodder vine grows toward any potential host plant, regardless of species.
- **D.** The dodder vine grows toward light bouncing off of a host plant.

16. A similar experiment is repeated, using the setup depicted below. What is the expected response of the dodder vine?

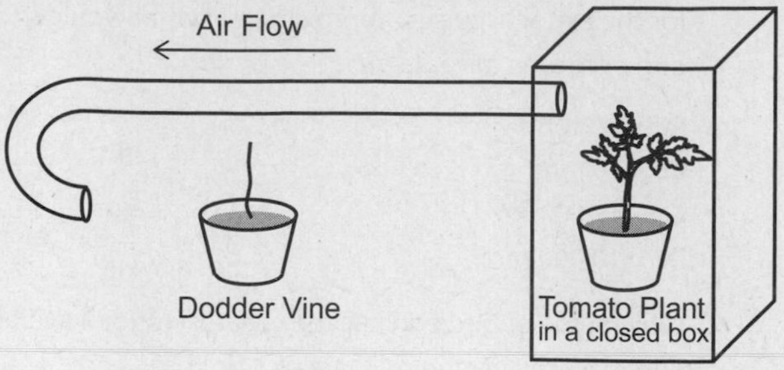

- **F.** To grow toward the tomato plant (right)
- **G.** To grow in the opposite direction of the tomato plant (left)
- **H.** To grow straight up
- **J.** To grow randomly left or right with no preference

PASSAGE IV

Before the late seventeenth century, most people and many scientists were convinced that some forms of life were generated from nonliving objects. This concept came to be called *abiogenesis*, or *spontaneous generation*. According to supporters of this idea, organisms such as maggots (fly larvae) arose spontaneously from decaying meat, earthworms were born from soil inundated with rain, and a soiled shirt left in the dark and sprinkled with grain could give birth to mice. Later, after microorganisms were discovered, proponents of abiogenesis proposed that these microscopic organisms arose spontaneously from spoiling broth.

Some scientists, however, took exception to this concept. They believed in the concept of *biogenesis*, that is, that life arises only from living things. Several noteworthy scientists performed experiments to support their position.

Some of the earliest experiments were performed by Italian physician Francesco Redi in 1688. Two of his experimental setups are shown in Figures 1 and 2.

FIGURE 1

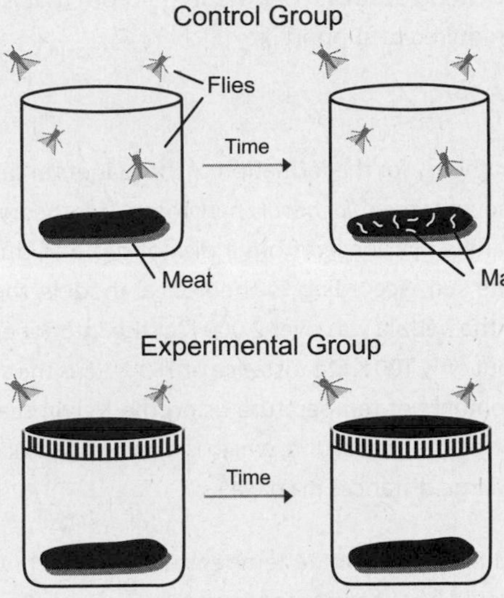

Redi's First Experiment

FIGURE 2

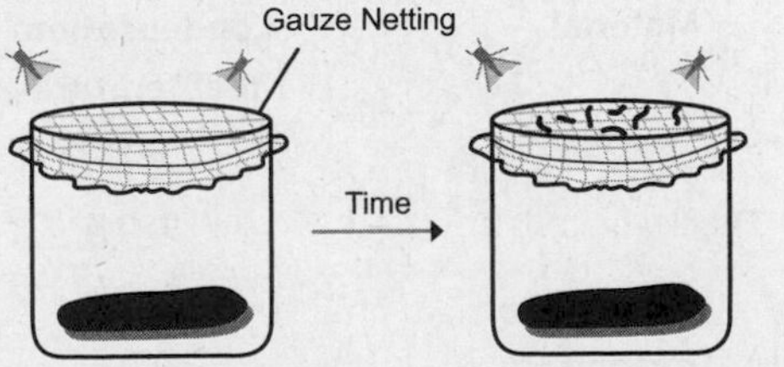

Redi's Second Experiment

In 1748, English naturalist John Needham performed the experiment shown in Figure 3. Needham believed that heating the meat for a short time to make broth would kill all living things in the broth.

FIGURE 3

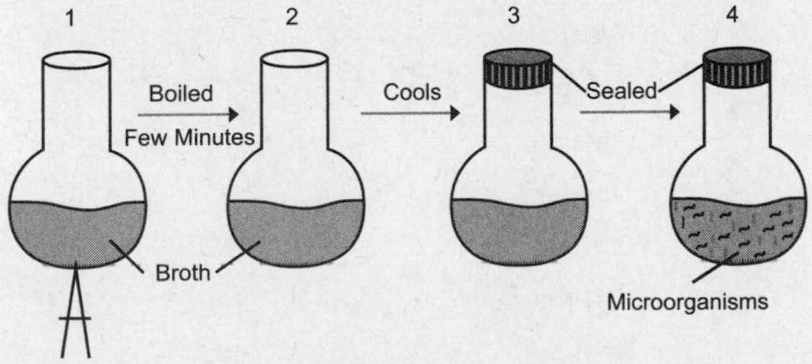

Needham's Experiment

Figure 4 shows an experiment performed in 1768 by Italian biologist Lazzaro Spallanzani. The broth he used was identical to that used by Needham.

FIGURE 4

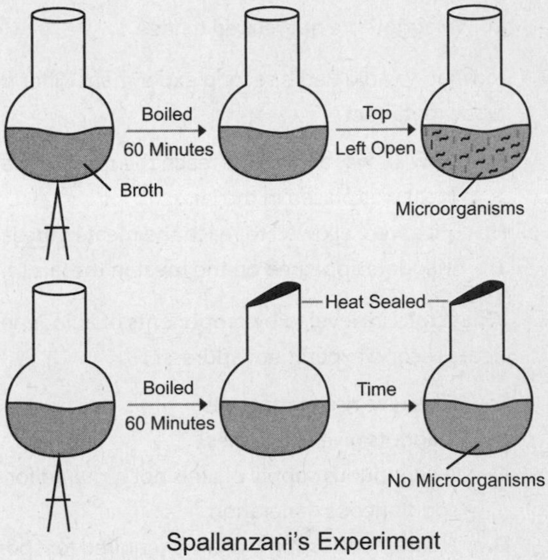

Spallanzani's Experiment

In 1860, French chemist Louis Pasteur addressed this question by performing the experiment shown in Figure 5.

FIGURE 5

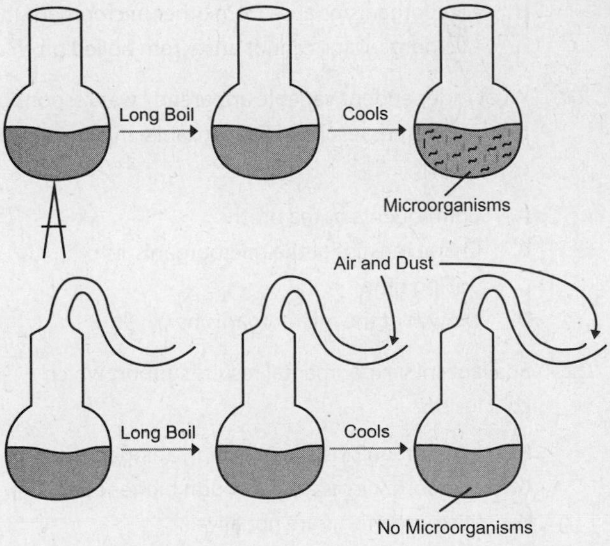

Pasteur's Experiment

CONTINUE

17. What conclusion can be drawn from Francesco Redi's first experiment?

A. Maggots arise spontaneously from decaying meat.
B. Air is required for maggots to arise spontaneously from decaying meat.
C. Maggots arise from decaying meat only if flies are able to reach the meat.
D. Maggots are not related to flies.

18. In what way did Redi's second experiment differ from his first experiment?

F. New air was allowed to reach the meat in the jars.
G. Meat was placed in the jars.
H. Flies were allowed to reach the meat in the jars.
J. Maggots appeared on the meat in the jars.

19. What criticism leveled by proponents of abiogenesis did Redi's second experiment address?

A. Flies give rise to maggots.
B. Maggots give rise to flies.
C. A continuous supply of air is not required for spontaneous generation.
D. A continuous supply of air is required for spontaneous generation.

20. What conclusion *seemed* to be supported by the results of Needham's experiment?

F. Air is needed for the growth of microorganisms.
G. Microorganisms arise spontaneously from broth.
H. Microorganisms arise from other microorganisms.
J. Microorganisms cannot arise from boiled broth.

21. What independent variable apparently was responsible for the different results of Spallanzani's and Needham's experiments?

A. Components of the broth
B. Characteristics of the microorganisms
C. Boiling time
D. Growth of the microorganisms

22. Spallanzani's experimental results support which conclusion?

F. Microorganisms arise through abiogenesis.
G. Microorganisms arise through biogenesis.
H. Microorganisms are not alive.
J. Broth is alive.

23. What conclusion could be reached by the results of Pasteur's experiment?

A. Dust particles, not air, carry microorganisms.
B. Air free of dust particles carries microorganisms.
C. Microorganisms arise spontaneously from broth.
D. Heating destroys a substance in broth that is required to support life.

PASSAGE V

One current theory for the formation of the planets in the solar system is known as the *solar nebula hypothesis*. This theory states that the planets condensed from a disk of gas and dust surrounding the sun. According to theoretical models, the temperature of the nebula was over 2,000 K at the interior edge of the cloud, but only 100 K at a distance of 10 AU. (K is the symbol for measurements of temperature using the Kelvin scale. AU stands for an astronomical unit, which is a unit of distance used to measure large distances in space.)

Table 1 lists the approximate temperatures at which various materials would have condensed from the solar nebula.

Table 1

Material	Approximate Condensation Temperature
Metals	1,600 K
Rocky materials	950 K
Water ice	270 K
Ammonia ice	100 K

Table 2 lists the distances at which several of the planets formed.

Table 2

Planet	Distance (AU)
Mercury	0.4
Venus	0.7
Earth	1
Mars	1.5
Jupiter	5.2
Saturn	9.5
Uranus	19.2
Neptune	30.1

Figure 1 compares the temperature of the nebula to distance from the sun.

FIGURE 1

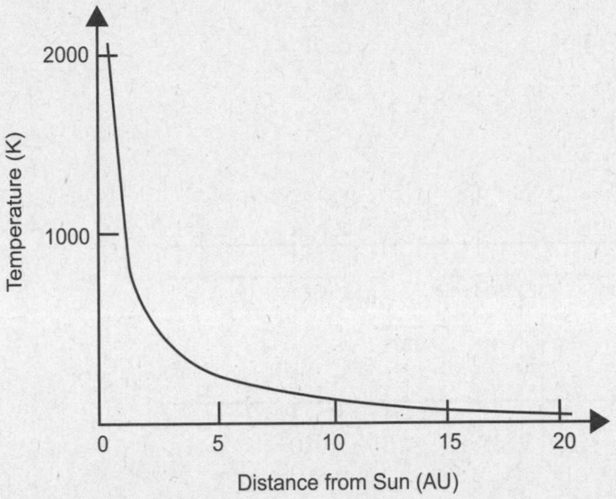

24. Earth is composed of primarily rocky material with a little metal, while Mercury is largely composed of metal, with a little rock. Based on the information in the passage, what is the most likely explanation for this difference?

- **F.** Mercury formed at higher temperatures than Earth.
- **G.** Mercury formed at lower temperatures than Earth.
- **H.** Mercury condensed before Earth, pulling in more metal.
- **J.** Mercury has a higher gravity than Earth, and is able to hold more metal..

25. Uranus and Neptune formed much farther from the sun than Earth did. What is the most likely composition of these planets?

- **A.** Mostly metal
- **B.** Mostly rock with some metal
- **C.** Mostly rock
- **D.** Mostly ice with some rock

26. Earth contains an iron core but consists mostly of rock. Mars formed a little farther out in the nebula, at approximately 1.5 AU. Which of the following is the most likely composition of Mars?

- **F.** Mostly iron
- **G.** Mostly rock with a little iron
- **H.** All rock with no iron
- **J.** Mostly ice

27. According to the theory, at approximately which temperatures did Saturn form?

- **A.** 0–100 K
- **B.** 100–500 K
- **C.** 500–1,000 K
- **D.** 1,000–2,000 K

28. If the solar nebula hypothesis is correct, how would the density of a planet in the solar system depend on its distance from the sun?

- **F.** The highest-density planets would be closest to the sun.
- **G.** The highest-density planets would be farthest from the sun.
- **H.** The density of the planets would reach a maximum around 1 AU.
- **J.** The density of the planets would reach a minimum around 1 AU.

CONTINUE

PASSAGE VI

Light, both visible and nonvisible, is described in terms of frequency (*f*) and wavelength (λ). Figure 1 shows the *electromagnetic spectrum*, which organizes types of light by frequency and wavelength.

FIGURE 1

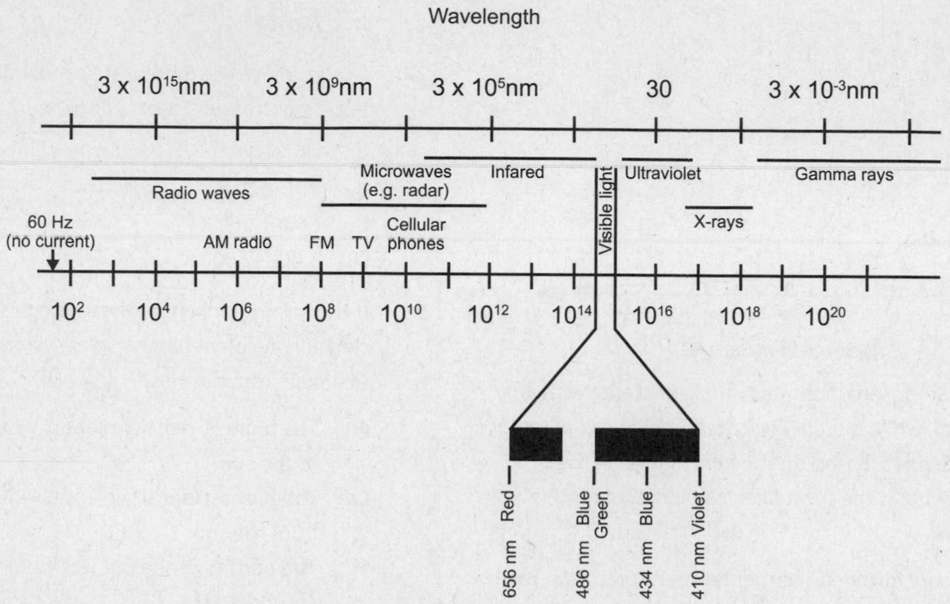

Under certain conditions, atoms can be made to emit light. When the light is analyzed through a spectroscope, a series of lines known as a *line spectrum* or *emission spectrum* is produced.

A great deal of research has been conducted on the emission spectra of different elements. The simplest line spectrum is produced by an atom of hydrogen. In 1885, a scientist named J.J. Balmer researched the spectrum of hydrogen. He discovered that the visible lines in the hydrogen spectrum followed a predictable pattern. Additional research by other scientists revealed a further series of lines in the hydrogen spectrum that also followed similar patterns.

FIGURE 2

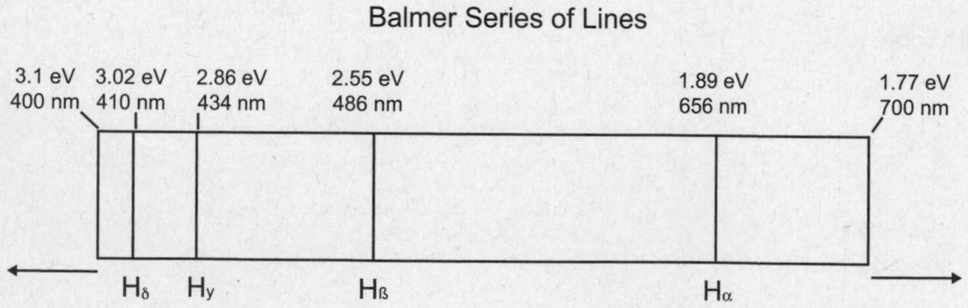

FIGURE 3

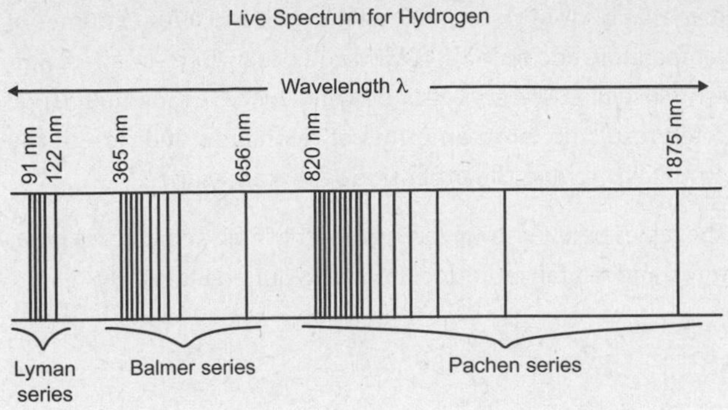

Why does an atom produce a line spectrum? The answer to this question came as a result of the research of Neils Bohr. Bohr suggested that electrons are found at discrete energy levels in an atom. When an atom is said to be excited, electrons jump to higher energy levels. This excited condition is not permanent. Eventually, the electrons return to their standard energy levels through one or more transitions. As electrons jump to lower energy levels, they release energy. The energy is not emitted in a continuous fashion, but instead in discrete amounts called *photons*. The amount of energy determines the nature of the light in the spectrum.

Table 1 lists the first six energy levels in a hydrogen atom.

Table 1

Level $n =$	Energy
1	0 eV
2	10.2 eV
3	12.1 eV
4	12.8 eV
5	13.1 eV
6	13.2 eV

29. The Balmer series is produced when excited electrons transition down to the first excited state ($n = 2$). The transition from the $n = 4$ level (H_β) involves an energy change of 2.6 eV. Which of the energies relate to the transition from the $n = 5$ level to the $n = 2$ level?

A. 1.9 eV
B. 2.9 eV
C. 3.0 eV
D. 13.1 eV

30. Each series in the hydrogen spectrum corresponds to transitions of excited electrons back down to a particular energy level (n). The lowest energy transition in each series corresponds to a transition back down to that level n from one level up ($n+1$). Based on the information provided in Figure 3, the Lyman series corresponds to transitions of excited electrons back down to which energy level?

F. 1
G. 2
H. 3
J. 4

31. According to Figure 1, the type of wave with the highest frequency is:

A. gamma ray.
B. infrared.
C. microwave.
D. radio wave.

32. In which portion of the electromagnetic spectrum does the Paschen series occur?

F. Infrared
G. Visible
H. Ultraviolet
J. X-ray

33. Which transition would most likely produce the H_γ line in the Balmer series?

A. $n = 3$ to $n = 1$
B. $n = 4$ to $n = 2$
C. $n = 5$ to $n = 2$
D. $n = 5$ to $n = 3$

34. Researchers confined excited hydrogen gas in a discharge tube. They found that it glows with a distinctive red color. This is probably due to which Balmer line?

F. H_α
G. H_β
H. H_γ
J. H_δ

CONTINUE

PASSAGE VII

The term *climate* refers to patterns of weather over time, including averages and extremes. In contrast, *weather* only describes short-term conditions. Climate includes measurements of temperature, precipitation and atmospheric pressure, which are affected by a region's geography. The amount and intensity of sunlight a region receives affects its temperature. Areas closer to the equator receive a consistent amount of sunlight year-round, while those at more northern or southern latitudes receive far less sunlight in the winter, and more in the summer. Proximity to a large body of water can buffer a region against extremes of temperature and humidity. Wind and ocean currents affect patterns in rainfall. Warm, wet air blowing toward a mountain range often results in large amounts of rainfall on one side of the mountain, leaving the other side significantly drier.

The tables below show average monthly high and low temperatures, and rainfall for four cities in the United States.

Table 1

Average High and Low Temperatures, °F

Month	Abilene, Texas	Bemidji, Minnesota	Los Angeles, California	Seattle, Washington
Jan	57, 33	26, 7	67, 51	47, 37
Feb	60, 37	31, 12	67, 51	50, 37
Mar	69, 44	43, 24	69, 51	54, 39
April	77, 52	58, 38	69, 53	58, 42
May	85, 61	71, 50	70, 56	65, 47
June	91, 69	80, 59	73, 58	70, 52
July	94, 72	85, 64	77, 62	76, 56
Aug	94, 72	82, 62	79, 62	76, 56
Sept	87, 64	73, 53	78, 62	71, 52
Oct	77, 54	59, 41	75, 59	60, 46
Nov	66, 43	42, 27	71, 55	51, 40
Dec	57, 34	29, 13	67, 51	46, 36

Table 2

Average Precipitation, inches

Month	Abilene, Texas	Bemidji, Minnesota	Los Angeles, California	Seattle, Washington
Jan	1.0	0.8	4.0	5.5
Feb	1.4	0.7	5.1	3.5
Mar	1.7	1.5	2.8	3.7
April	1.6	2.9	1.0	2.7
May	3.2	3.7	0.3	1.9
June	3.5	4.2	0.1	1.5
July	1.9	4.4	0.0	0.7
Aug	2.6	4.8	0.0	0.9
Sept	2.2	3.3	0.2	1.4
Oct	3.0	2.9	0.9	3.5
Nov	1.4	1.8	1.4	6.5
Dec	1.2	1.1	2.8	5.3

FIGURE 1

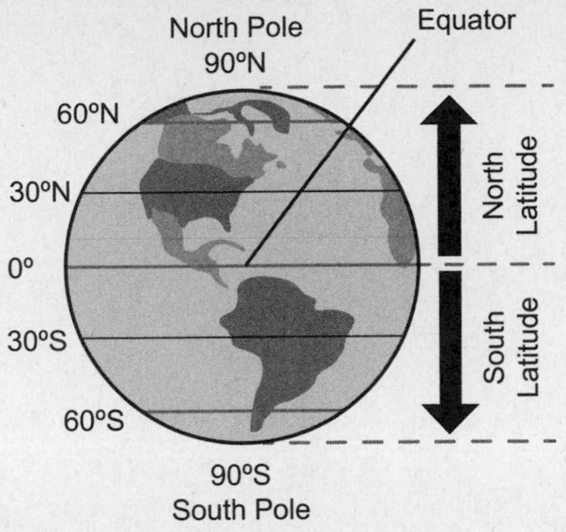

35. Which of the following statements describe climate as opposed to weather?

I. Los Angeles typically receives most of its annual rainfall in January and February.
II. Temperatures in downtown Los Angeles reached 104° on Friday.
III. Los Angeles has a warmer average temperature than Bemidji, Minnesota.

A. I only
B. II only
C. I and III
D. I, II and III

36. Which city experiences the smallest range of temperatures over the course of the year?

F. Abilene, Texas
G. Bemidji, Minnesota
H. Los Angeles, California
J. Seattle, Washington

37. Based on the information in the tables, which city is most likely to experience rain on July 10th?

A. Abilene, Texas
B. Bemidji, Minnesota
C. Los Angeles, California
D. Seattle, Washington

38. Seattle, Washington, and Bemidji, Minnesota, both lie between latitude 47° and 48° north. Based on the information in the passage, what most likely accounts for the difference in annual temperature between the two cities?

F. Being closer to the ocean gives Seattle a more moderate climate.
G. Being farther from the ocean gives Bemidji a more moderate climate.
H. Being closer to the mountain ranges gives Seattle a more moderate climate.
J. Being higher in altitude gives Bemidji a wider range of temperatures.

39. Bend, Oregon, and Saratoga Springs, New York, have a similar latitude and distance from an ocean. Based on information in the passage, what additional information would help explain why, on average, Bend receives 11 inches of annual rainfall and Saratoga Springs receives 45 inches of annual rainfall?

A. Altitude of both cities
B. Average annual temperature of both cities
C. Positioning of mountain ranges with respect to both cities
D. Distribution of rainfall over the year in both cities

40. Which of the following cities in the United States is likely to have the warmest summers and coldest winters?

F. A city located at low latitude, close to the Gulf of Mexico
G. A city located at high latitude, on the shore of one of the Great Lakes
H. A city located at low latitude, far inland
J. A city located at high latitude, far inland

STOP

WRITING TEST

40 Minutes

DIRECTIONS: This is a test of your writing skills. You have forty (40) minutes to write an essay in English. Be sure to carefully read the issue and three perspectives presented before planning and writing your essay so you understand clearly the task you are being asked to do. Your essay will be graded on the evidence it provides of your ability to analyze the issue; evaluate and analyze the perspectives; state and develop a personal perspective; and describe the relationship between the given perspectives and your own, while effectively using organization, logic, and language according to the conventions of standard written English.

A Dangerous Sport

Is football too dangerous a sport to keep playing? Media coverage regarding the increasing number of football-related injuries at every level—from youth football leagues to the NFL—has placed this issue in the national spotlight. Football injuries, often career-ending, life-altering, and even life-threatening, have placed the game under more scrutiny than ever before. Former professional players, worried parents, and politicians have become more vocal in their concern regarding player safety, raising questions about the future of the sport. The number of people calling for a ban altogether is on the rise. What are your thoughts regarding the future of football? How should we address the growing concerns regarding the safety of this sport? Should the game of football be banned altogether? Should serious reform, which might alter the way the game is currently played but would make the game safer to play, be considered?

Read and carefully consider these perspectives. Each suggests a particular way of thinking about how the dangers of football should be addressed.

Perspective One

Football should be banned immediately. It's simply too dangerous a sport to play, and people's lives should not be put at risk for a game. There have already been too many players who have been hurt, maimed, paralyzed, and even killed—and playing this game is not worth these risks. Professional football players whose careers aren't ended early due to injury are often saddled with a lifetime of pain and medical issues after retirement. Who wants to put their kids at risk of suffering a similar fate? Those who are interested in playing sports should choose to get involved in a safer one.

Perspective Two

The sport of football should be left alone! Generations of people have grown up on the game and have made following their favorite professional teams a big part of their lives—this shouldn't just be taken away from them. Football teaches discipline and teamwork, brings people together, and is a viable way for many individuals to succeed in their lives. Most players and organizations approach the game responsibly and carefully, and their lives are enhanced—not ruined—by their involvement with the game. Just because a few injuries have received media attention doesn't mean the game should be banned. Should everything that contains some level of risk be banned? If so, then add NASCAR, window washing, and mountain climbing to the list of things to ban. We live in a free society, and that includes the right to pursue athletic endeavors safely and responsibly.

Perspective Three

It's tough to deny that football is a dangerous sport. It's true, individuals who choose to get involved in this rough athletic activity are putting themselves at risk, even if they play carefully and responsibly and utilize the most current safety equipment. However, this doesn't mean that the sport should be banned altogether. There are lots of things in life that contain an element of risk, and banning them is against what a free society stands for. The fact is, people should have the right to choose whether or not they get involved in a rough sport like football, as adults or parents of children who play. The added media attention that football injuries have been receiving isn't a bad thing, but the conversation should turn to ways to make the game safer, such as improving safety equipment technology, greater information campaigns regarding the potential dangers of the game, and perhaps revising how the game is played to make it safer—not banning it altogether.

Essay Task

Write a unified, coherent essay in which you evaluate multiple perspectives on the future of football. In your essay, be sure to:

- examine and assess the perspectives given
- declare and explain your own perspective on the issue
- discuss the relationship between your perspective and those given

Your perspective may be in full or partial agreement, or in total disagreement, with any of the others. Whatever the case, support your ideas with logical reasoning and detailed, persuasive examples.

Plan and Write Your Essay

Use the first two pages of the Writing test answer sheet (found at the beginning of the test) to generate ideas and plan your essay. Then use the following four pages to write your essay. Consider the following as you compose your essay:

What are the strengths and weaknesses of the three perspectives provided?

- Identify the insights they present and what they fail to consider.
- Ascertain why a given perspective might persuade or fail to persuade.

How can you apply your own experience, knowledge, and values?

- Express your perspective on the issue, identifying the perspective's strengths and weaknesses.
- Formulate a plan to support your perspective in your essay.

English

1.	B	**20.**	F	**39.**	C	**58.**	F
2.	G	**21.**	D	**40.**	G	**59.**	D
3.	C	**22.**	G	**41.**	D	**60.**	F
4.	H	**23.**	A	**42.**	G	**61.**	A
5.	B	**24.**	J	**43.**	A	**62.**	J
6.	J	**25.**	D	**44.**	F	**63.**	C
7.	C	**26.**	H	**45.**	A	**64.**	G
8.	G	**27.**	B	**46.**	G	**65.**	B
9.	C	**28.**	H	**47.**	A	**66.**	H
10.	H	**29.**	C	**48.**	H	**67.**	A
11.	C	**30.**	G	**49.**	D	**68.**	H
12.	G	**31.**	B	**50.**	F	**69.**	A
13.	D	**32.**	H	**51.**	D	**70.**	H
14.	J	**33.**	D	**52.**	G	**71.**	B
15.	B	**34.**	G	**53.**	A	**72.**	F
16.	J	**35.**	C	**54.**	G	**73.**	D
17.	D	**36.**	G	**55.**	B	**74.**	G
18.	F	**37.**	A	**56.**	J	**75.**	C
19.	C	**38.**	J	**57.**	D		

1. **The correct answer is B.** As written, the sentence contains unnecessary commas and adds confusion. No commas or internal punctuation are needed here, so choice B is correct.

2. **The correct answer is G.** The sentence is written awkwardly, so look for a better construction, one in which *vaudeville* is the subject. Choice G is the best way, because *It was vaudeville* is simplified to the subject *vaudeville*; the simple past tense of the verb, *brought*, is more concise and effective in this sentence; and reordering the words in the second half is also a stylistic improvement. Choice H is awkward, and choice J is unclear, using a modifier (*in the millions*) that is far from the subject it modifies (*people*).

3. **The correct answer is C.** The sentence as written mistakes *a peel* for the similar sounding but correct *appeal* (choice C). Choices B and D also contain similar sounding but incorrect word choices.

4. **The correct answer is H.** The listed items in this sentence need to be separated by commas, which choice H does correctly. The other choices use incorrect internal punctuation to separate the items in this list.

5. **The correct answer is B.** The original sentence suffers from poor construction in that it lacks parallelism. The audience takes three basic actions in the sentence: laugh, join, and watch. In a correctly structured sentence, the form of each verb is parallel to the form of the other verbs. This answer choice states that the audience would laugh, join, and watch. The verbs are all in the same tense, controlled by the helping verb *would*. This corrects the parallelism problem. Choices C and D do not solve the problem.

6. **The correct answer is J.** Speaking is a form of verbal communication, so the phrase is redundant as written. The only way to correct the redundancy is to take out either "verbal communication" or "speaking." Choices G and H do not do that, but choice J does.

7. **The correct answer is C.** As written, the sentence ending in *inexpensive* is grammatically correct. However, the sentence beginning with *making* is a fragment, not a complete sentence, and therefore needs to be changed. Choice C corrects the fragment by joining it to the other sentence with a comma. Choice B is incorrect because it creates a comma splice (two complete sentences separated by a comma). Choice D is incorrect because the conjunction *yet* indicates contrast, which would be illogical in this sentence.

8. **The correct answer is G.** The appropriate verb tense here is the past tense, since it refers to vaudeville's popularity, which is in the past. Therefore, *was* (choice G) is the correct choice. The other answer choices utilize incorrect verb forms, given the context of the sentence.

9. **The correct answer is C.** There is an error in this sentence as written. The word *we* refers to the parents who took their children to vaudeville shows. Because *parents* is in the third person and *we* is in the first person, the sentence needs a different pronoun. *Parents* is plural, so it cannot be referred to with the singular *he or she* (choice B) or *one* (choice D). The only word that works is *they*.

10. **The correct answer is H.** While choice F is a true statement, it is not the main idea of the paragraph, which is the origin of vaudeville. Choice G, too, might be true, but it is too general and does not introduce the main idea of the paragraph. Choice H is correct because it is about the origins of vaudeville and leads logically into the sentence that currently begins Paragraph 3. Choice J would work if the paragraph presented various theories on the origin of vaudeville, but it does not.

11. **The correct answer is C.** It makes logical sense that as acts became more creative, they would attract larger audiences, so choice C is correct. As the sentence stands, the phrase "mostly creative" makes little sense; an act is by definition creative. Thus, choice A is incorrect. Choice B merely adds a misplaced comma, and choice D is illogical: how could the acts be *overly* creative, and if they were, why would that attract a wider audience?

12. **The correct answer is G.** The underlined portion of the sentence explains that the increasing popularity of vaudeville is the reason businesspeople began opening more theaters. Therefore, choice G is the best answer. The term *audience* is too vague to justify choice F. The underlined portion of the sentence only explains that vaudeville shows were attracting wider audiences; it does not explain why this happened, so choice H is incorrect. Since the underlined portion of the sentence does not provide specifics on how much the audience was growing, choice J cannot be correct.

13. **The correct answer is D.** It doesn't make sense for the paragraph to begin with examples, so eliminate choice A. Logically, examples should go after a statement of some kind. Since Sentence 3 begins by referring to *other famous vaudevillians*, this means that some vaudevillians were already mentioned. You can guess that Sentence 3 goes after Sentence 1. Sentence 2 is the topic sentence, referring in general to the performers who gained fame. It should be followed by Sentence 1, which lists several specific examples. Sentence 3 should end the paragraph by providing some additional examples. This is the most logical sequence. Choices B and C do not improve the logical flow of Paragraph 4.

14. **The correct answer is J.** This paragraph should be placed early in the essay because it gives introductory information, such as the origin and meaning of the word *vaudeville*. Nonetheless, the first paragraph should remain where it is because it is most effective as the introduction, so you can eliminate choice H. Therefore, Paragraph 3 should come directly after Paragraph 1. Choice G would place the introductory information at the end of the essay.

15. **The correct answer is B.** Paragraph 1 (choice A) mentions the laughter and joy that vaudeville brought to millions, but Paragraph 2 makes the author's argument more convincing. It provides many details—the diversity of the acts, vaudeville's appeal to non-English speakers, and its focus on family fun—to make the author's argument more convincing. This is the correct answer. Paragraph 3 (choice C) is mostly background information on the roots of vaudeville. This does not advance the author's argument. Paragraph 4 (choice D) focuses on performers who became famous on the vaudeville stage. This would not help the author's argument.

16. **The correct answer is J.** Although the meaning of this sentence is clear, it is awkwardly constructed, so eliminate choice F. The word order in choice G is also awkward, placing the phrase *to human life* right between the verb and its object. The construction in choice H changes the meaning of the original sentence. Word order is crucial to the meaning of a sentence. The sentence reads most effectively when *essential* is not separated from the phrase *to human life*, as it is in the other answer choices. Only choice J expresses the meaning more clearly and smoothly.

17. **The correct answer is D.** This sentence contains a nonrestrictive element. Think of a nonrestrictive element as a little bit of extra information in a sentence. When it appears in the middle, it must be set off by two commas, not one (as shown in choice D). So you can eliminate choice A, which uses only one comma, and choice B, which does not use any. Using *that* and no commas (choice C) makes the phrase suggest that there is more than one Huang He, one of which flows through China.

18. **The correct answer is F.** The sentence is correct as written. As a verb, *gets* should have no apostrophe, so choices G and H are incorrect. Additionally, *its* is correctly used here as a possessive; *it's* is a contraction for *it is*. *It's* is used mistakenly in choices G and J.

19. **The correct answer is C.** The verb in the sentence is in present progressive tense, which indicates that the action is taking place at the time it is written about. In this sentence, it creates an awkward, confusing sense of time and ignores that the river has been vital in the past as well. *It be* is incorrect, so eliminate choice B. Eliminate choice D because just saying *it is* ignores the role the river has played throughout history—*for centuries*, according to the passage. The only choice that works is choice C, which describes something that began in the past but still has an effect at the time of the writing.

20. **The correct answer is F.** The correct answer should provide a logical transition between the sentence about the river's importance to Chinese life and the sentence about the devastation caused by its flooding, as it includes and relates both topics. Eliminate choice G, because the river's propensity for flooding is not mentioned until the sentence that follows, so this answer choice creates an illogical sequence. Choice H just rephrases the idea in the previous sentence, that the river is crucial to life in China. It is a needless repetition and doesn't introduce the idea of the river's devastation. Eliminate choice J because a description of the river's physical characteristics does nothing to provide the needed transition between sentences. Only choice F makes sense.

21. **The correct answer is D.** The antecedent to the pronoun *their* is the Huang He. Since *Huang He* is a singular antecedent, *their* must be replaced with a singular possessive pronoun. The contraction *they're* means "they are." It makes no sense to say "with they are raging waters," so eliminate choice B. *Them* is not a possessive, so eliminate choice C. *Its* is the correct possessive to use here.

22. **The correct answer is G.** This sentence reads as if *caused* is modifying (or referring to) *devastating*, when it should refer to *flood*. In choice G, both *devastating* and *caused* correctly and clearly modify the noun *flood*. Choices F, H, and J are awkward and create confusion over which noun *caused* modifies.

23. **The correct answer is A.** The pronouns *who* and *whom* are frequently confused. *Who* is in the subjective case, which means that it functions as a subject. *Whom* (choice B) is in the objective case, which means that it functions as an object. Since *who* refers to *villagers and farmers*, which is the subject of the sentence, the pronoun must be in the subjective case. The sentence is correct as written. The pronoun *which* is not used to refer to people, so eliminate choice C. The pronoun *whose* shows possession, or ownership, which is not needed here, so eliminate choice D.

24. **The correct answer is J.** As written, the use of the word *content* indicates a sense of satisfaction, but it does not convey the stronger emotion that the villagers would have felt. Neither does *satisfied* (choice G) nor *pleased* (choice H). The word *elated*, which means "overjoyed," expresses the extreme happiness that the villagers would have felt. The sentence tells you that their crops and lives were in jeopardy, so they would have felt more than contentment or satisfaction at the end of the long drought.

25. **The correct answer is D.** The original sentence is wordy. This is a problem with style, not grammar, which is why wordiness can be easy to miss. In good writing, every word counts. A year *is* a period, so there is no need to state the obvious. Choices B and C simply reword the original unnecessary phrase; they do not correct the problem.

26. **The correct answer is H.** The original sentence is confusing and awkward. It sounds as though *the villagers working desperately to raise the dikes* modifies the second part of the sentence, and it doesn't make sense. Choice G contains a comma splice; it's grammatically incorrect, so eliminate it. Choice J changes the meaning of the sentence, so eliminate it. Choice H correctly shows the cause-and-effect relationship between the two parts of the sentence.

27. **The correct answer is B.** Eliminate choice A because the writer does not define other unfamiliar words in the passage. While it is true that the word is not the focus of the passage, writers do often define words and terms in their works, even if not crucial to the passage as a whole. Eliminate choice C. It is unlikely that most readers will know the word, so eliminate choice D.

28. **The correct answer is H.** Choice H provides specifics about the magnitude of the floodwaters and emphasizes their intensity since Niagara Falls is a well-known and very large waterfall. Choice F would be a fine answer if it did not repeat information already provided in the sentence. Choice G simply isn't specific enough. Choice J repeats information already given in the paragraph and fails to emphasize the floodwaters' magnitude or intensity.

29. **The correct answer is C.** Interesting details can enhance an essay. However, good writers are selective of the details they include in their writing. Just because a detail is interesting does not mean it belongs in the essay. The passage focuses on the flood of 1935. Paragraph 5 gives details of the tragic consequences of that particular flood. Throwing in one sentence about an earlier flood detracts from the unity of the paragraph and the passage, so choices A and B are incorrect. Choice D misidentifies the reason the sentence should be eliminated.

30. **The correct answer is G.** Choice G mentions the specific flood that the passage describes. It is the best summary of the passage as a whole. Choices F and H are too narrow, and choice J is too broad.

31. **The correct answer is B.** In order to determine the correct word choice we need to examine its context within the sentence. This part of the sentence is discussing the "things we need to have" in life—which word choice best describes these types of items? *Essential* (choice B) is the best fit. The other answer choices are inappropriate, given the context of the sentence.

32. **The correct answer is H.** As written, the sentence contains an incorrect possessive plural form of the underlined word. The correct fix for this word is *groceries* (choice H). The other answer choices all contain an incorrect plural form of *groceries*.

33. **The correct answer is D.** The underlined portion of the sentence contains a simple list of items, so they should be separated by commas, as choice D correctly does. Choice B utilizes parentheses, which should be used only for information that's an aside, or superfluous, which is not the case here. Items in a list should not be separated by asterisks, as they are in choice C.

34. **The correct answer is G.** The underlined portion of the sentence contains an incorrect word, *yore*, which is inappropriate here given the context of the sentence. The correct word given the context of the sentence is *you're*, which is a contraction of *you are*. Plug the word into the sentence to see if it makes sense: *Then there's the other category of purchases that I recently had an experience with, one that I have affectionately dubbed mistakes—if you're lucky, you'll have little or no experience with throwing your money away in this category, although if you do, make sure it's a real learning experience for you!*

35. **The correct answer is C.** Paragraph 3 contains a recollection of a memory about one night in the life of the author. Choice C would serve as the best opening for this paragraph.

36. **The correct answer is G.** As written, the words in the sentence are jumbled, which affects the clarity and narrative flow. Choice G fixes this issue, and makes the text clear and comprehensible. The other answer choices fail to fix the confusion and are therefore incorrect.

37. **The correct answer is A.** This question is asking you to examine the author's word choice in the underlined portion of the sentence. How can we determine how the customers are responding to Confidence in a Can? Scanning the sentence, we can see that the customers provided "stories of how the product completely changed their lives for the better." What word choice best fits here? The sentence is correct as written—the customers *endorsed* the product. The other choices don't fit, given the context of the sentence.

38. **The correct answer is J.** As written, the sentence contains an inappropriate contraction, *I'm*, and the incorrect form of the verb *to need*. As written, the sentence requires the pronoun *I* and the past tense, *needed*, so Choice J fixes the issue. You can check your answer by plugging it into the sentence to make sure it sounds correct: *And then, when the host said that if I called the toll-free number right now I could have not one but two full cans of Confidence in a Can for one low discount price—that was all I needed to hear!*

39. **The correct answer is C.** Without the statement in choice C, it would not be clear that the author actually decided to place the order. Choice A may show that the author was considering ordering Confidence in a Can, but it does not actually show that he placed the order. Choice B contradicts the fact that he found the host's pitch convincing. Choice D fails to show that the author placed the order for Confidence in a Can.

40. **The correct answer is G.** The sentence needs to begin with a transitional word indicating that the author went to Jackie's house as a consequence of needing to do something while allowing more time for the Confidence in a Can to work. *So* is a transitional word indicating a consequence. The transitional words *however* (choice F) and *nevertheless* (choice H) indicate contrast, not consequence. *In other words* indicates a clarification.

41. **The correct answer is D.** The underlined portion of the sentence contains a piece of dialogue spoken by a person in the story—a quote—so it should appear in quotation marks; therefore, choice D is correct. Putting the quote in parentheses (choice A), italicizing the quote (choice B), or underlining it (choice C) are not appropriate treatments for a quote.

42. **The correct answer is G.** Carefully analyzing the paragraphs in question, it seems that there's some disorganization. Paragraph 7 discusses opening the package, while paragraph 8 mentions waiting for the package to arrive. Logically, this information is out of sequence; reversing these two paragraphs, as choice G suggests, fixes the issue and is the correct answer.

43. **The correct answer is A.** An effective concluding sentence should tie up the themes and/or purpose of the written piece. This passage is all about the author learning that a purchase he made late at night while sleepy was a bad decision; choice A effectively captures the author's learned lesson and is the correct answer. Choice B is inappropriate, as only one product in a can is discussed, not everything sold in cans. Choice C is beyond the scope of the information contained in the passage; the value of confidence in achieving your goals is not discussed.

44. **The correct answer is F.** Deleting the first paragraph would delete essential details for understanding the passage, so it is not a good idea. The other choices don't reflect the best recommendation and reasoning here.

45. **The correct answer is A.** A careful reading of the passage reveals that it's a humorous recollection of an embarrassing yet funny learning experience in the life of the author, so choice A is correct. The other genres mentioned among the answer choices don't fit the tone and purpose of the passage.

46. **The correct answer is G.** This sentence requires two commas to set apart the two separate ideas of muscle power versus engine or sail power, and the original sentence is missing that comma. Choice G places the commas between the two ideas correctly. A conjunction such as *but* or *and* is not necessary and makes the construction of the sentence awkward, so choices H and J should be eliminated.

47. **The correct answer is A.** The sentence is correct as written. The conjunction *because* in choice B is incorrect since it changes the meaning of the original sentence (the popularity of rowing is illustrated by the number of clubs around the world). By adding *because*, the sentence indicates that rowing is popular due to the number of clubs. Choice C contains two unnecessary commas that splice and interrupt the flow of the sentence. Finally, because the aim of the original sentence is to illustrate just how popular rowing has become worldwide, choice D should be eliminated (although it is not grammatically incorrect) because separating the original sentence into two does not convey the meaning that the author intends.

48. **The correct answer is H.** The correct word for the underlined portion of the sentence is the adverb *as*, which is weighing a comparison between the effort given and its appearance. The other answer choices don't make sense, given the context of the sentence.

49. **The correct answer is D.** As written, there's an internal error in logic in this sentence: a "coordinated effort" is mentioned, but then an uncoordinated effort—body or mind—is referenced. Choice D corrects the error by showing that the coordinated effort mentioned refers to body *and* mind.

50. **The correct answer is F.** The sentence is correct as written. Choice G is incorrect because the semicolon divides the independent and dependent clauses. The period in choice H creates the sentence fragment "When rowing together in a team boat." Choice J is also a sentence fragment and can be eliminated.

51. **The correct answer is D.** Choice A is incorrect because it contains an unnecessary phrase *you see*. Choice B can be eliminated because adding *consequently* does not make sense; the author has not given a possible reason for the rowers getting out of synch. Therefore, there is no consequence to discuss. Choice C is incorrect because it is redundant. *Just a bit* repeats the idea behind *even for a moment*. Only choice D is written correctly.

52. **The correct answer is G.** The present participles of the verbs *to lose* and *to happen* are in agreement in choice G. Choice F is incorrect because *lost speed* does not really "happen" to an object, such as a boat. The addition of parentheses is inappropriate in choice H because the words contained in the parentheses are grammatically related to the rest of the sentence and should not be separated by this form of punctuation. Choice J should be eliminated because the infinitive *to lose* and the past participle *have happened* do not agree in tense.

53. **The correct answer is A.** Context is essential when determining the appropriate conjunctive adverb to begin this sentence. Answer choices B, C, and D reference a contrast between the sentence or independent clause it appears in and the previous sentence or independent clause—and are not appropriate here. The sentence is correct as written.

54. **The correct answer is G.** This is the appropriate compound preposition for this sentence. Choice F is incorrect because *additionally* is an adverb that is not modifying a verb in its current location. Choice H should be eliminated; the rowers do not spend time in the weight room as a result of training on the water. Choice J is incorrect because *since* is also an adverb and is grammatically incorrect.

55. **The correct answer is B.** The sentence as written doesn't make sense—who would train thousands of hours a year for a race that was inconsequential? Only a race that was significant would make sense for rowers to devote that much effort to it. Therefore, *important* (choice B) makes the most sense here and is the correct answer.

56. **The correct answer is J.** *Is* provides the proper tense of the verb *to be* for this sentence. Choice F should be eliminated because *are* is the second-person plural form of *to be*, while the subject of the sentence is third-person singular. Choice G is incorrect because it does not provide a verb for the sentence. Choice H can also be eliminated because it is partially in the past perfect tense and is an incomplete form of this tense.

57. **The correct answer is D.** The mention of longer races does not support the point the author is making about training time versus time spent racing. Choice A is incorrect because the placement of this sentence would be at the end of the paragraph where it would not help to further explain races themselves, a concept introduced in the very beginning of the paragraph. Choice B can be eliminated because the main point of this paragraph is that time spent racing is far less than the time spent training. Choice C is incorrect due to the fact that the World Championships are not the sole focus of this paragraph.

58. **The correct answer is F.** The comma precedes *or* and serves to join the two independent clauses. The colon in choice G is incorrect because it does not join the clauses. Choices H and J can be eliminated; they do not express the author's original intention of comparing one type of rower to another.

59. **The correct answer is D.** Without choice D at the beginning of Paragraph 5, the statement about watching possible Olympian rowers would not make any sense. The statement would make no sense if placed at the beginning of Paragraphs 2 (choice A), 3 (choice B), or 4 (choice C).

60. **The correct answer is F.** While the essay does mention that rowers train many hours, it is not composed entirely of specific details of racing and training. Choice G is incorrect because the essay does in fact illustrate that rowing requires both intense training and good technique. While the fourth paragraph discusses the distance and typical time of a rowing race, there is no other mention of this throughout the rest of the essay, so we may eliminate choice H. Choice J is similarly incorrect, as there was only a brief mention, not great detail, concerning weight training schedules.

61. **The correct answer is A.** The sentence is correct as written. It is most common in our language to say: "…studies indicate *that*." We would never hear "…studies indicate *for*" (choice B) or "…studies indicate *in*" (choice C). And while it might pass in ordinary conversation to say "…studies indicate *how*," this is not a proper construction, so choice D is incorrect.

62. **The correct answer is J.** Choice J pairs the singular verb *cites* with the singular subject *article*. Eliminate choice F since it offers a plural verb to match with the singular subject: "A recent article …cite experiments …." Eliminate choice G since it offers a noun instead of a verb, and a verb is most definitely required for this spot. Choice H proposes the gerund (*-ing*) form of the verb, which is inappropriate for this situation because the underlined word bears the responsibility of being the operative verb for the sentence. *Citing* could only be used if another verb bears the brunt of that work, as in: "A recent article citing several noted neurobiologists stated that …." In this example, *stated* becomes the operative verb.

63. **The correct answer is C.** Essentially, this question asks you to find the most common expression of the idea carried in this phrase. If a study is particularly interesting, how might you write that in an introduction to a sentence? Choices B and D offer roundabout constructions you would never hear spoken or see written. Choice A is a bit too colloquial for the written language, and the comma actually renders this choice grammatically incorrect.

64. **The correct answer is G.** Choice G proposes the best combination of proper punctuation and grammar to convey the meaning of the sentence. Choice F is a run-on sentence. There needs to be some sort of break in the prose after the word *discovery* since a new thought begins. Punctuation can be used, or perhaps an appropriate connecting word such as *and* or *because*. Choice H proposes the word *with*, but this is

inappropriate since it connects rather than separates the different thoughts in the sentence. Choice J turns *saturated* (an adjective) into *saturating* (a verb). This confounds the grammar in the sentence. Choice G appropriately uses a colon to signal the reader that information on the new discovery is forthcoming.

65. **The correct answer is B.** This question primarily tests your command of pronouns. *Each member* is the operative subject of the sentence. *Each member* is a singular construction. Pronouns are used to refer to previously established nouns. Singular pronouns must be used in reference to singular nouns. Plural pronouns must be used to refer to plural nouns. *They* is a plural pronoun; therefore, eliminate choice C. Choice D suggests no pronoun at all; it, too, can be eliminated because a pronoun is necessary to provide clarity in the sentence. Although *it* is a singular pronoun, it is not used to refer to people, so choice A is also incorrect. To some ears, choice B may sound cumbersome. It is, however, the only grammatically correct option available.

66. **The correct answer is H.** Choice H provides a grammatically correct descriptive phrase for the sentence. The underlined portion is essentially a phrase modifying the *period of four years*. Each option attempts to convey the idea that the referenced period occurred after the second research test was administered. A gerund (the *-ing* form of a word) is the most commonly used construction for this type of work, so choices F and J are incorrect. We frequently hear "a period following" in our language. There is no need to insert *that* as offered by choice G—it only interrupts the flow of the sentence.

67. **The correct answer is A.** The studies show that eating foods rich in saturated and hydrogenated fats can increase a person's chance of developing Alzheimer's disease. For clarification, the author chooses to list examples of these foods. The correct phrase for listing examples of a point is "such as." *Like* is often used incorrectly for this purpose. *Like* should be used when you are ascribing similar qualities to two things. Eliminate choice B since it offers *like*. Eliminate choices C and D since *with* and *because* are inappropriate words for listing examples of a concept.

68. **The correct answer is H.** This question asks you to find the most idiomatically acceptable expression of quantity. According to the author's information, a diet rich in saturated and hydrogenated fats will increase a person's chances of developing Alzheimer's disease. How much will it increase the chances? "More than twice." Why? Because *double* is either a verb or an adjective. It cannot stand in for "two times" like the word *twice* does. So eliminate choices F and G. Eliminate choice J because the word *plus* doesn't make sense there.

69. **The correct answer is A.** The sentence is correct as written because *attacks* offers the correct verb tense. Choice B offers a convoluted verb expression. While you may have heard a phrasing like *does an attack on* in English conversation, the rules of standard written language are more strict. Choice C proposes that the study *will attack* a theory in the future, but this doesn't hold up to the information contained in the rest of the essay: the study is currently being considered. Choice D's construction references the past tense—again, incorrect since the study is being considered in the present. Besides, *did attack* can be written more concisely as "attacked."

70. **The correct answer is H.** The passage says, "Many researchers have gone on record," and then we need to choose an underlined portion that describes their stance. Choice H offers a grammatically correct predicate phrase. Choice F, *in supporting the notion that*, is awkward. Similarly, choice G disrupts its own grammar by incorrectly pairing *to* with the gerund *supporting*. Choice J switches *that* to *which*. *Which* is used to establish a modifying clause, which does not exist in this case.

71. **The correct answer is B.** The subject of the sentence is *vitamins,* a plural noun. It must be coupled with a plural verb. Choice A offers *has*, which is a singular verb and can be eliminated. Choice C proposes *are*, which does not fit with the rest of the sentence—"are been singled out" is never a proper construction in English. Choice D proposes a repetition of forms of the verb *to be*: "will be been." The best option is choice B, which notes that *vitamins have been* singled out as agents that can reduce the risk of free radical damage. This answer choice has the correct subject-verb agreement.

72. **The correct answer is F.** Without the clause it would not be clear that the research subjects were being tracked to learn whether or not they developed dementia symptoms, so choice F is the best answer. Researchers would not be concerned about people who displayed no dementia symptoms, so choice G does not make sense. The clause may indicate that researchers were trying to learn about dementia developing in people with no previous symptoms, but it hardly explains how it develops (choice H). Treatment for

dementia would not begin before a person begins showing symptoms of the condition, so choice J does not make sense either.

73. The correct answer is D. Choices A and C can be eliminated immediately. They propose to begin the paragraph with "during that time" without previously establishing a point of reference. In fact, Sentence 2 contains the increment of time to which Sentence 1 refers. Therefore, any correct ordering of the paragraph must put Sentence 2 before Sentence 1, which choice B does not do. The only option that does this is choice D.

74. The correct answer is G. Eliminate choice F since it focuses only on antioxidant vitamins. Antioxidants are merely a point of reference in the author's narrative, which provides his readers with an outline of these new scientific studies. Delving into more detail concerning antioxidants would only harm the author's mission to provide an overview of the studies. Eliminate choice H since there is no need to provide counterpoints in order to offer an overview of the studies. Eliminate choice J on the basis that the author's inclusion of a quote from Jose A. Luchsinger in no way validates his success of creating an overview of the studies cited. Only choice G explains how the essay fulfills the assignment accurately.

75. The correct answer is C. Eliminate choices A and D since the second study mentioned by the author maintains that despite widely held beliefs concerning antioxidants, they are apparently ineffectual for decreasing the risk of contracting Alzheimer's disease or dementia. Eliminate choice B since it maintains the exact opposite of what the cited studies show. Saturated fats have been linked to an increased chance of contracting Alzheimer's disease or dementia. Increasing your dosage of saturated fats will only increase your chances of contracting these two ailments. Therefore, choice C is the best answer.

MATHEMATICS

1.	D	**16.**	G	**31.**	B	**46.**	G
2.	K	**17.**	D	**32.**	H	**47.**	D
3.	A	**18.**	H	**33.**	E	**48.**	K
4.	J	**19.**	A	**34.**	F	**49.**	B
5.	B	**20.**	K	**35.**	B	**50.**	J
6.	F	**21.**	E	**36.**	H	**51.**	C
7.	D	**22.**	H	**37.**	C	**52.**	J
8.	G	**23.**	B	**38.**	F	**53.**	D
9.	C	**24.**	J	**39.**	C	**54.**	H
10.	H	**25.**	D	**40.**	F	**55.**	E
11.	D	**26.**	F	**41.**	B	**56.**	F
12.	K	**27.**	B	**42.**	J	**57.**	E
13.	E	**28.**	H	**43.**	D	**58.**	J
14.	G	**29.**	C	**44.**	H	**59.**	B
15.	D	**30.**	G	**45.**	C	**60.**	F

1. **The correct answer is D.** If 20% equals 14 students, then 100% equals 70 students. 100% is five times 20%, so 100% of the class is 5 × 14, or 70 students. Choice A is 40%, not 100%, of the total class. In choice B, you added 20 and 14, but 20 is a percentage while 14 is a number of students—they cannot be added directly. Choice C is 80% of the total number of students in the class. In choice E, you added 14 to 100% of the class, which is actually 120% of the total class.

2. **The correct answer is K.** Solve the equation $4 - |2x - 16| = 0$. This is equivalent to $|2x - 16| = 4$, which generates two equations: $2x - 16 = 4$ and $2x - 16 = -4$. Adding 16 to both sides of these equations and then dividing by 2 yields the solutions $x = 10$ and $x = 6$. So the *x*-intercepts are (6, 0) and (10, 0). Choice F is incorrect because the equation $4 - |2x - 16| = 0$ has two solutions. Choice G is incorrect because this is when $2x - 16 = 0$, not 4. Choice H is incorrect because this is the *y*-intercept. Choice J is incorrect because you are missing one solution. Remember, an absolute value equation of the form $|x - a| = b$ generates two equations, namely $x - a = b$ and $x - a = -b$.

3. **The correct answer is A.** Solve for *x*:

$$1-\frac{3x}{2}=\frac{x+1}{6}$$
$$6-3(3x)=x+1$$
$$6-9x=x+1$$
$$5=10x$$
$$x=\frac{1}{2}$$

So the value of x^3 is $\left(\frac{1}{2}\right)^3=\frac{1}{2^3}=\frac{1}{8}$. Choice B is the value of *x*. In choice C, you multiplied base times exponent when computing $\left(\frac{1}{2}\right)^3$. Choice D is the reciprocal of *x*. Choice E is the reciprocal of the correct answer.

4. **The correct answer is J.** Since the three angles combine to form the straight line *GI*, the sum of the angles must equal 180°. You already know that $\angle JHI = 33°$ and $\angle KHJ = 22°$, so $\angle GHK = 180° - 33° - 22° = 125°$. Choice F is incorrect because the three angles form a straight angle, not a right angle. Choice G is incorrect because angle *GHK* is obtuse and cannot have measure equal to *KHJ* + *JHI* (which is 55 degrees). Choice H is too small—the sum of all three angles must be 180 degrees. Choice K is *GHK* + *KHJ*, not just *GHK*.

5. **The correct answer is B.** Calculate as follows:

$$\begin{aligned} f(2x+3) &= 1-2^{2x+3} \\ &= 1-2^{2x} \bullet 2^3 \\ &= 1-\left(2^2\right)^x \bullet 8 \\ &= 1-4^x \bullet 8 \\ &= 1-8 \bullet 4^x \end{aligned}$$

Choice A is incorrect because $a^{b+c} = a^b \bullet a^c$, not $a^b + a^c$, and $2^3 = 8$, not 6. Choice C is incorrect because you did not apply the exponent rules correctly. Choice D is incorrect because the power x does not apply to the 8 in the expression $8 \bullet 4^x$. Choice E is incorrect because $a^{b+c} = a^b \bullet a^c$ not $a^b + a^c$.

6. **The correct answer is F.** Each truck holds 11.4 tons, so all four trucks will hold $4 \times 11.4 = 45.6$ tons. With 45.6 tons in the trucks, there will be $55 - 45.6 = 9.4$ tons of sand left in the pile.

In choice G, you subtracted what three trucks can hold, not four trucks. Choice H is the amount that two trucks can hold. In choice J, you subtracted the amount one truck can hold, not four. Choice K is the number of tons the four trucks can hold combined.

7. **The correct answer is D.** Substitute the values of x and y into the expression and simplify:

$$\frac{1}{\sqrt{\left(\frac{2}{3}\right) \bullet \left(\frac{1}{6}\right)}} = \frac{1}{\sqrt{\frac{1}{9}}} = \frac{1}{\frac{1}{3}} = 3$$

Choice A is xy. Choice B is the reciprocal of the correct answer. Choice C is $\frac{1}{\sqrt{\frac{x}{y}}}$. In choice E, you did not take the square root.

8. **The correct answer is G.** Simplify using the order of operations:

$$\begin{aligned} -3^2\left|-6-(-4)\right| &= -3^2\left|-6+4\right| \\ &= -9\left|-2\right| \\ &= -9(2) \\ &= -18 \end{aligned}$$

In choice F, you computed $-6 - (-4)$ incorrectly as -10 instead of -2. Choice H is incorrect because $3^2 = 9$, not 6. Choice J has the wrong sign. Choice K has the wrong sign and you computed $-6 - (-4)$ incorrectly as -10 instead of -2.

9. **The correct answer is C.** The graph of $f(x)$ is a parabola opening upward (because the coefficient of x^2 is positive) with vertex $(-3, 2)$. The only graph that possesses these characteristics is the one in choice C.

10. **The correct answer is H.** The problem is asking you to find two consecutive integers, the first of which has a cube less than 80, and the second of which has a cube greater than 80. Use the answer choices to help you. The cubes of 2, 3, 4, and 5 are, respectively: 8, 27, 64, and 125. Since 80 falls between 64 and 125, you know that x is between 4 and 5, and you don't need to go any further—choices F, G, J, and K are not possible.

11. **The correct answer is D.** Solve for a:

$$\begin{aligned} 2a - 38 &= -26 \\ 2a &= 12 \\ a &= 6 \end{aligned}$$

So $3a = 3(6) = 18$. Choice A is incorrect because you should add 38 to both sides of the given equation, not subtract it. Choice B has the wrong sign. Choice C is the value of a. In choice E, you multiplied both sides of $2a = 12$ by 2 instead of dividing by it.

12. **The correct answer is K.** You can either solve algebraically or by choosing actual values for the ages. Algebraically, you know that Lina is x years old. Karen is twice as old, so Karen is $2x$ years old. Joel is 8 years older than Karen, so he is $2x + 8$ years old. Alternatively, you could choose a value for x. Let's say $x = 10$. Then Lina is 10, Karen is 20, and Joel is 28. Only choice K yields 28 when you substitute 10 for x, so this must be the correct answer. Choice F likely represents your calculation for Joel's age in relation to Karen, and choice G likely represents your equation for Karen's age in relation to Lina—both do not answer what the question asks. Choices H and J are untenable.

13. **The correct answer is E.** Looking at the coordinates given, you know that two of the points will have an x-coordinate of -4 and two will have an x-coordinate of 2. Likewise, two will have a y-coordinate of 5 and two will have a y-coordinate of -2. What is missing from the 3 points given? You see that you are missing an x-coordinate of 2 and a y-coordinate of -2. You could also draw a picture to help you visualize this. In order to have a chance at being the vertex, the points must lie on one of these lines: $x = -4$, $x = 2$, $y = 5$, or $y = -2$. The points in choices A and C do not. In choice B, the x-coordinate is wrong. In choice D, the y-coordinate is wrong.

14. The correct answer is G. Use the distributive property and then combine like terms:

$2(4y - 3z) - 4(2z - 3y) = 8y - 6z - 8z + 12y = 20y - 14z$

In choice F, you did not apply the distributive property to both terms of the parentheses. In choices H and J, you incorrectly added *y*-terms and *z*-terms; these are not like terms and so, cannot be combined. In choice K, you did not apply the negative to the second term of the second set of parentheses.

15. The correct answer is D. Since this is a parallelogram, the opposite angles are equal. Thus, $\angle WZY = \angle WXY$. You know that the angles in a triangle sum to 180°, so $\angle WXY = 180° - 45° - 30° = 105°$. Therefore, $\angle WZY$ also equals 105°. In choices A, B, and C, *WZY* is obtuse, so its measure must be greater than 90 degrees. Choice E is likely the result of an arithmetic error.

16. The correct answer is G. Substitute $y = 0$ into the equation $4y + 3x = 12$ to get $3x = 12$. So $x = 4$. The *x*-intercept is 4. Choice F is the *y*-intercept. In choices H and K, you solved the equation of the form $ax = b$ incorrectly; you should divide both sides by *a*. Choice J is just the constant term of the equation, not the *x*-intercept.

17. The correct answer is D. Solve for *x* using the radical method:

$$\begin{aligned}(3x+1)^2 + 9 &= 0\\ (3x+1)^2 &= -9\\ 3x+1 &= \pm 3i\\ 3x &= -1 \pm 3i\\ x &= \frac{-1 \pm 3i}{3} = -\frac{1}{3} \pm i\end{aligned}$$

Choice A is incorrect because $\sqrt{a+b} \neq \sqrt{a} + \sqrt{b}$. Choice B is incorrect because $\sqrt{-9} = 3i$, not 3. Choices C and E are incorrect because $(a + b)^2 \neq a^2 + b^2$.

18. The correct answer is H. Given the perimeter and the width of a rectangle, we can find the length by using the perimeter formula:

$$\begin{aligned}P &= 2l + 2w\\ 60 &= 2l + 2(12)\\ 60 &= 2l + 24\\ 36 &= 2l\\ 18 &= l\end{aligned}$$

Therefore the length is 18 units, and the area is $A = lw = (18)(12) = 216$.

Choice F is the length of the rectangle. If you chose G, you might have confused area for perimeter; if the area were 60 square units and the width 12 units, then the length would be 5 units and the perimeter 34 units. Choice J is double the area, and may be the result of forgetting to divide by 2 when solving for the length. Choice K is 4 times the correct area, which may be the result of forgetting to double the width when subtracting it from the perimeter, then forgetting to divide the difference by 2 to find the length.

19. The correct answer is A. Let *x* be the original price. Then, "70% of *x* is \$75.50" translates to the equation $0.70x = 75.50$. So $x = \frac{75.50}{0.70}$ dollars. In choice B, you divided by the wrong number. Choice C is incorrect because you should have divided by 0.70, not multiplied by it. Choice D is equivalent to choice C; you should divide 75.50 by 0.70. In choice E, you did not apply the percentage correctly.

20. The correct answer is K. FOIL the binomials to expand this expression:

$$\begin{aligned}(p^2q - 2pq^3)^2 &= (p^2q - 2pq^3)(p^2q - 2pq^3)\\ &= p^4q^2 - 2p^3q^4 - 2p^3q^4 + 4p^2q^6\\ &= p^4q^2 - 4p^3q^4 + 4p^2q^6\end{aligned}$$

Choice F does not include the middle term. In choice G, you should have doubled the middle term. Choice H is incorrect because when multiplying powers of the same base, you add the exponents, not multiply them. Choice J does not include the middle term and the last term should be added, not subtracted.

21. The correct answer is E. Solve the system using the substitution method. Substitute the expression for *x* given by the first equation into the second equation and solve for *y*:

$$\begin{aligned}y &= 2(2y - 1) - 1\\ y &= 4y - 2 - 1\\ y &= 4y - 3\\ -3y &= -3\\ y &= 1\end{aligned}$$

Substitute this value back into the first equation to determine the value of *x*: $x = 2(1) - 1 = 1$. Hence, $3^{x+y} = 3^{1+1} = 3^2 = 9$. Choice A is the value of *x* and of *y*. Choice B is $x + y$. Choice C is the result of multiplying the base times the exponent. Choice D is 2^3, not 3^2.

22. **The correct answer is H.** First convert the units so that you are working with ounces. Since each pound has 16 ounces, a 7.5 pound bag of rice has $7.5 \times 16 = 120$ ounces of rice in it. To determine the cost per ounce, divide the total cost ($4.80) by the number of ounces (120). That yields $4.80 ÷ 120 = $0.04. Choices F, G, J, and K are likely the result of an arithmetic error.

23. **The correct answer is B.** To calculate the total earnings, multiply the earnings per day, $23, by the number of days, in this case 6: (23)(6) = 138. Add this to $0.74 per bushel, multiplied by the number of bushels, which is represented by *x*.

Choice A multiplies both the $138 total of daily earnings and the rate per bushel by the number of bushels. Choice C multiplies the number of days by the earnings for bushels. Choice D is equivalent to choice A. Choice E is equivalent to choice C.

24. **The correct answer is J.** The problem is asking you to determine the area of the figure. There are a few ways to do this. You could break the figure into 3 rectangles and add their areas. However, a quicker method is to consider the figure a solid rectangle by drawing a line from one of the bottom "legs" to the other. The area of that rectangle would be 30 feet × 40 feet = 1,200 square feet. But that's too big; you have to subtract from this the area of the 12 foot × 12 foot square that isn't really part of the garden. That square is $12 \times 12 = 144$ square feet. 1,200 square feet – 144 square feet = 1,056 square feet (choice J).

Choice F is incorrect because the area of the large rectangle is 1,200, not 800. In choice G, you subtracted the areas of two such squares, not just one, from the area of the rectangle. In choice H, you subtracted the area of 1.5 such squares, not just one, from the area of the rectangle. Choice K is the area of the large rectangle; you did not subtract the area of the square portion that is not part of the garden.

25. **The correct answer is D.** Let $y = 2x - 6$. To find the inverse, switch the *x* and *y* and solve for *y*:

$$\begin{aligned} y &= 2x - 6 \\ x &= 2y - 6 \\ x + 6 &= 2y \\ y &= \frac{x+6}{2} \end{aligned}$$

So $f^{-1}(x) = \dfrac{x+6}{2}$. Thus, $f^{-1}\left(\dfrac{1}{2}\right) = \dfrac{\frac{1}{2}+6}{2} = \dfrac{\frac{13}{2}}{2} = \dfrac{13}{4}$.

Choice A is incorrect because this is $f\left(\dfrac{1}{2}\right)$. Choice B is incorrect because $f^{-1}(x)$ does not mean $\dfrac{1}{f(x)}$. Choice C is incorrect because $\dfrac{1}{2} + 6 \neq \dfrac{1+6}{2}$. Choice E is incorrect because $\dfrac{a+b}{c} \neq \dfrac{a}{c} + b$.

26. **The correct answer is F.** Compute the quantities in choices G, H, J, and K:

$$\begin{array}{ll} 36^0 = 1 & 36^0 = 1 \\ 1^{200} = 1 & 1^{200} = 1 \\ 3^2 = \dfrac{1}{3^2} = \dfrac{1}{9} & 3^2 = \dfrac{1}{3^2} = \dfrac{1}{9} \\ \left(\dfrac{1}{4}\right)^3 = \dfrac{1}{64} & \left(\dfrac{1}{4}\right)^3 = \dfrac{1}{64} \end{array}$$

Since $\sqrt{2} > 1$, it is the largest of the five quantities.

27. **The correct answer is B.** The area of a triangle is $\dfrac{1}{2} \times \text{base} \times \text{height}$. Since this is a right triangle, the height is the length of one of the legs of the triangle, and the base is the other leg of the triangle. Since the hypotenuse is always the longest side, the two legs of the triangle are the 15- and 20-meter sides. Using the formula shows the area to be $\dfrac{1}{2} \times 15 \times 20 = 150$ square meters.

Choice A is the perimeter, not the area. In choice C, you used the hypotenuse as one of the legs when computing the area. In choice D, you squared the hypotenuse to get the area, which is not the area formula. In choice E, you multiplied the lengths of all sides of the triangle, which is not how you calculate the area of a triangle.

28. **The correct answer is H.** Since the batteries can be evenly divided by 3, 4, 5, and 6, the answer will be the least common multiple of these numbers. The quickest approach is to consider the choices from smallest to largest. 15 is not a multiple of 4 or 6, so choice F is no good. 30 isn't a multiple of 4, so choice G is incorrect. 60, however, is evenly divisible by all four numbers. Choices J and K are divisible by 4, 5, and 6, but there is a smaller choice listed that also works.

29. **The correct answer is C.** The triangle law says that the sum of any two sides of a triangle must be strictly larger than the length of the third side. The triple in choice C does not satisfy this law because 1 + 1 is not strictly greater than 2.

30. **The correct answer is G.** Rewrite the first fraction as $\frac{ab}{b^2}$. Then, $\frac{a}{b}-\frac{a}{b^2}=\frac{ab}{b^2}-\frac{a}{b^2}=\frac{ab-a}{b^2}=\frac{a(b-1)}{b^2}$. Choice F is the result of canceling terms, not factors, common to the numerator and denominator. In choice H, you converted the first fraction to one with a denominator of b^2 incorrectly. In choice J, you multiplied the fractions instead of subtracting them. Choice K is the result of subtracting numerators and denominators, not determining a least common denominator.

31. **The correct answer is B.** Arrange the data in the second column in order:

0 0 1 1 2 2 3 4 4 4

The average of the 5th and 6th data values is 2. So the median is 2. Choice A is incorrect because you must first arrange the data values in increasing order before determining the median. Choice C is incorrect because this is the mean. Choice D is incorrect because you must include the 0s in the list of data values. Choice E is incorrect because it is the mode.

32. **The correct answer is H.** The width and length of the new rectangle are $1.30w$ and $0.75l$. So the perimeter of this rectangle is $2(1.30w) + 2(0.75l) = 2.6w + 1.5l$. Choice F is the perimeter of the original rectangle. In choice G, you did not apply the percentages to the width or length to get the new dimensions. In choice J you computed the percentages incorrectly. Finally, you should have multiplied choice K by 2.

33. **The correct answer is E.** By definition,

$$\cot\theta=\frac{\cos\theta}{\sin\theta}=\frac{-\frac{1}{2}}{-\frac{\sqrt{3}}{2}}=\frac{1}{\sqrt{3}}=\frac{\sqrt{3}}{3}.$$

Choice A is $\csc\theta$. Choice B is $\sec\theta$. Choice C is $\tan\theta$. Choice D is $-\tan\theta$.

34. **The correct answer is F.** The number line highlights the region between approximately –2.5 and 1. Thus, the best description of the range of numbers highlighted is choice F: the numbers greater than –2.5 but less than 1. The inequality in choices G and K do not make sense because 1 is not less than –2.5. Choice H is the exact opposite of the correct answer. Choice J is incorrect because the middle term of the double inequality should be x, not $|x|$.

35. **The correct answer is B.** The average is the sum of the terms divided by the number of terms—in this case, the sum of all the ratings divided by the number of tasters. You don't know how many tasters there were, but that's not a problem. Since you know all the percentages, simply pick a number for the number of tasters and use it. Since the percentages are in multiples of 5, you'll want a number that is easily divisible by 20, since 5% is one out of 20. Let's use 20 to keep things simple. (You could have used 100 or any other number divisible by 20.) 10% of 20 is 2, so 2 tasters gave a rating of 4. That's $2 \times 4 = 8$ points total. 15% gave a rating of 3. 15% of 20 is 3, so that is $3 \times 3 = 9$ points. Half the testers, 10 of them, gave a rating of 2, so that makes another $10 \times 2 = 20$ points. Finally, 25%, or 5 tasters, gave a rating of 1. That's $5 \times 1 = 5$ more points. Total points awarded = 8 + 9 + 20 + 5 = 42 points. Divide that by the number of tasters used, 20, and the average rating is $\frac{42}{20}=2.1$. Choices A, C, D, and E are close but likely the result of some small arithmetic error.

36. **The correct answer is H.** In an isosceles triangle, two sides have the same length, and the two angles opposite those sides have the same measure. Since sides $\overline{AB}$ and $\overline{BC}$ are marked as congruent, angles A and C are also congruent. The angle measures in any triangle add up to 180°. Therefore, you can subtract the known angle measure, 40° from 180°, and divide the difference by 2 to find the measure of each of the unknown angles:

$$180° - 40° = 140°$$
$$140° \div 2 = 70°$$

Choice F is the measure of angle B. Choice G is the measure of each angle in an equilateral triangle. This triangle is isosceles, not equilateral. Choice J would be correct if angle C were congruent to the given 40° angle, rather than to angle A. Choice K is the sum of the two unknown angles, which is double the measure of angle A.

37. **The correct answer is C.** The quickest way to do this is to find the pairs of factors that produce 36 and add them. The factors are: 36 and 1, 18 and 2, 12 and 3, 9 and 4, and 6 and 6. If you add the integers in those pairs, 6 + 6 gives the smallest sum, 12.

It is not possible to get these sums for choices A and B with factors of 36. Choice D comes from a viable pair (9, 4), but there is a pair with a smaller sum. Choice E comes from a viable pair (12, 3), but there is a pair with a smaller sum.

38. **The correct answer is F.** Line *d* forms a 180° angle, as does every line. If you look at the intersection of lines *b* and *d*, you can see that 3 different angles make up this 180°. Two of the angles are labeled: one is 115° and another is 40°. The third angle is the one you need to find. You can do that by subtracting the sum of the two known angles from 180°: 180° – (115° + 40°) = 25°. (Notice that the entire figure wasn't required to answer this question.) Choice G is the likely result of an arithmetic error. Choice H is the complement of the 40 degree angle, but when added to the sum of 40 and 115, the sum is not 180. Choice J is the supplement of the 115 degree angle, but when added to the sum of 40 and 115, the sum is not 180.

39. **The correct answer is C.** Solve for *y*:

$$6y - 12x = 1$$
$$6y = 12x + 1$$
$$y = 2x + \frac{1}{6}$$

So the slope is 2. Choices A, B, and E are the results of not solving for *y* before identifying the slope. Choice D is the coefficient *y*, but this is not the slope; solve for *y* and then identify the coefficient of *x* as the slope.

40. **The correct answer is F.** $\sqrt{6}$ is equal to approximately 2.449, so all the question is really asking is which point is closest to 2.449 on the number line. That number is just about halfway between 2 and 3, so the closest point is F. Since choices G, H, J, and K are larger, they are not the correct answers.

41. **The correct answer is B.** An obtuse angle is, by definition, one that measures between 90° and 180°. In order for angle *H* to fit this definition, its measure of (180 – *x*) must be more than 90 but less than 180. Algebraically, 90 < 180 – *x* < 180. Solving the inequality for *x*, –90 < –*x* < 0, and 90 > *x* > 0. This can also be written as 0 < *x* < 90, so choice B is correct.

Choice A is incorrect because *x* could be strictly between 60 and 90 degrees, and angle *H* would still be obtuse. Choice C would make angle *H* acute. Choice D would make angle *H* acute and negative. Choice E would make angle *H* acute.

42. **The correct answer is J.** Simplify as follows:

$$\frac{-x}{2-\frac{1}{2x}} = \frac{-x}{\frac{4x}{2x}-\frac{1}{2x}} = \frac{-x}{\frac{4x-1}{2x}}$$
$$= -x \div \frac{4x-1}{2x}$$
$$= -x \bullet \frac{2x}{4x-1} = \frac{-2x^2}{4x-1} = \frac{2x^2}{1-4x}$$

Choice F is the result of adding fractions incorrectly; $a - \frac{b}{c} \neq \frac{a-b}{c}$. Choice G is the result of canceling terms, not factors, in the numerator and denominator. Choice H is the result of subtracting fractions incorrectly; $\frac{a}{b-c} \neq \frac{a}{b} - \frac{a}{c}$. Choice K is the result of multiplying, not dividing.

43. **The correct answer is D.** Observe that $(g \circ f)(x) = g(f(x)) = \sqrt{(2x+1)^2 + 1 - 5} = \sqrt{(2x+1)^2 - 4}$. The *x*-intercept(s) are the solutions of the equation $\sqrt{(2x+1)^2 - 4} = 0$. Solve for *x*, as follows:

$$\sqrt{(2x+1)^2 - 4} = 0$$
$$(2x+1)^2 - 4 = 0$$
$$(2x+1)^2 = 4$$
$$2x+1 = \pm\sqrt{4} = \pm 2$$
$$2x+1 = 2 \text{ or } 2x+1 = -2$$
$$x = \frac{1}{2} \text{ or } x = -\frac{3}{2}$$

So the *x*-intercepts are $\left(\frac{1}{2},0\right)$ and $\left(-\frac{3}{2},0\right)$. Choice A is incorrect because you did not take the square root of 4 when solving for *x*. Choice B is incorrect because this is the *x*-intercept for *g*(*x*). Choice C is incorrect because this is the *y*-intercept for *f*(*x*). Choice E is incorrect because while *f*(*x*) itself does not have any *x*-intercepts, the composition $(g \circ f)(x)$ does.

44. **The correct answer is H.** Using the definition of slope, the slope of the described line is $\frac{4}{-5} = -\frac{4}{5}$. Using the point-slope form of the equation of a line with the point (3, –1) yields

$$y+1 = -\frac{4}{5}(x-3)$$
$$y+1 = -\frac{4}{5}x + \frac{12}{5}$$
$$y = -\frac{4}{5}x + \frac{7}{5}$$

So the *y*-intercept is $\frac{7}{5}$. In choice F, you used the slope as $\frac{4}{5}$ instead of $-\frac{4}{5}$. Choice G is the slope, not the *y*-intercept. Choice J is the *x*-intercept. In choice K, you identified the constant term as the *y*-intercept before completing combining like terms.

45. **The correct answer is C.** You know that the two numbers are both divisible by 6 and by no greater number. This eliminates choice D, as 12 is a common factor for 12 and 24. You also know that the least common multiple the two numbers share is 36. That knowledge eliminates choice A, as 12 is the least common multiple there. Choice B fails for the same reason, as 18 is a common multiple less than 36. Finally, choice E does not have 36 as a multiple of both numbers. Choice C has the only pair of numbers that fits the description.

46. **The correct answer is G.** The radius of the given circle is $\frac{x}{2}$ inches. So the radius of the new circle is $\frac{3x}{2}$ inches, and the area of the new circle is $\left(\frac{3x}{2}\right)^2 \pi = \frac{9\pi}{4}x^2$ square inches. Choice F is the circumference of the new circle. In choice H, you tripled the area of the original circle, but this is different from tripling the radius and then finding the area. In choice J, you used the diameter instead of the radius when computing the area. Choice K is the area of the given circle, not the new one.

47. **The correct answer is D.** The slope is $\frac{5-0}{0-(-3)} = \frac{5}{3}$. In choices A and E, you did not use both points to compute the slope. Choice B has the wrong sign. Choice C is the reciprocal of the slope.

48. **The correct answer is K.** The way to solve this is to compute the areas of both circles and subtract the area of the smaller from the area of the larger. The smaller circle has a radius of 2.5 inches. Using the formula Area = πr^2, you get area = $\pi(2.5)^2$, or 6.25π. The larger circle has an area of $\pi(5)^2$, which is 25π. Thus, the area of the shaded region is $25\pi - 6.25\pi = 18.75\pi$.

Choice G is the area of the small, unshaded circle. Choice F is the area of the small, unshaded circle if you used 2.5 as the diameter. For choice H, you just added the radii and multiplied the result by π. Choice J is the area of half the big circle.

49. **The correct answer is B.** To be a solution of a system, substituting the values of *x* and *y* must yield true statement for *both* equations. Substituting $x = 1$ and $y = \frac{1}{3}$ into both equations yields true statements. Choices A and D only satisfy the first equation of the system. Choice C and E only satisfy the second equation of the system.

50. **The correct answer is J.** The graphs intersect three times. The *x*-values of these points of intersection are the solutions of the equation $f(x) - g(x) = 0$. Choice F is incorrect because there are *x*-values for which the graph of $f(x)$ is above the graph of $g(x)$. Choice G is incorrect because there are *x*-values for which the graph of $f(x)$ is below the graph of $g(x)$. Choice H is incorrect because $f(0)$ itself equals 4, and 4 is not strictly greater than itself. Choice K is incorrect because eventually the graph of $g(x)$ will intersect the horizontal line $y = -2$ because the arrowhead on the left-part points downward.

51. **The correct answer is C.** Substitute $x = \frac{2}{3}$ into the given expression and simplify:

$$\left(\frac{2\left(\frac{2}{3}\right)+1}{2\left(\frac{2}{3}\right)-1}\right)^{-2} = \left(\frac{\frac{4}{3}+1}{\frac{4}{3}-1}\right)^{-2} = \left(\frac{\frac{7}{3}}{\frac{1}{3}}\right)^{-2} = 7^{-2} = \frac{1}{7^2} = \frac{1}{49}$$

Choices A and B involve multiplying base and exponent to compute a power. In choices B and D, you multiplied instead of dividing when simplifying the complex fraction. Choice E is the reciprocal of the correct answer.

52. **The correct answer is J.** For a function to be positive, its graph must be above the *x*-axis. This is true only on the interval (1, 5).

53. **The correct answer is D.** First label all the dimensions in the figure:

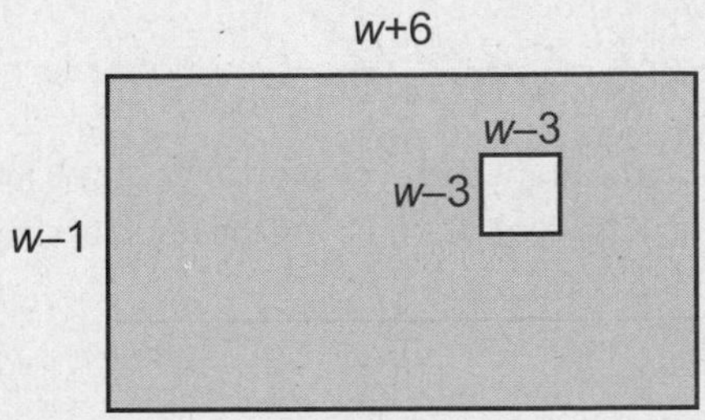

In order to find the shaded area, we need to subtract the area of the inner square from the area of the outer rectangle. The area of the outer rectangle is:

$$(w + 6)(w - 1) = w^2 + 5w - 6$$

and the area of the inner square is:

$$(w - 3)^2 = w^2 - 6w + 9$$

Subtracting these, we get:

$$w^2 + 5w - 6 - (w^2 - 6w + 9)$$

$$w^2 + 5w - 6 - w^2 + 6w - 9$$

$$11w - 15$$

Choice A is the area of the outer rectangle, which does not take into account the unshaded square. Choice B subtracts the *length* of the unshaded square from the area of the outer rectangle, rather than the area. Choice C adds the area of the unshaded square to the area of the outer rectangle. If you chose E, you might have distributed the subtraction sign incorrectly when simplifying the area of the unshaded square.

54. The correct answer is H. If the probability of drawing a classical CD is $\frac{4}{5}$, then the probability of drawing a jazz CD is $1-\frac{4}{5}=\frac{1}{5}$. This means that there are 4 classical CDs for each jazz CD. Since there are 3 jazz CDs, there are $3 \times 4 = 12$ classical CDs in the box.

Choices F, G, J, and K result from an error in determining the number of classical CDs per jazz CD in the collection.

55. The correct answer is E. This is a little trickier than it seems, because the numerator above the x is 2, not 1. You need to convert the other fractions so that they also have numerators of 2: $\frac{1}{12}$ becomes $\frac{2}{24}$ and $\frac{1}{8}$ becomes $\frac{2}{16}$. Now you can just list and count the fractions with 2 as a numerator that fall between $\frac{2}{24}$ and $\frac{2}{16}$ on the number line. There are 7 of them: $\frac{2}{23}, \frac{2}{22}, \frac{2}{21}, \frac{2}{20}, \frac{2}{19}, \frac{2}{18}, \frac{2}{17}$. If you didn't take note of the 2 in the numerator, you probably chose 3 (choice A), in error. Choices B, C, and D are the result of simple counting errors.

56. The correct answer is F. Use the distance formula:

$$\sqrt{\left(\frac{1}{2}a-\left(-\frac{1}{4}a\right)\right)^2+\left(-\frac{1}{4}a-\left(-\frac{1}{2}a\right)\right)^2}$$

$$=\sqrt{\left(\frac{1}{2}a+\frac{1}{4}a\right)^2+\left(-\frac{1}{4}a+\frac{1}{2}a\right)^2}$$

$$=\sqrt{\left(\frac{3}{4}a\right)^2+\left(\frac{1}{4}a\right)^2}$$

$$=\sqrt{\frac{9}{16}a^2+\frac{1}{16}a^2}$$

$$=\sqrt{\frac{10}{16}a^2}$$

$$=\frac{\sqrt{10}}{\sqrt{16}} \bullet \sqrt{a^2}$$

$$=\frac{\sqrt{10}}{4}a$$

In choice G you did not square the differences in the x- and y-coordinates in the radicand of the distance formula. Choice H is incorrect because you needed to take the square root. Choice J is the result of adding fractions incorrectly. Choice K is the result of computing a power of a fraction by multiplying the fraction by the exponent.

57. The correct answer is E. One way to visualize a rotation is by drawing a rectangle with one vertex at the center of rotation and the opposite vertex at the point to be rotated. Then rotate the entire rectangle to find the final location of the point P, as shown below.

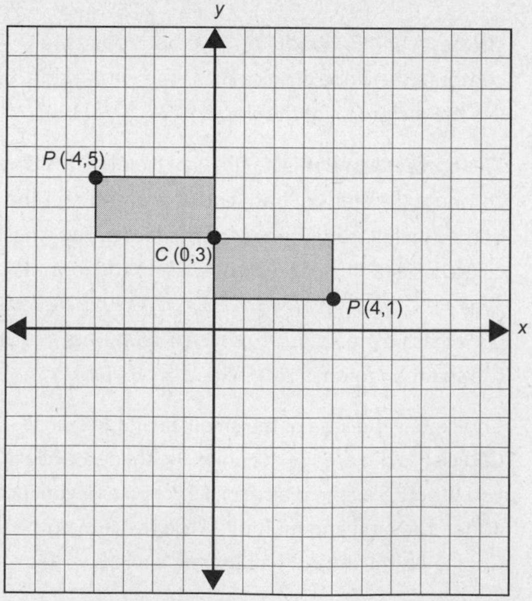

Choice A is the final location of point *P* after a 180° rotation centered at the origin. Choice B is the final location of point *P* after a 90° clockwise rotation centered at *C*. Choice C is the final location of point *P* after a 90° counter-clockwise rotation centered at *C*. Choice D is the final location of the point (4, 3).

58. The correct answer is J. It's easiest to give numbers to the question, since none are provided. Let's make the tin have 1 cherry candy. We're told it has twice as many grape candies, so there are 2 grapes. There are three times as many lemon candies as grape, so that means the tin has $2 \times 3 = 6$ lemon candies. So the bag has 1 cherry, 2 grape, and 6 lemon candies. Next, a number of apple candies equal to the number of cherry candies is added. That means 1 apple candy is added, and the tin has $1 + 2 + 6 + 1 = 10$ candies total. Six of the 10 are lemon, so the probability of selecting a lemon is $\frac{6}{10} = \frac{3}{5}$.

Choice F is way too low. There are 10 candies from which to choose, so the probability of any single outcome is $\frac{1}{10}$. Choice G is the probability of selecting an apple candy (or the probability of selecting a cherry candy). Choice H is the probability of selecting a grape candy. Choice K is the probability of selecting a lemon candy *before* adding the apple candy to the mix.

59. The correct answer is B. Let's get the total inches for each type of wire. Two 15 foot wires are $2 \times 15 = 30$ feet, which converts to $30 \times 12 = 360$ inches. Four 3.5 foot wires are $4 \times 3.5 = 14$ feet, which converts to $14 \times 12 = 168$ inches. And the last two wires are $2 \times 8 = 16$ inches. Now add up the inches: $360 + 168 + 16 = 544$ inches of wire per speaker. 544 inches per speaker × 9 speakers = 4,896 inches. That's the total amount of wire needed. At a cost of \$0.031 per inch, the job will require 4,896 × \$0.031 = \$151.776, or about \$152. Choice A is likely the result of an arithmetic error. Choice C is the number of inches in four 3.5-foot wires. Choice D is the number of inches in two 15-foot wires. Choice E is the number of inches per speaker.

60. The correct answer is F. How can you have two consecutive heads but not three? The first two tosses could be heads and the third could be tails. Also, the last two tosses could be heads while the first is tails. Those are the only ways to achieve the desired outcome. So what are the probabilities? For the first desired outcome, you need heads, heads, tails. The probability of that outcome is $\frac{1}{2} \times \frac{1}{2} \times \frac{1}{2} = \frac{1}{8}$. There's a one out of two chance of getting the outcome we want on each toss, so the chance of getting all three outcomes in a row is $\frac{1}{2} \times \frac{1}{2} \times \frac{1}{2}$. That's not the answer though. You could also get the tails, heads, heads outcome. This too has a $\frac{1}{2} \times \frac{1}{2} \times \frac{1}{2} = \frac{1}{8}$ probability. Since either outcome is acceptable, you add the probabilities: $\frac{1}{8} + \frac{1}{8} = \frac{2}{8} = \frac{1}{4}$.

For choice G, you included the outcome in which the two heads were not consecutive, namely HTH, but this does not satisfy the criterion. Choice H is the probability of getting HHT, but you forgot about THH. Choice J is too high; there are only 2 of 8 possible outcomes that satisfy the criterion. Choice K is the probability of the complement of the desired event.

Reading

1.	D	**11.**	D	**21.**	B	**31.**	C
2.	F	**12.**	J	**22.**	H	**32.**	F
3.	D	**13.**	C	**23.**	B	**33.**	B
4.	H	**14.**	G	**24.**	J	**34.**	G
5.	A	**15.**	B	**25.**	C	**35.**	A
6.	J	**16.**	G	**26.**	H	**36.**	H
7.	B	**17.**	B	**27.**	D	**37.**	C
8.	G	**18.**	H	**28.**	J	**38.**	G
9.	C	**19.**	B	**29.**	B	**39.**	D
10.	H	**20.**	J	**30.**	F	**40.**	F

1. **The correct answer is D.** If you were to replace the word *object* in line 10 with *purpose*, it would still make sense, so choice D is the best answer. Choices A and B have the same meaning, but *thing* and *item* do not make sense in the context of the sentence, so these words are incorrect. Choice C does not make sense in context either.

2. **The correct answer is F.** When his boss asks him to compare the sheet, Bartleby merely says, "I prefer not to." He gives no real reason for refusing the task, so there is no reason to reach the conclusions in choices G, H, or J.

3. **The correct answer is D.** The opening paragraph of the passage makes it clear that Bartleby has been working in the office for a while, so you can eliminate choice A. If Bartleby is in the middle of doing his own work, he clearly stops doing it when his boss asks him to compare the sheet, so choice C is incorrect. In fact, the boss stops insisting Bartleby compare the sheet after the third time Bartleby says he would prefer not to do it. Therefore, choice B can be eliminated and choice D can be confirmed as the correct answer.

4. **The correct answer is H.** After Aunt Polly confirms that Tom is only faking having a sore tooth, she says, "Tom, I love you so, and you seem to try every way you can to break my old heart with your outrageousness," which expresses loving exasperation (choice H). The love she expresses makes choice H a better answer than complete intolerance (choice F). She doesn't yell at Tom, so she hardly reacts with terrifying scorn (choice G). Since she expresses some emotion, it would be inaccurate to say she reacts with incredible boredom (choice J).

5. **The correct answer is A.** In the passage, Tom does not want to go to school, and the author states that Tom feels that going to school is like being in "captivity and fetters," which suggests something jail-like. The phrase is not meant literally, so choice B does not explain why the author uses it. There is no evidence that Tom does not want to go to school because he is claustrophobic, or has a fear of confining spaces (choice C). He does not seem to be very fearful at all, so choice D is not the best answer.

6. **The correct answer is J.** Sid seems to truly believe Tom is in pain and expresses true concern when he asks Aunt Polly to help Tom, so choice J is the best answer. That also means that choice F is incorrect. Tom does not force Sid to tell Aunt Polly that Tom is in pain, so there is no reason to conclude that choice G is correct. Also Sid does not seem to recognize that Tom is only faking having a sore tooth, so choice H is unlikely.

7. **The correct answer is B.** In Passage A, Bartleby does not want to do his job, and in Passage B, Tom Sawyer does not want to go to school, so choice B is the best answer. Only Bartleby works in an office, so you can eliminate choice A. You can eliminate choice C since only Tom Sawyer is trying to fool a relative. Bartleby's behavior confuses his boss, but Tom's aunt knows exactly what her nephew is trying to do, so choice D does not describe the main idea of both passages.

8. **The correct answer is G.** When Bartleby's boss asks him to do a task he does not want to do, Bartleby states "I'd prefer not to" clearly. When Tom Sawyer has to go to school but does not want to, he tries to trick his aunt by pretending he has a sore tooth. Bartleby's refusal to do his job may make him seem lazy, but the first paragraph of the passage contradicts this notion, so you can

eliminate choice F. The fact that Bartleby states his position clearly eliminates choice H. He also shows no signs of regret, so choice J can be ruled out too.

9. **The correct answer is C.** A nonconformist is someone who refuses to do what society expects of him or her. Society expects workers like Bartleby to do their jobs and young boys like Tom Sawyer to go to school, yet they both refuse to accept those expectations. However, to say they are lawbreakers (choice A) is an extreme and inaccurate conclusion. As a pair of nonconformists, Bartleby and Tom Sawyer are the opposite of followers (choice B). While Tom is somewhat clever, neither he nor Bartleby can really be described as a genius, so choice D is not the most sensible answer.

10. **The correct answer is H.** Bartleby's refusal to do his job takes his boss by surprise, yet Aunt Polly realizes that Tom is faking a sore tooth to get out of school, so she must expect this kind of behavior from him. Bartleby's boss and Aunt Polly are bothered by Bartleby and Tom Sawyer's respective behavior, so choice F does not explain how they are different. Bartleby's boss is probably as professional as he can be under the circumstances, but Aunt Polly is not in a workplace situation in Passage B, so describing her as "unprofessional" is not appropriate. Therefore, choice G is not the best answer. Bartleby's boss allows Bartleby to shirk his office duties, so he is hardly a firm and controlling boss. Aunt Polly is not particularly meek or easygoing, so choice J is incorrect.

11. **The correct answer is D.** This question is asking you to find the statement that is *not* true of a manor. According to the first paragraph, a town, not a manor, is a group of townships, so choice D is correct since it is not true. The paragraph also refers to a *rural manor*, so choice A is not the best answer. In that same line, the author explains that ". . . the town was a more defensible place than the 'township' or rural manor …, " so choice B is also true and must be eliminated. The passage notes that the word *manor* is the Norman name for the Saxon "townships," which confirms that choice C is true and should not be eliminated.

12. **The correct answer is J.** The answer to this question can be found in the second paragraph, which states that some towns " …grew up in the fortified camps of the invaders themselves [statement I] … ," and that "Others clustered round the country houses of some Saxon king or earl [statement III] … ." However, the passage says nothing about shops or stores, so the correct answer must include statements I and III and eliminate statement II. Only choice J does this. Choices F and H each only account for one of the true statements. Choice G only accounts for the false statement.

13. **The correct answer is C.** The answer to this question can be found in the third paragraph, which explains that *in demesne* means "in default of a lord," and later indicates that the towns that are "in demesne" *belong* to lords, so choice C is the best answer. This eliminates choices A and B, which both suggest that towns that are "in demesne" belong to someone other than their lords. While some towns that are "in demesne" may be shared, the passage shows that this is not true of all such towns, so choice D is not the best answer.

14. **The correct answer is G.** Throughout the passage, the author is primarily concerned with historical details about how English towns developed, so choice G is the best answer. The author does not spend much time comparing towns to manors (choice F) or proving that English towns evolved from marks (choice H). While the author does describe some of the qualities that define a town (choice J), this is mostly limited to the first paragraph, and the best answer should capture the purpose of the entire passage.

15. **The correct answer is B.** According to the fifth paragraph, "By the end of the Norman period all the towns had secured the *firma burgi*, and the right of assessing it themselves," so choice B is correct. While port towns enjoyed superior access to imports, this is not a feature of all towns, so choice A is not the best answer. Professor Freeman's quotation in the first paragraph contradicts the conclusion in choice C. The final paragraph states that towns ". . . had the right also of choosing a mayor of their own, instead of the king's bailiff or reeve," which contradicts choice D.

16. **The correct answer is G.** The author refers to a mound in terms of a town being defensible, so it must be something that protects, which makes choice G the best answer. Choice F describes a moat, which is also mentioned in line 7, rather than a mound, so this definition is both incorrect and redundant. Choices H and J could both be definitions of *mound* in another context, but they fail to imply something used to defend or protect a town.

17. **The correct answer is B.** In the fourth paragraph, the author writes that "London was of course a great port and trading center …, and the use of the phrase "of course" implies that this is something well known, so choice B is the best answer. At the end of the second paragraph, the author writes, "But all the English towns

were far less flourishing before the arrival of the Normans than they afterwards became," and since London was one such town, choice A is not the best answer. Choice C seems to refer to the quotation about how a town is "one part of the district where men lived closer together than elsewhere," but this is a statement made by Professor Freeman, not the author. While the author refers to the privileges of town life several times in the passage, the author implies that such privileges make *him* prefer town life, nowhere does the passage state that this was true in general, so choice D lacks sufficient support.

18. **The correct answer is H.** Throughout the passage, the author refers to specific, important details from town charters (choice J) and the Domesday Book (choice F) and calls William the Norman's survey (choice G) "our great authority" before referring to details in it. However, the author only refers to one very general observation that Professor Freeman made about towns, so choice H is the best answer.

19. **The correct answer is B.** In the fourth paragraph, the author states that London "had many foreign merchants in it" and that it was ". . . the centre of English national life, and the voice of its citizens counted for something in national affairs." This supports the conclusion in choice B. While London was a successful trading center (choice A), the author does not imply that this alone made London influential in national affairs. London also had a civic constitution (choice C), but this is not described as influential in the town's role in national affairs, either, and neither is the town's ability to distinguish itself from other towns (choice D).

20. **The correct answer is J.** The answer to this question can be found in the fifth paragraph, which describes ". . . the right of composition for taxation, i.e. the right of paying a fixed sum, or rent, to the Crown, instead of the various tallages, taxes, and imposts that might be required of other places." This fixed sum, or composition, was called the *firma burgi* (choice J). The fact that the author distinguishes the *firma burgi* from tallages and imposts eliminates choices F and G. The reeve was a person responsible for choosing a major, so choice H does not make sense.

21. **The correct answer is B.** In the eighth paragraph, the author writes, "The designer must be ready to respond at any time [statement I], and this implies a logical and balanced mind [statement II]. . . ." However, in the third paragraph, the author explains that "it is impossible to be original," so statement III must be false. Therefore, the correct answer must include statements I and II and eliminate statement III, and only choice B does this. Choice A only includes one of the true statements. Choice C includes a true statement and a false one. Choice D includes the two true statements as well as the one false statement.

22. **The correct answer is H.** This figurative phrase indicates that designers must follow the instructions of the people who pay them and cannot just follow their own artistic whims, so choice H is the best answer. This also contradicts choice J. Choice F is both inherently incorrect and too concerned with the role of music in the figurative phrase. The phrase refers to the employee/employer relationship and not the idea that true artists must be paid for their work (choice G).

23. **The correct answer is B.** In the seventeenth paragraph, the author refers to the fact that designers create work for commercial purposes, so choice B is the most sensible answer. While the seventeenth paragraph refers to manufacturers, this is distinct from designers, so choice A would not necessarily be true. The author also discusses how design should raise, rather than merely fit, contemporary tastes, so choice C is not the best answer either. Choice D is never discussed in the passage.

24. **The correct answer is J.** In the tenth paragraph, the author writes, "Design is therefore inseparable from consideration of material and process, with which the designer must be acquainted; without this technical knowledge it is impossible to take full advantage of the method of production either in the direction of economy or effect." This supports the conclusion in choice J. In the twelfth paragraph, the author writes that "mere utility is not in itself sufficient," which eliminates choice F. The author implies that public tastes tend to dictate which materials are used, so choice G is not the best answer. In the tenth paragraph, the author uses the word *economical* to mean *simple*, but choice H seems to mistakenly conclude that the word refers to costs.

25. **The correct answer is C.** As it is used in line 40, *fallacy* means an "untrue belief." While a fallacy might be popular, the fact that the idea in lines 38–39 is false is more significant than whether it is popular, so choice A is not the most logical answer. Choices B and D imply the opposite of an untrue belief.

26. **The correct answer is H.** The answer to this question can be found in the sixth paragraph, which states that, "... if inspired, design is rather in the nature of an accident [statement I] ... and that "What at first sight

suggests inspired thought may be accounted for by sub-consciousness [statement III]. . . ." The author downplays the role of inspiration in the artistic process, which makes statement II a false one. Choice F is incorrect because it only includes one of the true statements. Choice G is incorrect because it includes a true statement and a false one. Choice J includes both true statements as well as the false one.

27. **The correct answer is D.** The summarizing statement in the final paragraph captures the main idea of the entire passage perfectly. Choice A summarizes only the main idea of the section entitled "Human Limitations," while choice B is just one supporting detail from that section. Choice C is a supporting detail from the section titled "Process and Material."

28. **The correct answer is J.** As a whole, this passage is an analysis of what makes up effective design. There really are no historical details in this passage, so choice F is a misleading description. Choice G is basically a rewording of incorrect choice F, but which alters how comprehensive the passage is. The author is concerned with more than commercial design, so choice H is not the best answer.

29. **The correct answer is B.** The answer to this question can be found in the thirteenth paragraph, which states that the market "is governed by popular or individual demand." Therefore the correct answer must only include statement II, which choice B does. Choice A only includes a false statement. Choice C includes two false statements. Choice D includes the true statement as well as the two false ones.

30. **The correct answer is F.** The answer to this question can be found in the seventh paragraph, which states, "It would be beneficial to reject once and for all the idea of inspiration with its tendency to encourage the 'artistic temperament' in the belief that 'it does not feel like it.'" Since the author had already offered readiness as an important quality of the designer, choice F is the best answer. Choice G may be true in itself, but it is not an explanation the author proposes in this passage. Choice H seems to misinterpret the word *temperament*, since that word sometimes relates to anger, though it does not in this context. The author never suggests that the entire concept of artistic temperament is obsolete (choice J).

31. **The correct answer is C.** In the second paragraph, the author writes of *Ithomiines* that "the juices of their bodies are unpalatable" and that "A bird which had once attempted to eat one would find it little to its taste." Therefore, choice C is the best answer. The author refers to the *Ithomiines'* "weak powers of flight," so choice A is not a logical answer. The author only refers to the patterns on *Ithomiines'* wings, not their flight patterns, so there is no support for choice B. Since the author describes *Ithomiines* as "weak," choice D is not a likely answer.

32. **The correct answer is F.** *Pierines* actually have striking patterns so that predators will recognize them easily and know that *Pierines* probably do not taste good and are not worth eating, so choice F is the best answer. That fact also eliminates choices G and J. While those patterns are examples of protective resemblance, choice H implies that *Pierines* have those patterns for no other reason than this, which is incorrect.

33. **The correct answer is B.** Choice B captures the overall point of the first paragraph better than any other answer choice. Choice A is not the best answer because the first paragraph discusses more animals than just butterflies and more protective measures than just mimicry. Choice C is just one example of protective resemblance and not a statement that captures the main point of the paragraph as a whole. Choice D is the main point of the second paragraph, not the first one.

34. **The correct answer is G.** The word *contradistinction* is made up of the prefix *contra* meaning "in opposition" and the root word *distinction*, which means that protective resemblance and mimicry are distinct from one another. Therefore, choice G is the best answer. The author does not imply that protective mimicry is a branch of mimicry (choice F), but they are similar in that they are both ways that animals use appearance to protect themselves, so choices H and J can be eliminated.

35. **The correct answer is A.** The passage indicates that the *Origin of the Species* influenced H.W. Bates's interpretation of the similarities between *Ithomiines* and certain *Pierines*, so he must have read the book before he caught these butterflies. Therefore, statement I must come first. The passage also states that Bates noticed that *Ithomiines* and certain *Pierines* looked similar after catching some *Ithomiines*, so statement II must come before statement III. Therefore, the correct order is I, II, III (choice A) and choices B, C, and D can be eliminated. The fact that the author only mentions *Origin of the Species* after explaining how H.W. Bates caught some *Ithomiines* and noticed similarities between Ithomiines and certain *Pierines* may make choice B seem like a correct answer, but the events in which things are

discussed in a piece of writing should not be confused with the actual chronology of those events.

36. **The correct answer is H.** The author uses this phrase when explaining how information in *The Origin of Species* influenced Bates's conclusions, so choice H is the best answer. Choice F is too focused on wording and not concerned enough with information, so it is not the best answer. There is no strong indication that the information in *The Origin of Species* that influenced Bates was an argument, so choice G is not the best answer either. Choice J takes the word *lines* too literally and does not make any sense in this context.

37. **The correct answer is C.** As it is used in line 22, *distinguished* means "respected," so choice C is the best answer. While two distinctive theories might be distinguished from one another, choice A seems to make the error that *distinguished* and *distinctive* are synonyms, which they are not. While one might distinguish between two different things, choice B seems to make the similar error that *distinguished* and *different* are synonyms. A distinguished person might be charming, but *distinguished* and *charming* are not synonyms, so choice D is incorrect.

38. **The correct answer is G.** In the second paragraph, the author writes that most *Pierines* are very different from *Ithomiines* because of their white color (statement I) and their distinctive shapes (statement II). The author then refers to "the great bulk of their relations," but does not actually define *Pierines* as bulky, so statement III is false. Therefore, the correct answer must include statements I and II and eliminate statement III, which is what choice G does. Choice F only includes one of the true statements. Choice H includes one true statement and one false one. Choice J includes the two true statements as well as the one false statement.

39. **The correct answer is D.** The author's statement that "the names of the 'stick-' and 'leaf-' insects are in themselves an indication of their appearance" supports the conclusion in choice D. Since there is nothing particularly loop-like about most twigs, choice A does not seem logical. While some of these names may seem ridiculous to certain readers, choice B is not sufficiently convincing to be the best answer. While lines 5–9 do describe certain insects that resemble plant life, choice C is both much too extreme and factually incorrect.

40. **The correct answer is F.** In the second paragraph, the author states that H.W. Bates theorized that certain *Pierines* most likely came to resemble *Ithomiines* through the process of natural selection (choice F). Choice H misnames the process. While the author states that the butterflies' "patterns and colors are said to be of a 'warning' nature," choice G is an inaccurate explanation of how certain *Pierines* came to resemble *Ithomiines*. Certain *Pierines* came to resemble *Ithomiines* before H.W. Bates first captured some *Ithomiines*, so choice J is incorrect.

SCIENCE

1.	A	**11.**	D	**21.**	C	**31.**	A
2.	H	**12.**	H	**22.**	G	**32.**	F
3.	B	**13.**	C	**23.**	A	**33.**	C
4.	F	**14.**	G	**24.**	F	**34.**	F
5.	D	**15.**	A	**25.**	D	**35.**	C
6.	G	**16.**	G	**26.**	G	**36.**	H
7.	C	**17.**	C	**27.**	B	**37.**	B
8.	G	**18.**	F	**28.**	F	**38.**	F
9.	B	**19.**	D	**29.**	B	**39.**	C
10.	H	**20.**	G	**30.**	F	**40.**	J

1. **The correct answer is A.** In a fluorimetric assay, fluorescence intensity is directly related to enzyme activity. The display in Figure 1 shows a higher peak for fluorescence intensity in Setup A and a lower peak for fluorescence intensity in Setup B. Choice B would be correct if the setups for A and B were flipped. Choice C would be correct if they had the same fluorescence intensity. Choice D would be correct if neither setup gave any fluorescence intensity.

2. **The correct answer is H.** When the enzyme is more active, it converts more non-fluorescent substrate molecules into fluorescent product molecules, resulting in greater fluorescence intensity. The data point with highest fluorescence intensity corresponds to 47°C, which, of all the available choices, is closest to choice H. According to Figure 2, the fluorescence intensity is somewhat less at temperatures lower than 47°C, so choices F and G are incorrect. The fluorescence intensity drops off very quickly at temperatures higher than 47°C, so choice J is incorrect.

3. **The correct answer is B.** While there is no point on the graph that corresponds directly to 20°C, the fluorescence intensity should be between the point at 16°C (0.56) and the point at 25°C (0.69). Choice A would be correct if the question asked for the intensity at 10°C. Choice C would be correct if the question asked for the intensity at 30°C. Choice D would be correct if the question asked for the intensity at 40°C.

4. **The correct answer is F.** Adding more enzyme should increase the amount of substrate that is turned into to fluorescent product, increasing the fluorescence intensity. Choice G would be correct if the question had asked what would happen with half as much enzyme. Choices H and J are incorrect because temperature dependence should not be related to enzyme concentration.

5. **The correct answer is D.** Fluorescence intensity, and therefore enzyme activity, increases with increasing temperature from approximately 5°C to 50°C, and then decreases dramatically from 50°C to 80°C. The temperature dependence is not linear, so choices A and B are incorrect. Choice C would be correct if the shape of the plot in Figure 2 were inverted.

6. **The correct answer is G.** The kestrel has an average egg mass of 8.5 g and an average pore area of 0.2 mm^2; that corresponds to point 3 on the Figure. Choice F would be true for the redwing blackbird. Choice H would be true for the pigeon. Choice J would be true for the shearwater.

7. **The correct answer is C.** An egg mass of 10,000 g corresponds to the far right edge of Figure 1. Extrapolating the trend line gives a pore area greater than 1,000 mm^2 and less than 10,000 mm^2, which is consistent with a pore area of 1,200 mm^2. Choice A would be correct if an egg mass of 10 g were used. Choice B would be correct if an egg mass of 400 g were used. Choice D is incorrect, but the number corresponds to the gram weight of the elephant bird egg.

8. **The correct answer is G.** To find the answer, you must compare the average egg mass to the average pore area. For the rhea, the ratio is 820:5.0, or 164. Choices F, H, and J are 15, 70, and 7.5, respectively. These ratios are all less than that of the rhea.

9. **The correct answer is B.** The slope of the graph increases from bottom left to top right. This is characteristic of a direct relationship between two factors. As one rises, the other rises. From the graph, you can spot that choice A is incorrect. For the relationship to be inverse, the graph would have to

slope from top left to bottom right, which is not the case. Choice C is incorrect because a straight line graph always implies a linear relationship. If you chose D, reread the question. Choice D may be true, but it cannot be drawn from the data provided.

10. **The correct answer is H.** Trace horizontally from 15 mm^2 on the *y*-axis to the line and then trace down to the *x*-axis. The egg mass range in which this point falls is 100 to 1,000 g. The other three choices provide incorrect alternative mass ranges.

11. **The correct answer is D.** The vine is always located in the center between two stimuli. Choice A is incorrect because the light source is not specified in each experiment. Choice B is incorrect because in Experiment 3 the tomato plant (and its surrounding air) is isolated in a sealed box. Choice C is incorrect because Experiment 1 does not contain a wheat plant.

12. **The correct answer is H.** Chemotropism is directional growth in response to chemical signals. Based on information in the passage, the vine is bending toward airborne chemical signals released by the tomato plant. Phototropism is directional growth in response to a light stimulus; choice F would be correct if the vine grew toward the light source instead of toward the tomato plant. Gravitropism is directional growth in response to gravity; choice G is incorrect because it does not explain why the vine bends to the left or right. Thigmotropism is directional growth in response to touch; choice J is incorrect because there is no evidence of touch in any of the experiments.

13. **The correct answer is C.** In Experiment 2, the dodder vine preferentially grows toward the tomato plant. Choice A might be concluded from Experiments 1 and 2 but is not consistent with Experiment 3. Choice B might be concluded from Experiment 3 but is not consistent with Experiments 1 and 2. Choice D might be concluded from Experiment 3 but is not consistent with Experiment 2.

14. **The correct answer is G.** The dependent variable is the measured response to a change in experimental conditions (the independent variables). In the three experiments, the independent variables are the position and nature of the stimuli around the dodder vine, and the measured response is the direction of growth of the dodder vine. Choice F is incorrect because the length of the dodder vine is not specified. Choice H is incorrect because the length of time the dodder vine grows is constant in all experiments. Choice J is incorrect because the tomato plant is constant in all three experiments.

15. **The correct answer is A.** The dodder vine grows toward potential host plants, but only when it can sense airborne chemicals released by the host plant. Choice B is incorrect because it does not explain the direction in which the dodder vine grows. Choice C is incorrect because Experiment 2 shows clear preference for tomato plants. Choice D is incorrect because it does not explain why the dodder vine prefers tomato plants over wheat plants.

16. **The correct answer is G.** The dodder plant appears to sense airborne chemicals released by the tomato plant. The setup depicted in the question directs the airflow (including airborne chemicals) to the left side of the dodder vine, so the vine should bend in that direction. Choice F is incorrect because the closed box prevents airborne chemicals from reaching the dodder vine from the right. Choices H and J are incorrect because the dodder vine preferentially grows toward airborne chemicals from the tomato plant.

17. **The correct answer is C.** Maggots appeared on the meat only in the jars to which flies had access. Choice A can be eliminated because maggots did not arise from the meat in the sealed jars. The conclusion suggested by choice B cannot be reached because there is air in both the experimental and control jars, although no *new* air is allowed to enter the sealed jars. Eliminate choice D because the experiment implies that maggots are related to flies.

18. **The correct answer is F.** The jars of the experimental group in the first experiment were sealed tightly so that no new air could enter. The jars in the second experiment were covered with gauze through which air could enter. Choice G is incorrect because all the jars in both experiments contained meat. Choice H can be eliminated because flies were not allowed to reach the meat in the jars of the experimental groups of both experiments. Choice J should not be considered because maggots did not appear in the jars of the experimental groups in either experiment.

19. **The correct answer is D.** By allowing new air to enter the jars of the second experiment and showing that even under these conditions maggots did not arise from the decaying meat, the notion that a continuous supply of air was necessary for abiogenesis was refuted. Choice A is not correct because proponents of abiogenesis never suggested that flies gave rise to maggots. On the contrary, they suggested that decaying meat, not flies, gave rise to maggots. Choice B is incorrect for similar reasons. Proponents of abiogenesis did not

connect flies and maggots in any way. You should eliminate choice C because it states the opposite of what the proponents of abiogenesis suggested.

20. **The correct answer is G.** Needham believed that heating the broth would kill all living things in the broth. When such living things later appeared in the broth, he concluded that they arose spontaneously from the broth. Since air was not a variable in the experiment, the conclusion postulated in choice F cannot be drawn. Choice H is contrary to Needham's assumption that heating the broth killed microorganisms. Choice J is contrary to the experimental evidence, which showed that microorganisms could seemingly arise from boiled broth.

21. **The correct answer is C.** Both experimental setups were essentially identical. They differed primarily in the amount of time the broth was heated. Eliminate choice A because the broth used by Spallanzani was identical to that used by Needham. Since the microorganisms in both experiments were a mix of those ordinarily found in air, the characteristics of the organisms in both experiments were essentially the same. So eliminate choice B. Choice D can be eliminated because neither experiment measured or identified the growth characteristics of microorganisms.

22. **The correct answer is G.** Spallanzani's experiment showed that heating a broth for a relatively long period of time and then sealing the flask prevented microorganisms from reproducing. The contents of the flask did not contain living things. However, when the flask was left unsealed, living things entered and reproduced in the broth. The results support the concept of biogenesis. Microorganisms arise from other microorganisms. Choice F is contradicted by the experimental results. Microorganisms did not arise spontaneously in the heated and sealed flask. Choice H is incorrect because only living things can reproduce, and that is what occurred in the unsealed flask. The experiments provide no evidence to support the contention that broth is an organism. Eliminate choice J.

23. **The correct answer is A.** Air was free to move back into the broth in the swan-necked flask. Air also moved freely into the flask that had a straight neck. However, microorganisms grew only in the broth in the straight-necked flask. This can be explained if microorganisms riding on dust particles become trapped in the downward bend of the swan-necked flask. The air enters the broth, but the microorganism-carrying dust does not. Choice B can be eliminated because air free of dust particles entered the swan-necked flask but did not result in the growth of microorganisms in the broth. Choice C is incorrect because no microorganisms arose spontaneously in the broth of the swan-necked flask. Choice D is also incorrect since the broth in the straight-necked flask was heated, but microorganisms grew in it anyway.

24. **The correct answer is F.** Metals condense at higher temperatures than the other materials, so Mercury's higher metal composition is consistent with formation at higher temperature than Earth. Choice G is incorrect because this would result in less metal, not more. Choice H is incorrect because there is no mention of the order of planet formation, nor whether metals were limited during the process . Choice J is incorrect because the passage does not indicate which planet has more gravity. In reality, Mercury has less gravity than Earth because it has less mass.

25. **The correct answer is D.** Ice condenses at much lower temperatures than rock and metal. Since Uranus and Neptune are much farther from the sun, they probably condensed at much lower temperatures than Earth. Choices A and B would be correct if the question asked about planets that formed much closer to the sun than Earth. Choice C would be correct if the question asked about planets that formed at a very similar distance from the sun as Earth.

26. **The correct answer is G.** Mars formed farther from the sun, so it probably contains more rock and less iron than Earth. Choice F would be the best choice for a planet that formed much closer to the sun. Choice H suggests there would be no iron, but if rock materials condense, so would iron. Choice J would be correct for a planet much farther from the sun. At 1.5 AU, the solar nebula is too hot for ice to condense.

27. **The correct answer is B.** Saturn is approximately 10 AU from the sun. The corresponding point on Figure 1 is between 100 and 500 K. Choice A would be correct if the question asked about Neptune. Choice C would be correct if the question asked about Mars. Choice D would be correct if the question asked about Mercury.

28. **The correct answer is F.** According to the solar nebula hypothesis, metals would have condensed closest to the sun, rocks further out, then water ice, and then ammonia ice. So the density of the planets should decrease with distance from the sun (choice F). Choice G is reversed. Nothing in the passage indicates the kind of variation indicated by choices H or J.

29. **The correct answer is B.** The simple math equation is 13.1 eV – 10.2 eV = 2.9 eV. Choice A is the value for a transition from $n = 3$ to $n = 2$. Choice C is the value for a transition from $n = 6$ to $n = 2$. Choice D is the value for a transition from $n = 5$ to $n = 1$.

30. **The correct answer is F.** Using Figure 3, the Lyman series falls in the UV region of the spectrum, less than 125 nm. Using information in Figure 2, the UV wavelengths have energies greater than 3 eV. The only transition of $n + 1$ to n in Table 1 that gives an energy difference of greater than 3 eV is from $n = 2$ to $n = 1$. Using Table 1, the $n = 5$ to 4, $n = 4$ to 3, and $n = 3$ to 2 transitions have energy differences of less than 3 eV, making choices G, H, and J incorrect.

31. **The correct answer is A.** Using the bottom horizontal scale in Figure 1, gamma rays have the highest frequency. Choices B and C are incorrect because they fall in the middle of the scale. Choice D is incorrect because radio waves have the highest wavelength, not the highest frequency.

32. **The correct answer is F.** The Paschen series occurs in approximately the 800–1,800 nm range, which falls in the infrared portion of the spectrum. Choices G, H, and J are incorrect because they are all higher energy.

33. **The correct answer is C.** This transition involves 2.9 eV (13.1 eV – 10.2 eV). This corresponds most closely to the H_γ line, which is listed as 2.86 eV. Choice A would involve 12.1 eV. Choice B would involve 2.6 eV, which relates more closely to the H_β line. Choice D would involve 1.1 eV, which would be in the infrared region.

34. **The correct answer is F.** This value relates to H_α, which is near the red end of the visible spectrum. Choice G is incorrect because the H_β line is blue-green. Choice H is incorrect because the H_γ is blue, and choice J is incorrect because H_δ is violet.

35. **The correct answer is C.** Both statements I and III refer to long-term patterns. Choice A does not correctly identify both climate statements. Statement II refers to a short-term condition that is not specifically an extreme, so choices B and D are incorrect.

36. **The correct answer is H.** This question is answered by finding the difference between the highest average high and lowest average low in each city. The difference between the high (79, August) and low (51, January, February, March) in Los Angeles is only 28 degrees. Choice F is incorrect (94 – 33 = 61). Choice G would be correct if the question asked for the city with the greatest temperature range (85 – 7 = 78). Choice J has the second smallest temperature range (76 – 36 = 40) but is still larger than that of choice H.

37. **The correct answer is B.** According to Table 2, Bemidji, Minnesota, receives an average of 4.4 inches of precipitation in July, while the rest of the cities receive an average of less than 2 inches in the same month. Choice A is incorrect because Abilene's monthly average precipitation is never greater than that of the other three cities. Choice C would be correct if the question asked about a date in February. Choice D would be correct if the question asked about a date in January.

38. **The correct answer is F.** As described in the passage, proximity to a large body of water has a moderating influence on both average temperature and extremes. Seattle has a warmer winter and cooler summer than Bemidji. Choice G is incorrect because it has flipped the relationship. Choice H is incorrect because proximity to mountain ranges does not moderate climate, nor is information about Seattle's proximity to mountain ranges available in the passage. Choice J is incorrect because information about altitude is not included in the passage. In reality, increases in altitude result in colder average temperatures, but do not always increase the *range* in temperatures.

39. **The correct answer is C.** As described in the passage, location with respect to mountain ranges affects precipitation trends. Choice A is incorrect because altitude is not related to average rainfall. Choice B is incorrect because annual temperature is not related to average rainfall. Choice D is incorrect—while the distribution of rainfall over the year will help determine the average rainfall, it does not explain why one city receives a greater average rainfall than the other.

40. **The correct answer is J.** As described in the passage, regions at higher latitudes experience greater differences in sunlight received over the course of a year, resulting in greater temperature ranges. Regions far from large bodies of water also experience more extremes in temperature. Choice F is incorrect because it has flipped both relationships. Choice G is incorrect because the large body of water moderates temperature. Choice H is incorrect because lower latitudes tend to have less temperature variation.

Sample Essay: Score 1

Ideas and Analysis:	Score = 1
Development and Support:	Score = 1
Organization:	Score = 1
Language Use and Conventions:	Score = 1

Football is the best sport ever and I like baseball and basketball too but football is the best one by far. I'm going to keep playing even if I don't make it to the pros so why should I stop if I still get my homework done and keep doing everything else I need to be doing? Ive never been to a game but I like to go so if I can get tickets I would but I don't know they may cost too expensive and I got other thngs to pay for if I can just watch it on TV, right? Whoever gets hurt should wear a helmet and not be too crazy just to score some touchdowns and make the other team look bad but everyone who stops playing football can just let the rest of us to play and too watch but it shouldn't cost any more money than most people can afford to spend and that the truth.

Scoring Explanation

Ideas and Analysis: Score = 1

This essay is comprised of disparate ideas that don't address the essay task provided. Rather than an exploration of thoughts pertaining to the future of football and strategies for addressing related safety issues, the writer provides a loose amalgam of ideas on why he or she likes football and will continue to play and watch it (as long as it doesn't get "too expensive"). The result is an unsuccessful essay that falls off-task.

Development and Support: Score = 1

This largely confusing response demonstrates little ability to construct a cohesive argument that stays on topic. There is scant development and support of a clear perspective on the questions posed. There is also no sufficient exploration or on-topic analysis of the ideas that are provided by the writer, resulting in a piece of writing that is more a grouping of weak sentences than a cohesive argument.

Organization: Score = 1

This piece of writing is, at best, a loose and unstructured set of ideas that briefly touch on football (and other sports), with little regard to the topic of safety beyond "whoever gets hurt should wear a helmet and not be too crazy." There is no clear and obvious unifying theme or overarching perspective tying the essay to the given task; overall, it's an ineffective and unsuccessful essay attempt.

Language Use and Conventions: Score = 1

Beyond the deficits in idea development and organization, this essay suffers from numerous grammatical problems, limited word choice, and a weak grasp of standard conventions of English writing. It's clear that minimal effort was given to develop a convincing, nuanced argument; the end result suffers dramatically and is a deficient piece of writing.

Sample Essay: Score 6

Ideas and Analysis:	Score = 6
Development and Support:	Score = 6
Organization:	Score = 6
Language Use and Conventions:	Score = 6

On and off the athletic fields of America, the debate regarding the dangers of full-contact sports such as football rages on. Professional players, both active and retired, are more vocal about the physical perils and toll the game takes on players during their comparatively brief careers. Concerned parents across the country are thinking twice before allowing their children to play football, for fear of serious injury. Media outlets large and small are giving increased attention to the issue, helping to shape our national debate on this issue: Is football too dangerous? Should it be banned, or should the game change to satisfy the critics? Once posed, we shouldn't ignore these tough questions. And sometimes, tough questions require tough answers.

Should the sport of football be banned? No. Football is inexorably woven into the fabric of American culture, and attempting to ban the game would be an unfair and rash decision to say the least. It can be argued that football is now our primary national pastime, as evidenced by massive TV ratings and revenue generated by the game. Attempting to strip it from our collective hands would only demonstrate our inability to take a measured, careful approach to this issue. A blind, blanket ban on anything deemed somewhat dangerous, including football, stands in diametrical opposition to the tenets of a free and democratic society.

Yes, football is a dangerous sport. Injuries both major and minor, from sprains and concussions to broken bones and life-altering catastrophic trauma, occur at all levels of the game—from the NFL down to pee-wee football and everything in between. We should adopt a careful, phased approach to address this issue. Initially, there should be a collective acknowledgement of the sport's inherent dangers and a strict adherence to all accepted and available safety precautions. The game should simply not be played without the use of appropriate safety equipment. A thorough information campaign should be deployed, so anyone playing the game or interested in playing should be aware of the possible risks. Furthermore, I think a significant portion of the enormous profits generated by football at the professional and college levels should be invested in the exploration and development of enhanced safety equipment for players. We have come far from the days of leather helmets, but there is always room for improvement.

Does the game itself need to change? This question needs to stay at the forefront of our national discussion, and a serious review and exploration of ways to make the game safer needs to occur—even if this entails an alteration of the game's core structure in some way. Perhaps if there's a way to reduce the bone-crunching tackles and brutal pile-ups that occur in defense of a team's end zone, they should be considered and tested.

Anyone who defends football can no longer do so in ignorance. The tragic suicide of former NFL player Junior Seau brought media attention to chronic traumatic encephalopathy (CTE), a disease that occurs from repeated head trauma, which has affected numerous NFL players. We're all aware of the risks. Mature and realistic adults should accept the notion that football, like many facets of modern life, contains risks, and it is our responsibility to address them and do our best to minimize these risks whenever possible.

Take airplane flying for example. It is a mode of transportation with inherent risk, including loss of life, but that doesn't mean we should abandon it altogether. We approach it responsibly and carefully, we follow strict, evolving safety protocols, and we always look for ways to make flying even safer, even if it comes at a cost—whether it be money, time, or convenience. We should approach the sport of football in much the same way.

Informed compromise is often the best approach to any debate, and we cannot let blind devotion to tradition keep us from making progress. Perhaps a restructuring of football will not only make the game safer, but may also make it more enjoyable and accessible to everyone.

Scoring Explanation

Ideas and Analysis: Score = 6

This argument offers an impressive level of insight and analysis regarding the dangers of football and how the debate regarding the safety and future of the game should be handled. The writer calls for a "measured, careful approach" to address the issue, but clearly has considered both sides of the argument—those that defend the sport (arguably "our primary national pastime") and those who demand it to change or be banned ("a serious review and exploration of ways to make the game safer needs to occur")—resulting in a nuanced, effective essay that thoughtfully addresses the essay task.

Development and Support: Score = 6

The essay acknowledges cogent points on both sides of the football debate (football is dangerous but is "inexorably woven into the fabric of American culture"), develops a clear perspective on the topic (a stricter adherence to all safety protocols and a review of the game, with an eye towards making it safer), and makes a compelling argument for a considered yet aggressive march forward to make football safer. Support is provided to lend credence to the writer's argument, and prior research in the field of football-related injuries (chronic traumatic encephalopathy) is mentioned. The in-depth examination of both sides and skillful development and support of the writer's viewpoint leads to an essay that successfully tackles the task at hand.

Organization: Score = 6

This written response displays a strong command of effective essay structure and organization. It begins with a compelling call for action that asserts the seriousness of the topic, but wisely offers fair coverage of both sides of the debate in a clear, streamlined fashion. The writer's point-of-view on the topic is evident, and a sufficient level of support is provided. The writer even chooses to weave in examples of other dangerous activities (flying) that aren't banned but rather are carefully regulated, to help assert his or her concluding plea for a "careful, phased approach" and "informed compromise" to make the sport of football safer for everyone involved.

Language Use and Conventions: Score = 6

The writer displays a firm command of standard English-language use and conventions. The argument is well constructed and grammatically sound and contains a varied array of sentences, transitions, and word choices. The resulting essay is both compelling and effective and capably addresses the task provided.

Chapter 16: Scoring Your ACT® Practice Tests

OVERVIEW

After you take each ACT practice test in this book, you'll want to assess your score as accurately as possible. This chapter will explain how the ACT calculates your test score and will provide all the information you need to calculate your own score on each practice test. Using this information, you can measure your progress as you go and see where you need the most focus throughout your study plan.

But first, let's take a minute to discuss what the scores mean and how they relate to your official score report. The scores you will want to determine for each practice test (and that will be most prominently displayed on your score report) are the **composite score** and **scale scores**.

Your composite score represents how you performed on the ACT exam as a whole. Your scale scores represent how you performed in each subject area. Reporting categories, which highlight your specific strengths and weaknesses within each subject area, are also listed on the report.

When a college or university lists its preferred range of ACT scores for admission, it displays the composite score and the subject area reporting categories scores. These are the scores ACT, Inc., reports to you on your official report, to your high school, and to your requested colleges and scholarship agencies.

The goal of scoring your practice tests is to give you an idea of the composite and scale scores you would earn when you take the actual test. It's an important step in gauging your readiness to take the ACT exam, and it's not that complicated. Let's get started!

SCORING YOUR ACT® MULTIPLE-CHOICE QUESTIONS

We mentioned it before, and it bears repeating here—the ACT test counts *only* the questions you answer correctly. There is *no penalty* for guessing, which means you do not get any points deducted for wrong answers. Hopefully, as you gain a better understanding of how your score will be calculated, you'll be more inclined to make sure you don't leave many (if any) questions blank on test day.

We're going to begin with an overview of how to score your tests. Step-by-step instructions are also included in each scoring section, in case you need a reminder as you go through the process.

RAW SCORES

When scoring your exam, you will begin by counting the number of questions you answered correctly. The questions are assessed on two levels:

1) four ACT subject area tests (English, Mathematics, Reading, and Science), and

2) nine ACT reporting categories (listed in the chart below).

The number of test items you answered correctly within each section is your **raw score** for that section.

ACT Test Layout of Sections and Reporting Categories

Subject Area Tests	No. of Questions	Subscore Areas
English Test	75	• Production of Writing • Knowledge of Language • Conventions of Standard English
Mathematics Test	60	• Preparing for Higher Math ○ Number & Quantity ○ Algebra ○ Functions ○ Geometry ○ Statistics & Probability • Integrating Essential Skills • Modelling
Reading Test	40	• Key Ideas & Details • Craft & Structure • Integration of Knowledge & Ideas
Science Test	40	• Interpretation of Data • Scientific Investigation • Evaluation of Models, Inference & Experimental Results

Your first step to calculating your score on each ACT test is to figure out your raw score:

1) Take the tests, using the answer sheets provided.

2) Review your answers using the answer key and explanations at the end of every test.

3) Using the **Scoring Keys** starting on page 1101, score your practice tests. If you answered a question correctly, circle the correct number in the box next to the question number—every chart is already separated into the correct subscores for every subject test. Remember—do NOT place a mark of any kind if you left a question blank or answered it incorrectly.

The ACT scales raw scores uniquely for every test to adjust for small differences occurring among different versions.

4) Count the total number of questions you answered correctly for each ACT test section: English, Mathematics, Reading, and Science.

5) Write down your raw scores in the blanks provided on every chart.

Read on to find out how to turn these into recognizable ACT scores.

Scale Scores

After finding your raw scores for each subject area test, you then must convert each raw score to a **scale score**. The ACT converts raw scores for each subject area test into scale scores ranging from 1 to 36 using conversion tables that are unique for every test given.

For the practice tests in this book, you can convert your raw scores into scale scores using the scale score conversion charts at the end of this chapter, starting on page 1030. Each subject area has its own chart, followed by charts for individual subject area subsections. Take the following steps to convert your practice test raw score results:

1) Find your raw score result in the **Scale Score Conversion Chart** by locating the number of questions you answered correctly in the **Raw Score** row of the table. The number located below that number in the **Scale Score** row is your final scale score result (ranging from 1–36) for that test section.

   NOTE: Sometimes one raw score will correspond to one scale score, and sometimes a range of raw scores will correspond to one scale score. For example, in the chart below, if your English raw score is 6, your scale score is 4. If your English raw score is 21, your scale score is 10.

English Scale Score Conversion Chart

Raw Score	0–1	2–3	4–5	6–7	8–9	10–11	12–14	15–17	18–19	20–22	23–24	25–26
Scale Score	**1**	**2**	**3**	**4**	**5**	**6**	**7**	**8**	**9**	**10**	**11**	**12**

2) Enter your scale score number in the appropriate column in the **Multiple-Choice Scale Scores Chart** on page 1122.

3) Repeat steps 1–2 for every test section.

You now have your scale scores for each test section, which will give you a basic idea of which test sections are your strengths, which are your weaknesses, and where you should focus your study in the time leading up to the ACT exam. Compare your results after you take each new practice test to track your improvement!

Composite Score

The only time ACT combines scores is to calculate the **composite score** by adding together your English, Mathematics, Reading, and Science scale scores, dividing the resulting number by four, and rounding to the nearest whole number (to find the rounded average of the four subject area scores). Just like a scale score, a composite score can range from 1 to 36.

For example, say a student earned the following scale scores on each of the four subject area tests:

English: 21

Mathematics: 26

Reading: 20

Science: 24

First, add the scores: $21 + 26 + 20 + 24 = 91$.

Then, divide the result by 4: $91 \div 4 = 22.75$.

Finally, round the result to the nearest whole number: 22.75 rounds to 23.

The student's composite score in this case is 23.

Because your composite score is an average, even if you performed very well on one test section, a lower score can bring the total score down.

You can keep a record of your composite score for each practice test you take in the **Multiple-Choice Scale Scores Chart** on page 1122. Track how your composite score changes from test to test, especially if you put extra work into improving in test sections that give you trouble at the beginning of your study plan.

SCORING YOUR ACT® WRITING TEST ESSAY

Unfortunately, scoring an essay isn't as easy as simply checking a box to determine whether it is right or wrong. As you discovered in Chapter 14, there are many components that ACT Writing test graders look for when scoring and assessing individual student essays. The scoring rubric in Chapter 14 (page 587), which is based on the same grading scale official test reviewers use, will be your guide to determining your essay score.

You have a couple of options for calculating your score on your essay. The first, which is a difficult (but very useful!) exercise, is scoring your own essay using the official rubric to assign your work a score from 1–6 for each of the test's four domains:

1) Ideas and Analysis

2) Development and Support

3) Organization

4) Language Use and Conventions

The rubric clearly lays out the components an essay will have at each score level. While it's pretty hard to objectively read and evaluate your own work, doing so will ensure that you carefully and critically look at your work next to the criteria on which you will be graded. It's easy to write an essay and never look at it again—if you are forced to review it with a careful eye, you'll be able to see the crucial scoring areas that might be missing from your work. Becoming your own editor helps you grow as a writer and as a reader.

Another option is to also have someone else evaluate your essay for you in order to get an outside perspective—maybe a classmate, a tutor, a parent or other family member, or a teacher. If you prefer not to score your own essay, you could have two reviewers do it for you. Give your volunteer grader (or graders) your essay, the scoring rubric, and the sample graded essays on pages 603–609 to get a sense of what essays at different levels look like. Your reviewer should assign your practice essay a score of 1–6 for each of the four domains.

So let's say you're going to grade the writing test yourself, without another reader. To determine your score, assign your essay a score for each domain, for example: Ideas and Analysis: 4; Development and Support: 3; Organization: 4; and Language Use and Conventions: 3.

Then multiply each domain score by 2:

Ideas and Analysis:	$4 \times 2 = \mathbf{8}$
Development and Support:	$3 \times 2 = \mathbf{6}$
Organization:	$4 \times 2 = \mathbf{8}$
Language Use and Conventions:	$3 \times 2 = \mathbf{6}$

Finally, add the four domain score totals together:

$$8 + 6 + 8 + 6 = \mathbf{28}$$

Then divide the sum by 4:

$$28 \div 4 = \mathbf{7}$$

Your self-scored essay would receive a score of 7.

The average of your Writing score and your English and Reading scale scores is your English Language Arts (ELA) scale score, which ranges from 1–36, like the other test sections.

Remember—if someone helps you score your essay, simply add the reviewer's domain scores to yours instead of doubling your scores.

HOW TO USE YOUR TEST RESULTS

The purpose of taking the practice tests in this book is to familiarize yourself as much as possible with the format, timing, and content of the ACT exam. The more practice tests you take, the more comfortable you will be with the test, and the fewer surprises you will face on your actual test day.

As you score your tests, always take note of not only your final composite score, but also the individual test scores that comprise it. Your test results should help guide your study. Is there a specific test section giving you trouble? Is there an even more specific subsection within that section where you seem to get stuck, especially under timed conditions? Use the information you find when scoring your tests with the charts at the end of this chapter to target where you will focus the most work before you take your next practice test.

As much as possible, aim to take the practice tests in this book under the most test-like conditions you can: time yourself and take the test straight through in a quiet room. If you stick to the same methods for every test, you can really get a sense of whether or not you are improving.

If your score isn't as high as you expected, don't get discouraged—use the information you learn from scoring your tests to your advantage. You've taken a huge step by prepping with this book and committing to extensive practice!

SUMMING IT UP

- **ACT does not penalize you for wrong answers.** Your score is based only on the number of correct answers for every test section. There is no penalty for guessing.
- **Your raw score is the number of questions you answer correctly.** To calculate your score for each test section, figure out your raw score and then convert each raw score to a **scale score** using the charts at the end of the chapter. Your scale scores are featured on your official score report and range from 1–36 for each test section. No matter when you take the ACT exam, your scale score will accurately compare you to all other students who take the test.
- Your **composite score** is the average of your four test scale scores, rounded to the nearest whole number.
- Your **subscores** can help you to identify which specific areas within each subject test you need to work on.
- **You will have to calculate your essay writing score yourself or with the help of a volunteer grader**. Using the scoring rubric, assign yourself a score from 1–6 for each domain. Multiply each self-score by 2, or add it to the corresponding domain score from your grader. Take the average of the domain scores to get your Writing test score.
- **Use your test results to guide your study plan**. Take note of the test sections and subsections that give you the most trouble, and then focus on improving before you take your next practice test.

PRACTICE TEST 1: SCORING KEYS

Scoring Keys for Multiple-Choice Questions

To determine your raw scores using the Scoring Keys:

1) Circle the letter of the correct answer in the box next to each question you answered correctly.
2) Add the circled letters and put the number of correctly answered questions in the blank corresponding to each reporting categories.
3) Add the total number of questions you answered correctly. The total is your raw score.

Complete this process for all four tests (English, Mathematics, Reading, and Science). Simply put the number of correct answers in the blank provided to determine your raw score.

Practice Test 1 — English Scoring Key

	Reporting Category*				Reporting Category*				Reporting Category*		
Q#	**POW**	**KLA**	**CSE**	**Q#**	**POW**	**KLA**	**CSE**	**Q#**	**POW**	**KLA**	**CSE**
1.			C	**26.**			H	**51.**	A		
2.			H	**27.**		D		**52.**			G
3.			D	**28.**		G		**53.**	C		
4.			J	**29.**	C			**54.**			J
5.	D			**30.**	J			**55.**	B		
6.			G	**31.**	B			**56.**			G
7.		A		**32.**			H	**57.**	A		
8.			G	**33.**		B		**58.**			J
9.		A		**34.**			H	**59.**	B		
10.			G	**35.**			D	**60.**	H		
11.	B			**36.**		G		**61.**		A	
12.		J		**37.**			D	**62.**	H		
13.		D		**38.**			H	**63.**			B
14.	H			**39.**			B	**64.**	F		
15.	D			**40.**		F		**65.**			C
16.			J	**41.**			B	**66.**			G
17.		C		**42.**			F	**67.**			C
18.			F	**43.**			C	**68.**	J		
19.			C	**44.**	H			**69.**			D
20.	F			**45.**	A			**70.**			G
21.		B		**46.**			H	**71.**		A	
22.			J	**47.**			C	**72.**	H		
23.			A	**48.**			G	**73.**	A		
24.			H	**49.**		A		**74.**			G
25.	A			**50.**			J	**75.**	B		

***Reporting Categories**

POW = Production of Writing

KLA = Knowledge of Language

CSE = Conventions of Standard English

Raw Scores (Number of Correct Answers)		
Production of Writing (POW)	______________	**out of 23**
Knowledge of Language (KLA)	______________	**out of 14**
Conventions of Standard English (CSE)	______________	**out of 38**
Total Correct for English Test (POW + KLA + CSE)	______________	**out of 75**

Practice Test 1 — **Mathematics Scoring Key**

	Reporting Category*								Reporting Category*						
	PHM								PHM						
KEY	**N**	**A**	**F**	**G**	**S**	**IES**	**MDL**	**KEY**	**N**	**A**	**F**	**G**	**S**	**IES**	**MDL**
1.						D	D	31.					D		
2.						G		32.						G	G
3.						A		33.						D	
4.	H							34.				K			
5.						D	D	35.						C	
6.			H					36.						G	
7.		E						37.				C			
8.		H						38.						H	H
9.			E					39.						B	
10.					K			40.		G					
11.		C						41.				B			
12.						G		42.		G					
13.					E			43.	C						C
14.						G	G	44.						H	
15.			E					45.			E				
16.		G						46.					K		K
17.				E				47.						C	C
18.						H	H	48.	J						
19.			D					49.				A			
20.						H		50.				H			
21.						A		51.			E				
22.						F	F	52.						K	K
23.						C		53.		E					
24.				G				54.					H		
25.		B						55.	E						
26.	J							56.					J		J
27.						D		57.				D			D
28.			G					58.						H	H
29.						D		59.				D			D
30.		K						60.	G						

Add the total of the columns and put it in the **PHM** field below.

*Reporting Categories	Raw Scores (Number of Correct Answers)		
PHM = Preparing for Higher Math	**Preparing for Higher Math (PHM) (N + A + F + G + S)**	______	**out of 37**
N = Number and Quantity	**Integrating Essential Skills (IES)**	______	**out of 23**
A = Algebra	**Total Number Correct (PHM + IES)**	______	**out of 60**
F = Functions	**Modeling (MDL)** (Not included in test raw score)	______	**out of 15**
G = Geometry			
S = Statistics and Probability			
IES = Integrating Essential Skills			
MDL = Modeling			

Practice Test 1 — Reading Scoring Key

	Reporting Category*				Reporting Category*		
KEY	**KID**	**CS**	**IKI**	**KEY**	**KID**	**CS**	**IKI**
1.	B			**21.**		B	
2.	J			**22.**	H		
3.	C			**23.**			D
4.		J		**24.**	H		
5.	C			**25.**			A
6.	G			**26.**		J	
7.	A			**27.**	B		
8.			G	**28.**	F		
9.	D			**29.**			C
10.	F			**30.**		J	
11.	D			**31.**	A		
12.		F		**32.**		H	
13.	C			**33.**		D	
14.	J			**34.**	G		
15.			B	**35.**		D	
16.		J		**36.**	G		
17.		C		**37.**	D		
18.	F			**38.**	H		
19.		A		**39.**	B		
20.	J			**40.**	F		

***Reporting Categories**

KID = Key Ideas & Details

CS = Craft & Structure

IKI = Integration of Knowledge and Ideas

Raw Scores (Number of Correct Answers)		
Key Ideas & Details (KID)	________	**out of 24**
Craft & Structure (CS)	________	**out of 11**
Integration of Knowledge and Ideas (IKI)	________	**out of 5**
Total Correct for Reading Test (KID + CS + IKI)	________	**out of 40**

Practice Test 1 — **Science Scoring Key**

	Reporting Category*				Reporting Category*		
KEY	**IOD**	**SIN**	**EMI**	**KEY**	**IOD**	**SIN**	**EMI**
1.			C	**21.**		B	
2.	J			**22.**			H
3.	A			**23.**		B	
4.	G			**24.**			J
5.	B			**25.**			C
6.		G		**26.**	G		
7.			A	**27.**	A		
8.		J		**28.**			H
9.		B		**29.**	D		
10.		G		**30.**			G
11.			D	**31.**	C		
12.		H		**32.**			J
13.	C			**33.**			D
14.	F			**34.**			G
15.		C		**35.**		A	
16.	J			**36.**	F		
17.	D			**37.**	B		
18.	G			**38.**	H		
19.	B			**39.**	D		
20.			F	**40.**		J	

***Reporting Categories**

IOD = Interpretation of Data

SIN = Scientific Investigation

EMI = Evaluation of Models, Inferences & Experimental Results

Raw Scores (Number of Correct Answers)

Interpretation of Data (IOD)	______	**out of 18**
Scientific Investigation (CS)	______	**out of 10**
Evaluation of Models, Inferences & Experimental Results (EMI)	______	**out of 12**
Total Correct for Science Test (IOD + SIN + EMI)	______	**out of 40**

PRACTICE TEST 2: SCORING KEYS

Scoring Keys for Multiple-Choice Questions

To determine your raw scores using the Scoring Keys:

1) Circle the letter of correct answer in the box next to each question you answered correctly.
2) Add the circled letters and put the number of correctly answered questions in the blank corresponding to each reporting categories.
3) Add the total number of questions you answered correctly. The total is your raw score.

Complete this process for all four tests (English, Mathematics, Reading, and Science). Simply put the number of correct answers in the blank provided to determine your raw score.

Practice Test 2

English Scoring Key

	Reporting Category*				Reporting Category*				Reporting Category*		
KEY	**POW**	**KLA**	**CSE**	**KEY**	**POW**	**KLA**	**CSE**	**KEY**	**POW**	**KLA**	**CSE**
1.		B		**26.**	J			**51.**	D		
2.			H	**27.**		C		**52.**			G
3.		B		**28.**	G			**53.**			B
4.	H			**29.**	C			**54.**			F
5.	A			**30.**	G			**55.**			B
6.		J		**31.**			D	**56.**	J		
7.	B			**32.**	F			**57.**			B
8.			H	**33.**			C	**58.**			J
9.	B			**34.**			J	**59.**	A		
10.			G	**35.**			B	**60.**	H		
11.	C			**36.**	H			**61.**			B
12.		J		**37.**			A	**62.**			F
13.			B	**38.**			F	**63.**			C
14.	J			**39.**	B			**64.**			J
15.	A			**40.**			G	**65.**		C	
16.	F			**41.**			D	**66.**		J	
17.			B	**42.**			J	**67.**			B
18.			J	**43.**			A	**68.**			J
19.		B		**44.**		G		**69.**			C
20.	F			**45.**	C			**70.**		H	
21.		B		**46.**			G	**71.**			D
22.			H	**47.**			D	**72.**			J
23.		A		**48.**			J	**73.**			B
24.			G	**49.**			B	**74.**			H
25.		D		**50.**	F			**75.**			D

***Reporting Categories**

POW = Production of Writing

KLA = Knowledge of Language

CSE = Conventions of Standard English

Raw Scores (Number of Correct Answers)		
Production of Writing (POW)	________	**out of 22**
Knowledge of Language (KLA)	________	**out of 13**
Conventions of Standard English (CSE)	________	**out of 40**
Total Correct for English Test (POW + KLA + CSE)	________	**out of 75**

Practice Test 2															**Mathematics Scoring Key**
	Reporting Category*								Reporting Category*						
	PHM								PHM						
KEY	N	A	F	G	S	IES	MDL	KEY	N	A	F	G	S	IES	MDL
1.						A		31.						C	C
2.						G		32.					G		
3.						E		33.		E					
4.						F		34.						K	
5.						C		35.				C			
6.						J	J	36.	J						
7.		A						37.			C				
8.			J					38.			G				
9.						D		39.			C				
10.	G							40.				J			J
11.					D			41.		E					
12.		G						42.						G	G
13.	D							43.	E						
14.				F				44.		K					
15.	C							45.						E	
16.						J		46.				H			
17.			C					47.						B	
18.						K		48.						H	H
19.						A	A	49.						D	
20.		F						50.				G			G
21.						D		51.				E			E
22.						K	K	52.					H		
23.		D						53.						C	
24.					J			54.		F					
25.			C					55.					C		
26.						G	G	56.			K				
27.				B			B	57.						C	
28.						F		58.				K			K
29.					D			59.			C				
30.				G				60.						G	

Add the total of the columns and put it in the **PHM** field below.

***Reporting Categories**	**Raw Scores (Number of Correct Answers)**		
PHM = Preparing for Higher Math	**Preparing for Higher Math (PHM) (N + A + F + G + S)**	________	**out of 36**
N = Number and Quantity	**Integrating Essential Skills (IES)**	________	**out of 24**
A = Algebra	**Total Number Correct (PHM + IES)**	________	**out of 60**
F = Functions	**Modeling (MDL)** (Not included in test raw score)	________	**out of 12**
G = Geometry			
S = Statistics and Probability			
IES = Integrating Essential Skills			
MDL = Modeling			

Practice Test 2 — Reading Scoring Key

Reporting Category*				Reporting Category*			
KEY	KID	CS	IKI	KEY	KID	CS	IKI
1.	C			21.		D	
2.			J	22.			G
3.	D			23.		A	
4.		F		24.	G		
5.			B	25.	D		
6.		F		26.			J
7.	C			27.	A		
8.	G			28.	H		
9.			C	29.		B	
10.	F			30.			J
11.		A		31.	C		
12.	F			32.	F		
13.	C			33.	A		
14.	H			34.			H
15.	D			35.		D	
16.		F		36.	J		
17.		D		37.	B		
18.	G			38.	H		
19.	A			39.	D		
20.		J		40.	G		

***Reporting Categories**

KID = Key Ideas & Details

CS = Craft & Structure

IKI = Integration of Knowledge and Ideas

Raw Scores (Number of Correct Answers)		
Key Ideas & Details (KID)	______________	**out of 23**
Craft & Structure (CS)	______________	**out of 10**
Integration of Knowledge and Ideas (IKI)	______________	**out of 7**
Total Correct for Reading Test (KID + CS + IKI)	______________	**out of 40**

Practice Test 2	**Science Scoring Key**

	Reporting Category*				Reporting Category*		
KEY	**IOD**	**SIN**	**EMI**	**KEY**	**IOD**	**SIN**	**EMI**
1.	B			**21.**	A		
2.	G			**22.**	H		
3.			A	**23.**	B		
4.			G	**24.**	J		
5.		D		**25.**		A	
6.		F		**26.**	F		
7.	C			**27.**			C
8.			G	**28.**		J	
9.	B			**29.**		C	
10.	H			**30.**		J	
11.	D			**31.**		A	
12.	F			**32.**		G	
13.			B	**33.**			D
14.		J		**34.**	G		
15.			D	**35.**			D
16.	H			**36.**			G
17.			A	**37.**			C
18.	G			**38.**			G
19.	B			**39.**	B		
20.	H			**40.**		H	

***Reporting Categories**

IOD = Interpretation of Data

SIN = Scientific Investigation

EMI = Evaluation of Models, Inferences & Experimental Results

Raw Scores (Number of Correct Answers)		
Interpretation of Data (IOD)	________	**out of 18**
Scientific Investigation (CS)	________	**out of 10**
Evaluation of Models, Inferences & Experimental Results (EMI)	________	**out of 12**
Total Correct for Science Test (IOD + SIN + EMI)	________	**out of 40**

PRACTICE TEST 3: SCORING KEYS

SCORING KEYS FOR MULTIPLE-CHOICE QUESTIONS

To determine your raw scores using the Scoring Keys:

1) Circle the letter of correct answer in the box next to each question you answered correctly.
2) Add the circled letters and put the number of correctly answered questions in the blank corresponding to each reporting categories.
3) Add the total number of questions you answered correctly. The total is your raw score.

Complete this process for all four tests (English, Mathematics, Reading, and Science). Simply put the number of correct answers in the blank provided to determine your raw score.

Practice Test 3 — English Scoring Key

	Reporting Category*				Reporting Category*				Reporting Category*		
KEY	**POW**	**KLA**	**CSE**	**KEY**	**POW**	**KLA**	**CSE**	**KEY**	**POW**	**KLA**	**CSE**
1.			B	**26.**		F		**51.**			B
2.			F	**27.**	A			**52.**			G
3.			B	**28.**			H	**53.**			B
4.			F	**29.**	D			**54.**	F		
5.			C	**30.**	F			**55.**			C
6.			J	**31.**			B	**56.**			J
7.		C		**32.**	F			**57.**			A
8.	G			**33.**			B	**58.**	J		
9.	A			**34.**		G		**59.**	A		
10.			J	**35.**			D	**60.**	H		
11.			A	**36.**			J	**61.**		C	
12.			F	**37.**			C	**62.**	J		
13.			C	**38.**			G	**63.**			D
14.	G			**39.**			D	**64.**			H
15.	B			**40.**			H	**65.**			D
16.			J	**41.**			B	**66.**	F		
17.			B	**42.**	J			**67.**			C
18.			G	**43.**	C			**68.**			F
19.	B			**44.**	F			**69.**		B	
20.		J		**45.**	C			**70.**	J		
21.			D	**46.**			J	**71.**		A	
22.			G	**47.**			B	**72.**			H
23.			C	**48.**		H		**73.**			D
24.		G		**49.**		B		**74.**	F		
25.		B		**50.**			F	**75.**	C		

***Reporting Categories**

POW = Production of Writing

KLA = Knowledge of Language

CSE = Conventions of Standard English

Raw Scores (Number of Correct Answers)		
Production of Writing (POW)	______________	**out of 22**
Knowledge of Language (KLA)	______________	**out of 11**
Conventions of Standard English (CSE)	______________	**out of 42**
Total Correct for English Test (POW + KLA + CSE)	______________	**out of 75**

Practice Test 3 **Mathematics Scoring Key**

	Reporting Category*								Reporting Category*						
	PHM								PHM						
KEY	N	A	F	G	S	IES	MDL	KEY	N	A	F	G	S	IES	MDL
1.						E	E	31.					C		
2.				J				32.				F			
3.						C	C	33.					E		
4.			K					34.				J			J
5.						E	E	35.						C	
6.						F		36.						J	J
7.	E							37.						A	
8.						H		38.		G					
9.		C						39.						D	D
10.			F					40.			K				
11.			D					41.			D				
12.		H						42.						H	
13.						D	D	43.				E			
14.						J		44.		F					
15.				C				45.				B			
16.					J			46.						G	
17.						A		47.	A						
18.						J	J	48.	F						
19.						A		49.		B					
20.						H		50.						H	
21.		C						51.		D					
22.	K							52.				G			
23.					C			53.						D	
24.						J	J	54.						G	G
25.						C	C	55.				A			A
26.						F		56.		H					
27.						E	E	57.			B				
28.				J				58.						J	
29.	C							59.					D		
30.			G					60.						G	

Add the total of the columns and put it in the **PHM** field below.

*Reporting Categories	Raw Scores (Number of Correct Answers)		
PHM = Preparing for Higher Math	**Preparing for Higher Math (PHM) (N + A + F + G + S)**	______	**out of 34**
N = Number and Quantity	**Integrating Essential Skills (IES)**	______	**out of 26**
A = Algebra	**Total Number Correct (PHM + IES)**	______	**out of 60**
F = Functions	**Modeling (MDL)** (Not included in test raw score)	______	**out of 13**
G = Geometry			
S = Statistics and Probability			
Integrating Essential Skills			
MDL = Modeling			

Practice Test 3 — Reading Scoring Key

	Reporting Category*				Reporting Category*		
KEY	**KID**	**CS**	**IKI**	**KEY**	**KID**	**CS**	**IKI**
1.	D			**21.**		C	
2.		H		**22.**	F		
3.	B			**23.**		D	
4.	G			**24.**	H		
5.		B		**25.**			A
6.		J		**26.**	H		
7.	C			**27.**		C	
8.			F	**28.**	F		
9.	D			**29.**	D		
10.			H	**30.**		G	
11.	B			**31.**	C		
12.			J	**32.**	J		
13.	B			**33.**	C		
14.			H	**34.**			F
15.	A			**35.**		D	
16.		F		**36.**	H		
17.	D			**37.**	A		
18.		H		**38.**	H		
19.	D			**39.**	D		
20.	H			**40.**	G		

***Reporting Categories**

KID = Key Ideas & Details

CS = Craft & Structure

IKI = Integration of Knowledge and Ideas

Raw Scores (Number of Correct Answers)		
Key Ideas & Details (KID)	______	**out of 24**
Craft & Structure (CS)	______	**out of 10**
Integration of Knowledge and Ideas (IKI)	______	**out of 6**
Total Correct for Reading Test (KID + CS + IKI)	______	**out of 40**

Practice Test 3 — Science Scoring Key

KEY	IOD	SIN	EMI	KEY	IOD	SIN	EMI
	Reporting Category*				Reporting Category*		
1.	C			21.		C	
2.		H		22.		H	
3.	D			23.			B
4.		J		24.		G	
5.			D	25.			A
6.			F	26.		H	
7.	B			27.		D	
8.	G			28.		F	
9.			A	29.			C
10.	J			30.	J		
11.		D		31.	B		
12.		F		32.	F		
13.	C			33.		D	
14.	G			34.			J
15.	A			35.	D		
16.			G	36.	J		
17.		A		37.	D		
18.	J			38.	H		
19.	C			39.			B
20.	H			40.			J

***Reporting Categories**

IOD = Interpretation of Data

SIN = Scientific Investigation

EMI = Evaluation of Models, Inferences & Experimental Results

Raw Scores (Number of Correct Answers)		
Interpretation of Data (IOD)	________	**out of 18**
Scientific Investigation (CS)	________	**out of 12**
Evaluation of Models, Inferences & Experimental Results (EMI)	________	**out of 10**
Total Correct for Science Test (IOD + SIN + EMI)	________	**out of 40**

PRACTICE TEST 4: SCORING KEYS

Scoring Keys for Multiple-Choice Questions

To determine your raw scores using the Scoring Keys:

1) Circle the letter of correct answer in the box next to each question you answered correctly.
2) Add the circled letters and put the number of correctly answered questions in the blank corresponding to each reporting categories.
3) Add the total number of questions you answered correctly. The total is your raw score.

Complete this process for all four tests (English, Mathematics, Reading, and Science). Simply put the number of correct answers in the blank provided to determine your raw score.

Practice Test 4 — English Scoring Key

	Reporting Category*				Reporting Category*				Reporting Category*		
KEY	**POW**	**KLA**	**CSE**	**KEY**	**POW**	**KLA**	**CSE**	**KEY**	**POW**	**KLA**	**CSE**
1.			B	**26.**	H			**51.**			D
2.		G		**27.**	B			**52.**			G
3.			C	**28.**	H			**53.**		A	
4.			H	**29.**		C		**54.**			G
5.			B	**30.**	G			**55.**			B
6.		J		**31.**		B		**56.**			J
7.			C	**32.**			H	**57.**	D		
8.			G	**33.**			D	**58.**		F	
9.			C	**34.**			G	**59.**	D		
10.	H			**35.**			C	**60.**	F		
11.		C		**36.**		G		**61.**			A
12.	G			**37.**	A			**62.**			J
13.	D			**38.**	J			**63.**			C
14.	J			**39.**	C			**64.**			G
15.	B			**40.**		G		**65.**			B
16.			J	**41.**	D			**66.**			H
17.			D	**42.**			G	**67.**			A
18.			F	**43.**			A	**68.**			H
19.			C	**44.**		F		**69.**			A
20.		F		**45.**	A			**70.**			H
21.			D	**46.**			G	**71.**			B
22.			G	**47.**			A	**72.**	F		
23.			A	**48.**			H	**73.**	D		
24.		J		**49.**			D	**74.**	G		
25.			D	**50.**			F	**75.**	C		

***Reporting Categories**

POW = Production of Writing

KLA = Knowledge of Language

CSE = Conventions of Standard English

Raw Scores (Number of Correct Answers)		
Production of Writing (POW)	________	**out of 21**
Knowledge of Language (KLA)	________	**out of 12**
Conventions of Standard English (CSE)	________	**out of 42**
Total Correct for English Test (POW + KLA + CSE)	________	**out of 75**

Practice Test 4 — Mathematics Scoring Key

KEY	Reporting Category*							KEY	Reporting Category*						
	PHM								PHM						
	N	A	F	G	S	IES	MDL		N	A	F	G	S	IES	MDL
1.						D	D	31.					B		
2.			K					32.						H	H
3.		A						33.				E			
4.				J				34.						F	
5.			B					35.						B	
6.						F	F	36.				H			
7.	D							37.						C	
8.						G		38.				F			
9.			C					39.		C					
10.						H		40.	F						
11.						D		41.		B					
12.						K	K	42.						J	
13.						E		43.			D				
14.						G		44.		H					
15.				D				45.						C	C
16.		G						46.				G			
17.		D						47.		D					
18.						H		48.				K			
19.						A	A	49.		B					
20.						K		50.			J				
21.						E		51.	C						
22.						H	H	52.			J				
23.						B	B	53.						D	
24.						J		54.					H		
25.			D					55.	E						
26.	F							56.		F					
27.						B		57.				E			
28.					H		H	58.					J		
29.				C				59.						B	B
30.	G							60.					F		

Add the total of the columns and put it in the **PHM** field below.

***Reporting Categories**

PHM = Preparing for Higher Math
N = Number and Quantity
A = Algebra
F = Functions
G = Geometry
S = Statistics and Probability
IES = Integrating Essential Skills
MDL = Modeling

Raw Scores (Number of Correct Answers)

Preparing for Higher Math (PHM) (N + A + F + G + S) ________ **out of 36**
Integrating Essential Skills (IES) ________ **out of 24**
Total Number Correct (PHM + IES) ________ **out of 60**
Modeling (MDL) (Not included in test raw score) ________ **out of 10**

Practice Test 4 — Reading Scoring Key

KEY	KID	CS	IKI	KEY	KID	CS	IKI
	Reporting Category*				Reporting Category*		
1.		D		21.	B		
2.	F			22.		H	
3.	D			23.			B
4.	H			24.	J		
5.	A			25.		C	
6.	J			26.	H		
7.			B	27.	D		
8.			G	28.	J		
9.			C	29.	B		
10.			H	30.	F		
11.	D			31.	C		
12.	J			32.	F		
13.		C		33.	B		
14.		G		34.		G	
15.		B		35.	A		
16.			G	36.		H	
17.	B			37.		C	
18.	H			38.	G		
19.	B			39.		D	
20.	J			40.	F		

***Reporting Categories**

KID = Key Ideas & Details

CS = Craft & Structure

IKI = Integration of Knowledge and Ideas

Raw Scores (Number of Correct Answers)		
Key Ideas & Details (KID)	________	**out of 24**
Craft & Structure (CS)	________	**out of 10**
Integration of Knowledge and Ideas (IKI)	________	**out of 6**
Total Correct for Reading Test (KID + CS + IKI)	________	**out of 40**

Practice Test 4 — Science Scoring Key

	Reporting Category*				Reporting Category*		
KEY	**IOD**	**SIN**	**EMI**	**KEY**	**IOD**	**SIN**	**EMI**
1.	A			**21.**		C	
2.	H			**22.**			G
3.	B			**23.**			A
4.		F		**24.**			F
5.			D	**25.**	D		
6.	G			**26.**	G		
7.	C			**27.**	B		
8.	G			**28.**			F
9.			B	**29.**	B		
10.	H			**30.**	F		
11.	D			**31.**	A		
12.		H		**32.**	F		
13.			C	**33.**		C	
14.		G		**34.**			F
15.			A	**35.**		C	
16.		G		**36.**	H		
17.			C	**37.**	B		
18.		F		**38.**		F	
19.	D			**39.**			C
20.			G	**40.**			J

***Reporting Categories**

IOD = Interpretation of Data

SIN = Scientific Investigation

EMI = Evaluation of Models, Inferences & Experimental Results

Raw Scores (Number of Correct Answers)		
Interpretation of Data (IOD)	_______	**out of 18**
Scientific Investigation (CS)	_______	**out of 9**
Evaluation of Models, Inferences & Experimental Results (EMI)	_______	**out of 13**
Total Correct for Science Test (IOD + SIN + EMI)	_______	**out of 40**

SCALE SCORE CONVERSION CHARTS

Now that you know your raw scores for each test, you can convert them to scale scores using the following conversion tables. For each test section, find the number of questions you answered correctly in the **Raw Score** row of the table. The number located below in the **Scale Score** row is your scale score for that test. Enter your scale score in the **Multiple-Choice Scale Scores Chart** on page 1122.

The scale subscores tables immediately follow the test section in which they belong. Find the number of questions you answered correctly in each subsection in the Raw Score row of the table. The number located below in the **Scale Score** row is your scale score for that test. Enter your scale subscore in the **Multiple-Choice Scale Scores Chart** on page 1122.

SCALE SCORE CONVERSION CHARTS FOR MULTIPLE-CHOICE QUESTIONS

English Test

English Scale Score Conversion Chart

Raw Score	0–1	2–3	4–5	6–7	8–9	10–11	12–14	15–17	18–19	20–22	23–24	25–26
Scale Score	**1**	**2**	**3**	**4**	**5**	**6**	**7**	**8**	**9**	**10**	**11**	**12**
Raw Score	27–28	29–31	32–35	36–38	39–40	41–42	43–44	45–47	48–50	51–52	53–55	56–57
Scale Score	**13**	**14**	**15**	**16**	**17**	**18**	**19**	**20**	**21**	**22**	**23**	**24**
Raw Score	58–59	60–61	62	63–64	65	66	67	68–69	70	71	72–74	75
Scale Score	**25**	**26**	**27**	**28**	**29**	**30**	**31**	**32**	**33**	**34**	**35**	**36**

Mathematics Test

Mathematics Scale Score Conversion Chart

Raw Score	0	–	–	1	–	2	–	3	–	4	5–6	7
Scale Score	**1**	**2**	**3**	**4**	**5**	**6**	**7**	**8**	**9**	**10**	**11**	**12**
Raw Score	8–10	11–12	13–16	17–20	21–23	24–26	27–28	29	30–31	32–33	34–35	36–37
Scale Score	**13**	**14**	**15**	**16**	**17**	**18**	**19**	**20**	**21**	**22**	**23**	**24**
Raw Score	38–39	40–42	43–44	45–47	48–49	50–51	52–53	54	55–56	57	58–59	60
Scale Score	**25**	**26**	**27**	**28**	**29**	**30**	**31**	**32**	**33**	**34**	**35**	**36**

Reading Test

Reading Scale Score Conversion Chart

Raw Score	0	1	–	2	–	3	4	5	–	6–7	8	9–10
Scale Score	**1**	**2**	**3**	**4**	**5**	**6**	**7**	**8**	**9**	**10**	**11**	**12**
Raw Score	11	12–13	14	15–16	17	18	19–20	21	22–23	24	25–26	27
Scale Score	**13**	**14**	**15**	**16**	**17**	**18**	**19**	**20**	**21**	**22**	**23**	**24**
Raw Score	28	29	30	31	32	33	34	35–36	37	38	39	40
Scale Score	**25**	**26**	**27**	**28**	**29**	**30**	**31**	**32**	**33**	**34**	**35**	**36**

Science Test

Science Scale Score Conversion Chart

Raw Score	0	–	1	–	2	3	4	–	5–6	7	8	9
Scale Score	**1**	**2**	**3**	**4**	**5**	**6**	**7**	**8**	**9**	**10**	**11**	**12**
Raw Score	10	11	12	13	14–15	16	17–18	19–20	21	22–23	24–25	26–27
Scale Score	**13**	**14**	**15**	**16**	**17**	**18**	**19**	**20**	**21**	**22**	**23**	**24**
Raw Score	28–29	30–31	32	33	34	35	36	–	37	38	39	40
Scale Score	**25**	**26**	**27**	**28**	**29**	**30**	**31**	**32**	**33**	**34**	**35**	**36**

MULTIPLE-CHOICE SCALE SCORES CHART

Multiple-Choice Scale Scores Chart				
	Scale Score/Subscore			
	Test 1	Test 2	Test 3	Test 4
English				
Mathematics				
Reading				
Science				
Total Scale Scores				
Composite Score (sum ÷ 4)				

WRITING TEST SCORES

Writing Test Scores Chart

To determine your Writing Test scores:

1) Refer to the scoring rubric in Chapter 14 (page 587) and evaluate your essay based on the four domains.
   a. Each domain can be given a score ranging from 1–6. Enter the score you assign your essay in the Score 1 box.
   b. Since the writing test score is based on two ratings, enter either your score again or another reader's scores in the Score 2 box. The sum of Scores 1 and 2 is your domain score. Enter that number in the Domain Score field.
2) Calculate the average of your domain scores. Enter the total in the **Writing Test Scores** field.

Your ELA score is based on an average of your Writing score and English, Reading scale scores. ACT doesn't provide the exact formula for the ELA score, but you can rest assured that a Writing score above a 7 can raise your ELA score significantly.

Writing Test Scores				
Domain	**Test 1**	**Test 2**	**Test 3**	**Test 4**
Ideas and Analysis				
Score 1				
Score 2				
Domain Score (Score 1 + Score 2)				
Development/Support				
Score 1				
Score 2				
Domain Score (Score 1 + Score 2)				
Organization				
Score 1				
Score 2				
Domain Score (Score 1 + Score 2)				
Language Use/Conventions				
Score 1				
Score 2				
Domain Score (Score 1 + Score 2)				

Writing Test Score (Average of four Domain Scores)				

NOTES

NOTES

NOTES

NOTES

NOTES

NOTES

NOTES

NOTES

NOTES

NOTES

NOTES

NOTES

NOTES

NOTES